ADDISON-WESLEY
UNITED STATES
HISTORY

ADDISON-WESLEY
UNITED STATES HISTORY

The "Star-Spangled Banner," the flag that inspired Francis Scott Key to write the national anthem, is 30 feet wide and 42 feet long. A large portion of the banner was torn away "through the perilous fight" at Fort McHenry in the War of 1812. The odd red checkmark has never been explained.

IRVING F. AHLQUIST
GEORGE O. ROBERTS

DAVID C. KING
MARIAH MARVIN
DAVID WEITZMAN
& TONI DWIGGINS

ADDISON-WESLEY PUBLISHING COMPANY
Menlo Park, California   Reading, Massachusetts
London   Amsterdam   Don Mills, Ontario   Sydney

PROGRAM DIRECTORS

Irving F. Ahlquist is Professor of History, California State University, Long Beach. A recipient of the California State Colleges Distinguished Teaching Award, he has taught courses in American colonial history, the early national period, the Civil War and Reconstruction, United States history since 1900, California history, immigration history, and the history of the South. Since 1965 he has contributed to the preparation of high school history teachers.

George O. Roberts is Professor of Comparative Culture and Director of the Master of Arts in Teaching program at the University of California, Irvine. He has served as a member of the California Curriculum Development Commission, as a program administrator of the United States Office of Education Teacher Corps, and as a project evaluator and consultant for the United States Agency for International Development. He has been among the authors of *Social Sciences Education Framework for California Public Schools*.

AUTHORS

David C. King has taught high school English and social studies and has conducted workshops throughout the country in the teaching of American history. He is the author of several textbooks, including a high school world history and histories of the United States and California for middle-grade students. He has also served on committees to revise American history courses for the State Department of Education in New York as well as for school districts in California, New Mexico, Colorado, Nebraska, and North Carolina.

Mariah Marvin, a major author of the world history textbook *The Human Adventure*, has written extensively in the social sciences. Her contributions to education in the field of American history include scripts for a series of recorded dramatizations and narration for a series of filmstrips.

David Weitzman, long a teacher of United States history in the Oakland, California, public schools, served as a master teacher for the University of California, Berkeley, Division of Teacher Education. He has written a number of textbooks as well as books for young people on backyard history, on America's industrial past, and on industrial archeology. Under a grant from the National Endowment for the Humanities, he has developed curricular materials on the history of work in America.

Toni Dwiggins, a free-lance author, has written short stories as well as nonfiction works on psychology, engineering, sports, and travel. For high school students, she has contributed to textbooks in economics, psychology, biology, and political history.

FIELD TEST & REVIEW

Dr. Marion Casey, Fulbright Professor of History; Assoc. Professor, Rosary College, Illinois, and Fort Hays State University, Kansas
Dr. Hunter Draper, Coordinator of Social Studies, Charleston County School District, Charleston, South Carolina
Suzanne Kaufmann, George Washington High School, Philadelphia, Pennsylvania
Thomas Landers, Bay View High School, Milwaukee, Wisconsin
Alfred W. Lee, Strawberry Mansion High School, Philadelphia, Pennsylvania
Allen F. Long, La Sierra High School, Carmichael, California
Bonnie Tarta, Kenwood Academy, Chicago, Illinois

ACKNOWLEDGMENTS

The quotations on pages 678 and 684 respectively are from pages 59–61 and 112–113 of *Everything We Had*, by Albert Santoli. Copyright © 1981 by Albert Santoli and Vietnam Veterans of America. Reprinted by permission of Random House, Inc.

The information about "supertrees" on page 744 is adapted by permission of *Science '82* Magazine. © The American Association for the Advancement of Science.

ISBN 0-201-00103-9

ABCDEFGHIJKL-VH-89876543

CONTENTS

REFERENCE SECTION   754

MAPS

CHARTS

GRAPHS

AMERICAN OBSERVERS

CRITICAL ISSUES

SKILLS FEATURES

TO THE STUDENT

The historian Samuel Eliot Morison has said that history is "very chancy." He has observed that "America was discovered accidentally by a great seaman who was looking for something else; when discovered it was not wanted; and most of the exploration for the next fifty years was done in the hope of getting through or around it."

American history offers many further examples of risks and uncertainties. The English colonists who settled in 1587 on Roanoke Island, off the coast of what is now North Carolina, simply disappeared. The Jamestown Colony, founded in Virginia twenty years later, nearly failed to survive. Much later, when English colonies in North America were well established, the framers of the Declaration of Independence promised to risk "our lives, our fortunes, and our sacred honor" in an attempt to break away from Great Britain. There were good reasons to think that the attempt would not succeed.

The formation of the United States of America under the Constitution was itself a chancy step. Other nations were ruled by royal families. Could a nation endure under a republican form of government? "Let history answer the question," Thomas Jefferson said.

Despite conflicts about expansion and slavery, despite wars and periods of economic turmoil, history has answered Yes. The nation and the Constitution have endured through two centuries. Moreover, the United States has grown from a small nation to a great world power.

This book is organized to show the full sweep of American history—including the risks and uncertainties as well as the growth. Here is a guide to the book's organization.

UNIT ILLUSTRATIONS, TIMELINES

Each of the ten units in the book begins with a full-page **Unit Illustration.** It is a work of art that conveys a sense of the past. On the facing page is a **Unit Timeline,** as on page 1. At the top of the page, a mini-timeline displays the years of the unit in relation to all of American history. The timeline itself shows four main kinds of events and—for the years 1789 on—the presidencies as well.

CHAPTER ORGANIZATION

Each chapter begins with an opening quotation dating from the time of the chapter. The quotation—for example, the one on page 2—introduces ideas or events described fully in the chapter.

Beginning every section, there is a listing of **Read to Find Out** topics, as on page 3. It gives the main subjects of the section. These subjects also are covered by questions and brief assignments in the **Section Review,** as on page 9.

Each chapter ends with a **Chapter Survey** like the one on pages 26–27. It includes a summary of the chapter, review questions on main subjects, questions for essays or discussions, and assignments to develop skills. It also includes assignments relating the present to the past.

TEXT FEATURES

Each chapter includes an **American Observers** feature presenting one view of America. An example is "Anne Bradstreet—America's First Poet," on page 39. In addition, each unit includes a **Critical Issues** feature—focusing on a past issue of continuing importance—and a **Skills Feature.** An example of the former is "Freedom of the Press—the Trial of John Peter Zenger," on page 60. An example of a Skills Feature is "Map Reading—Spanish Exploration and Settlement 1519–1720," on page 23.

REFERENCE SECTION

The Reference Section, beginning on page 754, includes a **Resource Center** offering charts of the presidents and the states as well as other charts and graphs and maps. The Reference Section also contains **The Declaration of Independence, The Constitution of the United States** with notes about its meaning, **Suggested Readings** for each unit, and a **Glossary.** The Glossary words, chosen for their importance in the study of history, appear in heavy (boldface) type in the book. Other words that require definition appear in italic type and are defined in context or else are starred and defined at the bottom of the page where they appear.

AMERICANS OLD AND NEW

Prehistory–1763

Nicholas Vallard. *Cartier Map*, 1547.

1600	1700	1800	1900	2000

● Jamestown founded   ● Revolutionary War ● Civil War   ● Today

UNIT 1
Prehistory–1763

1550	1650	1750

AMERICA

● Cortés conquers Aztec in Mexico
● Pizarro conquers Inca in Peru
● League of the Iroquois
● First English colony at Jamestown
● First blacks in English colonies
● Mayflower Compact
● Navigation Acts
● New Orleans founded
● Georgia is thirteenth colony
● French and Indian War

SOCIAL

● Protestant Reformation
● Michelangelo: "Pietà"
● Shakespeare: *Hamlet*
● Harvard College founded
● Newton's theory of gravitation
● William and Mary College founded
● Bach: *Brandenburg Concertos*

EXPLORATION

● Columbus sails for Indies
● Balboa discovers Pacific Ocean
● Magellan's crew circles the earth
● Drake explores Pacific Coast
● Marquette and Joliet on Mississippi River
● Bering explores Alaska

INTERNATIONAL

● Elizabeth I rules England
● Spanish Armada fails
● Tokugawa, powerful Japanese shogun
● Charles II restores monarchy in England
● Czar Peter the Great visits western Europe
● Ashanti rise to power on Gold Coast

1550	1650	1750

1

BRIDGING TWO WORLDS

Prehistory–1700

THE FIRST AMERICANS
THE AGE OF EXPLORATION
SPAIN AND ENGLAND AS RIVALS

In 1519 the Aztec ruler Montezuma first met the Spanish explorer Hernando Cortés. A member of the Spanish expedition to Mexico wrote the story of this meeting:

"When we came close to Mexico . . . Montezuma descended from his litter while these great chiefs supported him with their arms. . . . He was richly dressed and wore shoes like sandals, with soles of gold covered with precious stones. . . . There were four other chiefs who carried the canopy and many other lords who walked before the great Montezuma, sweeping the ground where he would pass, and putting down mats, so that he would not have to walk on the ground. None of these lords thought of looking in his face; all of them kept their eyes down, with great reverence.

"When Cortés saw the great Montezuma approaching, he jumped from his horse and they showed great respect toward each other. . . . Then Cortés gave him a necklace he had ready to hand, made of glass stones. . . . He placed it around Montezuma's neck and was going to embrace him, when the princes accompanying him caught Cortés by the arm so that he could not do so, for they thought it an indignity."

The story ended with the fall of the Aztec empire. In its place would rise a Spanish empire. Spain's budding empire, however, covered only a part of the American continents. From the northern Arctic edge to the southern tip, this landmass was filled with other peoples. To them, this world was as old as their oldest ancestors.

The Spaniards, and other Europeans who followed, crossed an ocean to reach the Americas. To them, this was the New World—a land to be explored and conquered.

In the 1500s the countries of Europe, as if waking from a heavy slumber, were rising from villages and little land holdings into powerful nations. It was an age of inventions, discoveries, and explorations. One after another, explorers from Spain, England, Portugal, and France found their way to the New World.

THE FIRST AMERICANS

READ TO FIND OUT

— how early people might have come to the Americas.

— how the Eskimo survived on the tundra.

— how woodland tribes organized a confederacy.

— how the Plains people hunted buffalo.

— what ways of farming and settlement were practiced in the Southwest.

— how empires arose in Central and South America.

The very first Americans were probably immigrants, and their history was etched into the land. By studying fragments of that history—skeletons, fossils, etc.—people have tried to read the past.

According to one theory, the first Americans immigrated from Asia when the earth was in the grip of an Ice Age. The Ice Age would have caused the level of the Bering Sea to drop, making a land bridge almost 1,000 miles (1,600 kilometers) wide.

There is evidence that the Ice Age ended about 10,000 years ago. Glaciers began to melt as the climate warmed. The land bridge would have disappeared as the Bering Sea rose again.

Over the centuries, the people would have had to learn to adapt to changes in climate. Over the centuries, too, some of them would have experimented with growing plants from seeds and would have learned to cultivate crops. With the development of agriculture, the people would have stayed close to their fields, building semipermanent villages and moving on to hunt only after the harvest. Permanent settlements would have arisen later as some groups gave up hunting for the security of agriculture.

Isolated from each other, these American peoples, later called Indians, created different governments, religions, and ways of life. Eventually, the Indians established hundreds of different societies and developed from 1,000 to 2,000 separate languages.

PEOPLE OF THE ARCTIC

Stretching across the northern edge of the American continent is the Arctic, a land of vast frozen plains called tundra. A thin surface layer thaws briefly in summer. Afterward the Arctic locks the tundra back into ice. Only the hardy live here: a wiry plant called peat moss and a people called the Eskimo.

The Eskimo had no government or laws. Instead, they lived by rules of conduct, and the most important rule was that everyone cooperate in order to survive. The Eskimo organized into groups of whatever size was necessary to catch food.

Most groups lived near the sea, hunting seals with harpoons and fishing with forked spears and hooks made of bone. But these groups did not stay permanently on the coast. A seminomadic people, they wandered part of the time in their constant search for food. In summer and fall they left the sea and followed caribou, or deer, across the tundra.

Caribou and seals also were the source of clothing and shelter for the Eskimo. In the summer the people lived in tents covered with animal skins. In the winter, though, they built more permanent homes called igloos—dome-shaped houses made of tundra or blocks of snow.

PEOPLE OF THE EASTERN WOODLANDS

To the south of the Arctic, the land is more generous. Heavy forests run from southeastern Canada down through New England and far to the south. In these woodlands, dozens of tribes flourished.

Three groups of tribes that spoke similar languages dominated the region. Indians speaking Algonquian (al-GAHN-kee-uhn) were one group. They scattered through southern Canada, the Great Lakes area, and along the Atlantic coast to Virginia. The Algonquian had well-organized tribes whose names would mark American geography: the Huron, Narragansett, (NAYR-uh-GAN-sit), Delaware, and the strong Powhatan (POW-uh-TAN) tribes of Virginia.

The northern and southern Algonquian tribes were separated by the powerful Iroquois (IHR-uh-KWOI), who lived in the New York area. The Iroquois also had some southern relatives, like the Cherokee and Tuscarora. Farthest south, around the Gulf Coast, lived tribes speaking Muskogean (muhs-KŌ-gee-uhn)—the Creek, Choctaw, Seminole, and Chickasaw.

In thick woodlands the tribes lived well by hunting, fishing, gathering wild foods, and trading. Many also raised crops, creating farmland in the forest by burning trees and underbrush.

Many of the eastern tribes lived in villages protected by log stockades. Their shelters varied according to region, but the northeastern long-houses were among the most elaborate. Built by the Iroquois and the Algonquian, these sturdy, wood-framed structures housed several families.

For many years the Iroquois and the Algonquian warred with each other. Five of the Iroquois tribes—the Mohawk, Oneida (ōh-NĪ-duh), Onondaga (AHN-uhn-DAH-guh), Cayuga (kay-YOO-guh), and Seneca (SEN-ih-kuh)—dominated the land between the Hudson River and Lake Erie. These tribes went to war not only against the Algonquian but also against one another.

Around 1570, according to legend, the prophet Deganawidah (dee-gan-ah-WEE-dah) joined the Mohawk leader Hiawatha to urge unity among the Iroquois. Convinced, the five tribes then formed a **confederation**, or alliance, to end wars among themselves. This confederation became known as the League of the Iroquois, or the Five Nations.

The league was based on the political organization of the tribes. At the heart of the Iroquois village was the "fireside," made up of a woman and all of her children. Several firesides were combined into larger units, and a number of these units made up a clan. The many clans within the tribe formed the nation.

Women appointed men to represent the clan in tribal meetings. Women also named the 50 *sachems* (say-CHUHMS), or chiefs, who made up the ruling council of the league. Each summer the council met at an Onondaga village to make the laws, maintain the peace, and remind the tribes of the great power of unity.

PEOPLE OF THE GREAT PLAINS

To the west of the great woodlands, between the Mississippi River and the Rocky Mountains, lie the Great Plains. This is the heartland of the North American continent, stretching from Canada south to Texas. In the eastern part of the Plains, the grasses are tall, and streams and rivers are lined with woodland. The land becomes drier and the grass grows shorter to the west, and in some places the Plains shrivel to semidesert.

In the western Plains lived nomadic tribes like the Cheyenne and Sioux. These tribes depended on the buffalo and followed the great herds that roamed the grassland.

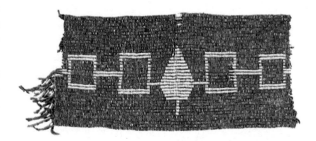

The founding of the Iroquois League was recorded on a wampum belt made of polished shells. In the center is the league's symbol—a tall tree to shelter the five nations.

The Dorset people of Greenland carved ivory images of the Arctic hare and the other animals that they hunted. The Dorset culture vanished a thousand years ago.

North American Indian Tribes and Culture Regions

ARCTIC OCEAN

BERING SEA

Eskimo
Koyukon
Eskimo
Tanana
Tanaina
Aleut

Hare

Tutchone

Tlingit

Kaska

Slave

Yellowknife

ARCTIC

Eskimo

Eskimo

Chipewyan

HUDSON BAY

Eskimo

Haida

Tsimshian

Bella Coola

Kwakiutl

Beaver

SUBARCTIC

Naskapi

Montagnais

NORTHWEST COAST

Nootka

Salish

PLATEAU

Blackfoot

Cree

Micmac

Chinook

Coeur d'Alene

Flathead

Assiniboine

Chippewa

Abnaki
Penobscot

Tillamook

Yakima
Spokane
Nez Perce
Cayuse

Gros Ventre

Ottawa

Algonquian

Nipmuc
Massachusett
Wampanoag
Narragansett
Pequot

Crow

Mandan
Teton
Arikara

Menomini
Sauk
Fox
Kickapoo
Winnebago

Huron

Seneca
Cayuga
Onondaga
Oneida
Mohawk
Mahican

Coos

Klamath
Modoc

Shoshone

Cheyenne

Sioux

Santee

Yurok
Hupa
Pomo Maidu
Miwok

Paiute

GREAT BASIN

Pawnee

Iowa

Missouri

Illinois

Erie

Susquehanna

Delaware

EASTERN WOODLAND

CALIFORNIA

Costanoan

Ute

Arapaho

Omaha

Powhatan

Yokut

Paiute

Kansa

Shawnee

PLAINS

Chumash

Cahuilla

Osage

Cherokee

Mohave
Yavapai
Hopi
Zuni
Acoma
Tewa

Navaho

Kiowa

Wichita

Chickasaw

Tuscarora

Catawba

PACIFIC OCEAN

SOUTHWEST

Papago
Pima

Mescalero

Comanche

Caddo

Creek

SOUTHEAST

ATLANTIC OCEAN

Seri

Concho

Yaqui

Tarahumara

Choctaw

Seminole

Guaicura

NORTHERN MEXICO

Coahuiltec

GULF OF MEXICO

Huichol

Tamaulipeco

Tarasca

Totonac

MIDDLE AMERICA

Maya

CARIBBEAN SEA

Aztec
Mixtec
Zapotec

Maya

N

0   1000 MILES

0   1000 KILOMETERS

Buffalo hunting was done on foot—horses were not native to the Americas—and men, women, and children took part. Children waved blankets, and men dressed in animal skins to frighten and stampede the herds. When some animals became trapped in a ravine or stampeded over a cliff, the men moved in with their spears and bows. Then the women went to work with stone scrapers and knives. Strips of meat were dried and stored in pouches. Hides were used for robes and cone-shaped houses called tepees.

Tribes of the eastern Plains also hunted buffalo, but most lived in large semipermanent settlements along the Missouri and other rivers. Here the soil was good, and tribes like the Osage, Missouri, Kansa, Omaha, and Iowa farmed.

The many tribes of the Plains usually had loosely organized governments. Men who had shown great courage, wisdom, or supernatural power became chiefs. These chiefs discussed major issues in council until they reached a unanimous decision.

PEOPLE OF THE WEST

Far from the grassy plains are the towering forests of the Pacific Northwest. Warm currents swirl along the coast, creating a mild, moist climate. Here, caribou, deer, and bear roamed forests rich with roots and berries. Coastal rivers swarmed with salmon. A tribe could catch all the salmon it needed to live for months.

The abundant food supply enabled the people of the Northwest Coast to live in large, permanent settlements even though they were not farmers. In this rich land, the Tlingit (TLIN-git), Kwakiutl (KWHA-kee-OOT-uhl), Chinook, Coos, and other tribes developed complex cultures.

The people of these tribes were skilled woodworkers. With tools made of stone and sharp-edged seashells, they built large wood-planked houses. Elaborately carved door posts called *totems* showed the symbols of the house owners—the animal spirits they relied on and the ancestors of their clan. The people also built large dugout canoes to reach trading partners and to follow offshore schools of halibut, cod, and even whales.

Wealth was highly valued in many of the tribes and was displayed in a ceremony called the *potlatch*. A chief gathered great treasures of blankets, furs, canoes, and sometimes even slaves captured from

enemy tribes. To prove his wealth, he gave the items to guest chiefs and their followers at a feast. The other chiefs would try to match or outdo his generosity, setting off contests of gift giving.

Trade was also of great importance to many of the tribes. Throughout the region there was brisk trading in furs, shells, copper, and slaves. Some traders even followed the coast south to trade with tribes in California.

In much of California there are warm summers and mild winters, and nearly everywhere oak trees grow. Acorns, then, became the main source of food of the Hupa, Pomo, Chumash, and other seminomadic California tribes. Their diet of acorns was supplemented by small game, fish, and berries.

Tribal members pounded acorns into a yellow flour, then rinsed it with water to leach out the bitter tannic acid. With the flour they made bread and gruel, which they cooked in baskets with fire-heated stones. These people, especially the Pomo,

The Kwakiutl and other Northwest Coast people used masks in their religious ceremonies. The skillfully carved raven mask is made of wood, brass, nails, and fiber.

Feathers from a duck and a blackbird are woven into the child's basketry cap. The cap was found in a cave in western Nevada. It is believed to be a thousand years old.

were among the finest basket makers in North America. Their baskets were so tightly woven that they held water.

To the east of the California tribes were other great basket makers—the Paiute (PĪ-yoot), Shoshone (shō-SHŌ-nee), and Ute of the Great Basin. This land was too dry for farming and had few game animals. The people of the Great Basin roamed in small bands from place to place, gathering wild plants and seeds and catching rabbits, snakes, and grasshoppers.

PEOPLE OF THE SOUTHWEST

South of the Great Basin is a vast, dry region known as the Southwest. In the northern part of the region, the mighty Colorado and other rivers have carved deep canyons and tall mesas* out of plateaus.

* mesa: a high plateau with a flat top and steep sides.

Pueblo Bonito in Chaco Canyon, New Mexico, was built a thousand years ago. The pueblo rose as high as five stories and included more than 800 rooms and several kivas.

Farther south, the Rio Grande has cut narrow valleys through rugged mountains. Beyond the Rio Grande lie the slopes of the Sierra Madre Oriental. They extend southwest, between the Gulf of Mexico and a vast desert.

The varied landscape of the Southwest has one common feature: It is dry. Scarcely 10 inches (25 centimeters) of rain, on the average, fall there in a year. In this parched land several tribes built remarkable societies. The earliest people, whose culture peaked between A.D. 1100 and A.D. 1300, eventually became known as the Anasazi (ahn-eh-SAH-zee), the "ancient ones."

The Anasazi were architects in stone. Lacking timber, they built homes of fitted stones on mesa tops and valley floors and in hollows in the faces of cliffs. Some of their buildings climbed four stories high. In the valleys they farmed, irrigating with rainwater trapped in reservoirs and canals.

For unknown reasons, the Anasazi abandoned their communities. Eventually, another southwestern culture arose, created by the Pueblo* (PWEB-lō) people. Pueblo tribes, such as the Zuñi, Acoma, and Hopi, traced their ancestry to the Anasazi. Like the Anasazi, the Pueblo were farmers and town builders. They built apartment-style villages atop mesas, in cliff faces, and on canyon floors.

The Pueblo community was bound tightly together by religion. At the center of each village was the *kiva* (KEE-vuh), an underground room used for religious ceremonies. Kiva leaders appointed people to govern and defend the village.

Men also did the farm work, planting crops in the moist riverbeds or in patches close to irrigation channels. Women did the cooking and made pottery and baskets. Women also owned all property—crops, homes, and furnishings.

Like their Anasazi ancestors, the Pueblo traded with one another as well as with neighbors like the Apache and Navaho. The Apache and Navaho were newcomers to the Southwest, arriving in the fourteenth or fifteenth century. Seminomadic people, they were fierce fighters. Eventually, the Navaho learned techniques of farming from the Hopi tribe and increasingly depended on crops. The Navaho also accepted much of the Hopi religion.

* *Pueblo* is the Spanish word for "village" and the word that the Spanish explorers also used to describe the Southwest Indians who lived in villages.

The Mayan athlete is wearing hand gauntlets, leggings, and a thickly padded belt. Players on a stone court used a hard rubber ball in a game widespread throughout Middle America.

CENTRAL AMERICAN EMPIRES

The land of Central America varies from plateaus and valleys to mountains and tropical jungles. The climate is generally warm year-round, and there is much fertile land.

As early as 2000 B.C., people in central Mexico farmed. Because of agriculture, the people had a steady supply of food. They could live in permanent villages and had the time to develop arts, trade, and government. The villages grew into cities, and eventually great empires arose.

One of these empires was located in the jungle of the Yucatán Peninsula, where the Maya built a highly complex civilization. For the most part, the Maya lived in farming villages that surrounded cities—the centers of trade and religion. In these cities Maya scientists and priests studied astronomy, created a highly accurate calendar, and developed a written language. Maya culture was at its height between A.D. 300 and A.D. 900, but then it began to decline.

As the Maya civilization declined, another people—the Toltec—were establishing an empire to the north, in the Valley of Mexico. By 1000 they had conquered the old Maya Empire. For nearly two hundred years Toltec civilization towered over Central America. Then civil war broke out and the empire began to topple.

Around 1200 the Valley of Mexico was invaded by another people—the Aztec. Conquering all peoples that they encountered, the Aztec claimed Toltec lineage and began their own empire in the early 1400s.

The Aztec built their capital, Tenochtitlán, in the marshes of a large lake near present-day Mexico City. Builders drained swamps to connect a series of islands and joined them to the mainland with earthen causeways.

The Aztec received crops and goods from trade within their empire, which spanned much of Mexico. But Tenochtitlán, a city of 300,000 people, was also fed by farmers who grew crops on terraced hillsides around the lake or on artificial islands called *chinampas* (chee-NAHM-pahs).

The Aztec had strict class lines, with religious leaders and nobles at the top. Ruling over all was the chief. When Montezuma II became ruler in the early 1500s, he was considered part god, like those rulers before him.

More than one hundred gods touched Aztec life. A major one was Quetzalcoatl (ket-SAHL-kō-AHT-ul), the feathered serpent, who had brought civilization to the people and then sailed away. Myths told that Quetzalcoatl would return someday out of the east.

THE INCA EMPIRE OF SOUTH AMERICA

Far to the south of Mexico, another magnificent empire existed. It extended some 2,000 miles (3,200 kilometers) in the Andes Mountains, which stretch along the western edge of South America.

In the 1400s these lands, populated by many tribes, had been conquered by a people called the Inca. Each great leader—also called the Inca—added to the empire until it ruled over some 6 million people. The Inca built on the achievements of earlier societies. They terraced mountainsides for farmland and created irrigation systems. They also constructed beautiful cities high in the mountains, linked by roads and bridges.

The Inca ruled as dictators over conquered tribes. Inca class structure was as rigid and peaked as the Andes. High up were nobles, military chiefs, and political and religious leaders. At the summit was the ruler, who held the structure together. Without him, the huge empire could quickly crumble.

Whether great empire builders like the Inca or nomadic hunters like the Eskimo, the peoples of the Americas believed that their world was a gift of the gods. If the gods were pleased, that world—and the peoples' ways of life—would pass to their children and grandchildren. The Maya had a prayer that could have been chanted in many tongues:

> Look at us, hear us! . . .
> Heart of Heaven, Heart of Earth!
> Give us our descendants, our
> succession, as long as the sun
> shall move and there shall be light.
> Let it dawn, let the day come!

A day would come, however, when other peoples reached the shores of the Americas. Traditional Indian ways of life that had been passed from generation to generation would be shattered.

SECTION REVIEW

1. Identify the following: League of the Iroquois, Anasazi, Montezuma II, Quetzalcoatl.

2. Define the following: tundra, seminomadic, potlatch, kiva, chinampas.

3. (a) What did the Eskimo have in place of government? (b) How did it work?

4. Describe some of the ways in which the tribes of the Eastern Woodlands obtained food.

5. Explain the importance of the buffalo to the Plains Indians.

6. (a) How did the climate affect settlement in the Pacific Northwest? (b) How did the climate affect settlement in the Great Basin?

7. Describe the architecture of Indians in the Southwest.

8. What were some of the achievements of the Maya? The Aztec?

High in the Peruvian Andes lie the ruins of Machu Picchu. The city covered more than a hundred acres. Without the use of the wheel or metal tools, Inca builders fit together huge granite stones so perfectly that a knife blade cannot be forced between them.

The people of the Andes region were skilled goldsmiths. The goblet was made in Peru sometime between A.D. 1000 and 1400. It was fashioned out of sheet gold hammered over a carved wooden form.

THE AGE OF EXPLORATION

READ TO FIND OUT

— how Europeans became interested in trade with Asia.

— how strong monarchies replaced the feudal system.

— how new technology enabled Portugal to sail along the coast of Africa.

— how the voyages of Columbus affected Europeans.

— what the voyage of Magellan proved.

— what Europeans learned from the search for the Northwest Passage.

Thousands of miles away from the Americas, from the Indian tribes and empires, there was the continent of Europe. Europeans, too, had built great empires—Greece, Macedonia, and mighty Rome. For hundreds of years much of Europe was governed by Rome and absorbed its culture. When the Roman Empire toppled in the fifth century A.D., Europe fractured into many small independent groups. Most traces of Greek and Roman culture faded in the ensuing thousand years known as the Middle Ages. But a time would come for great changes and exciting explorations.

FEUDALISM AND THE CRUSADES

During the Middle Ages a system known as *feudalism* emerged in Europe. Under feudalism most of the land was divided among wealthy lords, who then parceled out pieces of their holdings, or *manors*, to lesser lords called *vassals*. In exchange, the vassals served and fought for their lord, pledging "I will love what thou lovest; I will hate what thou hatest." In some places, lords also owed allegiance to a monarch.

Most of the people lived as peasant farmers in villages around a lord's castle. Many were *serfs*—servants permanently bound to the land and to the lord. With law and land supplied by the lord, crops and labor by the peasants, and religion by the local church, the feudal manor was almost an independent state.

Between the eleventh and fifteenth centuries, the feudal system gradually eroded. One of the first blows to feudalism was brought about by the Crusades.

The Christian Church had been the one unifying force in Europe since the Roman Empire. Christians revered the Middle Eastern land of Palestine, where Jesus Christ had lived. For centuries, this Holy Land had been ruled by Arabs, who were Muslims.* Christians were allowed to make pilgrimages there until around 1000, when a group of Muslims from Turkey conquered the Holy Land from the Arabs. The Turks began to harass Christians.

The Pope, Urban II, called on Europeans to wrest the Holy Land from the Turks. Across Europe cries of "God wills it!" rang out, and thousands embarked on the Crusades. From 1096 to the end of the 1200s, wave after wave of Crusaders swarmed into the Middle East. In the end, they failed to take Palestine.

The Crusades, however, had far-reaching consequences. Europeans discovered that Arab merchants traded freely with "the Indies"—China, India, and the East Indies islands. From these lands they obtained cloth and spices that were unknown in Europe. Europeans saw, appreciated, and quickly acquired a taste for these goods.

A brisk trade sprang up between Europe and the Middle East. Arabs controlled one part of the trade, bringing spices, perfumes, and cloth by ship and camel caravan to their ports on the Mediterranean Sea. Italian merchants controlled the other part, carrying the goods across the Mediterranean and selling them at high prices throughout Europe.

The spices preserved and flavored the food of wealthy Europeans. The perfumes and silks made life seem finer. And there were other prized goods—bright Persian rugs and Damascus steel, far superior to European iron or steel.

* Muslim: a believer in the religion known as Islam. Muslims believe in a supreme deity, Allah, and follow the teachings of the prophet Muhammad, the founder of the religion.

The arrival of European merchants is noted in this detail from a sixteenth-century Persian rug. Persian cities lay on the major trade route between Europe and China.

TRADE WITH ASIA

Europeans now knew what lay to the near east. But they wondered about the lands that lay even farther eastward. A seventeen-year-old Italian named Marco Polo listened to the tales of his father and uncle, who had visited the land called China. In 1271 the three set out from Venice to travel across the continent of Asia.

Twenty-four years later, the Polos returned. They astounded Venetians with their stories and their cargo—jewels, silky yak hair, a three-bladed sword, and other marvels. Marco Polo told of his experiences in a book called *The Travels of Marco Polo.*

The tales of Marco Polo spread throughout Europe and took hold in people's minds. Europeans were eager to obtain goods from these rich empires far to the east, but the Arabs controlled the only land routes into Asia. The only way to get these goods was to pay the high prices charged by the Italian and Arab merchants.

However, according to Marco Polo, China bordered the sea. If a route could be found, it would be possible to sail to China. But that meant venturing into unknown oceans—a danger that no one was willing to face. Throughout Europe, though, events were occurring that would lead some people to take the risk.

THE RISE OF NATIONS AND THE RENAISSANCE

The spread of trade and new ideas pierced the isolation of the feudal manors. Trade also spurred the growth of towns, many of which had begun as merchants' trading centers.

Gradually, towns blossomed into prosperous cities. There was plenty of work for weavers, metal workers, glass blowers, and carpenters. Craftspeople, merchants, and storekeepers were becoming a *middle class*—a class between the nobles and church leaders at the top and the peasants and serfs below.

Meanwhile, Europe's monarchs had been growing stronger. Trade could flourish only if there was law and order, a reliable money system, and safe trade routes. Strong rulers could provide these. For such protection, the middle class willingly paid taxes to monarchs. With tax money in their treasuries, monarchs hired officials to carry out royal business and built large armies to enforce their power.

As kingdoms grew stronger, the old feudal system declined. By the late 1400s, four strong, unified monarchies emerged in western Europe—Spain, Portugal, France, and England.

The monarchs of these nations were envious of the wealth that poured into Italian city-states* like Venice. They realized that expanding trade increased a nation's wealth and power. One way to expand trade was to support voyages of exploration and to set up trading outposts. And the new nations now had the resources to do this.

At the same time, the social and intellectual climate of Europe was changing, and many people were excited by the idea of exploration. The 1300s, 1400s, and 1500s were a period of great awakening called the Renaissance. The Renaissance was an era of fresh ideas and inventions in Europe.

* city-state: a state made up of an independent city and the territory it controlled.

For hundreds of years, the people of Europe had lived amid the ruins of the Greeks and Romans without wondering about those ancient civilizations. Then the Crusaders brought back from the Arab world the Greek and Roman learning that had been preserved there. They also brought back new mathematical and scientific theories developed by the Arabs. With new ideas and new interest in the great learning of the past, the Renaissance dawned in Europe.

Europeans plunged into a world of literature, sculpture, painting, and music. New technology aided the circulation of new ideas. In the early 1400s Europeans began printing books with wooden blocks, something the Chinese and Koreans had been doing for hundreds of years. By mid-century, a German named Johann Gutenberg developed movable type made of lead. He cast the type letter by letter and then set letters in rows to make up a page. With his press he could print about three hundred copies of a page a day. Printing replaced the copying of books by hand in Europe.

Ideas That Made Exploration Possible

A.D. 200	Ptolemy, a Greek Mathematician, devises a system of *latitude* and *longitude*
1000	*Magnetic compass* comes into use
	Mediterranean shipbuilders begin to adapt Arabic *triangular sails,* enabling them to sail into the wind
1200	The development of the *rudder* allows a ship to be guided by one person
1300	The *compass card* is added to the magnetic compass, allowing navigators to determine direction more accurately
	Cannons come into use aboard ships
1400	*Improved astrolabe* makes it possible to determine distance from the equator
	The swift, easily handled *caravel* is developed, combining the best features of Mediterranean triangular-sailed ships and square-rigged northern ships
1500	Gerhardus Mercator devises the first *map projection* to show the middle latitudes with little distortion
	A heavier ship with many masts, the *galleon,* or carrack, carries larger crews, heavier cargo, and more guns than previous ships

PORTUGUESE EXPLORATIONS

One of the most farsighted people of the Renaissance was Prince Henry of Portugal. Prince Henry was convinced that the Atlantic Ocean was the key to finding a direct route to India. To the south of Portugal lay the vast continent of Africa. If the Portuguese could sail south along its coast, they might find a way through Africa or around it to Asia. A sea route would be better for trade than any overland route. Then Portugal might replace the Italian city-states as leaders of trade.

In 1418 Prince Henry formed a school of navigation, assembling many of Europe's best sea captains, map makers, and shipbuilders. The Europeans borrowed Muslim inventions like the magnetic compass to tell direction and the *astrolabe.* The astrolabe was an instrument for sighting the stars to determine a ship's position. Europeans built an improved sailing ship called the *caravel.* The ship could sail into the wind rather than simply sailing with it. For the first time, European sea captains had the technology to sail in safety beyond the sight of land.

Year after year Prince Henry's ships pushed cautiously southward along the west coast of Africa. With each voyage they filled in their maps and established trading posts in African kingdoms along the coast. Ships returned to Lisbon with ivory, gold, and African slaves.

Prince Henry the Navigator died in 1460, but the Portuguese continued searching for a sea route to India. In 1487 Bartholomeu Dias (DEE-ahs) voyaged with three ships around the southern tip of Africa and into the unknown Indian Ocean. There, his crew panicked and Dias was forced to return to Portugal. Delighted that Dias had gone so far, Portugal's King John named the tip of Africa the Cape of Good Hope.

However, interest in African trade kept the Portuguese from pressing on to Asia for another ten years. Then, in 1497, a determined captain named Vasco da Gama followed the Dias route and crossed the Indian Ocean to the west coast of India. Da Gama returned to Portugal with spices and jewels purchased at remarkably low prices.

The Portuguese kept da Gama's route secret. Within a few years, Portugal had trading posts scattered from India to the Spice Islands. The small kingdom became the envy of Europe.

In 1535 an artist painted Portuguese carracks entering Lisbon harbor. More powerful and maneuverable than earlier ships, the carrack became the standard sailing vessel of the Age of Exploration.

No portrait of Columbus was painted during his lifetime. Sebastiano de Piombo painted this portrait of him in 1519.

THE VOYAGES OF COLUMBUS

Eleven years before the voyage of Vasco da Gama, Queen Isabella of Spain granted an audience to a sea captain and map maker named Christopher Columbus. Like most educated people, Columbus viewed the world as round. But he was also convinced that the earth was smaller than most scholars believed. Also, he thought that he could sail directly west from Europe to Asia. The short, direct voyage, Columbus believed, might take only a few days.

Portuguese explorers were sailing eastward, around Africa, to try to reach the Indies. Columbus had a different idea: The quickest way to reach the Indies was to sail west. Portugal, however, would not approve Columbus's plan for such a voyage, so he approached the Spanish.

Queen Isabella was concerned about Portugal's growing trade in Africa and eager for Spanish expansion. She listened to Columbus's plans. But she, too, was doubtful and kept him waiting for six years.

Finally, an advisor convinced Queen Isabella that Columbus's idea gave the Spanish an opportunity for expansion not to be missed. At last, Columbus had his chance. Spain would not only finance his voyage but would make him an admiral as well.

Isabella and Ferdinand gave Columbus supplies, a crew of ninety, and three caravels—the *Niña*, the *Pinta*, and the *Santa María*. The caravels had compasses but no astrolabes. Columbus would navigate by dead reckoning—compass readings and estimations of speed and distance.

On August 3, 1492, Columbus set out from Spain into the Atlantic, the "sea of pitchy darkness." Two months later, on October 12, a lookout yelled, "Land! Land!" The land sighted was a small island in the Bahamas, but Columbus was certain that it was an island of the Indies. He named it San Salvador, Spanish for "Blessed Savior." He called the people that he met Indians. The Europeans explored through the Caribbean, discovering Cuba, which they thought was Japan, and another island, which they called Hispaniola, "Little Spain."

Columbus returned to Spain in early 1493 as a hero. The Spanish court buzzed with excitement over the "Indian" captives and the strange fruits and plants that Columbus had brought. Within six months, a hopeful king and queen sent Columbus with a grand fleet of 17 ships to establish a colony and to find the coast of China.

Columbus charted more islands and planted a colony on Hispaniola, but he failed to find spices, gold, or China. On a third voyage, in 1498, he set foot on the mainland of South America. This, he believed, was another world to the south of China.

He sailed on to Hispaniola, bringing more settlers, including some women. He found the colony on the edge of rebellion. The colonists had found some gold, but not as much as they had expected. Columbus tried to restore order, but his skills lay in sailing, not in governing. A group of colonists seized ships and returned to Spain, where they complained of Columbus's rule.

Ferdinand and Isabella blamed Columbus for the rebellion, for the colonists' mistreatment of the Indians, and for the failure to find much gold. They sent a ship to Hispaniola, and Columbus was brought home in chains.

Columbus, however, pleaded for a last chance to find a route to India, and Ferdinand and Isabella finally agreed. In 1502 Columbus set out on his fourth voyage of exploration. On this voyage he combed the coastline of Central America, searching

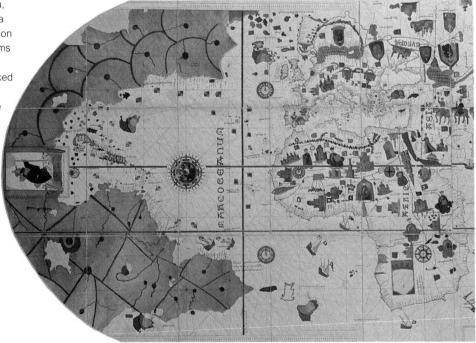

In 1500 Juan de la Cosa, Columbus's pilot, drew a world map. On this section of the map Spanish claims in the West Indies and South America are marked with Spanish flags. The Americas are green, the color used for the unknown.

for a passage that he thought would lead a little farther west to the Indian Ocean.

He did not find what he sought. He spent his remaining years in Spain, disappointed yet stubbornly claiming that he had reached the Indies. He never knew that his explorations had been a spectacular success. Instead of reaching Asia, Columbus had happened upon the American continents.

THE TREATY OF TORDESILLAS

Columbus's first voyages caused trouble between Spain and Portugal, both eager for trade with the Indies. Portugal's King John argued that Columbus had landed on the Azores, Atlantic islands already claimed by Portugal. But Spain insisted that Columbus had reached Asia.

AMERICAN OBSERVERS

The 230-foot long Bayeaux Tapestry illustrated the Norman conquest of England in 1066. Rivals Harold of England and William of Normandy were both descended from Viking chiefs. Norman dragonships followed Viking designs.

THE VIKING SAGAS
EARLY GLIMPSE OF NORTH AMERICA

"They found wild wheat . . . and grape vines. . . . Every stream was teeming with fish. . . . In the woods there were a great number of animals of all kinds." So the Viking tale, *Eric's Saga*, described a mysterious new land somewhere across the stormy North Atlantic. To the Viking sailors, who had come from the frozen shores of Greenland, it seemed a paradise. They named it Vinland, "land of grapes."

The great sea captain Leif Ericson was probably the first to explore the new land. He was a tall, strong, shrewd man, the sagas tell us, "very impressive in appearance." About the year 1000, he and his sea-weary sailors reached Vinland. "There was dew on the grass, and the first thing they did was to get some of it on their hands and put it to their lips, and to them it seemed the sweetest thing they had ever tasted."

The Vikings built houses and spent the winter in Vinland, tramping the woods and beaches and fishing for salmon. In the spring they returned to Greenland, laden with grapes and timber, and bearing tales of the rich new land.

Several years later, Viking colonists tried to settle in Vinland. But Indians, people in skin boats whom the Vikings called "Skraelings," drove them away. Eventually the new land was forgotten, except in the sagas told by the old folk on long winter evenings. By modern times, many people believed these sagas were myth, not history.

Then in 1960 Viking homes dating from the year 1000 were uncovered in Newfoundland. Because grapes do not grow there, scientists believe there may be other sites farther south, probably in New England. But the Newfoundland discovery shows that the sagas are probably based on fact. They give us our first glimpse of America as seen through the wondering eyes of Europeans who reached it five centuries before Columbus.

The Pope offered to settle the matter. In 1494 the two countries signed the Treaty of Tordesillas (TOR-day-SEE-yahs). Under the treaty, an imaginary line was drawn from north to south through the Atlantic Ocean. Spain could trade in and claim all lands to the west of the line. All lands to the east belonged to Portugal. It was believed that the line did not cross any land.

Then, in 1500, Portugal sent Pedro Álvares Cabral to India along Vasco da Gama's route. Cabral strayed far out into the Atlantic. He landed in South America, on a piece of land that stuck out into the Atlantic. That land was east of the Pope's imaginary line and thus in Portugal's area. Now Portugal, too, had a claim in America—Brazil.

CABOT AND VESPUCCI

Meanwhile, other sea captains began to explore north and south of the islands that Columbus had discovered. John Cabot, a navigator from Genoa, sailed for England's King Henry VII to find a route to the Indies. In 1497 he sailed a northern route across the Atlantic and most likely landed at Newfoundland.

On a second voyage a year later, Cabot explored the North American coastline as far south as New England. Like Columbus, Cabot believed that he had reached Asia and failed to understand the importance of his explorations. However, he established an English claim to whatever lands lay north of Spain's discoveries.

In 1499 an Italian navigator named Amerigo Vespucci (ves-POO-chee) was aboard a Spanish ship that touched the coast of South America. "These parts," Vespucci wrote, "we may rightly call a new world. I have found a continent more filled with people and animals than our own Europe or Asia or Africa."

Several years later, a German geographer drew a map of this new world. On the landmass he wrote the Latin version of Vespucci's name—*Americus*. The name took hold, and people began to speak of the New World as America.

BALBOA'S EXPLORATIONS

By 1510 the Spanish had established a settlement, later called Darién, in Panama, on the mainland of South America. A year later, Vasco Núñez de Balboa (bal-BŌ-ah), the acting governor, heard Indian tales of a great sea beyond the Isthmus of Panama.

In 1513 Balboa organized an expedition. He led about two hundred Spaniards and eight hundred Indians inland from the coast. For over three weeks, they hacked a path across the Isthmus of Panama, struggling through steaming jungles. Finally, the Spaniards made their way up a steep mountain slope. From the summit, they looked down on the "other sea." Calm as glass, it stretched into the haze of the western horizon.

A few days later Balboa—in full armor and with his sword drawn—planted the Spanish flag on the shore. He named the ocean the South Sea and claimed it and all of the adjoining lands for Spain.

THE VOYAGE OF MAGELLAN

The man most eager to see whether Balboa's South Sea would lead to the Indies was Ferdinand Magellan (muh-JEHL-uhn). Unable to gain support in his native Portugal, Magellan persuaded Spain to sponsor his voyage.

With five old ships and over two hundred sailors, Magellan set sail from Spain in the fall of 1519. The small fleet crossed the Atlantic and moved slowly south along the coast of Brazil, seeking a water route through the land. They almost reached the tip of South America before they had to stop for the winter. In that bleak land the crew of one ship turned back, and another ship sank.

In August 1520 Magellan set off again and finally found the water passage he had been seeking. For six desperate weeks, the ships threaded their way through jagged rocks in what became known as the Strait of Magellan.

The three ships finally sailed into Balboa's sea, an ocean so peaceful that Magellan renamed it the Pacific. The crews set a course for China, and as one torrid day melted into the next, they discovered the vastness of the Pacific Ocean. There was no sign of land. Food and water ran out. The sailors ate rats and gnawed on leather to ease their hunger.

At last they sighted islands and found water and fruit. They pushed on to a larger group of islands, the Philippines, and the crews found themselves caught in an island war. After journeying almost around the world, Magellan was killed in the clash.

The remaining sailors divided into two ships. One headed back across the Pacific, only to be cap-

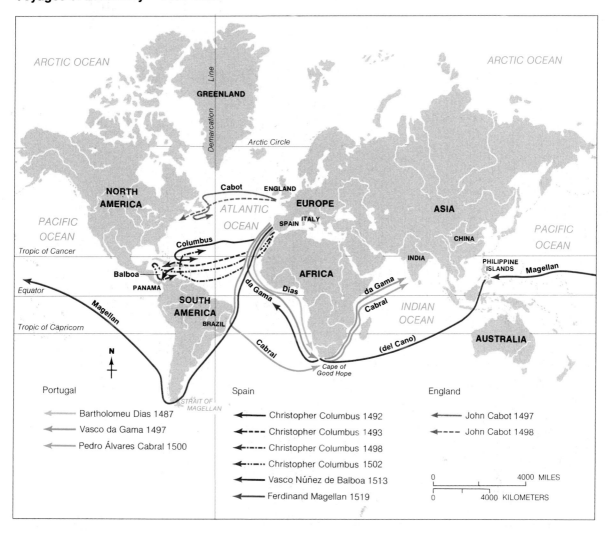

Voyages of Discovery 1487-1522

ARCTIC OCEAN · ARCTIC OCEAN · GREENLAND · Demarcation Line · Arctic Circle · NORTH AMERICA · Cabot · ENGLAND · EUROPE · ASIA · ATLANTIC OCEAN · PACIFIC OCEAN · SPAIN · ITALY · CHINA · PACIFIC OCEAN · Tropic of Cancer · Columbus · INDIA · PHILIPPINE ISLANDS · Magellan · Balboa · AFRICA · da Gama · Equator · PANAMA · Dias · Cabral · INDIAN OCEAN · SOUTH AMERICA · Magellan · da Gama · Tropic of Capricorn · BRAZIL · Cabral · (del Cano) · AUSTRALIA · N · Cape of Good Hope · STRAIT OF MAGELLAN

Portugal
Bartholomeu Dias 1487
Vasco da Gama 1497
Pedro Álvares Cabral 1500

Spain
Christopher Columbus 1492
Christopher Columbus 1493
Christopher Columbus 1498
Christopher Columbus 1502
Vasco Núñez de Balboa 1513
Ferdinand Magellan 1519

England
John Cabot 1497
John Cabot 1498

0   4000 MILES
0   4000 KILOMETERS

tured by the Portuguese. The other ship, under Juan Sebastián del Cano, finally reached the Indies, took on a load of spices, then followed da Gama's route around Africa to Europe. In September 1522, three years after leaving Spain, the ship *Victoria* limped into a Spanish harbor. The 18 sailors on board were the first to circle the earth.

The voyage ended any doubts that America was indeed a new world. And it showed that the earth was far larger than Columbus had believed. New maps and globes would now have to include the broad expanse of the Pacific Ocean.

However, the southwestern passage through the Strait of Magellan was a hazardous route to Asia. Explorers still hoped to find a better water route through America—a Northwest Passage.

THE SEARCH FOR A NORTHWEST PASSAGE

In 1524, two years after the completion of Magellan's voyage, the French began to explore North America. Giovanni da Verrazano (VAHR-rah-TSAH-noh), an Italian sea captain sailing for France, toured the American coast from the Carolinas to Newfoundland. He found no promising water routes, but he did claim land for France—much the same land that Cabot had already claimed for England in 1497.

Ten years later, another French explorer continued the search for a Northwest Passage. In 1534 Jacques Cartier (kar-TYAY) discovered the Gulf of St. Lawrence, and on his second trip he followed

The Search for a Northwest Passage

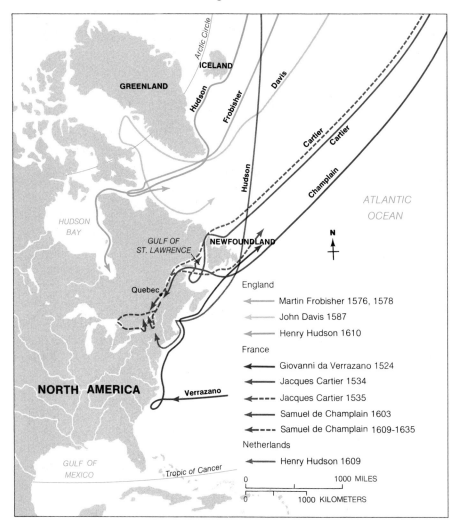

England
← Martin Frobisher 1576, 1578
← John Davis 1587
← Henry Hudson 1610

France
← Giovanni da Verrazano 1524
← Jacques Cartier 1534
←--- Jacques Cartier 1535
← Samuel de Champlain 1603
←--- Samuel de Champlain 1609-1635

Netherlands
← Henry Hudson 1609

0   1000 MILES
0   1000 KILOMETERS

The glazed earthenware figurine of Verrazano, discoverer of New York Bay, was made during his lifetime. Verrazano wrote the first description of the coast of North America from Georgia to Maine.

the St. Lawrence River far inland. He hoped it would lead to China. But on his third voyage, in 1541, he realized it was one more dead end. Still, Cartier claimed the land for France.

For the next half-century, France was torn by religious wars and no more voyages were launched. The search for the Northwest Passage was picked up by two English captains, Martin Frobisher and then John Davis, between 1576 and 1587. In every voyage, the explorers were turned back by Arctic ice packs. But these voyages enabled map makers to draw more accurate outlines of the eastern coast of North America.

By the early 1600s, a new generation of explorers began to probe the interior of the American continent. Between 1603 and 1635, Samuel de Cham-

plain (sham-PLAYN) made 11 trips for France. He traveled into the forests of the Northeast, using the lakes and rivers as pathways into the interior. In 1608 Champlain sailed up the St. Lawrence, established a town at Quebec, and made friends with many of the Algonquian tribes.

In 1609 English explorer Henry Hudson sailed to America for the Dutch East India Company. He found the harbor of New York and a broad river flowing into it from the north. In his ship, the *Half Moon*, he sailed up the river, lured onward by its broad sweep and the taste of salt in the water. Then, near present-day Albany, the river narrowed abruptly and the water no longer tasted of salt. Once more, hope for the Northwest Passage was dashed.

Hudson claimed the lands bordering the river for the Dutch, not knowing that both England and France claimed the same lands. The crew of the *Half Moon* found the Indians willing to trade handsome furs for goods made of metal. Within a short time, a Dutch company had set up a thriving trade.

In 1610 Hudson again sought the Northwest Passage, this time sailing for the English. He and his crew hit a dead end in Hudson Bay and were trapped there by ice for a desperate winter. In the spring, his crew mutinied and set Hudson adrift in an open boat, leaving him no chance for survival.

While all of these explorers were seeking a Northwest Passage, some people had different ideas for the New World. "We might inhabit some part of those countries," said English explorer Sir Humphrey Gilbert, "and settle there such needy people of our country which now trouble the commonwealth." Indeed, England, France, and the Netherlands were all considering colonies in the Americas. All three, though, lagged far behind their powerful neighbor Spain in colonization.

SECTION REVIEW

1. Identify the following: Marco Polo, Prince Henry, Bartholomeu Dias, Vasco da Gama, Treaty of Tordesillas, John Cabot, Amerigo Vespucci, Vasco Núñez de Balboa, Ferdinand Magellan, Giovanni da Verrazano, Jacques Cartier, Henry Hudson.

2. Define the following: feudalism, the Crusades, the Renaissance.

3. (a) What did European traders obtain from the Middle East? (b) Who controlled trade with the Middle East?

4. (a) How did the Crusades contribute to the Renaissance? (b) How did the development of a middle class contribute to the rise of strong monarchies?

5. (a) What Muslim inventions enabled Portuguese navigators to sail out of sight of land? (b) What were Portuguese navigators seeking?

6. List the areas explored by Columbus.

7. What two beliefs about the earth did Magellan's voyage confirm?

8. Why did Europeans search for a Northwest Passage?

SPAIN AND ENGLAND AS RIVALS

READ TO FIND OUT

— how Cortés and Pizarro built Spanish empires in the Americas.

— what legends brought Spanish explorers to Florida and the Southwest.

— how Spain governed its New World empire.

— why the Indians of the Southwest rose in revolt.

— how England challenged Spain's New World trade.

— how the English navy defeated the Spanish Armada.

One day in 1519 a messenger came to Montezuma II, ruler of the Aztec, with news that bearded white strangers were approaching from the east. According to Aztec legend, the bearded white god Quetzalcoatl would come one day from that direction. Montezuma ordered the people to prepare a grand welcome.

The strangers were not gods, but Spanish soldiers led by an adventurer named Hernando Cortés. Adventurers like Cortés would claim Indian lands and create a vast empire for Spain.

THE CONQUEST OF CENTRAL AND SOUTH AMERICA

Spain's first foothold in the New World was Columbus's settlement on the West Indies island of Hispaniola. From the home base of Hispaniola, the Spaniards fanned out onto other West Indies islands—Puerto Rico, Jamaica, and Cuba—and claimed them for Spain.

Some Spaniards who came to these islands were restless adventurers seeking wealth and fame. They found support from the Spanish government, which was interested in further exploration of the Americas for several reasons.

Catholic Spain felt it a duty to spread its religion to the people of the New World. Spain also wanted to discover new sources of wealth and to enlarge its empire. Finally, Spain still hoped to find a sea route to Asia. God, gold, and glory, then, were the driving forces behind the *conquistadors* (kohn-KEES-tah-DORZ)—the conquerors.

Hernando Cortés was a brash and clever conquistador. He had been ordered by the Spanish governor in Cuba to explore the mainland, but he had other ideas. In 1519 Cortés and about five hundred soldiers landed on the coast of Mexico. Ignoring the governor's orders, Cortés led his soldiers toward the Aztec capital, Tenochtitlán.

When Cortés and his soldiers reached Tenochtitlán, they were dazzled. It was, wrote Cortés, "the most beautiful city in the world." Then Montezuma greeted the Spaniards and presented Cortés with gifts of gold. This was what the conquistador sought.

The Spaniards steadily plundered the Aztec empire until the Aztec rose up in revolt. The revolt was followed by four months of war and the Aztec surrender of their city in August 1521. An Aztec poet wrote in anguish: "We have pounded our hands in despair against the adobe walls, for our inheritance, our city, is lost and dead."

Cortés ordered the beautiful city destroyed. A Spanish capital was built at Mexico City, not far from the ruins of Tenochtitlán. Spanish ships loaded with Aztec treasure sailed to Spain from its new empire in Central America.

The empire was expanded by another conquistador, an experienced soldier named Francisco Pizarro (pih-ZAHR-ō). Pizarro received permission from the Crown to conquer a rich Indian empire rumored to be south of Panama. In 1531 Pizarro and his soldiers landed on the Pacific coast of South America and trekked inland to scale the lofty Andes. Along the way, they learned that the Inca Empire in Peru gleamed with the riches they sought. They also learned that the Inca were at war with each other.

Playing on these rivalries, Pizarro's troops managed to capture the Inca ruler, Atahualpa (AHT-ah-WAHL-pah) in 1532. Pizarro demanded a ransom for Atahualpa's freedom. After the Inca provided great stores of treasure, the Spaniards executed their ruler. Then, for almost ten years, the Spaniards battled their way through the Inca Empire. They captured towns, set up outposts, and forced the Inca to work the gold and silver mines. Still more treasure ships headed for Spain.

EXPEDITIONS TO FLORIDA

Meanwhile, conquistadors were pushing north into what is now the United States. One of the first was Juan Ponce de León (POHN-say day-lay-OHN). He had sailed to the Americas on Columbus's second voyage and in 1508 claimed Puerto Rico for Spain. Drawn by Indian legends of a "Fountain of Youth," he explored in 1513 and again in 1521 a peninsula that he named Florida and claimed for Spain. On the basis of that claim, Spain would later establish St. Augustine. St. Augustine was the first permanent European settlement in the area that would eventually be the United States.

The next conquistador to explore Florida, in 1528, was Pánfilo de Narváez (nahr-VAH-ayz). For weeks he and his crew wallowed through the swampy Florida Everglades. Finding no gold, they returned to the coast and set sail for Mexico, but were shipwrecked off the coast of Texas.

For eight years the four survivors of the expedition wandered through Texas, New Mexico, and Arizona and finally reached Mexico City. One survivor, Álvar Núñez Cabeza de Vaca (kah-BAY-sah day VAH-kuh), told exciting tales of the people and places he had seen.

THE SEARCH FOR THE SEVEN CITIES

The Spaniards had heard legends of seven magnificent cities in the lands north of Mexico, and some believed that Cabeza de Vaca must have seen them. This prompted Spanish authorities to choose Marcos de Niza (NEE-sah), a priest, to lead an expedition into New Mexico and Arizona in 1539. Estevanico (es-tay-vah-NEE-kō), a black slave who was another survivor of the Narváez expedition, acted as guide.

Posing as a medicine man in bright robes and a plumed headdress, Estevanico was sent ahead to pave the way among the Pueblo Indians. He sent a message to Niza that he was hearing about cities full of turquoise and gold. Niza followed Estevanico's trail until he got word that his guide had been killed. Then he turned back.

The Spanish did not give up, however. A dashing officer named Francisco Vásquez de Coronado (KOR-uh-NAH-dō) was chosen to lead a grand expedition in search of the golden cities. Between 1540 and 1542, the company wandered through the southwestern desert and north into the Great Plains as far as Kansas. They found villages, "monstrous beasts" called buffalo, and "much very fine pasture land, with good grass." However, a discouraged Coronado reported, "there is not any gold . . . in all that country."

THE JOURNEYS OF DE SOTO AND CABRILLO

While Coronado was roaming the Southwest, two other Spaniards explored still more of the United States area. In 1539 Hernando de Soto, an imposing figure in gold-plated armor, sailed from Cuba to Florida.

For the next three years, de Soto and his soldiers explored the Southeast and traveled as far west as Oklahoma. In their travels they came upon the continent's mightiest river, the Mississippi. "A man standing on the shore could not be told," reported one of the explorers, "whether he were a man or something else, from the other side."

In 1542 Juan Rodríguez Cabrillo (kah-BREE-yō) who had been with Cortés in Mexico, sailed up the western coast of North America, seeking riches.

This seventeenth-century Spanish frontier guard was sent to protect New Spain both from the Indians and from rival European nations.

The red walls of Canyon de Chelly, Arizona, have been adorned with rock paintings for about two thousand years. One of the finest in the canyon is this Navaho painting representing Spanish soldiers with flintlock rifles. Nearby are many Anasazi paintings.

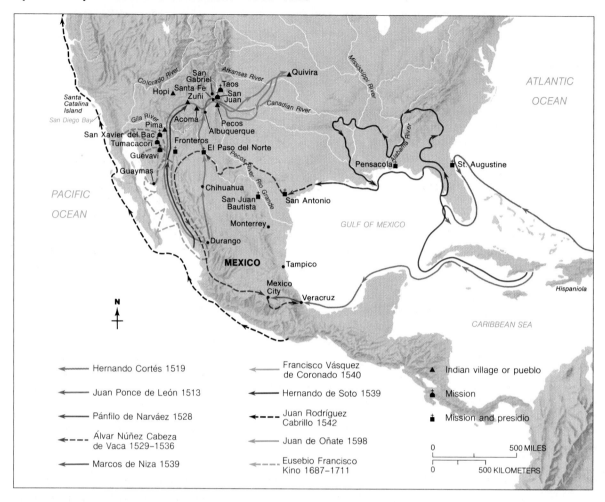

In 1598 Juan de Oñate led an expedition north along the Rio Grande. With Oñate came priests to convert the Indians and soldiers to maintain peace. Settlers came, too, bringing horses, cattle, and sheep. Oñate planted the first Spanish colony in New Mexico at San Juan.

For years, Spaniards had read of "an island named California," which abounded with gold and precious stones. Cabrillo did not find such wealth, but he claimed for Spain San Diego Bay, Santa Catalina Island, and other points along the California coast. More than two hundred years would pass, however, before Spaniards settled this coastland.

RULING THE SPANISH EMPIRE

As Spain's empire grew larger, the king wanted to make sure that the colonies were strictly managed. To safeguard the Spanish in America, military garrisons called *presidios* were established. Presidio sol-

diers not only fought Indians, but they also escorted wagons carrying gold and silver, delivered mail, and served as police for nearby towns.

The Spaniards also had to decide how to deal with the people they conquered. Many Spaniards took steps to spread their faith. By converting the Indians to Christianity, they believed, they were saving their souls. So from the beginning of Spanish colonization, Catholic priests came to the New World to establish *missions*.

Missions were self-sufficient little communities, much like the old European feudal estates. There were workshops filled with iron and steel hoes, pliers, clamps, and plows brought from Europe.

MAP READING
SPANISH EXPLORATION AND SETTLEMENT 1519–1720

Map reading is an important skill in studying history. A map is a visual tool that can give many different kinds of information about the earth.

In map reading, it is important to look first at the elements, or parts, of the map. Use the map entitled ''Spanish Exploration and Settlement 1519-1720'' to answer the following questions.

1. *Title and area.* What does the title tell you about the purpose of the map? What area of the world is shown on the map?

2. *Direction.* Look at the direction indicator. What information does it give? In which general direction did the Spanish conquistador Hernando Cortés travel to accomplish his bold journey of exploration in the year 1519?

3. *Scale.* The scale on a map shows how distances on the map relate to actual distances on the earth. A map scale may indicate that a line 1 inch long represents 500 miles. It may indicate that a line 2 centimeters long represents 12 kilometers. Use the scale indicator to give these approximate distances: Ponce de Leon's route, Cabrillo's route, the distance from Mexico City to Santa Fe.

4. *Topography.* Topography is the representation of the surface areas of the earth, including mountains, rivers, and lakes. What rivers were followed by Hernando de Soto? Which area might have been easier to explore—New Mexico or Florida? Why?

5. *Legend.* The legend tells the meaning of each symbol used on the map. Using the legend, give the name of one Indian pueblo, one Spanish settlement, one mission, and one presidio.

After you have looked at the elements of a map, you can interpret the map as a whole.

6. By 1720 what areas of North America had been explored by the Spanish? What areas had been settled, or colonized? As of 1720 what was the last area the Spanish had explored? What might have been the reason why this area was explored last?

Priests also brought foods and animals from Europe, and they proceeded to teach the Indians how to live like Europeans.

The priests taught the Indians to tend horses, cattle, and sheep and to plant European crops like sugar and wheat. They introduced cucumbers, artichokes, and a variety of fruits, including apricots and pears. They also doctored the Indians, especially after many were stricken with diseases brought to the Americas by the Europeans. But many of the priests forced the Indians to accept Christianity, sometimes whipping those who refused to change religions.

Other Spaniards were more interested in the Indians' strength than in their souls. Spanish settlers called for laborers to work the mines, to build cities and churches, and to tend crops. The Crown had forbidden slavery, but a system called *encomienda* (en-kō-mee-EN-dah) developed to fill Spanish needs in the Americas. The system let Spaniards maintain large numbers of Indian laborers.

Under this system, an expanse of land and the Indians who lived on it were entrusted to a Spanish settler, usually a conquistador or other privileged colonist. The settler was allowed to use the Indians as laborers, but also was expected to care for them and make sure they were taught Christian ways. In practice, though, the settler usually treated the Indians as mere slaves.

Bartolomé de Las Casas and other priests often protested bitterly against the settlers' treatment of Indians. In response, the government and the Crown made attempts to correct the abuses. But Spain was too far away to enforce policies made to protect the Indians.

Over time, the hardships of life under Spanish rule and the lack of immunity to European diseases took their toll on the Indian population. The number of native people in Central and South America was so greatly reduced that Spaniards turned to black slaves brought from Africa as a source of labor.

SPANISH NORTH AMERICA

In 1610 Pedro de Peralta founded a colony in a fertile valley in New Mexico and called the city Santa Fe, meaning "Holy Faith." This became the capital of the northern region of New Spain.

The establishment of Santa Fe brought decades of calm for the Spanish in New Mexico. But many Indians grew to resent their conquerors. As the Pueblo Indians' bitterness grew, a Tewa shaman named Pope (PŌ-peh) urged the people to rise up against the Spanish. In August 1680 Pope and his followers struck. Throughout the region, settlers and priests were killed and churches burned. After a courageous, but doomed defense, the Spaniards retreated from New Mexico.

Gradually, the Spanish edged back into New Mexico, and in 1692 they regained Santa Fe. This time, the Spanish government was determined not only to hold New Mexico, but also to expand its lands. While Spaniards regained New Mexico, a priest named Eusebio Francisco Kino (KEE-noh) was advancing into southern Arizona. Between 1687 and 1711, he explored and set up a chain of missions.

Spanish missions and settlements were also established in Texas in the early 1700s. But the Indians were determined to hold to their ways of life. The Pima and Papago rose in revolt, the Comanche and Apache raided, and many of the Spanish settlements in Arizona and Texas were abandoned.

CONFLICT WITH ENGLAND

In the sixteenth century, Spain was the only nation that had permanent settlements in the New World. In Europe, Spain controlled the Netherlands, parts of Italy, and in 1580 conquered the kingdom of Portugal and held it for 60 years. There was a common saying in Europe: "When Spain moves, the world trembles." Spain's King Philip II ruled over what was then the world's greatest empire.

Europe, however, was going through a period of great change in the 1500s. Some of those changes led other nations to challenge Spain's supremacy.

The Roman Catholic Church, based in Rome and headed by the Pope, had long controlled the religious and much of the political life of western Europe. However, in 1517 a German priest named Martin Luther protested what he felt were false doctrines and corrupt practices within the Church. Others, such as John Calvin in Switzerland, joined their voices of protest to Luther's, and the Protestant movement swept Europe.

The movement, known as the Protestant Reformation, shook Christianity to its foundations. It split the Church in two: the Roman Catholic religion and a growing number of Protestant denominations, including Lutheranism and Calvinism. The Reformation also broke the Catholic Church's hold in several nations, such as the Netherlands, which became Protestant.

In 1534 King Henry VIII of England officially cut England's church loose from Rome's control. Henry declared himself "pope, king, and emperor" of England. Over the years, the English church moved toward Protestantism. When Henry's daughter Elizabeth I took the throne, England's religion—by now a mixture of Catholicism and Protestantism—became known as Anglicanism.

Elizabeth ruled England from 1558 to 1603. Reared as a Protestant, she became the champion of the Protestant nations against the great defender of Catholicism—Spain. With the English queen's aid, Dutch Protestants in the Netherlands were able to throw off Spanish rule. This religious conflict alone would have been enough to cause trouble between Spain and England. But there were other sources of friction that fed the growing rivalry.

THE SEA DOGS

By the time of Elizabeth's reign, the English were fully ready to challenge Spain for a share in the New World trade. One determined English trader and sailor was John Hawkins. The shrewd Hawkins found that he could obtain slaves in Africa and sell them to Spanish landowners in Caribbean ports for gold, silver, and pearls. Soon Hawkins was sailing with a fleet of ships, some quietly supplied by Queen Elizabeth. When the Spanish government complained to the English queen, she coolly brushed off its protests.

Francis Drake, another English sailor, vowed to "singe the king of Spain's beard" and launched a career of plundering Spanish ships and towns in the New World. Drake and other "sea dogs" were often joined by groups of blacks who had once been slaves, but had escaped from the Spaniards and settled throughout the Caribbean.

In about 1593 an unknown artist illustrated the strong leadership of Elizabeth I. The queen is shown standing on a map of England.

In 1577, with Queen Elizabeth's unofficial backing, Drake set out to probe the Pacific coast of Spain's New World empire. He sailed his ship, the *Golden Hind*, through the Strait of Magellan and made his way up the Pacific coast of South America, raiding Spanish towns and ships. Drake continued as far northward as San Francisco Bay and claimed the area for England. Then, rather than face Spanish warships on the return voyage, he followed Magellan's route across the Pacific. Bulging with Spanish treasure, the *Golden Hind* sailed up England's River Thames in 1580. It was the second ship in history to sail around the world.

Drake's success and booty—including tons of silver and gold—enraged King Philip II of Spain. He demanded that Drake and his crew be punished. Instead, Queen Elizabeth made Drake a knight.

THE SPANISH ARMADA

For Philip of Spain, the English challenge had gone far enough. In 1588 Philip launched an invasion force to crush England and return it to Catholicism. His fleet of 130 ships, called the Invincible Armada, carried more than 19,000 soldiers and 8,000 sailors.

As the Armada reached the English Channel, the English fired their long-range guns, and the two sides fought for a week. Then, one night, the English filled eight ships with gunpowder, set them ablaze, and sent them toward the Spanish fleet. When the Armada scattered into open waters, the ships were easy prey for the English. The Armada then escaped to the North Sea, where a fierce storm destroyed more of Philip's ships than the English had.

The defeat of the Armada wounded a Spain already weakening from frequent wars and a poorly managed economy. Gradually, Spain's power began to decline in both Europe and the Americas. By the end of the 1500s, England, France, and the Netherlands were challenging Spain—and each other—for claims in North America.

SECTION REVIEW

1. Identify the following: Hernando Cortés, Francisco Pizarro, Juan Ponce de León, Álvar Núñez Cabeza de Vaca, Francisco Vásquez de Coronado, Pope, King Philip II, Martin Luther, Elizabeth I, Sir Francis Drake.

2. Define the following: conquistador, presidio, Protestant Reformation, sea dogs, Armada.

3. List four reasons for Spain's continued exploration of the Americas.

4. (a) What was the largest of the rivers observed by Hernando de Soto? (b) What areas of North America did Juan Rodríguez Cabrillo claim for Spain?

5. Explain the encomienda system. In what ways was it meant to be better than slavery?

6. Describe the extent of the Spanish empire in the 1500s.

7. How did religion cause conflict between Spain and England?

8. (a) Describe the defeat of the Spanish Armada. (b) What were two other causes for the decline of Spanish power?

SUMMARY

For thousands of years, different groups of people lived in North and South America without experiencing contact with people in other areas of the world. The cultures of these early Americans varied greatly. Some lived in small tribes, while others built huge empires.

In what is now the United States, Indian tribes flourished in all regions. South of the United States, the Maya, Aztec, and Inca lived in complex societies.

These early Americans did not know of the existence of Europe, nor did Europeans know of the Americas. In the 1400s Europeans were emerging from the feudal era, as villages gave way to towns and cities. Because of the Crusades and the travels of Marco Polo, Europeans had heard of the riches of the Far East and had become interested in exploration. The meeting of the two hemispheres—Europe and the Americas—became inevitable.

Portugal took the lead in the race for exploration with enlightened and daring sailors like Bartholomeu Dias and Vasco da Gama. But it refused to finance the dreams of the Genoese sailor, Christopher Columbus. Backed by Spain, Columbus reached the Americas.

France, the Netherlands, and England soon had explorers claiming lands in the new-found continents. Spain maintained its strong foothold in the New World, however. Cortés defeated the Aztec in Mexico, and Pizarro conquered the Inca in South America. Then Spanish interest turned to North America, as Ponce de León and Narváez explored Florida, and Coronado explored the Southwest. The Spanish not only explored. They established missions and presidios in New Mexico and, later, in Arizona, Texas, and California.

Spain and England emerged as the two strongest nations in Europe by the middle of the sixteenth century. The religious differences between them intensified their rivalry for power.

Conflicts led to a great sea battle in 1588. The Invincible Armada, which sailed from Spain to attack England, was defeated. Gradually, Spain's power declined in Europe and the New World. Other nations stood ready to fill the gap.

A sixteenth-century Indian drawing shows Cortés at the head of his army. With Cortés is Marina, an Indian woman who was his interpreter and his advisor on the affairs of Mexico.

CHAPTER REVIEW

1. Indian tribes were organized in many different ways. Describe the form of government practiced by each of the following: (a) the Eskimo (b) the Iroquois (c) the Plains tribes (d) the Pueblo.

2. Construct a chart to answer the following. Compare the location, environment, housing, and chief means of obtaining food of specific Indian tribes in each of these areas: Arctic, Eastern Woodlands, Great Plains, Northwest Coast, Southwest, Mexico, Peru.

3. (a) What was the original purpose of the Crusades? (b) How did the Crusades help to bring about the Renaissance? (c) How did the Renaissance help to bring about exploration?

4. (a) How did Marco Polo create widespread interest in Asia? (b) How did this interest in Asia eventually affect Prince Henry of Portugal? (c) What did Prince Henry do as a result?

5. Describe similarities and differences in the voyages of Christopher Columbus and Ferdinand Magellan with regard to the following. (a) the purpose of the voyage (b) difficulties encountered (c) discoveries (d) results

6. The European discovery of the Americas was the work of many explorers. Explain how the explorations of each of the following expanded knowledge of the Americas. (a) Amerigo Vespucci (b) Vasco Nuñez de Balboa (c) Ferdinand Magellan (d) Jacques Cartier (e) Martin Frobisher (f) Henry Hudson

7. (a) What was the result of Cortés's expedition to the Aztec empire? (b) What was the result of Pizarro's expedition to the Inca empire? (c) Explain why the expeditions of Cortés and Pizarro led finally to the exploration of the American Southwest. Give two examples.

8. Spain, England, France, and the Netherlands all claimed possessions in the Americas. (a) What parts of the American continents did each claim by the middle of the 1500s? On what was each claim based? (b) Which nation had the strongest claim? Why?

9. (a) How did the Protestant Reformation lead to tension between Spain and England? (b) How did Sir Francis Drake add to the tension between the two nations? (c) What was the eventual outcome of this struggle?

10. What brought each of the following to the North American continent? (a) the Vikings (b) Christopher Columbus (c) Giovanni da Verrazano, (d) Hernando Cortés (e) Eusebio Francisco Kino

ISSUES AND IDEAS

1. (a) If you were an Artec official in 1519, how would you justify Aztec claims to Tenochtitlán? (b) If you were a Spanish official in 1519, how would you justify Spanish claims to Mexico City? (c) Do the claims of each official necessarily lead to conflict? Explain your view.

2. Explain how each of the following developments led to the next: the Crusades, trade, cities, middle class, and strong, unified monarchies.

3. The times were right for Europeans to find the Americas. If Columbus had not, someone else would have. Agree or disagree with this statement, and support your opinion with evidence.

SKILLS WORKSHOP

1. *Maps.* Look at the map on page 17 of your text. Now find the route taken by da Gama. In which directions did he travel? About how far did he travel? In which directions did Magellan travel? Find Cabral's route. In which directions did he sail? About how far did he travel?

2. *Maps.* Look at the Resource Center at the back of your book. Find the map entitled "Physical Map of the United States." This map shows topography, or the physical features of the land. Name the major physical barriers faced by explorers of North America. These physical barriers may include large bodies of water, mountain ranges, deserts, etc.

PAST AND PRESENT

1. (a) How was discovery and exploration of the Americas made possible by advances in technology? (b) Find out about a recent technological advance. Explain how this new idea or invention is making great changes in our lives today. How might this idea or invention affect the future?

2. Indian tribes have left their influence in different parts of the United States. England, France, Spain, and the Netherlands also influenced different areas of the country. Describe the influence of one or more of these tribes and/or nations in the area where you live. Consider place names, foods, architecture, arts and crafts, clothing, and law.

A sixteenth-century geography book showed a sailor sighting his position by the stars. The sailor stood on shore because it was difficult to sight from aboard a tossing ship.

CHAPTER 2

PLANTING COLONIES

1500–1750

THE FRENCH, DUTCH, AND ENGLISH PLANT COLONIES
THE FOUNDING OF NEW ENGLAND
THE PROPRIETARY COLONIES

In 1623 Lady Margaret Wyatt wrote a letter to her sister in England. Wyatt had voyaged from England to the New World, and found the Atlantic crossing miserable. Her only defense against illness and crowding was a sense of humor:

"Dear Sister, ere this you should have heard from me, had not the extremity of sickness till now hindered me. For our ship was so pestered with people and goods that we were so full of infection that after a while we saw little but throwing folks over board. It pleased God to send me my health till I came to shore. . . . There never came [a] ship so full to Virginia as ours. I had not so much as my cabin free to myself. Our Captain seemed to be troubled at it, and . . . to make the people amends died himself. . . .

"This was our fortune at the sea, and the land little better, for as well our people as our cattle have died, that we are all undone, especially we that are newcomers, and unless our friends help us it will go hard with us next winter."

Colonists sailing for the New World needed more than money for the passage and provisions. They also needed a pioneering spirit. Crossing the Atlantic Ocean was like stumbling through a thick fog into the unknown, for few colonists had ever been to sea.

Yet people embarked in ship after ship from England and the continent of Europe. Many voyagers were fleeing religious persecution at home and found a haven in the New World. When the settlers arrived they found an untamed, often deadly wilderness. But they also found what they had left Europe to seek—land and opportunity.

Colonization of North America's eastern seaboard spanned more than a century. Four European nations planted flags there. Sweden and the Netherlands gained only brief toeholds in North America. France seeded the wilderness with fur traders. England, however, planted thirteen colonies that doggedly took root in the new land.

THE FRENCH, DUTCH, AND ENGLISH PLANT COLONIES

READ TO FIND OUT

— how colonies benefited the economies of European nations.

— how New France and New Netherland were established.

— what happened to England's first attempts to colonize North America.

— how English colonies were financed.

— how Jamestown survived and succeeded.

— how the House of Burgesses brought representative government to Virginia.

The Spanish had shown that fortunes could be made from the precious resources of the New World, especially gold and silver. This lesson was not lost on the French, Dutch, and English, who had their own hopes of getting a foothold in the New World. Their reasons varied, but the dream of riches was a vivid one that they all shared. This dream was acted out in an English stage comedy in 1605, in which a sea captain told his companion what awaited them in the New World:

> I tell thee, gold is more plentiful there than copper is with us . . . all the prisoners they take are fettered in gold; and for rubies and diamonds, they go forth on holidays and gather 'em by the sea-shore.

MERCANTILISM

Gold shone in the dream of sea captains. It also formed the heart of an economic system known as **mercantilism**, popular in Europe between the fifteenth and eighteenth centuries. Mercantilism was an economic approach to gaining national power.

As the European nations struggled for power, they realized that the strength of a nation depended directly on the strength of its economy. A strong economy was founded on a treasury full of gold and silver. With such wealth a government could build powerful armies and navies and strengthen its rule. Thus, mercantilists argued, a nation should manage its economy in whatever way was necessary to fill the treasury.

One way a nation could do this was to improve its **balance of trade**—the difference between the value of goods exported, or sold abroad, and the value of goods imported, or bought from other nations. If a nation could sell more goods to other nations than it bought from them, it would have a favorable balance of trade. Silver and gold would flow into the national treasury. To achieve this healthy balance, however, a nation needed plenty of customers. If it could not sell enough to other nations, which were also seeking a favorable balance of trade, then the national treasury would shrink.

A nation that had colonies had an advantage. Colonies provided a ready market for the goods of a nation. Also, colonies could be a new source of raw materials that had previously been imported from other countries. And, as Spain had found, colonies

It was not unusual for an expedition to include an artist. In about 1700 a French artist traveling with an exploring party made this sketch of various Indian fishing methods.

could be a treasure house of gold and silver. So, in the late 1500s and early 1600s, England, France, and the Netherlands all looked to the New World.

NEW FRANCE

Since the voyages of Verrazano and Cartier, in 1524 and 1534, the French had been fishing in an area off the Newfoundland coast called the Grand Banks. The French began landing along the coast to cure their fish so it would not spoil on the journey back to Europe. Soon they were trading guns and other metal items for furs trapped by Indians in the area. In Europe, these furs—especially beaver furs—were prized. The pelts were turned into expensive coats and stylish hats.

The French had found their golden dream in furs. It was to build up the fur trade that Samuel de Champlain established Quebec on the St. Lawrence River when he was exploring the Northeast in 1608. This was the first permanent French settlement in the New World.

It was Champlain, too, who probed the inland wilderness by traveling rivers and lakes—a pattern other French traders and explorers would follow. And it was Champlain who made friends with the Algonquian tribes in the Great Lakes region. On several occasions, he aided the Huron in their challenge to the stronger Iroquois. This gave the French valuable Huron allies—and Iroquois enemies.

Most of the French who came to Quebec and other parts of New France came for furs. They were known as *coureurs de bois* (koo-rur deh BWAH), "forest runners." They brought boatloads of goods to an Indian camp and traded until their boats were piled high with furs. Sometimes, they lived among the Indians, worked the trap lines with them, and married into the tribe.

Soon, forts were built along the major trade routes. Both Indians and traders often camped near these forts, which eventually grew into towns.

NEW NETHERLAND

The prospect of trade also led the Netherlands to establish its first New World settlement. The Dutch were excellent traders. In 1621 merchants set up the Dutch West India Company to trade in America. Sponsored by the company, 30 Dutch families settled in 1624 on the lands that Henry Hudson had earlier claimed for the Netherlands.

On the bank of the Hudson River they built a trading post called Fort Orange (now Albany). Smaller posts were strung along the Hudson, and along the Delaware and Connecticut rivers. Then in 1626 the colony's governor bought the southern tip of Manhattan Island from the Indians. This settlement, known as New Amsterdam, became the capital of the Dutch colony of New Netherland.

In 1629 the Dutch West India Company developed a plan to attract settlers to its fledgling colony. To anyone who would pay the cost of transporting 50 settlers to the colony, the company would grant a large estate along the Hudson or other navigable river in the area. These landlords, called *patroons,* were given feudal rights to the land, including the

NIEUW AMSTERDAM

The Dutch set up a trading post on the Hudson River near Albany. Dutch traders made friends with the Iroquois who controlled a land rich in furs. From the port of New Amsterdam, shown here as it appeared on a map in 1655, Dutch traders shipped furs to Europe.

right to hold court. Tenant farmers would work the land, paying the patroons rent in crops and livestock.

ENGLAND'S ATTEMPTS TO START COLONIES

Like the French and the Dutch, the English hoped to find the New World riches and expand their trade. The first English colony was established by Sir Walter Raleigh in Virginia, a vast area of land that stretched from Spanish Florida north to French claims in Maine. In 1585 Raleigh sent settlers to Virginia, and they landed on Roanoke Island, just off present-day North Carolina. But clashes with Indians and Spaniards soon drove these settlers back to England.

Finally, in 1587, another group of men, women, and children landed on Roanoke. The colony was again a failure. A visitor to Roanoke in 1590 found the colony deserted. There were no signs of a struggle and no evidence of what had happened to the colonists. The only clue left by this "lost colony" was the word CROATOAN carved on a doorpost.

Because the Crown did not have enough gold to finance colonies, the next step into North America was taken by the *joint-stock company.* This form of business organization had developed in the 1500s. Lured by the profits of trading with other European nations, particularly by selling English woolen cloth, English merchants had begun to operate on a larger scale. They pooled the money of investors by selling stock, or shares, in companies.

With dozens of people investing in an enterprise, more goods could be bought and sold. The company could even form its own trading fleet. And the Crown granted each company a charter, giving it control of trade in a certain geographic area.

In 1606, Elizabeth's successor, King James I, granted charters to two joint-stock companies to colonize North America. One group, which set up the London Company, was given rights to land along the coast of present-day North Carolina and Virginia. The other joint-stock company became the Plymouth Company, with rights farther north, around New England.

Deborah Glen, the daughter of prosperous Dutch parents, was seventeen when her portrait was painted by a Hudson River Valley artist, Pieter Vanderlyn, in about 1737.

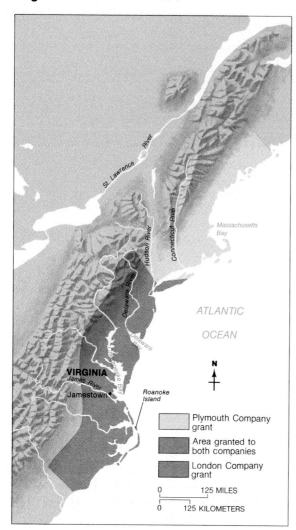

The Plymouth Company disbanded after a failed attempt to colonize Maine in 1607. Some of its members formed a new company which later leased land to the Pilgrims.

The London Company was the first to launch an expedition. In December 1606 the company sent out three ships for Virginia—the *Susan Constant*, the *Godspeed*, and the *Discovery*—carrying 105 men and boys. A ballad was composed for their venture, reflecting the hopes of all:

> And cheerfully at sea,
> Success you still entice,
>   To get the pearl and gold,
>   *And ours to hold*,
>   VIRGINIA,
> Earth's only Paradise.

JAMESTOWN

The settlers stood on the banks of a river that they named the James, for their king, and watched the three ships disappear on the homeward voyage. "Earth's only Paradise," in reality, was a rude shock. For their settlement, the colonists had chosen a low, swampy area because that site could be easily defended against Indians or Spaniards. However, the swamp swarmed with malaria-bearing mosquitoes.

Most of the settlers were "gentlemen," unused to work, anxious only to search for gold. There were gold refiners and perfume makers in the party, but few farmers or toolmakers, who would have had the skills to live in the wilderness. They survived their first weeks on a daily ration of wheat and barley.

During the first seven months, 73 settlers died of hunger and disease. The rest survived primarily because of the efforts of Captain John Smith, a seasoned soldier, explorer, and very practical person. Smith approached neighboring Indians, a united group of Algonquian tribes under the powerful rule of Chief Powhatan. "It pleased God (in our extremity) to move the Indians to bring us corn, ere it was half ripe, to refresh us," Smith wrote, "when we rather expected they would destroy us." The Indians taught the settlers to plant the corn and to use nets for catching fish.

Chances for survival looked stronger in 1608. Two ships arrived with fresh supplies and more colonists. And the company council that governed the colony placed Smith in charge. During the winter of 1608–1609, Smith tried to bring order to Jamestown. "You must obey this for a law," Smith declared. "He that will not work shall not eat." Soon the gentlemen were producing pitch, tar, and soap, tending the livestock, and readying the ground for crops.

The struggling colony suffered a major setback in the fall of 1609, when Smith was burned in a gunpowder explosion and returned to England. With his departure, discipline again declined and relations with the Indians soured. More colonists had arrived, but without the necessary provisions. The winter of 1609–1610 became known as the "starving time," and only 60 colonists survived it.

Many were ready to give up. If Jamestown did not make profits for the London Company, they figured, then surely it was doomed. But in 1610 one

In 1585 artist John White accompanied the Roanoke settlers. White's drawing of Pomeiooc, one of the first villages visited by the Roanoke colonists, shows the longhouses, the thatched construction, and the stockade typical of Atlantic coastal villages.

more ship of settlers arrived. It seemed the colony would struggle on. As one optimistic colonist wrote in *Newes from Virginia*:

> Let England knowe our willingnesse,
>   For that our worke is good;
> Wee hope to plant a nation,
>   Where none before hath stood.

JAMESTOWN TAKES ROOT

Very slowly, Jamestown crept toward prosperity. Around 1612 a colonist named John Rolfe planted some West Indies tobacco seeds in the fertile soil of Virginia. He also developed a method to cure the tobacco, so that it could be shipped long distances.

The sweet Jamestown tobacco was an instant success in England, despite King James's disapproval. Tobacco smoking, he said, was "loathesome to the eye, hateful to the nose, harmful to the brain, dangerous to the lungs." But to Jamestown, tobacco was an economic base on which the settlement could prosper. The old obsession with gold gave way to an obsession with tobacco. Colonists planted it everywhere, even in the streets.

Because tobacco crops quickly exhausted the soil, the planters were constantly looking for new fields. They began taking over Indian lands, and the settlement inched up the James River and other nearby rivers. This caused friction with the Indians, but John Rolfe improved relations when he married Pocahontas, daughter of Chief Powhatan.

The London Company saw that it might yet make a profit by controlling the Virginia tobacco trade. To give the colony a boost, the company started in 1618 the "headright" land system to attract settlers.

Previously, the settlers had labored on common land for the company. Under the headright system, people for the first time were lured to America by the promise of owning land. New colonists would receive 50 acres (20.2 hectares). Eventually, the headrights grew even more generous. Colonists could then get 50 acres (20.2 hectares) for each new settler whose passage they would pay. Wealthy colonists who paid enough headrights could own a plantation covering hundreds of acres.

By 1619 Jamestown was beginning to look like a proper English town, with shops, churches, schools, and inns. The main lack was women. Except for a handful of women who had earlier crossed over with their husbands, Virginia remained a colony of men and boys.

So London Company agents combed the English countryside, praising Virginia. Many poor farm families believed the agents' promises that their daughters could escape a life of poverty by going to Virginia. Many women signed marriage contracts, which they could break on arrival if the men did not meet with their approval. Others signed contracts as **indentured servants,** agreeing to work for a period of four to seven years for the colonist who paid for their passage. At the end of that period they would receive their own land. In 1619 the first shipload of women and girls arrived in Virginia.

Another ship arrived that year—a Dutch trading ship with a cargo of 20 blacks from Africa. The blacks joined the Jamestown settlement as indentured servants. They were promised a parcel of land after completing their period of service.

Universal Magazine explained tobacco production to its readers. The British government encouraged Virginians to plant other crops, but none were as profitable as tobacco.

STEPS TO REPRESENTATIVE GOVERNMENT

Because the settlers had come to Virginia as employees of the London Company, the company acted as government. The company-appointed council ruled until 1609, when John Smith returned to England. Since the council proved ineffective without Smith, the company then appointed a governor to run Jamestown.

Gradually, the company shifted its thinking as Virginia grew bigger and more self-sufficient. In 1619 company management suggested that the people of Virginia "might have a hand in the governing of themselves." Management ordered the governor to call an election.

In each of Virginia's settled districts, the adult males elected two representatives, called *burgesses,* to attend a legislative, or law-making, assembly. In August this general assembly—composed of the governor, his council, and 22 burgesses—met briefly at the Jamestown church. With this first session of the House of Burgesses, representative government took root in America.

The seeds of representative government had been planted long ago in feudal England, in a meadow called Runnymede by the River Thames. There, in 1215, a group of barons and Church leaders forced their monarch, King John, to approve a charter of rights they had drawn up. This *Magna Carta* (Latin for "Great Charter") placed the king under the supremacy of law.

Several articles in the Magna Carta limited royal power by stating that the king must gain the barons' consent in deciding important matters and in levying taxes. One article gave certain rights to all *freemen,* or property holders. It stated that no freeman would be imprisoned or deprived of property illegally or without a trial by jury.

In 1265 England took another step toward a constitutional government with the establishment of Parliament, a great council that advised the monarch. Over the decades Parliament gained the right to pass laws.

The Magna Carta and Parliament had set a foundation for government in England. Steps to representative government in Virginia set a foundation for government in England's colonies.

VIRGINIA BECOMES A ROYAL COLONY

This measure of self-government, however, did not solve Virginia's problems. For the next couple of years the colony struggled, losing hundreds of settlers to disease, accidents, and departures back to England. Then in 1622 disaster struck.

The Powhatan Indians had long resented the English crowding onto tribal lands. On March 22 the Powhatan attacked, killing more than 300 colonists—one third of the colony. Skirmishes between the Powhatan and the colonists continued for several years.

These events convinced King James I that the colony was being mismanaged. He sued the London Company, claiming that it had failed to accomplish what it intended. The king won the case in 1624, and the company's charter was taken away.

Virginia became a **royal colony.** The Crown, rather than the company, now appointed the governor and his council of advisors. Although the authority for an assembly had disappeared with the company, Virginians continued to meet. Their assembly—the House of Burgesses—passed laws as needed, which could be vetoed by either the governor or the king.

One of the first laws that the House of Burgesses passed forbade the royal governor or council to levy taxes on the colony, its land, or products without the authority of the assembly. England now had its first colony firmly planted on American soil. And clearly, England's colonists wanted to have some voice in governing it.

SECTION REVIEW

1. Identify the following: *coureurs de bois*, John Smith, Chief Powhatan, John Rolfe, Pocahontas, Magna Carta, Parliament, House of Burgesses.

2. (a) According to mercantilists, what made a nation strong? (b) Under mercantilism, how did a nation expect to benefit from its colonies?

3. What was France's main interest in North America?

4. (a) Describe the extent of Dutch settlement in North America. (b) Explain the patroon system.

5. How were joint-stock companies an advantage in colonization?

6. What four important changes took place in Jamestown from 1618 to 1619?

7. Describe the terms of an indentured servant's contract.

8. (a) Describe the House of Burgesses. (b) What was one of the first laws passed by this assembly?

THE FOUNDING OF NEW ENGLAND

READ TO FIND OUT

— **why people left Europe to settle in North America.**

— **how the Pilgrims established Plymouth Colony.**

— **how the Puritans established Massachusetts Bay Colony.**

— **how Massachusetts Bay Colony was governed.**

— **why people from Massachusetts settled Rhode Island, Connecticut, New Hampshire, and Maine.**

— **how war prompted colonists to organize.**

Many years passed between the planting of Jamestown and the next English foothold in North America. In 1614, while colonists struggled to survive in the hot, swampy wilderness of Virginia, the bold Captain John Smith voyaged to the coast of New England. He wrote:

> It is a country rather to frighten than delight one, and how to describe a more plain spectacle of desolation, or more barren, I know not; yet are those rocky isles so furnished with good woods, springs, fruits, fish and fowl, and the sea the strangest fish pond I ever saw, that it makes me think, the valleys and plains and interior parts may . . . be very fertile. But there is no country so fertile that hath not some part barren, and New England is great enough to make many kingdoms.

THE HUNGER FOR LAND

No one rushed to colonize Smith's New England. However, conditions in England—some longstanding and some new—would soon drive a flood of people across the Atlantic.

In England, the amount of available land had been shrinking for over 100 years. This was linked to England's growing strength in the European rivalry over trade.

Around the late 1400s, one of England's most profitable exports was woolen cloth. With the growing demand for wool, landowners enclosed, or fenced in, vast tracts of land to raise more sheep. The farmers who had rented that land were evicted.

Throughout the 1500s, thousands of farm workers roamed the countryside, searching for work or food. Others crowded into the cities, swelling their populations. Some were driven by desperation into begging or stealing. For many of these people, the chance for a fresh start would be worth the hardships of an unknown wilderness.

THE PURITANS

The land and opportunity promised in America were an attraction. But many in England had another vision of the New World—America as a refuge.

Ever since the Reformation, religious conflict had seethed around the Church of England. By law, all English people had to belong to the Anglican Church. Some people, however, kept their Catholic beliefs and hoped to practice freely their religion again someday. But some Protestant members of the Church of England argued fiercely that the Reformation had not gone far enough. These Puritans, or Dissenters,* wanted to "purify" the Anglican Church of all traces of Catholicism.

The Puritans called for several reforms in the Church of England. They wanted to do away with elaborate ceremonies and simplify the religious service. Some even wished to get rid of stained glass windows and church music.

During the seventeenth century, religious conflicts often went hand in hand with political changes. Queen Elizabeth, a practical and shrewd ruler, had seldom clashed with the Puritans.

Her successors, however, were very different rulers. Puritans and other Dissenters found life in England difficult during the reigns of James I and Charles I. Both kings were sympathetic to Catholics. Puritans were thrown out of universities, put into prison, and persecuted in many other ways.

During James's reign, some Puritans abandoned hope of reforming the Anglican Church. They separated from it completely. In 1608 one group of these Separatists fled to the Netherlands.

---

* Dissenter: a Protestant who refuses to accept the doctrines of the established Church of England.

THE PILGRIMS EMBARK

For years, the Separatists lived peacefully in the Netherlands. The Dutch allowed them to worship as they pleased, but life was not entirely satisfactory. The Separatists feared that Catholic Spain would once again seize control of the Netherlands. And the Separatists' children, growing up in a foreign country, lost touch with English ways.

Finally, a small group decided to find a new haven. They would make a pilgrimage across the ocean to America. They obtained from the London Company in England the right to settle in Virginia and set up a trading post.

On September 16, 1620, a ship named the *Mayflower* set out from England. On board were 101 passengers, one third of them Separatists from Holland. One of them, William Bradford, wrote of his friends, "They knew they were pilgrims."

After a stormy Atlantic crossing, the *Mayflower* reached the North American coast. The voyagers knew from the shoreline that they were not where they should be. They were not in Virginia at all but off the coast of John Smith's New England.

On November 21, two days after sighting land, 41 of the passengers crowded into the main cabin. They had to decide what to do next. The London Company had no authority over this area, and the Pilgrims had no charter to settle in New England.

One of the non-Separatists in the stuffy cabin declared that now "none had the power to command them." So they all agreed to create a government by "common consent," and drew up and signed the Mayflower Compact. In the compact they pledged to "combine ourselves together into a civil body politic" and to make "just and equal laws . . . for the general good of the colony." The Mayflower Compact was not a plan for a democratic form of government. But it was an agreement that people could govern themselves.

The colonists settled around a harbor named Plymouth by John Smith, and Plymouth became the name of their colony. The New England winter had already set in, and the settlers' first months in the New World were a trial of cold, hunger, and disease. Half of them died that winter.

In the spring the gaunt and ragged survivors were helped by neighboring Indians. One steadfast friend was a Pawtucket named Squanto, who brought food to the colonists. He showed them the best places to hunt and fish, and taught them to plant crops they had never seen before—corn, beans, squash, and pumpkins.

When the *Mayflower* set sail for the voyage home to England, none of the settlers asked to go back. They celebrated their small successes and first harvest in October 1621. Joined by Chief Massasoit (MAS-eh-SOYT) and 90 other Wampanoag (WAHM-puh-NŌ-ahg), the Plymouth colonists held a three-day Thanksgiving feast.

The colony, however, grew very slowly, with the people always struggling to survive. Yet Plymouth Colony's governor, William Bradford, was confident that these "small beginnings" would inspire others. "As one small candle may light a thousand," he wrote, "so the light here kindled hath shone unto many, yea, in some sort, to our whole nation."

THE PURITAN MIGRATION

Other people were inspired by the Pilgrims. In England, Puritans were being persecuted by the government for their refusal to conform to the Church of England. Many chose to go to America. In 1629 one group of Puritans formed the Massachusetts Bay Company and obtained a charter from the Crown to start a colony near Plymouth.

The charter said nothing about where the company was to hold its annual stockholders' meetings. If the meetings were held in England, the Puritans realized, their enemies might buy enough stock to control the company and then vote against Puritan colonial policies at the meetings. Legally, the location of the meeting was determined by the location of the company's charter. So the Puritans insisted on, and obtained, a clause that let them take the charter to America. Now they would be able to run their company—and their colony—as they wished. Massachusetts would be, in effect, a **self-governing colony**, largely free of royal control.

Massachusetts would also be a Bible Commonwealth, for the Puritans were determined to live by the teachings of the Bible. But their vision had a practical side, too. Most Puritans were also drawn to America by land and opportunity.

So began the flood of Puritans to America. In 1630 a total of 17 ships sailed for the new colony of Massachusetts. The thousand or so people who came that year were followed throughout the 1630s by 20,000 more. This became known as the "Great Migration."

On one of the first ships to cross in 1630 was a London lawyer named John Winthrop, who had been elected governor of Massachusetts. In a shipboard sermon, Winthrop voiced the Puritans' ideals:

> We must . . . rejoice together, mourn together, labor and suffer together, always having before our eyes our commission and common work. . . . For we must consider that we shall be like a City upon a Hill; the eyes of all people are on us.

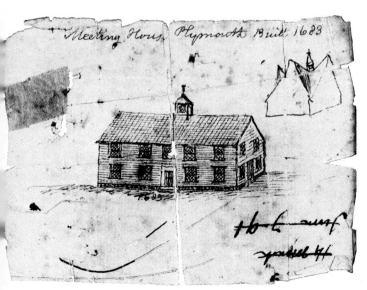

This meetinghouse was built in Plymouth in 1863. The meetinghouse served both as a church and a place where citizens met to vote on laws and choose officials.

Richard Mather was an influential minister in Massachusetts Bay. He helped compile the first book printed in the colonies—*The Bay Psalm Book.*

MASSACHUSETTS BAY COLONY

Massachusetts escaped the early hard times that Plymouth and Jamestown had suffered. The Puritans had planned well, bringing a good supply of provisions, equipment, and livestock with them. They knew the mistakes the first settlers had made and determined not to repeat them. After a short time, Massachusetts was growing robust on fur trading, farming, lumbering, and fishing.

The colony's economic independence was matched by its political independence. The colonists owed allegiance to the king. But because of the charter, they were really independent of royal control.

Massachusetts Bay was first run as a company. In England the stockholders, known as freemen, had held their annual meeting, or General Court, to elect the company's executive officers. These were Governor John Winthrop, a lieutenant governor, and a board of assistants. The only freemen to come to America were these executive officers.

This handful of leaders had sole authority over Massachusetts Bay, as long as they did not violate English law. For a year the leaders kept a firm hand on the colony, running all its affairs. But in 1631 many of the colonists demanded a voice in government. Under pressure, the leaders declared that all male church members were now freemen and had the right to vote.

However, becoming a church member was not all that easy. Most towns formed their own churches, and to be accepted into the congregation, people had to prove that they were worthy in God's eyes. The judging was strict. One person failed because of "speeches savoring of self confidence," and another was "too much addicted to the world."

Gradually, the colonists gained more rights. In 1632 they were allowed to elect the governor, and in 1634 the freemen could select representatives, or deputies, for their towns. Two deputies from each town sat in the General Court and took part in all legislation. Eventually, the deputies became a lower house in a two-house, or **bicameral**, legislature. And eventually any freeman, church member or not, who owned a certain amount of property could vote.

Town government differed from colony government. Freemen, and often nonfreemen, could vote and hold office. They gathered at "town meetings" to decide local affairs—fines for petty crimes, salaries for officials, whether to allow geese on the village green.

Despite these steps toward democracy, the Puritans of Massachusetts Bay strongly believed in church control over their lives. Both members and nonmembers were required to attend religious services, and the people were taxed to support the clergy. Colony leaders, both political and religious, believed that the government must always support the church. Thus Massachusetts began as a joint-stock company, but grew into the true Bible Commonwealth originally intended.

THE FOUNDING OF RHODE ISLAND

In 1631 a brilliant, personable minister named Roger Williams arrived in Massachusetts. Williams had studied religion at England's Cambridge University, and had grown to be a dedicated Separatist.

On his arrival in New England, he was offered a teaching post in a Boston church. But Williams found the church in Boston still too closely tied to the Church of England. Thus began Williams's troublesome stay in Massachusetts.

Williams had several quarrels with the Bible Commonwealth. He insisted that the settlers did not legally own the land because it belonged to the Indians. He also declared that the government had no right to dictate religious affairs. He felt that a government law ordering everyone to attend church simply brought in more sinners. Part of Williams's major quarrel was that he felt the church to be impure because sinners worshipped with God's elect.

Williams was a persuasive talker. Colony leaders feared that if his ideas caught on, the Commonwealth would crumble. In 1635 the leaders banished the minister.

Williams fled to the southern New England coast where he spent the winter with the Narragansett Indians. The next spring, he bought land from the tribe and, with some of his followers, began building a town called Providence. Now, Roger Williams had to decide who would worship at his church. He had to decide what made a person pure.

After wrestling with the question, Williams concluded that a truly pure church was an impossible ideal. The best that people could do was to work toward purity. Therefore, Williams welcomed people of all faiths, promising freedom of religion. As John Winthrop observed of Williams: "Now he would preach to and pray with all comers."

One who was to join Williams in dissent and exile was Anne Hutchinson. She was as brilliant and as troublesome to the Puritans as Williams. Shortly after her arrival in Boston in 1634, she set up weekly religious discussions that quickly became popular.

AMERICAN OBSERVERS

ANNE BRADSTREET
AMERICA'S FIRST POET

When eighteen-year-old Anne Bradstreet arrived in New England in 1630, she was dismayed by what she saw. "I found a new world and new manners at which my heart rose up," she said. The colonists lived a stark life on the edge of the wilderness. Food was scarce, and the weather harsh. Sickness and death stalked every family.

Anne Bradstreet had grown up on the pleasant estate of an English noble, whom her father had served as administrator. A bright and curious child, she had spent hours reading poetry in the castle library.

Anne Bradstreet's parents and her new husband were Puritans, and they had decided to join the Massachusetts Bay Colony. At first, Anne had rebelled, "but after I was convinced it was the way of God," she said, "I submitted to it."

She and her husband settled in North Andover, Massachusetts. There she raised eight children, yet somehow found moments to write. At first, her poems were an escape from pioneer life. She wrote of England—of kings and shepherds and nightingales. In 1650 she became the first colonist to have her poetry published.

As she grew older, her verse changed. She began to write about her own experiences. She wrote of her children, "my eight birds" she called them, and of her beloved husband. She told of her fears during childbirth. One poem described her grief when her house burned down.

She wrote, too, of the woods and cornfields and river near her home. She praised the elms and oaks of New England rather than the figs and pomegranates of English gardens. At times she found North Andover so beautiful it seemed "more heaven than earth." Anne Bradstreet had come to love the New World that had once disappointed her. She had become an American at last.

Although "The Fishing Lady" was embroidered in Boston a century after the publication of Bradstreet's poems, the picture echoes her concerns.

Hutchinson argued that people could receive God's grace whether or not they had led good lives. This challenged the Puritan belief that people could only achieve grace through years of prayer and good works. As a result, she was tried and convicted of heresy, and exiled from the colony.

Hutchinson and her family fled to Williams's settlement. Together with another exile, William Coddington, she founded the town of Portsmouth, not far from Providence.

In 1643 Williams sailed for England and obtained a charter to unite these and two other towns into the colony of Rhode Island. The charter, like that of Massachusetts, made Rhode Island largely a self-governing colony, with a general assembly composed of freemen. The charter also reflected Williams's religious beliefs: It promised separation of church and state and freedom of religion. Williams was able to boast that settlers in Rhode Island enjoyed "as great liberty as any people we can hear of under the whole heaven."

Anne Hutchinson had not intended to speak for religious freedom, yet her voice helped bring religious diversity to New England.

CONNECTICUT, NEW HAMPSHIRE, AND MAINE

There were other people in Massachusetts Bay who plunged into the wilderness to find havens for their beliefs. The liberal minister Thomas Hooker, who had fled to Massachusetts in 1633, found the colony too rigid. Hooker objected to the voting restrictions, believing that people should have more say in their government.

In 1636 Hooker led his congregation across the coastal hills to the broad and fertile Connecticut River valley. The settlers built several towns, including Hartford, and in 1639 they adopted rules for government called the Fundamental Orders of Connecticut. Although this government was similar to that of Massachusetts Bay, there was one important difference. The governor and other officials were to be elected "by the vote of the country." In practice, however, only freemen recognized by the General Court could vote.

By 1662 there were 15 towns scattered throughout the valley, and Charles II granted them a charter as the colony of Connecticut. The new colony absorbed a Puritan outpost by the sea called New Haven, founded earlier by the Reverend John Davenport. Connecticut also continued as a self-governing colony since the charter included the major provisions of the Fundamental Orders.

Massachusetts dissenters also fled northward to Maine and New Hampshire. An early explorer had described the region of New Hampshire: It had "goodly groves and woods and sundry beasts."

In 1622 John Mason and Sir Ferdinando Gorges (GOR-jehz) received a grant to settle in the northern region. Seven years later they divided the claim. Mason named his part New Hampshire, after his home in Hampshire, England. Gorges got the larger section, called Maine. (Early explorers called it *The Main*, meaning "mainland.")

However, after settlers from Massachusetts began edging into the region, Massachusetts Bay claimed that Maine and New Hampshire lay within its boundary. New Hampshire managed to throw off the Bay Colony's grasp in 1680, when it was granted a charter as a royal colony. In Maine, however, Massachusetts had better luck. It bought the land from Gorges's heirs, and in 1691 Maine became part of Massachusetts. Not until 1820 did Maine separate from Massachusetts.

CONFLICTS WITH INDIANS

The settlement of New England brought the English and the Indians into frequent, and often anxious, contact. As settlers pushed into the Connecticut Valley in the early 1630s, they entered the lands of the Pequot (PEE-kwaht) tribe. The situation quickly grew tense. A series of skirmishes was followed by a decisive battle in May 1637, when the English launched an attack against the heart of the Pequot nation, on the Connecticut coast. Hundreds of Pequot died by fire or musket-shot. The survivors fled, but the English trapped them near New Haven and killed most of the men.

The Pequot War convinced the colonists that they needed an organization to coordinate protection of New England. In May 1643 they formed the New England Confederation, containing representatives from Massachusetts, Plymouth, Connecticut, and New Haven. Confederation commissioners had the power to declare war and settle squabbles among the member colonies.

In 1675 conflicts arose again, this time with the Wampanoag tribe. The Wampanoag had lived peacefully alongside the New England settlers for a long time. Chief Massasoit and his tribe had shared the Pilgrims' Thanksgiving feast, helped them to survive the first hard years, and signed a treaty of friendship with them. The friendly feelings, however, had disappeared by the time Massasoit's son, Metacomet (MET-a-KAHM-eht), became chief in 1662.

Metacomet—called "King Philip" by the colonists—feared that the English would crowd the Wampanoag out of their homeland. Metacomet began to approach the Nipmuck and Narragansett and other neighboring tribes, and talked of an alliance against the English.

In June 1675 three of Metacomet's warriors were arrested by the English and were charged with the murder of a Christian Indian. The warriors were found guilty and executed. Metacomet was enraged. The countryside exploded into war, and Metacomet's forces raged through Massachusetts. One English town after another fell.

After 11 more months, King Philip's War finally ended. Both sides were worn out. Costs to the English were 600 dead, and 12 towns destroyed and many more badly damaged. Over 3,000 Indians were killed, including Metacomet. Many of the

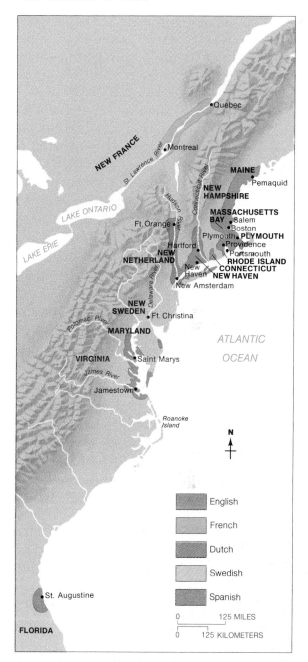

The Colonies in 1650

English
French
Dutch
Swedish
Spanish

0   125 MILES
0   125 KILOMETERS

surviving Wampanoag were shipped to the West Indies and sold as slaves. Metacomet's allies were broken.

Ten years later a French visitor to New England remarked of the Indians: "The last wars they had with the English . . . have reduced them to a small number, and consequently they are incapable of defending themselves."

This Iroquois chief was one of four whose portraits were painted during a visit to Queen Anne in London. The English were seeking allies among the powerful Iroquois.

SECTION REVIEW

1. Identify the following: Massasoit, William Bradford, Thomas Hooker, John Winthrop, Roger Williams, Anne Hutchinson, John Mason, Ferdinando Gorges, Metacomet.

2. (a) What reforms did Puritans want the Church of England to make? (b) How were the Separatists related to the Puritans? (c) How were the Pilgrims related to the Separatists?

3. What agreement was the basis of the Mayflower Compact?

4. Why did the Puritans insist on taking their charter to America?

5. How did Massachusetts colonists avoid the hard times that the Plymouth and Jamestown colonists suffered?

6. (a) Who held authority in Massachusetts Bay until 1631? (b) List the changes that took place in the government of Massachusetts Bay after 1631.

7. (a) How were Roger Williams's beliefs different from the beliefs of Massachusetts leaders? (b) How did Williams decide to welcome to Rhode Island people of all faiths?

8. Describe the Fundamental Orders of Connecticut.

THE PROPRIETARY COLONIES

READ TO FIND OUT

— how George Calvert began the colony of Maryland.

— how English nobles planned Carolina.

— how New Netherland became New York.

— why William Penn founded Pennsylvania.

— how political events in England affected colonial government.

— why James Oglethorpe founded Georgia.

George Calvert, first Lord Baltimore and owner of a large manor in Ireland, was very much interested in planting a colony in America. He had invested in the London Company and watched, from afar, as Virginia took root.

In 1625 Calvert went to Virginia. But he had converted to Catholicism and found a cool reception in Virginia. His refusal to take an oath of allegiance to the Anglican Church and his obvious interest in land roused suspicions.

Calvert returned to England still eager to plant a colony. Despite the unfriendliness in Virginia, he had been delighted with the climate and the profits that could be made from tobacco. He decided to colonize near Virginia.

MARYLAND

Charles I was willing to grant his friend Calvert a charter, and the two agreed on a site just north of Virginia. It included land around northern Chesapeake Bay, bounded on the southwest by the Potomac River.

The charter was for a **proprietary colony**. The Crown would give land to Calvert, who would be the proprietor, or owner. The proprietor would act much like a feudal lord and could distribute the land to others for annual fees called *quitrents*.

In return, the proprietor was to acknowledge the Crown's sovereignty. There was one check on the proprietor's power. The colony's laws must be made with the "advice, assent, and agreement of freemen," and must conform to the laws of England.

Charles proposed that the colony be named Maryland, in honor of his Catholic wife, Mary. This was fitting, since Calvert wished Maryland to be not only a moneymaking venture, but also a refuge for Catholics. For a generation English laws had forbidden Catholics to practice their religion.

However, before the charter was completed, Calvert died. It was Cecilius, his son and the second Lord Baltimore, who accepted the charter in 1632.

The first settlers arrived in Maryland in 1634. The wealthiest, mostly Catholics and friends of Lord Baltimore, leased sprawling tobacco plantations along Chesapeake Bay and the tidewater rivers, which received saltwater from the Atlantic. But the majority of settlers were Protestant artisans, laborers, and servants, who came to resent the Catholic aristocracy. At the bottom of Maryland society were black slaves, imported from Africa to work the tobacco farms and plantations.

At first, Maryland was ruled by a governor and three advisors. Within three years a representative assembly was meeting, and it soon began pressing for a strong voice in government. Gradually, the assembly gained the right to approve or modify the proprietor's legislation.

Then, in 1649, the colony was shaken by events in England. The Puritans, who had been gaining power, overthrew the Anglican government and beheaded Charles I.

Lord Baltimore knew he had to act to protect Maryland's Catholic minority against the increasingly hostile Protestants. He insisted on a Toleration Act, which the assembly passed in 1649. The act promised freedom of worship to all those who "believe in Jesus Christ." Thus Maryland remained a haven of religious freedom for all Christians.

Cecilius Calvert, the second Lord Baltimore, is portrayed with his grandson. Calvert never visited his colony, but he ruled it from England with care and good judgment.

THE CAROLINAS

When the English monarchy was restored in 1660, Charles's son and namesake took the throne. Charles II, the "Merry Monarch," came to power with a near-empty treasury and a host of debts. To reward and repay those who had helped him gain the throne, he thought of a plan that would cost the treasury nothing. He would grant to his friends lands in America.

Charles II had another motive for colonizing. Business interest in planting colonies had flagged around the 1630s as investors found more profitable ways to put their money to work. No new colonies had been planted since Maryland in 1634. With the Dutch wedged between Maryland and New England and the Spanish rooted in Florida, England's colonies were more outposts than empire. By granting land to proprietors, as his father had done with Maryland, Charles II could give a boost to England's fledgling empire.

Therefore, Charles II listened with interest when a group of eight English nobles suggested a proprietary colony south of Virginia. They hoped it would be settled by people from the established

Baltimore was a town of only 100 people when it was sketched by a resident, John Moale, in 1752. The harbor, however, was a busier port than the artist indicated. Tobacco and flax were brought from surrounding farms for shipment to Europe.

colonies and by planters from England's crowded West Indies islands, which had been captured from Spain. They imagined a rich colony with large estates raising olives, currants, and silk.

Charles II granted them a huge tract of land in 1663, with a charter modeled on the proprietary grant of Maryland. The colony was named Carolina, from the Latin *Carolana*, meaning "land of Charles."

The only restriction put on the proprietors was that they establish a government "agreeable to the laws and customs of England." In 1669 one of the proprietors drew up a plan for government with the aid of a well-known philosopher, John Locke.

Titled the Fundamental Constitutions of Carolina, this plan set up a strict hierarchy of nobles. At the top were the eight proprietors in England, and legislation flowed down from them. In Carolina were various levels of nobles. The top noble was the governor, aided by an assembly of property owners. The core of this government was ownership of property.

To encourage immigration to Carolina, the proprietors promised religious toleration and the opportunity to gain land under the headright system. In 1670 the first group of colonists, most of them from the West Indies, landed on the Carolina coast. Near a large bay fed by two rivers, they built the port of Charles Town, later called Charleston.

The people of Charles Town survived their first years by trading furs, raising livestock, and making barrel staves. Then, around 1690, someone tried rice, and a special strain from Madagascar turned out to be "Carolina gold." Eventually, the river-

banks in southern Carolina were lined with prosperous rice plantations, worked by slaves.

The northern section of the Carolina grant developed differently. With few good harbors or tidewater rivers, the north was not good for trans-Atlantic trade and did not attract planters. Most settlers were the poor from Virginia, who had trickled south to the Albemarle Sound area. They lived on small farms and traded with the Indians.

Over the years, many Carolina settlers became dissatisfied as the proprietors proved unable to defend the colonists against attacks by Indians and the Spanish. In 1729 the Crown finally ended proprietary rule and took over Carolina. North Carolina and South Carolina became separate royal colonies, each with an assembly elected by landowners.

THE ENGLISH TAKE OVER NEW NETHERLAND

Charles II had just begun his colonizing when he granted the Carolina charter in 1663. He also had his eye on the Dutch colony of New Netherland, which was blocking New England's westward expansion. Friction between the English and Dutch colonies had been increasing for years.

New Amsterdam had never grown large. In the mid-1600s it contained half the population of its neighbor Connecticut. New Netherland's director-general, Peter Stuyvesant, approached the New England Confederation. In 1650 Stuyvesant and the commissioners signed the Treaty of Hartford, drawing a boundary between the Dutch and English colonies.

However, the English government did not recognize this treaty. England and Holland had been quarreling for years over trade, and the rivalry was growing fierce. Dutch merchants traded extensively with the English colonies, and this undercut trade between England and the colonies.

In 1655 Stuyvesant alarmed the English when he sent an expedition into New Sweden—several Swedish trading forts around upper Delaware Bay. The Dutch seized Fort Christina, the capital of Sweden's tiny colony, and annexed the area.

By the time Charles II took the throne, England and Holland were on the brink of war. In 1664, as one of his prewar moves, Charles decided to pluck the Dutch colonial thorn from England's side. He made a proprietary grant of the land between the Delaware and Connecticut rivers, stretching from Delaware Bay north to Maine, to his brother James, Duke of York. Part of this grant was New Netherland—the "nest of interlopers," as Charles put it.

As admiral of the royal fleet, the Duke of York quickly dispatched four British warships to seize the Dutch colony. In August 1664 the ships sailed into New Amsterdam harbor, their gunports bristling with cannons. New Amsterdam surrendered, and by autumn the English had conquered the remainder of Holland's North American empire. Charles II noted with pleasure the capture of New Amsterdam: "A very good town, but we have got the better of it, and 'tis now called New York."

NEW JERSEY AND NEW YORK

The Duke of York found his proprietary grant too large. He decided to keep the northern part, named New York, and dispose of the land between the Hudson and Delaware rivers. He granted this province of New Jersey as a proprietorship to two friends, John Berkeley and George Carteret.

The proprietors of New Jersey offered religious and political freedom and a good price for land to attract settlers. The offer drew Puritans from New England and a religious sect called Quakers. Subsequently, different groups of Quakers bought out Berkeley and Carteret, and the colony was divided into East and West Jersey. However, through the years colonists clashed over disputed land claims, and the resentments flared into riots. In 1702 the monarchy stepped in and united New Jersey as a royal colony with a representative assembly.

Meanwhile, in New York, the duke continued his generosity to friends. He handed out large estates in the rich river valleys to English favorites, and allowed the Dutch patroons to keep their lands. Soon the families of the new English lords and of the old Dutch patroons were merging into a growing aristocracy.

The duke followed the Dutch system of selecting a governor and council who held tight control over the colony's affairs. When the people demanded a representative assembly, the duke claimed it "would prove destructive . . . to the peace of the government." However, to quiet protest, he finally allowed a popular assembly in 1683.

THE "HOLY EXPERIMENT" OF WILLIAM PENN

Among the many people to whom Charles II owed debts was Admiral Sir William Penn. When the admiral died, his son William inherited his father's claim against the royal treasury. William Penn, like earlier claimants, wanted to take his payment in American lands. A colony, he thought, would be both a good business venture and a religious haven.

Penn was a convert to a new religion—the Religious Society of Friends—that burst across Europe in the late 1640s. Its members were soon called Quakers because they "quaked" before the power of God. Quakers believed that neither a church nor even the Bible was the source of religious truth. Instead, people could experience truth, or the "inner light," directly from God. This light would guide them on the right path.

Many Quaker beliefs angered religious and government leaders in England. Quakers refused to take oaths, support the Anglican Church, pay taxes, or bear arms. They treated everyone as equals. And they persisted in trying to spread their faith. As a result, they were persecuted in England and in Massachusetts Bay Colony.

Despite England's attitude toward Quakers, Charles II was personally tolerant of these Dissenters. In 1681 Penn asked the king for, and was given, a proprietary grant in America as payment of the royal debt. The grant was for a vast tract of land west of the Delaware River. It was to be called Pennsylvania, meaning "Penn's woods." The following year the Duke of York, who also owed money to Penn's father, deeded to Penn "the three lower counties" of Delaware. Delaware remained part of Pennsylvania until 1701.

As proprietor, Penn drew up a Frame of Government that reflected his democratic sentiments. The governor, council, and assembly were all to be elected by freeholders, who included all adult males with property. The colony was to be a "holy experiment," welcoming all religions.

There were already settlers in Pennsylvania—English, Dutch, Swedes, Finns, and Germans. But Penn wanted to attract more, and he had pamphlets printed boosting Pennsylvania. Translated into French, Dutch, and German, they were distributed throughout Europe. Penn promised generous land terms: headrights of 50 acres (20.2 hectares) and tenant farms of 200 acres (80.8 hectares) that rented for one penny per acre. The response was enthusiastic.

In 1682 Penn arrived in Pennsylvania with his Frame of Government. He signed a treaty of friendship with the Indians, and paid them for most of the land granted by Charles II. On the banks of the Delaware and Schuylkill rivers, he founded Philadelphia, giving it the Greek name for "brotherly love." The "City of Brotherly Love" was laid out with broad streets in a checkerboard pattern, a design that other city builders would adopt.

By 1685 Pennsylvania was a thriving colony. Philadelphia boasted 350 houses and mills, kilns, tanneries, glassworks, and shops. As William Penn wrote with pride, "I have led the greatest colony into America that ever anyone did upon private credit."

THE DOMINION OF NEW ENGLAND

While Pennsylvania was taking root, Massachusetts Bay Colony was running into trouble with England. Massachusetts had been growing steadily more independent, defying royal authority. In 1684 the English courts finally lost patience with the stubborn colony and took away its charter.

Edward Hicks was both a Quaker minister and a folk artist. He expressed the spirit of William Penn's "holy experiment" in his 1840 painting, "The Peaceable Kingdom." In the background Penn is seen signing a treaty with the Delaware Indians.

In this 1732 engraving Lutherans prepare to leave Catholic Austria in search of freedom to practice their religion. This group settled in Georgia.

The following year, Charles II died and his brother, the Duke of York, took the throne as James II. One of his first moves was to extend royal rule to all the northern colonies. Massachusetts Bay, Maine, Plymouth, Rhode Island, Connecticut, New Hampshire, New York, New Jersey, and, later, Pennsylvania were combined under a single government. This government was called the Dominion of New England. James II appointed a royal governor, Sir Edmund Andros, and made no provision for a representative assembly.

The Dominion of New England was short-lived, for the King quickly ran into trouble at home. James II was a Roman Catholic, and England was by now overwhelmingly Protestant. Many feared that he would establish Catholic rule in England. When James and his wife had a son in 1688, the idea of a Catholic heir to the English throne proved too much.

Riots erupted throughout England, and James II fled the country. Parliament moved swiftly. Claiming that James had stepped down from the throne, Parliament asked his half-sister Mary to rule in his place. In February 1689 Mary took the throne with her husband William, who was ruler of the Netherlands.

Parliament gave William and Mary the throne with a condition attached—a Bill of Rights. In doing so, Parliament was building on the tradition of rights begun with the Magna Carta. The Bill of Rights was Parliament's declaration of power over the monarchy. It gave the legislators final say over taxation, lawmaking, and other powers of government. In addition, the Bill of Rights reasserted the right of all English subjects to trial by jury.

In America, colonists cheered what was called the Glorious Revolution. Authorities in the Dominion of New England were ousted, and the colonies returned to self-government. However, in 1691 Massachusetts was made a royal colony, incorporating Plymouth and Maine. The Puritan church lost considerable control over its Bible Commonwealth. The governor was now to be appointed by the Crown. Voting qualifications were to be determined by property ownership instead of church membership.

GEORGIA

Fifty years passed between the founding of Pennsylvania and the planting of England's thirteenth, and final, colony in North America. In 1732 some members of the English upper class, led by James Edward Oglethorpe, applied for a proprietary charter.

Oglethorpe had two motives. First, he was convinced that Spanish power in America must be controlled. A buffer colony between South Carolina and Florida, he concluded, would confine the Spanish to Florida.

Oglethorpe's second motive was a combination of mercantilism and idealism. He was keenly aware of the plight of England's debtors, thrown into jail for failure to pay their debts. A colony could be a haven for these jobless debtors, Oglethorpe reasoned. The debtors in turn could find work in the colony, and thus contribute to the welfare of England.

The king—at this time George II—granted the charter for a colony named Georgia in his honor. Oglethorpe and his 19 associates were appointed as trustees. They were not to profit from Georgia, but had total governmental power. The trustees, then, were like kindly parents guiding their offspring.

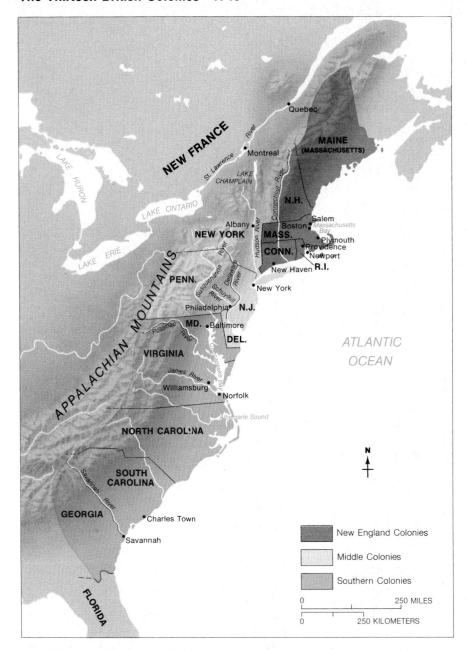

Wrought iron weather vanes like this one were made in Pennsylvania, the center of colonial iron production. At first iron products were imported from Britain. As ore deposits were discovered, colonial iron works were established. By the 1750s colonial iron merchants were competing with the British.

And Georgia, in the hands of the trustees, was the only colony denied a measure of self-government.

In 1733 Oglethorpe, as agent for the trustees, arrived in Georgia with the first colonists. They cleared a rectangular area of land in the pine forest and laid out Savannah, a town of straight streets and blocklike houses.

Each settler received a grant of 50 acres (20.2 hectares) of land. However, to prevent the growth of an aristocracy, each family was limited to 500 acres (20.2 hectares). Georgia's economy was to be based on silk, so the settlers were required to grow mulberry trees as food for silkworms. The silkworms would be imported into the colony.

This "Georgian Utopia" was to be guided by several principles. Freedom of religion was extended to all but Catholics. Slavery was banned. And settlers were not permitted to drink rum.

Most of the trustees' ideals faded in the blistering Georgia sun. Many settlers, unhappy with the restrictions, moved to other colonies. Those who stayed found that silkworms could not withstand the Georgia climate. They saw how their Carolina neighbors prospered on sprawling plantations maintained by slave labor, and wanted to make their own fortunes. Soon they were demanding self-government so they could live as they wished.

To keep the remaining settlers from deserting, the trustees relaxed the restrictions. By 1750 families could own 2,000 acres (808 hectares), rum was flowing, slavery was permitted, and Georgia had a representative assembly.

In 1752 the trustees' charter expired and Georgia became a royal colony, its economy much like South Carolina's. There were a few reminders of Oglethorpe's plans—plantations with such names as Mulberry Grove or Silk Hope.

THE THIRTEEN COLONIES

By the 1750s eight of the thirteen colonies were royal colonies, under direct control of the king and Parliament. The royal governor had considerable power in the colony. The governor was head of the militia, chief justice of the courts, and administrator of laws. The council, generally appointed by the Crown, served as an upper house of the colonial legislature. The lower house was the assembly, elected by the freeholders.

Three of the colonies remained proprietary— Maryland, Pennsylvania, and Delaware. These were similar to the royal colonies, except that the proprietors appointed the governors.

The other colonies, Connecticut and Rhode Island, were self-governing colonies. They had retained their original charters, which allowed them almost total independence from England. In both colonies, the freemen elected the governor, council, and assembly.

Over the years, there was continual squabbling for control in the proprietary and royal colonies. The governor had the power to **veto**, or reject, any law passed by the assembly. But the assembly generally had the power to levy taxes and decide how tax money would be spent—including how much should go toward the governor's salary. This control of the purse was a powerful weapon as the colonists practiced their skills in self-government.

In 1748 a visitor from Sweden named Peter Kalm toured the colonies. He was struck by this clash of authority in government:

> The King appoints the governor according to his royal pleasure; but the inhabitants of the province make up His Excellency's salary. Therefore, a person entrusted with this place has greater or lesser revenues according as he knows how to gain the confidence of the inhabitants. There are examples of governors . . . who, by their dissensions with the inhabitants of their respective governments, have lost their whole salary.

Thus, England ruled the colonies by "royal pleasure," either through royal governors or charters granted by the Crown. In England's view, the colonial governments could be dissolved by the stroke of a pen. But the colonists assumed that their right to self-government came from the English tradition of representative government, and was thus not to be violated.

SECTION REVIEW

1. Identify the following: George Calvert, Cecilius Calvert, Peter Stuyvesant, Duke of York, John Berkeley, George Carteret, William Penn, James Oglethorpe.

2. (a) Give two reasons for the founding of Maryland. (b) What was promised in Maryland's Toleration Act?

3. What hopes for Carolina did its proprietors have?

4. Give two reasons why England took New Amsterdam from the Dutch.

5. How did New Jersey become a separate colony?

6. Describe the main provisions of William Penn's Frame of Government.

7. (a) What was the Dominion of New England? (b) How did it come to an end?

8. What were James Oglethorpe's reasons for planting a colony?

9. What important power did colonial assemblies hold?

10. Explain how each of the following was governed: royal colony, proprietary colony, self-governing colony. Give two examples of each kind of colony.

SUMMARY

European mercantilists believed that colonies provided a source of raw materials and a market for goods produced by the colonizing nation. Thus, colonies helped a nation to establish a favorable balance of trade. European nations, then, began to look to the New World for colonies.

France established New France in the northern forests. New France became the center of a rich fur trade with the Indians. The Dutch established New Netherland, where merchants set up trading posts.

It was the English, however, who established permanent colonies. The first successful English colony was Jamestown, settled in 1607. By 1619 Jamestown had America's first representative assembly, the House of Burgesses.

The next English colonists were the Pilgrims, who settled Plymouth in 1620. Then, in 1630, the Puritans established Massachusetts Bay, the Bible Commonwealth. Dissent within Massachusetts Bay led to the settlement of Rhode Island and Connecticut. Next to be founded was New Hampshire. From 1632 to 1733, the last colonies were founded—Maryland, New York (taken from the Dutch), Delaware, the Carolinas, New Jersey, Pennsylvania, and Georgia.

Colonists came to the New World for a variety of reasons. To the Puritans, America offered a place in which they could practice their religion. To penniless or landless farmers, America offered an alternative to debtors' prison. To merchants, America promised wealth.

By the 1750s the Thirteen Colonies were well established. Eight were royal colonies, under direct control of the king and Parliament. Three—Maryland, Pennsylvania, and Delaware—remained proprietary. Connecticut and Rhode Island were self-governing colonies.

In all the British colonies the king remained the final authority. What was actually happening, however, was different from what anyone had planned or expected. Colonial assemblies were exerting power over royal governors, and colonists were building on the idea of free people making their own laws. The seeds of self-government were being sown.

CHAPTER REVIEW

1. (a) Explain the economic system known as mercantilism. (b) How did mercantilism affect rivalry between European nations?

2. (a) Why did France build an empire in North America? (b) What did the Netherlands seek in North America? What methods did the Dutch use to obtain their goal? (c) Why did England try to establish colonies in North America? What steps did the English take to obtain their goal?

3. To attract settlers, a new colony had to offer something people wanted. Describe the incentives offered by each of the following colonies: Jamestown, Plymouth, Pennsylvania, Rhode Island, Georgia. What kind of people settled in each of these colonies? Why?

4. (a) What religious conflicts in England prompted the settlement of Massachusetts and Maryland? (b) How did these religious conflicts relate to political conflicts?

Many people were swayed by persuasive pamphlets promoting settlement. The land was often described in enthusiastic terms as more abundant and beautiful than any yet known.

5. (a) With which Indian tribes did the French establish ties? What did each group of people gain? (b) With which Indian tribes did the Dutch establish ties? What did each group of people gain? (c) How did these alliances bring the French and the Dutch into conflict?

6. (a) What was the cause of conflict between the Pequot tribe and the New Englanders? (b) What was the cause of conflict between the Wampanoag tribe and the New Englanders? (c) How did these conflicts lead to the decline of Indians in New England?

7. In 1619 the House of Burgesses was established in Jamestown. What events in England had laid a foundation for the establishment of this assembly?

8. (a) Explain how a colony was organized as a business venture. Use the following terms in your explanation: charter, joint-stock company, shares, investors, profit. Give two examples of colonies established in this manner. (b) How was a proprietary colony also a business venture?

9. (a) How much control did the English Crown have over royal and proprietary colonies in 1750? (b) How much control did the Crown have over self-governing colonies in 1750? (c) How did England and the colonists differ in their views of colonial government?

10. List in chronological order steps taken toward religious freedom in the colonies. Include the date, the colony, and a brief explanation of each step.

ISSUES AND IDEAS

1. (a) If you were a member of the Wampanoag tribe in 1621, how would you try to persuade the tribal council to help the English settlers at Plymouth? What would you hope to achieve? (b) If you were a member of the Wampanoag tribe in 1621, how would you try to persuade the tribal council not to help the settlers? What dangers would you foresee?

2. John Winthrop told the Puritans, "We shall be like a City upon a Hill; the eyes of all people are on us." What did Winthrop mean? Why do you think Winthrop believed this?

In 1739 Elizabeth Blackwell published a book of drawings. *A Curious Herbal.* The book explained unfamiliar new world plants, such as the "love apple," or tomato, to Londoners.

SKILLS WORKSHOP

1. *Maps.* Look at the map on page 41 of your text. Then look at the map entitled "Political Map of the United States" in the Resource Center at the back of your book. What present-day states are in the territory once called New France?

2. *Writing.* Make an outline showing major steps toward self-government in the colonies. On your outline each step should be listed by a Roman numeral. Under each Roman numeral, write details that support the main idea. Use your outline to write three or four paragraphs. Underline main-idea sentences.

PAST AND PRESENT

1. The Pilgrims, Puritans, and other religious groups came to America with a mission. They wanted to establish communities in which they could worship as they wished. Do you think the American people today have a mission in the world? If so, what do you think it is?

2. Find out about Jamestown, Plymouth, or the Hudson River valley today. Describe buildings and other objects that have been preserved from the colonial period.

CHAPTER 3

BRITAIN'S AMERICAN EMPIRE

1600–1763

LIFE IN THE NEW ENGLAND COLONIES
LIFE IN THE MIDDLE COLONIES
LIFE IN THE SOUTHERN COLONIES
RIVALRY FOR EMPIRE

In 1759 Jean de Crèvecoeur (KREV-KOOR) left France to come to America. He later became an American citizen, and wrote of his new country:

"North America is divided into many provinces, forming a large association, scattered along a coast 1,500 miles long and about 200 wide. If America does not afford that variety which may be observed in Europe, we have colors peculiar to ourselves. For instance, it is natural to conceive that those who live near the sea must be very different from those who live in the woods.

"Those who live near the sea feed more on fish than on flesh. . . . The sea inspires them with a love of traffic, a desire of transporting produce from one place to another. . . . Those who inhabit the middle settlements, by far the most numerous, must be very different. . . .

As farmers, they will be careful and anxious to get as much as they can, because what they get is their own.

"Whoever travels the continent must easily observe those strong differences. . . . The inhabitants of Canada, Massachusetts, the middle provinces, the southern ones will be as different as their climates.

"Europe contains hardly any other distinctions but lords and tenants. This fair country alone is settled by freeholders, the possessors of the soil they cultivate, members of the government they obey, and the framers of their own laws by means of their representatives."

As different as the colonists were, they all shared one bond—the experience of living in the New World. The people in the Thirteen Colonies shared another experience. In 1754 they were pulled into a European war for possession of North America. The war would drive the colonists closer together and into the secure embrace of Great Britain.

LIFE IN THE NEW ENGLAND COLONIES

READ TO FIND OUT

— why the meetinghouse was the center of New England villages and towns.

— what trades were practiced in New England.

— what major New England industries depended on the sea.

— how triangular trade developed.

— how people were educated in New England.

The last Ice Age glacier had scoured the New England landscape, scraping off the topsoil and leaving behind rugged hills strewn with boulders. But the jagged seacoast offered good harbors, and, inland, the heavy forests were filled with timber. In this rich but severe land of bitter winters and quick summers, the New England colonists made their home.

America, unlike Europe, had abundant land. Colonists might lack money and tools and enough strong backs to do all the work. But they found what they could not find in the Old World—acres of land.

VILLAGE AND FARM

In New England, life was shaped as much by the church as by the land. The Puritan settlers were a tightly knit community, and the church was central to their daily affairs. Thus, early New England settlements were formed around church congregations.

The Massachusetts General Court granted a tract of land called a township, usually 36 square miles (93.6 square kilometers), to a church congregation. At the center of the township the colonists built their village. Some land was shared by everyone: for the meetinghouse, school, and village green, or *common*. The remainder of the village lots were distributed among the congregation.

The meetinghouse was the heart of the village. People gathered there to worship and to hold town meetings. Here they elected representatives to the General Court. Here, too, they discussed local matters, such as where to build roads, how much timber to cut, and when the cattle should be turned out to graze on the common land.

Families were allotted small patches of land outside the village in which to plant their corn, rye, barley, and oats. With the thin New England soil and hilly, wooded land, most farming was on a *subsistence level*. In other words, farmers could raise only enough to live on or to trade for necessities.

Everyone in the family shared in the chores. Men and women often worked together on the most difficult ones, like planting, butchering, and tanning hides. On other tasks they usually worked apart.

Over the years, villages swelled into towns, and the line of New England settlement advanced westward. Newcomers to the established towns often found that they could not afford to buy land, and so moved farther west. There, in hilly country, they carved out small farms. Also, some people in the old towns began to be uncomfortable with the tight community control. One New Englander declared, "If you persecute in one city, we must fly to another." And so the town–building went on.

PLYING A TRADE

A popular saying in the colonies was that anyone "that hath a trade hath an estate." The industrious New England towns were a prime market for the colonist with a trade. Towns often advertised for cobblers, blacksmiths, dressmakers, barbers—and even offered a house or bit of land to attract them.

Many of those with a trade or skills were women, often widows carrying on the family business. Women worked as innkeepers, lawyers, gunsmiths, shipwrights, and butchers. Several women owned printing presses, and a number of them published newspapers.

One enterprising woman was Sarah Kemble Knight. She set up shop in Boston, preparing legal papers for people. After many successful years in that business, Knight started a school to teach writing. In her fifties, energetic as ever, she speculated in land, bought several farms, and ran a tavern.

The most efficient way to learn a trade was through *apprenticeship*. Tradespeople taught their craft to young people who worked as assistants for a number of years. Some apprentices were indentured servants from Britain. They had agreed to work for masters in America to pay for their voyage.

Whether indentured or free, apprentices worked long, hard hours and received little except room and board. But in the process, they learned a skill that enabled them to make a living.

These industrious colonists illustrated proverbs in *Poor Richard's Almanac*. The widely read almanac was written and published by Benjamin Franklin every year for 26 years.

SEAFARERS AND MERCHANTS

Many New Englanders made their living from the sea. Off the Newfoundland coast, the cool water and broad underwater ledge known as the continental shelf made a good environment for fish, especially cod.

A New Englander named Frances Higginson wrote enthusiastically in 1629: "The abundance of sea fish [is] almost beyond believing; and sure I would scarce have believed it except I had seen it with my own eyes." Along the coast were great salt marshes, with salt so thick it caked on the rocks. Dried and salted, New England fish became a major export to England.

Some fishers roamed the whaling grounds that stretched from the Arctic Circle to Brazil. One of the many products of whales was oil for lamps, which was made by boiling down whale blubber. By the 1750s stately mansions built by shipowners and captains lined the streets of New England's whaling villages—Nantucket, Martha's Vineyard, and New Bedford.

Shipbuilding, too, became a major industry. Merchants in England found New England ships so well made that they often bought the ship along with its cargo. By the mid-1700s one out of every three ships in England's merchant fleet had been built in a New England shipyard. The New England ship and fishing industries were employing 10,000 people.

Above all else, New Englanders became known as shrewd merchants. With their fine sailing vessels they commanded shipping between the colonies, England, and the West Indies. There was always a market for New England products, like codfish, lumber, grains, salt pork, and barrel staves. And New Englanders found they could make a small fortune by transporting the goods of other colonies, like Virginia tobacco, and the products of other countries.

TRIANGULAR TRADE

One of New England's best markets was the British West Indies. In the 1700s a triangular trade developed involving the West Indies. The trade brought wealth to planters in the West Indies as well as traders in New England and slave dealers on the west coast of Africa.

Colonial Overseas Trade Routes

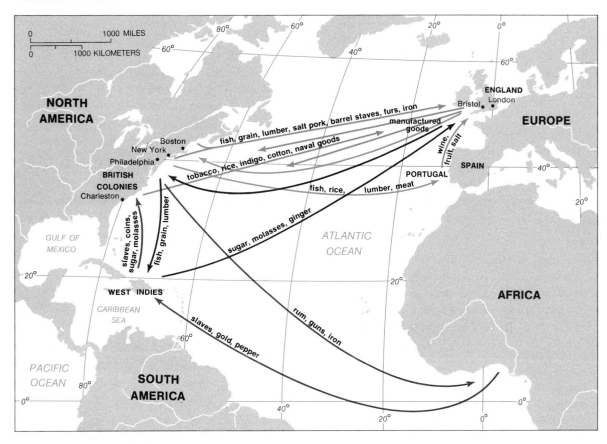

Although the major colonial ports were in the North, large quantities of goods were shipped directly from southern harbors such as Charleston. Colonists traded with Spain, Portugal, and other nations especially for products not available in British ports.

With West Indies molasses, a byproduct of sugar production, the New Englanders made rum. New England ships were loaded with barrels of rum, along with iron bars and muskets, and sent to Africa. The iron was used in some African kingdoms as money. The guns and the rum were traded for slaves or gold dust. The second leg of this route brought the slaves to the West Indies, where they were sold. More molasses was bought with the profits, and the ships finally returned to the American colonies.

This triangular trade was not always precise. New England shippers often crisscrossed the Atlantic Ocean, stopping at English, Spanish, and Portuguese ports as well as African ones. There were also other triangles of trade. Colonial vessels, bulging with lumber, fur, tobacco, and fish, headed directly for England or southern Europe. New Englanders

sold their products there, bought European goods, sailed for the West Indies to trade, and then returned home.

The prosperous trade turned some New England towns into bustling cities. The busiest, and the most devoted to commerce, was Boston. Boston's waterfront bristled with wharves, warehouses, and elegant homes of merchants. Its streets were lined with well-stocked shops and marketplaces.

SOCIAL CLASSES

Not everyone in New England was prosperous. There were class distinctions, but they could be overcome. Poor farmers, humble artisans, and indentured servants who had worked out their contracts could rise to wealth and power through hard work and a measure of luck.

The rise from lower to middle class, and even to upper class, was a goal almost all New Englanders could work for. However, there was one group of people rigidly kept at the bottom of society: blacks. From the beginning, blacks made up a very small percentage of New England's population, and almost all met with discrimination.

Most blacks in early New England were indentured servants, but over the years more and more black servants were treated as slaves. In 1641 the first Massachusetts legal code stated that those who were "sold to us," meaning blacks brought by slave ships, could be enslaved. Although large-scale slavery was impractical for New England's small farms, trade, and sea-based industries, there was some small demand for slaves.

Gradually, blacks were enslaved by the law. A 1652 Rhode Island law stated that English people could buy blacks and "have them for service or slaves forever." In 1690 Connecticut required all blacks to have "a ticket or a pass" to leave a town. In 1717 Connecticut forbade blacks to own land.

Free blacks, although discriminated against in many ways, occasionally managed to rise to success. A freed slave named Newport Gardner opened a music school in Rhode Island, and his former owner became one of his pupils. Another black Rhode Islander, Emmanuel Bernoon, set up shop as a caterer.

One of the most well-known blacks was Phillis Wheatley. Brought from Africa to New England as a slave in 1761, Wheatley was taught by her owners to read and write. Soon she was writing her own poetry. At 19 she was given her freedom and within a year had a book of poetry in print. She eventually gained international fame.

EDUCATION

Education was vital to the Puritans. Their society was based on religion, so they felt it necessary that everyone be able to read and understand the Bible and the laws of the Commonwealth. In 1647 Massachusetts ordered every town with 50 or more

The fanciful scene, *Bears and Pears*, once adorned a New England home. The oil painting was done on a fireboard, a board that covered the fireplace when it was not in use.

families to establish elementary schools to teach reading and writing. The schools were open to all children—boys and girls, rich and poor. Towns with 100 or more families also had to set up grammar, or secondary, schools "to instruct youths so far as they may be fitted for the university." Similar laws were passed in all the other New England colonies except Rhode Island, where education was strictly a family concern.

There were also vocational schools, sometimes called academies, in New England. These privately supported schools taught skills such as sewing, music, bookkeeping, shorthand, and navigation.

Most New England girls learned to write and read, either in elementary school or at home, but their scholarly education usually stopped there. Boys who successfully completed six years of grammar school could go on to college.

Until 1700, the only college in New England was Harvard. Named for a minister, John Harvard, it was the first college established in America. Its founders set high goals. Harvard would train ministers and would give New England children a classical education like that of English universities. Harvard offered courses in theology, logic, geometry, rhetoric, philosophy, Latin, Greek, and Hebrew. In the 1700s other colleges were founded in New England—Dartmouth in New Hampshire, Brown in Rhode Island, and Yale in Connecticut.

SECTION REVIEW

1. (a) How were New England communities formed? (b) What part did the meetinghouse play in New England village life?

2. Describe colonial apprenticeships.

3. What New England industries depended on the sea?

4. What were the chief products of New England?

5. Describe New England's triangular trade involving Africa.

6. (a) Why was education important to the Puritans? (b) Describe the school law passed by Massachusetts in 1647.

7. How did the education of girls usually differ from that of boys?

8. (a) What was the first college in America? (b) For what purpose was the college founded?

LIFE IN THE MIDDLE COLONIES

READ TO FIND OUT

—who settled the Middle Colonies.

—why the Middle Colonies were called the "grain colonies."

—what cities were centers of trade.

—how people were educated in the Middle Colonies.

Wedged between New England and the colonies in the South were the Middle Colonies—New York, New Jersey, Pennsylvania, and Delaware. A visitor to New York City reported that as he walked along the city's bustling docks, he identified 12 different languages. This coming together of cultures was common throughout the Middle Colonies. An English traveler, Andrew Burnaby, found the whole region "composed of people of different nations, different manners, different religions, and different languages."

The majority of all colonists were of English origin. English places, traditions, and kings and queens were remembered in colonial names—New Hampshire, New York, Maryland, Jamestown, New London, Elizabethtown. But in New York there were Dutch-named cities like Schenectady and Rensselaer. In New Jersey were Swedesboro and Finn's Point. And in Pennsylvania were Germantown and the Scotch-Irish town of Donegal.

The Dutch and the Swedish had been in America since the 1620s and 1630s. By the 1700s other non-English groups were arriving. The newcomers were of different religions—Catholic, Jewish, and a patchwork of Protestant sects.

GERMANS AND SCOTCH-IRISH

The most numerous of the non-English settlers were the Germans and the Scotch-Irish. In the 1680s William Penn's advertisements for Pennsylvania were spread throughout Europe, and Germans were quick to accept Penn's invitation.

Colonial Settlement by Nationality 1770

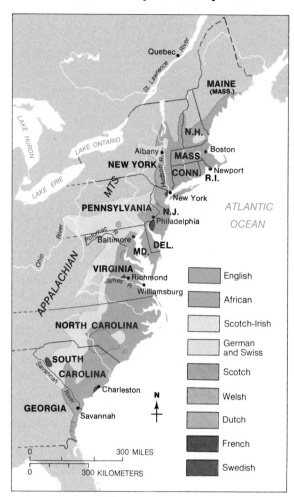

Map legend:
- English
- African
- Scotch-Irish
- German and Swiss
- Scotch
- Welsh
- Dutch
- French
- Swedish

Colonial Population by Nationality

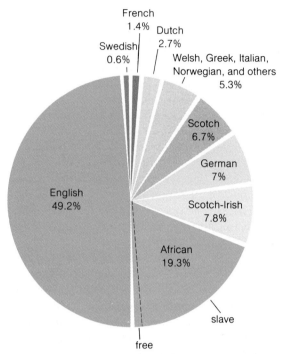

French 1.4%
Swedish 0.6%
Dutch 2.7%
Welsh, Greek, Italian, Norwegian, and others 5.3%
Scotch 6.7%
German 7%
Scotch-Irish 7.8%
English 49.2%
African 19.3%
slave
free

Estimates about the number of non-English colonists were made from names in the 1790 census. Many non-English colonists changed their names and thus may have been counted as English.

German families filled the Pennsylvania countryside with well-managed farms. German settlers developed the Conestoga wagon and the Pennsylvania (or Kentucky) rifle.

The first group of German immigrants settled north of Philadelphia on a piece of land they called Germantown. Their leader, Francis Pastorius, noted the settlers' many talents:

> There was a doctor of medicine with his wife and eight children, a French captain, a Low Dutch cakebaker, an apothecary, a glassblower, a mason, a smith, a wheelwright, a cabinetmaker, a cooper, a hatmaker, a cobbler, a tailor, a gardener, farmers, seamstresses, etc.

Settlers with such skills made Germantown thrive with orchards, farms, shops, mills, and even a bee colony.

Throughout the 1700s, waves of Germans poured into Pennsylvania, fanning out from Germantown into the surrounding Lancaster County. Many formed communities around religious sects—Quakers, Mennonites, and the colorfully named Dunkers, New Mooners, and the Society of the Woman in the Wilderness.

The Scotch-Irish, like the Germans, were fleeing troubles at home. They were people of Scottish blood whose ancestors had settled in northern Ireland. However, by 1700 England had put trade restrictions on Ireland and demanded that the Scottish Presbyterians conform to the Anglican Church. Many Scotch-Irish escaped to America, often entering through the port of Philadelphia.

AGRICULTURE

In New York, large land holdings still dominated the Hudson Valley. Thus, New York attracted few settlers interested in farming, since most people preferred to own rather than rent land.

To the south of New York, the coastal plain was far wider than in New England, and the Delaware, Schuylkill, and Susquehanna rivers watered the broad inland valleys. The soil was rich, deep, and easily plowed, and the good climate allowed a long growing season. Pennsylvania, especially, was blessed by an abundance of fruitful farmland. A German visitor exclaimed, "Pennsylvania is heaven for farmers."

The heavenly farmland produced rye, oats, barley, corn, and, most of all, wheat. The demand for grain increased steadily during the 1700s, and so did the price. More and more grain was sent to feed the other colonies. More and more of the ships sailing from Philadelphia and New York carried grain for the West Indies or Europe. By 1750 grain was second to tobacco as the leading export of the colonies. People began to call the Middle Colonies the "bread" or "grain colonies."

LIFE IN THE CITIES

The hub of Pennsylvania's commerce was Philadelphia. Philadelphia seemed a model city. It boasted street lights, a police department, a fire company, a newspaper, and America's first public library, hospital, insurance company, and philosophical society.

Most of these were the brainchildren of a remarkable man named Benjamin Franklin. He had come to Philadelphia at age 17. By the time he reached his fifties he had acquired a number of trades—printer, newspaper publisher, inventor, scientist, diplomat, and postmaster general of the colonies' postal system.

Philadelphia was also a paradise for artisans, merchants, and shippers. It held plenty of opportunity for the hard working to rise to success. Most of the city, and the colony, was dominated by Quakers who had made their fortunes in commerce.

The other great center of business in the Middle Colonies was New York City. New York had long been a magnet for people from many cultures, but it still retained much of the character of its Dutch founders.

The Dutch influenced the city's architecture. And their love of business flavored the city, which gained a reputation throughout the colonies for its interest in trade.

New York was also home to a thriving press—the New York *Gazette*, the New York *Weekly Journal*, and several other newspapers. New York was not the first city to have a paper. Boston had that distinction with its *News-Letter*. But New York was the site of the first clash between a newspaper and the government.

John Peter Zenger, publisher of the *Weekly Journal*, had printed a series of articles criticizing the governor of New York. Zenger's attacks landed him in jail, charged with libel,* and he went to trial in August 1735. What Zenger said about the governor, Zenger's lawyer claimed, could not be considered libelous because it was true.

* libel: any false and harmful statements written or printed in order to injure a person's reputation in any way.

Benjamin Franklin could not afford to go to college, but he never stopped learning. Skill as a printer, hard work, and intelligence brought him success. He became one of the most respected men in America.

FREEDOM OF THE PRESS
THE TRIAL OF JOHN PETER ZENGER

On the morning of August 4, 1735, the courtroom in New York's City Hall was jammed with people. They had come to see the trial of John Peter Zenger, a printer whose newspaper had dared to criticize the royal governor of New York. Soon the two judges, in crimson robes and great powdered wigs, entered the courtroom. Then the jury of 12 citizens was sworn in. Zenger's case had been the talk of New York for months. Yet as his trial began, few dreamed that it would make legal history.

Before Zenger started his New York *Weekly Journal* in 1733, there had been only one newspaper in the city. That newspaper was controlled by the royal governor, William Cosby, and printed only what he wanted it to say. Cosby was not a popular governor. He accepted bribes and fired officials who disagreed with him. New Yorkers complained bitterly about him among themselves, but until Zenger's *Journal* appeared, no one had done so in print.

Zenger's first issue contained a report about Governor Cosby's attempt to influence an election in a nearby town. It caused a sensation. Each week the paper continued its attack. Sometimes it opposed the governor in long, serious essays. Often it poked fun at him. The *Journal* was only a four-page weekly, but its impact was tremendous. It was the first politically independent newspaper in the American colonies.

Governor Cosby was furious. He ordered that copies of the *Journal* be burned in front of the public stocks. Finally, he had Zenger arrested for seditious libel—libel intended to stir up rebellion against the government.

Zenger languished in jail for eight months before his case came to trial. His newspaper, however, continued to appear. It was printed by his wife, Anna Catherine, who managed to talk business with her husband through a hole in the jailhouse door.

As Zenger's trial began that August day in 1735, a white-haired stranger unexpectedly stepped forward. His name was James Hamilton, and word soon spread through the courtroom that he was one of the best lawyers in America. He had come from Philadelphia to defend Zenger.

Because Zenger was accused of libel, his case turned around the meaning of this word. According to English law, any criticism of the government was called libel, whether it was true or false. James Hamilton disagreed with this view. He argued that people were guilty of libel only if they deliberately printed false information. Since Zenger had printed the truth, he had not committed libel. ''It is the truth alone,'' Hamilton told the court, ''that can excuse or justify anyone for complaining of a bad administration.''

When Hamilton saw that the judges believed Zenger was guilty, he turned his back on them and

spoke directly to the jury. In colonial times juries were usually controlled by the judges. But these 12 jurors were now Zenger's only hope.

Freedom of the press, Hamilton told them, should be a basic right. It was a necessary check on the power of the government. If people could not speak and write against their rulers, he warned, "the next step may make them slaves."

Hamilton was a powerful speaker. The crowd in the courtroom sat spellbound at his words. "The question before the Court and you of the jury is not of small nor private concern," he said. "It is not the cause of a poor printer, nor of New York alone. . . . It may in its consequence affect every free person that lives under a British government on the main of America. It is the best cause. It is the cause of liberty." If you find Zenger not guilty, he concluded, "everyone who prefers freedom to a life of slavery will bless and honor you."

The jurors took only a short time to reach a verdict. As the head of the jury came forward to announce the decision, the crowd stirred with excitement. "Not guilty," he said. The crowd cheered. The next day Zenger was released from jail.

Peter Zenger continued to print his newspaper. After his death, 11 years later, his wife, and later his son, carried on his work. Zenger also published an account of the trial, which featured James Hamilton's moving defense of freedom of the press. The account was reprinted 15 times during the century and became one of the most widely read books of its time. Peter Zenger's case later caught the imagination of Americans who resented English rule. It became a symbol of the freedom they desired. It was, said one Patriot of 1776, "the morning star of that liberty which subsequently revolutionized America."

1. Why did English colonial rulers try to prevent freedom of the press?

2. Why did the authors of the United States Constitution include freedom of the press in the Bill of Rights? What is its role in a democracy?

3. Can freedom of the press be carried too far? Are there times when even the truth should not be printed?

The spirited defense convinced the jury, which acquitted Zenger. Although the Zenger case did not end the struggle between the press and the government, it did have far reaching consequences. It was the cornerstone upon which the colonists established one of their most cherished rights: freedom of the press.

EDUCATION

The Middle Colonies, unlike New England, had no public school system. Schooling was usually privately funded, and it varied according to the educational aims of the diverse groups of settlers. New York, for example, had English, Dutch, French, and Hebrew private schools.

By the mid-1700s Philadelphia boasted an impressive array of private schools, both Quaker and non-Quaker. Students could study bookkeeping, surveying, natural science, crafts, sewing, music, dancing, and languages from English to Arabic.

The variety in the Middle Colonies also affected higher education. Princeton University was founded in New Jersey by Scottish Presbyterians, who wanted to ensure a steady supply of classically educated ministers. Another New Jersey college, Rutgers, was set up by members of the Dutch Reformed Church. And Pennsylvania's college, the University of Pennsylvania, stressed the practical side of education so popular in Philadelphia.

SECTION REVIEW

1. (a) Who were the most numerous non-English settlers in the Middle Colonies? (b) What skills did these settlers bring to their new home? List five.

2. Why did the Scotch-Irish come to America?

3. What were the main crops of the Middle Colonies?

4. (a) What did Benjamin Franklin contribute to Philadelphia? (b) What had Franklin accomplished by the time he had reached his fifties?

5. What were the consequences of the Zenger case?

6. (a) How did education in the Middle Colonies differ from education in New England? (b) What subjects were taught in schools in the Middle Colonies?

LIFE IN THE SOUTHERN COLONIES

READ TO FIND OUT

— what cash crops were grown on southern plantations.

— how slavery became part of the plantation economy.

— how people were educated in the Southern Colonies.

— how the back country was settled.

The rivers of the South laced the coastal plains and ran deep inland, and colonists scattered along these waterways. The soil was rich, the rain generous, and the climate warm almost year-round. This was planting land, fertile and plentiful, and it was soon dotted with farms and plantations.

Rivers became the arteries of the Southern Colonies, carrying the lifeblood of tobacco, rice, and other crops to market. Over the years, the river land filled up, and newcomers had to settle away from the waterways. Most made arrangements with the river planters to ship their crops and receive their imported goods. Thus, a settlement pattern developed in the Southern Colonies. There were few towns, most of the population was spread thinly, and each family was an island amidst its fields.

PLANTATIONS

The vast majority of southerners operated small farms, ranging from 50 acres (20 hectares) to a few hundred acres, and grew fruits, vegetables, and grains. A few had the help of an indentured servant, but most relied solely on the family to work the farm. With the region's good soil, the farmers grew enough to make a living. It was a modest living, without luxuries.

However, the kind of farming for which the South became noted was the large plantation. It produced a **cash crop**—a crop raised to be sold at a profit. In Virginia, Maryland, and part of North Carolina, tobacco was "king." Tobacco-growing quickly exhausted the soil, so planters had to obtain more and more land. Around 1700 prices for tobacco dropped, so only those planters with land enough to grow great quantities could profit. The planters became tied to merchants in England. The merchants bought the tobacco and advanced the planters credit to buy more land and support a growing supply of laborers.

Joshua Johnston painted ''the McCormick Family'' and other portraits of Baltimore's prosperous merchant families. A freeman, he was probably the first black portrait painter in America.

The eighteenth-century drawing shows skilled slaves harvesting, pressing, and drying indigo on a South Carolina plantation. Until the development of synthetic dyes in the mid-1800s, indigo was in great demand as the chief source of blue dye.

In South Carolina and Georgia the cash crops were rice and indigo, a plant used to make blue dye. Indigo was introduced to the South by Eliza Lucas Pinckney, the 17-year-old daughter of a South Carolina planter. During 1740, in her father's absence, she was left in charge of his plantations.

"I have the business of three plantations to transact, which requires much writing and more business and fatigue of other sorts than you can imagine," she wrote to a friend. Part of that business involved experimenting with crops suitable to Carolina. She noted "the pains I had taken to bring the indigo, ginger [and] cotton . . . to perfection, and had greater hopes from indigo (if I could have the seed earlier next year from the West India's) than any of the rest of the things I had tried." The hard work brought success. Pinckney developed a marketable indigo plant, which soon joined rice as a profitable export for the region.

Indigo and rice were good crops for the area, because each required a different type of land. Rice flourished in the swampy lowlands of Carolina and Georgia, and indigo grew well in loose, dry soil. With the introduction of indigo, thousands of previously unfarmed acres were put to use.

Like their tobacco-growing neighbors to the north, the indigo and rice planters depended on English merchants to buy their crops and to supply credit, supplies, and various "European goods fit for the season." The merchants, based in Savannah or Charleston, then shipped the crops to England. Rice and indigo exports soared, prices rose, and, as one resident of Charleston remarked, "The planters here all get rich."

Wealthy planters were the southern aristocracy and set the plantation way of life, which was followed by most planters with the necessary means. However, southern plantations came in several sizes. The average one had between 200 and 500 acres (80 to 200 hectares) and 10 to 12 slaves. From that size, plantations ranged down to 30 acres or less and no slaves or only one or two. On the other end of the scale, plantations ranged all the way up to sprawling estates of several thousand acres with hundreds of slaves.

The distance between neighbors meant that plantations became self-sufficient little worlds. Like a village, a good-sized plantation had its own blacksmith, miller, weaver, and butcher. Home became the substitute for the town church and school.

SLAVERY

Growing crops on such a huge scale called for a large pool of labor. At first most planters filled this need with indentured servants. However, after their period of service was over, these people were free to leave. To keep the plantation going, the planter then had to buy the contracts of new servants and train them.

In time, the planters relied more and more on another source of labor—black slaves. Although the cost of a slave was usually higher than the cost of a contract for an indentured servant, slaves provided nearly a lifetime of service. And the slaves' children belonged to the owner, which ensured a continuing labor supply.

The enslavement of blacks had developed slowly. Earlier, many blacks in the South had been indentured servants. Gradually, laws supporting the unofficial practice of slavery had been passed. In 1661 Virginia passed a law saying that some blacks were servants for life. By 1705 Virginia and South Carolina laws stated that slaves were "real estate." By the mid-1700s slavery was legal throughout the South. Slaves made up over 40 percent of Virginia's population and outnumbered whites in South Carolina by two to one.

The slave trade proved to be profitable for merchants. During the 1700s, New Englanders developed the triangular trade, making rum from West Indies sugar and selling it in Africa for slaves. The journey from Africa to the West Indies was the nightmarish "middle passage."

Hundreds of manacled Africans were jammed into the foul, airless hold of each ship. Many died on the crossing, perhaps 25 percent of them from disease. Some, during a brief period on deck, hurled themselves into the sea and drowned. The rest survived to be sold in the British West Indies, Latin America, or colonial slave ports like Newport, New York, Baltimore, and Charleston.

Not all slaves labored on the plantations. Many, along with free blacks, worked at trades in town. In Charleston, slaves could be found in all manner of occupations, from sweeping chimneys to shipbuilding.

Population of the Thirteen Colonies

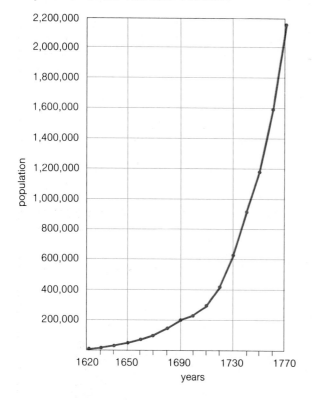

Black Population: Percent of the Total Population

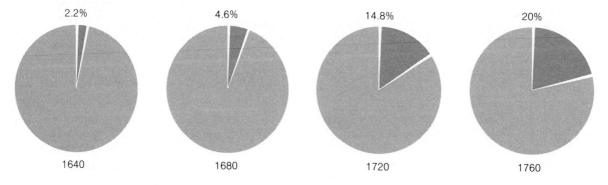

2.2%   4.6%   14.8%   20%

1640   1680   1720   1760

Many whites, fearing an uprising, kept an uneasy eye on the growing population of slaves. To keep the slaves under control, the whites adopted the restrictive *slave codes* used in the West Indies. Slaves could not hold religious meetings unless a white was present. They could not leave the plantation without a pass or assemble in groups away from the plantation.

However, slaves did revolt. In 1739 a slave uprising known as the Cato Conspiracy left some 75

AMERICAN OBSERVERS

OLAUDAH EQUIANO
AN EARLY PICTURE OF SLAVERY

"I had never heard of white men or Europeans, nor of the sea," wrote Olaudah Equiano of his childhood years in Africa. However, that soon changed. Born in 1745 in eastern Nigeria, Equiano was only eleven years old when he and his sister were kidnapped by slave traders. The two were quickly separated, never to see each other again. "I cried and grieved continually," Equiano remembered of that terrible time. "For several days I did not eat anything but what they forced in my mouth."

Taken to the African coast, he was put on a slave ship bound for the West Indies. The voyage was a nightmare. Equiano was thrust into the hot, stuffy hold, where slaves were chained so closely together that many died of suffocation. When the ship arrived in Barbados, young Equiano was sold to a Virginia planter.

At this point his luck changed. An English sea captain visiting the plantation took a liking to the frightened boy, purchased him, and took him to England. On board ship, Equiano was befriended by an American sailor, who taught him to read and write English. Later he was sold to a Philadelphia merchant, whose ships carried sugar, rum, and slaves between the West Indies and America.

Equiano was eventually able to buy his freedom, but his roving nature kept him traveling as a sailor. He journeyed to Turkey, the Arctic, and Central America.

In 1789 he published his own life story, *The Interesting Narrative*. A best seller, it went through eight editions in five years. By describing what it was like to be a slave, Equiano convinced many people to oppose the slave trade. "Surely this traffic cannot be good," he concluded, "which violates the first natural right of humanity, equality and independency, and gives one person dominion over another which God could never intend."

Godfrey Meynall's painting shows the crowded conditions aboard the slave ship *Albatross*. Some ships were so crowded that the slaves could not stand or sit up.

blacks and whites dead. Often, slaves ran away. Many runaways sought refuge with the Spanish in Florida, who promised freedom for slaves escaping England's colonies. Others fled to the Indians and were often accepted into tribal society. However, the vast majority remained in bonds. They could only develop their own society in the slave quarters.

Some whites sympathized with the blacks' plight and protested against slavery. The German Mennonites, a religious group with views similar to Quaker beliefs, made the first group protest in 1688. "There is a saying that we shall do to everyone like as we will be done ourselves, making no difference of what generation, descent, or color they are," their statement read. "To bring people hither, or to rob and sell them against their will, we stand against."

EDUCATION

Because the South had so few towns, there were few places to build schools. Most education, therefore, was left in the hands of families on farms and plantations. But there were some private elementary schools that taught reading, writing, arithmetic, and perhaps Latin.

Some people tried to educate Indians and slaves, although they were often blocked by southern laws that banned the teaching of reading and writing to slaves. In some places, though, slaves were allowed instruction so they could become Christians. In 1740 a Charleston school was set up to teach blacks to read the Bible.

Most of the South's private schools, however, were for the children of the wealthy. Often these schools were established by donors who left money in their wills. Perhaps the most successful was Virginia's Benjamin Symmes School, later Hampton Academy. The school was started in 1635.

Many wealthy planters brought schooling to the plantation, hiring tutors to teach their children at both elementary and secondary levels. Planters dissatisfied with education in America often sent their children to school in England.

The South did have one college, the second oldest in the colonies. In 1693 the English monarchs William and Mary granted a charter to the Reverend James Blair for a college in Virginia. Named for the king and queen, the College of William and Mary was similar to Harvard, offering classical instruction and training in the ministry.

Frontier schools had few books. A Georgia teacher, Thomas Perry, made his own schoolbooks. "The Hunter and the Buck" and the "Two Women and the Bear" illustrated his lessons.

THE BACK COUNTRY

There was a region to the west that colonists in the older, more settled areas called the *back country*. This slice of territory ran from the Pennsylvania-Maryland border southwest some 600 miles (966 kilometers) to Georgia, straddling the inland plateaus and hills of the Southern Colonies. This was the **frontier**, the place where the advancing line of settlers met the wilderness and began to tame it.

For many years hunters and fur traders had been trickling into the back country, which was home to Indians, deer, bear, wolves, and beaver. Then, beginning around 1730, the settlers began to come, traveling what became known as the Great Philadelphia Wagon Road. From Philadelphia, the road ran west through Lancaster County. Then it angled southwest into the hilly southern back country, following the route of an old Indian trail.

The settlers were mostly Germans and Scotch-Irish. They were driven to the back country by the high price of land in the eastern regions or sometimes by a desire for a more independent life. Eventually this tide from Pennsylvania met other

Settlement of the British Colonies

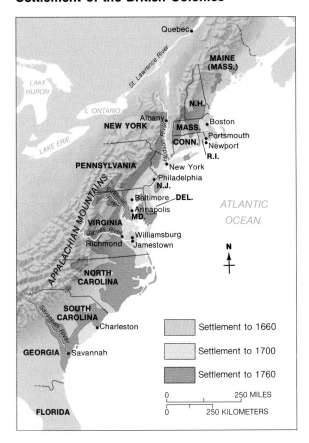

groups, "a mixed medley from all countries," flowing westward from the Virginia and Carolina lowlands. "The migrations of people are like the movements of a flock of sheep," observed one German on the road, "where one goes, the flock follows, without knowing why."

Although rich in soil, much of the back country was thickly forested and hilly. Many families simply cleared a few acres, built a rough log cabin, and planted their crops among the stumps. They were subsistence farmers, growing a few staples like corn, rye, barley, and vegetables.

In time, pockets of the back country grew crowded, villages sprang up, and local government was born. Government was generally arranged by eastern authorities, who extended the county system to the interior. Government officials filled a variety of needs: seeing that roads, bridges, and ferries were built, recording deeds, holding court, licensing taverns, paying bounties for wolves and bobcats. But government officials and rough pioneer folk did not always agree.

BACON'S REBELLION

In some areas, a rift developed between the back country and the lowlands, based in part on the small farmers' resentment of the aristocracy who controlled colonial affairs. As early as 1676, tensions had led to a clash on the Virginia frontier.

Settlements outside Jamestown had been terrorized by Indian attacks, but Virginia's governor, Sir William Berkeley, refused to order a counterattack. Frontier settlers were already annoyed at Berkeley's practice of giving political favors to friends. Now they accused him of protecting the fur trade at their expense.

Nathaniel Bacon, whose own farm was attacked, declared, "These traders at the head of the rivers buy and sell our blood." Bacon raised a force of angry farmers and led a series of attacks on Indian tribes, some of them friendly. Labeled a traitor by Berkeley, Bacon and 500 supporters then marched on Jamestown. The rebels took control of the government and forced the assembly to pass several reforms. Bacon's Rebellion collapsed, however, when Bacon suddenly died. But the tension between frontier settlers and easterners would continue over the years as the frontier line advanced westward.

SECTION REVIEW

1. Identify the following: Eliza Pinckney, "middle passage," slave codes, Cato Conspiracy, College of William and Mary, Bacon's Rebellion.

2. What advantage did southern river systems give southern agriculture?

3. (a) How large were most southern farms? (b) What large-scale system of farming developed in the South?

4. What was the status of blacks in the South before 1661?

5. (a) List the cash crops of the South. (b) Who bought most of these crops?

6. In what ways were plantations self-sufficient?

7. Describe two ways in which southern children were educated.

8. (a) Describe the extent and location of the back country. (b) Why were there conflicts between people in the back country and those in coastal areas?

RIVALRY FOR EMPIRE

READ TO FIND OUT

— how the Navigation Acts restricted colonial trade.

— how France extended its claims in North America.

— how the rivalry between France and Great Britain affected Indian life.

— how the French and Indian War began.

— how the Treaty of Paris divided land in North America.

"America has become the fountain of our riches," stated Great Britain's* *Gentleman's Magazine* in January 1755, "for with America our greatest trade is carried on." The colonies were fulfilling the mercantilist hopes of the early supporters of colonization.

To keep money flowing in, mercantilists called for a favorable balance of trade, in which a nation exported more goods than it imported. Colonies were ideal servants of mercantilism. They provided raw materials for the nation, reducing the quantity of materials that the nation had to buy from its competitors. The colonies also were a reliable market for the nation's exports.

However, the mercantilist system needed to be enforced. Some 90 percent of the colonists were farmers, and they needed markets in which to sell their crops. Since there was not much large-scale manufacturing in America, colonists also needed supplies and goods from other countries. Many colonists willingly traded with Britain's competitors, buying hats from the French or selling rice to the Spanish. Early in colonial history, therefore, Britain tried to keep the colonists in step with its mercantilist aims.

* In 1707 the Kingdom of England and Wales united with the Kingdom of Scotland under one government, called Great Britain. Colonists, however, continued to speak of "England" for some time. Even in Britain, the names "England" and "Great Britain" were used interchangeably.

THE NAVIGATION ACTS

Between 1660 and 1696 Parliament passed a series of laws to restrict colonial trade. The Navigation Acts ordered that all goods imported to the colonies or exported from them be carried in ships made or owned by the British or by colonists of British origin. Crews of these ships had to be 75 percent British. This action was directed, in part, against Dutch traders, who carried many colonial goods to market. Most goods from Europe bound for the colonies had to first pass through Britain and be taxed.

Further, the acts stated that certain *enumerated*, or listed, colonial goods—chiefly tobacco, sugar, indigo, and cotton—could be sold only to Britain or to another British colony. Enumerated goods shipped from colony to colony would be taxed in ports by newly appointed customs commissioners. Over the years, the British expanded the list of enumerated goods as the colonies developed more crops and raw materials. Added to the list were rice, furs, molasses, copper, iron, and naval goods like hemp, lumber, turpentine, tar, and resin.

In effect, the Navigation Acts gave Britain and British colonists control of colonial trade. Britain would not have to compete with other countries for

The schooner *Baltic* of Salem, Massachusetts, is greeted by a pilot boat. The *Baltic* and other merchant vessels built in the colonies were considered to be British ships.

American products, and the colonists had a sure market for their goods. Britain even encouraged production of goods it wanted, such as indigo, lumber, and hemp, by paying bonuses on delivery.

Vital to colonial trade was molasses, the basis of New England's triangular trade with West Indies planters and slave traders in Africa. The British West Indies could not supply enough molasses to meet the New England rum-makers' demand. So New England imported additional molasses from the French, Dutch, and Spanish West Indies. To give the British planters an edge, Parliament passed the Molasses Act in 1733. This levied high duties, or taxes, on molasses that was imported from the non-British West Indies.

New Englanders could not pay such ruinous charges and still make a profit. However, they managed to evade the duties by bribing customs officials or smuggling in the foreign molasses.

FRENCH CLAIMS IN AMERICA

While Great Britain was trying to control colonial trade, one of Britain's great rivals was staking claim to a huge slice of North America west of the colonies. The French had been established in New France since 1608. They had, however, a sparsely settled empire around the St. Lawrence River in northeastern Canada. The backbone of New France was the fur trade, which sent traders deep into the wilderness.

Then, in 1661, for the first time, the French encouraged immigration to North America. Settlers were even given land grants to farm. The grants, however, were assigned to army officers and gentlemen—people who were not farmers.

Not much came of French hopes for farming and for increasing the number of colonists in New France. The French did, however, expand the fur trade and, in the process, make more alliances with Indian tribes. Around 1670 French traders explored the Great Lakes country and claimed the area of Wisconsin for France. Indians there told of a great river to the west. This tale rekindled in the French their old dream of finding a Northwest Passage to the Pacific.

A fur trader named Louis Joliet (JŌ-lee-et) and a Jesuit missionary named Jacques Marquette (mahr-KEHT) were sent to find the great river. "The joy that we felt at being selected," wrote Mar-

quette, "animated our courage and rendered the labor of paddling from morning to night more agreeable to us." Marquette and Joliet traveled by canoe and portage* to the Wisconsin River, which carried them to the Mississippi. They paddled downstream for hundreds of miles, reaching an intersection with the Arkansas River. There, they learned from Indians that the Mississippi would carry them south into the Gulf of Mexico, not west to the Pacific.

In Quebec, Marquette and Joliet's report fired the imagination of two other people: Louis, Comte de Frontenac (FROHNT-NAHK), governor of New France, and a trader named Robert Cavelier, Sieur de La Salle (lah-SAHL). The Mississippi, the two men realized, could give France both control of America's interior and a fur-trading empire. They asked for and were granted permission by King Louis XIV to build a string of trading forts through the Great Lakes country and along the Mississippi.

Over the years the forts were built. Finally, in April 1682, La Salle followed the Mississippi all the way to the Gulf of Mexico. He claimed for France the entire region drained by the Mississippi and its tributaries, and named it Louisiana in honor of the king. Louisiana, noted a government memorandum of 1716, would serve as an "advance guard against the English colonies."

THE FRENCH AND INDIANS

By the 1720s French trading forts and settlements dotted the Gulf of Mexico at Biloxi, Mobile, and New Orleans and the Illinois country at Kaskaskia, Cahokia, and Vincennes. From the forts, the French continued their profitable fur trade with the Indians.

Even before the French arrived, the Algonquian tribes and the League of the Iroquois had fought over the St. Lawrence Valley. When the Algonquian became allies of the French, they also became enemies of the Dutch and British. Between 1642 and 1653, the Iroquois, armed by the Dutch, fought the Algonquian over the fur trade.

The tribes were also involved in a global conflict between Britain and France. Between 1689 and 1748, the two European nations fought three major

* portage (POR-tihj): carrying boats and supplies overland between navigable rivers.

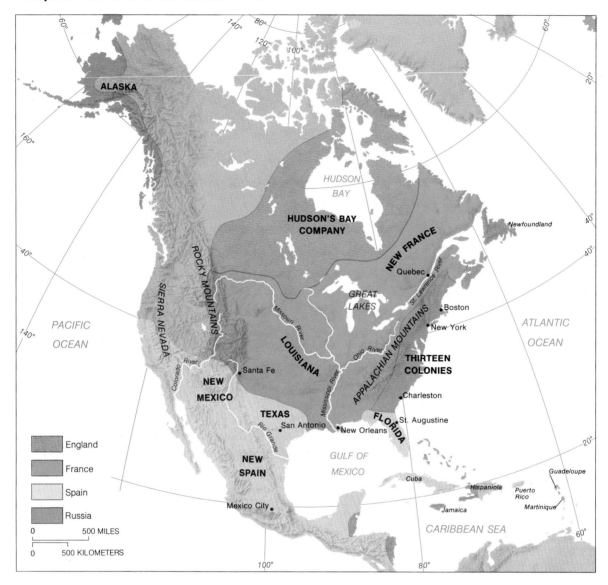

wars. The battles raged mainly in Europe, Asia, and the Pacific. In North America, far from the center of war, the British, French, and their Indian allies skirmished along the frontier.

None of the European wars was decisive. By mid-century France and Britain were technically at peace, but still competing for power. Their quarrel would explode again. It would be sparked by the conflicting claims of French and British colonists, each of whom wanted to settle in the fertile Ohio River valley.

RIVALRY OVER THE OHIO VALLEY

As the westward movement of settlers in the British colonies inched toward the Appalachian Mountains, land *speculators*—people willing to take a financial risk in the hope of making a huge profit—saw an opportunity. In 1747 a group of Virginia speculators formed the Ohio Company to gain ownership of land to the west. Two years later they obtained a royal grant for a huge amount of land in the Ohio River valley.

About the same time, other land companies obtained additional grants in the Ohio area. All planned to sell their land to settlers moving west.

The French, however, also claimed the Ohio Valley. They planned to build a line of forts across it to connect French Canada to Louisiana. Alarmed by the British plans, the French hurriedly sent troops to the region to support French claims.

The French also warned Indians in the region that the English were trying to "rob you of your country." This was precisely what many tribes feared. In the 1600s, in the Pequot War and King Philip's War, Indians had fought to halt English settlement and had lost. Now, the tribes hoped the Appalachians would prove a strong enough barrier to stop the tide of land-hungry settlers.

But it was the French, not the English, who first established themselves in the Ohio Valley. In 1753 the French began building their chain of forts, and English colonists began to worry. Some urged the Iroquois to take action against the French. Despite their own claims to the valley, the Iroquois stayed neutral. "We don't know what you Christians, English and French together, intend," they complained. "We are so hemmed in by both that we have hardly a hunting place left."

Meanwhile, the French forts were proving to be a real thorn in the side of the Ohio Company. The company asked for royal consent to build English forts in Ohio. In February 1754 a work party was sent to the Ohio Valley.

In April the lieutenant governor of Virginia sent out 120 Virginia militia* to protect the builders. In command was 22-year-old Major George Washington. A Virginia planter's son, Washington had worked as a surveyor. On the way to Ohio the militia met the work party, which had been forced by the French to retreat.

When Washington reached the Ohio site, he found the French building their own post, Fort Duquesne (doo-KAYN). Determined to force out the French, he had a stockade called Fort Necessity built about 40 miles (64 kilometers) away.

On a rainy July day, 1,000 French and their Indian allies attacked Washington's fort. After a nine-hour battle, the Virginians were driven out of the Ohio Valley.

*militia (muh-LISH-uh): an army of citizens rather than professional soldiers, to be called out in an emergency.

THE ALBANY PLAN OF UNION

While Washington was experiencing military defeat in Ohio, representatives from seven colonies were meeting at Albany, New York. They hoped to develop a program "for their mutual security and defense against the encroachment of their foreign neighbors." They had also been instructed by Britain to meet with Iroquois leaders.

The Iroquois had a list of complaints against the British, mostly about British settlers taking Iroquois land. The Iroquois were finally convinced by promises of better treatment. The alliance was renewed, but it was hasty patchwork.

Next, the Albany Congress turned to a plan proposed by Philadelphia's Benjamin Franklin. Franklin urged that the colonies form a union for their defense, to be headed by a royally appointed president and a legislature elected by the colonial assemblies. This government, which was given the power to tax, would be in charge of Indian relations, could raise an army and navy, declare war, and arrange peace treaties. The delegates adopted this bold Albany Plan, and it was sent to the colonial assemblies for approval.

However, not one colonial assembly approved the plan. No colony was willing to give up any of its power to a central government or to pay taxes for a common defense.

THE FRENCH AND INDIAN WAR BEGINS

The government in London, however, was determined to remove the French from the Ohio Valley. Since the colonies would not mount their own defense, Britain would pay for part of it and send British troops. The colonies, in turn, were expected to supply provisions and to raise several regiments of militia.

In April 1755 British General Edward Braddock arrived in Virginia as commander of the British forces in America. Braddock, military to the core but without much fighting experience, selected George Washington as his aide. Washington, who had retired to his plantation after the defeat in 1754, chose to serve as an unpaid volunteer.

On June 7 Braddock, Washington, and a force of 2,500 soldiers set out on a 110-mile (177-kilometer) march for Fort Duquesne. On July 9, only a few

Timelines show chronology, or the sequence of events, over a particular period of time. They can also show when different kinds of events took place or when events in different parts of the world took place in relation to one another.

Look at the two pages at the beginning of Unit 1 in your text. Use the timeline at the right to answer the following questions.

1. What period of history is covered in Unit 1? What four different kinds of events are shown on the timeline?

2. What is the earliest event shown on the timeline? What is the latest event?

3. What event was taking place in North America at the time Queen Elizabeth ruled England? What events were taking place in the colonies at about the time Peter the Great was visiting western Europe?

4. About how many years were there between the founding of Harvard College and the founding of William and Mary College? About how long after English colonists first settled Jamestown did Marquette and Joliet explore the Mississippi River?

5. What events that you have read about in Unit 1 would you choose to put on the timeline? Choose three to five events, and decide where you would put them.

---

miles short of the fort, disaster struck Braddock's expedition. About 900 French and Indians had marched out to meet the British, and the two forces came face to face. The French and Indians quickly scattered into the ravines that flanked both sides of the trail. The British were caught in a crossfire.

British casualties were large. Braddock was fatally wounded, and nearly two thirds of his force were killed or wounded. The French and Indians lost only about 60 of their number.

The British defeat laid open the Virginia, Maryland, and Pennsylvania western borders, and reports of Indian raids on frontier settlements became common. Meanwhile, British plans to capture other key French forts failed.

A campaign against Fort Niagara on Lake Ontario had to be given up when French reinforcements poured into that area. Then a colonial expedition against the French-held Crown Point on Lake Champlain failed. Thus, the French remained in command of Lake Champlain and even built another fort, Ticonderoga, to strengthen their hold.

The struggle that Americans called the French and Indian War continued to be a series of disasters for Britain and its colonies throughout 1756. In May of that year the conflict broadened when Britain declared war on France. Fighting between the British and French once more flamed across Europe, Asia, Africa, and on the seas. Other European nations lined up behind the two powers. The war begun in North America had become a world war, and it looked as if the British Empire might be lost.

THE BRITISH WIN

The tide began to shift against the French after William Pitt became secretary of state and leader of the British House of Commons in 1757. Pitt announced, "I am sure I can save this country, and nobody else can." Instead of tangling with the mighty French army in Europe, Pitt planned to seize the French colonies in North America.

Pitt poured money, supplies, and reinforcements into the British colonies. In 1758 he sent to America several generals who had been successful on European battlefields. Two of them—Jeffrey Amherst, a seasoned officer, and James Wolfe, a bold young fighter—quickly proved their worth.

In July 1758 Amherst and Wolfe led a force of 40 ships and 9,500 troops to Cape Breton Island, on the Gulf of St. Lawrence. There the two generals took Louisbourg, a French stronghold that commanded the entrance to the whole St. Lawrence region of New France.

The French and Indian War 1755-1763

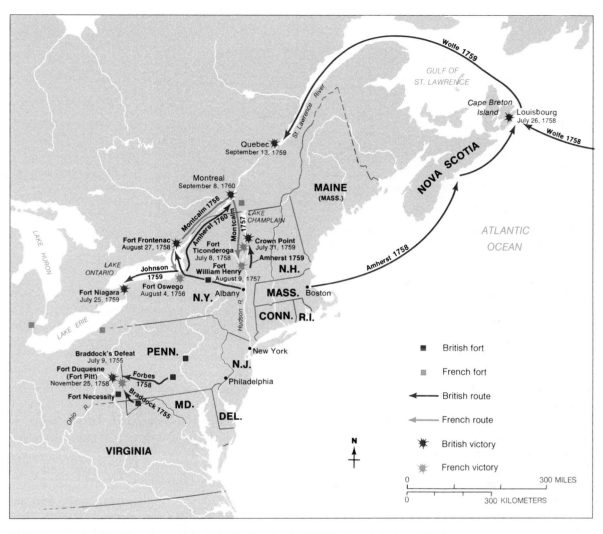

At first it seemed as if the French would win in North America. In 1756 the French destroyed Fort Oswego and other forts. In 1757 they took Fort William Henry, and a British attack at Fort Ticonderoga failed. Not until 1758 did a British victory seem possible.

This success was followed by two more British victories. In August the New England militia joined British regulars to take Fort Frontenac, located at the point where Lake Ontario feeds into the St. Lawrence. In November General John Forbes marched on Fort Duquesne, along a new road blazed by Washington and his militia. When Forbes reached Duquesne he found that the outnumbered French had burned and abandoned the fort. A new fort was built on the spot, named Fort Pitt in honor of the secretary of state.

The offensive against the French continued in 1759. Pitt developed a three-pronged attack against Niagara, Crown Point, and the French capital of Quebec. With the help of the Iroquois, Fort Niagara was taken in July. That same month Amherst broke through to Crown Point. By then, Wolfe and a fleet of 168 ships carrying 9,000 troops sailed along the St. Lawrence River outside Quebec.

Quebec was a walled city perched on rugged cliffs 200 feet (61 meters) above the St. Lawrence. The city and riverfront were defended by 14,000 French. Wolfe and his officers decided on a strategy. In the predawn hours of September 13, a group of small boats approached a cove beneath Quebec. From shore, French guards called out a

The English engraving shows in a single scene all the events leading to the capture of Quebec—British troops landing, scaling the cliffs, and fighting the battle.

challenge. A British officer who spoke French called back, *Vive le roi*! ("Long live the king!"). The British landed without any trouble.

Wolfe and his troops then scrambled up the cliffs and took control of the Plains of Abraham, a plateau around the city. By 8:00 A.M. more troops had arrived. When the French commander, Louis Joseph, Marquis de Montcalm, looked over the plains, he saw a double line of 4,500 British soldiers, or "redcoats."

Montcalm hurriedly assembled 4,500 French troops and marched on the British. The disciplined British troops waited until the French came within range, then unleashed a storm of musket and cannon fire. It was an overwhelming victory for the British. Both Montcalm and Wolfe were fatally wounded, but Wolfe realized that he died a victor: "Now, God be praised, I will die in peace."

With the fall of Quebec, the French lost the war in North America. The following year, Amherst captured Montreal and New France surrendered. In other parts of the world the fighting dragged on into 1762, as French forces crumbled on one battlefield after another.

THE TREATY OF PARIS

The French and Indian War came to an official end with the Treaty of Paris, signed in February 1763. Great Britain had at last defeated France in the great power struggle. The British navy was now ruler of the seas. The British army commanded Europe and North America. British ambassadors now outranked the representatives of France and Spain in the royal courts of Europe.

The treaty gave Britain vast new lands: all French territory in North America east of the Mississippi River except for two islands off the New-foundland coast and two in the Caribbean. From Spain, which had been France's ally, Britain received that troublesome land south of Georgia—Spanish Florida. To repay Spain, France gave to its ally the Louisiana territory west of the Mississippi.

The French had been driven from the continent of North America. American colonists joined the British in celebrating the great triumph. Statues were built to honor young King George III, who had become king in 1760. Americans composed a ballad to Wolfe, the hero of Quebec, who "did cross the ocean to free America from her invasion." Never had the colonies seemed so close to Great Britain.

SECTION REVIEW

1. Identify the following; Molasses Act, Louis Joliet, Jacques Marquette, Sieur de la Salle, William Pitt, Jeffrey Amherst, James Wolfe, Marquis de Montcalm.

2. (a) List the provisions of the Navigation Acts. (b) What colonial products eventually made up the list of enumerated goods? (c) How did the Navigation Acts benefit Great Britain? The colonies?

3. What did the French do to strengthen French claims in North America? What was the result?

European Claims in North America 1763

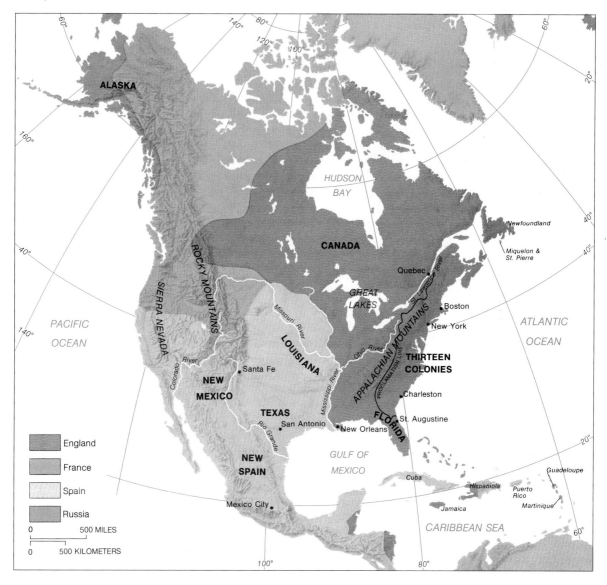

Following the defeat of the French in North America, British settlers began to move into the wilderness. To control westward expansion King George III proclaimed that for the time being colonists were forbidden to settle west of the crest of the Appalachian Mountains.

4. Explain ways in which the French affected Indian life.

5. (a) Why were the British interested in the Ohio River valley? (b) What plans did the French have for the Ohio River valley?

6. (a) Describe the Albany Plan of Union. (b) Why did colonial assemblies reject the Albany Plan?

7. How were the colonies expected to help Britain in the French and Indian War?

8. What were the results of Braddock's defeat in the wilderness?

9. Describe William Pitt's strategy against the French in 1759.

10. What were the provisions of the Treaty of Paris?

SUMMARY

By the 1750s regional characteristics began to develop in the Thirteen Colonies. Life in New England was shaped by the church and the land. The Puritans built villages around church congregations. These villages eventually swelled into cities. The land—rocky and hilly—discouraged large-scale agriculture. Thus, New Englanders became merchants, shipbuilders, and sailors.

The Middle Colonies represented a coming together of cultures. The majority of colonists were English, but there were also Germans, Scotch-Irish, Swedish, Dutch, and Finns. The land and climate in the Middle Colonies were suitable for agriculture. The settlers built prosperous farms that were soon able to supply far more wheat and corn than the farmers themselves could use. So they sold the remainder at home and abroad.

In the Southern Colonies the immigrants had a large area over which to spread. The warm weather proved ideal for the cash crops rice and indigo. Plantations developed, some of them sprawling over hundreds of acres. At first, workers in the fields were indentured servants. Soon, though, blacks were enslaved and forced to do field work. Strict control of the slaves became part of the plantation system. Beyond the plantations, some settlers began moving into the back country.

As the colonies prospered, they became an important part of Britain's empire. Between 1660 and 1696, Parliament tried to restrict colonial trade by passing the Navigation Acts. The Navigation Acts were an attempt to force the colonists to buy only British goods. Then, in 1733, Parliament passed the Molasses Act, designed to force colonists to buy molasses only from British planters.

The colonists' attention was directed away from Britain's actions by problems on the western frontier. Settlers from the colonies began to spill into the Ohio Valley and came into conflict with French fur traders. In 1754 this conflict exploded into war between France and Britain, who were already bitter enemies. In 1763 England emerged victorious from the French and Indian War. The French had been driven from North America, and the colonists' attachment to Britain had never been stronger.

A shipwright pounds pegs into a ship's hull. Fishing and commerce led to shipbuilding as a major colonial industry. Shipyards sprang up from the Carolinas to Maine.

CHAPTER REVIEW

1. (a) Compare farm life in the New England Colonies with farm life in the Middle Colonies and in the Southern Colonies. (b) Give reasons for the differences that you find.

2. (a) Compare education in New England with the education in the Middle Colonies and in the Southern Colonies. (b) Give reasons for the differences that you find. (c) How did the education available reflect farm and city life in each area?

3. New Englanders quickly earned a reputation for shrewdness. What New England activities might have caused this reputation to develop?

4. Southern farm families lived in isolation amidst their fields. How did this pattern of settlement develop?

5. (a) What were the main sources of income for the New England, Middle, and Southern colonies? (b) How did these sources of income affect the treatment of blacks in each area?

6. (a) Why did the hiring of indentured servants give way to the practice of buying black slaves in the South? (b) How did laws contribute to the growth of slavery in the South? (c) How did New England laws affect blacks?

7. (a) Not all settlers in the Thirteen Colonies came from England. From what other areas did colonists come? In what areas did each group settle? (b) The colonists also came from a variety of religious backgrounds. List five different religious groups. Tell in which colonies each could be found.

8. (a) What was the basis for French claims in the Ohio River valley? (b) What was the basis for English claims in the Ohio River valley? (c) Which nation had the stronger claim? Why? (d) How did each nation attempt to use the Indians in the region to gain their objectives?

9. (a) Why did the French win victories early in the French and Indian War? (b) Why did the tide turn in favor of the English? (c) What were the results of the war?

10. Why did the colonies seem closer to Great Britain in 1763 than at any time in the preceding century?

ISSUES AND IDEAS

1. To the Puritans, education was vital. Do you think that education is still very important to Americans today? In what ways?

2. (a) What might have happened to the English colonies if England had been defeated in the French and Indian War? (b) What might have happened in the Ohio Valley with an English defeat in the war? (c) What do you think America would have been like today? Why?

3. Jean de Crèvecoeur wrote that the inhabitants of "Massachusetts, the middle provinces, the southern ones will be as different as their climates." In what way was this true? False? Is this description still true today? Why or why not?

German settlers practiced the art of *Fraktur*, a handwritten script. Valentines, family documents, and house blessings were written in *Fraktur* on hand-decorated homemade paper.

Both fact and fancy appear in the picture embroidered early in the eighteenth century. The building in the picture is actually a composite of two buildings at Harvard College.

SKILLS WORKSHOP

1. *Timelines.* Make a timeline of the major events of the French and Indian War from 1755 to 1763. Put a brief description by each event.

2. *Maps.* Look at page 731 of your text. Find the map entitled "Agriculture and Industry 1980." Think of the products of the New England Colonies, the Middle Colonies, and the Southern Colonies. Are the products of those regions of the United States today similar to the products of the three regions in colonial times? Explain the similarities and the differences.

PAST AND PRESENT

1. Gather information about the ways that colonists made a living. What colonial occupations no longer exist? When did they disappear? Why? What present-day occupations do you think will cease to exist? When? Why?

2. By 1750 people from many nations had settled in America. Gather information about your ancestors. When did they immigrate? From where? Why? Compare their reasons for immigration with those of the colonists.

OUT OF MANY, ONE

1763–1801

Unknown artist. *Washington's Triumphal Entry into New York in 1783,* late nineteenth century.

1600	1700	1800	1900	2000
• Jamestown founded		• Revolutionary War • Civil War		• Today

UNIT 2
1763–1801

	1770	1780	1790	1800	1810
			Washington	Adams	Jefferson	

POLITICAL

• Proclamation of 1763
• Stamp Act
• Townshend Acts
• Boston Tea Party
• Intolerable Acts
• First Continental Congress
• American Revolution
• Declaration of Independence
• Northwest Ordinance
• Constitution ratified
• Bill of Rights
• Alien and Sedition Acts

SOCIAL

• *Encyclopaedia Britannica*
• Adam Smith: *Wealth of Nations*
• Noah Webster: *The American Spelling Book*
• Mozart: *The Marriage of Figaro*
• Boswell: *Life of Johnson*

TECHNOLOGICAL

• Mesmer introduces hypnotism
• Watt perfects steam engine
• First balloon ascension
• Dr. Benjamin Rush opens first free dispensary
• John Fitch launches first steamboat
• Eli Whitney: cotton gin
• Volta perfects battery

INTERNATIONAL

• Louis XVI: king of France
• Spain recovers Florida
• French Revolution
• Louis XVI and Marie Antoinette executed
• Napoleon seizes power in France
• Union of Great Britain and Ireland

1770	1780	1790	1800	1810

79

CHAPTER 4

THE STRUGGLE FOR INDEPENDENCE

1763–1783

BRITAIN ANGERS THE COLONIES
THE PATH TO WAR
THE BREAK WITH BRITAIN
FIGHTING FOR INDEPENDENCE

In 1766 the British Parliament wanted answers to some questions. Benjamin Franklin answered them, saying that the colonists' feelings toward England had changed:

"Q.—What is your name, and place of abode?

A.—Franklin, of Philadelphia.

Q.—Do you think it right America should be protected by this country, and pay no part of the expense?

A.—That is not the case. The colonies raised, clothed and paid, during the last war, near 25,000 men, and spent many millions. . . .

Q.—Do not you think the people of America would . . . pay the stamp duty, if it was moderated?

A.—No, never, unless compelled by force. . . .

Q.—What was the temper of America towards Great Britain before the year 1763?

A.—The best in the world. . . .

Q.—And what is their temper now?

A.—O, very much altered. . . .

Q.—What used to be the pride of Americans?

A.—To indulge in the fashions and manufactures of Great Britain.

Q.—What is now their pride?

A.—To wear their old clothes over again."

Once, most people in the English colonies saw themselves as loyal subjects of the Crown. Of course, not all were English. But those who were, remembered England, Parliament, and the Crown with deep affection and pride. Their children, born in the New World, learned of the old homeland at their grandparents' knees.

As the years passed, the old memories faded and a new generation of children heard different stories. They heard how their grandmother lived in three different colonies. Their grandfather talked of being elected to the colonial assembly. As the memories of the past changed, dreams of the future changed, too.

BRITAIN ANGERS
THE COLONIES

READ TO FIND OUT

— how Great Britain tried to strengthen its
  control of the colonies.

— why the colonists objected to the Stamp Act.

— how Great Britain planned to enforce the
  Townshend Acts.

— what the Boston Massacre meant to the colonists.

— how committees of correspondence linked the
  colonies.

— why the Tea Act angered the colonists.

The year was 1765. An angry crowd gathered in
Boston. A ship had arrived that morning with news
that Parliament had passed yet another tax act.

Soon, a speaker told the crowd, taxes would enslave the colonies. The angry colonists shouted in
agreement.

The colonists' anger had been growing since the
end of the war with France. Britain had passed law
after law that chipped away at their rights—the
rights guaranteed them as British citizens. The first
interference in colonial affairs had occurred two
years before, in 1763, after an Indian uprising in the
western lands.

THE PROCLAMATION OF 1763

After the French surrendered to the British, settlers
once again began flowing into Indian lands—the
lands of the Seneca, Delaware, Shawnee, Ottawa,
and others. In May 1763, only three months after
the Treaty of Paris was signed, Indian resentment
of settlers led to bloodshed. Eighteen tribes had
formed an alliance, with the Ottawa chief Pontiac
as their leader. Traveling over 1,000 miles (1,600
kilometers), they began attacking British forts and
settlements along the Great Lakes and Appalachian
Mountains.

The war, called Pontiac's Rebellion, dragged on
until August 1764, when Indian attacks on Fort Pitt
and Fort Detroit failed. Expected French supplies
never came, and the Indian alliance was eventually
broken. Pontiac's Rebellion had nearly succeeded,
however, for the Indians had captured every British
fort except Pitt, Detroit, and Niagara.

The rebellion convinced King George III and
Parliament that the costly fighting should not be
repeated. The British decided to keep the settlers
and the angry tribes apart. In October 1763 the king
proclaimed that all lands beyond the Appalachians
be closed to "any purchases and settlements."

The Proclamation of 1763 was designed to do
more than eliminate the cost of protecting settlers. It
would leave the western fur trade solely to the British. And it would stop the colonists from expanding
westward, away from British control.

A tide of anger swept through the colonies. The
colonists had fought and died for this land, and they
felt Britain was unfair in denying it to them. They
were further angered by the British decision to keep
an army of 10,000 soldiers in America to defend
Britain's empire. The colonists protested to Parliament. But Britain had its own troubles and
expected help, not protest, from its colonies.

Artist Richard Brunt portrayed Mrs. Reuben Humphreys of Connecticut with Eliza, one of her twelve children. Mrs. Humphreys' fashionable clothing was imported from England.

GRENVILLE TAXES THE COLONIES

Britain's victory in the French and Indian War expanded its empire, and Britain's victory in Pontiac's Rebellion strengthened its control over the western lands. Victory, however, proved costly.

Britain's latest war against the French had doubled its national debt. The newly won territories stretched across Canada and south through the eastern Mississippi Valley. This empire had to be protected and governed, and that cost money. In Britain people had already rioted over a new tax to raise revenue.

Britain's new chancellor of the exchequer* was George Grenville. He thought that the colonies should bear some of these costs. Up to this time Britain had levied customs duties to regulate colonial trade. The customs service levied lower duties on goods brought in from Britain than on goods imported from other nations. Thus, the colonists were encouraged to trade only with Britain. Duties often went uncollected, however, because Americans smuggled many goods into the colonies.

* chancellor of the exchequer (eks-CHEK-er): the minister of finance in the British government.

Grenville found that the British customs service in America cost more to operate than it collected in duties. A bold step was needed, he decided. New duties would be imposed to raise money.

In March 1764 Parliament passed the Sugar Act, which added or increased duties on foreign imports such as sugar, wine, cloth, and coffee. The act also reduced a previous duty on molasses, in the hope that colonists would pay it. They had evaded the earlier duty by smuggling in molasses from the French West Indies.

To stop the smuggling, Grenville strengthened the customs service. Collectors were encouraged to use warrants* called *writs of assistance* to search any building that might contain illegal goods. Furthermore, accused smugglers would no longer be tried in courts with juries of their fellow colonists. Instead, they would be tried in British admiralty courts* before a British judge. The right to a trial by a jury of their peers was thus denied the colonists.

That same year Parliament passed the Currency Act to control colonial printing of money. Over the years, colonists had spent much of their gold and silver to pay for British goods. More gold and silver flowed out of the colonies than came in to them. Because they did not have enough of this *hard currency*, the colonists printed paper money and used it to pay Britain.

The Currency Act ordered colonial legislatures to stop printing paper money. All duties and debts that colonists owed British creditors would now have to be paid with gold and silver. The colonists soon had trouble transacting their daily business.

Next, Parliament found a way to reduce Britain's costs for its troops in America. In March 1765 it passed the Quartering Act, which required colonial assemblies to provide the royal troops with barracks and supplies. The following year the act was expanded to include taverns, barns, and empty houses as troop quarters.

Britain's attempts to raise money infuriated many colonists. James Otis, leader of the Massachusetts assembly, said of the Sugar Act: "One single act of Parliament has set the people a-thinking in six months more than they have done in their whole lives before."

* warrants: legal documents authorizing some action.

* admiralty court: court dealing with laws of the sea and ships.

THE STAMP ACT

On October 31, 1765, the publisher of a Pennsylvania newspaper printed this statement:

> I am sorry to have to tell my readers that as the Stamp Act will have to be enforced after the first of November (the fatal tomorrow) the publisher of this paper is unable to bear the burden. I have decided it is better to stop printing for a while and to think about ways we can find to avoid the chains forged for us, and to escape this slavery.

On November 1, 1765, the Stamp Act went into effect. Under this act, written material such as newspapers, contracts, birth certificates, diplomas, and advertisements would have to be printed on a special stamped paper. Colonists could get the paper from local British tax agents, to whom they would pay a tax. Those who violated the Stamp Act would be tried in admiralty courts. Again basic rights of British citizens—such as the right to trial by a jury of one's peers—were violated.

Previous acts of Parliament had angered colonists, but this one began to unite them as well. The Stamp Act touched everyone. It was a *direct tax*, a tax levied on the people by the government to raise money. The Sugar Act also was designed to raise money, but it was an *indirect tax*, a tax designed as a duty.

Most colonists realized that they were not being taxed more than people in Britain, who also paid a stamp tax. But colonists objected to the *way* they were taxed. The colonial assemblies gave colonists direct representation, because the colonists themselves elected the delegates. These delegates then levied taxes.

The colonists, however, did not elect representatives to the British Parliament. Although Parliament claimed to represent all British subjects, the colonists felt they had no direct representation.

From New Hampshire to Georgia, a small but determined minority of Americans set to work. In town after town these Patriots* formed groups called the Sons of Liberty and the Daughters of Liberty. Patriotic merchants refused to trade with Britain. Women in the liberty groups organized to *boycott* British goods, refusing to buy or use them.

* Patriots: colonists who demanded British remedies for their grievances and, finally, complete independence from Britain.

Stamp Act protests occurred in every colony. Some were orderly; others were not. This etching of Bostonians burning stamped paper appeared in a German history book.

The Virginia House of Burgesses declared that only it had the "sole exclusive right and power to lay taxes . . . upon the inhabitants of this colony." Massachusetts, mirroring this mood, called for a Stamp Act Congress. In response, representatives from nine colonies met in New York in October 1765.

At the Congress, Representative Christopher Gadsden of South Carolina put the new spirit of unity into words: "There ought to be no New Englanders, no New Yorkers, known on the continent, but all of us Americans." In a petition to Parliament, the Congress urged repeal of the Stamp Act.

The petition reached an England already divided over the tax issue. The American boycott had hurt English merchants. Within a few months, exports to America had fallen about 40 percent.

In March 1766 the Stamp Act was repealed. In a goodwill gesture, Parliament even reduced the duty on molasses. However, Parliament did not want the colonists to get too headstrong. On the same day

Colonial Trade with Britain

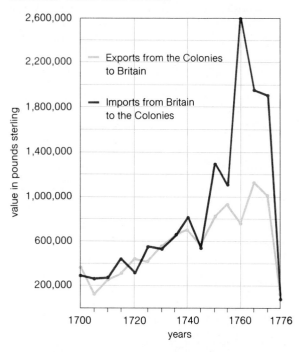

In the 1700s Britain turned increasing attention to colonial trade. The graph reflects mercantilism. Colonies provided raw materials and markets for the home country.

that it repealed the Stamp Act, Parliament passed the Declaratory Act, which upheld Parliament's power to make laws for the colonies "in all cases whatsoever."

THE TOWNSHEND ACTS

One year later, Britain's problem remained—it needed money. The country was now suffering through a **depression**, a time of declining business activity, falling wages and prices, and widespread unemployment. With Britons crying out for economic relief, Parliament cut their land taxes. The new chancellor of the exchequer, Charles Townshend, like Grenville, turned to the colonies for revenue.

In May 1767 Parliament passed the Townshend Acts. New duties were levied on imports such as paper, glass, paint, lead, and tea. The Townshend Acts provided for a supervisory board in Boston that would keep a close eye on the collection of duties. To

further curb smuggling and bribery, the acts gave customs officials greater power to use writs of assistance and provided for new admiralty courts to judge all offenders.

Townshend also enforced the Quartering Act, which the colonial assemblies had been evading. In December 1766 the New York assembly had refused to raise money to supply British troops, claiming that the Quartering Act was a tax. The third Townshend Act suspended the New York assembly for its defiance. Colonists worried that if New York's assembly could be suspended, no assembly was safe. Without assemblies, there would be no representative government.

John Dickinson, a Philadelphia lawyer, wrote essays in which he raised the three-year-old American complaint: The colonies would accept duties that regulated trade, but no taxes disguised as duties. People demonstrated across the colonies. Women organized spinning bees to make American cloth. Tea was smuggled in or brewed from raspberry leaves.

THE BOSTON MASSACRE

In September 1768 two regiments of British soldiers arrived in Boston and took up quarters in the hostile city. Throughout 1769 an uneasy standoff prevailed. Then, on March 5, 1770, an incident led to violence. A crowd gathered at the Boston customshouse, jeering and throwing snowballs at British troops guarding the place. Tempers exploded, and the troops fired. When the smoke cleared, three of the people in the crowd lay dead, and two were fatally wounded.

The British commander, Captain Thomas Preston, and eight soldiers were arrested and charged with murder. But Massachusetts lawyer John Adams worried that if the British could not get a fair trial in America, where liberty and justice were so highly prized, then the Patriots' ideals meant nothing. Joined by Josiah Quincy, John Adams himself undertook the defense of the British.

The two Patriot lawyers managed to prove that the crowd had provoked the shooting. Preston and six soldiers were acquitted, and two others were given light punishment.

Despite his cousin's defense of the British soldiers, Samuel Adams, a member of the Massachusetts assembly, saw the "Boston Massacre" as a

Paul Revere condemned the British for the "Boston Massacre" with this engraving. In fact, British Captain Preston was trying to stop the fight, not waving his sword. Revere added the sign, "Butcher's Hall," to the British customs-house. The engraving was widely circulated.

symbol of British tyranny. For years to come, his speeches, pamphlets, and newspaper articles would remind the colonists of that day. These reminders fed the fire of liberty, wrote one Patriot, "and kept it burning with an incessant flame."

COMMITTEES OF CORRESPONDENCE

In London a new prime minister, Lord Frederick North, felt that the Townshend Acts had been a mistake. The acts brought little money in duties, and worse, British trade to major colonial ports had already been cut in half by the boycott.

On March 5, 1770, the same day that the Boston Massacre occurred, Parliament repealed the Townshend Acts. Shortly after, the Quartering Act was allowed to expire. But Lord North did not want

American colonists to think that, by protesting, they could control Parliament. One Townshend tax was kept—the duty on tea.

Two years of calmness followed. Then, in June 1772, the British warship *Gaspee* went aground off Rhode Island while chasing a suspected smuggler. A crowd boarded the hated ship, chased off the crew, and burned the *Gaspee*.

Britain appointed a commission in America to investigate, and rumors quickly spread that anyone arrested would be sent to England for trial. The colonists were outraged by this threat to their cherished right to trial by a jury of their community. But the commission could find no evidence, and no one was arrested.

Shortly after the *Gaspee* incident, Thomas Hutchinson, the governor of Massachusetts, announced that his salary would hereafter be paid from cus-

Samuel Adams was a quiet man but he had the power to bring people together. He was dedicated to defending the rights that had been granted to colonists in their colonial charters.

toms revenues rather than by the Massachusetts assembly. A second announcement disclosed that judges would be paid in the same way. The one power that the assembly had had over the governor and judges had been "the power of the purse," and that power was now gone.

Samuel Adams saw a chance to unite the colonists against the British. He asked a Boston town meeting to appoint a *committee of correspondence* to communicate grievances against the British with colonists in other towns. Samuel Adams's idea spread throughout the colonies. By August 1774 all of the colonies were linked by committees of correspondence.

THE TEA ACT

In May 1773 Parliament unwittingly gave the colonists another reason to protest when it passed the Tea Act. The purpose of this act was simply to aid the failing British East India Company, which sold tea to America.

For years, British wholesale merchants had bought tea from the East India Company, then sold it to American wholesalers, who sold it to American retailers. By the time the tea reached the shops, its price was high, so most Americans bought cheaper tea smuggled in from Holland.

The Tea Act allowed the East India Company to sell its tea directly to American retailers, dispensing with all wholesale costs. The act also removed all duties, except the Townshend duty, on British tea exported to America. Now the price of East India Company tea was less than that of smuggled tea.

Soon American wholesale merchants were complaining that the Tea Act was causing them to lose business. Before long, they said, the East India Company would control all tea sales in America, and then everyone would have to buy British tea. And what, merchants asked, would keep the British from controlling other American businesses? The Tea Act set off a chain reaction that soon carried the colonies to open rebellion.

SECTION REVIEW

1. Identify the following: Pontiac, Sugar Act, Stamp Act, Sons and Daughters of Liberty, Townshend Acts, John Adams, Samuel Adams, *Gaspee*, British East India Company, Tea Act, Thomas Hutchinson.

2. Define the following: writs of assistance, hard currency, direct tax, indirect tax, boycott, committees of correspondence.

3. Why did King George III issue the Proclamation of 1763?

4. What actions did Grenville take to stop smuggling?

5. Why did the colonists object to the Currency Act?

6. (a) Why did the Stamp Act Congress object to the Stamp Act? (b) What had Patriots achieved by protesting the Stamp Act?

7. (a) What was the purpose of the Townshend duties? (b) How did Great Britain plan to enforce the duties? (c) Why did colonists object to the duties?

8. (a) Why did John Adams defend the British soldiers who had been involved in the Boston Massacre? (b) How did Samuel Adams view the Boston Massacre?

9. Why were committees of correspondence formed?

10. Why did colonists object to the Tea Act even though it lowered the price of tea?

THE PATH TO WAR

READ TO FIND OUT

— how Parliament responded to the Boston Tea Party.

— what the First Continental Congress did about the growing conflict.

— how the first shots were fired at Lexington and Concord.

— why the Battle of Bunker Hill elated Patriots.

— how the Patriots drove the British out of Boston.

The Sons of Liberty were ready when the first shiploads of East India Company tea arrived in late 1773. In Charleston the Patriots locked up the tea in a warehouse. In New York and Philadelphia they ordered ships' captains to leave without unloading. In Annapolis, Maryland, they burned a ship carrying tea.

In Boston the Sons of Liberty disguised themselves as Indians, boarded the ships, and dumped the tea into the harbor. This event—the Boston Tea Party—became the symbol of an angry people.

THE INTOLERABLE ACTS

The Boston Tea Party outraged the British—and many Americans. Destruction of valuable property could not be taken lightly. So, in May 1774 Parliament passed the four Coercive Acts. These acts were designed to punish Massachusetts, the heart of American patriotism. Massachusetts would be an example to other colonies where Patriots might be tempted to destroy British tea.

One of the acts, the Boston Port Bill, closed the harbor until the tea was paid for, cutting off the city's lifeline of trade. A second measure, the Ad-

Hundreds of people crowded the wharf to watch the Patriots "making salt water tea" in Boston harbor. The Sons of Liberty, some in disguise, were joined aboard the ship by several bystanders. In 1789 this engraving of the Tea Party was published in a British history of North America.

Colonial Tea Imports from England

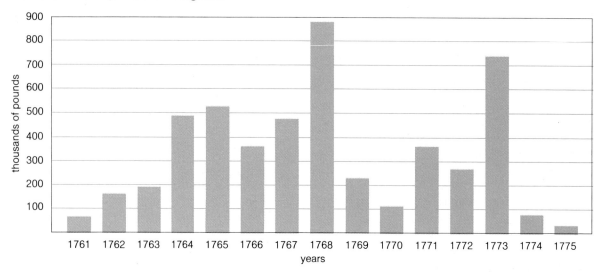

ministration of Justice Act, protected Crown officials in Massachusetts. If British officials were accused of committing an offense while collecting duties or putting down "riots and tumults," they could be tried in another colony or in Britain.

A third measure reorganized the Massachusetts government. The Massachusetts Government Act revoked most of the colony's independent rights under the Massachusetts charter. Members of the governor's council, previously elected by the assembly, were now to be appointed by the king. Sheriffs and many court officials would be appointed by the governor.

The Massachusetts Government Act reached to the heart of the colony's political rights. Juries would now be chosen by the sheriff, the governor's underling. Town meetings, the birthplace of Samuel Adams's committees of correspondence, could now meet only with the governor's consent and could discuss only what the governor approved.

The new governor of Massachusetts was General Thomas Gage, whose troops had been denied quarters and supplies by the New York assembly in 1766. Gage commanded the entire British army in North America. In Massachusetts civil authority had been replaced by military authority.

A fourth measure, the Quartering Act, applied to all colonies. The Quartering Act of 1765 and 1766 had directed colonies to house troops in barracks, taverns, or deserted buildings. The new Quartering

Act stated that if such quarters were not available, troops would be quartered in occupied dwellings—even homes.

Parliament then passed the Quebec Act. Although it was not part of the coercive program, colonists considered it in the same light. The Quebec Act gave Canada a permanent government, tightly controlled by Britain. Britain also granted religious freedom to Canada's Roman Catholics, and recognized privileges such as tithing,* claimed by the Catholic Church.

Many Protestant Americans had long distrusted the Catholic Church and objected to Britain's support of Catholicism in Canada. Equally worrisome to Americans was the Quebec Act's extension of Canada's boundary south to the Ohio River. Virginia, Massachusetts, and Connecticut all claimed land in that region. Colonists saw this as part of Britain's plan to punish them by cutting them off from western expansion.

The Coercive Acts shocked people throughout the colonies. Colonists called them the Intolerable Acts. Committees of correspondence spread news of Boston's plight from town to town. From as far away as South Carolina, wagonloads of supplies rolled into Boston. The committees soon adopted

---

* tithing (TĪTH-ing): to collect a portion of people's income or of the produce of their land as a contribution for the support of a church.

GRAPH READING
COLONIAL TEA IMPORTS FROM ENGLAND

Graphs, like maps, are a visual means of showing information. To read a graph, you must look first at the parts, or elements, of the graph. Look at the parts of the graph entitled "Colonial Tea Imports from England," on the facing page, to answer the following questions.

1. What kind of numbers are shown on the horizontal scale of the graph? What do the numbers on the left-hand, or vertical scale, indicate?

2. Find the bar for the year 1766. The top of the bar is more than half-way between 300 and 400 on the left scale. This shows that in 1766 more than 350,000 pounds of tea were imported from England. How many pounds were imported in 1763? How many pounds were imported in 1768? In what year did the total amount of tea imported from England first surpass 500,000 pounds?

After you have looked at the elements of a graph, you can interpret the information. Use the material in your text along with the graph to answer the following questions.

3. Britain passed the Stamp Act in 1765. What action did the colonists take in response? How did the colonists' response affect tea imports in 1766?

4. In 1767 the Townshend Acts went into effect. In 1768 the colonists agreed not to import certain goods, including tea. How are the effects of this agreement shown on the graph?

5. What act was passed by Britain in 1773? How did the colonists respond? Use the graph to explain how the colonists' response affected tea imports.

6. Why was so little tea imported from Britain in 1774 and 1775?

---

resolutions calling the acts "oppressive and tyrannous," but declaring their loyalty to King George. They urged colonists to meet at a continental congress to decide what to do.

In Virginia the House of Burgesses protested the Intolerable Acts, so the governor disbanded it. The representatives gathered at a tavern in Williamsburg. They, too, called for a congress of the colonies.

Parliament had not crushed the defiance in Massachusetts. Instead, the Intolerable Acts had made the colony a martyr, and spread the spirit of the Boston Tea Party. At a Massachusetts inn John Adams asked for a cup of tea—"provided it has been honestly smuggled." The innkeeper replied that "we have renounced all tea in this place." Adams approved: "Tea must be universally renounced. I must be weaned, and the sooner, the better."

THE FIRST CONTINENTAL CONGRESS

In September 1774 John Adams arrived in Philadelphia. In that city 56 delegates from all the colonies except Georgia were meeting in the First Continental Congress.

The Adams cousins and some other Patriots were already talking about independence—a complete break with Britain—if their demands were not met. Although they were a minority in the Congress, these Patriots were united and determined.

One of them was Patrick Henry, a member of the Virginia House of Burgesses. Unlike the aristocratic leaders of Virginia, Henry came from the frontier. He had failed as a storekeeper, gone into law, and discovered a talent for speechmaking. Another was Richard Henry Lee, a Virginia planter, who strongly believed in print as a means of spreading the Patriot viewpoint. Lee had a ready supply of pamphlets, letters, and articles to give to newspaper editors with space to fill. Also a member of the group considering independence was Christopher Gadsden, a plantation owner who was well known and well respected in South Carolina.

Other Patriots, including Virginia planter George Washington, took a more moderate view and wanted to compromise with Britain. Pennsylvania lawyer John Dickinson, for example, had written essays protesting the Townshend Acts. Nevertheless, he opposed a split with Britain, especially a violent one.

MERCY OTIS WARREN
PLAYWRIGHT OF THE REVOLUTION

Not long after the Boston Tea Party in 1773, John Adams asked Mercy Otis Warren, a Massachusetts housewife and mother of five children, to write a poem about it. "I wish to see a late glorious event celebrated by a certain poetical pen," he said, "which has no equal that I know of in this country." She agreed, and soon the colonists were enjoying her verses in a Boston newspaper.

Mercy Warren was a slender, intense woman with a keen wit. Like her brother, James Otis, and her husband, James Warren, she was deeply involved in the independence movement. She had never seen a play, because performances were prohibited in Boston. Yet, it was mainly as a playwright that she supported the cause.

Her first play, *The Adulateur*, (meaning "The Flatterer") had appeared as an unsigned pamphlet in 1772. The villain was a grasping tyrant named Rapatio, whom everyone recognized as the royal governor, Thomas Hutchinson. In later plays she continued her slashing attack on the British and American Loyalists, disguising them with such mocking names as Brigadier Hate-All, Hum Humbug, Simple Sapling, and Sir Sparrow Spendall.

Her plays delighted the revolutionaries, who eagerly passed them from hand to hand. At the height of her success, however, she began to worry that her work was too biting to be properly feminine. It was John Adams who reassured her. She had been blessed with exceptional talents "for the good of the world," he said. "It would be criminal to neglect them."

Mercy Warren continued to write. Throughout the Revolution, the British faced not only the ready gunfire of the American army, but also the satirical pen of Mercy Warren. In her hands, they found, it could be as piercing as a Patriot bullet.

THE CONGRESS TAKES ACTION

The First Continental Congress met in Carpenters' Hall in Philadelphia. There, the delegates drew up a list of resolves. In these resolves, passed on October 14, the delegates demanded an end to the Coercive and Quebec Acts, and denounced Britain's money-raising acts. The delegates also passed a declaration of colonial rights, including that of taxation and lawmaking. The declaration drew on the thoughts of Virginia legislator Thomas Jefferson and Pennsylvania lawyer James Wilson, two Patriots who had written pamphlets during the summer. Jefferson and Wilson claimed that Parliament had no right to tax or legislate for the colonies.

Finally, on October 18, the Congress set up the Continental Association. Delegates pledged that their colonies would suspend trade with Britain. To enforce the agreement, committees would be set up in towns to publish the names of violators and to seize any goods they imported. The committees also would organize boycotts against violators.

The First Continental Congress adjourned on October 26, 1774. Already, people in Massachusetts were preparing for war. Special militia units called *minutemen* were formed to "come in at a moment's warning" to defend the colony.

In Britain, King George took the colonial actions as open defiance. When the Congress's declaration was introduced in Parliament, some members were sympathetic to the Patriots. William Pitt, the former secretary of state, proposed removing the troops from Boston and accepting most of the demands, including the repeal of the Coercive Acts. But Parliament rejected Pitt's proposals and declared Massachusetts to be in a state of rebellion.

LEXINGTON AND CONCORD

While the colonists argued and debated, General Gage, the royal governor of Massachusetts, received orders from London. He was to capture Patriot leaders. Gage, knowing that such action would lead to war, delayed. But when he learned of a secret store of weapons in Concord, Massachusetts, he decided to act.

Gage ordered British troops to march to Lexington, then on to Concord to seize the weapons. The troops were to march at night in order to take the colonists by surprise. The soldiers may also have had orders to capture Patriot leaders Samuel Adams and John Hancock, who were in Lexington.

The British soldiers marched into Lexington on April 19, 1775. Early morning mists rose from the village green. On the green, facing the British, was an uneven line of 70 armed minutemen led by Captain John Parker. Paul Revere and William Dawes had ridden all night to warn them. The British had failed to surprise anyone.

The British major ordered the minutemen to leave. After a moment's confusion, someone fired a shot. Within seconds, bursts of gunfire came from both sides of the green. The colonists retreated, leaving eight minutemen dead on the field.

The British marched on to Concord, where at the North Bridge ". . . the embattled farmers stood, /And fired the shot heard round the world." After an exchange of gunfire at the bridge, the British turned and started back toward Boston.

At this point, the battle really began. The British were trapped. Militia from a dozen towns had been alerted earlier and now lined the road. Protected by

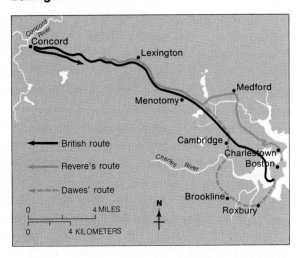

trees and stone fences, the militia fired into the ranks of the red-coated British soldiers. The British could only shoot back blindly at puffs of gun smoke, and then run. Finally, they reached Lexington, where they met fresh troops. Saved by these reinforcements, the British continued on to Boston. Two hundred forty-seven redcoats had been killed or wounded. The Patriots had 93 casualties.

The Massachusetts Provincial Congress called out 13,600 troops and asked other colonies for help. Patriots from Rhode Island, Connecticut, and New Hampshire rushed to join the Patriot camps ringing Boston. The British were under siege.

SECOND CONTINENTAL CONGRESS

Three weeks after the battle at Lexington, Connecticut sent a Patriot from the frontier, Ethan Allen, to capture a supply of weapons at British-held Fort Ticonderoga. The fort was on Lake Champlain, near the Canadian border. Allen and his volunteers, the "Green Mountain Boys," surprised the sleeping British early on May 10. News of the successful raid swept through the colonies.

On the day that Allen's raid took place, delegates gathered in Philadelphia for the Second Continental Congress. The colonists were at war with Britain and had to bring order to their scattered fighters. From the militias that surrounded Boston, the colonists created a Continental Army. They voted to raise more companies from Pennsylvania, Virginia, and Maryland to join the troops at Boston.

In John Trumbull's painting of Bunker Hill, Dr. Joseph Warren, a leading Patriot, lies dying (left) while the fatally wounded Major Pitcairn is held by two British officers (center). Pitcairn was shot by Private Peter Salem (extreme right, behind the Patriot lieutenant).

John Adams proposed George Washington of Virginia as commander in chief. Washington had fought in the French and Indian War and, said Adams, had "an easy, soldier like air." Equally important, he was a true Patriot, but a moderate, and so was acceptable to all the delegates. Congress approved Washington's appointment on June 15.

THE BATTLE OF BUNKER HILL

Before Washington could reach his troops in Boston, more blood was shed. Throughout May Americans had flocked to Boston. Three British generals—William Howe, John Burgoyne, and Henry Clinton—had brought in reinforcements to assist Gage. It was a standoff. Gage remained pinned down, and the Patriots could not take the city. However, the clash soon came.

Gage planned to seize Dorchester Heights, a hill strategically located above the city. When the Americans heard of this plan, they sent Colonel William Prescott to establish a military post nearby. American troops began fortifying Breed's Hill after dark on June 16. At dawn on June 17 the British discovered the work, and shortly after noon 2,400 British soldiers under General Howe prepared to attack. Waiting for them were 1,600 Americans.

While townspeople watched from nearby hills and rooftops, Howe sent half his force on a frontal attack up Breed's Hill. Weighted down by heavy packs, the British were driven back by staggering fire from Prescott's troops. Once more they attacked. Again, the Americans drove them back with a "continued sheet of fire."

Astounded at the Americans' strength but determined to win, Howe ordered a third assault. The troops, who had dropped their packs and had been strengthened by reinforcements, charged up the hill. By now the Americans had run out of ammunition, and the main force retreated. Some fought on, using their muskets as clubs, but the British could no longer be stopped. After capturing

Breed's Hill, the British went on to seize a second garrison at Bunker Hill. The day's fighting became known as the Battle of Bunker Hill.

The British victory at the Battle of Bunker Hill was a costly one. Whereas American losses were slight, nearly half the redcoats were killed or wounded. The colonists were joyful. They had stood up to a professional army and given more punishment than they received. Two weeks after the battle, Washington arrived to turn the enthusiastic fighters into an army.

THE OLIVE BRANCH PETITION

As the breach between the American colonies and Britain was widened by bloodshed, moderates in the Continental Congress again searched for a compromise with Britain. In early July the delegates sent a petition, written by John Dickinson, to King George. In the Olive Branch Petition they pledged their loyalty to the king and asked him to resolve colonial grievances, which they blamed on Parliament.

In November the delegates received their answer. The king had refused to read their Olive Branch Petition. He declared the colonies to be in a state of rebellion. In December the king closed the colonies to all trade and commanded that American ships under sail be seized. The king's actions unified Congress. And Congress was for the first time truly representative of all colonies—Georgia had sent delegates in September.

While Congress was waiting for the king's reply, it prepared to defend the colonies. It also seized a chance to act against the British. In the fall of 1775, not long after the Battle of Bunker Hill, American troops marched toward Canada.

QUEBEC AND BOSTON

Congress had received a report that the British commander in Canada, Sir Guy Carleton, was planning an invasion of New York from Quebec. If the Americans acted quickly, they could strike at British troops and prevent the invasion.

Americans still had a force at Fort Ticonderoga, and Congress authorized this northern army to invade Canada and march to Quebec. Led by young, British-trained General Richard Montgomery, about 1,200 Americans set out from Ticonderoga.

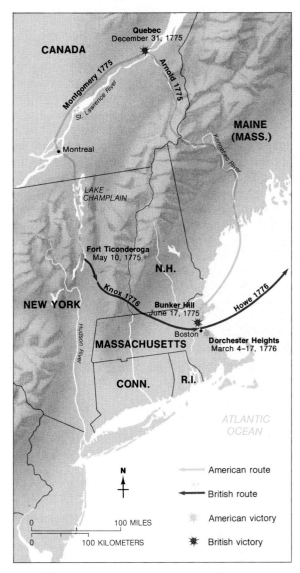

General Henry Knox delivered to George Washington cannons captured at Fort Ticonderoga. The cannons were hauled 300 miles on ox-drawn sleds in the dead of winter.

At the same time, a second American force was marching on Quebec from Maine. In command was General Benedict Arnold. For over a month, Arnold drove his 1,100 soldiers through 350 miles (560 kilometers) of thick wilderness and bad weather. At one point, the army survived by eating a mash of hair powder and shoe leather.

Arnold finally joined with Montgomery outside Quebec in the dead of winter. On December 30, in a raging blizzard, the two American forces attacked the city. The assault failed, leaving Montgomery dead, Arnold wounded, 100 colonial soldiers killed, and 300 taken prisoner. Still, the determined Arnold and his reduced force laid siege to the city until spring. Then British reinforcements arrived, and the Americans retreated to Ticonderoga on Lake Champlain.

Meanwhile, the Americans were having more success in Boston. Early in 1776 the Americans assembled artillery on Dorchester Heights, the hills above Boston. The British, already short of supplies, feared that they soon would be overpowered. On March 17 General Howe, now in command of the British troops in Boston, fled from Boston and sailed for Halifax, in Canada.

After America's disastrous defeat at Quebec, the British retreat thrilled the Patriots. In a letter to her husband, John, Abigail Adams wrote of her amazement that the Americans had peacefully regained "a town which we expected would cost us a river of blood." She continued, "Every foot of ground which they obtain now they must fight for, and may [they buy it at] a Bunker Hill price."

SECTION REVIEW

1. Identify the following: Boston Tea Party, Thomas Gage, Patrick Henry, Richard Henry Lee, Christopher Gadsden, John Dickinson, Paul Revere, Ethan Allen, Olive Branch Petition, Battle of Bunker Hill, Benedict Arnold.

2. (a) Describe the Intolerable Acts. (b) How did the colonists respond to the Intolerable Acts?

3. (a) At the First Continental Congress, what was the viewpoint of Patriots like Samuel and John Adams? (b) What was the viewpoint of Patriots like John Dickinson?

4. (a) What were the provisions of the resolves drawn up by the First Continental Congress? (b) List three actions taken by the First Continental Congress.

5. Why were British troops ordered to Lexington?

6. How did Patriots react to the outcome of the Battle of Bunker Hill?

7. (a) How did the king respond to the Olive Branch Petition? (b) What effect did the king's response have on the colonists?

8. Why did the British evacuate Boston in 1776?

THE BREAK WITH BRITAIN

READ TO FIND OUT

— why the American colonies declared their independence.

— what advantages and disadvantages the Americans had in the war.

— what problems the Loyalists faced.

— who contributed to the Patriot cause.

It was now 1776. In the 13 years since the Proclamation of 1763, blunders by the Crown and Parliament had driven the colonies closer together and away from Britain.

Although most Americans protested Parliament's oppressive acts, they were divided by issues of loyalty and independence. Even the American flag reflected the uncertainty. Thirteen stripes stood for the colonies, but the Union Jack of Britain was in the corner. As Washington trained his troops outside Boston, he still raised his cup each evening in a toast to King George.

COMMON SENSE

One person who helped Americans to define their loyalties was Thomas Paine, who had migrated to the colonies from England. In 1776 Paine published *Common Sense*, a pamphlet in which he called for independence. Paine wrote: "There is something very absurd in supposing a continent to be perpetually governed by an island. . . . England [belongs] to Europe. America to itself." Paine also attacked King George, calling him a "royal brute" who menaced American freedom. Within a few months 150,000 copies of *Common Sense* had been sold.

By now the mood in the Second Continental Congress, and in some colonial governments, mirrored John Adams's thoughts: "Britain has at last driven America to the last step, complete separation from her." First North Carolina, then Virginia, advised their delegates in Congress to vote for independence.

In a work by Edward Savage and Edward Pine, "Congress Voting Independence," Thomas Jefferson presents the Declaration of Independence to Benjamin Harrison, president of the Congress. Standing in the center are (left to right) Robert Livingston, Roger Sherman, and John Adams. Benjamin Franklin is seated in the foreground.

On June 7, 1776, Richard Henry Lee of Virginia offered a resolution to the Congress:

> These united colonies are, and of right ought to be, independent states. . . . All political connection between them and the State of Great Britain is, and ought to be, totally dissolved.

THE DECLARATION OF INDEPENDENCE

After three days of debate, Congress formed a committee to write a declaration of independence. The committee members were Thomas Jefferson, Benjamin Franklin, John Adams, Robert Livingston, and Roger Sherman. Thomas Jefferson, who had written on behalf of the Patriot cause, was chosen to do the actual writing of the document.

Thomas Jefferson had studied the political theory of John Locke, a philosopher of the previous century. Locke had written that government was a contract, or compact, between the government and the people. If government violated the people's natural rights, they could rebel and set up another government.

Jefferson applied Locke's theory to the preamble of the Declaration. All people, Jefferson wrote, had certain natural or God-given rights such as "life, liberty, and the pursuit of happiness." If a government did not protect these human rights, it lost its right to govern. When a group of people had failed in all peaceful ways to correct the abuses of their government, they then had the right to create a new government.

A second section explained to Britain and the rest of Europe why Americans were taking up arms and demanding independence. It listed, under 28 headings, the abuses of King George.

The last section of the Declaration pointed out that Americans had tried, and failed, to convince Britain to set right these wrongs. Therefore, the representatives of the United States of America, acting by the "authority of the good people of these colonies," solemnly declared their complete independence from Great Britain.

Congress debated what Jefferson had written, making several changes. Then on the evening of July 4, 1776, the delegates approved the final wording of the Declaration. All colonies voted for it except New York, which abstained.

In the weeks that followed, the Declaration was read in the streets of every town and village. A newspaper described the reaction in New York:

It was received everywhere with loud cheers, and demonstrations of joy. And tonight the statue of King George III has been pulled down by the Sons of Liberty. The lead with which the monument was made is to be run into bullets—a just end to an ungrateful Tyrant!

AMERICAN LOYALISTS

In spite of widespread celebrations, there were Americans in every colony who were indifferent about the Declaration of Independence. Others were actually opposed to it. These people came to be called Tories, after the Tory party in England, which was loyal to the Crown.

Loyalists, or Tories, could be found in every state. In Patriot centers like Virginia, Massachusetts, and Connecticut, Loyalists made up less than 10 percent of the population. In New York, though, almost half the population was Loyalist, and in the Carolinas and Georgia Loyalists were in the majority.

Loyalists were found in all social classes. Not surprisingly, Americans who held office under the Crown often stayed loyal. Benjamin Franklin's son William, the royal governor of New Jersey, was a confirmed Tory. Among the Loyalists, too, were many wealthy merchants, planters, and Anglican ministers. Support for the king also extended through the middle and lower classes.

About 60,000 Loyalists eventually fought with the British. Before the struggle ended, another 100,000 fled to Canada or England. State governments sold the property of those who fled.

THE BRITISH SIDE OF THE BALANCE SHEET

Americans had declared independence. The question remained, though, whether they could successfully defy Great Britain. The most powerful navy in the world belonged to Great Britain, and its well-disciplined army had gained valuable experience in the long war with France. In addition, most of the tribes of the strong League of the Iroquois sided with the British. The British, however, were used to fighting a certain kind of war. British soldiers were skilled at fighting "on equal terms," since battles in Europe were fought face to face in open fields. The British in America were fighting an enemy who did not follow European rules. Colonial warfare was unpredictable.

When armies marched in Europe, farmers and townspeople stayed out of the way. In America the farmers and townspeople *were* the army. As columns of British soldiers marched through forests and towns, bands of militia appeared from the countryside and disappeared just as quickly. One British officer summed it up: "The Americans are nowhere and they are everywhere."

Supplying the British army was a continual nightmare. Britain had to send everything across an ocean—arms, uniforms, tents, cooking equipment, food, wagons, and horses. Food often spoiled on the Atlantic crossing. As the army moved inland, away from British supply ships on the coast, problems worsened.

Throughout 1775 and 1776, British generals had requested more soldiers. But the recruiting officers had trouble in Britain. Many British people did not like the idea of fighting a "civil war" against fellow British subjects. Sympathy for the American Patriots led several high-ranking officers to resign their commissions. A leader of the Whig party—opposed to the ruling Tory party—selected blue and buff as his party's colors. They were the colors of George Washington's uniform.

In March 1776 Britain finally concluded negotiations with the German states for mercenaries—professional soldiers for hire. About 17,000 Hessians, from the German state of Hesse, were needed to fill out the British army.

Despite these problems, many in Parliament believed that most Americans would join Britain to put down the rebellion. And they knew that the Americans had to rely on only a tiny navy, a one-year-old army, and local militias.

THE AMERICAN SIDE OF THE BALANCE SHEET

When Washington took command of the American forces in Boston, he faced the task of forming independent militias into a Continental Army. Americans had never believed in a standing, or permanent, army. In times of trouble, they relied on their militias.

John Paul Jones fought his greatest battle as commander of the *Bonhomme Richard*. The *Bonhomme Richard* met the H.M.S. *Serapis* off the coast of England, and the two ships pounded each other for four hours. Although Jones's ship was badly damaged, he urged his crew on until the British commander surrendered.

The rough-and-ready Continental Army inherited weaknesses from the militias. There was little discipline. Officers were elected by the soldiers, who often simply ignored their orders. Most militia members had more allegiance to their home states and towns than to the Continental Army.

Washington also had trouble keeping citizens in the army long enough to make them into good soldiers. Soldiers signed up only when they were needed, and went home when the battle was over. Washington seldom had more than 17,000 soldiers in the army at one time. Often local militias had to back up the army troops.

If the army seemed weak, the navy barely existed. It had 13 warships, each of which usually operated alone to sneak past the British fleet off the coast. However, these few ships were often commanded by daring, able captains. The most successful and aggressive was John Paul Jones, who won several victories in the seas off Britain.

However, America's greatest success on the seas came from privateers.* Lured by rich prizes, hundreds of sea captains made privateering a wartime career. They raided British cargo and naval ships on both sides of the Atlantic, capturing $18 million worth of supplies.

---

* privateers: privately owned ships commissioned by a government to attack and capture enemy ships.

In a war that stretched across an ocean, any damage to the British supply line helped America. Still, America had its own money and supply problems.

Fighting the war cost money, and Congress did not have the power to tax. It did have the authority to ask each state for supplies, troops, and money, but it could not force a state to send them. Each state had its own economic problems and seemed to think the other states should do more. At best, states supplied their own soldiers. This left the army poorly paid and undersupplied.

Congress did have one source of money and supplies that proved vital throughout 1776 and 1777. Both France and Spain wanted to help America against their old enemy Britain, but they feared open help might lead to war. So each country secretly channeled $200,000 worth of guns, powder, and supplies to America.

America also received military advice, in the form of European officers. Many were poorly qualified, but a few gave the Americans priceless help.

From France came the 20-year-old Marquis de Lafayette (LAH-fee-EHT), who served without payment. He proved a skillful officer in several battles and became Washington's most loyal aide. From Prussia came Baron Friedrich von Steuben, who taught the Continental Army to drill with Prussian discipline. From Poland came Thaddeus

Kosciusko (кōs-ee-US-kō), a skilled engineer who had to borrow enough money to reach America. He planned fortifications for several key military sites, including a plateau above the Hudson River, called West Point.

Perhaps more important than the American balance sheet of strengths and weaknesses was the Americans' belief in their cause. They were fighting on their own soil, for their homes, and for their freedom. The British were fighting far from home, with no cause in their hearts.

CONTRIBUTORS TO THE CAUSE

Black Americans—both slave and free—played an important part in the Revolution. Early in the war, some blacks had joined the Patriots, fighting at Concord, Ticonderoga, and Bunker Hill. But late in 1775, Congress and General Washington decided not to enlist blacks. Americans feared that slaves who tasted freedom might start their own revolt.

The British had no such fear. The royal governor of Virginia promised freedom to slaves if they fought for the king. Over 14,000 American slaves eventually left the country, free, with the British at the end of the war.

By January 1776 Washington, noting the British recruitment, decided to enlist free blacks. Two years later, he decided also to accept slaves in the army, promising them freedom after the war in exchange for their service. About 5,000 blacks served in the Continental Army, fighting in regiments from every state but Georgia and South Carolina. Another 2,000 served in the navy, where they had been accepted from the beginning.

American women also worked for the Patriot cause. Many, including Abigail Adams, took over the running of farms and businesses while the men were gone. Others cared for the wounded, raised money for supplies, sewed uniforms, and melted lead into bullets. The Daughters of Liberty continued the boycott of British goods.

Some women followed their husbands to army camps, helping out with the camp work. A few became spies or took up arms. Sally St. Clair and Deborah Sampson dressed in men's clothing and marched off to battle. Margaret Corbin replaced her fallen husband at his artillery post, and later won a soldier's pension from Congress. A 16-year-old, Sybil Ludington, rode through the night

This sketch of Abigail Adams was made in 1812 by the painter Gilbert Stuart.

to summon militia troops to fight the British. Her ride of 40 miles was longer and more dangerous than the famous ride made by Paul Revere.

SECTION REVIEW

1. Identify the following: *Common Sense*, John Locke, Thomas Jefferson, John Paul Jones, Marquis de Lafayette, Friedrich von Steuben, Thaddeus Kosciusko, Deborah Sampson, Margaret Corbin.

2. Define the following: natural rights, standing army, Tory.

3. Before the Declaration of Independence was written, how did the Second Continental Congress prepare for a break with Britain?

4. According to the Declaration of Independence, under what circumstances do people have a right to set up a new government?

5. Describe two ways in which warfare in America was different from warfare in Europe.

6. Why was the American army poorly paid and undersupplied?

7. (a) When did black Americans first join in the fighting in the war? (b) When were blacks first enlisted in the Continental Army?

8. (a) How did most women Patriots serve their cause? (b) List three other ways women served in the Revolutionary War.

FIGHTING FOR INDEPENDENCE

READ TO FIND OUT

— how the British captured New York.

— why the battle at Saratoga convinced France to join the war.

— how hit-and-run tactics stopped the British in the South.

— how the war ended at Yorktown.

— what terms were agreed to in the Treaty of Paris.

On June 29, 1776, an American soldier looked out a second-story window on New York's Staten Island. To his amazement, he saw that "the whole bay was full of shipping as ever it could be. I declare I thought all London was afloat."

General William Howe and his British troops were returning from Halifax to American soil. On July 2, as Congress was debating the Declaration of Independence, the British landed unopposed on Staten Island. Shortly after, Admiral Richard Howe, William's brother, arrived with a huge British fleet.

THE BRITISH CAPTURE NEW YORK

The British planned to make their headquarters in New York City. New York was America's finest port, had a strong Loyalist population, and was strategically located in the middle of the states. Also, the Hudson River and Lake Champlain offered the British a water route to Canada. There, additional British troops were stationed under General Carleton.

Washington had foreseen the British move into New York. In April he had moved the Continental Army there from Boston and then fortified Manhattan Island and Long Island. Still, the two islands were open to the British from several directions, and the Americans were badly outnumbered.

On August 27 Howe attacked the Long Island fortification, and kept it under siege for two days. The Americans lost 1,500 in casualties. Washington, under cover of darkness and fog, managed to move his remaining troops to safety on Manhattan. But during the next month, Howe closed in. Washington realized he would be trapped, and on September 13 abandoned Manhattan.

TRENTON AND PRINCETON

Through the fall and winter of 1776 the British, under General Howe and General Charles Cornwallis, pushed Washington out of New York and across New Jersey. In December Washington's bat-

The "Battle of Princeton" was painted by William Mercer, deaf-mute son of an American general killed in the battle. After the victory at Princeton, Washington (center, on horseback) was able to persuade many soldiers to reenlist.

tered troops crossed the Delaware River into Pennsylvania. Instead of following Washington, the British withdrew to New York for the winter, leaving several garrisons in New Jersey.

At this point in the war, American despair matched the dark of winter. Congress had fled Philadelphia for Baltimore without authorizing reinforcements for Washington. Enlistments were running out, and many troops simply deserted. The months of retreat had worn down the army.

Washington knew he had to take action before he lost his army to expiring enlistments. On Christmas night he led his soldiers across the ice-clogged Delaware River, back into New Jersey. At Trenton the Continental Army surprised and captured a garrison of Hessian mercenaries.

A week later, Washington pushed deeper into New Jersey, and in a fierce battle forced the British to withdraw from Princeton. The battles at Trenton and Princeton cleared the British from much of New Jersey. Equally important, they boosted American morale.

Washington's successes, however, had exhausted the ragged Continental Army. The Americans pulled back to the hills around Morristown, New Jersey, for the winter.

SARATOGA—THE TURNING POINT

In February 1777 the British government approved a plan to isolate New England and split the colonies. The Hudson River provided an excellent natural boundary between New England and the rest of the states. The British already controlled the southern part of the Hudson River at New York City. Now they decided to gain control of the northern part, by capturing the city of Albany.

To carry out their plan, the British devised a three-pronged attack. The main army, under General John Burgoyne, would march south from Canada, through Lake Champlain and the upper Hudson. Lieutenant Colonel Barry St. Leger would lead a flanking army from the west, along the Mohawk River. From New York City, General Howe's forces would move north up the Hudson. All three armies were to meet at Albany.

Burgoyne and St. Leger set off as planned. But Howe took a side trip to Philadelphia. Counting on the support of the city's many Loyalists, he planned to capture the Patriot capital. Howe confidently

sailed up Chesapeake Bay into Pennsylvania, routed Washington's forces at Brandywine Creek, then occupied Philadephia on September 26.

Congress, having returned to Philadelphia in March, once again fled. Washington tried to secure the area around the city, but finally had to withdraw. He and his troops made their winter camp at Valley Forge, 20 miles (32 kilometers) outside Philadelphia.

Meanwhile, the two British armies to the north were running into trouble. St. Leger's force, made up mainly of Loyalists and Iroquois, stopped to besiege American-held Fort Stanwix on the Mohawk River. The Americans sent a relief force to Stanwix, under Benedict Arnold. St. Leger, who had gone only a third of the way to Albany, was forced to turn back.

Burgoyne, traveling south from Canada, had an early victory at Fort Ticonderoga. As he struggled farther south through New York's dense forests, though, his forces were continuously attacked by local militias. By October Burgoyne was desperate. Almost half his troops were killed or wounded, and he now realized that Howe would not be coming to his aid. For some reason, Howe had decided to remain in Philadelphia.

Battered by American attacks on his right and left flanks, Burgoyne was then attacked head-on by Benedict Arnold. The besieged British forces stopped at the town of Saratoga. For five days American troops under General Horatio Gates leveled a constant fire at them. On October 17 Burgoyne surrendered his entire army of almost 6,000 soldiers, 5 generals, and 300 other officers. It proved to be the turning point in the war.

American spirits soared with the victory at Saratoga. Across the Atlantic in Paris, American agents led by Benjamin Franklin had been urging Britain's old enemy, France, to enter the war. The smashing victory at Saratoga convinced the French that Americans could win the war.

America and France signed two treaties in February 1778. The first gave each nation special trade privileges. The second, a treaty of alliance, recognized American independence and declared that France was at war with Great Britain.

The Americans needed France's help. Well-equipped French troops would fill out the Continental Army. Badly needed supplies—blankets, muskets, ammunition, and cannons—would enable

The Revolutionary War 1776–1778

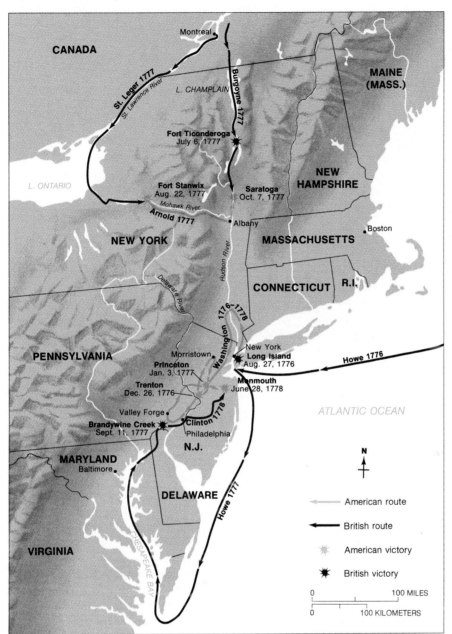

By mid-1778 the British held only New York City and Newport, Rhode Island, in the North. Washington stationed his army around New York to keep watch on the British and remained there until nearly the end of the war.

Drums were used to signal troops both in camp and on the battlefield. This drum bears the flags of France and the North Carolina militia.

Washington to continue the war. Furthermore, the French would be another enemy that the British had to fight.

MONMOUTH AND THE WEST

In June 1778 Washington's stay at Valley Forge ended. His army had camped there throughout a brutal winter, during which hundreds died from the cold, starvation, and typhus. On Thanksgiving the soldiers had rice and vinegar for dinner. During the winter Washington feared that the army would "starve, dissolve, or disperse." But the soldiers, maintaining their faith in Washington's leadership, survived through spring. By summer they were ready again to follow Washington into battle.

During the winter, the British army had remained in Philadelphia. In May Howe was re-

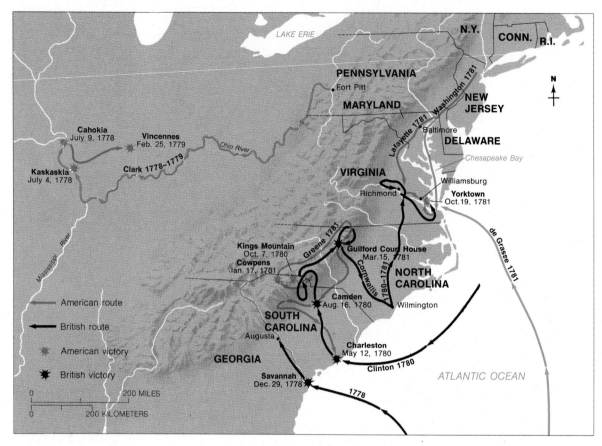

After Charleston, Congress sent Horatio Gates to lead the militia. At Camden his mistakes led to a Patriot defeat, and he was replaced by Nathanael Greene. Later in the midst of a second battle at Camden, Greene wrote, "We fight, get beat, rise and fight again."

placed by General Henry Clinton. Hearing that the French fleet was heading for America, Clinton decided to move the British troops to New York City. Washington's army set off in pursuit.

An advance American force under General Charles Lee met the British at Monmouth Court House in New Jersey on June 28. When British reinforcements arrived, Lee began to withdraw—just as Washington and the army arrived. In a rage at Lee as blistering as the day's heat, Washington turned the American retreat into a relentless attack. That night, the British slipped away and headed for New York. Washington followed, and encamped on the hills above the city to await French reinforcements.

Shortly after their victory at Monmouth, the Americans had some success in the West. George Rogers Clark, a young surveyor and Indian fighter,

led a frontier militia in the capture of three towns in Illinois and Ohio. Clark also rescued American settlers from attacks by Indian allies of the British.

The West, however, was not a major theater in the war. Nor was the North after the battle at Monmouth. For the next three years nearly every major battle would be fought in the South.

WAR IN THE SOUTH

Clinton, settled into his New York headquarters, planned the British offensive in the South. The British would capture southern seaports, ferry in troops, and sweep through the southern states. There, they believed, the large population of Loyalists would join them.

In December 1778 the British navy landed in Savannah, Georgia. The local militia, caught between the navy and a rear guard of British infantry, quickly collapsed. The British then stormed farther into Georgia, and within a month had reestablished a royal government. Throughout 1779 the Americans tried, and failed, to retake Savannah.

Early in 1780 the British struck the South's major port, Charleston. Clinton sailed south from New York to lead a massive army of 14,000 against the city, swamping the 5,000 American defenders. His victory won, Clinton returned to New York, leaving General Charles Cornwallis in command. Charleston was the worst Patriot defeat of the war.

In October Congress appointed Nathanael Greene as head of the southern militias. An outspoken general who had risen from the ranks, Greene planned to adopt the hit-and-run, guerrilla fighting style of the southern militias.

These guerrilla tactics had already stopped Cornwallis at the border between South Carolina and North Carolina. Assailed by Patriot bands, Cornwallis sent a Loyalist force out to cover his flank. At Kings Mountain, a frontier militia caught the Loyalists and crushed them in bloody fighting.

The British southern strategy was faltering. Clinton had not counted on the fierce bands of Patriots and their guerrilla tactics. And there were far more Patriots taking up arms than Loyalists. When Greene arrived in the South near the end of 1780, Clinton's southern offensive collapsed.

The Americans struck at Cornwallis again and again. In January 1781 at Cowpens, South Carolina, they routed the British. By March, when the armies clashed at Guilford Court House, Cornwallis had had enough. Although he won the battle, he lost more than a quarter of his army. He withdrew his weakened troops to Wilmington, North Carolina.

In Virginia a British force under a new ally was having more luck. Benedict Arnold had deserted to the British and was leading raids against the Americans throughout the state. In May Cornwallis marched into Virginia to join Arnold. The British raids continued into summer, but the American strength was growing.

By August 1781 the American troops, under the Marquis de Lafayette and Baron von Steuben, had driven Cornwallis to the city of Yorktown. Cornwallis felt secure in Yorktown, on Virginia's coast, because he now had a sea link to General Clinton in New York.

VICTORY

In New York, Washington at last received the French reinforcements for his planned attack on Clinton in the North. But Washington changed his mind about attacking Clinton. He had learned that Admiral de Grasse and the French fleet were headed

Francis Marion and his guerrilla band are shown crossing the Pee Dee River to harass British forces in North Carolina. One of the best guerrillas, Marion was known as the "Swamp Fox" for his ability to raid and disappear into the swamps. Guerrillas slowed Cornwallis's march.

for Chesapeake Bay, where they would be at Washington's service until October. At the mouth of Chesapeake Bay was Yorktown—and Cornwallis. Washington seized the opportunity.

On August 20 Washington and his French allies—5,000 soldiers under the Comte de Rochambeau (RŌ-shahm-BŌ)—set out on an overland march south. Ten days later, right on schedule, de Grasse and the French fleet arrived to blockade* Yorktown. The British navy sped south down the coast to rescue Cornwallis, but was soundly beaten by de Grasse.

The French then sailed north up Chesapeake Bay to Baltimore. They picked up Washington and Rochambeau, and sailed the armies south to Williamsburg, just outside Yorktown. The allied armies were joined by Lafayette. On September 28 a force of 9,000 Americans and 7,800 French marched on Yorktown.

Cornwallis and his army of 8,000 British and Hessians were trapped. The Americans and French besieged Yorktown for three weeks, hammering at the British with their cannons and guns. A jubilant American wrote of Cornwallis, "We have got him handsomely in a pudding bag."

On October 19, 1781, Cornwallis surrendered. The British soldiers stacked their weapons on the ground, then marched back to their camp. They were flanked on the right by the Americans in their tattered clothes, and on the left by the French in their elegant uniforms. Over the sound of marching boots, the British band played a popular song, "The World Turned Upside Down." The Americans sang "Yankee Doodle."

PEACE

Washington returned to New York to keep watch on Clinton's troops. With Cornwallis's surrender, however, the war in America was over.

In March 1782 Lord North—the prime minister—resigned. The new government quickly sent a peace commissioner to Paris to begin talks with the Americans. Congress had instructed the American negotiators, Benjamin Franklin, John Adams, John Jay, and Henry Laurens, to consult fully with the French during peace negotiations.

* blockade: to block, or shut off, a port or region by troops or ships in order to prevent passage in or out during war.

However, the negotiators worried that the French would block American claims to the western lands, despite the treaty of alliance. They began separate talks with the British, and worked out a preliminary peace treaty in November.

Most importantly, the British recognized American independence. American boundaries would stretch from the Atlantic to the Mississippi, and from the Great Lakes south to Florida. The Mississippi River would remain open to both American and British shipping, and Americans could still fish off the coast of Canada. Britain also agreed to withdraw its forces from America.

In turn, the Americans pledged that Congress would "recommend" that the states pay Loyalists for their lost property. And both sides agreed that citizens of either country could try to collect debts owed by citizens of the other country. This meant chiefly that British exporters could try to collect old debts from American merchants.

The Treaty of Paris was sent to Congress, which ratified it on April 15, 1783. Five months later, in a Paris hotel, the American and British commissioners signed the ratified treaty. At another meeting Britain concluded a peace with France—and with Spain, which had joined the French in 1779.

The "shot heard round the world" had touched off a war that lasted for six years. The peace negotiations took another two years. As Benjamin Franklin, America's representative at the Paris signing, observed: "There never was a good war or a bad peace." But there had never before been a war like this one, in which a group of people turned colonies into a self-governing nation.

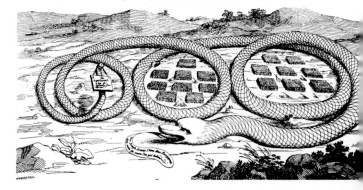

"The American Rattle Snake" has captured the armies of Burgoyne and Cornwallis, and still has room for more. The cartoon by James Gillray was published in 1782.

North America After the Treaty of Paris 1783

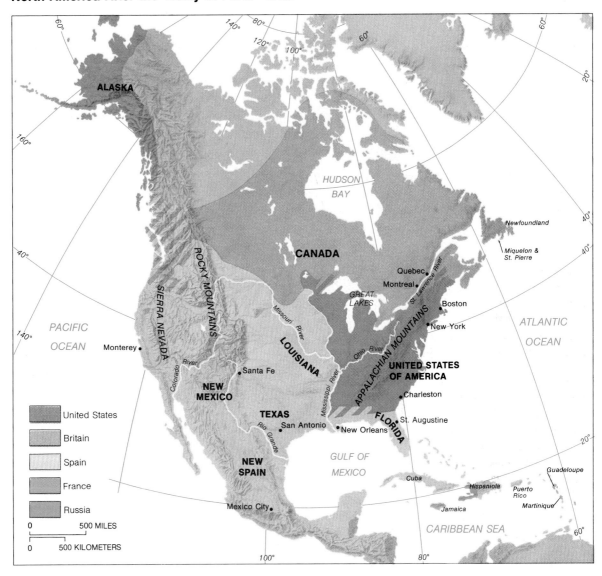

North America After the Treaty of Paris 1783

ALASKA

HUDSON BAY

CANADA

Quebec
Montreal
GREAT LAKES
Boston
New York

Newfoundland

Miquelon & St. Pierre

ROCKY MOUNTAINS

SIERRA NEVADA

PACIFIC OCEAN

Monterey

Colorado River

LOUISIANA

Missouri River

APPALACHIAN MOUNTAINS

Ohio River

St. Lawrence River

ATLANTIC OCEAN

Santa Fe

NEW MEXICO

Mississippi River

UNITED STATES OF AMERICA

Charleston

TEXAS

San Antonio

New Orleans

FLORIDA

St. Augustine

Rio Grande

NEW SPAIN

GULF OF MEXICO

Cuba

Guadeloupe

Hispaniola

Puerto Rico

Martinique

Mexico City

Jamaica

CARIBBEAN SEA

United States
Britain
Spain
France
Russia

0   500 MILES
0   500 KILOMETERS

SECTION REVIEW

1. Identify the following: Charles Cornwallis, Trenton, Valley Forge, Saratoga, George Rogers Clark, Savannah, Nathanael Greene, Yorktown, Admiral de Grasse.

2. Why did the British choose New York City as their headquarters?

3. What were the results of the battles at Trenton and Princeton?

4. Describe the three parts of the British plan to control the Hudson River.

5. Why is the battle at Saratoga called the turning point of the war?

6. What agreement did France and America make in their treaty of alliance?

7. Why did General Clinton decide to remove the British troops from Philadelphia?

8. Why did British strategy in the South falter?

9. How did Cornwallis become trapped at Yorktown?

10. (a) What terms did the British agree to in the Treaty of Paris (1783)? (b) What terms did the Americans agree to?

SUMMARY

After the French and Indian War, Great Britain took steps to control the colonies. These measures alarmed the colonists, who feared that they would lose their traditional liberties—the rights guaranteed English subjects. Such measures included acts designed to raise revenue from the colonies—the Sugar Act in 1764, the Stamp Act in 1765, and the Townshend Acts in 1767. The colonists argued that there should be "no taxation without representation."

Relations between Britain and the colonies worsened in 1774 when Parliament passed the Intolerable Acts. These acts were designed to punish Massachusetts for the Boston Tea Party. The First Continental Congress demanded an end to the Intolerable Acts.

The Revolutionary War began in April 1775 at Lexington and Concord, Massachusetts. The Second Continental Congress chose George Washington to form the Patriots into the Continental Army. Before Washington arrived in Boston, the Patriots fought the Battle of Bunker Hill.

Even though blood had been shed, Congress sent King George the Olive Branch Petition. The king refused to answer the petition, declared the colonies to be in a state of rebellion, and closed the colonies to all trade.

Thomas Jefferson wrote the Declaration of Independence, which was debated, then approved by Congress. As Congress acted, the war spread from New England to New York and New Jersey. The British planned to separate New England from the other colonies by taking control of the Hudson River. The plan failed when the British were stopped at Saratoga in October 1777.

When war in the North reached a stalemate, the British invaded the South. Patriots struck the British repeatedly as they marched north from Georgia through the Carolinas. Washington's forces, aided by French troops and a French naval blockade, trapped the main British army at Yorktown, Virginia. The British surrendered. Peace talks resulted in the Treaty of Paris in 1783, which gave America independence and boundaries that stretched to the Mississippi River.

CHAPTER REVIEW

1. (a) Why did Britain tighten its control of the colonies? (b) How did taxes under the Sugar Act, the Stamp Act, and the Townshend Acts differ from taxes that the colonists had paid before? (c) What argument did the colonists use against all three acts?

2. (a) What was the point of the Declaratory Act? (b) Why did Parliament keep the tax on tea when it repealed the other Townshend Duties?

3. (a) Explain how each of the following was an attempt to bring America and Britain together: petition by the Stamp Act Congress, Olive Branch Petition, William Pitt's speech to Parliament. (b) What was the response to each? Explain.

4. (a) Between 1763 and 1776, colonists took several measures to show their opposition to British policies. List five such measures and give an example of each. (b) Compare the ideas of the members of the First Continental Congress who wanted independence with the ideas of more conservative members.

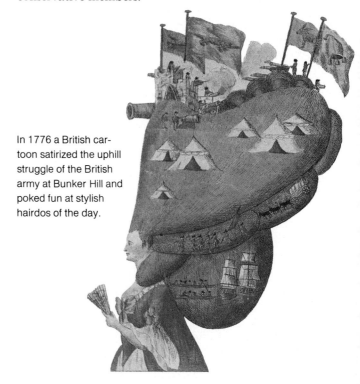

In 1776 a British cartoon satirized the uphill struggle of the British army at Bunker Hill and poked fun at stylish hairdos of the day.

5. (a) What principles of government are stated in the first part of the Declaration of Independence? (b) What was the purpose of the second part? (c) What is included in the last part?

6. (a) List three accomplishments of the First Continental Congress. (b) List two accomplishments of the Second Continental Congress.

7. Explain how each event led to the next: (a) Tea Act, Boston Tea Party, Intolerable Acts, First Continental Congress; (b) invasion of Charleston, appointment of Nathanael Greene, battle at Kings Mountain, battle at Guilford Court House.

8. (a) Why was the Continental Army undersupplied? (b) Name one battle in which a lack of supplies played an important part. Explain. (c) List three ways in which the Continental Army obtained supplies.

9. (a) Why did the Revolutionary War begin in New England? (b) How did the war spread to New York and New Jersey? (c) What were the positions of the main British and American armies late in 1778? (d) Why did the British plan a southern offensive?

10. How did each of the following contribute to British defeat: Nathanael Greene, guerrilla bands, Marquis de Lafayette, the French fleet?

ISSUES AND IDEAS

1. Conflict between the British government and the colonists often centered on the issue of taxation, but other issues also arose. For example, there was conflict over western lands, appointment of colonial officials, and the court system. (a) Evaluate one of these three issues as a member of Parliament might have. Cite examples of specific laws or situations in which the issue arose. (b) Respond to the member of Parliament's evaluation as a Patriot might have. Cite examples.

2. Explain what the British government intended to achieve by taking each of the following actions: Stamp Act, suspension of the New York assembly, British troops in Boston in 1768, Tea Act, Intolerable Acts, Lexington and Concord. Explain why each action increased colonial unity.

At the beginning of the Revolution America's few cannon were British-made. Charles Willson Peale, militia captain as well as artist, sketched this cannon between battles.

3. Describe what might have happened if each of the following took place. (a) George Washington had refused to be commander in chief. (b) The king had responded favorably to the Olive Branch Petition. (c) Moderate delegates had controlled the Continental Congress. (d) The British had won the battle at Saratoga.

SKILLS WORKSHOP

1. *Graphs.* Look at the bar graph on page 88 of your text. It shows colonial tea imports from Britain. Use the data on the bar graph to construct a line graph. Construct the line graph by making a point at the correct thousands of pounds of tea imported in each year. Then draw a line connecting the points. Which kind of graph shows the data better—a bar graph or the line graph? Give reasons for your opinion.

2. *Primary sources.* Look at the Declaration of Independence at the back of your text. Find three of the king's actions that the colonists thought were unlawful. Describe each of these actions.

PAST AND PRESENT

1. Gather information about a group or groups who strongly oppose a current policy of the local, state, or national government. What is the group protesting against? Compare their actions and methods with those of the colonists.

2. Each year thousands of people relive America's past by visiting Boston's Freedom Trail or Philadelphia's Independence National Historical Park. Explain what a visitor to historic sites in one of the two cities can see today.

CHAPTER 5

FORMING A GOVERNMENT

1777–1787

THE REINS OF GOVERNMENT
THE COUNTRY ADRIFT
A MORE PERFECT UNION

In 1775 Abigail Adams wrote a letter to her husband John, then a delegate to the Second Continental Congress:

"I wish I knew what mighty things were fabricating. If a form of government is to be established here, what one will be assumed? Will it be left to our assemblies to choose one? And will not many people have many minds? And shall we not run into dissensions among ourselves?

"The building up of a great empire may now I suppose be realized even by the unbelievers. Yet will not ten thousand difficulties arise in the formation if it? The reins of government have been so long slackened, that I fear the people will not quietly submit to those restraints which are necessary for the peace, and security, of the community.

"If we separate from Britain, what code of laws will be established? How shall we be governed so as to retain our liberties? Can any government be free which is not administered by general stated laws? Who shall frame these laws? Who will give them force and energy? . . .

"When I consider these things . . . I feel anxious for the fate of our monarchy or democracy or whatever is to take place."

The Revolution had taken place, and Americans had separated from Britain. But Abigail Adams's concerns were still valid. Americans had chosen a representative form of government, but the shape of that government was still unclear.

The national government had such few powers that it seemed barely able to govern. Most Americans gave primary allegiance to their state governments. These thirteen separate governments were rarely in agreement.

On the other hand, Americans did have a feeling of unity, born of the common fight for independence. Now this spirit of unity could carry Americans past their differences to work together. It could help them to answer Abigail Adams's questions.

THE REINS OF GOVERNMENT

READ TO FIND OUT

— how the colonies formed state governments.

— how Congress formed a government under the Articles of Confederation.

— how state claims to western lands delayed adoption of the Articles.

— how the limited powers of the Confederation weakened the nation.

— how people began to settle the frontier.

— why tension arose between the United States and Spain.

— how the Land Ordinance and Northwest Ordinance provided for western settlement.

The war was over. General Washington watched the British withdraw from New York City. Then he said an emotional farewell to his officers and rode home to his beloved plantation, Mount Vernon. The new flag of the United States flew from flagpoles, town halls, and upstairs windows.

But what, exactly, did this flag represent? In 1777 Congress had resolved that the flag should have thirteen stripes representing the thirteen states. For the Union there would be "thirteen stars, white in a blue field representing a new constellation." The Union, however, would have to be stitched together with more than thread on a flag. It would need to be secured by government.

STATE CONSTITUTIONS

In the following months, groups met in most states to write constitutions and to set up state governments. A sense of excitement, of experiment, filled the air. "You and I, my dear friend," John Adams wrote to Richard Henry Lee, "have been sent into life at a time when the greatest lawgivers of the past would have wished to live. How few of the human race have ever enjoyed an opportunity of making an election of government . . . for themselves or their children!"

Most of these meetings produced provisional, or temporary, legislatures that were not very different from the old colonial assemblies. But in Massachusetts and New Hampshire, the people demanded both a special convention to prepare a constitution and the right to ratify it.

Only in Connecticut and Rhode Island was there no constitution-making. Their colonial charters were so democratic that Connecticut and Rhode Island kept them, simply deleting mention of the British Crown.

The framers' experiences under British rule, and the rights they had claimed as British subjects, formed the basis of the new governments. Americans sought to lessen the power that the British King and colonial governors had exercised by separating governmental power into three independent branches. The **legislature** would make the laws, the **judiciary** would interpret the laws, and the **executive**—the governor—would enforce laws and manage the affairs of the state.

The British constitution was mainly unwritten traditions. Americans wanted their state constitu-

Busy State Street in Boston was depicted by the painter James B. Marston in the early years of the American nation. The steps lead up to the old State House, the center of government in Massachusetts until 1798. The state constitution, written in 1779, guided lawmakers there.

tions written down as a further guarantee that their rights would not be taken away. By 1777 ten states had constitutions in writing.

All of the new constitutions included a bill of rights defining the liberties of individuals. These were liberties that could not be taken away by government.

The state constitutions put most of the power into the hands of elected legislatures. In most states legislatures would elect the governor each year, and the governors would not have the power to veto bills or appoint officials. All legislatures, except Pennsylvania's, were bicameral, having two houses which would act as checks on each other.

State constitutions also ensured that the courts be as independent as possible. Most state legislatures appointed judges to serve permanently as long as they did not abuse their power. Once appointed, judges could decide cases without having to worry about being fired for offending the governor or legislature.

Most states continued their policy of allowing only men who owned a certain amount of property to vote or hold office. Property owners, it was thought, had some stake in the community. But the property qualifications for voting were reduced almost everywhere. In a few states all male taxpayers could vote. Voting rights almost never extended to women or blacks. However, unclear wording in New Jersey's constitution gave women the vote for a brief time, and the Massachusetts, Connecticut, and New Jersey constitutions did not exclude free blacks from voting.

Religious freedom was also written into many constitutions. All but three states—New Hampshire, Connecticut, and Massachusetts—abolished government-supported churches. Most states, though, continued to insist upon religious qualifications for officeholding.

Greater religious freedom and extended voting rights reflected the mood of equality rippling through America after the Revolution. In many

churches people were no longer seated according to their rank in society. States abolished inheritance laws designed to protect the large estates of the upper class.

Economic opportunity also seemed to spread in the wake of the Revolution. During the war, the states confiscated royal and Loyalist lands, then divided up and sold the large estates to raise money. Most often, these lands were split into still smaller parcels and sold to small landowners. Property ownership became so widespread that Charles Pinckney of South Carolina later boasted, "There is more equality of rank and fortune in America than in any other country under the sun."

THE ARTICLES OF CONFEDERATION

The state constitutions set up governments for the states but the national government was more of a problem. During those hot days in July 1776, when the members of Congress had voted for freedom, they had also considered a plan of union for the thirteen independent states. For over a year, the delegates debated a constitution—the Articles of Confederation—while waging war against Britain.

Most state constitutions limited the vote to men, but women too could cast ballots in New Jersey. This right was taken away after charges of irregularities in an election in 1806.

Lemuel Haynes became the first black minister of the Congregational Church in America in the 1780s. He guided parishioners in Connecticut and Vermont.

The delegates first argued over how states were to be represented in Congress. In the First and Second Continental Congresses, each state had been given a single vote. However, the large states had always been unhappy with this arrangement. In 1776 they demanded that state population be the basis for the number of representatives that each state send to Congress. Small states, fearful of being "swallowed" by the larger ones, insisted on an equal vote in Congress.

Finally, the delegates agreed that each state have one representative. Major measures, though, had to be passed by a two-thirds majority of states, and **amendments**, or changes, in the Articles of Confederation required the approval of every state.

The role of a central government also proved to be an issue. Most delegates feared that a strong central government would create a new tyranny, replacing the one they were fighting.

Thus, Congress, the only branch in the central government, was given important, but few, powers. Congress could wage war and make peace, regulate foreign affairs and Indian matters outside the states, and settle disputes among the states. It could coin and borrow money, request troops and money from the states, establish standards for weights and measures, and set up a postal service.

However, two traditional powers of government were withheld. Congress would not have the power to levy taxes or to set up **tariffs**, duties on imports or exports. The central government was further weakened because there was no executive branch to enforce the laws passed by Congress. Nor was there a judicial branch. This confederation of states, therefore, was little more than a "firm league of friendship."

RATIFICATION PROBLEMS

Congress finally adopted the Articles of Confederation in November 1777, but they still had to be **ratified**, or approved, by each state. During the following year, town meetings in Massachusetts and New Hampshire examined every clause of the Articles. Legislatures in other states debated them as thoroughly as Congress had. By the summer of 1778 nine states had ratified the Articles. But a few, led by Maryland, held back.

The stumbling block was the unsettled land west of the Appalachian Mountains. Seven states—Virginia, New York, Massachusetts, Connecticut, the two Carolinas, and Georgia—had claims there, most dating back to colonial charters. Often, the claims overlapped. Some states, with wild imagination, claimed land all the way to the South Sea, as the Pacific Ocean was sometimes called.

Six states—Delaware, New Hampshire, Pennsylvania, Rhode Island, New Jersey, and Maryland—had fixed western boundaries. These states feared that the states with claims to the West would come to overshadow them. No state "has a right to go to the South Sea," a member of Congress from Maryland argued. "It would not be safe to the rest." Maryland, Pennsylvania, and New Jersey demanded that the states with claims to western lands cede these lands to the Confederation.

There was another reason for the argument over western land claims. Before the Revolution, speculators had formed companies in these states and bought land in the Ohio Valley from the Indian tribes. But Virginia, with the oldest colonial charter, claimed what is now Kentucky and all the territory north of the Ohio River. Its legislature declared that only Virginia had the right to purchase from the Indians land in this territory and canceled the claims of outsiders.

Anxious to protect their investments, the land companies turned to Congress to demand cession of the western lands to the United States. Congress was unable to convince Virginia, but New York and Connecticut did cede their lands to the government. Still, this did not satisfy Maryland. Although the other states with definite boundaries had finally ratified the Articles of Confederation, Maryland refused to do so unless Virginia gave up its claims.

Finally, military affairs settled the matter. In 1780 British forces began winning major victories in the South. Completing the Confederation now seemed more important than arguing among states.

In January 1781 the Virginia Assembly agreed to cede all claims northwest of the Ohio River to Congress. But there were conditions. Virginia demanded that the land be formed into new states and that all purchases from Indians in the area be declared void. Eventually, all other states with land claims followed Virginia's example.

Although Virginia had met Maryland's demands, Virginia's conditions would take away the land that speculators had bought from the Indians. Again Maryland refused to ratify, and again a mil-

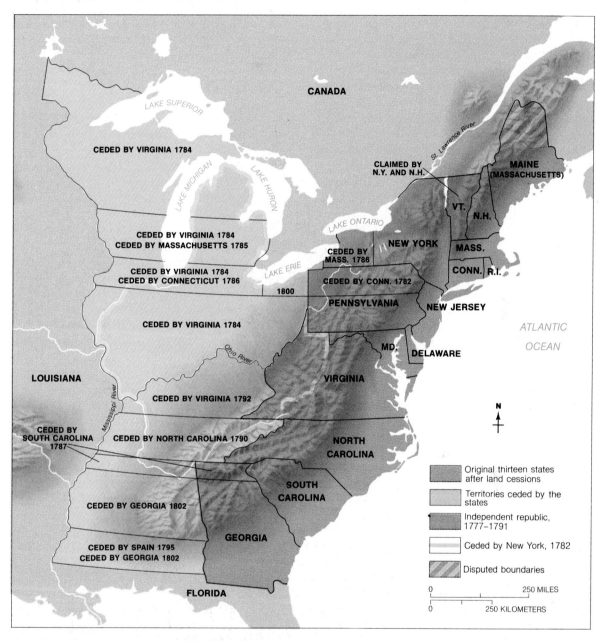

Map key:
- Original thirteen states after land cessions
- Territories ceded by the states
- Independent republic, 1777–1791
- Ceded by New York, 1782
- Disputed boundaries

0 250 MILES
0 250 KILOMETERS

Map labels:
CANADA
LAKE SUPERIOR
LAKE MICHIGAN
LAKE HURON
LAKE ONTARIO
LAKE ERIE
St. Lawrence River
Ohio River
Mississippi River
ATLANTIC OCEAN
LOUISIANA
FLORIDA

CEDED BY VIRGINIA 1784
CEDED BY VIRGINIA 1784
CEDED BY MASSACHUSETTS 1785
CEDED BY VIRGINIA 1784
CEDED BY CONNECTICUT 1786
1800
CEDED BY VIRGINIA 1784
CEDED BY MASS. 1786
CEDED BY CONN. 1782
CEDED BY VIRGINIA 1792
CEDED BY SOUTH CAROLINA 1787
CEDED BY NORTH CAROLINA 1790
CEDED BY GEORGIA 1802
CEDED BY SPAIN 1795
CEDED BY GEORGIA 1802

CLAIMED BY N.Y. AND N.H.
MAINE (MASSACHUSETTS)
VT.
N.H.
NEW YORK
MASS.
CONN.
R.I.
PENNSYLVANIA
NEW JERSEY
MD.
DELAWARE
VIRGINIA
NORTH CAROLINA
SOUTH CAROLINA
GEORGIA

itary crisis broke the deadlock. Threatened with a British invasion, Maryland appealed to the French to send ships to protect its shore. The French, believing that an American union would benefit France, suggested that ships might be available if Maryland signed the Articles of Confederation. Maryland's legislature accepted the suggestion. On March 1, 1781, its delegates ratified the Articles of Confederation, which then went into effect.

GOVERNMENT UNDER THE ARTICLES OF CONFEDERATION

The confederation government proved to be hardly the tyrant that some had feared. For its income, the government depended on the good will of the states, but they proved reluctant to send funds. Yet they also refused to give the government financial independence. When Congress tried to raise income by obtaining the right to levy a tax on foreign imports, the states defeated the plan.

Each state seemed to be following its own course. Each printed its own money and established its own trade regulations. Some states even engaged in tariff rivalries. When New York taxed incoming oysters from Massachusetts, Massachusetts struck back by levying a tariff on New York's nails.

State rivalry over land heated up. New York and New Hampshire were quarreling over Vermont, which had set up an independent republic during the war and would not join the Union until 1791. Settlers from Connecticut and Pennsylvania were warring with each other over land in northern Pennsylvania, which both states claimed. It soon became apparent that the league of friendship was not even firm.

To make matters worse, violations of the Treaty of Paris angered both Britain and America. Americans refused to pay debts owed British citizens, or to restore Loyalist property. When John Adams, minister to Great Britain, demanded that Britain remove its troops from army and fur-trading posts in the Northwest, the British paid no attention. The posts, they stated, would be held until British creditors received payment from the United States. They also refused to consider a commercial treaty with the United States. Any state, the British ambassador declared, could render such an agreement "totally fruitless and ineffectual."

MOVING WESTWARD

The British presence on American soil angered many Americans, but it did not curb their eagerness to settle the Northwest. Even before the Revolution, settlers hungry for land had begun trickling west, ignoring British efforts to keep them on the Atlantic seaboard. In the years after independence, that trickle became a torrent.

By whatever means of transport—by wagon train, on foot, or on river barges called flatboats—American pioneers reached the new frontier. This frontier included western New York, Pennsylvania, and Virginia, and the lands that would become the states of Kentucky, Tennessee, Ohio, Indiana, and Illinois. "The woods are full of new settlers," one traveler wrote. "Axes are resounding and the trees literally falling about us."

This "westering urge" drove people onward despite the dangers of the wilderness. It also drove them onto Indian land despite treaties with the tribes. To most settlers, the risks seemed worth it. One pioneer wrote, "I returned home to my family

Daniel Boone, shown in his old age, gained fame for trailblazing in Kentucky.

Settlers often gathered for work parties. The artist Linton Park showed flax scutching, in which pieces of stalk were scraped from the fibers.

with a determination to bring them as soon as possible to live in Kentucky, which I esteemed a second paradise."

Many settlers were guided into the frontier by long time explorers like Daniel Boone, who had first prowled the Kentucky wilderness in 1767. In 1775 Boone and others connected several Indian trails to form the Wilderness Road, a route that cut through the Cumberland Gap and led into Kentucky. This rough highway would open the West to thousands of pioneers.

By the mid-1780s thousands of Americans had spread out across the frontier. Most lived by farming and trapping, but their goods were too bulky to transport cheaply over the Appalachians to market. So they sent flatboats down the Mississippi River to New Orleans. From there, goods could be shipped to the Atlantic seaboard and to Europe. However, New Orleans was a Spanish possession.

Alarmed at America's westward expansion, Spain formed alliances with southern Indian tribes against the Americans. In 1784 Spain also closed the lower Mississippi to American shipping.

Spain later reopened the Mississippi to American trade—for a high fee. But tension continued over American rights on the river, over boundaries, and over Spanish intrigue with settlers and Indians in the Southwest.

THE LAND ORDINANCE OF 1785

Conflict with the Spanish in the Southwest and with the British in the Northwest spurred Congress to oversee the settlement of the West. In 1784 Virginia formally ceded to the government the Northwest—the area north of the Ohio River, west of Pennsylvania, and east of the Mississippi. A year later, Congress planned for the orderly sale and settlement of this area in the Land Ordinance of 1785. With these land sales, Congress expected to raise the money it badly needed to pay war debts.

The land was to be carefully surveyed and then divided into areas called *townships*, each 6 miles square (9.7 square kilometers). Each township was further divided into 36 *sections* of 1 square mile (2.6 square kilometers) each, 640 acres (259 hectares) to a section. Four sections in each township were set aside for the national government, and one was reserved to maintain public schools. The remaining sections would be sold to settlers.

The Northwest Territory 1787

Land Ordinance Survey System

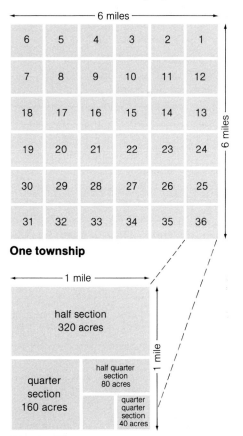

One township

One section

Hopes ran high as the first townships were surveyed and opened, but sales were slow. A settler had to purchase at least one section at a minimum price of $1.00 per acre—$640 total—and few had enough cash. Desperate for money, Congress had to compromise and sell large areas to land speculators at well below the legal price. The Ohio Company, organized by New Englanders, obtained 750,000 acres (304,000 hectares) in what was to become southeastern Ohio.

THE NORTHWEST ORDINANCE

In 1787 Congress, prodded by the Ohio Company, passed the Northwest Ordinance to establish a government in the land ceded by Virginia. The Northwest Territory was to be divided into no fewer than three and no more than five states. In the first stage of government, Congress would appoint a territorial governor, a secretary, and three judges. As soon as 5,000 "free male inhabitants of full age" lived in the territory, the people could elect their own legislature and nonvoting delegate to Congress. Any man who owned at least 50 acres (20.2 hectares) of land could vote. Finally, when the area had 60,000 free inhabitants, it could become a state.

The new states would join the Union "on an equal footing with the original states in all respects whatever." Their residents would enjoy the basic **civil rights**, or individual liberties, guaranteed to all citizens of the Confederation, such as religious freedom and trial by jury. The ordinance also planted two more seeds of democracy in the Northwest Territory. Slavery would not be allowed in the territory or in any state carved from it. And the state governments would "forever be encouraged" to support public education. Thus, a plan for the growth of the United States had been written.

One of the first settlers to strike out for the Northwest Territory after passage of the Northwest Ordinance was Colonel John May. He and a group of pioneers chose a river junction in Ohio as the site of their new town, Marietta. On July 4, May noted in his diary: "All labor comes to pause today in memory of the Declaration of Independence." Over a "handsome dinner" the pioneers raised their glasses in toast after toast. They saluted, among other things, the United States, Congress, General Washington, the memory of heroes, all human beings, and the Northwest Territory.

Settlers who moved into the Northwest Territory faced the risk of attack by Indians. Fort Franklin, a frontier outpost near Lake Erie, was built to protect settlements.

SECTION REVIEW

1. Identify the following: Daniel Boone, Wilderness Road, Land Ordinance of 1785, Northwest Ordinance.

2. What experiences under the British affected the way Americans formed state governments?

3. (a) Into what three branches were state governments divided? (b) Describe each branch.

4. (a) How did large states want to be represented in Congress under the Articles of Confederation? (b) How did small states want to be represented?

5. (a) What powers did Congress have under the Articles of Confederation? (b) What two traditional powers of government did Congress not have?

6. Explain why some states wanted western lands to be ceded to the Confederation government.

7. (a) In what ways did Americans violate the Treaty of Paris (1783)? (b) In what ways did Britain violate its treaty agreements with the United States?

8. What states would be carved out of the area that was the American frontier in the late 1700s?

9. What caused tension between the United States and Spain?

10. List three democratic ideals written into the Northwest Ordinance.

THE COUNTRY ADRIFT

READ TO FIND OUT

— how trade and currency problems damaged the nation's economy.

— what economic problems sparked Shays' Rebellion.

— how American leaders planned to strengthen the nation's government.

The Confederation Congress planned well for the Northwest Territory. Yet Congress lacked the means to solve many other problems. In 1780 George Washington was already worried about the weakness of the nation's government. "I see one head gradually changing into thirteen," he wrote.

The root of most of these problems was the economy. Although the war's end had brought prosperity, the good times proved to be short-lived. Soon merchants and artisans began to complain of falling prices and sluggish trade. Farmers, who had made great profits during the war, let their crops rot in the fields rather than sell them in oversupplied markets for low prices. People who worked for daily wages could no longer find work. By the mid-1780s the nation was in the grip of a depression.

While the nation stretched westward into the wilderness, the center of its commerce remained on the East Coast, in New York City. Merchants and shippers met every day at the corner of Wall and Water streets in Manhattan, pictured here, to exchange news and transact business.

TRADE PROBLEMS

Americans were proud of their independence, but they were not so pleased with the loss of their colonial trade privileges with Britain. The British still bought American raw materials, such as tobacco and timber, and even many of the manufactured goods Americans had begun producing during the war. But Britain struck at the states' rich triangular trade by banning Americans from trading in the British West Indies. Thus, the farmers, merchants, and fishers of New England and the Middle States lost their most important market.

At the same time, peace revived the American taste for British goods. British merchants, who had missed their American markets during the war, rushed to sell goods in the United States at prices so low that American manufacturers could not compete. Within a few years, the United States was buying much more from Britain than it sold to that country. And it was paying with its dwindling supply of gold and silver.

One solution to the unfavorable balance of trade would have been a tariff on imports. A tariff would raise the price of foreign goods, encouraging Americans to buy products made in the states. Some states did respond to the demands of American manufacturers and artisans for protection against British competition by levying duties on imported goods. But to be effective a tariff policy had to operate uniformly in all the states, and Congress had no authority to set tariffs. When Congress tried to obtain that right, one state or another, protecting its power, always defeated the proposal.

Merchants searched for ways to expand trade, at home and abroad. In 1784 the *Empress of China* sailed out of New York bound for Canton, China, halfway around the world. The Chinese wanted furs, so American sea captains set up a new triangle of trade. On their way to Asia, they stopped on the west coast of North America, where they traded cloth, beads, and iron to the Indians in exchange for furs. In China the traders exchanged furs for cargoes of tea, silk, porcelain, and *nankeen*, a popular cloth for men's trousers.

American merchants also expanded trade with France and Holland. But these markets were not large enough to tip the balance of trade in America's favor. The new nation still spent more on imports than it received for its exports.

CURRENCY PROBLEMS

American currency, the most visible symbol of the economy, was meanwhile steadily losing its value. During the war the Continental Congress had printed over $2 million in paper money but did not have gold to back it. People soon lost confidence in Continental dollars, and by 1781 the money was worthless. People began to say of any useless thing that it was "not worth a Continental." The states also had the power to print money. So, a dozen kinds of near worthless currency circulated along with the Continentals.

After the war Congress looked to the states for money to pay the nation's debts, but the states came up with only about one fourth of the amount requested. They, too, had war debts as well as war damage to repair, especially in the South. Seven states simply printed more money, again without gold backing. This caused **inflation**—a situation in which the paper money continued to decline in value and prices continued to rise.

A single national currency could have brought some order to the nation's finances. But Congress could not prevent the states from printing their own money. In fact, it seemed Congress could do nothing to help the economy, and many people were losing whatever confidence they had in the Confederation.

Free from British rule, many Americans hoped for prosperity like that shown in the needlepoint by Mary Woodhull of New England. Problems of trade and money crushed the hopes.

SHAYS' REBELLION

Most of the soldiers who fought in the war were farmers. In their pockets were papers from Congress, promising that they would someday receive their back pay. In Massachusetts, Captain Daniel Shays waited for his pay and almost went to jail because he could not raise $12 to pay a debt.

Throughout New England small farmers like Shays were hit hard by the loss of the market in the West Indies, and many slid into debt. Faced with low prices, they plowed their crops back into the ground. But that ground, now producing little cash income, was taxed, and in Massachusetts taxes had skyrocketed. The Massachusetts legislature was determined to pay its debts—and not in inflated currency as Rhode Island had done. So it voted for high taxes to raise the funds.

Some farmers borrowed money to pay their taxes or debts. They used their cattle or crop as collateral* for the loan. Sometimes they pledged the farm itself as payment by taking a mortgage on the property. Later, if they could not pay off the loan or mortgage, creditors took them to court. The judge ordered the crop or livestock sold to pay the debt, or the bank took the farm.

* collateral: anything pledged as security for a loan.

Many who could not pay debts or back taxes went to jail. "In 1786," one report said, "not a few of these poor creatures, blue with prison mould, were those who had fought for freedom." Throughout the summer of 1786, farmers asked the Massachusetts legislature for help. They wanted a law that would permit them to pay debts with their crops. Some even asked for a law that would allow them more time to pay their debts.

Farmers also asked for tax relief and the issue of paper money, as in Rhode Island. But the legislature, which was controlled by business interests, refused to act.

Some of the Massachusetts farmers decided to take action. If judges could not get to court, they could not foreclose mortgages or send debtors to prison. In county after county, groups of angry farmers gathered and broke up court sessions. Their number grew to about 1,000. Daniel Shays became their leader.

In January 1787 Shays and his followers marched on the Confederation arsenal at Springfield in order to obtain a supply of arms. Meanwhile, the governor of Massachusetts called out the state militia. When Shays' force moved to seize the arsenal, the troops fired. The farmers quickly retreated, leaving four of their band lying dead in the snow.

Despair led to bloodshed in Shays' Rebellion. The group of farmers at right retreated under a volley of shots at the Springfield, Massachusetts, arsenal.

By the end of February, Shays' Rebellion had been crushed. Also, the nation's economy was beginning to recover. But the rebellion sent waves of uneasiness through all of the states. More and more Americans came to believe that only a strong national government could maintain law and order and solve the economic problems that had caused the uprising in Massachusetts.

THE ANNAPOLIS CONVENTION

Even before Shays' Rebellion, worried American leaders were working to strengthen the Confederation by ending state arguments over commerce. In 1785 commissioners from Maryland and Virginia met to discuss problems of navigation on the Potomac River and on Chesapeake Bay.

In September 1786 delegates from five states met in Annapolis, Maryland. James Madison of Virginia was there, and so was Alexander Hamilton of New York. Both were young politicians who supported a strong national government.

James Madison, as a young man, had seemed destined for a life of scholarship and the ministry. Much of his childhood was spent in the company of tutors on the family plantation. When he went on to Princeton, he graduated from the university in just two years. His weak speaking voice, however, kept him from being a minister. And the brewing Revolution soon swept him into Virginia politics. In 1779 Madison was elected to the Continental Congress. During his three-year stay, he earned a reputation as a first-rate representative who worked to strengthen the weak government.

Alexander Hamilton was born in the British West Indies and was sent as a young child to New York for his education. Hamilton studied at Columbia but his career, like Madison's, was interrupted by the Revolution. A passionate Patriot and pamphlet-writer, Hamilton served as Washington's military assistant and fought at Yorktown. After the war he served for a year in Congress. He then studied law and built a thriving New York practice.

Both Madison and Hamilton argued that nothing could be done by the sparsely attended Annapolis meeting. The rest of the delegates agreed. Together, they called upon the states to send delegates to a new convention in Philadelphia in May 1787. There, delegates could discuss ways of strengthening the national government.

TOWARD A CONSTITUTIONAL CONVENTION

Five states, led by Virginia, quickly responded to the invitation by appointing delegates. Others held back, waiting for Congress's reaction. A congressional committee debated the plan during the winter of 1786 and 1787. During this time, depression raged throughout the nation, and Shays' followers rebelled in Massachusetts. In February 1787 Congress finally endorsed the proposed convention "for the sole and express purpose of revising the Articles of Confederation." Throughout the spring, seven more state legislatures elected delegates. Only Rhode Island refused to participate.

Benjamin Rush—Philadelphia physician, Patriot, signer of the Declaration of Independence—tried to encourage people to support the upcoming convention. In one speech he said that only the "first act of the great drama" was finished. The American Revolution would be completed when the government was perfected:

> Patriots of 1774, 1775, 1776—heroes of 1778, 1779, 1780! Come forward! Your country demands your services! . . . Hear it proclaiming, in sighs and groans, in its governments, in its finances, in its trade, in its manufactures, in its morals, and its manners, "The Revolution is not over!"

SECTION REVIEW

1. Identify the following: *Empress of China*, Daniel Shays, Annapolis Convention.

2. (a) What British actions created an unfavorable balance of trade for America? (b) What solution did manufacturers offer to correct the unfavorable balance of trade?

3. Describe briefly the American triangle of trade involving Asia.

4. (a) Define *inflation*. (b) Give two reasons why paper money lost its value after the Revolutionary War.

5. (a) Give one reason why New England farmers went into debt after the Revolutionary War.
(b) Why did Massachusetts levy high taxes?
(c) What often happened to people who could not pay debts or taxes?

6. How did Shays' Rebellion encourage Americans to change the national government?

A MORE
PERFECT UNION

READ TO FIND OUT

— what separation of powers the Constitutional Convention agreed upon.

— how the Constitutional Convention debated plans for a legislative branch.

— what compromises saved the Constitution.

— how the states and the national government share power under federalism.

— how the Constitution established a system of checks and balances.

— how the Constitution was ratified in the states.

— what liberties citizens were guaranteed in the Bill of Rights.

In May 1787, 55 delegates from 12 states gathered at Philadelphia's State House, where the Declaration of Independence had been signed more than a decade earlier. It was a dazzling assembly.

George Washington was there, and no one commanded greater respect from the American people. He was unanimously chosen president of the convention. Benjamin Franklin was also there, 81 years old now, but still radiating what one observer called "an unrestrained freedom and happiness." Other delegates, like Alexander Hamilton and James Madison, were veterans of the Revolution and state leaders in their thirties.

THE CONSTITUTIONAL CONVENTION

The convention opened on a note of urgency. Gunning Bedford of Delaware, warned, "The condition of the United States requires that something should be immediately done." Although the convention had been called to amend the Articles of Confederation, many delegates considered that document beyond mending and called for a new constitution and a new government.

The delegates generally agreed on the broad form of this new government. It had to have the powers that the Confederation Congress lacked: powers to tax, to raise and support armed forces, to regulate commerce, and to enforce laws. However, it had to be a **republic**—a nation with a government subject to the will of the people, who would directly elect their representatives.

In general, the delegates also agreed, following eighteenth-century political thought, that power should not rest in one branch of government. They could point to two different cases in which rule by legislature caused problems. Under the Articles of Confederation the government had operated only through a legislature. Without an executive or courts, the acts of Congress could not be enforced or interpreted. On the other hand, in some state governments too much power wielded by the legislature had produced tyranny. Separating governmental functions into independent executive, judicial, and legislative branches would balance power and at the same time provide for its effective use.

There the agreement ended. A long road stretched between the delegates and their destination. For four months, they argued over the details of the government-in-making.

THE VIRGINIA AND NEW JERSEY PLANS

On May 29, 1787, Virginia's governor, Edmund Randolph, presented the Virginia Plan of Union, outlining a new national government. Drafted by James Madison, the plan proposed a central government made up of three separate branches, each with clearly defined powers. The delegates considered the plan point by point.

On May 31 debate centered on the Virginia Plan's proposals for the legislative branch of government. The delegates agreed that the legislature ought to be bicameral. Then they took up the nature of the two houses. The Virginia Plan resolved that the members of the first house ought to be elected by the people of the states. After long argument, a majority of the convention agreed, approving the resolution. The convention next approved the proposal that the second, or senatorial, house should be made up of representatives chosen by the members of the first house.

The Virginia Plan also called for representation in both houses to be based on a state's population. Delegates from the smaller states disagreed angrily. New Jersey's William Paterson called for equal representation for all states. "If we are to be considered as a nation," Paterson declared, "all state distinctions must be abolished."

On June 15 Paterson presented the New Jersey Plan, which called for amending the Articles of Confederation rather than drafting a new constitution. Each state, regardless of its population, would still have one vote in Congress. And Congress would remain a single house with representatives elected by state legislatures. The plan gave most power to the states, although it did let Congress levy taxes and regulate foreign domestic trade.

In response, Governor Randolph of Virginia attacked the weakness of the Confederation government and a Congress not elected directly by the people. Only a national government, like that proposed in the Virginia Plan, would gain the people's trust. "The present is the last moment for establishing one," he said. "After this select experiment, the people will yield to despair."

AMERICAN OBSERVERS

CHARLES WILLSON PEALE
EARLY AMERICAN JACK-OF-ALL-TRADES

When young Charles Peale arrived at Mount Vernon in 1772, he was a little-known artist struggling to earn a living by his paint brush. Born in 1741 in Maryland, he had studied briefly in England, where he was already enough of an American Patriot to refuse to take off his hat to the king. As a painter, Peale was also thoroughly American, with a fresh, down-to-earth approach to his art.

Peale's subject at Mount Vernon was Colonel George Washington himself. A 40-year-old gentleman farmer, Washington had never had his portrait painted before, and he had trouble standing still. Nonetheless, the 6-foot-2, 200-pound colonel made an impressive figure. He was dressed in his French and Indian War uniform with its blue coat, red breeches, gold-braided vest, and pale purple sash. The portrait was a success. It was the first of 60 that Peale would do of Washington.

During the American Revolution, which began four years later, Peale served in Washington's army. Afterwards he settled in Philadelphia, where his interests soon included science. In 1786 he founded Peale's Museum, the first natural history museum in America. At its peak, it contained 200 kinds of animals, 1,000 birds, and 4,000 insects, the majority collected and mounted by Peale himself. He was proudest of his two mastodon skeletons, which he had dug up from a New York farm and painstakingly assembled.

Like America itself, Peale was practical, energetic, and boundlessly optimistic. He was interested in everything. A constant tinkerer, he invented a new kind of fireplace, butter churner, straw cutter, and windmill. He taught painting to many of his 17 children. Two of them, Raphael Peale and Rembrandt Peale, became famous artists themselves.

In 1822 Charles Willson Peale painted his own portrait in front of displays in his Philadelphia museum. The cases along the wall hold specimens of birds from the West.

Long deliberations led to the moment when the Constitution was written out and ready to be signed. The painter Thomas Rossiter, born thirty years after the convention, showed what that moment might have looked like. He rendered George Washington in a place of lone dignity.

THE GREAT COMPROMISE

By mid-July, weary of the humid weather, sharp arguments, and endless debate, the delegates were willing to compromise between the two plans. Roger Sherman of Connecticut proposed the Great Compromise, also called the Connecticut Compromise. He suggested that the legislative branch be organized in such a way that both large and small states would have a voice.

Every state legislature would elect two representatives to the Senate, giving the smaller states equal representation there. To satisfy the larger states, representation in the House of Representatives would be based on a state's population. Furthermore, members of the House would be directly elected by the people.

ADDITIONAL COMPROMISES

The next argument arose over which people would be counted as part of a state's population. Southern states, with a huge proportion of slaves, wanted to increase their representation by including slaves in the population count. Northern states disagreed, insisting that slaves were property and should not be represented. So the delegates compromised again, agreeing to count three fifths of a state's slaves to determine representation in the House.

An agreement on the two houses of Congress having been reached, the delegates turned to the executive branch. After long debate, they decided in favor of a president rather than an executive committee.

The delegates did not, however, agree on how the president would be chosen. Some felt that the people should not vote directly for an executive. They might be too easily swayed by personality and fail to make an informed choice. Others, however, feared the alternative, believing that an executive selected by the legislature could not be independent.

Once more, the delegates compromised. Each state would choose as many electors as it had members of Congress. The electors of each state, known altogether as the **electoral college**, would meet, cast votes, and elect a president and vice-president who would serve four years.

The necessity for compromise continued as the delegates considered the judicial branch. Delegates finally agreed that the president would choose judges of the Supreme Court, with the consent of the Senate.

It was late summer when the delegates took up government regulation of commerce—the issue that had prompted the Annapolis Convention. Their bitter experience under the Articles of Confederation had convinced northerners that the national government should control trade.

The merchants and manufacturers of New England and the Middle States wanted regulations to protect their businesses against foreign competition. But the South depended on the export of rice, indigo, and tobacco. Their delegates feared that Congress would use such a regulatory power to tax their exports. Again, the Convention hammered out a compromise. Congress would have the power to regulate foreign and interstate trade and to tax imports, but it was forbidden to tax exports.

Another type of trade—the slave trade—also provided heated argument. The First Continental Congress had called for a halt to this trade, and several states had responded with bans of one kind or another. In fact, some states had even freed their slaves. In 1780 New Hampshire and Pennsylvania had passed **abolition** laws—laws ending slavery. In Massachusetts a slave named Quock Walker sued the state of Massachusetts for his freedom. He won,

Although he was free, this black artisan lived in New England when slavery still was common there. The portrait was done by John Singleton Copley, colonial America's leading artist.

and because of the court decision all slaves in Massachusetts were freed in 1783.

Slaves remained an important part of the South's economy, and southern delegates would not consent to outlawing the slave trade. They were even more reluctant to consider **emancipation**, or freedom for slaves. John Rutledge of South Carolina advised the convention that "the true question at present is whether the southern states shall or shall not be parties to the Union."

Delegates from northern states were not willing to give up the Constitution and the Union over the slave trade. It was agreed that Congress would not have the power to prohibit the trade for 20 years, or until 1808. In addition, states were required to send fugitive slaves who had fled across state borders back to their owners. Many delegates believed that abolition societies and competition from immigrant white labor would end slavery in any case. Roger Sherman remarked that "abolition of slavery seemed to be going on in the United States and that the good sense of the several states would probably by degrees complete it."

FEDERALISM

The Constitution that was taking shape at summer's end was a complex document. It had to be. The delegates had to create a whole frame of government and decide its foundation—where its power came from.

"We the people of the United States" begins the Constitution. The people, then, were the source of government, but the question was whether their power was to be channeled into a national government or the state governments. Most delegates had come to Philadelphia favoring one idea or the other. They solved the problem by dividing powers between the state and national governments. This bold new system became known as **federalism**.

Under federalism, the states delegated, or gave over, to the national government powers that affected the nation as a whole—powers that the Confederation government had lacked. These **delegated powers** gave the new national government the authority to levy taxes, regulate foreign and domestic commerce, conduct foreign relations, and maintain an army and navy. Most important, the government was also given the power to "make all laws which shall be necessary and proper for

Federalism

National Government		State Government
DELEGATED POWERS	CONCURRENT POWERS	RESERVED POWERS
Maintain an army and a navy	Maintain law and order	Conduct elections
Admit new states	Establish courts	Establish schools
Establish post offices	Charter banks	Establish local governments
Coin money	Borrow money	Charter and regulate corporations
Declare war	Levy taxes	Regulate business within the state
Conduct foreign relations	Build roads	Regulate marriages
Regulate foreign and interstate commerce	Protect the health and safety of the people	Assume other powers not given to the national government or prohibited to the states
Makes all laws necessary and proper for carrying out the delegated powers		

carrying into execution the foregoing powers." This *elastic clause* in the Constitution would allow the government flexibility to adjust to changes in the nation over time.

Furthermore, Article 6 made the Constitution and the laws of Congress "the supreme law of the land." Both state and national courts were bound to enforce them. Thus, the states were no longer the link between the people and the central government, as they had been under the Articles of Confederation. Within its realm of powers, the national government would directly touch every person in the United States.

Powers not given to the national government, nor prohibited to the states, were reserved for the states. With these **reserved powers**, states retained the right to act on state-wide concerns. Thus, state governments would continue to build roads, regulate business, establish schools, charter companies, and control local governments within their borders.

The states also shared some authority with the national government. To function effectively, both the national and state governments needed certain powers, such as the power to maintain law and order and to levy taxes. These powers, called **concurrent powers**, were given to the states and the national government to use at the same time. As John Dickinson of Delaware explained, the new system would be like the solar system. "The states," he said, "were the planets and ought to be left to move freely in their proper orbits."

SEPARATION OF POWERS AND CHECKS AND BALANCES

A second cornerstone of the national government was the division of powers among three separate branches. Under the Articles of Confederation, the government had operated only through a legislature. Without an executive or courts, the acts of Congress could not be enforced or interpreted. On the other hand, in some state governments the legislature had wielded too much power.

Thus, the Virginia Plan adopted the principle of **separation of powers**—the separation of the government into executive, judicial, and legislative branches. The two-house legislature would pass laws regarding the national government's powers and duties. The executive would enforce those laws as well as conduct foreign relations and command the armed forces. The judiciary would interpret the laws.

The power of each branch was limited by the others in a complex system of **checks and balances**. One branch could not control the others. A law, for example, had to be passed by both houses of Congress, but the president could veto the law. Congress then could override the veto by a two-thirds majority vote in both houses.

Congress could also check other presidential powers. A treaty made by the president required the "advice and consent" of the Senate. Presidential appointments of ambassadors, federal judges, and other officials also needed Senate approval. The president commanded the armed forces, but only Congress could declare and finance war. In addition, Congress could **impeach**, or accuse and then try, the president for "treason, bribery, or other high crimes and misdemeanors." If convicted, the president would be removed from office.

The Supreme Court would check both Congress and the president by exercising its right to hear and decide cases "arising under this Constitution, the laws of the United States, and treaties made . . . under their authority." Supreme Court justices were to be appointed by the president for life, but had to be approved by the Senate. Like the president, justices could be removed from office by impeachment in Congress.

Another important idea was written into Article 5 of the Constitution. It provided for amendments, or changes, in the Constitution. Amendments could be proposed by a two-thirds vote in each house of Congress or by a convention called by two thirds of the state legislatures. To become part of the Constitution, an amendment had to be ratified by three fourths of the state legislatures or special ratifying conventions.

This complicated process ensured that an amendment could not be hastily adopted, and that a large majority in the federal and state governments found it vital to the country's welfare. At the same time, the right to amend gave the Constitution flexibility. It could be changed to meet people's changing needs.

Checks and Balances

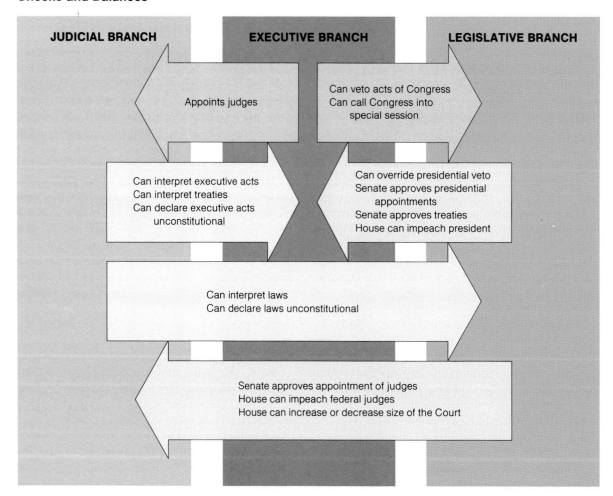

JUDICIAL BRANCH   EXECUTIVE BRANCH   LEGISLATIVE BRANCH

Appoints judges

Can veto acts of Congress
Can call Congress into
special session

Can interpret executive acts
Can interpret treaties
Can declare executive acts
unconstitutional

Can override presidential veto
Senate approves presidential
appointments
Senate approves treaties
House can impeach president

Can interpret laws
Can declare laws unconstitutional

Senate approves appointment of judges
House can impeach federal judges
House can increase or decrease size of the Court

THE CONVENTION ENDS

On September 17, 1787, the completed Constitution was read to the Convention. Although some unhappy delegates had already gone home, most agreed with Benjamin Franklin's assessment of the Constitution. "It will astonish our enemies," he said, "who are waiting with confidence to hear that our councils are confounded . . . . Thus I consent, sir, to this Constitution because I expect no better, and because I am not sure that it is not the best." Thirty-nine delegates signed the Constitution. Now it was up to the people to approve or reject the work of the Convention.

The delegates had known that when the Constitution was sent to the states it would meet strong opposition. So they set up a system to ease the way for ratification. The state legislatures, which stood to lose power under the proposed Constitution, would have no say. Instead, the people—the source of the government's power—would decide. People in every state would elect delegates to a convention, which would vote on ratification. As soon as nine of the thirteen states ratified the Constitution, the new government would be organized.

THE STRUGGLE FOR RATIFICATION

At the state conventions, feelings ran high. Federalists—people who favored the Constitution—argued that a strong national government was the only alternative to chaos and disunion. Opponents, called Anti-Federalists, feared that such a powerful national government would destroy not only the state governments, but also the "liberties of the people." They argued that the Constitution had no bill of rights as many state constitutions did.

The first vote was taken in December 1787 in Delaware, and it was a stunning victory for the Federalists. Delaware ratified by a unanimous vote. Soon after, New Jersey and Georgia also voted unanimously for the Constitution. Ratification did not come so easily in other states. However, by mid-1788 Pennsylvania, Connecticut, Massachusetts, Maryland, and South Carolina had followed Delaware.

The Federalist cause was almost lost in Massachusetts. A majority of delegates feared a strong federal government, which would, as one delegate complained, "swallow up all us little folks." To soothe the Anti-Federalists' fears, the Federalists promised that one of Congress's first acts would be to pass a bill of rights, listing the liberties of the people that the government could not violate. By a vote of 187 to 168, the Constitution squeaked through to ratification in Massachusetts.

By the end of May only one more state approval was needed to create a new government. "The plot thickens fast," Washington wrote to old comrade-in-arms Lafayette. "A few short weeks will determine the political fate of America." Then, in June 1788, New Hampshire became the ninth state to ratify. The Constitution was now the "supreme law of the land" among those nine states. Still, the remaining four states had nearly 40 percent of the nation's population.

In Virginia, Patrick Henry spoke intensely against the "horridly defective" Constitution. But some of the Federalists' brightest stars, like George Washington and James Madison, argued just as intensely for the Constitution. An able young lawyer named John Marshall stoutly defended it article by article. And Edmund Randolph, who had refused to sign in Philadelphia, was swayed by Federalist promises to enact a bill of rights. "I am a friend to the Union," Randolph declared. Virginia finally ratified by a vote of 89 to 79.

In New York, Alexander Hamilton waited anxiously for news from Virginia to spur the mostly Anti-Federalist convention toward ratification. For several months Hamilton, James Madison, and John Jay had been writing anonymous essays in New York newspapers to rally support for the Constitution. The essays, collected and published as *The Federalist* in May 1788, convinced many Americans of the need for a strong central government. In one essay Hamilton argued, "A nation without a national government is, in my view, an awful spectacle."

Word of ratification by New Hampshire, the ninth state, and then by Virginia in late June changed even more New York votes. Then Federalist New York City threatened to withdraw from the state and join the Union if the convention refused to ratify. Finally, after weeks of searing heat and bitter debate, New York ratified by three votes. Eleven states had now joined the Union. North Carolina did not enter the Union until November 1789, and Rhode Island waited until the spring of 1790.

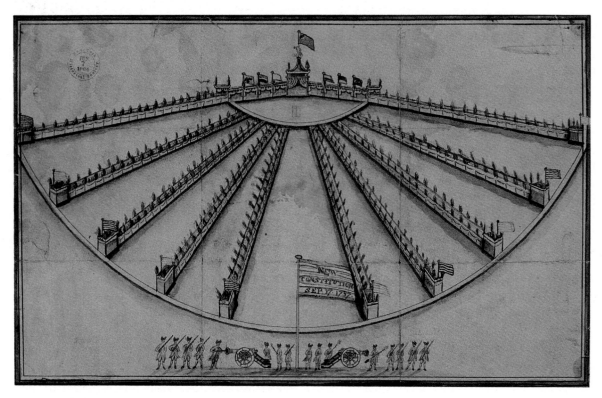

Six thousand citizens of New York City gathered at a huge banquet pavilion to celebrate the ratification of the Constitution. The flag in the foreground proclaims the day when the Constitutional Convention completed its work. The great banquet took place in July 1788.

GUARANTEES IN THE CONSTITUTION

At the ratifying conventions in Massachusetts, Virginia, and other states, Anti-Federalists had demanded that a bill of rights be added to the Constitution. Federalists had reluctantly agreed, arguing that this was unnecessary. The Constitution already protected individual rights from abuse by the government.

Citizens were given several guarantees in the Constitution that they would not be illegally imprisoned. Arrested people could obtain a *writ of habeas corpus*, a legal order requiring that they be charged with a crime or released. The Constitution forbade *ex post facto* laws, laws that punished actions that were not illegal when committed but became illegal after the action took place. Also outlawed were *bills of attainder*. These are laws that punish people accused of serious crimes, especially treason, without allowing them a trial. In addition, the Constitution provided for jury trials in all criminal cases, narrowed the charge of treason to making war against America or aiding its enemies, and prohibited religious tests as a qualification for holding office.

"The truth is," Hamilton wrote in one of *The Federalist* essays, "the Constitution is itself, in every rational sense, and to every useful purpose, a bill of rights." Many people, however, continued to think differently. Tirelessly, they demanded a list of the rights and freedoms guaranteed to Americans by the national government.

THE BILL OF RIGHTS

In the new Congress James Madison responded to that demand. He proposed a number of amendments to the Constitution, based on suggestions made by the state ratifying conventions.

Madison's amendments were approved by Congress and in September 1789 were presented to the states for approval. Over the next two years, the required three fourths of the states ratified them. Known as the Bill of Rights, these ten amendments clearly defined the rights of individuals. Some of the rights grew out of the British tradition of natural rights, adopted by Jefferson in the Declaration of Independence. Others grew out of America's colonial experience. Almost all of the rights carefully restricted the actions of the federal government.

The first four amendments listed the general rights of Americans. Under the First Amendment, citizens were guaranteed that the federal government would not interfere with religion. The First Amendment also guaranteed freedom of speech and freedom of the press. The Second Amendment said that because "a well-regulated militia [is] necessary to the security of a free State," Americans had the right to "keep and bear arms." The Third Amendment forbade quartering of soldiers in private homes. The Fourth Amendment protected citizens from "unreasonable searches and seizures" of "their persons, houses, papers, and effects."

The next four amendments protected the rights of people who were arrested. Under the Fifth Amendment, the accused was assured the right to a fair hearing and could not "be deprived of life, liberty, or property without due process of law." The amendment also stated that people could not be forced to testify against themselves or be tried twice for the same crime. The Sixth Amendment guaranteed the accused "a speedy and public trial by an impartial jury" and the right to have a lawyer. The Seventh Amendment guaranteed trial by jury in civil as well as criminal cases. Excessive bail and fines and "cruel and unusual punishments" were forbidden by the Eighth Amendment.

The last two amendments limited the scope of the new government. The Ninth Amendment declared that the Constitution and its amendments did not list all the rights of the people. There were other important rights, although unlisted, and they too would be protected. The Tenth Amendment assured the states that the powers not given to the federal government, or denied to the states, belonged to the states or to the people.

In December 1791 the Bill of Rights became part of the Constitution. Because of it, suspicion and criticism of the new government died down.

Most Americans were pleased with the work of the Constitutional Convention and Congress. Many would have agreed with the commonsense appraisal of a young farmer named Jonathan Smith. Speaking before the ratifying convention in Boston, Smith had this to say:

> Mr. President, I am a plain man, and get my living by the plow. I am not used to speak in public, but I beg your leave to say a few words . . . . I have lived in a part of the country where I have known the worth of good government by the want of it . . . . When I saw this Constitution, I found that it was a cure for these disorders . . . . I got a copy of it, and read it over and over. I had been a member of the convention to form our own state constitution, and had learnt something of the checks and balances of power, and I found them all here. I did not go to any lawyer, to ask an opinion, we have no lawyer in our town, and we do well enough without. I formed my own opinion, and was pleased with this Constitution.

SECTION REVIEW

1. Identify the following: Edmund Randolph, William Paterson, Roger Sherman, Federalists, Anti-Federalists, *The Federalist.*

2. Define the following: electoral college, federalism, concurrent powers, separation of powers, checks and balances, amendment, writ of habeas corpus, ex post facto law, bill of attainder.

3. On what points did the delegates agree at the start of the Constitutional Convention?

4. (a) How was the legislative branch of government set up under the Virginia Plan? (b) Under this plan how was representation in the legislature to be determined?

5. How was the legislative branch of government set up under the New Jersey plan?

6. Describe the compromise that ended debate over the structure of the legislature.

7. Explain the compromise that ended debate over each of the following: (a) the system of electing the president, (b) judicial appointments, (c) the slave trade.

8. (a) According to the Constitution, what powers does the national government have? (b) What powers are reserved for the states?

9. (a) By what system was the Constitution to be ratified? (b) Why was this system chosen?

10. Briefly list the rights guaranteed Americans in the Bill of Rights.

SUMMARY

At the end of the Revolutionary War, Americans had to form a national government. The Second Continental Congress had adopted the Articles of Confederation in 1776, but arguments between states with western land claims and those without such claims delayed ratification. Finally, in 1781, the Articles were ratified. They did not, however, provide for a strong national government. Congress, the only branch of the government, lacked the power to levy taxes and to set tariffs on trade goods.

The states were slowly nudged toward unity by problems too great for any one of them to handle. For example, Britain refused to remove its forts from the Northwest. Later Spain closed the lower Mississippi River to American shipping. Settlers from all the states were affected by these actions. The states again had a common cause. They worked together successfully to put into effect the Land Ordinance of 1785 and the Northwest Ordinance of 1787.

The need for unity became apparent, too, because of economic problems. There was an unfavorable balance of trade, different kinds of currency which were without value, and a depression. Reluctantly, the states agreed in 1787 to send representatives to Philadelphia to discuss ways to strengthen the national government.

Over the next several months the delegates argued, debated, and compromised. The result was the Constitution of the United States. The Constitution provided for three branches of government—the executive, legislative, and judicial branches. This division became known as separation of powers. The power of each branch was limited by a system of checks and balances.

Written into the Constitution was a provision for amendments, or changes. The first ten amendments to the Constitution are the Bill of Rights, guarantees of individual liberties.

Ratification of the Constitution did not proceed smoothly. Even the supporters of the new government had misgivings. They had, however, done their best, and they believed the document was sound. That document has served the nation for over 200 years.

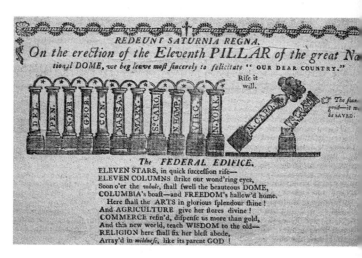

"Saturnia Regna," the reign of the Roman god Saturn, was supposed to be a golden age. An unknown poet foresaw another golden age when New York ratified the Constitution.

CHAPTER REVIEW

1. (a) How did new state governments protect the liberties of their citizens? (b) What liberties were included? (c) Why did state governments decide that such protection was necessary?

2. (a) What attempts were made by the states to deal with slavery and the slave trade during and after the Revolutionary War? Why? (b) How did these attempts differ in the North and South? Why? (d) How were these issues dealt with by the delegates to the Constitutional Convention?

3. How did each of the following lead to the Land Ordinance of 1785? (a) Spanish closure of the Mississippi to American shipping (b) Britain's refusal to abandon forts in the Northwest

4. (a) List the main weaknesses of the Confederation Congress. (b) How were these weaknesses reflected in each of the following problems: the unfavorable balance of trade, currency problems, Shays' Rebellion. Explain.

5. (a) Under the Constitution, what powers did the states give to the central government? Why? (b) What powers did the states retain? Why? (c) What did the states hope to gain from the new government?

6. Why was it important that New York and Virginia ratify the Constitution even though New Hampshire, the ninth state, had already ratified and thus put the Constitution into effect?

7. (a) How did each of the following influence the ratification of the Constitution? Delaware, Alexander Hamilton, the promise of a bill of rights (b) How successful was each?

8. (a) How did the Constitution reflect what was in state constitutions? (b) What principles were included in both?

9. Explain how each of the following limits the power of the national government. (a) a written constitution (b) checks and balances (c) bill of rights

10. Explain how each of the following allows the United States Constitution, written in 1787, to continue to be the supreme law of the land. (a) representative government (b) the amendment process (c) the elastic clause

ISSUES AND IDEAS

1. (a) As a Virginia Federalist, write a letter supporting ratification of the United States Constitution. Explain why arguments against the Constitution are not valid. Describe the benefits to be gained from the Constitution. (b) As an Anti-Federalist, write a letter opposing ratification. Explain why the new Constitution will not solve your state's problems. Explain why the states should remain sovereign.

Banned from the British West Indies, American traders sailed to China. There they exchanged furs for goods like this bowl, showing Chinese boats in Canton harbor.

An unknown engraver hailed the Declaration of Independence with these symbols. The thirteen hands represent the thirteen states, joined together and "Warm'd by one Heart."

2. (a) The President of the United States is elected by the electoral college. Why was this method chosen? (b) Why is the electoral college still used today? Should it be discarded? Why or why not?

3. In 1787 the Constitutional Convention divided the powers of government into three separate branches. Do you think this separation of powers still works as intended? Why or why not?

SKILLS WORKSHOP

1. *Timelines.* Make a timeline of the period from 1787 to 1790. Show when each of the original thirteen states ratified the Constitution.

2. *Primary sources.* Look at the Constitution, printed at the back of your text. Read Article 5. Explain four ways in which the Constitution may be amended.

PAST AND PRESENT

The constitutions of the American states were the first in the world to be officially written out. Find information on the constitution of your own state. When was it written and adopted? How many amendments have been added? How it is similar to the United States Constitution?

CHAPTER 6

THE FEDERALIST YEARS

1789–1801

A NEW GOVERNMENT
DOMESTIC POLITICS AND FOREIGN AFFAIRS
THE ADMINISTRATION OF JOHN ADAMS

In September 1789 Congress debated where the nation's capital should be located:

"Mr. Richard Bland Lee of Virginia—The House of Representatives is now called upon to decide a great national question. . . . A place ought to be selected as the permanent seat of government of the United States.

"Mr. Thomas Hartley of Pennsylvania—Many persons wish it seated on the banks of the Delaware, many on the banks of the Potomac. I consider the Susquehanna as the middle ground. It will suit the inhabitants to the north better than the Potomac could, and the inhabitants to the south better than the Delaware would.

"Mr. James Jackson of Georgia—Are the northern members to rule in this business? . . . I think the Potomac a better site.

"Mr. Theodore Sedgwick of Massachusetts—It is the opinion of all the northern states, that the climate of the Potomac is unhealthy.

"Mr. John Vining of Delaware—I am in favor of the Potomac. I wish the seat of government to be fixed there; because I think the interest, the honor, and the greatness of this country require it. I look on it as the center from which those streams are to flow that are to give life to the nation."

The issue at hand was more than the seat of government. It was also power. Many representatives argued that states closest to the capital would have greater say over laws that Congress passed. The issue would not be solved for almost a year.

The new government had many decisions to be made. Nearly every issue, however, caused an argument. Often the arguments centered on the role of the national government.

Meanwhile, news of war in Europe interrupted the work of building a nation. American leaders knew that their country needed breathing space to grow, and tried to steer clear of Europe's troubles. This would be a rough test for the young nation.

A NEW GOVERNMENT

READ TO FIND OUT

— what executive departments were created by the first Congress.

— how the Judiciary Act set up the federal court system.

— how Alexander Hamilton planned to fund the national debt.

— why Hamilton proposed federal assumption of state debts.

— why Hamilton proposed to establish the Bank of the United States.

— why Hamilton proposed a protective tariff.

— how the Whiskey Rebellion tested the authority of the new federal government.

In the spring of 1789 newly elected members of Congress made their way over mud-choked roads and swollen streams to New York City, the national government's latest home. George Washington, unanimously elected President of the United States by the electoral college, rode north from Mount Vernon toward his inauguration. Crowds cheered themselves hoarse as he retraced much of the route he had followed in his final assault on the British. He felt, he confessed to a friend, a bit like someone being led to his own execution.

New York City was noisy and festive, splashed with flags and decoration. No one seemed to mind that bad roads had delayed the ceremonies for almost two months. On the morning of April 30 George Washington, wearing a plain brown suit given to him by a Connecticut mill, stood on a balcony overlooking Wall Street. As he took the oath of office, the huge crowd cheered mightily.

Scattered throughout the crowd, clerks of the old Confederation were hoping that now they would receive their long-overdue pay. Indeed, the nation's empty treasury was only one of the problems in what Washington saw as an "ocean of difficulties."

The Confederation Congress had left huge debts. There was no money coming in and no means for collecting taxes. There was not even money for defense. The army had shrunk to 672 soldiers, and the navy no longer existed.

Most Americans took comfort in the knowledge that Washington's hand was on the tiller of government. Tall, broad-shouldered, red hair going gray, Washington represented the birth of the nation. Because of him, Americans pledged their loyalty to the new government.

THE EXECUTIVE BRANCH

With Washington's inauguration, Congress set about organizing the new federal government. The Constitution provided the framework, but the details had to be filled in.

One of Congress's first tasks was to organize the executive branch. President Washington and Vice-President John Adams, of course, had already been elected to their positions, for which the Constitution gave brief description.

Executive departments had first been created by the Confederation Congress to deal with foreign affairs, finance, war, and the postal service. Now

Congress created the Department of State, the Department of War, and the Department of the Treasury, along with the lesser office of postmaster general. President Washington would appoint the department heads, along with almost 1,000 minor federal employees.

Washington chose Thomas Jefferson, then minister to France, as secretary of state and lawyer-politician Alexander Hamilton for secretary of the treasury. Henry Knox, Washington's wartime artillery chief, became secretary of war, and Samuel Osgood was appointed postmaster general. During his two terms in office, Washington turned more and more to his major department heads for advice, and they became known as the president's *cabinet*.

THE JUDICIARY ACT

Next, Congress set the third branch of government into motion. For the judicial branch, the Constitution authorized the Supreme Court and whatever other courts Congress found necessary. In September 1789 Congress passed the Judiciary Act, which set up the federal court system and spelled out its powers.

The court system was like a pyramid, with the Supreme Court on top. Staffed by a Chief Justice and five associate judges, the Supreme Court had the power either to reverse or uphold state court decisions involving federal laws, treaties, and the Constitution. The Judiciary Act also provided for an attorney general to represent the United States in Supreme Court cases and to be legal advisor to the executive branch.

Further down the pyramid were three circuit courts, covering different regions of the country. These courts dealt mainly with disputes between citizens of different states, and they also heard appeals from district courts. The 13 district courts —one in each state—were at the base of the pyramid. Most federal cases would first be heard in the district courts.

Washington appointed and the Senate approved a judge, John Jay, to be Chief Justice of the Supreme Court. Edmund Randolph was chosen by President Washington to be attorney general. On February 2, 1790, six Supreme Court justices in black and scarlet robes first met in New York City. They had bowed to Jefferson's request to forego the "monstrous" wigs that English judges wore.

THE NATIONAL DEBT

While it was busily organizing the government, Congress also worked on the nation's most pressing problem—indebtedness. The government had no money to pay its debts and run the country, and it had no credit. The task of fund raising fell to the House of Representatives, which alone had the power to introduce bills involving revenue.

In July 1789 the House had its first success with a tariff bill, levying duties on some thirty imports. However, this money-raising bill was at best a stopgap measure. In September the House asked for advice from Secretary of the Treasury Alexander Hamilton.

The new secretary of the treasury was fiercely devoted to the new nation. Perhaps because he was born in the British West Indies, he gave his loyalty to no particular state. At the Constitutional Convention, he argued that the central government "must swallow up the state powers. Otherwise it will be swallowed up by them."

When Hamilton became secretary of the treasury, he saw a chance to strengthen the government. As a start, Hamilton planned to gain the support of wealthy Americans. People, he believed, would not be loyal to the new government unless they had "an active and constant interest in supporting it."

In January 1790 Hamilton gave to the House of Representatives his first Report on the Public Credit. It dealt with the nation's debt inherited from the Confederation—a whopping sum of over $50 million. During the Revolutionary War the Confederation had borrowed about $44 million from American citizens by issuing paper money and selling government *bonds*—certificates promising to pay back the buyers for their loans, plus interest, at a specified time. The state governments, too, had piled up a debt, borrowing about $25 million from Americans.

Hamilton believed that the war debt should be paid as soon as possible. If the United States did not honor its debts, it would lose the confidence of both its citizens and other nations. It would then have difficulty obtaining loans in the future.

To establish America's credit, Hamilton proposed that the government should fund, or provide money for, its national debt at *face value*—that is, call in the old war bonds that had lost value and ex-

NOAH WEBSTER
SPEAKING AMERICAN

When lanky, red-headed Noah Webster began to teach school during the Revolutionary War, he found the textbooks more English than American. They were laced with references to English geography, history, and literature.

Twenty-three-year-old Webster set out to change all this. During the 1780s he wrote a new series of schoolbooks that were American in every way. He included the European voyages to America and the history of the American Revolution for the first time in a textbook. He also Americanized the spelling. *Gaol* and *plough*, for example, became *jail* and *plow*. He even introduced the ABC's in a cheerful way. His reader began, "*A* was an apple-pie made by the cook."

Webster's books were eagerly accepted in American classrooms. His blue-covered speller became the country's first bestseller. By 1785, 75 million copies had been sold. The success of the speller allowed Webster to devote the rest of his life to another dream. That dream was a dictionary that would help to establish a uniform national language based on the unique way Americans spoke and wrote English.

For the next 25 years, Webster labored at his monumental task. Unlike other lexicographers—people who compile dictionaries—he worked alone. To find the origins of words, he taught himself 20 languages.

Webster's *American Dictionary of the English Language* appeared in 1828, when he was 70 years old. With nearly 70,000 entries, it was the largest dictionary ever published. It contained countless new words like *skunk, hickory, bullfrog, chowder, handy,* and *applesauce* that were not used in England.

Webster's dictionary was a revolutionary work because it made American speech the standard in the United States. Through it and his earlier schoolbooks, Noah Webster singlehandedly declared America's cultural independence from England.

Besides working on his spelling books and dictionary, Noah Webster played a role in politics. He edited two newspapers that supported the Federalist party.

change them for new federal ones. The government would regularly pay interest on these bonds and would redeem them at face value when they became due.

Although the House agreed that the national debt must be paid, the proposal for funding it raised a furor. The government had sold war bonds to private citizens or given them as pay to soldiers with the promise to pay at a future date. But many of these people had needed money and sold their bonds at a fraction of the face value. Speculators bought the bonds on the gamble that the government would survive and honor its obligations. That gamble would pay off handsomely if the government redeemed the bonds at full value. Furthermore, most of the bonds were now in the hands of northerners, but would be paid off from both northern and southern taxes.

Angry with Hamilton's plan, James Madison proposed a bill to distinguish between the purchasers of bonds. He suggested that only the original bond holders be paid in full.

Benjamin Banneker, author of a yearly almanac, helped survey Washington, D.C.

The nation's new capital grew slowly after Washington chose its site in 1791. The government moved there in 1800. Work on government buildings continued in the 1800s, largely directed by the architect Benjamin Latrobe. His sketch for the south wing of the Capitol is shown above.

Defending his program, Hamilton argued that it was unjust to distinguish between bond holders. Anyone who bought a bond risked not being repaid. If late buyers were denied the full value of the bonds that they bought in good faith, it would be "a breach of contract." Hamilton's argument carried the day, and the House approved his plan.

ASSUMPTION OF STATE DEBTS

Hamilton next recommended that the federal government assume, or take over, the unpaid war debts of the states. Then there would be one public debt for the entire nation. All of it would be paid in the same way and by one source—the federal government. Thus, all creditors would have a stake in the federal government, for only a strong government could pay them.

Hamilton's proposed assumption of state debts created an uproar in the House. New York, Massachusetts, Connecticut, and South Carolina, with the largest unpaid debts, favored assumption. But most southern states—Virginia, Maryland, North Carolina, and Georgia—had paid a large share of their debts. If assumption became law, southern taxes would be used to pay creditors of the debtor states, most of which were northern states. Moreover, assumption would saddle the nation with an even larger national debt. Most of this debt was owed to a small group of wealthy people.

The feud over the assumption of state debts tore through Congress. Led by Virginia's James Madison, southerners in the House rejected the assumption proposal by two votes in April 1790. The Senate, however, approved the measure.

Desperate, Hamilton kept the measure alive by connecting it with another controversy in the House—the permanent location of the national capital. Congress was deadlocked over the location of the capital. Northerners proposed New York City, which was the present capital, or Philadelphia. Southerners insisted on a southern site, on the Potomac River.

In June, Hamilton, Madison, and Jefferson met for dinner and settled on a compromise. Hamilton agreed that the national capital be moved to Philadelphia for ten years and then be given a permanent site on the Potomac between Virginia and Maryland. In return Madison and Jefferson agreed to obtain enough southern votes to pass the assumption bill. The compromise was successful. Within a month the House voted for a capital on the Potomac, at a site to be chosen by President Washington. The House also adopted the assumption plan.

THE BANK OF THE UNITED STATES

After Hamilton's plan for assumption had been accepted, the secretary of the treasury plunged into his next major project. In December 1790 he proposed to Congress a plan to establish a bank for the United States. The country had only three banks, Hamilton noted. A national bank with branches in major cities would help the government and strengthen the nation's economy.

Hamilton modeled his national bank on the Bank of England, a private company with public duties. He proposed that the bank be set up for 20 years and raise money by selling shares of stock—amounting to a total *capital stock*, or money value, of $10 million. Private investors would buy four fifths of the stock and choose four fifths of the bank directors, thus controlling the bank. The federal government would buy the remaining one fifth of the stock and appoint the remainder of the directors.

The government, businesses, and individuals could all deposit funds in the bank and borrow money from it. The bank would circulate its money in the form of paper currency, backed by gold or silver, and it would have the same value throughout the country.

The Senate found Hamilton's proposal sound and passed a bill to establish the Bank of the United States. The House passed the bank bill in February 1791. Washington, however, was concerned that the measure might be unconstitutional. Before signing the bill, he requested written opinions from members of his cabinet.

Secretary of State Jefferson strongly urged Washington to veto the bill, arguing that the Constitution did not give Congress the power to establish a bank. In Jefferson's view, the federal government had only the specific powers granted to it in the Constitution. All other powers belonged to the states or the people, according to the Tenth Amendment. This view came to be known as **strict construction**, or strict interpretation, of the Constitution.

In defending the bank, Hamilton presented his own view of the Constitution, which came to be called **loose construction**. Hamilton noted that the Constitution gave Congress the right to "make all laws necessary and proper for carrying into execution" the powers of the federal government. One of those powers was the right to collect taxes. Surely,

Hamilton argued, setting up a national bank to help collect taxes would be "necessary and proper." Washington was swayed by Hamilton's arguments and signed the bill on February 25, 1791. Jefferson, though, viewed Hamilton as an enemy.

THE TARIFF PROPOSAL

The nation now had a bank and a plan to restore credit. However, it had very little income to pay off the national debt and run the country. In December 1791 Hamilton submitted to Congress his Report on Manufactures. In it, he proposed to increase the duties laid on imported goods by the tariff of 1789.

Unlike the earlier tariff, this would be a **protective tariff**—that is, a tariff designed not to bring in revenue but to discourage Americans from buying foreign goods. Supposedly, as America became less dependent on other nations for essential goods, American industry would grow and prosper.

A protective tariff was unpopular with most Americans. Northern merchants feared that a high tariff would hurt international trade. Southern

Slater's Mill, the first cotton mill in America, competed with British factories. Samuel Slater, an immigrant, began setting up his mill at Pawtucket, Rhode Island, in 1790.

farmers, who sold much of their produce to Europe and bought European manufactured goods, also opposed it. They feared that Europe would strike back by slapping a high tariff on southern produce.

Reflecting the farmers' and merchants' fears, Congress rejected Hamilton's plan. However, in 1792 Congress finally did increase the duty on some imported goods in order to raise revenue, rather than to protect American manufacturers.

THE WHISKEY REBELLION

Hamilton had another plan to raise money. An *excise tax*—a certain tax on goods produced, sold, and consumed within the country—would be levied on "spiritous liquors." There were large-scale rum distillers in New England and New York, and the whiskey-making farmers in the West produced about a third of the nation's liquor. Many of the westerners had little respect for the new national government. The whiskey tax, Hamilton thought, would not only bring a steady income to the federal government but it would also show the back country that the power of the federal government reached across the Appalachians.

The excise tax became law in 1791 and immediately angered the farmers of western Pennsylvania. Whiskey was essential to their economy. It was their only marketable product and their medium of exchange. The tax would eat into farmer's profits, and they refused to pay it. Over the next three years, they harassed tax collectors and even threatened to attack Pittsburgh.

By the summer of 1794 President Washington had reached the limits of his patience. Alarmed by this defiance of federal authority, he sought advice from Hamilton. He then called out the militia from four states to put down the rebellion. In November an army of almost 13,000 troops marched into western Pennsylvania. There was no real fighting—the farmers simply stayed at home. Only 20 prisoners were captured. Jefferson commented that a rebellion "was announced and proclaimed and armed against, but could never be found."

To Hamilton, however, the government had passed a crucial test. Seven years earlier, the Confederation had been unable to act during Shays' Rebellion in Massachusetts. But the new government had called out the state militias, restored law and order, and upheld its authority.

Susanna Rowson made fun of the Whiskey Rebellion in her musical play *The Volunteers*, staged in 1795. She also wrote novels and founded a Young Ladies Academy in Boston.

SECTION REVIEW

1. Identify the following: Report on the Public Credit, Bank of the United States, Report on Manufactures, Whiskey Rebellion.

2. Define the following: strict construction, loose construction, protective tariff, excise tax.

3. (a) List the executive departments created by Congress. (b) What did the major department heads as a group come to be called?

4. Describe the court system as established by the Judiciary Act.

5. (a) According to Alexander Hamilton, what caused people to be loyal to their government? (b) From what group of people did Hamilton seek support for the government?

6. What were the two parts of Hamilton's plan for paying the nation's war debts?

7. (a) Explain the view of each side in the argument over federal assumptions of state debts. (b) What compromise ended the argument?

8. (a) Describe Hamilton's two proposals for increasing the nation's revenue. (b) How did Congress deal with each proposal?

9. Who favored a protective tariff? Why? (b) Who opposed it? Why?

10. To Hamilton, what was the importance of the government's actions during the Whiskey Rebellion?

DOMESTIC POLITICS AND FOREIGN AFFAIRS

READ TO FIND OUT

—how Thomas Jefferson and Alexander Hamilton differed in their view of government.

—how political parties began.

—why Washington issued the Proclamation of Neutrality.

—how France and Great Britain tested American neutrality.

—how Pinckney's Treaty settled disputes with Spain.

—what advice Washington gave the nation in his Farewell Address.

—what issues divided political parties in the election of 1796.

The financial program that Hamilton so painstakingly created had a successful beginning. However, Hamilton's program had also brought political squabbling, and that disturbed Washington. With the ratification of the Constitution, Washington had hoped that the division between Federalists and Anti-Federalists would disappear. Like most Americans, he worried that such factions would destroy national unity. To his dismay, the division was deepening. The issue was no longer the Constitution itself, but how it would be put into practice.

HAMILTON AND JEFFERSON IN OPPOSITION

From the beginning, Hamilton's plans stirred up opposition. America in 1790 was primarily a nation of farmers, and many of them resented Hamilton's support of business and his attempts to encourage manufacturing. Many of these farmers also favored a weak central government. They distrusted Hamilton's efforts to strengthen the federal government, and they were suspicious of his open admiration of the British system.

By 1791 critics of Hamilton's policies had formed an opposition group in Congress, led by Virginia's James Madison. And in the cabinet, Thomas Jefferson clashed openly with Hamilton. At first, the two department heads had worked together to end the stalemate over federal assumption of state debts. With their feud over the constitutionality of the bank, such cooperation ended.

Hamilton and Jefferson were a study in contrasts. With his pale sculpted features, rich brown hair, and fashionable clothes, Hamilton was an elegant figure. Jefferson, on the other hand, was tall, gangly, and rather untidy. He had warm hazel eyes, a shock of red hair, and, one observer noted, "his face has a sunny aspect."

The differences between the two men went deeper than appearances. To Jefferson, Hamilton's efforts to build a strong central government—especially his loose construction, or interpretation, of the Constitution—seemed like monarchy. Jefferson wanted the new government to have only those powers actually stated in the Constitution. Only a strict construction of the Constitution, he felt, would protect the liberty of the people.

Jefferson also thought that Hamilton's policy of favoring wealthy business interests was another step toward monarchy. He disagreed with Hamilton's programs to fund the national debt, assume state debts, and establish the national bank. Jefferson believed that these programs were creating an aristocracy of people in finance and business who were loyal to the treasury—and to Hamilton. Even members of Congress had been corrupted by the lure of money to be made in war bonds and bank stocks. The Department of the Treasury, Jefferson charged, would one day "swallow up the whole executive power."

To Jefferson, power in the hands of a few people threatened the republican form of government. Unlike Hamilton, he had great faith in the ability of the people to play a vital role in government. "The influence over government," he wrote, "must be shared by all the people." Only when power—and wealth that created it—was spread throughout the nation would government be safe from corruption by any person or any group.

So, while Hamilton favored merchants and bankers, Jefferson was the champion of the farmers. He wanted as many people as possible to own property and to take part in government. In Jefferson's

The elegant appearance of Alexander Hamilton matched his ideas. He believed in the importance of established wealth for individuals as well as for the national government.

eyes, a nation of small farmers, self-reliant economically and independent in their political views, would form a true republic.

THE RISE OF POLITICAL PARTIES

Jefferson once said, "If I could not get to heaven except with a political party, I would not go there at all." Nonetheless, in 1791 he began to work with Madison to organize national opposition to Hamilton.

Several months after Washington signed the bank bill, Madison and Jefferson set out on a nature-study trip to New York and New England. They may have looked for plants, but they also searched for political support in the upcoming 1792 presidential election. Washington planned to retire after one term and had even asked Madison to draft a farewell address.

Jefferson and Madison hoped to attract votes for candidates of the "republican interest," as opposed to the "Federalist interest" of Hamilton and his followers. They found support in Hamilton's state of New York, where United States Senator Aaron Burr and Governor George Clinton led an anti-Hamilton faction. The four met and formed a political alliance.

Four months later Jefferson and Madison established an anti-Hamilton newspaper, the *National Gazette*. Soon it was debating with the Hamilton-supported *Gazette of the United States*, a paper favoring the current administration.*

Supporters of Jefferson wrote violent attacks on Hamilton's policies and accused him of trying to set up a monarchy, with "drawing rooms" and "stately nods instead of shaking hands." Hamilton, using a variety of pen names, wrote editorials defending his actions and accusing Jefferson of opposition to the Constitution and the administration. Newspapers throughout the country chose sides and joined the battle. It extended to political factions in two new states, Vermont and Kentucky.

Except for President Washington, no one seemed above the quarrel. Vice-President John Adams was among those on the Federalist side. Once he had said that the country would be better off if ruled by "the rich, the well-born and the able."

The newspaper war and the constant clashes between Hamilton and Jefferson in cabinet meetings dismayed President Washington. He refused to take sides and tried to bring the two department heads together. He wrote to Jefferson, "I believe the views of both of you to be pure and well-meant. I have a great regard for you both, and wish that some line could be marked out by which both of you could walk." But there seemed to be no such line.

Washington had hoped to retire from the presidency, but the political rift made him pause. Hamilton and Jefferson, who could agree on little else, both urged the President to serve again, as did political leaders across the country. Reluctantly, Washington agreed. No one opposed him for the presidency in 1792.

By the time of the election in December, the political factions had hardened into more solid form—political parties. One, the Federalist party, was made up of Hamilton and his followers and favored a strong central government. The other was the Republican party, led by Jefferson and Madison, which wanted a weak central government.

When the electoral votes were counted, President Washington was reelected, as expected. John Adams was also reelected vice-president, in a close contest with New York's George Clinton, the Re-

* administration: the officials who make up the executive branch of a government and their policies.

This Federalist cartoon depicts President Washington firmly holding the reins of government while Jefferson clings to a wheel, vainly trying to halt the progress of the United States.

publicans' vice-presidential candidate. Other Republicans were more successful and won seats in Congress. Jefferson was optimistic. With Republicans in Congress, Republican ideas would now have a chance against Federalist ideas.

THE PROCLAMATION OF NEUTRALITY

When Washington decided to run for reelection, the nation's political divisions were not his only concern. More and more, he worried about upheavals in Europe.

Three years earlier, in 1789, revolution against the monarchy had broken out in France. In 1790 the French king accepted a constitution that provided for some representative government. Most Americans were delighted. They put up liberty poles, wore French-style hats, and called each other "citizen," the democratic form of address that had become popular in France.

The events of 1792 and 1793, however, showed that the revolution in France was not yet over. In November 1792 a new French legislature proclaimed France a republic and vowed to help other Europeans overthrow their governments. Two

months later, the French king, Louis XVI, was beheaded. Some 20,000 French citizens followed the king to execution, as enemies of the revolution.

France's revolutionary leaders had called for "a war of all peoples against all kings." Neighboring monarchs began discussing an alliance against France. By 1793 France was at war with much of Europe—Austria, Prussia, Great Britain, the Netherlands, and Spain. For the next two decades, war would engulf Europe—and vitally affect America.

The violence of the French Revolution and the spreading European war sent shock waves through America. Many Americans chose sides and, to no one's surprise, Republicans and Federalists had opposite views. The struggles in Europe led to new disputes in the United States.

Jefferson, Madison, and other Republicans remained enthusiastic friends of the French Revolution. To them, the overthrow of the monarchy was part of the struggle everywhere for democracy. It bound them in spirit to the French. Republicans also stressed that the United States was legally bound to France. One of the treaties of 1778, which brought French aid to the American fight for independence, was a treaty of "perpetual friendship and alliance."

Hamilton and the Federalists rejected these views. Although they had sympathized at first with the French Revolution, they became horrified by the mob rule and executions. Neither life, liberty, nor property was safe in such a revolution. Some Federalists even feared the spread of that spirit to American shores. Thus, the Federalists sided with Great Britain, which by contrast seemed stable, orderly, and well governed.

Britain also was a vital link in Hamilton's financial system. Most of the federal government's revenue came from import duties. And the majority of American imports came from the British Empire. If the United States supported France, it would be drawn into war against Britain. The ties of trade would be broken.

Although Hamilton favored the British and Jefferson the French, both realized that it would be disastrous for the young American nation to become involved in the war. Yet each tried to convince Washington to side with one of the two nations. Instead, Washington chose a middle course.

On April 22, 1793, he issued the Proclamation of Neutrality. The proclamation declared that the

United States would "pursue a conduct friendly and impartial toward the belligerent powers." It also warned Americans not to aid any of the warring nations. Washington's stand, however, did not still public debate.

CITIZEN GENÊT

In early April 1793, Edmond Genêt (zheh-NAY), the minister of the new French Republic, landed in Charleston, South Carolina, to the cheers of pro-French Americans. His government had instructed him to gain American support for the French Republic. Taking advantage of public enthusiasm, he also used the United States as a base for French action against its enemies.

In Charleston, Genêt recruited armies to free Louisiana and Florida from Spain. He also commissioned privately owned American ships to attack British merchant ships along the American coast. As "Citizen" Genêt traveled north to the capital, he heard of the Proclamation of Neutrality. But he ignored it.

By early August, Thomas Jefferson, a staunch supporter of the French, was sure that Genêt wanted to drag America into the war. He agreed with the administration that France must recall its minister. But there had been changes in France.

A new group had come to power and had sent another minister to the United States. The new minister had orders to arrest Genêt for "crimes" against the revolution. Washington, however, allowed Genêt to remain in America, and the French citizen wisely retired from politics. The whole affair prompted a surge of support for the President and his policy of neutrality.

BRITAIN ANGERS THE UNITED STATES

Neutrality was a tricky course to steer, and it was sorely tested not only by the French. It was also tested by the British on the open seas. Britain, determined to starve France into surrender, declared a blockade of France in June 1793. It would seize all neutral ships carrying *contraband*—war materials such as ammunition and weapons—to France. To America's outrage, Britain declared that food was contraband and began to seize American trade ships en route to France or the French West Indies.

The British also seized sailors on American ships. Service on British ships was so harsh that over 2,000 sailors deserted each year, and many turned to American shipping for work. So British captains searching for contraband on neutral ships also searched for British deserters, with orders to *impress*, or seize, them. Sailors who had become American citizens were not safe from impressment. Furthermore, British captains often made "mistakes" and took native-born Americans as well.

Angering America further, Britain still held a string of forts in the Northwest Territory although it had promised to withdraw ten years earlier. Americans were convinced that British troops armed Indian tribes in the region and encouraged attacks on settlers moving west.

Early in 1794 the American government learned that British officials in the Northwest had promised to aid the Indians in ridding the Ohio country of American settlers. The British had even built a new fort in the area. At the same time, news reached Philadelphia that the British navy had recently captured over two hundred American ships in the Caribbean.

Congress exploded with anti-British legislation. It approved a two-month **embargo**, or ban on trade, against Britain. It also authorized a navy, voted for funds to build six ships, and passed a number of defense measures. War fever raged through the country as Americans volunteered for the militia, attacked British sailors, and harassed pro-British Americans. Washington, however, did not want war. He sent Chief Justice John Jay to England to settle disputes between the two countries.

JAY'S TREATY

Jay's major goals were to talk the British into withdrawing from the Northwest Territory and to get them to agree to pay for the seized American ships. However, Jay had little bargaining power. America had no real army or navy. And it needed British trade. Jay's position was further weakened when Hamilton assured the British that the United States would not join a recently formed alliance of neutral nations against Britain.

Jay arrived in London in June 1794. After five months of talks, he signed a treaty. In March 1795 the treaty was made public. Jay himself expected it to cause some clamor. The treaty "will doubtless

An unknown artist painted General Anthony Wayne and his staff talking with Indian chiefs about the Treaty of Greenville. Twelve tribes signed the treaty in 1795, a year after Wayne's victory at the Battle of Fallen Timbers. The treaty forced the tribes to move farther west.

produce fresh difficulties," he wrote to President Washington from London. Jay added that the treaty also would "give occasion to much declamation." But the clamor caused by the treaty terms was louder and longer than Jay expected. Many Americans were disgusted by the agreement.

Britain promised to withdraw from its Northwest posts on or before June 1, 1796, but made no mention of relations with the Indians. Britain also agreed to pay Americans for seized ships, but did not give up its right to seize ships or sailors in the future. In turn, Jay promised to let a British-American committee decide whether Americans must pay their prewar debts to Britain.

Republicans called the treaty a sellout to Britain. Crowds burned "Sir" John Jay in effigy and hooted defenders of the treaty. When Hamilton tried to explain it to a crowd in New York City, he was pelted with stones. Nevertheless, Congress did approve the treaty. Despite its flaws, it kept the peace at a time when America was not prepared to wage war.

The treaty also would remove the British from the Northwest and separate them from their Indian allies. American troops, under General Anthony Wayne, had been battling the Miami, Shawnee,

and other tribes for almost two years. Finally, in August 1794, Wayne won a decisive victory at the Battle of Fallen Timbers. A year later the chiefs of 12 tribes met with Wayne and were forced to sign the Treaty of Greenville. In the treaty the Indians agreed to cede most of the Ohio country to the government and to move west. For the first time, the Northwest Territory was firmly in the hands of the United States.

PINCKNEY'S TREATY

Jay's Treaty also affected America's uneasy relations with the Spanish in the Southwest. Like the British, the Spanish had been fighting against France, but by 1794 they were losing. So Spain decided to end its alliance with Britain and ask France for peace, even though such a shift might result in war with Britain. News of Jay's Treaty convinced Spain that in such a war the United States would be Britain's ally. Fearful for its colonies in North America, Spain decided to gain favor with America and asked for a meeting.

In the summer of 1794 Washington sent Thomas Pinckney, America's minister in Britain, to Spain. Pinckney was instructed to settle all the boundary disputes and deal with the Spanish-Indian alliances that had bothered the United States for years. Also, Pinckney was to gain for Americans the right to navigate the Mississippi River "in its whole length and breadth, from its source to the sea."

The treaty that Pinckney signed in October 1795 made him as popular as John Jay was unpopular. At last, Americans would be able to travel freely on the Mississippi River through Spanish territory. Spain also granted Americans a three-year renewable *right of deposit*, allowing them to land their goods at New Orleans to await oceangoing ships. In addition, Spain accepted Pinckney's proposal of the thirty-first parallel as the boundary between the United States and Spanish Florida. Spain also promised not to support Indians against the United States. In turn, the United States agreed to prevent Indians living in American territory from attacking the Spanish.

In March 1796 the Senate unanimously approved Pinckney's Treaty. Between Pinckney's Treaty and Jay's Treaty, the United States had successfully smoothed relations with Spain and Britain. But war still raged in Europe, and the United States had conducted no talks with the revolutionary government in France.

THE ELECTION OF 1796

Washington was determined to retire at the end of his term in 1797. The nation was prosperous and at peace, and he felt that he could safely leave. Also, he would be glad to get away from party politics.

In September 1796 Washington's Farewell Address, written with Hamilton's help, was printed in the newspapers. Washington told the nation that he would not seek a third term and, as "a parting friend," warned of the "continual mischiefs" of party politics. Parties, especially those based on geographical regions, would divide the nation and threaten its unity.

Washington also warned Americans against political entanglements with Europe, because Europe's interests were different from America's. "Steer clear," he urged Americans, "of permanent alliances with any portion of the foreign world."

Three months after Washington gave his Farewell Address, the electoral college met to choose the next president. There were several candidates and disagreement about who should be president.

Leaving the capital in 1797, Martha Washington retired with her husband to Mount Vernon. The miniature portrait of her by Charles Willson Peale was shaped to fit a gold locket.

Without Washington, Federalists looked for a new leader. Hamilton, with his pro-British, strong-government views, was unpopular. Federalist leaders finally settled on John Adams as their presidential candidate. To gain southern support, they chose the popular Thomas Pinckney of South Carolina for vice-president.

Unlike the Federalists, Republicans who met in congressional *caucuses*, or conferences, knew who they wanted as a presidential candidate. They looked to Thomas Jefferson, who had happily retired to his plantation, Monticello, at the end of 1793. Jefferson, however, was reluctant to return to office. "The little spice of ambition which I had in my younger days," he told Madison, "has long since evaporated." Nonetheless he agreed to serve if elected. Aaron Burr of New York was chosen as the Republicans' vice-presidential candidate.

Neither Republican nor Federalist candidates campaigned in person. Instead, their supporters battled with pamphlets, newspapers, and mass meetings. All the issues that had divided the American people during the past seven years were debated again—assumption of debts, the national bank, the French Revolution, Jay's Treaty.

In December 1796 the electoral college voted. To Hamilton's dismay, his efforts failed. John Adams received the most votes, mainly from New England and the mid-Atlantic states. Adams was elected president. Thomas Jefferson received the second greatest number of votes, primarily from southern and western states, and was elected vice-president.

The government now had a Federalist president and a Republican vice-president. The cause lay with the rules of the electoral college. When the framers of the Constitution had established the electoral college, they had not foreseen the rise of political parties. Electors, choosing a president and vice-president, simply voted for two candidates. The candidate receiving the most votes became president. The candidate receiving the second most became vice-president.

As a result, electors in 1796 chose the Federalist Adams and the Republican Jefferson. Adams had worried about just such an outcome, predicting a "dangerous crisis in public affairs if the president and vice-president should be in opposite boxes."

SECTION REVIEW

1. Identify the following: Proclamation of Neutrality, Edmond Genêt, John Jay, Anthony Wayne, Thomas Pinckney.

2. Define the following: impress, embargo.

3. What were the results of Hamilton's efforts to build a strong federal government?

4. (a) What group of people did Jefferson feel should have influence on government? Why? (b) What was Jefferson's view of a true republic?

5. (a) What kind of government did the Federalist party favor? (b) What kind of government did the Republican party favor?

6. What was the result of the Genêt affair?

7. List four British actions that angered Americans in the 1790s.

8. (a) What were John Jay's goals in seeking a treaty with Britain? (b) What were the terms of Jay's Treaty? (c) From the viewpoint of the Republicans, what were the flaws in Jay's Treaty?

9. (a) What were Pinckney's goals in seeking a treaty with Spain? (b) What were the terms of Pinckney's Treaty?

10. (a) Who were the candidates in the election of 1796? (b) What issues divided the two political parties?

THE ADMINISTRATION OF JOHN ADAMS

READ TO FIND OUT

— why the XYZ Affair caused America to prepare for war.

— how Adams ended the threat of war with France.

— how the Alien and Sedition Acts silenced the Republicans.

— why Republicans protested with the Kentucky Resolution and the Virginia Resolution.

— why the election of 1800 was decided in Congress.

On March 4, 1797, John Adams stood in the crowded chamber of the House of Representatives and took the presidential oath of office. Like Washington, Adams had spent most of the last three decades striving to create the American nation.

Since 1765, when he spoke out against the Stamp Act, Adams had served in the Continental Congress and had helped to draft and defend the Declaration of Independence. He had also been a member of the group responsible for drawing up the peace treaty at the end of the American Revolution. Diplomatic missions to France, the Netherlands, and Britain provided Adams with considerable experience in foreign affairs. And eight years as America's first vice-president gave him a working knowledge of the young republic.

Like Washington, Adams was uncomfortable with party politics and did not want to be a party leader. But Adams did not come into office with Washington's popularity. He was not the unanimous choice of the nation, or even of his own party, and he won election by only three electoral votes.

Hoping to smooth divisions among the Federalists, Adams decided to keep Washington's cabinet. Only later did he discover that three department heads were loyal to Hamilton, now a private citizen practicing law. These "High Federalists" looked to Hamilton for advice.

John Adams resisted the pressures for an open war with France. This study for a portrait of Adams was the work of John Singleton Copley.

Determined to settle the disputes, Adams called a special session of Congress. He won Congress's approval to send a special commission to France for a fresh try at negotiation. As a precaution, however, Adams suggested that the nation build up its defenses.

American commissioners John Marshall, Elbridge Gerry, and Charles Pinckney reached Paris in October 1797. The French foreign minister refused to receive them officially. Instead, three of his agents visited the Americans. The agents demanded an apology for Adams's anti-French remarks in Congress, an American loan to France, and a bribe of $250,000. The Americans refused.

The French agents continued to demand the bribe and finally Pinckney insisted, "No, no, not a sixpence!" For six months the commissioners lingered in Paris, hoping to be received by the French government.

Meanwhile, the American commissioners' dispatches reached the American government in March 1798. The messages gave details of the ac-

Adams also tried to cross party lines and work with Republican Vice-President Jefferson, his old friend. But members of the cabinet and party leaders fought such gestures of good will. As a result, the President and Vice-President rarely met for consultation on public matters. "Party violence," Adams later recalled, "soon rendered it impracticable, or at least useless."

THE XYZ AFFAIR

Adams's first order of business was to deal with a hostile France. In his inaugural speech, Adams called for American neutrality. Yet French actions threatened this course. France had been furious over Jay's Treaty, suspecting an American-British alliance. To retaliate, France recalled its minister from the United States. It then refused to receive American minister Charles C. Pinckney, the older brother of diplomat Thomas Pinckney.

French warships were ordered to seize American ships trading with Britain and to treat as pirates any Americans serving under the British flag. Without a navy, the United States could offer little protection to its ships. French privateers even attacked them in sight of American land.

Pictured as a five-headed monster, the French government cries out for money in an American cartoon based on the XYZ Affair. An American coolly refuses the demand.

The ship on the left is a French privateer—a privately owned craft authorized by the French government to attack American shipping. American vessels such as the *Planter*, shown in close pursuit, captured dozens of French privateers in the "half war" between the two nations.

tions of the French agents, who were called simply Mr. X, Mr. Y, and Mr. Z. An angry President Adams told Congress of the dispatches. In April the House demanded to see the dispatches, and Adams sent them to both the House and Senate. Outraged, the Senate voted to publish the documents.

The XYZ dispatches set loose a tide of anger against the French. Federalists called for war. Across the country their slogan rang "Millions for defense, but not one cent for tribute." Congress acted, creating the Department of the Navy and the Marine Corps, and voting funds for new warships. It also authorized the President to expand the army. George Washington agreed to come out of retirement to lead it. Congress also voted a property tax to pay for the defense measures and repealed the 1778 alliance and trade treaties with France, which had been so important during the Revolution.

THE "HALF WAR"

The United States prepared for a full-scale war that never came. Instead, an undeclared naval conflict sputtered for two years, during which American ships captured 85 French privateers.

Adams was not unhappy with this "half war." Despite the initial furor, most Americans did not support open war and quickly tired of the expense. Republicans insisted that war was unnecessary and opposed most defense measures. Even Federalists were divided. Hamilton and his High Federalists demanded a declaration of war. But moderates thought it enough that the United States simply be prepared to defend itself.

The French government, however, had no intention of declaring war. It had misjudged America's pro-French feelings and, needing American

FREEDOM OF SPEECH
THE ARREST OF MATTHEW LYON

In the fall of 1798 Congressman Matthew Lyon of Vermont was fined $1,000 and thrown in jail. He had been convicted under the new Sedition Act of criticizing President John Adams and his administration.

Writing from jail, Lyon described the "loathsome dungeon" he shared with horse thieves and pickpockets. At night the cell was bitterly cold. "I was near four weeks without sight of fire, except my candle," he wrote, "in which time I suffered more with the cold than I had in twenty years before."

The Federalist party cheered Lyon's conviction. One Federalist newspaper called it "a noble triumph . . . over the unbridled spirit of opposition to government which is, at the present moment, the heaviest curse of America." Lyon's own party, the Republicans, disagreed. "I know not which mortifies me most," party leader Thomas Jefferson wrote, "that I should fear to write what I think or my country bear such a state of things."

Before his arrest, Irish-born Matthew Lyon had been known as one of President Adams's strongest critics. Like most Republicans, Matthew Lyon had long been sympathetic to the French Revolution with its cry of "Liberty, Equality, Fraternity." Then, in the early spring of 1798, the XYZ affair had exploded. Anti-French feeling swept the country. Many believed war was near. Some even suspected the Republicans of plotting to bring the French Revolution to America. A rumor spread that Philadelphia was to be set on fire and its citizens murdered.

Republicans like Matthew Lyon felt that the war fear was exaggerated. They believed peace terms could be worked out. To the Federalists, such views seemed dangerous and unpatriotic. The Congress acted to strengthen America's defenses. At the same time, Congress passed the Alien and Sedition Acts. The alien acts allowed the president to expel foreigners suspected of being disloyal to the nation. The Sedition Act made it a crime to write or speak in a "scandalous or malicious" way against the government. The Republicans protested the new law. "To laugh at the cut of a coat of a member of Congress will soon be treason," warned one.

The Federalists defended the Sedition Act as necessary in a time of national danger. "It was never intended that the right to side with the enemies of one's country in slandering and vilifying the government and dividing the people should be protected under the name of Liberty of the Press," declared a Federalist newspaper. "It is patriotism to write in favor of our government—it is sedition to write against it," announced another.

Three months later, Matthew Lyon became the first person to be jailed under the Sedition Act. In a letter published in a Vermont paper, he had criticized President Adams for his "ridiculous pomp" and attacked his policy toward France. In Congress, Republican leader Albert Gallatin charged that the real purpose of the Sedition Act was "to enable one party to oppress another." Congressman Lyon, he argued, had the right to express his opinions about President Adams. Thomas Jefferson agreed. "The basis of our government being the opinion of the people," he said, "the very first object should be to keep that right."

By the time Lyon was shivering in his jail cell, American relations with France had improved. Nonetheless, during the next two years, the Adams

administration sent ten political opponents to jail for sedition. Three were the country's leading Republican newspaper editors.

As the French war scare ended, more Americans protested the Sedition Act. The people of Lyon's Vermont district were so angry over his conviction that they reelected him to Congress while he was still in jail. Support for the Republicans rose. In 1800 Thomas Jefferson was elected president, with Matthew Lyon himself triumphantly casting the deciding vote in the House of Representatives.

During Jefferson's term, the Sedition Act was allowed to expire. What Jefferson called "the reign of witches" was over. But the question of opposition to government policy in a time of national danger was not resolved. It has arisen when Americans have felt threatened by opponents at home or abroad.

1. Why did the Federalists pass the Sedition Act? What arguments did the Republicans use against the Sedition Act?

2. Do you think the Sedition Act was necessary in 1798? Why or why not?

3. Are there ever times, such as a national emergency, when freedom of speech and the press should be limited? Explain.

Matthew Lyon was drawn as a cowardly lion wearing a wooden sword. This referred to a rumor spread by Federalists that Lyon had been a coward in the war. The porcupine in both drawings stood for a fierce Federalist editor, opposing Lyon in a "Beastly Action."

trade, now sought peace. France repealed its acts against American shipping and released American prisoners from French prisons. Then, in September 1798, France's foreign minister offered to receive an American representative in France.

In February 1799 Adams responded to France's offer. Adams proposed to the Senate that the United States send another mission to France. The High Federalists, who were in favor of war, were outraged and urged Adams to ignore French moves toward peace. The President refused. The Senate finally gave in, but Adams's victory widened the split in his party between high and moderate Federalists.

The American commission arrived in Paris in March 1800 to find a new government. Ruled by General Napoleon Bonaparte, this government was eager to negotiate. As instructed, the Americans demanded payment for the seized American ships. They also demanded French recognition that the treaties of 1778 were null and void. The French rejected both demands, and for six months the talks were deadlocked.

In September the two sides finally compromised. In the Convention of 1800, the French agreed to cancel the treaties, and the Americans dropped their claim for payment. Both countries also accepted the principle of *freedom of the seas*, the right of trade ships to travel freely the open seas at any time.

To President Adams, peace was worth the party bickering and the personal attacks he had endured. He later wrote, "I desire no other inscription over my gravestone than: Here lies John Adams, who took upon himself the responsibility of the peace with France in the year 1800."

THE ALIEN AND SEDITION ACTS

During the "half war" with France many Americans gave in to anti-French fears. The publication of the XYZ dispatches in April 1798 sparked not only anger against the French, but also suspicion of anyone who supported France.

Many Federalists, convinced that war was unavoidable, feared that French agents and sympathizers in the United States were endangering the young nation. Federalists used the threat of war as an opportunity to destroy the Republican party. They searched newspapers for Republican "treason" and kept watch on well-known Republicans, hoping to brand their activities as traitorous.

Because many immigrants tended to vote Republican, High Federalists were especially suspicious of them. Immigrants became associated with French sympathizers. During the summer of 1798, when fear was at its height, High Federalists proposed four laws to control "pro-French" factions. The Federalist-dominated Congress passed these laws, known as the Alien and Sedition Acts.

Three of the laws dealt with aliens, or foreigners. Previously, aliens had to live in the United States for five years before they could become citizens and vote. The Naturalization Act raised this period to 14 years, cutting off a source of Republican votes.

The Alien Act, aimed at suspected French agents, allowed the president to deport* aliens "dangerous to the peace and safety of the United States" or suspected of treason. A related law, the Alien Enemies Act, permitted the president to arrest, imprison, or deport enemy aliens, although only during a declared war or invasion. No aliens were deported under the Alien Act, but many were so fearful that they left the country.

The final law was the Sedition Act, designed to silence the Republicans and create a united front against France. The act imposed fines and imprisonment on both aliens and citizens convicted of sedition.* Under the act, sedition applied to people who opposed government measures or promoted riots. Sedition also included speaking, writing, or publishing anything "false, scandalous, and malicious" that could incite people against the government, Congress, or the President.

Republicans, and many others, charged that the Sedition Act violated freedom of speech. Between 1798 and 1800, twenty-five people were prosecuted under it. Ten Republicans, including newspaper editors and printers and one member of Congress, were convicted, fined, and sentenced to prison.

THE KENTUCKY AND VIRGINIA RESOLUTIONS

To Jefferson and Madison, the Alien and Sedition Acts were more than an attack on the Republican party. They were one more step toward Federalist tyranny. To oppose the laws, they decided to obtain support from state legislatures.

Because of his office—and the new laws—Jefferson acted secretly. He drafted a resolution that the legislature of the new state of Kentucky approved. The legislature then printed it and distributed it to Congress and the states in November 1798. Madison, now a private citizen, also secretly wrote a resolution, which the Virginia legislature printed in December.

Both the Kentucky Resolution and the Virginia Resolution declared that the United States of America was a compact, or agreement, between states bound together by the Constitution. Powers not specifically given to the central government in the Constitution belonged to the states. According to the Bill of Rights, Congress did not have the power to pass such laws as the Alien and Sedition Acts. Thus, the states had the right to **nullify** these federal laws—to declare them void and refuse to enforce them.

The argument could be carried even further. Because the federal government was created by the states, the states had the right to nullify any federal law they considered unconstitutional. This **states' rights**, or compact, theory of the Constitution jolted Hamilton. He warned that it could "destroy the Constitution of the United States."

No other states joined Kentucky and Virginia in their fight against the acts, although many Americans petitioned Congress to repeal the laws. The Alien and Sedition Acts stayed on the books for several years, until they expired or were repealed.

THE ELECTION OF 1800

As Adams's term drew to a close in 1800, the young nation was suffering from political strife. As it had done four years earlier, the Republican caucus nominated Thomas Jefferson for president and Aaron Burr of New York for vice-president. The party was growing strong, and this time it was unified.

The Federalists nominated John Adams for president. Charles C. Pinckney, whose brother Thomas had been the candidate in 1796, was nominated for vice-president. But there was no party unity. When Adams had sent his peace commission to France in 1799, the High Federalists, led by Hamilton, had broken with him and tried unsuccessfully to find

---

* deport: to force an alien to leave a country by official order.

* sedition: speech or action causing discontent or rebellion against the government.

another candidate for the upcoming election. Before the campaign ended, Adams and Hamilton and their followers were attacking each other more fiercely than they fought their Republican opponents.

On December 3, 1800, electors assembled in each of the states and cast their ballots. When the votes were later counted at the capitol, Jefferson and Burr each had 73 votes and Adams had 65. Furthermore, Republicans won a majority in both houses of Congress.

Adams had lost the presidency, but it was not clear whether Jefferson or Burr had won. Because separate ballots were not cast for president and vice-president, the candidate with the most votes became president.

According to the Constitution, the House of Representatives would decide electoral ties, with each state having one vote. Thus, the Federalist-dominated House met to determine which Republican would be president and which would be vice-president.

Although Jefferson was his party's presidential candidate, Federalists were determined to support Burr. Then a surprising ally rode to Jefferson's defense—Alexander Hamilton. "Jefferson is to be preferred," he wrote Federalists in the House. "He is by far not so dangerous a man."

The House took its first vote on February 11, 1801, but neither side gained the necessary majority. Eighteen more roll calls were called during that day and night. For 6 days—and 35 more ballots—the House remained deadlocked. On February 17, on the thirty-sixth ballot, Jefferson was chosen president, and Burr vice-president.

Two years later Congress proposed the Twelfth Amendment to the Constitution, providing for separate balloting for the president and vice-president in the electoral college. With this amendment, ratified in 1804, two-party politics became a part of the Constitution.

In March 1801 the new president was inaugurated, and John Adams returned to private life. In his four years as president, Adams had strengthened the young nation and preserved peace with France, despite his party's cry for war. "In your administration," his son John Quincy wrote him, "you were not the man of any party but of the whole nation."

SECTION REVIEW

1. Identify the following: High Federalists, Charles Pinckney, XYZ Affair, Alien and Sedition Acts, Twelfth Amendment.

2. What French actions caused John Adams to send a special commission to France in 1797?

3. What congressional actions resulted from the XYZ dispatches?

4. Describe the "half war" with France.

5. (a) What terms did Adams's second commission to France demand? (b) What compromise was reached in the Convention of 1800?

6. Describe two Republican arguments against the Sedition Act.

7. What theory of the Constitution was set forth in the Kentucky and Virginia Resolutions?

8. Who were the candidates for each party in the election of 1800?

9. Describe the split in the Federalist party in the election of 1800.

10. Why was the election of 1800 decided by the House of Representatives?

Since the bald eagle was chosen as the national emblem in 1782, it has been the most widely used symbol in the United States. This eagle graced the customhouse in Salem, Massachusetts.

CHAPTER SURVEY

SUMMARY

In 1789 George Washington was inaugurated as President, and the new government was set in motion. Congress soon organized the executive branch by setting up executive departments. The heads of these departments became the president's cabinet. Next, Congress passed the Judiciary Act, setting up a Supreme Court and circuit and district courts.

The nation faced economic problems, especially a large war debt. To pay off this debt, Treasury Secretary Alexander Hamilton planned that the national government fund war bonds at face value and that it assume the states' war debts. To strengthen the nation's economy, Hamilton established the Bank of the United States.

Hamilton's actions met strong opposition. Many Americans feared that the government was becoming too powerful. Thomas Jefferson and James Madison argued for strict limitations on the national government. Hamilton disagreed.

Out of this conflict emerged the nation's first political parties. The Federalist party, following the beliefs of Hamilton, supported a strong national government, and favored manufacturers. The Republican party, led by Jefferson and Madison, favored a weaker national government, with power distributed widely among the people.

Divisions between the two political parties deepened in 1793 over war between France and Great Britain. The Federalists supported Britain, and the Republicans supported France. Washington wisely steered a middle course by issuing the Proclamation of Neutrality.

After Washington retired, John Adams became president. He, too, urged neutrality. Yet French actions, including the XYZ Affair, brought the United States to the brink of war with France. The anti-French fears in the United States led to passage, in 1798, of the Alien and Sedition Acts, supported by the Federalists. The Republicans opposed these acts by drawing up the Kentucky and Virginia Resolutions, which argued that states had the right to nullify federal laws.

Adams's term ended in 1800 with his defeat for reelection. In a confused and bitterly fought election, Thomas Jefferson became the next president.

CHAPTER REVIEW

1. (a) Why did Congress create executive departments? (b) What executive departments had Congress created by 1800?

2. (a) Explain how each of the following was an attempt to improve the nation's economy: funding the nation's war debt, assumption of state debts, the Bank of the United States, excise tax on liquor, Tariff of 1789. (b) How did each of these measures affect the economy? Explain.

3. (a) Why did Hamilton favor a loose construction of the Constitution? (b) How did his proposal to set up a national bank reflect this view? (c) Why did Jefferson favor a strict construction of the Constitution? (d) How did he support his view?

4. Compare the views of Jefferson and Hamilton regarding the ability of the average person to participate in government.

5. How did each of the following contribute to the development of two political parties? (a) passage of the national bank bill (b) Jefferson and Madison's visit to New York (c) establishment of the *National Gazette* (d) the election of 1792

6. (a) Why was Washington's policy of neutrality an advantage for the young nation? (b) Explain how each of the following tested Washington's policy: Britain, France, Spain.

7. (a) Why was Jay's Treaty unpopular? (b) Why was Pinckney's Treaty popular? (c) Why was

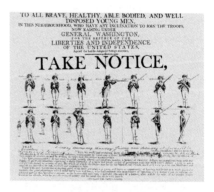

In 1798 George Washington agreed to end his retirement and lead American troops if the French declared war. This recruiting poster invited young men to join him.

Pinckney able to receive such favorable terms from Spain? (d) Why was Jay unable to gain favorable terms from the British?

8. (a) Explain how each event led to the next: Jay's Treaty, the XYZ Affair, the "half war," the Alien and Sedition Acts. (b) How did the Alien and Sedition Acts cause political strife?

9. In his Farewell Address Washington warned against permanent alliances with foreign nations. (a) With what European nation did the United States have a treaty of alliance? (b) Why did the United States end the alliance? (c) How did the United States end it?

10. (a) List the major problems of Washington's administration. (b) How did the administration respond to each problem? Explain. (c) What was the major accomplishment of John Adams's administration? Explain.

ISSUES AND IDEAS

1. In 1793 England and France were at war. (a) As a Federalist, present arguments why America should support the British. (b) As a Republican, present arguments why America should support the French. (c) Support Washington's opinion that neutrality is the best policy.

2. James Madison called the people who had first bought government bonds to support the Revolution the "original sufferers." What do you think he meant? Do you think his proposal to repay the money or Hamilton's proposal was the fairest? Why?

3. What might have happened if the Twelfth Amendment had not been added to the Constitution? Use information about the last presidential election. Explain how the original rules for the electoral college would have affected the choice of a president and vice-president.

SKILLS WORKSHOP

1. *Charts.* Make a chart comparing the ideas of members of the Federalist party and members of the Republican party. Under each of your two headings—"Federalists" and "Republicans"—list

Signed by Alexander Hamilton, a United States Treasury note served to raise money for the young nation. The note promised to pay interest of 6 percent to the lender.

ideas about the role of the national government, the role of state governments, the importance of manufacturing and agriculture, etc. Include attitudes toward Great Britain and France.

2. *Maps.* Look at page 209 of your book. Find the map entitled "Agriculture and Industry 1840." By 1840 was the United States a nation of manufacturers or a nation of farmers? What sections of the country were primarily agricultural? Where were the major manufacturing areas? Whose viewpoint predominated—Hamilton's or Jefferson's?

PAST AND PRESENT

1. The Whiskey Rebellion was a revolt against taxes that farmers thought were too high. Gather information about a group or groups who are protesting local, state, or federal taxes today. What remedies do they seek? What methods do they use to gain attention?

2. Using the elastic clause in the Constitution, Hamilton persuaded Washington to approve the Bank of the United States. Today what kinds of federal legislation are passed by Congress on the basis of this clause? Give three examples.

UNIT 3

BUILDING
A NATION

1801–1850

Susan Merrett. *Fourth of July Picnic at Weymouth Landing* (detail), c. 1845. Collection of The Art Institute of Chicago.

1600 | 1700 | 1800 | 1900 | 2000

• Jamestown founded • Revolutionary War • Civil War • Today

UNIT 3
1801–1850

1810 | 1820 | 1830 | 1840 | 1850

Jefferson | Madison | Monroe | Adams | Jackson | Van Buren | Harrison | Tyler | Polk

POLITICAL

- Louisiana Purchase
- Lewis and Clark expedition
- War of 1812
- Florida purchased
- Missouri Compromise
- Monroe Doctrine
- Republic of Texas
- Trail of Tears begins
- California Republic

SOCIAL

- Jane Austen: *Pride and Prejudice*
- Francis Scott Key: "The Star-Spangled Banner"
- Washington Irving: *The Sketch Book*
- Mount Holyoke: first women's college
- John Audubon: *Birds of America*
- Frederick Douglass: *Autobiography*
- Seneca Falls Declaration

TECHNOLOGICAL

- Fulton's steamboat: *Clermont*
- Erie Canal completed
- McCormick: reaper
- Charles Babbage: early computer
- John Deere: steel plow
- Morse: telegraph
- Goodyear: rubber process
- Howe patents sewing machine

INTERNATIONAL

- Modern Egypt established
- Napoleon defeated at Waterloo
- Brazil gains independence
- Bolívar: ruler of Peru
- Victoria: queen of England
- Liberian independence

1810 | 1820 | 1830 | 1840 | 1850

CHAPTER 7

JEFFERSON AND THE REPUBLICANS

1801–1815

JEFFERSON AS PRESIDENT
AMERICA'S EXPANDING BORDERS
THE WAR OF 1812

In March 1801 Margaret Bayard Smith described the inauguration of Thomas Jefferson:

"I have this morning witnessed one of the most interesting scenes a free people can ever witness. The changes of administration, which in every government and in every age have most generally been eras of confusion, villainy and bloodshed, in this our happy country take place without any . . . disorder. This day, has one of the most amiable and worthy men taken that seat to which he was called by the voice of his country.

"If doubts of the integrity and talents of Mr. Jefferson ever existed in the minds of any one, methinks this address must forever destroy them. The Senate chamber was so crowded that I believe not another creature could enter. On one side of the house the Senate sat, the other was resigned by the representatives to the ladies. The roof is arched, the room half circle, every inch of ground was occupied. It has been guessed by several people whom I've asked, that there were near a thousand persons within the walls."

The day was quite a cause for celebration. The nation was still young, and the government still vulnerable. Yet the Federalists had transferred power peacefully, according to law, to their most bitter foe. It was a triumph for the Constitution.

Over the following years, Jefferson moved the government in a new direction, toward his vision of a Republican nation. He also purchased Louisiana, pushing the country's western boundary all the way to the Rocky Mountains.

Still, the young nation faced problems, especially with Europe. Because of the conflict between Britain and France, the shadow of war edged across the Atlantic. By the time Jefferson's successor took office, the United States had become enmeshed in the British-French conflict. In the end it would mean war for Americans.

JEFFERSON AS PRESIDENT

READ TO FIND OUT

— how Jefferson put Republican ideals into practice.

— how decisions of the Supreme Court affected the government.

— how the United States stopped paying tribute to pirates.

On March 4, 1801, Thomas Jefferson was inaugurated in the nation's new capital on the Potomac River. "Washington City" was far from finished. In fact, the capital was merely a cluster of uncompleted buildings, a few rooming houses, and broad avenues that reached out like spokes from wheels. Clouds of reddish dust rose as people traveled over the unpaved streets, and the ground turned into swamps after every rain.

John Adams and many other Federalists did not attend the inauguration. Indeed, the change of power filled staunch Federalists with dread. Jefferson, they feared, would lead a revolution in the United States like the one in France. Perhaps he would even destroy the American nation itself.

Jefferson did look on his election as a revolution, but not one of radical change. To him, it meant the end of Federalist tinkering with the Constitution and a return to the "spirit of 1776."

REPUBLICAN PRINCIPLES

In his inaugural address, Jefferson tried to soothe Federalist fears. He called upon all citizens to unite to end party strife. He reminded them that as loyal Americans "we are all Republicans, we are all Federalists."

Jefferson then told the country what to expect under his administration. At home, he said, he wanted a limited government. This government would leave people free to go about their business and would not "take from the mouth of labor the bread it has earned." Abroad, Jefferson called for "peace . . . with all nations, entangling alliances with none."

The machinery of government had been running for 12 years on Federalist policy, and Jefferson did not try to stop it. He let stand the economic system built by Hamilton to repay federal and state debts. Even the national bank, which Jefferson had fought, remained in existence until its charter expired in 1811.

Jefferson did, however, take several actions to put his principle of limited government into practice. The number of federal officials was cut. The budgets for the army and navy were slashed. And the national debt was reduced by almost a third during the next eight years.

Jefferson's administration also ended tax laws passed by the Federalists. The excise tax on whiskey and the tax on property were repealed. For income, the federal government would depend primarily on its import duties.

Finally, Jefferson allowed the Alien and Sedition Acts to expire. He also pardoned people still imprisoned under the acts and paid their fines. In 1802 Congress repealed the Naturalization Act and restored the nation's original five-year residence requirement for citizenship.

THE REPUBLICANS AND THE JUDICIARY

In his effort to simplify government, Jefferson was backed by the Republican majority in Congress, elected in 1800. The executive branch also became Republican territory as Republicans gradually replaced Federalists in many government positions. However, there were no Republicans in the judiciary. The federal courts were staffed by Federalists—and judges served for life.

The new Chief Justice of the Supreme Court was John Marshall of Virginia. Marshall had served in the Revolutionary War and had then become a lawyer. He joined the Federalist party and served in the House of Representatives. In 1800 Adams appointed him secretary of state. In 1801, as Adams was leaving office, he appointed Marshall Chief Justice of the Supreme Court. Marshall and Jefferson had distrusted each other for years.

Adams used other methods, too, to make sure that the judiciary stayed in Federalist hands. Less

---

AMERICAN OBSERVERS

WASHINGTON IRVING
AMERICA'S FIRST PROFESSIONAL WRITER

"Who the whole world over reads an American book?" sneered an English critic in 1820. Yet that very year, for the first time, an American book did become a bestseller in England. Its author was Washington Irving. Born at the close of the American Revolution, he was named after its hero.

Irving was the youngest child of a New York hardware merchant. Irving grew into an elegant

Irving disliked this portrait taken after his final return from Europe. In later years he refused to sit for photographers.

In a painting illustrating Irving's tale, Ichabod Crane, hero of "The Legend of Sleepy Hollow," flees from the Headless Horseman. The picture was painted about 1835.

than three weeks before Jefferson was inaugurated, the Federalist Congress had passed the Judiciary Act of 1801 to reform the federal courts. The bill corrected real problems of organization. It reduced the number of Supreme Court justices from six to five and created many new positions in the judiciary.

Adams promptly nominated Federalists for the new positions, and the Senate began confirmation hearings. Adams signed the commissions, or authorizations, of those confirmed by the Senate up until the night before Jefferson's inauguration. Republicans angrily called these new officials "midnight judges."

No other action by Adams angered Jefferson more than this last-minute use of presidential power. The appointees, Jefferson later wrote, were "among my most ardent political enemies, from whom no faithful cooperation could ever be expected." Republicans in Congress agreed. In March 1802 they repealed the Judiciary Act after a two-month battle with Federalists.

young man-about-town. He left school when he was sixteen and dabbled in law, but preferred to attend the theater or dash off an essay for a local paper. At twenty-one he went to Europe because of his poor health. For two years he traveled in France, Italy, and England. By now he was keeping a notebook, where he practiced the craft he would make his profession.

Irving returned home an aristocrat. A lover of the past, he was deeply suspicious of American democracy. His first book, *Knickerbocker's History of New York*, was a gentle spoof of New York's early Dutch settlers. It also made fun of Americans like Thomas Jefferson, with their faith in the common people. To Irving, such faith was hopelessly idealistic.

Irving returned to Europe, staying seventeen years. His bestseller, a collection of essays and stories called *The Sketchbook*, was published there in 1820. Though mainly about Europe, it did contain two fine American tales, "The Legend of Sleepy Hollow" and "Rip Van Winkle." Irving would never again equal these two masterpieces. Both stories are based on tales of the Dutch New York in which Irving grew up.

Like many cultured Americans of his time, Irving looked to Europe for inspiration. Even when he wrote about the western fur trade, he could not help comparing the shape of a frontier tree to a Spanish arch. Like Rip Van Winkle after his twenty-year sleep, Irving felt out of place in the crude, bustling United States. He was, however, the first American to earn his living by his pen and the first American writer to gain worldwide fame.

John Marshall served as Chief Justice of the Supreme Court for thirty-five years. William James Hubard painted his portrait in 1832.

MARBURY v. MADISON

Before the Judiciary Act was repealed, Jefferson took another step to block Adams's midnight appointments. When the government changed hands, some commissions had not yet been delivered to the prospective judges. Jefferson forbade the State Department to send the undelivered commissions.

One of those commissions belonged to William Marbury, who had been nominated as a justice of the peace two days before Adams left office. Marbury obtained a lawyer and went to the Supreme Court to force Secretary of State James Madison to deliver his commission. The Judiciary Act of 1789, Marbury claimed, gave the Court power to enforce delivery.

In February 1803 the Supreme Court heard the case of *Marbury* v. *Madison*. In the Court's decision, Chief Justice John Marshall declared that Marbury had "a legal right to the office," and his commission should not have been withheld. However, Marshall also ruled that the section of the Judiciary Act of 1789 under which Marbury sued Madison was unconstitutional and therefore void. Thus, the Court did not have the power to act in this kind of case.

Marbury lost his appointment, but the Supreme Court gained in authority. With this case, it asserted for the first time the power of **judicial review**—the right of the Supreme Court to determine whether an act of Congress was constitutional.

IMPEACHING JUDGES

The Court's ruling worried Jefferson. He wanted to stem the growing power of the judiciary, and its weakest links were judges. The Constitution gave only one way to remove judges—"impeachment for, and conviction of, treason, bribery, or other high crimes and misdemeanors." Soon after the Marbury case, Jefferson marked for impeachment several federal judges.

The most well-known of these judges was Associate Justice Samuel Chase of the Supreme Court. A signer of the Declaration of Independence, Chase was also a strong Federalist. He had denied fair trials to Republicans prosecuted under the Sedition Act. He was openly hostile to Jefferson's administration and condemned it in the Court. In 1804 the House of Representatives, at Jefferson's urging, impeached Chase for "high crimes and misdemeanors."

The next year the Senate, with Vice-President Aaron Burr presiding, tried Chase. Republicans, however, could not muster the necessary two-thirds majority for a guilty verdict, and Chase was acquitted. Many senators—including some Republicans—believed that Chase's actions had been improper, but not impeachable.

The Barbary States

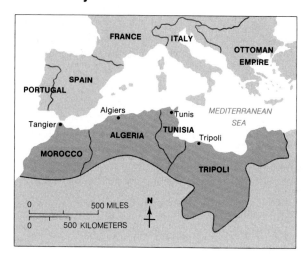

After Chase's acquittal, the Republican attack on Federalist judges ended. Still, the case served as a warning to judges, and open bias in the courts began to disappear. Even more important, the case set a precedent, or example, for the future. Judges could not be removed from office simply because they differed politically with Congress or with the president.

WAR WITH TRIPOLI

While affairs at home took up much of Jefferson's attention during his first term, foreign problems did intrude. In his inaugural address, Jefferson had pledged strict economy at home and peace abroad. With his approval, Treasury Secretary Gallatin cut the army by one third and reduced the navy to six ships. But less than three weeks after Jefferson took office, his pledges were threatened by events overseas.

Since the 1780s, American trade ships sailing the Mediterranean Sea had risked capture by pirates of the Barbary States of North Africa. To protect American ships, presidents Washington and Adams had followed the European lead and paid tribute* to the rulers of Morocco, Algiers, Tunis, and Tripoli. During the 1798 XYZ Affair—while Federalists shouted "millions for defense, but not one cent for tribute"—the United States was paying the four Barbary States a yearly bribe of $100,000.

---

* tribute: money paid by one nation to another for peace or protection.

In May 1801 the ruler of Tripoli demanded more money and declared war on the United States by chopping down the flagpole at the American consulate. Jefferson hated war, but he hated paying tribute even more. He sent several warships to the Mediterranean.

During the next two years, the small naval force protected American traders and blockaded Tripoli. Then, in October 1803, the U.S.S. *Philadelphia* ran aground on the shore of Tripoli while chasing pirates. The captain and crew were captured and held for a ransom of $3 million. A few months later, a daring young naval lieutenant named Stephen Decatur sailed into Tripoli harbor and burned the *Philadelphia* so it could not be used by the enemy. But its crew remained prisoners for another two years. Meanwhile the United States tightened its blockade.

In 1805 Tripoli agreed to a peace treaty with the United States. The hostages were released for a ransom of $60,000—a bargain compared to the $3 million first demanded. In addition, American tribute was no longer required, although "gifts" were still expected.

As soon as Jefferson withdrew the navy, the pirates resumed plundering American ships. Finally, in 1815, an American naval force led by Stephen Decatur joined Europeans to destroy the pirate bases.

SECTION REVIEW

1. Identify the following: John Marshall, William Marbury, Samuel Chase, Aaron Burr, Barbary States, U.S.S. *Philadelphia*, Stephen Decatur.

2. Define the following: "midnight judges," judicial review.

3. (a) List three ways that Jefferson cut government spending. (b) Which taxes were repealed?

4. How did the timing of the Judiciary Act of 1801 cause anger?

5. (a) Give two reasons why the House of Representatives impeached a Federalist judge. (b) What was the outcome of the trial? (c) What effect did it have on the judicial branch of government?

6. List the main events, and their approximate dates, in the American conflict with the Barbary States.

AMERICA'S EXPANDING BORDERS

READ TO FIND OUT

— why Louisiana was important to France and to the United States.

— how the United States doubled in size.

— what constitutional problem the Louisiana Purchase created for Jefferson.

— how the vast new territory was explored.

— how some Federalists planned to withdraw from the Union.

— why Aaron Burr was tried for treason.

Thomas Jefferson was a man of many talents. Besides being a statesman, he was a planter, musician, inventor, and scientist. He was also an architect and designed his own plantation at Monticello, in Virginia. He placed the house on a hilltop, facing west. In his boyhood, Jefferson had been drawn to stories of the West and Indians and exploration. As an adult, he continued to look west with boyish enthusiasm.

Many Americans shared Jefferson's yearning. Already settlers were streaming westward to the Mississippi River. The territory of Mississippi, including the present state of Alabama, was organized in 1798. Kentucky and Tennessee became states in time to help elect Jefferson president. Ohio entered the Union in 1803. Over the next six years Indiana, Michigan, and Illinois were organized as territories.

Beyond the Mississippi River, however, lay an unknown wilderness. Jefferson decided to discover what could be seen in the western half of the continent. Early in 1803 he persuaded Congress to fund an expedition to explore all the way to the Pacific Ocean. Two army officers—Captain Meriwether Lewis and Lieutenant William Clark—were placed in charge.

There was a political barrier to the expedition. Much of the land Lewis and Clark would be crossing was the Louisiana Territory, which did not belong to the United States. Then, by a strange combination of events, that barrier was removed.

FRENCH DREAMS OF EMPIRE

The land called Louisiana, stretching from the Mississippi River to the Rocky Mountains, was first claimed by France in the 1680s and named in honor of King Louis XIV. With defeat in the French and Indian War, France ceded Louisiana to Spain in 1763. But the French never forgot Louisiana or their dreams of empire in North America. In 1800 France's ruler, Napoleon Bonaparte, demanded that Spain cede Louisiana back to France. Spain debated about returning the territory. Finally, deciding that Lousiana "costs us more than it is worth," Spain signed a secret treaty, and the territory was returned to France.

Napoleon had restored French power in Europe, and he meant to do the same in North America. Control of Louisiana was part of his plan. But the key was Santo Domingo, a Caribbean island that Napoleon wanted as a naval base.

Santo Domingo had been France's most important "sugar island" until 1795. At that time, black slaves in Santo Domingo revolted and freed the island from French rule. Before Napoleon could build his French empire overseas, he had to reconquer Santo Domingo. Therefore, the French decided to wait to take actual possession of Louisiana, even though they now secretly controlled it.

AMERICAN FEARS

When word of the transfer of Louisiana to France reached Jefferson, it filled him with alarm. Spain, peaceful and weak, might have held the territory

Christopher Columbus first brought sugarcane to the western hemisphere. He planted it on Santo Domingo where sugar refining became a valuable industry. Juice from sugarcane was boiled and skimmed several times. The liquid was then cooled until the sugar crystallized.

A French explorer planted the city of New Orleans on Mississippi delta lands sheltered from gulf storms. By 1803 New Orleans was a valuable port. The painting, "A View of New Orleans from the Plantation of Marigny," celebrates America's acquisition of the city.

quietly for years. France, however, would be a powerful, ambitious neighbor, and a threat to American security and expansion.

Jefferson was especially worried about French control of New Orleans, at the mouth of the Mississippi River. American settlers beyond the Appalachians moved their goods to market down the Mississippi and through the port of New Orleans. To these westerners, the river was "the Hudson, the Delaware, the Potomac, and all the navigable rivers of the Atlantic states, formed into one stream." Jefferson feared that the French would close the Mississippi to Americans.

In April 1802 Jefferson asked Robert Livingston, the American minister in France, to find out if France would sell New Orleans and Florida, which he believed France had also acquired. If France refused, Jefferson would consider an alliance with Britain, France's old enemy. "The day that France takes possession of New Orleans," he warned Livingston, "we must marry ourselves to the British fleet and nation."

Livingston made little progress with the French. Jefferson then sent James Monroe, ex-governor of Virginia, to France to aid Livingston. Congress voted $2 million for Monroe and Livingston to offer the French for New Orleans and Florida. If necessary, they were to offer as much as $10 million. If the French still refused to sell, the envoys were to go to London to seek an alliance with Britain.

THE LOUISIANA PURCHASE

In April 1803 Monroe arrived in Paris and found a surprising turn of events. Instead of planning a colonial empire in North America, Napoleon now wanted to sell the whole territory of Louisiana.

Two events had prompted Napoleon's abrupt change of plans. First, French troops had failed to retake Santo Domingo. The French did capture the rebel leader, Toussaint L'Ouverture, but his followers fought on. By 1803 Napoleon could not afford to invest more troops and money in Santo Domingo, and he lost interest in empire building in North America.

At the same time, France and Britain were edging closer to war. In such a war, Napoleon knew that Britain's powerful navy could easily seize New Orleans. Britain might even make an alliance with the United States to push France out of North America.

To keep America neutral and Louisiana out of British hands, Napoleon offered the territory to the United States for $25 million. Monroe and Livingston had no instructions covering such an offer, but this was an opportunity they could not resist. "We

Pierre Toussaint L'Ouverture's followers fought for freedom. If they had not rebelled when France tried to retake Santo Domingo, Napoleon might never have sold Louisiana.

shall do all we can" to bring down the price, Livingston wrote to Secretary of State Madison, "but . . . we shall buy."

After a few weeks of bargaining, the Americans and the French struck a deal. In a treaty signed on April 30, 1803, the United States bought New Orleans and all of Louisiana for about $15 million. Two weeks later, France and Britain went to war.

CONSTITUTIONAL QUESTIONS

Although its boundaries were vague, the Louisiana Territory doubled the size of the United States. It added over 800,000 square miles (2,000,000 square kilometers) of land as well as some 200,000 people—Indian, French, and Spanish.

Jefferson also gloried in the purchase of this vast territory. However, the purchase treaty created a problem for him. Republicans stood for a strict interpretation of the Constitution. The Constitution did not grant the government power to buy foreign territory and bring it into the Union.

A constitutional amendment granting that power would have solved the problem, but there was no time. The treaty had to be ratified by the United States within six months. Also, as Livingston wrote from Paris, Napoleon was having second thoughts about the sale.

With no time to lose, Jefferson submitted the treaty to the Senate for approval. Jefferson deeply believed in a strict reading of the Constitution. However, he reasoned, keeping France out of Louisiana was necessary for American safety and thus of higher importance.

Federalists did not look at the purchase in quite that way. "We are to give money of which we have too little," a writer complained in a Boston newspaper, "for land of which we already have too much." Before, Federalists had favored a loose interpretation of the Constitution. Now they took a strict constructionist stand and questioned the government's right to buy Louisiana.

Still, the heavily Republican Senate easily approved the Louisiana treaty. On December 20, 1803, the Louisiana Territory became part of the United States. A delighted Tennessean wrote Jefferson: "You have secured to us the free navigation of the Mississippi. You have procured an immense and fertile country: and all these great blessings are obtained without war and bloodshed."

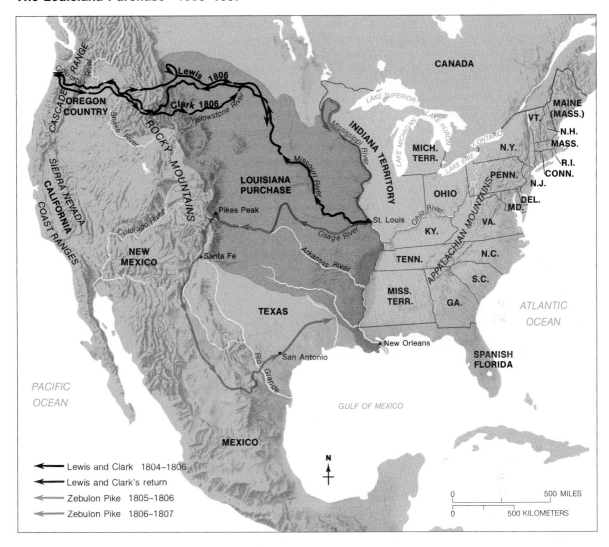

Lewis and Clark 1804–1806
Lewis and Clark's return
Zebulon Pike 1805–1806
Zebulon Pike 1806–1807

THE LEWIS AND CLARK EXPEDITION

With Louisiana in American hands, Meriwether Lewis and William Clark could freely probe the western half of the continent. Jefferson gave them instructions to explore the rivers of the West and to find a route to the Pacific and the fur trade of Canada. The explorers were to establish friendly relations, and perhaps trade, with the Indians they met. And they were to seek knowledge. "Other objects worthy of notice," Jefferson instructed, "will be the soil and face of the country, the animals, the mineral production of every kind . . . the winds prevailing at different seasons."

In May 1804 the 45-member expedition plunged into the wilderness from St. Louis, a frontier center of the fur trade. They followed the Missouri River into what is now North Dakota, and made their winter camp in a Mandan Indian village. In the spring they shipped home by keelboat crates of bones and skins and horns of strange animals. They also shipped pieces of Indian clothing and even a live prairie dog.

In April 1805 they again set out westward. Joining them as guides and interpreters were a 17-year-old Shoshone woman named Sacajawea and her French-Canadian husband. In their journey the explorers fought wild waters, snakes, grizzlies, sickness, and mosquitoes the size of flies—and

Lewis stands while Clark is seated near his servant, York. Sacajawea is seen in the tent. Both explorers praised her bravery and skill as a "pilot through this country."

mapped half a continent. Only once did a tribe meet them with weapons. Indeed, the Indians and explorers usually met in curiosity. Sacajawea, commented Clark, was an excellent guide.

Back east, months passed with no news. Some people thought the explorers had died in the wilderness. Meanwhile, another explorer began probing the new American territory. Lieutenant Zebulon Pike led expeditions to the upper Mississippi and along the Arkansas River into Colorado.

Then, in September 1806, Jefferson opened a letter sent from St. Louis and read:

> It is with pleasure that I announce to you the safe arrival of myself and party at twelve o'clock today at this place with our papers and baggage. In obedience to your orders, we have penetrated the continent of North America to the Pacific Ocean.
> —Meriwether Lewis

THE FEDERALIST THREAT TO THE UNION

Most Americans applauded Jefferson's purchase of Louisiana. Even in the Federalist Northeast, his policies were gaining support. But a few High Federalists from New England, led by Senator

Clark's journals contained many detailed descriptions and drawings of wildlife. He sketched the salmon trout and the prairie bird near the Columbia River.

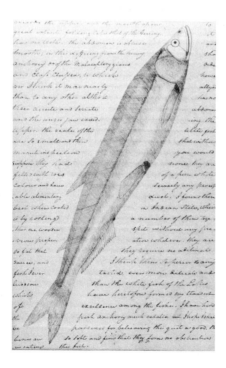

Timothy Pickering of Massachusetts, violently opposed the Louisiana Purchase. This group feared that the commercial Northeast would lose its power as new agricultural states sprang up west of the Mississippi.

In desperation, they decided to form a new nation. In their plan, the New England states and New York would **secede**, or withdraw, from the Union to become a "new confederacy." Most Federalist leaders, however, would have nothing to do with the plan. For support, Pickering turned to Vice-President Aaron Burr, who had accepted Federalist backing in the presidential electoral tie in 1801.

Jefferson distrusted Burr and gave him little part in the administration. For the upcoming 1804 election, the Republicans replaced Burr with George Clinton as the vice-presidential candidate. Burr promptly decided to run for governor of New York. Pickering promised Federalist support in the election, but Burr made no commitment.

New York was Alexander Hamilton's home. Alarmed by Burr's entry into the governor's race, Hamilton actively opposed Burr's election. Hamilton considered Burr "a dangerous man, and one who ought not to be trusted with the reins of government."

Burr lost the election. He blamed his defeat on Hamilton and challenged him to a duel. In July 1804 the two met in the morning mists by the Hudson River in New Jersey. Hamilton was killed, and Vice-President Burr fled New York to escape murder charges.

With Burr's election defeat and Hamilton's death, Pickering's plan for secession collapsed. Indeed, it had never really gained much support. In 1804 Jefferson was reelected in a landslide win over Federalist Charles C. Pinckney. In this first election with separate ballots for president and vice-president, Jefferson and Clinton carried every state but Connecticut and Delaware.

BURR AND THE SOUTHWEST

With Hamilton's death, Burr's political career died, and he turned to intrigues in the lands of the West. He talked to the British, then to the Spanish about a plan to separate the West from the United States, but without much success. In 1805 he traveled throughout the West and conferred with his friend General James Wilkinson, who was commander of American forces in Louisiana. Wilkinson was also in the pay of the Spanish. Rumors of Burr's suspicious actions spread.

A year later, Burr organized a mysterious military expedition and led it down the Mississippi. But Wilkinson warned Jefferson of Burr's actions. The President, convinced that Burr was acting against the United States, ordered his arrest. Burr tried to flee to Spanish Florida, but was captured.

In 1807 Burr was accused of plotting war against his country and tried for treason in the United States Circuit Court at Richmond, Virginia. On the bench as presiding judge was Chief Justice John Marshall. Marshall insisted on a strict reading of the Constitution's definition of treason. To be convicted, he ruled, Burr had to be guilty of an "overt act" against the United States, not just words or plans. The prosecution could not prove that Burr had committed such an act. As a result, the jury quickly reached a verdict of not guilty.

Acquitted, Burr searched for new adventures abroad. He would spend five years in Europe, watching France and Britain war for empire.

SECTION REVIEW

1. Identify the following: Napoleon Bonaparte, Santo Domingo, Robert Livingston, Toussaint L'Ouverture, Sacajawea, Zebulon Pike, Timothy Pickering, James Wilkinson.

2. (a) Why were Americans worried about French control of Louisiana? (b) What two events changed Napoleon's plans for Louisiana?

3. What constitutional problem was raised by the Louisiana Purchase?

4. Besides the constitutional problem, why were some Federalists opposed to the Louisiana Purchase?

5. (a) Who were Meriwether Lewis and William Clark? (b) What instructions were they given by Jefferson?

6. Why did some Federalists plan to secede from the Union?

7. What was the outcome of Aaron Burr's failure to be elected governor of New York?

8. (a) What charge was brought against Aaron Burr in his trial? (b) What was John Marshall's ruling in the trial?

THE WAR OF 1812

READ TO FIND OUT

— how war in Europe affected the United States.

— what steps Jefferson and Madison took to protect American neutrality.

— how trouble in the Northwest pushed the United States closer to war.

— how Americans felt about war in 1812.

— what happened to American forces in early battles.

— how Andrew Jackson defeated the British at New Orleans.

— what agreements were made in the Treaty of Ghent.

United States Frigate *Chesapeake*, Chesapeake Bay, June 22, 1807. 6 a.m., wind favorable, weighed anchor and stood to sea. . . .

As these words were entered in the ship's log, the U.S.S. *Chesapeake* sailed out of the harbor at Norfolk, Virginia. Commodore James Barron spotted two British warships, but was not concerned. British warships often cruised off the United States coast to keep watch on the movements of American and French ships.

One of the British ships, H.M.S. *Leopard*, signaled that it had a message and pulled alongside. A small boat brought a British admiral to the *Chesapeake*. The admiral ordered Barron to allow his ship to be searched for British deserters. Barron refused to allow the British on board his ship.

The British officer returned to the *Leopard*. Then, without warning, the *Leopard*'s gunports swung open, and three broadsides ripped into the *Chesapeake*. Barron knew his crew had no time to ready their cannons, so he surrendered.

A party of British officers boarded the *Chesapeake*. The crew was mustered and their papers were examined. Then the British left, taking four sailors. Only one was a British deserter. The other three were native Americans.

The *Chesapeake* limped back to Norfolk. Amidst the splintered rigging and timbers on deck lay 21 Americans dead or wounded.

NEUTRALITY THREATENED

The attack on the *Chesapeake* climaxed a two-year test of American neutrality by the British and the French. When France and Britain had gone to war in 1803, Americans wanted no part of the struggle. However, as a neutral nation the United States claimed the right to trade with both nations.

By the end of 1805, the war had reached a stalemate. Britain was supreme on the seas, and France controlled much of Europe. Desperate for victory, each tried to damage the other's war effort by cutting off its trade.

In 1806 and 1807 the British blockaded Europe's coast and banned all neutral trade in ports under French control. Napoleon quickly struck back. He declared Great Britain under blockade and vowed that the French would seize any ship that traded with the British.

As the world's leading neutral trader, the United States was caught between these two powers. Even worse, Britain's navy returned to its old policy of halting American ships and impressing sailors. In one year alone, 781 Americans were impressed into the Royal Navy.

British and French abuse of American neutrality—seizing ships and impressing sailors—angered Americans. "Free trade and sailors' rights!" became a popular slogan. But when the British fired on the *Chesapeake*, cries for war began to ring out.

THE EMBARGO ACT

Jefferson was reluctant to go to war. Instead, he turned to economic pressure. In December 1807 he recommended and Congress passed the Embargo Act, which forbade all American ships to leave for foreign ports. By cutting off American exports, Jefferson hoped to force Britain and France to come to terms. The embargo also would keep American ships and sailors at home and protect them from seizure.

The embargo, however, backfired. The French barely felt it. The British suffered, but not nearly as much as the Americans. Before, American traders had made large profits by running the blockades of

Amid banners the ship *Fame* was launched in Salem, Massachusetts in 1802. Merchant ships from Salem and other prosperous ports carried tea, carpets, and spices from Asia to Europe. America's foreign policy was aimed at protecting this flourishing foreign trade.

Britain and France. But the embargo kept ships at home and thus choked off most trade. Merchants and farmers everywhere grumbled over the loss of their foreign markets. Federalists accused Jefferson of trying to destroy New England shipping, which was hit hard by the ban on trade.

As the economy plunged into depression, some Americans, especially in the Northeast, actively opposed the embargo. Some began to smuggle goods into Canada. New England legislatures claimed that the embargo was unconstitutional, and some New England governors refused to enforce it. Threats of secession sprang up.

Amid this furor, Jefferson ended his second term. Following Washington's example, he refused to run for a third term. Instead, he supported for president Secretary of State James Madison. In the election of 1808, Madison and his running mate, George Clinton, defeated their Federalist opponents. But the Republicans lost all of New England except Vermont.

On March 4, 1809, three days before he left office, Jefferson signed a congressional bill repealing the embargo. This bill—the Nonintercourse Act—allowed Americans to resume trade with all countries but Britain and France.

American Exports   1803–1815

American trade with Britain was usually greater than its trade with France. At different times, however, trade with both nations was disrupted by political events.

MADISON AS PRESIDENT

James Madison, who had served Jefferson for eight years as secretary of state, was now president. Jefferson's handpicked successor was the third Virginian to become president.

Like Jefferson, Madison searched for a solution short of war. He hoped the Nonintercourse Act would bring Britain and France to American terms, but neither power would change its actions on the high seas. Also, American shippers, eager for profit, sailed to Britain and France regardless of American restrictions.

By 1810 Madison was ready to try another approach. The Nonintercourse Act was allowed to expire, and in May he signed a new measure. This law removed all restrictions on trade, and offered something more to tempt Britain and France into agreeing to American terms. If either country agreed to respect the neutral rights of the United States, the President would cut off trade with the other.

Napoleon quickly announced that he would end restrictions against American shipping. Madison accepted Napoleon's word. He then warned Britain to repeal its restrictions or lose American trade. Britain doubted Napoleon's promise and refused, so Madison prohibited trade with the British. Indeed, Napoleon did not live up to his words, and the French continued to violate American neutrality. Madison was left with a broken promise from the French and worsening relations with the British.

By late 1811 Madison was convinced that only one choice was left—war with Great Britain. Most Republicans came to share this view. Two of the most outspoken Republicans were newcomers to Congress: Henry Clay of Kentucky and John C. Calhoun of South Carolina. Clay was a young lawyer with a westerner's pride in the growing nation. He angrily denounced British actions. Clay quickly attracted a following, and he was named Speaker of the House.

One of Clay's closest allies was John Calhoun, a serious young man with a razor-sharp mind. Calhoun had grown up in the southern back country, where memories of bloody Revolution battles still remained strong. Both Calhoun and Clay believed that the United States must go to war or submit to Britain. Federalists began to call Calhoun, Clay, and the Republicans who shared their beliefs "War Hawks."

THE BATTLE OF TIPPECANOE

Soon after Congress met in 1811, trouble in the Northwest added to the growing clamor for war. As settlers poured into Indiana, Michigan, and Illinois, they forced the Indians to cede land. The tribes were pushed farther and farther west.

A powerful Shawnee chief named Tecumseh (tuh-KUHM-suh) and his brother, known as the Prophet, were furious at the loss of Indian lands. To resist the settlers, they began organizing a confederacy of all tribes east of the Mississippi.

The Shawnee brothers quickly built a following and set up a camp called Prophetstown on Tippecanoe Creek in Indiana. Alarmed settlers demanded that William Henry Harrison, the governor of the Indiana Territory, take action. In November 1811, while Tecumseh was away, Harrison led a force to Prophetstown and clashed with Tecumseh's warriors. It was a bloody fight with no clear victory.

Among the weapons Harrison found after the battle were some made in Britain. Westerners were sure that the British in Canada were aiding Tecumseh. The conquest of Canada, then, would end Indian troubles in the Northwest and give the United States the fur trade of the entire continent.

Westerners also joined southerners in a call to seize Florida from Spain. Florida was a haven for runaway slaves, and the Spanish were suspected of encouraging Indian raids on American settlements. Americans were also worried that Britain—Spain's ally—could land troops in Florida and attack the United States from the south.

These cries for war were echoed by the War Hawks in Congress, most of whom were from the West or the South. The Federalists, however, continued to oppose war. They argued that France, not Britain, was the real threat and that British trade was vital to the United States.

WAR WITH BRITAIN

Throughout early 1812 American patience with Britain continued to decline. Then, late in May 1812, Madison received word that the British stand on neutral rights remained unyielding. Seeing no choice, President Madison asked Congress on June 1 for a declaration of war.

The House quickly approved the declaration. In the Senate, however, opposition to war was far stronger. The New England states, as well as New York, New Jersey, and Delaware, all voted for peace. The southern and western states voted for war, and had the numbers to win.

Meanwhile, Britain was having second thoughts. The American embargo, along with Napoleon's blockade and a British crop failure, had hurt the nation. Faced with depression, Britain decided to repeal the restrictions on neutral trade.

Britain's change of heart, however, came too late. Two days later—on June 16, 1812—President Madison officially declared war on Great Britain.

The United States was not prepared for war. The army was poorly equipped and had only 7,000 troops and few experienced officers. The navy, which had experienced officers and crews, had only 16 ships. The government had no central banking

This beaded belt is thought to be the one Tecumseh brought to a meeting with British officials in 1810. He asked for their support.

In 1812 Tecumseh joined the British army. The daughter of a British officer stationed near Detroit painted him wearing British military trousers.

system since the charter of Bank of the United States had lapsed in 1811. To raise money, the government issued war bonds. Only half were sold, and the treasury was soon empty.

Especially damaging was the lack of national unity. New England Federalists bitterly opposed what they called "Mr. Madison's War." It was, they claimed, "a war of conquest." They also feared it would destroy trade and tie the nation to France.

The presidential election of 1812 reflected the strength of this opposition. New Yorker De Witt Clinton, the candidate of antiwar Republicans and Federalists, won every northern state except Vermont and Pennsylvania. Madison won a second term only because he carried the South and West.

EARLY CAMPAIGNS

The United States began the war with a string of defeats on land. Westerners were eager to conquer Canada, declaring that this would simply be a "matter of marching," even though the British controlled the Great Lakes.

In the late summer and the fall of 1812, American troops launched a three-pronged attack against Canada. In the West, General William Hull marched from Detroit into upper Canada. But he decided that the British were too strong and returned to Detroit. A few days later the British followed, and Hull surrendered Detroit without a fight. This left the British in control of Lake Erie and the Michigan country.

In the second prong of the attack, General Stephen Van Rensselaer crossed the Niagara River to seize a Canadian village. However, the New York militia refused to follow the army across the river, and the invasion failed. Soon after, General Henry Dearborn led a large force along Lake Champlain toward Montreal. His militia also refused to cross the border, and the army returned to base without accomplishing anything.

On the seas, however, the United States triumphed for a time. Privateers harrassed British trade ships. And in brilliant battles, the small American navy captured several British ships. Still, the United States Navy was no match for the large British fleet. By 1813 Britain had tightly blockaded the American coast from Long Island to Georgia. This stopped both overseas trade and trade among the states, which depended on coastal water routes.

A SEASON OF VICTORY

In September 1813 the United States finally had success in its Canadian campaign. Captain Oliver H. Perry was ordered to prepare for battle on Lake Erie, but he had few ships. With lumber from oak trees and iron from barn door hinges, he had several ships built. When the British challenged Perry, his makeshift navy won the battle. Afterward, Perry sent this message: "We have met the enemy, and they are ours! 2 ships, 2 brigs, 1 schooner, and 1 sloop." With this victory, the United States gained control of Lake Erie and forced the British to leave Detroit.

Cheered by the news, General William Henry Harrison led his militia north into Canada. Fleeing ahead of them were the British and their Indian allies, led by Tecumseh. The American troops caught them on the Thames River early in October. In the American victory, Tecumseh was killed. Without him, the Indian confederacy collapsed, and the tribes began to abandon the British.

About six months later, Americans gained another major victory, this time in the Southwest. In March 1814 General Andrew Jackson of the Tennessee militia led his troops against the Creek Indians, who had been attacking settlers. The Battle of Horseshoe Bend was costly for both sides, but Jackson won. The Creek were forced to cede to the United States about two thirds of their lands, part of present-day Georgia and Alabama. Jackson became a general in the United States Army.

THE BRITISH STRIKE BACK

In April 1814 the British finally defeated Napoleon in Europe and could now send experienced troops to America. Before those troops could arrive, however, Americans tried once more to invade Canada. An army under General Jacob Brown crossed the Niagara River in July, captured Fort Erie, and smashed British troops at the Battle of Chippawa. Later that month Brown's force tangled with the British at Lundy's Lane, near Niagara Falls. The five-hour battle ended in a draw, and the Americans returned to Fort Erie and held it against British attacks.

By August veteran British troops began to arrive. One British force swept down from Canada along Lake Champlain. Just below Plattsburgh, New York, the British paused to await vital naval

The War of 1812

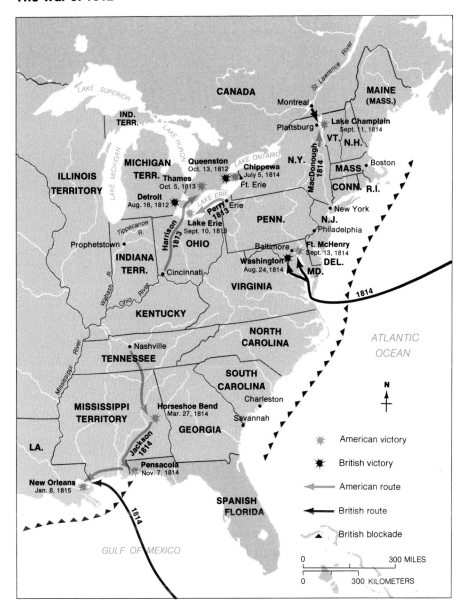

"The Impressment of an American Sailor Boy" was first sung on the Fourth of July, 1814. American sailors aboard a British prison ship sang the lament, according to the printed sheet of lyrics.

The War of 1812 was a series of small, widely scattered skirmishes on land and at sea. American and British ships clashed near Nova Scotia, Britain, Morocco, and even in the China Sea. American victories at sea did not win the war, but they filled Americans with pride.

support. Their wait was in vain. Young Captain Thomas Macdonough of the United States Navy destroyed that support on Lake Champlain with a quickly built fleet of warships. The victory gave the Americans control of the lake and forced the British to retreat to Canada.

Meanwhile, a second British force landed at Chesapeake Bay and marched toward Washington.

As the British entered the American capital in late August, the volunteer defenders fled. The British put torches to the White House, the Capitol, and other government buildings in retaliation for the American sacking of Canadian towns. All that was saved from the White House was a portrait of George Washington, which Dolley Madison had ordered removed to safety.

In "The Bombardment of Fort McHenry" the flag flying above the fort at the center is the one that inspired Francis Scott Key. American gunboats on the river face the British fleet. The Americans sank some of their own boats in the river so that British ships could not enter.

From the capital, the British marched to take Baltimore. Here, at last, they were stopped by American troops at Fort McHenry. An American lawyer named Francis Scott Key was on board a British ship trying to arrange an exchange of prisoners. From the deck, he watched the British bombardment of the fort through the night. The sight moved him to write "The Star-Spangled Banner."

THE HARTFORD CONVENTION

Despite the victory on Lake Champlain and the standoff at Baltimore, the American cause seemed hopeless in the fall of 1814. More British troops were on the way to America, and the American treasury was empty.

High Federalists, mostly from New England, had opposed the war from the beginning. New England bankers refused to loan the government money to fight the war. Federalist governors would not allow their militias to serve outside their own states. Then, in October, the Massachusetts legislature called a convention of New England states to discuss "a radical reform in the national compact."

On December 15, Federalist delegates from Connecticut, Rhode Island, Massachusetts, New Hampshire, and Vermont met in Hartford, Connecticut. The delegates proposed several constitutional amendments that would give New England a stronger voice in government. They also declared that if the national government threatened people's liberty or states' rights, the states then had the duty to resist.

In early January the convention closed. The delegates planned to present their proposals in Washington, but their timing could not have been worse. The nation's attention was riveted on New Orleans.

THE BATTLE OF NEW ORLEANS

Since the summer of 1814, two British forces had invaded the United States—one from Canada and one along Chesapeake Bay. In December a third British force cut through the Gulf of Mexico for an assault on New Orleans.

General Andrew Jackson, now commander of American forces in the Southwest, heard the rumors of invasion. When British troops landed in Pensacola, he invaded Spanish Florida and seized the city. Then he moved on to defend New Orleans.

Jackson set to work to arm New Orleans, and sent out a call for volunteers. Into the city poured fighters and pirates who were granted Jackson's personal protection. There were also local militias, including two battalions of free blacks. A few miles from New Orleans, Jackson determined to make a stand. His troops built a line of trenches and rolled naval guns into place.

Meanwhile, British troops had landed near the city. On the frosty dawn of January 8, 1815, they attacked Jackson's defenses. Protected by the trenches, Jackson's gunners waited until the British came into range, then unleashed a withering fire. Line after line of redcoats toppled in the field. After half an hour of battle, the British surrendered.

The American victory at New Orleans was stunning. However, the soldiers who fought that day would soon get a surprising piece of news. The war was already over. Two weeks earlier a treaty had been signed in Europe. Still, the rousing victory made Andrew Jackson a national hero and filled Americans with pride.

THE TREATY OF GHENT

In 1814 American and British commissioners had begun peace talks at Ghent in Belgium. After years of war with France and then war with the United States, the British longed for peace. Americans were just as eager to end the fighting.

In December the commissioners agreed to the Treaty of Ghent. The issues that had led to war— neutral rights on the high seas and impressment— were ignored. The treaty simply provided for the return of all occupied territory and restored the prewar boundaries between the United States and Canada. Since part of this boundary was disputed by both sides, the treaty set up a commission to settle the claim.

On Christmas Eve, 1814, the Americans and British signed the Treaty of Ghent. John Quincy Adams, son of John Adams and one of the commissioners, wrote in his diary, "I hoped it would be the last treaty of peace between Great Britain and the United States."

SECTION REVIEW

1. Identify the following: U.S.S. *Chesapeake*, Nonintercourse Act, War Hawks, Tecumseh, Tippecanoe Creek, Oliver H. Perry, Thomas Macdonough, Dolley Madison, Francis Scott Key, Hartford Convention.

2. Explain the meaning of the slogan "Free trade and sailors' rights."

3. Describe the Embargo Act. (a) What effect did Jefferson hope the Embargo Act would have? (b) What were its actual effects?

4. (a) What offer did Madison make to Britain and France in 1810? (b) What was Napoleon's response to Madison's offer? (c) How did Madison act upon Napoleon's response?

5. (a) What caused Indians to band together at Prophetstown? (b) How did westerners react when they learned how Indians had obtained some of the weapons found at Prophetstown?

6. (a) Which sections of the United States favored war in 1812? (b) How did the government raise money for war?

7. Describe the three-pronged attack against Canada in 1812.

8. (a) How were the British forced to give up Detroit? (b) What led the Indian tribes to desert the British? (c) What was the result of the Battle of Horseshoe Bend?

9. (a) What was Andrew Jackson's plan for defending New Orleans? (b) How did the plan work?

10. (a) What were the terms of the Treaty of Ghent? (b) What issues were ignored in the treaty?

CHAPTER SURVEY

SUMMARY

When Thomas Jefferson took office in 1801, he dedicated his presidency to the Republican ideal of limited government. The change from Federalist rule was smooth—Jefferson kept many Federalist programs. Yet there were some areas of conflict, especially with the judicial branch of government. In several landmark court cases, the authority of the Supreme Court became more clearly defined. Jefferson also had to deal with the issue of piracy against American ships in the Mediterranean. This issue had existed since the 1780s.

As American settlers pushed west as far as the Mississippi, Jefferson considered exploring even farther. He planned an expedition, led by Lewis and Clark, to explore all the way to the Pacific Ocean. The land did not belong to the United States. However, an unforeseen series of events persuaded France to offer to sell to the United States all of the Louisiana Territory. Jefferson accepted the offer. The Senate approved the treaty just before France and Britain went to war.

The United States tried to remain neutral in the European conflict, but British and French actions made neutrality difficult. Jefferson tried to stop trade altogether with the Embargo Act. Then he tried to limit trade by putting into effect the Nonintercourse Act. These and later measures taken by James Madison, Jefferson's successor, had little effect in keeping the United States from drawing closer to war. The issue of free trade and the fear of Indian uprisings sparked demands for war by congressional leaders. In June 1812 the United States declared war on Britain.

Neither Britain nor the United States was eager for the war. The United States was badly prepared, and Britain was busy fighting France. The early battles of the war were inconclusive. American forces began to achieve some success in 1813. Then the European war ended, and Britain could send more troops to fight Americans. Lack of money in the treasury and the opposition of many New England Federalists made the outlook bleak for the United States. But by the time America won a big victory at New Orleans, both sides had signed a treaty to end the war.

CHAPTER REVIEW

1. (a) Describe Jefferson's principles of government. (b) Explain how each of the following was an attempt by Jefferson to put those principles into practice: cutting the federal staff and budget, reducing the national debt, repealing taxes on whiskey and property, allowing the Alien and Sedition Acts to expire.

2. (a) Why did Adams and other Federalists distrust Jefferson and the Republicans? (b) How did Adams attempt to maintain some Federalist control of the national government? (c) Was Adams successful? Explain.

3. (a) Explain why William Marbury took Secretary of State James Madison to court. (b) In what way was the Supreme Court ruling in *Marbury* v. *Madison* a victory for the Republican administration? (c) In what way did the ruling give additional authority to the Supreme Court?

4. How did the trial of Samuel Chase establish the independence of the judicial branch of government?

5. (a) Describe two accomplishments of Lewis and Clark. (b) Did these accomplishments fulfill Jefferson's instructions? Explain.

OGRABME, or The American Snapping-turtle.

In 1807 Alexander Anderson's cartoon showed the "ograbme, or, American Snapping-turtle" catching a smuggler disobeying the Embargo Act. "Ograbme" is embargo spelled backwards.

William and Thomas Birch entitled their etching "Preparation for WAR to defend Commerce." The scene depicts the building of the frigate *Philadelphia* in 1799.

6. (a) Why did Jefferson favor a loose construction of the Constitution in the trial of Aaron Burr? (b) How did Marshall's view differ from Jefferson's? (c) What effect did Marshall's ruling have on the definition of treason in the United States?

7. (a) Explain how each of the following was an attempt to force Britain and France to recognize American neutrality: the Embargo Act, the Nonintercourse Act, Madison's offer of 1810. (b) How did each of these affect French and British actions? Explain.

8. (a) Twice during his administration, Jefferson faced threats of secession. Who threatened secession each time? Why? (b) How did such threats affect the Republicans in the elections of 1804 and 1808? Why?

9. How did each of the following contribute to the American declaration of war against Britain? (a) the seizure of American ships (b) impressment (c) the battle of Tippecanoe (d) the fur trade (e) American interest in Spanish Florida

10. (a) List the major problems of the United States in the War of 1812. (b) Why did the war end in 1814? (c) Did the United States gain its objectives in the Treaty of Ghent? Explain.

ISSUES AND IDEAS

1. What do you think Jefferson meant when he said to Americans, "We are all Republicans, we are all Federalists"? Could Americans today say "We are all Republicans, we are all Democrats"? Explain.

2. After the repeal of the Judiciary Act of 1801, Jefferson commented, "We have restored our judiciary to what it was while justice and not Federalism was its object." What do you think he meant?

3. Is it necessary for the Supreme Court to have the power of judicial review? Why or why not?

4. Give arguments for or against declaring war in 1812 by a Massachusetts merchant, an Indiana settler, a sailor, and a Georgia slaveholder. Then present Madison's argument for war.

SKILLS WORKSHOP

1. *Maps.* Look at page 173 of your book. Find the map entitled "The War of 1812." In what area were most of the battles of the war fought? Why?

2. *Graphs.* Look at page 170 of your book. Find the graph entitled "American Exports." When did American trade with these two nations rise to an all time high? Why? When did trade sharply decline? Why?

PAST AND PRESENT

1. In 1793 and 1803 the United States declared its neutrality in the war between Britain and France. Do you think the policy could have succeeded? If so, how? Do you think such a policy for the United States could be successful today? Why or why not?

2. In the 1960s Congress established the Lewis and Clark Trail Commission to honor the explorers and mark their trail. Through which present-day states would the trail be marked?

CHAPTER 8

THE GROWTH OF THE NATION

1815–1828

POSTWAR PRIDE
THE INDUSTRIAL REVOLUTION
THE MONROE YEARS
POSTWAR DIPLOMACY
THE JOHN QUINCY ADAMS YEARS

In 1832 Frances Ann Kemble toured the United States. She found travel by coach over roads jolting. In contrast, gliding along the Erie Canal by boat was a delight:

"Oh, these coaches! . . . Away we went, bumping, thumping, jumping, jolting, shaking, tossing and tumbling, over the wickedest road, I do think, the cruellest, hard-heartedest road, that ever wheel rumbled upon. Through bog and marsh, and ruts, wider and deeper than any christian ruts I ever saw, with the roots of trees protruding across our path, their boughs every now and then giving us an affectionate scratch through the windows . . . Bones of me! what a road! . . .

I like traveling by the canal boats very much. Our's was not crowded, and the country through which we passed was delightful. The placid moderate gliding through it, at about four miles and a half an hour, seemed to me infinitely preferable to the noise of wheels, the rumble of a coach, and the jerking of bad roads, for the gain of a mile an hour. The only nuisances are the bridges over the canal, which are so very low, that one is obliged to prostrate oneself on the deck of the boat, to avoid being scraped off it; and this humiliation occurs, upon an average, once every quarter of an hour."

Roads and canals were apt symbols of the United States after the War of 1812. These were building years—of roads, canals, steamboats, machines, and factories. The nation was in the grip of a new force known as the Industrial Revolution.

However, the postwar years were also troublesome times. The war left the economy shattered, and leaders labored to rebuild it. Meanwhile, in foreign affairs, the young nation was mastering the tools of diplomacy.

Yet the United States somehow won the war. Out of the ashes, Washington D.C. sprang back. Buildings were repaired and refurnished. The president's official residence—called the White House because of its whitish sandstone walls—was painted white to cover the sooty marks left by flames.

As the capital put on a fresh face, Americans felt a new surge of pride in their country. Albert Gallatin, treasury secretary and a peace commissioner at Ghent, wrote: "The war has renewed and reinstated the national feelings which the Revolution had given and which were daily lessened." He noted that people "are more American. They feel and act more like a nation." Back again in the White House, President Madison was now the nation's victorious leader.

THE AMERICAN SYSTEM

With the celebration of the Treaty of Ghent, people tended to forget the problems of the war years. But American leaders did not. The conflict had given the nation a painful lesson about its ability to finance and to wage war. And although the war was over, there were still problems with the economy. Both President Madison and Congress were determined to solve these problems. Then, a strong United States could face any future threat.

In December 1815 Madison submitted to Congress his annual message, the last one of his presidency. The message dealt primarily with Madison's suggestions for improving the economy.

Madison asked Congress to reestablish a national bank, to pass a protective tariff, and to build roads and canals. The bank would give the nation a uniform financial system. The tariff would protect American industries from foreign competition. The roads and canals would increase trade between the industrial North and the agricultural South and West.

Madison's suggestions found support in Congress. Like the country, Congress was basking in warm feelings of *nationalism*, or patriotism. Led by the chief War Hawks of 1812—House Speaker Henry Clay and Representative John C. Calhoun—Congress set to work to hammer out legislation. Clay named the program that emerged the American System. It was designed to benefit each part of the country while making the whole nation self-sufficient.

POSTWAR PRIDE

READ TO FIND OUT

— how Madison planned to spur the economy.

— how the new national bank benefited the economy.

— how the Tariff of 1816 was intended to help American industries.

— how roads and canals stimulated trade.

For the United States, the worst time of the War of 1812 had been the burning of Washington. As flames hissed through the White House and other buildings, James and Dolley Madison fled into the hills of Virginia. The British soldiers, riding out of Washington, joked that they would catch Madison and bring him to England "for a curiosity."

The furniture industry began to grow rapidly in the early 1800s. Duncan Phyfe was one of the first furniture makers to develop a distinctive American style. The watercolor depicts his shop and warehouse.

THE BANK OF THE UNITED STATES

The first issue that Congress took up was the Bank of the United States. Only five years earlier the charter for the national bank, created by Hamilton, had expired.

Between 1811 and 1816 the government had no central bank to handle its money, so it turned to "state banks," private banks chartered by state legislatures. Originally, the national bank had supervised these banks, but when its charter expired, state banks were left on their own.

The number of state banks grew rapidly, and the banks became reckless in their money policies. They issued increasing amounts of paper money, called bank notes. Often the banks notes were issued without gold or silver to back them up. Thus, the paper money declined in value.

Furthermore, there was no national currency, so each bank issued its own notes, which circulated locally. The result, Treasury Secretary Gallatin complained, was "a baseless currency varying every fifty miles and fluctuating everywhere." The lack of a uniform national currency made commerce between the states very difficult.

In his message to Congress, Madison stressed the nation's need for a uniform national currency. "If the operation of the state banks cannot produce this result," he wrote, "a national bank will merit consideration."

In January 1816 Calhoun introduced a bill to charter the second Bank of the United States for a period of twenty years. Within three months Congress passed the bill, and the President signed it into law. The new national bank was much like Hamilton's original. It would serve as a safe place in which the federal government could deposit its funds. It would also provide a uniform national currency. In addition, it would regulate credit. If farmers and manufacturers needed to borrow money, the money loaned would not be worthless currency but would be backed by gold and silver.

THE TARIFF OF 1816

Although the war had shown that the United States had banking troubles, it gave the economy a solid push. Because of Jefferson's embargo and Britain's blockade, the nation was unable to import the British manufactured goods that it was so dependent on, particularly cloth and iron. Americans, especially in New England and the middle states, began to make these goods themselves. With wartime demand and no foreign competition, America's "infant industries" flourished.

After the war, however, things quickly changed. British manufacturers, cut off from their American market during the war, had stored up a huge surplus of products. When peace came, they flooded the United States with their goods. The British prices were so low that the new American industries could not compete and faced extinction.

President Madison was determined to prevent that. If America had healthy industries of its own, the nation could be less dependent on European markets. Thriving industries also would create jobs, wealth, and goods that the United States could sell abroad. To give the infant industries a chance to grow, Madison asked Congress to pass a protective tariff. This would set high duties on imported goods, and thus prompt Americans to buy goods made at home.

The tariff proposal set off a heated debate in Congress. The mid-Atlantic states of New York, New Jersey, and Pennsylvania, with their manufacturing interests, gave the bill support. So did the western states. Westerners thought that with tariff protection industry would prosper in both North and South. Then cities would grow around industries. These cities, westerners reasoned, would need western produce.

However, there were disagreements over the issue in both New England and the southern states. New England wanted protection for its manufacturing, but feared that a tariff, in damaging British trade, would hurt its shipping interests. Most southern states, which had little manufacturing, also opposed the bill.

Finally, supporters pushed the bill through Congress, and the nation had its first protective tariff. The Tariff of 1816 was aimed mainly at the foreign imports that competed with major American manufactures. Foreign manufacturers would have to pay import duties of 20 percent to 25 percent of the value of their goods. Now, Congress hoped, British imports would be more costly than American-made goods.

In reality, however, the tariff was not high enough to be effective. Imports still cost less than domestic goods. The British continued to sell their goods in America, and American manufacturers faced hard times in the postwar years.

INTERNAL IMPROVEMENTS

President Madison's third request to Congress was to consider a national plan for building roads and canals. The War of 1812 had shown that the nation needed better transportation. Bad or nonexistent roads had hindered the movement of troops and supplies and hurt the war effort as much as had the nation's poor finances. Actually, Congress had voted funds for a National Road in 1806, but progress on the road had been slow.

In February 1817 Calhoun sponsored the Bonus Bill, calling for the government to fund an entire network of roads and canals. The persuasive Calhoun pleaded for these "internal improvements" not only for military reasons, but also to bring the regions of the country into closer union. He feared that the nation was growing so fast that the Union might be fragmented by the great distances. He urged the Congress, "Let us then bind the Republic together with a perfect system of roads and canals. Let us conquer space."

Calhoun's forceful speech did not convince New Englanders or even his fellow southerners. New England already had good roads and feared that it would lose trade to Philadelphia, Baltimore, and New York if roads there were improved. The southern states agreed. They too had a good transportation system—their rivers—and saw no advantage in building routes between the North and West.

Calhoun managed to get the bill passed over the opposition, only to have Madison veto it. Although the President had proposed such internal improvements, he was having second thoughts. He still believed that the government should fund roads and canals, but felt that a constitutional amendment was needed before Congress could act in this area. Madison hoped that one would soon be passed, but it never was.

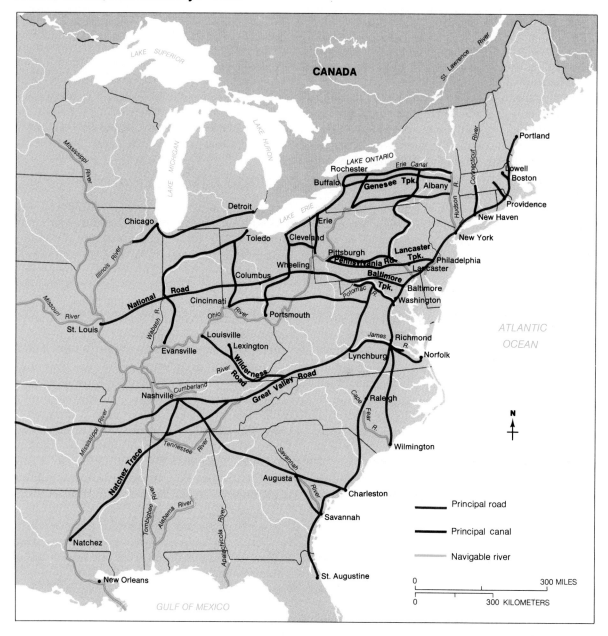

EARLY ROADS AND CANALS

Although Calhoun's Bonus Bill was vetoed, work on the National Road continued. Construction had begun in 1811, five years after Congress voted funds for the project. By 1818 this "permanent turnpike" stretched from Cumberland, Maryland, to Wheeling, Virginia, on the Ohio River. By the 1830s the road was extended through Ohio, and it reached Illinois a decade later.

Most road building, however, was done by the states to connect their cities and towns. Pennsylvania led the way as early as 1790 by chartering a private company to build a road between Lancaster and Philadelphia.

People using the Lancaster Turnpike, completed in 1794, were charged *tolls*, or fees, to pay the building costs. This system was so successful that it sparked a flurry of toll-road building by states and cities eager to draw trade.

Rebecca Lukens' ironworks benefited from internal improvements. Iron ore and coal were moved cheaply by water. Lukens' works made iron plates for steamboat boilers.

By the 1820s, New England and the middle states were crisscrossed with toll roads. Toll roads, however, were not much help to merchants who needed an inexpensive way to move heavy freight over long distances. A team of horses took an hour to haul a loaded wagon two miles (three kilometers), and the tolls were often high. Waterways were more efficient for transporting freight. Thus many states and cities began to build canals.

In 1817 Governor DeWitt Clinton prodded the state of New York to fund work on the Erie Canal. Construction on "Clinton's Big Ditch," as the Erie Canal came to be known, was started on the Fourth of July in 1818. The building of the canal would take eight years and present countless difficulties. Much of the territory through which the canal was built was unsettled wilderness. In addition, there were no trained engineers. Able, untrained people, mainly lawyers, worked on the canal.

When completed, the canal sliced from Albany to Buffalo, connecting the Hudson River to Lake Erie. Barges, pulled by horses or mules walking along a towpath beside the canal, moved people and goods at low prices.

Before, goods had cost a hundred dollars a ton to be hauled by wagon between Buffalo and Albany. Now they could be moved by water for a tenth of that cost. The canal created a new link between the West and the Northeast through the Great Lakes. Since the Hudson River flowed from the eastern end of the canal to New York City, that old commercial center had a new outlet to markets.

The Erie Canal's success set off a canal-building craze across the nation. Over 3,000 miles (4,800 kilometers) of canals were built, many in the northwestern states. These canals connected the Great Lakes to the Ohio and Mississippi rivers. In this way the states began to answer Calhoun's call for roads and canals to bind the nation together.

SECTION REVIEW

1. Identify the following: Bonus Bill, National Road, DeWitt Clinton.

2. Define the following: American System, nationalism, tolls.

3. (a) Describe one way in which state banks had become reckless in their money policies. (b) How did the reestablished national banking system correct the problem?

4. During the War of 1812 how had Jefferson's embargo and Britain's blockade helped the growth of American industries?

5. (a) How was a protective tariff supposed to help American industries after the war? (b) Why were mid-Atlantic and western states in favor of a protective tariff but New England and southern states opposed to it? (c) Explain why the Tariff of 1816 did not help American industries.

6. Why did the New England states, the southern states, and President Madison each oppose the Bonus Bill?

7. How did the building of the Lancaster Turnpike in Pennsylvania lead to the building of roads in other states?

8. (a) In what two ways were canals better than toll roads for transporting goods? (b) List four effects of the building of the Erie Canal.

THE INDUSTRIAL REVOLUTION

READ TO FIND OUT

— how the Industrial Revolution came to the United States.

— how factory owners solved the problems of finding labor and raising capital.

— how the Industrial Revolution affected the West, the South, and the North.

— what effect steam power had on transportation, industry, and western settlements.

In January 1801 a dozen people gathered in the White House around a table piled with musket parts. Inventor Eli Whitney had arranged a demonstration. Whitney asked each person to select a part from each pile. Then he took the parts and quickly put together a musket. Again and again he fitted together parts until he had ten finished muskets. The entire demonstration took only minutes.

The people around the table must have been amazed. They knew that a gunsmith took weeks to craft a single musket, making one part at a time and then fitting it to the next. Because no two guns were exactly alike, their parts could not be interchanged. But Whitney's muskets set a new standard. With machine tools called dies and molds, he could make identical, **interchangeable parts** that could be put together easily by unskilled workers.

Whitney's system of interchangeable parts marked the beginning of **mass production**—the production of goods in large quantities. In the years to come, the art of crafting would gradually give way to the business of manufacturing. Hundreds of other people would follow Whitney's example, using machine tools to produce quickly and cheaply almost anything having parts—furniture, wood stoves, carriages, clocks. As manufacturing became profitable, investors were attracted. As factories were built, they drew workers from homes, farms, and small shops. Once more there was a revolution in the United States. This revolution was called the Industrial Revolution.

MANUFACTURING BY MACHINE

In the Revolutionary War Americans replaced one government with another. The battle continued for six years. In the Industrial Revolution, Americans began to shift from one way of life—farming—to another—manufacturing. The shift was as gradual as a river changing course. Once underway, however, it could not be stopped. Industrialization was made possible by two major developments, power-driven machinery and factories. Both had first appeared in Great Britain.

In Britain the Industrial Revolution had been underway since the mid-1700s. Workers in British textile factories, or mills, had become accustomed to using machines powered by water or by steam engines. Some machines spun thread, allowing one worker to spin a dozen threads at once. Other machines wove the thread into cloth. Britain, fearing competition, kept the plans for its machines and factories highly secret.

Americans, faced with a shortage of labor, were eager to switch to machine power and were willing to borrow ideas from the British. In 1789 Samuel Slater, a former apprentice in a British textile mill, reached the United States. With his own good memory for detail and with financial backing from Rhode Island merchant Moses Brown, Slater reproduced the British cotton-spinning machinery.

In 1790 Slater set up a textile mill in Pawtucket, Rhode Island—the first factory in the United States. The factory's water-powered machines enabled 9 children to operate 72 spindles at once. The mill flourished, and others soon sprang up in villages along New England rivers. The rivers provided power for the machines.

Slater's mill produced only thread. The cotton thread was woven into finished cloth by people in their homes. In 1810 Francis Cabot Lowell, a Massachusetts merchant, visited British cotton manufacturers and memorized their design for a power loom, which wove cloth. When Lowell returned home, he and other merchants formed the Boston Manufacturing Company.

In 1813, at Waltham, Massachusetts, the company built a mill where raw cotton fiber was made into thread and then woven into cloth. This was the first mill in the United States in which all steps of producing finished cotton from raw fiber were done under one roof.

As the Industrial Revolution spread, mill wheels became a familiar sight. "The Red Mill near Yellow Springs, Ohio" pictures one of the many mills that sprang up.

Lowell died in 1817, but the success of the Waltham mill spurred his partners to expand. They chose a site on the Merrimack River in Massachusetts for a new mill and named it in honor of their late partner. The first five-story mill at Lowell was established in 1822. In time, eighteen more mills would be built.

LABOR AND CAPITAL

The new factories needed a large pool of labor, but many Americans shunned work in factories. Artisans had always worked at home or in small shops, spinning thread, weaving cloth, or making hats, shoes, or other goods. They were skilled, well paid, and reluctant to give up their independent status. Farmers also cherished their independence. With cheap land to the west, they worked for others only until they earned enough to buy property of their own.

Factory owners had to find people willing to work for wages away from home. They found that work force primarily in the women and children of New England. Many of these women and children came from poor farm families and were eager to earn money, so they worked for lower wages than men demanded. Later, in the 1830s, factory owners tapped an endless supply of cheap labor in the tide of immigrants coming to the United States from Europe.

Setting up factories, paying workers, and building machines all required money. Raising the money, or the *capital*, required investors, people who would risk their money on a new venture. An old form of business organization, called the **corporation**, helped manufacturers attract investors. In the 1600s the British had organized joint-stock companies, or corporations, to finance some settlements in America.

In the 1820s, Americans turned to this form of organization. Businesses large and small became corporations and sold stock to investors to raise the money to take advantage of business opportunities. The investors who bought the stock had the assurance of limited risk. The investors hoped to make profits, of course. But if the company lost money or went out of business, laws said that the investors could not be held responsible for the corporation's debts. The investors could not lose their personal fortunes. The worst that could happen was the loss of their investments.

THE EFFECTS OF INDUSTRY

The Industrial Revolution touched sections of the United States in different ways. The West remained agricultural, specializing more and more in livestock and crops that easterners, southerners, and Europeans wanted. Wheat and corn, for example, became the main crops in Ohio and Indiana.

As westerners turned their land to commercial crops, they relied on better tools and machines. Cyrus McCormick's reaper and John Deere's steel plow, both invented in the 1830s, would become a necessary part of the business of farming. In addition, the once self-sufficient farmers gradually came to rely on factories for clothing, furniture, and new farm machinery.

The southern states also relied on commercial agriculture and needed farm machinery. Tobacco production spread from Virginia to Kentucky, Tennessee, and Missouri. Rice continued to be cultivated in South Carolina and Georgia. Sugarcane became profitable in Louisiana, and hemp was grown in sections of Kentucky and Missouri.

However, none of these crops matched the profitability of cotton. The rise of cotton was linked to a machine. Originally, colonists had grown cotton only for their own use. After the Revolutionary War farmers began to export it to Britain, where it was made into cotton cloth. As the British textile industry grew, the demand for cotton became greater and greater. The United States could not meet the demand because of the difficulty in separating cotton fiber from the seeds.

Then in 1793 Eli Whitney, who later introduced interchangeable parts, invented the cotton gin. The cotton gin was a machine that removed cotton seeds from fibers. The cotton gin could clean fifty times as much cotton in a day as a worker could by hand. Suddenly cotton became a crop that could earn huge profits.

Land on one-horse farms and on huge plantations was turned over to this cash crop. The cotton gin made the South the world's leading producer of cotton. The South's cotton fed the mills of Britain as well as those of New England.

The Industrial Revolution played a far different role in the North. That region hummed with new industrial activity. Here were the factories that made the machinery and goods needed by the South and West. Textile mills sprang up throughout New England. Ironworks and machine shops multiplied in the Middle Atlantic States. By the 1830s machine tools made in the United States rivaled those of Europe.

STEAM POWER

A significant invention of the Industrial Revolution was the steam engine, perfected by James Watt of Scotland in the 1780s. The steam engine powered most of Britain's factories. In the United States, which had miles of rushing rivers, factories were powered by water as well as steam. In the United States, too, the hissing steam engine would be put to a brand-new use.

Since the 1780s American inventors had been tinkering with steam power to propel boats. Then an inventor named Robert Fulton put together a steam-powered engine and huge paddlewheels and produced the steamboat. At first Americans scorned "Fulton's Folly." But Fulton proved that steamboat transportation could move goods and people profitably.

In August 1807 his *Clermont* churned its way up the Hudson River against the current at a remarkable five miles (eight kilometers) per hour. Four years later, Fulton's *New Orleans* successfully steamed down the Ohio and Mississippi rivers, from Pittsburgh to New Orleans. Builders next developed steamboats to navigate the treacherous shallows of western rivers like the Missouri. By the 1820s

The power-driven loom allowed inexperienced workers to make cotton cloth cheaply. New England's textile mills were able to compete with the British for markets in both the United States and Europe.

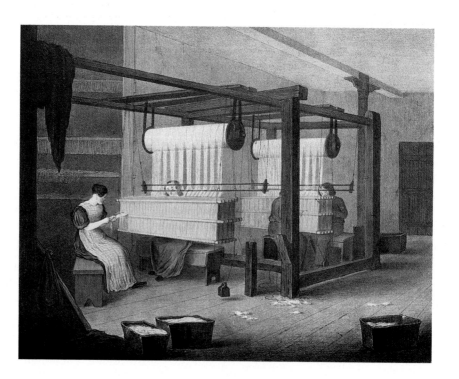

On a trip up the Missouri River, artist George Catlin painted a scene showing the *Yellowstone* passing the city of St. Louis. With the coming of steamboat travel, St. Louis developed into a major transportation center.

hundreds of steamboats traveled the nation's rivers, turning them into highways that flowed in two directions.

Just as the steam engine benefited transportation, improved transportation in the form of steamboats and canals and roads helped industry. Many northeastern manufacturers made use of raw materials, such as cotton, that were produced far from their factories. They needed to receive those materials and then transport the finished goods to market. Thus roads, canals, and rivers were the factories' very lifeline.

Steamboats and canals also had a vital effect on settlements in the West. Towns might live or die, depending on how close they were to a river or canal. Cincinnati became a mighty trade center nicknamed "Porkopolis," thanks to its shipments of pork by steamboat. A Richmond, Indiana, newspaper commented on a planned canal:

> With it our course will be upward, and without it our city will become a deserted village. . . . With it our streets will be the avenues of traffic; without, grass will grow upon the sidewalks. With it we will rival and outstrip surrounding towns; without it they will leave us in the background.

SECTION REVIEW

1. Identify the following: Eli Whitney, Samuel Slater, Francis Cabot Lowell, James Watt, Robert Fulton.

2. Define the following: interchangeable parts, mass production, cotton gin.

3. (a) Which country was the first to build factories that used power-driven machines? (b) How did Americans learn about cotton-spinning machinery?

4. (a) Where was the first factory in the United States? What did it produce? (b) How were its machines powered?

5. (a) Why did some people shun work in factories? (b) What groups of people were willing to do factory work?

6. Explain how capital was raised to set up factories, pay workers, and build machines.

7. What effect did the Industrial Revolution have on the agricultural West? the South? the North?

8. (a) How did the steam engine benefit transportation? Industry? (b) How did improved transportation benefit industry?

THE MONROE YEARS

READ TO FIND OUT

— what effect Monroe's election had on the Federalist party.

— how John Marshall strengthened the power of the federal government.

— what problems led to the Panic of 1819.

— why the issue of Missouri's statehood threatened the Union.

— what the Missouri Compromise achieved.

While the United States hummed to the new tune of the Industrial Revolution, the presidency passed to James Monroe. Monroe, who was a Republican and Madison's secretary of state and successor, took office on March 4, 1817. Monroe was tall and lanky like Jefferson, with a rough-hewn face that resembled Washington's. Known as the "last of the Revolutionary farmers," Monroe would sometimes go about in his faded officer's uniform from the Revolution. He was the fourth Virginian—the third in a row—to gain the presidency.

Monroe's election victory had been a crushing defeat for the Federalists. The Federalist candidate, Senator Rufus King of New York, gained only 34 out of 221 electoral votes. His party was near death. Many of its ideals and programs had been taken over by the Republicans. Its sponsorship of the Hartford Convention during the War of 1812 had thoroughly discredited it. One-time Federalists now supported Monroe. When he toured New England after his inauguration, so many people greeted him warmly that a Boston newspaper called the times an "era of good feelings."

Monroe hoped to keep that mood alive. He tried to choose cabinet members that reflected all sections of the country. In his solemn, matter-of-fact way he worked to keep political harmony. Like Washington, he distrusted political parties and hoped they would disappear. Monroe's wish was granted in the presidential election of 1820. He was reelected without opposition. During his two terms, only the Republican party existed.

THE SUPREME COURT UNDER JOHN MARSHALL

Since Jefferson's election in 1800, the nation had been led by Republicans in the presidency and Congress. But all that time a Federalist had headed the Supreme Court.

Chief Justice John Marshall, too, was a Virginian and a veteran of the Revolution. He had served in Congress and in the cabinet but found his home in the Supreme Court, where his career spanned 34 years. A witty man who made jokes about lawyers, Marshall nevertheless took the law quite seriously. In many of his court decisions, he strengthened the federal government and broadly interpreted the Constitution.

In the 1803 case of *Marbury* v. *Madison*, Marshall had first asserted the Court's power to review acts of Congress and to declare them void if they violated the Constitution. Seven years later, in *Fletcher* v. *Peck*, he extended this power of judicial review. The Georgia legislature had made several land grants to companies. However, a new legislature found the grants tainted by bribery and canceled them. Marshall ruled that Georgia had no right to cancel the grants, because they were contracts and thus protected by the Constitution.

The thorny issue of federal and state powers came up again in 1819. The New Hampshire legislature had altered the colonial charter of Dartmouth College. Lawyer Daniel Webster argued the college's case before the Court. Some observers said that Webster moved Justice Marshall to tears. In *Dartmouth College* v. *Woodward*, Marshall declared that charters were contracts, protected by the Constitution, and could not be changed by the states. Once more, he affirmed the Court's power to overturn a state action that it considered unconstitutional.

That same year, a case involving the second Bank of the United States reached the Supreme Court. In *McCulloch* v. *Maryland*, the Court overruled an act of the Maryland legislature to tax the national bank's branch in Baltimore. Marshall declared that "the power to tax involves the power to destroy." No state could be allowed to destroy an agency of the federal government.

In the same decision, Marshall strengthened the federal government by ruling that Congress had acted constitutionally in chartering the bank.

Harking back to Hamilton's loose construction of the Constitution, Marshall noted that the government's authority to tax, regulate commerce, conduct war, and raise and support armies and navies implied the power to establish a bank. All actions within "the letter and spirit of the Constitution," he stated, "are constitutional."

In 1824 the Court once more upheld the supremacy of federal over state powers. In *Gibbons v. Ogden*, Marshall declared unconstitutional a contract that New York State had granted for steamship service between New York and New Jersey. A state could regulate commerce within its borders, Marshall ruled, but the Constitution gave Congress the sole authority over commerce between states. By defining interstate commerce to include transportation as well as all kinds of trade, Marshall gave Congress a broader range of authority.

When lawyer Daniel Webster argued for Dartmouth College in 1819, he stressed the significance of the issue. "The case before the Court," he argued, "is not of ordinary importance, nor of everyday occurrence." The decisions of John Marshall were of such importance as to affect everyday occurrences for many years to come.

THE PANIC OF 1819

John Marshall's Supreme Court made many controversial decisions during the years after the war, but none was more unpopular than *McCulloch* v. *Maryland*. The ruling in favor of the second Bank of the United States was handed down in the midst of the Panic of 1819. Many blamed this financial panic on the bank.

The panic and the depression that followed grew out of the economic boom of the postwar years. With the end of the Napoleonic Wars, Europeans clamored for more American corn, beef, pork, flour, tobacco, and cotton. Crop failures in Europe during the next few years increased the demand, and Americans rushed to meet it and reap the profits their products brought. The market for cotton seemed endless. By 1819 cotton made up over one third of America's total exports.

Land values soared as Americans scrambled to buy new land to the southwest and west so they could plant cotton or other cash crops. The land also attracted speculators who hoped to profit from the land itself. Most people, however, did not have the ready cash to buy land or farm equipment, so

In 1829 distinguished Virginians met to rewrite the state constitution. In the group portrait marking the event, James Madison, standing, is addressing the meeting. From his position in the tall chair, chairman James Monroe listens intently. John Marshall also attended the convention.

they turned to state banks for loans. The banks, especially those in western areas, readily extended easy credit. In the process, they issued paper money without having enough gold or silver to back it up.

Instead of curbing the state banks, the Bank of the United States encouraged the extension of credit. It was backed by the Department of the Treasury, which urged settlers without cash to buy government land on credit. Like the state banks, the national bank gave generous loans and issued a flood of paper money without enough gold or silver to back it. Everyone seemed caught up in the spiral of prosperity. Prices for American exports continued to rise, land speculation boomed, and credit was expanded further and further.

Then in 1818 this spiral collapsed. European agriculture revived, producing a series of bumper crops. British manufacturers switched from buying expensive American cotton to buying cheaper cotton from India. As the demand for American exports fell, so did prices. American farmers and speculators could not pay their debts for land and equipment.

At the same time, the national bank grew concerned about its lax credit policies. The president of the bank, faced with a congressional investigation, resigned. In 1819 the bank was placed under new management and strictly curbed credit. It called in loans, and demanded gold and silver from state banks in exchange for their notes. It also ordered state banks not to renew mortgages.

The response was panic. States banks called in their loans. People could not pay their debts, and many farmers and merchants went bankrupt. Workers lost their jobs. Prices plunged. Many state banks collapsed. The national bank foreclosed on mortgages and became the owner of homes, farms, and shops, especially in the West and the South.

Senator-elect Thomas Hart Benton traveled from Missouri to Washington in 1820 and heard the same story of despair everywhere. "No employment for industry—no demand for labor—no sale for the product of the farm—no sound of the hammer, but that of the auctioneer," he recalled. *"Distress*, the universal cry of the people; *Relief*, the universal demand thundered at the doors of all legislatures, state and federal."

Some western states did pass laws to help debtors. But most federal leaders did not believe in interfering in the economy, and those who did could not agree on what should be done.

Rebecca Gratz pioneered in founding private institutions to aid women and children during hard times. The Hebrew school she organized became a model for many other schools.

The depression lasted through the early 1820s and soured America's optimism and spirit of unity. People everywhere, particularly in the West, blamed the Bank of the United States for creating the depression and the federal government for failing to provide relief.

CONFLICT OVER SLAVERY

In 1819, while most Americans were concerned with the depression, Congress began to debate over Missouri's entry into the Union. The debate divided the nation as much as the depression had.

The Territory of Missouri applied to Congress for statehood in 1818. Missouri was part of the Louisiana Purchase, and under French and Spanish rule slavery had been allowed in Louisiana. When Americans began to settle in the territory after the War of 1812, many brought slaves. As a result, Missouri's proposed constitution allowed slavery.

In February 1819, as the House discussed the bill to admit Missouri, Representative James Tallmadge of New York offered an amendment. Missouri would be admitted to the Union if no more slaves were brought into the state and the children of slaves were set free at age 25. After a fierce debate the House adopted the bill, but the Senate dropped Tallmadge's amendment. That session of Congress ended in a stalemate.

The bitterness over the amendment reflected a deep division in the nation. Ever since the Constitutional Convention, the states of the Northeast had resented the Three-fifths Compromise, which allowed southern states to count three fifths of their slaves for representation in Congress and for votes in presidential elections. This, northerners felt, added unfairly to the political power of the South. If Missouri was admitted as a slaveholding state, that would give the South even more power.

Power was not the only issue, however. Many people simply opposed slavery. Even before the nation's birth, a number of both northerners and southerners had looked on slavery as immoral. Antislavery societies, some as old as the Revolution, existed in most parts of the country.

In 1787 the Northwest Territory had been closed to slavery. By 1804 every state north of Delaware had provided for its abolition, usually by a gradual method similar to Tallmadge's proposal for Missouri. In 1808 the African slave trade had been prohibited. And in 1817, when the American Colonization Society was formed to send emancipated slaves and free blacks to Africa, southern leaders Madison and Monroe gave it their support.

However, as opposition to slavery grew in the Northeast, the South became more and more dependent on slaves. Since colonial times, slaves in the South had cultivated tobacco, rice, cotton, and indigo. After the American Revolution, depression hit the prosperous tobacco industry of Virginia and Maryland. Prices for tobacco dropped, and slave labor became expensive. Many southern leaders, including Thomas Jefferson, hoped that this might mean the end of slavery.

While tobacco was becoming less profitable, however, cotton was becoming more profitable—thanks to the cotton gin and an increase in British demand. Cotton was first grown in South Carolina and Georgia. However, when the War of 1812 pushed cotton prices skyward, farmers hoping to make even greater profits looked for new lands to plant. Cotton spread southwest—to Alabama, Mississippi, and Louisiana.

Wherever cotton spread, slavery followed. And as the demand for cotton continued to rise, so did the demand for slaves. Despite the ban on the African slave trade, Africans were still smuggled into the United States. Meanwhile, a domestic slave trade sprang up, as the Upper South sold slaves to the Deep South.

The driver and field slaves were photographed in the cotton fields of South Carolina in 1860. The living conditions of slaves had changed little since earlier times. The life of field slaves was strictly regulated. They were not even allowed to leave the farm or plantation without a pass.

Free state or territory

Territory closed to slavery

Slave state or territory

THE MISSOURI COMPROMISE

When Congress reopened in December 1819, it took up the touchy issue of Missouri's statehood. At that time, there were 22 states in the Union—11 slave and 11 free. If Missouri entered the Union as a slave state, the balance would be destroyed. Congress, claimed the northeasterners, had the constitutional right to forbid slavery in Missouri.

Southerners replied that Congress did not have the right to restrict a state's actions. They too were worried about political power. Even with the Three-fifths Compromise, the slave states had only 81 votes in the House compared to 105 for the free states.

Furthermore, the population of the free states was growing faster than that of the slave states. The South did have an equal vote in the Senate, but if Missouri entered the Union as a free state, that balance would be destroyed.

The words that were flung back and forth were so fiery that Henry Clay feared the Union was threatened. Under his guidance, a compromise was finally worked out in March 1820. The people of Maine had recently asked for statehood. So Maine was admitted to the Union as a free state and Missouri as a slave state. Thus the balance of free and slave states was retained. In addition, slavery was "forever prohibited" from the rest of the Louisiana Purchase north of latitude 36° 30'. This latitude line was the southern boundary of Missouri.

The Missouri Compromise was generally accepted in both slaveholding and free states. Northerners were pleased that most of the lands in the Louisiana Purchase could never be made into slave states. Southerners thought that there was little chance for slavery to develop there anyway, since they believed the land was barren prairie unsuitable for growing cotton. But in the North and the South, *sectionalism*, or devotion to a section's interests, was not buried with the compromise. The balance between slave and free states would have to be carefully maintained.

President Monroe signed the compromise after talking to Secretary of State John Quincy Adams. Yet Adams felt uneasy, and confided in his diary:

> I have favored the Missouri Compromise, believing it to be all that could be effected under the present Constitution and from extreme unwillingness to put the Union at hazard. But perhaps it would have been a wiser as well as bolder course to have persisted in the restriction upon Missouri, till it should have terminated in a convention of the states to revise the Constitution. . . . If the Union must be dissolved, slavery is precisely the question upon which it ought to break. For the present, however, this contest is laid asleep.

SECTION REVIEW

1. What was the status of the Federalist party after Monroe's election?

2. How did the decisions of the Supreme Court under Chief Justice Marshall affect federal and state powers in the case of *Dartmouth College* v. *Woodward*? In the case of *McCulloch* v. *Maryland*? In the case of *Gibbons* v. *Ogden*?

3. (a) How did crop failures in Europe affect agriculture, land values, and credit in the United States? (b) How did revived crop production in Europe affect American exports, farmers, and speculators?

4. (a) What action by the national bank contributed to the Panic of 1819? (b) What did the federal government do during the depression that followed?

5. How did statehood for Missouri threaten the balance of political power in the United States Congress?

6. List the terms of the Missouri Compromise.

POSTWAR DIPLOMACY

READ TO FIND OUT

— how the United States and Britain resolved boundary disputes.

— how problems concerning Spanish Florida were resolved.

— how the Monroe Doctrine expressed America's independence from Europe.

While the United States went through economic trials and was divided over statehood for Missouri, President Monroe concentrated on foreign affairs. Monroe had a valuable aide in Secretary of State John Quincy Adams. The son of the second president, Adams had served as foreign minister to four different countries and was a member of the peace talks at Ghent.

ANGLO-AMERICAN TREATIES

In the War of 1812 the United States had rewon its independence. From that time on, Great Britain accepted the United States as a nation. For its part, the United States gradually came to accept Canada as a permanent part of the British Empire.

In 1817 Britain's minister to the United States, Charles Bagot, worked out a treaty with Richard Rush, who was acting as secretary of state until John Quincy Adams arrived from London. In the Rush-Bagot Agreement, the two nations limited their ships and weapons on the Great Lakes and agreed to build no more warships there. The treaty became the basis for later disarming the entire frontier between Canada and the United States.

A year later, in the Convention of 1818, Britain and the United States settled some issues left unresolved by the Treaty of Ghent. Americans were permitted to fish in Canadian waters off the coast of Newfoundland. Also, the boundary line between the United States and Canada was drawn farther westward, setting the northern limit of the Louisiana Purchase. The boundary, fixed at the 49th parallel, ran from the Lake of the Woods in what is now Minnesota to the crest of the Rocky Mountains.

Beyond that point was the vast region of Oregon—west of the Rockies, north of Spanish California, and south of Russian Alaska. Since the 1790s the United States, Britain, and Spain had claimed Oregon. Ignoring the Spanish claim, Britain and the United States also agreed in 1818 to occupy Oregon jointly for ten years. Later, the joint occupation was renewed for an unlimited time.

The Hudson's Bay Company of London established Fort Vancouver as a fur trading post. Competition among commercial hunters led to conflicting land claims in the Northwest. America's claims were based partly on the voyage, in 1791, of the trading ship, *Columbia*.

The United States in 1822

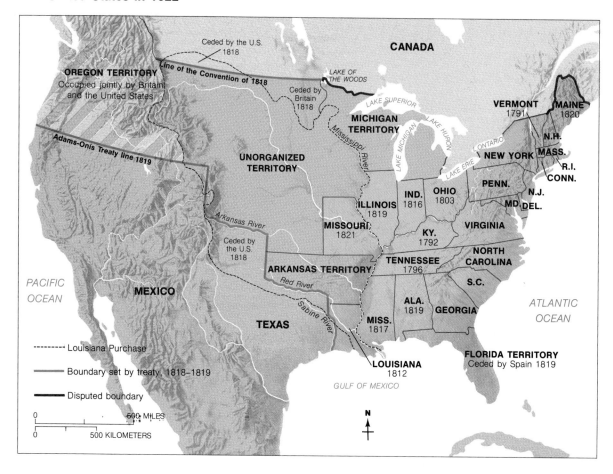

The United States in 1822

Ceded by the U.S. 1818
CANADA
OREGON TERRITORY
Occupied jointly by Britain and the United States
Line of the Convention of 1818
LAKE OF THE WOODS
Ceded by Britain 1818
VERMONT 1791
MAINE 1820
Adams-Onís Treaty line 1819
MICHIGAN TERRITORY
LAKE SUPERIOR
LAKE HURON
N.H.
MASS.
R.I.
CONN.
UNORGANIZED TERRITORY
LAKE MICHIGAN
LAKE ONTARIO
NEW YORK
Mississippi River
LAKE ERIE
PENN.
N.J.
IND. 1816
OHIO 1803
MD DEL.
ILLINOIS 1819
MISSOURI 1821
Arkansas River
VIRGINIA
KY. 1792
Ceded by the U.S. 1818
TENNESSEE 1796
NORTH CAROLINA
ARKANSAS TERRITORY
Red River
S.C.
PACIFIC OCEAN
MEXICO
ALA. 1819
GEORGIA
ATLANTIC OCEAN
Sabine River
MISS. 1817
TEXAS
-------- Louisiana Purchase
LOUISIANA 1812
FLORIDA TERRITORY
Ceded by Spain 1819
Boundary set by treaty, 1818–1819
GULF OF MEXICO
Disputed boundary
0   500 MILES
0   500 KILOMETERS
N

THE ADAMS-ONÍS TREATY

With harmony established between the United States and Britain, Monroe turned to another long-standing problem—Spanish Florida. Since 1793, Spain had been too involved in the Napoleonic Wars to watch over Florida. Florida's Seminole Indians and American settlers in neighboring Georgia often raided each other across the border. At the same time, Florida was a haven for runaway slaves from Georgia. Angered by the raids and the loss of slaves, Georgians demanded government action.

Jefferson tried to buy Florida, which was actually divided into East and West Florida. He failed. His successor, James Madison, used more forceful diplomacy. Between 1810 and 1813, the United States annexed West Florida. Busy in Europe and declining in power, Spain could only protest.

When James Monroe took office, he and John Quincy Adams tried both Jefferson's and Madison's

approaches. In December 1817 Adams and Spanish minister Don Luis de Onís (ō-NEES) began talks on the fate of Spanish Florida. At the same time, Monroe tried to end the conflicts between the Seminole and the Georgians. He sent General Andrew Jackson—the hero of New Orleans—into Florida to pursue the Seminole bands.

While Adams and Onís talked in Washington, the headstrong Jackson and his force marched into Florida. They seized the Spanish fort of St. Marks, and captured the Spanish colony's capital of Pensacola. Adams, whose talks with Onís had been unsuccessful, saw that with Florida in American hands his bargaining position was much stronger.

Spain realized it could not hold Florida and decided to give it up, hoping to obtain something in return. In the Adams-Onís Treaty of 1819 Spain gave both East and West Florida to the United States, and renounced its claim to Oregon. In return, the United States agreed to pay up to $5

Revolution in Latin America 1804-1825

When Latin American colonies revolted against Spain, Henry Clay led the movement to grant recognition to the new governments. He and others looked forward to an expanding trade with Latin America. The United States was the first nation to recognize the independence of Latin American nations.

million of the claims Americans had made against Spain for the border raids. The United States also gave up its claim to Texas, which it had considered part of the Louisiana Purchase.

With the treaty, the United States reached its longtime goal of acquiring all land east of the Mississippi. The day the treaty was signed, Adams noted in his diary, was "the most important day of my life."

THE MONROE DOCTRINE

By 1819 Spain had lost not only Florida but also most of its empire in the Western Hemisphere. When Spain became a battlefield during the Napoleonic Wars, it lost control of its restless colonies in Latin America. After the war Spain tried to put its empire back in order, but rebellion broke out from Mexico to Argentina.

People in the United States watched these revolutions with a good deal of sympathy. Most European rulers were not as sympathetic. In 1822 France, where the monarchy had been restored, joined Prussia, Austria, and Russia in the Quadruple Alliance. They planned to crush any revolutions in Europe, and talked of French aid to Spain to help recover its colonies.

This alliance worried Britain. In the years since Napoleon's final defeat, British trade with the new Latin American nations had flourished. If Spain regained its empire or if France claimed it, Britain would lose this trade. Determined to prevent that, Britain approached the United States and proposed a joint warning to Europeans to stay out of Latin America.

Britain's proposal came at a time when Secretary of State Adams was already worried about European activity in the Western Hemisphere. In 1821 Russia enlarged its claim on the Pacific Coast south into Oregon.

The Russian and French threats in the Americas prompted Monroe and Adams to consider carefully the British proposal of joint action. However, they finally decided that the United States should act alone.

Monroe's announcement of United States foreign policy in December 1823 became known as the Monroe Doctrine. However, it bore the strong imprint of Adams, who wrote part of it. As secretary of state, Adams continually strived to make the United States a strong nation, separate from Europe. The Monroe Doctrine set forth that principle—and included the entire Western Hemisphere.

"The American continents," the doctrine stated, "by the free and independent condition which they have assumed and maintained, are henceforth not to be considered as subjects for future colonization by any European powers." The doctrine also warned European nations not to impose their system of government in any part of the Western Hemisphere.

For its part, the United States vowed to continue its long-time policy toward Europe. It would not interfere in European affairs or with existing European colonies in the Americas. Finally, the doctrine warned Europe to let alone the newly independent nations in Latin America.

Now that the United States had so firmly declared its foreign policy, Adams turned to the Rus-

St. Michael's Cathedral was built when Sitka, Alaska, was the center of Russia's fur trade in America. The Russians founded Sitka, originally called New Archangel, in 1799.

sian boundary claim. Earlier, the czar had refused to discuss it. By April 1824, however, the Russians changed course and agreed to withdraw their claim.

SECTION REVIEW

1. Identify the following: Charles Bagot, Richard Rush, Don Luis de Onís, the Quadruple Alliance.

2. What experience did Secretary of State John Quincy Adams bring to politics and foreign affairs?

3. What territorial issues were resolved by the United States and Britain in the Rush-Bagot Treaty? In the Convention of 1818?

4. (a) What problem existed between Georgia and Spanish Florida? (b) What two steps did Monroe take to resolve the problem?

5. What did the United States gain through the Adams-Onís Treaty?

6. Describe what interest each of these countries had in the Western Hemisphere in 1819: Spain, France, Russia.

7. Why did Britain propose that other European nations be warned to stay out of Latin America?

8. What principle of foreign policy did the Monroe Doctrine declare?

THE JOHN QUINCY ADAMS YEARS

READ TO FIND OUT

— how John Quincy Adams was elected president in 1824.

— why Adams's administration encountered problems.

— how Andrew Jackson and the Democratic Republican party came to power in 1828.

During the early postwar years America basked in a spirit of unity. Then, suddenly, the Panic of 1819 jolted the nation. The spirit of unity sank beneath the gloom of the depression.

There was only one party that could take credit or blame for all this—the Republicans. By 1824 it seemed that everyone was a Republican, and yet party unity, like national unity, was tattered. Republican voices were raised in favor of rival candidates, and the candidates represented different regions of the country.

THE ELECTION OF 1824

As in the past, Republicans met in caucus to choose a candidate. They nominated Secretary of the Treasury William H. Crawford of Georgia, who was supposedly Thomas Jefferson's choice. However, Crawford was in ill health and did not have strong backing. Only a third of the Republicans had attended the caucus. They, like many Americans, considered the caucus an undemocratic way to choose a presidential candidate.

Secretary of War John C. Calhoun led the attack on the caucus and announced that he would run. Later, he changed his mind and ran successfully for vice-president. A Boston meeting nominated Secretary of State John Quincy Adams, and New England rallied behind him. The Kentucky legislature nominated Henry Clay, Speaker of the House of Representatives. "Gallant Harry of the West," as Clay was known, became the choice of many western states.

The daguerrotype of John Quincy Adams was taken in 1848, the year of his death. After his term as president, Adams served as a representative to Congress for 17 years.

As early as 1822, the Tennessee legislature nominated United States Senator Andrew Jackson for president. Jackson's political views were unknown, but he was the popular hero of the Battle of New Orleans, and he was independent. The Southwest was Jackson territory, but support for him arose in other regions. In Pennsylvania the people forced the Republican convention to endorse him for president. In Ohio a visitor wrote, "Strange! Wild! Infatuated! All for Jackson! . . . It is like an influenza."

Such strong support brought Jackson a majority of the popular vote and 99 electoral votes. Adams was second with 84, Crawford third with 41, and Clay fourth with 37. But no candidate had a majority of the electoral college votes. This deadlock sent the election, according to the Constitution, to the House of Representatives. Each state could cast one vote for one of the three leading candidates.

Although Clay was eliminated from the contest, he still had great influence. Since Adams shared his beliefs and supported the American System, Clay persuaded Kentucky, Ohio, and Missouri to back the New Englander. When the House voted, Adams

JOHN JAMES AUDUBON
ARTIST OF AMERICAN WILDLIFE

"My best friends solemnly regard me as a madman," wrote John Audubon when he decided to devote his life to drawing birds. Even as a child, his passion had been nature. Born in Haiti in 1785, Audubon had grown up in France. "Almost every day, instead of going to school . . . I usually made for the fields," he remembered. There he collected "birds' nests, birds' eggs, curious lichens, flowers of all sorts, and even pebbles." He also discovered that he could draw with extraordinary skill.

When he was eighteen, Audubon immigrated to the United States. He married and settled in the frontier village of Louisville, Kentucky, where he opened a store. However, Audubon was more interested in roaming the woods to draw birds than tending to business or his growing family.

When he was thirty-five, Audubon made his decision. He quit his job to create a book of life-size drawings of American birds. He journeyed from the Florida swamps to the Texas plains and to the northern forests in search of specimens. At night he often slept in the open air, rolled in a buffalo robe.

Audubon was fifty-four and his hair gray when he finished his monumental *Birds of America* in 1839. It was a masterpiece. Its 435 color plates were both accurate and stunningly beautiful.

After years of poverty, Audubon found himself rich and famous. Yet, he was not ready to retire. Working 14 hours a day, he began a series of drawings of American animals. But his health failed. He died in 1851, surrounded by the wildlife he had collected and still longed to preserve on paper.

won 13 states, Jackson won 7, and Crawford won 4. John Quincy Adams became president, thanks in part to Clay's help.

The results led John Randolph of Virginia to declare, "It was impossible to win the game, . . . the cards were packed." Jackson and his followers came to agree. Soon after the election, Adams appointed Clay secretary of state, a position that traditionally was a stepping stone to the presidency. Outraged Jackson supporters cried "bargain and corruption." Furious, Jackson resigned from the Senate in 1825 to prepare for the next presidential election.

THE ADAMS ADMINISTRATION

Adams's presidency was stormy from the beginning. He had been elected by the smallest of margins, and admitted that two thirds of the people were unhappy with the result.

Also, Adams's program was out of step with the times. He and his supporters, now calling themselves National Republicans, believed in a strong central government that had broad powers. But Americans' mood was to limit, not expand, the federal government. Adams's strongest opposition came from Jackson's supporters. They called themselves Democratic Republicans to emphasize their bond with the common people. For four years they blocked the President's program in Congress.

THE ELECTION OF 1828

Adams's four-year term was wracked with conflict and failure. Even Vice-President John Calhoun, who had become a strong supporter of states' rights, challenged the President's program. Still, in 1828 the National Republican Convention nominated Adams for a second term. Secretary of the Treasury Richard Rush of Pennsylvania became his running mate.

Jackson and his Democratic Republicans had been busily campaigning since the election of 1824. In the congressional elections of 1826, the Democratic Republicans won control of both houses of Congress and of a majority of state governments. As the presidential contest sharpened, the party took no clear-cut stands on major issues such as the tariff, land policy, and internal improvements. Instead, it stood for change from Adams and offered Andrew Jackson, military hero and friend of the people. Jackson's running mate was John Calhoun.

By 1828 the two parties were locked in a bitter contest of name-calling not seen since the election of 1800. Both went directly to the people, organizing huge rallies and sending officials on campaign tours.

The fierce rivalry fired up people's interest. Voter turnout in 1828 was double that of 1824. Jackson and Calhoun won soundly, taking both the popular vote and the electoral vote. The West, the South, New York, and Pennsylvania gave Jackson 178 votes in the electoral college. Adams gained 83, carrying all of New England, New Jersey, Delaware, and Maryland. Adams had expected the defeat, but it was still a bitter end to his labors for his country. He left Washington, convinced that he would never return to public office.

John Quincy Adams had been elected in 1824 in the midst of Republican discord. After the election of 1824, the Republicans split apart, creating new parties and new groups. Thus the Republican party of Thomas Jefferson died. As the party was dying, the era of the old fighters for independence was also drawing to a close.

July 4, 1826 was a special Independence Day. It was the fiftieth anniversary of the Declaration of

The Elections of 1824 and 1828

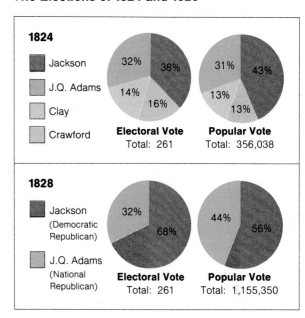

Independence. At Monticello, his Virginia plantation, Thomas Jefferson lay dying. Hundreds of miles away in Quincy, Massachusetts, John Adams was also dying. The second and third presidents of the United States had become fast friends in their old age and had kept in touch by letter. Both had hoped very much to live until this special Fourth of July.

As dawn broke on the Fourth, Jefferson asked a friend who was attending him, "This is the Fourth?" The friend said yes and Jefferson murmured "Just as I wished." In Massachusetts, Adams was asked to join the day's celebration. Too ill to attend, he did send a toast: "Independence forever!" Both men died that day, their hopes fulfilled.

SECTION REVIEW

1. List the presidential candidates in the election of 1824.

2. How was the president finally elected in 1824?

3. Why did Andrew Jackson resign from the Senate in 1825?

4. Why was Adams's presidency a failure?

5. (a) How did the rival parties campaign in the election of 1828? (b) By what margin did Jackson win?

SUMMARY

As national pride revived after the War of 1812, President Madison tried to improve the economy. The national bank was reestablished to regulate funds, currency, and credit. The Tariff of 1816 attempted to protect American industries from foreign competition. Transportation improved as the states built miles of roads and canals.

The Industrial Revolution reached the United States. Borrowing ideas from Britain, Americans built factories and machines to mass produce textiles. Manufacturers found laborers among the women and children of New England. The manufacturers raised capital by forming corporations and selling stock to investors.

Farmers in the West and South began specializing in cash crops to ship to the East and to Europe. The South relied on northern factories for farm machinery and clothing. The North became more industrialized as mills, ironworks, and machine shops multiplied. With the invention of the steamboat, transportation expanded and western settlements grew into cities.

Beginning in 1817, James Monroe's administration faced serious domestic and foreign problems. When the economy collapsed after a period of reckless expansion, the federal government tightened restrictions on state banks. The result was panic and depression.

Then, in 1819, the balance of power between free states and slave states was threatened by Missouri's application for statehood. Congress responded by passing the Missouri Compromise.

Through treaties Monroe settled territorial issues with Britain and gained Florida from Spain. To halt European countries from further colonizing the Western Hemisphere, Monroe issued the Monroe Doctrine.

The election of 1824 marked the decline of the Republican party. Andrew Jackson and John Quincy Adams were the leading candidates. When neither won a majority in the electoral college, the House elected Adams. An unpopular president, Adams failed to win support for his programs. Jackson and the Democratic Republicans swept into office in 1828.

CHAPTER REVIEW

1. (a) List the parts of the program known as the American System. (b) How was each part expected to benefit the United States? (c) Which parts were put into effect? Were they successful? Explain. (d) Which parts were rejected? Why?

2. How did each of the following contribute to the Industrial Revolution in the United States? (a) Whitney's muskets (b) water and steam power (c) Slater's textile mill (d) the Boston Manufacturing Company (e) women and children workers

3. (a) How are corporations organized? (b) What advantage do corporations have over individually owned businesses? (c) Why do corporations appeal to investors?

4. Compare the changes that occurred in the North, the South, and the West as a result of the Industrial Revolution.

5. (a) Describe the following Supreme Court cases: *Dartmouth College* v. *Woodward*, *McCulloch* v. *Maryland*, *Gibbons* v. *Ogden*. (b) In what way did the Court's ruling in each case strengthen the power of the federal government?

In 1794 Eli Whitney drew plans for a cotton gin and applied for a patent. That year the South produced 10,000 bales of cotton. By 1825 production had risen to a half-million bales.

Improvements in agriculture, industry, and transportation are represented in Terence Kennedy's "Political Banner." The painting illustrates pride in American achievements.

ISSUES AND IDEAS

1. In 1816 and 1817 Congress debated a protective tariff and internal improvements. (a) As a western farmer, write a letter to your representative in Congress, supporting both proposals. (b) As a southern farmer, write a letter to your representative, opposing both proposals. (c) As a New Englander, write a letter to your representative, expressing your concerns about both proposals.

2. In *McCulloch* v. *Maryland,* Marshall declared that all actions within "the letter and spirit of the Constitution are constitutional." What might have happened in the nation's economic affairs if Marshall had not supported a loose construction of the Constitution? Cite two examples.

SKILLS WORKSHOP

1. *Charts.* Make a chart of events that tended to unify the nation and events that tended to divide the nation between 1815 and 1828. Make two columns—"Nationalism" and "Sectionalism." In each column list economic policies and events, political issues, judicial decisions, and foreign policy.

2. *Timelines.* Do research, and make a timeline of inventions and developments that changed American industry, agriculture, and transportation between 1790 and 1840. Briefly describe each event on the timeline.

PAST AND PRESENT

1. In the early 1800s the Supreme Court, under Chief Justice Marshall, asserted its right to overturn state actions that it considered unconstitutional. Do research, and give two other examples of the Supreme Court's use of this power. Briefly describe the cases and the rulings.

2. After the War of 1812, the United States gradually began to shift from farming to manufacturing. What advantages of this shift do you see today? What disadvantages? Explain.

6. (a) Explain how land speculation and easy credit contributed to the Panic of 1819. (b) Why was the Bank of the United States blamed for the panic and depression that followed? (c) How did the depression affect Americans' feelings toward the government?

7. (a) Why did the North favor the Tallmadge amendment to the Missouri statehood bill? (b) How did the spread of cotton affect the South's reaction to the amendment? (c) How did northerners and southerners differ regarding Congress's power to restrict a state's actions?

8. (a) Why did northerners accept the Missouri Compromise? (b) Why did southerners accept the compromise? (c) Why did the compromise fail to resolve permanently differences between the northern and southern sections of the country?

9. Explain how each of the following contributed to the United States' new sense of strength and independence from Europe: Rush-Bagot Agreement, Convention of 1818, Adams-Onís Treaty, the Monroe Doctrine.

10. (a) Why did the United States have only one political party between 1817 and 1824? (b) How did party unity shatter in the election of 1824? (c) How did the election of John Quincy Adams lead to political conflict?

CHAPTER 9

JACKSON AND REFORM

1828–1850

THE ERA OF ANDREW JACKSON
JACKSON AND THE BANK
REFORMING SOCIETY
MOVEMENTS FOR PEOPLE'S RIGHTS

In 1850 a few women began wearing bloomers, a loose short dress worn over full trousers. When Elizabeth Cady Stanton put on bloomers, her son asked her not to come to his school in "the short dress." She replied:

"You do not wish me to visit you in a short dress! Why, my dear child, I have no other. Now suppose you and I were taking a long walk in the fields and I had on three long petticoats. Then suppose a bull should take after us. Why, you, with your arms and legs free, could run like a shot, but I, alas! should fall . . . my petticoats would be caught by the stumps and the briars, and what could I do at the fences? Then you in your agony, when you saw the bull gaining on me, would say, 'Oh! how I wish mother could use her legs as I can!' Now why do you wish me to wear what is uncomfortable, inconvenient, and many times dangerous? I'll tell you why. You do not like to have me laughed at. You must learn not to care for what foolish people say. Such good men as Cousin Gerrit and Mr. Weld will tell you that a short dress is the right kind. So no matter if ignorant silly persons do laugh."

Stanton and other women wanted more than just clothing in which they could run from a bull. They wanted the chance to go to college, to speak out in public, to own property, to vote. Their calls for change stirred up a movement for women's rights. The time was right, for the United States between the 1820s and 1850s was alive with the spirit of reform. The crusade for women's rights grew with other crusades—for better schools, against alcohol, and most of all, to abolish slavery.

While some people tried to perfect society, others tackled politics. This grass-roots democracy spread like wildfire. In 1828 the democratic spirit swept the land, when a hero of the people became president. Andrew Jackson suited the times.

from a western state. "People from the West and South seemed to have thrown themselves on the North and overwhelmed it," one observer wrote. "Everyone seemed bent on the glory of shaking the President's hand."

Not everyone, however, was thrilled by Andrew Jackson. With his election, the West was now a political force to be reckoned with. Some people also worried about what to expect from this westerner. Senator Daniel Webster of Massachusetts jotted a note to friends:

> Nobody knows what he will do when he does come. . . .
> My opinion is
> That when he comes, he will bring a breeze with him.
> Which way it will blow I cannot tell . . . .
> My *fear* is stronger than my *hope*.

THE DEMOCRATIC SPIRIT OF THE TIMES

The breeze that worried Webster was the spirit of democracy that was sweeping the country. People were demanding—and winning—greater participation in government than ever before.

Part of this change was in **suffrage**, or the right to vote. In the early 1800s only New Hampshire, Vermont, New Jersey, and Maryland allowed all adult white males to vote. Then, after the War of 1812, the democratic momentum increased. New states—Indiana, Illinois, Alabama, Missouri, and Maine—entered the Union with constitutions allowing all white males to vote. Older states, such as Connecticut, Massachusetts, and New York, dropped property qualifications for suffrage.

Most states did not allow women, Indians, and blacks to vote. However, by Jackson's time, most adult white males in the United States could do so. Voter participation rose throughout the 1820s and 1830s and reached a high of 78 percent in 1840.

Other political procedures also were becoming more democratic. In the past, state legislatures had usually chosen the electors who would vote for president. By 1828 the people chose the electors in all but two states. Also, in most parts of the country, people now voted on paper ballots rather than voting openly by voice in front of election officials. However, the colored ballot of each party still identified the vote.

THE ERA OF ANDREW JACKSON

READ TO FIND OUT

— why Andrew Jackson was called the people's president.

— how Indian tribes were moved to the West.

— how the North, South, and West reacted to protective tariffs.

— why the Tariff of 1828 led to conflict over states' rights.

— how the nullification crisis was settled.

It was a raw, blustery day in February 1829. Washington was packed with visitors. They had come to see the arrival of the new president—General Andrew Jackson of Tennessee, the first president

The Duration of Property and Tax Restrictions on Voting   1776–1860

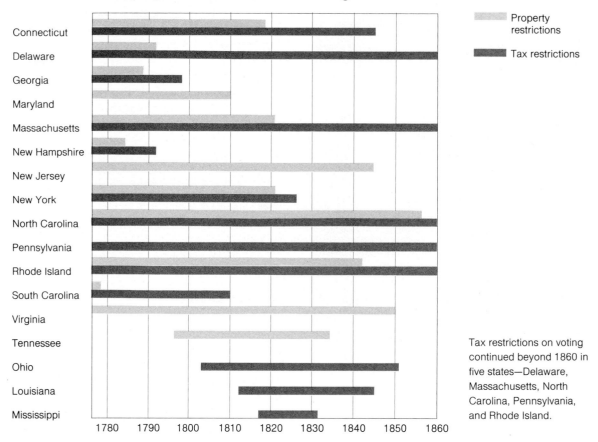

Property restrictions

Tax restrictions

Tax restrictions on voting continued beyond 1860 in five states—Delaware, Massachusetts, North Carolina, Pennsylvania, and Rhode Island.

Since Jefferson's time, presidential candidates had been chosen by congressional leaders at secret party caucuses. In the 1820s people began to condemn the rule of "King Caucus." As a result, by 1832 party delegates met in open, national conventions to nominate candidates for president and vice-president. And political parties began to adopt *platforms*—statements of their beliefs—to lure the growing numbers of voters.

Andrew Jackson's election in 1828 reflected the democratic spirit of the times. Here was a man who had risen above his frontier origins and who lacked a formal education. Yet he became a lawyer, built a prosperous cotton plantation, and served on the Tennessee supreme court and in the United States Congress. He became a military hero fighting the Creek in 1813–1814 and later the Seminole in Spanish-owned Florida. Most impressive of all, he had won the American victory at the Battle of New

Orleans. With Andrew Jackson in the White House, the West was now a political force that would require special reckoning.

The story of Jackson's success seemed to many the American dream come true. His election, a Kentucky editor declared, was "a proud day for the *people*—General Jackson is *their* own president." So the common people turned his inauguration into their own party. It did not matter that they were not invited to the White House reception. They stormed the building—yelling, crowding, and drinking toasts. The President, reported a bystander, was "almost torn to pieces by the people in their eagerness to shake hands."

Some people fretted over the "reign of 'King Mob.'" Others celebrated the progress of democracy. "It was the People's day," one woman declared, "and the People's President and the People would rule."

THE SPOILS SYSTEM

Andrew Jackson demanded frank opinions from his advisors and then, he said, "I do precisely what I think just and right." Admirers of Jackson's strong will called him "Old Hickory." His enemies came to call him "King Andrew."

Jackson used the executive office as no other president had. Defying tradition, he rarely met with his cabinet. Instead, he relied on a handful of unofficial advisors, whom critics of Jackson called the "Kitchen Cabinet."

Jackson also removed almost 20 percent of all government officeholders and filled their jobs with his supporters. Senator William L. Marcy of New York defended this action. "To the victor," he declared, "belong the spoils of the enemy." Critics promptly called this practice the **spoils system**. However, Jackson believed that any intelligent citizen was fit to hold public office. Besides, he argued, "rotation in office" involved more people in government.

Andrew Jackson was forty-seven years old when this charcoal sketch was drawn. Thomas Sully, a leading portrait painter, captured the rugged strength of America's new hero.

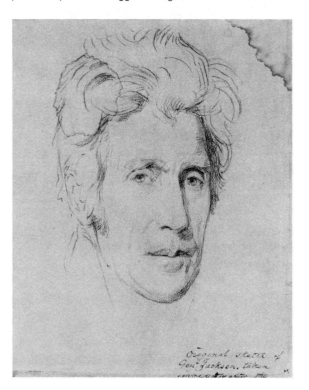

THE INDIAN REMOVAL ACT

In 1830 Jackson took the offensive against the Indians of the South. As Americans pushed westward, Indian tribes in their path generally retreated or were driven to resettle on the Great Plains. But five tribes—the Cherokee, Creek, Choctaw, Chickasaw, and Seminole—clung to their ancestral lands in the Southeast.

These Indians became known as the Five Civilized Tribes. They accepted the teachings of white missionaries, setting up schools, Christian churches, and even plantations. One Cherokee, Sequoyah, developed an alphabet so his tribe could write down and preserve its history. Using Sequoyah's alphabet, the Cherokee published their own books and newspapers.

To many whites, the five tribes were a barrier to expansion. Some of the most valuable farmland in the Southeast was in Indian hands, and settlers pressed state governments to take it over. The pressure became more intense in 1829 when gold was discovered on Cherokee land. Jackson came up with a solution, which had been proposed earlier by Presidents James Monroe and John Quincy Adams.

Jackson believed that the Indians would be better off separated from whites, and suggested removing the tribes to lands west of the Mississippi River. Americans had little interest in those lands, which were considered too arid for farming. Congress responded with the Indian Removal Act of 1830. This act gave the president power to exchange land west of the Mississippi for eastern lands held by Indians. Later, in 1834, Congress set up a special Indian territory in the Arkansas Territory.

INDIAN REMOVAL

Throughout the 1830s, Jackson's administration forced the Indians to sign treaties ceding, or giving up, their lands. In the winter of 1831 the first band of migrants, the Choctaw, began the long journey westward. Without experience in such matters, the government did not make adequate plans for the migration. In addition, government agents were often indifferent to Indian needs. So the Choctaw made the journey without warm clothing in freezing temperatures and heavy snows.

Jackson hoped that all the Indians would move voluntarily, but many resisted. The Cherokee felt

Robert Lindeux painted "The Trail of Tears" about a hundred years after the journey. In autumn of 1838, over 15,000 Cherokees started westward, most of them on foot.

that they were protected by earlier treaties with the federal government. These treaties recognized the Cherokee as a nation within Georgia with their own laws and lands. The Cherokee tried to further protect themselves in 1828 by writing a constitution that set up an independent Cherokee Nation within Georgia. Georgia was bound to honor the federal treaties, but refused to recognize the Cherokee nation.

Under pressure from Georgia to sell their land, the Cherokee turned to the United States Supreme Court for protection. The Court upheld the Cherokee land claim in two decisions. Jackson, however, would not enforce the Court's ruling. With no place left to appeal, the Cherokee ceded their eastern lands to the United States in 1835. Three years later, they were forced to set out for the West.

Jackson placed General Winfield Scott in charge of the Cherokee removal. Scott asked the troops to be kind, but they rarely were. One soldier wrote, "I saw the helpless Cherokee arrested and dragged from their homes. In the chill of a drizzling rain, I saw them loaded like cattle or sheep on 645 wagons." Nearly one fourth of the tribe died on the trail. Many of the survivors arrived on their new lands sick and weak. To the Cherokee, the journey became known as "the Trail of Tears."

A few tribes fought removal with weapons, not law. In 1832 a group of Sauk and Fox Indians, led by Chief Black Hawk, returned from Iowa to their old lands in Illinois and the Wisconsin area to plant corn. When they refused to leave, army troops pur-

Four days after the sittings for his portrait ended, Osceola died, dressed in this costume. George Catlin's portraits are a treasured memorial to the American Indian.

sued them to Bad Axe River in southern Wisconsin. Few Indians escaped alive. As punishment for this Black Hawk War, the Sauk and the Fox were forced to cede eastern Iowa to the United States.

In Florida the Seminole, led by Chief Osceola (os-ee-Ō-lah), refused to move west and retreated

Indian Removal 1830-1850

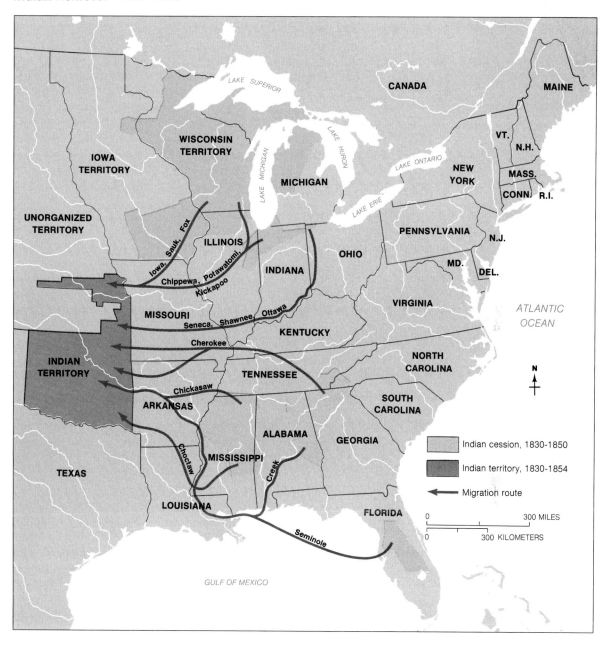

The Indians of Georgia and Florida were not the only ones to be moved west of the Mississippi between 1830 and 1850. Numerous northern tribes that also migrated offered less resistance. Many of them had already had to leave their original homelands.

into the Everglades in 1835. Osceola was captured by army troops in 1837, but the fierce struggle continued for seven years. In the end, the Seminole were forced to surrender and were moved to Oklahoma. Hundreds, however, avoided capture and continued to live in the swamps.

By the early 1840s the Indian removal was completed. The tribes were promised that the western lands would be theirs "as long as the grass grows, or water runs." But even as the Indians were getting settled on their new lands, pioneers were crossing the Mississippi.

Delegates from the Pawnee, Ponca, Potawotomi, Sauk, and Fox tribes posed for this photograph, taken at the South Portico of the White House in 1857.

Much southern cotton was sold in Britain, and southerners bought manufactured British goods in return. But the Tariff of 1816 added about 25 percent to the prices of certain goods, making them expensive. Angry southerners argued that the tariff protected the manufacturing North at the expense of the agricultural South. The Constitution, they declared, provided no authority for such favoritism.

Eight years later, Congress narrowly passed another tariff with support from northern and western states. This Tariff of 1824 raised average duties to 37 percent. Still, northerners and westerners cried out for more protection for their products against British competition. Congress responded in 1828 with another tariff.

The Tariff of 1828 raised average duties to an all-time high of 45 percent. Cotton states angrily labeled it the "Tariff of Abominations." Georgia, Mississippi, Virginia, and South Carolina passed resolutions attacking the tariff as "unconstitutional, oppressive, and unjust."

CALHOUN'S DOCTRINE OF NULLIFICATION

South Carolina also issued a report, the "South Carolina Exposition and Protest." It was secretly written by Vice-President Calhoun, now an outright opponent of tariffs. The report gave the most full blown argument for states' rights yet to appear.

The Constitution, Calhoun maintained, was a compact, or agreement, among sovereign, or independent, states to form the Union. The states delegated only limited powers to the federal government, so only they could judge whether the government exceeded those powers. If a state judged an act of Congress to be unconstitutional, it could nullify, or refuse to enforce, the act within its borders. The national government must then withdraw its act, unless three fourths of the states amended the Constitution to grant it such power.

The government, Calhoun declared, had exceeded its power with the tariff. It had the power to tax only to raise revenue, not to purposely protect certain interests or groups. Protective tariffs, in effect, were an extra tax upon the people of the South to benefit the North. And Calhoun called on the national government to obey the Constitution or South Carolina would use its right of nullification.

Jackson's treatment of the Indians was condemned by some religious groups, such as the Quakers and Methodists. But most people supported Jackson's Indian policy. They also approved his firm action when conflict over the tariff threatened national unity.

CONFLICT OVER THE TARIFF

In 1827 an angry crowd gathered in Columbia, South Carolina. One speaker raised the question that burned in everyone's mind. "Is it worth our while," he asked, "to continue this Union of States, where the North demands to be our masters and we are required to be their tributaries?"

The issue was the series of protective tariffs that the government had passed on imported goods. Jackson and Vice-President Calhoun, who was from South Carolina, were caught in the conflict. Calhoun was one of the few southerners who had supported the tariff passed in 1816 to protect American industry from British competition. However, southern states had not developed industry as he had hoped. When depression struck the country in 1819, the price of cotton dropped and never fully recovered.

Agriculture and Industry 1840

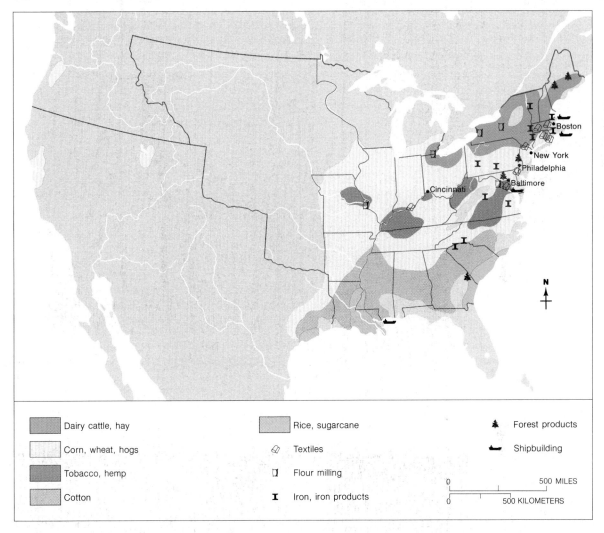

Dairy cattle, hay	Rice, sugarcane	Forest products
Corn, wheat, hogs	Textiles	Shipbuilding
Tobacco, hemp	Flour milling	
Cotton	Iron, iron products	

0 — 500 MILES
0 — 500 KILOMETERS

In 1840 the United States was primarily an agricultural nation. Nearly 70 percent of the nation's labor force worked on farms. However, rapid growth was taking place in industry. Products were no longer made by artisans working at home, but by workers in factories. By 1840 more goods were produced in mills and factories than in home workshops.

THE UNION DEFENDED

The "South Carolina Exposition and Protest" was published in December 1828, just after the presidential election. Southerners hoped that Jackson, a cotton planter himself, would work to reduce the tariff. But Jackson's first message to Congress said little of tariff reform and nothing about South Carolina's protest.

The Senate, however, paid close attention to Calhoun's doctrine of nullification. In January 1830 a Senate discussion on public land turned into a fierce debate on the Union when Robert Y. Hayne of South Carolina proclaimed the sovereignty of the states. Daniel Webster, a strong nationalist from Massachusetts, rose to answer him

For six days, Webster and Hayne debated the powers of state and federal governments. Webster forcefully defended the Union. The states, he declared in his most famous speech, did not create the government—the people made it.

Like Webster, Jackson saw nullification as a threat to the Union. In April he was invited to a dinner celebrating Jefferson's birthday. Knowing that Hayne, Calhoun, and others supporting states' rights would be there, he wrote a toast beforehand. He went prepared for "the field of battle" rather than a celebration.

Twenty-four toasts were made at the dinner, many to states' rights. Then Jackson stood and offered his toast: "Our federal Union. It must be preserved." There was a sudden silence. Calhoun raised his glass next. "The Union," he challenged, "next to our liberty, most dear. May we always remember that it can only be preserved by distributing equally the benefits and burdens of the Union." This dinner further loosened the weak political tie between Jackson and Calhoun.

★ ★ ★ ★ ★ ★ ★ CRITICAL ISSUES ★ ★ ★ ★ ★ ★ ★ ★ ★ ★ ★

The daguerreotype was at the height of its popularity in America when Daniel Webster posed for camera operators. His fame as champion of the Union was long established.

In 1832 South Carolina adopted the Ordinance of Nullification against tariff laws. Senator Robert Y. Hayne then resigned from the Senate to become governor of his state.

STATES' RIGHTS
THE GREAT DEBATE

On January 19, 1830, Robert Y. Hayne of South Carolina, one of the ablest debaters in the Senate, rose to speak. The question at hand was the sale of public lands on the frontier. Hayne supported the West's position on the issue. Then, almost as an aside, he went on to condemn the growth of federal power. "I am one of those who believe the very life of our system is the independence of the states," he declared. "I am opposed, therefore, in any shape, to all unnecessary extension of the power or the influence . . . of the Union over the states."

As Hayne spoke, Senator Daniel Webster of Massachusetts strolled through the Senate chamber. Alarmed by Hayne's words, he leaned against a pillar to listen. Finally, he sat down to hear every word. The next day Webster took the floor to answer Hayne. It was the beginning of one of the most famous debates in Senate history.

The question of states' rights—whether the states or the federal government had final authority—was not new. When Congress passed the Sedition Act in 1798, many Americans believed that it violated the right to free speech guaranteed in the Bill of Rights. In resolutions written by Thomas Jefferson, the Kentucky legislature declared the act unconstitutional. A state, wrote Jefferson, could disobey a federal law that violated its rights under the Constitution. During the War of 1812, New Englanders also questioned federal power. At the Hartford Convention, some even threatened to secede from the Union if the government continued a war they opposed. Now, in 1830, the southern states were most concerned with the question. They were disturbed because a northern majority in Congress had pushed through a tariff bill they hated but were forced to obey.

Webster began his answer to Hayne by discussing the issue of public lands. Then he skillfully used Hayne's brief remarks on federal power to change the subject. The real question, Webster said, was not the sale of public lands in the West, but the fate of the Union. To him, the Union was "essential to the

THE NULLIFICATION CRISIS

For two years South Carolina simmered with talk of nullification. Meanwhile, Jackson called for a revision of the tariff. In July 1832 Congress passed a new, lower tariff. Jackson signed it into law, sure that it would end southern discontent.

The lower tariff, however, did not satisfy the people of South Carolina. Protest meetings shook the state, and a convention was called in November.

The convention quickly adopted an ordinance, or a law, of nullification, declaring the tariffs of 1828 and 1832 null and void.

The ordinance banned the collection of duties in South Carolina after February 1, 1833. It also declared that the state would secede from the Union if the federal government forced South Carolina to collect the duties. To back the ordinance, the legislature voted money to buy arms and called for volunteers.

★ ★

prosperity and safety of the States." Hayne's questions about federal power had bothered him. Did Hayne think the Union was a temporary thing? Was it to exist only "while it suits local and temporary purposes to preserve it; and to be sundered whenever it shall be found to thwart such purposes?"

Over the next few days, Hayne answered Webster in several brilliant speeches. If, he asked Webster, northern members of Congress valued the Union so much, why had they passed a tariff that had brought "ruin and devastation" to the South? Was the South always to be a minority upon whom Congress forced its will? "Is this the spirit in which this Government is to be administered?" he asked, his voice ringing with emotion. "If so," he warned, "the seeds of dissolution are already sown, and our children will reap the bitter fruit."

To Hayne, the Union was a compact, an agreement among independent states. Each state, he argued, remained sovereign. Each could interpret the Constitution for itself and set aside any national law that violated its rights. To allow the federal government to interpret its own laws would be tyranny.

As Hayne spoke, Webster sat nearby, taking careful notes. The next day, impressive in a blue swallow-tailed coat with brass buttons, he began his famous second reply. By now news of the debate had spread. "Everyone is thronging to the Capitol to hear Webster's reply," wrote a Washington woman who attended. To her, the blond and graceful Hayne and the dark-haired, heavyset Webster were like two noble gladiators engaged in a great battle.

With his notes in his hand, Webster began slowly and calmly. Steadily, hour after hour, he built his case. The great question, he said in his rich, deep voice, was who had the right "to decide on the con-

stitutionality or unconstitutionality of the laws." If each state could accept or reject national laws as it pleased, the result would be chaos. The Union would fall apart like "a rope of sand." If there was a conflict between a state and the federal government, Webster declared, it was the Supreme Court, not the state, who should decide the issue.

The United States, he declared, was not a group of independent states, each free to act as it chose. It was a federal union whose real authority was the people. "It is, sir, the people's constitution, the people's Government; made for the people; made by the people; and answerable to the people," he said. If each state demanded sovereignty, the nation would be "rent with civil feuds, or drenched in blood." Webster ended his speech with a moving tribute to the Union: "Liberty *and* Union, now and forever, one and inseparable!"

In the years ahead, countless Fourth of July speakers quoted Webster on the Union. Thousands of schoolchildren, including a lanky frontier lad named Abraham Lincoln, memorized his final words. But many felt that Hayne had the better case. The question of who had the final power, the federal government or the states, was far from settled.

1. How did Hayne view the relationship between the federal government and the states? How did Webster's view differ?

2. Do you think a state should have the right to disobey a federal law it opposes? Why or why not?

3. What are some of the issues today that involve state versus federal power? How do you think they should be decided?

Jackson was outraged, but he moved cautiously. He asked Congress to reduce the tariff again. He also called on the people of South Carolina to reject nullification. "Disunion by armed force is *treason*," he warned. Then he alerted the armed forces.

By January 1833 Calhoun had resigned from the vice-presidency and had become a senator for South Carolina. Soon after, Jackson asked Congress to pass the force bill giving him the power to use the armed forces if necessary to collect duties in South Carolina.

Then Henry Clay broke the deadlock. He proposed a compromise tariff that reduced the duties to a uniform 20 percent over the next 10 years. Calhoun, torn between his native state and his beloved Union, readily accepted. Jackson, too, preferred this peaceful solution.

In early March Congress passed the Tariff of 1833 as well as the Force Act, which Jackson had still demanded. South Carolina accepted the new tariff, but furiously nullified the Force Act. Slowly, cries for secession died out. Calhoun, exhausted, went home to his plantation to recover. However, he feared that "the struggle, so far from being over," had just begun.

SECTION REVIEW

1. Identify the following: Daniel Webster, Kitchen Cabinet, Sequoyah, Trail of Tears, Chief Black Hawk, Chief Osceola, Robert Y. Hayne.

2. Define the following: suffrage, party platform, spoils system, nullification.

3. List four ways that political procedures became more democratic between 1800 and 1840.

4. (a) What did the Cherokee do to protect themselves from the Removal Act of 1830? (b) How did the Sauk and Fox react to the Removal Act? How did the Seminole react?

5. Why did southerners feel that the tariffs of 1816, 1824, and 1828 were unfair to the South?

6. Explain Calhoun's doctrine of nullification as he applied it to the Tariff of 1828.

7. (a) How did South Carolina react to the 1832 tariff? (b) What action did Jackson take in relation to South Carolina?

8. (a) What was Henry Clay's solution to the tariff conflict? (b) Why did his solution work?

JACKSON AND THE BANK

READ TO FIND OUT

— how Jackson destroyed the Bank of the United States.

— why the Whig party was formed.

— how Van Buren became president in 1836.

— how the United States slid into a depression in 1837.

— why Tyler was expelled from the Whig party.

During his first term, Andrew Jackson had fought against the Indians of the Southeast and a defiant South Carolina. Perhaps the most hard-fought battle, however, was the one that dominated much of his second term. Andrew Jackson was at war with the Bank of the United States.

The bank was the brainchild of Alexander Hamilton. First chartered in 1791, it existed until 1811. Later, in 1816, the bank was given a second charter, to run for 20 years. Then came the Panic of 1819, and many people, especially debtors, blamed the bank.

Many of these debtors lived in the West. Later they found a champion against the bank in Senator Thomas Hart Benton of Missouri. "All the flourishing cities of the West are mortgaged to this money power," Benton thundered. "They may be devoured by it at any moment. They are in the jaws of the monster! A lump of butter in the mouth of a dog! One gulp, one swallow, and all is gone!" To many people, the Bank of the United States became known as "the Monster."

THE BANK WAR

The Bank of the United States had great power. Also it was controlled mainly by wealthy eastern investors. Jackson believed that the bank benefited only "the rich and powerful."

Since 1823 financier Nicholas Biddle had run the national bank as its president. Under him, the bank had maintained sound currency and spurred economic growth. Jackson, however, heard stories that the bank had interfered in state politics in the election of 1828. It also loaned money as a favor to influential people, including members of Congress. The stories convinced Jackson that the bank was dangerous and should be destroyed.

Early in 1832 Biddle prepared to defend the bank against Jackson. The bank's charter was due to expire in 1836. Biddle asked Henry Clay and Daniel Webster about the best time to apply for its recharter. Both agreed to introduce immediately a bill in Congress. The 1832 presidential election was in December. Jackson, Clay reasoned, would be forced to approve the bill because a veto would hurt his campaign. In July Congress passed the bank bill.

Clay, however, had now miscalculated. Jackson promptly returned the bill to Congress with a stinging veto message. He swept aside the earlier Supreme Court decision in *McCulloch* v. *Maryland* that the bank was constitutional. To Jackson, the bank was "unauthorized by the Constitution, subversive of the rights of the states, and dangerous to the liberties of the people."

Congress failed to override Jackson's veto of the bill, and the bank became the major issue in the election of 1832. The National Republicans nominated Henry Clay for president and called for the recharter of the bank. The Democrats, as the Democratic Republicans now were called, nominated Jackson for a second term. Martin Van Buren was chosen to run for vice-president. Andrew Jackson campaigned on his record, proudly stressing the bank veto.

Jackson won a stunning victory. He carried 16 of the 24 states, receiving 219 electoral votes to Clay's 49. Jackson saw his reelection as a call from the people to destroy "the Monster."

The bank's charter had four more years to run, but Jackson decided to end its power immediately. However, this was not as easy as he expected. He requested the secretary of the treasury to stop depositing the government's funds in the bank. His treasury secretary opposed the step, so Jackson shuffled his cabinet and chose a new treasury chief. When his new appointee also refused, Jackson finally selected someone who shared his views. In September 1833 the new treasury secretary, Roger B. Taney, announced that government funds would no longer be deposited in the national bank. The money would be placed in private or "pet banks" in major cities.

In this 1836 cartoon General Jackson and aides battle the Bank of the United States—the "Many-Headed Monster." The largest head is Nicholas Biddle, the bank's president.

During the winter and spring of 1833 and 1834, Biddle fought back. He called in the bank's loans and tightened credit. The economic distress this caused would force Congress, he hoped, to recharter the bank. But Jackson and his supporters held firm. "I never will restore the deposits," Jackson declared. "I never will recharter the United States Bank, or sign a charter for any other bank, so long as my name is Andrew Jackson." When the bank's charter ran out in 1836, it was not renewed.

THE ELECTION OF 1836

Jackson's bank war united his opponents. National Republicans, who were angry about the bank's destruction, joined states' righters, who were angry about Jackson's stand on nullification. Democrats unhappy with Jackson's bank policy also moved into this camp.

In 1834 this new group, led by Clay and Webster, formally took the name of Whigs. Whigs protested against the policies of "King Andrew," just as American Whigs had earlier opposed the rule of George III. The party attracted a wide variety of people—manufacturers, bankers and merchants, workers and conservative farmers in the North, and big planters in the South. The force binding together the Whigs was their distrust of Jackson. But the party also supported Clay's American System. In the election of 1836, the nation once again had two national parties—Democrats and Whigs.

In May 1835 Democrats met in convention to choose a presidential candidate. Jackson refused to run for a third term. He threw his support to Vice-President Martin Van Buren, who was nominated by the convention. Van Buren pledged to "tread generally in the footsteps of President Jackson."

The Whigs were unable to agree on a single candidate, so they nominated three who had strong regional support. They hoped to split the total vote, throwing the election into the House. The major Whig candidate was William Henry Harrison of Ohio, hero of the Battle of Tippecanoe. Massachusetts nominated Daniel Webster while Tennessee chose Hugh L. White, an anti-Jackson Democrat.

Jackson's popularity was still strong enough to bring the Democrats victory on election day. Van Buren carried 15 of the 26 states, but he received only 25,000 more popular votes than his combined

opponents. In the House, Whigs and conservative Democrats held the balance of power.

As president, Martin Van Buren lived in the shadow of Andrew Jackson. He reappointed almost all of Jackson's cabinet. At the inauguration, more people came to see "Old Hickory" than the new president.

THE PANIC OF 1837

Van Buren also reaped the destructive results of Jackson's bank war. The trouble started while Jackson was still president. As Jackson deposited government funds in "pet banks," the Bank of the United States lost its power to regulate the nation's currency. "Pet banks" as well as new banks, especially in the West and South, printed and loaned money that was not backed by gold or silver. Good times and easy credit led to feverish speculation in canal building and land.

With the flow of paper money, the purchase of public lands soared. In 1836 people bought over four times the acreage that was sold two years earlier. Prices also skyrocketed.

Jackson tried to stop the wild speculation and inflation. In 1836 he issued a "Specie Circular,"

French artist Edgar Degas painted "Cotton Merchants in New Orleans" after a visit to America. When the cotton market was healthy, bargaining took place in settings like this.

The continuing popularity of campaign commemoratives is seen in this 1840 banner. The log cabin, famous in Harrison's campaign, symbolizes virtue, while he is shown as a hero.

ordering the government to accept only specie—gold or silver coins—in payment for public lands. The order sharply slowed land sales. It also strained the resources of banks as people tried to convert their paper money to specie.

In 1837, at the time that Van Buren took office, a financial crisis hit Britain. The British had invested heavily in the United States. Now they called in their loans, causing a wave of bankruptcies. British demand for American cotton also dropped, causing prices to fall 50 percent.

In March, cotton brokers in New Orleans began to go out of business. In May, depositors withdrew at least $1 million in gold and silver from New York City banks in two days. The banks promptly suspended coin payments, and banks in other cities followed New York City's example. Many banks simply failed. Factories closed and unemployment spread. Land prices plunged as much as 90 percent. By autumn, the United States was in a severe depression that would last for the next six years.

In September 1837 Van Buren called Congress into special session. He blamed the depression on "overbanking," and argued that treasury funds should not be kept in state banks. Instead, he wanted to set up in major cities treasury vaults that would store federal money. Almost three years later, Congress would pass the Independent Treasury Act. But Van Buren would not interfere with the economy or provide government relief for people hurt by the depression.

THE ELECTION OF 1840

By 1840 prosperity had not returned to the nation. In that electoral year many Americans blamed Van Buren for the depression. Still, the Democratic convention renominated him for president.

The Whigs, sensing victory, met in convention and chose William Henry Harrison of Ohio. Harrison, a military hero, had made a strong showing in the election of 1836 and had few political enemies. To balance the ticket, the Whigs chose Virginia legislator John Tyler for vice-president. An ex-Democrat, Tyler had broken with Jackson over nullification.

The campaign sizzled with name-calling. Whigs blamed Van Buren for the depression and criticized him for not helping workers. They claimed his policy was "fifty cents a day and French soup" while Whig policy toward workers was "two dollars a day and roast beef."

Democrats responded in kind. A Democratic newspaper scoffed: "Upon condition of his receiving a pension of $2,000 and a barrel of cider, General Harrison would no doubt consent to . . . spend his days in a log cabin on the banks of the Ohio." The Whigs simply made the log cabin and the cider barrel symbols of Harrison's link to the people and victory at Tippecanoe. They adopted the Democrats' campaign tools—parades, rallies, slogans, and songs. Soon people were singing "Tippecanoe and Tyler too."

The log cabin campaign swept the Whigs to victory, in the largest voter turnout yet seen. Harrison carried 19 of 26 states, winning 234 electoral votes to Van Buren's 60. The Whigs also won majorities in both the House and the Senate.

Harrison did not live long enough to put Whig ideals into action. Soon after his inauguration, he became ill with pneumonia and died. On April 6, 1841, John Tyler became president.

Once again there was a Virginian in the White House. John Tyler, said an acquaintance, was "approachable, courteous, always willing to do a kindly action, or to speak a kindly word." Whigs were pleased when he kept Harrison's cabinet. They expected him to support their goals of internal improvements and a national bank. But Tyler believed in states' rights and a strict interpretation of the Constitution.

Within three months, Tyler vetoed two bills for a national bank that the Whigs pushed through Congress. Outraged, every cabinet member but one resigned. Tyler also vetoed every bill for internal improvements that Congress passed. The Whigs expelled him from the party. A political loner, Tyler simply continued on his chosen path.

SECTION REVIEW

1. Identify the following: "the Monster," Nicholas Biddle.

2. Define the following: "pet banks," depression, specie.

3. (a) List three reasons why Jackson wanted to destroy the Bank of the United States. (b) What steps did he take to achieve this goal?

4. (a) List two reasons why Jackson's opponents united against him. (b) What was the result of this union?

5. How did Jackson's popularity affect the presidential election of 1836?

6. (a) Why did Jackson issue a "Specie Circular" in 1836? (b) List two results of the circular.

7. (a) How did Van Buren propose to overcome the depression? What was the result of this proposal? (b) What actions did Van Buren refuse to take?

8. (a) What did the Whigs expect of John Tyler? (b) How did Tyler anger his party? (c) How did the Whigs react?

REFORMING SOCIETY

READ TO FIND OUT

— **how religious revivals swept the United States.**

— **why reformers organized the American Temperance Union.**

— **how reformers improved public education.**

— **how Dorothea Dix helped the mentally ill.**

The democratic breeze that swept the United States during the Jacksonian era was not the only movement to stir Americans. Between the 1820s and the 1850s, a spirit of social reform caught hold of the nation. Reformers bubbled with optimism and faith in progress. While some people were busy developing cities and building roads and machines, reformers wanted to build a better society.

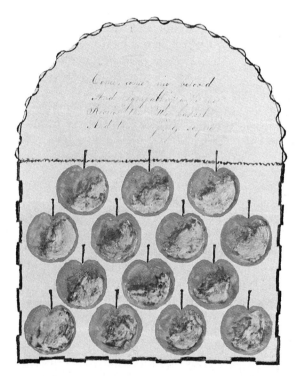

The first Shakers came to America in 1774. Today there are fewer than twenty Shakers left. Shaker art and crafts, simple and beautiful in line, speak of their orderly lives.

Artist Olof Krans felt privileged to record the accomplishments of Bishop Hill Colony in western Illinois. "Women Planting Corn" shows how labor was organized for maximum efficiency.

REVIVALS AND UTOPIAS

Religious faith spurred Americans in their drive to improve society. Around 1800 Protestant leaders launched a series of *revivals*. The goal of these public meetings was to renew interest in religion among Americans who seemed to have grown indifferent to Bible teachings. The ministers preached with such force that they awakened religious fervor from New England to the South and West.

For the next fifty years, waves of religious revivals swept the nation. The "Godless West" was a special target because it lacked houses of worship and ministers. But, Presbyterian, Congregational, Methodist, and Baptist churches sent preachers, often called revivalists, to the frontier. At "camp meetings" they preached to thousands about accepting God's love and wiping out sin.

The revivals also kindled new religious movements that set out to establish *utopias*, or perfect communities. Joseph Smith said that he had been given new revelations from God in *The Book of Mormon* and gathered followers into a tightknit community. Ann Lee Stanley, known as "Mother Ann," led English Shakers to the United States to escape persecution. The Shakers, who praised God in song

and dance, drew converts and created communities based on their beliefs. Eventually they spread to seven states.

Utopias based on economic and social ideals were also built during these years. Fruitlands and Brook Farm in Massachusetts were experiments in sharing property. Fruitlands, which refused to "enslave" horses for farm work, faced starvation and failed within a year. Novelist Louisa May Alcott, whose father planned the experiment, later wrote, "Poor Fruitlands! The name was as great a failure as the rest." Brook Farm lasted several years longer, then collapsed from debt.

However, a few of the more than fifty utopias created did survive. John Humphrey Noyes created a utopian community at Oneida, New York. By manufacturing goods, including silverware, it grew strong, and in 1880 reorganized as a corporation.

CRUSADING FOR TEMPERANCE

The impulse for perfection that led some Americans to build utopias led to others to try to reform society. One of the first evils that reformers, especially revivalists, attacked was drunkenness. Revivalist James Finley noted that "a house could not be raised, a field of wheat cut down, nor could there be a log rolling, a husking, a quilting, a wedding or a funeral without the aid of alcohol." Reformers believed too much drinking led to violence and poverty and called for *temperance*, or moderation.

In 1833 delegates of state temperance societies met at a national convention. They declared "traffic in ardent spirits" to be "morally wrong" and formed the American Temperance Union. Although they kept "temperance" in the title, they now preached abstinence, or no drinking at all. Thirteen years later, in 1846, Maine passed the first statewide law prohibiting alcohol. In the next decade, most other northern states also passed prohibition laws.

IMPROVING PUBLIC EDUCATION

While many reformers fought the "Demon Rum," others joined the movement to improve public education. Massachusetts led the way. Since colonial times, New England's town-supported schools had been teaching people to read and write. But by the early 1800s, the public schools suffered from lack of funds. Teachers were paid little and often were

With education, women proved their ability in many fields. Sometime around 1850 this daguerreotype was taken at the George Barrell Emerson School in Boston.

not qualified to teach. Conditions were even worse in other parts of the country where there were few public schools.

In 1837 Horace Mann of Massachusetts gave up his career in politics to accept the position of secretary of the new state board of education. He was convinced that only educated citizens could make a democratic government work. For the next dozen years, Mann tirelessly campaigned to improve Massachusetts schools. His efforts succeeded. State funds for public education were doubled, school buildings were improved, and the school year was extended to a minimum of six months. Also, teachers' salaries were increased, and three schools were set up to train teachers.

Mann toured the country, spurring reformers in other states to fight for publicly supported schooling for all. Reformers were aided by workers who demanded education for their children. "We want a *common* and *equal* education," a Jacksonian newspaper declared. "It is in the *interest of all*, that ALL should be equally well educated."

Such proposals sparked opposition. Taxpayers did not want to pay taxes to educate "other people's children." Families often resented the idea of compulsory attendance, especially when children could be working in the fields or in factories. Some people even denied that it was necessary that everybody should be able to read and write.

Despite such protests, states across the country gradually moved toward free public schooling. By the 1860s most northern states offered elementary education that was free and open to all white children. Separate schools were generally established for black children.

States also began to set up tax-supported high schools, which were first introduced by Massachusetts in 1821. The numbers of these schools grew slowly, since many private academies already existed to provide secondary education. However, by 1860 the nation had some 300 public high schools.

Unlike high schools, colleges multiplied quickly during the first half of the 1800s. Some were state universities—a total of 17 by 1860. Most, however, were founded by churches for the education of young men. Many of these were little more than academies and did not last long. Others, however, became very influential. Oberlin College in Ohio, for example, led the way in the education of women and blacks.

MARGARET FULLER
A NEW VIEW OF WOMEN

Even as a child, Margaret Fuller was different. Born in Massachusetts in 1810, she was reading Latin by the time she was six. In an age when women were expected to be pretty and helpless, she was brilliant, independent, and plain. "I made up my mind to be bright and ugly," she said.

While most women looked forward only to marriage, she wanted an education and a career. Yet no colleges admitted women, and there were few jobs open to them. Margaret Fuller tried teaching, writing, and editing a literary journal. She held a famous series of "Conversations" with Boston women, in which they discussed history, literature, and women's roles. Eventually she became the first woman on the staff of the New York *Tribune*.

During these years, her ideas about women developed. In 1845 she wrote *Women in the Nineteenth Century*, the first defense of women's rights published in the United States. Women's natural talents, she said, were stifled.

Margaret Fuller argued that girls, like boys, should be encouraged to develop freely. "Some little girls like to saw wood, others to use carpenters' tools," she noted. When parents forbid such activities because they are "not proper for girls," their growth is stunted.

In the same way, all jobs should be open to women. "Let them be sea-captains, if you will," she wrote. "We would have every path laid open to Woman as freely as to Man."

Many Americans found Margaret Fuller's ideas shocking. Yet, she had planted a seed. That seed would sprout three years later, when the first women's rights convention at Seneca Falls proclaimed that "all men and women are created equal."

HELP FOR THE MENTALLY ILL

Many reformers tried to help people who were ignored by society. Some, like Margaret Fuller of the New York *Tribune*, tried to improve conditions for prisoners. Others worked to help the poor and to abolish imprisonment for debt. A few, such as Thomas H. Gallaudet and Samuel G. Howe, founded the first schools in the United States for the deaf and the blind. Others helped the mentally ill.

In 1841 teacher Dorothea Dix visited a prison near Boston, Massachusetts, to teach a Sunday school class. Among the prisoners she found mentally ill people, treated as criminals. Outraged, she spent the next two years investigating jails and poorhouses throughout the state.

In 1843 she presented her findings to the Massachusetts legislature and convinced the members to vote funds for a hospital for the mentally ill. Dix then turned her attention to other states and eventually to Europe. In the next ten years she traveled thousands of miles, visiting jails, planning hospitals, and winning support for her cause. She refused to be discouraged. "They say nothing can be done here," she wrote. "I reply, 'I know no such word in the vocabulary I adopt!' "

From 1843 to 1880 the number of mental hospitals in the United States grew from 13 to 123. Dorothea Dix was directly involved in the founding of 32 state mental hospitals.

SECTION REVIEW

1. Identify the following: "Mother Ann," Fruitlands, John Humphrey Noyes, Horace Mann, Dorothea Dix.

2. Define the following: revival, utopia, temperance.

3. Why were revivalists interested in the West?

4. (a) List three utopian communities formed between the 1820s and 1850s. (b) Were these communities successful? Why?

5. (a) What was the aim of the American Temperance Union? (b) In what way was the union successful?

6. (a) What did public education reformers want? (b) What opposition did they meet? (c) What did they achieve?

7. (a) When were tax-supported high schools first established? (b) Why did they spread slowly?

8. What did Dorothea Dix achieve in 1843?

MOVEMENTS FOR PEOPLE'S RIGHTS

READ TO FIND OUT

— how abolition became the nation's major reform movement.

— how blacks worked for the abolitionist cause.

— how northerners and southerners reacted to the abolitionist movement.

— how the movement for women's rights began.

— how higher education became available to women.

— how women organized to gain their rights.

One Sunday in 1833, a young man stood on the shore of Chesapeake Bay. As he watched the passing boats, he said to himself:

> You are loosed from your moorings, and are free; I am fast in my chains and am a slave! . . . You are freedom's swift-winged angels, that fly round the world; I am confined in bands of iron! . . . O God, save me! God, deliver me! Let me be free!

The young man was Frederick Lewis Douglass and he had been born into slavery. Slaves were forbidden to read and write, but Douglass taught himself. He escaped to freedom at the age of twenty-one. Before he turned thirty, he had written his autobiography. The *Narrative of the Life of Frederick Douglass* revealed to the world what it was like to be a slave in the United States.

THE MOVEMENT TO ABOLISH SLAVERY

Opposition to slavery had been stirring in the United States since the 1780s, but the movement was small. Quakers had always opposed slavery as an evil. They formed abolition societies, and several Quakers, such as Benjamin Lundy, printed antislavery newspapers around the 1820s.

The American Colonization Society was founded in 1817 by northerners and southerners. It urged slaveowners to free their slaves and to send them to Liberia, a tract of land in West Africa that the society had bought. The society was just as eager to persuade free blacks to migrate, believing they would never fit into American society. However, the society was short of funds, and most slaveowners and free blacks opposed the plan.

A convention of free blacks in New York City stated that America was their home, their country. For it, some of their fathers had fought and died. They also intended to die here. By the 1830s the society realized that colonization was not the answer to slavery.

One of the most single-minded workers against slavery was William Lloyd Garrison. Garrison was a Massachusetts printer who had been an assistant to Benjamin Lundy. In 1831 Garrison published the first issue of the *Liberator*, a newspaper that demanded an immediate end to slavery. "I am in earnest," Garrison thundered in print, "I will not excuse—I will not retreat a single inch—*and I will be heard."*

As young journalist, William Lloyd Garrison edited the world's first temperance newspaper. His stand on abolition and women's rights disturbed more moderate supporters.

Few white northerners, however, listened, and the antislavery movement remained small. Then came a thunderbolt from across the Atlantic. In 1833 Great Britain abolished slavery at home and throughout its colonies. The British action spurred American reformers, and the small antislavery groups were swept into a major movement. In fact, abolitionism became the foremost movement of the whole reform era.

In 1833 the American Anti-Slavery Society was born, modeled on Britain's successful Abolition Society. The American group was founded by Garrison and two wealthy New York silk merchants, brothers Arthur and Lewis Tappan. Slowly, the society grew to some 200,000 members.

The Abolitionist movement grew even stronger when some revivalists turned their fervor against slavery. In Theodore Dwight Weld, a Garrison-like hatred of slavery was combined with a preacher's eloquence. While a student at Cincinnati's Lane Seminary, Weld preached abolition among his fellow ministry students. The result was an 18-day debate on slavery that converted almost the whole student body to the antislavery movement.

In 1835 Weld and many of his Lane converts opened a school of theology at Ohio's Oberlin College. Under Weld's prodding, Oberlin agreed to admit blacks. Oberlin soon became the center of the western abolition movement, and Weld was its leader.

Weld lectured tirelessly to bring people to the cause. He would speak as many as thirty times in one town, he said, to win the "hearts and heads and tongues" of the townspeople. Slavery, he told people, was a sin and contrary to American ideals of equality.

BLACKS IN THE ABOLITION MOVEMENT

Many blacks—both free and escaped slaves—worked for the abolitionist cause. Frederick Douglass traveled through the North speaking out against slavery. He also wrote against it in his newspaper, the *North Star*. Others, like Harriet Tubman and Jane Lewis, worked with whites in an underground movement to help slaves escape from the South. The black "conductors" in the Underground Railroad risked their freedom and their lives by traveling south to guide slaves to freedom.

Frederick Augustus Washington Bailey, a runaway slave, changed his name to Frederick Douglass to avoid capture. Douglass lectured, protested, and wrote for black rights.

Harriet Tubman was the most famous of the black conductors. She was called "Moses" by blacks and "General Tubman" by white abolitionists. From Canada, where she had taken refuge, she made nineteen trips south to bring over three hundred slaves out of bondage.

Some blacks called for a more extreme response to slavery. David Walker was a free black who sold clothing in Boston. In 1829 he published an angry pamphlet titled *Appeal to the Colored Citizens of the World*. It urged slaves to revolt. The South reacted instantly.

Savannah's mayor demanded that the mayor of Boston arrest Walker. But Walker had not violated the law, so he could not be arrested. Many southern states made it a crime to circulate pamphlets like Walker's, and forbade blacks to travel without a white or to meet in large groups. Black sailors on ships docking in Georgia harbors were warned not to go ashore.

REACTIONS TO ABOLITIONISTS

Most moderate abolitionists in the North condemned the radical stand of David Walker and William Lloyd Garrison. Like poet James Russell Lowell, they wished to end slavery, but felt "the world must be healed by degrees."

Many northerners, however, had no desire to end slavery. Opposition to the abolitionist movement took a nasty turn in the mid-1830s. A mob wrecked the presses of Garrison's *Liberator* and set his house afire. In 1837 Elijah Lovejoy, an Illinois minister who published an antislavery paper, was shot dead by rioting anti-abolitionists.

Many Americans were shocked by the murder of Lovejoy and the attacks on the press. Suddenly the argument went beyond the issue of slavery to the issue of free speech. And many abolitionists now took up a double cause—slavery and civil liberty.

The free speech issue also exploded in Congress. Abolitionists had launched a drive to outlaw slavery and the slave trade in the nation's capital, and petitions were flooding Congress. Representatives from slave states were already alarmed by the spread of the abolitionist movement. They did not want a debate on slavery in Congress. In 1836 the proslavery group pushed the "gag rule" through Congress, barring debate on antislavery petitions.

The gag rule aroused the wrath of ex-president John Quincy Adams, now a Massachusetts representative in the House. Adams was not an abolitionist, but he saw the rule as a violation of free speech. He doggedly fought the rule for months and then years. In 1844, the gag rule was repealed.

THE ANTI-SLAVERY SOCIETY SPLIT

While antislavery sentiment was growing, a rift was opening in the Anti-Slavery Society. Garrison and his followers continued to demand immediate abolition. They were not willing to work through politics, since they believed Congress would do nothing to offend the slave states. Moderate society members, however, were quite willing to take any sort of political action they could.

In 1840 the moderate abolitionists left the society to form their own group. They included the Tappan brothers, Theodore Weld, and James G. Birney. Birney had been a wealthy planter in Alabama until Weld persuaded him to join the abolitionist cause. Birney freed his slaves and moved to Ohio to work against slavery.

The moderates organized the Liberty party, and presented Birney as a candidate for president in the 1840 election. Birney attracted only 7,000 votes. He did better in the 1844 election, gaining 60,000 votes.

One of the issues that helped to split the Anti-Slavery Society was the role of women in the movement. Garrison and his followers believed women should play an active part in the society. They also wanted the society to support the new women's rights movements, but felt that the society should concentrate on ending slavery.

THE MOVEMENT FOR WOMEN'S RIGHTS

In 1838 Angelina Grimké—born of a slaveholding family in South Carolina—stood before the Massachusetts legislature. She and her sister Sarah, now Quakers and abolitionists, had brought to this meeting a petition demanding an end to slavery. It bore the names of 20,000 women.

Few members of the legislature had ever heard a speech by a woman. Grimké knew this, so she spoke not just about the evils of slavery. She also demanded the right of women to be heard on this or any other subject:

> These petitions relate to the great and solemn subject of slavery. . . . And because it is a political subject, it has often tauntingly been said, that women had nothing to do with it. Are we aliens, because we are women? Are we bereft of citizenship because we are mothers, wives and daughters of a mighty people? Have women no country?

Grimké's talk about political rights for women was something new. But the restrictions against women that sparked such talk were not new. Many people believed that women were suited for only certain roles, and owning a business or speaking in public were not among them. These beliefs were often translated into law. In some states, for example, when women earned wages, the money belonged to their husbands. Women could not vote, own property, or keep custody of their children after a divorce.

Women also found barriers in education. Although elementary schools were usually open to girls, there was little opportunity for schooling beyond that level. And without college training, women could not hope to enter a profession.

During the 1820s and 1830s concerned women became active in reform movements. They worked for temperance, abolition, public education, and other causes. And slowly they began to work for women's rights.

In the 1830s women petitioned the New York legislature to grant married women the right to own property. The legislature finally passed such a law in 1849, and some other states followed. Women later had success in changing other laws. In 1860 New York gave women joint guardianship with their husbands of children. The state also granted women the right to sue and be sued, and the right to keep their own wages.

EDUCATION AND THE PROFESSIONS

The doors to higher education were also opening to women. The first high school for girls, Troy Female Seminary in Troy, New York, began classes in 1821. Troy was established by Emma Hart Willard, who wrote her own textbooks and offered her students "male" subjects like physics and geometry.

In 1833 Oberlin College admitted women and became the nation's first coeducational college. Four years later Mary Lyon opened Mount Holyoke in Massachusetts. It was the first women's college in the United States. Its entrance requirements were as difficult to meet as those in any men's college. The women were expected to study hard *and* do the school's housework. On Thanksgiving, one student wrote, "we all had the privilege of sleeping as long as we wished in the morning, provided we were ready for breakfast by 8 o'clock."

As higher education opened to them, women began to venture into new fields, such as the ministry, journalism, and medicine. A determined young woman named Elizabeth Blackwell entered the medical school of Geneva College in New York, and graduated first in her class in 1849. Eight years later Dr. Blackwell opened the nation's first school of nursing. Antoinette Brown, who married one of Blackwell's brothers, was the first woman to graduate from Oberlin's theological school. And Maria Mitchell followed in the footsteps of her astronomer father, and at age twenty-eight discovered a comet.

Lucretia Mott was the daughter of a Nantucket sea captain. In her Quaker home, regard for women's intelligence and for their capability in practical affairs was a matter of course.

Warm and cheerful, Elizabeth Cady Stanton won people over. She spoke for the right of women to serve on juries, to own property, and to be legal guardians of their children.

WOMEN ORGANIZE

The successes of Blackwell and others were milestones, but by no means was every path open to women. In the 1840s two women—Elizabeth Cady Stanton and Lucretia Mott—decided that only an organized movement for women's rights was likely to clear the path.

Elizabeth Cady Stanton was the daughter of a New York judge. She was moved by women's complaints to her father that the law did not protect women's rights. As an adult, she married an abolitionist named Henry Stanton, and the two plunged into reform work.

Lucretia Mott was a strong-willed Quaker, who would speak against slavery to an unfriendly crowd with calm courage. She, too, married a man committed to reform and women's rights. When she challenged a speaker at one meeting, her husband, James, advised him, "If she thinks thee is wrong, thee had better look it over again."

In 1848 Stanton, Mott, and Mott's sister, Martha Coffin Wright, called a convention at Seneca Falls, New York, to discuss women's rights. A large crowd of men and women gathered to hear Stanton read the Declaration of Sentiments. This was based on the Declaration of Independence, but presented women's complaints against "man" rather than colonists' complaints against King George. Stanton asked that women be given the rights of citizens, including the right to vote. With the help of Frederick Douglass, Stanton convinced the convention to accept the declaration.

After the Seneca Falls Convention, women set out on speaking tours to win support for the struggling movement. To this campaign came a few strong women. Susan B. Anthony was a schoolteacher, converted to the cause by Elizabeth Cady Stanton. Anthony devoted her life to the drive for women's rights. She and Stanton formed a close team. Anthony supplied statistics, Stanton wove them into fiery speeches, and Anthony gave them in town after town. Henry Stanton remarked to his wife, "You stir up Susan and she stirs up the world."

Another tireless campaigner was Lucy Stone, a graduate of Oberlin and an abolitionist. She married Henry Blackwell, abolitionist and brother of Dr. Elizabeth Blackwell, and the two spent their lives working for abolition and women's rights.

Lucy Stone—abolitionist, suffragist, feminist—was the first Massachusetts woman to take a college degree. She kept her own name after her marriage to Henry Blackwell.

In 1864 Sojourner Truth visited President Lincoln at the White House. In 1870 she presented President Grant a petition for public land in the West for blacks.

Once, Stone refused to pay property taxes because "women suffer taxation, and yet have no representation." The government sold her furniture at auction to pay the tax bill.

Stone and Blackwell were not the only ones to combine the drive for women's rights with the abolition movement. The Grimké sisters, Lucretia Mott, and many others worked for both goals. To Sojourner Truth, these goals were especially important.

Sojourner Truth had been a slave for half her life. When New York abolished slavery in 1817, she gained her freedom. Truth became a leading speaker for abolition and women's rights. "I want women to have their rights," she told one audience. "I have been forty years a slave and forty years free, and would be here forty more to have equal rights for all."

SECTION REVIEW

1. Identify the following: Frederick Lewis Douglass, American Colonization Society, William Lloyd Garrison, Underground Railroad, Harriet Tubman, Angelina Grimké, Elizabeth Blackwell, Elizabeth Cady Stanton, Susan B. Anthony, Sojourner Truth.

2. (a) What happened in Great Britain in 1833 that affected the abolitionist movement in the United States? (b) What American group was formed because of Great Britain's action?

3. Why did Oberlin College become the center of the western abolition movement?

4. What was the South's reaction to the pamphlet *Appeal to the Colored Citizens of the World*?

5. List two incidents in the 1830s that turned the issue of slavery into an argument on free speech.

6. (a) What was the "gag rule"? (b) Why was John Quincy Adams opposed to it?

7. (a) Why were some abolitionists unwilling to work through politics? (b) Why was the Liberty party formed?

8. (a) List four legal restrictions on women in the 1830s. (b) What success did women have in changing those restrictions?

9. (a) What was the first coeducational college in the United States? When did it first admit women? (b) What was the first women's college in the United States?

10. (a) What declaration was made at the Seneca Falls Convention? (b) After the convention, how did the movement spread?

CHAPTER SURVEY

SUMMARY

In the early 1800s the American people demanded and received greater participation in their government. Many restrictions on voting were lifted, and voter participation greatly increased. The election of westerner Andrew Jackson to the presidency in 1828 reflected the spirit of the time. His election was heralded as a victory for the common people.

The new spirit of democracy extended only so far. Indians were excluded from it. The Five Civilized Tribes and other Indians were forced to give up their lands and move west.

A controversy over the protective tariff threatened to split the North and South during Jackson's administration. Southerners claimed that states could nullify certain acts of Congress. Northerners disagreed, claiming that states' rights undercut the powers of the federal government. Only a compromise by Henry Clay averted a headlong clash over states' rights.

Jackson's destruction of the Bank of the United States and his stand on nullification united his opponents into a new political party, the Whigs. The new party could not defeat Martin Van Buren, the presidential candidate backed by Jackson in 1836. Four years later, however, the Whigs triumphed. They elected the first Whig president, William Henry Harrison, thus ending the Jacksonian era.

A spirit of reform swept through the United States during the Jacksonian era. Reformers were intent on bettering society as well as government. Revivalists took religion to the West, and many religious communities were founded. Revivalists and reformers preached temperance. Some reformers fought for public education. Others campaigned for humane care of the mentally ill.

Reformers organized to abolish slavery and were joined by revivalists. Blacks worked for the abolitionist cause. Women became involved in various reforms, including abolition. They sought reforms in their legal status. Women admitted to the field of education and the professions distinguished themselves. As it became clear that an organized movement for women's rights was needed, strong leaders, such as Elizabeth Cady Stanton and Lucretia Mott, dedicated themselves to this work.

CHAPTER REVIEW

1. (a) Why did Americans demand a greater voice in government? (b) Explain how each of the following allowed Americans more participation in government: white male suffrage, popular election of electors, national political conventions. (c) What were two results of such changes? (d) How did Jackson expect his practices regarding officeholding to give Americans a greater voice in government?

2. (a) Why did whites consider Indian tribes in the Southeast a barrier to expansion? (b) Why did Jackson favor a plan of Indian removal? (c) How did Jackson's administration proceed with Indian removal? (d) What were the results of removal for the tribes involved?

3. (a) Why did northerners and westerners support the protective tariffs of 1824 and 1828? (b) How did southerners react to these tariffs? Why? (c) Why was the Tariff of 1828 called the "Tariff of Abominations"?

4. Explain how each event led to the next. (a) Tariff of 1828 (b) "South Carolina Exposition and Protest" (c) Tariff of 1832 (d) South Carolina nullification ordinance (e) the force bill (f) Tariff of 1833

"Indian Seated Overlooking a Lake" is a pencil sketch by the early American landscape painter Thomas Cole. Cole never painted on the spot; he relied on sketches and memory.

5. (a) How did Jackson's view of the Bank of the United States differ from the Supreme Court ruling in *McCulloch* v. *Maryland*? (b) How did Biddle, Clay, and Webster's defense of the bank backfire? (c) What action did Jackson take to end quickly the bank's power? (d) In what way was Jackson's action a success? In what way did it hurt the nation?

6. (a) How did two-party politics return to the nation in the election of 1836? (b) In what ways did the parties differ? (c) What part did Jackson play in this election? Cite two examples.

7. How did each of the following contribute to the Panic of 1837? (a) "pet banks" (b) canal and land speculation (c) "Specie Circular" (d) economic problems in Britain

8. (a) Between 1800 and 1850, Americans launched reform movements to improve society. List five such movements and explain their goals. (b) How did religion affect these movements? (c) What tactics did these reformers use to gain support? (d) In what ways did these reform movements succeed?

9. Explain how each of the following affected the abolitionist movement: the *Liberator*, British abolition of slavery, the Lane Seminary debate on slavery, the *North Star*, David Walker, the murder of Elijah Lovejoy, the "gag rule," the Liberty party.

10. (a) What were the first goals of women in their work for women's rights? Why? (b) Why was education so important to women? (c) Why did women begin an organized movement for their rights? What steps did they take?

ISSUES AND IDEAS

1. After Jackson's inauguration, a woman wrote, "It was the People's day and the People's President and the People would rule." How does this quotation summarize political beliefs in the Jacksonian era?

2. What might have happened if each of the following had taken place? (a) Jackson had enforced the Supreme Court's ruling on Cherokee

For many years nearly all American children used McGuffey readers. More than 120 million copies were sold. The lessons, poems, and drawings encouraged good conduct.

land claims. (b) The doctrine of nullification had been accepted in 1828 by the federal government. (c) Congress had succeeded in overriding Jackson's veto of the bank bill.

SKILLS WORKSHOP

1. *Maps.* Look at page 207 of your book. Find the map entitled "Indian Removal 1830–1850." Which tribes had been forced to move west by 1850? Where were their old lands? What lands did they now hold? How do you think these lands differed from the tribes' ancestral lands?

2. *Diagrams.* Make a diagram of the changes in political parties between 1828 and 1840. Include the National Republicans, the Democratic Republicans, the Democrats, and the Whigs. Also include elections, presidential candidates, and presidents.

PAST AND PRESENT

1. Does the United States make use of protective tariffs today? Give examples.

2. Between the 1820s and the 1850s, the United States bubbled with movements to reform society. What do you think are the nation's most important reform movements today? Why?

CHAPTER 10

WESTWARD TO THE PACIFIC

1820–1850

TRAILS TO THE WEST
GONE TO TEXAS
MANIFEST DESTINY

James Beckwourth fled St. Louis and slavery to become a mountain man in the untracked West. In 1850 he blazed a trail that thousands would follow into California:

"We proceded in an easterly direction, and all busied themselves in searching for gold; but my errand was of a different character; I had come to discover . . . a pass.

"It was the latter end of April when we entered upon an extensive valley at the northwest extremity of the Sierra range. . . . Deer and antelope filled the plains, and their boldness was conclusive that the hunter's rifle was to them unknown. We struck across this beautiful valley to . . . the eastern slope of the mountain range. This, I at once saw, would afford the best wagon-road.

"While thus busily engaged I was seized with an infection, and abandoned all hopes of recovery; I was over one hundred miles away from medical assistance, and my only shelter was a brush tent. I made my will, and resigned myself to death. Life still lingered in me, however, and a train of wagons came up, and encamped near to where I lay. . . . [They] came to my assistance, and through their kind attentions and excellent nursing I rapidly recovered . . . until I was soon able to mount my horse, and lead the first train, consisting of seventeen wagons, through 'Beckwourth's Pass.'"

Between the 1830s and the 1850s, pathfinders like Beckwourth roamed country that was shrouded in mystery to most Americans. These were the lands that would become Oregon, California, Utah, New Mexico, and Texas. Most of these lands belonged to Mexico, which had won them along with independence when it threw off Spain's rule in 1821.

Eventually, the trails west would be rutted by wagon wheels. Eventually, too, the United States would go to war with Mexico to win the western lands.

Along that route today, there are still traces of the past. Here and there among the fields of corn and wheat are deep ruts in the ground, carved a hundred and fifty years ago by countless wagons. Thousands of traders and settlers followed this trail across the plains beyond the Missouri River.

From the 1830s to the 1850s, Americans were pushing farther westward than ever before. The trails tell the story of this migration "from civilization to sundown."

TRADERS

Since the Lewis and Clark expedition and the explorations of Zebulon Pike, few Americans had ventured beyond the Mississippi River into the western wilderness. Some traders traveled southwest to Spanish Santa Fe, but the government there was suspicious of foreigners and jailed them. Then, in 1821, Mexico won its independence from Spain, and the Mexicans welcomed American traders in Santa Fe.

Missouri trader William Becknell was one of the first to accept the welcome—and the first to bring wagons to Santa Fe. He set out from Franklin in 1822 with three wagons piled with cloth and household goods. Instead of following the steep Rocky Mountain route of earlier traders, he blazed a trail across forbidding desert. When the weary Becknell finally reached Santa Fe, he sold his goods for huge profits.

Other traders heard about Becknell's good fortune and set out to follow Becknell's Santa Fe Trail. They found markets in Santa Fe and nearby Taos, and brought back furs, hides, Spanish mules, and gold and silver coins. A few traders stayed on in these towns, and tiny American outposts took root in New Mexico.

FUR TRAPPERS

Fur trappers, called mountain men, also headed west. They were an independent and a mixed lot—Americans, French, Spaniards, Mexicans, and even some British army officers who had enjoyed service on the frontier. The main quarry of these trappers was beaver. Beaver fur was made into fashionable hats for European and American gentlemen.

The mountain men hunted and trapped from Canada to Mexico and from the Missouri River to

TRAILS TO THE WEST

READ TO FIND OUT

— **how traders and trappers led the way west.**

— **what settlers faced on the Oregon Trail.**

— **how the Spanish founded missions throughout California**

— **how the California Trail was opened.**

— **how Salt Lake City was founded.**

West of St. Louis on the Missouri River lies the small town of New Franklin. On the main street a historical marker reads:

Franklin
"Cradle of the Santa Fe Trail". . . .
This trail
one of the great highways of the world
stretched nearly one thousand miles from
Franklin, Missouri to Santa Fe, New Mexico

the Great Basin and beyond. Usually traveling alone, they roamed the West for months at a time, working traps along streams and ponds and living mainly off the land. They came to consider these lands their "home in the wilderness."

Of course, their "home" was often home to local Indian tribes. Some trappers met tribes in friendship and occasionally lived with them. Other trappers fought Indians, and even stirred neighboring tribes into war. Whether the trappers met Indians as friends or enemies, they left their mark. They brought diseases to the Indians and killed game.

After months of trapping, the mountain men paddled down the Missouri River to sell their furs in St. Louis, the center of the fur trade. Sometimes, traders moved west to meet the trappers. As early as 1807, Manuel Lisa of St. Louis built a trading post at the mouth of the Bighorn River and hired his own trappers. A year later, John Jacob Astor started the American Fur Company, and his posts and forts soon dotted the Missouri River and its tributaries.

Still later, in the 1820s, the young Rocky Mountain Fur Company pushed farther into the wilderness. To compete with the successful Astor, the company sent trappers into the Rocky Mountains to find untouched fur country. Instead of setting up permanent trading posts, company traders met the trappers in the summer at a designated spot in the mountains. At such a rendezvous,* trappers exchanged their fur pelts for supplies and wages.

The annual rendezvous freed trappers from journeying east to trading posts and left them time to explore. And explore they did. Mountain men such as Joe Walker, Tom Fitzpatrick, Jedediah Smith, and James Beckwourth wandered high plains, explored passes in the Rocky Mountains and the Sierra Nevada, and trekked across blistering deserts.

Some pathfinders made their way into the Mexican-owned land of California and eventually settled there. Others wandered into the Oregon country, which was claimed by the United States and Britain. There they found the British trappers and traders of Hudson's Bay Company.

Then, around 1840, fashion changed and gentlemen turned from beaver hats to tall silk ones. By then, too, the mountain men had trapped the

*rendezvous (RAHN-duh-voo): a meeting place.

James Beckwourth's autobiography, *Life and Adventures of James P. Beckwourth,* describes the life of a mountain man. Beckwourth was a trapper, an Army scout, and a rancher.

beaver almost to extinction. Most mountain men turned to trading, buffalo hunting, scouting for the army, or guiding others through the wilderness that they had explored.

THE OREGON COUNTRY

The mountain men's tales of Oregon trickled eastward, enticing Americans. Business people thought about opportunities in trade and fishing. Farmers were eager to plow the fertile Oregon valleys. Missionaries prepared to convert tribes to Christianity. But all these seekers would have to cross a continent to reach Oregon. And there was an obstruction—the Rocky Mountains.

Nathaniel J. Wyeth, a Massachusetts ice merchant, organized expeditions to Oregon in 1832 and 1834. Wyeth traveled with horses and mules. With Wyeth went Methodist minister Jason Lee and four other missionaries. Once in Oregon, the Reverend Lee explored the Willamette River valley, chose a homestead, and established a mission and school.

Other missionaries soon followed. Marcus Whitman, a Presbyterian, decided not only to go to Oregon but also to prove that wagons could make the trip. Wagons, Dr. Whitman felt, were the way to bring families to Oregon and to set up missions.

In 1836 Marcus and Narcissa Whitman and another missionary couple, Eliza and Henry Spalding, joined a fur-trade caravan and set out for Oregon with two wagons. One wagon was soon abandoned. The other also became troublesome. "Wagon was upset twice," Narcissa Whitman noted in her diary one day. "Do not wonder at all this. It was a greater wonder that it was not turning a somersault continually." This wagon, too, was left behind, and the missionaries traveled to Oregon on horseback.

In the next few years, more missionary men and women made the long overland journey to Oregon the same way. Still other missionaries took ships that sailed around Cape Horn at the southernmost tip of South America and up the Pacific Coast. Then, in 1840, trappers succeeded in bringing a few wagons through the mountains. Marcus Whitman said that they had "broken the ice." He was right.

OREGON FEVER

The missionaries who went west wrote glowing reports of the warm climate and rich soil of Oregon's Willamette Valley. Restless Americans eagerly read them and envisioned a "pioneer's paradise." So did Americans suffering from the long-lasting depression which began in 1837. By the early 1840s, "Oregon fever" was sweeping the country.

In 1841 the first wagon train of 12 wagons and about 70 men, women, and children set out on the Oregon Trail. Other trains soon followed, and between 1841 and 1845 some 5,000 "overlanders" trudged that trail.

At first the town of Independence, on the Missouri River, was the "jumping-off place" for wagon trains. Then other river towns sprang up farther west—Kansas City, St. Joseph, Council Bluffs.

From the Missouri River towns, the wagon trains set out in late April or early May. The timing was critical, for they had to cross the Rockies before the winter snows. The bulky wagons—pioneers called them prairie schooners—were usually pulled by sturdy, but slow, oxen.

The Oregon Trail stretched 2,000 miles (3,200 kilometers) through deserts, canyons, and several mountain ranges. It took at least four months, sometimes six, to reach the end of that trail. The pioneers had to conquer hunger, disease, numbing winter cold, and searing summer heat. Many of them died along the way.

Tabitha Brown, who traveled to Oregon at age sixty-six, found the journey a nightmare. The wagon train's guide robbed the pioneers, leaving them lost in the wilderness. "We had sixty miles of desert without grass or water," she wrote, "mountains to climb, cattle giving out, wagons breaking, emigrants sick and dying."

Still, the trail did end for Brown and for others. The now-hardy pioneers fanned out into Oregon's Willamette Valley. They cleared land, built cabins, and laid out towns. Brown started a school for children orphaned on the trek west. Later she founded Pacific University.

As Oregon grew, American settlers decided to form a government. In 1843 settlers drafted a constitution and drew up a bill of rights, assuring religious freedom and trial by jury and banning slaveholding. They elected a governor and set up a legislature and judicial system. They also petitioned Congress to make Oregon a United States territory.

The more the settlers made themselves at home, the more the British and the Indians worried. Friction grew as pioneers claimed Indian land, and missionaries tried to change tribal ways of life. Conflict erupted in the late 1840s between the Cayuse and the settlers.

The British also feared the Americans in Oregon. Under the Convention of 1818, Britain and the United States jointly occupied Oregon. The British in Oregon, however, were now outnumbered, and Americans had their eyes on statehood.

CALIFORNIA

South of Oregon, along the Pacific Coast, lay Mexican-owned California. Claimed by Spain in the 1500s, California had remained largely unexplored for over two centuries. Then in the 1760s the British as well as the Russians, who claimed Alaska, began to expand southward toward California. Alarmed, Spain set out to protect this slice of its empire from foreign powers.

In early 1769 a Spanish expedition of soldiers and Indians was organized to occupy California. In command was Gaspar de Portolá (POR-toh-LAH), accompanied by a Franciscan priest named Father Junipero Serra (SEHR-rah). From Mexico, the expedition headed north for California, a grueling journey across mountains and deserts. When they

Spanish California

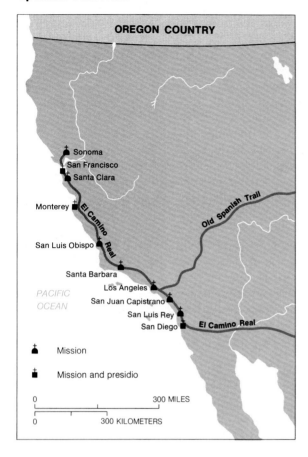

OREGON COUNTRY

Sonoma
San Francisco
Santa Clara
Monterey — El Camino Real
San Luis Obispo
Santa Barbara
Los Angeles
San Juan Capistrano
San Luis Rey
San Diego — El Camino Real
Old Spanish Trail

PACIFIC OCEAN

✝ Mission

✝ Mission and presidio

0   300 MILES

0   300 KILOMETERS

The Indians, though, did not prosper. They lost their independence and fell prey to European diseases such as measles and smallpox. With no immunity, Indians died in great numbers.

The mission system was doomed when Mexico won its independence from Spain in 1821. Thirteen years after California became a Mexican province, the new government began to take over the mission lands. The lands had been held in trust for the mission Indians by Spanish law, but Mexico broke up the lands into large ranches and granted them to favored settlers.

Abandoned, the missions slowly fell into ruin. Mission Indians, left with neither land nor the protection of the Catholic Church, scattered. Some went to the hills, returning to old ways of life. Others continued to herd and tend cattle, now on the Mexican ranches formed from mission lands.

THE CALIFORNIA TRAIL

When Mexico became independent in 1821, it welcomed trade between California and the United States. More and more American traders sailed to California to obtain its major product—huge herds of cattle. Cattle hides were made into shoes, and the animals' fat, called tallow, became candles and soap. Hides, in fact, were so vital to commerce that they were used, like silver, as money. American sailors called them "California banknotes."

A few American trappers found their way into California by a different route—overland. Twice, in 1826 and 1827, Jedediah Smith and some fellow mountain men wandered into California searching for beaver streams. They explored the San Joaquin (wah-KEEN) and Sacramento valleys and returned home by blazing a trail east through the Sierra Nevada and the Great Salt Lake basin.

Other trappers soon followed Smith, exploring, trapping, and returning east with tales of California's "perennial spring and boundless fertility." Two people who listened eagerly were Missourians John Bidwell and John Bartleson.

In 1841 the Bidwell-Bartleson expedition joined the first wagon train that set out on the Oregon Trail. These 34 overlanders traveled with the train as far as Soda Springs, in Idaho, then headed off on their own—south to California. They plodded through the deserts of Utah and Nevada, abandoning their wagons and eating their oxen to survive.

reached San Diego Bay, Father Serra stopped to begin construction of Mission San Diego de Alcalá—the first of nine missions that he would build in California.

While Serra's work party labored, Portolá and his soldiers pushed northward. Wherever they camped, they named the sites—Los Angeles, Santa Barbara, San Luis Obispo. They discovered a large bay, which they named San Francisco. On a second expedition north, in 1770, Portolá found Monterey. He and Serra began work there on a fort and a mission.

The Spanish missions survived and grew. Between 1769 and 1823 Father Serra and his successors built 21 missions, most of them close to the sea. Like links in a chain, they stretched from San Diego north to San Francisco. The missions were planned so that they were about a day's march apart. At each of these self-sufficient communities, priests worked to convert the Indians to Christianity and to teach them Spanish ways of life.

Early explorers of San Francisco Bay saw war-dance costumes like these at Mission San Francisco de Assis. Paint, feathers, and shells provided ornament.

Mission San Carlos Borromeo de Carmel was founded in Monterey on June 3, 1770. Father Serra moved the mission to Carmel in 1771 and used it as his headquarters. Because of its beautiful features and setting, this mission is considered the gem of the California chain.

When the party reached the towering Sierra Nevada, they plunged ahead on foot and horseback. Young Nancy Kelsey, with her husband and infant child, was the only woman along. Walking barefoot because her feet were blistered, Kelsey carried her child while she led her horse down steep cliffs.

The party made it through the mountains and emerged into California's San Joaquin Valley. This journey and the others that followed opened the California Trail. A small but steady stream of Americans flowed into California, and the fertile San Joaquin and Sacramento valleys were soon dotted with their settlements.

THE MORMON TRAIL

The California Trail was not the only one to branch out from the Oregon Trail. Another route angled off through a high pass in the Rocky Mountains, then dropped down to the Great Salt Lake. This was carved by a religious group called Mormons, and became known as the Mormon Trail.

The Mormon Church, or Church of Jesus Christ of Latter-Day Saints, was founded in New York in 1830 by Joseph Smith. Mormons lived in a theocratic, or church-governed society. Everyone worked for the common good and, at first, each person's property was considered the common property of the Church. Mormons also came to practice polygamy, which allowed men to have more than one wife at the same time. Many people reacted to Mormon beliefs with hostility.

The Mormons tried settling in Ohio and then Missouri to build their "Kingdom of God in the wilderness." When anti-Mormon Missourians turned to violence, the Mormons fled to Illinois. On the Mississippi River they built the city of Nauvoo, meaning "beautiful place" in Hebrew. Business and industry flourished, a university was planned, and a Mormon militia guarded the city. By 1844 booming Nauvoo had almost 15,000 people. But again, conflict between Mormons and non-Mormons erupted into rioting, and Joseph Smith and his brother were killed.

Brigham Young became the Mormons' new leader. As so many others had done, Young looked west for religious freedom and a new home. Meeting with church leaders, he determined to lead the Mormons to the Great Salt Lake valley, a region owned by Mexico.

Trails to the Far West

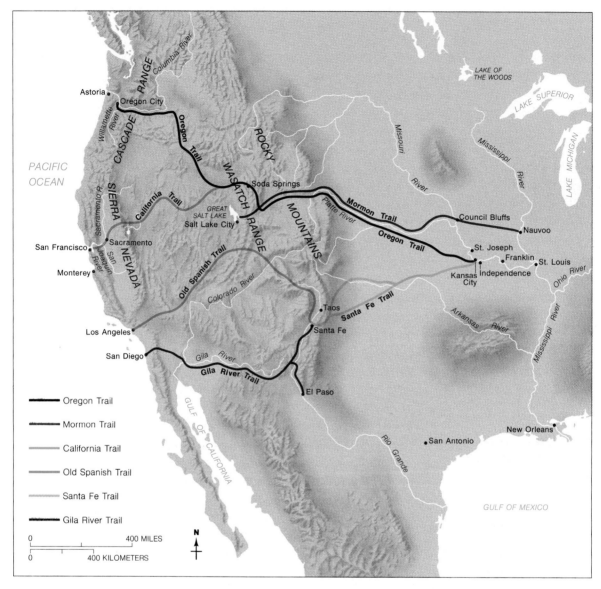

Spanish missionaries following old Indian trails opened parts of the Old Spanish Trail. American fur trappers blazed the rest. The Gila Trail was also traveled first by missionaries, then by trappers. In time both trails became routes for emigrant wagons.

Early in the spring of 1846, the first groups left Nauvoo and crossed the Mississippi. Day by day, other groups followed until some 15,000 Mormons were on the move. By late fall most of the Mormons had crossed the Missouri River. On its banks they camped for the winter. It was a harsh winter of hunger and disease, and hundreds of Mormons died. But when spring came, the survivors still looked west.

In April 1847 the first Mormon wagon train, consisting of 148 people, resumed the westward journey under the leadership of Brigham Young. They followed the north bank of the Platte River, joined the Oregon Trail through the Rockies, then cut southwest through the rugged Wasatch Range. From one mountain peak an advance party of Mormons "looked out on the full extent of the valley where the Great Salt Lake glistened in the sunbeams."

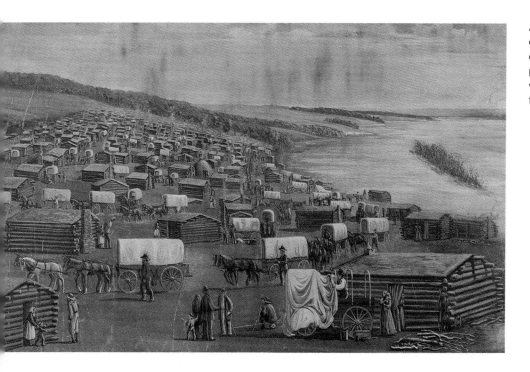

At their winter quarters on the Missouri River, determined Mormons prepared to resume their westward flight to a land free from persecution.

In July 1847 the first Mormon wagons entered the valley of the Great Salt Lake. Few places could have seemed less promising for settlement. The Mormons' new refuge was a dry, flat plain baked by the summer heat and populated by crickets, coyotes, and rattlesnakes. "I don't remember a tree that could be called a tree," one Mormon later said. Yet snow-fed streams from the surrounding mountains wandered the plain. A day after their arrival, the group offered prayers of thanksgiving. Then they began to plow and sow grain and parsnips, and even built a small dam to irrigate the soil.

In time, the Mormons constructed complex irrigation systems, laid out a magnificent city, and prospered. Salt Lake City became a beacon for further migrations of believers, and European converts poured steadily into the valley. Within the next ten years, over ninety separate settlements were planted in the valley. Mormon outposts reached west to Nevada and southern California and north to Idaho.

In 1849 the Mormons applied to Congress for statehood. The issue of polygamy, or plural marriages, proved to be a stumbling block, however. Instead, Congress granted the area territorial status in 1850 and gave it the name of Utah, after the Ute Indians living there.

SECTION REVIEW

1. Identify the following: Santa Fe Trail, Nathaniel Wyeth, Jason Lee, Oregon Trail, Tabitha Brown, Gaspar de Portolá, Junipero Serra, California Trail, Joseph Smith, Nauvoo, Brigham Young.

2. Define the following: mountain men, rendezvous, "California banknotes," polygamy.

3. (a) Describe the roles of William Becknell, Manuel Lisa, and John Jacob Astor in the westward movement. (b) How did Joe Walker, Tom Fitzpatrick, Jedediah Smith, and James Beckwourth open the way to the West?

4. What was the purpose of the Whitmans' and the Spaldings' journey to Oregon?

5. (a) What Missouri River towns were starting points for westward-bound wagon trains?
(b) What area in Oregon was the final destination of the pioneers on the Oregon Trail?

6. What was the effect of the Spanish mission system on California Indians?

7. (a) By what two routes did American settlers reach California? (b) What was the significance of the Bidwell-Bartleson expedition?

8. Why did the Mormons keep moving west?

GONE TO TEXAS

READ TO FIND OUT

— why Americans began to settle in Texas.

— what issues caused tension between Mexicans and Americans in Texas.

— how Texans rebelled against the Mexican government.

— how the Alamo became a symbol to Texans.

— how the Lone Star Republic grew and prospered.

Couples perform a Spanish dance in a candlelit room. The home had been a Spanish governor's palace. A French visitor painted the scene in San Antonio in 1840.

To the southwest of the United States was a land called Texas. It bordered Louisiana, and some Americans argued that it was part of the Louisiana Purchase. It was, however, owned by Spain.

Texas seemed big enough to hold everybody's dreams. There were vast prairies matted with buffalo grass, high mesas whipped by the wind, blistering deserts, rolling hills sprouting thick woods of cypress and pine. In east Texas, cane plants grew to 25 feet (7.6 meters) high.

Into this land came an American named Moses Austin, in the winter of 1820. Austin had a dream of settling Americans in Texas. The Connecticut-born Austin had settled in Missouri when it was Spanish territory, had pledged his loyalty to Spain, and had prospered. Now, though, he was bankrupt—ruined in the Panic of 1819—and determined to recover his losses. Like so many other Americans, Austin looked west for land and opportunity.

EARLY TEXAS

Texas had been claimed by Spain in the early 1500s, but remained unoccupied by Spaniards for almost two centuries. Then, in the late 1600s, French probes into eastern Texas stung Spain into action. Anxious to protect their claim, Spaniards rode north from Mexico into Texas.

The land that they found impressed them. So did the Caddo Indians, whom the Spaniards called *Tejas*, (TAY-hahs), from an Indian word meaning "friends." They also called the land *Tejas*, or Texas.

In the early 1700s, New Spain, still concerned with French invasion, sent priests and soldiers to eastern Texas. They built missions to bring Christianity to the Indians and built presidios to defend the Spanish frontier. To provide a way station between Mexico and Texas, priests, soldiers, and settlers established the mission and presidio of San Antonio in 1718.

To Spain's dismay, the settlements did not prosper. The Caddo rejected Christianity and mission life. The eastern Apache—and later the Comanche—also refused to settle at the missions and raided Spanish settlements, driving off herds of horses.

By the early 1800s Spain had new worries in Texas caused by its neighbor, the United States. Ignoring boundaries, Americans drifted from newly purchased Louisiana into eastern Texas. Some were fugitives and runaway slaves, seeking a haven. Others were farmers, who illegally settled along the Red River to plow the rich soil. All were unwelcome to Spain. The Spanish had forbidden such immigration, but lacked the power to enforce the ban.

THE DREAM OF MOSES AUSTIN

In December 1820 Moses Austin requested a land grant in Texas and promised to populate it with 300 responsible American families who would become

Spanish subjects. The settlers would have a legal right to their land, he argued. Thus, they would defend Texas against illegal American immigrants as well as the Apache and Comanche.

Early in 1821, Spanish officials agreed to Austin's proposal, promising to grant him 200,000 acres (81,000 hectares) of his choice. Austin, however, never had a chance to put his plan into action. Back in Missouri, he died of pneumonia in June 1821. Austin's last wish was that his son Stephen carry on in his place.

Stephen F. Austin explored along the Colorado and Brazos rivers and found an area for settlement. He requested the area for his colony, and by 1822 settlers, mostly from southern states and territories, had arrived. Then, Austin received dismaying news. Mexico had won its independence from Spain in 1821, and Texas was now part of Mexico.

Nevertheless, in April 1823 Mexico approved Austin's land grant. He could bring into east Texas 300 American families. They would not have to pay for the land or pay taxes for 6 years, but there was a condition. They must agree to become Mexican subjects and to accept the Catholic religion. As chief official and land agent, Austin received his own land and the right to charge settlers to cover his costs for the colony. Once more, Moses Austin's dream was on track.

TEXAS FEVER

The Mexican state of Coahuila-Texas (kō-ah-WEE-lah), of which Texas was a part, soon opened Texas to immigration. It issued land grants to agents like Austin and even to individual settlers of "Christian and good moral character." As before, settlers had to become Mexican subjects and were promised tax exemptions.

"Texas fever" quickly swept the Mississippi Valley, which was still suffering the aftereffects of the Panic of 1819. Would-be land agents poured into Texas for grants. Some were conscientious and honored their contracts by recruiting settlers. Many, though, were speculators who sold their grants for a quick profit without bringing in any settlers.

Still, their advertisements about cheap land in Texas lured Americans, mostly southerners searching for good cotton land. Many brought their slaves—one planter arrived with 100 slaves. Free blacks also came to Texas to start a new life. All over the South the words "Gone to Texas"—or just plain "GTT"—were scrawled on abandoned shacks and barns.

By 1830 some 16,000 Americans had settled in Texas, outnumbering Mexicans by 4 to 1. For many years corn was the major crop, but then cotton, grown on plantations with slave labor, began to challenge corn's lead.

AMERICAN-MEXICAN TENSIONS

Most American settlers were initially loyal to the Mexican government, but relations soon deteriorated. To own land, Americans had formally accepted Mexico's national religion—although the government did not demand that settlers actually practice Catholicism. But later settlers, especially illegal ones, wanted their own churches and eventually built them.

Slavery also became an issue between Mexicans and Americans. In 1829 the president of Mexico abolished slavery everywhere in the nation. Most Americans in Texas were southerners who had brought slaves or hoped to buy them. Under American pressure, Texas was exempted from that law, but the issue of slavery caused ill will.

Besides Mexico's stand on religion and slavery, Americans also resented the Mexican government. The capital of Coahuila-Texas was 500 miles (800 kilometers) from Austin's land grant, so quick enforcement of the law was impossible. Most court cases were decided there, and the court system was different from that of the United States. In addition, Texas had only one seat in the state legislature, and Americans wanted more representation.

For its part, Mexico feared that the United States planned to annex the province. Presidents John Quincy Adams and Andrew Jackson had offered to buy Texas. Mexico turned down the offers. Furthermore, it encouraged Mexicans to settle in Texas and banned further American immigration. Americans, however, continued to cross into Texas, now illegally.

Tension between Americans and Mexican soldiers led to violence in 1832. Mexico offered to settle the Texans' grievances. The government repealed the anti-immigration law in 1833, and the state of Coahuila-Texas increased Texan representation in its legislature. Calm returned to Texas, and more settlers than ever poured across the border.

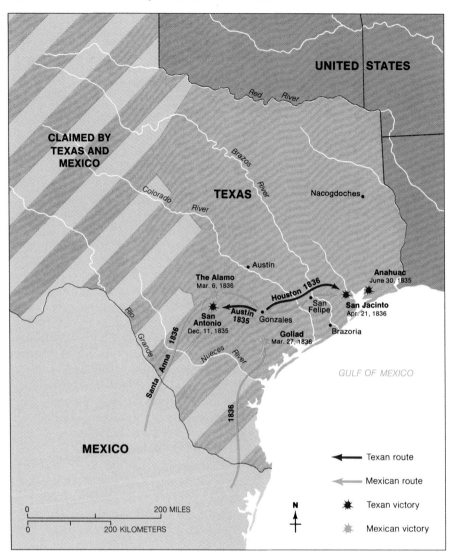

With the end of the Texas War for Independence, a new dispute began. Texas announced the Rio Grande as its boundary. Mexico replied that the Texas boundary had always been the Nueces River. When Texas joined the Union, the boundary was still in dispute.

THE TEXAS REVOLUTION

Changes in Mexico's government soon shattered peace in Texas. In 1834 the president of Mexico, General Antonio López de Santa Anna, made himself dictator. He planned to create a strong central government under his tight personal control. In 1835 he established military rule in Texas.

In June a young lawyer named William B. Travis heard that Santa Anna was sending troops to garrisons in Texas. Travis gathered some fighters and a cannon and captured the Mexican garrison at Anahuac (ah-NAH-wak) on Galveston Bay. Four months later, Texans rushed to Gonzales (gohn-ZAHL-ehs) and stopped Mexican troops from taking the city's sole cannon. Next, a small group of Texans descended on Goliad (GŌ-lee-AHD) and forced Mexican troops there to surrender. Finally, in late October, Stephen Austin and a frontier fighter named Jim Bowie led Texas volunteers in a march on San Antonio. After laying siege to the city for a month, Austin's troops captured the city.

While Austin's volunteers laid siege to San Antonio, Texans met at San Felipe to draft a Declaration of Causes for taking up arms. They were loyal to Mexico but not to the dictator Santa Anna, they declared, so they were setting up their own temporary state government. For commander of the army they settled on a relative newcomer to Texas. Sam Houston was the adopted son of a Cherokee chief, an ex-member of Congress, an ex-governor of Tennessee, and a friend of President Andrew Jackson.

A few months later, on March 2, 1836, the Texans adopted a declaration of independence. They also drew up a constitution for the Republic of Texas based on that of the United States.

"REMEMBER THE ALAMO!"

Meanwhile, Santa Anna was gathering his army. In early February, Santa Anna and over 5,000 troops crossed the Rio Grande and headed for San Antonio. Only 100 Texans were still there, at a fort called the Alamo. Jim Bowie vowed, "We will rather die in these ditches than give it up to the enemy."

Over the following days, others—Texans, Mexicans, Americans, and several slaves—joined the small force at the Alamo. William Travis arrived with 25 volunteers, among them Juan Seguin (SAY-geen), a Mexican whose valiant fighting for the Texans had earned him a place in the Texas army. Davy Crockett, pathfinder and former member of Congress, soon followed.

On February 23 Santa Anna arrived at San Antonio. The next day, Mexican cannons began bombarding the Alamo.

Travis, joint commander with Bowie, sent message after message for help to "the people of Texas and all Americans in the world." There was no help. The Texans' position was hopeless. At dawn on March 6, 1836, Mexican soldiers swarmed over the walls, killing every defender of the Alamo.

USING PRIMARY SOURCES
A MEXICAN ACCOUNT OF THE ALAMO

A *primary source* is a document written by a person involved in an event. All secondary sources, such as textbooks, make use of primary sources.

Read the following primary source. It is part of an account written in 1849 by Vicente Filisola, a Mexican soldier involved in the attack on the Alamo.

> On the morning of March 6, the Mexican troops were stationed at 4 o'clock, a.m., in accord with Santa Anna's instructions. The artillery, as appears from these same instructions, was to remain inactive, as it received no order; and furthermore, darkness, and the disposition made of the troops which were to attack the four fronts at the same time, prevented its firing without mowing down our own ranks. . . .
>
> Our loss was very heavy. . . . Our own men were exposed not only to the fire of the enemy but also to that of our own columns attacking the other fronts; and our soldiers being formed in close columns, all shots that were aimed too low, struck the backs of our foremost men.
>
> The official list of casualties, made by General Juan de Andrade, shows: officers 8 killed, 18 wounded; enlisted men 52 killed, 233 wounded. Total 311 killed and wounded.
>
> In our opinion the blood of our soldiers as well as that of the enemy was shed in vain, for the mere gratification . . . and guilty vanity of reconquering

Bexar [San Antonio] by force of arms, and through a bloody contest. . . . The massacres of the Alamo, of Goliad, of Refugio, convinced the rebels that no peaceable settlement could be expected, and that they must conquer, or die, or abandon the fruits of ten years of sweat and labor, together with their fondest hopes for the future.

After you have read a primary source, you can interpret the information.

1. First, consider who wrote the document. Was the person writing it closely involved in the event described? When was it written? Would you expect that the person who wrote it had a particular viewpoint toward the conflict between Texans and Mexicans? What might that viewpoint have been? Answers to questions like these help you to determine whether the source is reliable.

2. Now try to separate *fact* from *opinion*. What parts of the document seem to deal with fact? What parts give the writer's opinion of the event? What is the writer's opinion of Santa Anna's decision to attack the Alamo?

3. From this primary source, what did you learn about the fighting at the Alamo that you did not learn from your text?

A woodcut from the *Crockett Almanack* depicts Davy Crockett's death at the Alamo. These almanacs were popular from the mid-1830s to the mid-1850s. They included illustrated tall tales about Crockett as well as the usual almanac contents.

Texans received a second defeat a few weeks later. A force of over a thousand Mexican troops trapped some four hundred Texans near Goliad. The Mexican soldiers, following Santa Anna's orders, executed them.

As the Mexicans advanced eastward across Texas, Houston and his army retreated steadily. Finally, on April 21, 1836, Houston's army stopped near the San Jacinto (SAN hah-SEEN-toh) River. Eight hundred Texans turned to meet the Mexican force. Screaming "Remember the Alamo! Remember Goliad!" the Texans quickly won the battle. Later, the Texans captured Santa Anna.

The president of Mexico signed two treaties with the Texans. One called for an *armistice*, or truce, and ordered all Mexican troops to leave Texas. In the other, Santa Anna promised to support an independent Texas with a boundary at the Rio Grande.

The Mexican Congress, however, rejected the treaties and would not recognize Texan independence. For years, Texans and Mexicans clashed over boundaries, warring in all but name. The distrust between most Mexicans and Texans, based on cultural and political differences and inflamed by warfare, ended any hope of harmony.

THE LONE STAR REPUBLIC

With victory at the Battle of San Jacinto, Texans set about making their temporary government permanent. In September 1836 Texan voters approved the constitution drafted earlier that year. Like the United States, the Republic of Texas would have a president, a two-house legislature, and a supreme court. Sam Houston was elected president.

Texans also voted on another matter that September. By a large majority, they favored annexation* to the United States. President Jackson refused to push for annexation. Such an act, he thought, would lead to war with Mexico.

The issue of slavery was also troubling. Texas allowed slavery and would enter the Union as a slave state, upsetting the balance between slave and free states. Northerners, especially abolitionists, already strongly opposed the admission of new slave states. Jackson feared that annexing Texas would tear apart the Union. Instead, on his last day in office in March 1837, Jackson recognized Texas as an independent nation.

For the next eight years Texas, with its lone star flag, went its own way. To lure settlers, it offered free land to all newcomers. Americans suffering from the depression that began in 1837 eagerly responded.

Farmers steadily pushed inland from the coast, turning fertile plains into fields of corn and riverside land into acres of cotton. Gradually, too, Texans learned from Mexicans how to raise cattle on the open range. Ranchers adopted Mexican methods and equipment, such as using hot irons to mark the

* annexation: the joining of a state's or country's territory to another state or country.

ranch's brand on its cattle. A new American figure was born, based on the Mexican *vaquero* (vah-KEHR-ō)—the cowboy.

In 1839 a site on the Colorado River was chosen for the new capital of Texas. It was named in honor of Stephen Austin, who had died shortly after the Battle of San Jacinto.

SECTION REVIEW

1. Identify the following: Caddo Indians, San Antonio, Stephen Austin, William Travis, Jim Bowie, Sam Houston, Juan Seguin, Davy Crockett.

2. What problems did the Spanish encounter in trying to settle Texas?

3. (a) What was Moses Austin's dream? (b) What was his plan for carrying it out?

4. (a) What were the terms of the land grants offered by Mexico? (b) What two major crops did Americans plant?

5. What were three sources of friction between the settlers and the Mexican government?

6. (a) Who was Antonio López de Santa Anna? How did his actions lead to war in Texas? (b) Name three towns captured by Texans.

7. (a) Describe the battles at the Alamo, Goliad, and the San Jacinto River. (b) What were the two terms agreed to by Santa Anna?

8. Explain two problems that prevented Texas from becoming part of the United States in 1836.

The new capitol of the Republic of Texas in Austin in the 1840s was a simple building. The present capitol, Austin's chief landmark, resembles the United States Capitol.

MANIFEST DESTINY

READ TO FIND OUT

—**how President Tyler settled the Canadian-American border dispute.**

—**how the issue of Texas annexation affected the election of 1844.**

—**how President Polk planned to acquire Oregon and California.**

—**how a boundary dispute led to war with Mexico.**

—**what America gained in the Treaty of Guadalupe Hidalgo.**

—**what effects the gold rush had on life in California.**

By the 1840s Americans were streaming across the continent, settling in Texas, Utah, Oregon, and California. Land hunger set many of them in motion. But other feelings also drove them west. Many Americans wanted to secure their borders against the Mexicans to the south and the British to the north. Fiercely proud of their republican form of government, they wanted to spread it across the continent.

It seemed clear, or manifest, to many people that the nation's destiny was to extend from the Atlantic to the Pacific. This belief became known as *manifest destiny.* Representative Richard Yates of Illinois later told the House:

> The time is not distant when the seat of empire, the stronghold of numerical power, will be west of the Alleghenies. The handwriting is on the wall. It is *manifest destiny.* It is written on the signs of the times in clear, fresh, and unmistakable lines.

Those lines drew a new map of the United States.

THE WEBSTER-ASHBURTON TREATY

When Vice-President John Tyler succeeded to the presidency after William Henry Harrison died in 1841, he had a chance to play a part in American expansion. Tyler was something of an unknown.

The Whigs had expected him to continue Harrison's—and the Whigs'—domestic program. But the independent Tyler followed his own course, ignoring the outraged Whigs.

Under Tyler, a longstanding border dispute with Britain was finally settled to American advantage. The peace treaty at the end of the American Revolution had only vaguely defined the boundary between Maine and Canada. Some 12,000 square miles (31,000 square kilometers) of land were in question, and both the United States and Britain claimed them. Conflict there between Canadians and Americans even raised talk of war in the late 1830s.

Tyler's administration and the British government calmed the uproar with a treaty in 1842. Worked out by Secretary of State Daniel Webster and Britain's Lord Ashburton, the Webster-Ashburton Treaty divided the land between Canada and Maine. Maine received some 7,000 square miles (18,000 square kilometers), over half the disputed territory.

In addition, a Canadian-American boundary was established further west, between Lake Superior and the Lake of the Woods. With this new boundary, Britain gave up a huge chunk of land, which it considered "of little importance to either party." Britain was wrong. The land, in northern Minnesota, contained a range of mountains called the Mesabi—rich in iron ore deposits.

ANNEXATION OF TEXAS

Clearly, Tyler had a knack for foreign affairs. At one critical point in the Canadian boundary talks, he had stepped in to smooth the bargaining. But Tyler's main interest was Texas.

Both Jackson and Van Buren had rejected annexation. In 1843, however, the United States and Texas began talks—despite Mexican warnings that annexation would mean war. By April 1844 Tyler had a treaty to present to the Senate for approval, but the Senate was cautious. Annexation of Texas was a very sensitive subject because of the issue of slave states and free states.

To Tyler's dismay, his new secretary of state, John C. Calhoun, played up that issue. Calhoun insisted that Texas must be annexed to assure the survival of slavery. Northern senators, convinced of a southern plot to create new slave states, were out-

raged. And some senators believed, along with Henry Clay, that "annexation and war with Mexico are identical."

While the Senate debated, the political parties met to choose presidential candidates for the election of 1844. The Whigs turned away from Tyler, who had opposed their policies, and unanimously chose Henry Clay. Clay opposed annexation of Texas without Mexico's consent. The abolitionist Liberty party ran James G. Birney, who had been their candidate in 1840. The party made no mention of Texas, but denounced the spread of slavery.

In late May the Democrats gathered in Baltimore. Former president Martin Van Buren was the leading candidate, but he opposed the Texas treaty because of the danger of war with Mexico. His stand angered southern and western Democrats. Van Buren could not gain a majority, and the convention deadlocked.

Then an unexpected candidate was nominated. James K. Polk, former governor of Tennessee and member of Congress, had Jackson's support. He was also an **expansionist**, who favored expanding the nation's territory. On the ninth ballot, the delegates unanimously chose him as their candidate.

On this campaign banner, Polk is shown with vice-presidential nominee George M. Dallas. Dallas was chosen after Senator Silas Wright, an admirer of Van Buren, rejected the offer.

In "Dance on a Sequoia Stump" artist F.R. Bennett did not exaggerate the size of the giant trees settlers found in northern California and southern Oregon.

The Democratic platform was boldly expansionist, calling for occupation of Oregon and annexation of Texas. Between the Democrats and the Whigs, voters had a clear-cut choice on expansion. In the election that December, Polk won 170 electoral votes to Clay's 105. The popular vote, however, was very close.

To Tyler, the election showed the nation's wishes. Still, Tyler knew that he could not get the needed two-thirds majority in the Senate to approve a treaty for annexing Texas. Instead, he called for annexation by joint resolution of Congress, which required only a simple majority in both houses.

Tyler's plan worked. In February 1845 both houses approved a resolution inviting Texas to enter the Union as a state, not a territory. In fact, Texas was allowed to form as many as four states out of its territory. Furthermore, the resolution extended the Missouri Compromise line of 36°30′, thus permitting slavery in Texas. In October Texans voted to join the United States. Two months later Texas formally entered the Union.

THE OREGON SETTLEMENT

James K. Polk was a man of discipline. In college he had studied both mathematics and the classics. In his 14 years in the House of Representatives he missed only one day of work. When he took office as president, his mind was clearly fixed on his goals and would not let go. Admirers called him "Young Hickory."

Polk came to the presidency with two campaign promises to fulfill—the annexation of Texas and of Oregon. Thanks to Tyler, Texas was already in the Union, so Polk turned his attention to Oregon. He sternly warned Britain that joint occupation of Oregon was no longer enough for Americans.

Polk asked for all of Oregon up to the southern tip of Russian Alaska at boundary line 54°40′. His supporters promptly adopted the slogan "Fifty-four forty or fight!"

Earlier administrations had offered to divide the Oregon country at the 49th parallel, which was the boundary between the United States and Canada to the east. Polk was willing to compromise. He had his secretary of state, James Buchanan, renew the offer of 49°.

British leaders reluctantly agreed. The British were already outnumbered in Oregon, and the once-prosperous fur trade was dying. Most of all, the British wanted peace, not war. In June 1846 Britain and America signed a treaty.

The Oregon treaty made the 49th parallel the boundary between Canada and the United States west of the Rocky Mountains. It settled a bitter British-American quarrel peacefully. And it opened the way for Oregon to become an American territory, which it did in 1848. Now Polk was free to concentrate on another matter in the West: California.

AMERICAN AMBITIONS IN CALIFORNIA

Since the 1830s, American leaders had been eager to expand trade in the Pacific. The bay of San Francisco was a powerful lure. When Polk took office he, like Jackson and Tyler, wanted California. His interest was sharpened when rumors reached Washington of British plans to seize California. In 1845 Polk sent Captain John C. Frémont, an explorer and a skilled map-maker, to survey a route to the Pacific Coast. The journey would take Frémont and his well-armed company into California. If Britain tried to seize the province or war broke out between Mexico and the United States, Polk would have an armed force in the area.

Finally, Polk harked back to the Monroe Doctrine to warn Europe, especially Britain, not to interfere in North America. In his message to Congress in December 1845, Polk declared that "the people of this continent alone have the right to decide their own destiny."

THE BREAK WITH MEXICO

Polk's efforts to acquire California, however, were complicated by Mexico's anger over Texas. The Mexican minister to Washington called the annexation of Texas in 1845 "an act of aggression, the most unjust . . . of modern history." In May 1845 Polk sent troops under General Zachary Taylor to the area "on or near the Rio Grande" to defend Texas. Taylor set up camp 150 miles (241 kilo-

meters) north of the Rio Grande, on the Nueces (nu-AY-sehs) River.

The border between Texas and Mexico had long been disputed. Texans said that the Rio Grande was the boundary, and Polk supported them. Mexico insisted that the southern border of Texas was at the Nueces River. Texas, the Mexicans flatly stated, had never extended as far south as the Rio Grande. Although neither Texas nor Mexico had occupied the land between the two rivers before annexation, both sides now claimed it.

Other issues set Mexico and the United States at odds with each other. During Mexico's revolt against Spain, Americans had sold the Mexicans supplies and arms. Mexico promised to pay later, but the continued upheavals there and an empty treasury kept it from paying its debts. In addition, American property had been destroyed and American lives lost in the revolt. The United States pressed its citizens' claims for damages.

Aware that Mexico had no money, Polk hoped to persuade the Mexican government to pay its debts in land. In November 1845 he sent John Slidell of Louisiana to Mexico with his offer. If Mexico would accept the Rio Grande as the southern border of Texas, the United States would pay off Americans' claims against Mexico. Slidell was also to offer $5 million for the territory of New Mexico, and another $25 million for California.

Slidell never presented these terms to the Mexican government. Mexico refused to negotiate with Slidell and vowed that no concessions would be made to the United States.

On January 12, 1846, Polk learned of the Mexican reaction. He ordered General Taylor to march from his camp on the Nueces River to the Rio Grande. In late April, Mexican cavalry crossed the Rio Grande and clashed with American soldiers.

News of the clash on the Rio Grande reached Washington on May 9. Two days later, Polk asked Congress to declare war. "Mexico," he declared, "has passed the boundary of the United States, has invaded our territory and shed American blood upon the American soil." Congress approved the message, and Polk declared war on May 13.

Not all Americans, however, supported the war. Northern Whigs and abolitionists considered it a plot by southerners to gain new land for slave states. John Quincy Adams called it "a most unrighteous war" and voted against it in the House.

The Mexican War 1846-1848

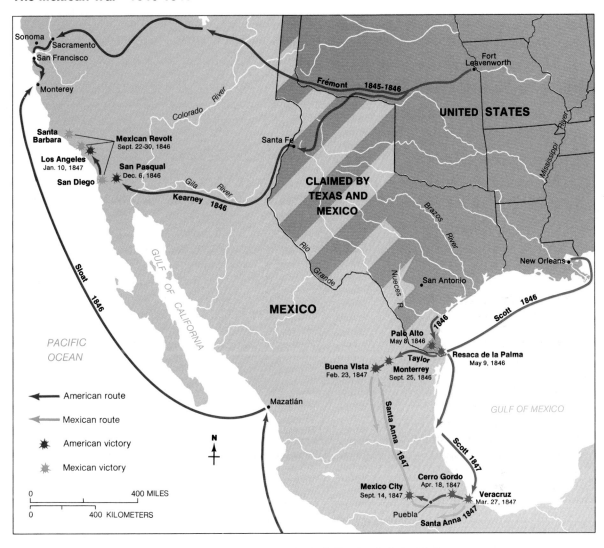

Mexico won no battles in the Mexican War. But Mexican colonists in California rebelled against an American takeover. The Mexican Californians struck and quickly retook garrisons at Santa Barbara, Los Angeles, and San Diego. They were not driven out for three months.

WAR WITH MEXICO

Polk planned to launch a three-pronged attack against Mexico. General Zachary Taylor would push into northern Mexico, and a second force would travel by sea to southern Mexico. The third army would head for New Mexico and then California.

In June, General Stephen W. Kearney started out from Missouri, leading the "Army of the West." Two months later, Kearney and his army reached New Mexico and proclaimed it to be part of the United States. The Americans occupied Santa Fe without opposition and raised the American flag.

Meanwhile, the war had already begun in California. In mid-June a group of American settlers in the Sacramento Valley, encouraged by Captain John C. Frémont, had seized the small town of Sonoma. They declared American settlements independent and lowered the Mexican flag. Replacing it was the flag of the "Republic of California," showing the name of the republic, a grizzly bear, and a star. Frémont soon joined the "Bear Flag Revolt" and was voted leader of the republic.

In 1842, four years before war began, an American naval officer led a premature invasion at Monterey in Mexican California.

About a month later the Americans reached the last barrier to Mexico City—Chapultepec (chah-pool-tay-PEHK). In wave after deadly wave, the Americans stormed the fortress there. Chapultepec fell to the Americans. After another day's bitter fighting, the capital itself fell. Although Mexicans still fought on in scattered groups, the war was over.

THE TREATY OF GUADALUPE HIDALGO

In February 1848 Mexico and the United States made their formal peace. The treaty, signed in the town of Guadalupe Hidalgo (GWAH-dah-LOO-pay ee-DAHL-goh), recognized American conquests during the war.

Mexico renounced all claims to Texas north of the Rio Grande. It also ceded California and an area including New Mexico, Arizona, Utah, Nevada, and parts of Wyoming and Colorado. Altogether, Mexico lost one half of its territory to the United States. In return, Americans agreed to pay $15 million and assume some $3 million in debts owed by Mexico to American citizens. Also, the United States guaranteed the religious, civil, and property rights of Mexicans living in the ceded area.

Five years later, both Mexico and the United States disputed the southern border of New Mexico drawn by the treaty. Americans, especially southerners, wanted to build a railroad to the Pacific Ocean across some of the Mexican land. In 1853 James Gadsden, the American minister to Mexico, warned the Mexican government to give up the land or risk a fight.

Mexico unhappily agreed to a treaty. For $10 million, it sold to the United States a strip of territory south of the Gila (HEE-lah) River as well as a disputed region near El Paso. The Gadsden Purchase angered Mexicans.

It also angered many Mexicans living in the new United States territories. Their ancestors—Spanish and Indian—had been the first to make the West their home. Names of mountains, rivers, and cities and ways of life all reflected their long presence in these lands.

Yet they were treated as an "alien culture" by Americans moving west. "Our unfortunate people," Mexican diplomat Manuel Crescencio Rejón declared, "will have to wander in search of hospitality in a strange land."

In early July, a naval force under Commodore John D. Sloat joined Frémont's "California Battalion," and the Americans swept first into northern California coastal towns.

Then Stephen Kearney and a company of 100 joined the naval force to capture San Diego, Los Angeles, and other southern towns. By January 1847 the war in California was over.

Meanwhile, Zachary Taylor—called "Old Rough and Ready" by his troops—relentlessly tracked the Mexican army through northern Mexico. He captured Monterrey in mid-September.

On February 22, 1847, the armies of Taylor and Santa Anna collided at Buena Vista (BWAY-nah VEES-tah), in the hilly country south of Monterrey. The Americans soundly defeated the Mexicans, causing 1,800 casualties. The Americans were left victors of northern Mexico.

In early March 1847, General Winfield Scott put into action his plan to invade Mexico by sea. Scott and 10,000 troops landed near Veracruz (VER-ah-KROOZ), on the east coast of Mexico. By the end of March, Veracruz had been captured.

Next, Scott's army turned inland. After a series of skirmishes, Scott's army of 14,000 set out for Mexico City in August. Santa Anna tried to stop Scott's forces short of the capital, in bloody battles at Contreras (kohn-TRAY-rahs) and Churubusco (CHOO-roo-VOOS-koh). Still, Scott pressed onward.

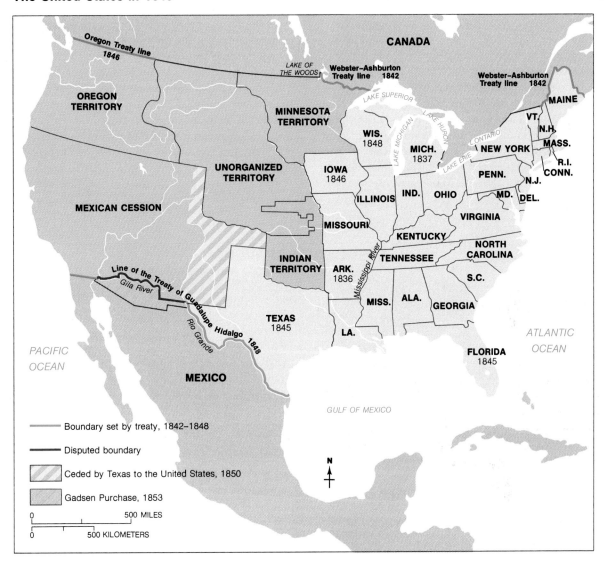

Boundary set by treaty, 1842–1848

Disputed boundary

Ceded by Texas to the United States, 1850

Gadsen Purchase, 1853

THE GOLD RUSH

The ink on the Treaty of Guadalupe Hidalgo was scarcely dry when news of gold in California began to spread across the nation. Gold had been discovered in late January 1848 by James W. Marshall as he worked on John A. Sutter's sawmill at Coloma, on the American River. Word leaked out, and a gold rush erupted in northern California.

"Gold fever" raged eastward. By 1849 crowds of gold seekers were heading west on the trails, making "helter-skelter marches" for California. Others went by sea, sailing around the cape of South America or crossing the Isthmus of Panama.

These "forty-niners" turned California into a land of untamed mining camps and booming towns. Prices soared—coffee cost $4 a pound and flour $400 a barrel—and miners paid in gold dust.

The few women easily earned a living cooking, doing laundry, and running shops. While Luzena Wilson's husband searched for gold, she made the family fortune in Nevada City, California.

> With my own hands I chopped stakes, drove them into the ground, and set up my table. I bought provisions at a neighboring store, and when my husband came back at night he found, amid the weird light of the pine torches, twenty miners eating at my table.

Soon, Wilson was running a prosperous hotel. Charlotte Parkhurst took a different sort of job. Disguised as a man, "Charley" became a fearless stagecoach driver along the narrow mountain trails.

Boom-town California was without real government and soon became a land of violence. Gold fever led to claim jumping, ambushing, and murder. Gold fever also heated up prejudices. American miners from different sections of the country looked on each other with dislike and distrust. They also looked upon the Mexicans and, especially, the Chinese with dislike.

Perhaps the ones to suffer most were California's original residents, the Indians. Disease cut a deadly swath through the tribes. Indians also found their prime food sources—fish and acorns—disappearing.

The gold boom did not last long. Few ever made the fortunes that they dreamed of, but many found California to their liking and stayed on. In 1849 a constitutional convention met to form a state government, and its work was ratified by the people.

By early 1850 California was ready to apply for statehood, and its constitution did not allow slavery. This raised an old, nagging question. Would the

AMERICAN OBSERVERS

One method of sifting gold from the soil was to run water through a sluice, or trough, over the dirt. The many streams of northern California supplied the water very conveniently.

DAME SHIRLEY
GOLD-RUSH CHRONICLER

Among those who caught the gold-rush fever that swept the United States in 1849 were a young doctor, Fayette Clapp, and his wife, Louisa. They were not a promising pair for the rugged life. The doctor himself was sickly, while Louisa confessed to being a "half-dying invalid." Blonde, pretty, and frail, she was a well-educated lady accustomed to the genteel parlors of New England. Yet this unlikely individual would prove to be a brilliant reporter. She produced what historians now consider the best accounts of gold-rush life ever written.

The Clapps sailed around Cape Horn to San Francisco, then headed to Rich Bar, a boom town in California's mining country. Arriving by muleback in 1851, Louisa Clapp set up housekeeping in a tent. Then, signing herself "Dame Shirley," she began to write.

She described Rich Bar, from its single fancy hotel with bar and gambling tables to its crude

miners' huts made of pine branches covered with red calico shirts. She told how the miners lived and worked, and reported their adventures and their tragedies.

She also described the violence. "In the short space of twenty-four days," she wrote in July of 1852, "we have had murders, fearful accidents, bloody deaths, a mob, whippings, a hanging, an attempt at suicide and a fatal duel."

Twenty million dollars in gold were mined at Rich Bar, but by late 1852, the gold was running out. Still, "Dame Shirley" hated to leave. Like many women who had gone west, she had changed. "And only think of such a shrinking, timid, frail thing as I *used* to be," she exclaimed. The once delicate Victorian lady had become a strong woman. "I *like* the wild and barbarous life," she said. "I go from the mountains with a deep sorrow. . . . Here, at last, I have been contented."

San Francisco Bay could easily accommodate the ships that brought gold seekers to early California, as seen in this 1851 lithograph. The dress of the people tells the story of their varied origins and backgrounds. Mexican and Chinese are prominent among the townspeople.

new territories and states being formed in the West be slave or free? Years earlier, Thomas Jefferson had cautioned that the slavery issue was "like a fire bell in the night." As the United States entered the 1850s, that clanging fire bell could be heard as never before.

Mariano Vallejo, one of Mexican California's leading citizens, concluded that California's future lay with the United States. In 1849 he helped draw up the state constitution.

SECTION REVIEW

1. Identify the following: Webster-Ashburton Treaty, John C. Frémont, John Slidell, "Bear Flag Revolt," Treaty of Guadalupe Hidalgo, Gadsden Purchase.

2. Define the following: manifest destiny, expansionist.

3. (a) What issue made the annexation of Texas a hotly debated subject in the election of 1844? (b) Name the three parties involved in the election, their candidates, and their stand on that issue.

4. (a) Explain the slogan "Fifty-four forty or fight!" (b) How was the Oregon boundary dispute settled?

5. Describe the boundary dispute between the United States and Mexico.

6. Name two groups and two individuals in the United States who were against the war with Mexico.

7. List the three parts of Polk's plan for war with Mexico. Who were the leaders of the three forces? Describe the results of each campaign.

8. (a) When was gold discovered in California? (b) What were some of the results of the gold rush?

SUMMARY

In the 1820s and 1830s, Americans pushed farther and farther west. First trappers and traders, then settlers with wagons, opened trails to New Mexico, Oregon, Utah, and California. Ultimately, the United States began to claim the land.

Land claims were settled peaceably by treaty with Britain. Boundary disputes between Texas and Mexico, however, were fueled by cultural and political differences. Eventually these disputes led to war.

At first Texas seemed big enough for everyone, even to Mexico. Mexico agreed to grant land to Americans, provided they become Mexican subjects and accept the Catholic religion. On this basis thousands of Americans streamed westward into the vast lands of Texas.

The Americans did not always follow the rules set out for them, however. In 1830, when Americans in Texas outnumbered Mexicans by four to one, Mexico banned further American immigration. Tensions increased, and in 1832 the first actual fighting broke out. After two particularly bloody battles—at the Alamo and Goliad—American forces defeated the Mexicans at San Jacinto. But the treaties signed by Santa Anna were not recognized by the Mexican government. Texas remained the Lone Star Republic until 1845, when it became a state.

Mexico recognized neither the independence of Texas nor its annexation to the United States. An offer of negotiation over boundaries was refused. Fighting broke out again on the banks of the Rio Grande, and in May of 1846 the United States declared war on Mexico. The war ended with the fall of Mexico City to the Americans late in 1847.

In the Treaty of Guadalupe Hidalgo Mexico lost Texas north of the Rio Grande. Mexico also gave up California along with an area including New Mexico, Arizona, Utah, Nevada, and parts of Wyoming and Colorado.

Shortly after the United States acquired California, gold was discovered there, and the gold rush began. In 1849 a constitutional convention met to form a state government. By 1850 California was ready to apply for statehood.

CHAPTER REVIEW

1. How did each of the following motivate Americans to move west? (a) trade (b) beaver fur (c) rich farmland (d) Indian tribes (e) economic depression (f) religious freedom. Cite examples.

2. (a) List three reasons why many Americans reacted to Mormon beliefs with hostility. (b) How did events in Nauvoo determine the Mormons' new home? (c) How did the Mormons build their "Kingdom of God in the wilderness"?

3. (a) Why were Americans drawn to Texas in the early 1800s? (b) What prompted Spanish officials to accept Moses Austin's plan of settlement? (c) What caused "Texas fever"? How did it affect population in the South? In Texas?

4. (a) Explain how each of the following led to war in Texas: religion, slavery, government, American offers to buy Texas, military rule in Texas. (b) How did Americans in Texas justify their resistance to Mexican rule?

5. (a) Why did the results of the election of 1844 spur Tyler to annex Texas? (b) How did Tyler gain Senate approval of annexation? Why did he choose this approach? (c) What were the provisions of Texas annexation?

Flags of six nations have billowed in the Texas winds through its history. The lone star flag was adopted in 1839. The red, white, and blue stand for loyalty, strength, and bravery.

Searching for beavers, trappers opened new trails through the West. In a good year fur companies paid about four dollars a pound for pelts. Beaver hats sold for five dollars.

6. (a) How did "Oregon fever" begin? (b) What did American settlers demand in 1843? How did this conflict with the Convention of 1818? (c) How did Polk acquire Oregon without war?

7. (a) Why did the Spanish finally settle California? How? (b) What caused American interest in California in the 1830s and 1840s? (c) Why did Polk send Frémont to California? (d) How did the American annexation of Texas complicate Polk's attempts to acquire California?

8. (a) How did each of the following cause tension between the United States and Mexico: the annexation of Texas, the border between Texas and Mexico, Mexican debts, American claims? (b) What offer did Slidell carry to Mexico? (c) How did Mexico's response influence Polk?

9. Compare the views of Polk and northern Whigs and abolitionists on war with Mexico.

10. (a) How did Polk's plan of attack reflect his goals in the war with Mexico? (b) What were the provisions of the Treaty of Guadalupe Hidalgo? (c) How did the Gadsden Purchase affect the provisions? How did Mexicans react to both the treaty and the purchase? Why?

ISSUES AND IDEAS

1. (a) What American beliefs and concerns made up the idea of manifest destiny? (b) Do you think this idea was always important to Americans? Consider the Louisiana Purchase, the War of 1812, and the Adams-Onís Treaty of 1819.

2. Give arguments for or against annexing Texas in 1844 by a northern Whig, a liberal party member, and a western Democrat. Then give the arguments of Andrew Jackson and John C. Calhoun.

SKILLS WORKSHOP

1. *Writing.* Stories, letters, and advertisements praising Oregon, California, and Texas lured many Americans west. Write such a story, letter, or advertisement about Oregon, California, or Texas. Include information that you think easterners would want to know.

2. *Primary sources.* In 1848 Thomas Larkin, the American consul in California, wrote to Secretary of State James Buchanan regarding the gold rush:

> Three fourths of the houses in the town on the Bay of San Francisco are deserted. Every blacksmith, carpenter, and lawyer is leaving; brickyards, sawmills, and ranches are left perfectly alone. A large part of the volunteers at San Francisco and Sonoma have deserted. Vessels are losing their crews. Both our newspapers are discontinued. San Francisco has not a justice of the peace left.

Do you think Larkin is a reliable source of information on events in northern California? Why? What parts of this letter seem to deal with fact? What parts might be opinions? From this letter, what did you learn about the effect of "gold fever" on people, businesses, and government?

PAST AND PRESENT

1. Many people are still moving west. Do you think that their reasons are similar to those of people in the 1830s and 1840s? Why or why not?

2. Using a modern road map, find out what highways follow the old Santa Fe, Oregon, California, and Mormon trails. What present-day states do these trails cross? Do the Missouri River towns that were "jumping-off places" still exist? What new, large cities have developed along the routes of the old trails? Name several of them.

A HOUSE DIVIDED

1850–1900

Kurz and Allison lithograph after a painting by an unknown artist. *Battle of Antietam*, 1888.

1600
1700
1800
1900
2000
• Jamestown founded
• Revolutionary War
• Civil War
• Today

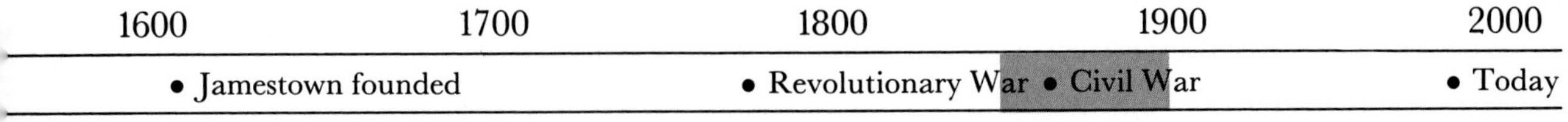

UNIT 4
1850–1900

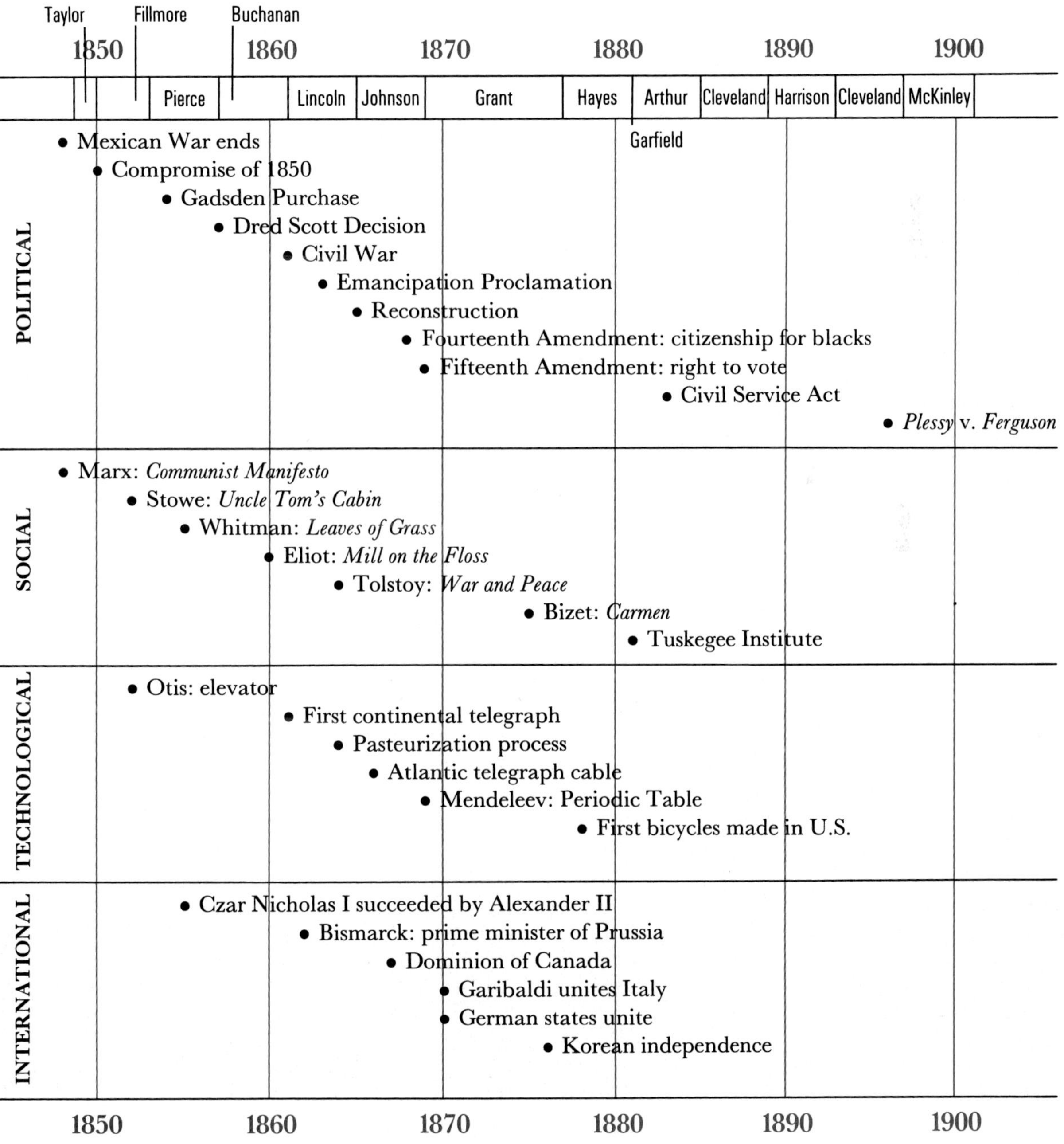

Taylor
Fillmore
Buchanan
1850
1860
1870
1880
1890
1900
Pierce
Lincoln
Johnson
Grant
Hayes
Arthur
Cleveland
Harrison
Cleveland
McKinley
Garfield
POLITICAL
• Mexican War ends
• Compromise of 1850
• Gadsden Purchase
• Dred Scott Decision
• Civil War
• Emancipation Proclamation
• Reconstruction
• Fourteenth Amendment: citizenship for blacks
• Fifteenth Amendment: right to vote
• Civil Service Act
• *Plessy* v. *Ferguson*
SOCIAL
• Marx: *Communist Manifesto*
• Stowe: *Uncle Tom's Cabin*
• Whitman: *Leaves of Grass*
• Eliot: *Mill on the Floss*
• Tolstoy: *War and Peace*
• Bizet: *Carmen*
• Tuskegee Institute
TECHNOLOGICAL
• Otis: elevator
• First continental telegraph
• Pasteurization process
• Atlantic telegraph cable
• Mendeleev: Periodic Table
• First bicycles made in U.S.
INTERNATIONAL
• Czar Nicholas I succeeded by Alexander II
• Bismarck: prime minister of Prussia
• Dominion of Canada
• Garibaldi unites Italy
• German states unite
• Korean independence
1850
1860
1870
1880
1890
1900

NORTH AND SOUTH IN CONFLICT

1850–1861

LIFE IN THE NORTH AND THE SOUTH
SLAVERY IN THE WEST
THE NATION DIVIDES

In 1854 Charlotte Forten saw the capture of an escaped slave named Burns. A new law allowed fugitive slaves to be captured in the free North and returned to their southern owners.

"Friday, June 2. Our worst fears are realized; the decision was against poor Burns, and he has been sent back to a bondage worse, a thousand times worse than death. Even an attempt at rescue was utterly impossible; the prisoner was completely surrounded by soldiers with bayonets fixed. . . . Today Massachusetts has again been disgraced. . . . With what scorn must that government be regarded, which cowardly assembles thousands of soldiers to satisfy the demands of slaveholders; to deprive of his freedom a man, created in God's own image, whose sole offense is the color of his skin! . . . This, on the very soil where the Revolution of 1776 began. . . .

"Sunday, June 4. A beautiful day. The sky is cloudless, the sun shines warm and bright, and a delicious breeze fans my cheek as I sit by the window writing. How strange it is that in a world so beautiful, there can be so much wickedness; on this delightful day, while many are enjoying themselves in their happy homes, not poor Burns only, but millions beside are suffering in chains."

Forten was luckier than most other blacks. She was free. She was, however, familiar with slavery, an issue dividing North and South. Indeed, by the 1850s the North and South were two different worlds. Factories outlined the North, and seemingly endless fields of cotton spread over the South. The needs of industry and the needs of agriculture were to underlie a great conflict.

To the west were lands to be settled. New states would be carved from these lands. Should these states be slave or free? On the eve of the 1860s, this issue threatened to break the bonds that held the Union together.

LIFE IN THE NORTH AND THE SOUTH

READ TO FIND OUT

— what effects the railroad system had on the North.

— how expanding industry changed working conditions.

— how the labor movement began.

— how the tide of immigrants affected American society.

— how free blacks were treated in the North and West.

— how agriculture shaped the economy and society of the South.

— how slavery became a major issue dividing North and South.

By the 1850s factory and cotton field had become symbols of the different ways of life in the North and the South. In the North, new factories hummed to the tune of industry. In the South, life working on the land continued as rhythmically as the seasons.

Of course, factory and field were only symbols. Many northerners still earned their living by farming, and there were industries in the South. North and South often worked together. Southern cotton fed northern mills, and Yankee ships moved southern crops to market. In fact, the two regions were bound together by the ties of commerce.

THE RAILROAD ERA

Commerce could not exist without transportation. In the 1820s and 1830s canals, roads, and river-going steamboats had spurred the growth of both trade and industry. Now, there was a new way to move people and goods—travel over rails.

For years, passenger and freight cars had been pulled along rails by horses or mules. Then, in 1828, the city of Baltimore set about enlarging its western market by granting a charter to the Baltimore and Ohio Railroad. A New York manufacturer named Peter Cooper hoped to convince the railroad to hitch its cars to his steam-powered locomotive instead of to a horse.

In 1830 the owners of the Baltimore and Ohio staged a race to see which was faster—horse or locomotive. Each pulled a railroad car. Cooper's *Tom Thumb* chugged to an early lead, then broke down. The horse then pulled ahead and won. Still, the Baltimore and Ohio took up the idea of the locomotive. The railroad era had begun.

Other railroads soon followed. By 1833 a line stretched 130 miles (209 kilometers) from Charleston, South Carolina, westward across the state. In Pennsylvania, which soon took the lead in railroad building, lines brought coal straight from the mines to the blast furnaces of industry.

By 1840 over 400 railroads had laid some 3,000 miles (4,800 kilometers) of track, and cities from New England to Georgia had rail service. Then, in 1850, Congress began giving federal land to the states to build railroads in unsettled areas. One line was built from Chicago to the Gulf of Mexico at Mobile, Alabama.

By 1860 over 30,000 miles (48,300 kilometers) of track linked cities of the eastern seaboard, and

With the growth of transportation came growth in the technology of bridge building. John Roebling designed this two-level bridge built over Niagara chasm in 1855. Roebling later designed one of the world's most famous suspension bridges—the Brooklyn Bridge.

reached out westward like fingers to the Mississippi River. Almost 70 percent of the track was in the North, and railroads and industry quickly became necessary to each other. Railroads helped industry to grow by moving goods quickly and cheaply. Freight cars moved raw materials to factories, and products to market.

As Daniel Webster said at the opening of a line in New Hampshire: "Fellow citizens, this railroad may be said to bring the seas to your door. You cannot, indeed, sniff its salt water, but you will taste its best products."

THE MERCHANT MARINE

While the railroads moved goods within the United States, ships were carrying goods across the seas. Between the 1820s and 1850s America's merchant marine—ships used in commerce—grew tremendously. New England designers built swift sailing vessels called *clipper ships*, which set speed records between ports of America, Europe, and Asia. With its fleet of clippers and other sailing ships, the United States captured over half the highly profitable China trade by 1860.

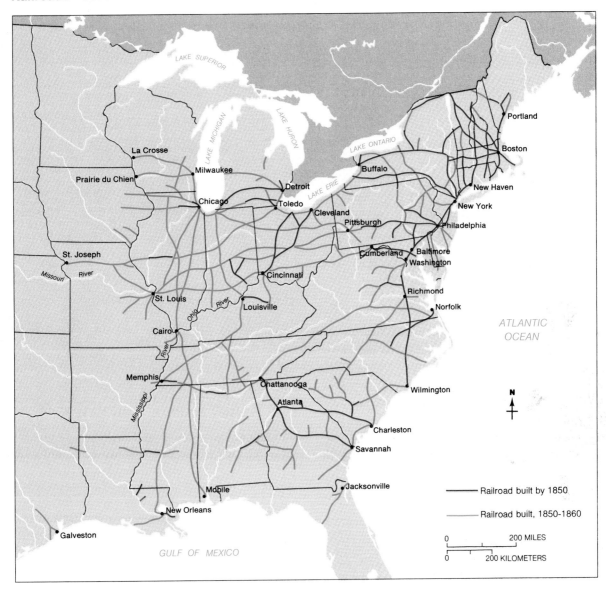

Railroad built by 1850

Railroad built, 1850-1860

0   200 MILES

0   200 KILOMETERS

However, steam power soon made sailing ships obsolete. Britain had built a fleet of fast steamships with huge cargo holds, and it took the lead in ocean trade. The United States belatedly built some steamships and mounted a challenge, but its infant steamship industry could not match that of Britain.

THE INDUSTRIAL NORTH

In the North, industry grew side by side with improved transportation. Throughout the region, factories churned out goods. Cotton goods led the way, but other industries were growing quickly. By 1850 wool products were being produced by 1,500 mills. Factories large and small produced countless other goods—plows, clocks, rubber goods, shoes. By 1860 the North boasted a total of 74,058 factories producing a variety of goods.

This burst of industry brought new factories to cities. And the factories recruited workers, many of whom left the farm for a paycheck and a better life in industry. Some smaller cities like Newark, New Jersey, and Lowell, Massachusetts, simply grew up around industry.

During the 1860s about 58 percent of workers in cotton mills were women, and about 7 percent were children under twelve. Winslow Homer shows their prominence in this drawing of laborers at a New England textile mill.

In the 1820s Lowell had been a small farming village on the Merrimack River. In two decades it became an industrial city of 30,000 people, and was built around busy textile mills. People called Lowell "the mile of mills on the Merrimack."

Most mill employees, known as the "Lowell girls," were young women from farming families. They earned decent wages, lived in clean boarding houses, and were encouraged to continue their schooling.

However, conditions changed at Lowell after 1840. As the textile companies grew and competition became greater, the original owners lost control. Managers were hired to run the mills, and their first duty was to cut waste and increase profits. Wages were cut, the long hours stayed the same, and workers had to handle more looms. If the workers complained, they were fired. Often, they also were "blacklisted," which meant that employers at other factories agreed not to hire them.

Working conditions grew harsh in all industries during the 1830s and 1840s. One factory manager remarked: "I regard my work-people just as I regard my machinery. . . . When my machines get old and useless, I reject them and get new, and these workers are part of my machinery."

THE EARLY LABOR MOVEMENT

As industries grew larger and working conditions worsened, some workers tried to change conditions. This small labor movement began in the 1820s.

Skilled workers, such as printers, shoemakers, and carpenters, realized that the old system of apprenticeship was breaking down. As more and more goods were made in large factories, there was less opportunity to learn a trade and then open a small shop. Since their future seemed to lie as wage earners rather than business owners, many skilled workers tried to band together.

Some joined *workers' parties*, which called for such changes as free education and an end to imprisonment for debt. Some skilled workers formed *craft unions*, groups of people who tried to improve working conditions in their trade. The first goal of unions was to shorten the work day, which averaged 12.5 hours in 1830. To get a 10-hour day, workers went out on **strike**. In other words, they stopped working in order to force employers to meet their demands.

However, both strikes and labor unions were illegal. Workers involved in them could be fined and arrested. When 21 tailors went on strike in 1836, they were fined $1,150 for striking and for

WALT WHITMAN
CELEBRATING AMERICA

On the Fourth of July, 1855, a thirty-seven-year-old Brooklyn newspaper reporter and part-time carpenter named Walt Whitman published his first book of poetry. He called it *Leaves of Grass*. The author's picture set the tone. Dressed in rough workclothes and a broad-brimmed hat set at a rakish angle, Whitman stared challengingly out at the reader.

The poetry was startlingly different. Unlike most verse of the day, it had no rhyme and no set rhythm. Moreover, Walt Whitman had rejected what he called "delicate lady words" and "gloved gentleman words" to write in everyday language. "I am not a bit tamed," he announced in one poem. "I sound my barbaric yawp over the roofs of the world."

Critics pounced on the book. It sounded like "some escaped lunatic raving," said one. "Walt Whitman is as unacquainted with art as a hog is with mathematics," wrote another.

Yet a few recognized its stunning originality. New England philosopher Ralph Waldo Emerson called it "the most extraordinary piece of wit and wisdom that America has yet contributed. He told Whitman, "I greet you at the beginning of a great career."

Though today many consider Whitman America's greatest poet, his work was never accepted during his lifetime. Still he continued to write. He celebrated ordinary people and common things.

Walt Whitman's main subject was the United States in all its variety. "The United States themselves are essentially the greatest poem," he said. In a time of conflict between North and South, he held

In "I Hear America Singing" Whitman expressed his admiration for the citizens of America who made up a great chorus, "each singing what belongs to him or her and to none else."

fast to his faith in "the democratic wisdom underneath, like solid ground for all." In Walt Whitman, America had found its voice.

---

forming "into an unlawful club or combination to injure trade." The fledgling labor movement was dealt an even harsher blow by the Panic of 1837. As the economy deteriorated and unemployment lists grew, workers eager to hold their jobs would not risk joining unions or striking.

Then, when the economy improved in the 1840s, many of the craft unions came back to life. In 1842 the Massachusetts Supreme Court, in *Commonwealth v. Hunt*, ruled that unions were legal organizations. Demand for the 10-hour day resumed, and this time spread rapidly among factory workers.

Cotton mill workers in Pittsburgh struck twice for the shorter day. Both times they were unsuccessful. In 1848 textile workers in western Pennsylvania won the 10-hour day, but at the price of a 16 percent wage cut. Many craft unions won the 10-hour day, and by 1853 laws were passed in most northern states upholding it.

However, the flurry of labor activity again died out. In 1857 another depression killed many unions. By 1860 under 1 percent of American workers belonged to unions. Meanwhile, a new supply of labor was flooding the market.

THE IMMIGRANT TIDE

From the 1830s through the 1850s, over 4 million immigrants landed at American ports. Almost half of them came from Ireland, where a blight ruined the potato crop and led to widespread famine. About one third were Germans fleeing political turmoil and hard times.

Nearly all the immigrants arrived in the North and stayed there. Most were penniless, and quickly lined up for factory jobs. Since they were willing to work for low wages, many employers lowered wages for all their workers. Those who complained or went on strike could be replaced by immigrants.

Immigrants were accused of taking jobs from "native-born" Americans. Also, many Protestant Americans disliked Irish and German Catholics. And many Americans feared that the newcomers would change the American way of life.

The immigrants' accents, language, and traditions were different. Most groups settled together, retaining their old culture in the new world. Anti-immigrant feelings led to street fights and riots in many northern cities.

In the 1840s *nativists*, or those who opposed unrestricted immigration, formed secret societies to keep immigrants out of American politics. Members had to pledge to vote against any immigrant or Catholic candidate for office. In one such society, the Supreme Order of the Star-Spangled Banner, members had to claim "I know nothing" if questioned about the order. By 1849 the order had spread throughout the country and established itself as a political party, the American party. It was popularly called the Know-Nothing party.

FREE BLACKS IN THE NORTH

Others who faced resentment and discrimination throughout the North were free blacks. By 1840 about 90 percent of northern blacks lived in states that excluded them from voting. Blacks often could not find unskilled, much less skilled, work. When they did find work, it was usually for low wages.

Factory workers did not like competing for jobs with blacks any more than with immigrants. Blacks were barred from membership in most unions. When white workers went on strike, employers hired blacks to replace them. This hardened white bitterness toward blacks.

Many free blacks headed west, looking for a better life. However, most discovered that prejudice was just as strong in the West. In the early 1850s Iowa, Illinois, Indiana, and Oregon all passed laws making it a crime for blacks to settle there. In Oregon blacks could not own property or make contracts. In California blacks could not testify in court against whites.

Most northerners ignored the plight of blacks, immigrants, and workers. If there were problems, they were considered merely a part of the progress that was going on all around. And while the North moved to the clang and clatter of the Industrial Revolution, the South was being shaped by different forces.

THE SOUTHERN ECONOMY

In 1845 William Gregg, president of the company that owned the South's first cotton mill, urged South Carolina to develop more industry. "At every village and crossroad in the state," he wrote, "we should have a tannery, a shoemaker, a clothier, a hatter, [and] a blacksmith."

Northern resentment led to the removal of blacks and abolitionists from Fremont Temple in Boston—the subject of an 1860 wood engraving published in *Harper's Weekly*.

Agriculture in the South 1860

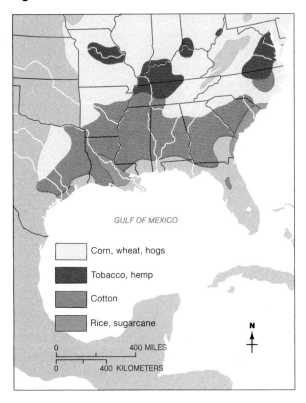

GULF OF MEXICO

Corn, wheat, hogs

Tobacco, hemp

Cotton

Rice, sugarcane

0   400 MILES

0   400 KILOMETERS

N

The South did begin to be involved in manufacturing. By 1860 the region had over 20,000 small factories, mainly producing cotton textiles, flour, and tobacco products. However, these factories made up only 15 percent of the nation's manufacturing establishments. Clearly, most of the southern economy rested on agriculture.

Louisiana grew 95 percent of the South's sugarcane. Virginia was the chief tobacco producer, followed by Kentucky, Tennessee, and North Carolina. Rice was grown in the coastal regions of Georgia and South Carolina. The states in the Deep South produced about 30 percent of America's corn, and those in the Upper South grew from 20 percent to 25 percent of its rye, oats, and wheat. Still, the king of crops was cotton.

Ever since Eli Whitney's invention of the cotton gin in 1793, more and more southern land had been turned over to cotton. Around 1800 most of the South's cotton was grown in South Carolina and Georgia. Then, after the War of 1812, fertile lands to the west attracted cotton planters. The cotton kingdom spread to Alabama, Mississippi, Louisiana, and eventually Texas.

A riverboat fully loaded with bales of cotton settles low in the water. This scene was common in Southern ports as products of plantations were moved to distant markets.

Cotton Production 1800–1860

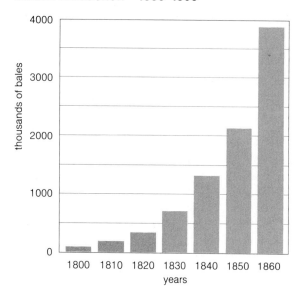

Mills in the North and in Britain could use as much cotton as could be grown. Between 1800 and 1850 the demand doubled, then doubled again. Cotton became America's major export, making up nearly two thirds of all exports.

FREE SOUTHERN SOCIETY

About three fourths of the southerners who worked the land were whites who owned small farms. They grew their own food and a few acres of cotton or tobacco as cash crops. They were not rich, but they were not very poor either.

Poor whites made up barely 10 percent of the population. Some settled on abandoned, worn-out lands and scraped by as best they could. Others were the hill people of the Appalachian back country. Isolated from the rest of the South, these independent people lived by hunting, fishing, or herding wild cattle and hogs.

There was another minority of southerners at the bottom of free society—some 250,000 free blacks. They worked as servants, as hired farm workers, in factories, and in unskilled jobs in the cities. A few managed to become artisans, merchants, or farmers.

The group that had the most striking influence on the South was also a minority—the slaveholding planters. They farmed the richest soil and produced most of the South's cash crops. In 1850 about one southern family out of four held slaves.

Slaveholders had a rigid hierarchy. Most held only 5 or 6 slaves and were considered farmers rather than planters. To be considered a planter, a person had to own at least 20 slaves, and only about 12 percent of the slaveholders qualified. At the peak of the hierarchy were some 3,000 families who owned 100 or more slaves.

SLAVERY

The poor southerners, the small farmers, and the rich planter class all had counterparts in other areas of the country. But only in the South was there slavery. In 1800 there had been about 900,000 slaves in the South. By 1860 the number had soared to 4 million. Slaves could be found working in factories, on construction gangs, in mines, even as assistants to artisans. Many labored on plantations.

Most plantation slaves were field hands. They worked the cotton fields in a *gang system*. Groups of thirty or forty men, women, and children plowed, hoed, planted, and harvested the cotton. With crops like tobacco, rice, and sugar, a *task system* was used. Each slave was assigned to a specific job.

Somewhat better off were the slaves who learned crafts such as carpentry or bricklaying. Household

Black Population 1820–1860

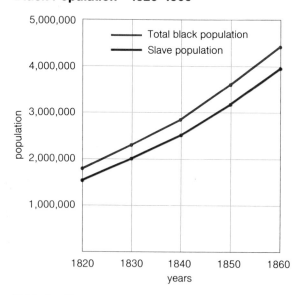

Blacks lived in every state of the Union. After 1790 the total population of the United States doubled every twenty-five years, but the black population did not grow as rapidly.

slaves sometimes had easier work and better food, too. Best off of all was the driver, who saw to it that every order was carried out.

Some slaves were well treated while others suffered miserable living conditions. "Scarce a week passed without [the overseer] whipping me," Frederick Douglass wrote of his days as a field hand. But no matter how slaves were treated, they still lacked what other Americans enjoyed—freedom. As a North Carolina field hand said, "If I had my life to live over again, I would die fighting rather than be a slave."

Although their chances of fighting to freedom were small, a few slaves did revolt. In 1822 a revolt plotted in Charleston, South Carolina, was revealed to whites by an informer. The leader, a free black named Denmark Vesey, and 35 others were hanged. In 1831 a slave named Nat Turner led a band of slaves on a two-day sweep of revenge through the Virginia countryside, killing 57 whites. The state militia tracked down Turner's band, killing between 40 and 100 blacks. Turner was tried and executed.

Revolts like these had a strong effect. Northern abolitionists saw them as further proof of the evils of slavery. The southern states, fearing more uprisings, began passing *slave codes*, or laws to control both free blacks and slaves. Blacks could not vote, move freely from state to state, or meet in large groups.

In addition, white southerners felt they had to defend slavery. Many insisted that slavery was a positive good. Southerners proudly pointed out that a slave was cared for for life—unlike a factory worker in the North. John C. Calhoun compared southern civilization to the civilizations of ancient Greece and Rome, which also had rested on slave labor.

THE GULF BETWEEN NORTH AND SOUTH

Slavery was a major issue dividing North and South, but it was not the only issue. Southerners feared the growing power of the North.

The North's economic strength was part of the problem. The North was benefiting from its trade ties to the West. Trains and canal barges carried immigrants, farm machinery, and factory goods from the North to the rich farmlands of the Midwest. On the return trip, they carried the grain, hogs, and corn of the farms to northeastern cities. From the southern view, the North now stretched from Boston to Chicago and beyond.

Southerners depended on the banking, industry, and trade of the North. One southern writer complained:

> In one way or another, we are dependent on the North every day of our lives. In infancy, we are wrapped in northern muslin. In childhood, we are

Southern White Families Holding Slaves   1850

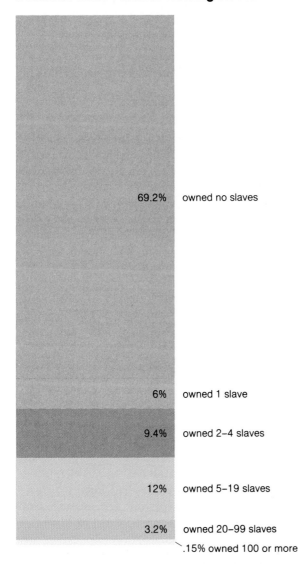

69.2%   owned no slaves

6%   owned 1 slave

9.4%   owned 2–4 slaves

12%   owned 5–19 slaves

3.2%   owned 20–99 slaves

.15% owned 100 or more

On the graph a family represents five persons. In 1850 the total white population of the South was about 6 million.

humored with northern toys. In youth, we are instructed out of northern books. In the decline of our life, we remedy our eyesight with northern spectacles. In old age, we are drugged with northern medicine. And, finally, when we die, our bodies, shrouded in northern linen, are borne to the grave in a northern carriage, entombed with a northern spade, and memorialized with a northern slab.

The North seemed about to overpower the South politically, too. In the House of Representatives, where representation was based on population, the North had long held an advantage. The hopes of the South rested in the Senate. Because each state could have only two senators, the Senate was balanced between North and South in 1850. However, the admission of one more free state would destroy that balance in the Senate.

Some southern leaders began to insist on the South's right to extend slavery into the territories won from Mexico. Politician Jefferson Davis explained, "We of the South are an agricultural people, and we require an extended territory."

SECTION REVIEW

1. Identify the following: Peter Cooper, *Tom Thumb*, *Commonwealth* v. *Hunt*, Know-Nothing party, Denmark Vesey, Nat Turner.

2. Define the following: craft union, strike, nativist, slave codes.

3. How did improvements in transportation affect cities and industries in the North?

4. (a) What was the first goal of craft unions? (b) Why did many craft unions die out in the 1850s?

5. Why did factory workers resent immigrants?

6. (a) Why were free blacks resented in the North? (b) How were free blacks treated in the West?

7. Why was more and more land turned over to cotton by 1793?

8. (a) What effect did slave revolts have on the attitude of Northern abolitionists? (b) How did slave owners react to the revolts?

9. What two major issues divided North and South?

10. How were North and South bound together by commerce?

SLAVERY IN THE WEST

READ TO FIND OUT

— how the Free-Soil party affected the election of 1848.

— what the Compromise of 1850 accomplished.

— how the Fugitive Slave Law caused resentment in both North and South.

— how the Ostend Manifesto angered northerners.

— how the Kansas-Nebraska Act provoked violence.

— what the new Republican party represented.

Toward the end of the war with Mexico, in 1846, David Wilmot of Pennsylvania added a clause to a House bill that provided funds to buy Mexican territory. The Wilmot Proviso banned slavery in any lands acquired during the war. The proposal passed in the House of Representatives and then lost in the Senate. But the Wilmot Proviso set off arguments across the nation. Was slavery to be extended to the new territories?

Senator John C. Calhoun of South Carolina claimed that the Wilmot Proviso would be unconstitutional and led the battle against it. Slaves were property, he claimed, and the Constitution protected property rights. People could take their property wherever they pleased. Calhoun's argument became known as the "Doctrine of the South."

Many northerners argued just as fiercely against the extension of slavery onto free soil. Some, agreeing with abolitionists, condemned the immorality of slavery. Many others feared competition from slave labor in the western lands.

Between these positions were two moderate proposals. One, backed by President Polk, would extend the Missouri Compromise line to the Pacific. The 1820 compromise banned slavery in all areas of the Louisiana Purchase north of the 36°30′ line, and allowed it south of the line.

Two senators—Lewis Cass of Michigan and Stephen A. Douglas of Illinois—had another solution.

The people of each territory would decide whether to allow slavery in that territory. This idea became known as *popular sovereignty*.

THE ELECTION OF 1848

The issue of slavery in the West was dividing the nation, but both major parties tried to avoid it in the 1848 presidential election. Since Polk had decided not to run again, the Democrats chose another moderate, Senator Lewis Cass. The Whigs chose General Zachary Taylor, hero of the war with Mexico. A southerner and a slaveholder, Taylor was silent on the question of extending slavery.

Northern abolitionists, labor unionists, and other opponents of the spread of slavery were dissatisfied with both parties. They met in Buffalo, New York, in the summer of 1848 and formed the Free-Soil party. Under the slogan "Free Soil, Free Speech, Free Labor, and Free Men," the party opposed any extension of slavery. The Free-Soilers chose ex-president Martin Van Buren as their candidate.

The Free-Soil party showed surprising strength in the election, sending ten members to the House. Since the House had been evenly split between Democrats and Whigs, these ten would wield some power. The Free-Soilers also polled enough votes in the key state of New York to keep the Democrats from winning there. Whig Zachary Taylor won the state and the presidency.

Free-Soilers not only affected the election, they kept the issue of slavery in the territories alive in Congress. Democrats and Whigs could no longer avoid the question.

THE COMPROMISE OF 1850

The Congress that met on December 3, 1849, was deeply divided. Members took 59 ballots to elect a Speaker of the House acceptable to both northerners and southerners. When the question of statehood for California arose, southern members refused to consider it. And Congress found it just as difficult to organize the rest of the territory gained from Mexico.

Throughout the South, people backed their representatives in Congress. State legislatures, newspapers, and public meetings gave the same warning. If the government limited the spread of slavery, the southern states would leave the Union.

The Compromise of 1850

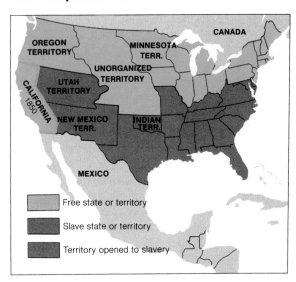

Henry Clay was a leading American statesman for nearly forty years. His efforts toward compromise between North and South won him admiration but never the presidency.

Henry Clay of Kentucky, who had preserved unity in 1820 with the Missouri Compromise, once more thought of a plan to bridge these differences. Clay, called "the Great Compromiser," offered concessions to both North and South. California would be admitted as a free state. Utah and New Mexico would become territories, and the slavery question would be decided there by popular sovereignty. In the District of Columbia, the slave trade—but not slavery—would be abolished. Congress would not interfere with the slave trade between existing slave states. A strict fugitive slave law, strengthening a 1793 law, would provide for the return of escaped slaves to their owners.

Clay's proposal touched off seven months of dramatic debate in the Senate. It was a time of brilliant speeches by the grand old debaters. John C. Calhoun—aging, sick, close to death—had to have a friend read his speech. He bitterly opposed Clay's plan. He warned that agitation over slavery and the North's actions would snap "the cords which bind these states together . . . nothing will be left to hold the states together except force." He would rather see the South secede from the Union, and prayed that the separation would be peaceful.

Three days later, Calhoun was carried into the Senate chamber to hear Daniel Webster's speech. "Peaceable secession!" Webster thundered. "What states are to secede? What is to remain American? What am I to be? An American no longer? Where is the flag of the republic to remain?" He claimed that there was no need for the North to exclude slavery from the territories—it would not prosper there anyway. Webster would support Clay's proposals.

President Taylor, who was furious at the South's threat of secession, would not consider a compromise. For months Clay and Webster, aided by Senator Stephen Douglas of Illinois, worked to pass the proposals. Then, in midsummer, President Taylor became ill and died. He was succeeded by Vice-President Millard Fillmore, who gave his support to Clay's plan. By September 1850, a majority of Congress had been convinced that the compromise was necessary to save the Union. The proposals passed and were signed into law.

FEELINGS DEEPEN OVER SLAVERY

By 1851, the issue of slavery arose again. In October 1851 a group of southern slave-catchers, hired to track down fugitive slaves, arrived in Syracuse, New York. Citing the new Fugitive Slave Law, they asked federal marshals to seize one Jerry McHenry, who they claimed was an escaped slave. People in Syracuse were shocked to see someone in chains marched through the streets to the federal courthouse.

An angry crowd of more than 2,000 gathered. Led by abolitionist ministers, the crowd mobbed the courthouse and battered down the door. McHenry was taken from the marshals and spirited away by members of the Underground Railroad.

This and other slave-catching incidents brought the issue of slavery to the very doorsteps of northerners. People who had thought little about slavery before were now stirred to anger. Ministers, newspaper editors, and political leaders railed against the law as "a hateful statute of kidnappers." Some northern states passed "personal liberty laws," forbidding officials to help slave-catchers.

Southern leaders resented the northern resistance to the Fugitive Slave Law. This proved, they said, that the North did not intend to live up to the Compromise of 1850 and that abolitionists were gaining control of the North.

The law also inspired Harriet Beecher Stowe to write *Uncle Tom's Cabin*, a dramatic novel showing the plight of plantation slaves. Published in 1852, it caused a greater sensation than any work since Thomas Paine's *Common Sense*. More than 300,000 copies were sold the first year, and it was soon adapted to the stage. Newspaper writers in the South complained heatedly that *Uncle Tom's Cabin* gave a twisted view of slavery. Stowe, they said, lived in the North and had no firsthand knowledge of the system. But to thousands, Stowe's work was a compelling judgment against slavery.

THE ELECTION OF 1852

As northern antislavery sentiments grew and southern fears hardened, political leaders had trouble holding their parties together. The Free-Soil party had opposed the Compromise of 1850 and lost many of its moderates to the Democrats. For the 1852 presidential election, the weakened Free-Soilers chose John P. Hale as their candidate.

Both the Democrats and Whigs were divided into northern and southern factions, and both had to compromise to pick their candidates. The Whigs chose General Winfield Scott, hero of the Mexican War. The Democrats settled on a politician from New Hampshire named Franklin Pierce. Pierce soundly defeated his Whig and Free-Soil rivals.

The publication of *Uncle Tom's Cabin* by Harriet Beecher Stowe caused strong antislavery feeling. Some thirty anti-Uncle Tom novels followed within three years.

Forests, streams, and swamps were far safer than open fields for escaping slaves. Once, while leading an escape, Harriet Tubman waded into a stream of uncertain depth. At one point only her head was visible. When she emerged safely on the opposite shore, her followers crossed.

Although Pierce was a northerner, he often favored southern goals. Pierce wanted to acquire more territory for the United States. But would such new territory be slave or free?

Southerners, in search of a new slave territory, had set their sights on the Spanish colony of Cuba. In 1854 the American ministers to Britain, France, and Spain met in Ostend, Belgium. With Pierce's approval, they were to devise a plan to acquire Cuba.

In their statement, called the Ostend Manifesto, the ministers recommended that the United States offer to buy Cuba. If Spain refused to sell, the manifesto said, the United States should take Cuba by force.

Pierce denied that he had played any part in the preparation of the Ostend Manifesto, but northerners were outraged. The South, they charged, would risk war to extend the boundaries of slavery.

THE KANSAS-NEBRASKA ACT

That same year another political move caused anger. Senator Stephen Douglas was promoting a plan to build a transcontinental railroad from Chicago to the Pacific. It would cut across a stretch of land that had not been organized into a territory. Douglas thought that the railroad could be built only if the land had some political organization. So, he proposed a bill to organize the land west of Iowa and Missouri into the Nebraska Territory.

Southerners promptly demanded that the territory be open to slavery. The land, however, was north of the Missouri Compromise line, and therefore closed to slavery. Douglas was willing to compromise. He proposed that the territory be divided into Nebraska and Kansas. The issue of whether slavery would be allowed would be decided by popular sovereignty—by the people in the territories rather than by Congress. The Kansas-Nebraska Act was passed by Congress in May 1854. The Missouri Compromise line existed no longer.

Northern reaction was harsh. Many said that the act opened the new territories to slavery. The day after Congress passed the Kansas-Nebraska Act, troops had to hold back a Boston mob protesting the capture of a fugitive slave.

After the Kansas-Nebraska Act went into effect, both proslavery and antislavery people raced to settle the Kansas Territory. Many of these "settlers" stayed just long enough to vote for the territory's new legislature in March 1855, because this legislature would decide whether slavery would be allowed in Kansas. "We are playing for a mighty stake," a southern senator said. "If we win, we carry slavery to the Pacific Ocean."

On voting day, thousands of proslavery people rode from Missouri across the border into Kansas so they could cast their ballots in the election. The proslavery forces won, and the new legislature began passing laws to protect slavery. The penalty for aiding a fugitive slave was death. Even those speaking against slavery could be fined and jailed.

The legislature also expelled the few antislavery members who had been elected. The antislavery forces responded by proclaiming Kansas a free territory. They set up their own government in the nearby town of Lawrence.

Both sides resorted to violence in early 1856. A band of proslavery supporters rode into Lawrence, threw printing presses into the river, set a hotel on fire, and killed one man. Three nights later, John Brown, an antislavery agitator, led a small band into a proslavery area. Brown and his band dragged five proslavers who had had nothing to do with the attack on Lawrence from their homes and put them to death.

The fighting between the proslavery and antislavery groups raged for weeks, taking more than two hundred lives. Only the arrival of the United States Army created an uneasy peace in what people were now calling "bleeding Kansas."

The issue had even provoked violence in the United States Senate. Senator Charles Sumner of Massachusetts blamed the Kansas trouble on slaveholders, including several in Congress. Angered, Representative Preston Brooks of South Carolina attacked and beat Sumner with a heavy cane as he sat at his desk. Sumner never fully recovered.

The Kansas-Nebraska Act   1854

Free state or territory

Slave state or territory

Territory opened to slavery by Compromise of 1850

Territory opened to slavery by Kansas-Nebraska Act

THE NEW REPUBLICAN PARTY

While the Kansas-Nebraska bill was being debated in the summer of 1854, groups of Whigs and Democrats were meeting across the country. Dissatisfied with their parties, they wanted to create a third party that would take a strong stand against slavery in the territories.

These conventions brought together Free-Soilers, abolitionists, northern Whigs, and northern Democrats. At one convention in Jackson, Michigan, delegates adopted the name of Thomas Jefferson's party—the Republican party.

By the fall of 1854, the Republicans were already in a strong position for the congressional elections. They won 108 seats in the House, to the Democrats' 83. The anti-immigrant Know-Nothing party reached the peak of its power, winning 43 seats. The splintered Whigs had practically disappeared as a party. The great Whig leaders—Daniel Webster and Henry Clay—had both died in 1852.

The presidential election of 1856 represented a mixture of parties on the rise and parties on the decline. The Republicans nominated John C. Frémont, western explorer and hero of California victories in the Mexican War. The Know-Nothings split over slavery. Northern members supported Frémont. Southern Know-Nothings and southern Whigs, meeting in separate conventions, chose expresident Millard Fillmore. The Democrats chose

James Buchanan of Pennsylvania, who had been a United States senator. Buchanan supported the Kansas-Nebraska Act and popular sovereignty.

The real contest was between the Republicans and Democrats. The Democrats supported popular sovereignty as "the only sound and safe solution of the slavery question." The Republicans, who used the slogan "Free Soil, Free Speech, and Frémont," wanted to keep slavery out of the territories.

James Buchanan won a sound victory, carrying all of the southern states except Maryland, as well as 5 states in the North. John C. Frémont won 11 free states. Millard Fillmore took only the slave state of Maryland.

The election showed a new alignment in American politics. The Democrats had become primarily a party of the South, although they retained key areas of power in the North. The Republicans were purely a party of the North. They had not even appeared on the ballot in most southern states. In fact, several southern leaders had warned that the South would secede if Frémont won.

Positions on both sides of the slavery issue had hardened. Now that the Democrats and Republicans each represented separate regions of the country, the possibility of settling differences became more remote. The compromisers, such as Clay and Webster, were gone.

SECTION REVIEW

1. Identify the following: Wilmot Proviso, Free-Soil party, Jerry McHenry, Harriet Beecher Stowe, Ostend Manifesto.

2. (a) Name the three political parties that participated in the election of 1848. (b) What position did each party take on slavery in the West?

3. (a) Who proposed the Compromise of 1850? (b) List the terms of the compromise.

4. (a) How did people in the North react to the arrests of fugitive slaves? (b) Why did people in the South resent that reaction?

5. How did antislavery sentiments affect the presidential election of 1852?

6. (a) Explain how a plan to build a railroad brought about the Kansas-Nebraska Act. (b) List the terms of the act.

7. How did the principle of popular sovereignty lead to violence between northerners and southerners in Kansas?

8. (a) What groups made up the new Republican party? (b) On the issue of slavery how did Republicans and Democrats differ in the election of 1856? (c) How did the states align politically after the election?

An 1856 election cartoon shows the monster, slavery, being pulled into Kansas by Democrats. Republican Frémont orders it back while Whig Fillmore straddles the fence.

THE PRESIDENTIAL CAMPAIGN OF '56.

THE NATION DIVIDES

READfrom TO FIND OUT

—how the Dred Scott case affected the extension of slavery.

—how the Lincoln-Douglas debates affected the election of 1860.

—how John Brown's raid at Harpers Ferry heightened southern fears.

—why the election of 1860 brought about secession.

—how the Civil War began at Fort Sumter.

The new president, James Buchanan, had spent much of his life in office. He served 10 years in the House and 11 in the Senate, acted as Polk's secretary of state, and was appointed minister to Russia and to Britain.

Buchanan had reached his country's highest office at a critical time. The issue of slavery was sending shock waves through North and South. Clearly, the country needed a leader who could calm the angry voices—a new compromiser.

In his inaugural speech, Buchanan mentioned an upcoming decision of the Supreme Court. The decision, Buchanan said, would settle the question of slavery in the territories. He hoped all Americans would abide by it.

Neither Buchanan's advice nor the Supreme Court's decision would calm the country. In fact, it would cause more conflict in a tense nation.

THE DRED SCOTT CASE

The Supreme Court case mentioned by Buchanan involved Dred Scott, a man who had been the slave of an army surgeon from Missouri. For four years Scott and his owner had lived in the free state of Illinois, and then in the free territory of Minnesota. After they returned to Missouri, the owner died. Scott, supported by abolitionists, sued in court for his freedom. His lawyers argued that the years living on free soil made Scott a free man. A series of appeals carried the case to the Supreme Court.

The court decided against Scott, ruling in 1857 that blacks—free or slave—were not United States citizens and therefore had no right to sue in any federal court. Scott, therefore, was still subject to Missouri laws.

The Supreme Court also declared the Missouri Compromise unconstitutional because it banned slavery in certain territories. Under the Fifth Amendment, persons could not be deprived of property without due process of law. The Court declared that slaves were property. Congress, ruled the Court, could not forbid owners to take their slaves—their property—into the free territories.

Southerners were joyful over the Dred Scott decision. The Supreme Court had, in effect, upheld Calhoun's "doctrine of the South." All territories were now open to slavery.

The decision struck the North like a thunderbolt. The Republican party had dedicated itself to preventing the extension of slavery. Now, it seemed, slavery could be extended throughout the country. Frederick Douglass called the decison "an attempt to blot out forever the hopes of an enslaved people."

The decision also was a blow to Senator Stephen Douglas, since the issue of slavery could no longer be decided by popular sovereignty. The doctrine of popular sovereignty was one that Douglas intended to promote in the upcoming reelection contest for his Senate seat.

The Supreme Court decision in the Dred Scott case, a personal defeat for Scott, had great effects on the nation. Scott was soon freed by his new owner.

THE LINCOLN-DOUGLAS DEBATES

By 1858 northern Democrats were unhappy with their party and their president. President Buchanan had appointed a majority of southerners to his cabinet and favored the admission of Kansas as a slave state. Many northern Democrats split from the party and formed an opposition wing under Stephen Douglas.

Douglas entered the 1858 Senate race in Illinois. Concerned with national unity, he wanted to find a compromise between proslavers and free-soilers. He also wanted a solid reelection victory, for he hoped to win the presidential election in 1860.

Douglas's opponent was Republican Abraham Lincoln. Lincoln was an Illinois lawyer with little political experience. He had served one term in the House of Representatives. In 1858 Lincoln did not seem to be a rising politician.

Lincoln challenged Douglas to a series of public debates about slavery. The two met seven times in different parts of Illinois, and newspapers throughout the country gave detailed coverage. Crowds gathered from miles around for each debate. Douglas always arrived in grand style in a private railroad car. Lincoln arrived by regular train.

The opponents seemed a study in contrasts. Lincoln, who had been born in a log cabin in Kentucky, retained a folksy manner. He slept in a homemade flannel undershirt, and he often told jokes to make a point. Beneath the folksy manner, however, there was a shrewd politician. Lincoln, wrote his law partner, was "a great big—angular—strong man—limbs large and bony. His mind was tough—solid—knotty—gnarly, more or less like his body."

The short, sturdy Douglas was known as the "Little Giant." Douglas was famous in the Senate as a brilliant debater with an aggressive style. Both Lincoln and Douglas opposed slavery and wanted to maintain the Union at all costs. Their ideas, however, were very different. Lincoln hewed his position out of the Republican opposition to the extension of slavery. He refined it in his opening campaign speech in June 1858:

> A house divided against itself cannot stand.
> I believe this government cannot endure
> permanently half slave and half free. I do not
> expect the Union to be dissolved; I do not expect
> the house to fall; but I do expect it will cease to be
> divided.

Stephen A. Douglas felt that slavery was a political, not a moral, question. The doctrine of popular sovereignty and the Kansas-Nebraska Act resulted from this belief.

Lincoln and the Republicans promised to stop the expansion of slavery and to allow slavery in the South to die a "natural death." The alternative was to allow slavery to expand "till it shall become alike lawful in all the states, old as well as new, North as well as South."

Douglas did not believe that slavery was a crucial issue. The best way to protect the Union, he thought, was to let each state rather than Congress make a decision about slavery. "If each state will only agree to mind its own business, and let its neighbors alone," he argued, "this republic can exist forever divided into free and slave states."

At a debate in Freeport, Illinois, Lincoln challenged Douglas and the doctrine of popular sovereignty. Lincoln noted that in the Dred Scott case the Supreme Court had ruled that slavery could not be forbidden in territories. "Can the people of a United States Territory in any lawful way," Lincoln asked, "exclude slavery from its limits?"

Douglas's reply became known as the Freeport Doctrine. He claimed that, although it was legal for an owner to bring a slave into any territory, citizens could refuse to enact laws protecting slavery. Without slave codes, slavery simply could not exist. Many voters were impressed with Douglas's logic.

In the Freeport Doctrine, however, Douglas angered northern abolitionists by dismissing the moral issue of slavery. Furthermore, Douglas lost southern support by suggesting a way to get around the Dred Scott decision and thus stop the extension of slavery. Douglas was reelected to the Senate. In the upcoming presidential election, however, southerners would not forget his stand.

THE RAID ON HARPERS FERRY

A year and a day after the last Lincoln-Douglas debate, the slavery issue again provoked violence. On the night of October 16, 1859, a small band of blacks and whites marched on the federal arsenal at Harpers Ferry, Virginia. Leading them was John Brown, the abolitionist who had taken bloody revenge on proslavers in Kansas. Brown, with financial backing from radical abolitionists, planned to arm the slaves of Virginia and bring about a mighty slave rebellion.

Brown and his raiders seized the arsenal at Harpers Ferry with no difficulty. When the arsenal employees arrived for work in the morning, Brown took them as hostages. Meanwhile, news of the raid spread. Local militia moved in, followed by federal troops under Colonel Robert E. Lee. Almost half of Brown's men were killed, and Brown and the survivors were taken prisoner.

Within a matter of weeks Brown and six raiders were tried and convicted of murder, treason, and conspiracy. All were hanged. The swift punishment, however, did not ease southern fears. Not since Nat Turner's slave revolt in 1831 had people in the South been so shaken.

Southerners found little comfort in the fact that no slaves had joined Brown, or in northern newspapers' shocked reactions to Brown's raid. Instead, their suspicions were deepened by some northerners who approved of Brown's actions. Philosopher Ralph Waldo Emerson even declared Brown "a new saint" who would "make the gallows as glorious as the cross."

THE ELECTION OF 1860

In April 1860 the Democratic party met in Charleston, South Carolina, to choose a presidential candidate. Southerners wanted a platform promising that the federal government would uphold slavery in the territories. That demand was too much for northerners. The convention broke up.

Two months later delegates met again, this time in Baltimore, Maryland. The northern faction nominated Stephen Douglas for president and adopted popular sovereignty as a platform. Southern delegates stormed out of the convention. They met separately, nominated John C. Breckinridge of Kentucky, and adopted a proslavery platform.

The Republicans nominated Abraham Lincoln. He was the only Republican who could challenge Douglas in the Midwest and satisfy both moderates and abolitionists. The Republican party platform opposed the extension of slavery and declared that the Dred Scott decision violated the Constitution's protection of personal liberty.

The Republicans also supported the building of a transcontinental railroad. They favored a new protective tariff, a homestead law to give western land to settlers, and immediate admission of Kansas to the Union as a free state.

Some people in both the North and the South— former Whigs, unhappy Democrats, Know-Nothings—still hoped for compromise. They formed the Constitutional Union party and nominated John Bell of Tennessee for president. Their platform supported patriotism, the Constitution, and the Union, and avoided any mention of slavery.

The split in the Democratic party gave Lincoln the election. He received only 39 percent of the popular vote, but he gained a solid majority of the electoral votes. He won all of the free states but New Jersey. Although Douglas was close to Lincoln in popular votes, he carried only Missouri. Bell won Virginia, Kentucky, and Tennessee, while Breckinridge carried the rest of the South.

To southerners who voted for Breckinridge or Bell, the next president of the United States was a president of the North. Neither Lincoln nor any other Republican had ever campaigned in the South. Indeed, Lincoln had not even appeared on the ballot in many southern states.

SECESSION

In the weeks following Lincoln's election, many southerners thought that they saw their way of life disappearing. Alexander H. Stephens of Georgia wrote that in the South "the people run mad. They are wild with passion, doing they know not what. . . . The truth is our leaders and public . . . do not desire to continue the Union on any terms."

The Election of 1860

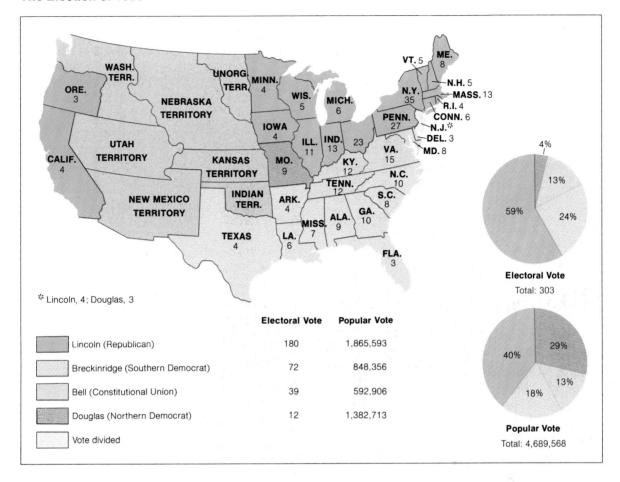

* Lincoln, 4; Douglas, 3

	Electoral Vote	Popular Vote
Lincoln (Republican)	180	1,865,593
Breckinridge (Southern Democrat)	72	848,356
Bell (Constitutional Union)	39	592,906
Douglas (Northern Democrat)	12	1,382,713
Vote divided		

Electoral Vote
Total: 303

Popular Vote
Total: 4,689,568

In South Carolina, the legislature called a statewide convention to vote on secession. Southerners had threatened to leave the Union before. In the nullification crisis of 1832, they had claimed that the Union was a voluntary contract, or compact, among states, and that any state could withdraw if it wished. Lincoln and most Republicans thought that the southerners were bluffing.

President Buchanan, serving the final months of his term, reacted cautiously. He warned that no state had the right to secede, but said that he had no constitutional power to force states to stay in the Union. Buchanan turned to Congress, asking for yet another compromise. Senator John J. Crittenden of Kentucky suggested that the Missouri Compromise line be restored and that slavery be permitted in all states and new territories south of it. But Republicans—Lincoln included—would not consider any plan that allowed slavery to expand. The spirit of compromise was exhausted.

On December 20, 1860, the South Carolina convention voted unanimously to secede from the Union. South Carolina opened the floodgate. By February 1861 Mississippi, Florida, Alabama, Georgia, Louisiana, and Texas had also seceded.

Throughout the South, state troops seized federal forts, arsenals, and shipyards. A few forts remained in federal control. Fort Sumter in South Carolina's Charleston harbor became an island of federal resolve, held by Major Robert Anderson and a small force.

Early in February, delegates from six of the seven states that had seceded met in Montgomery, Alabama, to form a new union—the Confederate States of America. They chose former senator Jefferson Davis of Mississippi as president, selected a flag of stars and crossed bars, and drafted a constitution modeled after the United States Constitution. This constitution, however, gave ultimate sovereignty to states and guaranteed the existence of slavery.

FORT SUMTER

A month later, Lincoln took office as president of a shattered Union. Seven states had seceded. Slave states in the West and southern states still in the Union were discussing secession. Lincoln asked the Confederate states to return to the Union and repeated his promise not to forbid slavery where it already existed. But he took a firm stand against the states' right to secede, warning the Confederacy:

In your hands . . . and not in mine, is the momentous issue of civil war. The government will not assail you. You have no conflict without being yourselves the aggressors. You have no oath registered in Heaven to destroy the Government, while I shall have the most solemn one to "preserve, protect and defend it."

One day after taking office, Lincoln received a request from Major Robert Anderson for more troops and supplies to hold Fort Sumter. Lincoln's

AMERICAN OBSERVERS

As the wife of a military aide to Jefferson Davis, diarist Mary Boykin Chesnut knew personally most of the South's military and civil leaders. Her record of the personalities, events, and suffering of the South is invaluable.

MARY BOYKIN CHESNUT
RECORDING THE END OF AN ERA

On the night of April 11, 1861, Mary Chesnut could not sleep. "Things are happening so fast," she wrote in her diary. Her husband, James Chesnut, had gone with other Confederate representatives to demand the surrender of Fort Sumter, the federal base in Charleston harbor. Alone in her room, Mary Chesnut waited in dread. Then at four-thirty in the morning, a cannon boomed. She knew it meant that the Union forces had not surrendered. Hurrying to the rooftop, she watched southern shells burst against the fort. The Civil War had begun.

Mary Chesnut had started her diary just a few months before. A bright and lively woman married to a prominent southern politician, she sensed that she was a witness to history. She had been with her husband in Montgomery when the Confederate government was formed. Soon she would live in Rich-

mond, where her husband would assist President Jefferson Davis. "It was a way I had," she noted, "always to stumble on the *real show*."

Mary Chesnut loved the South and believed deeply in states' rights. "I was a rebel born," she wrote. Yet she branded slavery "a monstrous system" and thought most southern women felt the same way. An early feminist, she also saw parallels between the lives of slaves and women.

All during the Civil War, Mary Chesnut kept her diary. Published after her death, it brilliantly documented southern life during these dramatic years. In vivid detail, she described the battles and the balls, the gaiety and the destruction. Yet from the beginning she felt a sense of doom. She knew she was watching "our world, the only world we cared for, literally kicked to pieces."

The flag of the Confederacy, with seven stars for the seceding states, flies over Fort Sumter after its surrender. In February 1865 the United States flag was once again raised there.

cabinet warned that if he sent a supply ship, the South would consider it an act of war. But Lincoln feared that if Fort Sumter surrendered, the Confederacy would take that as recognition of its independence.

For six weeks, Lincoln delayed. Tension mounted in the North as the public and the press began to demand action. Lincoln at last decided to send food—but not troops—in an unarmed ship. He assured the governor of South Carolina that no troops would be sent "without further notice, or in case of an attack upon the fort."

Still, Confederate leaders took the sending of the supply ship as an act of war. Under orders from Jefferson Davis, the Confederate general P. G. T. Beauregard demanded that Anderson surrender Fort Sumter. Anderson refused. At 4:30 in the morning, on April 12, 1861, Confederate cannons opened fire on the fort. Anderson returned the fire. The supplies sent by Lincoln had to remain outside the harbor. On April 13, his ammunition exhausted, Anderson lowered the United States flag. He and his troops were allowed to retreat to the Union relief ships.

The North and South were now at war.

SECTION REVIEW

1. Identify the following: Major Robert Anderson, Jefferson Davis, General P. G. T. Beauregard.

2. What did the Supreme Court rule in the Dred Scott case? How did the decision affect the Missouri Compromise?

3. (a) About what did Abraham Lincoln and Stephen Douglas agree? (b) Explain the position of each on the extension of slavery.

4. (a) What was the purpose of John Brown's raid at Harpers Ferry? (b) Why did Brown's conviction and death fail to ease southern fears?

5. (a) Name the presidential candidates and their parties in the election of 1860. (b) List six goals of the Republican party platform.

6. Why did South Carolina call a statewide convention? What was the outcome?

7. How did the Confederate constitution differ from that of the United States?

8. Explain Lincoln's dilemma over sending troops and supplies to Fort Sumter. What did he decide to do? What was the result?

SUMMARY

By the 1850s the nation seemed to be divided into two worlds—North and South. In the North railroads spurred the growth of industries and cities. But as factories and competition increased, working conditions deteriorated. Many workers formed unions and organized strikes. When immigrants and free blacks willingly replaced striking workers, the labor movement weakened. Resentment toward immigrants and free blacks led to the start of a nativist political party, the Know-Nothing party.

The South's economy rested on agriculture, principally cotton. Cotton was America's major export and the main crop of five states. Agriculture also shaped the social hierarchy. At the very bottom were 4 million slaves. At the top were the land-owning, slave-holding planters. Many northerners were neutral about slavery, but abolitionists viewed it as evil.

Commercially, North and South benefited each other. Southerners, however, feared that the North was growing too strong and sought to extend slavery into the West. When statehood for California was proposed, the issue of slavery in the West threatened the Union. Southerners began to talk of secession.

The Compromise of 1850 was an attempt to satisfy both North and South by providing for popular sovereignty in new territories and by establishing the Fugitive Slave Law. Both popular sovereignty and the slave law provoked violence. The issue of slavery reshaped political alignment. The Democrats became the party of the South. The new Republicans became the party of the North.

When the Supreme Court's decision in the Dred Scott case upheld slavery in new territories, the bonds holding together the Union were strained. Competing for a seat in the Illinois state senate, Republican Abraham Lincoln and Democrat Stephen Douglas eloquently debated the issue of slavery. Douglas, supporting popular sovereignty, won the state election. Two years later, however, Lincoln won the presidency, and seven southern states seceded from the Union. They formed the Confederate States of America. On April 12, 1861, war began between North and South.

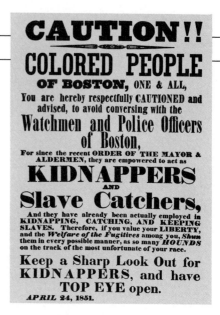

Northern discrimination and resentment against blacks was balanced by the efforts of sympathetic abolitionists. This 1851 poster warns blacks in Boston of danger.

CHAPTER REVIEW

1. (a) How did the use of steam power lead to the railroad era? (b) What was carried to factories over railroads? What was moved from factories over railroads? (c) How did improved transportation lead to the growth of industry?

2. How did each of the following affect factory workers? (a) increased business competition (b) craft unions (c) the case of *Commonwealth v. Hunt* in 1842 (d) the increase in immigrants

3. (a) Why did some Americans resent immigrants? (b) What was the Know-Nothing party? (c) In the North how were attitudes toward free blacks similar to attitudes toward immigrants?

4. (a) What effect did slave revolts have on northern abolitionists? On white southerners? (b) What similarities existed between southern slave codes and the voting laws of many northern states? (c) What laws regarding free blacks did Iowa, Illinois, Indiana, and Oregon pass in the 1850s? How were these laws similar to slave codes?

5. How did each of the following cause conflict between North and South? (a) the extension of slavery (b) the Fugitive Slave Law (c) *Uncle Tom's Cabin* (d) the Ostend Manifesto

6. (a) List the provisions of the Compromise of 1850. (b) What events led up to the compromise?

7. (a) What were the provisions of the Kansas-Nebraska Act? (b) How did the act lead to violence in the Kansas Territory?

8. (a) What did the Democratic party support in the election of 1856? What did the new Republican party support? (b) How did the results of the election show a new alignment in American politics?

9. (a) What did the Supreme Court rule in the Dred Scott case? (b) How did this ruling affect the Missouri Compromise? The doctrine of popular sovereignty?

10. Compare the viewpoints of Lincoln and Douglas on each of the following issues. (a) slavery (b) the extension of slavery (c) the implications of the Dred Scott decision

11. (a) What were the provisions of the Republican platform in the election of 1860? (b) What helped Lincoln to win the election? (c) How did the southern states react to Lincoln's victory?

12. Describe the events that took place at Fort Sumter.

ISSUES AND IDEAS

1. Compare the economies of the North and the South in the 1850s. How did economic differences contribute to conflict between the two regions of the country?

2. Are there circumstances in which a state has the right to secede from the Union? Defend your answer by referring to the Constitution and by giving examples.

3. Some people have said that the Civil War was the most unavoidable war in history. Do you agree? Defend your answer.

4. Comment on John Brown's raid on Harpers Ferry from the viewpoints of a southern planter and a northern abolitionist.

SKILLS WORKSHOP

1. *Graphs.* The following figures give the number of immigrants coming to the United States at five-year periods from 1820 to 1850: 1820—8,385; 1825—10,199; 1830—23,322; 1835—45,374; 1840—84,066; 1845—144,371; 1850—369,980. Make a graph showing this information. Decide which kind of graph—line or bar graph—would present the data better.

2. *Maps.* Look at the map on page 273 showing the election of 1860. What does it show about sectionalism? With what region—North or South—did westerners vote? Give a reason for this. In what states was the new Constitutional Union party successful? Give a reason for this.

PAST AND PRESENT

1. What were the chief products of your state in the 1850s? What cities, towns, or posts were the main centers of trade? Describe one main route used in the 1850s in transporting products to a trading center in your state.

2. Sectionalism was a major cause of the Civil War. Is there sectionalism in the United States today? Why are there fewer differences among regions of the United States than there were in the 1800s?

By 1860, thirty years after the race between Cooper's *Tom Thumb* locomotive and a horse, the locomotive had become indispensable to northern industry.

CHAPTER 12

THE CIVIL WAR

1861–1865

THE CALL TO ARMS
FROM BULL RUN TO ANTIETAM
FREEDOM FOR SLAVES, PROBLEMS AT HOME
FROM GETTYSBURG TO APPOMATTOX

In April 1861 an Indiana teenager named Theodore Upson heard some shocking news:

"Father and I were husking out some corn when William Cory came across the field and said, 'Jonathan, the Rebs have fired upon and taken Fort Sumter.' Father got white and couldn't say a word.

"We did not finish the corn and drove to the barn. Father left me to unload. . . . After I had finished I went in to dinner. Mother said, 'What is the matter with Father?' He had gone right upstairs. I told her what we had heard. She went to him. After a while they came down. Father looked ten years older.

"We sat down to the table. Grandma wanted to know what was the trouble. Father told her and she began to cry. 'Oh, my poor children in the South! Now they will suffer! God knows how they will suffer! I knew it would come!'

"'They can come here and stay,' said Father.

"'No, they will not do that. There is their home. There they will stay.'

"Mother had a letter from the Hales. Charlie and his father are in their army. I wonder if I were in our army and they should meet me would they shoot me. I suppose they would."

North and South were at war. Northerners put on the blue uniform of the United States Army. Southerners wore the gray for the Confederate States of America.

For many thousands of Americans, the war brought a special tragedy. Family ties and friendships did not stop at state borders. Mary Todd Lincoln, the wife of the President, had three brothers in the southern army. All were killed. Varina Davis, the wife of President Jefferson Davis of the Confederacy, had relatives who wore Union blue. Theodore Upson, the Indiana teenager, had glimpsed what was to come. This would be a war of American against American.

THE CALL TO ARMS

READ TO FIND OUT

— what part the border states played in the Civil War.

— how a long war would affect each side.

— how the Confederacy attempted to obtain British support.

— how the North and the South raised money for the war.

— what causes each section was fighting for.

"War! and volunteers are the only topics of conversation or thought," wrote an Ohio student. "The lessons today have been a mere form. I cannot study. I cannot sleep, I cannot work, and I don't know as I can write."

Three days after the firing on Fort Sumter, President Lincoln called for 75,000 state militia members to enlist for 90 days. Confederate President Jefferson Davis asked for a volunteer army of 100,000. North and South, volunteers rushed to join the cause. Both sides predicted a short war, an easily won war. Northerners talked of quickly putting down the southern "insurrection." One southerner promised to wipe up all the blood spilled with his handkerchief.

THE BORDER STATES

Sandwiched between the Union and the Confederacy were the border slave states that had not yet decided whether to secede. Lincoln was acutely aware of their importance. If Maryland seceded, Washington, D.C., would be surrounded by Confederate states.

In addition, through Maryland and western Virginia ran the Baltimore and Ohio Railroad, the major rail link between East and West. Along the border of Kentucky ran the Ohio River, and along the border of Missouri flowed the Mississippi. The Union needed these rivers and the railroad to supply and move its troops. To keep these slave states from joining the Confederacy, Lincoln assured them that he was fighting to preserve the Union, not to free southern slaves.

The Confederacy, too, valued these border states. It needed their population, their factories, their resources. Without at least some of these states on its side, the Confederacy would be a poor match for the Union. By May 1861 four border states—Virginia, Arkansas, Tennessee, and North Carolina—had joined the Confederacy. This brought its total to eleven states and almost doubled its population.

Of all fifteen slave states, only Delaware unanimously rejected secession. The western counties of Virginia refused to recognize their state's secession and declared their loyalty to the Union. These counties formed a new state of West Virginia and joined the Union in 1863. However, three states— Maryland, Kentucky, and Missouri—seemed hopelessly divided between unionists and secessionists.

Division in Maryland was so bitter that pro-Confederate mobs attacked a Massachusetts regiment on its way to Washington in April 1861. Lincoln sent federal troops to keep order and suspended habeas corpus, the right to a trial before imprisonment. Suspected Confederate sympathizers, including members of the legislature and the mayor of Baltimore, were arrested and jailed without trial. In the fall a pro-Union governor was elected, and Maryland remained loyal to the Union.

Kentucky, also torn between the Union and the Confederacy, at first declared its neutrality. Lincoln promised Kentucky that it could keep its slaves, and that he would not send in troops if it remained peaceful. But then, in September 1861, Confederate forces crossed into Kentucky and occupied Columbus. The Union countered by sending in troops. Its policy of neutrality dead, Kentucky expelled the Confederates and stayed with the Union.

Conflict in Missouri between unionists and secessionists led to open warfare. Two major battles were fought there before the Union gained control of the state in 1862. But guerrilla warfare continued for the next few years, forcing the Union to put Missouri under martial law.*

STRENGTHS OF NORTH AND SOUTH

If numbers told the whole story, the Confederate cause looked hopeless. The 23 Union states, including California and Oregon, had a total population of about 22 million people. The Confederacy had only 9 million people. Of this total, 3.5 million were

* martial law: rule by the army in time of trouble or war instead of by civil authorities.

AMERICAN OBSERVERS

JULIA WARD HOWE
"THE BATTLE HYMN OF THE REPUBLIC"

When Julia Howe arrived in Washington in late 1861, the city looked like an armed camp. Troops were everywhere. From her hotel window, she could see a grim billboard for a funeral company. The company embalmed and shipped home the bodies of soldiers killed in battle or by disease.

Julia Howe had come to Washington with her husband, Dr. Samuel Gridley Howe, who was helping with war relief work. She herself believed deeply in the Union cause. But as the mother of six young children, she felt there was little she could do to help. A tiny, red-haired woman with a gift for poetry, she could only watch in horror and fascination.

One crisp November day she went with friends to see a military parade outside of town. Suddenly southern troops attacked a nearby regiment. Hurriedly, Julia Howe's group started back to Washington, but the road was crowded. To pass the time, they began to sing. As they finished the popular camp song, "John Brown's Body," someone suggested that she write new words to the rousing tune.

"I went to bed that night as usual, and slept . . . soundly," Julia Howe recalled. She woke before daybreak. "As I lay waiting for dawn, the long lines of the desired poem began to twine themselves in my mind." She fumbled for pen and paper, then began to write: "Mine eyes have seen the glory of the coming of the Lord. . . . His truth is marching on."

The *Atlantic Monthly* paid her five dollars for her five-verse poem. Soon Union soldiers were singing it as they marched into battle. When Abraham Lincoln heard it, his eyes filled with tears. "Sing it again," he said. Julia Ward Howe had put the spirit of the northern cause into words, creating one of the most enduring songs in American history.

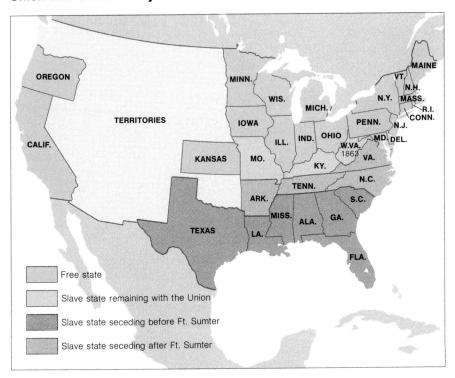

Free state

Slave state remaining with the Union

Slave state seceding before Ft. Sumter

Slave state seceding after Ft. Sumter

It is not known whether this young Confederate soldier was a volunteer or a draftee. A primary aim of the draft in April 1862 was to persuade first-year veterans to re-enlist.

slaves, and slaves were barred from fighting. However, at the beginning of the war the Confederate army found it easy to fill its ranks with volunteers. Therefore, the smaller southern population seemed to make little difference.

Indeed, Confederate leaders felt they had many advantages in a short, defensive war. The North would have to invade and occupy the South. Union troops would have longer distances to travel, and the North's long supply lines would be vulnerable.

Almost all southern soldiers were comfortable on horseback and familiar with guns. Many northern recruits were city youths—thousands of them fresh off immigrant ships—who would need months of training. The South could also count on nearly all of the nation's best generals. Most were trained at West Point or Virginia Military Institute and were experienced in battle from the Mexican War.

But the North had its own advantages. In this war, railroads would be vital to move troops and supplies. The North had more than twice as many miles of track as the South. Supplying troops with war materials was also crucial. Over 80 percent of the nation's factories and most of its coal and iron were in northern states.

The North also had overwhelming sea power, and it was preparing to blockade the southern coast. It boasted one of the world's largest merchant fleets. Furthermore, its navy grew from 42 to 671 ships during the war. In 1861 the Confederate secretary of the navy did not have a single ship to command.

EUROPE AND THE WAR

Southern leaders hoped to force the British into aiding the Confederacy. Convinced that Britain was dependent upon southern cotton, the Confederacy imposed a ban on cotton exports in 1861. Rather than lose the cotton supply, they believed, Britain would recognize the South's independence and even help as the French had done during the American Revolution.

The southern strategy failed. Britain had stockpiled cotton in the years before the war and later found other suppliers in India and Egypt. Also, British trade with the North in wheat and munitions, or military supplies, was flourishing. By the time Confederate leaders decided to ship cotton to Europe in exchange for supplies, the North's blockade of the southern coast made it almost impossible.

FINANCING THE WAR

Raising money for the war was a difficult task for both sides. At the war's outbreak, both Confederate and Union treasuries were empty.

To finance the war, the Union government sold war bonds and laid heavy taxes and tariffs. In 1861 Congress passed manufacturers' and sales taxes. It also passed the nation's first income tax. By the end of the war, incomes between $600 and $5,000 were being taxed 5 percent. Incomes of over $5,000 were being taxed 10 percent. In 1861 Congress also passed the Morrill Tariff Act, raising duties on imports to about 30 percent of their value. Later acts pushed the duties even higher.

In early 1862 Congress passed the Legal Tender Act, allowing the government to print treasury notes. These notes, called "greenbacks" because of their color, were backed only by the government's

The youthfulness of the armies impressed poet Walt Whitman. Posing for a Richmond photographer, these southern volunteers try to look hardened in spite of their youth.

Mathew Brady and his assistants, traveling with the Union armies, photographed thousands of battle and camp scenes such as this encampment on the James River in Virginia, 1864.

promise to redeem them in gold or silver some day. Ultimately, the Union printed some $450 million worth of greenbacks. Since they were not backed by gold or silver, their value declined about 50 percent during the war.

Part of the Union's money troubles stemmed from the chaotic banking system. Since the closing of the second Bank of the United States in 1836, state banks had multiplied.

To provide sound currency and to boost the sale of war bonds, Congress passed a National Banking Act in 1863 and in 1864. These acts set up federal banks, which were required to invest one third of their capital in United States bonds. The banks could then issue paper money up to 90 percent of the value of the bonds they bought. The federal money began to drive the state money out of circulation, giving the Union a standard currency.

The Confederacy also resorted to tariffs and taxes and sold bonds. The Union blockade, how-

After the war Jefferson Davis was imprisoned for two years, then released without trial. In defense against his critics he wrote *The Rise and Fall of the Confederate Government.* Though Lincoln never wrote a book, the words of his speeches and letters are famous.

ever, cut into southern trade and income from duties. And southerners, like northerners, had little gold or silver to buy bonds. As a result, the Confederacy relied mainly on its printing presses, issuing about $2 billion in paper money. Like greenbacks, these dollars were not backed by gold and silver, and the South suffered disastrous inflation.

CAUSES AND LEADERS

The hard numbers that showed money and resources and soldiers certainly played a major role in the war effort of both sides. Perhaps as vital as hard numbers, however, was morale. Northerners were fighting to save the Union, and to many this cause was sacred. The Confederate cause was independence. Moreover southerners would be fighting to defend their own soil and their own homes.

Both northern and southern morale would be sorely tested by war. People needed leaders who could keep their cause alive through the war's darkest hours. In Abraham Lincoln and Jefferson Davis, the Union and Confederacy had strong leaders.

Jefferson Davis was born in Kentucky in 1808. He had served the United States during the Mexican War as commander of the Mississippi Rifles. During peace, he had been a member of Congress and in the presidential Cabinet. He accepted the presidency of the Confederacy, reluctantly, because he felt it was his duty.

Having made the decision to lead the Confederacy, Jefferson Davis vowed to "redeem my pledge to the South by shedding every drop of my blood in its cause." He was confident enough of his military skills to plan the Confederate war strategy.

Abraham Lincoln was born in 1809, also in Kentucky. In 1832 he served briefly in the Black Hawk War against the Sauk and Fox Indians, although he never saw action. He said his biggest battle had been with the mosquitoes. Although his military experience was slight, Lincoln, like Davis, took personal command of military strategy. He, too, vowed "not to shrink, not even to count the chances of [my] own life."

SECTION REVIEW

1. Identify the following: Morrill Tariff Act, Legal Tender Act, National Banking Acts of 1863 and 1864.

2. Define the following: martial law, greenbacks.

3. Name four resources of the Border States that the Union and the Confederacy both needed in the war.

4. (a) List three advantages the North would have in a war against the South. (b) List three advantages the South would have in a war.

5. (a) Describe the intended results of the South's cotton embargo in 1861. (b) What were the actual results?

6. (a) How did the Union government finance the war? (b) How did the Confederacy finance the war?

7. (a) Explain how the printing of paper money caused problems for the North. (b) How did it cause problems for the South?

8. (a) What were Jefferson Davis's qualifications for leadership? (b) Abraham Lincoln's?

A solitary Union soldier sits beside his tent in "At the Front." George Cochran Lambdin is noted for his flower paintings and for portraits and scenes of the Civil War.

FROM BULL RUN TO ANTIETAM

READ TO FIND OUT

— **what strategies were planned by the North and by the South.**

— **how new kinds of ships fought the naval war.**

— **what battles led to Union control of most of the Mississippi River.**

— **how Confederate forces defended Richmond.**

— **what effect Antietam had on the war.**

In the Union and Confederate capitals, presidents Lincoln and Davis planned their strategies. Davis, a West Point graduate, followed West Point textbook advice. Davis planned to fight a defensive war. The South would try to hold territory, hoping to convince the North that the Confederacy could not be conquered.

President Lincoln's commander, General Winfield Scott, proposed a war plan based on southern geography. The Appalachian Mountains and Mississippi River divided the Confederacy into three regions. Scott planned to cut these regions off from one another. Meanwhile, the Union naval blockade of the southern coast would keep much-needed supplies from reaching the Confederacy. Then, the Union could crush each region—just as the anaconda snake crushes its victims.

Scott's proposal became known as the "anaconda plan." It depended on a slow steady pressure. Many northerners, however, wanted a hard strike and quick victory.

THE FIRST BATTLE OF BULL RUN

By the early summer of 1861, some 30,000 Union volunteers were camped near Washington, D.C. The public, the press, and Lincoln's cabinet eagerly called for an attack on Richmond, Virginia, the new Confederate capital. It was only about 100 miles (161 kilometers) from Washington. The war could be over in a few weeks.

A Mathew Brady photograph of the 31st Pennsylvania Regiment shows how camp life for a soldier is softened by the presence of his family.

In July 1861 the Union troops were ordered to advance, under the command of General Irvin McDowell. With cheerful cries of "Forward to Richmond!" the troops crossed the Potomac into Virginia. Hundreds of civilians followed along on horseback or in carriages, hoping to get a view of the fighting.

About 25 miles (40 kilometers) from Washington, the Union columns met the Confederate army. There were about 30,000 troops under General P.G.T. Beauregard, the Confederate hero of Fort Sumter. They were camped at the town of Manassas Junction, near a stream called Bull Run.*

The Union troops advanced, but Confederate General Thomas J. Jackson—standing "like a stonewall"—kept his brigade's line firm. From that time on, Jackson was known as "Stonewall."

In late afternoon Confederate reinforcements arrived. McDowell, realizing he was outnumbered, ordered a Union retreat. Panic shot through the soldiers. The entire Union force bolted, scrambling in haste to get back to Washington. The

* The battle is generally known as the Battle of Bull Run. The Confederates, however, named battles after the nearest town, so this became for them the Battle of Manassas Junction.

Confederate army, surprised and confused, did not follow. One southern general explained that "the Confederate army was more disorganized by victory than that of the United States by defeat."

In the South, the news of Bull Run made people confident of victory in the war. News of the Union army's disastrous retreat stunned the North. The dream of a short, heroic war began to fade. After Bull Run, the Union followed Scott's anaconda plan.

There were two major theaters of war. In the eastern theater, east of the Appalachian Mountains, the Union concentrated on taking the Confederate capital of Richmond. In the western theater, west of the mountains, fighting centered in the Mississippi Valley. The Union fought to control the river, its arteries, and vital railroad lines.

Beyond the Mississippi lay a third theater of war—the states of Louisiana, Arkansas, and Texas. Neither North nor South, however, sent large forces to this theater, and it had little effect on the war. The Union strategy, then, rested on the eastern and western theaters and its naval blockade.

THE NAVAL WAR

In 1860, the last year of peace, some 6,000 ships sailed into and out of southern ports. Bringing in manufactured goods and leaving with cotton and tobacco, the ships connected the South to crucial northern and European markets. With war, the South lost its northern markets. After Union warships blockaded Confederate ports and set up bases on the Atlantic coast, the South also began to lose its trade with Europe.

The Confederacy was desperate for weapons and supplies. Daring sea captains in swift, small ships ran the blockade, but Union ships captured more and more of them. Only about eight hundred ships evaded the Union blockade in its first year of operation.

At first, the Confederates had no warships, so they improvised. When Union forces had abandoned the navy yard in Norfolk, Virginia, they sank the steam-powered U.S.S. *Merrimac*. The Confederates raised the *Merrimac* and covered its sides with iron plate. An iron battering ram was projected from the prow of the ship.

On March 8, 1862, the *Merrimac*, renamed the *Virginia*, lumbered into Chesapeake Bay to attack

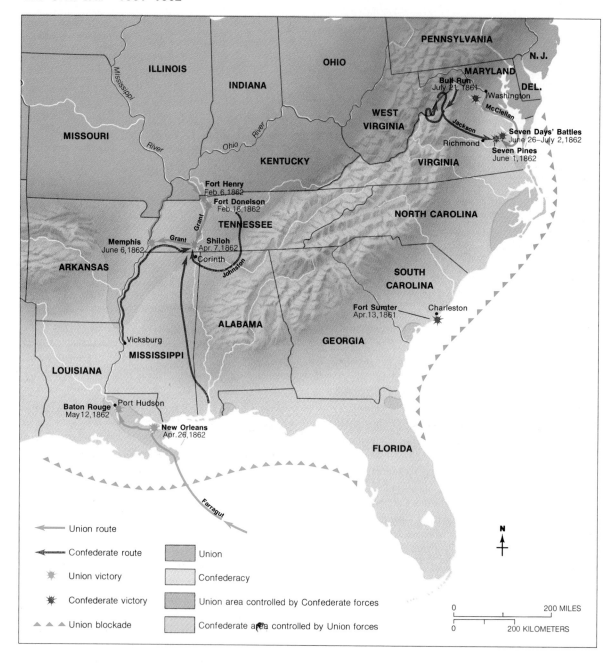

the blockading Union fleet. In one day the ironclad ship destroyed two of the wooden Union ships and ran a third aground.

The Union navy, however, had been building its own ironclad, with a revolving gun turret. The Union's *Monitor* was waiting when the *Virginia* reappeared on March 9. The two ships met in a noisy five-hour battle that ended in a draw. Neither ship could sink the other. The battle dashed southern hopes that the *Virginia* could rule Chesapeake Bay and help blockade runners reach the open sea.

The Confederate government also took advantage of Britain's wavering neutrality. It had powerful frigates built in English shipyards. The first two, the *Alabama* and the *Florida*, went to sea in 1862 to attack northern shipping. Along with other

In the encounter between the *Monitor* and the *Virginia*, the *Virginia* won a strategic victory for the South. It bought time for the Confederacy to shift forces from the Potomac to defend Richmond.

Confederate ships, such as the *Shenandoah*, they sank over two hundred fifty Union merchant ships throughout the war.

Southern inventors also tried schemes, including torpedoes and submarines. Four crews perished during unsuccessful trial runs of the submarine *H.L. Hunley.* Then, in 1864, a fifth crew took the submarine into Charleston harbor and sank a Union warship with a torpedo. But the explosion also blew up the submarine, killing the crew.

THE WAR IN THE WEST

After the Battle of Bull Run, Lincoln appointed the dashing, popular General George B. McClellan as commander of the Union armies. General Scott, old and in poor health, had retired. For months McClellan drilled the eastern wing of the Union forces—the Army of the Potomac. The troops became sharp and well disciplined. But throughout the fall and winter of 1861 and into 1862, Lincoln was unable to get McClellan to move his army. Fed up, Lincoln wrote: "My dear McClellan: If you don't want to use the army I should like to borrow it for a while. Yours respectfully, A. Lincoln."

While McClellan endlessly drilled troops, however, Union forces in the western theater were on the move. In early 1862 General Ulysses S. Grant led an army of 17,000 soldiers south into Tennessee. They were heading for the crucial Mississippi River, but first they would have to take Confederate forts on the Tennessee and Cumberland rivers. With the help of Union gunboats, Grant easily captured Fort Henry on the Tennessee River on February 6.

Grant immediately pushed on to the second barrier—Fort Donelson on the Cumberland River. After four days of a Union siege, the Confederate commander asked for an armistice. Grant demanded "unconditional and immediate surrender." The fort surrendered on February 16. U.S. Grant earned a nickname, "Unconditional Surrender" Grant.

Forts Henry and Donelson had been the center of the Confederate western defense. With their surrender, General Albert S. Johnston withdrew his southern army farther south to regroup. The Confederates made their camp in Corinth, a major railroad center near the Tennessee-Mississippi border.

Grant continued his relentless advance south along the Tennessee River to Pittsburg Landing. But the Confederates had decided to attack Grant, and they now marched north from Corinth. On April 6 in the Tennessee countryside near a meetinghouse called Shiloh Church, the Confederates struck. The attack caught Grant's force by surprise, and the fighting raged fiercely for 13 hours.

At a trench dubbed the "hornet's nest," the Union soldiers made a desperate stand. The Union line held that first day, and the Confederacy lost General Albert Johnston, who was killed. On the second day, Union reinforcements arrived, and the outnumbered Confederates withdrew to Corinth. Union troops were too exhausted to pursue.

The Battle of Shiloh left the Union in control of Kentucky and much of Tennessee, but at a high cost. On each side, over 10,000 soldiers were killed or wounded. Many northerners called for Grant's removal because of the large Union losses. But Lincoln replied, "I can't spare this man—he fights!"

Meanwhile, a powerful Union naval force under Flag Officer David G. Farragut struck northward from the Gulf of Mexico. In late April, the force captured New Orleans. Then part of Farragut's fleet moved upriver and took Baton Rouge, Louisiana, in early May. A few weeks later, Union troops drove the Confederates out of the railroad center of Corinth. Next, a joint force of army troops and gunboats took Memphis, Tennessee. By June Union forces controlled much of the Mississippi River. The only forts on the river still in southern hands were Vicksburg and Port Hudson.

THE WAR IN THE EAST: RICHMOND CAMPAIGNS

In the eastern theater, McClellan was at last ready to lead his army against Richmond. He decided to attack the Confederate capital from the south. In March 1862 his force of some 100,000 soldiers moved by ship through Chesapeake Bay and landed on the Virginia peninsula below Richmond.

McClellan, however, did not march directly on Richmond. Instead, he advanced cautiously, giving Confederate General Joseph D. Johnston time to rush reinforcements to Richmond. When McClellan's forces finally approached Richmond, Johnston struck. At the Battle of Seven Pines, near the Fair Oaks Station, Johnston stopped the Union advance, but casualties on both sides were high. Johnston himself was severely wounded, so command of the southern army passed to General Robert E. Lee.

Lee was a superb soldier who was fiercely loved by his troops. He had been schooled at West Point, and had seen action in the Mexican War. At the outbreak of the Civil War, Lincoln offered Lee command of the United States Army. Although he loved the Union, the Virginian refused. "I have not been able to make up my mind to raise my hand against my relatives, my children, my home," Lee wrote.

Robert E. Lee and Ulysses S. Grant were unlike in many ways. But each general was a brilliant military strategist, fully trusted by the president who appointed him.

Lee's first move was to keep reinforcements from reaching McClellan. He sent Confederate troops to reinforce Stonewall Jackson in the Shenandoah Valley of western Virginia. With some 18,000 troops, the daring Jackson raided up and down the valley, seizing supplies and keeping over twice as many Union troops tied up. Lincoln feared that Jackson meant to take Washington and sent the reinforcements intended for McClellan to stop him. Jackson and his soldiers easily escaped the Union troops and joined Lee at Richmond.

In late June, Lee launched an offensive to drive McClellan out of Virginia. He unleashed his best officers on the Union—Stonewall Jackson and the lively cavalry leader James E.B. ("Jeb") Stuart. From June 26 until July 2 the Confederates struck again and again at the Union army. But McClellan skillfully retreated, inflicting heavy casualties on the Confederates.

At the end of these battles, called the Seven Days' Battles, McClellan was on the banks of the James River, protected by Union gunboats. The Confed-

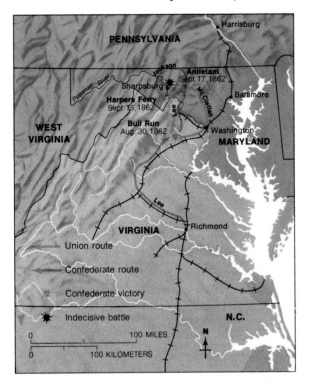

PENNSYLVANIA

Harrisburg

Jackson

Antietam
Sept. 17, 1862

Sharpsburg

Harpers Ferry
Sept. 15, 1862

Baltimore

WEST
VIRGINIA

Bull Run
Aug. 30, 1862

Washington

MARYLAND

Potomac River

Lee

McClellan

VIRGINIA

Richmond

Lee

Union route

Confederate route

Confederate victory

Indecisive battle

N.C.

0   100 MILES
0   100 KILOMETERS

N

join the Confederacy. His ultimate aim was to capture Harrisburg, Pennsylvania, from which he could cut railroad lines and isolate Washington, D.C. Lee sent Jackson with part of the army to capture the Union arsenal at Harpers Ferry. With his remaining 50,000 troops, Lee took up a defensive position at Antietam (an-TEE-tahm) Creek near Sharpsburg.

On September 17 McClellan attacked—once, twice, and a third time. With each blow the Confederate line reeled and then held, strengthened finally by troops returning from Harpers Ferry. "The air was full of the hiss of bullets and the hurtle of grapeshot," said a Union volunteer. "The mental strain was so great that . . . the whole landscape for an instant turned slightly red."

By the end of that long, bitter day's battle there were over 18,000 wounded and almost 5,000 dead. Antietam was the bloodiest day of the war. When McClellan did not attack the next day, Lee led his mauled troops across the Potomac, back to Virginia. McClellan's battered soldiers did not pursue Lee's army.

The Battle of Antietam was not decisive, but it had a vital effect on the war. It shattered the Confederate offensive in the East. It made the British, who were on the verge of recognizing the Confederacy, hold back. And it was enough of a Union victory to enable Lincoln to take steps to end slavery.

SECTION REVIEW

1. Identify the following: anaconda plan, Stonewall Jackson, *Virginia*, *Monitor*, George McClellan, David G. Farragut, Robert E. Lee, Jeb Stuart.

2. Describe the first Battle of Bull Run. How did its outcome affect northern plans for the war?

3. (a) What was the effect of the northern blockade of southern ports? (b) How did the South get warships?

4. List the three battles fought by General Grant in his push toward the Mississippi River. What was the outcome of each one?

5. What were the results of the Seven Days' Battles? The Second Battle of Bull Run?

6. (a) What were Lee's goals in the fall of 1862? (b) What were the results of his strategy?

erates withdrew. They had not crushed McClellan as hoped, but Richmond still stood as the Confederate capital.

McClellan did not attempt another drive up the peninsula. Instead, the troops were slowly evacuated by sea to northern Virginia, where they were to join another force under General John Pope. The combined armies, under McClellan's command, would then march overland to Richmond.

Aware of the Union moves, Lee decided to strike Pope before McClellan joined him. Leaving a small force at Richmond, Lee and Jackson hurried north. On August 29 and 30 the two forces clashed at Manassas Junction, the site of the Battle of Bull Run a year before. The outcome of the Second Battle of Bull Run was the same as the first—a Confederate victory. The stunned Union army crept back to Washington.

ANTIETAM

The Union retreat gave the Confederates a tempting opportunity. In the East, Lee's army crossed the Potomac and invaded Maryland in the fall of 1862. His immediate goal was to persuade Maryland to

FREEDOM FOR SLAVES, PROBLEMS AT HOME

READ TO FIND OUT

— how fugitive slaves aided the Union side.

— how the Emancipation Proclamation boosted northern morale.

— how the cause of blacks was furthered by their performance in battle.

— how opposition to the war damaged morale on both sides.

— why the southern economy declined while the northern economy grew.

— how women contributed to the war effort.

In 1863 the North began enlisting black soldiers. A dignified Sergeant J.L. Balldwin, Company G, 56th Colored Infantry, posed for this picture.

On August 19, 1862, abolitionist editor Horace Greeley criticized Lincoln in the New York *Tribune*. Many Americans, Greeley told Lincoln, "are sorely disappointed and deeply pained by the policy you seem to be pursuing with regard to the slaves of the Rebels."

Lincoln promptly wrote a letter in reply to Greeley's editorial. In the letter Lincoln wrote, "My paramount object in this struggle *is* to save the Union, and is *not* either to save or destroy slavery."

BLACKS AND THE WAR

At the start of the war Lincoln had resisted abolitionist pleas to enlist blacks in the Union army. After Fort Sumter, free blacks in Boston held a huge rally and pledged "to raise an army in the country of fifty thousand . . . ready to go at a moment's warning." This offer—and others—were turned down. Lincoln did not dare anger the border states by using blacks as soldiers. There was also fear that prejudice against blacks would create problems within the army. Frederick Douglass complained, "Colored men were good enough to fight under Washington, but they are not good enough to fight under McClellan."

However, blacks slowly forced the North to change its policies. As federal forces entered the South, thousands of slaves fled to Union lines. There was no government policy toward such fugitives, so commanders made their own decisions. Some tried to return the slaves to their owners or keep them out of Union camps.

General Benjamin F. Butler, in command of Fortress Monroe in Virginia, took a different approach. The fugitive slaves in his lines had been building Confederate fortifications. In May 1861 Butler declared them to be "contraband of war" and forbade anyone to return them to the South. He gave them noncombat work and paid them wages.

Ultimately, nearly 200,000 fugitive slaves worked for the Union as carpenters, cooks, nurses, scouts, teamsters. Many brought valuable information about Confederate troop movements. A few even brought valuable supplies. In 1862 Robert Smalls and seven of his fellow slaves from South Carolina seized the Confederate steamer *Planter* on which they had been forced to serve. With their wives and children, they sailed it out of Charleston harbor and turned it over to Union ships blockading the coast.

In March 1862 Congress officially adopted General Butler's contraband policy, forbidding the Union army to return fugitive slaves. Later that spring and summer, Congress went further. It abolished slavery in the District of Columbia and in all of the territories and allowed the President to use blacks in the army.

THE EMANCIPATION PROCLAMATION

With momentum building for emancipation, Lincoln decided to act. In July, Lincoln outlined an emancipation plan to his cabinet. Secretary of State William Seward urged him to wait until the North won a battle. The proclamation, Seward said, should be "borne on the bayonets of an advancing army, not dragged in the dust behind a retreating one." The limited Union victory at Antietam gave Lincoln his opportunity. On September 22, 1862, he issued a preliminary proclamation, warning states "in rebellion against the United States" to surrender or their slaves would be freed the first day of the new year.

The Confederate states ignored the warning, so on January 1, 1863, Lincoln issued the Emancipation Proclamation. It stated that all slaves in any state still at war were from that moment "forever free." The proclamation did not free slaves in the Union border states or in Confederate areas occupied by Union armies. Because it abolished slavery only in areas not under Union control, no slaves were immediately freed.

Lincoln justified his action as a "fit and necessary war measure." But it was more than that. As he signed the proclamation he said, "If my name ever goes into history, it will be for this act, and my whole soul is in it."

The proclamation achieved all that Lincoln had hoped. Most abolitionists were satisfied. In Europe, people hailed the measure. Public opinion was so strongly in favor of the Union that British leaders ended all talk of recognizing the Confederacy.

Not everyone in the North was pleased. Many northern soldiers did not feel that they were fighting to free blacks. Some Democrats renewed their opposition to Lincoln. In much of the North, however, the feeling grew that the Union cause had become more noble. People were now fighting both for national unity and for human freedom.

BLACK TROOPS

The Emancipation Proclamation not only pledged that the Union would free the slaves. It also authorized the enlistment of black troops in the Union

The Union army had twelve black heavy artillery units. This Brady photograph shows an all-black battery encamped in Tennessee, dressed in heavy coats against the winter cold.

PRESIDENTIAL POWER
LINCOLN IN THE CIVIL WAR

In 1863 several newspapers printed this bitter attack on President Abraham Lincoln:

Q.—What is the meaning of the word "law"?
A.—The will of the President. . . .
Q.—Have the people any rights?
A.—None, except what the President gives.
Q.—What is the habeas corpus?
A.—It is the power of the President to imprison whom he pleases.

The newspapers were, in effect, calling Lincoln a dictator. While most Americans would have disagreed, many were concerned about Lincoln's use of presidential power. The Constitution gave Congress the right to declare war. Yet in April 1861, Lincoln had not waited for Congress to meet before declaring an "insurrection" in the South, ordering a naval blockade, and calling for volunteer troops. He had also ordered the writ of habeas corpus suspended in parts of Maryland. As a result, people suspected of aiding the South were jailed without formal charges or trials.

Lincoln himself pondered the question of presidential power. Since the Constitution named the president "Commander in Chief of the Army and Navy," Lincoln felt that in wartime the president had the power to do whatever was necessary to save the nation. "I conceive that I may in an emergency do things on military grounds which cannot be done constitutionally by Congress."

In 1863 Lincoln decided that anti-draft riots and criticism of government policy were hurting the

The cares of the presidency aged Lincoln rapidly. Deep lines and hollows mark his face in this photograph, taken on April 20, 1864, just a year before his death.

northern war effort. He suspended habeas corpus for all who resisted the draft, spoke out against it, or were suspected of "any disloyal practice affording aid and comfort to the rebels." During the next two years, more than 13,000 people were jailed for suspected disloyalty, many without charges or trial. The government also opened private mail and telegrams, and shut down newspapers.

During the 1864 presidential campaign, Lincoln's use of power became a major issue. "Crush the tyrant Lincoln before he crushes you," proclaimed one slogan. "By whom and when was Abraham Lincoln made dictator of this country?" asked an opposition newspaper. "The administration has vio-

army. Some blacks, both free and ex-slave, were already in uniform as soldiers of the 1st South Carolina Volunteers, the Kansas Colored Volunteer Regiment, or the Native Guards of Louisiana. They had been enrolled by commanders in 1862 without permission from the government. But with the proclamation, enlistment soared, especially in the Union-occupied South.

By the end of the war, some 186,000 blacks had fought in the Union armies and 30,000 in the navy. Black troops saw action in some 450 engagements, 39 of them major battles. And 16 black soldiers and 4 black sailors received the Congressional Medal of Honor for bravery.

Despite their bravery and willingness to serve, blacks suffered discrimination, especially in the army. They were confined to all-black regiments. They were usually commanded by white officers, many of whom were prejudiced.

Black troops were assigned more than their share of building bridges, fortifications, and trenches. They often were given poor weapons and inade-

lated the rights of the people in a manner which, in any other country, would have provoked a revolution," charged another.

Despite such protests, Lincoln was reelected. He continued to use what he called "broader powers" during the war. Senator John Sherman of Ohio may have best expressed the feelings of many Americans about the problem. "I do not believe the President of the United States has the power to suspend the writ of habeas corpus, because that power is expressly given to Congress, and to Congress alone; I do not believe the President of the United States has the power to increase the regular army, because that power is expressly given by the Constitution to Congress alone," he said. Nevertheless, Sherman backed Lincoln's actions during the war. "I believe the President did right," he said. "He did precisely what I would have done if I had been in his place—no more, no less; but I cannot here, in my place, as a senator, under oath, declare that what he did was legal."

1. Do you think Lincoln exceeded the powers given to him by the Constitution? How did he justify his actions?

2. During a war or other national emergency, should a president assume greater power? Who should judge when a national emergency exists?

3. Can you think of other cases when presidents may have exceeded their constitutional powers?

quate training for battle, and suffered very high casualties. There were few camp hospitals or doctors for blacks. Black soldiers also faced a threat that no white soldier had to fear. Black soldiers who were taken prisoner could be enslaved or executed rather than put in prison.

Especially annoying to black troops was the unequal pay that they received. Blacks were paid as laborers, not as soldiers, and they all received the same amount regardless of rank. The troops of the 54th Massachusetts Regiment refused to accept any money unless they received equal pay. When the Massachusetts legislature voted state funds to make up the difference in pay for their black regiments, the troops refused it. They said that they would serve for free until they were treated as free people. Finally, in 1864, Congress granted retroactive,* equal pay for all black soldiers. The troops of the 54th Massachusetts Regiment at last accepted their pay.

EXPANDING THE RIGHTS OF BLACK AMERICANS

Colonel Thomas W. Higginson, abolitionist commander of the 1st South Carolina Volunteers, believed that the conduct of blacks in uniform "shamed the nation into recognizing them" as equals. During the war, abolitionists and black leaders fought against racial discrimination and slavery.

Susan B. Anthony and Elizabeth Cady Stanton formed the National Woman's Loyal League. The members of the League urged Congress to pass a constitutional amendment ending slavery in all of the United States. Anthony and Stanton collected 400,000 signatures on their petition.

Laws against black immigration in Illinois, Iowa, and Ohio were repealed. Rhode Island voted to end school **segregation**—the practice of separating one racial group from another. New York City ended segregation in its public transportation.

On the national level, the Dred Scott decision was nullified. The attorney general declared that free blacks born in the United States were citizens. In 1864 black calls for the right to vote were ignored, but the wall of discrimination was beginning to crack.

Corporal Thomas Long of the 1st South Carolina Regiment believed that black soldiers would win the fight against discrimination:

> If we hadn't become soldiers, all might have gone back as it was before; our freedom might have slipped through the two houses of Congress, and President Lincoln's four years might have passed by and nothing been done for us. But now things can never go back, because we have showed our energy and our courage.

* retroactive: going into effect as of a specified date in the past.

DISCORD WITHIN

As black Americans were gaining their rights, the leaders of the Confederacy and the Union were facing problems at home. Neither Abraham Lincoln nor Jefferson Davis had total support.

Jefferson Davis presided over a cabinet of officials as independent as the seceded states. Davis also had to deal with outspoken critics in the Confederate Congress.

Some state governments, too, distrusted the centralized power of the Confederacy. Before the war, these states had resented the federal government's power over their affairs. Now, they did not intend to let the Confederacy meddle with states' rights. Alabama's governor would not even let the Confederacy collect taxes in the state.

Furthermore, not everyone in the Confederacy was loyal to the cause. Some Union supporters in the South joined the United States Army or spied on southern troop movements for the North. To quiet opposition to the war, Davis suspended the right to the writ of habeas corpus. People suspected of being disloyal were arrested and jailed without trial. Such problems weakened the Confederacy's ability to wage war. The Union, however, suffered similar problems.

Like Davis, Lincoln clashed with many of his advisors. Several cabinet members were Republican rivals of Lincoln. Secretary of State William H. Seward tried to control policy, until Lincoln overruled him.

Before he issued the Emancipation Proclamation, Lincoln had faced die-hard opposition from abolitionists within his own party. But opposition was not limited to Republicans. A faction of Democrats actively opposed the war and demanded a peaceful settlement with the South. For such opposition they were called by the name of a poisonous snake—*Copperheads*. Like Davis, Lincoln suspended the right to the writ of habeas corpus to suppress opposition.

In both North and South nothing aroused more opposition than the draft. The Union tried, with some success, to attract volunteers by paying *bounties*, or rewards, to those who would enlist. However, some of these volunteers were "bounty jumpers." Bounty jumpers went from place to place, enlisting, receiving their bounties, and then deserting from the army.

In April 1862 the Confederacy had to resort to America's first draft. The wealthy could hire substitutes to serve for them. Angry southerners began to call it "a rich man's war and a poor man's fight," and in some states officials refused to enforce the draft. Two years later the Confederacy, desperate for troops, passed a tighter draft law. It ended most exemptions and drafted all white males between the ages of seventeen and fifty.

In March 1863 the Union also resorted to a draft. As in the Confederacy, people with money could hire substitutes. They could also pay three hundred dollars to exempt themselves from the draft. Northerners bitterly complained that these provisions benefited the wealthy, and antidraft riots broke out in a few cities. In New York City, the drawing of the first draftees' names in July led to four days of rioting.

Despite these problems, the Union army not only filled its ranks but also received a boost from another source. During the war, immigrants poured into the North, and 400,000 eventually served in the Union army. At war's end, the Union had reserves of almost 2 million soldiers. The Confederacy, however, grew more and more desperate.

THE ECONOMIES OF THE SOUTH AND NORTH

The South suffered more than just the shortage of troops. As the war continued, the Union blockade tightened into a stranglehold. With its lifeline to outside markets cut off, the Confederacy turned inward to fill its needs. Instead of growing cash crops, farmers—mostly women and slaves—grew enough grains and other food to feed the armies and the people at home. Victoria Clayton of Alabama wrote, "We were blockaded on every side, could get nothing from without, so had to make everything at home."

Because most of the fighting took place in the South, invading Union armies destroyed crops and occupied valuable farmland. Also the inadequate southern railroad system hindered distribution of food and caused shortages. In 1863, when this transportation system broke down, people in some cities faced near starvation. Food shortages—and inflation—sent prices soaring.

The Confederacy turned to manufacturing to produce what it could not import. Most industries,

A nurse from the United States Sanitary Commission sits among patients at a Fredericksburg hospital in May 1864. The Commission was set up in June 1861 to care for sick and wounded Union soldiers.

however, lacked the capital and skilled workers to fill the needs of the army and civilians in a long war. Railroads were needed for moving troops and supplies. Throughout the war, however, they began to wear out because of lack of new equipment.

In contrast to the Confederacy, the northern economy slowly, steadily responded to the demands of war. To link further the Union, some 5,000 miles (8,000 kilometers) of railroad track were laid. By 1863 northern industries were pouring out so many war supplies that Union soldiers often left coats and blankets behind when they advanced.

The war also stimulated northern agriculture. Farmers began to produce more grain, and bought machinery to take over from farm workers who had become soldiers. One of Cyrus McCormick's reapers could do the harvesting work of four to six farmhands, and 165,000 of these reapers were sold during the war.

Lincoln's administration, divided in other areas, united to keep the farm boom going. In May 1862 the Republicans fulfilled a campaign promise and passed the Homestead Act, offering any citizen 160 acres (64.8 hectares) of public land. That same year, the government created the Department of Agriculture. It also passed the Morrill Land Grant Act, by which public lands were given to states for agricultural colleges.

WOMEN AND THE WAR

Franklin Thompson of Michigan served two years in the Union army. Harry B. Buford of Louisiana fought on the Confederate side and was wounded twice. Buford wore a false moustache, and Thompson deserted on the way to the hospital to keep a secret. Both were women.

Most women, however, served the war effort behind the lines as "soldiers without guns." Some were spies. An ex-slave named Elizabeth Bowser became a Union spy, placed in the Confederate White House in Richmond. Rose O'Neal Greenhow, a Confederate spy, was questioned in prison by Union generals. One questioner confronted her: "General McClellan, madam, charges you with having obtained a thorough knowledge of his plans, and of forcing him consequently four times to change them."

Many women—black and white, in North and South—shouldered the work of men in fields and factories. Thousands of women organized aid societies to collect, make, and distribute food and supplies to the soldiers.

Northern women in the United States Sanitary Commission raised millions of dollars to train nurses, to staff and supply hospitals, and to transport the wounded. Teacher Clara Barton started

For three years Harriet Tubman served as a Union spy and scout in South Carolina. She often contacted black informants behind Confederate lines for military information.

and giving them water. The men are laying all over the house, on their blankets, just as they were brought from the battlefield. . . . We have to walk, and when we give the men anything, kneel, in blood and water.

Black women and men, slave and free, often formed the core of the nursing staff in Confederate hospitals. Two well-known abolitionists, Sojourner Truth and Harriet Tubman, divided their time between nursing and scouting for the Union army.

Women's war efforts did not go unnoticed in the White House. "All that had been said by orators and poets since the creation of the world in praise of women," commented President Lincoln, "would not do them justice for their conduct during the war."

SECTION REVIEW

1. Identify the following: 54th Massachusetts Regiment, Thomas W. Higginson, National Women's Loyal League, Cyrus McCormick, Clara Barton, Sally Tompkins.

2. Define the following: Copperheads, "bounty jumpers."

3. Describe General Benjamin F. Butler's contraband policy. What roles did fugitive slaves play in the Union army as a result?

4. (a) What did the Emancipation Proclamation state? (b) What was the general feeling in the North about it?

5. (a) Name three organized groups of black troops. (b) List four burdens black soldiers faced because of discrimination.

6. (a) Give two examples of southern opposition to Jefferson Davis's policies during the war. (b) Give two examples of northern opposition to Abraham Lincoln's policies.

7. (a) How could some men in both North and South avoid being drafted? (b) What was a large source of troops for the North?

8. List three causes of food shortages in the South.

9. List three actions taken by Lincoln's administration to encourage the farm boom.

10. (a) List five kinds of contributions to the war effort made by women. (b) Name five women and the contribution each made in the Civil War.

volunteer nursing groups to care for sick and wounded Union soldiers behind the lines and on battlefields. After the war she headed a government-sponsored search for missing soldiers. Reformer Dorothea Dix was appointed superintendent of women nurses, in charge of hospital nursing for the Union forces.

In the South, many women used their homes as medical shelters and a few, such as Ella Newsom, headed hospitals. Nurse Sally Tompkins even set up her own hospital in Richmond and later was commissioned a captain by the Confederacy. Kate Cummings of Alabama wrote of her first day in a Confederate hospital:

Nothing that I had ever heard or read had given me the faintest idea of the horrors witnessed here. . . . I sat up all night, bathing the men's wounds,

FROM GETTYSBURG TO APPOMATTOX

READ TO FIND OUT

— how the Confederate offensive ended with the Battle of Gettysburg.

— how Union forces gained complete control of the Mississippi River.

— how General Grant put his philosophy of war into practice.

— what happened when Sherman marched through Georgia.

— what events brought the Civil War to a close.

By late 1862 Union forces were bogged down in the East. Lincoln was sorely disappointed in his commander. George McClellan had watched the Con-federates slip back into Virginia, stubbornly refusing to follow. He needed more soldiers and supplies, he claimed, before he could chase Lee.

To the President, this was too much. In November Lincoln relieved McClellan of his command. "He has got the 'slows,'" Lincoln explained. As the new Commander of the Army of the Potomac, Lincoln chose General Ambrose E. Burnside.

THE BATTLE OF GETTYSBURG

In December 1862 Burnside tried to take Richmond. His larger army was soundly defeated by Lee's forces at the town of Fredericksburg, about 40 miles (64 kilometers) short of the Confederate capital. Lincoln promptly replaced Burnside with General Joseph Hooker.

"Fighting Joe" Hooker took over the Union drive toward Richmond, but he too was stopped by Lee. Lee's victory at Chancellorsville, Virginia, in May 1863 was costly. The Confederacy lost over 1,600 soldiers and a brilliant general. Stonewall Jackson was accidentally shot by Confederate troops and died soon after.

John Richards' painting of the Fredericksburg battle-field reflects the horrors of that encounter. Union losses numbered about 9,000; Confederate losses were over 1,500.

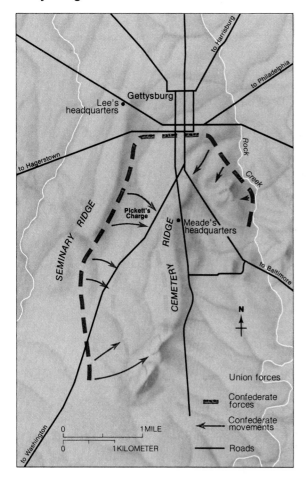

With the southern victories, Lee decided to try a second invasion of the North. As in 1862, his goal was Pennsylvania, where he could cut off the Northeast from the Northwest. Both Lee and Davis hoped that a successful invasion would win foreign recognition of the Confederacy and force the Union to negotiate for peace.

In June 1863 Lee led 75,000 troops up the Shenandoah Valley, across the Potomac River, and north into Maryland and Pennsylvania. The Army of the Potomac moved forward to challenge him with 90,000 troops. The Union army had yet another commander. General George G. Meade had replaced Hooker. The armies met at Gettysburg, Pennsylvania, on July 1, 1863.

The Union troops established a line along Cemetery Ridge, just outside the town. The Confederate army drew up opposite them on Seminary Ridge, about a mile to the west. Time after time,

Confederate troops poured around the ridge to attack the Union army's flanks, but the Union line held firm.

On the third day of fighting, Lee ordered a frontal attack against the center of the Union line. Supporting artillery pounded the Union position first. Then a force of 15,000 Confederate soldiers under General George E. Pickett charged across the open ground. "More than half a mile their front extends," wrote a Union officer. "The arms . . . gleam in the sun, a sloping forest of flashing steel. Right on they move, as with one soul." Union cannons and rifles responded with a withering fire that mowed down the attacking Confederates. A fraction of the soldiers managed to reach the crest of Cemetery Ridge, only to be captured or killed.

The battered Confederates did not attack again. Both sides were stunned by the battle. Over 25 percent of the soldiers were killed or wounded. Lee gathered the remains of his army and retreated into Virginia. Despite Lincoln's urging, Meade did not pursue.

Several months later, a cemetery was dedicated at the Gettysburg battlefield. In a short speech, Lincoln expressed his feeling about the battle and the war. Honoring the Union troops, he said:

> The world will little note, nor long remember what we say here, but it can never forget what they did here. It is for us the living, rather, to be dedicated here to the unfinished work which they who fought here have thus far so nobly advanced. . . . We here highly resolve that these dead shall not have died in vain—that this nation, under God, shall have a new birth of freedom—and that government of the people, by the people, for the people, shall not perish from the earth.

The Battle of Gettysburg proved to be a turning point in the war. The Confederacy would not invade the North again. Furthermore, its final hopes for foreign recognition and aid died with the soldiers on Cemetery Ridge.

VICKSBURG, PORT HUDSON, AND CHATTANOOGA

While Lee's and Meade's forces battled at Gettysburg, the Union was marching to victory in the West. Since mid-1862 General Ulysses S. Grant had tried to capture Vicksburg, one of the last major cities on the Mississippi River still in Confederate

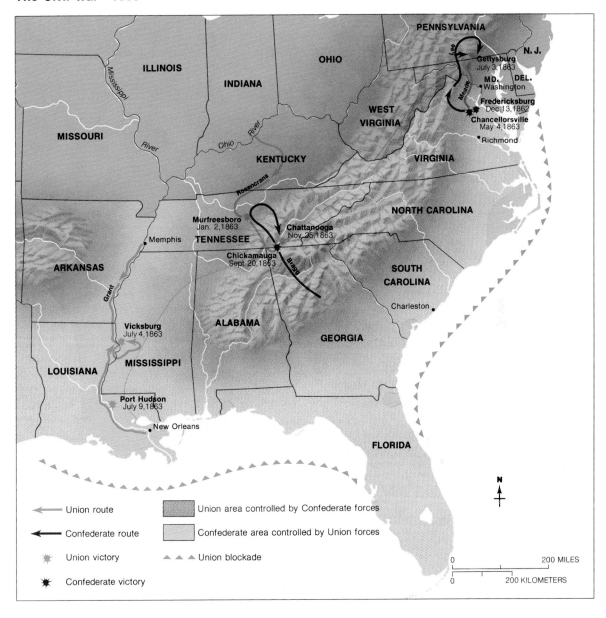

hands. Vicksburg perched on sheer cliffs and was partly surrounded by impassable marshland. The best assault would be from the east across dry ground, but that was enemy territory.

Finally, in March 1863, Grant tried a bold new plan. From Memphis, he led about 20,000 troops to a point southwest of Vicksburg. There, Union gunboats, which had slipped along the Mississippi past Vicksburg's deadly cannon, ferried the troops to the east bank of the river. Grant's army then fought its way northeastward, and finally circled Vicksburg.

After two attempts to storm the city, Grant besieged it while Union gunboats bombarded it from the river. For over six weeks Vicksburg held out. Civilians hid in caves for safety and ate mules and horses for food. "We are utterly cut off from the world, surrounded by a circle of fire," one girl wrote in her diary. Finally, on July 4, 1863—the day after Gettysburg—General John C. Pemberton surrendered the city and over 30,000 troops.

Five days later, the last Confederate stronghold on the Mississippi fell to Grant. Port Hudson, Louisiana, surrendered to Union troops after a six-week siege. The Union now controlled the entire river, and the Confederacy was split in two.

That same month, another Union army in the West was marching on Chattanooga, a key city on the Tennessee River and the gateway to Georgia and Alabama. As the Union force under General William Rosecrans approached Chattanooga, Confederate forces under General Braxton Bragg evacuated the city. Rosecrans followed, and in September the two armies clashed near the stream of Chickamauga (CHIK-ah-MAH-gah), an Indian name meaning "river of death."

On the second day of fighting, the Union line broke. Only the forces under General George H. Thomas stood their ground, holding off the Confederate army. Thomas finally was forced to follow the rest of the Union forces into Chattanooga. Bragg, too, followed, and the Confederates laid siege to the city.

A month later, Lincoln placed General Grant in command of all the troops in the West. Grant's first task was to save the starving Union army trapped in Chattanooga. Grant assembled a mighty force and in late November swept down on the Confederates surrounding the city. After a rough two-day battle, the Confederates crumbled. With victory at the Battle of Chattanooga, Union forces were now in position to move into Georgia and divide the eastern states of the Confederacy.

GRANT'S STRATEGY

In March 1864 Lincoln made his final change in commanders, putting Grant in charge of all the armies of the United States. Grant, like Lee, had been educated at West Point and had fought in the Mexican War. Grant, however, did not present the heroic figure that Lee did. A soldier noted that Grant had "rough light-brown whiskers, a blue eye, and rather a scrubby look."

Nevertheless, Grant saw war with a clear cold eye. "The art of war is simple enough," he wrote. "Find out where your enemy is. Get at him as soon as you can. Strike at him as hard as you can and as often as you can, and keep moving on." Grant's war was total war, fought not only on battlefields, but in the fields and cities of the enemy.

Noting the Union's superior numbers, Grant planned two major offensives at the same time. He would lead the Army of the Potomac against Lee's army—the major Confederate force—and take Richmond. Meanwhile, an army under General William Tecumseh Sherman would push into Georgia. Sherman's orders were to destroy the Confederate army under General Joseph E. Johnston. He was also to seize Atlanta, the Confederacy's major industrial and railroad center.

TOWARD RICHMOND

In early May, Grant began his drive toward Richmond, with over 100,000 troops. But as they marched into the Wilderness, a desolate forest in northern Virginia, Lee appeared with 60,000 Confederates to stop him. For two days, the armies clashed in the heavily wooded terrain, and Lee checked Grant's advance. Despite heavy casualties, Grant did not retreat as other Union generals had done. As the Union troops realized that Grant would not turn back, the old rallying cry rang out—"On to Richmond!"

Grant marched south, and the armies next clashed at Spotsylvania Court House. In five days of bloody trench warfare Grant was once again battered. Still, he refused to retreat. "I propose to fight it out along this line," he advised Washington, "if it takes all summer."

Grimly, Grant pushed southward, and Lee tracked him. By the first of June the two armies reached Cold Harbor, just outside Richmond. Again, they battled and the casualty list grew longer. In the first month of his campaign, Grant lost nearly 60,000—about Lee's total strength. But Grant had replacements, and his army swelled back to its original size. Lee's army, with some 30,000 casualties, never recovered its strength.

Shocked at Union losses, northerners began to call Grant "a butcher." He ignored the charges and headed south once more. His goal was Petersburg, a key railroad center about 20 miles (32 kilometers) south of Richmond. Lee moved to defend Petersburg—and Richmond—and Grant dug in to besiege the city. Hoping to divert Grant, Lee sent troops under General Jubal A. Early north through the Shenandoah Valley to threaten Washington.

Keeping a tight hold on Petersburg, Grant sent General Philip H. Sheridan to the Shenandoah Valley after Early. Sheridan was also ordered to lay waste to the valley so that Confederate forces could

A watercolor by British artist Frank Vizetelly, an eyewitness, shows the Union assault on Fort Fisher in January 1865. The fort was the principal defense of the port of Wilmington, North Carolina. With its fall the South lost its last major port on the Atlantic.

not use it again. The aggressive Sheridan carried out his orders to the letter. Lee remained trapped at Petersburg, and the siege would go on for nine months.

THE GEORGIA CAMPAIGN

In May 1864, as Grant had moved into the Wilderness, General Sherman launched the second part of the Union offensive. A hardened veteran of Shiloh and Vicksburg, Sherman slashed into northwestern Georgia with 100,000 troops.

Sherman was met by an army of 60,000 Confederates under General Joseph Johnston. They made the Union pay for every advance, but by mid-July Sherman was outside Atlanta. He battered the Confederates, now under John B. Hood, and occupied the city on September 2, 1864.

The news was wired to Washington just before the presidential election. Lincoln had been renominated by the Republicans, with Democrat Andrew Johnson of Tennessee as his running mate. However, he expected to lose to his Democratic opponent, General George McClellan. The North was weary of war, and many were calling for an armistice. Atlanta's capture, though, convinced northerners that the war could yet be won. Lincoln was swept into a second term by an electoral vote of 212 to 21.

In Atlanta, Sherman now proposed to sweep across Georgia to destroy the South's resources and will to fight. "I can make the march," he promised Grant, "and make Georgia howl!" In November

Sherman's troops destroyed all supplies in Atlanta that the enemy could use. Then they set fire to the city. From Atlanta they marched almost unopposed toward the sea, cutting a path 60 miles (97 kilometers) wide through Georgia. Eliza F. Andrews wrote of the results:

> About three miles from Sparta we struck the "burnt country," as it is well named. . . . There was hardly a fence left standing all the way from Sparta to Gordon. The fields were trampled down and the road was lined with carcasses of horses, hogs, and cattle that the invaders . . . had wantonly shot down. . . . Here and there, lone chimney stacks, "Sherman's sentinels," told of homes laid in ashes.

Sherman reached the sea in December and crowned his campaign by taking Savannah. Then he set off north to join Grant. In early 1865 his army drove into South Carolina, destroying even more than it had in Georgia, and then rolled on into North Carolina. The two states fell to the Union.

UNION VICTORY

In Petersburg, Lee's besieged army could not hold out much longer. In early April Grant's army broke through Confederate lines and marched triumphantly into Petersburg and then Richmond. Lee was forced to flee. With fewer than 30,000 troops and scant rations, he soon realized that more fighting would be useless.

On April 9, 1865, Lee and Grant met at the village of Appomattox Court House to discuss the

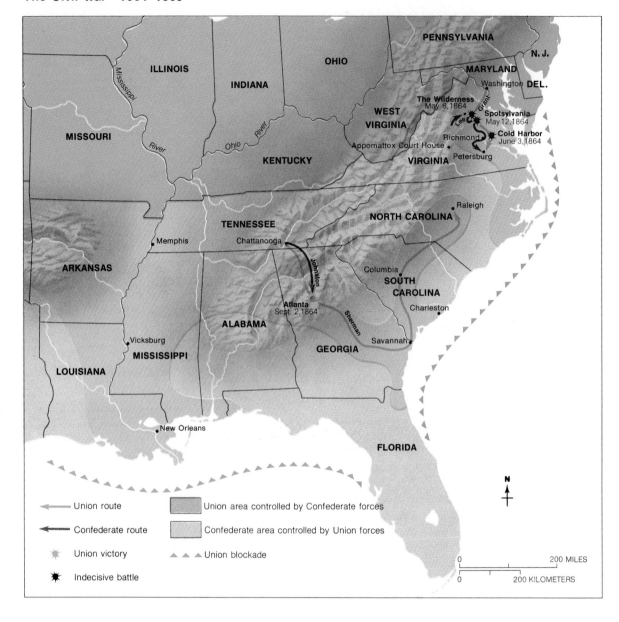

Union route

Confederate route

Union victory

Indecisive battle

Union area controlled by Confederate forces

Confederate area controlled by Union forces

Union blockade

0   200 MILES

0   200 KILOMETERS

Confederate surrender. "General Lee was dressed in a full uniform which was entirely new," Grant wrote later. "In my rough traveling suit, the uniform of a private with the straps of a lieutenant-general, I must have contrasted very strangely with a man so handsomely dressed, six foot high and of faultless form."

Grant wrote out the terms of surrender, keeping in mind the generous instructions of Lincoln. Lee's soldiers could return home if they promised to fight no more. The officers would be allowed to retain their swords and pistols. All soldiers could keep their own horses and mules. Lee agreed to the terms, and both generals signed the document. As Lee left, the two longtime foes saluted each other.

The Union victory ended one of the bloodiest wars in the nation's history. More than 600,000 Confederate and Union soldiers had died. Hundreds of thousands more were wounded, many disabled for life.

Three days later Lee's army formally surrendered. At the surrender Grant appointed General

The Final Days

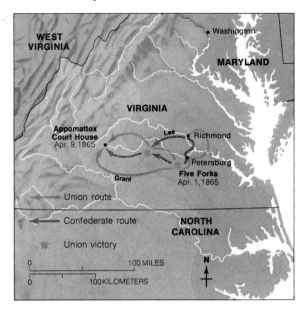

cheer, nor word nor whisper," he wrote. "Here pass the men of Antietam . . . and Cemetery Hills at Gettysburg; these survivors of the terrible Wilderness." As the long lines passed by, he thought, "It is by miracles we have lived to see this day."

SECTION REVIEW

1. Identify the following: George Meade, Cemetery Ridge, Chickamauga, Petersburg, Appomattox Court House.

2. (a) What were the two goals of the Confederate invasion of the North in 1863? (b) How was Gettysburg a turning point in the war?

3. Explain why control of each of the following was important: Vicksburg, Port Hudson, Chattanooga. What Union general captured all three cities?

4. Explain Ulysses S. Grant's policy of total war.

5. After Grant was placed in charge of all Union armies, what two offensives did he plan?

6. List four battle sites in Grant's drive to Richmond.

7. (a) What was the immediate result of the capture of Atlanta in 1864? (b) What was Sherman's purpose in burning houses and killing livestock as his army moved through Georgia?

8. What were the terms of surrender? Who signed the document?

Joshua Chamberlain, a former college professor, to represent the Union. Chamberlain watched the Confederate troops march forward with their flags flying. As they approached the Union line, Chamberlain ordered his own ranks to shift to the "marching salute," the highest honor soldiers could give one another. The Confederates returned the salute.

Chamberlain was deeply moved. "On our part not a sound of trumpet more; nor roll of drum; not a

Throughout the war the North had the advantage in supplies and the means to move them. Here, near the end of the war, Union supply wagons leave Petersburg to provision Grant's troops.

SUMMARY

When the Civil War began in 1861, neither North nor South foresaw that the fighting would take four long years, a tremendous amount of money and resources, and the lives of over 600,000 soldiers. The South had dedicated, well-trained soldiers, who would be fighting on their home ground. The North had the ability, however, to outlast the South because of larger population and greater industrial power.

Northern war strategy rested on the anaconda plan. The advance of Union troops in the west under U.S. Grant was relentless. By June of 1862 much of the Mississippi River was in Union hands. In the east, however, George McClellan moved more cautiously. Confederate troops under Robert E. Lee were able to prevent the capture of Richmond, and win the Second Battle of Bull Run. Then a Confederate offensive in 1862 was unsuccessful, and ended with the bloody Battle of Antietam.

Northern morale was boosted by Lincoln's Emancipation Proclamation early in 1863. Many blacks fought valiantly on the Union side. The struggle to end slavery and discrimination slowly advanced. Women, too, were vital to the war effort. They worked on farms and in factories, especially as these flourished in the North. On both sides they worked as nurses.

General Lee attempted a second invasion of the North in June of 1863. His drive into Pennsylvania ended at Gettysburg, where both sides suffered huge losses. Besides soldiers the South lost all hope of foreign aid. From that time on, the offensive belonged to the North.

In the West, Grant gained complete control of the Mississippi River and a clear path to Georgia and Alabama. Heavy casualties did not halt his drive toward Richmond. Grant's troops outlasted Lee's diminishing army to take Petersburg and then Richmond in April of 1865. Meanwhile Sherman had captured Atlanta and led a devastating march across Georgia to Savannah. With the fall of Richmond, Lee surrendered. Although Lincoln's terms were generous, the national wounds caused by this violent and destructive Civil War would be a long time in healing.

CHAPTER REVIEW

1. (a) Why were the border states valued by both the North and the South? (b) What happened in each of the border states at the beginning of the Civil War?

2. Discuss the strengths and weaknesses of each side in the Civil War from the standpoint of each of the following. (a) population (b) supply lines (c) military experience (d) industry (e) sea power (f) finances (g) morale

3. (a) Describe the South's military strategy. (b) Describe the North's military strategy.

4. Explain how each of the following military actions helped Union forces to gain control of the Mississippi River. (a) Forts Henry and Donelson (b) the Battle of Shiloh (c) New Orleans and Baton Rouge (d) Memphis (e) Vicksburg (f) Port Hudson

5. Describe how each of the following military actions helped Confederate forces to hold Richmond. (a) the Battle of Seven Pines (b) Stonewall Jackson's raids in the Shenandoah Valley (c) the Seven Days' Battles (d) the Second Battle of Bull Run

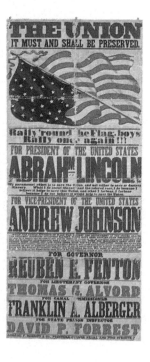

When Lincoln ran for re-election in 1864, he had little confidence of winning. However, Union victories restored the voters' faith in him and gave him the election.

6. (a) What was the result of the Battle of Antietam? (b) What long-range effects did this battle have?

7. (a) Describe events prior to the Emancipation Proclamation that helped blacks to win rights. (b) Describe events taking place after the Emancipation Proclamation that helped blacks to win rights.

8. (a) Give the provisions of the Emancipation Proclamation. (b) How did the British react to the proclamation? (c) How did northerners react?

9. (a) Describe issues that brought about conflict within the North during the Civil War. (b) Describe issues that brought about conflict within the South.

10. (a) Describe the Battle of Gettysburg. (b) Why was it a turning point in the war?

11. (a) Describe these two major offensives planned by Grant: the capture of Richmond and the capture of Atlanta. (b) What were the results?

12. (a) What happened at Appomattox Court House? (b) What were the terms of the surrender?

ISSUES AND IDEAS

1. General Sherman's march through Georgia represented what is called a "scorched earth policy." What does this mean? Sherman's march also showed that the Civil War was a total war. How has total warfare made war more devastating than before? Give several ways. Is there any way to wage war today and avoid total war? Defend your answer.

2. In the Civil War more soldiers died of disease than were killed in battle. What were some reasons for this? Why is this not as great a problem today?

3. What might have happened if England had come to the aid of the South in the Civil War? Give your ideas about the effects and the possible outcome of the war.

4. The Emancipation Proclamation had several purposes. Discuss these purposes, and comment on Lincoln's timing in issuing the proclamation. Why did Lincoln issue the proclamation at that particular time? What were the results?

SKILLS WORKSHOP

1. *Primary sources.* Find and read a copy of the Gettysburg Address. What can you tell about Lincoln's viewpoint on government from this speech? What is his attitude toward the rights of states in relation to the national government?

2. *Maps.* Trace a map of the United States. Draw in state boundaries as they existed in 1861. Show major rivers and cities. With arrows, show the North's war strategy, called the anaconda plan.

PAST AND PRESENT

1. There was opposition to the draft in both the North and the South during the Civil War. In recent years, there has been opposition to the draft in the United States. Did people in the 1860s have the same reasons for opposing the draft as they do now? How have reasons changed? What were arguments in favor of the draft in the 1860s? Now?

2. Plan a visit to the sites of at least three major battlefields of the Civil War. Explain why you chose these sites, and describe what you would find there today.

An unknown Union soldier drew this interior view of the Confederate submarine *H.L. Hunley.* He mistakenly showed eleven men rather than eight turning the ship's crankshaft.

CHAPTER 13

RECONSTRUCTION AND POST-WAR POLITICS

1865–1900

**REBUILDING THE UNION
THE SOUTH UNDER RECONSTRUCTION
BLACKS IN THE NEW SOUTH
THE GILDED AGE**

In August 1875 *Scribner's Monthly* ran an article about the nation's one-hundredth birthday:

"We are to have grand doings next year. . . . The Centennial is expected to celebrate in a fitting way the birth of a nation.

"The great point is to recognize the fact that . . . these United States constitute a nation; that we are to live, grow, prosper, and suffer together, united by bands that cannot be sundered. Unless this fact is fully recognized throughout the Union, our Centennial will be but a hollow mockery.

"A few weeks ago, Mr. Jefferson Davis, the ex-president of the Confederacy, was reported to have urged an audience to be as loyal to the old flag of the Union now as they were during the Mexican War. If the South could know what music there was in these words to the northern ears. . . .

"People of the South, we want you. We would see . . . all causes and all memories of discord wiped out forever. You do not believe this? Then you do not know the heart of the North. Have you cause of complaint against the politicians? Alas! So have we. Help us, as loving and loyal American citizens, to make our politicians better. There is nothing that the North wants so much today, as that the old relations between you and us are forever restored—that your hope, your pride, and your destiny are one with ours."

The Centennial, *Scribner's* hoped, would celebrate not only the birth of the nation but also its rebirth. A nation divided by civil war needed to be united in peace.

The task would not be easy. In the chaotic postwar years the United States needed strong, wise leadership. Many leaders tried hard to meet that need, but others gave Americans much "cause for complaint."

disabled for life. Because the war had been fought almost entirely on southern soil, northern factories, farms, and cities escaped damage. But much of the South lay in ruins.

When Confederate soldiers marched home, most were penniless. Many reached home to find their houses, farms, and plantations destroyed and their livestock killed.

Plantation owners faced bankruptcy, having lost a major portion of their wealth—their slaves. In southern cities and towns, banks and businesses failed. Damaged factories stood empty.

For the former slaves, problems accompanied freedom. The freed slaves were homeless and without a means of making a living. Many ex-slaves took refuge in camps set up by the Union army. The camps were plagued with food shortages and disease, and thousands of blacks died.

The South needed to be rebuilt. The question was, How could this be done?

RECONSTRUCTION PLANS

Even during the war, northern leaders had thought about the difficult task of rebuilding the Union. One group of Republicans, called Radicals, especially differed with Lincoln over **Reconstruction**—the plan by which the Confederate states would be readmitted to the Union.

Radicals felt that the Confederate states had lost their statehood by seceding. They were "conquered provinces" without state governments, under the control of Congress. Lincoln, however, believed that the states had never left the Union because they did not have that right. In December 1863 he had presented his plan for Reconstruction, based on his authority to grant pardons.

Lincoln would pardon any southerner, except high Confederate leaders, who took an oath of loyalty to the Constitution and the Union. When a certain number of people in any state took the oath of loyalty and accepted emancipation, that state could set up a government and be welcomed back into the Union. The number of people needed to fulfill these requirements was set at 10 percent of those who had voted in 1860.

Radicals as well as many moderate Republicans disliked the "ten percent plan." They felt that the price of secession should be far higher. They watched angrily as Lincoln's plan was carried out in

REBUILDING THE UNION

READ TO FIND OUT

— how Lincoln and Radical Republicans disagreed over the Reconstruction of the Union.

— how President Johnson tried to reconstruct the Union.

— how Radical Republicans gained the support of moderates.

— what legislation was enacted by Radical Republicans.

— why President Johnson was impeached.

Four years of war left 360,000 Union soldiers and 258,000 Confederate soldiers dead. Many thousands more on both sides were wounded—many

the occupied states of Tennessee, Arkansas, and Louisiana. When representatives arrived from these states, Congress refused to seat them.

In July 1864 Congress passed a much harsher Reconstruction plan, proposed by Radicals Benjamin F. Wade and Henry W. Davis. The Wade-Davis bill called for a *majority* of those who had voted in 1860 to declare loyalty to the Union before the state could be readmitted. Only those who vowed that they had been loyal to the Union during the war could vote or hold office. The bill also said that state constitutions must abolish slavery, bar Confederate officials from holding office, and agree not to pay Confederate war debts.

Lincoln would not sign the bill. He especially objected to its provision regarding slavery. He believed that slavery should be ended by an amendment to the Constitution.

Congress had already taken action against slavery in 1862. It had abolished slavery in the District of Columbia and in the territories. In February 1865 it proposed the Thirteenth Amendment, outlawing slavery throughout the United States. The amendment would be ratified by three fourths of the states and become part of the Constitution by the end of the year.

THE ASSASSINATION OF LINCOLN

In March 1865 Lincoln gave his second inaugural address, making a plea for a generous peace: "With malice toward none, with charity for all," he urged, "let us . . . bind up the nation's wounds." But Lincoln would never bring about that peace.

Six weeks after his inauguration and just a few days after the Confederate surrender at Appomattox, Lincoln went to see a comedy at Ford's Theater in Washington, D.C. As the play unfolded, John Wilkes Booth burst into the presidential box and shot Lincoln. "The South is avenged!" he reportedly shouted. Booth, a former actor and unstable proslavery supporter, hoped to save the Confederacy by murdering Union leaders. Lincoln died the next morning, April 15, 1865.

John Wilkes Booth escaped but was tracked down. He was hiding in a barn in Virginia. There, he either shot himself or was killed by his pursuers. He died on April 26.

Booth's death, however, did not compensate for the loss of Lincoln. "Never before that startled April morning," wrote author James Russell Lowell, did so many "shed tears for the death of one they had never seen, as if with him a friendly presence

Women in mourning gaze at the ruins of Richmond in 1865. Atlanta and Charleston also lay in ruins. In the South, industrial and farm buildings, crops, livestock, and miles of railroad had been destroyed.

had been taken away from their lives, leaving them colder and dark." North and South now faced the difficult task of Reconstruction without that friendly presence.

ANDREW JOHNSON'S PLAN

Andrew Johnson succeeded Lincoln as president. Johnson was a Democrat and a southerner. He had modeled himself on another politician from Tennessee, Andrew Jackson. Like his hero, Johnson saw himself as a champion of the people.

Johnson took office when Congress was not in session. At first, he seemed an ally of the Radicals. He declared that "traitors must be punished" and called for the arrest of Confederate leaders.

However, the Radicals soon discovered that Johnson was not an ally. He wanted to bring the workers and small farmers of the South to power through his party—the Democratic party. To do so, he would have to bring the southern states back into the Union as quickly as possible. Johnson adopted Lincoln's "ten percent plan."

In May 1865 Johnson recognized Louisiana, Tennessee, Arkansas, and Virginia—the four states organized under Lincoln's plan. He set up provisional, or temporary, governments for the remaining seven states. They would be readmitted to the Union if they ratified the Thirteenth Amendment, rejected their acts of secession, and repudiated* Confederate war debts. Johnson also offered *amnesty*, or a general pardon, to former Confederates willing to pledge their loyalty to the Union.

Throughout the summer and fall of 1865, the provisional governments held conventions to consider Johnson's terms. Mississippi would not ratify the Thirteenth Amendment. South Carolina and Mississippi would not cancel their war debts. A few states would not reject secession. Despite such actions, Johnson accepted the governments as reconstructed.

THE RADICALS' ANGER GROWS

The Radical Republicans fumed over Johnson's plan for Reconstruction. However, Congress would not convene until December, so they could do nothing to stop the President.

* repudiate: refuse to acknowledge or pay.

The photograph of Andrew Johnson was taken by Mathew Brady. Brady's original negative, brittle with time, is now cracked. The crack is seen as a slash across the print.

Meanwhile, the new southern legislatures were meeting. They elected many former Confederate leaders to Congress and passed laws known as the **black codes** to clarify the status of the freed slaves. The codes differed from state to state. Some codes protected blacks' rights. For example, blacks could own property, make contracts, sue, and be sued. But many measures restricted blacks' rights, especially in states where blacks were a majority. Black codes barred blacks from voting, bearing arms, serving on juries, or holding office. Blacks could be arrested and fined if they were unemployed.

Most of the North did not feel strongly about rights for blacks. Many northerners were, however, shocked by passage of the black codes and the election of Confederate leaders. In Congress, moderate Republicans began to agree with the Radicals.

Both Representative Thaddeus Stevens and Senator Charles Sumner, Radical leaders in Congress, insisted that blacks be granted full rights as citizens. "I am for Negro suffrage in every Rebel state," Stevens declared. "If it be just, it should not be denied; if it be necessary, it should be adopted; if it be a punishment to traitors, they deserve it."

When Congress finally met in December 1865, the Radicals had gained the support of the moderate Republicans. This coalition* was now a majority in Congress. Then the new delegates from the southern states arrived, and Republicans were furious. Many of the southerners were former Confederate leaders, and most were Democrats. Congress refused to seat the southern delegates.

CITIZENSHIP RIGHTS

In late December, Congress set up a Committee on Reconstruction. After several months, the committee reported that all 11 states were "disorganized communities" without government. Congress then created its own Reconstruction program. President Johnson's response to the different parts of this program was usually a veto.

Congress's first act, in February 1866, was to extend the life of the Freedmen's Bureau* and increase its powers. Congress had created this bureau a year earlier to care for blacks as they moved from slavery to freedom. The Freedmen's Bureau issued clothing and food to former slaves and organized schools for blacks. Johnson vetoed the bill to retain the Freedmen's Bureau, saying that the Constitution did not allow the creation of a federal agency to support the needy. Congress eventually managed to pass the bill over the President's veto.

Congress next moved to protect blacks from discrimination of the kinds found in the black codes. In April it passed a civil rights bill. This bill granted citizenship to blacks and outlawed discrimination based on race or color. Again, Johnson vetoed Congress's bill. He believed that blacks should be "well and humanely governed," but the states, not Congress, should make such policy. Congress overrode Johnson's veto.

However, Republicans feared that the Supreme Court, which had denied black citizenship in the Dred Scott case, might declare the Civil Rights Act unconstitutional. In June it proposed the Fourteenth Amendment to protect the act from the Court and from future Congresses.

The amendment said that anyone born in the United States is a citizen. No state could deprive a citizen of equal protection of the laws, or of life,

---

* coalition: an alliance of politicians or political parties formed for a special purpose.

* freedmen: the term used to refer to all former slaves—men, women, and children.

Fully equipped black soldiers stand in Arlington, Virginia, near a store sign reading "Dealers in Slaves." Later, under the black codes, freed slaves could not bear arms.

liberty, or property without due process of law. Any state violating the amendment would lose some of its representation in Congress and the electoral college. It stated further that no Confederate official, unless pardoned, could hold federal office.

A month later, race riots erupted in Memphis and New Orleans over black voter registration. More than eighty blacks were killed. Tennessee and Louisiana were two of the states Johnson had recognized. The riots there convinced many northerners that Johnson's plan would not work. The riots also dramatized the Republican position that the Fourteenth Amendment was necessary to protect black rights.

RADICAL RECONSTRUCTION

Before the fall congressional elections, President Johnson set out on a speaking tour across the country to gain support for his plan. He urged southern states not to ratify the Fourteenth Amendment. He also campaigned for congressional candidates who opposed ratification. Johnson's speeches angered many voters, but his fight against ratification succeeded in the South. Ten of the southern states rejected the Fourteenth Amendment, which was eventually ratified in 1868. Only Tennessee ratified and was readmitted to the Union in July 1866.

Still, Republicans won large victories in the elections of 1866, gaining a two-thirds majority in the House and the Senate. They were now in a strong position. In March 1867 Congress passed, over Johnson's veto, the Reconstruction Act.

The act suspended the governments of the ten unreconstructed southern states. The South was then divided into five military districts. In each district, a United States Army commander would oversee the formation of new governments. Blacks and loyal whites would be registered to vote. Then, voters would choose delegates to state conventions to write new constitutions, guaranteeing black suffrage. Finally, these new state governments would have to ratify the Fourteenth Amendment to be readmitted to the Union.

The Radicals had achieved their goal. The southern states were now conquered territories. Radical Reconstruction would guide them back into the Union. Some states protested. Georgia and Mississippi declared the Reconstruction Act unconstitutional, but the Supreme Court refused to hear their suit. Over the next four years, one after another of the states eventually met the Radicals' terms and was readmitted.

IMPEACHMENT OF JOHNSON

During this period Radicals feared that Johnson, as Commander in Chief, would block military Reconstruction. To limit his power, in 1867 Congress passed two laws over his veto. The Command of the Army Act restricted Johnson's control of the army. The president would have to issue all military orders through the General of the Army, Ulysses S. Grant. The Tenure* of Office Act stated that the president could not dismiss any appointed officials who had been approved by the Senate, unless the Senate agreed to the dismissal.

Johnson decided to test the Tenure of Office Act in February 1868 by firing his secretary of war, Edwin M. Stanton. The Radicals reacted quickly. The House voted to impeach Johnson because he had violated a federal law.

---

* tenure: the length of time during which an individual has the right to hold an office or position.

From March to May 1868 Johnson stood on trial before the Senate. His lawyers defended him by insisting that a president could be impeached only for "high crimes and misdemeanors," not for actions unpopular with Congress. If Johnson were convicted and dismissed from office, they argued, any future president could be removed for political reasons.

When it was time to vote, seven Republicans defied the Radical leaders by voting to acquit the President. They believed that the Tenure of Office Act was unconstitutional and that Johnson had not committed a crime. The Senate could not muster the majority of votes needed for a guilty verdict. Johnson was kept in office by the margin of a single vote.

Johnson served out his term, powerless. He did not obtain the Democratic nomination for a second term. Still, he did not forsake politics. Five years later he returned to Washington as a senator from Tennessee. He died a senator, shortly thereafter, and was buried with a copy of the Constitution.

SECTION REVIEW

1. Identify the following: Benjamin F. Wade, Henry W. Davis, John Wilkes Booth, Thaddeus Stevens, Charles Sumner.

2. What was Lincoln's plan for Reconstruction? How did Radical Republicans disagree with it?

3. What were the provisions of the Thirteenth Amendment?

4. (a) What was Andrew Johnson's plan for Reconstruction? Why did Radical Republicans oppose it? (b) How was Johnson, without the approval of Congress, able to readmit states to the Union?

5. (a) Describe the black codes. (b) Why did Congress refuse to seat the southern delegates in December 1865?

6. (a) What were the provisions of the Fourteenth Amendment? (b) Why did Congress pass it? (c) Why did Johnson speak against it?

7. (a) What were the terms of the Reconstruction Act of 1867? (b) What were the results?

8. (a) How did Congress limit the president's powers? (b) Why did the House vote to impeach Johnson? What was the result?

THE SOUTH UNDER RECONSTRUCTION

READ TO FIND OUT

—how tenant farming and sharecropping came about.

—why carpetbaggers and scalawags were resented in the South.

—how the political rights of blacks were extended.

—how some southerners reacted to Reconstruction.

—how Reconstruction came to an end.

Radical Reconstruction went into effect in the South in 1867, welcomed by some and despised by others. To those who had taken pride in the Confederate cause, military occupation by northerners was deeply humiliating.

Many southerners bitterly protested the political changes taking place in the South. The massive registration of black voters gave blacks a strong voice in state politics. Radical rule also welcomed poor southern whites into the new Republican governments in the states.

For the states, the period of Reconstruction was also time for rebuilding. The new state governments faced the task of repairing war-torn cities, industries, and railroads.

THE POOR

During Radical Reconstruction, the black codes were removed. Blacks discovered that they could move about as they pleased. They could vote and sit on juries and be elected to office. Despite this greater freedom, blacks still struggled with the basic question of survival. Most blacks could not read or write because it had been illegal in most southern states to teach slaves these skills. Most blacks knew how to farm but did not have the money to buy land.

Some former slaves looked for work in southern towns or northern factories. Some joined the move-

ment westward. Most blacks, however, stayed in the South. They worked out arrangements with landowners, often their old masters. Landowners did not have money to hire workers, so many blacks—and poor whites—became tenant farmers. They farmed parcels of the owner's plantation, supplying their own tools and seed. Rent was paid in cash or with part of the tenant farmer's crop.

Others became **sharecroppers.** They farmed the land, and the owner provided food and supplies. When the crop was sold, the sharecropper and the owner split the profits.

For both white and black sharecroppers, the system created a new kind of bondage—a life of debt. The sharecroppers had to buy clothing and other necessities. Because they had no cash, they borrowed from the landowner, the bank, or a local merchant. Landowners, too, often had to borrow to supply the sharecroppers. Outrageous interest rates were charged—as high as 30 percent—and often more than doubled the debt of the borrowers.

Many lenders insisted that cash crops like cotton be planted. But cotton depleted the soil, leaving it almost useless for sharecroppers who wanted to grow their own food. When the cotton crop was sold and the debts paid, little remained of the profits.

The cotton gin owned by a group of black farmers is one example of the cooperation that grew after Reconstruction. Blacks united to form hundreds of self-help organizations.

Sharecroppers could have to borrow again next year and the next and the next. By the 1870s, the share-cropping system was used throughout the South.

Many poor whites and blacks received aid from the Freedmen's Bureau. It helped many find jobs. And between 1865 and 1870 it handed out over 21 million rations.

The bureau also opened 4,300 schools and started the first colleges for blacks. Blacks flocked to the new schools. Charlotte Forten, a black teacher, wrote:

> I never before saw children so eager to learn, although I had had several years' experience in New England schools. Coming to school is a constant delight and recreation to them. They come here as other children go to play. The older ones, during the summer, work in the fields from early morning until eleven or twelve o'clock, and then come to school, after their hard toil in the hot sun, as bright and as anxious to learn as ever.

Mathematics students at Hampton Institute in Virginia were photographed by Frances Benjamin Johnston. Hampton was founded in 1868, funded in part by the Freedmen's Bureau.

CARPETBAGGERS AND SCALAWAGS

Large numbers of northerners began moving to the South. Thousands, many of them women, came as teachers. Business people came, talking of railroads and factories. The new South could be an industrial South, they said.

Many southerners came to resent these north-erners and called them *carpetbaggers*. Carpetbags were small handbags, and thus carpetbaggers were those who traveled fast and light in search of a quick dollar. Some northerners did come to fill their car-petbags with southern money. But many arrived with money to invest, and others came to create opportunities for blacks.

Even more hated by former Confederates were the *scalawags*, southern Republicans who had re-mained loyal to the Union and now supported Re-construction. Many were poor whites from the back country who had always disliked the plantation and slavery systems. Others were merchants and busi-ness people who opposed the Democrats. But most white southerners saw the scalawags purely as trai-tors to the memory of the Confederacy.

Carpetbaggers and scalawags—good and bad of both groups—worked with blacks and sympathetic whites to create the new state governments. Many of these Reconstruction legislatures worked hard to build a new South. Some built schools and hos-pitals, repaired railroads, and established public services.

However, many officeholders were inexperi-enced, and some were corrupt. Legislatures were often swindled by dishonest carpetbaggers. Law-makers spent large sums on phony schemes—on railroad tracks that were never laid and factories and bridges that were never built. Southern news-papers publicized these problems.

These scandals, however, were small compared to the kind of corruption that plagued the nation in the postwar years. Corruption in New York City in this period involved greater sums than in all the southern states combined.

BLACKS IN POLITICS

During Reconstruction, blacks turned out in large numbers to vote. In the presidential election of 1868, the Democratic candidate, Horatio Sey-mour, opposed Radical Reconstruction and what he referred to as "Negro supremacy." The votes of nearly 500,000 blacks helped to swing the election to the Republican candidate, Union war hero Ulysses S. Grant.

Hiram R. Revels was the first black to serve in the U.S. Senate. From 1870 to 1871 he completed the unfinished term of Jefferson Davis.

Blanche K. Bruce was the first black to serve a full term in the U.S. Senate. He represented Mississippi from 1875 to 1881.

"The Great Epoch in the history of our race has at last arrived," wrote one black. "Today the colored citizens of these southern [states] are casting their votes for presidential candidate U.S. Grant . . . their votes are going in like snowflakes, silently and surely."

Blacks also began serving in elected and appointed offices in the South. From 1868 to 1876, fourteen blacks served in the House of Representatives, and two in the Senate. Blacks were more numerous in state and local governments. However, they never gained a majority in a state legislature, and no black was elected a governor.

The late 1860s were a triumph for black voting rights. In July 1868 the Fourteenth Amendment, assuring blacks' citizenship, was ratified by the necessary number of states. The following year Congress safeguarded black voting rights. It passed the Fifteenth Amendment, which said that a citizen's right to vote "shall not be denied . . . by the United States or any State on account of race, color, or previous condition of servitude." By March 1870, the amendment had become law.

ANTIBLACK FEELING

Among southern whites, resentment hardened against Radical Reconstruction. Many Confederate veterans lost the right to hold office while blacks were gaining their political rights. Many whites hated the governments that supported black rights and that some thought were dominated by carpetbaggers and scalawags.

Although they resented Reconstruction and black suffrage, many whites of the upper classes felt they could control the votes of the former slaves. They would gain blacks' trust, win them to the Democratic party, and return to power aided by black votes.

Many poorer whites, however, felt threatened by blacks' new power. A northerner wrote, "There is at this day more prejudice against color among the middle and poorer classes . . . who owned few or no slaves than among the planters who owned them by the scores and hundreds."

As early as 1866, some southerners combated both black rights and Republican influence. They formed secret societies like the Knights of the White Camelia and the Ku Klux Klan. All of these societies shared the goals of the Ku Klux Klan—"to oppose Negro equality, both social and political," and to work for a "white" government.

Klan members wore long hooded robes, pretending to be ghosts of Confederate soldiers. Hooded "nightriders" roamed the countryside to discourage black and white Republicans from voting. They burned crops and houses, and beat both blacks and their white supporters. Flaming crosses set the nighttime sky ablaze with warnings. Soon those flames outlined corpses hanging from trees and telegraph poles.

Many southerners condemned these terrorist acts. In 1869 Nathan B. Forrest, the head of the Klan, formally disbanded the organization. The Knights of the White Camelia was disbanded in 1870. However, local groups continued to be active.

ANALYZING CONFLICTING PRIMARY SOURCES
BLACK RIGHTS

A primary source gives a description of an event or the viewpoint of someone involved in an event.

Read these two primary sources. The first is taken from testimony given in 1866 to the congressional Joint Committee on Reconstruction. The speaker was James D.B. DeBow of New Orleans, a white newspaper editor. The second is taken from a speech made in 1868 by the black leader Henry MacNeal Turner, a member of the Reconstruction legislature of Georgia.

> I think if the whole regulation of the negroes, or freedmen, were left to the people of the communities in which they live, it will be administered for the best interest of the negroes as well as of the whites. I think there is a kindly feeling towards the freedmen. They are not held at all responsible for anything that has happened.
> In talking with a number of planters, I remember some of them telling me they were succeeding very well with their freedmen. . . . The sentiment prevailing is that it is for the interest of the employer to teach the negroes, to educate their children, to provide preachers for them, and to attend to their physical wants. . . .
> Leave the people to themselves and they will manage very well. . . .
> I think there is a willingness to give them [blacks] every right except the right of suffrage. . . .The idea is entertained by many that they will eventually be endowed with [given] that right. It is only a question of time; but it will be necessary to prepare for it by slow and regular means, as the white race was prepared. I believe everybody unites in the belief that it would be disastrous to give the right of suffrage now.
> —James D.B. DeBow

> . . . We are told that if blacks want to speak, they must speak through white trumpets; if blacks want their sentiments expressed, they must be . . . sent through white messengers.
> The great question, sir, is this: Am I a man? If I am such, I claim the rights of a man. Am I not a man because I happen to be of a darker hue than honorable gentlemen around me?
> We have pioneered civilization here; we have built up your country; we have worked in your fields, and garnered your harvests for two hundred and fifty years! . . . We are willing to let the dead past bury its dead; but we ask you now for our rights.
> —Henry MacNeal Turner

After you have read the primary sources, you can analyze them.

1. First compare the backgrounds of the speakers. How might the background of each speaker have affected his viewpoint on black rights?

2. Did both speakers express opinions? Look for phrases like ''I believe'' or ''I think.'' Such phrases signal opinions. Are there facts in either speech ?

3. How did the speakers differ on the issue of black rights? What arguments did each speaker give for his position?

4. Each speaker attempted to express not only his own viewpoint but also the viewpoint of a large group of people. Do you think that all white southerners agreed with DeBow? Explain. How could you learn more about other viewpoints on the rights of blacks during Reconstruction?

In 1870 and 1871 President Grant's administration responded to the terrorism with the Force Acts. The acts allowed Grant to declare martial law and to suspend habeas corpus. Those who interfered with anyone's voting rights could be fined or arrested. Although about 7,400 persons were indicted under these acts, there were few convictions and only once did Grant re-establish military rule on a large scale.

Still, the violence continued. In South Carolina, Louisiana, and Arkansas, whites rebelled against the Reconstruction government, and federal troops were sent to keep order.

A DISPUTED ELECTION

While southern whites worked to restore the old Democratic governments, northerners were losing interest in Reconstruction. A New York merchant complained that Reconstruction damaged southern business: "As merchants we want to see the South gain her normal condition in the commerce of the country." Northern business people believed that southern Democrats could restore order, and thus encourage commerce. They urged Republicans to withdraw support from the Reconstruction govern-

The Election of 1876

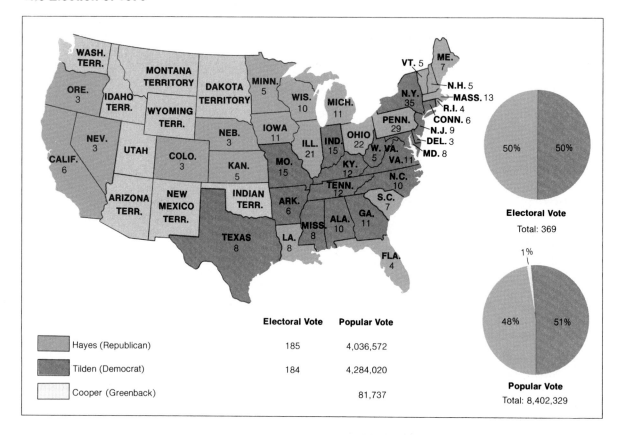

	Electoral Vote	Popular Vote
Hayes (Republican)	185	4,036,572
Tilden (Democrat)	184	4,284,020
Cooper (Greenback)		81,737

Electoral Vote
Total: 369

Popular Vote
Total: 8,402,329

ments. At the same time, northern Republicans realized that they could stay in power through their strength in the North and the West. The votes of southern Republicans—including blacks—were no longer vital. As northerners wearied of Reconstruction, Radicals lost influence in Congress.

In 1872 Congress passed the Amnesty Act, restoring the right to hold office to all Confederate veterans except the top leaders. Rallying under the banner of the Democratic party, southern whites began to regain control of state and local governments. By 1875, eight southern states were in their power. Reconstruction governments remained only in Florida, Louisiana, and South Carolina. The end of Reconstruction was in sight. The presidential election of 1876 sealed its fate.

By 1876 the Democrats were in a strong position. In the congressional elections two years earlier, a Democratic majority had swept into the House of Representatives. And now the Democrats had a campaign theme with which to attack the Republicans—reform. Some of President Grant's appointees had used their offices for personal gain, and the scandals shook the Republicans. The Democrats chose Samuel J. Tilden, governor of New York, as their candidate. Their slogan was "Tilden and Reform."

Republicans argued among themselves over a candidate who could beat the Democrats, and the party split into two factions. The "Stalwarts," old-line Republicans who supported Radical Reconstruction, stayed loyal to Grant. The "Half-breeds," known for their half-hearted support of Reconstruction, insisted on a reform candidate. Finally, the Republican party settled on Rutherford B. Hayes, three-time governor of Ohio. The *San Francisco Chronicle* wrote, "His character and career make up a party platform in themselves. He has not been touched by the breath of scandal."

The Republicans also reminded voters that they were the party of the Union in the Civil War. They urged veterans to "vote as they shot." This type of campaigning became known as "waving the bloody shirt."

To the voters, Tilden and Hayes must not have seemed very different. Both supported reform, and both wanted to end Reconstruction in South Carolina, Louisiana, and Florida. The election results were as close as the two candidates' promises.

Tilden received some 250,000 more popular votes than Hayes, and he won 184 electoral votes to Hayes's 165. There was no clear winner, but there were 20 disputed electoral votes. Tilden needed only one of these to win the necessary majority.*

RECONSTRUCTION ENDS

One of the disputed votes was from Oregon, which had sent in two sets of ballots. The Oregon dispute was settled quickly, and its electoral vote went to Hayes.

The rest of the disputed votes were from Florida, Louisiana, and South Carolina. These southern states, still under Reconstruction, had each sent in two sets of ballots. Tilden had won a majority of the popular vote in each state, but the Republicans charged that the Democrats had won through fraud and by keeping blacks from voting. Thus, Republican electors had voted for Hayes. A rival set of Democratic electors in those states had voted for Tilden.

To decide which set of electoral votes should be counted in the three southern states, Congress set up an electoral commission. The 15 members were senators, representatives, and Supreme Court judges. There were to be 7 Democrats, 7 Republicans, and an independent, but the independent was disqualified and replaced by a Republican. The commission accepted the ballots for Hayes by an 8 to 7 margin. Of all 20 contested votes, Tilden gained none. Rutherford B. Hayes became president.

Democrats were furious over what they called "the stolen election." The Republicans responded quickly by trying to soothe southern Democrats. Hayes promised funds for internal improvements in the South. He also promised to remove all remaining federal troops from the South. Southern Democrats were willing to accept Hayes on those terms. It meant an official end to Reconstruction.

* When one candidate does not receive a majority of the electoral votes, the choice of president is made by the House of Representatives, with each state casting one vote.

The Nation Reunites

	Readmitted to the Union	Reconstruction government ended
Tennessee	1866	1869
Alabama	1868	1874
Arkansas	1868	1874
Florida	1868	1877
Louisiana	1868	1877
North Carolina	1868	1870
South Carolina	1868	1877
Georgia	1870	1871
Mississippi	1870	1875
Texas	1870	1873
Virginia	1870	1870

In April 1877, after Hayes's inauguration, federal troops were pulled out of the South. The last Radical Republican governments in the South fell. Reconstruction had come to an end.

SECTION REVIEW

1. Identify the following: Charlotte Forten, Horatio Seymour, Nathan B. Forrest, Samuel J. Tilden.

2. (a) Why did many poor southerners work as either tenant farmers or sharecroppers? (b) Describe the disadvantages of the sharecropping system.

3. Describe the work of the Freedmen's Bureau.

4. (a) Who were carpetbaggers and scalawags? (b) What problems did some of these people cause in the South?

5. (a) How was the black vote important in the presidential election of 1868? (b) How were blacks politically active in government?

6. (a) Why did Congress pass the Fifteenth Amendment? (b) What does that amendment safeguard?

7. (a) Describe the violence that resulted from the increased activity of blacks in politics. (b) What were the Force Acts of 1870 and 1871?

8. (a) Why did northern business people and Republicans lose interest in Reconstruction? (b) What did the Amnesty Act of 1872 restore?

9. Explain how Hayes won the election of 1876.

10. When did Reconstruction come to an end? How?

BLACKS IN
THE NEW SOUTH

READ TO FIND OUT

— **how Conservatives met the challenge to their power.**

— **how blacks were disfranchised.**

— **how Jim Crow laws set up segregation.**

— **why a black migration took place.**

— **how Booker T. Washington and William E.B. Du Bois provided leadership for blacks.**

In 1877 President Hayes promised that the South would be "let alone by the general government." The southern Democrats, now known as Conservatives, worked to increase their power in the South. One of their primary goals was to strengthen the southern economy. They would build a "new South." A newpaper editor described this South: "thrilling with new life . . . the home of fifty millions of people; her cities vast hives of industry."

This vision of the South did not take into account some problems. In the hill country of states like Georgia, South Carolina, and Mississippi, many whites were very poor. Small farmers were suffering from a nationwide depression and the "daily defeats of crumbling barn and fence." Many blacks were sharecroppers and tenant farmers and shared the plight of the whites.

POLITICS IN THE NEW SOUTH

Conservatives worked to defeat opposition to the Democratic party. They did so with the help of black votes. They courted black voters, pledging to protect their rights. In many places, blacks were given minor posts like constable or jury commissioner, and occasionally a seat in the state legislature. Indeed, black rights generally were protected, and blacks faced less discrimination in the South than in the North.

Then, in the 1890s, the Conservative dependence on black votes was shaken. Another group was courting the blacks. Hit hard by the depression of 1893, farmers across the country organized *farmers' alliances*. They demanded government aid and a change in political leaders. One farmers' alliance tried to unite southern white and black farmers. Organizers hoped that such an alliance would enable farmers to gain political power in the South.

The Conservatives felt their position challenged. They were willing to sacrifice black support to split such an alliance. Conservatives now began to woo white farmers, appealing to their simmering resentment of blacks. Many white southerners were suffering from the depression as much as blacks, but they saw blacks as competitors for jobs.

However, many southerners also had a long list of complaints against the Conservative leaders. To gain support, the Conservatives adopted programs based on "white supremacy," or racial hatred. Blacks were now presented as a threat to white rule, and Conservatives began a campaign for *disfranchisement*—denial of black voting rights.

DISFRANCHISEMENT

Beginning in 1890, one southern state after another passed laws that effectively blocked blacks from voting. Voters were now required to pay *poll taxes*—taxes that had to be paid at the polls, or place of voting, in order to vote. Voters also had to pass *literacy tests*—examinations to determine whether a person can read or write. Few blacks could afford the taxes, and many were former slaves who had not yet learned to read or write.

However, these laws also made it difficult for some whites to vote. Many states, then, adopted *grandfather clauses*. Such clauses made a person eligible to vote if the person's father or grandfather had voted in 1867. The clause helped whites only, because blacks had not been eligible to vote in 1867.

Disfranchisement laws had the desired effect. By the turn of the century, few blacks could find a way to exercise their right to vote. The Fourteenth and Fifteenth amendments did not seem to protect the civil rights of blacks. In 1898, for example, in *Williams* v. *Mississippi*, the Supreme Court ruled that grandfather clauses did not violate the Fifteenth Amendment because they did not "on their face discriminate between the races." (The Supreme Court did, however, rule in 1915 that such clauses were unconstitutional.)

JIM CROW LAWS

Blacks also faced new forms of discrimination in their everyday lives. From the 1880s on, dozens of state and local legislatures passed laws that set up segregation, or separation of the races. These were called Jim Crow* laws. The laws set up separate areas for blacks and whites in railroad and trolley cars, hotels, restaurants, and theaters. Even drinking fountains were segregated. In some states, textbooks for blacks and whites were segregated in warehouses.

Not all southerners supported the antiblack laws. Opposition was strong enough in South Carolina to delay passage of the laws until 1898. The editor of the Charleston *News and Courier* ridiculed segregation. "If there must be Jim Crow cars on the railroads," he scoffed, "there should be a separate Jim Crow dock and witness stand in every court—and a Jim Crow Bible for [blacks] to kiss."

Despite such opposition, Jim Crow took solid hold. In 1896 the Supreme Court upheld a Louisiana law that called for segregated railroad accommodations. This decision, in *Plessy* v. *Ferguson*, set up the "separate but equal" doctrine. Blacks could be segregated from whites as long as the facilities were equal. In practice, however, facilities were almost never equal. Many more Jim Crow laws were passed following the Court's decision.

Meanwhile, the atmosphere of racial hatred was growing. Segregationists turned out antiblack propaganda, and newspapers warned of black crime. Fanned by such cries, white resentment exploded into violence. Blacks were attacked, burned, and lynched. Lynching in the 1890s took place across the nation, but most of it took place in the South. Most victims in all parts of the United States were black. From 1885 to 1900, about 2,500 blacks were lynched.

THE BLACK MIGRATION

Some blacks fled the prejudice or the hardships of sharecropping. Many went to the cities of the North, while others went to the West. A former slave named Benjamin "Pap" Singleton led a large group

---

* Jim Crow was the name of a song and dance character created by a white entertainer in the 1830s. The term came to refer to blacks in a negative way.

of blacks from Tennessee to Kansas in the "Exodus of 1879." In the following years, thousands of blacks packed up and moved westward to Kansas, Colorado, and Nebraska. In Oklahoma black pioneers founded several all-black towns.

Still, most blacks stayed in the South. If they could not make a living on the land, they migrated to the cities. There, they clustered in Jim Crow areas—Beale Street in Memphis, Tennessee, and Cotton Row in Macon, Georgia. They hoped to find jobs, better schooling, a new start. Most looked to their own black communities for a helping hand. Black schools, churches, clubs, and newspapers sprang up in the cities in response.

Now, more than ever, blacks needed leaders who could voice their concerns to the nation, who could give them a vision of hope. They would find bold new leaders in Booker T. Washington and William E.B. Du Bois.

BOOKER T. WASHINGTON

Booker Taliaferro Washington was born into slavery in Virginia. Washington bore the backbreaking labor with the help of a dream. He once followed his owner's child to school and peeped inside this place forbidden to blacks. "I had the feeling that to get into a schoolhouse," he wrote, "would be about the same as getting into paradise."

Freed by the Civil War, Washington finally had the chance to go to school. He went on to attend Hampton Institute, a black industrial-arts college set up after the war. Washington became a teacher and, in 1881, was picked to head a new black school at Tuskegee, Alabama. At Tuskegee Institute, thousands of blacks improved their farming skills and learned occupations such as carpentry and nursing.

In 1895 Washington gave a speech in Atlanta, telling blacks to remain in the South and work the land:

> No race can prosper till it learns that there is as much dignity in tilling a field as in writing a poem. It is at the bottom of life we must begin, and not at the top. Nor should we permit our grievances to overshadow our opportunities.

Washington's speech, which became known as the Atlanta Compromise, was printed in papers throughout the country. It caused a sensation.

George Washington Carver spent his life teaching agricultural chemistry at Tuskegee Institute. He developed hundreds of products from the peanut and the sweet potato. His research had a direct influence on the shift of Southern agriculture from single-crop to diversified farming.

Many whites and blacks saw him as a great new leader for blacks. Others criticized him for asking blacks to adjust to Jim Crow. They disagreed with his idea that black people should work for economic progress and ignore political and social equality.

WILLIAM E.B. DU BOIS

Blacks who found Washington's approach too moderate found an outspoken leader in the late 1890s. William E.B. Du Bois (doo BOYCE) was born shortly after the Civil War, in a small Massachusetts town. Like Washington, Du Bois was eager for schooling. The only black in his high school, he graduated at the head of his class. He went on to attend Harvard University in Boston. Prejudice in the South and rebuffs at Harvard left a bitter stamp on Du Bois.

Like Washington, Du Bois went on to teach college, at Atlanta University. As he studied the problems of blacks, he decided that he must argue against Booker T. Washington's approach. He would ask blacks to fight discrimination and prejudice and demand their political rights.

In 1905 at Niagara Falls, Du Bois organized a group of black professionals into the Niagara Movement. The next year, members met at Harpers Ferry—the site of abolitionist John Brown's raid in 1859. Du Bois addressed the nation about the

The powerful portrait of William E.B. Du Bois was drawn in 1925. For twenty-five years a magazine editor, Du Bois encouraged promising black thinkers, writers, and artists.

movement's purpose: "We claim for ourselves every single right that belongs to a freeborn American, political, civil, and social; and until we get these rights we will never cease to protest and assail the ears of America."

A FAREWELL SPEECH

On January 29, 1907, George H. White of North Carolina addressed Congress. He was the last black member of the House of Representatives from the South, and he was giving his farewell speech. Proudly, he detailed the accomplishments of blacks during their 40 years of freedom.

Blacks, he said, had published almost 300 newspapers and 500 books. Over 4,000 blacks were lawyers and doctors. Blacks operated several banks and businesses in the South, including a silk mill and a cotton factory. They supported 7 colleges, 10 law and medical schools, and 25 seminaries. Blacks owned over 600,000 acres (1.5 million hectares) of land in the South alone.

Blacks now bid Congress farewell, but they would return. "These parting words," concluded White, "are in behalf of an outraged, heart-broken, bruised, and bleeding, but God-fearing people, faithful, industrious, loyal people." The chamber rang with loud applause.

SECTION REVIEW

1. Identify the following: Benjamin "Pap" Singleton, Booker T. Washington, Hampton Institute, Atlanta Compromise, William E.B. Du Bois.

2. Define the following: disfranchisement, poll tax, literacy test, grandfather clause, segregation, Jim Crow laws.

3. Why did Conservatives feel that their position was challenged?

4. List three methods used to block blacks from voting.

5. Name four places in which blacks were segregated from whites.

6. (a) What did the Supreme Court rule in *Plessy* v. *Ferguson*? (b) How did the decision affect segregation?

7. (a) What was the "Exodus of 1879"? (b) Where did blacks migrate in the following years? (c) Where did they look for help?

8. Compare Booker T. Washington and William E.B. Du Bois with regard to the following: background, education, ideas about how blacks could best improve their lives.

THE GILDED AGE

READ TO FIND OUT

— **how corruption became an issue during Grant's administration.**

— **how the issue of corruption split the Republican party.**

— **how Hayes attacked the spoils system.**

— **how Garfield expected to deal with reform.**

— **how Arthur supported civil service reform.**

— **what issues overshadowed reform during the terms of Cleveland and Harrison.**

The years between 1865 and 1900, which were so stormy for blacks and the South, were confusing years for the nation's government. After the war the president and Congress had argued over the issue of Reconstruction, and Congress had won. That was a sign of times to come. It would be an era in which presidents lost much of their power to Congress.

The presidency would change hands with bewildering frequency. In 30 years America would have 7 presidents. Except for Ulysses S. Grant, not one president won enough support from the public to stay in office for a second term. Not one president could count on his party's control of both houses of Congress for his full term.

More than confusion marked the nation's politics during this era. On every level, politics was tainted by corruption. During the war, fortunes had been made supplying the Union army. Money was invested in new industry, such as railroads. As industry expanded, so did opportunities for profit. People were tired of the sacrifices of the war years, and disillusioned by Reconstruction.

Many—including politicians—became caught up in the new age of fast money. Corruption seemed to spread like seeds on the wind, taking root wherever the soil was rich. Humorist Mark Twain wrote:

> Why, it is telegraphed all over the country and commented on as something wonderful if a [member of Congress] votes honestly and unselfishly and refuses . . . to steal from the government.

To Twain, these years were the Gilded Age—golden with growth on the surface, but corrupt on the underside.

SCANDALS UNDER GRANT

Corruption first became a major issue during Grant's administration. Grant had been elected in 1868 as the "saviour of the Union." Yet Grant himself later admitted, "It was my fortune, or misfortune, to be called to the office of Chief Executive without any previous political training."

Although he had been a brilliant general, as president he showed poor judgment. Many of those he appointed to office took advantage of their positions and Grant's trust to enrich themselves. Grant seldom realized what was going on, but he was hurt by others' schemes.

In 1869 two speculators named James Fisk, Jr., and Jay Gould tried to corner the gold market. "Jubilee Jim" Fisk, who built his own private opera house, was used to big risks and big payoffs. Gould had made his fortune in railroads. "I don't build railroads," he once said, "I buy them." The two planned to buy all the gold for sale by the government, then convince the government not to sell any more. A nationwide gold shortage would drive the price up, and the pair could then sell at a handsome profit.

Gould and Fisk bought the help of the President's brother-in-law, who asked Grant to withhold gold from the market. Grant would not agree, but Fisk and Gould spread rumors that he opposed the sale of gold. The price shot up, reaching a high on September 24—"Black Friday." Grant finally acted, ordering the Department of the Treasury to sell $4 million worth of gold. The price soon plunged, but scores of investors had already been ruined. Many people linked Grant to the whole scheme.

A greater scandal broke in 1872, involving the Union Pacific Railroad. Railroad officials had set up a construction company called Crédit Mobilier to lay track. The company was paid $73 million but did only $50 million worth of work. The extra money went into the pockets of the officials.

Because the government was funding the railroad, Crédit Mobilier had to be sure Congress did not ask questions about the missing money. The company bribed members of Congress and Grant's vice-president with millions of dollars worth of stock.

Word of the affair soon leaked out, another blow to Grant's administration. Of the scandals during Grant's second term, this was the most notorious.

Corruption did not stop at the national level. Many state and city governments had their own scandals. In 1868 New York state legislators received a visit from Jay Gould. Gould needed a bill passed to legalize some fake railroad stock he had issued. He was carrying two suitcases stuffed with money. He left with empty suitcases, and obtained the legislation he wanted. On the city level, William Marcy Tweed, called Boss Tweed, was perhaps the most famous example of political corruption. From 1868 to 1871, Tweed and his associates robbed New York City of millions of dollars.

THE ELECTION OF 1872

"It looks," said one senator in 1870, "as though the Republican party were going to the dogs. . . . It has become corrupt." Indeed, Republicans themselves were sensitive to the issue of corruption. By the end of Grant's first term the issue had split the party. A group of reform-minded Republicans, joined by some Democrats, organized the Liberal Republican party.

Belva Lockwood was the first woman to practice law before the Supreme Court. She was twice a candidate for president, in 1884 and in 1888. Her portrait is by Nellie Horne.

TWO GREAT QUESTIONS.

WHO STOLE THE PEOPLE'S MONEY ? — DO TELL . N.Y.TIMES.

'TWAS HIM.

Thomas Nast's cartoon, "Who stole the People's Money," was one of a series of cartoons attacking politician William Marcy Tweed. Tweed was so disturbed by Nast's cartoons that he once offered Nast $500,000 to leave the country.

THOMAS NAST
POLITICAL CARTOONIST

During the dark days of the Civil War, *Harper's Weekly* published a series of drawings by a young war correspondent named Thomas Nast. One of the most powerful was called "Emancipation." It showed Nast's vision of life for blacks after the war, when they would have equal rights with other Americans. Nast's work electrified the North. To many it made the Union cause concrete. His message was so effective that Abraham Lincoln called him "our best recruiting sergeant."

Born in Germany in 1841, Nast had come to New York City with his family when he was six. He showed an early talent for drawing. At fifteen, he became an illustrator for *Leslie's Weekly*. Soon the magazine sent him to sketch a prize fight in England and a revolution in Italy. When the Civil War began, he was hired by *Harper's*. At its close, he was twenty-five and famous.

For the next twenty years, Nast continued drawing for *Harper's Weekly*. During Reconstruction, he supported Radical Reconstruction. In one cartoon he protested the pardoning of Confederates while blacks were still denied the vote. In others he pictured President Andrew Johnson as a traitor to the northern cause.

Nast invented the Republican elephant and the Democratic donkey as party symbols. During the 1870s he exposed New York's corrupt political boss, William Tweed. Everyone could understand Nast's drawing of a giant thumb labeled "Tweed," about to squash New York City. Nast was unmoved by Tweed's offer of a huge bribe to leave him alone.

By the time he was forty, Nast's cartoons had lost their fire. Disillusioned with politics, he turned to oil painting but had little success. In 1902, to earn money for his family, he became the American consul in Ecuador. Six months later he died of yellow fever, far from the nation he had loved and scolded in the passionate political cartoons of his youth.

Most of these reformers were intellectuals, politicians, and newspaper editors. In 1872 the reformers chose as their presidential candidate newspaper editor Horace Greeley. Greeley was a longtime crusader for issues like abolition, land reform, and even vegetarianism.

In the 1872 election, Democrats supported the Liberal Republicans because they felt that it was the only way to defeat Grant. But Grant still enjoyed popular support, and many scandals had not yet come to light. Grant won the election by a wider margin than he had in 1868. The Liberal Republican party soon fell apart.

GRANT'S SECOND TERM

Although the reform party died, the issue of corruption grew larger during Grant's second term. Early in 1873 the House of Representatives began a series of investigations into reported scandals.

News of each new scandal stunned the public. Contracts for building ships went to the company that paid the most to certain officials in the War Department. Secretary of War William W. Belknap sold rights to trade on Indian lands in the West—receiving up to $25,000 for each trading post.

One scheme was concocted by a group of whiskey distillers in St. Louis, Missouri. They avoided paying millions of dollars in excise taxes by bribing Treasury officials. Even Grant's private secretary, Orville Babcock, was involved in this "Whiskey Ring." Grant promptly called for the arrest of the guilty, but managed to protect his secretary. Babcock was acquitted.

Meanwhile, another issue was surfacing, not as shocking as the scandals. This was the spoils system. Under the system, government jobs in the civil service* were given as rewards, or spoils, to loyal party workers. When a new party came to power, it fired political opponents in the service and appointed supporters to those jobs. Employees who were appointed to return political favors were often unqualified to perform their jobs.

The system had begun under Andrew Jackson and had grown along with the federal government. As the spoils system grew, the civil service became

_____
* civil service: all those employed in government administration except in the armed forces, legislature, or judiciary.

more and more inefficient. Reformers put pressure on Grant to appoint a commission to improve the service. In 1875 the commission presented its plan.

However, Senator Roscoe Conkling of New York led the "Stalwarts"—the old-line Republicans who supported Radical Reconstruction—in a fight against such reform. Congress ignored the commission's suggestions and the commission disbanded. The grip of the spoils system tightened. New York newspaper editor Whitelaw Reid wrote: "There is an utter surrender of the civil service to the coarsest use by the coarsest men."

By 1876 the Republicans were sorely wounded by "Grantism," as political corruption was now called. They had lost control of the House in the congressional elections of 1874 and barely retained a majority in the Senate. But they would keep their hold on the presidency with the election of reform candidate Rutherford B. Hayes.

HAYES ATTACKS THE SPOILS SYSTEM

On the basis of his election, Rutherford B. Hayes seemed an unlikely reformer. There was some question whether he had really defeated his Democratic opponent Samuel Tilden. Rather, he had won a disputed election in a way that left people talking of a "stolen election."

Above all, however, Hayes believed in doing what he saw as right. He had fought bravely in the Civil War, accepting the risk of death for a "just and necessary war." He served two terms in Congress and three as governor of Ohio, earning a reputation as an honest hard-working public servant. His motto was that people could best serve their party by serving their country.

Hayes quickly tried to put into practice his campaign promises about government reform. He did not make use of the spoils system. Instead, he chose members of the cabinet for their abilities, not for their party loyalty. Several appointments went to reformers. Carl Schurz was appointed secretary of the interior, John Sherman secretary of the treasury, and William Evarts secretary of state.

Republican leaders were outraged at this attack on their control of government appointments. The Senate withheld confirmation of the nominees, but public outcry soon forced it to accept the President's cabinet.

In 1876 Americans celebrated with a great exposition in Philadelphia. At Independence Hall a parade, fireworks, and bells marked the centennial Fourth of July.

Hayes next started an investigation into the New York Customs House, which collected two thirds of the nation's duties on imported goods. Customs officials were regularly embezzling large amounts of this money, and many did not work to earn their salaries. These officials were appointed by state Republicans who controlled policy and had the power to give political jobs or favors. Senator Roscoe Conkling and his allies in Congress bitterly fought the investigation. Hayes, however, managed to dismiss the Collector of Customs, Chester A. Arthur, and another official.

Hayes's battle with Conkling and his allies further split the Republican party between Stalwarts and Half-breeds. Conkling's Stalwarts kept Hayes from accomplishing any other reforms. Since Hayes did not intend to run for a second term, civil service reform would be left to his successor.

By the 1880s more job seekers than ever tried to obtain civil service jobs by any means. Some took out ads in newspapers: *Wanted*—a government clerkship at salary of not less than $1,000 per annum. Will give $100 to any one securing me such a position."

REFORM UNDER GARFIELD

In the 1880 election Republican Stalwarts and Half-Breeds divided over candidates. They finally settled on James A. Garfield, a Half-Breed and longtime member of Congress. But Stalwart boss Roscoe Conkling succeeded in having his friend Chester A. Arthur—who had lost his New York customs post—named as candidate for vice-president. The Republican ticket defeated the Democratic candidate, General Winfield Scott Hancock of Pennsylvania, by a slim margin.

Garfield, like Hayes, had a distinguished record in the war and in Congress. As head of the House Appropriations Committee, he had shown a keen sense of duty. "If I find out where every dollar goes and how it is used," he wrote, "I shall understand the apparatus thoroughly, and know if there are useless or defective parts."

However, when Garfield took office he was quickly caught up in the conflict between the Half-breeds and Stalwarts. Each group sought from Garfield jobs for their supporters. Garfield complained of the spoils system, saying that job seekers were "lying in wait" for him. His efforts—whether to reform or to strengthen the Half-breeds—were directed against Roscoe Conkling's machine.

First, Garfield appointed Half-breed leader James G. Blaine as secretary of state. Then he challenged Conkling's control of New York by appointing a political enemy of Conkling's as collector of the port of New York. But Garfield's efforts ended after he served only four months of his term. On July 2 Charles Guiteau, a Stalwart who had been refused a government appointment by Garfield, shot the President at the Washington railroad station. Garfield died on September 19.

ARTHUR AND THE CIVIL SERVICE ACT

Shocked by the killing, people across the country began to support reformers' demands. Yet many doubted that Chester Arthur, Garfield's successor, would act. His lack of experience and his part in the New York Customs House scandal seemed a poor background for a reformer.

Arthur had begun his career as an abolitionist lawyer in New York. During the Civil War, he became New York's quartermaster general, in charge of supplying Union troops. By the time he became head of the customs house, he was known as a good administrator and a faithful machine politician. As president, however, Arthur shocked the party machine. He soon recommended civil service reform.

Congress could not ignore the public outcry for reform. In January 1883 it passed the Civil Service Reform Act, also known as the Pendleton Act. The act stated that certain government jobs were to be classified as civil service positions and filled by a "merit system."

A Civil Service Commission was established. Its purpose was to find qualified people. It would give competitive examinations to people to determine their merit, or worth. People who passed these tests would be appointed to the classified jobs. The act protected qualified officeholders from being fired for failing to support the party in power. Originally only about 10 percent of federal offices were filled by the merit system. However, the act allowed presidents to increase the number of classified jobs. Within fifteen years over half of the federal employees were included.

Arthur's efforts at reform angered many Republicans. Although he worked hard for the Republican nomination, Arthur was not chosen as the party's candidate at the convention in 1884. Instead, the Republicans chose a person who did not actively seek the nomination, James G. Blaine. Blaine was a senator from Maine and the leader of the Half-breed faction of his party.

Blaine, who had once been accused of dishonest dealings with railroad officials, aroused the suspicions of reform-minded Republicans. Carl Schurz remarked that Blaine "wallowed in spoils like a rhinoceros in an African pool." He and other reformers walked out of the Republican convention, believing Blaine would not support civil service re-

form. They said that they would support a liberal Democrat if one were chosen.

Regular Republicans ridiculed the rebels by calling them *Mugwumps*, an Algonquian word meaning "important people." The reformers proudly accepted the name.

The Democrats nominated Governor Grover Cleveland of New York, who had gained a reputation as a city reformer. The campaign was bitterly fought, and the election of 1884 was one of the closest in the history of the nation. Grover Cleveland won the presidency, gaining 219 electoral votes to Blaine's 182. In addition, the Democrats took control of the House of Representatives, and the Republicans kept a majority in the Senate.

By the turn of the century business and industry had created enormous wealth for a few. Wealthy, fashionably dressed women stroll in John Sloan's "Fifth Avenue."

CLEVELAND

Grover Cleveland was a big, bluff man who had little use for the art of compromise. As mayor of Buffalo and then governor of New York, Cleveland had worked to destroy corrupt machine politics. As one humorist remarked, Cleveland "sailed through American history like a steel ship loaded with monoliths of granite."

The first Democratic president in almost thirty years, Cleveland was besieged by Democratic office seekers. "The Washington hotels are crowded, and office seekers are as thick as shells on the beach," wrote one journalist. "The city will be overrun with these office seekers until Cleveland has firmly established that civil service reform is to prevail, not only in spirit but in *fact*."

Cleveland tried. He announced that he would enforce the Civil Service Act. Even Republican workers not protected by classified jobs, he said, would be replaced only for cause. Although he hated wasting time on appointments, he devoted hours to the task. He carefully read all job applications, even for minor posts like fourth-class postmaster.

Mugwumps were pleased, but Democrats continued to demand the spoils of victory. Cleveland had stated that officeholders who "used their places for party purposes" should be fired. High Democratic officials used these words to dismiss many Republicans in the civil service. Senator Benjamin Harrison, a Republican, began collecting a file of bitter letters from fired civil servants. Cleveland's talk of civil service reform, he charged, was hypocrisy.

HARRISON

In the presidential election of 1888, Harrison defeated Cleveland. The new president came from a famous family. His grandfather was the ninth president of the United States, and his great-grandfather had signed the Declaration of Independence.

Benjamin Harrison had devoted years to public service, in Indiana politics and then in the Senate. As a senator, Harrison had called for civil service reform. But he won the presidency on a platform of a high tariff and pensions for war veterans. As president, he had little interest in reform. Under Harrison, Republicans fired many Democrats in unclassified jobs from the civil service.

In 1892 the Democrats again chose Cleveland as their presidential nominee. Cleveland had changed his economic policies and had won back the support of business. In their second presidential election, Cleveland defeated Harrison. By then, the economy was a much larger issue than reform.

The cry for political reform would surface again in the next century. During the final decades of the 1800s, however, reform seemed just out of reach. As an issue, it surfaced in seven presidencies. Yet this was an era of politics adrift, as parties came in and out of power. In 1883 a visitor to America asked someone to explain an instance of political corruption. "Why," the citizen answered, "what can you expect from the politicians?"

If many Americans did not expect much from the politicians, perhaps it was because they were absorbed in other matters. The economy flourished and then worsened. Industry was coming of age, symbolized by mighty engines. The United States was rapidly exploring its frontier—the West.

SECTION REVIEW

1. Identify the following: James Fisk, Jr., Jay Gould, Horace Greeley, Roscoe Conkling, Mugwumps.

2. (a) Describe two major scandals that occurred during Grant's first term as president. (b) What was Grant's part in those scandals?

3. (a) Why was the Liberal Republican party formed? (b) How successful was it?

4. (a) Describe the spoils system. (b) How was it used by those involved in political corruption?

5. (a) Describe two reforms begun by President Hayes. How successful were they? (b) What group of Republicans fought against Hayes efforts?

6. (a) What conflict affected Garfield's efforts at reform? (b) How was Garfield's term ended?

7. (a) How did President Arthur support reform? (b) Describe the purpose of the Civil Service Commission.

8. How did Cleveland support reform during his first term?

9. What happened to efforts at reform during Harrison's administration?

10. What issue was larger than reform during Cleveland's second term?

CHAPTER SURVEY

SUMMARY

Presidents Lincoln and Johnson wanted to readmit the Confederate states to the Union as quickly and as simply as possible. Radical Republicans disagreed. Congress prevailed and passed the Radical Reconstruction plan. It proposed the Thirteenth Amendment, which outlawed slavery. The amendment was ratified in 1865. Congress also passed laws limiting the president's powers. When Johnson challenged those laws, the House impeached him.

During Radical Reconstruction, blacks' rights were protected. The Civil Rights Act was passed and the Fourteenth Amendment, guaranteeing blacks the right of citizenship, was ratified. The Fifteenth Amendment safeguarded black voting rights.

Efforts to rebuild the southern economy caused problems and resentment. Slavery was replaced by sharecropping and tenant farming. Carpetbaggers, many of them unscrupulous, poured in from the North to start businesses. Together with scalawags—southern Republicans loyal to the Union—they formed new state governments. Among many southern whites, resentment hardened against Radical Reconstruction and was expressed in violent attacks on blacks. Then northerners began to lose interest in Reconstruction, and Radical Republicans' influence in Congress declined. By 1877 Reconstruction had ended, and the Democratic party had regained power in the South.

At first, Southern Democrats called Conservatives supported black rights. When their political power was threatened, however, Conservatives began to adopt an antiblack program. Jim Crow laws were passed to segregate the races. Antiblack violence increased. Many blacks fled to the North and the West. Many more formed black communities within southern cities. Black leaders, like Booker T. Washington and William E.B. Du Bois, expressed their concern to the nation.

The late 1800s were also years of corruption throughout government. Major scandals threatened the financial stability of the nation, and the spoils system rendered the civil service inefficient. The public demanded reforms, a few of which were made. True reform, however, was not achieved.

CHAPTER REVIEW

1. What tasks did Americans face in rebuilding the nation after the Civil War? Answer by giving examples of two problems in each of the following areas: industry and agriculture, government, relationships between blacks and whites or northerners and southerners.

2. How did each of the following divide the Republican party? (a) a plan for Reconstruction (b) the branch of the government responsible for Reconstruction (c) the status of Confederate states

3. (a) Compare Lincoln's "ten percent plan" and the Wade-Davis bill. (b) In what ways was the Wade-Davis bill a harsher plan? (c) How did Lincoln react to the bill? Why?

4. (a) Explain how each of the following united Radical Republicans and moderate Republicans against Johnson: election of Confederate leaders, black codes, control of Congress. (b) What action did Congress take in 1865 in opposition to Johnson's Reconstruction policy? (c) How did Johnson react to the extension of the Freedmen's Bureau and a civil rights bill? Why?

5. (a) Explain how each event led to the next: the Congressional elections of 1866, the Reconstruction Act, the Command of the Army Act,

Carpetbags were made by sewing two squares of carpet together. Many people looked down on carpetbaggers, who seemed to carry all their possessions in one bag.

In 1865 an anonymous artisan worked a hooked rug honoring Abraham Lincoln. Lincoln's initials and the dates of his birth and death are in the lower left corner.

and the Tenure of Office Act, the impeachment of Johnson. (b) What precedent did the Johnson trial establish regarding the impeachment of a president?

6. (a) Why were tenant farming and share-cropping both solutions to landowners' financial problems as well as farm workers' problems? (b) Why was debt a built-in part of these systems?

7. (a) How did blacks participate in the Reconstruction governments in the South? (b) When did northern business and political concerns weaken the Grant administration's support for the Reconstruction governments? Why? (c) What effect did the election of 1876 have on Reconstruction and the Democratic party in the South?

8. How did each of the following contribute to disfranchisement and segregation of blacks in the South? (a) interracial farmers' alliances (b) the idea of white supremacy (c) poll taxes and literacy tests (d) *Williams* v. *Mississippi* (e) Jim Crow laws (f) *Plessy* v. *Ferguson*

9. (a) Why was political corruption called "Grantism"? Cite examples. (b) How did such corruption affect Republican party unity in 1872?

How did it affect Republican control of Congress in 1874? The presidential election in 1876?

10. (a) How did the spoils system affect the civil service in the 1870s? Why? (b) Describe how each of the following presidents dealt with the spoils system and civil service reform: Grant, Hayes, Arthur, Cleveland, Harrison.

ISSUES AND IDEAS

1. Charles Sumner said, "I am for Negro suffrage in every Rebel state. If it be just, it should not be denied; if it be necessary, it should be adopted; if it be a punishment to traitors, they deserve it." How do these words reflect Radical Republican attitudes on Reconstruction?

2. Compare the position of blacks in the South in 1865 and in 1896. Describe the changes.

SKILLS WORKSHOP

1. *Charts.* Make a chart showing major legislation affecting blacks that was passed by the federal government between 1862 and 1871. Indicate the date of passage, the provisions of the legislation, and the results.

2. *Writing.* Assume that you are President Lincoln or President Johnson. Write a Reconstruction plan for the South. Note your goals and ways to achieve them. Take into account relations with Congress, relations between whites and blacks in the South, and northern eagerness to return to normal.

PAST AND PRESENT

1. In what ways was Radical Reconstruction radical for the times? How would Radical views on black rights be viewed by most people today? Explain.

2. Political corruption was a major issue in the nation after the Civil War. Is it an issue today at the local, state, or national level? Explain. What actions are people seeking to correct the problem? Compare these methods with the actions of earlier reformers.

NEW HORIZONS

1865–1900

John Kane. *Homestead,* c. 1929? Collection of The Museum of Modern Art, New York.

1600	1700	1800	1900	2000

• Jamestown founded	• Revolutionary War	• Civil War	• Today

UNIT 5
1865–1900

1870	1880	1890	1900

Johnson	Grant	Hayes	Arthur	Cleveland	Harrison	Cleveland	McKinley	

POLITICAL

• U.S. buys Alaska

Garfield

• Battle of Little Bighorn

• Haymarket riot
• Dawes Act
• Interstate Commerce Act
• Oklahoma Territory organized
• Sherman Antitrust Act
• Pullman strike

SOCIAL

• Grange founded
• Knights of Labor
• Mark Twain: *Tom Sawyer*
• Large tide of immigration begins
• Standard Oil trust
• Jane Addams opens Hull House
• Jacob Riis: *How the Other Half Lives*
• Klondike gold rush

TECHNOLOGICAL

• Transcontinental railroad completed
• Bell: telephone
• Edison: phonograph
• Edison: light bulb
• Brooklyn Bridge
• Eastman: the box camera
• Hollerith: computer card
• Henry Ford's first car

INTERNATIONAL

• Disraeli: prime minister of Britain
• Japanese reform courts of law
• Porfirio Díaz: dictator of Mexico
• Belgian king takes over the Congo
• Britain takes over Uganda
• Ethiopians defeat Italians

1870	1880	1890	1900

CHAPTER 14

THE SHIFTING FRONTIER

1865–1900

THE BOOMING WEST
THE PLAINS INDIANS
THE PRAIRIE FARMERS

The Cheyenne woman Iron Teeth wrote of her life on the Great Plains. Born in 1834, she lived to see many changes sweep her homeland:

"We used to plant corn, when I was a little girl. With sharpened sticks we punched holes in the ground, dropped in the grains of corn, went hunting all summer, then returned to gather our crops. . . .

"The first issue of government presents to the Cheyenne was when I was fifteen years old. . . . We were given beef, but we did not eat any of it. Great piles of bacon were stacked on the prairie and distributed to us, but we used it only to make fires or to grease robes for tanning. . . .

"I was married to Red Ripe when I was twenty-one years old. . . . My husband was a good hunter and did not need my help for gathering meat for his family, but I often went hunting with him.

"Soldiers built forts in our Powder River country when I was about thirty-two years old. The Sioux and the Cheyenne fought against them. After a few years, peace was made. The Cheyenne settled at the White River agency, in our favorite Black Hills country. This was to be our land forever, so we were pleased. But white people found gold on our lands. They crowded in, so we had to move out. . . . The only thing we could do was go to other lands offered to us. We did this."

When Iron Teeth was a girl, her homeland was barely touched by the pioneers trudging across the Great Plains to Oregon and California. One explorer called those plains the "Great American Desert." Many believed that such an area could never be settled, and it was promised forever to the Indians.

By the 1860s, however, railroad tracks crept across the vast plains. Soon America's greatest westward migration began. The grass could fatten cattle and sheep, the soil could be farmed, and the hills could be mined for gold. Here, on the land that Iron Teeth and other Indians called home, was America's newest frontier.

magnificent distance—1,600 miles (2,575 kilometers) from the Missouri River to the Pacific Ocean.

Americans who had first jolted over that distance in wagons spent four to six months on the journey. During the California gold rush, people looked for a faster way west. In 1858 John Butterfield's Overland Mail Company began a stagecoach service to meet that need. Butterfield's stagecoaches ran from Missouri south through Texas, skirted the Mexican border, and rumbled north into California.

Other companies, notably the Central Overland, also established routes to the West. The stagecoaches of the Central Overland followed the old Oregon Trail and then branched off to California. The stagecoach era, however, was short-lived. Steam-powered engines would soon replace the stagecoach and change the frontier forever.

THE TRANSCONTINENTAL RAILROAD

In the 1840s a newspaper editor had written that a railroad could never be built across the continent. The barriers of mountains and rivers made construction too difficult. Also, the cost would be more than railroad companies could afford. Then, in 1862, Congress and President Lincoln approved plans to build just such a railroad.

The Union Pacific Railroad planned to build westward from Omaha, Nebraska, while another company, the Central Pacific Railroad, worked eastward from Sacramento, California. To help finance the work, the federal government gave the companies long-term loans. The government also gave the companies land along the route. Much of this land had been acquired in treaties with Indian tribes. The railroad would obtain as much as 20 square miles (52 square kilometers) of land for every mile of track laid. State and local governments, eager to connect their tracks to the proposed line, also granted land to the companies.

Work on the transcontinental railroad began in 1863. Union Pacific workers—mainly Irish immigrants—overcame blizzards, burning heat, and Indian raids to lay track across the vast prairie. The Central Pacific construction crew, made up mostly of Chinese immigrants, dynamited a path through the rugged Sierra Nevada. In the harsh Sierra winters they also cut paths through snowdrifts as high as 50 feet (15 meters).

THE BOOMING WEST

READ TO FIND OUT

— how the first transcontinental railroad was built.

— how cattle ranching became big business.

— how gold and other valuable metals lured people to the West.

— how towns boomed in the West.

— how justice was administered on the frontier.

— why the open range ended.

"A railroad, fellow citizens, is a machine, and one of the most beautiful and perfect of labor-saving machines. It well suits the energy of the American people. They love to go ahead fast, and to go with power. They love to annihilate the magnificent distances." So said one railroad booster. In the 1850s and 1860s people talked of laying track across a

After six years of work, this amazing project was completed. In 1869 the two sets of tracks met at Promontory Point, in the Utah desert north of Salt Lake City. The last spike, solid gold, was driven into place, and locomotives from both companies met. Western author Bret Harte wrote:

> What was it the Engines said,
> Pilots touching, head to head,
> Facing on a single track,
> Half a world behind each back.

A RAILROAD NETWORK

There was a flurry of railroad building in the East and the Midwest. Smaller railroads knitted together key cities, creating a great rail system. There had been over 30,000 miles (48,000 kilometers) of track in the United States in 1860. That figure more than doubled over the next 15 years. By 1890 it topped 166,000 miles (267,000 kilometers)—roughly one third of the world's total miles of track.

The federal government supported the construction of three more transcontinental lines: the Southern Pacific; the Northern Pacific; and the Atchison, Topeka and Santa Fe. A fourth line, the Great Northern, was built without government aid.

To create a working rail network, companies had to standardize their tracks. By 1886 all the nation's tracks conformed to a standard gauge so that their rails were laid the same distance apart. In 1883 the American Railway Association improved train scheduling by dividing the nation into four time zones: Pacific, Mountain, Central, and Eastern. In each zone, clocks were set to the same time. That way, train schedulers knew exactly what time it was throughout the country.

The age of railroad building was also the age of the booming West. Long trains rumbled over the trail that Lewis and Clark had taken months to cover. People poured into the West to take up mining, farming, and ranching. Their products rumbled by railroad back to the East. Between the 1860s and the 1890s, the railroads pried open the frontier and helped to fill it.

THE CATTLE BOOM

The longhorn steer also helped to open the frontier. Longhorns had roamed the open range of the Southwest ever since the land had belonged to the Spanish. Then under Mexican rule in 1821, Americans began to settle there. They learned from the Mexicans how to raise cattle on the open range.

Americans adopted all the Mexican tools of ranching. They used the lasso to rope cattle, the saddle with a horn on which to hang the lasso, and chaps to protect their legs from cactus and sagebrush. They branded their cattle with hot irons, with each rancher using a different design. This custom went all the way back to the sixteenth century, when Hernando Cortés used a brand of three crosses. A new American figure came to life on the Texas range—the cowboy. "Cowboy" was a translation of the Spanish word *vaquero*.

By 1860 about 5 million cattle grazed the Texas plains. Still, ranching was not a big business. The longhorn beef was tough, and there was no way to ship it to markets. Ranchers sold the cattle primarily for their hides.

After the Civil War, the fate of the longhorn abruptly changed. The growing eastern population demanded more beef than eastern herds could supply. A steer that sold for four dollars in Texas could bring ten times that amount in the East. And the new transcontinental railroad could transport cattle to that market.

First, the steers had to be driven to the railhead at Abilene, Kansas. They were then herded onto cattle cars bound for Chicago stockyards. From Chicago, the beef was shipped east in refrigerated cars.

CATTLE DRIVES

About 10 million head of cattle were driven north from Texas between 1867 and 1888. The long drives began each spring. Cattle scattered over the plains were rounded up and branded. About 3,000 longhorns were chosen for the drive.

For the next two or three months, two dozen or more cowboys rode beside long lines of cattle plodding over the prairie grasslands. The drive covered about 15 miles (24 kilometers) a day, with stops to graze the cattle. Cowboys spent the cold nights swapping stories around a campfire.

The peacefulness of the night camp, however, could shatter. Mattie Huffman, a fifteen-year-old girl who worked on her family's drive, wrote:

> A cow came up to the salt barrel near the camp; in taking a nibble of salt she in some way got a sack fastened on to her horns. Of course she went mad

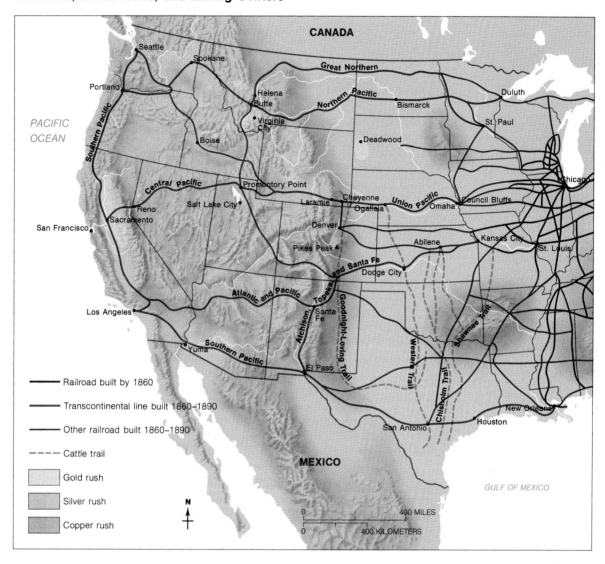

with fear and spread terror among the entire bunch by dashing among them. A stampede was on in no time.... It took about a week to get all the cattle together again.

During the long drives, cattle fattened on the hardy buffalo grass of the Great Plains. Ranchers began to realize that the prairies were good range land. Soon, they were grazing their herds across the unclaimed public lands, or *public domain*, that stretched from Texas through the Great Plains to the Canadian border. Then, as more railroads were built across the plains, new railheads emerged—Dodge City in Kansas, Cheyenne and Laramie in Wyoming.

All the elements of a profitable business merged on the plains. There was plenty of open land, a steadily multiplying product, and transport to a growing market. Soon the cattle business attracted investors from the East and Britain, and their companies came to control huge spreads of land. A great cattle empire was rising from the prairie.

RANCHERS AND COWBOYS

Ranchers had a busy life—keeping account books, buying and selling cattle, housing and feeding hired hands, and caring for the stock. Most ranch owners were men, but their wives and children usually

Nat Love, a well-known and adventuresome cowboy, became a rodeo celebrity.

Two vaqueros of early California display their skill in capturing wild horses with the riata, or lasso. Spanish and Mexican vaqueros were the West's first cowboys.

shared the work. Sometimes women ran ranches alone, having inherited or bought them. Agnes Morley recalled how her mother learned the "role of cattle queen."

> Cattle-raising on a grand scale was the Great Adventure of the hour. . . . Faced with the supervision of a well-stocked cattle range of a good many thousand acres, she rode and did her indomitable best to keep herself informed about what was happening to her livestock.

If ranchers were the head of the cattle empire, cowboys were its backbone. Most cowboys were young, on their way from one life to another. Some had been soldiers who chose not to go home after the Civil War. Some were running from the law. Some were easterners who came seeking adventure.

Many of these cowboys were Mexican Americans following the *vaquero* tradition. And many were blacks, some of them ex-slaves. "It was the great West I wanted to see," wrote Nat Love, a freed slave from Tennessee. "The wild cowboy, prancing horses of which I was very fond, and the wild life generally, all had their attractions for me."

After a few years on the range, most cowboys settled on their own ranches or headed back home. But while they rode the range, they were part of a growing legend. The cowboys on their horses became the nation's new heroes.

THE MINERS

While the grasslands of the West attracted ranchers and cowboys, discoveries of gold and other metals lured treasure seekers by the thousands. The first gold rush had been the California strike in 1849. When that ended, mining shifted eastward across the Great Basin to the Rocky Mountains. The first big gold strike there came near Pikes Peak, in what is now Colorado, in 1859. About 100,000 "yondersiders" from California and "greenhorns" from the East poured into the area in just six months.

Other strikes kept the mining fever burning. Gold and silver were found in Nevada, and copper gleamed in Montana. More gold was struck in Idaho, in Wyoming, and in the Black Hills of the Dakota Territory. Prospectors—and townspeople who served them—poured into these areas. By 1870 Colorado, Nevada, Idaho, Montana, and Wyoming had been organized into territories.

Some prospectors found the fortunes they dreamed of, but large mining companies reaped most of the profits. The Comstock Lode in Nevada, for example, was discovered in 1859. Its major wealth of silver and gold, however, remained deep underground until a large company dug a mine in 1870.

The company had the money to pay for the latest engineering knowledge and the machines that could bore through rock and extract the minerals. The company also could hire large work crews, mainly unsuccessful prospectors. In 20 years, the Comstock produced $306 million, mostly in silver.

Still, prospectors continued to follow the strikes. These people were drawn to places where settlers might otherwise not have gone. Settlement here did not follow the old pattern of the search for fertile land. Here it was the glint of minerals—gold, silver, copper, lead, iron—that drew the newcomers. On such hopes, towns boomed.

BOOM TOWNS

Late in 1877 writer Helen Hunt Jackson arrived in Garland City in the Colorado Territory. She stepped down from the stagecoach amid deafening noise and asked a bystander what was happening. "The building of the city," he said. "Twelve days ago there was not a house here. Today there are one hundred and five. And in a week there will be two hundred."

All over the West, towns were bursting into life. Some, like Garland City, grew up along the railroads. Others, like Virginia City in the Nevada Territory, grew up around the mines. Still others, like Laramie in the Wyoming Territory, were cowboy towns.

Many of these new towns lived up to the eastern image of the "Wild West." Mark Twain visited Virginia City in the 1870s and called it "the 'livest' town . . . that America had ever produced."

> The sidewalks swarmed with people. . . . There was a glad, almost fierce, intensity in every eye, that told of the money-getting schemes that were seething in every brain and the high hope that held sway in every heart.

Some of these rough towns kept on booming. Others were smoothed into respectable communities. Still others faded quickly and seemed to blow

Chinese laborers worked as drillers, graders, masons, and track layers for the Central Pacific Railroad. Laying track through the rugged Sierra Nevada required a store of grit and energy.

Caldwell, Kansas, in the 1880s was a noisy, dirty, exciting western boom town. A marshal who kept the peace here died holding up a bank in another town.

away. Mining towns often became "ghost towns" when the mines were no longer profitable. The same thing happened to some railroad towns. A shift in railroad company plans could turn one of these settlements into an "air town." A writer for *Harper's Monthly* told how that had happened to a place called Coyote, Kansas:

> On every side the dreary rolling plains lay up against the cloudless horizon. . . . Canvas saloons, sheet-iron hotels, and sod dwellings [were] surrounded by tin cans and scattered playing-cards. . . . In one short week not a house but that of the railroad section people remained.

FRONTIER JUSTICE

Most western towns boomed without government or laws, often before a territory was organized. Gradually, an unwritten set of rules evolved known as the "code of the West."

Hospitality and honesty were the heart of the code. On isolated ranches, strangers were usually welcome to stay to dinner. Cowboys took off their sharp spurs when visiting someone else's house. A rancher would buy cattle without looking them over. The word and handshake of the seller was enough.

However, when arguments arose or someone broke the code, punishment was swift. The worst crime on the range was horse theft because it left a person on foot in a harsh country. Horse thieves, robbers, and murderers were usually hanged—executed legally or illegally by "lynch law."

The illegal executions were usually the work of **vigilantes** (vij-ih-LAN-teez), who were members of "vigilance committees." In many places, these committees sprang up to control lawlessness and keep order in a town. Such groups, however, operated outside the law. Vigilante justice had none of the safeguards of due process of law. The innocent were often hung with the guilty.

Often, justice in the West was administered by cattle ranchers. Ranchers often competed for land and water, and sometimes hired gunfighters to settle their differences. To control the rivalry and to stop cattle rustling, ranchers formed stock-growers' associations. These groups created rules for the range, sometimes called "cow custom." The associations often became informal governments that regulated whole territories.

END OF THE OPEN RANGE

However, the cattle ranchers could not keep the prairie all to themselves. By the 1870s farmers had penetrated the cattle empire. And by the 1880s the "Great American Desert" was marked off in chunks by barbed-wire fences.

Barbed wire had first been marketed in 1874. A wire with "thorns," it would stop the most determined steer from wandering off its owner's land or onto farmland. Barbed wire was especially valuable on the treeless plains, where wood fences could not be built. So farmers unrolled barbed wire by the mile, fencing their property and breaking up the open range.

Sheep ranchers also moved to the prairie in the 1870s and 1880s and challenged cattle ranchers' hold on the open range. Cattle ranchers complained that longhorns would not drink from waterholes where sheep had drunk. They also complained that the sheep ate the grass down to the roots and killed it. Bitter range wars were fought between cattle ranchers and sheep ranchers over these issues.

By the mid-1880s two other problems beset the cattle ranchers—overgrazing of the land and falling beef prices. The final blow to the open range came in the winter of 1886–1887. It brought blizzards that buried the grass under mountains of snow. Only about 10 percent of the cattle on the range survived.

After that winter, most of the remaining independent ranchers sold out to big companies. Cattle companies learned from the great blizzard that they could no longer depend on the open range. They drilled wells for water, stored hay to feed the cattle in winter, and fenced their land. They also brought in fatter breeds of cattle to cross with the tough, lean longhorns.

The change spelled an end to a way of life on the plains. But the story of the plains was not simply the story of ranchers. It was also the story of Indians and farmers.

SECTION REVIEW

1. Identify the following: the "Great American Desert," John Butterfield, time zones, long drives, *vaquero*, Nat Love, "the code of the West."

2. (a) How was the first transcontinental railroad financed? (b) Where did it begin in the East? In the West?

3. (a) How did cattle ranching change after the first transcontinental railroad was built? (b) Why did Abilene, Kansas, and Chicago, Illinois, become important?

4. How did ranchers discover that the prairies were good range land? How did that discovery affect cattle raising?

5. (a) Name four places besides California where big mineral strikes occurred. (b) Who made the most profits from mining? Why?

6. List three reasons why towns boomed in the West.

7. (a) What led westerners to form vigilance committees? (b) Why was vigilante justice dangerous?

8. (a) How did farmers change the open range? (b) Why did range wars erupt between cattle ranchers and sheep ranchers? (c) What did the winter of 1886–1887 teach cattle companies?

THE PLAINS INDIANS

READ TO FIND OUT

— why the Fort Laramie Treaty led to warfare.

— how reservations were established.

— how the Sioux and Cheyenne won the battle at the Little Bighorn.

— how the army ended Indian resistance.

— how the fight for Indian legal rights began.

— why the Dawes Act failed.

In 1834 a baby boy was born on the northern plains in a camp of the Sioux. He was given the name Tatanka Yotanka by his father. Tatanka Yotanka became a great Sioux leader, known to whites as Sitting Bull.

The year Sitting Bull was born, Cyrus McCormick patented his reaping machine. When Sitting Bull was three, John Deere manufactured a plow with a hard steel blade. The new plow could cut through the tough soil of the plains with ease, and the reaper could harvest seas of wheat.

By the time Sitting Bull became chief of his tribe, the long drives were bringing cattle to the plains. The transcontinental railroad sliced across land that had once been Indian land. When Sitting Bull was forty, gold was discovered on Indian land in the Dakota Territory.

The fate of Sitting Bull and that of all Plains Indians became tangled with the plow and the reaper, with the longhorn, with the railroad, and with the earth's metals.

THE FORT LARAMIE TREATY

When the western lands were still thought of as the "Great American Desert," they were promised in treaties to the tribes "as long as the rivers shall run and the grass shall grow." About 250,000 Indians, in dozens of tribes, roamed the Great Plains, the mountains, and the Great Basin.

Most tribes were native to those lands—the Arapaho, Comanche, Sioux, Blackfoot, Crow,

Cheyenne, Osage, Pawnee, Navaho, Apache. Other tribes—the Cherokee, Creek, Chickasaw, Choctaw, Seminole—had been driven west in the 1830s.

By the 1850s, however, pioneer trails and United States Army forts were strung out across the plains. As settlers moved into Indian country, the tribes and newcomers often met in conflict. The United States government needed to develop a policy that would enable settlers and tribes to share the land.

In 1851 government agents met with 10,000 Indians from 9 tribes in a great council at Fort Laramie, Wyoming. After 20 days of talks, tribal leaders and agents signed the Fort Laramie Treaty. The United States was given the right to build more roads and forts in Indian territory in exchange for yearly payments to the tribes.

The treaty also set boundaries for each tribe's hunting grounds to reduce conflicts over hunting areas. Also, the boundaries were intended to keep settlers and Indians apart.

Albert Bierstadt painted "Indians near Fort Laramie" in 1859. At this time Bierstadt served as the artist-illustrator for a government team surveying the West.

WARFARE AND RESERVATIONS

The treaty proved a path to war, not peace. The Indians continued to follow the buffalo across hunting boundaries. And settlers, lured by gold or fertile land, readily entered Indian country.

The government tried to solve the problem by buying more Indian land. In treaty after treaty between 1853 and 1856, the government acquired 174 million acres (70 million hectares) of land. In some of these treaties, areas of land, called **reservations**, were set aside for Indians. Reservations were usually located within Indians' former hunting grounds.

In 1859 gold was discovered on Cheyenne and Arapaho land in the Colorado Territory. The government acquired the land, and the tribes were removed to a reservation on barren land. In the early 1860s miners built roads through Sioux lands in the Wyoming and Montana territories. To halt the ceaseless invasion of their homelands, many tribes went to war.

During the 1850s and 1860s, warfare spread like wildfire across the plains. Although outnumbered by the army soldiers, the Indians were skilled warriors and were fighting to save their way of life. Some soldiers remarked that Indians were "the best fighters the sun ever shone on."

The fighting was often savage. In 1862 Sioux chief Little Crow led warriors through southern Minnesota, killing hundreds of settlers. Two years later a Colorado volunteer regiment killed several hundred Cheyenne and Arapaho men, women, and children encamped at a place called Sand Creek.

The continuing warfare brought government agents in 1868 to Medicine Lodge Creek, Kansas, to negotiate the Medicine Lodge treaty. Two large reservations were set up—one for northern tribes in Dakota's Black Hills, another for southern tribes in the Oklahoma Territory. The government promised to build reservation schoolhouses and to supply food, clothing, and farming tools. With the Indians concentrated in these two areas, a wide belt of land through the plains was left to the settlers.

THE PEACE POLICY

Throughout this period, a few reformers and religious groups like the Quakers had been urging humane treatment of the Indians. In 1869 President Grant responded by establishing a "peace policy." Reservation agents would be chosen by churches and would help Indians learn the ways of white people. Some agents cared about the Indians, but many did not. Corrupt agents kept most of the government money that they were supposed to use for supplies for the tribes. As a consequence, Indians received spoiled food and tattered clothing.

Such corruption increased Indian bitterness at the reservation system. Many Indians tried to return to their old lands and way of life. Most were caught and brought back. By this time, something besides treaties chained the Indians to the reservations. The buffalo were nearly extinct.

To live on the plains, the Indians needed buffalo. A Kiowa woman named Old Lady Horse said, "Everything came from the buffalo. Their teepees were made of buffalo hides; so were their clothes and moccasins. They ate buffalo meat."

White hunters, however, shot buffalo for sport, and railroad construction crews slaughtered them for food. When a way was found in 1871 to tan buffalo hides, hunters raced for the kill. Buffalo-hide coats became fashionable in the East. By 1875, no more than a thousand buffalo remained.

THE LITTLE BIGHORN

The Medicine Lodge Treaty had promised that no persons but members of the tribes "shall ever be permitted to pass over, settle upon, or reside in" the Black Hills of Dakota. But when gold was discovered in 1874, miners flocked to those hills. The army tried to keep the miners out, but failed.

In response, angry Sioux raided white settlements in the Dakota and Montana territories. The government ordered the Sioux back to the reservation, but they refused. For months, the Sioux bands fought with the army, winning several battles.

In the summer of 1876, about 7,000 Sioux and Cheyenne—1,800 of them warriors—gathered in a great encampment at a bend in the Little Bighorn River in the Montana Territory. They were led by Sitting Bull and a chief called Crazy Horse by whites.

The chaos and confusion at the Little Bighorn is shown in a pictograph by Red Horse, who witnessed this last Sioux victory. Red Horse said that during the battle the soldiers became confused and threw away their guns, asking to be taken prisoner.

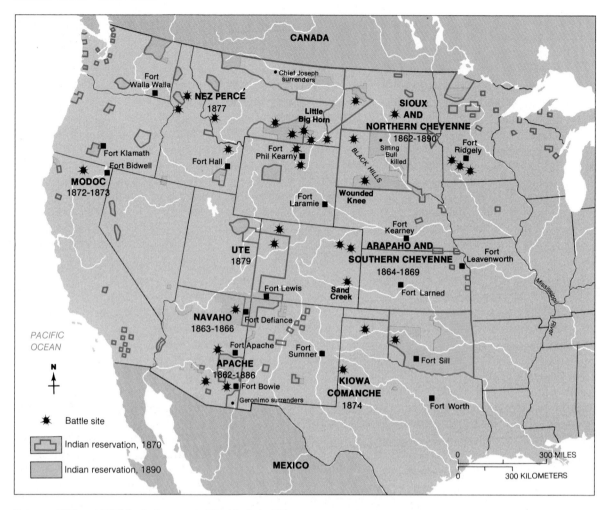

Between 1860 and 1890 the Indians west of the Mississippi River were moved onto reservations.
Major battles in the ensuing conflicts are shown on the map. The area set aside for reservations
was 166 million acres in 1875, 78 million acres by 1900, and 39 million acres by 1930.

Three columns of army troops had tracked the Sioux and were preparing an attack. However, they did not realize how many Indians were camped by the river. General George Armstrong Custer led one column of 264 soldiers. Without waiting for the other two columns, Custer led his troops in a charge toward the Indian camp.

The soldiers rode straight into a band of warriors. The Indians charged into the lines of troops, splitting them off. When the battle ended, not one soldier was left alive. For the Indians, victory at the Little Bighorn was their greatest triumph. But it was also to be their last victory in the struggle to save their lands and way of life.

THE END OF INDIAN RESISTANCE

In October 1876 government agents concluded yet another treaty with reservation chiefs. As a result, the Black Hills, rich in metals, were no longer part of the Sioux reservation. One chief signed the treaty holding a blanket in front of his eyes.

Meanwhile, the government increased its drive to force Plains Indians back to the reservations. The Sioux broke up into bands to evade the army. Sitting Bull escaped with some of his people into Canada. Crazy Horse and his followers remained on the plains and fought bitterly into the winter of 1877. Then, near starvation, they surrendered.

Tribes in other areas tried to escape life on the shrinking reservations. The Nez Percé (NEHZ per-SAY) of Idaho, led by Chief Joseph, hoped to reach safety in Canada. For more than three months in 1877, the army chased the Nez Percé over 1,700 miles (2,736 kilometers), stopping them just short of the Canadian border. Looking at the half-starved band, an army officer said: "I think that in his long career Joseph cannot accuse the Government of the United States of one single act of justice."

Throughout the West, tribes were forced into surrender. In 1863 army troops led by explorer Kit Carson ended Navaho resistance in the Arizona Territory. The Modoc of California and Oregon held out for six months amid the lava beds of an extinct volcano before they were captured in 1873. The fierce Apache of the Southwest, led by Geronimo, were finally defeated in 1886.

Even Sitting Bull in Canada could not hold out. Canadian tribes could not share their crowded hunting lands, so the Sioux sent hunting parties across the border into the United States. Many of the hunters were killed by the army. Finally, in 1881 Sitting Bull and his people climbed into wagons and headed south for the reservation.

WOUNDED KNEE

Some Indians, resisting the changes, tried to bring back their lost freedom with a new religion—the "Ghost Dance." The movement began in 1889 when a Paiute leader named Wovoka claimed to have had a vision.

Wovoka said that the whites would disappear, dead Indians would return with Christ, and vast herds of buffalo would once more roam the prairie. This would happen in 1891, and those Indians who danced the Ghost Dance could see the world to come. In the meantime, "ghost shirts" with special markings would keep them from harm.

The faith spread rapidly among Plains Indians. Government and military officials became worried about this new force. When Sitting Bull became a leader of the Ghost Dance, they decided that he must be arrested.

On a December morning in 1890, Indian police employed by the government surrounded Sitting Bull's cabin. When they tried to arrest him, a young Sioux shot an officer. In the gunfire that followed, Sitting Bull was killed.

Sitting Bull (left) was a great medicine man. Though he gave advice, he did not actually fight at the Little Bighorn. To the Nez Percé, Chief Joseph (right) was a guardian in times of great trouble. He was a powerful voice in the council of leaders.

Fear of a Sioux uprising swept through settlements, and the army began arresting Indians considered troublemakers. Ten days after Sitting Bull's death, the army put under guard 350 Sioux, who were camped on the banks of Wounded Knee Creek in South Dakota. As soldiers were disarming the warriors, a shot was fired. The soldiers opened fire. When the firing stopped, 290 men, women, and children of the Sioux were dead or dying.

The Ghost Dance, too, died at Wounded Knee. A woman survivor allowed doctors to remove her ghost shirt to examine a wound. "Yes, take it off," she said. "They told me a bullet would not go through. Now I don't want it anymore."

INDIAN RIGHTS

One group of Indians won a small victory fighting with words rather than with arrows and guns. In 1877 the government moved the small Ponca tribe from the Dakota reservation to the one in Oklahoma where many died from hunger and disease. Chief Standing Bear promised his dying son that he would be buried on the old lands.

Standing Bear and 30 followers returned home. Shortly after, the army arrested the Ponca. However, the Ponca had two strong allies. One was Thomas Tibbles, a Nebraska journalist who took up

CHARLES EASTMAN
A BRIDGE BETWEEN TWO WORLDS

When fifteen-year-old Ohiyesa was first sent to school, he wanted to run away. "They might as well try to make a buffalo build houses like a beaver," he thought, "as to teach me to be a white man."

Ohiyesa was a Sioux Indian, born in Minnesota in 1858. When his tribe had been forced off their lands, his father had joined Little Crow's rebellion and had been captured by soldiers. Believing him dead, his family had fled to the Canadian woods.

Ohiyesa spent the next ten years in the wilderness. "It was," he remembered, "the freest life in the world." Wild animals became his pets. His uncle taught him to fish, trap, ride, and hunt. In the evenings he learned the legends of his tribe.

When Ohiyesa was fifteen, his father suddenly appeared. Jailed for years, he was now convinced that the Indians were doomed unless they accepted white ways. He renamed his son Charles Eastman and sent him to a mission school in the Dakota Territory. Bewildered at first, Charles proved an able pupil. Eventually he attended Boston University Medical School.

In 1890 he became the doctor at South Dakota's Pine Ridge Reservation. A month later, 290 Sioux were killed at a nearby camp at Wounded Knee. Eastman worked desperately to save the victims.

Eastman devoted the rest of his life to his people's cause. In books like *Indian Boyhood* and *From the Deep Woods to Civilization*, he explained the Indian way to white Americans. Although he believed most Indian problems were caused by land hunger and broken treaties, he tried to be a bridge between the two groups. "I am an Indian," he said. "Nevertheless, so long as I live, I am an American."

Charles Eastman received the first Indian Achievement Award in 1933 for his work.

About 4,000 Sioux camped near Pine Ridge, South Dakota, in January 1891.

the Ponca cause in a series of articles. The other was Susette La Flesche, daughter of the Omaha chief.

They made a powerful pair. Tibbles was an aggressive crusader who had earlier championed slaves and poor farmers. La Flesche had been educated in white schools and could defend Indian rights in fluent English. She wrote a document detailing the Ponca's plight, and Tibbles used it to draw up a suit of habeas corpus to free the Ponca.

In April 1879 Tibbles, La Flesche, and a church group of supporters gathered in court. Tibbles based his suit on the Fourteenth Amendment, which guaranteed citizenship to people born in the United States. He argued that the Ponca had been illegally jailed and were entitled to protection under the Constitution. The judge decided that "an Indian is a person within the laws of the United States." Standing Bear and the Ponca were set free.

For Tibbles and La Flesche, this was only the beginning of a fight for Indian rights. They went east to plead the Indian cause.

A young writer named Helen Hunt Jackson was so moved that she devoted her life to helping the Indians. In *A Century of Dishonor*, she would tell the story of the broken treaties. In a novel called *Ramona*, she would write of the California mission Indians. She hoped *Ramona* would help Indians as *Uncle Tom's Cabin* had helped blacks.

Another person moved by La Flesche was Senator Henry L. Dawes of Massachusetts. In 1887 he introduced a bill in Congress to reform the government's Indian policy. It passed partly because of public feelings stirred up by *Ramona*.

THE DAWES ACT

The Dawes Act tried to bring Indians fully into American life. To do so, the government would have to stop dealing with Indians through their tribes. As long as Indians clung to tribal customs, many reformers believed, they could not become part of American culture. The Dawes Act intended to turn the Indian into a small farmer.

Under the act, tribes were no longer recognized as legal groups and could not hold their reservation lands in common. Those lands would be divided among individual Indians to farm—160 acres (395 hectares) for families and 80 acres (198 hectares) for single adults. Reservation land not allotted to Indians—almost 90 million acres (222 million hectares)—would be sold. Money from the sale would finance schools to teach Indians new ways. Those who abandoned tribal ways could one day become United States citizens.

Although Dawes and the reformers had good intentions, the act did little to help the Indians. Indian tradition did not recognize private ownership of land, and many Indians did not understand the new arrangement. Speculators moved in quickly. Some Indians sold their land for as little as fifty cents an acre. For decades to come, acres and acres of land would steadily pass out of Indian hands.

Susette La Flesche married Thomas Tibbles in July 1881. She continued her work for Indian rights, testifying with her husband several times before Congressional committees.

SECTION REVIEW

1. Identify the following: Cyrus McCormick, John Deere, Crazy Horse, George Custer, Chief Joseph, Kit Carson, Geronimo, Wovoka, Helen Hunt Jackson, Henry L. Dawes.

2. (a) What was the purpose of the Fort Laramie Treaty? (b) Why did settlers and Indians break the treaty? (c) How did the government try to solve the problem? What were two results of the government's actions?

3. What was President Grant's "peace policy"? Why did it fail?

4. What events led to the battle at the Little Bighorn? Who led the army troops? Who led the Indian warriors? What was the outcome?

5. (a) How did the army force Plains Indians to return to reservations? What happened to Indians who resisted? (b) Why did Sitting Bull go to Canada? Why did he return?

6. (a) What was the Ghost Dance? Why did it worry government and military officials? (b) Describe the arrest of Sitting Bull. (c) How did that event lead to the killing of Sioux at Wounded Knee?

7. How did Tibbles defend the Ponca in court? What was the judge's decision?

8. What did the Dawes Act attempt to do? Why did the act fail to help Indians?

THE PRAIRIE FARMERS

READ TO FIND OUT

— how the Homestead Act encouraged settlement of the plains.

— how advertising lured people to the plains.

— why plains farming was difficult.

— how the last land rush took place in Oklahoma.

— how Alaska became the new frontier.

On his way to California's gold fields in 1849, Jasper Hixson took a good look at the land he was crossing—the Great Plains. "In the best map we can get hold of, this is all marked the Great American Desert," he wrote in his diary. But Hixson saw something else. In another entry he remarked, "The land is too fertile and it possesses too many inducements for settlement to remain in possession of the Indians forever. Now that so many from the older states begin traveling over this fine land . . . they must write to their friends to 'Go West.'"

Guidebooks to Oregon and California had warned that little water and no trees existed on that vast grassland. When pioneers like Hixson saw the soil of the plains, however, they realized it could be farmed. Their reports reached the East—and Europe—where farmland was in short supply. People responded, heading west to try prairie farming.

At first, homesteaders claimed the fertile river valleys on the fringes of the prairies, but that midwestern land filled up fast. Then, after the Civil War, homesteaders streamed into the lands farther west. They settled on the prairies, finding endless acres of soil and grass and little else. It was not farming as they had ever known it, and many fled their homesteads in despair. Yet, many stayed, met the challenges, and transformed grasslands into farms, and solitary homesteads into communities.

Pioneer Edwin Bryant in 1846 predicted of the Great Plains: "At some future day it will be the Eden of America." With plow and seed and labor and grit, the prairie pioneers slowly began to build it.

THE HOMESTEAD ACT

In 1862 Congress encouraged the settlement of the plains by passing the Homestead Act. Any citizen, or immigrant who planned to become a citizen, could claim 160 acres (64 hectares) of public land. All a homesteader had to do was pay a small registration fee, improve part of the land, build a house, and live on the land for five years.

Between 1862 and 1900, 80 million acres (32 million hectares) were claimed under the Homestead Act. But only about 17 percent of this land was settled by homesteaders. Speculators acquired much of it through various schemes and often sold it off at high prices. Thus, some farmers ended up paying as much as $6,000 for their homesteads.

The Homestead Act also ignored the nature of prairie farming. In the East, where rainfall was plentiful, a 160-acre (64-hectare) farm could produce enough crops to support a farmer. In the West there was little rainfall. Thus many crops that thrived in the East would not grow well on the plains. Homesteaders found it hard to support themselves on farms of this size. One woman who went to Kansas in 1879 wrote:

> Methods of farming, farm tools even, the western way of handling stock, all were so different from eastern ways that my father, who had always been successful with sheep, soon found his first venture in Kansas a disastrous failure.

Nevertheless homesteaders came, drawn not only by the stories of fertile land and the Homestead Act, but also by promoters with land to sell.

LAND FOR SALE

Railroad companies, which had been granted about 128 million acres (51 million hectares) of public land, wanted farmers to settle along their routes. To attract settlers, the companies often sold the land at low prices. Thus, the railroad would have a steady supply of customers in the homesteaders, who would pay the railroad to ship farm crops east. The homesteaders would also be a market for eastern merchants, who would pay the railroad to ship manufactured goods west. Soon, towns would be booming along the railroad lines.

The railroads spent millions on advertising to lure people to the prairies. In western Kansas, the ads promised, crops practically raised themselves,

Land in Farms by Region 1850–1900

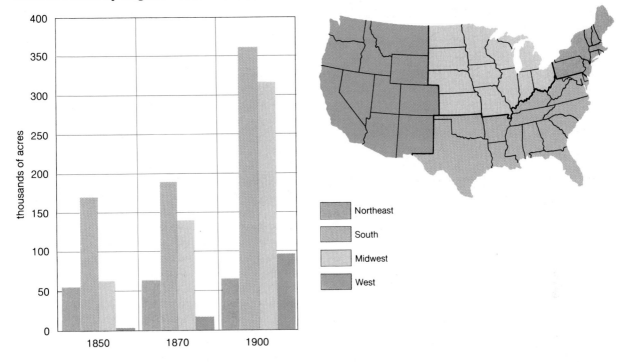

and rain fell in just the right amount. Settlers could travel there easily on the railroad.

Each railroad had agents in eastern seaports to meet immigrants off ships and to arrange their travel west. The Northern Pacific Railroad even had offices in England, Germany, Holland, and the Scandinavian countries. The Europeans came by the thousands. A Minnesota newspaper editor wrote, "It seems as if the Scandinavian kingdoms were being emptied into this state."

Territorial and state governments added to this "boomer" literature. They, too, had land to sell. They persuaded newspapers to print glowing reports about the soil, the climate, the crops, and the people. Easterners were told to give their gardens a boost by ordering a sack of rich Minnesota soil. The Nebraska Immigration Association advertised in Europe: "Land for the landless! Homes for the homeless!"

The advertising, along with some boom crop years, worked. Between 1870 and 1890 the populations of Kansas and Nebraska each grew by about a million people. The Dakota Territory, sparsely settled in 1870, was filled with over 500,000 newcomers within 20 years. By 1912, eight new plains states

entered the Union. Nebraska joined in 1867, Colorado in 1876, North Dakota, South Dakota, and Montana in 1889, Idaho and Wyoming in 1890, and New Mexico in 1912. Four other states also joined during that time—Utah in 1896, Washington in 1889, Oklahoma in 1907, and Arizona in 1912.

HOMESTEADS ON THE PRAIRIE

Homesteading the prairie tested the pioneers' courage and cleverness. One young girl wrote of arriving on her family's new homestead:

> We had barely gotten unloaded when a neighbor man rode up on a donkey and brought us the key to our house. You are no doubt wondering what was locked in the house. Well, it was something very precious—a plow. Father had stored it there after he had located the place. It was to be our means of support. Not a single tree was there; just bare prairie.

Since there were few trees for timber, most homesteaders learned to make houses of earth. Under the prairie buffalo grass lay a thick mat of tangled roots. Homesteaders sliced up chunks of this sod

Women in the early West worked hard alongside their families. They also enjoyed a release from some of the restrictions of more settled communities. These two young women gallop across open land riding astride instead of sidesaddle.

with a special plow. With the sturdy sod bricks they built "soddie" houses, barns, and some of their first schools and churches.

Most homesteaders had to dig for their water, sometimes as deep as 300 feet (91 meters). They erected windmills over the wells to pump up the water. The windmills had vanes, or rudders, which held the wheel of blades toward the wind. These vanes were specially designed not to break in the strong prairie winds. Enough well water might be pumped in this manner to irrigate a few acres of vegetables, but large-scale irrigation was not practical.

To use every drop of the scarce ground water, many homesteaders tried "dry farming." With steel-tipped plows they dug until they reached soil that held some moisture. That moisture would rise through the plowed soil to reach the plants' roots. To keep the moisture from rising to the surface and evaporating, homesteaders packed the topsoil into a firm layer. With dry farming, farmers could cultivate more land and grow grain crops like wheat, oats, and corn. Eventually these became the cash crops of plains farming.

Many new tools and machines boosted the harvest on the plains. Some were old implements, like plows and windmills, that were adapted to new conditions. Some were inventions, like barbed wire.

New machines mechanized labor. Steam-powered rigs drilled wells, threshers beat the grains from their husks, and binders gathered wheat into bundles. Most of the equipment, however, was ex-

pensive. Homesteaders could not afford to buy it unless they farmed larger tracts and planted more cash crops.

Congress tried to help by passing acts that allowed homesteaders to claim more land. But most of the measures were impractical. Under the Timber Culture Act of 1873, a settler who planted trees on 40 acres (16 hectares) could claim another 160 acres (64 hectares). Yet trees would not grow and thrive without water, and water was scarce. Under the Desert Land Act of 1877, farmers also could get more land by irrigating part of their claim. Few had the money or machines to do so.

For most homesteaders, plains farming remained a hard life and a risky business. Bitter winters, baking summers, drought, floods, loneliness, and an endless moaning wind all took their toll. In addition, some years grasshoppers came like the plague and devoured crops. In 1884, the "grasshopper year," the insects ate everything growing in Kansas.

People who stayed on the plains did so because they belonged there. In *O Pioneers!* Willa Cather, a writer who grew up on the prairie, wrote:

It's a queer thing about that flat country. It takes hold of you, or it leaves you perfectly cold. A great many people find it dull and monotonous; they like a church steeple, an old mill, a waterfall, country all touched up and furnished, like a German Christmas card. I go everywhere. . . . But when I strike the open plains, something happens. I'm home. I breathe differently.

THE LAST LAND RUSH

Throughout the nation's history, land had been a resource without limits. People could always head west in search of new land. Now, as the 1880s came to a close, Americans were beginning to feel that this era was ending. The western land was filling up.

In the late 1880s, land-hungry settlers demanded that the Oklahoma District be opened to settlement. This was an unoccupied area in the middle of Indian Territory in Oklahoma. At noon on April 22, 1889, the government opened up the district to homesteaders. Within hours, almost 2 million acres (800,000 hectares) were claimed. Oklahoma gained about 50,000 people in a single day.

A year later, in 1890, the Oklahoma Territory was organized. That same year the Bureau of the Census declared that "there can hardly be said to be a frontier."

Land, however, remained, most of it belonging to Indians. In 1891 Sauk, Fox, and Potawatomi (pot-ah-WAT-o-mee) tribal lands in the Oklahoma Territory were offered to settlers. The following year, 3 million acres (1.2 million hectares) of the Cheyenne-Arapaho reservation in Colorado were settled. Then, in 1893, the government bought from the Cherokee a strip of the Oklahoma Territory called the Cherokee Outlet. It, too, was opened to homesteaders.

The last land rush took place at noon on September 16, 1893. Thousands of people gathered at the starting lines—100,000 on the Kansas border alone. One young pioneer was making the run by bicycle, for the fun of it, and watched the start:

> First in the line was a solid bank of horses; some had riders, some were hitched to gigs, buckboards, carts, and wagons, but to the eye there were only the two miles of tossing heads, and restless front legs of horses. . . . While we stood, numb with looking, the rifles snapped and the line broke with a huge, crackling roar. That one thundering moment of horseflesh by the mile quivering in its first leap forward was a gift of the gods, and its like will never come again.

A mad race for land was on. People scrambled over each other to get a stake and flag into the ground. Within a few hours, the land was all taken up.

The sod house in its lonely setting, the farm animals, and tools tell the story of the settlers' daily lives. The little wagon suggests that even toys were practical.

THE FRONTIER IN AMERICAN HISTORY
ANALYZING HISTORICAL INTERPRETATIONS

Historians do not simply report events. They also analyze and interpret them. Often, the interpretations differ. One issue that has long divided historians is the importance of the frontier in American history.

In 1893 Frederick Jackson Turner, a young historian from the University of Wisconsin, wrote a paper titled "The Significance of the Frontier in American History." "The true point of view in the history of this nation is not the Atlantic Coast," Turner wrote, "it is the Great West." Turner believed that the frontier, with its available land, made possible American economic development and shaped the American character. In addition, Turner said, "The frontier individualism has from the beginning promoted democracy."

> To the frontier the American intellect owes its striking characteristics. That coarseness and strength . . . that practical inventive turn of mind . . . that masterful grasp of material things . . . that restless nervous energy; that dominant individualism, working for good and for evil . . . these are the traits of the frontier, or traits called out elsewhere because of the existence of the frontier. Since the days when the fleet of Columbus sailed into the waters of the New World, America has been another name for opportunity. . . . But never again will such gifts of free land offer themselves. . . . Now, four centuries from the discovery of America, at the end of a hundred years of life under the Constitution, the frontier has gone, and with its going has closed the first period of American history.
>
> —Frederick Jackson Turner

Many later historians thought that Turner had overemphasized the importance of the frontier. Historian David M. Potter of Stanford University did not believe that the frontier was the most significant factor in American history. He felt that another factor was more important.

"Many of the traits which have been attributed to the frontier influence . . . could equally be accounted for by the impact of abundance," wrote Potter in 1954 in his book *People of Plenty*. "Thus abundance, rather than the frontier [has produced] what have been regarded as frontier aspects of American culture." To Potter, economic abundance included not only fertile and available land but also available goods. Abundance, said Potter, encouraged democracy because people believed that they could all share in the nation's riches.

> In the first place, then, by making the frontier the one great hopeful factor in our experience, Turner gave us every cause to feel alarm and pessimism about the conditions that would follow the disappearance of the frontier. . . . To [Turner] the frontier remained the polar force until it was exhausted. . . . Yet, in fact, what happened was that, as early as the mid-century, if not earlier, American industrial growth, relying upon the use of other forms of abundance than soil fertility, began to compete with the frontier in the opportunities which it offered, and the migration of Americans began to point to the cities rather than to the West. Later this same industrial growth provided a general standard of living so high that people were no longer willing to abandon it for the sake of what the frontier promised. . . . In short, the frontier ceased to operate as a major force in American history not when it disappeared . . . but when the primary means of access to abundance passed from the frontier to other focuses in American life.
>
> —David M. Potter

In analyzing historical interpretations, it is important to answer several questions.

1. How do the interpretations differ? According to Turner, what American characteristics were formed by the frontier? How was democracy affected? To Potter, how was industrial growth an important factor in American development? Why did Potter feel that Turner's interpretation led to "alarm and pessimism"?

2. In what year did each historian publish his work? How might the difference in time have affected the historians' conclusions? Frederick Jackson Turner was born in Wisconsin. David M. Potter was born in Georgia. Why might the western frontier have seemed more important to Turner than to Potter? Questions like these concern a historian's *frame of reference*, the standards and values that help to shape his or her outlook.

3. In this and other chapters, can you find evidence that supports either of the interpretations? Can you find evidence that makes either interpretation seem false?

Chilkoot Pass, Alaska, led to the Klondike. Everyone walked, traveling light, in this group nearing the summit in 1898. Rest stops were brief because of the extreme cold.

A NEW FRONTIER

Most of America's expansion before the Civil War was fueled by settlers' desire for land. Settlers crossed the frontier first, then the government followed. But in 1867 the United States acquired about 500,000 square miles (1.3 million square kilometers) of land without settlers demanding it. Secretary of State William H. Seward arranged the purchase from Russia for $7.2 million. The new territory was Alaska, called the "great land" by Indians who lived on the coastal Aleutian Islands.

Most Americans scoffed at the purchase, calling Alaska "Seward's icebox" or "Seward's folly." A few miners drifted up that way, since many western mines were giving out. They found a little gold here and there, but few struck it rich.

One young Californian, George Washington Carmack, wandered into Alaska and then over the border into Canada's Yukon Territory. In the summer of 1896 he found gold in a creek that flowed into the Klondike River. The news traveled quickly. Before the end of summer, most of the ground around nearby creeks was staked out. A boom town called Dawson sprang up. The gold rush was on.

Most of the miners heading for the Yukon went through Alaska. Then, a few years later, gold was discovered in Alaska, too. The stream of gold seekers set off dreams for Alaska—dreams of gold, furs, coal, timber, silver, copper, platinum. Back in Washington, D. C., interest in Alaska stirred, and a homestead act encouraged its settlement. "Seward's folly" would be America's last land frontier.

SECTION REVIEW

1. Identify the following: "soddie" houses, "dry farming," Timber Culture Act, Willa Cather, the Oklahoma District, William H. Seward.

2. Why did Congress pass the Homestead Act? How did it help settlers? What weaknesses did it have?

3. (a) Why did railroad companies want farmers to settle along their routes? (b) How did the railroads try to attract settlers to the plains? Were they successful? Why or why not?

4. Describe four problems that homesteaders faced on the plains.

5. (a) Where was the last land rush? (b) How did the government obtain the land that it offered to settlers? (c) Describe the start of the land rush.

6. What was America's last land frontier? How did the United States acquire it?

CHAPTER SURVEY

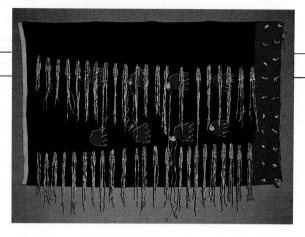

An Omaha or a Pawnee artist fashioned the Bear Society flag in about 1865. Each element of the flag—the fringe, the paw prints, and the color—had a special meaning.

SUMMARY

By 1869 the first transcontinental railroad stretched across the Great Plains, and people began pouring into the West. Beef raising became big business as ranchers drove cattle from Texas to railheads in Kansas and Wyoming. From there, trains carried the cattle east. Soon huge herds were grazing across the unclaimed grasslands between Texas and Canada. In the 1870s farmers and sheep ranchers challenged the cattle ranchers for a share of the rich prairie land.

Meanwhile, discoveries of gold and other metals drew people to Colorado, Nevada, Montana, Idaho, Wyoming, and the Dakota Territory. Towns boomed beside the railroads and around the mines.

The fate of the Plains Indians became tied to the westward migration. Early treaties had promised the Great Plains to the tribes. But settlers moved into Indian country, and the tribes and newcomers clashed. To resolve differences, the government signed treaty after treaty with the Plains Indians.

Treaties, however, often led to warfare. President Grant created a peace policy, which, in the end, led to additional resentment. A series of Indian wars were fought. The eventual result of these conflicts was the end of Indian resistance.

During this period, Indians and non-Indians worked on behalf of Indian rights. The Dawes Act, too, was passed in an attempt to change policy toward Indians.

The government, through the Homestead Act of 1862, and the railroads encouraged people to settle on the plains. Easterners and immigrants responded by the hundreds of thousands. Homesteading proved to be a harsh life. As the 1800s ended, the last unoccupied land, most of it belonging to Indians in the Oklahoma Territory, was opened to homesteaders. By 1912, eight new plains states entered the Union.

In 1867 the United States acquired the territory of Alaska. The area was ignored, however, until gold was discovered in Canada's Yukon Territory. Prospectors heading for the gold fields traveled through Alaska. Interest in Alaska grew stronger when gold was discovered there, and it became America's last land frontier.

CHAPTER REVIEW

1. Answer the following questions to describe the nature and extent of the United States rail system in 1890. (a) How much and what kind of track was there? Where did it extend? (b) How were the railroads financed? (c) Where did the labor come from?

2. Summarize the changes that occurred in the cattle industry after the building of railroads.

3. (a) Compare the life and work of cowboys and mining prospectors. (b) Describe boom towns, telling how they were related to cowboys and prospectors.

4. (a) What were considered the most serious crimes on the frontier? How were they punished? (b) What was the nature of the groups that administered justice?

5. Explain the changes that were brought about on the range by each of the following. (a) barbed wire (b) sheep-raisers (c) overgrazing, falling beef prices, and bad weather

6. Explain how each of the following caused conflict between the Indians and the settlers: the plow, the transcontinental railroad, gold.

7. Explain how the following agreements were alike and how they were different: the Fort Laramie Treaty, Grant's peace policy, the Dawes Act.

8. Summarize the warfare that occurred between Indians and army soldiers between 1850 and 1880. Describe major conflicts, and name leaders.

Let the traveler beware this poster's advertising. The BEAUTIFUL, BOLD, GRAND, PICTURESQUE SCENERY would be seen from a stagecoach. In fact, such a ride was often BUMPY, DUSTY, LONG, and TIRESOME.

9. (a) What were the purpose and results of the Homestead Act? (b) How did the railroads encourage settlement? (c) What was life like for the homesteaders?

10. Describe the two events—the settlement of the Oklahoma Territory and "Seward's folly"—that opened up the last land frontiers.

ISSUES AND IDEAS

1. You are a representative of the United States government under President Grant. Defend your position to an Indian council with regard to the purchase of Indian land, the setting up of reservations, the killing of buffalo.

2. You are an Indian tribal leader. Defend your position to a representative of the United States government with regard to your right to possess land, the role of the buffalo in your culture, your religion and customs.

3. The Homestead Act, the Timber Culture Act, the Desert Land Act, the settlement of the Oklahoma District, and the purchase of Alaska were all government efforts to encourage settlement of the frontier. Comment on the beneficial or harmful results of each.

SKILLS WORKSHOP

1. *Maps.* Refer to the map "Railroads, Cattle Trails, and Mining Centers" in this chapter. (a) Choose a cattle trail, describe its course, and indicate how it is served by a railroad. Where did the railroad take the cattle? (b) Do the same with the relationship between a mining center and

the railroad. (c) What were some cities that developed near the railroad as a result of the cattle industry or mining?

2. *Maps.* Refer to the map "Settlement of the United States" in the Resource Center at the back of your book. Using information from this chapter, give reasons for the changes shown between 1850 and 1870 and between 1870 and 1890.

PAST AND PRESENT

1. At the turn of the century, trains delivered freight and passengers to nearly every town. How has that picture changed today? Find out what has happened to railroad service in your community since 1900. Do people who remember the railroad service of the past approve or disapprove of the changes?

2. So-called Westerns have been popular movies and television shows for many years, with their portrayals of life on the frontier, of conflicts between cowboys and Indians, and of frontier justice. Select a Western with which you are familiar. From your reading in this chapter, tell whether the Western is true to life.

A Ute Indian drew this petroglyph on a rock near Vernal, Utah. The solid, boxy train with its standing figure has endured though its model is probably long gone.

CHAPTER 15

THE AGE OF INDUSTRY

1865–1900

INDUSTRY AND BUSINESS
THE IMMIGRANTS
THE CITIES

Around 1900 Lee Chew wrote the story of his life. He had been born and lived in China, until tales of a faraway place called America sent him halfway around the world:

"I worked on my father's farm till I was about sixteen years of age, when a man of our tribe came back from America. . . . The man had gone away from our village a poor boy. Now he returned with unlimited wealth, which he had obtained in the country of the American wizards. . . .

"The wealth of this man filled my mind with the idea that I, too, would like to go to the country of the wizards and gain some of their wealth. . . .

"My father gave me $100, and I went to Hong Kong with five other boys from our place and we got steerage passage on a steamer, paying $50 each. Everything was new to me. All my life I had been used to sleeping on a board bed with a wooden pillow, and I found the steamer's bunk very uncomfortable, because it was so soft. The food was different from that which I had been used to, and I did not like it at all. . . . When I got to San Francisco, . . . a few days' living in the Chinese quarter made me happy again. A man got me work as a house servant in an American family, and my start was the same as that of almost all the Chinese in this country."

During the 1880s and 1890s millions of immigrants like Lee Chew came to the United States to find jobs, land, fortunes, and freedom. They came from China and Japan, from Mexico, and from southern and eastern Europe.

Within the United States itself, farmers were also leaving home, seeking a better life. The rapidly growing cities were magnets to farmers as well as to immigrants.

In some ways, the United States that the immigrants found was the "country of the wizards" that Lee Chew sought. Almost like magic, inventors were transforming the nation. It was a noisy, busy age for the United States—an age of industry.

INDUSTRY AND BUSINESS

READ TO FIND OUT

— how industries grew between 1865 and 1890.

— how steel and railroads were vital to the growth of industry.

— why corporations were formed.

— how competition among railroads led to consolidation.

— how John D. Rockefeller obtained a monopoly in the oil industry.

— how Andrew Carnegie became a leader in the steel industry.

— how John Pierpont Morgan succeeded in banking.

— why the Sherman Antitrust Act was passed.

America's hundredth birthday celebration in 1876 showed just how much the nation had changed since its birth. However, the grand Centennial Exposition in Philadelphia was not simply an occasion for looking back. It was also a glimpse into the future.

About 8 million people visited the exposition. That was nearly double the total colonial population at the time of the Declaration of Independence. The nation's population had now passed 40 million, and the rate of immigration was increasing steadily.

A visit to the Centennial Exposition made it clear that the United States was not only a nation of farmers. It was also a nation of industry. In Machinery Hall the visitor passed row upon row of machines for farming and manufacturing.

The giant of all the machines was the Corliss steam engine. It towered over 30 feet (9 meters) above the crowds. The great engine produced enough horsepower to run every machine at the exposition. One awed visitor wrote:

> The Corliss engine does not lend itself to description. Its personal acquaintance must be sought by those who would understand its vast and almost silent grandeur. . . . In the midst of this powerful mechanism is a chair where the engineer sits reading his newspaper. Now and then he lays down his paper and clambers up one of the stairways that cover the framework. He touches some irritated spot on the giant's body with a drop of oil. He then goes down again and takes up his newspaper. . . .

As quietly as a watch, the Corliss hummed along. With a whir of machinery, the United States entered its second century.

GROWING INDUSTRIES

Between 1865 and 1890 the United States saw a tremendous growth in industry. The Industrial Revolution had created the building blocks needed for modern industry—machines, steam engines, standardized parts, mass production, and the factory system. Now these elements were brought together on a larger scale. Small shops and businesses developed into industries to meet the needs of the growing nation.

Between 1860 and 1890 the value of the nation's manufactured goods leaped from about $2 billion to $9 billion. In 1890, for the first time, the value of

Agriculture and Industry 1890

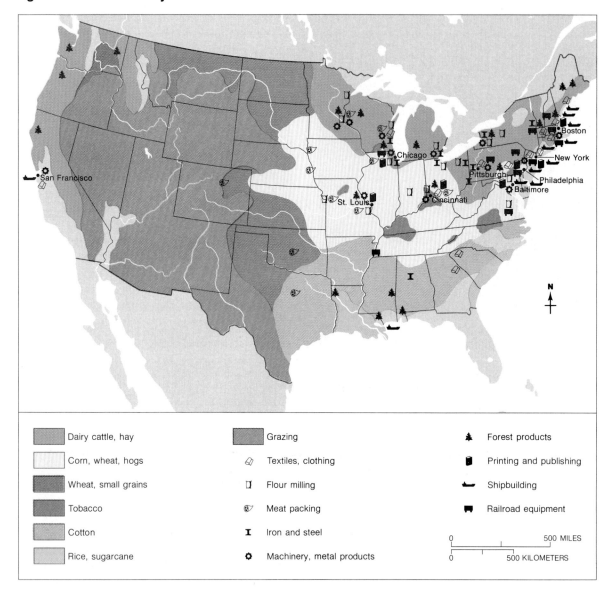

Between the Civil War and the early 1900s, the United States became the world's greatest industrial nation. The importance of agriculture did not end with the spread of industry. Between 1860 and 1900 the number of acres under cultivation more than doubled.

America's industrial goods was greater than that of its agricultural goods. Factories expanded. Machine power did more kinds of work. And industry, once found mainly in the North, spread across the nation.

California, which had first boomed on gold, became a major manufacturing state. Its factories churned out leather, lumber, flour, shoes, tobacco products, and refined sugar. Illinois became known for its farm tools and meat industry, Minnesota for its flour milling, and Michigan and Wisconsin for their lumber.

The growth of industry was particularly striking in the South. Near Birmingham, Alabama, large deposits of iron ore had been found in the 1850s. By 1890 Alabama was the nation's third largest iron producer. Ironworks in neighboring Tennessee were

Joseph Pickett painted "Manchester Valley" to celebrate the coming of the railroad to the valley in 1891. The railroad company's name, Philadelphia and Reading, can be read on the side of the coal car. The town represented in the painting is New Hope, Pennsylvania.

almost as busy. Virginia and North Carolina prospered on tobacco. The lumber, cottonseed oil, and textile industries also strengthened the southern economy.

Still, the Northeast remained the nation's industrial heart. In 1890 the region produced over 85 percent of the United States' manufactured goods.

STEEL AND RAILS

Two of the nation's leading industries—steel and railroads—were vital links in the spread of American manufacturing. Railroads moved goods to more people, and steel gave industries a strong new building material.

Steel had been made in the United States before the Civil War by adding carbon to melted iron. The process was expensive, however, because it took a great deal of coal to keep the iron heated to a liquid state. Then, in 1859, William Kelly in the United States and Henry Bessemer in Britain independently developed a faster and cheaper way to make steel. In this new process, a blast of air was forced into the melted iron, causing the impurities to burn. This produced the heat to keep the iron liquid, so less coal was needed.

Most American steelmakers soon adopted the *Bessemer process* and the output of steel rose from 2,000 tons (1,800 metric tons) in 1867 to 3.7 million tons (3.3 million metric tons) in 1890. As output rose, the price dropped, and steel was used in products from nails to barbed wire to bridge beams.

Railroad companies realized that steel would last longer than iron, and they began using steel rather than iron rails. By the mid-1880s almost all the rails laid were steel, which had become cheaper than iron. And by that time, other developments were improving both freight and passenger railroad service.

George M. Pullman's sleeping cars made rail travel more comfortable, and George Westinghouse's air brakes made it safer. Gustavus F. Swift and Philip D. Armour developed refrigeration for railroad cars. The refrigerated cars brought beef from midwestern slaughterhouses to butcher shops in the East.

Indeed, America's industry moved on rails. Huge deposits of iron ore lay on the western rim of the Great Lakes. Railroads carried the ore to factories in Chicago, Cleveland, Buffalo, and Pittsburgh. Coal from the mines of Pennsylvania and West Virginia was carried by rail to the same cities. The coal fired the blast furnaces that turned the ore into steel— steel for more tracks, engines, cars, and tools.

INVENTIONS TRANSFORM THE NATION

One measure of industry's vigor was the increased number of inventions. Many of these inventions took over tasks once done only by hand. Water-driven machines of the early 1800s spun thread and wove it into cloth. Now, with sewing machines, factories could turn the cloth into ready-made clothes. Machines plowed, sowed seed, and harvested and threshed wheat on the vast American prairies. Machines drilled wells for oil, gas, or water deep in the earth. Machines also molded metal cooking pots, printed newspapers, milled locomotive parts, and added and subtracted figures.

The typewriter challenged inventors for over a hundred years. Finally, in 1867 a group of Milwaukee inventors designed the first successful American typewriter.

There was even a machine to type letters. Humorist Mark Twain tried the new typewriting machine and wrote: "One may lean back in the chair and work it. It piles up an awful stack of words on one page. It [doesn't] muss things or scatter ink blots around."

Every invention affected the way Americans lived. More and more people, including farmers, were no longer self-sufficient. They relied on factories for clothing, tools, and household goods. As people bought more manufactured goods, production increased and prices dropped. New items came on the market, and American industry boomed. As industry boomed, business grew larger and business leaders became more important.

THE GROWTH OF CORPORATIONS

Before the Civil War, most American businesses were run by single owners, called proprietors, or by partners. As industry expanded—and businesses needed more capital, labor, and equipment— owners began to form corporations.

A corporation is the ideal framework on which to build a large business. Corporate owners can sell shares of stock to hundreds of investors, who then own part of the business and share in the profits. This brings in large sums of money to finance expansion of the business or new ventures.

Legally, the corporation is an "artificial being," created by a charter from the state government. It exists as a legal "person," independent of its owners. The corporation can make contracts, own property, sue, and be sued. If owners die, their shares of stock are sold or pass to heirs, and the corporation continues. If the corporation fails, stockholders are protected by *limited liability*. In other words, they lose only the money they invested. They are not responsible for the corporation's debts, as proprietors and partners are if the business that they own fails.

In some industries, many corporations were involved in the headlong rush to do business and make profits. During the 1880s about a thousand separate companies competed in the railroad business, and a thousand different plants were making steel. Americans had always believed in such business competition. It was the basis of the system known as **free enterprise**—the system in which private companies could freely compete with one another with little or no regulation by the government.

However, the fierce scramble convinced some people that something must be done to create order. In three major industries—oil, steel, and railroads—corporate leaders tried to control competition.

COMPETITION ON THE RAILS

Railroading was an exciting business that hummed with opportunity. But it attracted so many competing companies that they had to battle for survival. This cutthroat competition often led to questionable business practices.

Railroad rates varied widely throughout the country. In areas where a railroad had no competition, it would charge "all the traffic can bear." But wherever railroads competed for customers, they tried to charge less than their rivals. When one railroad won a rate war and its competitors went bankrupt, it promptly raised its rates. Also, many railroads charged more per mile for hauling freight a short distance than they did for long hauls over the same route.

The competition often led to still more abuses. To raise funds, many owners sold *watered stock,* which was not backed by railroad money or property. It paid no **dividends**, or shares of the company's profits. In addition, many railroads offered **rebates** to large companies. Under such an agreement, a company promised all its freight business to a railroad. The railroad then rebated, or returned, part of the shipping costs to the company. Thus the company paid lower freight rates, and the railroad had control of a big chunk of business. Rebates were seldom offered to smaller shippers.

Many railroads could not survive such competition. As a protective measure, competing railroads sometimes formed a *pool.* All the companies in the pool agreed to share freight business, to set standard rates, and to divide profits.

The pools did not always work. Companies often ignored agreements and returned to cutthroat tactics to make a quick profit. There was, however, another way to end competition. Several companies could *consolidate,* or combine into one large company. A railroader named Cornelius Vanderbilt was a master at such consolidation.

Vanderbilt began his career as a ferryboat operator, built a fortune in steamboats, then switched to

George Bellows was another American painter fascinated by industry. In "Pennsylvania Station Excavation," done in 1909, Bellows painted the actual construction of buildings.

railroads after the Civil War. He bought up several small railroads in New York, but the New York Central would not sell its line to him.

In 1867 Vanderbilt stopped service between his lines and the Central, thus isolating it. Losing freight and passenger business, the Central finally was forced to sell to Vanderbilt. The shrewd railroader went on to build a rail network that stretched from New York City to Chicago.

Railroad lines could often be run more efficiently when consolidated in a single company. If the new company was successful, passengers usually paid lower rates and investors received higher stock dividends. However, the companies continued to use rebates and variable rates. Small shippers complained that the railroads discriminated against them by not giving them rebates and by charging them higher prices.

REGULATING THE RAILROADS

Railroad abuses provoked cries of outrage from injured groups. Farmers, shippers, and business people were all threatened by the unfair rates and demanded laws to regulate railroads. By 1874 Illinois, Iowa, Minnesota, and Wisconsin had passed laws against discriminatory railroad practices.

The railroads argued that states had no legal right to regulate them. The issue eventually reached the Supreme Court. In 1877 the Court, in *Munn* v. *Illinois*, upheld the Illinois law regulating railroads.

However, nine years later, the Court changed its view and ruled against state regulation. In *Wabash, St. Louis and Pacific Railroad Co.* v. *Illinois*, the Court ruled that states could not set the rates of railroads that crossed state lines. Only the federal government could regulate interstate commerce.

Despite the Court's ruling, pressure for regulation continued. Congress responded in 1887 by passing the Interstate Commerce Act. This act declared that rates of railroads crossing state lines must be "reasonable and just." It forbade rebates, higher charges for short hauls, and pooling. A five-member Interstate Commerce Commission (ICC) was created to enforce the act.

In practice, though, the ICC had little success. Railroads often ignored its rulings, so the Commission had to go to court. By 1897 sixteen cases had reached the Supreme Court, and the railroads won fifteen of them.

ROCKEFELLER AND OIL

Railroading was not the only industry affected by the drive toward business consolidation. The oil industry became controlled by a business genius named John D. Rockefeller.

In his twenties, Rockefeller had started a partnership in Cleveland, Ohio, selling farm goods. The Civil War boom helped him save several thousand dollars. A visit to the oil fields of Pennsylvania convinced him that this was the place to invest.

Before the mid-1800s, oil had been little more than a nuisance to the farmers of western Pennsylvania. The smelly, greenish ooze ruined their water and splattered over their cows. However, in 1855, Yale chemistry professor Benjamin Silliman, Jr., pointed out that oil could be refined into petroleum and used to fuel lamps and heaters. Suddenly, oil was in demand, but people wondered if enough of it could be taken from the ground.

Then, in 1859, the Seneca Oil Company hired "Colonel" E.L. Drake to drill a well near Titusville, Pennsylvania. With three helpers, Drake drilled the first successful well, which pumped 10 to 35 barrels a day. Other wells were soon pumping. The frantic rush for "black gold" began.

By the end of the Civil War, wildcatters* were as common as prospectors for gold. Oil fields dotted Pennsylvania, Ohio, and West Virginia, and produced 40 million barrels each year. Dozens of companies competed for wells, refineries, and markets.

John D. Rockefeller and his business partners were in the midst of the competition and were determined to succeed. Besides refining his own oil, Rockefeller had his own wagons and barrels built to control its transportation. Soon Rockefeller controlled 20 percent of the oil business in Cleveland, Ohio.

THE RISE OF THE TRUST

In 1870 Rockefeller reorganized his partnership as a corporation—Standard Oil of Ohio—with stock worth $1 million. Because the railroads needed Rockefeller's business, they agreed to give rebates to Standard Oil and to raise shipping rates for rival refineries. Rockefeller then sold his oil for less than

---

*wildcatter: a person who drills for oil in an area not previously known to have oil.

The profits from oil were not wasted on beautifying the oil fields. An 1865 photograph shows the realities of life at Pioneer Run in the Oil Creek district of Pennsylvania.

his rivals could manage, and many of them were forced out of business. By 1872 Standard Oil controlled 25 percent of the nation's oil refining.

In a depression that began in 1873, many of the remaining oil companies failed. With large amounts of cash that he kept on hand, Rockefeller bought the bankrupt companies. Standard was thus expanding in one area of the oil industry—refining. This is called *horizontal integration*.

Then, throughout the 1870s, Rockefeller extended Standard's reach into all areas of the oil industry. Standard bought ships, docks, barrel companies, and even built its own pipelines. This control of each step of production, from start to finish, is called *vertical integration*.

By 1876 Rockefeller could say, "The coal-oil industry belongs to us." By 1879 Standard controlled 90 percent of the refining business and almost all oil transportation. It had nearly exclusive control—a **monopoly**—of the oil industry.

To control efficiently the companies he had acquired, Rockefeller formed the Standard Oil Trust in 1882. The **trust** was a new form of business combination. Stockholders of Standard's companies still owned their stock, but they gave control of it to a single board of trustees, or managers—the Standard Oil Trust. In exchange, stockholders received "trust certificates" that paid them dividends from Standard's profits. The trustees, by controlling all the stock, managed all the corporations.

Voting Trust

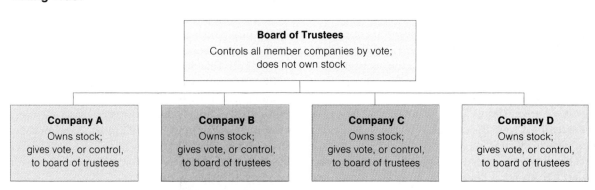

John D. Rockefeller built a huge fortune by skillfully organizing an oil empire. With the same careful planning, he disposed of millions for public benefit.

Rockefeller felt that he had created order out of industrial chaos. In many ways he had. The oil industry operated more efficiently, with lower production costs. Thus Standard could lower selling prices and raise workers' wages.

Other companies saw the advantages of trusts. Trusts were soon formed in the cottonseed oil, linseed oil, whiskey, sugar, and lead industries. By 1904 a government survey revealed that 319 trusts had combined 5,300 companies that had once been independent.

CARNEGIE AND STEEL

While Rockefeller was creating his empire out of oil, an immigrant from Scotland named Andrew Carnegie saw his future in steel. Carnegie began his career in a Pennsylvania cotton mill, earning $1.20 per week. At age 28, he was a manager for the Pennsylvania Railroad. He saved his money and invested it wisely. By the age of 30, he was earning nearly $50,000 a year.

While others were struggling to control the railroad industry, Carnegie saw that railroads needed metal for tracks, locomotives, and bridges. He started a company to build bridges in 1864, and he soon expanded it to include several plants producing iron. During a trip to England, Carnegie saw the Bessemer process for turning soft crude iron into hard steel. So Carnegie moved into steel.

In 1873 Carnegie built the nation's largest Bessemer plant near Pittsburgh—the Homestead Steel Works. Like Rockefeller, Carnegie received railroad rebates and undersold his competitors. During the depression in the 1870s he, too, bought failing companies in a process of horizontal integration.

Carnegie also set out to integrate his company vertically. He bought freighters and railroads to ship his ore, and coal fields to supply his furnaces. He even leased part of the Mesabi Range in Minnesota, which held the country's largest deposit of iron ore. By 1900 the Carnegie Steel Company produced 25 percent of American steel.

MORGAN AND BANKING

Money was the lifeblood of business, and by 1900 investment bankers controlled its flow. They acted as money managers for companies. They sold corporate stocks and bonds, arranged loans, and advised clients how to run their businesses.

John Pierpont Morgan was a magician in the field of investment banking. He bought failing railroads, then combined competing lines into profit-making businesses. He felt that cutthroat competition was wasteful and worked to end it in the railroad industry. Indeed, Morgan had more success in regulating the railroads than the government did. But his determination to end competition alarmed many people, who feared the free enterprise system was in danger. This fear was stirred by the rapid creation of trusts.

It was Morgan who helped to put together many of the huge trusts that would dominate the American economy—General Electric, American Telephone and Telegraph, International Harvester. In 1901 Morgan bought Carnegie's steel company and combined it with steel companies that he already controlled. Thus Morgan created the mightiest trust of them all, the United States Steel Corporation. It owned 1,000 miles (1,600 kilometers) of railroad track, 112 blast furnaces, 78 ore boats, and employed 170,000 workers.

J.P. Morgan was pleased with his photograph by Edward
Steichen. Light reflecting from the chair arm has sometimes
been mistaken for a dagger in Morgan's hand.

No business venture seemed too large for Morgan. His reputation was such that President Cleveland came to him for help in 1895. The United States, in the midst of a depression, needed a loan of $65 million in gold and could not get it from Europe. Morgan made the loan, earned a profit, and helped out the government.

THE GOSPEL OF WEALTH

Morgan, Rockefeller, Carnegie, and many others made fortunes from their businesses. In 1890, according to *The New York Times*, there were over 4,000 millionaires in the United States. Many lived in a world of mansions, yachts, 12-course dinners, and uniformed servants.

Yet some of the rich business leaders felt a need to explain how they had obtained such wealth. In 1900 Andrew Carnegie published a book called *The Gospel of Wealth*. He described the growth of trusts and the wealth they created as "triumphant democracy." He felt justified in earning such wealth, but believed it carried a social responsibility. "The man who dies rich," he wrote, "dies thus disgraced."

After selling his steel interests, Carnegie retired to a castle in Scotland. He spent his last years giving away most of his $400 million fortune "to help those who will help themselves." The money went to build libraries, universities, concert halls, and hospitals. Carnegie also set up foundations to serve the cause of international peace.

SOCIAL DARWINISM

Rockefeller, too, found a philosophy to explain his success: "The growth of a large business is merely a survival of the fittest. . . ." The notion of the "survival of the fittest" was taken from the writing of Charles Darwin, an English naturalist. Darwin believed that animals that were adapted to their environment survived, while those that were not adapted died. The English philosopher Herbert Spencer applied Darwin's theory to society and business.

The philosophy of *Social Darwinism* soon took root in the United States. Social Darwinists believed that companies struggled for survival in the economic world and that government should not tamper with this natural process. In the struggle for survival, the fittest business leaders would survive and would improve society.

Social Darwinism fit well with another principle popular throughout the 1800s—**laissez-faire** (LEHS-ay FEHR) economics. A great number of people, including many in government, believed that businesses should be run without government regulation or control. Government regulation, they thought, would hinder the natural laws of supply and demand.

THE SHERMAN ANTITRUST ACT

Many Americans argued against the consolidation that led to monopoly. The free enterprise system, they said, was endangered by the lack of competition. These people blamed corporate leaders—the "captains of industry"—for business abuses and economic troubles. In 1869 editor E.L. Godkin compared Cornelius Vanderbilt to "the medieval baron" who took money from everyone on the manor. Soon critics were calling the fast-rising business leaders "robber barons."

By the 1880s people were crying out for the government to step in and regulate business. Their

Holding Company

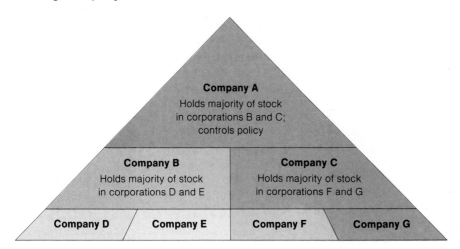

cries against the trusts awoke the political parties in the election year of 1888.

Both Republicans and Democrats suddenly opposed trusts. Outgoing president Grover Cleveland said people were being "trampled to death beneath [the] iron heel" of trusts. Newly elected president Benjamin Harrison said trusts were "dangerous conspiracies against the public good."

In this atmosphere, Congress passed the Sherman Antitrust Act in 1890. The law declared that any business combination, including trusts, operating "in restraint of trade" was illegal. The vague wording of the law, however, made it difficult to enforce.

The Sherman Antitrust Act was weakened in 1895 by a Supreme Court ruling in *United States* v. *E.C. Knight Company*, a case against the sugar trust. The trust, said the Court, had a monopoly only on the production of sugar. Because it did not control the shipping of sugar across state lines, it therefore did not restrain trade.

Meanwhile, companies that were ordered to break up their trusts were shifting to a new form of business combination—the **holding company**. The first holding company was set up in New Jersey in 1889. Whereas a trust controlled but did not own stock in other companies, a holding company owned stock in other corporations. A holding company held enough stock to control the policies of its flock of companies as effectively as did the trust.

Although the Sherman Antitrust Act and the earlier Interstate Commerce Act proved ineffective,

they signaled a new role for government. People were now asking government to set up rules for business and the economy. Still, it would be years before government regulation was effective.

SECTION REVIEW

1. Identify the following: William Kelly, Henry Bessemer, George M. Pullman, George Westinghouse, Gustavus F. Swift, Philip D. Armour, Benjamin Silliman, Jr., Herbert Spencer.

2. Define the following: corporation, consolidation, horizontal integration, vertical integration, trust, holding company, Social Darwinism, laissez-faire.

3. (a) Explain the Bessemer process. (b) How did it affect railroads?

4. Why were corporations formed?

5. Describe each of these practices: rate wars, the giving of rebates, the forming of pools.

6. What were the advantages of consolidation? The disadvantages?

7. (a) Why did Congress pass the Interstate Commerce Act? (b) How effective was it?

8. Why did John D. Rockefeller combine his oil companies in a trust?

9. Trace Andrew Carnegie's career from mill worker to leader in the steel industry.

10. (a) Why did Congress pass the Sherman Antitrust Act? (b) What new role for government did its passage signal?

THE IMMIGRANTS

READ TO FIND OUT

—when the largest tide of immigration began.

—what nations the new immigrants came from.

—what problems the immigrants faced.

—why people immigrated from China.

—what problems Chinese immigrants faced.

—why people immigrated from Japan.

—how Congress tried to limit immigration.

America began as a nation of immigrants, and has remained so. The first Americans—the Indians—immigrated from Asia. Some Americans immigrated from lands to the south of the United States. Other Americans have the shadow of an ancestor standing on a shore or on a dock in New York, San Francisco, Charleston, or some other port of entry.

WAVES OF IMMIGRATION

Immigration to the United States came in waves that peaked in different periods. In the colonial period, most newcomers were English. Of course, many were German, Dutch, Swedish, French, and of other European nationalities. Also, thousands of blacks from Africa were brought to the colonies as servants and slaves. On the whole, however, the language, customs, and political system of the English had strongly influenced America.

The 1830s and 1840s saw a second wave of immigration to the United States. Most of these newcomers were from northern European countries such as Ireland, England, Germany, and Scandinavia. Some Swiss, French, and a few Chinese also came at this time.

Beginning in the early 1880s, the largest tide of immigration began. During the next 20 years, almost 9 million people set foot on American soil for the first time. The 20 years after that brought 14.5 million more people. Some of these immigrants came from Mexico, China, and Japan, but most were from southern and eastern Europe.

These immigrants came to the United States for the same reasons earlier groups had come. They were fleeing poverty, drought, high taxes, persecution, or a scarcity of jobs. They were seeking opportunity in a land, wrote a Polish girl, that had "plenty for all."

NEW IMMIGRANTS

The Italians made up a majority of the newcomers. Most were fleeing southern Italy, which was stricken by cholera epidemics, drought, and a poor economy. Many Italians planned to stay in the United States only long enough to earn what would be a fortune back home. Some succeeded and returned home, and some changed their minds and stayed in the United States.

Italians settled mainly in the Northeast and Pennsylvania, and in lesser numbers throughout the rest of the country. Entire villages left Italy and formed their own communities in the United States. Many Italians worked in industry and mining. On the east and west coasts they farmed fruits and vegetables.

A family of Italian immigrants arrives in New York sometime around 1900. The parents and children seem to be absorbed with what lies beyond the camera's eye.

Origin of Immigrants to the United States   1840–1910

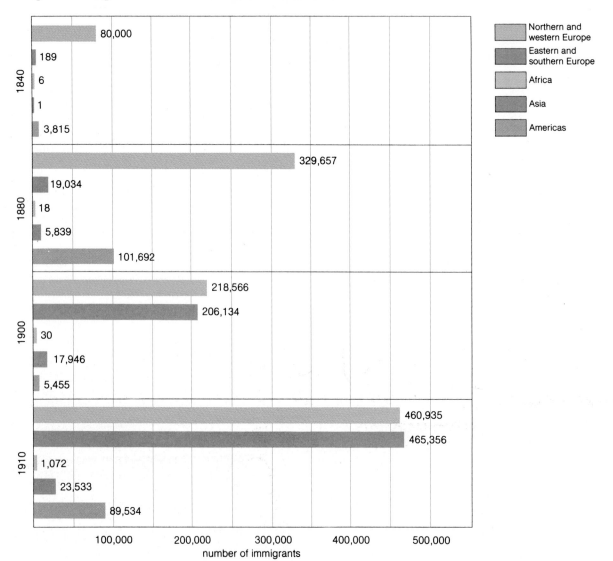

Legend:
- Northern and western Europe
- Eastern and southern Europe
- Africa
- Asia
- Americas

1840
- 80,000
- 189
- 6
- 1
- 3,815

1880
- 329,657
- 19,034
- 18
- 5,839
- 101,692

1900
- 218,566
- 206,134
- 30
- 17,946
- 5,455

1910
- 460,935
- 465,356
- 1,072
- 23,533
- 89,534

number of immigrants

The Jews formed the second-largest group of immigrants. In colonial times many had come from Portugal and Spain, and in the 1830s from Germany. Now Jews came mainly from Slavic countries like Russia and Poland. Most left home to escape religious persecution and pogroms.*

Other immigrants from Slavic countries—Russians, Poles, Serbs, Slovaks, Croations, Czechs—made up the third-largest group. Like the Italians,

many planned only a temporary stay. The Slavic peoples clustered in the mining and industrial centers of the Midwest and Northeast. More Slavs settled in Pennsylvania than in any other state, finding work in the iron, steel, and coal industries.

Still more groups—Hungarians, Spanish, Dutch, Portuguese, Lithuanians, and Greeks—came in lesser numbers. Many Greeks flocked to the big cities and struggled to start their own businesses. Other Greeks scattered throughout the nation, herding sheep in the Rockies or working mines and mills in Wyoming.

* pogrom: organized persecution and massacre of a minority group.

MARY ANTIN
THE PROMISED LAND

In May 1894 a large-eyed, painfully thin thirteen-year-old girl named Mary Antin arrived in Boston harbor on a packed immigrant ship. She and her family had come from Russia, where as Jews they had led a desperate hand-to-mouth life in a small village. The six-week rail and steamship journey to the United States had also been hard. "We emigrants were herded at the stations, packed in the cars, and driven from place to place like cattle," Mary remembered.

The family settled in a crowded Boston slum. Yet to Mary everything seemed beautiful. She was dazzled by the tall brick buildings, the paved streets, the lights, and even a "queer, slippery kind of fruit" called a banana.

The best thing, however, was school. In Russia schools were open only to the rich and well born.

Few Jewish boys and no girls could attend. In the United States, however, "education was free." To Mary's father it was "the essence of American opportunity, the treasure that no thief could touch, not even misfortune or poverty. It was the one thing that he was able to promise us . . . surer, safer than bread or shelter."

Because she spoke no English, Mary was put in first grade. But she quickly skipped ahead. Soon she was writing so well that her poetry was published in a Boston newspaper. Later she attended college, married, and became a writer. In 1912 she wrote *The Promised Land*, which described her experiences as a young immigrant. A bestseller, the book reaffirmed that the United States was indeed a land of freedom and opportunity. It showed that for at least one small girl, the promise had come true.

Mary Antin was committed to defending immigration. She said that immigrants were not "refuse"; rather, they were the "sinew and bone of all the nations."

All immigrants had to be processed at their port of entry. This group arrived in 1907. There is a solemn look on many faces as the immigrants wait their turn.

Not all the new immigrants were from Europe. From the Middle East came Armenians, Syrians, and Lebanese. Mexicans crossed the United States border into the Southwest, finding work in towns and cotton fields. Chinese and Japanese came to California and worked in mines, on farms, and on construction crews.

Most of the newcomers settled in towns and cities, where there were industries and jobs. By 1900 New York City had a foreign-born population of 1,260,924, more than a third of its total population. Chicago had more Germans than any German city except Hamburg and Berlin, and more Swedish than any Swedish city except Stockholm. Smaller American towns had even larger percentages of foreign-born residents. In Lawrence, Massachusetts, most of the textile workers were immigrants. Among these there were people of 25 nationalities who spoke 40 different languages.

IMMIGRANT LIFE

Most immigrants tried to bring some of their old world to their new home. People who spoke the same language and followed the same customs were naturally drawn together. City neighborhoods were known by names such as Little Italy, Second Warsaw, and Chinatown. The sculptor Jacob Epstein recalled growing up as the son of Jewish immigrants in New York City in the 1880s:

> My earliest recollections are of the teeming East Side where I was born. This Hester Street and its surrounding streets were the most densely populated of any city on earth. And, looking back on it, I realize what I owe to its unique and crowded humanity. Its swarms of Russians, Poles, Italians, Greeks, and Chinese lived as much in the streets as in the crowded tenements. And the sights, sounds, and smells had the vividness and sharp impact of an Oriental city.

Many immigrants saw education as the key to their children's future success. Public schools operated day and night in many cities, giving lessons in English and citizenship to immigrants and their children. Often, as the children learned English, they tried to escape their parents' language and old-country customs. Most struggled to be as American as possible.

Some immigrants resented this process of *assimilation*, of being absorbed into American culture. They saw schooling as a threat to their religion and customs. They thought their children would be better off learning skills on the job—and keeping to the old ways. Still, the old and the new, the foreign and the American steadily mixed.

George Luks frequently roamed the Lower East Side of Manhattan. "Hester Street," 1905, is his bold and realistic painting of the busy marketplace.

These Jewish immigrant women found employment in a clothing factory. Every dollar they earned in the long hours of labor helped toward starting anew in the United States.

NATIVIST FEELINGS

Becoming American was difficult for the latest immigrants. Their customs were not northern and western European customs, which had become the "American way."

Many of these immigrants were Catholics and Jews and met religious prejudice. Their languages, clothing, and food seemed strange to Americans. Many also came from countries without democratic governments, where ideas like **socialism, communist,** and *anarchism* were beginning to spread.

Communists wanted society as a whole, rather than individuals, to own property, and wanted to give everyone an equal share of goods. Socialism was a stage between **capitalism,** America's system in which property was privately owned, and communism. Many socialists wanted government to own major industries. And anarchists wanted to do away with government entirely. Some immigrants came to the United States with these ideas, and many Americans began to fear that their system of government was in danger.

In addition, many immigrants arrived during harsh depression years in the 1870s, 1880s, and 1890s. Wages were low, and workers were on strike. Immigrants who were unskilled, who had spent their last money on passage to America, needed jobs quickly. They accepted lower wages than other workers or even accepted jobs of workers on strike.

American workers fiercely resented such competition. And as hard times lengthened, nativism—the practice of favoring the native-born—once more grew strong.

IMMIGRANTS FROM CHINA

The western gateway into the United States was Angel Island in San Francisco Bay. Beginning in 1849, thousands of Chinese entered California through the strait known as the Golden Gate.

These Chinese were young men seeking fortunes in California's "golden hills," or simply jobs in the gold rush camps. They came from a wounded China, where crops were failing and a civil war raged. Most Chinese planned only a temporary stay in America. They promised their families they would work hard, send money home, and eventually return.

From the first they were set apart by their appearance and customs, and they met prejudice. Those who found gold had to pay an annual miners' tax, levied only on foreigners. In some places Chinese were not even allowed to stake claims. Most Chinese ended up working in mining camps, cooking, cutting hair, and washing clothes.

By 1860, the Chinese were a vital part of the labor force in California's mining, construction, agriculture, clothing, and fishing industries. When the railroad boom began in the 1860s, the Chinese filled the work crews. The Central Pacific Railroad, in its race to meet the Union Pacific in Utah, hired about 10,000 Chinese laborers.

Some Chinese moved eastward to other mining areas, and to jobs in eastern cities. In Chicago and New York, as in San Francisco, they formed Chinatowns—pockets of home in a strange land.

OPPOSITION TO CHINESE IMMIGRATION

By the end of the 1860s the Chinese population in California had reached 75,000. Many Chinese had never earned enough to return home, and their communities were becoming permanent. Chinese had become owners of factories, laundries, hotels, and restaurants. "This portion of our pop-

Chinese immigrants preserved their language and customary diet, dress, and celebrations. A Chinese parade in Los Angeles includes the traditional dragon.

ulation," a newspaper stated, "is a pattern for sobriety, order and obedience to laws, not only to other foreign residents, but to Americans themselves."

However, in 1873 a depression hurt the nation's economy. It lasted through the decade. Americans, out of work or laboring for lowered wages, no longer welcomed workers from China. But still they came, at the rate of about 4,000 per year.

The Workingmen's Party of California was formed in 1877 out of the anger of jobless workers. Its leader, Denis Kearney, raged that the Chinese were stealing jobs from whites.

By July 1877 anti-Chinese feelings were strong. One night, groups of unemployed workers stormed through San Francisco's Chinatown. They wrecked stores and homes, and soon Chinatown was burning. The rioting lasted for three days.

Anti-Chinese violence spread to other places. In 1878 all the Chinese in Truckee, California, were driven from the town. And in 1885, the worst rioting took place in Rock Springs, Wyoming, where 28 Chinese were killed.

LIMITING IMMIGRATION

From the Golden Gate to Ellis Island, many towns and cities echoed with nativist voices. Politicians heard, and the federal government responded. Denis Kearney's Workingmen's Party had the first

success when Congress passed the Chinese Exclusion Act in 1882. This act banned the immigration of Chinese workers for ten years. Later laws renewed the ban and even prohibited the return of Chinese who had gone home for a visit.

However, even as the Chinese were excluded, Japanese immigrants were allowed to enter the United States. California farmers depended heavily on the Chinese for farm labor. Cut off from that labor source, farmers demanded that the government admit Japanese workers. The Japanese came, many with their families, to work the farms. Like the Chinese, they also worked in mines and on railroads. By 1900 there were 24,000 Japanese in the country.

Old fears and prejudices eventually erupted against the Japanese, too. In 1905 the Japanese Exclusion League was formed. The following year San Francisco's school board proposed to place Japanese and Chinese students in a school separate from other children. The Japanese government protested, and President Theodore Roosevelt became involved. He worked out the "Gentlemen's Agreement" with Japan in 1908. Japan agreed not to issue passports to laborers, unless they were joining a family already in the United States.

Not all regulations were directed against Asians. After the Chinese Exclusion Act, there was a flurry of restrictions passed against all immigrant groups.

IMMIGRATION DEBATE IN CONGRESS

In March 1896 Henry Cabot Lodge of Massachusetts addressed the Senate. Lodge's subject was immigration. He was concerned about the number of immigrants arriving from southern and eastern Europe. Lodge believed that the newcomers were threatening America's traditional way of life. "Their thoughts and their beliefs . . . are wholly alien to ours," he claimed. Moreover, he argued, they were taking jobs away from American workers.

To stop the flood of immigration, Lodge had a solution. Immigrants would have to pass a literacy test to prove that they could read and write either in their own language or in English. Since more northern than southern European immigrants were literate, such a test would "bear most heavily upon Italians, Russians, Poles, Hungarians, Greeks, and Asiatics."

From the first days of the Republic, most Americans had welcomed immigrants. By the time Lodge spoke in 1896, however, there were problems. Good frontier land had become scarce. Poverty spread as immigrants crowded into eastern cities. Some Americans also blamed growing troubles between workers and management on immigrants who brought radical ideas from Europe. Then, in 1893, a depression gripped the nation. No longer were there jobs or land for all.

Lodge's speech touched off a great debate on immigration. Representative Charles Buck of Louisiana disagreed with Lodge. An immigrant himself, Buck had come from Germany with his family when he was eleven years old. "This country . . . has grown great by absorbing more than 40 million foreigners," he said. "We are big enough to take in all who want to come."

Representative Rowland Mahany of New York, an Irish immigrant, supported Buck. "I would like to ask how many there are upon the floor of this House," he said to fellow members of Congress, "whose ancestors would have been admitted to this Republic" if there had been a literacy test. Senator Lodge should not try to limit immigrants to people like himself, Mahany added. Representative Samuel McCall of Massachusetts replied that the United States was not "an international soup kitchen for the benefit, primarily, of the rest of the world."

When the Lodge literacy bill was put to a vote in the House, it passed by a large majority. Although most members of Congress did not want to stop all immigration, they were alarmed about slums, labor unrest, and the depression. Soon afterward the Senate approved the bill.

When the bill reached the White House, however, Grover Cleveland vetoed it. Until now, he said, Americans "have encouraged those coming from foreign countries to cast their lot with us and join in the development of our vast domain, securing in return a share in the blessings of American citizenship." This "generous and free-handed" immigration policy has worked for a hundred years, he declared. It has made the nation strong and prosperous.

Meanwhile, the depression had lifted. Suddenly there were jobs for all. Argument over immigration was forgotten.

Unlimited immigration continued until the end of the First World War, when a literacy bill became law. By 1924 restrictions had been passed that strongly favored northern European immigrants.

1. Why did Lodge and his supporters want to restrict immigration?

2. What reasons did Buck, Mahany, and Cleveland give in favor of open immigration?

3. Do you think the United States today should admit all who want to enter? Why or why not? If you think there should be restrictions, what should they be?

To keep jobs open for Americans, Congress passed the Contract Labor Act of 1885. This barred entry to immigrants whose passage had been paid by American employers. In 1891 Congress passed a law allowing immigrants who were illegally in the country to be deported, or expelled from the country. And a series of regulations made it harder for immigrants to enter the country.

More antiforeign groups were formed. The American Protective Association was launched in 1887 to protest against Catholic and southern and eastern European immigrants. The Immigration Restriction League was formed in the mid-1890s and worked for a literacy test that would ban immigrants who could not read or write. Such a bill passed Congress and was vetoed by presidents four times, but it finally became law in 1917.

At the height of this nativist feeling, in 1886, workers in New York City's harbor put in place the last bronze sections of the Statue of Liberty. The statue became a symbol of hope for immigrants as they approached the United States. On the base would later be carved the words of Emma Lazarus:

Give me your tired, your poor,
Your huddled masses yearning to breathe free,
The wretched refuse of your teeming shore.
Send these, the homeless, tempest-tossed to me:
I lift my lamp beside the golden door!

Stretching into America's future, as it stretched into the past, was a tide of immigrants seeking the golden door.

SECTION REVIEW

1. Identify the following: Jacob Epstein, Denis Kearney, Emma Lazarus.

2. (a) From 1880 to 1900 how many immigrants came to the United States? (b) For what reasons did these immigrants come?

3. (a) Name the three largest groups of immigrants from Europe. (b) Name four other groups of immigrants, and tell in what areas they settled.

4. Where did most immigrants settle? Why?

5. Why did nativism grow strong as the depression lengthened?

6. (a) Why did Chinese and Japanese immigrants come to the United States? (b) What kinds of work did they do?

7. Why was the Workingmen's Party of California formed?

8. Tell the purpose for each of the following: the Chinese Exclusion Act, the "Gentlemen's Agreement" with Japan, the Contract Labor Act, the American Protective Association, the Immigration Restriction League.

THE CITIES

READ TO FIND OUT

— how improved transportation changed cities and the way people lived.

— how the inventions of Edison, Westinghouse, and Bell changed cities and city life.

— what problems resulted from the rapid growth of cities.

— how political machines helped people but also lead to corruption.

— how settlement workers, churches, and writers tried to improve conditions in the cities.

Immigrants were not the only people who poured into American cities in the 1880s and 1890s. Many farmers abandoned plow and soil for the jobs and excitement of the cities. One young farmer was thrilled to go "from the farm to a new and shining world, a town world where circuses, baseball games, and county fairs were events of almost daily occurrence." A few years later he moved on to a large city, and saw another side of that shining world:

With all my pay in my pocket, and my trunk checked, I took the train to Chicago. I shall never forget the feeling of dismay with which, an hour later, I perceived from the car window a huge smoke-cloud, which embraced the whole eastern horizon . . . this I was told, was the soaring banner of the great and gloomy inland metropolis.

That smoke cloud was also a signpost of industry. Cities thrived on industry, and their populations swelled as people turned to work in industry. By the late 1880s many cities sprawled into **metropolises**, huge urban centers of business and industry.

Cities in key locations grew fastest. There were port cities like San Francisco, New York, and New Orleans, river cities like Pittsburgh and St. Louis, and railroad hubs like Chicago and Memphis. All were crossroads at which the flow of people and goods and money met.

By 1890 one person in three lived in cities of more than 8,000 people. And over 80 percent of all city dwellers lived in the Northeast and Midwest. Chicago, the world's grain and cattle market, had a population of 300,000 in 1870. The next year, more than half of the city's buildings were destroyed by fire and had to be rebuilt. Twenty years later, Chicago's population passed a million, making it the second largest city in the country.

Cities were booming all over the United States. Mark Twain visited some cities along the Mississippi River in 1882. He reported that Minneapolis and St. Paul were alive with "newness, briskness, swift progress, wealth, intelligence . . . and general slash and go and energy." Perhaps that was the lure of the cities.

The splendor of New York is caught in "Fifth Avenue at Twilight" by Birge Harrison. Elevators and iron girders made the soaring skyscrapers possible.

INVENTIONS AND CITY LIFE

Much of the energy came from inventions. Some inventions solved existing problems, and some provided new and better ways of doing things. But they always changed the way people lived.

Most American cities had grown as "walking cities," small enough to cover on foot from one side to the other. As transportation improved, city borders expanded. By 1880 horse-drawn streetcars carried people beyond the old city limits. Then, in 1887, Frank J. Sprague, building on the ideas of European inventors, installed a system of electric streetcars run on overhead trolley lines in Richmond, Virginia.

Within 3 years, electric streetcars hummed in 51 cities. Americans could live farther and farther from their places of work. Cities spread outward, engulfing smaller towns.

Each new idea that succeeded spurred the growth of cities by creating new jobs, services, or products. A rich source of ideas was Thomas Alva Edison, who applied for over a thousand patents. Edison invented the phonograph and the motion picture camera, and built America's first research laboratory in Menlo Park, New Jersey.

The "Wizard of Menlo Park" vowed to produce "a minor invention every ten days and a big thing every six months or so," and he did. Edison made the first successful electric light bulb in 1879. Then he took the first steps in bringing electricity to all of the United States. Out of his laboratory came sockets for the light bulbs, switches, fuse boxes, underground cables, and the dynamo to produce electricity.

ELECTRICITY AND THE TELEPHONE

In 1882 Edison built the nation's first central power station in New York City. Soon other cities had stations—even the 600 citizens of Sheridan, Wyoming, had electric lights. But Edison's electrical system, using direct current, could bring power only to nearby places. Then George Westinghouse, who had invented air brakes for railroads, introduced alternating current. Alternating current was a practical and inexpensive way to send electricity over long distances. By 1900 Westinghouse's electrical system was lighting 25 million electric bulbs.

Another inventor changed the way that people communicated. In 1876 Alexander Graham Bell invented the telephone. It was one of the curiosities at the Centennial Exposition that year. Europeans scoffed at this "electrical toy," but American cities had telephone service by 1880. By the end of the century, a giant web of telephone wires connected the nation's cities.

Like Sprague's trolley and Edison's light bulb, Bell's telephone created a new industry. Occupations that had not existed a few years earlier—operators, assemblers, installers—employed thousands.

The inventions not only created jobs and wealth, but they also added to the magic of city life. One visitor to Chicago described the amazing Otis elevator, which serviced the new tall buildings called skyscrapers:

> The slow-going stranger . . . [is] loaded into one of those . . . baskets . . . and the next instant . . . up goes the whole load as a feather is caught up by a gale. The descent is more simple. Something lets go, and you fall from ten to twenty stories as it happens.

CITY PROBLEMS

The cities' grand magic—skyscrapers, electric lights, telephones—were usually out of reach of the poor. These people crowded closer and closer together in the inner cities.

The noise, smoke, and dirt of the factories, railroads, shipyards, and warehouses made the inner cities undesirable places to live. As workers earned enough to escape these conditions, they abandoned the area and moved away from the city center. Into the blighted, run-down city neighborhoods poured immigrants and Americans fleeing rural poverty. They had to live closer to the docks, factories, and mills where they hoped to find work.

Almost every foot of ground in these neighborhoods was taken for living space. Thousands of people found shelter in ramshackle houses, subdivided into one room per family. Most lived in *tenements*, new housing hastily constructed to relieve the housing shortage. Tenements were usually wood buildings four to six stories high. Many were built cheaply and lacked safety or comfort.

In 1905 trolley cars turned around where Front Street met Market Street in San Francisco. About a year after W.N. Jennings made this print, the whole business district was destroyed. An earthquake, fire, and dynamite used to control the fire left a pile of ruins.

In pictures as well as words, Jacob Riis recorded the grim sights of tenement life. The photograph of Baxter Street Court shows a "gap between dingy brick walls."

To stay alive, desperately poor immigrant families used all available hands. A three-year-old child helps her family make artificial wreaths to sell.

Good sanitation was impossible for most tenement occupants. Many tenements had no water, except perhaps a faucet in the yard. Garbage that piled up rotted in boxes on the streets. Sewage ran in the gutters. In the late 1870s a charity worker visited a tenement in New York:

> This building is six stories high. Its middle rooms throughout receive almost no daylight. In one room servant girls out of employment find board at 10 cents per night. On the fourth floor in a rear room lives a widow, who takes five boarders. On the sixth floor lives a laborer; he has a wife and four children. . . . In this house live 90 persons; of these 17 are men, 36 women, and 37 children.

Many tenements were even worse. Some became extensions of the factory. In crowded rooms men, women, and children worked at sewing clothes or rolling cigars.

Sewage dumped in rivers, piles of garbage, and poor water supplies all bred diseases such as typhoid and cholera. Disease spread most quickly in crowded tenements. Because of unsanitary conditions, claimed an 1882 report, one half of the children born in Chicago died before reaching five years of age.

Cities, which had grown with little planning, had to find a way to deal with these problems. At great expense, many cities began building sewage systems and water treatment plants and setting up garbage disposal. Boston spent 30 percent of the city's funds on such projects between the 1870s and 1890s. Over the years, most cities did make progress. By 1898, for example, about 3,500 cities had public water works.

POLITICAL MACHINES

As cities tried to improve services, they were in a constant race with the influx of people. Often, officials simply could not keep up with the demand for help. In many cities **political machines** formed a link between the people and the city government.

A political machine was run by a "ring" of leaders headed by the "boss." Ring members sel-

Before reforms were effected, children as young as six sold papers on the street. This child probably worried daily about unsold papers on which he lost money to the dealer.

dom were elected officials. Instead, they gained power by exchanging favors with officials. City officials gave the machine the right to hand out city jobs, contracts, and political favors. In return, the machine delivered votes to the officials. Machine workers helped people, especially immigrants, who gratefully voted as the machine directed.

In poor neighborhoods, one observer noted, "souls and bodies were saved by the parish priest, the family doctor, and the local political [machine worker]." A machine worker listened to neighbors' problems. A landlord refused to heat a tenement, for example. The worker then made the rounds of city hall. Within days, there would be action, and the landlord would find a way to fix the heating.

Although this give-and-take system helped people, it also bred corruption. Often the machine could be bribed by job seekers, budding politicians, and companies who wanted contracts. And the machine sometimes delivered phony votes. One reporter wrote of voting lists with the names of "dead dogs, children, and non-existent persons."

The most well-known machine was in New York City. Between 1869 and 1871 it was run by boss William Tweed. The Tweed Ring plundered the city treasury of at least $75 million, perhaps more. Then newspapers aroused the public, and reform politicians were elected. In 1871 Tweed and many of the ring were arrested.

Still, machine politics remained in New York and other cities. St. Louis was run by the Butler Ring, Minneapolis by the Ames Ring, and Philadelphia by the Gas Ring. And, claimed one writer, "every little municipality in our whole land has to struggle with some 'boss' who has learned his trade or taken his cue from successful rascals in our larger towns."

HELP FOR THE CITIES

In the 1880s and 1890s reformers began to tackle both the political and social problems of the cities. In 1887 a young American woman named Jane Addams traveled to London and found slums that rivaled those in the United States. In the midst of the slums she found Toynbee Hall, a community center where the poor came for schooling, child care, and various forms of aid.

When she returned home, Addams and a friend named Ellen Starr decided to conduct their own "Toynbee Hall experiment." They bought an old building in Chicago, called it Hull House, and in 1889 opened their settlement house. With other volunteers, mostly well-educated young women, they set to work. "From the first," Addams wrote, "it was understood that we were ready to perform the humblest neighborhood services. We were asked to wash new-born babies, and to prepare the dead for burial, to nurse the sick, and to 'mind the children.'"

The settlement workers tried to improve the lives of the poor. They taught classes in English, health, and nutrition. They helped the poor to deal with city agencies. Jane Addams even became a neighborhood garbage inspector and convinced the city to improve service. By 1895 there were 50 settlement houses in major cities in the United States.

Churches also tried to help the poor. Protestant ministers dedicated themselves to the Social Gospel—a movement for the improvement of working and living conditions in the slums. Catholic clergy and Jewish synagogues set up schools, hospitals, and welfare agencies. The Salvation Army, established in 1879 to bring people back to Christianity, joined in the welfare work. By the late 1880s it was running soup kitchens, employment agencies, and rooming houses for the poor.

However, these early efforts showed reformers that they needed government on their side to create lasting change. Jane Addams had learned through her work at Hull House that charity work was "totally inadequate to deal with the vast numbers of the city's disinherited."

In 1890 Jacob Riis, a New York reporter, campaigned for the poor in his book *How the Other Half Lives*. Riis described a tenement:

> This gap between dingy brick walls is the yard. That strip of smoke-colored sky up there is the heaven of these people. . . . What sort of an answer, do you think, would these tenement house dwellers give to the question, "Is life worth living?"

Riis stirred up the public, including a New York politician named Theodore Roosevelt. Roosevelt sent Riis a note: "I have your book and I have come to help." Eight years later Roosevelt became governor of New York and appointed a tenement house commission. Its report led to a law in 1901 that set strict building codes for tenements. In the years that followed, many more people would come to help.

SECTION REVIEW

1. Identify the following: Frank J. Sprague, Thomas Alva Edison, George Westinghouse, Alexander Graham Bell, William Tweed, Jane Addams, Jacob Riis.

2. Tell what effect each of these inventions had on cities and city life: electric streetcars, the central power station, alternating current, the telephone, the Otis elevator.

3. Why did many cities begin building sewage systems and water treatment plants and setting up garbage disposal?

4. (a) What was a political machine? (b) How did it form a link between the people and the city government? (c) How did political machines also breed corruption?

5. (a) What did Jane Addams and Ellen Starr do to improve the lives of the poor? (b) How did church groups help? (c) How did Jacob Riis help?

Jane Addams believed in finding the causes of crime and poverty. In recognition of her social work, she received the Nobel peace prize in 1931.

To avoid the dirty, crowded streets, tenement dwellers often crossed the rooftops. A settlement house nurse takes this route as she brings help to the poor.

CHAPTER SURVEY

SUMMARY

Between 1865 and 1890 industry grew rapidly. Increased steel output and improvements in railroads aided the spread of manufacturing. Machines took over tasks once done by hand. Many businesses formed corporations to raise the large sums of money needed for expansion or investment. Then, consolidation took place in some industries—notably in railroads, oil, and steel.

Cornelius Vanderbilt consolidated companies in the railroad industry. John D. Rockefeller combined his oil companies in a trust. Andrew Carnegie amassed a fortune in the steel industry. Banker John Pierpont Morgan formed huge trusts in several industries. As consolidation led to monopoly—the elimination of competition—many Americans began to argue for government regulation of business. In 1890 Congress passed the Sherman Antitrust Act.

The workers who, to a large extent, made possible the growth of industry were immigrants. From the early 1880s to the early 1900s—a twenty-year period—almost 9 million immigrants came to the United States. The newcomers were mainly from southern and eastern Europe. As immigration increased and the economy underwent problems, nativist feelings arose. Attempts were made to limit immigration.

On the West Coast, Chinese immigrants arrived by the thousands. The Chinese worked in California's mining, construction, agriculture, clothing, and fishing industries. The Japanese immigrated to the West Coast, too, and worked in similar jobs, particularly in agriculture. Nativist feelings arose against these immigrants, too, and attempts were made to limit immigration.

As cities grew, inventions changed people's lives. In the inner cities, however, the poor faced crowded living conditions and lack of sanitation. A new kind of organization, the political machine, helped the poor because of its connection with city government. In time, however, the machines themselves led to corruption. Reformers—settlement workers, clergy, and writers—began working to improve conditions in the cities and to stir public interest in reform.

CHAPTER REVIEW

1. Describe the following technological developments and their effects. (a) Bessemer's process in the steel industry (b) the inventions of Pullman, Westinghouse, Swift, and Armour in railroads (c) Silliman's contribution in oil (d) Sprague's streetcars (e) Edison's work in electricity

2. Between 1865 and 1890, what was occurring in industry in the South? In California? In the Midwest and Northeast?

3. (a) Explain how each of the following led to consolidation: horizontal integration, vertical integration, trusts, holding companies. (b) What effects did consolidation have on competition? Give a detailed answer.

4. Compare the development of John D. Rockefeller's Standard Oil Company with that of Carnegie's steel company. Note the percentage of the industries controlled, the structures of the two corporations, and methods of controlling competition.

5. J.P. Morgan was not an industrialist but a banker. Describe how his banking activities affected the industry of the period. How did Morgan's attitudes toward competition compare with those of Carnegie and Rockefeller?

6. How were the philosophies of Social Darwinism and laissez-faire different from the ideas of those people who supported the Sherman Antitrust Act?

7. Summarize the nature of the first and second waves of immigration that occurred before the Civil War. How did these first two waves differ from the great tide of immigration that began in the 1880s? List the major groups in each period.

8. (a) List factors that contributed to anti-immigrant feelings. (b) Describe actions taken or laws passed to restrict, or limit, immigration.

9. (a) Summarize the history of Chinese immigration to this country between 1849 and 1882. Include the numbers of people that came, where they settled and what kinds of work they did, and what actions were taken for or against them. (b) Summarize the history of Japanese

immigration from the 1880s to 1908. Include the same points covered in your summary of Chinese immigration.

10. Compare a boom town of the western plains with an industrial city in the Northeast or Midwest around 1890.

ISSUES AND IDEAS

1. Carnegie, Rockefeller, and Morgan argued that competition in industry was wasteful. They believed that consolidated companies were more efficient than numerous small, competing companies in the same industry. As the owner of a small business, what might have been your point of view on this subject?

2. The United States has often been called a "melting pot." This means that as different immigrant groups came to this country they gradually became assimilated into the existing culture. On the other hand, the country has been described as "pluralistic." This means that various ethnic groups live side by side and retain their individual cultures. Which condition do you think was generally true in the period between 1870 and 1900? Which condition do you think is generally true today? Is one or the other—a melting pot or a pluralistic society—preferable? Defend your opinion.

SKILLS WORKSHOP

1. *Diagrams.* Standard Oil and Carnegie Steel both had vertical and horizontal integration. Set up two diagrams side by side that show the similarities in the way these two corporations were organized. Include each aspect of the industry that was controlled by these giant trusts.

2. *Graphs.* Look at the line graph on page 762 of the Resource Center to analyze the following trends. (a) In what decades was immigration greatest? (b) In the seven peak years shown, how many people were immigrating? (c) Immigration from four continents is shown—Europe, Asia, South America, and North America (Canada). Do you see any trends in the pattern of people immigrating from these four continents?

PAST AND PRESENT

1. The Sherman Antitrust Act was an early attempt by the government to regulate business. Today the government has regulatory powers over many industries. Government regulation of industry is the subject of constant debate. Choose a local industry, and determine to what extent it is regulated by government. Do you agree or disagree with this regulation? Defend your answer.

2. How does your community compare with an industrial city of 1890? Compare the living conditions, the methods of transportation and communication, the political system, and the social services.

In an Edward Kemble cartoon, the vulture trusts thrive on a Senate whose members could be bought. Both trusts and senate appointments by state legislatures were destined for change.

CHAPTER 16

THE RESPONSE TO INDUSTRIALIZATION

1865–1900

WORKERS ORGANIZE
THE PLIGHT OF THE FARMERS
THE POPULISTS

Bessie Van Vorst was a writer from the upper class who wanted to find out what life was like for the factory woman. Around 1900, she entered the world of the American worker:

"Before leaving New York I assumed my disguise. . . . With the aid of coarse woolen garments, a shabby felt sailor hat, a cheap piece of fur, a knitted shawl and gloves I am transformed into a working girl of the ordinary type. . . . I am going over now into the world of the unfortunate. . . .

"I have become with desperate reality a factory girl, alone, inexperienced, friendless. I am making $4.20 a week and spending $3 of this for board alone. . . .

"My shoulders are beginning to ache. My hands are stiff, my thumbs almost blistered. . . . Cases are emptied and refilled; bottles are labeled, stamped and rolled away; jars are washed, wiped and loaded, and still there are more cases, more jars, more bottles. Oh! the monotony of it, the never-ending supply of work to be begun and finished, begun and finished, begun and finished! Now and then someone cuts a finger or runs a splinter under the flesh; once the mustard machine broke— and still the work goes on, on, on! . . . Once I pause an instant, my head dazed and weary, my ears strained to bursting with the deafening noise. Quickly a voice whispers in my ear: 'You'd better not stand there doin' nothin'. If *she* catches you she'll give it to you.'"

In the United States, during the last three decades of the 1800s, industry was reshaping the world of the workers. As machines grew more complex, working conditions often worsened. Many mine, factory, and other unskilled workers earned low pay for long hours. Finally, workers united to make their voices heard.

Farmers, too, were making little money for long hours of labor. They planted more and watched in desperation as prices for their harvests dropped. In mutual need, farmers began to unite. In the late 1800s, then, both farmers and workers were demanding change in the industrial United States.

From Stefan Lorant's *The Glorious Burden,* Author's Edition.

WORKERS ORGANIZE

READ TO FIND OUT

— why workers began to organize in the late 1800s.

— what the National Labor Union tried to accomplish.

— how the railroad strikes of 1877 showed the power of labor.

— how the Haymarket riot affected the Knights of Labor.

— how the American Federation of Labor was organized.

— how the Homestead and Pullman strikes affected the labor movement.

In the 1700s and early 1800s, a worker could become a shoemaker's apprentice, learn the trade, and someday open a small shop to make and sell shoes.

Then, the Industrial Revolution changed the role of the average worker. Shoes, and most other products, were made in large factories.

Workers did not craft a product from start to finish. Most did one small job, over and over, and few ever dreamed of owning the factory. One observer wrote of workers in the 1860s, 1870s, and 1880s: "They no longer carried the keys of the workshop, for workshop tools and keys belonged not to them, but to their master."

In the factory system, however, workers' output did increase. Also, between 1870 and 1890, wages inched upward while the cost of living dropped. Still, not many workers moved into skilled jobs or were able to own their own businesses. Few even earned enough to support a family. When depressions hit, many lost their jobs.

Many workers felt that they had to do something to improve their situation. They did not have the power that business owners did, but they did have numbers. United, workers could become powerful. They could force owners to improve conditions.

THE WORK PLACE

Workers could not effectively organize until they agreed on some common goals. What did a textile worker, a coal miner, and a railroad conductor have in common? From industry to industry, from state to state, working conditions varied a great deal.

A 6-day work week of 10 hours per day was common. Hours, however, ranged from an 8-hour day for workers in the building trades to a 12-hour day, seven days a week, for blast-furnace operators in steel plants.

Brewery workers generally received higher wages than steelworkers, who, in turn, earned more money than textile workers. Northern tobacco workers earned more than their southern counterparts. Skilled workers earned up to 50 percent more than unskilled. For the same work, men made around 75 percent more than women and almost 300 percent more than children. Blacks and immigrants almost always were paid less than other Americans.

In many industries, working conditions were unhealthy, or even dangerous. Cigarmakers and garment workers usually labored where they lived— in dark, crowded, dirty tenements. Factories were often just as bad, with poor lighting, heating, and ventilation.

By the early 1900s, at least 1,700,000 children under 16 were employed in factories and fields. These child laborers in a hosiery mill in 1910 had to stand on boxes to do their work.

An 1877 newspaper described the working conditions in the sorting room of a Pennsylvania coal mine. The workers were children:

> In a little room . . . forty boys are picking their lives away. . . . They work here, in this little black hole, all day and every day, trying to keep cool in summer, trying to keep warm in winter, picking away among the black coals, bending over till their little spines are curved, never saying a word all the livelong day.

No one paid much attention to the health or safety of the workers. Whistles shrieked after a bad accident—an arm caught in the machinery or a child buried in an avalanche of coal. Then work went on. There were also quieter ways of dying, like breathing in coal dust or clouds of cotton lint.

Workers might be able to agree that they wanted shorter hours, higher pay, and safer working conditions. What they could not agree on was how to win their goals. Should they go out on strike until employers gave in, or should they work to get labor laws passed? One worker said, "Keep down strikes and rioters." Another said, "Abolish child labor and [pass] any other act that capitalists say is wrong."

Labor was so divided that railroad owner Jay Gould could boast: "I can hire one half of the working class to kill the other half."

THE STRUGGLE TO ORGANIZE

The workers' search for power, known as the labor movement, led them in many directions. Some people in the labor movement wanted to form **industrial unions**. Industrial unions organized all the workers in a given industry. Some people wanted to form **trade unions**, or craft unions, which organized all workers with a particular skill. Others hoped to unite all workers into one huge union.

In 1866 representatives of many unions joined to form the National Labor Union (NLU). The major goal of this nationwide association of unions was an eight-hour work day. Members pledged not to strike except as a last resort.

As time went by, the NLU expanded its goals. It called for civil service reform, temperance, and an end to child labor. In the late 1860s the union welcomed black delegates and women's suffrage groups. However, as its goals expanded, the NLU began to lose the support of member unions. Most of these unions wanted to achieve practical economic gains rather than to bring about social reform.

The labor movement faced another problem—the economy. Workers were more likely to join unions in times of prosperity. When business boomed, labor was in demand, and owners were reluctant to fire workers who joined unions. In hard times, the idea of strength through unity collapsed.

In 1873 a depression began which dragged on until 1877. By the end of that bleak time, over half a million people were unemployed. Those with jobs were eager to keep them, accepting wage cuts and dropping their union membership. Most unions that remained were badly weakened. The faltering NLU did not survive.

THE RAILROAD STRIKES

The depression that harmed the labor movement in general had the opposite effect on labor in the railroad industry. Hurt by the failing economy, railroad after railroad began cutting wages. Then, in the summer of 1877, railroad workers' frustration flamed into anger.

In mid-July workers on the Baltimore and Ohio Railroad walked off their jobs. One group seized a station in Martinsburg, West Virginia, vowing that no trains would move until the owners canceled wage cuts. The Baltimore *Sun* noted the part taken in the strike by the wives and mothers of the workers:

> They look famished and wild, and declare for starvation rather than have their people work for the reduced wages. Better to starve outright, they say, than to die by slow starvation.

At the request of the railroad president, 400 federal troops were sent to Martinsburg. Meanwhile, the strike spread from line to line, even reaching railroads in the West. The nation's railroad network was paralyzed, and many people were outraged. The New York *Sun* recommended "a diet of lead for the hungry strikers."

Local police, state militias, and federal troops were called out to break up the strikes. In New York, the militia refused to fire on the angry crowds. One officer explained that members of the militia might be soldiers, but they were workers first. Still, fighting erupted in other places.

After the local militia joined the strikers in Pittsburgh, officials called in 600 troops from Philadelphia. A battle between the troops and strikers left 26 dead. The enraged workers then ripped apart $5 million worth of railroad property.

At the end of July, President Rutherford B. Hayes sent thousands of federal troops into the worst trouble spots. The Pittsburgh-to-Philadelphia line was opened by four troop trains, one pushing a flatcar that held a rapid-fire gun. Under the combined force of the troops, militias, and local police, the strikes collapsed.

The country was stunned. More than a hundred people had been killed. To many Americans, the strike echoed labor unrest in Europe. There, socialists and communists were demanding that the governments take over ownership of railroads and other industries. Anarchists were calling for violent attacks on political and business leaders. From this time on, many Americans saw labor unrest as a communist conspiracy.

The railroad strikers had lost, but they had shown their power. They had also drawn support from other workers. In sympathy, workers in St. Louis had called a **general strike**, a strike against all industry. St. Louis had been shut down for five days. Many in the labor movement saw, and would remember, the power of a general strike.

THE KNIGHTS OF LABOR

The great strike of 1877 had an immediate effect on a union called the Noble Order of the Knights of Labor. The Knights had been founded by Uriah S. Stephens in 1869 as a garment-cutters' union, and it soon opened to other trades.

However, Stephens felt that trade unions were "too narrow" to be effective. What was needed, he said, was to join all workers into one "great brotherhood." The railroad strikes gave many workers the same idea. Thousands rushed to join the Knights of Labor.

Then, in 1879, Terence V. Powderly took over leadership of the union. Powderly was a machinist, and had been president of his trade union before joining the Knights. Like Stephens, he called for "one common brotherhood" of workers.

Within six years after Powderly became its leader, the Knights of Labor attracted over 100,000 new members. Powderly opened the ranks to women, blacks, immigrants, and unskilled workers.

The Knights, like the earlier National Labor Union, called for an eight-hour day and improved working conditions. They also wanted to form cooperative worker-owned businesses. Their goal was "to secure to the toilers a proper share in the wealth that they create."

However, the Knights soon had problems. Many skilled workers found it hard to join with the unskilled. Many also resented the acceptance of women and blacks.

Dividing the union even further was the question of strikes. "Strikes are a failure," Powderly said. "I shudder at the thought of a strike and I have good reasons." Many in the union disagreed. Powderly's antistrike position grew more unpopular.

Throughout 1883 and 1884 there raged a "great upheaval" of unorganized workers and those in other unions. Miners, telegraphers, glassblowers, and railroad workers went on strike. When the strikes were settled, many of these workers joined the Knights.

Then, in 1885, railroad workers belonging to the Knights struck the southwestern railroad system over a pay cut. The Knights worked out a settlement with railroad owner Jay Gould, who agreed to recognize the union. The strike's success over the powerful Gould electrified workers. Membership soared from 100,000 to 700,000 in one year.

THE HAYMARKET RIOT

In 1886 a series of disasters hit the Knights of Labor. In March, a strike against another Gould railroad failed, and the union suddenly did not seem so powerful. On May 1, many Knights joined a nationwide general strike for the eight-hour day. But this was overshadowed by a separate strike in Chicago.

Workers at the Chicago McCormick Harvester plant had been on strike since February over the firing of union workers. On May 3, the McCormick workers clashed with strikebreakers and police. Four strikers were killed and several were injured.

The next night, a small band of anarchists protested the killings by holding a rally in Chicago's Haymarket Square. When police were called in to break up the rally, someone hurled a bomb. The police opened fire on the crowd. A battle erupted that left 70 wounded and 7 police officers dead.

The violence terrified the public. Eight anarchists were arrested and tried, and four of them were hanged. One anarchist had belonged to the Knights of Labor. Powderly and his union quickly condemned the bombing. In the public's mind, however, the Knights of Labor became associated with the anarchists and the violence.

The American Federation of Labor owed its success to an immigrant, president Samuel Gompers. However, the AFL opposed immigration as a threat to unionization.

As a result of the failed strike against Gould and the Haymarket riot, the Knights of Labor rapidly declined. By 1900 the union was nearly extinct. The Illinois Bureau of Labor Statistics concluded that "the explosion of the bomb on the Haymarket Square abruptly ended" the movement for the eight-hour day.

THE AMERICAN FEDERATION OF LABOR

The year 1886, such a disaster for the Knights, saw the birth of a rival union. In December representatives of many trade unions—with total membership of 300,000—met at Columbus, Ohio. They formed a new nationwide union called the American Federation of Labor (AFL). Samuel Gompers, a longtime union organizer, was elected president.

Gompers was a Jewish immigrant from London who had come to the United States with his parents when he was thirteen. Like his father, he became a cigarmaker. Although he labored for long hours at low wages, he took pride in his craft and the feeling of unity that developed among the workers.

It was this sense of unity that Gompers felt was essential to a union's success. "The employer fixed wages until he shoved them down to a point where human endurance revolted," Gompers later said. "Often the revolt started by an individual whose personal grievance was sore, who rose and declared:

'I am going on strike. All who remain at work are scabs.' Usually the workers went out with him."

Gompers' personal experience in the cigar-makers' union made him a devoted union member. When he joined the AFL, he was the natural choice for president. With the exception of one year, he led the AFL until his death.

The AFL operated somewhat like the union of American states. Each member union made its own day-to-day decisions. Each union decided whether to strike or to sign a contract. The federation kept the unions working together toward common goals.

The AFL was a narrower organization than the Knights of Labor had been. Immigrants and unskilled laborers were not admitted. Unions with blacks and women as members were accepted in the AFL, but not encouraged. In practice, the AFL seldom recruited women's craft unions. By 1900 it allowed its member unions to exclude blacks.

Gompers wanted to make the AFL "the business organization of the workers." It stressed bread-and-butter issues, not political and social reform. "Our labor movement," Gompers said, "has no system to crush . . . nothing to overturn."

The AFL set practical, clear-cut goals. The federation worked for the eight-hour work day, the six-day work week, higher wages, and better working conditions. The AFL also supported **collective bargaining**, the right of unions to represent groups of workers. Member unions were encouraged to negotiate goals with management. If talks failed, however, the unions could strike. Unlike the Knights of Labor, the AFL found strikes a useful weapon if all else failed.

Management had its own weapons to deal with workers. Strike organizers were often *blacklisted*, or denied employment in an entire industry. Employers forced workers to sign "yellow-dog contracts," in which workers promised not to join a union. Workers on strike could be kept out of their work place by an employer's *lockout*, and allowed to return only if they agreed to management's terms.

Furthermore, management could usually find workers willing to fill strikers' jobs. These workers were often the poor, immigrants, and blacks, who were barred from many unions. By taking strikers' jobs, these people were acting as strikebreakers and were called "scabs" by union supporters.

Sometimes, employers used strikebreakers to fight the strikers. One group of immigrants killed two strikers on orders from a coal mine owner. The immigrants were jailed for murder and the owner was fined five dollars.

THE HOMESTEAD STRIKE

In the 1890s two strikes showed the grim determination of both management and labor. The first strike occurred in July 1892, at Andrew Carnegie's Homestead steelworks in Pennsylvania.

At Homestead, Carnegie had built a *company town*. Housing was provided for workers, and there were company-owned schools and stores. Although the company town gave workers some degree of comfort in their living conditions, there were disadvantages. Workers bought food at high prices from the grocery store. They worshipped at the company church and sent their children to the company school.

At the Homestead plant, there was a 12-hour work day, 6 days a week. People worked so close to molten steel that fatal accidents were not unusual.

In 1892 when the steel company announced a wage cut, the Amalgamated Association of Iron and Steel workers went on strike. Only a minority of the plant's steelworkers belonged to the union, but

When strikers gained ground at the Homestead steelworks in Pennsylvania, the state militia was called in. After their intervention, the strike failed completely.

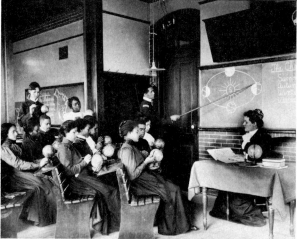

The beautiful precision of Frances Johnston's work is evident in her photograph entitled "Geography. Studying the Seasons."

Collection of The Museum of Modern Art, New York.

FRANCES JOHNSTON
EARLY DOCUMENTARY PHOTOGRAPHER

When young Frances Johnston became a professional photographer in the 1890s, she took two pictures of herself. In the first, she is gazing out from under a frilly hat topped with two feathery plumes. In the second, she is daringly showing her ankles—something forbidden a Victorian lady.

The two pictures—one proper and one boldly independent—reflect the two sides of Frances Johnston. On the one hand, she was President Grover Cleveland's niece, who earned her living by photographing fashionable Washingtonians. On the other, she was an adventurous documentary photographer who wasn't afraid to travel alone into slums and factories to take her pictures.

Though she was born in West Virginia in 1864, Johnston spent much of her childhood in Washington, D.C. She studied art in Paris, then discovered photography. By the time she was twenty-six, she had a thriving portrait studio. But her most lasting

works were the carefully composed and beautifully detailed photographs she took of ordinary Americans. She traveled to the Pennsylvania coal mines to photograph the miners, including the young boys who worked underground. She also photographed iron workers in Michigan and women at their machines in a Massachusetts shoe factory.

In 1898 she toured the South, documenting the poverty of rural blacks. She also took pictures of students at two new black schools, Tuskegee Institute in Alabama and Hampton Institute in Virginia. Simply by putting the two sets of photographs together, she told a story of what blacks were doing to change their lives.

Only recently have Frances Johnston and her work been rediscovered. One of America's first career women, Johnston shows us through her brilliant camera eye both the hope and hardship of late nineteenth-century life.

plant manager Henry Frick was determined to crush it. He hired a private police force from the Pinkerton agency to take control of the plant. Once control was established, strikebreakers would be brought in to fill the strikers' jobs.

On the night of July 6, strikers on watch saw barges moving down the river toward the plant. On

board were 300 armed Pinkerton guards. The alarm was sounded. Armed workers met the Pinkertons when they landed, and the battle began. Some 13 hours and 10 deaths later, the Pinkertons waved a white flag. The strikers had won—so far.

Six days later, however, the state militia moved in and stayed until most jobs had been filled by strikebreakers. One enraged striker tried to kill Frick. The attempt failed, and it ended much public sympathy for the strike. Four months later the starving strikers gave up, but few got their jobs back. Most were blacklisted. Wages at Homestead were cut even lower than had been expected.

Emboldened by the Carnegie Steel Company's victory, other steel companies refused to recognize the steelworkers' union, and it was destroyed. The failed Homestead strike ended most union activity in the steel industry for years.

THE PULLMAN STRIKE

Two years after the Homestead strike, there was another violent showdown between labor and management. It occurred at the railroad town of Pullman, Illinois, in May 1894.

For years, workers at the Pullman sleeping-car works had lived in a company town that George Pullman had built near Chicago. One worker said:

> We are born in a Pullman house, fed from the Pullman shop, taught in the Pullman school, catechized in the Pullman church, and when we die we shall be buried in the Pullman cemetery.

After working 10 hours a day for 12 days, one worker had 7 cents left, once his rent and charges at the company store had been taken out.

When a depression began in 1893, Pullman cut wages by 25 to 40 percent. But the rents and store prices stayed the same. About 4,000 workers then joined the American Railway Union, led by Eugene V. Debs.

In May 1894 the American Railway Union called a strike. Union railroad workers refused to move any train that had a Pullman car. By June 30, there was almost no movement of goods and mail across the country.

Strikebreakers were brought in, and the state militia responded to outbreaks of violence, but the shutdown continued. Then a new weapon was used against the strikers. On July 2 a federal court issued a stop-action order, called an **injunction**, against the striking workers.

The injunction ordered the strikers to stop interfering with the trains. The court based its decision on the Sherman Antitrust Act, which banned business combinations that were "in restraint of trade." Because the strike stopped delivery of mail and goods, the court decided, the American Railway Union was acting in restraint of trade.

When the workers ignored the injunction, President Grover Cleveland sent in federal troops to break the strike. Furious, the strikers fought the troops and destroyed railroad property. By July 20 the strike was broken, and Debs was arrested and convicted for defying the injunction.

With the failure of the Pullman strike, workers felt more powerless than ever. The government had used the Sherman Antitrust Act—a law intended to control trusts—to break a labor strike. Many workers lost faith in the labor movement. By 1899, out of 17 million workers, only half a million still belonged to unions. The workers' struggle to organize had just begun.

SECTION REVIEW

1. Identify the following: National Labor Union, Uriah S. Stephens, Terence V. Powderly, the Knights of Labor, Samuel Gompers.

2. Define the following: general strike, collective bargaining, blacklist, "yellow-dog contract," lockout, "scab," company town, injunction.

3. (a) How did the Industrial Revolution change the role of the average worker? (b) Before workers could organize, they had to agree on common goals. List three goals many workers agreed on.

4. What two factors caused the National Labor Union to fail?

5. (a) Why did the workers on the Baltimore and Ohio Railroad strike in 1877? (b) What effect did this strike have on other railroads?

6. (a) What were the goals of the Knights of Labor? (b) What two factors caused problems within the Knights' organization?

7. Explain how the Haymarket riot affected the Knights of Labor and the labor movement.

8. (a) Describe how the American Federation of Labor was organized. (b) What were the goals of the AFL?

9. (a) Describe the events of the Homestead and Pullman strikes. (b) What were the results of each of these strikes?

10. How was an injunction used during the Pullman strike?

THE PLIGHT OF THE FARMERS

READ TO FIND OUT

— how technology and science changed farming in the late 1800s.

— how crop surpluses and weather affected American farmers.

— how national economic conditions affected farmers.

— why farmers left their farms.

For many prairie families, life was basic and uncluttered. No trees or flowers intrude on the bare landscape. Simple necessities of food, conveyance, and shelter are evident.

Those who labored in mines and shops and factories for unfair and inadequate wages were not the only Americans affected by the growth of industry. Farmers, too, had trouble adjusting to the changes brought by industrialization.

In the 1830s a Michigan pioneer wrote, "We moved into a house of our own, had a farm of our own, and owed no one." That summed up the American dream. It was the dream that brought millions of people to America and sent so many waves of pioneers westward.

Fifty years later, pioneers still set out to farm the West. Farmers throughout the country were producing record harvests, but this did not mean that all farmers were prospering. To produce the rich harvests, farmers went into debt to buy new equipment. Droughts and blizzards ruined crops. Competition drove prices down. Inventions changed the nature of farming. The Michigan pioneer of the 1830s would hardly recognize his dream in the farm of the 1880s.

TECHNOLOGY AND FARMING

As I look back over my life on that Iowa farm, the song of the reaper fills a large place in my mind. We were all worshippers of wheat in those days. Farmers thought and talked of little else between seeding and harvest, and you will not wonder at this if you have known and bowed before such abundance as we then enjoyed. . . . Our fields ran to the world's end.

Hamlin Garland was writing of his youth on a farm in the 1870s and 1880s. The reaper and wheat were perfect symbols of farming in the prairie states. Machines and science were turning the small farm into a big business.

New strains of wheat, brought from Europe and Asia, withstood the harsh prairie winters. A new milling device, developed in Minnesota, produced inexpensive high-quality flour from the wheat.

Cyrus McCormick, inventor of the reaper, developed a new machine called the combine. It handled every step of harvesting wheat. It cut, gathered, threshed, and even bagged the grain. By the 1880s giant combines rumbled through the fields of the prairies. Thirty to forty horses or mules were needed to pull each one.

However, the cost of such machinery was high. Farmers sometimes pooled their money to buy or rent a combine, and moved it from farm to farm during the harvest. Combines enabled farmers to plant more acres and obtain bigger harvests. Bigger harvests led to increased profits. However, farmers needed more money to pay for equipment, so they kept planting more acres.

Farms on the Plains grew larger and larger. Farmers began growing a single crop that would bring more money, usually a cash crop like wheat. By the 1880s the prairie states were America's leading grain producers. It seemed certain that expanding markets, at home and abroad, would keep the price of wheat at a dollar per bushel or even send it higher.

In other parts of the country, farmers were also growing huge crops. In the South cotton was harvested in record-breaking crops, and there were also good yields of wheat, corn, sugar, tobacco, and rice. Farmers in the West grew wheat, fruits, and vegetables. The Northeast churned out huge quantities of corn, milk, butter, fruits, and vegetables.

Machinery affected agriculture in these regions, too. A dairy centrifuge, marketed in 1880, separated cream from milk. Soon many dairy farmers in the Northeast were sending their milk to creameries, where it could be processed quickly and cheaply.

Scientific advances also changed farming. Researchers created pesticides to kill insects that damaged crops, and found ways to combat plant diseases. One scientist saved California citrus groves by making use of ladybugs, which ate pests.

New fertilizers enriched the soil. Because of fertilizers, said a North Carolina agricultural expert, cotton had spread "forty or fifty miles up the slopes of the Blue Ridge and northward across the Virginia line."

OVERPRODUCTION

The abundance created by farmers was hailed by business interests and local boosters. "Do not be afraid of going into debt," a Kansas newspaper advised farmers on the Great Plains. "Do all you can for Belle Plaine regardless of money . . . and Belle Plaine will boom."

Many easterners, too, believed that the plains would boom and were eager to loan money to farmers. A farm mortgage, they hoped, would be a good investment. The manager of an eastern loan company was busy in 1886: "My desk was piled high every morning with hundreds of letters each enclosing a draft and asking me to send a farm mortgage from Kansas or Nebraska."

However, the increased production brought problems. Farmers grew more than the American market demanded, so the surplus was sold in international markets. Other countries—Australia, Canada, Russia, Argentina, Brazil—were also flooding the world market with their crops. The surplus sent prices plunging.

Wheat prices dropped from $1.19 per bushel in 1881 to 49 cents by 1894. Corn fell from 63 cents in 1881 to 28 cents in 1890. Cotton had sold for 31

In a field in eastern Washington, horse-drawn harvesters cut and bundle grain. Such machines greatly increased the acreage that could be planted. Because of this, farmers found profit in replacing small, diversified crops with large-scale plantings of a few crops.

Overproduction, mortgages, low prices, and bad weather were not the only problems farmers faced. Soil depletion caused by poor farming methods was also becoming a problem in some parts of the country.

cents per pound in 1866, but prices after 1870 began a steady decline, reaching 6 cents in 1893. Cotton cost more to produce than the price received for it. In some communities grain was so difficult to sell that farmers burned it as heating fuel.

Weather also caused problems for farmers. Southern farmers in the Mississippi Valley saw acres of land destroyed by floods. Beginning in 1887, a series of droughts ruined harvests on the plains. A Nebraska woman wrote of one: "The drought exceeded all probability. Corn did not sprout . . . buffalo grass was started and browned before the first of May."

THE BURDEN OF DEBT

By the 1880s most farmers had become links in a commercial system. No longer were farms little self-sufficient worlds. Farmers' survival was no longer a matter of growing their own food and producing their own goods. If the price for cash crops dropped, farmers were in serious trouble.

Farmers became locked into a grim cycle, as endless as the cycle of the seasons. To make enough money, they needed to plant more crops. They mortgaged their land to buy additional machinery. They went to banks and merchants for credit, and fell deeper into debt.

Many farmers were still in debt to the railroad companies that had sold them their land. Furthermore, prairie farmers complained that the rates railroads charged for carrying goods were three times higher for mid-westerners than for easterners. In the East, river and canal transportation competed with railroads, keeping rates down.

Any farmer in debt was hurt by the general decline of prices from 1865 through the 1880s. In this period of **deflation**, the value of money—that is, its purchasing power—rose. Every dollar farmers owed in debt was worth more than the dollar they had borrowed. A farmer who borrowed $1,000 in the late 1860s could have repaid that debt by selling about 1,200 bushels of wheat. By the 1880s it took almost twice as many bushels to repay that same number of dollars.

Since costs of farming were rising, fewer people could afford to become independent farmers. Many became tenant farmers and sharecroppers instead, especially in the South. Tenants and sharecroppers rarely had goods to pledge for credit, or land to mortgage. To get credit they gave merchants a lien, or claim, on their future crops. If they could not pay back the merchant, the merchant took the crops in payment. Under this crop-lien system, tenants and sharecroppers piled up debts and had little hope of ever owning land.

FLIGHT FROM THE LAND

There seemed to be no solution to the farmers' troubles. Farmers needed the railroad system to carry their goods, the industrial system to make machinery, and the banking system to lend money. Profits dropped, harvests were ruined, but debts remained.

Thousands of farms failed and banks foreclosed on mortgages. Between 1889 and 1893, there were 11,000 foreclosures in Kansas alone. In some prairie counties of that time, 90 percent of the farms were sold or lost to foreclosures.

The farmers' troubles had produced a bitter harvest—a migration away from the land. Between 1888 and 1892 half the population of western Kansas left the prairie. Scattered counties in Michigan, Illinois, Indiana, and Ohio lost as much as half their populations between 1880 and 1890. New England was also hit hard. Half of its townships lost population and entire villages were abandoned.

Wagons heading east from the Plains carried signs like "In God we trusted, in Kansas we busted." A sign on an empty Texas farmhouse said, "250 miles to the nearest post office—100 miles to wood—20 miles to water. . . . God bless our home! Gone to live with the wife's folks."

Still, flight from the land was not the only way to escape debts and falling profits. Those who stayed on the farms found another answer.

SECTION REVIEW

1. Define the following: deflation, crop-lien system.

2. List seven technological and scientific advances that changed farming in the 1870s and 1880s.

3. (a) Why were easterners eager to loan money to farmers? (b) Why did farmers need money?

4. (a) How did the production of surplus crops affect the prices in the international market? (b) How did international prices affect American farmers in the late 1800s?

5. Explain why, in the 1880s, farmers mortgaged their land and fell into debt.

6. Why did deflation hurt farmers who were in debt?

7. List two factors that caused farmers to remain in debt.

8. What caused the migration away from the farms in the 1880s and 1890s?

THE POPULISTS

READ TO FIND OUT

—how farmers united into a strong nationwide organization.

—why farmers wanted to increase the amount of money in circulation.

—how Farmers' Alliances affected the congressional election of 1890.

—what proposals were made in the Populist party platform in 1892.

—how economic conditions led to controversy over free silver and the gold standard.

—how the presidential election of 1896 affected the Populist party.

When the banker says he's broke,
And the merchant's up in smoke,
They forget that it's the farmer feeds them all.
It would put them to the test
If the farmer took a rest,
Then they'd know that it's the farmer feeds them all.

In this song of the 1890s, farmers declared a revolt. The country, they reminded Americans, could not get along without farmers. And farmers were in trouble.

Farmers protested unfair railroad rates and high costs of farm machinery, while their crops sold for less and less. They blamed the banks and the government for an economic policy that hurt debtors. And the farmers, trying to pay off crushing mortgages, were the nation's angriest debtors.

From the farmers' anger a movement was born. It began with local groups meeting to share problems, then grew into nationwide groups that sought political solutions. Finally, it fused into a new political party, calling for widespread reform.

THE GRANGE

The farmers' movement began with a group called the Patrons of Husbandry, better known as the Grange. Founded in 1867 by a postal worker named

Workers at a grain depot in Washington sometime around 1900 posed on a pyramid of bagged grain. In orderly progression, a loaded wagon arrived, bags were passed from hand to hand, and the empty wagon moved on.

Oliver Kelley, the Grange sought to improve the social lives of rural Americans.

Faced with loneliness and hard times, farmers began flocking to the Grange. The movement steadily spread across the nation. By 1875 about 20,000 local Granges had a combined membership of 800,000.

The Grange grew especially strong in the Midwest, where it provided a welcome relief from the isolation of prairie farming. "New friendships are formed, and old ones strengthened," wrote a farmer in 1875. "The farmer is taught that the world does not end . . . at the boundaries of [the] farm."

Men and women were equal members in the local Grange. The group held picnics and meetings, and talked over common problems.

Some of the talk led to the formation of new businesses. Grangers started their own farm supply stores and formed organizations, called cooperatives* to run warehouses and granaries. This cut out the wholesalers who had charged farmers high prices to store grain.

An admiring Kansas senator wrote of the Grange: "It lacks but one element of strength, and that will come in due time—namely, the uniting with other bodies of organized farmers in one great political movement."

* cooperative: a store or building owned collectively by its members, who share in its benefits and profits.

THE GREENBACK-LABOR PARTY

While the Grange satisfied many of the farmers' needs, it could not alter the deflation that made it difficult for farmers to pay their mortgages. During the Civil War, Congress had issued paper money ("greenbacks") that was not backed by gold. After the war, farmers wanted to keep the greenbacks in circulation. They said that more currency was needed to match the country's growth.

The greenbacks stayed, but in 1874 Congress limited the amount in circulation. The nation slipped into depression and deflation. Money became scarce, so it rose in value. And the value of the money farmers owed in debts also rose.

Farmers urged the government to put more greenbacks into circulation to inflate the economy. This would cause the value of money to decrease. With the "cheap money," people could buy more farm goods, causing farm prices to go up. Furthermore, farmers could pay their mortgages and other bills.

Farmers and others hurt by the government's tight money policy were drawn to the Greenback-Labor party. In 1878 it managed to get over a million votes in state and local elections. However, the depression ended that year and farmers enjoyed a sudden burst of prosperity. They lost interest in the political activities of the Grange and the ideas of the Greenback-Labor party.

Only with a return of falling prices in the 1880s did farmers renew their political efforts. And this time, they created one of the most vital movements in the nation's history.

FARMERS' ALLIANCES

The movement began as farmers in the South and West formed Farmers' Alliances. Like the earlier Granges, the alliances were both social and political.

Speakers toured farm areas, urging farmers to unite to solve their problems. Members received newspapers and magazines, local branches held picnics, and cooperatives set up warehouses and stores. And the talk at meetings was becoming more and more impatient.

The Southern Farmers' Alliance began as a ranchers' association in the 1870s. In the 1880s it merged with other southern farmers' groups. Some members tried to unite their group with the Colored Farmers' Alliance. However, these initial stirrings of black and white unity soon died.

There was no question of the cooperative spirit of this group of apple pickers. Men, women, and children took part in the harvest, carefully identified as YORK IMPERIALS.

The Northwestern Farmers' Alliance was started in 1880. The group wanted to "unite the farmers of America for their protection against . . . the tyranny of monopoly." The alliance flourished in the plains states, attracting thousands of mortgaged farmers and tenants.

In 1889 the two alliances met in St. Louis, Missouri. Prices for farm crops were plummeting, and the meeting rang with cries for federal help. Farmers wanted more money in circulation, and lower taxes. There was talk that the government should take over railroads. Farmers called for low-interest government loans. Both alliances adopted platforms based on these demands.

In the congressional elections the next year, the alliances campaigned vigorously. The Southern Alliance ran candidates for Democratic seats, since the Democrats controlled the South. Alliance members won control of 8 state legislatures, elected 3 governors, and sent 44 representatives to Congress.

The Northwestern Farmers' Alliance distrusted the Democrats and Republicans, believing them to be controlled by business interests. So the plains farmers formed third parties. In Kansas, Minnesota, Nebraska, and South Dakota, the farmers' parties swept into state legislatures. Kansas, where the campaign reached fever pitch, elected several members to Congress.

The fever was fanned by Mary Lease, preaching the farmers' cause throughout Kansas:

> Wall Street owns the country. It is no longer a government of the people, by the people and for the people, but a government of Wall Street, by Wall Street and for Wall Street. The great common people of this country are slaves, and monopoly is the master. The West and South are bound and prostrate before the manufacturing East. Money rules, and our Vice-President is a London banker.

The farmers were in revolt. Many were ready to unite in a single national party. At a meeting of Farmers' Alliances in May 1891, the People's Party of the U.S.A. was launched. It soon became known as the Populist party.

THE POPULIST PARTY

They came from everywhere, crowding the hotels and rooming houses of Omaha, Nebraska, in the hot July of 1892. Most were members of Granges and Farmers' Alliances, but there were also remnants of

This meeting of the Grangers took place in the woods near Winchester, Scott County, Illinois, in 1873. Banners stating grievances and goals reinforced the speaker's words.

the Knights of Labor and the Greenback party. This was the first national convention of the Populist party.

A sense of excitement and hope filled the crowded meeting room. It was a presidential election year, and the delegates hoped to do what the Republicans had done in the 1850s. They would make their party a major force in the land.

The Populist platform called for many of the changes that the Granges and Farmers' Alliances had been suggesting for years. The government should own and run railroads, banks, and telephones and telegraphs "in the interest of the people." The government should set up warehouses where farmers could store their crops, and loan them money until the crops were sold. To gain support of city workers, the Populists called for an eight-hour day.

The Populists supported taxes on personal income, rather than on land. They proposed the **graduated personal income tax**—a system by which people were taxed at a rate proportional to their income. In addition, they demanded that the government not limit the amount of silver coined. Farmers had failed in their efforts to make the

government increase the amount of paper money. They now wanted the federal government to enlarge the money supply by placing more silver in circulation.

The convention adopted the platform, reported a journalist, with cheers that "rose like a tornado from four thousand throats and raged without cessation for thirty-four minutes." The convention then nominated a former Grange and Greenback leader, James B. Weaver of Iowa, as the Populist presidential candidate.

Political reform was also a part of the platform. Populists wanted people to be able to participate more directly in politics. Senators should be chosen by the people, not by state legislatures. People should vote on secret ballots. People should have the right to propose legislation and to vote their approval of laws.

In the months that followed, populism swept the farm states like a prairie fire. Leaders traveled the country roads and farm villages, making speeches. Populist leaders were colorful people who were given colorful names.

Jerry Simpson of Kansas had once scorned rich politicians who wore silk socks. A reporter then wrote that the rustic-looking Simpson probably did not wear any kind of socks. Thus, he became "Sockless Jerry." Mary Lease, the fiery crusader for farmers, was known as the "Kansas Pythoness." Other leaders were "Cyclone" Davis of Texas and "Calamity" Weller of Iowa.

The Populist campaigners spoke the language of rural America. They offered help to farmers, who felt that they had not received much help from either the Democrats or the Republicans. Many farmers listened and joined the Populist movement.

THE ELECTION OF 1892

The results of the election of 1892 were mixed. James B. Weaver won more than a million popular votes and 22 electoral votes, all from states west of the Mississippi. Over a dozen Populists were sent to Congress, and Populist governors were elected in Kansas, North Dakota, and Colorado. It was a strong showing for a third party.

Weaver's 22 electoral votes could not, however, stop Democrat Grover Cleveland from winning his second term. In the South, many members of the Southern Alliance had voted Democratic, still hop-

Mary Lease was an energetic and fiery speaker for the Farmers' Alliance and the Populist party. In 1890 alone, she gave over 160 speeches for the farmers' movement.

ing to reach power through that party. City workers had simply ignored the Populist cause, despite its call for an eight-hour day. The Populists emerged solely as the party of the plains farmers.

Some Populists reacted with despair. One who lost a race for governor wrote in his diary, "Beaten! Whipped! Smashed! . . . Our followers scattered like dew before the rising sun." There were others, however, who were encouraged by the strong showing and began planning for the election of 1896.

THE DEPRESSION OF 1893

As Grover Cleveland took office in 1893, the nation was struck by its third depression within twenty years. People argued angrily over economic cures.

On one side were those who saw salvation in silver. They were people with a stake in silver—silver miners, and most people in debt, like the farmers. Many of these "silverites" were Populists or Democrats disillusioned with the Democratic party. The silverites wanted free, or unlimited, coinage of silver in order to increase the money supply. This would help people in debt and, they believed, end the depression.

Standing firmly against them were business leaders, conservatives in Congress, and President Cleveland. All were defenders of the **gold standard**—currency based on the amount of gold in the nation's treasury. Under the gold standard, a paper dollar was equal to a certain amount of gold, and could be exchanged for it. Therefore, there could be no more currency in circulation than there was gold in the nation's treasury to back that currency.

Until the Civil War, the country had used a **bimetallic standard** of both gold and silver. In other words, currency was based on both gold and silver. The Civil War, however, set off a raging inflation. One southerner said, "We used to go to the stores with money in our pockets and come back with food in our baskets. Now we go with money in baskets and return with food in our pockets. Everything is scarce except money!"

DEPRESSION DEEPENS

To control inflation after the war, the government tightened the money supply with the Coinage Act of 1873. Silver would no longer be coined, leaving gold the sole standard.

The money supply shrank, and deflation followed. Those in debt, along with western silver miners, demanded that silver be coined again. Buffeted between gold and silver backers, Congress twice passed acts to coin silver.

The Bland-Allison Act of 1878 required the government to buy a certain amount of silver each year to be minted into coins. The Sherman Silver Purchase Act of 1890 increased the amount of silver bought each year and allowed the government to issue paper money backed by silver. Both laws limited the amount of silver that could be coined, and the money supply was not much affected.

President Cleveland was sure that the Sherman Silver Purchase Act was at the root of the depression. Because of the act, the treasury was using up its gold to buy silver. Shortly after he took office, Cleveland led a successful fight in Congress to repeal the Silver Purchase Act.

The depression did not end. In fact, by 1894, the farmers' plight grew worse, and thousands of industrial workers lost their jobs. That year—the year of the Pullman strike—hundreds of the unemployed marched on Washington. They were led by Jacob Coxey, a Populist who wanted the government to employ the jobless on public works. When "Coxey's Army" tramped onto the Capitol grounds, they were arrested for trespassing.

The depression was turning many voters against Cleveland. In the congressional elections that fall, thousands of voters flocked to the Populists. They won 42 percent more votes than they had in 1892, and elected 8 people to Congress and almost 500 to state offices.

The voters' mood also helped elect many Republicans and Democrats with Populist leanings. The discontent especially affected the Democratic party. It was split between silverites—mostly from the South and West—and backers of gold and President Cleveland.

WILLIAM JENNINGS BRYAN

By the presidential election of 1896 the Democratic silverites had gained control of the party. Cleveland was abandoned, and the party searched for a new candidate.

"All the silverites need," the New York *World* reported, "is a Moses. . . . They have the brass bands and the buttons and the flags, they have the howl and the hustle, they have the votes. But they are wandering in the wilderness like a lot of lost sheep." They found their leader at the Democratic convention—a silverite from Nebraska named William Jennings Bryan.

Bryan was guided by his faith in the Bible and by the democratic ideals of Thomas Jefferson and Andrew Jackson. Early in life, he had wanted to be either a minister or a farmer. Instead, he carried his speaking skills into politics and became a champion of the people.

Bryan served four years in Congress as a representative from Nebraska. "I don't know anything about free silver," he confessed during that time. "The people of Nebraska are for free silver and I am for free silver." By 1896, however, Bryan had schooled himself in the politics of silver.

Bryan electrified the Democratic convention with a speech that summed up the feeling of the silverites. Without silver, Bryan said, the farmers would be lost. Without farmers, the nation would be lost.

> You come to us and tell us that the great cities are in favor of the gold standard; we reply that the great cities rest upon our broad and fertile prairies.

> Burn down your cities and leave our farms, and your cities will spring up again as if by magic; but destroy our farms and the grass will grow in the streets of every city in the country. . . .

> We will answer their demand for a gold standard by saying to them: You shall not press down upon the brow of labor this crown of thorns, you shall not crucify mankind upon a cross of gold.

The convention exploded into wild cheers, shouting for Bryan and for "free" silver. The Democrats had taken over the Populist cause and made it their own.

THE ELECTION OF 1896

When the Populist convention met shortly after, it was bitterly divided. Many wanted to support Bryan, since he supported a vital Populist issue. Others argued that if they endorsed the Democratic candidate, the Populists would be doomed as an independent third party. Finally, the Bryan supporters won, and the Populist party endorsed him.

Bryan stormed across the country in an amazing campaign tour. He visited 21 states, made some 600 speeches, and traveled over 18,000 miles (29,000 kilometers). Meanwhile, Republican candidate Senator William McKinley of Ohio stood on his porch and spoke to crowds brought in by train for the occasion.

The Republicans tried to reach the supporters of the gold standard and unite them behind McKinley. Campaign literature flowed across the country. McKinley said nothing to offend anyone, trusting that the smooth-running operation of the Republican party would get him elected.

The Republicans counted not only on business support, but also on eastern Democrats who feared the Populist-inspired Democratic platform. Middle-class Americans, such as lawyers, small business owners, merchants, and office workers, felt the same way.

"Billy" Bryan gained the support of labor leaders Samuel Gompers of the AFL and Eugene V. Debs of the American Railway Union. Many workers, however, did not support Bryan and the Democrats. They were afraid the Democratic policies would lead to inflation, which would decrease the value of their wages.

On election day, only the farmers and the silver interests voted for Bryan. But theirs was a loud voice

William McKinley campaigned from his own front porch, refusing to leave his invalid wife. Still, he defeated Bryan, who campaigned across the country. Outgoing President Cleveland (in top hat, center left) walked with McKinley (center right) to the inauguration in 1897.

of protest—about 6.5 million votes. Bryan carried more states than McKinley, but they were the less populous states of the South and West.

McKinley, with 7 million votes, won all the industrial states from New England to the Great Lakes. *The Nation* wrote, "The silver lining no longer adorns the Western sky."

The election all but destroyed the Populist party, and movement began to fade. Still, a new voice had been heard in the land, the voice of farmers speaking together. Like the voice of labor, it would be heard again.

SECTION REVIEW

1. Identify the following: the Grange, Oliver Kelley, Greenback-Labor party, Farmers' Alliances, Mary Lease, James B. Weaver, Jerry Simpson, Jacob Coxey.

2. Define the following: cooperatives, greenbacks, free silver, gold standard.

3. (a) Why was the Grange formed? (b) In what part of the country were Granges strongest?

4. Why did farmers want the federal government to put more greenbacks into circulation?

5. (a) In 1889, what did the Farmers' Alliances demand at their St. Louis Convention? (b) What effect did the Alliances have on the Congressional election of 1890?

6. List seven provisions in the Populist platform of 1892.

7. How were the Bland-Allison Act of 1878 and the Sherman Silver Purchase Act of 1890 supposed to help the economy?

8. (a) What caused voters' discontent in 1894? (b) How did this discontent affect the Democratic, the Republican, and the Populist parties in the election that year?

9. (a) In the presidential election of 1896, what was the Democratic position on the issue of free silver? (b) What was the Republican position on the issue of free silver?

10. (a) What was the result of the election of 1896? (b) How did the result affect the Populist party?

CHAPTER SURVEY

SUMMARY

During the last three decades of the 1800s, the role of the average worker changed from one of independent craft or trade worker to one of factory worker. Under the factory system, there was an increase in the amount of goods manufactured. Industrial workers, however, became discontented. Wages were poor, hours were long, and working conditions were unhealthy.

To improve their lives, workers began to unite, and the labor movement began. Small specialized unions were formed. These led to the formation of large labor organizations representing many unions.

Labor organizations were undecided about the way to win shorter hours, higher wages, and better working conditions. Some favored legislation; others favored the strike. Eventually, however, increased labor unrest led to several violent strikes. When these strikes failed, industrial unions declined. By the end of the century, the labor movement was still in its infancy.

Changes brought by industrialization also affected farmers. Technological and scientific advances had turned farming into big business. Farmers planted more and more crops, and surpluses caused prices to drop in the international market. Farmers borrowed and mortgaged their land to finance the purchase of additional machinery and land. Poor harvests, declining prices, and deflation in the economy made it impossible for farmers to pay their debts.

Angered, farmers began to unite. Granges and Farmers' Alliances were formed. Farmers became a national political force with the formation of the Populist party. A change from the gold standard to a bimetallic standard of currency seemed to Populists and to some Democrats a way to solve economic problems.

The issue of whether silver should have free and unlimited coinage dominated the presidential election in 1896. The farmers and the silver interests were defeated when Republican William McKinley won the election. By the end of the century, however, it was apparent that the voices of farmers and of industrial workers would be heard again.

CHAPTER REVIEW

1. Describe the working conditions common to many factories between 1870 and 1890. Include wages, hours, and health and safety conditions.

2. (a) Compare the National Labor Union with the Knights of Labor. (b) Explain how the American Federation of Labor differed from both the NLU and the Knights.

3. Summarize the events of each of the following. (a) strike that began in Martinsburg in 1877 (b) Haymarket riot (c) Homestead strike (d) Pullman strike

4. What factors contributed to the growth and prosperity of American farming in the 1870s and 1880s?

5. List factors that became problems for American farmers in the 1870s and 1880s.

6. Compare the Granges with the Farmers' Alliances.

7. What were the objectives of the Greenback-Labor party? How did these objectives differ from those of the Granges and Farmers Alliances?

8. (a) Explain how the Populist party grew out of the Granges and Farmers' Alliances. (b) What were the objectives of the Populist party?

9. Explain the nature of the controversy between the silverites and those people who supported the gold standard.

Harvesting machines in 1870 were wonders of teeth and wheels. Combines would later replace these separate machines.

The benefits of Grange membership are depicted in this 1873 lithograph entitled "The Purposes of the Grange." The small scenes show different aspects of farm life.

10. Describe the presidential election of 1896, giving the candidates and their platforms, as well as the results.

ISSUES AND IDEAS

1. In Chapter 14 you read about events and conditions on the western frontier from 1870 to 1900. This chapter is largely about the East, the Midwest, and the South during the same period. Choose an area in the West and one in the East, and compare and contrast what was happening in a given year or decade.

2. What was the importance of the strike in the early labor movement? Determine how many of the five major strikes described in this chapter were successful. Give evidence of what they did or did not accomplish.

3. William Jennings Bryan said, "You shall not crucify mankind upon a cross of gold." Take a position as a silverite or as a supporter of the gold standard and defend it.

SKILLS WORKSHOP

1. *Timelines.* Construct a timeline from 1866 to 1900. Show the major events that were occurring in (a) the labor movement and (b) the farmers' attempts to organize. Include the dates that various organizations, such as unions and Farmers' Alliances, were founded and that strikes occurred, as well as any other pertinent date.

2. *Writing.* Take the position of a Populist candidate for president in 1896. Outline your platform. Use a formal outlining procedure, with Roman numerals for the main "planks" of your platform, and capital letters and Arabic numerals for subordinate ideas. Include positions on labor, farmers, and money.

PAST AND PRESENT

1. Today about 25 percent of the work force is unionized. Find out if there is an industry or industries in your community in which there are union members. What kind of a union is it? What does it do for its members? How are its objectives similar or different from the objectives of one of the early unions described in this chapter?

2. The Granges and the Farmers' Alliances were partly political and partly social. The Greenbacks and the Populists were political parties. From your knowledge of current events, are there any political parties today other than the Republican party and the Democratic party? What are some social or political action groups? List five such groups and explain their special interests.

This anarchist handbill announced in English and German a rally in Chicago's Haymarket Square. The rally ended in a riot.

QUESTIONS OF POWER

1865–1920

Childe Hassam. *Allies Day, May 1917* (detail), 1919.

1600	1700	1800	1900	2000
• Jamestown founded		• Revolutionary War	• Civil War	• Today

UNIT 6
1865–1920

1890	1900	1910	1920
Harrison	Cleveland	McKinley	Roosevelt	Taft	Wilson	

POLITICAL

- U.S. annexes Hawaii
- Spanish-American War
- U.S. annexes Philippines
- Open Door policy
- NAACP formed
- Roosevelt Corollary
- Sixteenth Amendment: income tax
- Clayton Antitrust Act
- *Lusitania* sunk
- Puerto Rico becomes U.S. territory
- U.S. at war with Germany
- Fourteen Points

SOCIAL

- First pro football game
- H.G. Wells: *War of the Worlds*
- Beatrix Potter: *Peter Rabbit*
- First teddy bears
- Mother's Day established

TECHNOLOGICAL

- John Loud: ballpoint pen
- Wright brothers: first airplane flight
- First crossing of U.S. by car: 65 days
- Peary reaches North Pole
- Marie Curie: Nobel prize for chemistry
- Zippers used in clothing
- Panama Canal completed

INTERNATIONAL

- First modern Olympic games, Athens
- Russo-Japanese War
- Jim Thorpe: Stockholm Olympics, gold medalist
- Mexican Civil War
- World War I
- Czar Nicholas II and family executed
- Treaty of Versailles

1890	1900	1910	1920

CHAPTER 17

THE UNITED STATES AS A WORLD POWER

1865–1916

THE UNITED STATES REACHES OUTWARD
THE SPANISH-AMERICAN WAR
NEW RESPONSIBILITIES
DIPLOMACY IN LATIN AMERICA
DIPLOMACY IN ASIA

In 1900 vice-presidential candidate Theodore Roosevelt, on William McKinley's presidential ticket, addressed the Republican convention:

"We stand on the threshold of a new century big with the fate of mighty nations. It rests with us now to decide whether in the opening years of that century we shall march forward to fresh triumphs or whether at the outset we shall cripple ourselves for the contest. Is America a weakling, to shrink from the work of the great world-powers? No. The young giant of the West stands on a continent and clasps the crest of an ocean in either hand. Our nation, glorious in youth and strength, looks into the future with eager eyes and rejoices as a strong [athlete] to run a race."

Roosevelt wanted to turn the nation's eyes outward, beyond its borders. In 1867 the United States had bought Alaska, but that was the last territorial expansion for nearly a quarter of a century. Americans had been busy at home, settling their western frontier, adjusting to industrialization.

As the new century approached, however, the nation plunged into world affairs. Some people opposed America's new interests. Others looked outward and saw new markets, a new frontier, and a new role for the United States as a world power.

To the south of the United States was the island-dotted Caribbean Sea, and embracing the Caribbean were Central and South America. To the west, spanning the Pacific, were the islands of Hawaii, Samoa, Guam, and the Philippines. Just beyond the Philippines loomed Asia. Each of these places—next door and halfway around the world—would become familiar to Americans.

THE UNITED STATES REACHES OUTWARD

READ TO FIND OUT

— how expansionists viewed a strong navy and a growing foreign trade.

— how the United States acquired territory in the mid-Pacific.

— how Hawaii became part of the United States.

While the United States was settling its western frontier, the industrial nations of Europe were engaged in a race to gain ownership or control of lands around the world. Within twenty years, Europe had established colonies in almost all of Africa. Colonies were also established in Asia and among the Pacific islands.

As economic competition among the world powers grew more intense, a few Americans urged the United States to seek more territory. For years these people's voices failed to arouse interest in acquiring territory. Eventually, however, the voices grew in number. From their clamor came territorial growth for the United States.

EXPANDING TRADE AND NAVAL POWER

One of the earliest Americans to acquire territory for the nation was William H. Seward, secretary of state to presidents Lincoln and Johnson. In 1867 Seward's efforts resulted in the planting of the American flag in the icy north. For $7.2 million, he purchased Alaska from Russia. Russia had found Alaska unprofitable, but Seward thought that the area had potential.

Until the 1880s, however, most Americans were not interested in acquiring new lands for the United States. Britain, France, Belgium, and the Netherlands might follow policies of **imperialism**—of building empires by conquering other countries and establishing colonies. Americans, however, had once been part of a colonial empire themselves and had fought a long war for independence. Americans, too, had vast open territories within their own nation. There was no reason to look outward while the American frontier remained unsettled.

By the 1880s, however, Americans were beginning to talk of the closing frontier. Although there were still huge amounts of open land, the availability of good land was shrinking. Some people began to look to lands beyond the nation's borders.

America's interest in the rest of the world began to grow, too, because of its expanding economy. The products of America's farms and factories were flooding the country, and spilling over into international markets.

American exports soared, from $281 million in 1865 to $1.4 billion by 1900. But other nations, too, sold their products abroad in competition with America. Many farmers and manufacturers hoped that more foreign markets would open up to them. They believed that increased exports could free the United States from economic depressions.

Captain Alfred Thayer Mahan of the Naval War College agreed that the country must expand its trade. He was dismayed that trading ports around

This family of goldseekers pulled its possessions across Alaska in 1898. Thousands flocked to Alaska when gold was discovered in Canada's Klondike and then in Alaska.

EXPANSIONIST IDEAS

Young politicians like Senator Henry Cabot Lodge of Massachusetts and Theodore Roosevelt of New York were strongly influenced by Mahan's ideas. Lodge wrote: "Commerce follows the flag, and we should build up a navy strong enough to give protection to Americans in every quarter of the globe." By the beginning of the new century the United States had a navy second only to that of Britain and France.

Mahan and people like Lodge and Roosevelt were expansionists. The construction of a strong navy and the expansion of trade led naturally to the expansion of the United States itself. If the country acquired new territories, it would have both naval bases and new markets which would increase trade.

Other expansionists had different goals. Josiah Strong, a Congregational minister, believed that America had a mission to spread Christianity throughout the world. In his popular book, *Our Country*, published in 1885, Strong wrote, "The Anglo-Saxon* is the representative of two great ideas. One . . . is that of civil liberty. . . . The other . . . is that of pure spiritual Christianity." According to Strong, Americans, as representatives of the Anglo-Saxon race, would "civilize" the world.

The theory of Social Darwinism also appealed to Strong and other expansionists. John Barrett, an American diplomat, wrote, "The rule of survival of the fittest applies to nations as well as to the animal kingdom." Strong agreed, arguing that because Americans were the fittest, they were destined to build a great empire.

the world were being taken over by the Europeans. Furthermore, foreign ships carried over 80 percent of America's exports and imports.

In 1890 Mahan published *The Influence of Sea Power Upon History*. Mahan argued that every great nation in history grew through naval power. The United States needed a bigger merchant marine to carry its goods. It needed a strong navy to protect the merchant marine, and naval bases around the world to protect its trade. To acquire naval bases, the United States should acquire or control islands in the Caribbean and Hawaii and Samoa.

At the end of the Civil War, the country had had an able navy. But Confederate warships had damaged the merchant marine. Many Confederate ships, such as the *Alabama*, had been built by the British, so the United States asked Britain to pay for the damages. In 1872 an international court settled the so-called *Alabama* claims according to terms spelled out in the Treaty of Washington, signed by the United States and Britain in 1871. Britain was ordered to pay $15.5 million in damages.

However, Congress was not interested in a strong peacetime navy. It set aside very little money for shipbuilding. Then, in the 1880s, Congress realized that several South American navies could defeat the United States fleet.

This revived Congress's interest in naval power, and within a few years 22 modern steel ships were built. In 1890, then, Mahan's book fueled an already strong interest in a powerful navy.

FIRST INVOLVEMENT IN THE PACIFIC

William Seward had, in 1867, annexed, or acquired, the Midway Islands, in the middle of the Pacific Ocean. For years, the United States showed no more interest in Pacific lands.

Then, in the 1870s, another group of mid-Pacific islands, Samoa, caught the interest of American land speculators and President Grant. Samoa, with its superb harbor of Pago Pago, had long been a stopover for American ships.

* Anglo-Saxon: descendant of the early peoples who settled England—the Angles, Saxons, and Jutes.

In the early 1870s, island chiefs and the interested Americans agreed on a proposal for annexation. The Senate rejected the proposal but did approve a trade treaty in 1878. The United States gained the right to build a naval base at Pago Pago.

Twenty years later, however, the antiexpansionist climate in the United States had changed. When civil war began in Samoa, the United States and Germany—which also had claims there—intervened. For months, the threat of conflict hovered over the two nations. Finally, in 1899, the United States, Germany, and Great Britain (which also had interests in Samoa) agreed to share control of the islands. The United States received the harbor of Pago Pago.

CONFLICT OVER HAWAII

In May 1897 Assistant Secretary of the Navy Theodore Roosevelt wrote to Captain Mahan: "As regards Hawaii I take your views absolutely. . . . If I had my way we would annex those islands tomorrow." Not everyone, however, shared those views. Argument over Hawaii had gone on for years.

American interest in the Hawaiian Islands dated back to the early 1800s. The British sailor, James Cook, had been the first European to learn of the Islands. He had landed on them in 1778. The people Cook traded with were descendants of immigrants from the Polynesian islands, who had settled in Hawaii 2,000 years earlier. Shortly after Cook's visit, in 1795, the individual islands were united under one ruler, King Kamehameha I (kah-MAY-hah-MAY-hah).

During the 1800s, traders from China, France, Spain, and the United States stopped in the Hawaiian Islands. Honolulu's Pearl Harbor became a favorite stopover for American whaling ships and traders on the route to China. Then missionaries from New England arrived to bring Christianity to the natives. The American missionaries settled there, and many of their offspring turned to sugar growing.

In 1875 Hawaii and America signed a treaty allowing sugar into the United States duty-free. Over the following years Hawaiian sugar poured into the United States. Hawaii became economically dependent on the United States and controlled by the sugar planters on the Islands.

Then, in 1890, the United States passed the McKinley Tariff Act. The act raised many duties but removed duties on all foreign sugar. Hawaii lost its special advantage. Now Cuban sugar, shipped only a short distance, sold in America more cheaply than Hawaiian sugar. The act protected planters in the United States by giving them a bonus of two cents on each pound of sugar they produced.

Hawaii's sugar economy was ruined. The foreign planters appealed to President Harrison to annex the Islands, so that the protection of the tariff act would apply to them too. Harrison and his minister for Hawaii, John L. Stevens, were eager for annexation.

In 1891, however, Hawaii's throne passed to a strong new ruler—Queen Liliuokalani (lih-LEE-oo-oh-kuh-LAH-nee). Over the next two years she tried to end foreign influence in Hawaii. She also tried to restore the power of the Hawaiian monarchy.

When Kamehameha I united the islands of Hawaii, about 300,000 Hawaiians lived there. By the time of Liliuokalani's reign, the Islands had become a melting pot of Hawaiians, Americans, British, Germans, Chinese, and Portuguese.

ANNEXATION OF HAWAII

American business interests, together with wealthy Hawaiians, were threatened by Queen Liliuokalani's actions. In January 1893 they began a revolution. Stevens called in United States marines, arguing that he had to protect American lives and property in the Islands, and the sugar planters quickly set up a provisional, or temporary, government. Queen Liliuokalani protested at this use of force but had to surrender her throne.

Representatives of the new Hawaiian government signed a treaty of annexation, which Harrison submitted to the Senate. Before the Senate could act, however, Grover Cleveland became president. Cleveland was enraged at the sugar planters and thought that the United States had behaved dishonorably by sending the marines into Hawaii. He withdrew the treaty.

For the next four years, expansionists badgered the government to annex Hawaii before another interested nation could. Antiexpansionists repeatedly blocked their efforts. By 1898 Americans, agreeing with expansionists, had become concerned that some other nation would take control of the Hawaiian Islands. In July 1898 Congress annexed the Islands, in the midst of a war that would bring the United States even more territory.

SECTION REVIEW

1. Identify the following: Alfred Thayer Mahan, Josiah Strong, *Alabama* claims, Henry Cabot Lodge, King Kamehameha I, John L. Stevens, Queen Liliuokalani.

2. Define the following: imperialism, expansionists.

3. Describe Alfred Thayer Mahan's theory about the importance of naval power.

4. (a) What effect did the McKinley Tariff Act have on the Hawaiian economy? (b) How would the annexation of Hawaii have solved this problem?

5. Explain how the United States came to have control of the harbor of Pago Pago.

6. (a) Give two reasons why Cleveland withdrew the treaty of annexation of Hawaii. (b) Give one reason why, in 1898, the United States annexed Hawaii.

THE SPANISH-AMERICAN WAR

READ TO FIND OUT

— how Cleveland applied the Monroe Doctrine in Venezuela.

— how yellow journalism affected American attitudes toward events in Cuba.

— how the Spanish-American War was won in the Pacific.

— how the Spanish-American War was won in the Caribbean.

In the mid-1880s Canadians and Americans were arguing over fishing and seal-hunting rights. American newspapers fanned the flames of the conflict. The Detroit *News* rephrased a popular British song of the 1870s to suggest that Americans and Canadians might go to war. In the song, the words "by jingo" were used.

The dispute was settled peacefully, but the word "jingo" was remembered. *Jingoism* came to refer to an intense national pride and support of a warlike foreign policy. By the 1890s, jingoism flourished in the American press.

APPLYING THE MONROE DOCTRINE

In 1891 the crew of an American warship joined a riot in Valparaiso, Chile, and two of the Americans were killed. Newspapers in the United States demanded action, and thousands of Americans volunteered to fight. The flare-up ended quietly when Chile apologized and paid an *indemnity*, or compensation for damages, to the United States.

The United States came even closer to war in 1895 over a border dispute between Venezuela and Britain's colony, Guiana (gee-AH-na). For decades the two nations had claimed the same slice of jungle. Claims became more important when gold was discovered there.

Venezuela asked the United States for help, and Congress urged the two countries to negotiate. The

British refused Venezuela's demand to submit the dispute to arbitration* by a neutral third party.

President Cleveland felt that he had to defend the Monroe Doctrine. The doctrine, issued in 1823, had warned European powers not to colonize further in the Americas and not to interfere with independent nations in the Western Hemisphere.

Cleveland's secretary of state, Richard Olney, sent a strong note to Britain declaring that the United States would not permit Britain to interfere in Venezuela. Furthermore, the United States demanded that the British submit the dispute to arbitration. Four months later, the British replied, saying that the Monroe Doctrine had not been violated and was, in any case, not part of international law.

Cleveland, Congress, and the country were furious. Congress voted for an American commission to investigate and then draw the boundary. Britain was enraged by this challenge to its power.

The real threat of war encouraged both nations to act responsibly. Britain, too, was encouraged to compromise because it was facing problems in Africa and did not want additional conflict. It agreed to submit the dispute to arbitration. In 1899 the conflict over the border was settled peacefully. As that crisis was passing, however, newspaper headlines turned Americans' attention to Cuba.

REVOLUTION IN CUBA

Cuba, only 90 miles (145 kilometers) off the Florida coast, was a colony of Spain. The Cubans had long chafed under Spanish rule, and from 1868 to 1878 had fought a war for independence. The revolution failed, but the Cuban anger remained.

In 1894 the United States, in the middle of a depression, imposed a high duty on Cuban sugar. Cuba depended on its sales of sugar to the United States. Because the new duty increased prices, sales fell sharply. The Cuban economy reeled. As Cubans sank deeper into poverty, their old resentment of the Spanish rulers exploded. In February 1895 they revolted once more.

Cuban revolutionaries stormed across the island, killing Spanish loyalists, tearing up railroad depots, and burning villages and sugar plantations. By Feb-

ruary 1896 the rebels were clearly winning. Spain responded by sending General Valeriano Weyler to force the colony back to order. Under Weyler's orders, thousands of men, women, and children were herded into prison camps, called *reconcentration camps*, in Spanish-held towns. Many died of hunger and disease.

Two New York newspapers—William Randolph Hearst's New York *Journal* and Joseph Pulitzer's New York *World*—were competing bitterly for circulation. Each tried to outdo the other with sensational accounts of the rebellion. Other papers rushed to increase their readership by printing stories sympathetic to the Cuban revolutionaries.

Headlines screamed that the Spanish were "feeding prisoners to sharks." The *World* warned: "American citizens are imprisoned or slain without cause." The stories became more and more distorted. Hearst said to one of his illustrators. "You furnish the pictures. I'll furnish the war."

A new kind of journalism was being practiced—a journalism based on emotional appeal rather than on facts. It became known as *yellow journalism*—a reference to the color of the paper on which newspapers were printed.

Yellow journalism helped to bring the United States to the brink of war. Americans probably would have been sympathetic to the Cubans in any

The cartoon favoring United States involvement in Cuba appeared in the New York *World*. Its caption read, "Peace, by jingo, if I have to fight for it."

---

* arbitration: the settlement of a dispute by a person or persons chosen to hear both sides and come to a decision.

event. The United States, after all, had undergone its own revolution and struggle for independence from a colonial power. Yet, the slanted newspaper coverage made many Americans feel that the United States had only one choice. It had to assume moral responsibility and bring order to Cuba.

TOWARD WAR

Antiwar Americans had an ally in President Cleveland, who wanted to keep the United States out of the conflict. As the presidential election of 1896 approached, however, expansionists managed to insert the Cuban revolution into the campaign. But the expansionists were to be disappointed with their candidate, William McKinley.

When he became president, McKinley announced, "We want no wars of conquest." In September 1897 McKinley's offer to help Spain negotiate peace in Cuba was refused. Spain was making its own gestures of peace by removing Weyler and doing away with its reconcentration policy.

The peace feelers came too late. Spanish loyalists in Cuba rioted, demanding Weyler's reinstatement. The revolutionaries wanted nothing short of independence. In the United States, two events pushed McKinley toward intervention.

The Spanish minister to America, Dupuy de Lôme (doo-PWEE duh-LOME), had written to a friend that McKinley was "weak and a bidder for the admiration of the crowd." A Cuban spy stole the letter, and it soon appeared on the front page of the New York *Journal*. Americans were outraged at this Spanish criticism of the President.

A few days later, on February 15, 1898, the American battleship *Maine* blew up in Havana's harbor, killing 260 sailors. McKinley had stationed the ship there to protect Americans in Cuba. The cause of the explosion remained a mystery, but the American press immediately blamed Spain. The battle cry "Remember the *Maine*!" rang throughout the country.

In March McKinley asked for a cease-fire between the Spanish troops and the Cuban revolutionaries. McKinley offered to arbitrate the dispute, making it clear that he was in favor of independence for Cuba. The Spanish agreed, in general, to these terms.

Despite the chance for a peaceful resolution, McKinley, on April 11, asked Congress to declare war. Apparently, the pressure for war had simply become too great for him to withstand. On April 20 Congress passed a resolution recognizing Cuba's independence and declaring war. Antiexpansionists, however, managed to add the Teller Amendment to this resolution. The Teller Amendment stated that the United States would not annex Cuba.

VICTORY IN THE PACIFIC

Even before war was declared, Assistant Secretary of the Navy Theodore Roosevelt had secretly cabled Commodore George Dewey in Hong Kong. Dewey was to prepare to attack Spain's Pacific fleet in the Philippine Islands.

On May 1, just 11 days after Congress's resolution, Dewey's fleet steamed into Manila Bay.

The Japanese print shows Admiral Dewey's forces bombarding the Spanish fleet in Manila Bay. All ten Spanish warships were destroyed, disabled, or captured.

The Spanish American War in the Caribbean 1898

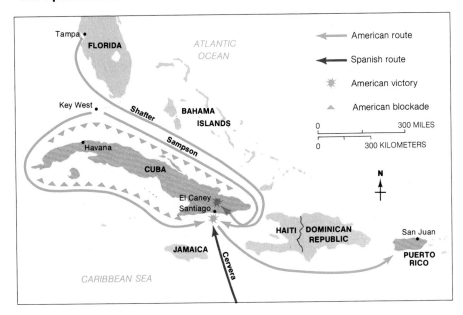

While Admiral Sampson's fleet blockaded Cuba on the north, Commodore Winfield Scott Schley's squadron patrolled to the south. Schley's squadron joined Sampson's in the battle against the Spanish fleet in Santiago harbor.

America's modern "steel navy" defeated the old-fashioned Spanish warships in a matter of hours, with no loss of American lives. Dewey then blockaded the bay and waited for reinforcements to attack the Spanish stronghold on the island.

Dewey's reinforcements arrived in August. The American force was swelled by Filipino rebels led by Emilio Aguinaldo (AH-gwee-NAHL-doh). The rebels wanted independence from Spain. On August 13 the combined American and Filipino forces attacked Manila and forced the Spanish to surrender the Islands.

VICTORY IN THE CARIBBEAN

On May 7, news of Dewey's victory at Manila Bay reached an America preparing for war. By June troops that had assembled in Florida had sailed and landed in Cuba.

General William Shafter led one group of Americans northward along the Cuban coast toward the Spanish stronghold of Santiago. On July 1 they were stopped just outside the city. At the village of El Caney about 600 Spaniards, concealed behind their fortifications, held off the 7,000 Americans. It took the Americans most of the day to dislodge the Spanish.

Nearby, another force of 8,000 Americans trudged through the jungle beneath San Juan Hill. The Spanish, atop the hill, sprayed the Americans with gunfire. Theodore Roosevelt, who had resigned from his government post to form a group called the Rough Riders, was among the pinned-down Americans. He saw that their best chance was to try to take the hill.

Roosevelt led the Rough Riders and black soldiers of the 9th Cavalry on foot in a charge up the hill. Individual soldiers from other regiments joined in the charge. Under withering Spanish fire, the Americans managed to reach the top and seize the Spanish garrison. "The battle simply fought itself," Roosevelt later commented.

America's armed forces numbered more than 200,000 during the war, but the Rough Riders received the most publicity.

STEPHEN CRANE
WRITING ABOUT WAR

"It was a fine morning and everybody—the doomed and the immunes—how could we tell one from another?—everybody was in the highest spirits." War correspondent Stephen Crane wrote these words just before the Rough Riders charged San Juan Hill. As the fighting began, "the crash of the Spanish fire became uproarious," he reported, "and the air simply whistled."

A tall, lean, watchful man, Crane was in Cuba covering the Spanish-American War for Joseph Pulitzer's *World*. At twenty-seven, he was already famous as the author of *The Red Badge of Courage*.

A preacher's son from New Jersey, Crane had dropped out of college to write. For the next three years, he lived in the New York slums. There he developed a realistic style of writing that was revolutionary for the time. While reading about the Civil War, Crane saw that no one had ever described how soldiers really felt in battle. He decided to try. The result was a novel about a young man in the Civil War. Crane's *The Red Badge of Courage* is perhaps the finest war story ever written.

When Crane wrote his brilliant novel about fear and courage under fire, he had never seen a battle. Now he repeatedly risked his life to get his story. He seemed almost ready to die in order to find out what war was like. Yet Crane had mixed feelings about the Spanish-American War. Though he felt caught up in a glorious adventure, he saw clearly the role that yellow journalism had played in the war.

Two years later Stephen Crane was dead of tuberculosis and malaria caught in Cuba. But his masterpiece—*The Red Badge of Courage*—survived. As Crane himself admitted after seeing his first battle, he had imagined war truly. *"The Red Badge,"* he said, *"is all right."*

The army had few lightweight uniforms so the 9th Cavalry and other American units in Cuba wore heavy dark blue wool.

Meanwhile, Admiral William Sampson and a squadron of American ships had trapped the Spanish Atlantic fleet in the harbor at Santiago. On July 3 the Spanish, led by Admiral Pascual Cervera (pas-QUAHL sayr-VAYR-ah), tried to fight their way out. In a four-hour battle, Spain's wooden ships were burned or run aground by the modern American fleet.

The 24,000 Spaniards in Santiago were trapped. American ships commanded the harbor, and American soldiers encircled the city. On July 17, the Spanish surrendered.

Shortly thereafter, an American force landed on the neighboring island of Puerto Rico. The Spanish put up a brief, unsuccessful, fight. Within a few weeks Spain had lost both of its Caribbean colonies.

PEACE

In a peace treaty signed in Paris in October 1898, Spain surrendered its claim to Cuba. It also ceded to the United States Puerto Rico, Guam (an island in the Pacific), and the Philippines. For the Philippines, the United States agreed to pay Spain $20 million. In addition, the United States acquired another Pacific possession—Wake Island.

The Spanish-American War lasted only four months and cost less than 400 American battle deaths. Thousands more died of dysentery, yellow fever, malaria, and typhoid.

This short little war had, however, far-reaching consequences. Until 1898, the United States' only overseas possession was the Midway Islands. After the Spanish-American War, the United States became a world power.

SECTION REVIEW

1. Identify the following: William Randolph Hearst, Joseph Pulitzer, the Teller Amendment, Theodore Roosevelt, George Dewey, Emilio Aguinaldo, Rough Riders, William Shafter, William Sampson.

2. Define the following: jingoism, yellow journalism.

3. What was the reason for American involvement in a dispute between Venezuela and Great Britain in 1895? How was the dispute settled?

4. (a) What was Spain's purpose in sending General Weyler to Cuba? (b) How did he carry out his mission? (c) How were his actions reported in the American press?

5. (a) How did an indiscreet remark by a Spanish minister to the United States come to the attention of the American public? What effect did the news have on Americans? (b) How did the explosion of the *Maine* affect relations between the United States and Spain?

6. (a) Describe Dewey's victory in Manila Bay. (b) Describe the American attack on Manila.

7. (a) Describe the attack on San Juan Hill. (b) Describe the American victory in the harbor of Santiago.

8. List four provisions of the formal peace treaty ending the Spanish-American War.

NEW RESPONSIBILITIES

READ TO FIND OUT

— why Americans argued over annexation of the Philippines.

— what rights were guaranteed people in incorporated and unincorporated territories.

— what steps were taken toward independence for the Philippines.

— how Puerto Rico became a Commonwealth.

— what status Cuba had in relationship to the United States.

The Spanish-American War made the United States a world power. Yet, it left the nation sharply divided. Expansionists were delighted to receive the new territories.

However, a small but vocal group of Americans opposed annexing territory. They formed an Anti-Imperialist League, attracting such people as Andrew Carnegie, Samuel Gompers, Mark Twain, Jane Addams, Grover Cleveland, and William Jennings Bryan.

The argument between the two groups soon centered on the Philippines. What happened in those islands would set the foreign policy course that the United States was to steer.

ANNEXATION OF THE PHILIPPINES

Early in 1899, the peace treaty ending the Spanish-American War was sent to Congress. Americans chose sides on the question of annexing the Philippines. Business leaders had opposed the war, but now they saw the territories gained as vast new markets. Church leaders saw the territories as opportunities for missionary work. And the navy saw the Philippines as an ideal Pacific base.

During the peace talks, McKinley had at first wavered over the question of annexation. However, he finally decided to annex the Islands. Many in

The United States in the Pacific 1865-1900

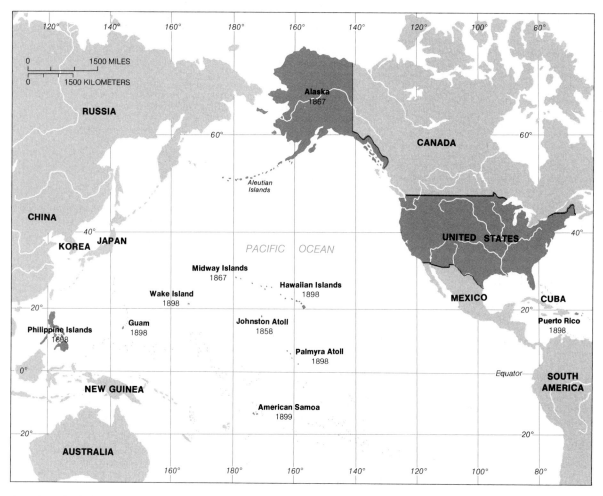

As early as the 1850s the United States claimed several small uninhabited coral reefs and atolls between Hawaii and Samoa. Wake Island was claimed by Dewey on his way to Manila. By 1900 U.S. possessions stretched across the Pacific to the Philippines.

Congress were bitterly opposed to annexation. Among them were Democrats, Populists, and some New England Republicans.

William Jennings Bryan, however, persuaded Democrats to vote for the treaty. Bryan was anxious to conclude the peace. He told Democrats that if they won in the election of 1900, they could then set the Philippines free.

The treaty was ratified in the Senate on February 6, 1899, by a margin of one vote. It was, said Senator Henry Cabot Lodge, the "hardest fight I have ever known."

While Americans argued over the treaty, Filipinos set up their own temporary, or provisional, government. Emilio Aguinaldo and the rebels had expected the United States to recognize Philippine independence. When Aguinaldo realized that the Islands were to be annexed, he led a revolt against American rule.

Aguinaldo's 80,000 rebels waged a bitter war of resistance against some 70,000 American soldiers. In the three-year struggle, over 4,000 Americans and 20,000 Filipinos were killed. Aguinaldo was captured in the spring of 1901, and took an oath of loyalty to the United States. The rebellion was over, although scattered fighting continued in the Philippines for years.

During the war in the Philippines, Bryan opposed McKinley in the election of 1900. Bryan thundered in one speech: "When we made allies of the Filipinos and armed them to fight against Spain . . . we had full knowledge that they were fighting for their own independence."

The Republican slogan was expansionist: "Don't haul down the flag." It was voiced loudest by McKinley's running mate, Theodore Roosevelt, in campaign tours across the country. The public listened. McKinley won the election by a bigger vote than he had in 1896.

Thus Americans approved their new empire, which had been born of the Spanish-American War. The Philadelphia *Record* wrote: "Our war in aid of Cuba has assumed undreamed of dimensions . . . willy nilly we have entered upon our career as a world power."

RULING THE NEW TERRITORIES

The United States now had territory on both sides of the globe. It would have to assume an unfamiliar role. Americans would have to create a policy toward the Filipinos, Puerto Ricans, and Cubans. Were these peoples to become independent, or colonial subjects, or American citizens?

Many Americans felt that a colonial role did not suit the United States. If people in the new territories could not be given independence, they should at least be given American citizenship rights. "The Constitution follows the flag," these Americans said. Others rejected this idea. The argument reached the Supreme Court in 1901. In a series of decisions known as the Insular Cases, the Court settled the argument.

New territories, the Court decided, would either be incorporated or unincorporated. People in *incorporated territories*—Hawaii and Alaska—would be given all the constitutional rights of American citizens. Furthermore, these territories could eventually become states. *Unincorporated territories*—the Philippines, Guam, Samoa, and others—would not become states. People in these territories were not entitled to all constitutional rights. However, certain fundamental rights, such as protection of life, liberty, and property, would be guaranteed in the unincorporated territories. Ultimately, these territories might be given independence.

The Supreme Court had made a decision about the legal status of the islands. McKinley and Congress, however, faced the practical task of governing them.

GOVERNING THE PHILIPPINES

On July 4, 1901, government of the Philippines passed from the American military to a civil commission sent by President McKinley. William Howard Taft, who had been a judge and law school dean, headed the commission and became the Islands' governor. The efficient Taft quickly set about building a government for the Filipinos. In time, they were promised, they could become self-ruling.

The commission became fairly popular with the islanders. Filipinos were soon taking part in the civil government, and three eventually joined the commission. The Americans built roads and schools and gave to peasants lands previously held by the Church. The islanders, who spoke various languages, began to learn English. However, they still brought up the subject of independence.

In 1902 Congress passed the Organic Act, which made the Philippines an unincorporated territory. The act approved the commission's work and gave some encouragement toward Filipino self-rule. Filipinos could now elect a lower legislative house, and the commission would become the upper house.

The Islands inched toward independence. A major step came in 1916 when Congress passed the Jones Act. The commission was replaced by a Filipino senate, but the American governor remained. Philippine independence would come as promised, but not for over thirty years.

This photo of a Philippine school class was taken in 1916. Under American occupation Filipinos developed their first public school system and a government-supported university.

GOVERNING PUERTO RICO

While Americans were governing the Philippines in the Pacific, they were also occupied in the Caribbean with Cuba and Puerto Rico. Puerto Ricans had welcomed the American overthrow of their Spanish rulers. After the war, the United States promptly established a military government, which set out to fight the island's terrible poverty.

Although some Puerto Ricans hoped for independence, many others set their sights on statehood. The United States proceeded slowly, as in the Philippines.

In April 1900 Congress passed the Foraker Act, organizing a civil government for Puerto Rico. The island would be run by an executive council appointed by the United States president, and a popularly elected lower house. Over the years, this tight control was loosened.

In 1917 a second Jones Act was passed. This one gave Puerto Rico control over both houses, retained an American governor, and made Puerto Rico an unincorporated territory. Here the similarity to the Philippines ended. Puerto Ricans were not slated for independence. Rather, they were granted American citizenship. Puerto Rico would remain under United States protection, until it became a self-governing commonwealth* 35 years later.

The photograph was taken in San Juan, Puerto Rico, in the early 1900s. A crowd gathered to watch the festivities as Puerto Rican soldiers marched in a Fourth of July parade.

GOVERNING CUBA

The status of Cuba was far different from that of the Philippines and Puerto Rico. Annexation was forbidden by the Teller Amendment, which Congress had passed in 1898 when it declared war on Spain. Still, the United States felt it must have some hand in governing Cuba. The war had left Cuba a ruins of scorched land, dead livestock, and disease. There was no government. Bandits ran the Island.

To help Cuba recover, the United States set up a military government under General Leonard Wood. What Cuba needed, Wood said, was "clean government . . . legal and educational reform."

---

*commonwealth: Puerto Rico's special status under the United States government allows it to make its own laws and handle its own finances. The United States provides for Puerto Rico's defense, allows unrestricted immigration from the island into the United States, and gives it a place in the American tariff system.

The Americans set political prisoners free, distributed food, built roads and schools, and improved sanitation. A team of army doctors under Dr. Walter Reed discovered that the insect carrier of yellow fever was a mosquito and thus were able to end a terrible epidemic.

In November 1900 the United States ordered Wood to arrange a constitutional convention in Havana. Cuban leaders were to write a constitution that guaranteed a special relationship between Cuba and the United States. The Cubans ignored the instruction. They framed their constitution on independence for Cuba.

Early in 1901 Congress attached an amendment, written by Senator Orville H. Platt, to an army funding bill. The Platt Amendment spelled out the terms by which Cuba could become independent. Cuba could not make foreign treaties that threatened its independence. It must never go deeply into debt. Cuba must sell or lease land to the United States for navy bases.

Most important, the United States could intervene in Cuba to maintain law and order and guarantee independence. In effect, Cuba became a protectorate* of the United States. Congress insisted that military forces would not be withdrawn until Cuba added the Platt Amendment to its constitution. The Cubans grudgingly agreed to add the amendment.

Then, in September 1901, McKinley was assassinated and Theodore Roosevelt, a devoted expansionist, took office. Europe and Latin America watched, expecting the United States to annex Cuba. However, in May 1902, Roosevelt upheld the promise that was part of the Platt Amendment and ordered American soldiers out of Cuba.

Cuban resentment lingered, however, and eventually boiled into rebellion. In September 1906, making use of the Platt Amendment, Roosevelt sent troops and an American governor back to the island.

When the rebellion ended, Roosevelt withdrew the troops. However, the United States would intervene three more times before Congress finally repealed the amendment in 1934.

SECTION REVIEW

1. Identify the following: Anti-Imperialist League, William Howard Taft, Organic Act, Foraker Act, Leonard Wood, Walter Reed, Orville Platt.

2. (a) Name three groups in the United States that favored annexing the Philippine Islands. Why did each group favor annexation? (b) What groups opposed annexation? Why?

3. Why did Filipino rebels fight American soldiers?

4. What did voters approve in the election of 1900?

5. What did the Supreme Court decide in the Insular Cases?

6. What major step came for the Philippines in 1916?

7. What provisions were made for Puerto Rico in the Jones Act of 1917?

8. List the four provisions of the Platt amendment.

* protectorate: a state or territory controlled and protected by another state.

DIPLOMACY IN LATIN AMERICA

READ TO FIND OUT

— **how a crisis in Venezuela was resolved.**

— **how the Roosevelt Corollary signaled a major shift in foreign policy.**

— **how the United States built the Panama Canal.**

— **how "dollar diplomacy" and "moral diplomacy" affected Latin America.**

— **how Wilson responded to a revolution in Mexico.**

— **how the United States and Mexico were brought to the brink of war.**

The month that he became president, September 1901, Theodore Roosevelt gave a speech at the Minnesota State Fair. He told the fair-goers:

> There is a homely adage which runs, "Speak softly and carry a big stick; you will go far." If the American nation will speak softly and yet build and keep at a pitch of the highest training a thoroughly efficient navy, the Monroe Doctrine will go far.

That homely saying was a West African proverb that Roosevelt had adopted as his own. Within a few years, Roosevelt's state fair message was put into action in the Caribbean.

STANDOFF IN VENEZUELA

In December 1902 British, German, and Italian warships sailed into the Caribbean and blockaded the coast of Venezuela. The British and Germans seized four Venezuelan gunboats. The British fired on one of Venezuela's ports and landed soldiers at another.

Venezuela owed all three countries a considerable amount of money. The Europeans had earlier tried negotiating with Venezuela's ruler Cipriano Castro. When Castro refused to pay the long-overdue debts, the Europeans decided to use force.

Mindful of the Monroe Doctrine, however, Germany and Britain first checked with the United States. Roosevelt approved, so long as the Europeans did not seize any territory.

Many Americans worried about European warships in the Caribbean. Newspaper headlines warned darkly that Europe was violating the Monroe Doctrine. Pressure mounted on Roosevelt to defend the doctrine.

Tension increased on all sides. Admiral Dewey, commanding the American fleet in the Caribbean, put his ships on alert. A Venezuelan fort fired on a German ship and the Germans struck back and destroyed the fort. Roosevelt warned the Germans that the United States would not allow them to seize territory in Venezuela or anywhere else in the Caribbbean.

Roosevelt, at Castro's request, urged the Europeans to agree to arbitration. Eager to avoid a confrontation with the United States, they agreed. The warships withdrew, and the claim was submitted to the International Court at The Hague, in the Netherlands.

The incident had significance for both Latin America and the United States. Latin Americans worried that such armed intervention might be repeated. For the United States, the Monroe Doctrine had been applied successfully. Yet, it, too, worried that European nations would again intervene in Latin America.

THE ROOSEVELT COROLLARY

Venezuela was not the only Latin American country to borrow money abroad. Its island neighbor, the Dominican Republic, owed Europeans over $20 million. The country had pledged its customs duties to pay the debts. Yet the Dominican Republic was paralyzed by civil war, nearly bankrupt, and clearly very close to *defaulting*, or failing to pay, its debts.

It seemed likely that European warships would reappear in the Caribbean. The International Court at The Hague had decided the Venezuelan case in favor of the Europeans. Thus, forceful intervention had brought results.

In May 1904 Roosevelt decided that it was time to defend the interests of the United States in the Western Hemisphere. "If we intend to say 'Hands off' to the powers of Europe," he wrote, "sooner or later we must keep order ourselves." Consequently, the United States would exercise "international police power" in Latin America.

This policy became known as the Roosevelt Corollary to the Monroe Doctrine. It signaled a major shift in American foreign policy. The Monroe Doctrine was designed to prevent European powers from intervening in Latin America. The Roosevelt Corollary announced that the United States alone could intervene in Latin America.

Early in 1905 Roosevelt took action in the Dominican Republic. Fearful of European intervention, the Dominicans agreed to let the United States run their customhouses and handle the debts.

Roosevelt then asked Congress to approve the agreement with the Dominican Republic in the form of a treaty. Democrats, already furious about the Roosevelt Corollary, blocked approval. Roosevelt did not press for a treaty but went ahead with his plan.

Roosevelt's plan worked. For two years the United States ran the Dominican customhouses and paid off the debts. With the American navy offshore, the Dominican civil war ended. In February 1907 the Senate at last approved Roosevelt's agreement with the Dominican Republic and signed it into law as a treaty.

PLANS FOR A CANAL

Roosevelt was successful, too, when he turned his attention to a strip of land called Panama. Shaped like a curved finger, Panama joins Central and South America and separates the Caribbean from the Pacific. That geography posed a problem during the Spanish-American War.

The U.S.S. *Oregon* had left San Francisco, steamed around the tip of South America, and north to the Caribbean to join the blockade of Cuba. The long journey—69 days—was not forgotten. Did the United States need a navy in each ocean, or was there another answer?

One possibility was to build a canal through Panama—a waterway to join the two oceans. A French company had tried to build such a canal in the 1880s but was defeated by the mountains and disease-infested jungle. Now Roosevelt was determined to build the canal despite all obstacles.

One obstacle was the Clayton-Bulwer Treaty, which the United States had signed with Britain in

1850. Each nation had agreed to joint control of a future canal. In 1901, Roosevelt's secretary of state, John Hay, met with the British ambassador, Sir Julian Pauncefote (PAWNCE-fote). The British agreed in the Hay-Pauncefote Treaty to let the United States proceed independently to build a canal.

There were two likely canal routes—one across Panama, the other through Nicaragua. Congress argued over the choice, but nature decided the issue in May 1902. Not far from the proposed Nicaraguan route, a volcano began rumbling and an earthquake leveled a town. Roosevelt and Congress chose Panama.

Because Panama was ruled by Colombia, Secretary Hay began talks with the Colombian minister. By the summer of 1903 there was a proposed treaty, but the Colombian government rejected the terms. Furious, Roosevelt said that the Colombians were barring "one of the future highways of civilization."

The discord prompted some Panamanians to think of revolting against Colombia. The rebels had a French ally named Philippe Bunau-Varilla (fil-EEP BOO-now var-EE-yah), a stockholder in a company owning rights to the Panama route. He secretly spoke to Roosevelt and Hay on behalf of the rebels. Roosevelt did not commit himself, but Bunau-Varilla believed that the United States would support a revolution.

The American warship, the U.S.S. *Nashville* arrived at Panama on November 2, 1903. The revolution took place the next day. American troops seized Panama's railroad, preventing Colombian soldiers from entering the country. The rebels—mostly railroad workers and members of Panama's fire brigade—won a quick victory. That evening, the Americans cabled Secretary Hay: "Uprising occurred tonight 6; no bloodshed. Government will be organized tonight."

THE PANAMA CANAL

The United States quickly recognized the new government and worked out a treaty with Panama's new minister, Bunau-Varilla. The Hay-Bunau-Varilla Treaty guaranteed Panama's independence and gave the United States control, "in perpetuity,"* of a Canal Zone 10 miles wide (16.1 kilometers). The United States agreed to pay Panama $10 million plus an annual fee of $250,000—the terms originally offered to Colombia.**

Some Americans called Roosevelt's action "piracy," and much of Latin America bitterly resented it. Yet Roosevelt had public support, and the treaty was approved by Congress.

Roosevelt was anxious to "make the dirt fly" on the Panama Canal. However, it was a slow beginning. First, plans had to be drawn. The swampy jungle had to be cleared of mosquitoes carrying yellow fever. This work was carried out under the direction of Dr. William Gorgas, who had worked with Dr. Walter Reed in Cuba. Gorgas helped not only to build the Panama Canal. His work also helped to eliminate the disease around the world.

Finally, in 1907, the Army Corps of Engineers let the dirt fly. Led by Colonel George Goethals, the engineers and some 43,000 workers dug the big ditch from sea to sea—a distance of 40.3 miles (64.8 kilometers). The canal was opened in August 1914 and hailed as one of the greatest engineering feats in the world.

In Charles Sheeler's painting, "Panama Canal," one of the canal's pairs of locks is clearly seen. Ships traveling in opposite directions may enter the locks at the same time.

*perpetuity: unlimited time.

**In 1921 the United States paid Colombia $25 million as partial compensation for its loss of Panama.

The United States in the Caribbean 1898-1941

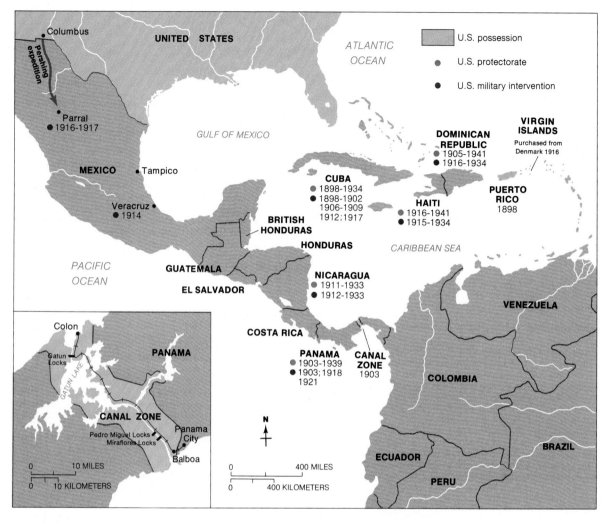

In the early 1900s the United States attempted to keep order in the Caribbean. For this reason the United States established unofficial protectorates or, at times, sent military units. Many Latin Americans viewed U.S. actions as interference.

DOLLAR DIPLOMACY

The presidents who followed Roosevelt inherited a delicate situation in the Western Hemisphere. Latin American leaders were growing acutely uneasy over American influence. No matter how American diplomacy in the Caribbean shifted, American influence continued to grow.

President William H. Taft, elected in 1908, had his own version of Roosevelt's "big stick" diplomacy. Taft's policy, which became known as "dollar diplomacy," was that Americans should use dollars rather than bullets: "The United States shall extend

all proper support to every legitimate and beneficial American enterprise abroad." American investments abroad, Taft believed, would both profit the United States and help Latin American countries to gain stability and peace.

Nicaragua, like many Latin American countries, had borrowed heavily from Europeans and pledged its customs duties to cover the loans. A year-long revolution shook the country in 1910 and gave it a pro-American president—a bookkeeper named Adolfo Díaz. Díaz asked the United States for help in sorting out his country's finances, and a treaty was drawn up.

It was agreed that the United States would give Nicaragua enough money to pay its debts. To protect its loan, the United States would operate the Nicaraguan customhouses. When the Senate refused to approve the treaty, Taft encouraged American bankers to make the loan and appointed an army officer to collect the duties.

Many Nicaraguans heartily disliked the American control of their finances. When a revolt flared in August 1912, Díaz asked Taft for armed help. Taft sent marines, on the grounds that American interests had to be protected. Troops remained until 1933, helping to make Nicaragua stable but also making it an unofficial American protectorate.

MORAL DIPLOMACY

Woodrow Wilson, who succeeded Taft in 1913, tried yet another kind of diplomacy—"moral diplomacy." Wilson courted Latin America: "We must prove ourselves their friends," he said, "and champions upon terms of equality and honor."

Wilson hoped to end the seemingly endless revolutions in Latin America and promote democracy. In practice, however, this meant using the marines to protect the governments in power and American interests. Wilson's diplomacy, like Roosevelt's and Taft's, came to depend on United States arms.

Wilson sent the marines to Haiti in 1914 and to the Dominican Republic in 1916. He kept a force in Nicaragua and sent another to Cuba. American newspapers became accustomed to printing, "The marines have landed and have the situation well in hand." Moral diplomacy, although well-intentioned, had the same effects as earlier forms of diplomacy. Increasingly, Latin America became dotted with United States protectorates.

REVOLUTION IN MEXICO

Wilson's diplomacy faced perhaps its toughest test in Mexico. For more than thirty years, Mexicans had suffered under the dictatorship of Porfirio Díaz. A small upper class owned almost all the land while most people lived in poverty. In 1911 Francisco Madero led a revolution that overthrew Díaz, then embarked on a series of reforms. Two years later, Madero was overthrown and shot by General Victoriano Huerta (WEHR-tah).

Many countries, both European and Latin American, quickly recognized Huerta's government. However, President Wilson would not, he said, recognize "government by murder." He was dismayed by the death of Madero's short-lived democracy and by a new government that he felt did not represent the people.

Huerta's control was not firm, and Mexico quickly became involved in a bloody civil war. General Venustiano Carranza, the leader of thousands of Mexicans, pledged to overthrow Huerta and continue reforms begun by Madero. One of Carranza's most daring generals was a former bandit named Francisco "Pancho" Villa (VEE-yah).

Wilson waited, futilely, for Carranza to break Huerta's hold. Finally Wilson urged Huerta to resign, asked other countries to withdraw diplomatic recognition, and offered to supply arms to Carranza. Huerta remained. By spring 1914, Wilson reluctantly decided that only American intervention could topple Huerta. The opportunity came in April.

Some American sailors, trying to buy gasoline in Tampico (tam-PEE-koh), Mexico, were arrested by Huerta's forces. Although the sailors were quickly released, with an apology, Wilson put the American navy on alert off the Mexican shore.

Shortly after the Tampico incident, Wilson learned that a German ship, loaded with arms for Huerta, was headed for Veracruz. Under Wilson's orders, marines poured into Veracruz and seized the town. The battle cost the lives of 19 Americans and over 400 Mexicans.

Outraged protest rang around the world, even in Carranza's rebel stronghold. The American intervention had backfired, and Wilson was eager to retreat. When Argentina, Brazil, and Chile offered to arbitrate, Wilson and Huerta quickly agreed. Carranza, however, refused. Not surprisingly, the mediation conference at Niagara Falls, Canada, solved nothing.

Huerta's power was badly eroded, and he resigned in July. No sooner had Carranza assumed the presidency, however, than his ally Pancho Villa turned against him. Wilson was unsure about whom to recognize. He supported Villa briefly, then switched to neutrality. In October 1915 he ended his policy of "watchful waiting" and, along with six Latin American countries, recognized Carranza's government.

In the Mexican Revolution women cooked for soldiers, nursed the wounded, and gathered weapons and ammunition as well as food. Many fought. The women of the Revolution came to be called *Adelitas*, after the heroine of a popular song.

The sight of American troops in Veracruz in 1914 angered both the followers of Huerta and the followers of Carranza.

TO THE BRINK OF WAR

Pancho Villa was furious at Wilson. He began a series of attacks against Americans. Perhaps, too, he hoped that by fighting against an unpopular foreign power, he would draw thousands of Mexicans to his cause. Early in 1916 his band murdered 16 American engineers who were traveling through Mexico. A few weeks later he crossed the border into New Mexico and burned the town of Columbus, leaving 19 Americans dead.

Wilson, supported by a stirred-up American public, told Carranza that he wanted to stop Villa. Carranza agreed to let the Americans pursue Villa into Mexico. Wilson ordered 150,000 members of the National Guard to the border. Then General John J. Pershing and a force of 15,000 chased Villa 300 miles (483 kilometers) through the heart of Mexico. To Carranza, the United States had far exceeded the agreement. He asked for an end to the "invasion."

The conflict quickly worsened. Villa struck again across the border, this time in Texas. The American forces massed along the border increased tensions. Wilson prepared for war.

However, neither Wilson nor Carranza wanted war. The United States and Mexico began negotiations late in 1916. Although the two nations could not agree on a settlement, war fever gradually cooled.

By early 1917 Wilson had a graver concern than Mexico. A war that had been raging for three years in Europe seemed likely to entangle the United States. In February Wilson ordered the Americans to withdraw from Mexico, and the two neighbors settled into a restored peace.

SECTION REVIEW

1. Identify the following: Cipriano Castro, Clayton-Bulwer Treaty, John Hay, Sir Julian Pauncefote, Hay-Pauncefote Treaty, Dr. William Gorgas, George Goethals, Adolfo Díaz, John J. Pershing.

2. (a) What three European countries were involved in a dispute with Venezuela? (b) What was the role of the United States in resolving the dispute?

3. (a) Explain the Roosevelt Corollary to the Monroe Doctrine. (b) How did Roosevelt practice this policy in the Dominican Republic?

4. (a) What was Philippe Bunau-Varilla's role in making the Panama Canal possible? (b) What were the terms of the Hay-Bunau-Varilla Treaty?

5. Describe "dollar diplomacy," and tell which president practiced it.

6. Describe "moral diplomacy," and tell which president practiced it.

7. List and identify five Mexican leaders during the time of the revolution.

8. (a) Describe Pancho Villa's actions following Wilson's recognition of the Carranza government. (b) What was the United States' response?

DIPLOMACY IN ASIA

READ TO FIND OUT

— how European nations partitioned China into spheres of influence.

— why the United States announced the Open Door policy.

— how Japan became a modern industrial nation.

— how conflict over Chinese territory brought Japan and Russia to war.

— why the Gentlemen's Agreement was negotiated.

— how Taft's actions damaged Japanese-American relations.

The Spanish-American War had left the United States a world power. The world powers eagerly traded in Asia, and competed to invest in railroads and mining and raw materials. The United States, with its own small Asian trade, paused at the edge of the competition. If it did not act soon, the door to Asia's trade might swing shut.

THE PARTITIONING OF CHINA

The United States had opened trade with China in 1784. The *Empress of China* sailed to China with raw cotton and furs. The ship returned to Boston with a cargo of tea, silk, porcelain, and jade that dazzled Americans. But China, cautious of trade with the West, sold more than it bought.

Foreign ships were allowed only in the port of Canton. In the 1790s, when Britain tried to expand its China trade, the Chinese emperor refused. "There is nothing we lack," he wrote.

Through the first half of the nineteenth century, however, foreign merchants and missionaries made inroads into China. A British-Chinese war flared over trade in the 1840s and China was forced to open more ports to Britain. Other nations, including the United States, soon made their own treaties to trade with China. As the years passed, Chinese ports filled with foreign merchants—and foreign navies.

In the 1890s China lost a war to Japan, and the Chinese helplessness emboldened the foreigners. The foreign powers carved China into **spheres of influence**, areas in which each had exclusive rights to trade and to invest. Japan's sphere of influence was the island of Formosa. Russia claimed Manchuria, in northern China. Germany's sphere was the Shantung (Shandong)* Peninsula on the Pacific coast, and France's was Kuangchou (Guanzhou) Bay in southern China. Britain held the ports of Hong Kong and Shanghai and, inland, the Yangtse (Jinsha Jiang) Valley.

At first, the United States was not concerned about this *partitioning*, or dividing, of China. But then traders and missionaries began to fear that the United States would lose its access to China. Although Chinese-American trade had never been large, Americans were now talking of expanding it. After all, sprawling China covered almost one fourth of Asia, with a population of some 400 million.

THE OPEN DOOR POLICY

Throughout the 1800s all nations had enjoyed equal opportunity in China—paying the same port fees and duties, and trading freely. But this "open door" was threatened by the partitioning of China into European spheres of influence.

President McKinley and Secretary of State John Hay agreed that the door to China must not be closed on the United States. In the fall of 1898 Hay sent letters to the nations involved in China, urging them to follow the Open Door policy. The letters asked that, in each sphere, ports remain open to trade of all nations and that the nations cooperate in establishing equal railroad rates and port fees. Hay also suggested that the Chinese collect duties in each sphere.

Britain liked the idea, Russia did not, and the other nations would not commit themselves. Still, in May 1900, Hay announced that the Open Door policy was in effect.

As Hay was making his announcement, a secret society that opposed all "foreign devils" was gath-

---

* As of January 1, 1979, the People's Republic of China started using a new system of translating Chinese words into the Roman alphabet. Words in the new system—called Pinyin—are shown in parentheses on maps and in the text.

Foreign Influence in China 1900

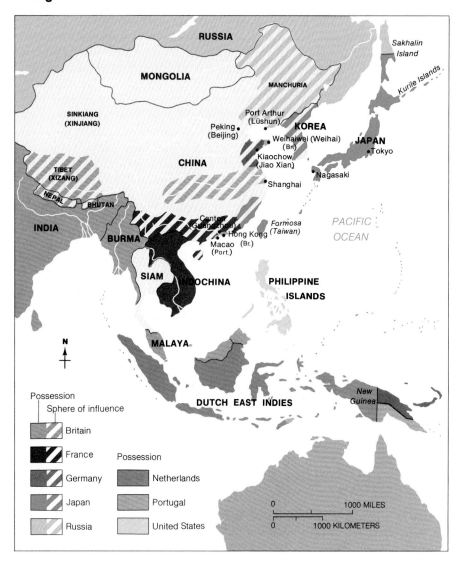

ering strength in China. In June 1900 the *Boxers*—a poor translation of their society's name—rampaged through the city of Peking (Beijing). They killed over 200 foreigners and laid seige to the city's foreign headquarters. In mid-August soldiers from Japan, Russia, Europe, and the United States poured into Peking, crushed the rebellion, and rescued their trapped citizens.

In the midst of the Boxer Rebellion, Hay sent out a second Open Door letter. Hay was worried that the powers would use the rebellion as an excuse to seize Chinese territory. In his letter, Hay said that the United States wanted to preserve both China's territory and its government. In addition, he wrote,

the United States wished to "safeguard for the world the principle of equal and impartial trade with all parts of the Chinese empire."

This letter, unlike the earlier one, was not a request. It was a statement of American foreign policy. Great Britain, France, and Germany accepted the policy. The other powers, wary of a fight over territory, observed it.

In September 1901, as a settlement of the rebellion, China agreed to pay indemnities amounting to $332 million. Of the $24.5 million that the United States received, most was returned to China to finance Chinese scholars studying in the United States.

The photo of foreign businessmen was taken in China in 1875. By the end of the century many Chinese angrily blamed all foreign merchants for treaties unfavorable to China.

Although China did not lose lands in the Boxer settlement, Chinese territory was still threatened. Off the Chinese coast was a powerful neighbor who had already clashed with China over territory. Japan, land-poor, would soon reach for more.

THE OPENING OF JAPAN

Japan was a newcomer to world affairs. For over two centuries, from the 1600s to the mid-1800s, the Japanese had pursued an antiforeign policy. Japan's only contact with the world came at its port of Nagasaki, where Dutch trading ships were allowed infrequent stops.

On July 8, 1853, an American naval squadron, led by Commodore Matthew Perry, dropped anchor off Japan. Perry asked Japan to open trade with the United States. He also presented the Japanese with a show of American force, including two steam-powered frigates. Perry then sailed on to China and returned eight months later to receive Japan's answer.

The Japanese were impressed with the American ships and with Perry's gifts, including several farm machines. They would, however, agree only to limited trade. Still, the American-Japanese treaty caused a shift in Japan's policy, opening the islands to the rest of the world.

Japan later signed treaties with other nations. Foreigners flooded the country, causing turmoil. In 1868, Japan's turmoil produced a new government intent on "obtaining knowledge in the world."

The artists also made portraits of each officer, including this likeness of Commodore Perry.

Before the use of the camera, artists' sketches provided important records. Japanese artists recorded Commodore Perry's visit, one artist showing special interest in the uniforms and weapons worn by the American officers. The Perry expedition introduced the camera to Japan.

Japanese scholars and officials toured the world, learning from other countries. Japan turned to British experts to learn about democratic ways and shipbuilding. Americans gave advice about industry, banking, and education. German military officers trained a modern Japanese army. Within thirty years, Japan leaped from isolation to become a modern industrial nation.

THE RUSSO-JAPANESE WAR AND THE AMERICAN PEACE

Industrialization, however, brought Japan problems. With new medicine and better sanitation, the death rate dropped and the population soared. Japan began importing food. It also began to look for a source of raw materials for its growing industry. By the 1890s, Japan had decided that it needed more territory.

Japan began competing with Russia for two nearby areas. Both nations had plans for Chinese-controlled Korea and China's northeastern province of Manchuria. Japan had strong influence in Korea after defeating China in the war in 1894. Russia, however, also wanted control of Korea, and had long-standing claims in Manchuria.

After the Boxer Rebellion, Russia showed increased interest in Manchuria. Japan appealed to the United States, pointing out that Russia was threatening the Open Door policy. Secretary Hay urged the Russians to leave Manchuria alone.

Japan then decided to stop Russian advances into Manchuria and Korea on its own. In February 1904 Japan attacked a Russian naval base at Port Arthur, Manchuria. The surprise attack launched the Russo-Japanese War.

President Roosevelt soon grew worried that Japan, if it won this war, might then develop an interest in the Philippines. In July 1905 he sent Secretary of War William Taft to meet Japan's foreign minister. The two countries agreed that the United States would not interfere with Korea, and that Japan would stay out of the Philippines.

Meanwhile, Roosevelt offered to arrange a peace conference between Japan and Russia. Exhausted by the costly war, both accepted. In September 1905 they signed a treaty at Portsmouth, New Hampshire. Japan, acknowledged as the victor, gained a good deal. It received recognition of its claims in Korea, control over southern Manchuria, and part of Russia's Sakhalin Island. But Roosevelt asked Japan to give up its demand that Russia pay an indemnity for Japanese war losses.

Roosevelt's peacemaking won him worldwide praise and a Nobel peace prize. The Japanese, however, felt cheated. Thanks to the Treaty of Portsmouth, Japan was now a world power. Losing the indemnity, however, was a heavy blow to Japan's economy, and the Japanese blamed Roosevelt.

SOURED RELATIONS

In the aftermath of the war, good will between the United States and Japan soured. One reason for this was the treatment of Japanese immigrants in the United States. Resentment of Japanese was especially strong in California, where Japanese were accused of working for low wages and thus taking jobs from other workers. In October 1906 the San Francisco school board placed the city's Japanese students in a segregated school. Japan was outraged, and Roosevelt was furious at "the infernal fools" who had done this.

Roosevelt invited the schoolboard to the White House, where an agreement was reached. The school-

These Japanese children were attending school in California in 1910. By then many Japanese immigrants had developed lush farms on lands once considered unproductive.

board would end the segregation if Japanese immigration was restricted. Roosevelt next negotiated the "Gentlemen's Agreement" with Japan. Japanese wouldn't be barred from entering the United States, but Japan would discourage emigration.

Still, the crisis had caused talk of war in both countries. Roosevelt decided to display American power as a warning to Japan. In December 1907 he sent the American fleet, including 16 new battleships, on a world tour with a stopover in Japan.

Roosevelt also used diplomacy to ease the tension. In May 1908 his secretary of state, Elihu Root, concluded an agreement with the Japanese ambassador, Baron Kogoro Takahira (tah-kah-HEE-rah). Both countries agreed to maintain the balance of power in the Pacific, respect one another's territories, and support China's independence. Although the Root-Takahira Agreement guaranteed the Open Door policy in China, Japan still had control of southern Manchuria.

RAILROAD DIPLOMACY

By 1910 Roosevelt's successor, President Taft, was trying to enforce the Open Door policy in Asia through dollar diplomacy.

A group of French, German, and British bankers was preparing to finance railroads in central and southern China. Taft, believing that American investment would strengthen United States policy, urged the Europeans and China to accept American participation. The American bankers were eventually admitted. Meanwhile, dollar diplomacy centered on Manchuria.

Taft wanted all of China to be open to American investment, but Japan had shut the United States out of southern Manchuria. So Taft and Secretary of State Philander Knox tried to persuade American bankers to finance a railroad in Manchuria to compete with Japan's South Manchuria Railroad.

Knox also had an alternate plan. China, financed by an international group of bankers, would buy all the Manchurian railroads. Either plan, Knox believed, would "smoke Japan out" of Manchuria and restore the Open Door there.

The American actions alarmed the other powers, who feared any shift in the balance of power. They rejected Knox's scheme. Next, old enemies Japan and Russia allied to hold on to Manchuria. Thus, dollar diplomacy damaged the Open Door policy.

When Woodrow Wilson succeed Taft, he reinforced the Open Door with his moral diplomacy. He asked the American bankers to withdraw from the international group, because it threatened China's independence. Soon after Wilson repaired relations with China, he had to deal with a new Japanese-American crisis.

In 1913 California passed a law barring immigrant Japanese from owning land. Wilson refused to act. Japan objected loudly, considering the law an insult. Then Wilson asked the California governor and legislature to change the law. California refused. Again, talk of war flared, then died down.

The United States policy in Asia remained bound to the Open Door policy, but the door hinged on a delicate balance of power. Roosevelt, in a letter to Taft, had warned:

> The "open-door" policy in China was an excellent thing . . . but as has been proved by the whole history of Manchuria, alike under Russia and under Japan, the "open-door" policy, as a matter of fact, completely disappears as soon as a powerful nation determines to disregard it, and is willing to run the risk of war rather than forego its intention.

Roosevelt's warning about the Open Door policy could have been applied to other areas of international conflict. In the future, as well as in the past, powerful nations would all too willingly risk war.

SECTION REVIEW

1. Identify the following: Boxer Rebellion, Elihu Root, Kogoro Takahira, Philander Knox.

2. List the countries that had spheres of influence in China, and the areas that each claimed.

3. (a) Describe the Open Door policy. (b) Why did its authors feel it was necessary?

4. Describe Matthew Perry's visit to Japan and its effects.

5. (a) Why did Japan and Russia go to war? (b) List the terms of the Treaty of Portsmouth.

6. (a) What was the "Gentlemen's Agreement"? (b) Why was it negotiated?

7. Describe the Root-Takahira Agreement. What did it guarantee?

8. What was the result of Knox's plans for Manchuria?

SUMMARY

With the purchase of Alaska and the Midway Islands in 1867, the United States began to expand beyond its borders. By the 1880s, many Americans had a new vision of the United States. They wanted the nation to take its place among the world powers. Expansionist ideas led to involvement in Samoa. Then, in 1898, Hawaii became part of the United States.

In the Western Hemisphere, the United States used the Monroe Doctrine to prevent European nations from intervening in Latin American affairs. Then, in the late 1890s, revolution in Cuba caused conflict between the United States and Spain. Yellow journalism helped to ignite war fever in the United States. The Spanish-American War, lasting only four months, gave the United States control of Puerto Rico, Guam, the Philippines, and Wake Island, and made the nation a world power.

After the war, the United States had to decide how to govern the new territories. The Philippines became an unincorporated territory, slated for future independence. Puerto Rico became a Commonwealth. Grudgingly, Cuba, which had become independent from Spain, became, in effect, a protectorate of the United States.

A new attitude toward foreign policy was expressed, in 1904, in the Roosevelt Corollary to the Monroe Doctrine. Roosevelt stated that the United States could intervene in Latin America. This policy led to American involvement in the Dominican Republic and Panama. Further involvement came under Taft and then Wilson, in Nicaragua, Haiti, Cuba, the Dominican Republic, and Mexico. As the United States faced problems in Latin America, it built the Panama Canal, which connected the Atlantic and Pacific Oceans.

The United States also looked to the East—to Asia. European powers had partitioned China for purposes of trade and investment. The United States worked, through the Open Door policy, to keep China open to trade for all nations. It also established trade with Japan, which in the late 1800s, became a modern industrial nation. When Japan and Russia went to war, the United States helped to bring peace.

CHAPTER REVIEW

1. What did William H. Seward and Captain Alfred Thayer Mahan have in common? Discuss the influence of each on the foreign policy of the period.

2. Compile a list of events that led to the American annexation of the Hawaiian Islands in 1898.

3. (a) What role did yellow journalism play in shaping the attitude of the United States toward the Cuban revolution? Toward the blowing up of the battleship *Maine*? Toward de Lôme's letter to a friend? (b) What happened at San Juan Hill and at Santiago? At Manila Bay?

4. Describe the status of Cuba and Puerto Rico after the Spanish-American War. Include reference to unincorporated territories, the Jones Act, the Foraker Act, the Teller Amendment, and the Platt Amendment.

5. Compare the status of the Philippines after the Spanish-American War with that of Cuba and Puerto Rico.

6. Explain how the Monroe Doctrine was applied in each of the following incidents: (a) the dispute between Venezuela and British Guiana in 1895; (b) the confrontation between British, German, and Italian warships and Venezuela in 1902; (c) the affair of the Dominican Republic in 1905-1907.

Rapid urban growth meant a rapid rise in newspaper circulation. Big-city papers brought their readers banner headlines, inside stories, and advertisements for the products of industrial America.

The famed Japanese artist, Hiroshige, made this print showing Commodore Perry's flagship. The ships commanded by Perry were the first U.S. naval vessels to enter Tokyo Bay.

7. Compare the results of Roosevelt's "big stick diplomacy" in Panama, Taft's "dollar diplomacy" in Nicaragua, and Wilson's "moral diplomacy."

8. Summarize the sequence of events in Mexico from the overthrow of Díaz to the negotiations between the United States and Mexico in 1916.

9. (a) What was the relationship between spheres of influence in China and the Open Door policy? (b) What was the Boxer Rebellion, and how was it settled?

10. Trace the relations between the United States and Japan, beginning with Commodore Perry's arrival through the Root-Takahira Agreement.

ISSUES AND IDEAS

1. The following ideas appear in this chapter: spheres of influence, expansionism, Social Darwinism, and jingoism. Give a brief definition of each, and discuss how they are related.

2. What was Theodore Roosevelt's role or viewpoint in each of the following events: the annexation of Hawaii, Dewey's attack on Manila Bay, Cuban self-governance, the incident off Venezuela in 1902, and the agreement with Panama over the canal? Write a one-paragraph statement, as Roosevelt might have done, expressing his position on foreign policy.

3. Roosevelt was preceded as president by William McKinley. Find events in this chapter in which McKinley's influence affected events. How did McKinley differ from Roosevelt regarding expansionist policy?

SKILLS WORKSHOP

1. *Chart.* Make a chart, or table, summarizing the results of United States intervention in the following areas in the period described in this chapter: Cuba, Puerto Rico, the Philippines, Panama, Nicaragua, Mexico.

2. *Map.* Using the map, "Foreign Influence in China 1900," list the countries involved and estimate the percentage of China in which each had a sphere of influence. Also list the European countries with possessions in Asia, and name their possessions. Arrange the list according to the amount of territory held, from most to least.

W.A. Rogers' cartoon comments on Theodore Roosevelt's policies. One toy ship is named "The Receiver," a reference to America's role as customs collector for other countries.

PAST AND PRESENT

1. For decades, the United States owned and operated the Panama Canal. In 1978 the Senate ratified two treaties that would eventually give Panama control of the Canal. Find out about the terms of these treaties.

2. Until the mid-nineteenth century, Japan had very little contact with any other country, either culturally or with regard to trade. How has that situation changed today? Give examples.

CHAPTER 18

THE PROGRESSIVES

1900–1917

**THE IMPULSE FOR REFORM
REFORM IN CITY HALL AND STATEHOUSE
ROOSEVELT, THE PRACTICAL REFORMER
TAFT AND WILSON**

In 1911 a fire raged through New York's Triangle Shirtwaist Company. Frances
Perkins, an eyewitness, described the scene:

"It was a fine, bright spring afternoon. We
saw the smoke pouring out of the building.
We got there just as they started to jump. . . .
They came down in twos and threes, jumping
together in a kind of desperate hope.

"The life nets were broken. The fire-
fighters kept shouting for them not to jump.
But they had no choice; the flames were right
behind them. . . .

"Out of that terrible episode came a self-
examination . . . in which the people of this
state saw for the first time the individual
worth and value of each of those 146 people
who fell or were burned in that great fire. . . .

"There was a stricken conscience of public
guilt and we all felt that we had been wrong,
that something was wrong with that building
which we had accepted or the tragedy never
would have happened. Moved by this sense
of stricken guilt, we banded ourselves together to find a way by law to prevent this
kind of disaster."

The workers were trapped in that blazing building because exits were locked, fire
escapes collapsed, and stairways were narrow. "Out of the ashes of the tragedy,"
wrote Perkins, rose the Factory Investigating Commission. It stirred the state legislature
to pass tough protective laws. This was one response in one state to a single disaster.
But all across the United States, people were stirring to correct injustices.

The stirring began before 1900 in the hearts and minds of a few thousand people.
It flared into a reform movement, whipping through the cities, the states, and straight
into the heart of the nation and the minds of presidents. It was a movement of hope
and optimism, and it became known as progressivism.

THE IMPULSE
FOR REFORM

READ TO FIND OUT

— how the progressive movement began.

— how muckrakers spread progressive ideas.

— why the NAACP was formed.

— what part women played in the progressive movement.

— how progressives became associated with the labor movement.

The United States, in the first years of the twentieth century, was changing profoundly. In foreign affairs, the nation grew from an inexperienced young country to a major world power. At the same time, a new spirit was taking hold at home.

While the United States won victory in the Spanish-American War, a wave of prosperity cleansed the nation of the 1893–1897 depression. Business was booming again. Inventions—automobiles, airplanes, cameras, X-rays—continued to dazzle Americans. Booming industry and rapid change, however, heightened problems, such as political corruption, poverty, crowded cities, and monopolies.

PROGRESSIVISM

Populism—the upheaval of the 1890s—had ended when William Jennings Bryan lost to McKinley in the election of 1896. The spirit of reform passed on to others. The new reformers, however, were markedly different from the populists.

Populism had been a movement of farmers, growing desperate as the economy dove into depression. The new movement was born in the cities, during a surge of prosperity, and took root in the middle class. The reformers saw poverty and corruption as problems that *could* be solved, and therefore *should* be solved. They were confident that they could redirect progress toward reform. They became known as progressives.

The progressives were middle-class lawyers, doctors, merchants, ministers, office workers, homemakers, writers, manufacturers—Democrats as well as Republicans. Many had special concerns, such as giving women the vote, ending child labor, improving education, banning alcohol. Others were business people rebelling against corporate giants. Often people became progressives simply for practical reasons. Railroad rates were hurting their businesses, for example, or the slums were spreading disease.

A strong backbone of the movement, however, was idealism. "It is natural to feed the hungry and care for the sick, it is certainly natural to give pleasure to the young, [and] comfort the aged," wrote Jane Addams, the founder of Hull House. Social workers like Addams and thousands of others became progressives out of compassion.

Although progressives had dozens of different concerns, the movement soon focused on three major aims. Progressives wanted to help the poor by improving working conditions and cleaning up the slums. They hoped to end business abuses that concentrated wealth among the few and destroyed

Susan B. Anthony had begun working for women's suffrage in the 1850s. Her influence led many progressives to view women's suffrage as a necessary political reform.

free enterprise. Third, they wanted to pry government out of corruption's grip and return it to the hands of the people.

THE MUCKRAKERS

Books helped to ignite progressivism. Jacob Riis' account of the slums, *How the Other Half Lives* (1890), converted many to progressivism. In 1886, in *Progress and Poverty*, Henry George described how monopolies destroyed economic opportunity. The book sold over 2 million copies.

It was magazine articles, however, that brought progressivism to most Americans. Samuel Sidney McClure, an editor who wanted to increase the readership of his magazine, assigned some of his best writers to investigate corruption.

One of these writers was Ida Tarbell, who had studied history at the Sorbonne in Paris. McClure asked her to find out the true story of Standard Oil. The result was a series of articles that revealed in detail Standard Oil's cutthroat methods.

In January 1903 *McClure's* magazine ran three articles on corruption. Among them was one of Tarbell's Standard Oil pieces. Also featured was an article on police corruption in Minneapolis by Lincoln Steffens, a former newspaper editor. The third story, on dishonest leaders in the mine workers' union, was by Ray Stannard Baker. In an editorial, McClure wrote, "Capitalists, workers, politicians, citizens—all breaking the law, or letting it be broken. Who is left to uphold it? . . . There is no one left," he continued, "none but all of us."

That ten-cent issue of *McClure's* caused a sensation. Other monthly magazines rushed into print their articles exposing crime and scandals. Steffens collected his articles into a book, *The Shame of the Cities*. Tarbell did the same, and the *History of the Standard Oil Company* stunned the public.

Journalists investigated slums, poor working conditions, child labor, lynching, false advertising, bribery in the Senate, and a host of other evils. Novelists brought these problems to life in fiction. Frank Norris exposed railroad abuses in *The Octopus*. Theodore Dreiser wrote of a ruthless tycoon in *The Financier*.

Most of the journalists were from small towns and were truly shocked by the big-city problems they found. Some, however, overstated their findings for effect. In 1906 Theodore Roosevelt compared them to a character in John Bunyan's *Pilgrim's Progress*, who did nothing but rake filth and muck. Such people, said Roosevelt, "are often indispensable to the well-being of society, but only if they know when to stop raking the muck."

The name "muckrakers" took hold. Although the muckrakers offered few solutions to the problems they uncovered, they made Americans aware of society's flaws. Thousands of their readers were stirred and called for reform.

THE RANGE OF REFORM

Most progressives did not blame impersonal powers like Wall Street or Congress for society's ills. "We are responsible," wrote Lincoln Steffens, "not our leaders, since we follow them." This personal urge to reform seeped into the heart of society.

Church leaders urged their congregations to live their daily lives as Jesus would, helping the needy. Painters portrayed workers and machines, the tenements and rooftops of city life. Their realistic style became known as the "Ashcan School." Professional societies of engineers, doctors, and lawyers turned their talents to improving society.

Progressivism especially influenced education. Since the Civil War, the United States had been building schools at a dizzying rate. In 1870, only 57 percent of school-age children (5 to 17 years old) went to elementary and high schools. By 1900 attendance had jumped to 72 percent.

Most people now supported tax-funded public schools. Most states had passed laws requiring school attendance. The nation was growing devoted to its children's education, and people had new ideas about how students should be taught.

The traditional teaching method stressed memorization. To show what they had learned, students recited lessons in subjects like arithmetic, history, and geography. But a group of progressive educators wanted to broaden teaching methods and subjects.

The founder of progressive education, John Dewey, believed that children should learn by doing. In laboratories, kitchens, gymnasiums, and gardens—as well as in classrooms—students would work on projects, learning at their own pace. They would relate learning to their interests and to current problems. Teachers would have more time for individual instruction.

The ferment in schooling also reached colleges and universities. College enrollment was exploding, from 52,000 students in 1870 to 600,000 in 1890. Thousands of women attended both women's and coeducational colleges.

The progressive spirit was ranging throughout society. However, it touched certain groups more than others.

TO BE BLACK AND AMERICAN

Rights for blacks were not part of progressivism. It was left to black leaders like Booker T. Washington and W.E.B. Du Bois to explain, and try to remedy, the blacks' plight. Du Bois had organized the Niagara Movement to protest discrimination, but this group never attracted widespread support.

In 1903, Du Bois wrote of blacks' despair in his book, *The Souls of Black Folk*:

One ever feels his two-ness—an American, a Negro; two souls. . . . He simply wishes to make it possible . . . to be both a Negro and an American, without being cursed and spit upon by his fellows, without having the doors of opportunity closed roughly in his face.

William E.B. Du Bois, seated center, edited the NAACP journal, *The Crisis*. Du Bois defined the magazine's purpose: "to set forth facts which show the danger of race prejudice."

The doors, however, were slammed—by Jim Crow laws in the South and similar discrimination through the rest of the country. One of the most violent results of prejudice was lynching. Between 1885 and 1905 more Americans were lynched than were legally executed. Most victims were black.

One black, Ida Wells Barnett, began a campaign against lynching. In 1892 her Memphis newspaper charged white people in a lynching of three blacks. Her presses were wrecked, and her life was threatened. She continued her campaign.

Antiblack violence, like lynching, began to be noticed by some progressives. In 1908 a lynch mob in Springfield, Illinois terrorized a black neighborhood. Shocked, progressives Jane Addams and John Dewey and muckrakers Lincoln Steffens and Ray Stannard Baker offered their help. Du Bois and other blacks welcomed the white support. The group of blacks and whites called for a new black rights organization, and said, "If Mr. Lincoln could revisit this country in the flesh, he would be disheartened and discouraged."

In 1909 the group formed the National Association for the Advancement of Colored People (NAACP). The NAACP worked through the courts to battle lynching and protect blacks' civil rights.

While the NAACP combated prejudice, another organization aided blacks who moved to the cities. The National Urban League, founded by physician George E. Haynes, helped blacks to find housing and jobs.

PROGRESSIVE WOMEN

Unlike blacks, women were in the midst of the progressive movement. Women had marched and organized for reform since the early 1800s. They began the settlement house movement in the 1890s.

These reformers were a minority of women, but their numbers were growing. "For me," said one woman, "and for many others, Hull House and Jane Addams opened the door to a larger life." By the new century, doors began opening for many women.

During the progressive years, people began to speak of the "new woman." She was from the middle or upper class. She had been freed from day-long housework by canned foods, factory clothing,

---

HENRY OSSAWA TANNER
BLACK AMERICAN IN PARIS

When twelve-year-old Henry Tanner was walking in the park one day, he saw an artist painting a picture of a magnificent elm tree. Young Tanner was entranced. "It was this simple event," he said later, "that set me on fire."

Tanner had always loved to draw. He had never thought, however, that he could make it his profession. "But after seeing this artist at work for an hour, [I] decided . . . that I would be one, and I assure you it was no ordinary one I had in mind." So began the career of one of America's most important black painters.

Henry Tanner was born in 1859 in Pittsburgh, Pennsylvania. His father was a scholarly and deeply religious man, who served as a bishop of the African Methodist Episcopal Church. It was from him that Tanner learned the Bible stories that he would later depict in his most famous paintings.

Although it was difficult for a black to become an artist, Tanner did not give up. He studied at the Pennsylvania Academy of Fine Arts. In 1891 he set out for Europe. The tall, serious young man had encountered prejudice in the United States. When he later recalled his experiences, "my heart sank," he said, "and I was anew tortured by the thought of what I had endured."

In Paris, Tanner found a new life. He was soon recognized as an outstanding painter, particularly of landscapes and of religious subjects. His work was shown at major French exhibitions.

Tanner returned to the United States for visits, but Paris became his home. As a black artist, he found he did his best work there. Yet the choice was pain-

Henry Ossawa Tanner depicted a quiet moment shared by a grandfather and his grandson in "The Banjo Lesson."

ful. "I am sometimes sad," he wrote a friend not long before his death in 1937, "that I cannot live where my heart is."

The increasing freedom of women is reflected by the energetic tennis player. By the 1900s the urban middle class—both men and women—found the leisure time to participate in sports. Golf, tennis, cycling, swimming, basketball, and gymnastics grew in popularity. Baseball and football rapidly became national spectator sports.

indoor plumbing, washing machines, and other labor-saving devices. With more free time, she pursued interests outside the home.

Women would be found exercising at the local YWCA (Young Women's Christian Association) or studying in a college classroom. Thousands worked as secretaries and teachers. Some managed to enter fields like law, medicine, and architecture.

Amid all this change, a group of women continued to press for the vote. Many progressives saw women's suffrage as simply a means to an end. Women's votes could help elect reform candidates. To suffragists, however, women's right to vote was a reform in itself. By 1896 four western states—Wyoming, Colorado, Utah, and Idaho—had granted full voting rights to women.

One of the leaders of the suffrage movement was Carrie Chapman Catt. A college graduate, Catt had risen through the Iowa school system, from teacher to principal to superintendent of schools. As she faced and broke barriers against women, she was drawn to the women's movement. When she married, she and her engineer husband drew up a contract. He could take whatever time he needed for business trips, and she could devote several months each year to winning suffrage.

WOMEN'S ORGANIZATIONS

Many women used their free time for good works. They joined clubs organized around special issues—tenements, education, child labor, temperance. By 1898 the General Federation of Women's Clubs counted over 50,000 members.

One organization, the Women's Christian Temperance Union (WCTU), worked to outlaw liquor. Since the nation's birth, some Americans had believed that liquor led to social problems. Churches worked for temperance throughout the 1800s. In 1874 the WCTU joined the movement. By 1900 liquor was banned in five states.

The temperance movement drew many progressives who felt that the outlawing of liquor would reduce crime and poverty. The WCTU, led by former college president Frances Willard, attracted hundreds of thousands of members. Following Willard's motto, "Do everything," the WCTU set up reform schools and clubs for orphans. It gave textbooks to schools. And it campaigned for causes from suffrage to public drinking fountains.

Liquor still flowed, however, from states where it was legal to states where it was banned. Supporters of temperance realized that nationwide action was needed if liquor was to be outlawed effectively. That would come, but not for almost twenty years.

Another women's organization, the National Consumers League, had more immediate success. It was organized in 1899 by a Hull House worker named Florence Kelley. In addition to her social work, Kelley had been a factory inspector in Illinois. She brought her concern for safe working conditions to the league.

The National Consumers League, said writer Rheta C. Dorr, cared about "the human side of industry." Companies that treated their workers well earned the league's white label. Consumers were asked to buy only labeled goods. Indeed, concern for workers—men and children as well as women—was a major progressive issue.

CONCERN FOR WORKERS

The millions of workers in factories and mills wanted better pay, shorter hours, and safer working conditions. A writer named Robert Hunter sympathized. In 1904, in his book, *Poverty*, he wrote:

> On cold, rainy mornings, at the dusk of dawn, I have been awakened, two hours before my rising time, by the monotonous clatter of hobnailed boots on the plank sidewalks. . . . Heavy, brooding men; tired, anxious women; thinly dressed, unkempt little girls; and frail, joyless little lads passed along, half-awake, not one uttering a word as they hurried to the great factory.

Few of these workers belonged to unions. They began, however, to obtain help from the progressives. Progressives used tactics different from the strikes and collective bargaining of the labor unions. They asked government to pass laws protecting workers.

One of their first goals was to end child labor. In the early 1900s, about 1.5 million children under 16 years of age toiled in America's factories and mines. They worked 10 to 13 hours a day, earning as little as 60 cents a day. Many of these children, along with adult workers, faced unsafe conditions. Industrial accidents killed or gravely injured over 1.5 million workers in only one year—1900.

In 1901 an Alabama minister named Edgar Murphy organized the first Child Labor Committee to demand government action. Within three years the committee became national.

The committee had an ally in a longtime union worker named Mary Harris Jones. A widow in her seventies who wore a black bonnet and knitted shawl, she became known as "Mother" Jones. In 1867 she had lost her union-leader husband and her four children in a yellow fever epidemic. Jones carried on her husband's union work.

Mother Jones was especially concerned about child workers. In 1903 she organized a march from Pennsylvania to New York to spread her message. Leading the 300 marchers were three children dressed like Revolutionary soldiers. They carried signs that said "We Want to Go to School" and "Prosperity, Where Is Our Share?"

Thousands witnessed this "March of the Mill Children." And many thousands more learned of the child worker's life from the Child Labor Committee. Their cries for reform joined the cries of the muckrakers, the social workers, and others asking for change.

Government began to listen. The progressive movement made inroads in a few city governments, and then in a few more. It spread from the city to the state governments.

SECTION REVIEW

1. Identify the following: Jane Addams, Ida Tarbell, Lincoln Steffens, *McClure's*, W.E.B. Du Bois, NAACP, Carrie Chapman Catt, Florence Kelley, Mother Jones.

2. Define the following: progressives, muckrakers, temperance movement.

3. (a) List five special concerns of the progressives. (b) What were the three major aims of the progressive movement?

4. How did muckrakers advance the progressive cause?

5. How did progressives influence education?

6. (a) Why was the NAACP formed? (b) What actions did it take?

7. Why did progressives support women's suffrage?

8. Why did many progressives support the temperance movement?

9. Why was the National Consumers League formed?

10. What labor reforms did progressives support?

REFORM IN CITY HALL AND STATEHOUSE

READ TO FIND OUT

— **what changes progressives brought about in city living and city government.**

— **how Robert La Follette's ideas reformed Wisconsin's state government.**

— **what reforms progressives brought about in other states.**

By the late 1800s, America's cities had become tarnished. City services could not keep up with population growth. Government was often inefficient and corrupt. If the cities were to shine again, thought many reformers, citizens themselves would have to take action. Political leaders, wrote muckraker Lincoln Steffens, "will supply any demand we may create. All we have to do is to establish a steady demand for good government."

REFORM IN TOLEDO

In city after city, progressives formed civic groups to demand better sewers and lighting and police protection. These groups also worked to rid cities of political machines. Toledo, Ohio, was one of the first to be touched by reform.

In 1897 Toledo voters elected Samuel M. Jones as mayor. In Jones's office hung a sign bearing the Golden Rule: "Do unto others as you would have them do unto you." His golden-rule government, he promised, would be honest and effective. "Golden Rule" Jones kept his promises.

Toledo's public utilities—trolleys, waterworks, electricity plants, telephones—were almost all privately owned. Companies that had monopolies often charged high rates and gave poor service. Jones believed that services "necessary to the welfare of the whole family . . . can only be successfully operated by the family," and he fought to place these public services under city control.

Jones changed Toledo in other ways. Citizens listened to free concerts in public parks. Their children played in tax-supported kindergartens and playgrounds. City employees were hired on the merit system and worked an eight-hour day.

William Glackens' "Park on the River" pictures urban dwellers enjoying a park in the midst of a crowded city. In the early 1900s in almost every city, reform leaders worked to have land set aside for parks and playgrounds.

REFORM IN OTHER CITIES

Other cities were changed by reform mayors. In San Francisco, New York, Jersey City, St. Louis, and Cleveland, progressive mayors battled corruption. In Detroit, Hazen S. Pingree, a wealthy manufacturer like Samuel M. Jones, fought privately owned utility companies. He also developed the "garden plot" plan, allowing the poor to plant gardens in vacant city lots. The "Pingree Potato Scheme" spread to several cities.

Sometimes reforms changed more than the people in city government. Sometimes the actual form of government changed. Galveston, Texas, devised one method in 1900, after a flood ruined the city and killed hundreds of people. The task of rebuilding the city was placed in the hands of five commissioners. Each commissioner was responsible for a separate function, such as safety, finance, or public health. The *commission system* proved so effective that some two hundred cities adopted it over the next twelve years.

In 1914 another flood led Dayton, Ohio, to adopt a different form of government. A commission was set up, which then appointed a *city manager* to act as executive. The city manager acted more like a corporation president than a mayor. The city manager was not directly involved in city politics and stayed in office only as long as he or she did a good job. The city manager system spread to hundreds of cities.

Many reformers wanted to end the states' control of the cities. They had often found their city reforms blocked by state codes. States, however, did not willingly give up control of cities. So reformers had to broaden their goals. One goal was to defeat the states' political machines.

LA FOLLETTE'S WISCONSIN IDEA

Wisconsin's political machine, controlled by railroads and lumber companies, ran the state legislature. One observer wrote that "politics was a privileged trade, into which ambitious people entered only when approved by the state machine." The machine's fiercest opponent was Robert M. La Follette. "Battling Bob" was a lawyer with strong convictions and a taste for Shakespeare.

La Follette ran for governor of Wisconsin twice. Twice, the machine helped to defeat him. Unfazed,

"Battling Bob" ran a third time in 1900. By now he had his own machine—small farmers and city workers. He swept into office on the progressive tide. He wanted, he said, to "go back to the first principles of democracy. Go back to the people."

Through three terms, Governor La Follette fought against the Wisconsin machine. His major victory was in establishing the **direct primary**. The machine had been able to nominate candidates for office at party conventions. In the direct primary, voters chose candidates directly in a primary election.

La Follette turned to the University of Wisconsin for advice on a variety of subjects. The university president helped him to draw up a plan to keep lumber companies from overusing the forests. University experts sat on commissions to regulate the railroads and public utilities.

In 1906 La Follette moved on to the United States Senate. But the Wisconsin Idea—La Follette's movement to reform state government—continued. Wisconsin, for example, accepted La Follette's proposal of a graduated personal income tax, an idea first suggested by the populists. "Battling Bob" had turned Wisconsin, said Theodore Roosevelt, into a "laboratory of democracy."

REFORM IN OTHER STATES

The Wisconsin Idea inspired progressives in other states. New Yorkers elected Charles Evans Hughes as governor after he exposed corruption in that state's insurance companies. Californians made Hiram Johnson governor because he would fight the powerful Southern Pacific Railroad. To appeal to the poor, "Little Jeff" Davis campaigned through Arkansas coatless and with unpolished shoes. When he became governor, Davis fought for the cause of compensation for injured workers. He also effectively drove the insurance companies from the state and obtained improved budgets for charitable institutions.

Many of the new state reforms, like the direct primary, were designed to give people greater participation in government. The **initiative** allowed voters to propose a new law by collecting on a petition a required number of signatures for registered voters.

The **referendum** let them approve or discard a proposed bill. If voters collected a required number of signatures on a petition, the state legislature had to place the bill before all the voters of the state for approval or disapproval.

With the **recall**, voters could remove an elected official from office before his or her term expired. This could be done by collecting a required number of signatures on a petition. The state then had to hold a special election so people could vote for or against the official.

All these reforms had been part of the Populist platform in the 1890s. By 1916 most states adopted at least one of these reforms. Another reform, the Australian **secret ballot**, was first adopted in Massachusetts in 1888. By 1910 every state, because of action by progressives, allowed voters to mark their ballots in a private booth. In addition, a few more states had given women the vote.

Many states also made social reforms. Laws were passed to make factories safer and cleaner. Workers' compensation laws provided income for disabled workers. Women workers were guaranteed a minimum wage, and limits were set on the number of hours they could work.

Several laws protected children. Children who committed crimes had always been treated the same as adults in court or in jail. Jane Addams and other progressives pressed for more humane treatment of juvenile and adult offenders. In 1899 Illinois set up special juvenile courts, and the idea spread to other states.

The campaign to protect child workers began to produce results. In the wake of Mother Jones's "March of the Mill Children," Pennsylvania, New Jersey, and New York passed child labor laws. Between 1902 and 1909, laws limiting or banning the hiring of children were passed in 23 states.

Not all states, however, passed reform laws. Furthermore, laws that were passed were not always enforced. Florence Kelley reported on state labor laws in 1907. She described a large sign put up by reformers in Philadelphia:

Pennsylvania—Children employed, 40,140.
Children Illegally Employed, 3,243.
Prosecutions, 22.

"The next step which we need to take," wrote Kelley, "is to insist that this is a national evil, and we must have a national law abolishing it." In fact, across the nation, progressives were looking toward Congress and the White House.

Judge Benjamin Barr Lindsey was a pioneer in the field of juvenile law. For 27 years he served as judge of the Denver Juvenile Court, one of the nation's first.

SECTION REVIEW

1. Identify the following: Samuel M. Jones, Robert M. La Follette, Hiram Johnson.

2. Define the following: direct primary, secret ballot.

3. List five of the reforms brought about in Toledo under Mayor Samuel Jones.

4. Explain the following forms of city government. (a) commission system (b) city manager system

5. Why did city reformers turn to reform of state governments?

6. What was Robert La Follette's major victory?

7. In what way did each of the following give people greater participation in government? (a) initiative (b) referendum (c) recall

8. Near the turn of the century several laws were passed to protect children. List two such laws.

ROOSEVELT, THE PRACTICAL REFORMER

READ TO FIND OUT

— how Roosevelt tried to regulate the trusts.

— how Roosevelt involved government in the settlement of labor disputes.

— what laws were passed under the Square Deal.

— what laws were passed to protect the nation's natural resources.

— why Roosevelt was blamed for the depression in 1907.

Audiences enjoyed Theodore Roosevelt's enthusiastic and dynamic approach. He is shown speaking on Decoration Day (Memorial Day) at the tomb of Ulysses S. Grant.

In the election of 1900, President William McKinley had defeated Bryan and the Democrats. Theodore Roosevelt became McKinley's vice-president. Six months into McKinley's term, on September 6, 1901, McKinley visited the Pan-American Exposition in New York. There he was shot by an anarchist named Leon Czolgosz, and died eight days later. Roosevelt was thrust into the presidency.

Energetic and popular, the 42-year-old Roosevelt was the youngest president in history. Most of his ideas were the opposite of McKinley's.

ROOSEVELT BECOMES PRESIDENT

Roosevelt came from a wealthy family. He had private tutors, was sent to tour Europe and Egypt, and graduated from Harvard. Near-sighted, asthmatic, and weak, he determined to be physically active. He played tennis—91 games in a single day. He took up boxing at Harvard. He hunted, and dreamed of battling a grizzly bear with a hunting knife.

After his marriage, and a honeymoon climbing the Alps, Roosevelt entered politics as a member of the New York assembly. When his wife suddenly died, he fled to the West, took up ranching, and made himself into a cowboy.

Eventually Roosevelt returned to New York, a second marriage, and politics. He served as police commissioner of New York and on the United States Civil Service Commission. He went from New York to Washington as assistant secretary of the navy under McKinley. During the Spanish-American War, Roosevelt charged up San Juan Hill. Then he became governor of New York.

Inside the athletic Roosevelt was a scholar who wrote history books, read science and literature, and occasionally yearned to be a professor. As he studied and thought, he developed a strong moral code. His religion, he said, would consist of "good works." Roosevelt, however, was a shrewd politician who had little patience with "impractical reformers."

TAKING ON THE TRUSTS

Roosevelt believed firmly in business and in the free enterprise system. He saw a difference between "good" and "bad" trusts. According to Roosevelt, the bad trusts had grown out of control, stifling competition and misusing their power. He wanted the government to regulate trusts in a way that would stop abuses without destroying corporations. He asked Congress to create a Department of

Commerce and Labor, whose secretary would be a member of the cabinet. The new department would include a Bureau of Corporations to watch over the conduct of those corporations.

In March 1902 Roosevelt ordered his attorney general to file suit, under the Sherman Antitrust Act, against the Northern Securities Company. The Northern Securities Company was a huge holding company that had been created in 1901 by the merger of three railroads—the Northern Pacific, the Great Northern, and the Chicago, Burlington, and Quincy. The company had a monopoly on a large part of the national railroad system.

Northern, headed by J. P. Morgan, fought the suit for two years. In 1904, however, the Supreme Court upheld the government and broke up the holding company. This enforcement of the Sherman Antitrust Act put other trusts on notice.

The government, under Roosevelt, went on to file 44 suits against such giants as the beef, tobacco, and oil trusts. Although Roosevelt continued to urge that trusts be regulated rather than broken up, he gained a reputation as a "trustbuster."

THE COAL MINERS' STRIKE

In the spring of 1902, over 140,000 Pennsylvania coal miners walked off the job. They were striking for a 10 percent to 20 percent pay raise, an 8-hour day, and recognition of their union, the United Mine Workers. Leading the strikers was John Mitchell. Mitchell shepherded the strikers, keeping them orderly and winning public sympathy.

Management refused to negotiate. The strike dragged on through the summer and fall. Coal supplies for industry, homes, and even hospitals grew dangerously low. As winter and cold weather approached, the problem became worse.

On October 1 Roosevelt invited the owners and union leaders to Washington. The daylong meeting stalled. Mitchell agreed to arbitration, but the mine owners refused to "deal with outlaws."

Furious at the owners, Roosevelt threatened to send federal troops to seize and run the mines. The owners backed down and agreed to federal arbitration. The miners went back to work. In March 1903 the arbitration board announced its verdict. The miners were given a 10 percent raise in pay and a 9-hour day. There was, however, no recognition of the union.

The nation had its coal in time for winter. Furthermore, Roosevelt had done something new. He had made government a participant in labor disputes.

The following year, while running for reelection, Roosevelt referred to his role in the strike. He had simply been trying, he said, to give both the miners and owners a "square deal."

THE SQUARE DEAL

Roosevelt wanted to win the election of 1904 and become "president in his own right." His Democratic opponent was Judge Alton B. Parker, a conservative from New York who campaigned against government interference in the economy. Roosevelt said nothing to anger corporate leaders. His campaign button spoke to all Americans. Surrounding a white-on-red "TR" was the slogan "A square deal all around."

Roosevelt triumphed, winning by the largest margin in history. Encouraged by the victory, he deluged Congress with proposals for economic and social reforms. First on his program was regulation of the railroads.

Roosevelt wanted to strengthen the Interstate Commerce Commission (ICC), which Supreme Court decisions had weakened to the point where it was totally ineffective. Roosevelt's ICC proposals

Most homes in the East were heated with coal. When the coal strike led to shortages in 1902, people waited in long lines to purchase a share of the limited supply.

survived, slightly battered, an 18-month battle in Congress. In June 1906 Congress passed the Hepburn Act, which allowed the ICC to set a ceiling on railroad rates. It also expanded the ICC's jurisdiction to include railroad terminals, bridges, ferries, oil pipelines, and sleeping-car companies.

That same year Roosevelt read *The Jungle*, by muckraker Upton Sinclair. Sinclair described the Chicago stockyards and meatpacking plants. To kill rats, Sinclair wrote, "the packers would put poisoned bread out for them; they would die, and then rats, bread, and meat would go into the hop-

★ ★ ★ ★ ★ ★ ★ ★ **CRITICAL ISSUES** ★ ★ ★ ★ ★ ★ ★ ★ ★ ★ ★ ★ ★

LABOR-MANAGEMENT CONFLICT
THE CLOAKMAKERS' STRIKE

Shortly after two o'clock on July 7, 1910, the streets of New York City's garment district began to fill with workers. They streamed out of hot, dingy workrooms, where they spent their days cutting, stitching, and pressing cloaks and suits. Before the afternoon was over, more than 50,000 workers had left their jobs. It was the beginning of a long and bitter strike that would make labor history.

Conditions in the clothing industry were harsh. The workers, mainly new immigrants, labored long hours in crowded, poorly lit shops that were often infested with cockroaches and rats. During the slow season the workers sat at their jobs nine or ten hours a day, but in rush periods they were required to work up to sixteen hours. Wages were barely enough to live on. Men earned from ten to twenty dollars a week, women as little as three or four.

"At seven o'clock we all sit down to our machines," one young woman said. "The machines go like mad all day because the faster you work the more money you get. Sometimes in my haste I get my finger caught and the needle goes right through it. . . . At the end of the day one feels so weak that there is a great temptation to lie right down and sleep."

In the hot summer of 1910, the workers were determined to act together. They were striking for higher wages, a forty-eight-hour week, and extra pay for overtime. Most important of all, they wanted recognition for their union.

When the strike began, the employers refused to deal with the union. The workers, most believed, should realize that "their employers were their best friends." As the summer wore on, the employers became alarmed. The workers refused to give in. Meanwhile the employers were losing millions of dollars in business. Some smaller firms were forced to close. By late July they were ready to talk.

Louis Brandeis, a brilliant Boston-based lawyer who would later become a Supreme Court justice, was called in to bring the two sides together. With Brandeis' help, they settled wage and hour questions. Then they reached a deadlock.

The workers demanded a closed shop, where only union members could be hired. But the employers felt this would give the union too much power. They insisted on an open shop, where they would be free to hire anyone they pleased. The open shop, they argued, gave every person the freedom "to work for whom he will for such prices as he is willing to accept."

The strikers disagreed. "Should we accept your proposition," said one union leader, "that is having non-union [people] working hand-in-hand with us,

Louis Brandeis came to be called the "people's attorney" because of his concern with economic and social reform. As an attorney he argued cases in favor of workers' compensation, minimum wage laws, and nine-hour and eight-hour work day laws.

pers together." Out of that, sausage was made for "the public's breakfast."

Roosevelt doubted some of Sinclair's charges, but he ordered an investigation of the meatpacking industry. The report shocked him, and he demanded congressional action. In June 1906 Congress passed the Meat Inspection Act. Sanitary regulations for the meatpacking industry would now be enforced. Any meat sold across state lines would be examined by a federal inspector.

The Jungle also focused Americans' attention on drugs and canned foods. A chemist found that an

then we will lose our organization, as every organization was lost that went into deals like you are trying to make us go into."

Brandeis agreed with the employers that the closed shop was "contrary to the American spirit." Yet he also recognized that the open shop could be used to force out the union, leaving the workers unprotected. To settle the issue, Brandeis proposed a compromise. He called it the "preferential union shop." Under this plan, management would hire union people first and non-union workers only if there were no qualified union members available.

At first the union was suspicious of the plan. It was merely "the open shop with honey," said one leader. The union members were afraid that the employers would use it to break the union.

Through the steamy days of August the deadlock continued. Finally in early September the union accepted the Brandeis plan. The two sides put their agreement in writing. They called it the Protocol of Peace.

The protocol was a major victory for the workers. It gave them higher wages, a fifty-hour week, and extra pay for overtime. It set up a board of inspection to check on sanitary conditions in the shops. The protocol also set up worker-management committees to settle disputes. The workers agreed to take their complaints to these committees rather than to strike. And both sides agreed to Brandeis' preferential union shop.

As word of the settlement spread through the city, workers poured into the streets, singing and shouting. "Everywhere, men and women, young and old, hugged and kissed and congratulated each other," one striker remembered. Although the issue of the open and closed shop was only temporarily settled, each side had learned to give and take. A vital process had been established. In one of the first instances of true collective bargaining in American history, labor and management had sat down together to work out their differences.

1. What were the main issues in the 1910 strike?

2. The issue of the open and closed shop is still unsettled today. Describe the open shop (often called "right to work"), the closed shop, and the preferential union shop. Which do you think is best for labor? For management? For the general public?

3. How does collective bargaining work? Do you think it is an effective way of settling labor disputes? Why or why not?

average day's meals contained forty different chemicals and dyes. Advertisements promised that drugs could do such things as remove freckles and ensure love.

Along with the meat act, Congress passed the Pure Food and Drug Act. This act outlawed the manufacture, sale, or transportation of foods and drugs that were impure. It also forbade misleading statements in advertisements.

ROOSEVELT AND CONSERVATION

Roosevelt had been a hunter, a rancher, a bird watcher, and an amateur naturalist. He knew the joys of the wilderness and the difficulties in preserving it. Already, three quarters of the nation's forests were being logged. Careless farming was destroying the topsoil. Mining and manufacturing were scarring the land and ruining waterways.

Roosevelt was deeply influenced by naturalist John Muir, who knew every peak and valley of the western mountains. In 1903 Roosevelt and Muir camped in California's Yosemite Valley and mapped out plans to protect the Grand Canyon, the Petrified Forest, and other natural treasures.

Two earlier presidents, Harrison and Cleveland, had set aside forest areas as reserves. But during his presidency, Roosevelt and Gifford Pinchot, chief of the United States Forest Service, created a national policy. They doubled the number of national parks. They increased the national forest land from 45 million to 195 million acres (18 million to 79 million hectares).

Roosevelt believed not only in preserving resources. He also believed in conserving them—using them efficiently. In 1902, at his prodding, Congress passed the Newlands Reclamation Act. This act authorized money from the sale of public lands to be used for irrigation projects for the arid West. In 1906 the Forest Homestead Act allowed certain forest lands to be used for agriculture.

In 1908 Roosevelt called political leaders to the White House Conservation Conference. "The time has come to inquire seriously what will happen when our forests are gone," he said, "when the coal, the iron, the oil, and the gas are exhausted, when the soils . . . [are] washed into the streams." The conference led to the formation of the National Conservation Commission, devoted to studying and protecting these natural resources.

John Wesley Powell, head of the U.S. Geological Survey from 1881 to 1894, fought for scientific management of western lands. Many of his ideas were carried out under Roosevelt.

THE PANIC OF 1907

Toward the end of his second term, Roosevelt's popularity was hurt by a sudden depression. Throughout 1907, stock prices fell, production of goods slowed, and business leaders worried.

In October crisis struck the nation's financial community. Banks, low on funds, could not make loans. Some simply closed their doors. Several big companies went bankrupt. Then J. P. Morgan, the longtime "Doctor of Wall Street," took charge.

Morgan bailed out a failing company, then a bank, then the city of New York. He made or arranged loans. He warned speculators to stay out of the stock market. He also directed the flow of federal loans, arranged by Roosevelt.

The Panic of 1907 ended amid a shower of criticism of Roosevelt. Corporate leaders blamed the depression on Roosevelt's regulatory reforms, especially the Hepburn Act. Roosevelt blamed "certain malefactors of great wealth," who wished to "discredit the policy of the government." Most business leaders were now thoroughly convinced that Roosevelt was their enemy.

ROOSEVELT'S RECORD

While big business protested Roosevelt's regulatory policies, some progressives argued that his regulations did not go far enough. Despite the numerous antitrust suits, there were more trusts in 1908 than when Roosevelt had taken office.

To many other progressives, however, Roosevelt was a hero. Robert La Follette, now a senator, said that Roosevelt had "made reform respectable in the United States." Roosevelt had prodded Congress to pass national conservation laws, to regulate corporations, and to protect public health.

Still, for Roosevelt, there was much left undone. In the 1904 campaign he had said he would not challenge the tradition of the two-term presidency by running again. So, in his final message to Congress in December 1908, he spoke freely, with no need to court support for reelection.

Asking that government help workers, he proposed the eight-hour day, abolition of child labor, a federal workers' compensation act, and federal investigation of major labor disputes. Industry, he said, must be even further regulated. He also called for federal inheritance and income taxes.

Roosevelt did not really expect to see his proposals accepted and made into law during his final months in office. He had decided, however, that he would not quietly wait out his term. He would, he said, continue "to rage with uninterrupted violence."

SECTION REVIEW

1. Identify the following: Northern Securities Company, United Mine Workers, John Mitchell, Hepburn Act, Upton Sinclair, Pure Food and Drug Act, John Muir, Gifford Pinchot.

2. Explain Roosevelt's attitude toward trusts.

3. (a) Why did Pennsylvania coal miners strike in 1902? (b) What role did Roosevelt play in the strike?

4. (a) What caused Roosevelt to order an investigation of the meatpacking industry? (b) What was the result of the investigation?

5. What problems caused Roosevelt to work toward preserving the wilderness?

6. List the steps Roosevelt took to conserve the nation's natural resources.

7. Why did corporate leaders decide that Roosevelt was an enemy of business?

8. Why was Roosevelt considered a hero by many progressives?

TAFT AND WILSON

READ TO FIND OUT

—why Taft's position on the tariff angered the progressives.

—why a dispute over federal lands caused progressives to distrust Taft.

—what progressive measures Taft supported.

—why Roosevelt's position split the Republican party.

—why Wilson won the election.

—how the progressives amended the Constitution.

—how Wilson lowered the tariff.

—how a new banking system regulated the nation's money supply.

—how Wilson's administration attempted to regulate the trusts.

—what social reforms Wilson supported.

Roosevelt had handpicked his successor, Secretary of War William Howard Taft, and announced that Taft would carry on "my policies." Taft, however, was a very different person from the vigorous, dramatic Roosevelt. A large easygoing man who preferred playing golf and bridge to hunting grizzlies, Taft had served ably as governor of the Philippines. He had then proved to be a sound member of Roosevelt's cabinet.

The Republican convention followed Roosevelt's wishes and nominated Taft. The Democrats returned to William Jennings Bryan. Bryan, too, ran on a progressive platform, but he had lost his vote-getting appeal. The campaign, wrote a newspaper, was "loaded down with calm." Taft won comfortably, obtaining 321 electoral votes to Bryan's 162.

Assured that Taft would follow his policies, Roosevelt left for some big-game hunting in Africa. He thought it might be his "last chance for something in the nature of a great adventure."

THE PAYNE-ALDRICH TARIFF

Taft began his presidency with a political mistake. Progressive Republicans were trying to pry Joseph Cannon out of his position as speaker of the House of Representatives, or at least reduce his power.

As speaker, Cannon appointed all House committees. He made himself head of the Rules Committee, which could introduce bills to the House or hold them back. Thus Cannon controlled all bills.

Taft let Congress know that he, too, would like to see Cannon replaced as speaker. Then, Cannon went to the White House and proposed a deal to Taft. If Taft would support him, he would support a tariff-reduction bill that the President wanted. Taft agreed. Cannon retained his position, although progressives eventually pared down his powers. The Rules Committee began work on the tariff bill.

Progressives had long demanded a lower tariff, and Taft had made it a campaign pledge. With a tariff reduction, Americans would pay less on imported goods. Furthermore, American industry would have to compete with foreign industry and thus would charge lower prices.

The tariff bill, however, emerged from Congress weighted down with some eight hundred amendments. These actually increased rates on hundreds of imports. Progressives in Congress called on Taft for help to kill the bill. Taft was torn. He didn't want to anger the conservative Republican majority. He chose to work with the conservatives to try to decrease some of the rates.

The resulting Payne-Aldrich Tariff was a compromise, which Taft termed "the best bill that the Republican party ever passed." To the progressives, however, the bill was a high-tariff measure. They were outraged when Taft signed it into law and disgusted with his earlier support of Cannon.

THE BALLINGER-PINCHOT DISPUTE

A feud between two of Taft's officials caused more difficulties between the President and the progressives. Gifford Pinchot had been chief of the United States Forest Service under Roosevelt and continued in his position under Taft. Pinchot was a strong conservationist who stood for Roosevelt's policies.

Richard Ballinger had been Roosevelt's land office commissioner, and became Taft's secretary of the interior. Soon he and Pinchot clashed over wilderness areas in Wyoming and Montana. These lands had been removed from sale under Roosevelt. Then, in mid-1909, Ballinger claimed that the removal was illegal and reversed it.

Pinchot wrote a letter to Congress, calling Ballinger's actions "a national danger." Taft fired Pinchot for disloyalty. A congressional investigation concluded that Ballinger had done nothing wrong. Nevertheless, progressives called Taft and Ballinger "despoilers of the national heritage."

TAFT'S PROGRESSIVISM

Despite progressives' distrust of him, Taft remained a progressive himself. When Ballinger resigned to quiet the protest, Taft replaced him with a strong conservationist. Taft eventually set aside more public lands as forest reserves than Roosevelt had.

Taft also fought the railroad monopolies. The Mann-Elkins Act of 1910, which he proposed and nursed through Congress, tightened regulation of the railroads. The Interstate Commerce Commission could now make rate changes, and regulate telephone and telegraph companies.

In addition, Taft was twice the trustbuster that Roosevelt had been. His attorney general filed 90 suits against monopolies. Roosevelt had used the Sherman Antitrust Act as a means to an end— the federal control of trusts. Taft used the Sherman Act to break up the monopolies. When corporate leaders complained, Taft replied, "We are going to enforce that law or die in the attempt."

Under Taft, a great many social reforms were enacted. New laws set up safer conditions in mines and railroads. Federal workers received the eight-hour day. The Children's Bureau in the new Department of Labor was formed to look into child labor. Members of Congress had to make public all campaign contributions they had received. Still, whatever Taft did, his presidency was overshadowed by the figure of Roosevelt.

THE NEW NATIONALISM

In mid-1910, Roosevelt returned from Africa to a hero's welcome. Roosevelt was deeply disappointed in Taft, believing that the President had "twisted around" his policies. He set off on a speaking tour of the West, calling for a New Nationalism.

The family portrayed in John Sloan's "Gray and Brass" seems justifiably proud of their shiny new 1907 automobile. From the beginning of the twentieth century, automobiles, along with trucks and buses, began to compete with the railroads.

The New Nationalism, Roosevelt said, would give government new powers to guard the American people. The president should be "the steward of the public welfare." Congress should supervise industry, pass reform laws, and revise the tariff.

Roosevelt's views split the Republican party. Conservatives supported Taft. Moderate progressives were drawn to a new group of Democratic leaders. In the congressional elections of 1910, the Democrats regained control of the House while the Republicans barely held on in the Senate. Everyone began preparing for the campaign of 1912.

THE ELECTION OF 1912

There were a number of candidates in the presidential campaign of 1912. All of them were progressives of one kind or another. Parties ranged from the Democrats and Republicans to Socialists.

The Socialist party had been formed in 1901 with the basic goal of doing away with capitalism. The Socialist platform called for several of the standard progressive demands. But it also argued for government ownership of banks and major businesses. Eugene V. Debs—union leader and cofounder of the party—was its presidential candidate.

The Republican party was splintered, with Taft, Roosevelt, and La Follette all trying to obtain the nomination. Then La Follette grew ill, leaving it a two-way race. Taft's supporters were in the majority in the convention, and Taft was nominated.

Roosevelt and his supporters held another convention and formed the Progressive party. The party's candidate, of course, was Roosevelt, who announced, "I feel as fit as a bull moose." The group quickly became known as the "Bull Moose" party.

The Democrats, too, chose a progressive—New Jersey's reform governor, Woodrow Wilson. Wilson had first taught political economy at Princeton University. He had then gone on to serve as university president. "I should be complete," he wrote before becoming governor, "if I could inspire a great movement." In 1912 presidential candidate Wilson named his movement the New Freedom. The New Freedom, Wilson said, would attempt to free Americans from the rule of monopolies.

The leading parties—Democrats, Republicans, and Progressives—all supported banking and currency reform, a lower tariff, conservation, and an end to the abuses of the trusts. However, the heated battle between Roosevelt and Wilson over how to reform the trusts became the focus of the campaign.

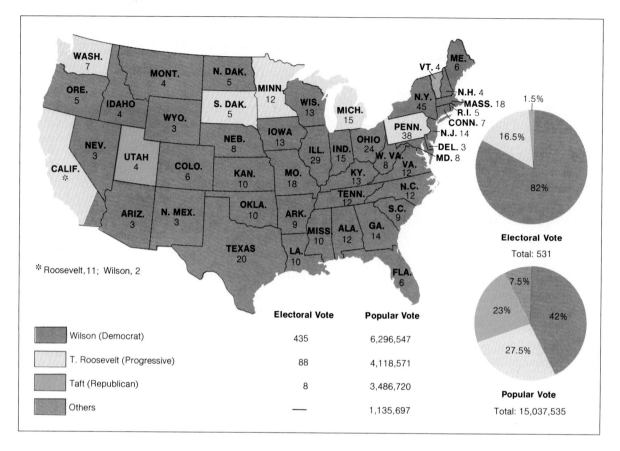

WASH. 7
ORE. 5
MONT. 4
N. DAK. 5
MINN. 12
WIS. 13
MICH. 15
VT. 4
ME. 6
N.Y. 45
N.H. 4
MASS. 18
R.I. 5
CONN. 7
IDAHO 4
S. DAK. 5
WYO. 3
IOWA 13
PENN. 38
N.J. 14
NEV. 3
UTAH 4
NEB. 8
ILL. 29
IND. 15
OHIO 24
W. VA. 8
VA. 12
DEL. 3
MD. 8
CALIF. *
COLO. 6
KAN. 10
MO. 18
KY. 13
N.C. 12
ARIZ. 3
N. MEX. 3
OKLA. 10
ARK. 9
TENN. 12
S.C. 9
TEXAS 20
LA. 10
MISS. 10
ALA. 12
GA. 14
FLA. 6

* Roosevelt, 11; Wilson, 2

Electoral Vote
Total: 531

1.5%
16.5%
82%

Popular Vote
Total: 15,037,535

7.5%
23%
27.5%
42%

	Electoral Vote	Popular Vote
Wilson (Democrat)	435	6,296,547
T. Roosevelt (Progressive)	88	4,118,571
Taft (Republican)	8	3,486,720
Others	—	1,135,697

Roosevelt insisted that monopolies were not harmful if properly regulated by a powerful federal government. Wilson claimed that monopolies were "intolerable," because they strangled free enterprise. But he did not think that the government should police the trusts. He wanted to lower the tariff that gave monopolies an advantage over small business and to break up the trusts. Roosevelt's New Nationalism would increase government power, and Wilson's New Freedom would limit it.

Wilson had two vote-getting advantages. Virginia-born, he could count on the support of the Solid South. More important, the Republicans were split between Roosevelt and Taft. At election time, the Democrats sailed to victory. Wilson won 435 electoral votes, and Democrats won control of both houses of Congress.

However, the popular vote was closer, revealing the nation's attraction to all the progressive candidates. Over 6 million people voted for Wilson, over 4 million for Roosevelt, and about 3.5 million for Taft. Debs received nearly 900,000 votes, the largest

showing yet for the Socialists. Woodrow Wilson was elected president, but the biggest winner of the election was an idea—progressive reform.

CONSTITUTIONAL AMENDMENTS

At the same time that the country elected one more progressive president, the Constitution received two more amendments—both inspired by progressives. The Sixteenth Amendment, passed by Congress in 1909 and finally ratified by three fourths of the states, became law in February 1913.

The amendment allowed Congress to levy taxes on incomes. Progressives thought such a tax would help to raise the money to pay for reforms like workers' compensation.

The Seventeenth Amendment was adopted in May 1913, a year after it was proposed. It provided for the election of United States senators by the people, rather than by state legislatures. During the recent progressive years, the Senate had consistently been slower than the House, whose members were popularly elected, to consider reform. Progressives hoped that if senators' election depended on the people, the Senate would warm to reform.

THE UNDERWOOD TARIFF

President Wilson's first task was to lower the tariff. Lowering or removing protective tariffs, he said, would force American businesses to compete.

Where Taft had failed, Wilson was determined to succeed. He conferred with Oscar Underwood, an authority on tariff reform and the leader of a powerful House committee. Underwood produced a bill that reduced the average tariff by 11 percent.

The Underwood bill removed entirely duties from imports like food, clothing, and farm machinery, and from all products that would compete with those of the trusts. For example, with imported steel duty-free, the American steel trusts would have to compete with foreign producers.

The bill eased through the House, with one important amendment. To replace lost customs duties, progressives added a provision for a graduated personal income tax, in which the rate of tax increased according to a person's income. The bill now had to pass the strongly conservative Senate.

Into the capital swarmed **lobbyists**—people acting for special interests in order to influence legislation. The lobbyists demanded that high duties be restored on imported wool or sugar or cotton. In a shrewd move, Wilson appealed to the public. He argued that lobbyists were spending "money without limit" to support special interests, while no lobby protected the interests of the public.

The public spotlight and a Judiciary Committee investigation into lobbying moved the Senate to pass the Underwood Tariff Act in October 1913. Supporters in the Senate had managed to lower the tariff rate to an astonishingly low 26 percent. The success, said a London newspaper, boosted Wilson "from the man of promise to the man of achievement." Encouraged, Wilson moved on to his next task—banking and currency reform.

THE FEDERAL RESERVE ACT

The nation's banking system had been set up during the Civil War and by now was as outdated as Confederate dollars. Individual banks estimated what demand would be and kept enough money on hand to meet the demand. The banks' estimations could be wrong. In the Panic of 1907, when companies suddenly needed a steady flow of cash, many banks ran out of money.

Bankers, business people, and political leaders all agreed that the banking system must be changed, but they disagreed as to how this should be done. Conservatives wanted a system organized around a central bank—controlled by bankers. Progressives, fearing that a central bank would give Wall Street control of the money supply, demanded government control over the banking system.

For six months, Congress argued over banking reform. Wilson, encouraged by progressives, decided that only government control would make banks serve "individual enterprise and initiative." He entered the congressional battle and finally emerged with a compromise. On December 23, 1913, the Federal Reserve Act was signed into law.

Under the act, local banks would deposit cash reserves with a district Federal Reserve Bank. All national banks in the district became members of the Reserve Bank, as did any local or state banks who wished to join. The Reserve Bank could increase or decrease the district's money supply according to business needs. Acting strictly as a bank for bankers, the Federal Reserve Bank would not serve businesses or private citizens. There would be 12 of these district banks, privately run but supervised by a Federal Reserve Board.

The board—with headquarters in Washington and with members appointed by the president—controlled the national money supply by raising or lowering the interest rates that the district banks charged. The system was set up to keep the value of money stable and the supply flexible.

TACKLING THE TRUSTS

Wilson had promised to break up the trusts and rescue free enterprise. At the end of 1913 he met with congressional leaders to work out the details. Some urged a new law to strengthen the Sherman Antitrust Act. Others, including many business people, called for a commission to supervise business practice.

Wilson decided to ask Congress for an antitrust law. The proposed Clayton antitrust bill breezed through the House. Meanwhile, however, Wilson was having second thoughts.

A group of progressives told him that an antitrust law could not define all possible business abuses, since business practices kept changing. They suggested instead a trade commission with broad authority to deal with any abuses that occurred.

This had been Roosevelt's policy, but Wilson became convinced that it was the only practical course. He supported a trade commission bill and abandoned the Clayton bill, which was now in the Senate. Consequently, what emerged from Congress in the autumn of 1914 was a strong trade commission and a weakened antitrust law.

The Clayton Antitrust Act covered certain business practices overlooked by the Sherman Antitrust Act. A company could not buy stock in another company, sell goods at lower prices to preferred customers, or make contracts forbidding customers to deal with its competitors. A person serving on one company's board of directors could not, at the same time, be a director of a competing firm. However, all these practices were forbidden only *if* they would "tend to create a monopoly."

Labor leaders, remembering how the Sherman Antitrust Act had been used against unions in the 1890s, had demanded that unions not be subject to antitrust laws. The Clayton Act said that unions would not be prosecuted *if* their activities, such as strikes and picketing, were lawful. However, in order to prevent major property damage, courts could issue an injunction against strikers.

The newly created Federal Trade Commission (FTC), replacing Roosevelt's Bureau of Corporations, could patrol businesses involved in interstate trade. The commission would look into business activities and publish its findings. If it uncovered unfair practices, it would order the company to stop the practices. If necessary, it could enforce the order through the courts. The companies, in turn, had the right to appeal the order in court.

Progressives had high hopes for the trust regulation, and they congratulated Wilson on another victory. These laws, said Wilson, would help small business succeed as easily as big business did, and would "kill monopoly in the seed."

WILSON AND REFORM

Wilson's New Freedom had not included social reforms. Wilson believed that social reform was the responsibility of the states. By 1915 he faced a

Big business grew out of the Industrial Revolution. Small business changed. By the late 1800s people could buy thousands of small, manufactured items from the new mail-order houses and department stores. By the 1900s five-and-ten cent stores began to appear.

strengthened Republican party and a reelection campaign, and progressives were urging him to support welfare legislation. Between 1915 and 1916 he steered social reform bills through Congress.

Two laws—the Federal Farm Loan Act and the Warehouse Act—helped farmers to obtain loans. The Seamen's Act improved working conditions and wages in the merchant marine. The Adamson Act gave railroad workers the eight-hour day. The Workingmen's Compensation Act gave financial help to injured federal workers. The Child Labor Act limited the number of hours children could work, and outlawed the interstate shipment of goods made by children.

With the tariff, banking, and trust bills and this latest burst of reform, Wilson took the leadership of progressivism from Roosevelt. In September 1916 Wilson said with pride:

> This record must equally astonish those who feared that the Democratic party had not opened its heart to comprehend the demands of social justice. We have in four years come very near to carrying out the platform of the Progressive party as well as our own; for we also are progressives.

THE BALANCE SHEET

In a period of a little less than twenty years, progressivism had grown from a small movement into a national force. The movement did not achieve all that its followers wanted. Progress through government action was often slow, and many reforms worked better on paper than in practice.

The direct primary, for example, gave people the hope of greater control over politics. But the primary forced candidates to run in two elections—one for the nomination and another for the election. That was expensive. To obtain money, candidates needed strong party support. Therefore, party leaders still played a major role in selecting candidates.

Social legislation was not always enforced. Factory and mine owners often ignored laws involving workers' welfare. The Child Labor Law was declared unconstitutional. If children agreed to work a 12-hour day, ruled the Supreme Court, they had the right to do so.

Regulatory agencies sometimes became too friendly with the industries they were to regulate. Sometimes the bosses returned to city hall. The slums did not disappear.

Black rights were not an issue for progressives. Roosevelt supported some blacks who sought federal office, but he was not interested in ending segregation. During Wilson's administration, segregation in government offices steadily increased until the NAACP protested. Only then did the trend begin to reverse.

Many reforms, however, did accomplish what the progressives wanted. Also, the progressives made popular a new idea—the idea that government could solve social and economic problems. That idea would be a source of argument among Americans from the progressive era to the present.

In 1917 the progressive era ended, and the great energy that Americans had poured into reform was abruptly diverted. The United States was soon to be involved in a world war.

SECTION REVIEW

1. Identify the following: Payne-Aldrich Tariff, Mann-Elkins Act, Progressive party, Sixteenth Amendment, Seventeenth Amendment, Underwood bill, Clayton Antitrust Act, Federal Trade Commission.

2. Define the following: lobbyist, Federal Reserve Bank.

3. Why did progressives want to lower the tariff?

4. Compare Taft's use of antitrust laws with Roosevelt's.

5. List three social reforms enacted under Taft.

6. Explain Roosevelt's New Nationalism.

7. (a) In the 1912 election what ideas did all the leading parties support? (b) Compare Roosevelt's and Wilson's ideas about trusts.

8. What prompted the passage of the Seventeenth Amendment?

9. How did the Underwood bill provide for the money lost because of the decrease in customs duties?

10. Explain how the Federal Reserve Board controlled the national money supply.

11. (a) Under what circumstances were business practices forbidden by the Clayton Antitrust Act? (b) How did the Clayton Act deal with labor?

12. List five social reform bills passed during Wilson's administration. Briefly explain each.

SUMMARY

After populism disappeared, a new reform movement—progressivism—was born. Progressives wanted to deal with the problems brought about by rapid growth in industry and cities. They were concerned about poor working and living conditions, business abuses, and corruption in government. Journalists, social workers, businesspeople, educators, leaders of women's groups, and workers all joined in a call for reform.

The progressive movement began in the cities. People began to demand improvements in city services and less corruption in city government. To improve city government, reformers introduced the commission system and the city manager system.

Progressives also worked to make changes in state government. Under Governor Robert La Follette, Wisconsin became a model for reform in other states. Many states adopted new practices—the initiative, referendum, recall, and the secret ballot— to allow people greater participation in government. States also passed laws to protect both adult and child workers.

The spirit of reform reached the White House when Theodore Roosevelt became president. Roosevelt supported business, but he applied the Sherman Antitrust Act to control the trusts. Under Roosevelt, Congress passed laws to conserve natural resources, to regulate corporations, and to protect public health.

Roosevelt was followed as president by William Howard Taft. Taft became unpopular with progressives, but he continued government action against trusts. He strongly supported conservation and social reforms.

Roosevelt returned to politics in 1912 as the presidential candidate of the newly formed Progressive party, but it was Woodrow Wilson who was elected. Wilson first worked to lower the tariff. Under Wilson banking laws were reformed, and new antitrust laws were passed.

The progressive era came to an end with World War I. Many progressive reforms had not worked as well as reformers had hoped, but in just two decades progressivism had changed the role of government.

CHAPTER REVIEW

1. (a) How did the progressives get their name? (b) What factors caused progressivism to become an influential movement?

2. Throughout the progressive era, private citizens worked hard to influence public affairs. Describe one method used by each of the following. (a) black leaders (b) women's groups (c) nonunion workers (d) union members

3. (a) What reforms did progressives make in city government? (b) Explain the commission and city manager systems. (c) What caused progressives to shift their attention from city government to state government?

4. (a) Roosevelt called Wisconsin a "laboratory of democracy." What facts might be used to support his opinion? (b) What reforms did progressives make in state governments as a whole?

5. (a) Theodore Roosevelt saw himself as a friend of business. Why, then, did he enforce antitrust laws? (b) Why did many businesspeople eventually consider Roosevelt their enemy?

6. (a) How did Theodore Roosevelt become president in 1901? (b) What factors contributed to the election of each of the following presidents: Roosevelt, 1904; Taft, 1908; Wilson, 1912?

The Pure Food and Drug Act required companies to list on medicine labels ingredients that might be harmful. The sellers could be prosecuted for misleading advertising.

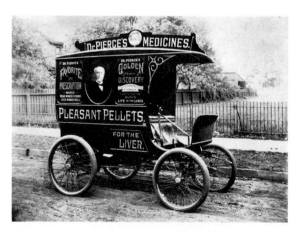

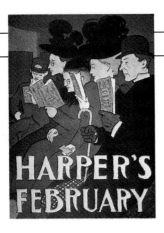

The writings of muckrakers were published in widely circulated magazines. Large-scale circulation of magazines was made possible by lower postal rates, improved printing equipment, and national advertising.

7. (a) Give one example of the way Roosevelt put progressive ideas into practice in dealing with each of the following: trusts, labor, railroads, manufacture of food and drugs, resources.
(b) Give one example of the way Taft put progressive ideas into practice in dealing with each of the following: trusts, labor, railroads, resources.

8. (a) What groups favored a low tariff? (b) What groups favored a high tariff? (c) Compare the results of Taft's and Wilson's attempts at tariff reform.

9. What constitutional amendments were adopted as a result of the progressive movement?

10. (a) What were the failures of the progressive movement? (b) One progressive goal was direct democracy—the direct participation of people in government. List at least four reforms designed to increase citizens' participation in government.

ISSUES AND IDEAS

1. (a) In what way were journalists and other writers important throughout the progressive era? (b) Describe the works of one writer and the reforms that writer may have helped to bring about. (c) Give several reasons why writers had such a strong influence on public affairs.

2. (a) According to Samuel McClure, who was responsible for upholding the law? (b) Use McClure's statement as the topic sentence for a paragraph. Complete the paragraph with arguments for or against the statement.

3. (a) Compare Roosevelt's idea of big government with Wilson's idea of limited govern-

ment. Give examples. (b) What are the advantages and disadvantages of each viewpoint?

4. Evaluate the Clayton Antitrust Act as each of the following might have evaluated it. (a) President Wilson (b) a labor union member (c) the owner of a small business (d) a leading industrialist

SKILLS WORKSHOP

1. *Graphs.* (a) Study the graph of educational statistics on page 766 of the Resource Center. How many students were enrolled in public elementary and secondary schools in 1870? In 1900? (b) Compare the graph of educational statistics with the population graph on page 755. What percentage of the total population was attending school in 1870? In 1900? In 1950? In 1980?

2. *Writing.* (a) Make an outline showing changes that took place during the administrations of Roosevelt, Taft, and Wilson. Choose one of the following topics for your outline: labor conditions, conservation of resources, or regulation of business. Outline key events during each administration. Include only events related to the topic. The main headings should be phrases that express the general attitude of each president toward the topic. The subheadings under each main heading should list laws passed and other government actions taken by that administration. (b) Write a concluding paragraph summarizing the changes you have outlined.

PAST AND PRESENT

1. Do research to find a political reform made in your state during the progressive era. Possibilities are the direct primary, the initiative, the referendum, and the recall. Find out the names of the people responsible for the law. Does the law still exist? If so, how does it affect government in your state?

2. Describe a recent management-labor dispute either in your area or on a national level. How was it settled? Was collective bargaining used?

CHAPTER 19

THE FIRST WORLD WAR

1914–1920

WAR IN EUROPE
FROM NEUTRALITY TO WAR
MOBILIZING FOR WAR
THE UNITED STATES IN THE WAR
THE DIPLOMACY OF PEACE

In June 1918, in a wooded patch of France that had once been a hunting preserve, Private Elton Mackin of the 5th Marine Regiment faced the guns of the German army:

"We left the firing line on our bellies snaking away into the trampled wheat . . . . From time to time, the Sergeant would motion us down while he surveyed the terrain ahead and to our right, where things were getting hot. . . .

"We began to fret some because we were really in no man's land, far . . . from our battalion line. . . .

"Baldy, the most assured of us (none were at all brave) finally ventured to question, 'Hey, Sarge?' He got no answer—not even the grunt we expected. The Sergeant was full-length out of the ditch, snuggled down in a patch of shrubs and weeds; his chin rested on his folded arms, and he was peering under the brim of his helmet. His field glasses lay in front of him.

"'Hey, Sarge?' Baldy shook one foot to get his attention. There was no response. We knew better. We should not have left him there, but the evening star was glowing against the east and we were suddenly a bunch of lost, scared kids—a long way from home."

American soldiers were getting their first taste of battle, in a war that had raged in Europe since 1914. At first the war was called the "European War." But, as if to the steady beat of a drum, nations from around the world were drawn in. In spring 1917 the United States entered the war and Americans crossed the Atlantic to join the fighting. This would be, they told each other, the "war to end all wars."

Later, veterans recalled the "Great War." Finally, when people realized that this war had not ended all wars, it became simply World War I.

WAR IN EUROPE

READ TO FIND OUT

— **what events made possible World War I.**

— **how an assassination set off a chain reaction of nations declaring war.**

— **how the United States tried to stay neutral.**

— **how a quick victory for Germany disappeared at the Battle of the Marne.**

— **how Britain and Germany used propaganda in the war.**

It was Sunday, June 28, 1914. Factories were closed, farmers finished their chores early, and sermons rang through churches. It was a day of relaxation for Americans.

Many Americans settled down with the Sunday newspaper. The comics had the latest pranks of the Katzenjammer Kids and Buster Brown. For sports fans, there was news about America's first black heavyweight boxing champion, Jack Johnson. On the front page, the nation's concerns were reflected in headlines like "Suffragettes March on Capitol" and "Plain Facts about Tariff."

Something else happened that Sunday, but it occurred thousands of miles away and seemed to have little to do with Americans. Nevertheless, Americans awoke on Monday to read about it in the headlines. *The New York Times* splashed it over half the front page:

> Heir to Austria's Throne Is Slain With His Wife by a Bosnian Youth To Avenge Seizure of His Country

THE BALANCE OF POWER

Few Americans knew that Bosnia was a region within Austria-Hungary on the Balkan Peninsula. This mountainous peninsula lies in the southeast corner of Europe. Six nations—Serbia, Montenegro, Albania, Romania, Bulgaria, and Greece—were sandwiched between Austria-Hungary and the Ottoman Empire. Both Austria-Hungary and the Ottoman Empire were land-hungry neighbors. For years the peninsula had been torn by wars, earning it a nickname—"the powder keg of Europe."

Europe itself was something of a powder keg. In many countries there had developed a fierce sense of nationalism—the belief that one's language, customs, and homeland are better than one's neighbor's. Some countries exhibited this nationalism by displaying their armies and weapons and urging conquest of more territory.

Wars of conquest encouraged still more nationalism. In 1871 Germany won a war with France and annexed the French provinces of Alsace and Lorraine. France yearned to regain its provinces and reunite the French-speaking peoples. The Austro-Hungarian Empire expanded, engulfing Italians, as well as Slavic peoples like the Czechs, Slovaks, and Serbians. The Balkan countries, when they were not fighting off their neighbors, fought among themselves for more territory.

Nationalism also fed the rivalries among the European powers—Britain, France, Russia, and Germany—in their competition for colonies, new markets, and raw materials. These rivals, however,

Otto von Bismarck (center, with the walrus moustache) approaches the castle of Kaiser Wilhelm II, the last emperor of Germany. Wilhelm, who dismissed Bismarck in 1890, remained kaiser through World War I.

feared each other. Britain worried that the other European powers would expand their spheres of influence in China and damage British trade. Germany feared that France would attack to win back Alsace-Lorraine.

Germany had been a loose federation of states until 1870. At that time Otto von Bismarck united the states into a powerful nation. Anxious to protect his country, the "Iron Chancellor" looked for allies. Bismarck found them in Austria-Hungary and Italy, which feared the other European powers. Thus began the Triple Alliance.

Britain, France, and Russia were aware of the threat to them from the Triple Alliance. They saw that Germany, Austria-Hungary, and Italy were three strong nations committed to mutual defense. In addition, Russia was a rival of Austria-Hungary for control of the Balkans. Although Britain, France, and Russia had territorial disputes among themselves, they formed their own alliance, the Triple Entente (ahn-TAHNT).

Peace in Europe now hinged on a delicate *balance of power* in which one alliance was poised against another. Or, as the German ambassador to France said in 1914, "Peace remains at the mercy of an accident."

OUTBREAK OF WAR

The gunshot on that Sunday in June 1914 destroyed the balance of power. The assassin was a Bosnian revolutionary trained in neighboring Serbia. The Serbians claimed Bosnia because both peoples were Slavic.* Bosnia, however, was part of the Austro-Hungarian Empire. By killing the Austrian heir, Archduke Francis Ferdinand, the young revolutionary hoped to frighten Austria-Hungary into recognizing Serbia's claim to Bosnia.

Austria-Hungary claimed that the Serbian government was behind the assassination. On July 28, with encouragement and support from Germany, Austria-Hungary declared war on Serbia. Russia, a rival of Austria-Hungary, called up troops to defend its fellow Slavs in Serbia and declared war on Germany. Russia's ally France supported Russia's actions.

On August 1, 1914, Germany declared war on Russia, and on August 3 it declared war on France. Germany and Austria-Hungary planned to defeat France rapidly and then turn east to attack Russia. The shortest route to France was through Belgium, a neutral nation. Germany asked for permission to move troops through the nation, and Belgium refused. On August 4 Germany invaded Belgium. Britain was committed to defend neutral Belgium. That same day, Britain declared war on Germany, and on August 12 it declared war on Austria-Hungary.

By the second week in August the five major European nations were at war. Only Italy temporarily held back. Month after month, nation after nation joined the war. Japan declared war on

---

* Slavic: a language group including East Slavic (Russian), South Slavic (Bulgarian, Serbo-Croatian, etc.), and West Slavic (Polish, Czech, Slovak).

Allies and Central Powers

Allies		Central Powers
Belgium	Japan	Austria-Hungary
Brazil	Liberia	Bulgaria
British Empire	Montenegro	Germany
China	Nicaragua	Ottoman Empire (Turkey)
Costa Rica	Panama	
Cuba	Portugal	
France	Romania	
Greece	Russia	
Guatemala	San Marino	
Haiti	Serbia	
Honduras	Siam	
Italy	United States	

Germany in late August. Japan wanted to seize German colonies in the Pacific and to invade the Shantung (Shandong) Peninsula, Germany's sphere of influence in China.

The Ottoman Empire—now called Turkey—sided with Germany and Austria-Hungary. Italy eventually broke with the Triple Alliance in May 1915, and declared war on Austria-Hungary. The Italians hoped to win provinces in southern Austria and to unite Italians living there with Italy.

Now, replacing the alliances of peace were alliances of war. Germany, Austria-Hungary, Turkey, and the Balkan country of Bulgaria became the Central Powers, because they were in the center of Europe. Britain, France, Russia, Italy, and their allies—eventually a total of 24 nations on 6 continents—became the Allies.

As the nations tumbled into war, most people counted on a quick victory, but a few felt a grim foreboding. Sir Edward Grey, the British foreign minister, looked out his window at the street lamps. "The lamps are going out all over Europe," he said, "We shall not see them lit again in our lifetime."

AMERICAN NEUTRALITY

On August 4, 1914, President Wilson issued a proclamation of neutrality and urged Americans to be "impartial in thought as well as in action." Wilson was concerned about his program of reform and was working with Congress to get trust legislation passed. War, he knew, could only turn American attention away from reform.

Wilson, a minister's son, did not see war in terms of glory and empire. He did, however, see a role for the United States in the war. Neutral America could be an impartial mediator and bring peace to Europe.

Many Americans who supported neutrality found it hard to be "impartial in thought." About one third of all Americans were immigrants or first-generation children of immigrants. Many still had family and friends in the Old World. Their sympathies were stirred by memories of Germany or Britain or whatever their country of origin.

Some Irish-Americans sided with the Central Powers because of their dislike for Britain, which ruled Ireland. Even President Wilson, with his Scottish and English ancestry and love of English literature, could not be impartial in thought. Like the majority of Americans, Wilson sympathized with the Allies.

THE INVASION OF BELGIUM

For years Germany had prepared for war with France, and it now had the best army in Europe. On August 4 the German army had invaded its small neighbor, Belgium, to reach France. An American war correspondent in Belgium reported watching an unending column of German soldiers in gray:

The Belgian town of Termonde shows damage from German shells. In 1914 Germany gave Belgium a choice—allow the German army to pass or fight. Belgium chose to fight.

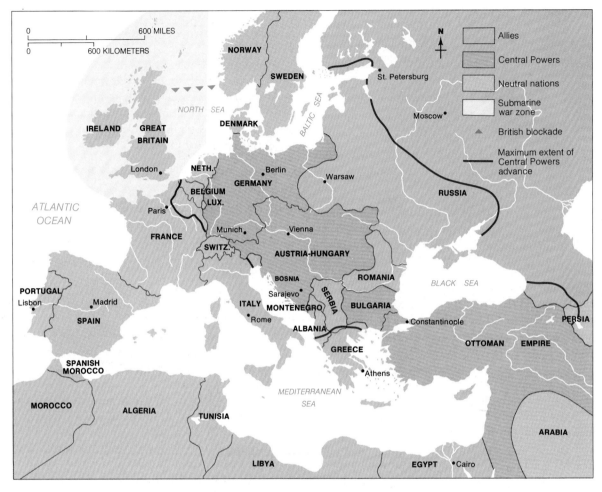

While opposing forces were stalemated along the western front and the Italian-Austrian border, the Turks held off the Allies in the Middle East. However, war raged along the eastern front. Twice Russia attacked Germany and Austria, and twice the Russian armies were driven back.

"It is a gray-green, not the blue-gray of our Confederates. It is the gray of the hour just before daybreak, the gray of unpolished steel."

Belgian cities fell to the steel-gray army, and the army rolled into France. It was not stopped until it reached the Marne River, about 40 miles (64 kilometers) from Paris. There the Allies had assembled a huge force, including 6,000 French troops driven to the Marne in Paris taxicabs.

The Battle of the Marne forced the Germans into a northward retreat to the Aisne (AYN) River, where they halted and dug trenches for protection. The Allies followed but could not dislodge the Germans, so the Allies also dug in. There would be no quick victory, only a bloody, drawn-out stalemate.

War broke out on many fronts—Italy, Austria, Russia, the Middle East, even in the European colonies in Africa. To most Americans, however, the war was in France, in the trenches along the western front.

PROPAGANDA

Britain and Germany waged another kind of war, each flooding the United States with propaganda designed to win public opinion to its side. Britain cut Germany's transatlantic telegraph connection to the United States. The remaining telegraph cables belonged to the Allies. This meant that Germany's only communication with the United States was by mail or by a new, still imperfect invention—the radio. The news that hummed to the United States, not surprisingly, favored the Allies.

Americans learned of the German style of warfare. The Germans preferred to strike hard and fast and terrorize the enemy, including civilians, into surrender. When Belgians in one town interfered as the Germans repaired a bridge, the soldiers lined up 600 civilians in the town square, men on one side and women on the other. The firing squad shot until no one was left standing. The Germans made an example of another Belgian city, Louvain, burning it and its famed library to the ground.

As shocking as these reports were, Americans soon heard even more horrid details of actions supposedly committed by German soldiers. The Germans, charged the Allies, cut off the hands of Belgian children and sent battlefield corpses to Germany to be made into soap and fertilizer. The Germans, in turn, accused the Allies of blinding captured soldiers and using cholera germs to poison wells in German-occupied areas.

Few Americans were swayed by the unproved stories. However, the invasion of Belgium—a small neutral nation—wrung American hearts and swept American sympathies to the Allies.

SECTION REVIEW

1. Identify the following: Bosnia, Alsace-Lorraine, Balkan nations, Otto von Bismarck, Archduke Francis Ferdinand, Marne River, Louvain.

2. Define the following: balance of power.

3. Describe two ways in which nationalism was an underlying cause of World War I.

4. Name the nations in each of the following: the Triple Alliance, the Triple Entente. What was the main reason both alliances were formed?

5. (a) Which nation declared war first? Against whom? (b) Which nations made up the Central Powers? Which main countries made up the Allies?

6. Give two reasons why President Wilson wanted to keep the United States out of war.

7. What was the German plan for winning the war? Where was the German army first stopped?

8. How did Britain and Germany each use propaganda in the war?

FROM NEUTRALITY TO WAR

READ TO FIND OUT

— **what effect the British blockade had on American trade.**

— **how naval warfare threatened American neutrality.**

— **how Americans reacted to the sinking of the *Lusitania*.**

— **how peace attempts failed and preparedness for war began.**

— **why the United States declared war.**

The stalemate on the western front was draining Germany and the Allies nearly dry. Every day some 7 million soldiers went through tons of food and supplies. Each side had to have supplies, and each was grimly determined to stop the other from getting them. Whoever controlled the seas and the ports had a lifeline to trade. Under international law, neutral nations could trade with countries at war as long as the neutral ships did not carry contraband—forbidden cargoes like guns and ammunition. Neutral ships could be searched, but only at sea.

The major neutral country trading with Europe was the United States. Both the Allies and the Central Powers tried to cut off American trade with their enemies without turning the United States into an enemy.

THE BLOCKADE OF TRADE

Early in the war British ships began stopping neutral merchant ships headed for Germany, or even for Germany's neutral neighbors Holland, Sweden, and Denmark. The British illegally brought the neutral ships into Allied ports, searched them, and seized even noncontraband cargoes like food. The United States, touchy about freedom of the seas, quickly complained to Britain, saying that this was an illegal blockade.

American industry, however, was profiting as it sold food, steel, oil, and other supplies to the Europeans. Because of the British blockade American trade with the Central Powers fell off sharply while trade with the Allies soared. Sales to the Allies more than tripled within two years. When the Allies eventually ran short of money, American bankers made them loans.

As more and more American goods flowed to the Allies, the Germans decided to break the British blockade. "England wants to starve us!" said the head of the German navy.

SUBMARINE WARFARE

The seas of Europe soon grew dangerous. In November 1914 both Britain and Germany planted mines in the North Sea. Britain declared the sea a military area and warned neutral ships that they would be safe only under Allied protection.

Germany could not match Britain's mighty navy, but it did have a tiny fleet of submarines, called U-boats. Small and light, submarines were designed to travel unseen underwater. A submarine could close in on a surface ship, fire a torpedo, and slip away.

Submarines, however, could not obey the rules of international law. Under international law, a warship must not fire on an enemy merchant ship without giving warning. After sinking an enemy ship, it must rescue the passengers and crew. Submarines, however, were slow on the surface and could be easily rammed. They could not, then, give warning. Furthermore, they had no room to carry survivors.

In February 1915 the Germans announced a war zone in the waters around Britain. Enemy ships would be sunk on sight. Even neutral ships might be sunk, the Germans said, because British ships sometimes disguised themselves with neutral flags. Wilson protested to Germany. If an American ship was sunk or an American killed, the United States would consider it a violation of neutrality. The Germans, in turn, warned Americans not to travel on enemy ships.

While warnings were being exchanged, an American, Colonel Edward M. House, was trying to negotiate a peace settlement. House was Wilson's adviser and closest friend. Through the early months of 1915, House shuttled from London to

This poster, designed by a prominent German artist, Hans Erdt, may have been planned as an advertisement for a book or movie. The poster reads, "The U-boats are out!"

Paris to Germany and back again. "Everybody seems to want peace," he wrote home, "but nobody is willing to concede enough to get it."

THE *LUSITANIA*

On March 28, 1915, a U-boat sank the British liner *Falaba* in the Irish Sea. An American was killed. Then on May 7, a U-boat torpedoed the *Lusitania*, a British liner traveling from New York to London. Explosions ripped apart the passenger ship. Within 18 minutes it rolled over and sank. The sinking of the *Lusitania* cost the lives of 1,198 men, women, and children—128 of them American citizens.

Americans were stunned. Not since Belgium had German actions horrified so many Americans. But President Wilson said that the United States must remain an example of peace, adding, "There is such a thing as . . . being too proud to fight."

Nevertheless Wilson sent a letter of protest to Germany and asked for reparations, or payment for damages. Germany replied that the *Lusitania* had carried arms and that Americans had been warned to stay home. Thus began a year-long "*Lusitania* correspondence" between the two nations.

THE PREPAREDNESS CAMPAIGN

Despite German actions, most Americans favored peace. Still, some Americans thought that the United States should be prepared for war. Since late 1914 a small group, led by Theodore Roosevelt and Henry Cabot Lodge, had been urging "preparedness." After the *Lusitania* crisis, they stepped up their campaign and won thousands of supporters.

Finally President Wilson, frustrated by the *Lusitania* correspondence, saw the need for a defense plan. In November 1915 he publicly announced his program to build up the army and navy. The program, however, was set aside in Congress.

In January 1916 Wilson began a tour of the country to obtain support for his defense plan. At the same time he sent Colonel House on a second tour of the European capitals, offering an American-arranged peace conference. Both tours failed.

In March 1916 a German submarine torpedoed the unarmed French passenger liner *Sussex*, injuring several Americans. After carefully thinking through his response, Wilson sent a final demand, or ultimatum, to Germany. Unless the Germans abandoned their methods of warfare against merchant and passenger ships, the United States would "have no choice but to sever diplomatic relations" with Germany.

Not wanting to push the United States too far, the Germans pledged to give warning before sinking merchant ships. Germany, however, attached a condition. The United States must force Britain to end its illegal blockade or Germany would feel free to change its policy. Wilson simply accepted Germany's pledge and replied that he could not accept the condition.

Although the tension eased with Germany, the *Sussex* sinking broke the deadlock over preparedness. Congress passed several defense measures. The National Defense Act more than doubled the size of the army. The Naval Appropriations Bill set shipbuilders to work on cruisers, battleships, and submarines. A Council of National Defense was established to prepare the nation's industry and resources in case of war.

As the presidential election of 1916 approached, Wilson campaigned on a platform of reform and peace. The Democrats' message to the voters was "He Kept Us Out of War." The Republicans also ran a peace candidate, Justice Charles Evans Hughes of the Supreme Court. Wilson defeated Hughes by a very narrow margin.

Wilson tried one more time to lead the Europeans into peace talks. In January 1917 he proposed "a peace without victory," in which neither side would lose territory or gain power. But the Europeans felt they had fought too hard and too long to give up victory now.

THE LAST STEPS TO WAR

On February 1, 1917, Germany announced that it would begin again its unrestricted submarine warfare. The Germans knew that this was likely to bring the United States into the war, but they were hopelessly stalled on the western front. They planned to break the British control of the seas with their U-boats—now numbering over one hundred—and win before the United States joined the fight.

Wilson immediately cut off diplomatic relations, but he hoped that Germany would back down. In late February his hope died. Britain had gotten hold of a message from the German foreign minister, Arthur Zimmermann, to his minister in Mexico. The "Zimmermann note" suggested a German-Mexican alliance if the United States entered the war. "It is understood," the note continued, "that Mexico is to reconquer the lost territory in New Mexico, Texas, and Arizona."

The preparedness campaign stirred American patriotism. Textile workers at a New Hampshire factory expressed pride in their nation by producing a flag four stories high.

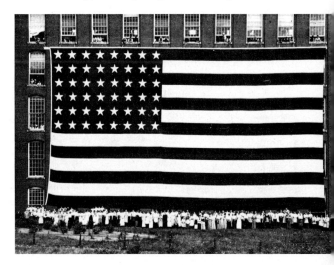

Wilson released the note to the press on March 1. Americans were at first unbelieving, and then furious. The public uproar increased when Germany unleashed its submarines against several American merchant ships. Each German outrage brought war closer.

War was brought still closer by another event in March. Revolutionaries in Russia overthrew the monarchy, replacing the dictatorship of Czar Nicholas II with a democratic government. The preparedness group had long claimed that this war was between the democracies of the Allies and the dictatorships of the Central Powers. The revolution made Russia an acceptable ally.

Those in favor of war and those in favor of peace were vocal, but the majority of Americans watched quietly to see what Wilson would do. Wilson accepted the unanimous advice of his cabinet. On April 2, 1917, Wilson addressed a special session of Congress and asked for a declaration of war against Germany.

The United States, said Wilson, was not going to war for conquest or territory, but for the cause of human rights everywhere and the freedom of all nations. Then, in one phrase, Wilson expressed the heart of his war message: "The world must be made safe for democracy." On April 6 Congress voted for the declaration of war.

SECTION REVIEW

1. Identify the following: North Sea, Edward M. House, National Defense Act, Naval Appropriations Bill, Council of National Defense.

2. (a) How did the war in Europe aid the American economy? (b) With which side did the United States trade more? Why?

3. According to international law, what rules were involved in firing on merchant ships? Why couldn't German submarines obey this law?

4. Who were the leaders of the war preparedness movement in the United States? What event helped them to convince Congress to pass defense measures?

5. Describe the election of 1916. Who were the candidates, and what was the main issue?

6. (a) What three events brought Wilson to the decision that war was unavoidable? (b) How did Wilson justify the United States going to war?

MOBILIZING FOR WAR

READ TO FIND OUT

— **how the United States recruited soldiers.**

— **how the United States raised money for war.**

— **how peacetime industries were converted into suppliers of war materials.**

— **how the United States fed the Allied armies.**

— **how American workers contributed to the war effort.**

— **how dissent was controlled and support built for the war.**

The Allies were overjoyed when they heard that the United States was entering the war. Paris was decorated with American flags, the British Parliament cheered President Wilson, and the Allied soldiers on the western front managed a smile of hope. The Allies needed help desperately. Russia was in chaos after the revolution. Despair had driven some French units to mutiny. German U-boats were sinking Allied ships faster than the Allies could replace them.

THE DRAFT

Large-scale mobilization* would have to be directed by the federal government. Government had expanded during the progressive era, to look after the nation's welfare. It would grow still stronger in getting the nation ready for war.

In April 1917 the army counted about 200,000 soldiers, most of them not yet trained. Wilson and Congress would have preferred to build up the army with volunteers, but they realized that volunteer enlistments could never fill the ranks. The alternative was *conscription*—the draft.

On May 18 Congress passed the Selective Service Act. The act required all men between the ages of twenty-one and thirty (and later, between eighteen

---

*mobilization: the organization of people and other resources for immediate use in war.

and forty-five) to register for military service. From this pool the army would take those who were physically fit and claimed no exemptions, such as necessary war work in a shipyard.

In response to the government's appeals, over 9 million Americans registered in the first draft call. During the war over 24 million registered, and almost 3 million of them served in the army, along with 2 million volunteers. There was at no time any significant resistance to the draft. Draftees and volunteers fought with equal bravery.

Among those serving were some 360,000 blacks, inspired by W.E.B. Du Bois' words: "Let us, while this war lasts, forget our special grievances and close ranks shoulder to shoulder with our own fellow citizens." Blacks, however, found discrimination in military service. They were placed in segregated units that usually had white officers. Only after strong protests from groups like the NAACP were several hundred blacks made officers.

Once overseas, most blacks were assigned tasks like cooking and moving equipment. However, some did see combat. One black regiment, the 369th Infantry, was under enemy fire for a record-breaking 191 days. Two blacks, Henry Johnson and Needham Roberts, fought off a German attack and received France's highest combat honor, the Croix de Guerre.

RAISING MONEY

The massive mobilization eventually cost about $36 billion. Congress passed two measures to raise the money. The Liberty Loan Act, passed in April 1917, made it possible for the government to borrow money by selling Liberty bonds to the public. The government could also make loans to the Allies so they could buy food and supplies from the United States.

Wilson's secretary of the treasury, William McAdoo, took charge of the Liberty Loan drives. He gave speeches and lined up artists and film stars to support the drive. Americans eventually bought over $20 billion worth of bonds.

Congress also raised taxes by passing the War Revenue Act of October 1917. Previously, people earning under $3,000 per year were not taxed, and the tax rate on incomes above $3,000 ranged from 1 percent to a high of 7 percent. The Revenue Act lowered the taxable income to $1,000 and above,

and raised the tax rate to range from 4 percent to 67 percent on the highest incomes. Taxes were also raised on corporations, and on goods like alcohol and tobacco.

INDUSTRY GOES TO WAR

"War is no longer Samson with his shield and spear," said Secretary of War Newton Baker, "it is the conflict of smokestacks now." Industry's smokestacks burned to produce rifles, artillery, ships, airplanes, and gas masks.

Industry, like the armed forces, had to be mobilized for war, and the government took on the task. Congress had already set up the Council of National Defense to direct the overall war effort. During 1917 and 1918 Congress gave Wilson broad new powers to coordinate war-related agencies and to make wartime regulations.

During World War I records were set in almost every industry. Before the war it had taken almost two years to build a destroyer. This ship was built in just seventeen days.

The War Industries Board was set up in July 1917 to spur production and stop waste. By spring of 1918, however, it was snarled in red tape. To cut the tape, Wilson appointed Bernard Baruch as head of the board. Baruch was a stockbroker so at ease with the statistics and workings of business that Wilson called him "Dr. Facts."

Baruch faced the difficult task of setting priorities for vital goods and of making sure that they were delivered on time. He also had to build new factories and convert old ones to wartime needs. Rather than force industry to comply, Baruch explained war needs to business owners, and they usually cooperated with him.

Piano builders turned to making airplane wings. Corset manufacturers made belts and gas masks. The steel they would have used in corsets went to build trucks or guns. To cut waste and save labor, the board regulated the products and the quantities that could be made.

Guided by the board, industry poured out shipload after shipload of war supplies. Meanwhile, other agencies were reaching even deeper into American life. The Railroad Administration took over the country's railroads to move troops and supplies speedily to seaports. The Fuel Administration increased the production of coal and oil, and rationed the amount of fuel Americans could burn in their homes. Even the clock was managed when the fuel board followed Great Britain's example and established daylight-saving time. The extra hour of daylight enabled people to conserve energy by turning their lights on later.

FOOD CONSERVATION

A major war need was food for both the American military and the Allied armies and civilians. The United States and the Allies, said Wilson, were now "eating at the common table." But American grain harvests had been poor for two years and food prices were rising. How could the country put food on the table for everyone?

To deal with this problem, Wilson appointed Herbert Clark Hoover head of the Food Administration. Hoover was a mining engineer who had lived in London when the war started, and volunteered to head the relief efforts for Belgium. The American ambassador in London later wrote Wilson, "But for Hoover Belgium would now be starved."

Hoover and the Food Administration were given authority to set prices on crops, determine which farm products would be sent to Europe, and punish people who hoarded food or obtained unfair profits on food sales. But Hoover, like Baruch, preferred to rely on voluntary efforts. He began a campaign to persuade Americans to adopt "food conservation." A poster urged Americans to "Use all left-overs."

The Allies most needed four basic foods—sugar, fats, meat, and wheat. Soon there were meatless Tuesdays, wheatless Mondays and Wednesdays, and porkless Thursdays and Saturdays. The campaign was a great success, and the United States more than tripled its prewar shipments of basic foods to the Allied countries.

The food conservation campaign also gave new life to the movement to ban alcohol. Grain used to make alcohol was needed to make bread. In December 1917 Congress passed the Eighteenth Amendment, prohibiting the manufacture, sale, or transportation of alcohol. However, the amendment was not ratified until after the war. It went into effect in January 1920. Meanwhile, in December 1917 Wilson ordered reductions in the alcohol content of beer and the amount of grain used in malt liquors.

LABOR HELPS THE WAR EFFORT

To keep relations between owners and workers running smoothly and to settle labor disputes, Wilson set up the National War Labor Board in April 1918. Another agency, the War Labor Policies Board, had the power to set standard wages, hours, and working conditions. Labor leaders served on most of the war boards, including the Council of National Defense. The fruits of this cooperation were high productivity and few strikes. There was also an increase in union membership, from 2.75 million in 1916 to 4.25 million in 1919.

It was a boom time for workers, especially for women. When men moved from the factory to the military, women took their places. Women operated trolleys, directed traffic, delivered mail, cared for the wounded, worked in munitions factories, and served on war boards. Some 11,000 did office work for the navy and 269 served in the marines.

Leaders of the women's suffrage movement supported the war effort but did not abandon the fight for the vote. Suffragists picketed the White House day and night, holding banners insisting that "democracy should begin at home."

The demonstrations—and the sight of thousands of women doing jobs previously considered men's work—began to sway the public. Wilson told Congress that women's suffrage "is vital to the winning of the war." In January 1918 the House passed the Nineteenth Amendment to give women the right to vote. Ratification of the amendment, however, was almost three years away.

For blacks, too, the war brought change. America's supply of immigrant labor stopped with the war. The shortage prompted northern business people to send recruiting agents to the South. The agents promised blacks good wages and plenty of jobs, and hundreds of thousands of blacks streamed to the North.

Edward Hopper's study for a poster emphasizes labor's place in the war effort. The final poster won first prize in a competition conducted by the United States Shipping Board.

They found the jobs, many of which had been earlier closed to blacks. Blacks worked in gas stations and garages, in steel mills, automobile factories, and railroads. They delivered goods and unloaded ships. But they also found poor housing and discrimination.

BUILDING SUPPORT FOR THE WAR

Most, but not all, Americans supported the war. Opponents ranged from individuals to groups like the peace societies and the Socialist party. Some opponents claimed that they would fight to defend the United States but wanted no part of the "European war of aggression." Others, true pacifists,* objected to the agony of any war, whatever the cause. Still others felt the war benefited the bankers who made loans to the Allies and the industries that turned out war supplies.

Most government leaders did not want anything to damage the war effort. Congress quickly moved to quiet dissent. In June 1917 Congress passed the Espionage Act. Anyone found guilty of helping the enemy, hurting recruitment, or causing disloyalty in the military could be fined up to $10,000 or imprisoned up to 20 years. The act also allowed the postmaster general to ban from the mails any materials, such as newspapers, that he judged treasonable. The Trading with the Enemy Act of October 1917 outlawed trade with Germany and called for censorship of publications exchanged between the United States and foreign countries.

Finally, the Sedition Act, passed in May 1918, imposed severe penalties on those who said anything that interfered with the war effort, or used "disloyal . . . or abusive language" about the American government, Constitution, flag, or "uniform of the Army or Navy." The earlier Espionage Act was aimed at disloyal activities. The Sedition Act was aimed at disloyal words, even an antiwar opinion.

The government was also interested in winning people's support. In April 1917 Wilson set up the Committee on Public Information and appointed newspaper editor George Creel to head it. Creel's committee used speeches, pamphlets, articles, movies, and posters to build support for the war.

* pacifists: people who, for reasons of conscience, refuse to fight in any war.

The committee built support for the war, but its efforts sometimes heightened fears and suspicions. Some Americans unleashed their fury at Germany on German-Americans. The governor of Iowa banned the speaking of German in public, or even on the telephone. Sauerkraut became known as "liberty cabbage." Some German-Americans found it dangerous to appear in public. Despite these unhappy effects, Creel's committee accomplished what it intended.

Actually there was little disloyalty during the war. Most Americans fully supported the Allied cause. Soldiers set off for Europe with a marching song on their lips:

Over there, over there,
Send the word, send the word over there,
That the Yanks are coming, the Yanks are coming,
The drums rum-tumming everywhere.
So prepare, say a prayer,
Send the word, send the word to beware,
We'll be over, we're coming over,
And we won't come back till it's over over there.

SECTION REVIEW

1. Identify the following: 369th Infantry, Railroad Administration, Fuel Administration, National War Labor Board, War Labor Policies Board.

2. What was the Selective Service Act?

3. What two measures did Congress pass to pay for the war? List the provisions of each.

4. Who was the head of the War Industries Board? What four tasks were he and the Board supposed to accomplish?

5. (a) Who was head of the Food Administration? (b) What four foods were especially needed? How was conservation of these foods accomplished?

6. (a) How was the women's suffrage movement affected by the large number of women in the labor force? (b) How were blacks affected by the mobilization for war?

7. What three acts were passed in 1917 and 1918 to keep Americans from speaking out against the war or hurting the war effort? List two provisions of each.

8. Who was George Creel, and what was his job during the war? How did he carry it out?

THE UNITED STATES IN THE WAR

READ TO FIND OUT

— how the United States shipped troops and supplies to France.

— what preparation American troops needed for war.

— how the German offensive of 1918 split the British and French armies.

— what difference American troops made to Allied military power.

— what the war cost in human life.

On June 26, 1917, a large group of troop and supply ships sailed into the small port of St. Nazaire on the west coast of France. French citizens turned out to watch as the ships crowded into the docks. The American commander of this operation, Vice-Admiral Albert Gleaves, described the effect on the French:

The population gathered along the quays looked on in whispering wonderment at the young khaki-clad strangers who had appeared, almost overnight, from over the seas. There was no cheering, no patriotic demonstration, only the respectful silence of the women and children, the old men and the broken soldiers.

THE AMERICAN NAVY

That June day was the beginning of America's military participation in the war. The first American troops had arrived "over there." It was also the United States Navy's first success in a plan to defeat the deadly U-boats.

To transport American troops and supplies safely across the Atlantic, ships had to navigate sea lanes patrolled by German submarines. Admiral William S. Sims of the United States Navy suggested that the ships be accompanied by a guard of British and American destroyers and submarine chasers.

This plan to use *convoys* worked beautifully, from the first landing at St. Nazaire to the last landing of the war. Over 2 million soldiers and 4 million tons of supplies crossed the sea on this "bridge of ships." There was little loss of life, and only 24 out of 1,500 ships sunk.

The British and American navies also cooperated in a massive operation in the North Sea, laying a barrier of over 50,000 mines between Scotland and Norway. German submarines had great difficulty in crossing the barrier to reach open sea. By October 1918 Allied shipping losses declined by almost 90 percent. The United States Navy—with a wartime strength of some 2,000 ships and 500,000 sailors—made up almost a third of the convoy escorts and laid 80 percent of the North Sea mines.

THE AMERICAN EXPEDITIONARY FORCE

On July 4, 1917, the French invited troops of the American Expeditionary Force (AEF) to join in an Independence Day celebration. American and French officials and soldiers paraded through Paris, stopping at a national shrine, the tomb of Lafayette.

The Marquis de Lafayette, and thousands of French soldiers, had come to help America during the Revolutionary War. Now Americans could repay that debt. Colonel Charles E. Stanton spoke for his country: "America has joined forces with the Allied Powers, and what we have of blood and treasure are yours. . . . Lafayette, we are here."

However, only a fraction of the AEF—about 14,000 troops—had reached France by July. These inexperienced *doughboys*, as soldiers had been called since the Civil War, were not ready for battle. The commander of the force, General John J. Pershing, realized this and rushed them to a training camp outside of Paris.

Pershing was a soldier in every inch of his six-foot frame. He had received his discipline and education at West Point, and had fought in the Indian wars, the Philippines, and the Spanish-American war. His service in the conflicts between Mexico and the United States had won him Wilson's admiration and the AEF appointment.

Pershing had strict orders to make the AEF a distinct unit, separate from the other Allied armies. He resisted pressure from Britain to use Americans in British divisions, and he awaited the arrival of the

By 1918 two million American troops had reached France, and an equal number were prepared to follow.

main body of the AEF. The doughboys would see little fighting in 1917, but their training with French units introduced them to trench warfare.

TRENCH WARFARE

Ever since the Battle of the Marne in September 1914, the armies on the western front had fought from trenches. Each side tried to outflank, or go around, the other by extending its trenches. Eventually, the trench line extended 600 miles (966 kilometers) across Belgium and France, reaching from the North Sea to Switzerland.

The trenches were about 5 feet (1.5 meters) deep and 2 feet (.6 meters) wide. Barbed wire stretched in front of the firing line. Beyond that was "no man's land"—deadly open ground.

American army nurses received training in the use of gas masks. Air enters the mask through a charcoal filter.

Each side used the newest weapons to try to break through the other's line. An attack began with hours of heavy artillery fire from howitzers and field guns. Then the attacking infantry charged across no man's land, hoping to get through holes in the barbed wire to the enemy's trench.

There was another, silent, weapon used by both sides—chlorine or mustard gas. The clouds of gas sometimes floated down into the trenches, choking, blinding, and killing anyone without a gas mask.

Most battles were remembered by the number of lives lost. In February 1916 the Germans launched an attack on the city of Verdun. In six months the German army advanced 4 miles (6 kilometers) and lost over 300,000 in casualties, while the French defenders lost over 350,000. The ground was battered by 40 million artillery shells into a landscape of mud, craters, and burned husks of trees.

THE GERMAN ADVANCE BEGINS

The Allies hoped that the addition of the American Expeditionary Force would at last give them enough troops to break the stalemate on the western front. But upheavals on the eastern and southern fronts in the winter of 1917 gave Germany the advantage. On the southern front, the Italians were crushed by German and Austrian troops in a bloody battle at Caporetto. The Allies had to rush troops from the western front to save Italy.

Then, in November, the eight-month-old democratic government in Russia fell to the Bolsheviks, a wing of the radical Communist party. The leader of the Bolshevik revolution, Nikolai Lenin, began peace talks with Germany. In March 1918 Germany and Russia signed the Treaty of Brest-Litovsk (BREST lih-TOFSK). Shortly after, Romania decided it could not continue fighting without its powerful neighbor and ally Russia. It too signed a peace treaty.

With its army freed from the eastern front, Germany began a massive offensive in France and vowed to take Paris. On March 21, 1918, the Germans struck at the Allied lines along the Somme River, and split the British and French armies.

Desperate, the Allies decided to coordinate their armies under a "supreme Allied commander," France's General Ferdinand Foch. Foch and Pershing seemed ready to clash over Pershing's desire for a separate American army. The grimness of the Allied position, however, moved Pershing to tell Foch, "There is at the moment no other question but of fighting. Infantry, artillery, aviation—all that we have are yours. Use them as you will."

ALLIED DEFENSE ALONG THE MARNE

By the end of May the Germans had pushed to the banks of the Marne River along a 40-mile (64-kilometer) front. As in September 1914, the Allies would have to stop them at the Marne or lose Paris. This time, however, three American divisions joined the Allied troops marching to the front.

The doughboys entered the front at the town of Château-Thierry (shah-TOH teh-REE) on the Marne, and they helped the French to stop the German advance. Then the Americans were ordered into their first offensive, to recapture a square-mile patch of woodland known as Belleau (BEL-loh) Wood.

On June 6 a brigade of American marines, most of them fresh volunteers, charged across the field. "The air was full of red-hot nails," wrote a correspondent with the troops' brigade, and the marines were mowed down by the hundreds. Still, they managed to obtain a foothold. Throughout June they launched attack after attack, each time gaining a bit of ground. After suffering nearly 8,000 casualties, the marines at last won Belleau Wood.

World War I: The Western Front 1918

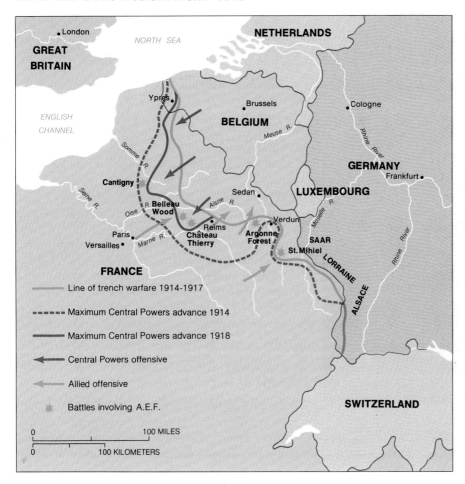

In the spring of 1918 Germany launched a massive campaign in an attempt to end the war before more American troops could arrive. The German forces gained ground with fierce fighting near Ypres, the Somme River, and Reims. But by August, the Allied armies, reinforced with American troops, began to push the Germans back.

In mid-July the Germans made a massive attack at Reims (REEMZ) in a final attempt to cross the Marne River. But General Foch turned the Second Battle of the Marne into the beginning of an Allied counteroffensive. From July 18 through August 6 the Allies forced the Germans into a northward retreat, and the Germans lost ground they had held since 1914.

About 270,000 Americans fought in the offensive, suffering heavy casualties. But as one American wrote home, "Folks, we have them on the run."

THE ALLIES TAKE THE OFFENSIVE

By late summer over a million American soldiers had reached France, and thousands more arrived with each convoy. General Pershing drew up plans for an American attack against the last German stronghold that bulged into the French line, at the town of St. Mihiel (SAN mee-YEL). Meanwhile, Foch was planning a final Allied campaign to force the Germans out of France.

Foch and Pershing finally agreed on a compromise plan. Foch would give Pershing artillery and air support for St. Mihiel. In turn, Pershing and his army would join in an offensive around the Meuse (MYOOZ) River and the Argonne (ahr-GUN) Forest.

For the attack on St. Mihiel, Pershing assembled 9 American and 3 French divisions, some 3,000 field guns, about 1,400 airplanes, and 267 tanks. Tanks, resembling giant armored tractors, had been developed by the British to cross land torn by shell holes. Airplanes had had to be adapted to warfare. At the war's outset pilots had fired pistols at each other. Eventually planes were fitted with radios, bombs, and machine guns.

In 1914 French photographer Jacques-Henri Lartique focused on a biplane flying above French soldiers. Early in the war airplanes were used primarily to scout enemy positions.

In 1916 a band of American volunteers had joined France's Lafayette Escadrille, a squadron of fliers. Several Americans, such as Eddie Rickenbacher and Billy Mitchell, became skilled at shooting down enemy planes and earned their reputation as "aces." In 1917 they transferred to the AEF air service.

In the foggy predawn hours of September 12, 1918, the Americans launched a heavy artillery bombardment at St. Mihiel. The artillery was supported by airplanes, which spotted the enemy and dropped bombs. Then, at 5:00 a.m., the infantry and tanks rolled into the German trenches, and by nightfall had routed the enemy. After three more days of mopping up, the Americans had successfully taken St. Mihiel and 16,000 prisoners.

Buoyed by their splendid victory, the doughboys immediately set out for the Meuse-Argonne front. The American goal was the Sedan railroad in northern France. This railroad was the Germans'

main line of supply and communication on the western front. Meanwhile, French, British, and Belgian troops would attack at other spots along the German line.

The way to Sedan was 35 miles (56 kilometers) through the Argonne Forest. For 47 days over a million Americans made their way through the dense forest, which was laced by barbed wire, German trenches, machine-gun nests, and bunkers. In the fog and rain the Germans were an invisible enemy.

American casualties were grim, almost 120,000. Finally, in early November, the weary Americans pushed through to Sedan and broke the German communications line. All along the western front, the Germans were crumbling under Allied blows. Germany's allies had already sensed defeat. Between late September and November, Bulgaria, Turkey, and Austria-Hungary each signed an armistice. Germany, alone, remained at war with the Allies.

ARMISTICE

Germany's military leaders, too, had realized that the war was lost. In September they had advised the German emperor, Kaiser Wilhelm II, to seek an armistice. Meanwhile, however, morale in Germany had plunged. A mutiny by some German sailors sparked a series of revolts against the kaiser. On November 9 a group of German socialists proclaimed "the German Republic." Kaiser Wilhelm stepped down from the throne and fled to Holland. Two days later delegates of the new government met with Foch to sign an armistice. On a cold, rainy day—November 11, 1918—the Great War ended.

The terms of the armistice were harsh. Germany had to leave immediately all occupied territory. It had to surrender its arms and equipment. It had to promise to acknowledge Allied rights to claim damages, return all prisoners of war, and allow Allied troops to occupy German land around the Rhine River. The armistice, in fact, amounted to a German surrender.

The costs of the war were far harsher. Each side lost about 50 percent of its troops in casualties—killed, wounded, or missing. Over 5 million of the Allies and over 3 million from the Central Powers died in battle or from wounds or disease. There was a total of some 8.5 million dead.

Collection of The Museum of Modern Art, New York.

Edward Steichen was placed in charge of developing aviation photography for military use. The aerial photo shown here was taken in France in 1917. The wiggly white line is a trench. Other lines reveal roads and railroads. The small white splotches are shell craters.

EDWARD STEICHEN
PHOTOGRAPHING THE HUMAN FAMILY

When World War I ended, army photographer Edward Steichen did not feel like celebrating. "I went into my room at the barracks and flung myself on the bed," he remembered. "The whole monstrous horror of the war seemed to fall down on me and smother me. I smelled the rotting carcasses of dead horses, saw the three white faces of the first American dead that I had seen. . . . How could men and nations have been so stupid? What was life for if it had to end like this?"

Born in Luxembourg in 1879, Edward Steichen had come with his family to the American Midwest when he was only two. Although his parents were poor, they had encouraged his interest in art. At sixteen he had taken his first photographs. Later in New York City he had become a founding member of the Photo-Secession group of experimental young photographers. These young people were eager to make their work a serious art.

Steichen's war experiences changed his approach to photography. He no longer wanted to create pictures for an educated few. "I wanted to reach out into the world, to participate, to communicate," he said. Through photography he hoped to do what he could to heal the wounds of war.

Steichen went on to become one of America's most distinguished photographers. But he was most proud of his "Family of Man" exhibit, created for the Museum of Modern Art in 1956. For it he selected 503 photographs from 68 countries, showing ordinary people at work and play, singing, dancing, marrying, grieving. Shown throughout the world, the "Family of Man" became the most popular photographic exhibit of all time. Millions of people were deeply touched by it. Steichen had achieved what he set out to do after World War I: to make photography "a mirror of the essential oneness of [humanity]."

France and Germany suffered the greatest losses, losing approximately one out of every 30 people to war-related deaths. France figured out that between August 1914 and February 1917 one French soldier was killed every minute. American losses were far less but still frightful. About 116,000 Americans were killed, and twice that many wounded or missing.

For many of those left alive, memories would long remain. Novelist F. Scott Fitzgerald wrote in *Tender Is the Night* about a group of friends looking at a battlefield years after the war. One says:

> See that little stream—we could walk to it in two minutes. It took the British a month to walk to it—a whole empire walking very slowly, dying in front and pushing forward behind. And another empire walked very slowly backward a few inches a day, leaving the dead like a million bloody rugs.

SECTION REVIEW

1. Identify the following: Verdun, Bolsheviks, Nikolai Lenin, Ferdinand Foch, Eddie Rickenbacker, Billy Mitchell, Kaiser Wilhelm II.

2. Define the following: convoy, doughboy.

3. (a) What was meant by the "bridge of ships"? (b) What was the purpose of placing mines in the North Sea?

4. Who was the commander of the American Expeditionary Force? What were his qualifications?

5. (a) What was the general effect of trench warfare on the progress of the war? (b) What new and deadly "silent weapon" was used in World War I?

6. What was the Treaty of Brest-Litovsk? What advantage did it give the Germans?

7. (a) Where did American troops join the front? Name the nearby area where the Americans won their first offensive. (b) What happened in the Second Battle of the Marne?

8. What plan did Generals Pershing and Foch agree on to force the Germans out of France?

9. Name two inventions that were new to World War I.

10. List the five terms required of Germany in the armistice.

THE DIPLOMACY OF PEACE

READ TO FIND OUT

— what plans President Wilson had for a peace settlement.

— how foreign and domestic leaders reacted to Wilson's peace plan.

— what compromises were made in the Treaty of Versailles.

— how the League of Nations was organized.

— how the Senate refused to ratify the peace treaty.

The long-awaited news of the armistice reached the United States at 3:00 a. m. Edith Wilson, the President's wife, had been up all night decoding messages for him. Excitedly she woke him: "The armistice is signed! The guns are still!"

The news flashed across the United States, and the country joyfully celebrated. For Woodrow Wilson, there was little time to rejoice. When he greeted the wild, cheering throng in front of the White House, he talked of the responsibilities that lay ahead. "Everything for which America has fought has been accomplished," he told the crowd. Now the nation had a special mission—to "aid in the establishment of just democracy throughout the world."

THE FOURTEEN POINTS

Woodrow Wilson had firm ideas about how this "just democracy" should be built. Even before the war had ended, he had suggested a peace settlement that he hoped would benefit the world. His plan had been prompted by events in Russia.

When the Bolsheviks took power in Russia in November 1917, they asked the warring countries to make peace without demanding any territory or reparations. The Bolsheviks also published "secret treaties" that the Allies had made in 1915. In these treaties, the Allies had agreed on the territory that

An American veteran views an Armistice Day parade. More than 200,000 Americans were wounded. The British and French suffered much greater casualities.

Early in the morning of November 11, news of the German surrender reached the United States. Fire and factory whistles blew. Thousands poured into the streets to celebrate, some thoughtfully quiet, others enthusiastic. In New York and other cities parades were organized.

each would gain from the war. France, Britain, and Japan would divide up Germany's colonies, Austria-Hungary would be parceled out, and so on.

The United States was not involved in these treaties, but Wilson realized that their existence hurt the Allied cause. He decided to propose an American plan for peace. On January 8, 1918, Wilson outlined his fourteen-point program to Congress.

The first five points were designed to remove the causes of conflict that led to war. First, nations would practice diplomacy openly and make no secret treaties. Second, ships could move freely on the seas, during peace and war. Third, tariff barriers would be removed to allow free international trade. Fourth, nations would reduce their armaments. Finally, the colonial claims of nations would be settled impartially, in the best interests of the colonial peoples.

Points six though thirteen dealt with *territorial integrity*—the protection of national boundaries—and *self-determination*—the right of people to be independent or to decide in which country they want to live. Thus Wilson asked that all countries regain territory lost during the war. Furthermore, he called for Europe's boundaries to be redrawn along the lines of nationality. For example, the Italian-speaking areas of Austria-Hungary would become part of Italy. Peoples ruled by Austria-Hungary, Turkey, and Russia would form their own independent nations.

The fourteenth point was the key to a permanent peace. It called for a "general association of nations"—a League of Nations. The League of Nations would have the power to guarantee the independence and territory of "great and small states alike."

RESPONSE TO THE FOURTEEN POINTS

Thousands of copies of Wilson's speech were dropped from airplanes over enemy areas. Both soldiers and civilians read the leaflets and saw hope for a favorable peace settlement.

In October 1918 German leaders, hoping to avoid a humiliating defeat, asked Wilson for an armistice. Wilson spelled out his terms. Germany must accept the Fourteen Points, get rid of the kaiser, and set up a democratic government. As talks with Germany got underway, Wilson talked to

Maps can represent the same land area at different time periods. In this chapter there are two maps of the same land area that show political boundaries at different times. Look first at the map on page 456 entitled "World War I: 1914–1918." Use the legend on the map to answer the following questions.

1. List the names of the nations that made up the Central Powers.

2. Give the names of the Balkan nations. Tell on which side each nation fought. Was any of the Balkan nations neutral?

Now look at the map entitled "Europe After World War I." Look first at the legend. Then compare this map with "World War I: 1914–1918" to answer the following questions.

1. Give the name of the Central Power that changed its name during World War I. What territory did this nation lose? What nation or nations received this territory?

2. What new nations came into being after the war? From whose territory were these nations carved?

3. Describe changes in Germany's territory.

4. What happened to each of the Balkan nations that existed before World War I? Did the boundaries of any Balkan nation remain precisely the same as they were before the war?

---

the Allies. Reluctantly, they agreed to an armistice based on the Fourteen Points, with two exceptions. They would not accept the second point, which assured freedom of the seas. They also demanded that Germany pay reparations for war damages suffered by Allied civilians.

Thus, the war came to an end almost entirely on Wilson's terms. However, those terms were not acceptable to all Americans, especially Republican leaders. The Republicans were afraid that the Democrats would take the credit for peace in the upcoming congressional elections. Many of them also felt that Wilson's terms were too easy on Germany.

In response, Wilson asked Americans to show the world that they supported him by electing Democrats in the November elections. Although most Americans approved of Wilson's program, they were angered by his appeal to party politics. The Republicans won control of both the House of Representatives and the Senate in the election. They claimed that their victory showed the voters' disapproval of Wilson's policies.

Wilson then made two more political mistakes. Determined to build his "association of nations," he announced that he would personally attend the upcoming peace conference in Paris. No president

had ever gone to Europe while in office. Many Americans felt that the president's place was at home, helping the nation to adjust to post-war conditions.

Criticism was even stronger when Wilson named the American delegation to the peace conference. There were no leading Republicans in the group. Ex-president Taft seemed a logical choice because he supported Wilson's plan, but he was not chosen. There were no senators, even though the peace treaty would have to be ratified by the Senate. Wilson had chosen as delegates only loyal friends and advisers like Colonel House and Secretary of State Robert Lansing.

THE PEACE CONFERENCE

The peace conference opened in Paris in January 1919. Delegates from 27 Allied countries attended. The major decisions, however, rested with four people—Wilson, British prime minister David Lloyd George, French premier Georges Clemenceau (ZHORZH klay-mahn-SŌ), and Italian prime minister Vittorio Orlando.

Lloyd George was concerned about maintaining Britain's naval superiority. He also wanted to crush Germany's naval power. Lloyd George did not,

Europe After World War I

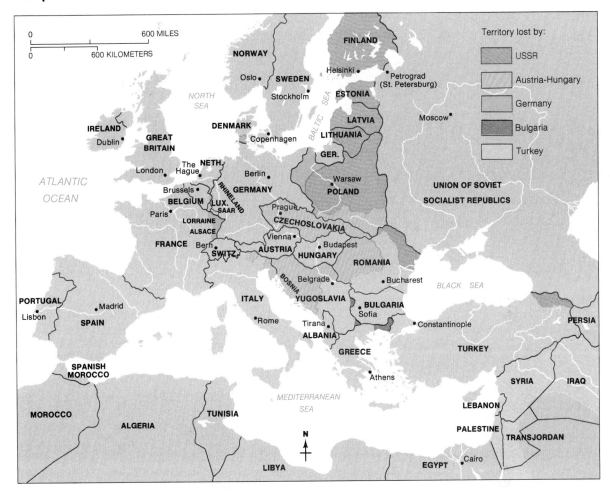

World War I altered borders in the Middle East as well as in Europe. The Ottoman Empire was eventually replaced by a new Turkish government. Syria and Lebanon were placed under French supervision. Transjordan, Palestine, and Iraq were placed under British supervision.

then, support Wilson's idea of "freedom of the seas." Clemenceau had lived through the German siege of Paris in 1871 and had seen France become a scarred battlefield in the world war. He was bitterly determined to disarm Germany and protect France. Clemenceau demanded that there be a security line between the two countries along the Rhine River. Orlando wanted Italy to be given territory secretly promised to it when it joined the Allies in 1914.

Obviously, many of Wilson's Fourteen Points clashed with the Europeans' aims. The final peace treaty bore the marks of both the Allies' demands and Wilson's ideals. It included an agreement for a League of Nations, it punished Germany, and it redrew the map of Europe.

THE TREATY OF VERSAILLES

Poland, which had been divided among Austria, Germany, and Russia, was made an independent nation. It was given access to the Baltic Sea through German territory, placing some Germans under Polish rule. The former Russian territories of Finland, Estonia, Latvia, and Lithuania became independent. The Austro-Hungarian empire was divided into four countries—Austria, Hungary, Czechoslovakia, and Yugoslavia. United at last in Yugoslavia were the Serbians and Bosnians, whose fierce nationalism had touched off the war.

The new borders were not drawn entirely along national lines. Italy, for example, received territory

Woodrow Wilson was the first American president to travel to Europe while in office. In 1918 and again in 1919 he sailed to Paris to participate in the peace negotiations.

occupied by Austrians. Never before, however, had Europe's political boundaries more clearly reflected the independence of national groups.

Although Wilson managed to keep Germany from being dismembered, Germany lost one eighth of its territory. German colonies, along with Turkish-ruled territories, were distributed among Japan, France, and Britain. These nations, however, had only *mandates* over the colonies. In other words, they were required to account for their rule of the colonies to the League of Nations. The suggestion for mandates had been Wilson's.

France regained Alsace-Lorraine and obtained control of Germany's coal deposits in the Saar Valley. Clemenceau received security for France. A buffer zone 31 miles (50 kilometers) wide was established along the Rhine, to be occupied by Allied troops for 15 years.

The Europeans also obtained their revenge. Germany would be disarmed, losing much of its armed forces and all of its submarines. The Germans would have to pay for the damages in France and Belgium. Germany, too, would have to pay for disabled Allied soldiers and dependents of those killed. In effect, Germany would be forced to sign a blank check. (Later, the damages were fixed at a staggering $33 billion.) Finally, Germany had to accept full responsibility for causing the war.

In early May German delegates joined the conference at the palace of Versailles (ver-SĪ), just outside Paris. The Germans, expecting generous terms based on the Fourteen Points, read the treaty in shock and refused to sign. Only after a threat of renewed fighting did Germany reconsider.

On June 28, 1919, Germany finally signed the Treaty of Versailles. The Allied commander, Ferdinand Foch, remarked about the treaty, "This is not peace. It is an armistice for twenty years."

Among the bitter people in the defeated nation was a thrice-wounded corporal, recovering from blindness caused by mustard gas. Germany's humiliation would burn in Adolf Hitler's mind for the rest of his life.

THE LEAGUE OF NATIONS

Woodrow Wilson had finally agreed to the treaty's terms because he felt that any injustices would be worked out by the League of Nations. "A living thing is born," Wilson had said at the creation of the League. He pinned his hopes on the League to heal war wounds and keep the peace.

The League would be a world organization devoted to maintaining peace. Member nations—Allies who signed the treaty and other nations yet to be chosen—would have an equal voice in making policy in a General Assembly. However, the real power lay in the Council, consisting of the United States, France, Britain, Italy, and Japan. These nations were permanent members. Other nations joined on a rotating basis. The day-to-day administrative work would be done by the Secretariat, permanently located in Geneva, Switzerland.

Members of the League were required to pledge that they would reduce armaments and that they would let the League settle all disputes that could lead to war. If a member did declare war, the others would stop trade with or even use force against the aggressor. The key to peace-keeping was Article Ten of the Covenant* of the League of Nations. In this article members pledged to respect and preserve each other's territorial and political independence against "external aggression."

The League actually had no means of fighting aggression. Because it had no army and no way of

* covenant: a solemn agreement between two or more persons or groups.

enforcing policy, it had to depend on the members' honor to uphold their pledges. It excluded Russia and the defeated Central Powers from membership. There were also several compromises that had been demanded by the United States Senate during the negotiations. The League had little say in the matter of tariffs, and no say in "regional understandings like the Monroe Doctrine."

DEFEAT OF THE TREATY

A number of Republican senators opposed the League of Nations. These senators, led by Henry Cabot Lodge of Massachusetts, especially objected to Article Ten. That article said that member nations could take military and economic actions against any nation violating the territorial integrity of a member nation.

To the Republican senators, this sounded as though the League could make decisions about foreign policy for the United States. Furthermore, they felt that the United States could all too easily be drawn into European conflicts. Because the League of Nations was part of the peace treaty, opponents of the League began to fight the entire peace settlement.

Desperate to save the peace treaty—and the League of Nations—President Wilson began a speaking tour of the nation. He traveled to 29 cities in 22 days. Everywhere, he was followed by opponents of the treaty who often drew larger crowds than he did. After a speech in Colorado Wilson suddenly collapsed from exhaustion and was hurried back to Washington. A few days later, a stroke left him half-paralyzed.

By now the Senate was debating the treaty. It had adopted 14 amendments proposed by Lodge to protect American interests. One of the amendments changed Article Ten.

Wilson, from his sickbed, directed Democrats to vote against the revised treaty. He thought that the proposed amendments dangerously weakened the League and believed that the treaty would eventually be ratified without them. On November 19 the revised treaty was defeated in the Senate.

Many Americans were dismayed. The British and French feared that the League would be ineffective without the United States. They said that they would accept American participation on the basis of the amendments.

Amid the public uproar, the treaty was sent back to Lodge's committee—the Foreign Relations Committee—which returned it to the Senate floor with 15 amendments. Wilson again refused to compromise, although that was clearly the only way to see the treaty passed. On May 20, 1920, the treaty was defeated for the second, and final, time. Five months later the United States concluded a separate peace with the Central Powers. In Geneva, the League of Nations began its struggle to keep the peace, without the United States.

On Armistice Day of 1923 a small crowd assembled outside the house of ex-president Wilson, and a band struck up "Over There." As Wilson stepped out his door, a member of the crowd said some sympathetic words about the Senate rejection of the League of Nations. Tears glinted in Wilson's eyes, but he turned his gaze to the veterans in the crowd and replied, "I am proud to remember that I had the honor of being the Commander-in-Chief of the most ideal army that was ever thrown together."

SECTION REVIEW

1. Identify the following: David Lloyd George, Georges Clemenceau, Vittorio Orlando, General Assembly, Council, Secretariat, Article Ten of the Covenant of the League of Nations.

2. List eight of Wilson's "Fourteen Points."

3. In drawing up the armistice, what two exceptions did the Allies make to the Fourteen Points?

4. What three political mistakes did Wilson make in trying to get his peace plan accepted by Americans?

5. (a) At the peace conference, what was the main concern of each of these nations: Britain, France, and Italy? (b) How did these concerns clash with some of Wilson's Fourteen Points?

6. (a) What nine new countries were formed by the Treaty of Versailles? (b) How were the Germans punished?

7. List two reasons why the League of Nations had no actual means with which to fight aggression.

8. (a) Who was the leader of the opposition to the peace settlement? (b) What was the final result of the opposition?

SUMMARY

In the early 1900s many European nations were developing a strong sense of nationalism. The competition for colonies, markets, and raw materials also led to rivalry among nations. The nations began to look for allies and to draw up treaties for protection. The treaties—an attempt to maintain a balance of power—plunged all of Europe, plus Turkey and Japan, into war in 1914.

The policy of the United States was neutrality. At first, American industry sold goods to both sides in the war. As the British blockade became effective, however, the overwhelming bulk of supplies went to the Allies. Germany countered with submarine warfare. Americans became enraged at the sinking of nonmilitary ships and the loss of American lives. In April of 1917 the United States declared war on Germany.

As the United States entered the war, there was little opposition. Most Americans voluntarily saved food and fuel, worked where needed, and registered for military service. Money was raised through bonds and taxes, and industries were converted to turn out war materials.

The Allies badly needed help, and American troops provided necessary reinforcements. Finally, in 1918, the Allies were able to break through German lines all along the western front. On November 11, 1918, an armistice was signed. The Great War—World War I—was over.

The terms of the armistice were harsh, but the terms of the peace treaty drawn up at Versailles were harsher. President Wilson had outlined a plan for peace, which included removing causes of friction that led to war, safeguarding nations' rights, and establishing a League of Nations to keep the peace. But the Allies demanded war reparations and greater national protection written into the peace treaty.

The United States Senate suggested amendments to the treaty and finally defeated it when Wilson refused to compromise. The United States concluded a separate peace with the Central Powers. Wilson lost his dream of American leadership in the League of Nations. Germany was resentful of what it considered a humiliating treaty.

CHAPTER REVIEW

1. (a) Group the following countries as either Allies or Central Powers: Austria, Britain, Bulgaria, France, Germany, Hungary, Italy, Russia, Turkey. (b) State two or three reasons why the Allies and the Central Powers were in dispute.

2. What relationship, direct or indirect, did each of the following have with the entry of the United States into the war? (a) the invasion of Belgium (b) the British blockade of ships heading toward Germany (c) German submarine warfare

3. (a) Describe the way in which troops were mobilized after the United States entered the war. (b) By what methods was money raised to finance the war?

4. Industry and labor had to be mobilized, and food resources had to be distributed. Explain what role each of the following had in these efforts. (a) the War Industries Board (b) the Food Administration (c) the National War Labor Board

Citizens could buy liberty bonds over a period of time by first buying war savings stamps. A booklet filled with savings stamps could be applied to the purchase of a bond.

Ammunition—
Don't waste it!

The Food Administration campaigned to persuade Americans to be less wasteful. As a result, during the war America was able to ship the Allies three times more food than usual.

5. Summarize changes occurring in the roles of women and blacks during World War I. Include reference to the suffrage movement.

6. (a) Summarize actions taken, including laws passed, to control dissent during the war. (b) Summarize actions taken to build support for the war.

7. Compare the following battles. Include information about when each battle occurred, the armies involved, and the results and numbers of casualties. (a) the First Battle of the Marne (b) the Second Battle of the Marne (c) the Meuse-Argonne offensive

8. (a) Summarize the intent of Wilson's first five points. (b) Summarize points six through thirteen. (c) What was the significance of point fourteen?

9. (a) Describe how each of these nations or areas was affected by the Treaty of Versailles: Poland, Finland, Latvia, Lithuania, the Austro-Hungarian Empire, Turkey. (b) List the terms of the treaty for Germany.

10. (a) Describe the organization and intent of the League of Nations. (b) Summarize the battle over its ratification and the result of that battle.

ISSUES AND IDEAS

1. In this chapter pre-World War I Europe, and particularly the Balkan Peninsula, is referred to as a "powder keg." Explain some of the complex economic and political factors that make this a vivid image.

2. Addressing Congress just before the United States entered the war, Wilson said, "The world must be made safe for democracy." What did he mean by this statement? Was Wilson's peace plan consistent with this statement? Explain your answer.

3. Assume the role of a senator who is for or against the League of Nations. What arguments would you use?

SKILLS WORKSHOP

1. *Timelines.* Construct a timeline of the major battles of the western front. For each battle indicate briefly the immediate results and, if possible, the long-term effects.

2. *Writing.* In three short paragraphs, write a summary of the major causes of World War I. The main-idea sentence for each paragraph should give a major cause. The two or three sentences supporting the main idea should give examples, including the names of the nations involved.

PAST AND PRESENT

1. During World War I newspapers were a powerful factor in shaping public opinion. Because of television, there are fewer newspapers today and they are of lesser importance. Prepare a discussion of the role television plays in reporting today. Discuss some of the differences in the effects of the two media, especially during wartime.

2. The League of Nations no longer exists, but another world organization does—the United Nations. Compare the purposes and the organization of the League of Nations and the United Nations.

PROSPERITY AND DEPRESSION

1919–1939

Stuart Davis. *Garage Lights* (detail), 1931–32.

UNIT 7
1919–1939

	1920	1925	1930	1935	1940	
		Harding	Coolidge	Hoover	Roosevelt	

POLITICAL

• Steel and mine workers' strikes
• Eighteenth Amendment: prohibition
  • Nineteenth Amendment: women's suffrage
    • Quota Law
      • Fordney-McCumber Tariff Act
        • Teapot Dome scandal exposed
      • Snyder Act
              • Hawley-Smoot Tariff Act
                • Bonus Army
                  • Agricultural Adjustment Act

SOCIAL

  • Fitzgerald: *The Great Gatsby*
  • Crossword puzzles
      • Gertrude Ederle swims English Channel
        • First talking movie: *Jazz Singer*
          • Stock market crash
            • Dashiell Hammet: *The Maltese Falcon*
              • Langston Hughes: *The Dream Keeper*
                • Picasso: "Guernica"

TECHNOLOGICAL

• Coast-to-coast airmail flights
    • King Tut's tomb discovered
      • George Washington Carver: Spingarn medal
        • Charles Lindbergh: first nonstop Atlantic flight
          • Amelia Earhart: nonstop Atlantic flight
        • Vitamin C

INTERNATIONAL

• Gandhi emerges as Indian leader
      • Germany joins League of Nations
        • Chiang Kai-shek rises to power
          • Jane Addams: Nobel prize for peace
          • Haile Selassie: emperor of Ethiopia
              • Jesse Owens: Berlin Olympics, gold medalist

1920	1925	1930	1935	1940

CHAPTER 20

THE ROARING TWENTIES

1919–1928

UNREST IN THE UNITED STATES
THE REPUBLICANS TAKE CHARGE
PROSPERITY AND CHANGE
THE JAZZ AGE

In the 1920s James A. Rogers, a journalist for the black newspaper *The Messenger*, reported on a phenomenon called jazz:

"Jazz reached the height of its vogue at a time when minds were reacting from the horrors and strain of war. Humanity welcomed it because in its fresh joyousness [people] found a temporary forgetfulness. . . .

"Jazz has a popular mission to perform. Joy, after all, has a physical basis. Those who laugh and dance and sing are better off . . . than those who do not. Moreover, jazz with its mocking disregard for formality is a leveller and makes for democracy. The jazz spirit demands more frankness and sincerity. . . . This new spirit of joy and spontaneity may itself play the role of reformer.

Jazz is rejuvenation, a recharging of the batteries of civilization with . . . new vigor. It has come to stay, and they are wise, who instead of protesting against it, try to lift it and divert it into nobler channels."

To Rogers, jazz was more than music. It was a spirit, "a joyous revolt from convention, custom, authority, boredom, even sorrow." Rogers believed jazz could heal the United States.

In 1920 Americans were poised between two worlds. The past had been nearly destroyed in the spasms of war, and the future looked uncertain. Many people, feeling cut off from past and future, welcomed the spirit of jazz and decided to live for the moment. Others, meanwhile, wished only to return to a normal life and get on with their business.

As the wounds of war healed, often painfully, Americans entered the new decade. Like the explosive sounds of jazz, the years were full of change and unexpected turns. They became known as the "Roaring Twenties."

UNREST IN THE UNITED STATES

READMENT TO FIND OUT

READ TO FIND OUT

— how the postwar economy hurt workers.

— why labor strikes raised fears of revolution.

— why terrorist activities by a few led to the arrest of many.

— how immigration was restricted.

— why a revival of the Ku Klux Klan failed.

In 1919 a *Life* magazine cartoon featured Uncle Sam and a soldier returned from overseas. "Nothing is too good for you, my boy! What would you like?" asked Uncle Sam. "A job," replied the soldier. Some 4 million ex-soldiers looking for work found America a nation in economic distress.

Prices, boosted by the war, continued to soar. Americans grumbled about the cost of rent, clothing, and food. There were no more meatless Tuesdays, and foods like butter were now available. The cost of steak and butter, however, had nearly doubled since 1914. Also, companies that had geared up for war now saw contracts for airplane wings and gas masks canceled. While some companies converted to producing peacetime goods, others laid off workers or shut down for an overhaul.

Then, in late 1920, the economy slid into depression. Prices dropped, businesses failed, and farm profits vanished. Wages dropped along with prices, and unemployment tripled in one year.

Hurt by the economy, Americans became resentful. They had done their part during the war, but victory had not brought the secure world they had worked for.

THE SEATTLE STRIKE

The wartime truce between labor and management ended in 1919 as unions called strikes for higher wages and shorter workdays. Over 4 million workers walked off their jobs that year.

One of the first strikes hit Seattle, Washington. In January 35,000 shipyard workers protested housing shortages and the high cost of living by laying down their tools. In February the unions in the city decided to support the shipyard workers in a general strike—a strike against all industry. Work in Seattle nearly came to a stop for four days.

To many Americans, a general strike seemed to be a step toward revolution. Mayor Ole Hanson of Seattle saw the strike that way and called in federal troops to end the walkout. The strikers, he warned, were revolutionaries who "want to take possession of our American government and try to duplicate the anarchy of Russia."

Mayor Hanson's words touched a nerve in the United States—fear of the Russian Bolsheviks. After the overthrow of the monarchy in March 1917, the revolution in Russia took a sharp turn to the left. In November 1917 Bolsheviks, or Communists, seized power from the new parliamentary government. They took control of Russia's major industries. They also urged workers in the rest of the world to overthrow the ruling classes. Many Americans looked suspiciously for the influence of "Reds"—as Bolsheviks were called—in the Seattle strike.

THE STEELWORKERS' STRIKE

The failure of the Seattle strike did not stop other workers. Railway workers left their jobs in New Jersey. Carpenters laid down their hammers in Chicago. Actors closed down New York theaters. The year's longest strike hit the steel industry, in which one half of the workers labored 12 hours a day, 7 days a week.

The disastrous Homestead, Pennsylvania, strike of 1892 had killed the steelworkers' union, but now it was reorganized. When the union asked for one day off per week, management refused. In September 1919 almost 300,000 steelworkers struck at a plant in Gary, Indiana. Within a week the walkout spread to other areas. Violence erupted between the strikers and plant guards, and federal troops were called into Gary.

Newspapers ran stories of Bolsheviks among the strikers. Soon the public lost its sympathy for the steelworkers. The strike ended in some three months, with 20 dead, and no gains for workers.

OTHER STRIKES

Other workers with grievances were police, most of whom had received no pay raise since before the war. Police in several cities successfully formed unions. When Boston police organized, however, their union leaders were fired. On September 9, 1919, about 75 percent of the police force walked out.

The strike left Boston virtually unprotected. Looting and rioting by townspeople broke out. On the third day of the strike, Massachusetts governor Calvin Coolidge called in state troops, and recruits began to fill the police force. When the striking police asked for their jobs back, Coolidge refused. "There is no right to strike against the public safety by anybody, anywhere, any time," he declared. Coolidge's tough stand delighted the nation.

The great wave of walkouts crested in November 1919 as some 400,000 members of the United Mine Workers (UMW) struck for higher wages for miners of soft coal. Miners of hard coal, which was used in the heating of homes, had earlier received pay raises. The strike closed soft coal mines and threatened the nation's transportation and manufacturing, which depended on soft coal.

With a court order in hand, United States Attorney General A. Mitchell Palmer ordered the miners back to work. UMW leader John L. Lewis reluctantly bowed to the order, but the miners stood fast. The strike finally ended in December when President Wilson intervened to arrange a wage increase.

The miners were among the few workers to gain from strikes. After labor's failures in 1919, unions steadily lost members, shrinking from 5 million to 3.4 million in 8 years. Despite their basic demands, union members had been linked in the public's mind with Reds.

THE RED SCARE

In the tense atmosphere of 1919, resentments often flared into terrorism. Late in April a package wrapped in brown paper was mailed to Mayor Ole Hanson of Seattle. Inside was a bomb, which failed to go off. A similar package arrived at the home of a senator who was trying to restrict immigration. The bomb exploded in the hands of his maid.

Across the nation, postal workers searched their offices for brown-paper packages. They found 34, addressed to people like John P. Morgan and John D. Rockefeller. Terrorists struck again in June, setting off bombs at the same hour in eight different cities. One bomb wrecked Attorney General Palmer's house and killed the bomber.

The public blamed Bolsheviks. To many Americans, Reds included anarchists, socialists, communists, and many immigrants from eastern Europe. The spread of Russian communism, or bolshevism, heightened American fears. In March 1919 there were Communist-led uprisings in Germany and Hungary. Six months later the Communist party was formed in the United States. However, its members numbered only about 40,000.

Fearful Americans believed that revolution was on their doorstep, and some decided to counterattack. In New York City soldiers and sailors beat the editors of a socialist newspaper. Books that were considered radical were banned from libraries. Teachers had to sign oaths declaring their loyalty to the government of the United States.

This "Red Scare" peaked in November when Attorney General Palmer ordered mass arrests and deportations of immigrant "agitators," or troublemakers. One of Palmer's young assistants, J. Edgar Hoover, had gathered information on radicals in the United States, and this guided the Palmer raids.

In December a ship sailed for Russia carrying 249 aliens. Few of them were charged with crimes, but they were all deported.

On January 2, 1920, raids in 33 cities netted 4,000 suspected Reds. The aliens were deported, and the American citizens were handed over to state authorities. Many of the suspects were held without warrants and were denied a lawyer.

These unconstitutional actions began to bring serious protests from the American public when, in January, the New York state legislature expelled five legally elected socialists. Americans from all political parties protested. Public criticism grew throughout the year as revolution in the United States failed to break out. Slowly, the Red Scare began to subside.

Ben Shahn. *Bartolomeo Vanzetti and Nicola Sacco*, 1931–32.
Collection of The Museum of Modern Art, New York.

"The Passion of Sacco and Vanzetti" series by Ben Shahn includes this portrait. The 23 paintings in the series are a protest against the executions.

THE SACCO-VANZETTI CASE

Then, in May 1920, two Italian immigrants were arrested and charged with stealing the payroll of a shoe factory and killing two of its employees. The Italians were Nicola Sacco and Bartolomeo Vanzetti. They were anarchists—people who wanted to do away with government entirely—and they had been active in several strikes. The criminal evidence against them was open to question. Still, the two were found guilty and sentenced to death.

Liberals and many others felt that the Italians had not received a fair trial and started a "Save Sacco and Vanzetti" committee. However, all legal appeals failed, and Sacco and Vanzetti were put to death in the electric chair in 1927. Their supporters charged that they were convicted "by atmosphere, not evidence."

RESTRICTING IMMIGRATION

Sacco and Vanzetti had come to the United States with the great prewar tide of immigrants from southern or eastern Europe. After the war immigrants again poured into America. The majority once more were Italians, Hungarians, Poles, Russians, Austrians, and Greeks. Many of them were fleeing the postwar chaos of Europe.

Many jobless Americans resented the newcomers. Americans, they felt, had saved Europe. Now Europeans were arriving to take jobs away from Americans. There were other complaints. A number of the strikers in 1919 were foreign-born, and many immigrants caught in the Palmer raids were from Russia. Thus, people suspected all new immigrants of being Reds.

Congress heard the complaints and in 1921 passed the Quota Law. This law limited the number of immigrants from Europe, Africa, the Near East, Australia, and New Zealand to a yearly total of 357,000. Each nation's limit was 3 percent of the number of people born in that nation who were living in the United States in 1910. The law's purpose was to favor immigrants from northern and western Europe.

Still, Americans clamored for stricter limits, especially against southern and eastern Europeans. Many business leaders joined the chorus. Black migration to the North had created a large pool of cheap labor, and more jobs were done by machine. Thus, fewer employers depended on immigrant workers.

Congress responded with the Immigration Act of 1924, further restricting the number of immigrants from southern and eastern Europe. As a temporary measure, the 1921 quota was reduced to 2 percent of the Census of 1890. This census had been taken before the great wave of immigration from southern and eastern Europe. Later, in 1927, an even stricter system would replace the 2 percent quota.

Under this system the United States would accept unlimited immigrants from Canada and Latin America, but would accept only 150,000 immigrants per year from the rest of the world. Each nation's quota would be based on the national origins of all whites, native and foreign-born, living in the United States in 1920. Britain's quota, for example, was large because so many Americans were of British descent. Italy's quota was much smaller, although more Italians than Britons wished to come to America. In addition, the law broke the 1907 Gentlemen's Agreement with Japan by prohibiting all Japanese immigration.

RETURN OF THE KLAN

On a summer day in 1923 over 100,000 people thronged a park in Kokomo, Indiana. The arrival of an airplane stirred the crowd. David C. Stephenson, robed in purple silk, stepped from the plane. This was his inauguration day as head of the Indiana branch of the Ku Klux Klan.

This Klan was a revival of the original Klan that arose in the South after the Civil War and faded away with the end of Reconstruction. It was reborn in 1915 at Stone Mountain, Georgia, with an expanded list of enemies. In addition to being antiblack, the new Klan members were opposed to Roman Catholics, Jews, and immigrants, who they feared were destroying America's Anglo-Saxon, Protestant heritage.

The new Klan grew slowly until 1919, when the nation was plagued by antiblack violence. As blacks

Black artist Jacob Lawrence depicted the current history of black Americans in several series of paintings. The migration of blacks to the North was his first subject.

moved to the North, they sometimes settled in white neighborhoods and sought jobs held by whites. Many whites resented the competition for homes and jobs.

When whites stoned a black who was swimming near a segregated beach in Chicago, the incident touched off a 3-day race riot that took over 30 lives. Riots also flared in St. Louis, Charleston, Omaha, Washington, D.C., and many other cities as tension

In the early Twenties Klan membership skyrocketed. In an eerie nighttime rite new members were sworn in. This ceremony took place at South Mountain near Brunswick, Maryland, on June 28, 1922.

between blacks and whites increased. In 1919 at least 78 blacks were lynched, a few of them still wearing their soldier's uniforms.

The Klan played on racial conflict and on American fears of immigrants. Its membership soared. In the early 1920s the Klan reported 4 million members. Klan members swept into politics. They helped to elect senators from 10 states and governors in 11 states—places like Oregon, Colorado, Indiana, and Maine, as well as southern states.

However, the Klan's power brought it wide publicity, which exposed political corruption and campaigns of terror. Hooded bands of the Klan beat, tarred and feathered, and sometimes murdered their enemies.

In 1925 Indiana Klan leader David C. Stephenson was convicted of murder, and the scandal shook the Klan. Membership dropped. By 1930 fewer than 10,000 still belonged to the group. Ten years later the head of the failing Klan sold its Atlanta headquarters to the Roman Catholic church.

SECTION REVIEW

1. Identify the following: A. Mitchell Palmer, John L. Lewis, J. Edgar Hoover, Nicola Sacco, Bartolomeo Vanzetti.

2. Define the following: anarchy, agitator.

3. What economic conditions led to the series of labor strikes in 1919?

4. Explain the decline in union membership in the 1920s.

5. Explain how terrorism in 1919 contributed to fears that communism would spread in the United States.

6. What Red hunt tactic provoked loud criticism from all political parties?

7. Give two reasons why many Americans were suspicious of immigrants after World War I.

8. (a) What was the intent of the Quota Law of 1921? (b) How did the Immigration Act of 1924 differ from the Quota Law ? (c) Explain how both of these laws worked to discriminate against immigrants from southern and eastern Europe.

9. What groups were targets of the new Ku Klux Klan?

10. Why did Klan membership decline in the late 1920s?

THE REPUBLICANS TAKE CHARGE

READ TO FIND OUT

—**how postwar problems caused voters to seek "normalcy."**

—**how Harding planned to restore the nation's economy.**

—**why farmers and veterans faced special problems after the war.**

—**what scandals rocked the Harding administration.**

—**what issues arose in the election of 1924.**

—**how the Coolidge Era brought an end to progressive policies.**

In June 1920 delegates to the Republican national convention met in Chicago to choose a presidential candidate. There were many candidates, including Senator Warren G. Harding of Ohio.

Harding was not well known, and his chances for nomination seemed slim. However, Harry Daugherty, his manager, was not worried.

There will be no nomination on the early ballots. After the other candidates have failed, . . . the leaders, worn out and wishing to do the very best thing, will get together in some hotel room about 2:11 in the morning. Some fifteen men, bleary-eyed with lack of sleep, and perspiring . . . will sit down around a big table. I will be with them and present the name of Senator Harding. When that time comes, Harding will be selected, because he fits in perfectly with every need of the party and nation.

Daugherty was right. Harding won approval in the hotel room and the next day won the convention's nomination. Governor Calvin Coolidge of Massachusetts, known for his stern dealing with the Boston police strike, became Harding's running mate. The friendly Harding and the aloof Coolidge had one thing in common—they were both conservative.

Women's Suffrage Before the Nineteenth Amendment

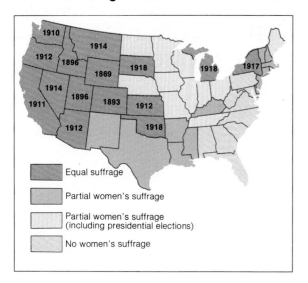

Equal suffrage

Partial women's suffrage

Partial women's suffrage
(including presidential elections)

No women's suffrage

In partial suffrage states women were granted the right to vote in certain elections, usually elections involving local schools. In some states women could vote on tax issues.

In 1869 the National Woman Suffrage Association was set up to secure a constitutional amendment granting suffrage to women. In 1920 many women cast their first vote.

THE ELECTION OF 1920

The national convention of the Democrats was in San Francisco. Like the Republicans, the Democrats selected a candidate from Ohio—progressive Governor James M. Cox. Their nominee for vice-president was Franklin Delano Roosevelt, assistant secretary of the navy and a distant cousin of Theodore Roosevelt.

The third major candidate was Eugene V. Debs, running once more as head of the Socialist party. Debs was still serving his ten-year prison sentence under the 1917 Espionage Act for protesting against the war, so he campaigned from jail.

Democrat Cox campaigned on the road. His first trip was a visit to President Wilson, still in poor health from his collapse during the peace treaty fights. The popular president who had led his nation to war was now unpopular.

People blamed Wilson for the economic depression following the war. Many also feared that Wilson was trying to entangle the nation in international troubles by urging it to join the League of Nations. Still, Wilson insisted that the League was the issue of the 1920 election, and Cox declared himself in favor of it.

Harding, campaigning from his front porch, tried to avoid any stand on the League. Instead, he talked about getting back to everyday life. He even invented a word for it—"normalcy." As he explained in one speech, "America's present need is not heroics, but healing; not nostrums but normalcy; not revolution but restoration . . . not surgery but serenity."

Harding hit the right note, for most Americans also wanted to return to "normalcy." They gave Harding over 16 million votes, compared to some 9 million for Cox and 900,000 for Debs. Harding swept the electoral vote, gaining 404 votes to Cox's 127.

There were millions of newly eligible voters in this election. The Nineteenth Amendment, giving women the vote, had passed the House in January 1918 and the Senate in June 1919. The amendment then was ratified by the states and became law in August 1920.

HARDING AND HIS CABINET

One journalist remarked that Warren G. Harding "looked more like a president than any president who ever lived." Harding's home was Marion, Ohio, a small, pretty town, surrounded by rolling farmland. In Marion, Harding had progressed from typesetter on a local newspaper to owner and editor of his own paper. Along the way, he had become the town's leading citizen. Then, advised and encouraged by Harry Daugherty, he entered politics and moved from state offices to the United States Senate.

Harding's good nature, good looks, and loyalty to friends made him popular. However, he worried about the job of president. He admitted to the listeners of one campaign speech his "limited ability to meet your full expectations."

Harding began his term well by choosing several experienced politicians to serve in his cabinet. The new secretary of state was Charles Evans Hughes, who had an outstanding political record. Secretary of commerce was Herbert Hoover, the popular head of the Food Administration during the war. Henry Wallace, a progressive and friend to farmers, was made secretary of agriculture. But Harding's most vital appointments were in the Department of the Treasury, for the economy was his main concern.

REVIVING THE ECONOMY

The nation's finances were in difficulty. Between 1914 and 1921, America's national debt exploded from about $2 billion to over $26 billion. The United States had run up the huge debt during the war, borrowing over $20 billion from citizens. About half that amount was loaned to the Allies, and it seemed they would have trouble repaying the loans.

Harding was determined to revive the stricken economy. He promised to do so by having "less government in business as well as more business in government." Toward this end, he appointed Andrew W. Mellon as secretary of the treasury. Mellon, who had earned a fortune in the aluminum industry, seemed to be the perfect choice to bring business skills into government.

Mellon thought that the high taxes passed during the war were one cause of the ailing economy. He proposed to end a profits tax on industry and to reduce the income taxes paid by the wealthy. Thus, Mellon argued, the wealthy would have more money to invest in business, which would create more jobs.

The majority in Congress agreed. However, a group from the farm states in the Midwest and South—called the "Farm Bloc"—joined with progressives to fight what they considered preferential treatment for the rich. Still, a changed version of

Mellon's plan passed in the Revenue Act of 1921. The act reduced the maximum income tax rate from 65 percent to 50 percent.

Many business and government leaders believed that tax cuts had to go hand in hand with reduced government spending. In June 1921 Congress passed the Budget and Accounting Act to put the nation's finances in order. Previously, Congress had spent money as the need arose and hoped there would be enough income to cover it. According to the new act, the Bureau of the Budget in the Department of the Treasury would study the estimated costs of various government departments, and draw up a budget. This would balance spending and income. The President was required to submit the budget to Congress, which had to keep as strictly to the budget as possible.

Harding named Chicago banker Charles G. Dawes as director of the budget. As purchasing agent for the American Expeditionary Force in France, Dawes had expertly balanced income and expenses. Now he promptly worked out a budget for the coming fiscal year* of $3.5 billion, a cut of about $2 billion from the current spending level.

Together, Congress, Dawes, Mellon, and Harding seemed to perform miracles. Taxes dropped and Congress stayed within the budget. The Treasury had enough of a surplus to make payments on the national debt. By the end of 1922, business was back on its feet, unemployment was dropping, and the economy became healthier. Most Americans thanked the Republicans for the return of good times.

FARMERS AND VETERANS ASK FOR HELP

Farmers, however, took little comfort in the tax cuts or the new budget. Farming had tumbled into a deep depression by 1920. This was more than just "hard times," said Secretary of Agriculture Henry Wallace, it was a "financial catastrophe."

Farm problems, like so many others, could be traced to the war. During wartime, both Europe and the United States needed all the food farmers

---

* fiscal year: a 12-month period that is considered a year for purposes of budgeting and accounting. The fiscal year of the federal government begins October 1 and ends September 30.

could grow. The government had even guaranteed high prices for crops like wheat in an effort to stimulate production. With the boom market, farmers went into debt to buy more land and new machinery.

When the war ended, the dream collapsed. The government ended its wartime farm policy, and European farmers returned to normal production. American farmers kept planting vast crops in order to earn money to pay their debts. However, the market continued to shrink, and prices dropped. Wheat that had sold for over two dollars a bushel in wartime sold for sixty-seven cents by 1921. Across the nation, banks took over farm properties and equipment and sold them at auction. Between 1920 and 1924, over 100,000 people lost their farms this way.

In Congress, the Farm Bloc pushed for legislation to aid farmers. The bloc was particularly interested in a high tariff on agricultural products. Congress also wanted to protect American business from foreign competition. In the Emergency Tariff of 1921, Congress placed high tariffs on 28 agricultural imports. The following year, the Fordney-McCumber Tariff Act set the highest tariffs in history on man-

ufacured goods and kept the 1921 levels of protection on farm goods.

The steep tariffs choked off most foreign trade. European nations could not profitably sell their goods in the United States, and in turn, bought fewer American goods. This did not hurt American manufacturers. They sold almost everything they produced to a public hungry for consumer goods after the lean war years. Farmers, however, needed foreign markets for their surplus crops. For them, hard times had just begun.

Veterans also came out of the war with an economic complaint. While they had served in the armed forces for about thirty dollars per month, civilians had earned as much as twelve dollars a day in industry. Many veterans insisted on some form of "adjusted compensation," or bonus.

In 1922 Congress passed a bill that would give each veteran a bonus. However, President Harding vetoed the bill because it would cost the taxpayers too much. Veterans had better luck with their demand for compensation for war injuries. In 1921 Congress set up the Veterans Bureau to handle such claims. Harding appointed a friend, Colonel Charles R. Forbes, to direct it.

Warren G. Harding's genial, kindly manner and handsome appearance are evident in this photograph. His public appeal, resting too strongly on these bases, crumbled when the public learned of his weaknesses as president.

SCANDALS IN THE HARDING ADMINISTRATION

Forbes soon had veterans' hospitals under construction. However, he pocketed a large portion of the bureau's annual budget through illegal deals. He even sold needed hospital supplies to private businesses in return for a share of the price. The scandal eventually came to light, and Forbes was sent to prison.

Harding was shocked by this betrayal. He had trusted his friends. When people warned him that friends might abuse that trust he replied, "They won't cheat me." Harding had appointed several of his Ohio friends to offices such as White House physician and head of the Federal Reserve. His longtime friend and adviser Harry Daugherty became attorney general. Yet Daugherty sold Justice Department favors.

The worst scandal involved Secretary of the Interior Albert B. Fall, an old Senate colleague of Harding's. Fall persuaded the secretary of the navy to transfer to the Department of the Interior control of two oil fields. These fields held the navy's reserve supply of fuel. Fall then leased one reserve, in California's Elk Hills, to oilman Edward L. Doheny and the other, at Teapot Dome in Wyoming, to oilman Harry F. Sinclair. In return, Fall received stocks, Liberty bonds, and cash equaling about $400,000.

When Fall started spending freely, suspicious senators launched an investigation. Late in 1923 Congress made public the Teapot Dome scandal. Fall was eventually convicted of bribery and conspiracy. He became the first cabinet officer in United States history to go to jail.

Harding was spared the full details of this disgrace. Upset by rumors of corruption, he left Washington to go on a speaking tour in the summer of 1923. Exhaustion and stress overtook him in San Francisco, California, where he died on August 2.

CALVIN COOLIDGE

In a Vermont farmhouse, at 2:30 a.m. on August 3, Calvin Coolidge took the oath of office from his father, a local official. The ceremony had to be repeated in Washington, because Coolidge's father did not have the authority to swear in a president. Nevertheless, the homey touch appealed to the nation. Americans saw in Coolidge the virtues of small-town New England: solid common sense, honesty, hard work, and simple living.

Coolidge got rid of the most corrupt of Harding's appointees, and retained Mellon, Hoover, Hughes, and Wallace in his cabinet. With that housecleaning done, he was content to let business keep the economy booming. As he tersely explained, "The business of America is business."

THE ELECTION OF 1924

By the Republican convention in 1924, the business community was solidly behind Coolidge, and he easily won the presidential nomination. His running mate was budget-cutter Charles G. Dawes. The Republican platform supported tax cuts, a tight budget, a high tariff, and restricted immigration. It also courted farmers and veterans with promises of help.

The Democrats, meeting in New York City, could agree on nothing. Convention delegates argued over whether the United States should join the League of Nations and whether the Ku Klux Klan should be condemned. They deadlocked over candidates. The arguments divided the convention. After 103 ballots, delegates settled on a compromise ticket. For president, they nominated corporate lawyer John W. Davis and for vice-president, Nebraska's Governor Charles W. Bryan. The Democratic platform sidestepped the League and Klan issues, and supported a lower tariff, tax cuts, aid for farmers, and unions.

For Americans unhappy with the Democratic and Republican platforms, there was an alternative. In July 1924 progressives, union members, socialists, and farmers united to protest the politics of normalcy. They launched a new Progressive party and nominated Senator Robert M. La Follette of Wisconsin for president. The party platform called for low tariffs, aid for farmers, trustbusting, collective bargaining, public ownership of railroads and water power, and a ban on war.

Over 15.5 million Americans, however, voted to "Keep Cool with Coolidge." Davis pulled in only half as many votes, and La Follette gained about 5 million. Although this was a strong showing for the Progressive party, followers trickled back to the major parties, and the movement fell apart. One progressive concluded that people might just as well "lay a wreath" on progressivism.

An abundant harvest, the reward of good farming, is the focal point of Grant Wood's carefully detailed "Fall Planting." But such harvests were mixed blessings for America's farmers in the Twenties.

VETERANS AND FARMERS

During the next four years, Coolidge acted on his belief in limited government. He particularly opposed federal aid to "special interest" groups, and in May 1924 he vetoed a second bonus bill for veterans. Congress, however, overrode the veto. The bill did not give veterans an immediate cash bonus. Instead, the bonus was made in the form of a 20-year life insurance policy. Veterans holding the policy for 20 years would receive its full cash value. Veterans also could borrow up to 25 percent of the value of their policies.

About the same time, the Farm Bloc thought of a plan to aid farmers, who were still being hurt by surplus crops and by low prices. The McNary-Haugen farm relief bill proposed that the government support prices for certain crops in order to maintain the purchasing power of farmers. For example, in the boom years of 1910 to 1914, farmers had received a good price for wheat and with that money could buy a certain amount of goods. Now, although wheat prices had dropped, the government would buy up surplus wheat at the earlier, higher price. Thus, farmers would have the same purchasing power that they had in 1914. The government would either store the surplus until the market improved or sell it abroad. This system of government-supported farm prices was known as **parity.**

The parity bill passed Congress twice, in 1927 and 1928, but Coolidge vetoed it both times. The bill, he believed, would send food prices soaring. Thus farmers would be encouraged to overproduce. The whole plan, said Coolidge, "is bureaucracy gone mad."

COOLIDGE'S SUPPORT OF BUSINESS

Coolidge also opposed agencies that regulated business, such as the Interstate Commerce Commission and the Federal Trade Commission. He felt that the agencies should be helpful to business, and his conservative appointments turned the watchdog agencies into friendly advisers. Coolidge's choice to supervise the FTC was corporate lawyer William Humphrey, who criticized his agency as "an instrument of . . . injury instead of help to business." Under Humphrey, the FTC allowed hundreds of business combinations.

Business was supported again when Congress passed the tax-cut plan of Secretary of the Treasury Andrew Mellon. The Revenue Act of 1926 reduced inheritance taxes and lowered the maximum income tax rate to 20 percent. A person who formerly paid about $600,000 in taxes on a yearly income of $1 million would now pay under $200,000. People in support of tax cuts believed that a large part of the money saved would be invested in business. Thus the economy would be stimulated.

The economic program, begun under Harding, continued to produce dazzling effects. Many observers thanked the partnership of government and business for the ongoing prosperity. "Never before, here or anywhere else," wrote the *Wall Street Journal*, "has a government been so completely fused with business."

SECTION REVIEW

1. Identify the following: Harry Daugherty, Nineteenth Amendment, Henry Wallace, Andrew W. Mellon, Farm Bloc, Bureau of the Budget, Charles G. Dawes, Veterans Bureau, Albert B. Fall, Teapot Dome.

2. Define the following: normalcy, fiscal year, parity.

3. (a) Why had President Wilson become unpopular by 1920? (b) What was the main concern of voters in the 1920 election?

4. What was Harding's main concern as president?

5. What problem was each of the following laws intended to correct? (a) Revenue Act of 1921 (b) Budget and Accounting Act

6. Explain the chain of events that led farmers from the prosperity of World War I to the hard times of the early 1920s.

7. (a) What legislation did the Farm Bloc favor in 1921? (b) What was the result of this legislation on foreign trade?

8. Compare the platforms of the three political parties in the 1924 election. On what issue did all three agree?

9. Explain how the McNary-Haugen farm relief bill was expected to aid farmers.

10. What was Coolidge's attitude toward federal agencies that regulated business?

PROSPERITY AND CHANGE

READ TO FIND OUT

— how Henry Ford revolutionized industry.

— how the automobile changed the face of America.

— how the automobile encouraged a building boom.

— why industrial productivity increased rapidly.

— what increased productivity meant for women and blacks.

— how the changes of the Twenties affected Mexican Americans and Indians.

The glow from the business boom lighted the whole decade, which became known as the "Golden Twenties." There were clear signs of prosperity. By the end of the 1920s, almost one third of the national debt was paid off. Production in industry leaped, sending corporate profits up 62 percent between 1923 and 1929. The postwar economy, shaky at first, was skyrocketing.

One of the most important measures of economic health was the **gross national product** (GNP). This was the dollar value of all the goods and services produced in the United States each year. The GNP had slumped in the postwar depression. Then it bounced back, climbing from $75 billion in 1922 to over $100 billion in 1929.

Even muckraker Lincoln Steffens was impressed with the boom. "Big business in America," he declared, "is producing what the Socialists held up as their goal: food, shelter, and clothing for all." But not quite all Americans shared the bounty. Farmers, workers in ailing industries, and the unemployed saw little that was golden in the Twenties. Still, many workers made substantial gains.

While the average worker's income rose 11 percent during the decade, the cost of living began to fall after 1925. More and more workers had money to spend on luxuries. By saving or borrowing, they might even be able to buy a new car.

HENRY FORD AND THE MODEL T

America's romance with the motorcar began about 1900. There were only about 8,000 cars on the road then, and most were custom-built for wealthy buyers. Roads were bad and cars often broke down. Sensible drivers carried a huge kit of supplies, including electrical wire, axes, and food.

One of the pioneers in the new industry was engineer Henry Ford, who dreamed of building a low-priced, dependable car. In 1903 he formed the Ford Motor Company, and by 1908 his Model T Ford was on the market. It sold for about $900—a bargain compared to the average $2,000 price tag on other cars. But it was too expensive for most workers.

Ford set out to mass-produce Model T's and bring down the price. To streamline his automobile factory, Ford adopted the system popularized in the 1890s by another engineer, Frederick W. Taylor.

Taylor had worked out a "scientific management" system to teach workers machinelike efficiency. One of his methods was a "time-and-motion study." In this study, Taylor would diagram the movements of a worker performing a task. He also would time the number of seconds required for each movement. Then Taylor told the worker the proper motions to use to complete a task in the proper amount of time. If Taylor judged the tools or working conditions to be faulty, those elements also would be changed.

When Henry Ford studied his workers, he found that they brought car parts to one area in the factory and built the car there. Ford decided to take "the work to the workers." In 1913 he tried out his new scheme—the **assembly line**. A worker stood in one place and did one task while a conveyor belt moved the partly finished car along. The time required to produce a Model T was cut from 12 hours to 90 minutes.

The next year Ford astounded the nation by reducing the workday in his factory to eight hours and doubling his workers' daily wage to five dollars. The workers, he reasoned, would spend more money, especially on Fords.

The Ford plan was a wild success. Between 1908 and 1926 Ford sold more than 15 million cars. The price of the Model T dropped to $290 in 1926, when the average car cost $700. More and more Americans could afford a Ford.

At the Ford Plant in Highland, Michigan, the conveyor belt was introduced to bring materials to workers. This made possible assembly lines, mass production, and reduced costs.

THE AUTOMOBILE BOOM

Ford did not have the booming automobile market all to himself. General Motors Corporation, a competitor of Ford's since 1908, offered Buicks, Cadillacs, Oldsmobiles, and Chevrolets. The Chrysler Corporation was formed in 1925 by Walter Chrysler.

In the 1920s these competitors began to catch up with Ford. Each year, they brought out stylish new models. Ford scorned the fashionable cars, declaring that people could buy his Model T in "any color you choose so long as it's black."

However, the public demanded new models, and in 1928 Ford gave them what they wanted. His new Model A cars came in 7 major styles and sold for an average of $430. While Ford was switching from Model T to Model A, General Motors took the lead in the automobile market with its Chevrolet.

No one, though, would forget that it was Henry Ford whose efforts had "put America on wheels." As humorist Will Rogers put it, "Good luck, Mr. Ford. It will take a hundred years to tell whether you have helped us or hurt us, but you certainly didn't leave us like you found us."

Indeed, little in the United States was untouched by the car. The riches of the automobile industry swelled the GNP by some $2 billion per year and spilled over into many areas. Steel production rose to supply steel for automobile bodies. The rubber industry grew to supply new tires and replace worn-out ones. Gasoline production quadrupled during the 1920s. And people were needed to work the assembly lines, sell cars, pump gasoline, repair tires, and do other jobs to keep motorists happy.

By the end of the 1920s many American families owned a car. The face of America changed. Gasoline stations replaced stables, and over 100,000 miles (161,000 kilometers) of paved highways replaced dirt roads. Along those highways sprouted

In a 1931 Walker Evans photograph, automobiles, like beads on a chain, line Main Street in Saratoga Springs, New York. A trip to resorts like this grew easier with the automobile.

hot dog stands, "tourist homes," and billboards. Mobile Americans moved to new homes and new jobs, and many left the farm for the city. Those who stayed on the farm were no longer so isolated. An interviewer asked one farm woman why she owned a car instead of a bathtub. "You can't go to town in a bathtub," she answered.

THE LAND AND BUILDING BOOM

As Americans on wheels poured into cities, the population balance in the nation changed. In the 1920s, for the first time, more Americans lived in cities of 2,500 or more people than in small towns and on farms. All these new arrivals needed housing, which meant good times for the construction industry.

Builders proudly advertised "dream houses" with modern appliances like electric stoves and refrigerators, and most dream houses were in the suburbs. Motorists loved the suburbs. They could live near open country and drive to jobs in the city. Elegant Grosse Pointe, just outside the auto capital of Detroit, Michigan, grew 700 percent during the 1920s. A suburb called Beverly Hills that nestled near the movie town of Hollywood, California, grew 2,500 percent.

Housing construction began to slow after 1925, but commercial building soared throughout the decade. The brick, cement, lumber, and plumbing industries boomed as more factories, hospitals, schools, and offices were built. And wherever Americans were building, the price of land surged, drawing investors eager to become rich on real estate.

The most amazing real estate story was in Florida. People began to flee the harsh northeastern winters by driving or riding a bus south to Florida's sunny beaches. Soon there was a rush to buy land there for housing developments in oceanside cities like Miami and West Palm Beach.

In the stampede to buy, some lucky people made fortunes. One woman bought a slice of land for $2,500 and sold it a short time later for $35,000. Then, in 1926, the dream soured. Sellers outnumbered buyers, and speculators failed to make their payments. In addition, a fierce hurricane leveled many of the new buildings. *The Nation* reported, "The world's greatest poker game, played with building lots instead of chips, is over."

ELECTRIC POWER

While land values rose and fell, there were other booms to keep the 1920s golden. Productivity in industry was increasing, due in part to Frederick Taylor's efficiency studies and Henry Ford's assembly line. Delighted Americans snapped up new products like kitchen gadgets, cigarette lighters, cosmetics, refrigerators, vacuum cleaners, dry ice, and Clarence Birdseye's frozen foods.

Many of these products were made in factories run on electric power. Before the war, only 30 percent of industry used electricity, but by 1929 close to 70 percent did. The use of electricity jolted industry into a new age. Electric power could be cheaply and easily transmitted long distances. Thus, factories no longer had to be built near coal fields or rivers, their old sources of power. They could be built where land was cheap, or labor plentiful, or at the source of raw materials.

The electric power companies themselves were changing. Power stations that had served only one town linked their lines to power whole regions. With design improvements, stations doubled their output. As the price of electricity declined, more Americans had their houses wired. By 1929 almost 70 percent of the nation's homes had electricity.

BREAKTHROUGHS IN INDUSTRY

Other young industries came of age during the 1920s. Some, like chemicals, had been helped by the war. Earlier, the United States had imported German dyes and chemicals used in fertilizers. When the war cut off that source, the American chemicals industry took over. By 1929 new companies were producing about $4 billion worth of chemical products.

Researchers did wondrous things with chemicals. Chemist George Washington Carver turned surplus crops like sweet potatoes and peanuts into paste, shaving lotion, axle grease, ink, and even instant coffee. Physicist Robert H. Goddard built the world's first rocket fueled by liquid ether and oxygen. It roared 184 feet (56 meters) into the air at 60 miles (97 kilometers) per hour on its first launch.

Industries often overlapped. The electrochemical industry improved the gasoline-powered engines used in cars. The *synthetics* industry produced artificial, or chemically produced materials—plastics and fibers like rayon. When the industry produced lacquer, a quick-drying paint substitute, automakers quickly adopted it. The Du Pont Company produced cellophane in 1924, and Americans were soon wrapping their food in the filmy material.

In the 1920s electrical appliances became big business. This sales force in Louisville, Kentucky, would gladly demonstrate and explain the merits of vacuum cleaners, washing machines, and other appliances.

However, there were no success stories to tell about the "sick" industries of soft coal and textiles. Coal was being replaced by newer forms of energy—gasoline, natural gas, and especially electricity. Most of the textile industry had fled New England for the South's cotton fields and supply of cheap labor. But the industry was rocked by the up-and-down price of raw cotton, competition from rayon, and the quickly changing fashions of the 1920s.

WOMEN IN THE 1920s

In 1923 the average worker made about $30 for a 47-hour week. By 1928 the wages inched up to $33 and the workweek slipped to 45 hours. Of course, there was no "average" worker, and wages varied wildly. While steelworkers earned about $35 per week in the late 1920s, southern textile workers scraped by on $12 per week. Even within the same industry, wages differed by region. New England textile workers, for example, earned $18 per week. Wages even differed for the same job if some of the workers happened to be women.

In 1923 women workers earned about twenty-three cents per hour less than men, and the gap widened throughout the decade. Low wages, however, did not stop women from pouring into factories and offices. By 1930 they made up 25 percent of the labor force. Most worked in mills, on assembly lines, and in clerical jobs. An independent few, however, conducted orchestras, ran baseball teams, drove taxis, and continued to enter professions like medicine and engineering.

Lillian Moller Gilbreth made a name for herself as the first woman in scientific management. Gilbreth and her husband, Frank, both engineers, ran a company that did time-and-motion studies for industry. They also applied scientific management theories to running their own home and raising their 12 children.

BLACK AMERICANS IN THE 1920s

Throughout the 1920s black workers also streamed into the work force, especially into office jobs and the steel, meatpacking, and auto industries. Working conditions had not really changed, though. Blacks were poorly paid and were barred from most unions. They were given the tasks nobody else wanted and were likely to be fired in hard times.

Still, northern industry was a magnet to poor southern blacks. Sharecropping, always a risky living, had been hit hard by the agricultural depression. Sharecroppers who planted cotton faced more than an unstable market. Hardy insects called boll weevils were wiping out whole fields of cotton. Many sharecroppers were among the one million blacks who migrated to the North in the 1920s.

In a decade when America's business was business, many blacks became involved in business ventures. Engineer Archie Alexander headed a firm that built sewage systems and bridges. C. C. Spaulding was president of the North Carolina Mutual Life Insurance Company and guided it to $35 million in sales. Inventor Garrett Morgan produced an automatic stoplight in 1923 to cope with America's newest headache—traffic jams. Almost 70,000 blacks had gone into business for themselves by the end of the decade.

MEXICAN AMERICANS IN THE 1920s

The lure of jobs also encouraged the migration of Mexican workers into the United States. This large-scale migration had begun about 1910 as thousands fled Mexico's poverty and political turmoil. In the 1920s some 500,000 Mexicans crossed the border into the United States. Immigration from Mexico was not limited by quotas. Still, many Mexicans simply avoided red tape and immigration officials and became illegal aliens.

The immigrants found a bit of home in the American Southwest, with its Spanish place names, architecture, and cooking. Mexican Americans found work, but it was generally low-paid, back-breaking work. About half the newcomers became *migrant workers*. They moved from place to place to harvest seasonal crops and lived in crude barracks in migrant farm worker camps. Others labored for the railroads and lived in boxcars.

Word of jobs in industry drew still others deeper into the United States. Mexican Americans worked in cement factories in the West and steel mills in the East. They canned fruit in California and salmon in Alaska. They crowded into barrios* in towns and cities, and soon these became Mexican communities.

* barrios (BAHR-ee-ōs): Spanish word for "district in a city."

Mexican American migrant workers harvest grapes in a California vineyard. The state's great agricultural industry relied heavily on the cheap and readily available labor force they provided.

INDIANS IN THE 1920s

The framers of the 1887 Dawes Act had hoped to bring Indians into the mainstream of American life by breaking up the tribes and giving tribal land to individual Indians to farm. The Dawes Act, however, did not work. Indians had always been members of a close-knit community, and preferred that way of life. Also, those who tried to live by farming had a difficult time, especially on barren reservation land.

Meanwhile, speculators bought up land from Indians and, under the Dawes Act, thousands of acres were opened to homesteaders. By the 1920s Indians had lost 86 million acres (34.4 million hectares), over half the land they owned when the Dawes Act was passed.

Finally, reformers sparked a public outcry against the treatment of Indians, and Congress moved into action. Partly as a gesture to Indians who had fought in World War I, Congress passed the Snyder Act in 1924. The act granted full citizenship to all Indians born in the United States. Ten years later, in the Indian Reorganization Act, Congress reversed its policy of breaking up tribes. The act provided for tribal self-government and returned some lands to tribal ownership.

SECTION REVIEW

1. Identify the following: Henry Ford, Frederick Taylor, George Washington Carver, Robert Goddard, Lillian Moller Gilbreth, Garrett Morgan, Snyder Act, Indian Reorganization Act.

2. Define the following: gross national product, assembly line, synthetics, illegal aliens, barrio.

3. How did Henry Ford reduce the cost of building an automobile?

4. (a) List three industries that grew rapidly because of the auto industry. (b) Describe three changes in the landscape because of the car.

5. Why did the price of land rise rapidly in the Twenties?

6. How did the use of electricity encourage the growth of industry?

7. What jobs did most women workers hold in the Twenties?

8. Why did many southern blacks migrate to the North?

9. Give two reasons why immigration from Mexico increased between 1910 and 1930.

10. Give two reasons for the failure of the Dawes Act of 1887.

THE JAZZ AGE

READ TO FIND OUT

— why the Eighteenth Amendment was repealed.

— how movies and radio brought new sights and sounds to the Twenties.

— who the heroes and heroines of the era were.

— how writers of the Twenties pictured America.

Nothing stood still in the Twenties. Farmers raced to plant enough and sell enough to live on. Workers crossed the nation for jobs. Business people rushed to put their newest dreams into production. Meanwhile, the Twenties generation lived faster and harder than Americans had every lived before.

Jazz was their music, and the golden-haired F. Scott Fitzgerald recorded their lifestyle. "We were tired of Great Causes," Fitzgerald wrote. "Scarcely had the staider citizens of the republic caught their breaths when the wildest of all generations, the generation which had been adolescent during the confusion of the War, . . . danced into the limelight."

A new age had begun, and Fitzgerald called it the "Jazz Age."

THE SOUND OF THE JAZZ AGE

Jazz, said one listener, "is a release of all the suppressed emotions at once, a blowing off of the lid." Its roots were in African rhythms, American folk songs, gospels, ballads, and ragtime music. New Orleans claimed to be the cradle of jazz. Wherever it was born, however, jazz soon set the whole Twenties generation dancing.

The heart of jazz was improvisation—composing music on the spur of the moment. While the band played a steady background beat, a horn blower sent notes leaping and wheeling, creating a melody on the spot. The kings and queens of jazz were blacks. Pianist and composer Duke Ellington and his band played at the Cotton Club in Harlem, a black section of New York City. Bessie Smith sang slow, melancholy pieces and became known as the "Empress of the Blues." Trumpeter Louis Arm-

Charles Demuth's "In Vaudeville (Dancer with Chorus)" captures the frenzied atmosphere of Jazz Age nightlife. His use of wavy lines and vivid color creates a restless mood.

Recording preserved the genius of these jazz greats. Louis Armstrong's records with the "Hot Five" and the "Hot Seven" and all of Bessie Smith's records are jazz treasures.

strong was the first great soloist in jazz, and his wife and fellow band member, Lil Hardin, became a star pianist.

White musicians added their own improvisations to the ever-changing jazz. Cornet player Bix Beiderbecke was an inventive musician with a subtle tone. He played in the popular Paul Whiteman band, which brought jazz to millions of new listeners. According to Whiteman, jazz was "the folk-music of the machine age."

FLAPPERS AND SHEIKS

Young Americans looked for excitement in the Jazz Age. They read Fitzgerald's glittering stories and saw movies of adventure like *The Sheik*. They studied John Held, Jr.'s magazine drawings of flashily dressed young people. They adopted any style that defied tradition. A deep gap stretched between them and their parents—a gap called the Great War—and it seemed to have swallowed up the prewar world. The Jazz Age youth tried to live the words of poet Edna St. Vincent Millay:

> My candle burns at both ends;
> It will not last the night;
> But ah, my foes, and oh, my friends,
> It gives a lovely light.

Jazzy young women turned themselves into "flappers." They bobbed, or cut, their hair short and abandoned corsets for short dresses and stockings rolled below the knees. They draped themselves with beads and bracelets and carried long cigarette holders and large compacts to hold rouge and lipstick. Young men slicked down their hair to look like Rudolph Valentino, star of *The Sheik*, and wore raccoon coats and loose galoshes.

Decked out as daring sheiks and flappers, they roared off in motorcars to parties and to clubs called "speakeasies." In speakeasies, they could defy the nation's law against alcoholic drinks.

PROHIBITION

With passage of the Eighteenth Amendment during the war, Congress had made **prohibition**—the ban on the manufacture and sale of alcoholic drinks—a national goal. Early in 1919 the states ratified the amendment. Congress then passed the Volstead Act to enforce the ban on liquor, beginning in January

"The Bootleggers" by Thomas Hart Benton shows the sinister aspects of the trade. It was a business of dark places, smugglers, guns, bribery, and secret exchange of money.

1920. Thus, the Twenties received yet another nickname, the "Dry Era."

It was against the law to sell liquor, transport it, produce it, or smuggle it into the country. However, "bootleggers" did all these things. They were named for earlier smugglers who hid whiskey bottles in their boot legs when entering the dry states of Oklahoma and Kansas.

Bootleggers smuggled West Indian rum or Canadian whiskey from "rum row," a line of ships anchored off the Atlantic coast. Onshore, they loaded the liquor into trucks or touring cars with heavy-duty springs. The liquor was delivered to private buyers or to the illegal speakeasies.

By the mid-1920s bootlegging was a big business of $2 billion per year. For the Federal Prohibition Bureau, it was a big headache, costing $12 million per year for enforcement that was seldom effective. Many bureau agents were incompetent or corrupt. There were not nearly enough capable agents to police all the people who broke the law.

The big profits to be made from illegal liquor attracted organized crime. A gang would move into a city district and control the distribution of liquor throughout the area. Often, rivalries led to bloody gang wars, and the victors then expanded their business. "I call myself a businessman," said gangster Al Capone, who ran a good part of Chicago. "I make my money by supplying a popular demand. If I break the law, my customers are as guilty as I am."

By the end of the 1920s, few people still believed that prohibition would end the social problems caused by alcohol. Americans, angry about the costs and the crime, let the government know their feelings. In 1933 the Twenty-First Amendment was adopted. It repealed the Eighteenth Amendment and thereby ended prohibition.

THE MOVIES

If prohibition was one of the decade's great failures, the motion picture industry was one of its dazzling successes. This booming business began in the early 1900s in little theaters called nickelodeons.

In a converted New York cigar store, 200 customers crowded together on kitchen chairs and faced a white canvas screen. The lights went out, a piano player pounded out a flurry of chords, and onscreen a band of robbers galloped after a speeding train. The fifteen-minute movie, *The Great Train Robbery*, was made in 1903 and was shown thousands of times in the next ten years. The former cigar store was a typical nickelodeon, charging a nickel for admission. By 1907 there were as many as 5,000 of these theaters in the United States.

After 1910 the movie industry changed rapidly. Producers discovered that people would pay to see their favorite actors and actresses on the silent screen, and the "star system" was born. A passenger in *The Great Train Robbery* became America's first cowboy star, "Broncho Billy" Anderson. Mary Pickford, "America's Sweetheart," played the innocent heroine, and her evil counterpart was played by Theda Bara, "the Vamp." Douglas Fairbanks starred as a romantic hero, and Charlie Chaplin was a comic tramp.

Meanwhile, movie lengths stretched from 15 minutes to 90 minutes and more. Nickelodeons gave way to larger, more luxurious theaters. Most movies were now made in Los Angeles, which had sunny days and outdoor settings that could serve as deserts or steamy jungles. And in 1927 a movie was produced with a new dimension—sound. Al Jolson talked and sang in the first talking movie, *The Jazz Singer*, and opened the era of the "talkies."

THE RADIO

Sound was the sole attraction of another wonder of the Twenties—the radio. The groundwork for radio was laid in the late 1800s, when radio signals were sent through the air on electromagnetic waves. Then, in the early 1900s, electrical engineers created vacuum tubes, which could pick up and amplify radio signals. By 1920 radio had grown out of its childhood, and millions of Americans were catching the "radio bug."

Regular commercial broadcasts began in 1920, when stations WWJ in Detroit and KDKA in Pittsburgh went on the air. That year, in the first radio broadcast of election returns, Americans learned that Harding was president. Within two years, more than five hundred local stations had been set up.

Two stations, WJZ in New York City and WGY in Schenectady, New York, linked up by telephone lines and formed the first network in 1922. Four years later, a nationwide network called the National Broadcasting Company (NBC) was flashing news to every corner of the nation.

NEWS OF HEROES

Americans were especially eager to hear news of heroic deeds. They heard about Gertrude Ederle, who in 1926 became the first woman to swim the English Channel. She completed the crossing from France to England in 14 hours and 31 minutes, breaking the existing men's record.

Sport-loving Americans also devoured accounts of sports stars like golfer Bobby Jones and tennis player Helen Wills. In 1927 over 40 million people listened to a blow-by-blow radio account of a boxing match between Gene Tunney and Jack Dempsey. Americans were thrilled by football player Jim Thorpe, a Sauk-Fox Indian, who played until he was 40 years old. They made a hero of Babe Ruth, the "Sultan of Swat," who hit 60 home runs in 154 games in 1927.

That same year a shy young pilot from Michigan named Charles A. Lindbergh became the hero of the decade. Early on May 20 he took off from a New York airfield and headed his plane, *The Spirit of St. Louis*, toward Paris. Other aviators had crossed the Atlantic, but no one had done it alone or flown nonstop from New York to Paris. Newscasts of

Lindbergh's progress electrified Americans. Word of his landing, after almost thirty-four hours in the air, stirred them deeply.

WRITERS IN THE TWENTIES

F. Scott Fitzgerald was 24 years old when he published his first novel, *This Side of Paradise*. The book describes college-age youths who are tired of the past and ready to seek romance and pleasure in their own way. Appearing in 1920, the book helped to set the style of the decade. So did Fitzgerald himself. He and his wife Zelda were called "the prince and princess of their generation."

Other writers in the Twenties worked out new styles of prose. In lean, brisk language, Ernest Hemingway wrote about people traveling and enduring war. *The Sun Also Rises*, his first major novel, describes American *expatriates*, Americans who chose not to live in their homeland after World War I. For many of these people, the war, with its slaughter, destroyed faith in progress. Many of these people also did not feel comfortable in postwar America, with its emphasis on business and wealth.

Hemingway's book was published in 1926, when he was an expatriate based in Paris. That city was the longtime home of Gertrude Stein, an American who influenced Hemingway and many other writers. She understood the withdrawal, or alienation, of these writers. "You are all a lost generation," she remarked. Stein's own writing often was as inventive as jazz.

AMERICAN OBSERVERS

ZORA NEALE HURSTON
WRITER AND FOLKLORIST

Zora Hurston had only $1.50 and a stack of manuscripts to her name when she arrived in New York City in 1925. Still, she was a joyous young woman, with hope, energy, and a gift for words. She had spent the last few years at Howard University in Washington, D.C., but her real home was Eatonville, Florida.

Eatonville was a self-governing black town. It had its own charter and laws, written by Hurston's father, a Baptist preacher. It also had a rich folk culture. Zora often sat on the porch of Joe Clarke's general store, listening to folk tales and to music played on the guitar and mouth harp. She was an adventurous child, whose mother encouraged her to "jump at the sun." When she was fourteen she joined a traveling musical company as wardrobe girl.

In New York City she soon became known as a fine writer. She was also known as an extraordinary storyteller, who could entertain people for hours with Eatonville tales. She became a leader of the Harlem Renaissance, an outpouring of work by talented black writers.

While studying anthropology at Columbia University's Barnard College, she came to understand the value of her heritage. Soon she was traveling to Eatonville and other southern and West Indian

towns to collect tales, songs, games, sermons, and sayings. "I needed my Barnard education to help me see my people as they really were," she said. The result was *Mules and Men*, the first popular book about black culture by a black scholar.

During the next decades, Zora Hurston used black folklore in pageants, stories, and novels. Still, she barely made a living, and died penniless in 1960. Yet today she is recognized as an outstanding writer of her time.

F. Scott and Zelda Fitzgerald themselves mirrored the lives of Scott's Jazz Age characters. Glamorous at times, their life style was also hectic and destructive.

John Dos Passos presented rapid flashes of city life in *Manhattan Transfer*, published in 1925. Like a subway train, the novel moves jerkily from scene to scene. In poetry T. S. Eliot, an American living in England, used similar quick changes to express his view of modern experience.

When writers chose to use more ordinary styles, they still could break with the past. Eugene O'Neill brought powerful writing to the American stage, where most plays had been mere entertainment. Nearly all of O'Neill's plays were tragedies. Sinclair Lewis wrote novels criticizing everyday Americans. His books *Main Street* and *Babbitt* did more than any writings of the time to make Americans take a critical look at themselves and their nation.

THE HARLEM RENAISSANCE

Literature also flowered in the 1920s in the Harlem area of New York City. This area was the center of a new movement in black writing known as the "Harlem Renaissance." James Weldon Johnson, one leader of the movement, wrote *God's Trombones*, a series of sermons in verse that celebrated the eloquence of black preachers. Claude McKay, an immigrant from Jamaica, told of a young black soldier returning from the war in *Home to Harlem*. Countee Cullen celebrated his heritage in his first collection of poems, *Color*, and many others. Perhaps the most

famous black writer was Langston Hughes, who published over twenty books of poetry and prose.

It was during the 1920s that an immigrant from the West Indies named Marcus Garvey urged blacks to go "back to Africa," where they could find a sense of belonging. Garvey's movement fizzled, but it forced many blacks to think hard about their place in America. They found encouragement in Langston Hughes' poem "I, Too, Sing America." Hughes praised blacks who had the pride and strength to be Americans.

ECHOES OF THE JAZZ AGE

In 1931 F. Scott Fitzgerald wrote an article called "Echoes of the Jazz Age." He looked back at the Twenties and remembered the best of the age:

> Sometimes, though, there is a ghostly rumble among the drums, an asthmatic whisper in the trombones that swings me back into the early Twenties . . . and it all seems rosy and romantic to us who were young then, because we will never feel quite so intensely about our surroundings any more.

SECTION REVIEW

1. Identify the following: F. Scott Fitzgerald, Duke Ellington, Bessie Smith, Louis Armstrong, Charles Chaplin, Rudolph Valentino, *The Jazz Singer*, Gertrude Ederle, Jim Thorpe, Babe Ruth, Ernest Hemingway, Langston Hughes.

2. Define the following: flapper, speakeasies, prohibition, bootlegger, expatriate, nickelodeon.

3. What are the roots of jazz?

4. In what ways did jazz match the mood of the Twenties?

5. What did the Eighteenth Amendment and the Volstead Act prohibit?

6. Give three reasons why the Eighteenth Amendment was repealed.

7. What three changes took place in movies between 1910 and 1930?

8. Describe Charles Lindbergh's feat.

9. Explain how each of the following writers reflected the mood of the Twenties: Sinclair Lewis, John Dos Passos, T.S. Eliot.

10. What was the Harlem Renaissance?

SUMMARY

The American economy of the early postwar years declined rapidly. Union-organized strikes across the nation attempted to gain better conditions for workers. Fear of communism grew as strikers were compared with Russian revolutionaries. Terrorists' activities provoked a Red hunt in which mass arrests and deportation of "agitators" became common. New immigration laws and the revival of the Ku Klux Klan further reflected America's unrest.

In 1920 American voters, including women for the first time, elected Warren G. Harding. Harding revived the nation's economy by lowering income taxes and budgeting government spending. He failed to provide much help for troubled farmers and veterans. Shocked by scandals involving his appointees, Harding died suddenly on August 2, 1923. His successor, Calvin Coolidge, opposed aid to "special interest" groups—veterans and farmers—and supported business by cutting income taxes further.

As the economy prospered, Americans had money for luxuries. In 1902 Henry Ford formed the Ford Motor Company to produce an inexpensive automobile. From Ford's assembly line emerged millions of Model T's. The automobile industry expanded and related industries grew. Americans moved out and away on their wheels. The construction industry provided suburban housing and commercial buildings. The electric, chemical, and synthetic industries flourished. Increasing numbers of women and blacks entered the job market. Mexicans crossed the border into the United States to find jobs. The lives of American Indians were improved by new laws.

Jazz proclaimed the spirit of the Twenties. Flappers in daring styles and young men groomed like movie idol Rudolph Valentino raced in motorcars to speakeasies. Defeated by bootleggers' activities, the government ended prohibition. In entertainment, silent films gave way to the "talkies" and the "radio bug" caught on. News of heroes' feats thrilled the nation, climaxing in Charles Lindbergh's flight to Paris. Writers, black and white, in style and subject, recorded the Golden Twenties, the Jazz Age.

Many Spanish-speaking immigrants settled in sections of big cities. A small segment of their lives is suggested by "New York Street Scene" by Joaquin Torres-Garcia.

CHAPTER REVIEW

1. How did each of the following contribute to unrest in the United States after World War I? (a) the depression of 1920 (b) the Seattle strike (c) terrorist bombings (d) Communist uprisings in Europe (e) race relations

2. Harding promised to have "less government in business as well as more business in government." (a) What did he mean? (b) In what ways did he follow this policy? (c) In what ways did Coolidge follow this policy?

3. (a) Why did farmers and manufacturers support the Emergency Tariff of 1921 and the Fordney-McCumber Tariff Act? (b) How did the tariffs affect manufacturers? Why? (c) How did the tariffs affect farmers? Why?

4. (a) Why was the Progressive party formed in 1924? (b) In what ways did the party offer voters an alternative to the Democrats and Republicans? (c) Why did the Progressive party collapse?

5. (a) What demands did veterans make after World War I? (b) Explain how their demands were met during the administrations of Harding and Coolidge.

6. (a) Compare Calvin Coolidge's attitude toward the Federal Trade Commission with the attitude of Woodrow Wilson. (b) How do these attitudes reflect different views of the role of government?

7. (a) Summarize Andrew Mellon's views on taxation and the economy. (b) How did Mellon plan to improve the economy? (c) How did legislation passed in the Harding and Coolidge administrations further Mellon's goals?

8. Explain how each of the following contributed to the business boom of the 1920s. (a) decline in the cost of living (b) the assembly line (c) the auto industry (d) the construction industry (e) the synthetics industry

9. (a) Describe the problems of each of the following groups in the 1920s: women, blacks, Mexican Americans, and Indians. (b) Did any of these groups have problems in common? Explain.

10. (a) Summarize the reasons why Americans supported prohibition. (b) Explain how speakeasies, bootleggers, and organized crime affected prohibition.

ISSUES AND IDEAS

1. During the Boston police strike, Governor Calvin Coolidge of Massachusetts declared, "There is no right to strike against the public safety by anybody, anywhere, any time." What did he mean? Do you agree with his statement? Why or why not?

2. Many Americans opposed prohibition as a violation of their personal freedom. The con-

Political cartoonists found a rich subject in the oil scandals of the Harding administration. This cartoon put the right lid on the pot.

sumption of alcohol, they felt, should be an individual decision rather than a matter of government legislation. Do you agree? Defend your answer.

3. Some American writers in the 1920s felt that people in postwar America were too materialistic—too concerned with wealth and material things. Do you think that Americans became more materialistic in the 1920s? Why or why not? Cite examples.

SKILLS WORKSHOP

1. *Graphs.* Study the graphs of immigration on pages 762 and 763 of the Resource Center. (a) During what decades was immigration highest in the twentieth century? Why was immigration high then? (b) From what areas of the world did the immigrants come? (c) When did immigration drop sharply? Why?

2. *Timelines.* Construct a timeline of inventions and developments that changed American industry and communication between 1900 and 1930. Describe briefly each invention or development on the timeline, and explain its effects.

PAST AND PRESENT

1. In the 1920s jazz reflected the mood of many Americans. Do any forms of modern music seem to express the feelings of Americans today? Explain, citing examples.

2. Americans in the 1920s made heroes out of sports stars and movie stars. Who do you think are heroes today? List several examples and explain the reasons for your choices.

Charles A. Lindbergh won a nickname, "The Lone Eagle," a $25,000 prize, and international fame and admiration for his solo transatlantic flight in May, 1927.

CHAPTER 21

BOOM AND BUST

1928–1932

THE GOOD TIMES GO ON
THE CRASH ON WALL STREET
YEARS OF SUFFERING

The 1920s were mainly years of glory for American business leaders. They received praise from writers like Edward E. Purinton, an efficiency expert and a popular lecturer:

"What is the finest game? Business. The soundest science? Business. The truest art? Business. The fullest education? Business. The fairest opportunity? Business. The cleanest philanthropy? Business. The sanest religion? Business.

"You may not agree. That is because you judge business by the crude, mean, stupid, false imitation of business that happens to be located near you.

"The finest game is business. The rewards are for everybody, and all can win. There are no favorites—Providence always crowns the career of the [person] who is worthy. And in this game there is no "luck"—you have the fun of taking chances but the sobriety of guaranteeing certainties. The speed and size of your winnings are for you alone to determine; you needn't wait for the other fellow in the game—it is always your move. And your slogan is not 'Down the Other Fellow!' but rather 'Beat Your Own Record!' or 'Do It Better Today!' or 'Make Every Job a Masterpiece!'"

To Purinton and others, business leaders provided more than goods and services and earned more than mere wealth. Rather, these executives offered the best example of art, science, education, and religion in action. They earned the spiritual reward of service to humanity. American business, thought Purinton, could bring about "the salvation of the world."

The glory of business touched humble clerks just beginning their careers. It attracted the best efforts of sales representatives and advertising people. They and the great executives alike were players in "the finest game." The glory lasted as long as the business boom. Then it faded quickly as business turned into a game in which everyone lost.

THE GOOD TIMES GO ON

READ TO FIND OUT

— why Herbert Hoover won the election of 1928.

— how medicine and education benefited from business prosperity.

— how advertising changed during the Twenties.

— why chain stores and brand names were successful with American buyers.

— how credit changed Americans' buying habits.

While the nation's factories poured out new products, the Republicans looked on proudly. Their party had encouraged the quick growth of American business, and now business was responding. The economy was overflowing with new automobiles, electric stoves, and refrigerators, and a hundred other items.

In their campaign speeches the Republicans took credit for the business boom. They asked the voters to keep the good times going by choosing the Grand Old Party, the GOP. Most voters did just that. The Republicans won the majority of seats in the House of Representatives and the Senate in every election from 1920. Confident that the boom would go on, the GOP looked forward to more election victories.

HOOVER AND SMITH

Republican confidence was shaken briefly in the summer of 1927, when President Calvin Coolidge made a surprise announcement. He told the nation simply, "I do not choose to run for president in 1928." With Coolidge out of the running, Republicans needed an acceptable candidate to take his place.

The party soon turned to Herbert C. Hoover, Coolidge's secretary of commerce. Business leaders liked Hoover. The public respected him as an able administrator. Farmers, however, opposed Hoover for his stand against government-supported farm prices. They worked hard to block his nomination, but with no success. In June 1928 Hoover became his party's candidate for president. A few weeks later, the Democrats chose their candidate, Alfred E. Smith, the four-time governor of New York.

Smith and Hoover both had risen from humble beginnings to high political office, though by very different routes. Smith came from the tenements of New York City. Instead of completing school, he went to work in the Fulton Fish Market to help support his family. Then he entered big-city politics within Tammany Hall, the New York City Democratic organization. His political know-how won him steady advancement in the city. Smith made the jump from city to state office in his first race for the governorship, in 1918.

Hoover was born in Iowa farm country and grew up there and in Oregon. He completed high school and then studied engineering at Stanford University in California. After graduating he directed engineering projects all over the world. His skills as a project director helped him win appointment as head of the nation's Food Administration during World War I. Working efficiently, Hoover shipped millions of tons of food to Allied troops and starving civilians in Europe. He worked just as efficiently as secretary of commerce from 1921 on.

Politicians use various ways to help voters identify with them. Honoring a favorite American pastime, Herbert Hoover threw a ball for a group of pleased onlookers.

What better place than a baseball game to meet the public? Al Smith, derby in hand, started a game for the New York Giants. Mrs. Smith stood at his left.

THE ELECTION OF 1928

Hoover, with his broad face and high stiff collar, was the picture of a responsible business leader. Smith, sporting a brown derby hat and smoking a cigar, looked the part of a shrewd big-city politician. He spoke with a strong New York accent, and his campaign song was "The Sidewalks of New York." Voters outside New York wondered whether he belonged in the White House.

Voters had other reasons to doubt Al Smith. His party stood for prohibition, but Smith personally hoped for repeal of the Eighteenth Amendment. That hope troubled Americans who supported prohibition. Smith and the Democrats also proposed greater government regulation of some public utilities. That proposal worried Americans who opposed government interference in business. Finally, Smith's religion was troublesome. He was a Roman Catholic—the first to run for the presidency—and many voters were anti-Catholic.

Realizing his disadvantages, Smith campaigned vigorously to overcome the voters' doubts. Hoover, meanwhile, stressed that his party was defending "the American system of rugged individualism." After the war, Hoover said, the Republican party "restored the government to its position as an umpire instead of a player in the economic game."

Now, warned Hoover, the Democrats threatened to spoil the system by bringing on "a huge program of government in business."

Hoover won the election easily, gaining 444 electoral votes to Smith's 87. The Republicans also won increased control in Congress. The national government was firmly in Republican hands.

A SURGE OF CONFIDENCE

On the day after the election the stock market moved up sharply. Investors felt confident about prices and profits while the Republicans stayed in power. To Hoover, the prospects of continued business success raised grand hopes for the entire nation. "We in America today are nearer to the final triumph over poverty than ever before in the history of any land," he had said before the voting. "The poorhouse is vanishing from among us."

The nation also seemed nearer than ever to conquering disease. Typhoid fever, an epidemic disease from colonial days, was swiftly vanishing in the United States. Diphtheria, feared as a killer of children, was becoming rare. Even tuberculosis, long a major cause of death, was slowly being controlled. Babies born in 1900 were expected to live forty-seven years on the average. By 1929 the life expectancy of newborn children was ten years higher.

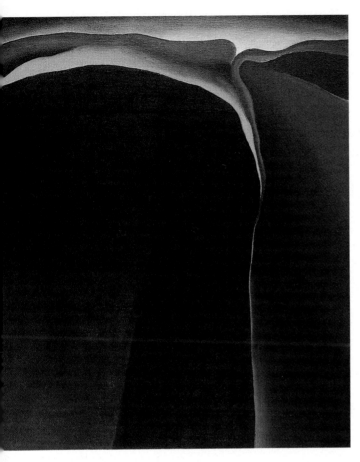

In the Twenties Georgia O'Keeffe was beginning her long, influential career. In "Dark Abstraction" 1924, she painted large, bold color areas with careful edging.

Every advance in medical research and treatment needed money, and the nation's thriving businesses helped to provide it. Education also was benefiting from business success. In earlier times children had often dropped out of school to help support their families. In 1900 only about 6 percent of all students completed high school, and about 4 percent went on to college. By 1929 more than 25 percent received high school diplomas, and about 12 percent of all young people entered college. Their families could afford the extra years of schooling.

THE POWER OF ADVERTISING

"Advertising," said a writer of advertisements around the turn of the century, "is sales [ability] in print." By the 1920s that was only part of the truth. Printed advertisements still sold goods, but so did electric signs, painted billboards, and voices on the radio. Even airplanes bore sales messages.

Advertisements also were growing bolder. Company buildings once were marked with the firm's name carved in stone. Now electric lights blazed the company's name and message. The Cleveland Credit Company placed a huge electric display on top of its building. Thousands of lights proclaimed, "This sign burns more current than the entire town of Elyria." Elyria, Ohio, then had 30,000 residents.

For a time, radio stations did not allow direct sales messages. The sponsors could only present programs, paying the stations to broadcast music by

By 1930 the nation had more than 100,000 miles of paved roads spawning tourist cabins, filling stations, diners, and billboards. The motto of American business might have been "Never lose a chance to advertise."

groups such as "The A & P Gypsies" or "The Ipana Troubadors." That restraint did not last long. By 1928 sponsors were pouring more than $10 million a year into selling by radio. Their messages were now direct, loud, and frequent.

Printed advertisements also grew bolder. Old-fashioned magazine and newspaper advertisements were small and wordy. The stylish new ones featured large drawings and simple slogans. One advertisement showed a fox terrier beside a record player. Titled "His Master's Voice," it promoted the products of the Radio Corporation of America (RCA).

Salespeople were just as direct. Trainees in selling were told to look a prospective customer "straight in the eye." Then the customer would have "no chance to reason or reflect. An idea is planted. . . . It is not analyzed. . . . It is taken as truth."

CHAIN STORES

While advertisements lured buyers, guarantees of high quality reassured them. The guarantees came especially from chain stores, groups of stores owned by the same company. Chain stores spread across the nation by offering reliable products at reasonable prices.

The chain of stores founded by James Cash Penney applied the golden rule to selling. "Golden Rule principles are just as necessary for operating a business profitably as are trucks, typewriters, or twine," he said. Similar attention to fair dealing guided the expansion of the Sears, Roebuck Company, as well as Montgomery Ward and other chains selling general merchandise.

Chain pharmacies spread through the cities and suburbs. Among them were Walgreen and Rexall drugstores. The Woolworth "five and ten cent stores" crowded out local stores selling small, useful articles. The Great Atlantic and Pacific Tea Company opened thousands of A & P grocery stores in the 1920s. Chain banks also grew in number. Chains such as the Bank of America in California flourished.

Chain stores took much of the risk out of buying, and so did brand-name products. A new Ford carried with it the company's reputation for building reliable cars. In prepared foods the name H.J. Heinz stood for dependability. The Heinz Company advertised "57 Varieties" of foods, including pickles and chili sauce. Some large companies purchased many different brand names. By the end of the decade, General Foods owned Swansdown flour, Jell-O, Log Cabin syrup, Birds Eye frozen vegetables, and other food companies.

Such business combinations grew rapidly in the 1920s as companies acquired other companies. *Mergers*, in which two or more independent companies combined into one, were also common. Most of the firms that had stock which was traded on the New York Stock Exchange owned other companies.

In the Twenties and Thirties shoppers had many choices of small articles priced at five or ten cents. This view of a New York Woolworth store shows how the merchandise was organized.

CREDIT BUYING

Even the most confident buyers needed some way to pay for the new products that industry produced. When the products were expensive, buyers might save for months to acquire them.

To let buyers purchase a product right away, a seller could offer them *credit*. Buyers would need some cash as a down payment. Then they would make monthly payments to the seller until the product was paid for.

Credit buying extended the purchasing power of Americans for a while, and it helped business keep booming. But credit payments could also prevent further purchases. Buyers with monthly payments for a new electric stove and a new car usually could not afford other large items at the same time. By early 1929 the business boom was slowing. Despite vigorous advertising, the sales of cars, ranges, refrigerators, and furnishings were leveling off.

SECTION REVIEW

1. Identify the following: GOP, Tammany Hall, James Cash Penney.

2. Define the following: sponsor, chain store, merger, brand-name product, credit.

3. (a) List two reasons why Hoover was an acceptable candidate for the Republican nomination in 1928. (b) Who opposed his nomination and for what reason? (c) List three reasons why voters doubted Al Smith's suitability for the presidency.

4. (a) Name three diseases that were largely brought under control during the Twenties. (b) How did the life expectancy of children change over two decades? (c) How were the advances in medicine related to business?

5. Explain how education benefited from business success.

6. (a) List five ways products were advertised in the Twenties. (b) Explain how radio advertising changed in this decade.

7. (a) Name five chain stores that were founded in the 1920s. (b) Explain what brand names had in common with chain stores.

8. (a) Explain how credit buying got its start in America. (b) Explain why credit buying was or was not totally successful as a business practice.

THE CRASH ON WALL STREET

READ TO FIND OUT

—how buying on margin enabled Americans to speculate in stocks.

—why the stock market in 1928 was primarily a bull market.

—how dreams of wealth captured the imagination of stock buyers.

—how a prediction of a decline in the stock market came true.

—how wealthy investors attempted to save the stock market.

—what happened in the crash of 1929.

During the late 1920s the business boom took a new turn. An increasing number of Americans realized that they could buy not only the products made by a company. They also could buy shares, or stock, in the company itself. Buying and selling company stock became a national craze.

Stock certificates were traded in several cities, but the chief market was the New York Stock Exchange. It did more business than all the nation's other stock markets combined. Founded in 1817, the exchange was the heart of Wall Street, New York City's financial district. On each workday, stockbrokers met on the floor of the exchange to buy and sell shares in the ownership of the nation's leading companies.

Like merchants who set up chain stores, large New York brokerage firms opened branch offices during the 1920s. Some offices looked like the barrooms of preprohibition days. Even at noon the lights were low. People entered through swinging doors and sat in mahogony chairs. While the latest stock prices were posted on a board, the brokers and clients swapped stories. By 1929 about 1,200 brokerage offices were scattered across the United States in big cities and in towns such as Steubenville, Ohio, and Storm Lake, Iowa.

BUYING ON MARGIN

Poor Americans or Americans struggling to make credit payments could scarcely hope to take part in stock-market trading. Some wealthier people chose not to. But about one family in twenty placed money in the market. Conservative buyers paid cash in full for their shares.

Buyers willing to speculate bought shares *on margin*. There buyers paid some percentage, or margin, of the share's selling price in cash. They borrowed the rest of the money from the stockbroker, who held the shares as collateral, or security for the loan. The stockbroker in turn borrowed money from banks to cover loans to buyers.

When stock prices moved up, buying on margin proved to be a splendid way to make money. Someone with an extra $1,000 in 1925 could buy 10 shares of General Motors at $99 each, for cash. Another person with exactly the same amount of money could buy twice as many shares on a margin of 50 percent. Each $99 share of General Motors reached a price of $212 at one point in 1928. The cash buyer could then sell all 10 shares for more than $2,000, a gain of more than $1,000. However, the buyer on margin could sell 20 shares for more than $4,000, pay back the broker's loan (about $1,000), and still gain more than $2,000. So far, buying on margin seemed a very good plan.

If stock prices stayed level, the buyer on margin might lose a little money. Interest payments due on the broker's loan usually wiped out whatever company dividends, or shares of profit, the buyer received as a stockholder. If stock prices fell, the buyer could be asked for more margin money. If the buyer did not pay a large enough margin, the broker could sell the stock to cover the loan. In that case the buyer would lose the stock and perhaps part or all of the margin money. Buying on margin paid off only when stock prices started rising. People who accepted brokers' loans were speculating that the market would continue to go up.

The speculators' outlook seemed reasonable at the end of 1927. Except for setbacks early in 1926, stock prices had been rising steadily for three and a half years. That rise reflected the increasing value of American companies in a business boom. Because of business know-how, the boom seemed likely to go on forever, and stock prices seemed likely to keep on rising.

Telephones, a ticker tape, and a wallsize board kept information circulating in this broker's office. When large volumes of stocks traded rapidly, the tape fell behind.

THE BIG BULL MARKET

In Wall Street's vocabulary a "bull" is someone who expects the stock market to rise. A "bear" is someone who expects the market to fall and who arranges to profit from lower prices. In March 1928 the bulls dominated Wall Street. Radio Corporation of America (RCA) was selling at just under $95 per share on March 3. By March 20, RCA shares were $178 each.

Other companies posted strong gains in heavy trading. Toward the end of March more than 4.5 million shares changed hands in one day's trading on the New York Stock Exchange. It was an all-time record.

The bears had their turn on June 12. More than 5 million shares changed hands in a sharply falling market. Because of the heavy volume of trading, the ticker tapes* in brokerage offices ran two hours late. Owners of RCA had to wait to find out that each of their shares had dropped by $23 that day. However, the market recovered during the summer and reached new highs. A share of RCA costing $95 in March was worth $420 at the end of the year. The gain was all caused by speculation. RCA stock paid no dividends to its stockholders in 1928.

* ticker tape: a paper tape on which a ticker, a telegraphic instrument, prints stock market reports.

DREAMS OF WEALTH

Stories spread of waiters and window washers who made fortunes in stocks. A nurse was supposed to have profited by $30,000 from following the market advice of well-to-do patients. Every surge in stock prices was described in glowing news stories.

People in country villages could call or write a broker and buy a few shares on margin. At the height of the Big Bull Market, half a million people or more were speculating in stocks. Each one dreamed of future wealth.

The stock-buyers' dreams rested partly on the rising market and partly on brokers' loans. These loans had increased from a total of $3.5 billion at the start of 1928 to nearly $6 billion at the end of the year. The rate of interest on the loans had gone up too, from 5 percent to 12 percent or more. Such high interest rates attracted money from bankers and other big investors.

While speculators were busy buying on margin, investors were pouring cash into Wall Street to be used for brokers' loans. The loans looked safe. They were secured, or protected, by stocks that normally were easy to sell if the market dropped.

THE MARKET CONTINUES TO RISE

Early in 1929 the bull market slipped, then recovered. Coolidge, nearing the end of his term as president, was reassuring. Stocks, he said, were "cheap at current prices." When Hoover was inaugurated on March 4, the market surged higher.

Late in March the market dropped sharply. Brokers began calling for extra margin money from buyers. Speculators worried that loan money was drying up. If that happened, the bears would take over on Wall Street. Then Charles E. Mitchell of the National City Bank in New York City promised that his bank would provide up to $25 million for new brokers' loans. That news sent the bulls off and running again.

Through the summer of 1929 the speculators could keep on dreaming of great wealth. They were aided by business executive John J. Raskob, who wrote an article titled "Everybody Ought to Be Rich." Published in the *Ladies' Home Journal*, the article told how as little as fifteen dollars a week invested in stocks could produce a small fortune over the years.

THE BABSON BREAK

In June, July, and August of 1929, many stock prices increased by a third or more. Brokers' loans kept pace, reaching a total of more than $7 billion. After a year and a half, the Big Bull Market still looked strong.

"Sooner or later a crash is coming, and it may be terrific," warned economist Roger Babson on September 5. He and others had made similar predictions of doom before. However, on September 5 the market seemed to pay attention. It fell in what became known as the "Babson Break." For the rest of the month and into October, stock prices were uneven but mostly down.

Speculators waited impatiently for stock prices to turn around. They heard assurances from experts like Professor Irving Fisher of Yale University. "Stock prices have reached what looks like a permanently high plateau," he announced.

Stock prices fell off that plateau on Saturday, October 19. The next day brokers sent out many calls for more margin money. Trading was ragged on Monday and Tuesday. The market fell again on Wednesday, and brokers sent out more margin calls.

Investors clinging to the falling market in October 1929 had a wild ride to the bottom. A cartoon from early October illustrates their situation.

On the morning of Thursday, October 24, prices began to drop rapidly. "Fear struck the big speculators and little ones, big investors and little ones," said a newspaper account. "Thousands of them threw their holdings into the whirling Stock Exchange pit for what they would bring. Losses were tremendous."

That afternoon a group of bankers stopped the panic selling. The group included Mitchell and Thomas W. Lamont, senior partner of J.P. Morgan and Company. "There has been a little distress selling on the Stock Exchange," Lamont told reporters. However, the market was "susceptible to betterment."

Then a trader acting for the bankers placed large orders for more than a dozen different stocks. The market promptly rebounded, making up some of the morning's losses. Some 13 million shares were traded on the New York Stock Exchange that day. It was a new record.

The market held steady on Friday and Saturday. By then the mood on Wall Street was hopeful. Thanks to the bankers, the awful slide in prices seemed to be over.

THE CRASH

On Monday the hopefulness vanished. Stock prices dropped sharply, and this time the bankers did not try to save the day. Tuesday, October 29, was far worse. *The New York Times* reported the turmoil on Wall Street:

> Stock prices virtually collapsed, . . . swept downward with gigantic losses in the most disastrous trading day in the stock market's history. Billions of dollars in open market values were wiped out as prices crumbled under the pressure of liquidation of securities which had to be sold at any price.

As large amounts of stock were sold, prices dropped further. This triggered more calls for margin money and more forced selling. Huge amounts of stock were thrown into the market. The volume on the New York Stock Exchange exceeded 16 million shares. The ticker tapes ran hours late.

Tuesday's disaster was followed by words of assurance. "Believing that fundamental conditions of the country are sound," said John D. Rockefeller, "my son and I have for some days been purchasing sound common stocks." The market rallied for a few days and then sank again. It reached its low for the year on November 13. By then stock values had been cut in half. Investors and speculators had lost billions.

Rumors spread that speculators were jumping from high windows to escape the shame of their losses. Very few did, in fact. What fell along with the market was the decade's sense of hope. By the end of 1929 few could dream of glorious new opportunities just around the corner.

SECTION REVIEW

1. Identify the following: Wall Street, "Everybody Ought to Be Rich," Roger Babson, November 13, 1929.

2. Define the following: share, margin, collateral, dividend, "bull," "bear," ticker tape, secured loan.

On this day in 1929 a large, apparently happy crowd gathered outside the New York Stock Exchange. On October 29 a larger, stunned crowd witnessed the grim news.

3. (a) How did Americans without cash for full payment purchase shares of stock? (b) What happened to an investment in stock bought on margin when prices moved up? (c) What could a buyer on margin expect when stock prices fell?

4. (a) What was the outlook for speculators at the end of 1927? (b) Describe the condition of the market in March 1928, June 1928, December 1928. Use the term "bear" or "bull."

5. (a) Name the two economic bases on which stock buyers' dreams rested. (b) How did interest rates affect investors' loans? (c) Why did investors' loans look safe in 1928?

6. (a) Explain how Charles E. Mitchell saved the bull market in March 1929. (b) Where could Americans find cheap advice from an expert on how to turn fifteen dollars a week into a small fortune in the future?

7. (a) What was the "Babson Break"? (b) How was the panic selling on October 24 stopped?

8. (a) How did *The New York Times* describe the October 29 conditions on Wall Street? (b) How did John D. Rockefeller try to reassure panic-stricken stockholders? (c) How was the American mood of the 1920s affected by the events on Wall Street in late 1929?

The crash caused many Americans to reorder their values. As the sign indicates, a former stock investor found that basic necessities did not include an automobile.

YEARS OF SUFFERING

READ TO FIND OUT

— how Hoover attempted to improve the economy.

— why economists opposed the Hawley-Smoot Tariff Act.

— how the crash hurt the world economy.

— how unemployment affected the lives of Americans.

— what efforts were made to relieve the needy.

— how veterans demanded help.

After the crash, Wall Street was a place of shattered fortunes and reputations. Bankers and stockbrokers who once appeared to be business geniuses now seemed powerless and confused. Americans looking for economic leadership turned away from Wall Street and toward the White House.

In his public statements, President Hoover was reassuring. Although the crash had wiped out billions in paper profits, it had not damaged the nation's factories. It had not changed highways or railways or farms across the land. It had not even taken money from the average American. Some 95 percent of all families had stayed out of the stock market, and they did not lose a cent when the crash came.

Nonetheless, there were reasons to worry. After years of increasing prosperity, the economy had slowed down. Industry was producing more goods than Americans could buy. People who had already bought on credit could not afford further purchases.

In addition, many products, such as cars and stoves, were durable goods, made to last for a relatively long period of time. As sales leveled off and factory surpluses grew, industry cut back production and laid off workers. This reduced the purchasing power of more Americans, which in turn further cut production and employment in industry.

Hoover feared that the economy might be going into a sharp decline. If so, he could simply wait for the economy to reach bottom. In private, Secretary of the Treasury Andrew Mellon advised him to do this. Let prices and wages fall, suggested Mellon. Sooner or later the economy would start to recover.

Hoover refused this advice. He did not want the economy to drift into a long recession, or decline in business activity, after the crash. He still believed that government should be "an umpire instead of a player in the economic game." But like an umpire, he could ask the players to keep the game moving quickly.

HOOVER'S VOLUNTARY PROGRAM

On the morning of November 21, Hoover met with Henry Ford, Pierre du Pont, and many other business leaders. After the meeting he announced their promise not to cut wages. That afternoon Hoover met with labor leaders. They promised not to seek wage increases.

On November 23 Hoover sent telegrams to governors and mayors throughout the nation. He asked them to speed up their spending for highway projects and other public works. Such projects, Hoover believed, would provide jobs and pour money into the economy.

In December he made the same request of Congress. In response Congress in 1930 voted funds for new harbors, roadways, public buildings, and the Boulder Dam project. Located on the Colorado River, the dam later was renamed Hoover Dam.

Before 1929 ended, Hoover also asked businesses to maintain or to increase spending for new construction. To most business leaders, however, new construction did not seem wise. Unless the economy improved, they owned more than enough buildings and machines. Indeed, some business leaders were closing plants. In January 1930 reporter Beulah Amidon toured one of these plants, a huge automobile assembly line in Toledo, Ohio. It reminded her of a ghost town in the desert:

> There was the same sense of suspended life, as I moved among silent, untended machines or walked through departments where hundreds of half-finished automobile bodies gathered dust while they waited for the next cleaning or finishing process.

By and large, business leaders did not lower wage rates right after the crash. But they did reduce the number of hours worked, thereby lowering the average take-home pay. They also cut expenses by

Business Failures 1918–1932

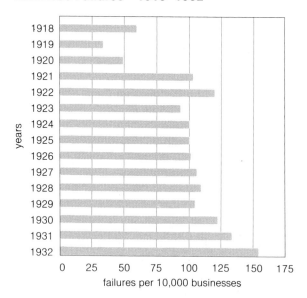

The information on the graph does not apply to railroads, banking, insurance, or real estate. Farming, professional services, and some other services are also excluded.

A group of unemployed gathered by an open fire on a city street, trying to keep warm. Hunger, cold, and homelessness created many scenes like this during the depression.

firing unneeded workers. At the time of the crash, about a half million workers were unemployed. That number jumped to more than 4 million early in 1930.

FARM PRICES

Long before the crash, farmers complained about the low prices they were receiving. Many of them wanted the government to buy crops to support prices. Hoover rejected this idea. However, in June 1929 he accepted legislation setting up the Federal Farm Board. It was intended to help private groups improve sales of cotton, wheat, or other farm products. The board could not buy crops directly, but it could make loans to be used for crop purchases.

Despite the loans, farm prices sank rapidly in 1930. Farmers who had received a dollar a bushel for wheat the year before now received an average of

---

AMERICAN OBSERVERS

GEORGE SANCHEZ
SPEAKER FOR A FORGOTTEN PEOPLE

In 1923, when George Sanchez was just seventeen, he became a teacher in a one-room country school near Albuquerque, New Mexico. Like Sanchez himself, most of his pupils were descendants of the Southwest's early Spanish settlers. For more than three hundred years, these people had made a meager living, grazing cattle and sheep and growing crops in remote mountain valleys. By the 1920s they made up half of the population of New Mexico. Yet they were isolated from a booming United States by language and geography.

Sanchez's own childhood had also been hard, as his family struggled to survive on his father's pay as a miner. But Sanchez was a gifted student. He mastered English and graduated from high school in Albuquerque. For the next seven years, he taught in country schools to earn his way through the University of New Mexico. Later he received a Ph.D. in education from the University of California at Berkeley.

Sanchez's years in country schools shaped his career as an educator and writer. He saw that the Mexican American people of the Southwest—both descendants of the early settlers and later immigrants from Mexico—had little share in the American dream. For the rest of his life, he worked to change that situation.

To Sanchez, education was both the problem and the cure. In *Forgotten People*, he showed that the schooling Mexican American children were receiving was not adequate. Teachers were poorly trained and poorly paid. Often they did not speak Spanish. As a result, the drop-out rate of students was alarming.

Sanchez hoped to broaden American democracy to include his people. Through good schools, he

A young Mexican American farm girl posed in her Texas home. Handsomely framed pictures in the background show an effort to preserve family ties and proud memories.

believed, they could become a true part of the United States while preserving their special heritage. "Democracy," Sanchez said, "must not only be *thought*—it must be *done*."

Farm Income 1918–1932

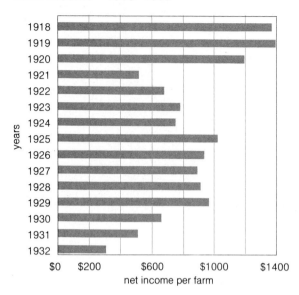

net income per farm

Food Prices 1925–1932

	Bread 1 lb.	Eggs 1 doz.	Milk ½ gal.	Chuck roast 1 lb.	Navy beans 1 lb.
1925	9.3	55.4	27.8	22.8	10.3
1926	9.3	51.9	28.0	23.7	9.4
1927	9.2	48.7	28.2	25.2	9.4
1928	8.9	50.3	28.4	29.6	11.8
1929	8.8	52.7	28.8	31.4	14.1
1930	8.6	44.5	28.2	28.6	11.7
1931	7.7	35.0	25.2	22.7	8.1
1932	7.0	30.2	21.4	18.5	5.2

Prices given in cents

only 68 cents. The price of cotton fell from 17 cents a pound to less than 10 cents. The Farm Board gave up its loan program and simply asked farmers to cut production. That also proved ineffective. Farm prices kept dropping.

In June 1930 Hoover accepted another piece of legislation intended to help farmers. The Hawley-Smoot Tariff Act raised United States import duties to an all-time high. The act placed new duties on foreign sugar, citrus fruit, and many other farm products. The act also placed new duties on a wide range of manufactured goods. Industrialists as well as farmers favored the tariff act. It offered them protection against foreign competition.

Experts warned that the act also would cause problems. "Countries cannot permanently buy from us unless they are permitted to sell to us," declared a group of a thousand economists, all opposed to the act. They warned that other nations would strike back by levying duties against American goods.

A Ben Shahn photograph of a restaurant menu sometime in the mid-Thirties shows many items available for 25 cents or less. Even at these prices, thousands of Americans could not afford to buy a meal.

The economists' prediction proved correct. Other nations raised their tariffs and cut their imports. The Hawley-Smoot Tariff Act did not keep farm prices from falling. Instead, the act contributed to serious problems in the world economy.

FOREIGN DEBTS

The United States had loaned about $10 billion to the Allies during World War I and the years just following. The Allies agreed to repay the loans gradually, over more than sixty years. Germany meanwhile was obliged to pay reparations to the Allies for war damages.

Private American investors had loaned another $12 billion to foreign governments and businesses. This money helped to support the world economy. Nations in Latin America and Europe imported goods from the United States. The nations usually did not export enough to the United States to pay for all their imports. Often they paid the balance with money loaned by American investors.

The crash sharply reduced the flow of American loans. As a result, nations had to reduce their imports from the United States or increase their exports. However, it was almost impossible to increase exports to the United States when the United States imposed higher tariffs. As trade declined, a number of foreign governments defaulted, or failed to pay, on their loans. The higher tariffs, then, hurt American investors as well as American exporters.

Lack of loan money threatened the world's banking system. In the spring of 1931 the largest bank in Austria collapsed, setting off a chain reaction. Panicky investors then withdrew their loans from Germany, forcing the German government to stop paying reparations. There was fear that the German government would fall.

In June, Hoover eased the problem by calling for a one-year *moratorium*, or delay, on both reparations and the Allies' debt payments. Yet the world economy continued to slow down, and Hoover faced increasingly hard problems in his own country.

UNEMPLOYMENT

For a long time, business leaders kept their promise to Hoover to maintain wage rates. The rates held through the summer of 1930, and they did not slip much for a year after that. Then they fell along a wide front. The United States Steel Corporation announced a 10 percent wage cut in the autumn of 1931. Other firms announced cuts of 15 percent to 25 percent.

Employees grumbled, but not too loudly. By then one out of every six workers had no job at all. The first workers fired usually were unskilled laborers. Next came skilled workers, clerks, and even managers. From January 1930 to January 1931, unemployment jumped from 4 million to 8 million.

A study of jobless workers in Philadelphia showed that about half had not saved any money while they were working. They had nothing to fall back on. Families with savings usually had put away only a few hundred dollars. Even large savings were not a guarantee against hard times. When banks failed, depositors lost most or all of their savings.

THE SPREAD OF POVERTY

After savings were gone, people turned to friends and relatives. When friends and relatives were out of work and out of money, people appealed to public charities for help. In 1930 and 1931 charities distributed millions of dollars in food, clothing, and cash to keep jobless Americans and their families alive.

Hoover applauded the charities. They demonstrated, he said, the spirit of "mutual self-help through voluntary giving." He backed their efforts by setting up the President's Organization on Unemployment Relief (POUR). In advertisements it appealed for more aid to charities like the Community Chest.

Hoover's call for voluntary giving might have been all that was needed in easier times. However, another 3 million people lost their jobs in 1931.

Unemployment 1918–1932

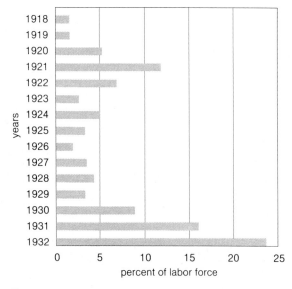

The unemployment figures are estimates from various sources. To be counted as unemployed a person must be available for work and actively seeking a job, or temporarily laid off.

Wages of Workers in Manufacturing 1918–1932

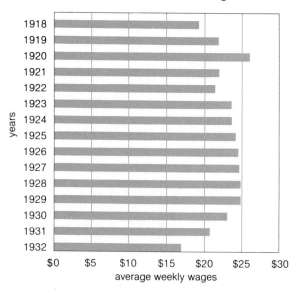

From 1928 to 1932 even employed workers experienced declining incomes. In factories average hourly wages decreased from $.56 to $.44, and weekly hours of employment fell from 44.4 to 38.3.

Soup kitchens saved hundreds of thousands of America's unemployed from starvation during the Great Depression. This Chicago kitchen was opened by Al Capone.

Big-city charities could not raise enough money to feed all the people who needed help. By autumn most city charities were bankrupt.

The number of unemployed workers reached 12 million in March 1932 and 13 million in June. Fathers, ashamed of being jobless, deserted their families. Older sons left home so they would not burden their parents. They joined thousands of drifters, young and old, begging for rides and food. As the Great Depression deepened, young women also became drifters. One was asked where she was going. "Going?" she snapped. "Just going."

Young people who stayed at home postponed marrying. If they did marry, they postponed having children. The cost of rearing children seemed too high. Jobless parents fed their youngsters steady diets of potatoes, beans, or rice. Thousands of children suffered from undernourishment, and many went to hospitals because they were starving.

The humorist Will Rogers spoke about hunger. "We used to be told that depression was a state of mind but starvation has changed that impression. Depression is a state of health. It's moved from the mind to the stomach."

THE CALL FOR RELIEF

When most charities failed in 1931, cities were forced to step in. In New York City the Board of Education provided hot lunches. The schools offered the three R's plus the "three C's: clothing, coal, and cash." The city also set up a program of work relief, giving part-time jobs to thousands of people. Yet the city's relief efforts did not reach all the needy.

Detroit, Michigan, tried to feed thousands of unemployed auto workers. By January 1932 the task outpaced the city's ability to raise taxes or to borrow. Mayor Frank Murphy said that "there ought to be federal help, as at present the assistance we are able to render is inadequate. . . ." In Chicago, Illinois, the demands for assistance also reached a crisis point early in 1932. Relief programs in Chicago survived through a $20 million emergency loan approved at the last minute by the Illinois legislature.

A few other states also provided some relief money. The first was New York. Its governor, Franklin D. Roosevelt, said that citizens who could not find work because of the depression deserved aid "not as a matter of charity but as a matter of social duty."

There is a feeling of great desolation in Jacob Vavak's painting "Women of Flint." Flint, Michigan, a center of the automobile industry, was hit especially hard by the depression.

Before the winter of 1932 was over, more than half the states had set up emergency relief programs. But local needs kept increasing. More and more local officials agreed with Gifford Pinchot, governor of Pennsylvania. "The welfare of the working people," he said, was "a national responsibility and a national duty."

HOOVER'S RELIEF EFFORTS

Hoover disagreed with Pinchot's argument. He thought that direct relief from the national government would strike "at the roots of self-government." People would begin to rely upon "government charity in some form or other."

Early in 1932 Hoover won congressional approval for a new agency, the Reconstruction Finance Corporation (RFC). The RFC made loans totaling more than $1.5 billion to banks, mortgage companies, railroads, and insurance firms. Hoover hoped that the loans would boost industrial investments, creating more jobs and more consumer spending.

Pressured by the Democrats and the worsening depression, Hoover then went a bit further. He still opposed direct relief to needy people from the national government. But he approved RFC loans to the states to be used for relief. Early in the summer of 1932, Congress passed the Emergency Relief and Construction Act, giving the RFC up to $300 million for relief loans. The new act also gave money to the RFC to loan to the states for public works. States, however, often needed more money than the RFC was willing to loan.

VETERANS PROTEST

Widespread suffering led to demands for government action. In May 1932 a group of veterans from Oregon set out for the nation's capital. They meant to press Congress for a bill to pay veterans' bonuses. As approved by Congress in 1924, the bonuses were not payable in full until 1945, The "Bonus Expeditionary Force" wanted the money right away.

Publicity about the Oregon group prompted some 22,000 other veterans to join them. From all over the nation, jobless veterans poured into Washington, D.C. Many brought their wives and children. Some veterans set up housekeeping in abandoned buildings. Most built shacks outdoors, using

cardboard boxes, packing crates, and whatever else they could find. The police chief of Washington, D.C., Pelham D. Glassford, helped to raise money to feed them all.

In June the House voted for immediate bonus payments. The Senate, however, voted the measure down. After hearing the Senate's decision, many veterans chose to leave the city. Still, thousands remained because they had no place else to go.

Tension rose in the capital, and Hoover ordered that the "Bonus Army" be disbanded. On July 28 the police swept veterans out of the abandoned buildings. Then soldiers, cavalry, and tanks of the United States Army under Chief of Staff Douglas MacArthur advanced on the outdoor camps. The soldiers used tear gas to force out the veterans and fire to destroy their shacks. The Bonus Army dispersed.

Many Americans felt sympathy for the veterans. A reporter spoke of July 28: "It was an experience that stands apart from all others in my life. So all the misery and suffering had finally come to this—soldiers marching with their guns against American citizens."

Of the 15,000 to 20,000 veterans who came to Washington in the Bonus Army, half stayed on. They had nowhere to go. Their makeshift shack homes were burned on July 28, 1932.

THE ELECTION OF 1932

The President's reputation had sunk along with the economy. The groups of shacks that poor people built near city dumps were called "Hoovervilles." The newspapers that drifters used for covers at night were called "Hoover blankets." Hoover's use of force against the veterans' Bonus Army caused more bitter remarks about him. Although he once again was his party's candidate for president, Hoover seemed to have little chance to win. The Democratic candidate appeared likely to become the next president.

Meeting in Chicago late in June, the Democrats nominated Governor Franklin D. Roosevelt of New York. It was a custom for the nominee to wait for formal notice before giving an acceptance speech. Roosevelt did not wait. He flew from Albany, New York, to Chicago and spoke directly to the convention. The main issue of the election, he said, was "a depression so deep that it is without precedent in modern history." He went on to promise "a new deal for the American people."

During the election campaign, Hoover warned that the Democrats wanted government to become a player in the economic game. "They were proposing changes and so-called new deals which would destroy the very foundations of our American system," Hoover said. He said that the Democrats, if elected, would bring ruin to the land.

In November the voters chose Roosevelt. He won 472 electoral votes to 59 for Hoover. It was a victory even more sweeping than Hoover's triumph over Al Smith four years before. Yet the vote was more a mark of blame for Hoover than of confidence in Roosevelt.

SECTION REVIEW

1. Identify the following: Boulder Dam, POUR, RFC, the "three C's," "Bonus Army," "Hoovervilles."

2. Define the following: durable goods, recession, default, moratorium.

3. (a) List three assurances Hoover gave Americans that the economy would be all right. (b) List four reasons why there was cause for worry.

4. (a) Name two promises about wages that Hoover got from business and labor leaders. (b) What requests did Hoover make of governors, mayors, and Congress in late 1929? (c) How did business leaders react to Hoover's request for new construction?

5. (a) What was the purpose of the Federal Farm Board? (b) Describe the changes in wheat and cotton prices in 1930.

6. (a) What was the purpose of the Hawley-Smoot Tariff Act? (b) Explain how economists' prediction about the tariff proved correct.

7. (a) Why were American loans important to Latin American and European nations? (b) How did the crash affect American loans? (c) How did Hoover try to ease the problems in the world banking system?

8. (a) Name three places needy Americans could look for help in 1930 and 1931. (b) Why did big-city charities stop helping people?

9. What was Hoover's attitude toward relief from the national government?

10. (a) What was the Bonus Expeditionary Force? (b) Describe the reaction of many Americans to Hoover's treatment of the Bonus Army.

For over thirty years Dorothea Lange recorded the social history of America with her cameras. "Man Beside Wheelbarrow" documents the despair of the Great Depression.

SUMMARY

In the 1920s business boomed in the United States. Americans gave the Republican party the credit for prosperity. Voters returned Republican majorities to Congress throughout the decade. In the presidential election of 1928 voters also showed their approval of Republican policies. They elected Herbert C. Hoover, the Republican candidate, by a large margin.

As American business grew in the 1920s, it changed. Businesses found new ways to advertise their products, using neon signs and radio messages as well as paint and ink. Companies opened chain stores across the nation. Business combinations grew rapidly as companies acquired other companies.

Many firms also offered credit to their patrons. Thus, Americans went into debt to buy more of the large, expensive products that business was producing.

In the late 1920s more and more Americans also began to buy shares of stock on margin. They were speculating that stock prices would continue to rise. Throughout most of 1928 and 1929, the stock market fulfilled their hopes. Then, late in October 1929, stock prices dropped sharply, causing the stock market crash.

President Hoover tried to prevent the economy from declining. However, businesses closed, unemployment rose, and farm prices dropped. The administration's tariff policies also hurt the United States as well as the world economy.

The United States slid into depression. Unemployment spread across the nation. Depositors lost savings as banks closed. Hoover called on public charities to help needy Americans, but the problem was too widespread for charities to manage. Relief programs set up by cities and states also were inadequate.

Hoover opposed direct relief from the national government to the needy. Instead, he set up a government agency to make loans to businesses. States also received loans to be used for relief. However, widespread suffering led to demands for government action. In the election of 1932, Americans turned from Hoover and elected Franklin D. Roosevelt by a sweeping margin.

A humorous headline announced the tragedy on Wall Street to readers of *Variety*, the theatrical newspaper. The bad show on Wall Street needed a complete rewrite.

CHAPTER REVIEW

1. (a) Compare Al Smith's attitude toward the government's role in relation to business with the attitude of Herbert Hoover. (b) What did Hoover mean when he spoke of "the American system of rugged individualism"?

2. (a) Explain how advertising, chain stores, and credit buying helped businesses to find buyers for their products in the 1920s. (b) Describe how credit buying eventually affected the business boom.

3. (a) Why did Americans buy stock on margin? (b) Where did stockbrokers obtain money to loan to people who bought on margin? (c) What collateral did stockbrokers receive for such loans?

4. Explain how each event led to the next: the business boom, the bull market, stock speculation.

5. How did each of the following influence the stock market in 1928 and 1929? (a) news stories of fortunes made in stocks (b) new brokers' loans (c) John J. Raskob

6. What led to the stock market crash? Include each of the following in your explanation. (a) the Babson Break (b) calls for margin money (c) stock buying by J.P. Morgan and Company and other bankers (d) panic selling

7. (a) How was Hoover's response to the economic decline after the crash different from government responses to earlier economic declines? (b) What was Hoover's approach to the economy in 1929? In 1932?

8. How did each of the following contribute to problems in the world economy? (a) the Hawley-Smoot Tariff (b) the crash (c) foreign defaults on loans (d) the Austrian bank collapse

9. (a) Why did unemployment begin to rise after the crash? (b) How were wages affected by the crash? By the depression? (c) Describe how unemployment affected Americans' lives.

10. Explain how each of the following contributed to the election of Franklin D. Roosevelt in 1932. (a) the length of the depression (b) failure of local relief efforts (c) Hoover's views on direct relief (d) "Hoovervilles" (e) the "Bonus Army"

Whatever the causes of the Great Depression, its effects were to ruin millions of helpless Americans. Heroic efforts to avoid dependence on charity failed. There was no work.

ISSUES AND IDEAS

1. Al Smith's campaign for president was hurt by his religion. Why do you think this was so? Consider other periods in American history to support your conclusions.

2. During the depression, Governor Gifford Pinchot of Pennsylvania declared that "the welfare of the working people" was "a national responsibility and a national duty." What evidence could Pinchot use to support his argument? Do you agree with him? Why or why not?

3. Hoover feared that direct relief from the government to Americans would strike "at the roots of self-government." What did he mean? Do you agree with Hoover? Why or why not?

SKILLS WORKSHOP

1. *Statistics.* Use the following statistics to make a table of the dollar value of durable goods and of nondurable goods, such as food or clothing, produced in the United States between 1929 and 1932. Value of durable goods: 1929—$17.5 billion; 1930—$11.4 billion; 1931—$7.7 billion; 1932—$3.6 billion. Value of nondurable goods:

1929—$38.5 billion; 1930—$35.5 billion; 1931—$29.7 billion; 1932—$23.1 billion. What do these statistics tell you about economic conditions in these years? From these figures, what can you conclude about consumer demand? About production? About employment?

2. *Charts.* Construct a chart of activity on the New York Stock Exchange from March 1928 to November 1929. Include dates and events. Below the chart, briefly describe each event included and its effects.

PAST AND PRESENT

1. Hoover wanted the national government to be "an umpire instead of a player in the economic game." Do you think that Hoover's view of the government's role would work today in the United States? Why or why not?

2. Business continued to boom in the 1920s partly because of credit buying and stock buying on margin. Do you think such credit buying plays a major role in today's economy? Why or why not? If so, do you think it is dangerous? Explain.

THE NEW DEAL

Years later, Jessie Lopez De La Cruz remembered the Great Depression in California. She talked to interviewers of her experiences as a teenager.

"In '33, we came up north to follow the crops because my brothers couldn't find any work in Los Angeles during the depression. I remember going hungry to school. I didn't have a sweater. I had nothing. I'd come to school and they'd want to know, 'What did you have for breakfast?' They gave us a paper, to write down what we had! I *invented* things! We had eggs and milk, I'd say, and the same things the other kids would write, I'd write. . . . You know: glasses of milk, and toast, and oranges and bananas and cereal. I'd never had *anything*. My grandmother couldn't work, we couldn't work, so we went hungry. One of my friends at school said, 'Jessie, why don't you eat with us?' And I said, 'I don't have any money.' . . .

"We weren't feeling sorry for ourselves: We didn't know there was anything better than we had. Everybody that came into the camp and stayed there lived the way we did."

About 13 million workers in the United States were unemployed in 1933. Among those millions were Jessie Lopez De La Cruz's brothers and grandmother. Once they had lived in southern California. Now they were migrant workers, moving from farm to farm to harvest crops. They were joined by other desperate Americans, some from as far away as Oklahoma and Arkansas.

In 1933 President Franklin D. Roosevelt, confident and optimistic, took office and launched the New Deal. Soon Congress, meeting in hurried sessions, was passing legislation to provide relief for needy Americans and to speed the economic recovery of the nation. Critics argued against the "alphabet agencies" that Roosevelt established. To most Americans, however, the New Deal offered action, aid, and most of all, hope.

THE FIRST NEW DEAL

READ TO FIND OUT

— why states declared bank holidays.

— how Roosevelt ended the bank panic.

— how the National Recovery Administration worked to revive business.

— how the Agricultural Adjustment Administration helped farmers.

— how new rules were set for bankers and brokers.

— how relief programs helped the nation's needy.

— how the Tennessee Valley Authority was established.

In 1932 the New Deal was only a campaign slogan. Franklin D. Roosevelt promised to aid "forgotten" Americans "at the bottom of the economic pyra-

mid." However, he did not announce to the anxious public how he planned to do this.

Roosevelt's background provided few clues to his plans. A distant cousin of Theodore Roosevelt, Roosevelt grew up in Hyde Park, New York. In 1905 he married Anna Eleanor Roosevelt, another distant cousin. Beginning in 1913, he served as assistant secretary of the navy in the Wilson administration. He campaigned as the Democratic candidate for vice-president in 1920 and lost. The next year he was stricken with polio, which left his legs permanently paralyzed. However, he was able to win election as governor of New York in 1928 and again in 1930.

During the campaign for president, Roosevelt sometimes appeared to be making far sighted plans to end the Great Depression. He sought the advice of experts in economics and law. Three of them— Raymond C. Moley, Rexford G. Tugwell, and Adolph A. Berle, Jr.—were professors at Columbia University. They and others became known as Roosevelt's "brain trust."

At other times Roosevelt seemed ready to proceed on a hit-or-miss basis rather than by long-term plans. "It is common sense to take a method and try it," he remarked. "If it fails, admit it frankly and try another. But above all, try something."

Most Americans agreed with Roosevelt. They had elected him president by an overwhelming margin. Now they waited anxiously for his inauguration.

THE LAME DUCK AMENDMENT

Roosevelt could not be inaugurated until March 4, 1933, four months after election day. In the meantime Hoover was a "lame duck" president—a public official who had been defeated for reelection and was serving the last part of his or her term. Because of this Hoover had little power to make political bargains. Many members of Congress also were due to be replaced. One complained, "We're milling around here utterly unable to accomplish anything of real consequence."

In February 1933 the states ratified the Twentieth Amendment to the Constitution. It had been proposed to the states a year before. Known as the "lame duck amendment," it reduced the time in which defeated officials waited to be replaced. After 1933 each new Congress and each new president took office in January, not March.

However, the amendment did not go into effect in time to reduce Roosevelt's long wait in 1933. In February, while he prepared for his inauguration, the nation's banking system began to collapse.

BANK CLOSINGS

The nation's bankers held $41 billion in deposits early in 1933. The bankers kept about $6 billion of that sum in cash. The rest of the money was secured by bankers' investments in home mortgages, business loans, and company stocks.

Even in the boom times of the 1920s, some bankers had made bad investments. Each year, hundreds of banks lost money and closed. When the Great Depression began, homeowners could not keep up their mortgage payments. Businesses failed, and stock prices continued to decline. In the crash, General Motors stock fell from $73 to $36 per share. In 1932 it reached $8.

As the value of their investments shrank, more and more banks went out of business. Some depositors received part of their money back. Others re-

A large crowd gathered outside the closed Bank of United States after its failure. This was one of more than 6,000 bank failures from 1930 through 1933.

ceived none. A woman in the Midwest worked for 52 years, saving for retirement. When her bank failed, she lost every cent.

Worried people began hoarding currency, especially gold coins. They withdrew their savings from banks and hid the money. As a result, banks began running out of cash.

On February 14, 1933, the governor of Michigan declared a "bank holiday." He closed all the banks in the state for several days in order to let the banks obtain more cash. News that banks had closed their doors in Michigan caused panic in other states. Frightened depositors lined up to withdraw their money while they still could. By March 2 banks had been closed or had limited withdrawals in 23 states.

Still the "run" on banks continued. Before dawn on March 4, Inauguration Day, the governors of New York and Illinois declared bank holidays in their states. The New York Stock Exchange also closed that day. The world, said journalist Agnes Meyer, was "literally rocking beneath our feet."

ROOSEVELT TAKES OFFICE

In his inaugural speech Roosevelt called on Americans to regain their confidence. "Let me assert my firm belief," he said, "that the only thing we have to fear is fear itself." Roosevelt promised speedy action. If necessary, he would ask Congress for emergency power "as great as the power that would be given to me if we were in fact invaded by a foreign foe."

On March 5 Roosevelt announced a four-day national bank holiday. He also called Congress into an emergency session, beginning March 9. And he ordered his secretary of the treasury to complete an emergency banking bill by the time Congress met.

ENDING THE BANK PANIC

On March 9 Congress hurriedly passed the Emergency Banking Relief Act. The act allowed the reopening of banks that the Department of the Treasury declared sound. It also gave the government the power to call in all gold. People who continued to hoard gold could be sent to jail.

Before any banks reopened for regular business, they accepted gold from the people who had been hoarding it. In a few days millions of dollars in gold flowed back into bank vaults across the nation.

Bank Closures   1928–1938

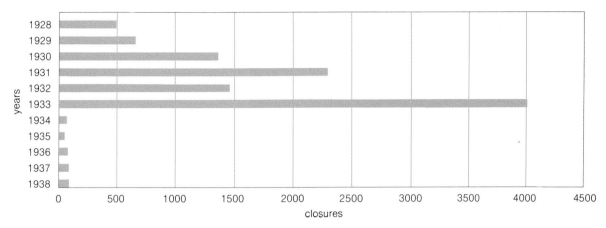

The graph includes banks closed either temporarily or permanently. Because of changes in the banking system in 1933, figures for 1933 do not compare exactly with figures for other years.

On Sunday evening, March 12, Roosevelt made the first of his "fireside chats" on radio to the American people. He said that banks would reopen the next day. Only banks in grave difficulty would stay closed for a while. "I assure you," he told Americans, "that it is safer to keep your money in a reopened bank than under the mattress."

By the end of the next week, three fourths of the nation's banks were again doing business. Money was circulating freely. Within two weeks stock prices rose 15 percent.

Roosevelt transformed the mood in Washington. The city had been a place of deep despair. Within days it was charged with energy, like an army command post in wartime. Congress, prompted by Roosevelt, stayed in emergency session for exactly 100 days in the spring of 1933. It passed more than a dozen major bills, giving meaning to Roosevelt's promised "New Deal."

After passing the Emergency Banking Relief Act, Congress approved the Economy Act. This act cut the salaries of government workers. It also reduced pension payments to veterans.

Congress then passed the Beer-Wine Revenue Act. It changed the Volstead Act to make some beers and wines legal once again. Even before Roosevelt took office, the Twenty-first Amendment had been passed by the lame duck Congress. The amendment would repeal prohibition, thus allowing the sale of all alcoholic drinks. The amendment was ratified by the states late in 1933.

REVIVING BUSINESS

One of the most ambitious bills of the "Hundred Days" was the National Industrial Recovery Act, passed in June 1933. The act set up the National Recovery Administration (NRA) in an effort to revive American business.

The goal of the NRA was simple. It would see that *every* major business shortened working hours and raised wages. That way no one business could gain an advantage by paying low wages for long hours of work. Because of shorter working hours, firms would hire more workers. Because of higher wages, workers would buy more products.

Achieving the NRA goal was another matter. Each industry had its own patterns of wages, prices, and work. Each had its own guidelines.

Roosevelt appointed an energetic cavalry veteran, General Hugh S. Johnson, to head the NRA. Early in the summer of 1933, Johnson and the directors of major cotton mills agreed on a code of fair practices in the manufacture of cotton cloth. The code set maximum working hours and minimum wages and ended child labor in the mills.

Johnson then drew up codes of fair practice for other industries. He also started a campaign to gain support for the codes. Employers who honored minimum NRA standards or who signed codes could display a new symbol, the NRA Blue Eagle. On it was the motto "We do our part." The Blue Eagle, said Roosevelt, would be "a badge of honor."

Johnson soon managed to complete codes for the nation's ten largest industries. The Blue Eagle appeared in coal mines, lumber mills, and oil rigs. It also appeared in small factories and shops. A new professional football team, the Philadelphia Eagles, was even named for the NRA symbol.

CRITICS OF THE NRA

Not all Americans applauded the work of the NRA. Union leaders charged that the NRA did not honor Section 7a of the National Industrial Recovery Act. That section recognized labor's right "to organize and bargain collectively through representatives of their own choosing."

Under the NRA codes, companies could agree to limit production, thereby raising prices. Blacks claimed that the prices they paid were increasing more than the wages they earned. To one black writer, the NRA meant "Negroes Ruined Again."

Owners of small businesses charged that the NRA prevented healthy competition. The codes, they said, gave unfair power to a few giant companies in each industry. Business leaders in minor industries complained that they were being tied up in red tape. One NRA code regulated the dog-food industry. Another code governed the manufacture of shoulder pads for suits.

In 1934 Roosevelt ended the agency's control of some minor industries. Still, by 1935 the NRA was administering over five hundred industrial codes.

HELPING FARMERS

During the Hundred Days, Congress also sought to help the nation's farmers. In May 1933 the Agricultural Adjustment Act was passed. This act set up the Agricultural Adjustment Administration (AAA) to increase the purchasing power of farmers. One of its methods was to adjust farm production to demand. "We have been producing more of some crops than we consume or can sell in a depressed world market," said Roosevelt in a fireside chat. "The cure is not to produce so much."

The AAA planned to reduce production through payments to farmers. The agency would pay farmers to restrict the number of acres that they planted or the number of animals that they raised. Money for the payments would come from a special tax on firms that processed farm products.

In the summer of 1933 agricultural agents set out to convince farmers to reduce their crop acreage. The farmers were hard to persuade. Many of them had planted their fields before the AAA began operating. Yet that summer the agents persuaded farmers to destroy 10 million acres (4 million hectares) of growing cotton. In return, the farmers received more than $100 million.

The AAA also arranged the slaughter of 6 million small pigs to prevent a surplus of pork. News stories about the pigs upset many people. The slaughter seemed cruel and wasteful at a time when people were hungry.

In later years, though, the agency had time to arrange payments *before* crops were planted or farm animals were bred. In 1934 payments from the AAA kept farmers from planting acreage more than equal to all the land in Illinois.

When crop production fell, farm prices rose. From 1933 to 1934 the price of wheat and cotton doubled. For the first time in years farmers had money to pay debts and to buy supplies. This money circulated through the economy.

The new farm program also helped to prevent the ruinous cycle of surplus crops, lower prices, and farm bankruptcy. However, the program caused unexpected hardship to tenant farmers and sharecroppers. To cut crop acreage, farmers could simply evict the tenants or sharecroppers who worked part of their land. Most of these workers became migrants, people on the move to find any kind of job.

THE DUST BOWL

Nature increased the number of migrants who once lived on farms. Dust storms swept over the Great Plains, burying crops and farm buildings. The first large storm struck South Dakota in the fall of 1933. The storm was "a wall of dirt," one writer said. When the storm was over "fences, machinery, and trees were gone, buried." The next day dust from that storm darkened the skies over Chicago.

The dust storms were caused by years of large-scale plowing followed by severe drought. The plowing began at the time of World War I, when crop prices were high. Farmers started cultivating vast areas of the Great Plains.

For years enough rain fell to maintain the farms. Then no rain fell in 1933 and again in 1934, 1935, and 1936. The dry, loose prairie soil was swept up by

The Dust Bowl storms blew away millions of tons of soil. Dorothea Lange photographed the bleak effects of dust storms on a Texas farm in 1938.

the wind. Dust storms battered farms in the Dakotas, Nebraska, Kansas, Oklahoma, and the Texas Panhandle. The Great Plains became a "Dust Bowl."

On many prairie farms the drought and the dust storms cut production to zero. Year after year, desperate families were forced to leave their homes and take to the road as migrants.

CREDIT FOR HOUSING

Both farmers and townspeople found it hard to continue paying for their homes in the Great Depression. Many farmers already were deeply in debt. They could not keep up mortgage payments when crop prices fell. Townspeople faced the same problem when they lost their jobs or received lower wages. Early in 1933 more than a thousand families were losing their homes every day.

By executive order Roosevelt set up the Farm Credit Administration (FCA) in March 1933. It helped farmers borrow money they could use to pay off mortgages. The new government loans had low interest rates and could be repaid over a long period of time. Eventually the FCA arranged refinancing of one fifth of all farm mortgages.

The Home Owners Loan Corporation (HOLC) did the same for townspeople. Created during the Hundred Days, the HOLC eventually helped to refinance one fifth of all mortgages for urban homes. In 1934 Congress also set up the Federal Housing Administration (FHA) to insure bank loans for home repairs or for new construction.

RULES FOR BANKERS AND BROKERS

Throughout the 1920s, hundreds of banks made unsound investments, lost money, and closed. The Glass-Steagall Banking Act, passed by Congress in June 1933, provided new rules to reduce the number of bank failures. The act prevented wild speculation by bankers. It also set up the Federal Deposit Insurance Corporation (FDIC). The FDIC guaranteed individual bank deposits in FDIC-insured banks up to $5,000. This guarantee increased depositors' confidence in banks and ended frantic runs on bank assets.

During the Hundred Days, Congress also passed legislation to regulate the stock market. The Federal Securities Act allowed investors to gain reliable information about new issues of stock. Later, in 1934, Congress voted for a stricter law governing stock sales. The Securities Exchange Act was designed to limit speculation and to end secret stock market deals. The act created the Securities and Exchange Commission (SEC). It was given authority to license each of the nation's stock exchanges.

RELIEF PROGRAMS

The FDIC and the SEC were examples of *reform*. Both agencies enforced new rules to eliminate old problems. The NRA and the AAA, in contrast, were set up to aid *recovery*. They were supposed to revive business and agriculture in order to lift the United States out of the Great Depression. Besides attempting reform and recovery, the New Deal offered programs of *relief*. They were to ease human suffering until recovery was achieved.

The key figure in the relief programs was Harry L. Hopkins, who had directed relief efforts in New York State. In May 1933 he became head of the newly created Federal Emergency Relief Administration (FERA). The FERA provided direct relief to needy Americans. Money went from FERA to state and local agencies. They investigated relief applicants and helped the neediest.

However, Hopkins worried that direct relief would harm people's sense of self-reliance. He persuaded many states to set up programs to provide work. Work relief cost more and was more difficult to administer than direct relief. But Hopkins believed that only by having jobs would people feel that they were productive. Hopkins also convinced Roosevelt to request a huge new program of work for the jobless. Winter was coming, and some 12 million people still were unemployed.

WORK RELIEF

Following Roosevelt's lead, Congress approved the Civil Works Administration (CWA) in November. In two months under Harry Hopkins' direction more than 4 million workers were hired to build or repair roads, schools, and parks. Each worker received a minimum wage averaging $15 a week.

That winter the CWA pumped almost $1 billion into the economy. However, the high cost alarmed Roosevelt. He ordered Hopkins to phase out the program. The CWA ended early in 1934.

Roosevelt had other reasons to halt the CWA. He feared that workers would come to depend on government employment. He also was waiting for a more permanent public-works program to get underway. It was run by the Public Works Administration (PWA).

Heading the PWA was Harold L. Ickes, nicknamed "Honest Harold." He and Hopkins were alike in their dedication. But Hopkins tried to put the most people to work with the least delay. Ickes planned slowly and was thorough. He wanted the PWA to supervise well-planned projects with no wasted money. Started in June 1933, the PWA did not have much impact for more than a year.

Once the PWA began rolling, though, it made an impressive record. From 1933 through 1939 the agency gave or loaned $6 billion for public works.

The First New Deal

Date	Agency or Program		Purpose	Status
March 31, 1933	CCC	Civilian Conservation Corps	Provide employment for men 18–25 years of age	Ended in 1941
May 12, 1933	AAA	Agricultural Adjustment Administration	Advise and assist farmers	Program largely ended in 1936
May 12, 1933	FERA	Federal Emergency Relief Administration	Provide direct relief to needy Americans	Ended in 1936
May 18, 1933	TVA	Tennessee Valley Authority	Help develop resources of Tennessee Valley	Still in operation
June 13, 1933	HOLC	Home Owners Loan Corporation	Help townspeople refinance mortgages	Ended in 1950
June 13, 1933	NRA	National Recovery Administration	Revive American business	Ended in 1935
June 13, 1933	PWA	Public Works Administration	Provide employment on public works	Ended in 1937
June 16, 1933	FCA	Farm Credit Administration	Set up a credit system for farmers	Became part of Dept. of Agric. in 1939
June 16, 1933	FDIC	Federal Deposit Insurance Corporation	Set up a system to guarantee individual bank deposits	Still in operation
Nov. 8, 1933	CWA	Civil Works Administration	Provide employment at federal expense	Ended in 1934
June 6, 1934	SEC	Securities and Exchange Commission	Protect public and private investors in stocks	Still in operation
June 28, 1934	FHA	Federal Housing Administration	Insure bank loans for home construction and repair	Still in operation

Major River Basin Development Projects

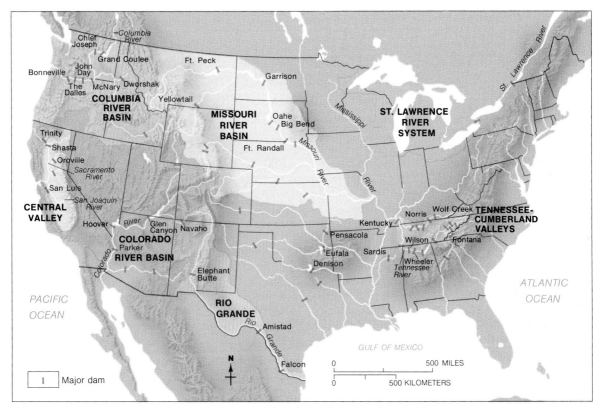

Dams in the Tennessee Valley are managed by the TVA. Less controversial river valley projects also provide flood control and soil conservation as well as electric power.

The CCC could point with great pride to its reforesting record. It was responsible for more than half of the forest planting in the nation's first 175 years.

The money allowed states and private firms to build hospitals, city halls, courthouses, and public gardens. PWA dollars financed more than half of all the school buildings constructed in those years.

The early New Deal offered one other program of work relief. The Civilian Conservation Corps (CCC) was set up in March 1933 and hired jobless young men to work in forest camps. The workers were known as Roosevelt's "Tree Army." Besides planting trees, the CCC workers cleared trails, built shelters, and battled forest fires. Their wages were $30 per month, part of which went to their families.

The CCC was limited to single men, aged 18 through 25. From 1933 through 1942, the corps hired more than 2 million men.

THE TVA

The Tennessee Valley includes a system of rivers extending from the Great Smoky Mountains to the Mississippi River. The longest river, the Tennessee,

THE ROLE OF GOVERNMENT IN THE ECONOMY
THE TENNESSEE VALLEY AUTHORITY

Harry Ransley, a member of Congress from Pennsylvania, was alarmed about the Tennessee Valley Authority bill. This vast plan for the poverty-stricken Tennessee Valley would put the government in the electric power business. "It is the entering wedge," he warned members of the House of Representatives in April 1933. "Continue along these lines and you will have a socialist government, destroying the initiative that has made this country great."

Tennessee Representative Gordon Browning disagreed. "Members who are complaining about . . . putting the government into competition with private enterprise seem not to distinguish between what belongs to private enterprise and what belongs to the public." The electric power from the nation's rivers should not be used for private profit, Browning declared. "The little fellow who tills his farm on the hillside near the Tennessee Valley is just as much entitled to the use of this public resource for a reasonable charge as the man who runs a great manufacturing establishment."

While Congress discussed the true meaning of TVA, President Roosevelt avoided labels. He was asked how he planned to explain the political philosophy behind the project. He replied, "I'll tell them it's neither fish nor fowl. But, whatever it is, it will taste awfully good to the people of the Tennessee Valley."

The President's plan called for a public corporation, the Tennessee Valley Authority. It would be "clothed with the power of government but possessed of the flexibility and initiative of a private enterprise." The TVA would provide low-cost electric power to valley residents through dams on the Tennessee River. It would use two World War I plants to make low-cost fertilizer. It would also establish projects to control flooding, to plant forests, and to conserve the soil.

Opponents of the TVA believed that the government should stay out of business. "I am against government competition with business as a matter of principle," said one Massachusetts representative. When the government took over the railroads during World War I, explained John Taber of New York, it ran them very badly. "That is a sample of the way government does business. . . . What can we expect," he concluded, "if the government now tries to run power and fertilizer plants?"

Representative John Rich of Pennsylvania argued that the government's job was to regulate business, not to own it. "Business and politics don't mix," he said. "If you want efficient business, it must not be controlled by politicians."

Others, however, pointed out that the state commissions set up to regulate private power companies

This TVA photograph documented the poverty of the Tennessee Valley. The purpose of the soil conservation and power programs was to remedy such conditions.

runs by the town of Muscle Shoals, Alabama. During World War I the government built two plants at Muscle Shoals to make explosives. It also started work on a dam to produce electricity.

After the war the two nitrate plants and the dam brought Muscle Shoals to the center of controversy.

Henry Ford wanted to buy the plants, but Senator George W. Norris of Nebraska blocked the sale. He wanted the government to use the dam to provide low-cost electrical power for the people of the Tennessee Valley. Twice Congress passed bills for government operation of the dam. However, the

had failed to do the job. Such commissions, said Senator George Norris of Nebraska, could no more control utility rates "than a fly could interfere with the onward march of an elephant." To him, the only solution was public ownership.

Another supporter agreed. "I look upon the power in the river as I do the sunshine, air, and the water of the seas and oceans," he said. "It is a right that is inherent to our people and should be used for the welfare of all the people and not in the interests of a few."

To many supporters of TVA the issue boiled down to the price of electricity. Much of the public believed that utility companies charged whatever they could get away with, reaping huge profits at the expense of ordinary citizens. "Eighty-five percent of the farmers of the nation do not have electric power," said one

Norris Dam, completed in 1936 and named for Senator George Norris, was the first dam built by TVA. It is located on the Clinch River in east Tennessee.

representative. "No one can deny that if the power was cheaper, thousands of farmers throughout the nation would be using it."

A representative from Tennessee pointed out that the people of his district were paying ten cents a kilowatt-hour for electricity from a private company. In Canada, where the power company was publicly owned, the rate was one and a half cents a kilowatt-hour. "Let us now insist," he concluded, "that our people have a right to as low a rate as those people in Canada."

The battle over public versus private power ended temporarily when Congress approved the creation of TVA. "It was a glorious fight, right up to the very end," said one elated supporter. But the issues that it evoked were far from decided. TVA successfully brought low-cost electric power and fertilizer to one of the most depressed regions of the United States. However, the question of what part the government should play in the economy remains as controversial today as it was in 1933.

1. Why did opponents of TVA think that the government should stay out of the electric power business? What reasons did its supporters give for public ownership?

2. In some cities and towns in the United States, the public owns the local electric power and gas facility. In others it is owned by a private company. Which type of ownership do you think works best? Why?

3. Who do you think should own such natural resources as rivers, forests, or coastlines? Should their use be controlled for the public good? If so, how? By whom? What rights should business have in their use or control?

measures were vetoed, first by Coolidge, then by Hoover.

In May 1933 Congress created the Tennessee Valley Authority (TVA). Norris's plans became part of a vast new program of economic improvement. The TVA took over the dam and the two

plants and sold power directly to homes and businesses. It also planned a series of dams to produce additional power and to control flooding.

Private power companies opposed the TVA, arguing that it was unfair competition. Defenders of the TVA replied that the competition would help to regulate the electric-power industry. The TVA rates for electricity, they said, would be a "yardstick" for judging the fairness of rates charged by private companies. The power companies, however, claimed that the TVA could charge less because it enjoyed special privileges.

Electric rates were only one concern of the TVA. It built a series of special dams that made it possible for barges to navigate for 650 miles (1,000 kilometers) along the Tennessee River. The TVA also planted new forests where old ones had been cut down. It produced fertilizers, encouraged conservation, and brought new industries into the valley.

SECTION REVIEW

1. Identify the following: brain trust, fireside chats, Hugh S. Johnson, Dust Bowl, FCA, Harry L. Hopkins, Harold L. Ickes, Tree Army, TVA.

2. Define the following: lame duck president, bank holiday, NRA codes, drought.

3. (a) Why were the four months following the election of 1932 difficult for both Hoover and Roosevelt? (b) What was the purpose of the Twentieth Amendment?

4. (a) Why were banks running out of money early in 1933? (b) How did states handle the banking crisis?

5. (a) Name two provisions of the Emergency Banking Relief Act. (b) List two results of the passage of this act.

6. (a) Explain the goal of the National Recovery Administration. (b) Explain the complaints of each of the three groups that were dissatisfied with the NRA.

7. (a) How did the Agricultural Adjustment Administration plan to achieve its goal? (b) What negative results did the program have?

8. Explain the causes and results of the Dust Bowl.

9. (a) How did Congress increase depositors' confidence in banks? (b) What controls were put on the stock market?

10. (a) Why did Harry L. Hopkins favor work relief rather than direct relief? (b) Name three work programs established by the New Deal. (c) Describe the accomplishments of each program.

THE SECOND NEW DEAL

READ TO FIND OUT

— how three leaders challenged Roosevelt.

— how the Works Progress Administration helped jobless Americans.

— how the Social Security Act provided security for Americans.

— how the National Labor Relations Board protected workers' rights.

— why conservative opposition to Roosevelt grew.

— how Roosevelt won the election of 1936.

Roosevelt won wide praise during the Hundred Days. "The admirable trait in Roosevelt is that he has the guts to try," said a Republican senator. "How do you account for him?" asked a newspaper reporter. "Was I just fooled in him before the election, or has he developed?"

Another journalist was convinced that Roosevelt had changed. "Roosevelt the candidate and Roosevelt the President are two different men," he said. "The oath of office seems suddenly to have transfigured him from a man of mere charm and buoyancy to one of dynamic aggressiveness."

Yet not all Americans were pleased. Some felt that the New Deal, with its "alphabet agencies," was leading to overcontrol by the government. Others wanted government to do still more to end the Great Depression. Out of these conflicting demands, a second New Deal would be born.

THE TOWNSEND PLAN

In 1934 three leaders challenged Roosevelt and his New Deal. Each of the three demanded more government action to help the American people.

Dr. Francis R. Townsend, a retired California physician, offered "a quick cure for this depression." He proposed a plan for an old-age pension, or regular payment, that would help both the elderly and the government.

Hundreds greeted President Roosevelt when he visited the Pine Mountain Valley Resettlement Administration project in Georgia. He clearly enjoyed their welcome.

In the plan, the government would pay two hundred dollars each month to every citizen who was sixty years old or older. There were, however, two conditions. The person could not hold a paying job and had to spend the entire amount each month. Such spending, Townsend believed, would stimulate "every avenue of commerce and trade."

Economists pointed out that the Townsend Plan would require $24 billion each year, more than half the national income. However, Townsend's ideas sparked a mass movement in 1934. More than a thousand Townsend Clubs sprang up, mostly in western states. Club members collected more than 10 million signatures on petitions to Congress to enact the pension.

FATHER COUGHLIN

Father Charles E. Coughlin, known as the "Radio Priest," also challenged Roosevelt. Coughlin began broadcasting sermons in Detroit in 1926. By 1933 he was reaching more than 30 million listeners each week. By 1934 he was receiving more mail than any other American, including the President.

Coughlin at first supported Roosevelt. However, he soon grew critical of the New Deal. In 1934 he charged that the policies of the NRA and the AAA were failing. He lashed out at the government's money policies. He also attacked Roosevelt for not expelling bankers from positions of power. Bankers, Coughlin believed, had brought ruin to average working people.

Late in 1934 Coughlin formed the National Union for Social Justice. Its goal was to reform America's economic system. Within 2 months, more than 5 million of Coughlin's listeners joined the organization.

HUEY LONG

Senator Huey Long of Louisiana, nicknamed the "Kingfish," also set up a political organization in 1934. Its motto was "Share Our Wealth." Long proposed that the government take money from the rich and give it to the needy. He wanted every family to have a home, an automobile, and a radio.

Long also called for a minimum annual income of $2,500 for every family, free college education for young people, and bonuses for veterans. Long publicized his program in press stories and radio talks.

During the depression Ben Shahn worked as an artist and a photographer for the Farm Security Administration. This 1937 painting suggests the sad life of drifters.

Ben Shahn. *Scotts Run, West Virginia*, 1937. Collection of Whitney Museum of American Art.

Other agencies besides the CCC had youth training programs. At this Farm Security Administration Workers Community in Arizona, Russel Lee photographed boys learning to garden in a vocational training class.

Within a year he claimed to have 7 million followers in his Share Our Wealth Society.

Of the three leaders, only Long could think seriously about becoming president someday. Townsend's main support came from older voters, who were only a fraction of the electorate. Coughlin was a native of Canada, and therefore could not run for the presidency. Long, though, was an able candidate with strong support.

EXTENDING THE NEW DEAL

After starting in a burst of energy, the New Deal faltered in the summer of 1934. The economy stopped improving. Some 11 million people—more than 20 percent of the work force—remained unemployed. One year after they were established, New Deal programs seemed powerless to produce a quick recovery.

In June 1934 Roosevelt announced that he would seek sweeping new legislation from Congress in 1935. His first objective would be "the security of the men, women, and children of the nation." Voters approved Roosevelt's goal. In the congressional elections in November, they strengthened the Democratic majority in Congress.

When Congress met in January 1935, Roosevelt outlined a vast new program of relief and reform. In the following months, Congress enacted a variety of new laws. They were called the second New Deal.

THE WORKS PROGRESS ADMINISTRATION

In April Congress passed the Emergency Relief Appropriation Act. It allowed Roosevelt to set up the Works Progress Administration (WPA) to offer work relief to able-bodied, unemployed Americans. Harry L. Hopkins was appointed head of the WPA.

Hopkins launched a massive work-relief campaign. By March 1936 the WPA was employing nearly 3.5 million people. They built roads, playgrounds, schools, airports, and hospitals.

Hopkins also found work for writers and artists. "They've got to eat just like other people," he said. Writers working for the WPA prepared guidebooks to states and cities. Artists painted murals in government buildings. Actors presented plays in local parks and theaters.

The actors were part of the WPA's Federal Theatre Project, led by Hallie Flanagan. Hopkins warned her about the pressures of WPA spending. "If you try to hold down wages, you'll be accused of union-busting and of grinding down the poor; if you pay a decent wage, you'll be competing with private industry and pampering a lot of no-accounts. . . . Whatever happens you'll be wrong."

In 1936 Hopkins started a wage policy that silenced some critics of the WPA. He paid average hourly wages for fewer-than-average hours of work. Typically a WPA worker was on the job for 30 hours or less each week. The wage rate was high enough to satisfy most unions. The total take-home pay was low enough to ease most private employers' fears of unfair competition.

Still, one group of Americans remained jobless. These were students who needed part-time jobs. They were helped by the National Youth Administration (NYA), set up as part of the WPA. High school and college students, ages sixteen through twenty-five, found jobs in NYA projects. The NYA also offered work relief to needy young people who had left school.

Hopkins became known as "the world's greatest spender." From 1935 until its end in 1943, the projects of the WPA cost $11 billion. About 85 percent of that money paid workers' wages and salaries.

THE SUPREME COURT ACTS AGAINST THE NEW DEAL

While Congress was creating more agencies, the Supreme Court struck one down. In May the Court ruled in the case of *Schechter* v. *United States*. The Schechter brothers ran a poultry slaughterhouse in Brooklyn, New York. When they were convicted of breaking NRA rules, they appealed their case.

The Supreme Court ruled unanimously in favor of the Schechters. It found that the National Industrial Recovery Act, which set up the NRA, was unconstitutional. Congress, the Court declared, had given too much power to the executive branch. Further, the power had been used to regulate intrastate*, not just interstate, commerce.

Roosevelt was stunned. The nation, he claimed, was being handed a "horse-and-buggy definition of interstate commerce." Yet he could not maintain the NRA. The Blue Eagle soon disappeared from American businesses.

THE SOCIAL SECURITY ACT

Congress was near adjournment in June 1935, but Roosevelt insisted that major new bills be passed first. The Senate then completed work on a Social Security Act, and Congress passed it in August. The act created a system of government aid to workers who lost their jobs or who retired. It also helped children, the handicapped, and the aged.

* intrastate: within a state

Workers covered by the act received retirement pensions when they were too old to work. Payment of the pensions would begin in 1940. Money for the pensions came from taxes on workers' wages and on employers' payrolls, beginning in 1937. The pension plan was involuntary—every covered worker had to take part. The taxes were collected and the pension checks were sent out by the federal government only, not by the states.

Needy people already over sixty-five years of age could not qualify for the federal pension. Instead, they were helped by federal money added to state pension plans. The Social Security Act worked in the same way to aid homeless children as well as the handicapped. It gave federal money to assist state programs.

If workers covered by the Social Security Act were fired or laid off, they could collect *unemployment compensation*. This payment of a certain amount of money for a fixed period of time gave workers some income between jobs. Unemployment compensation also was a federal-state program. Most of the money came from federal payroll taxes on businesses, but the money was paid out by the states.

The Social Security Act was the result of long planning by presidential advisers. They were led by Secretary of Labor Frances Perkins, the first woman

Frances Perkins dedicated her life to improving workers' conditions. She believed that change should come through legislation rather than through union activity.

ever to hold a cabinet position. She and the others expected the act to give "the greatest practical degree of economic security" to the people covered.

THE NATIONAL LABOR RELATIONS BOARD

Between 1935 and 1938 labor unions in the United States more than doubled their membership. One reason was the National Labor Relations Board (NLRB), created by Congress in July 1935. It supervised elections in which workers could vote to become union members.

The National Labor Relations Act that created the NLRB was introduced by Senator Robert F. Wagner of New York. Thus, the measure was also known as the Wagner Act. The act reaffirmed Section 7a of the National Industrial Recovery Act, which had been struck down by the Supreme Court. Once again the right of workers to join labor unions and to bargain collectively was guaranteed.

The act also encouraged union elections and blocked "unfair labor practices." The NLRB could take action against companies that refused to bargain with unions or that fired workers because of their union activities.

OTHER NEW DEAL MEASURES

Three other major bills became law during the summer. The Banking Act of 1935 gave the government more power to regulate the nation's banks. The Public Utilities Holding Company Act allowed the government to break up the large holding companies that dominated the gas and electric industry. For years these companies, which controlled other companies by buying their stock, had forced consumers to pay high rates and had evaded state laws. The Revenue Act of 1935 raised taxes on high personal incomes and on high company profits.

Another bill greatly changed the way Americans lived. The Emergency Relief Appropriation Act, passed in the spring, allowed Roosevelt to set up the Rural Electrification Administration (REA). At the time, only one eighth of all farm homes had electric service. The REA loaned electric companies money to construct power lines to farm areas. By 1940 electricity was flowing to about one third of all farm homes, and by 1945 to almost one half.

OPPOSITION TO THE NEW DEAL

Many people of wealth began to oppose Roosevelt, especially after the Revenue Act of 1935. Some people called it the "Soak the Rich" program. William Randolph Hearst, owner of a chain of newspapers, told his editors to use the words "Raw Deal" in place of "New Deal."

Some opponents of Roosevelt joined the American Liberty League. It had been formed in 1934 by conservative Republicans and Democrats who believed that the New Deal was too extreme. Among its leaders was Alfred E. Smith, the Democratic candidate for president in 1928.

Early in 1936 Smith delivered a slashing attack on the New Deal. A few weeks before his speech, the Supreme Court had struck down the Agricultural Adjustment Act, the major New Deal farm legislation. Smith said he knew why. Roosevelt's policies, he claimed, were disguised socialism. "That is the reason why the United States Supreme Court is working overtime throwing the alphabet out the window three letters at a time."

Roosevelt was undismayed. Congress quickly passed a new law to allow limits on crop production.

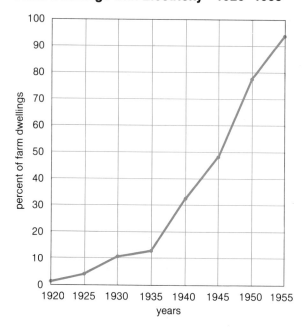

Farm Dwellings with Electricity   1920–1955

Nearly half of the nation's rural electric systems are operated by cooperatives and financed by REA loans.

The Second New Deal

Date	Agency or Program		Purpose	Status
April 8, 1935	NYA	National Youth Administration	Provide jobs and training for Americans 16–25 years of age	Ended in 1942
April 8, 1935	WPA	Works Progress Administration	Provide employment on public works projects	Ended in 1942
May 11, 1935	REA	Rural Electrification Administration	Aid farmers to electrify homes	Became part of Dept. of Agric. in 1939
July 5, 1935	NLRB	National Labor Relations Board	Guarantee rights of workers	Still in operation
August 14, 1935	SSB	Social Security Board	Provide a sound social security system	Still in operation

THE ELECTION OF 1936

Roosevelt went on the offensive in his 1936 election campaign. He criticized his opponents, especially rich conservatives who backed the American Liberty League. He scarcely mentioned his Republican opponent, Governor Alfred M. Landon of Kansas.

Landon faced a difficult struggle. His party was burdened with the public's memory of the crash and early depression. Landon lacked Roosevelt's skills as a campaigner. Moreover, the New Deal seemed to be working. After a year of stagnation, the economy had started moving again. Since the spring of 1935 a million more people had found jobs.

Republican leaders hoped that a new third party would take votes away from Roosevelt. The Union party, backed by Father Coughlin's National Union for Social Justice, was formed in the summer of 1936. William Lemke, a member of Congress from North Dakota, was its candidate for president.

The Union party appealed to the many followers of Coughlin, Townsend, and Long. However, the party never developed organized leadership. Long was shot and killed by a political enemy in the Louisiana capitol in September 1935. Townsend, Coughlin, and Lemke did not cooperate well enough to run an effective campaign.

In earlier elections the returns from Maine often matched the national voting. People believed in the saying, "As Maine goes, so goes the nation." In 1936 Roosevelt carried all but two states, Maine and Vermont. They went to Landon. Victorious Democrats now joked, "As Maine goes, so goes Vermont."

SECTION REVIEW

1. Identify the following: Townsend Clubs, NYA, Frances Perkins, Public Utilities Holding Company Act, REA, American Liberty League.

2. Define the following: intrastate, interstate, unemployment compensation.

3. (a) What were the provisions of the Townsend Plan? (b) List three criticisms Charles E. Coughlin had of the New Deal. (c) Explain the proposals of Huey Long's Share Our Wealth Society.

4. (a) Why did Roosevelt ask Congress for new legislation in 1935? (b) List eight kinds of projects WPA employees worked on. (c) How did the Second New Deal help America's needy youth?

5. (a) Explain why the Supreme Court declared the National Industrial Recovery Act unconstitutional. (b) How did Roosevelt react to the ruling?

6. (a) Name five groups of people who would benefit from the Social Security Act. (b) Who provided the money for the different parts of this plan?

7. (a) How did the creation of the National Labor Relations Board affect union membership? (b) Name two "unfair labor practices" blocked by the Wagner Act.

8. (a) Why did many people of wealth oppose the Revenue Act of 1935? (b) Why did the Union party fail to hurt Roosevelt's chances of reelection?

THE LAST YEARS OF THE NEW DEAL

READ TO FIND OUT

— how black Americans fared under the New Deal.

— how labor unions expanded in the 1930s.

— how government programs helped rural Americans.

— how Roosevelt tried to change the federal court system.

— why the Democratic coalition ended.

— how Roosevelt fought the recession of 1937-1938.

In 1936 Roosevelt won the greatest electoral majority since James Monroe's victory in 1820. Roosevelt gained 523 electoral votes to Landon's 8 and received more than 60 percent of the popular vote. The Democratic party increased its power in Congress for the fourth straight time since 1930.

Roosevelt could now work with a mighty coalition, or alliance, of Democrats in Congress. The coalition included southern conservatives and big-city liberals from the North. Behind the Democrats' election victories were many different voting groups. Some had long been loyal Democrats. Others, such as black voters, were transferring their loyalty to the Democratic side.

BLACK VOTERS AND ROOSEVELT

When the depression began, some 80 percent of all blacks lived in the South. There the Democratic party controlled most state and local governments. The party used its control to try to maintain all-white rule. Blacks often were prevented from voting, despite the Fifteenth Amendment.

To many blacks, the Republican party—the party of Lincoln—represented the old hopes of Reconstruction. Yet the Republicans offered no new policies to assure the rights of blacks as citizens. As the depression grew worse, blacks saw no purpose in

remaining loyal to the Republican party. Black voters, especially in the North, began supporting the Democrats.

Roosevelt welcomed the support, but he also needed the support of southern whites. After an outbreak of lynching in 1933, he would not push for an antilynching bill.

Roosevelt's economic programs did aid needy people, both black and white. Some of the programs practiced discrimination. The CCC, for example, restricted the number of blacks allowed in Roosevelt's "Tree Army." The WPA, though, offered work relief without such quotas. The NYA provided part-time jobs for thousands of young blacks as well as whites.

Roosevelt also opened his administration to black leaders. One was Mary McLeod Bethune, a noted educator. Beginning in 1936, she directed the Division of Negro Affairs of the NYA. She and others formed Roosevelt's "black cabinet," an informal group of advisers to the President. They tried to lessen discrimination in New Deal programs. So did Harold Ickes, head of the PWA.

Eleanor Roosevelt, the President's wife, also urged fair treatment for black Americans. An ex-

Mary McLeod Bethune influenced the course of black history for decades through education and politics. She worked especially for the rights of black women.

It was said of Marian Anderson, "A voice like hers comes once in a century." Her autobiography, *My Lord, What a Morning*, tells the story of her remarkable career.

most people who voted for Democratic candidates in the 1920s maintained their party loyalty in the 1930s.

Old-line Democrats had different backgrounds and motives. They included opponents of prohibition and believers in Woodrow Wilson's League of Nations. They also included big-city politicians and people who favored the Democrats simply through family tradition.

White voters in the states that once formed the Confederacy were old-line Democrats. Since the end of Reconstruction in 1877, these voters had elected Democrats in most elections. The pattern of southern voting almost broke in 1928. Majorities in five of the Old South states chose Herbert Hoover over Al Smith. But in the 1930s the voters resumed their usual party loyalty. Their region remained the Solid South, strongly Democratic.

Other old-line Democrats lived in big cities in the East and Midwest where Democratic political machines, or organizations, were in control. Such machines, whether Democratic or Republican, had developed the power to deliver votes on election day. In the 1930s Tom Pendergast ran the Democratic machine in Kansas City, Missouri. A foreigner once asked him to explain how he did it. Pendergast replied, "There's people that need things, lots of 'em, and I see to it that they get 'em."

UNION WORKERS

In the 1932 election John L. Lewis of the United Mine Workers backed the Republicans. In 1936 Lewis backed Roosevelt and the Democrats. By then Lewis's support meant a lot in election campaigns. His union had been growing, and he had become a key figure in the Committee for Industrial Organization (CIO). Later it was renamed the Congress of Industrial Organizations.

The CIO was formed following a bitter quarrel between Lewis and other leaders of the American Federation of Labor (AFL). For years the AFL had organized craft unions, which were composed of skilled workers such as machinists. Each of these unions represented one craft, or skill. Lewis demanded that the AFL organize industrial unions. Each industrial union represented workers, skilled and unskilled, who all held jobs in one industry.

Lewis's demand was rejected at the AFL convention in October 1935. The next month Lewis

ample of her concern was her support for singer Marian Anderson. In 1939 Anderson was denied permission to sing in a private hall in Washington, D.C. because she was black. In protest, a group of Americans sponsored a free concert by her at the Lincoln Memorial. The sponsors included artists, politicians, and Eleanor Roosevelt.

TRADITIONAL DEMOCRATIC VOTERS

Roosevelt lost the support of some old-line, or traditional, Democrats in 1936. Al Smith and others believed the New Deal had gone too far. However,

Through open windows at the General Motors plant in Flint, Michigan, strikers studied the activity outside. At this point the large crowd seemed quiet and orderly.

and seven other union leaders formed the CIO within the AFL. However, in the summer of 1936 the AFL and CIO split. The CIO unions showed their strength by giving more than $750,000 to the Democrats' campaign fund in 1936. Its workers helped Roosevelt win the vote in Illinois, Indiana, Ohio, and Pennsylvania.

EXPANDING LABOR UNIONS

Ambitious to expand the CIO, Lewis set up the Steel Workers Organizing Committee in 1936. Its prime target was the giant of the industry, the United States Steel Corporation. If that company could be unionized, other steel companies were likely to follow.

Before the steelworkers were ready to strike, another CIO group acted. Auto workers in Flint, Michigan, suddenly took over several plants owned by General Motors. The workers refused to leave the factories until the company agreed to bargain with the United Auto Workers, a CIO union.

Like other auto makers of the time, General Motors fought the growth of labor unions. The company hired private detectives to scare away union organizers. It also encouraged workers to spy on one another and to report union sympathizers. Workers had long resented the high speed of assembly lines at General Motors. However, if they complained or talked about organizing a union, they were likely to be fired.

Yet the strikers in Flint had one special advantage. Instead of walking out, they were staging a *sit-down strike* inside the General Motors plants. If

the company tried removing them by force, it risked damaging its own property.

The sit-down in Flint, which started on December 30, 1936, was the first large-scale strike of its kind in the United States. The strikers wanted the public to know what the strike was about. "We don't aim to keep the plants or try to run them," a striker told a reporter. "But we want to see that nobody takes our jobs."

Pickets outside the plant passed food to the strikers inside. At night some of the strikers kept watch while the others slept on car seats. "It was like we were soldiers holding the fort," a worker said. In January city police tried unsuccessfully to force the strikers out of one plant.

The sit-down strike went on until February 11, 1937. Then the two sides signed an agreement allowing the union to organize General Motors workers. By the end of April the union had reached similar agreements with other auto makers. Ford, however, resisted the union until 1941. In that same month, Lewis's Steel Workers Organizing Committee won recognition from the United States Steel Corporation. By the end of 1937, CIO unions had organized much of American industry.

RESULTS OF UNION GROWTH

The success of the CIO tended to strengthen the Democratic party. Hundreds of thousands of industrial workers joined the CIO unions. The workers were grateful to the party that had passed the Wagner Act and had created the NLRB to oversee union growth.

At the same time, many voters worried that the unions were going too far. The success of the Flint strike set off a wave of sit-downs. Alarmed by the increasing takeover of private property, people lost sympathy with the strikers. Many people blamed Roosevelt for allowing the wave of strikes to continue.

The number of sit-down strikes declined after 1937. These strikes were outlawed in 1939 when the Supreme Court ruled that they were a violation of property rights.

RURAL VOTERS

Roosevelt's coalition of Democrats in Congress required the support of many rural voters. These voters made up nearly 45 percent of the total electorate in the 1930s. In many states the percentage was much higher.

Rural voters judged the New Deal mainly by the success of its farm agencies. When the AAA was able to increase the prices of major crops, the voters were impressed. Many changed their party loyalty to support New Deal Democrats.

The Democrats' standing with rural voters was threatened in January 1936. That month the Supreme Court halted the work of the Agricultural Adjustment Administration. Money paid to farmers by the agency had come from a special tax on businesses that processed farm products. The court ruled that the tax took "money from one group for the benefit of another." Thus the act authorizing the AAA was unconstitutional.

In February Congress acted to replace the AAA crop programs. It passed the Soil Conservation and Domestic Allotment Act. This act allowed the government to pay farmers for limiting their crops for the purpose of conservation. Farmers would receive money for growing soil-conserving plants such as clover instead of growing soil-depleting plants such as wheat and cotton. The new act, however, proved ineffective. Not enough farmers took part, and surplus cotton and wheat sent farm prices tumbling.

After two years, Congress revived the old law with some changes. The Agricultural Adjustment Act of 1938 called for farm payments from the federal treasury, not from a special tax. In years of good harvests the government would buy and store surplus crops. In lean years the government would release the crops for sale. In this way crop prices would stay close to parity—government-supported prices that gave farmers about the same buying power that the sale of the crops had given them in the good years from 1909 to 1914.

TENANT FARMERS AND MIGRANTS

The new agricultural act affected only farm owners. In 1937 Congress passed a separate law to help those who were renting farmland. The Bankhead-Jones Farm Tenant Act set up the Farm Security Ad-

An Oklahoma family, too poor to own an automobile, carted their meager possessions down a highway in 1938. Like thousands of other migrants, they had no special destination. Many simply headed "west."

ministration (FSA). It made long-term, low-interest loans to qualified tenants and sharecroppers who wanted to buy their own farms.

The FSA also helped the migrant farm workers who crowded the highways and farmlands of the West. Some, including people from Arkansas, were called "Arkies." They had been evicted from the farmland they rented. Others, including people from Oklahoma, were called "Okies." They had abandoned their farms in the Dust Bowl, the area stuck hardest by drought and dust storms.

Okies and Arkies traveled west to Washington, Oregon, and California, looking for any kind of work. The farm jobs that they found usually lasted for a few weeks only and paid low wages. "This is a hard life to swallow," an Okie said, "but I just couldn't sit back there and look to someone to feed us."

By the late 1930s a million migrants were seeking work. Their plight was not widely known until John Steinbeck wrote about them. His novel *The Grapes of Wrath*, published in 1939, opened people's eyes to

AMERICAN OBSERVERS

DOROTHEA LANGE
DOCUMENTING THE DEPRESSION

When the depression began, Dorothea Lange was a successful portrait photographer in San Francisco, California. However, her work seemed unimportant in such difficult times. From her studio window she often watched a breadline, where people without jobs waited for food. "I looked as long as I could," she remembered. Finally, grabbing her camera, she went outside to photograph the scene.

During the next years, Lange continued to photograph the victims of the Great Depression. Working mainly for the United States Farm Security Administration, she traveled throughout rural California, the South, and the Dust Bowl.

From the first Dorothea Lange had a special rapport with the people that she photographed. They trusted her and wanted her to know their stories. Lange had had polio as a child and walked with a limp. In school in New York City, she had always been an outsider, painfully conscious of her lame leg. Now it became a link with these proud, often desperate people, who were crippled in a different way.

Lange's most famous photograph came at the end of a month's travel to California migrant camps. Exhausted, she was driving home at last, when she glimpsed a crude sign, "Pea Pickers' Camp." She hurried on, but the sign stayed in her mind. Twenty miles beyond, she turned around. "I was following instinct, not reason," she said.

At the camp she was drawn to a woman sitting in a ragged tent. The woman told Lange that the pea crop had frozen, so there was no work. She and her

children were living on wild birds and frozen peas from the fields.

"Migrant Mother"—the picture Lange took of this worn young woman with her hungry children—became the most published photograph of the time. Through it, Lange brought home to all Americans the tragedy of the depression.

Occupants of migrant camps fought a constant battle against the weather and poor sanitary conditions. Uncertain work, poverty, and sickness plagued these families.

the suffering of these displaced families. The FSA provided some medical care and clean camps for the migrants.

The migrant workers in the West included American citizens with Mexican backgrounds. Many had been forced to give up farms of their own during the hard times. Immigrant workers from Mexico were a smaller group. Although a large number entered the United States in the 1920s, the Great Depression caused a reverse migration. Some 300,000 Mexican workers and their families left the United States in the 1930s.

THE INDIAN REORGANIZATION ACT

Indians living on reservations were also rural voters. All Indians enjoyed full United States citizenship following the Snyder Act of 1924. However, their traditional ways of life were not respected. The federal government had tried for years to make them give up tribal ways.

Policy changed in the 1930s as the Indian Reorganization Act of 1934 halted the breaking up of tribes and tribal lands. Indian Commissioner John Collier encouraged self-government on the reservations. He expressed the heart of the new policy: "We find the Indians, in all the basic forces and forms of life, human beings like ourselves. . . . Just as we yearn to live out our own lives in our own ways, so, too, do the Indians, in their ways."

ROOSEVELT'S SECOND TERM

Roosevelt's first term produced sweeping new programs. The New Deal was established by the laws of the Hundred Days in 1933. It was extended by the laws of the second New Deal in 1935. After the Democrats' great election victory in 1936, it seemed that the New Deal would be extended still further in Roosevelt's second term.

"I see one-third of a nation ill-housed, ill-clad, ill-nourished," Roosevelt proclaimed in his inaugural speech in January 1937. He promised to meet this challenge. However, Roosevelt faltered as a leader in 1937. His great coalition in Congress fell apart. His popularity slipped sharply. And the laws he called for failed to appear.

One cause of his problems was the wave of sit-down strikes which began in the auto plants in Flint, Michigan. The strikes soon spread to industries producing rubber, steel, oil, ships, and textiles. Some people feared that the strikes were a step toward communism. Others simply believed that the sit-down strikes were unfair to employers. Roosevelt disliked the strikes, but he would not call out troops to stop them. As a result he lost some support in Congress and in the nation.

THE SUPREME COURT CONTROVERSY

A more direct cause of Roosevelt's problems was his attempt to change the federal court system. He planned to modify court procedures, to add extra judges to the federal courts, and to increase the number of justices on the Supreme Court. He kept his plan secret until February 1937. Then he sent the plan to Congress as a measure to increase court efficiency.

Under the plan, Roosevelt would be able to add an extra justice to the Supreme Court for each one who reached the age of seventy and did not retire. The plan limited the extra justices to a total of six. Thus if Congress approved, the President might increase the number of Supreme Court justices from nine to as many as fifteen.

Few in Congress believed that efficiency was Roosevelt's true motive. The Supreme Court had struck down the NRA in 1935 and the AAA in 1936. It seemed likely to strike down the NLRB and the Social Security Act. What Roosevelt really wanted, opponents declared, were more justices who shared his ideas about the constitutionality of the New Deal.

Roosevelt's plan shocked many members of Congress. It also upset many voters. The opponents of the plan called it a scheme for "packing" the Supreme Court to favor the executive branch. They warned that it would destroy the balance of powers established by the Constitution.

Roosevelt argued that his plan must pass to save the New Deal and economic recovery from an old-fashioned Supreme Court. However, two events weakened the President's argument. In April the Supreme Court upheld the Wagner Act. The decision allowed the NLRB to continue operating. The decision also made it doubtful that Roosevelt's court plan was necessary to protect New Deal legislation. In fact, in the next weeks the Supreme Court upheld other New Deal laws, including the Social Security Act.

In May Supreme Court Justice Van Devanter announced his retirement from the bench. That allowed Roosevelt to name a new justice without the passage of the court plan. However, Roosevelt kept on fighting for the plan. He did not give up until August, when Congress passed a much weaker bill than he had asked for. The bill changed court procedures, but it did not allow Roosevelt to appoint extra judges to the lower courts or extra justices to the Supreme Court.

THE END OF THE DEMOCRATIC COALITION

The "court-packing" controversy split the Democratic coalition. Conservative Democrats, many from the South, joined Republicans in blocking the President's plan.

The controversy also wasted Roosevelt's time. He did not push for many new bills until October. Then he called Congress into special session, just as he had in 1933 and 1935. Congress met for five weeks in November and December of 1937, but it did not pass any bill that Roosevelt recommended. Again conservative Democrats joined with Republicans to thwart the President's wishes.

Although Roosevelt lost his court fight, he was able to appoint a majority of Supreme Court justices before long. Vacancies on the court let him name five new justices during his second term.

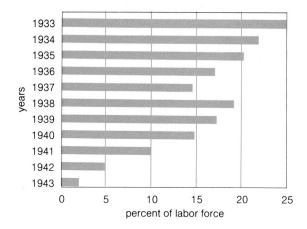

Unemployment   1933–1943

THE RECESSION OF 1937–1938

As the court-packing controversy was ending in August 1937, a worse problem appeared. Instead of continuing its slow rise out of the Great Depression, the economy slumped badly. The stock market fell, and in four months it lost all the gains of two years.

One reason for the slump, or decline, was Roosevelt's decision to reduce federal spending. In June 1937 he cut funding for the WPA. He also cut PWA funds. Both steps led to reduced consumer spending. So did the new social security taxes on workers as well as employers.

When the government cut its spending, business did not take up the slack by making new investments. In order to reduce the amount of money in circulation, the Federal Reserve Board had raised interest rates on loans. This "tight money" policy made business loans expensive. Wage increases won by labor unions also worried businesses.

Instead of expanding, business cut back on spending. Just one year after the sit-down strike at Flint, Michigan, General Motors laid off 30,000 workers. The company put other workers on a 3-day week. All in all, 2 million workers lost their jobs during the recession. The unemployment rate soared close to 20 percent.

As unemployment grew, so did relief rolls. In Chicago the number of people on relief more than doubled in the first five months of 1938. The Democrats, who had taken credit for the recovery, now were blamed for the "Roosevelt depression."

In April 1938 Roosevelt decided to fight the economic decline with **deficit spending**—a policy of spending more money than the government received in taxes. The President asked Congress to pump money into the economy. In June Congress approved almost $1.5 billion for the WPA and almost $1 billion for the PWA.

A few days after it approved the billions in spending, Congress passed the Fair Labor Standards Act. This act affected large groups of workers who were paid by the hour. It set a minimum hourly wage and a maximum number of hours per workweek, with time-and-a-half pay for overtime. When the act took effect in August, it raised the wages of 750,000 people.

CONGRESSIONAL ELECTIONS OF 1938

In the summer of 1938 the economy resumed its slow recovery. Roosevelt then set out to stage a recovery of his own. His authority with Congress had declined because of the recession, the sit-down strikes, and the court controversy.

The President campaigned actively in certain Democratic primaries in 1938. He gave speeches for liberal Democrats in half a dozen states, mostly in the South. He hoped to bring about the defeat of conservative Democrats who opposed the bills that he sent to Congress. However, in about half the campaigns, Roosevelt's candidates lost. The primary results were another blow to his prestige.

In the regular elections in 1938 the Democrats lost 7 seats in the Senate and 80 in the House of Representatives. A defeated Democrat explained: "The prosperity for which the American people have been yearning for more than a decade has failed to make its appearance. It is still around the corner."

Despite their losses, the Democrats retained large majorities in both the House and the Senate. Yet the real power in Congress was balanced between liberal Democrats and conservative Democrats plus Republicans. The liberals passed the Administrative Reorganization Act of 1939, giving Roosevelt a streamlined executive branch. The conservatives passed the Hatch Act in 1939. It resulted from charges that some WPA workers tried to influence votes in the 1938 elections. The act declared that most government workers could not take an active part in political campaigning.

For the most part, though, liberals and conservatives faced each other in a standoff. Roosevelt, two years after his great election victory, could not achieve further reforms. Conservatives could not undo the major programs he had already established. And by 1939 politicians on both sides were turning away from domestic worries. They were increasingly concerned with the distant rumblings of war.

SECTION REVIEW

1. Identify the following: Mary McLeod Bethune, Marian Anderson, CIO, AFL, old-line Democrats, Fair Labor Standards Act.

2. Define the following: coalition, craft union, industrial union, sit-down strike, deficit spending.

3. (a) Why did black voters turn away from the Republican party in the 1930s? (b) Explain how some of Roosevelt's economic programs helped blacks while others did not.

4. (a) Why was the CIO organized within the AFL? (b) What caused the split between the two organizations?

5. (a) What special advantage did the strikers at the Flint, Michigan, General Motors plants have? (b) Why was the success of this strike so important?

6. (a) Why were CIO members loyal to the Democratic party? (b) What worries did many voters have about unions? (c) Why did the Supreme Court outlaw sit-down strikes?

7. (a) Why was the Soil Conservation and Domestic Allotment Act ineffective? (b) What were the provisions of the Agricultural Adjustment Act of 1938?

8. (a) How did the Farm Security Administration help farm renters and migrant workers? (b) What caused the reverse migration of Mexican workers in the 1930s? (c) What was the purpose of the Indian Reorganization Act of 1934?

9. (a) Name three ways in which Roosevelt planned to change the federal court system. (b) What did many members of Congress believe was Roosevelt's real motive for changing the system? (c) Explain the effects of the "court-packing" controversy on the Democratic coalition.

10. (a) Why did the economy begin to slump in mid-1937? (b) How did Roosevelt fight the economic decline?

SUMMARY

The months between Franklin D. Roosevelt's election and his inauguration were difficult ones for Americans. Early in 1933 banks began to go out of business, causing depositors to panic. By the time of the inauguration, many states had closed their banks. In his inaugural speech, Roosevelt promised speedy action against the Great Depression. The next day he called Congress into an emergency session.

During the first Hundred Days, Congress passed legislation to aid the nation's banking system. To help business and agriculture, Congress set up the National Recovery Administration and the Agricultural Adjustment Administration. Direct relief was provided for needy Americans. Jobs were also provided. Finally, Congress set up the Tennessee Valley Authority.

Some Americans believed that the New Deal was too extreme. Others thought that it was not extreme enough since it had not ended the Depression. In 1935 Congress passed a new program of legislation, known as the second New Deal.

The Works Progress Administration was set up to provide jobs for Americans. The Social Security Act was passed to give government aid to the unemployed, children, the handicapped, and the aged. The National Labor Relations Board was created to protect workers' rights. Other legislation led to regulation of banks and public utilities and to expansion of electric service.

With the second New Deal, opposition to Roosevelt became stronger. Also, the Supreme Court struck down two major pieces of New Deal legislation. Still, Roosevelt won reelection in 1936. He was supported by a coalition of southerners, northerners, blacks, union workers, and rural voters.

New Deal laws helped unions to expand during the 1930s. Farmers, tenant farmers, sharecroppers, and migrants also were aided by New Deal legislation in 1937 and 1938. However, Roosevelt's attempt to change the federal court system split the Democratic coalition. In addition, Americans blamed the recession of 1937–1938 on Roosevelt. In the congressional elections of 1938 many candidates who had Roosevelt's support lost. Roosevelt was not able to achieve further reforms.

The Blue Eagle symbolized fair practices for business and industry. It lost its impact in 1935 when the NRA was declared unconstitutional.

CHAPTER REVIEW

1. (a) Explain how each event led to the next: poor banking investments, bank failures, currency hoarding, bank holidays, runs on banks. (b) During the Great Depression what conditions made banks likely to fail?

2. (a) Why was little done to help Americans in late 1932 and early 1933? (b) Describe three ways in which Roosevelt attempted to restore Americans' confidence during his first ten days in office.

3. (a) How did the National Recovery Administration and the Agricultural Adjustment Administration seek to revive American business and agriculture? (b) What methods did each agency use? (c) How successful were the agencies? (d) Why did the Supreme Court declare both agencies unconstitutional?

4. How did each of the following change American business practices? (a) the Glass-Steagall Banking Act (b) the Federal Securities Act (c) the Securities Exchange Act (d) the Public Utilities Holding Company Act

5. (a) Describe two kinds of relief that the New Deal offered to needy Americans. (b) How did the programs differ? Cite examples of each. (c) How did the programs affect the economy?

6. Explain how each of the following affected Roosevelt's plans in 1935. (a) Francis R. Townsend (b) Charles E. Coughlin (c) Huey Long (d) the economy

7. In 1934 Roosevelt called for legislation to provide for "the security of the men, women, and children of the nation." In what ways did the

RESETTLEMENT ADMINISTRATION
Rescues Victims
Restores Land to Proper Use

A Ben Shahn poster captures the despair of the Dust Bowl victims. The loss of valuable top soil in thick, choking dust storms prompted federal soil conservation programs.

Works Progress Administration and the Social Security Act satisfy that goal?

8. (a) How did the National Labor Relations Act protect workers and unions? (b) Describe the expansion of the Congress of Industrial Organizations in 1936 and 1937. (c) How did Americans react to union tactics?

9. Explain why each of the following contributed to Roosevelt's reelection in 1936. (a) the economy (b) black voters (c) old-line Democrats (d) union workers (e) rural voters

10. In 1936 Roosevelt was reelected by an overwhelming majority, Two years later, he was unable to gain reform legislation from Congress. Describe three reasons for this change.

ISSUES AND IDEAS

1. Roosevelt advised farmers that the cure to the cycle of surplus crops, low prices, and farm bankruptcy was "not to produce so much." Why was this cure difficult for farmers to accept? Consider farmers' goals in earlier times, such as the 1860s and 1870s and the World War I years.

2. Some historians think that the aims of the New Deal were not new. Instead, these aims were part of previous reform movements, such as populism and progressivism. Do you agree? Why or why not? Cite examples to support your conclusions.

3. In the presidential campaign of 1932, Hoover warned that the Democrats were proposing "changes and so-called new deals which would destroy the very foundations of our American system." What did Hoover mean? Do you think that Hoover's fears were justified? Why or why not?

SKILLS WORKSHOP

1. *Timelines.* Make a timeline of labor advances during the 1930s. Include legislation that affected workers and events that affected the union movement. Describe briefly each piece of legislation or event, and explain its effects.

2. *Charts.* Make a chart of New Deal legislation. Use three headings—"Recovery," "Reform," and "Relief"—and list each piece of legislation in the appropriate category. Some items might fit in more than one category. Below the chart describe briefly the particular laws that vastly changed the role of the federal government.

PAST AND PRESENT

1. Find out whether the Works Progress Administration or other New Deal work-relief agencies were active in or near your community. If so, what projects did the agencies undertake? How did the projects affect the people of the community?

2. What New Deal programs are still functioning today? How would you and your family be affected if the programs did not exist?

The design quality of poster art was raised to a new high by members of the WPA Federal Art Project Poster Divisions. This poster is a good example of their work.

SHADOWS OF WAR

1920–1945

Felix de Weldon, after a photograph by Joseph Rosenthal. *Marine Corps War Memorial,* dedicated 1954. Photo by William Weems.

1600	1700	1800	1900	2000

- Jamestown founded
- Revolutionary War
- Civil War
- Today

UNIT 8
1920–1945

1925	1930	1935	1940	1945

Harding | Coolidge | Hoover | Roosevelt

POLITICAL

- Dawes plan
- Kellogg-Briand Pact
- Good Neighbor policy
- Selective Training and Service Act
- Lend-Lease Act
- Office of Price Administration
- Office of War Mobilization

SOCIAL

- Sinclair Lewis: Nobel prize for literature
- "Star-Spangled Banner" named national anthem
- Orson Welles: "Invasion from Mars"
- Pearl Buck: Nobel prize for literature
- Richard Wright: *Native Son*
- Ernie Pyle: *Here Is Your War*

TECHNOLOGICAL

- Planet Pluto discovered
- First TV broadcasts
- First jet planes
- Self-sustaining nuclear reaction
- Streptomycin
- Atomic bomb developed

INTERNATIONAL

- Washington Naval Conference
- Mussolini: premier of Italy
- Japan invades Manchuria
- Hitler: chancellor of Germany
- Spanish Civil War begins
- Japan invades China
- Germany annexes Austria
- Germany attacks Poland
- World War II begins
- U.S. enters World War II
- D-Day

1925	1930	1935	1940	1945

CHAPTER 23

A FRAGILE PEACE

1920–1941

THE SEARCH FOR PERMANENT PEACE
A WORLD CHANGED BY WAR
EUROPE GOES TO WAR
THE END OF ISOLATION

On March 12, 1938, German ruler Adolf Hitler took the first step toward annexing Austria to Germany. An American journalist named Dorothy Thompson wrote an urgent cry of warning to Americans.

"Write it down. On Saturday, February 12, 1938, nazism started on the march across all of Europe east of the Rhine.

"Write it down that the world revolution began in earnest—and perhaps the world war. . . .

"And it never needed to have happened. One strong voice of one strong power could have stopped it.

"Tomorrow, one of two things can happen. Despotism can settle into horrible stagnation. . . . Perhaps, then, all of Europe east of the Rhine will become, eventually, a no-man's land of poverty, militarism and futility. But nonetheless a plague spot.

"More likely the other law of despotism's nature—the law of perpetual aggressiveness—will cause it to move . . . onward, emboldened, and strengthened, by each success.

"To the point where civilization will take a last stand. For take a stand it will. Of that there is not the slightest doubt.

"Too bad that it did not take it this week."

To Thompson, the world in the 1930s was threatened by dictators on a march of conquest. Nations in Europe, Africa, and Asia were crushed by invading armies.

In the United States, few Americans heeded Dorothy Thompson's warning that they would have to take a stand. After World War I, they had sworn that never again would American lives be lost in someone else's war. World War I, however, had thrust the United States to the center of the world stage. Would Americans accept the leading role?

THE SEARCH FOR PERMANENT PEACE

READ TO FIND OUT

— why the arms race grew after World War I.

— how efforts were made to end the arms race.

— how the Kellogg-Briand Pact sought to prevent future wars.

— how the United States began to withdraw from Latin American affairs.

In 1917 Americans had gone to war for ideals like democracy, honor, and freedom. The world had not seemed very interested in these ideals. Now, most Americans wanted only to forget the war and the problems of Europe. They preferred to avoid all foreign entanglements—a policy that became known as **isolationism**.

However, the United States had emerged from the war as the world's leading economic power. Ties of trade linked the nation to many corners of the globe. It would not be easy to isolate the United States from the world.

THE ARMS RACE

The United States had turned down membership in the League of Nations by rejecting the Treaty of Versailles. Slowly, however, American distrust of the League began to soften. By 1923 American experts unofficially attended League meetings on issues such as health and international trade. The United States did not intend to withhold its support of the good that the League would accomplish.

The United States never did join the League, but it did consider joining the League's judicial arm. The Permanent Court of International Justice, known as the World Court, was open to nonmembers of the League. The Senate considered resolutions for membership several times, but every time rejected the idea.

In rejecting membership in the League of Nations, the United States did not reject the cause of peace. On the contrary, most Americans were horrified by the idea of another war. They wanted peace and prosperity. Both aims, however, conflicted with an **arms race**—a race to build weapons—that began after the war.

In 1918 Britain had the world's largest navy, the United States had the second largest, and Japan had the third largest. Japan had emerged from the war with a good deal of territory—the Shantung (Shandong) Peninsula in China, the eastern part of Siberia in Russia, and several islands in the Pacific.

To Americans, Japanese moves in Asia seemed to be a threat to the Open Door policy that guaranteed China's independence. American naval experts worried that the Philippines, America's possession in the Pacific, might be Japan's next target. To protect their interests, both Japan and the United States launched a huge shipbuilding program.

By 1921 many Americans feared that the arms race would lead to war. Furthermore, the cost of building ships was a crushing burden to taxpayers, who were calling for tax relief. Neither Britain nor Japan could afford the naval race either. The three nations cautiously searched for a way to end the race.

WILL ROGERS
THE COWBOY PHILOSOPHER

When Will Rogers was growing up in Indian Territory, he was already known for his wit. "I never saw him get up in front of a class without making them laugh," a schoolmate remembered. Born in 1879, the eighth child of a properous rancher, Rogers was part Cherokee Indian. "My ancestors didn't come on the *Mayflower*," he said, "but they met the boat."

As a boy Rogers dreamed of becoming a champion rope twirler. In his teens he performed in roping contests, rodeos, and Wild West shows. Eventually he had his own vaudeville act, complete with a pony named Teddy.

When Rogers added talk to his routine, he found that his audiences enjoyed his down-to-earth humor even more than his skill with a lasso. His material changed daily, according to the news. He poked fun at politicians and commented on the international scene. "I don't make jokes," he said. "I just watch the government and report the facts and I have never found it necessary to exaggerate." Soon he was doing radio shows, movies, and a newspaper column.

His warm humor made his name a household word in the 1920s and early 1930s. Like most Americans, he thought that the United States should stay out of world affairs. "We never lost a war and we never won a conference," he noted after an international meeting. "Who is the next country wants their affairs regulated?" he joked when he felt that the United States was too involved in Latin America. He traveled to observe the Japanese-Chinese war in Manchuria. "America could hunt all over the world and not find a better fight to keep out of," he warned.

On a trip to Alaska in 1935, Will Rogers was killed in a plane crash. The whole nation mourned his death. "A smile," said a friend, "has disappeared from the lips of America."

THE WASHINGTON NAVAL CONFERENCE

In July 1921 President Harding called a conference to discuss both naval limitations and the situation in Asia. Nine nations—naval powers and others with interests in Asia—sent delegates to Washington, D.C. in November.

Chairing the Washington conference was the American secretary of state, Charles Evans Hughes. Hughes stunned the delegates by calling for a 10-year halt in shipbuilding. He also proposed that the United States, Britain, and Japan scrap a total of 66 armored battleships.

For 12 weeks the delegates labored to work out the details, and produced several treaties. The Five-Power Treaty followed Hughes's plan to reduce the numbers of battleships. For every 5 United States ships, Britain was allowed 5, Japan 3, and France and Italy 1.75 ships each. Britain, Japan, and the United States would scrap whatever ships were necessary to achieve their 5:5:3 ratio. No new battleships would be built for 10 years.

In the Four-Power Treaty, Japan, Britain, France, and the United States agreed to respect one another's rights in their island colonies in the Pacific. They also agreed to consult if there was any "aggressive action" in the Pacific. Japan, however,

Pacifists urged the use of international law and diplomacy to settle disputes among nations. Pacifist groups were most active between the two world wars.

signed the treaty with a condition. The United States and Britain had to pledge not to fortify any of their island colonies in the Pacific, except Hawaii and islands near British territory.

Other agreements dealt with Asia. In the Nine-Power Treaty, all of the nations at the conference agreed to uphold the Open Door policy. All pledged to respect China's independence. In other negotiations, Japan promised to withdraw from China's Shantung (Shandong) Peninsula and from Russian Siberia.

The Washington Naval Conference did not guarantee peace. Naval limits applied only to heavy battleships, not to submarines and light surface ships. Furthermore, enforcement of the treaties was left up to the good faith of the signing nations. Still, the conference eased tension in Asia.

THE GENEVA CONFERENCE

In February 1927 President Coolidge proposed that the nations that had signed the Five-Power Treaty meet again to limit further naval building. France and Italy both refused.

Therefore, only the United States, Britain, and Japan attended the conference, which opened in June 1927 in Geneva, Switzerland. For weeks, the delegates argued over details. In early August, the conference ended in failure.

Because the other powers seemed intent on continuing the naval race, the United States decided to build up its own strength. In February 1929 Congress authorized the construction of 15 cruisers. It was the largest naval bill since the war.

THE KELLOGG-BRIAND PACT

While peace through disarmament was proving a failure, people were exploring other paths to peace. One idea was simply to make war a crime.

In 1927 an American peace leader interested the French foreign minister, Aristide Briand (bree-AHN), in the idea. Briand promptly announced that France was ready to sign such an agreement to outlaw war. American Secretary of State Frank B. Kellogg also agreed to the proposal. In August 1928 delegates from 15 nations met in Paris to sign the Kellogg-Briand Pact. They agreed to renounce war "as an instrument of national policy" and to solve all their disputes peacefully. Eventually, a total of 64 nations signed the pact.

Critics, however, complained that the pact was worthless. Indeed, most powers added reservations to the pact, stating their right to go to war in self-defense. Also, the pact did not set up any means of enforcing the pledges to renounce war.

UNITED STATES INTERESTS IN LATIN AMERICA

America's search for a way to preserve peace was not its only interest in foreign affairs in the 1920s. In fact, there was one area of the world that was an exception to the American policy of isolation. This was Latin America.

Ever since the early 1900s, the United States had been involved in Latin America. Theodore Roosevelt's Corollary to the Monroe Doctrine in 1904 promised the world that the United States would keep order in Latin America. And so it did. When problems arose in Latin American nations, the United States stepped in.

When President Harding took office in 1921, United States troops remained in the Dominican Republic, Haiti, and Nicaragua. By 1924 the United States was managing the treasuries of ten Latin American nations.

Also, a web of business ties linked the United States with its neighbors. Yankee companies had branches in Latin American factories and mines. Latin America was a good market for Yankee machines and automobiles. In return, the United States bought Latin American coffee, sugar, bananas, rubber, tin, copper, and oil.

Charles Evans Hughes, secretary of state to both Harding and Coolidge, intended to protect the interests of the United States in Latin America, under the Roosevelt Corollary. Still, he tried to reassure Latin Americans, saying, "We covet no territory; we seek no conquest." Hughes and the leaders of the Dominican Republic worked out plans to hold elections there, and in 1924 United States troops left that nation.

NICARAGUA

The United States had particular interest in Nicaragua because of its closeness to the Panama Canal. President Taft had first intervened in that nation in 1912 to help Nicaraguan president Adolfo Díaz (DEE-ahs) stay in power and to aid the nation in paying off its debts. By 1925 Nicaragua had paid off its debts and seemed to be stable, so Coolidge withdrew the marines.

However, rebel forces immediately mounted a fresh attack on the Nicaraguan government. Coolidge rushed troops back to Nicaragua to protect United States property, and sent arms to Díaz to keep the regime in power. The intervention set off protests in the United States and Latin America against Coolidge's "private war."

Finally, in 1927, Coolidge dispatched a representative to Nicaragua to bring about an agreement between the government and the rebels. Coo-

lidge's representative managed to arrange a truce and an election. United States troops stayed in Nicaragua until 1933 to help keep order in the country.

MEXICO

The United States also had to mend relations with Mexico. President Wilson's interference in 1916 in the Mexican Revolution had left bitter feelings on both sides of the border. Then, during World War I, Mexico's friendship with Germany had angered the United States.

Even more annoying to the United States was a section of Mexico's new constitution. It limited foreign buying of property in Mexico. It also stated that the Mexican government could take control of all oil lands, some of which were owned by Americans. The United States demanded that the property of American citizens in Mexico be protected. For years, successive governments on both sides argued over the issue.

Then, in 1927, relations were further strained when Mexico backed the rebel forces in Nicaragua. In addition, oil companies were demanding that the United States send troops into Mexico to protect their property. Neither Congress nor Coolidge wanted war.

In the fall of 1927 Coolidge named an old college friend, lawyer Dwight W. Morrow, as ambassador to Mexico. Morrow proved to be a skilled diplomat and worked with the Mexicans to solve the dispute over oil rights. Mexico decided to let United States companies keep all oil lands that they had owned before 1917. Thanks to Morrow, relations between the two nations improved a good deal.

American marines drew little attention on this Nicaraguan street in 1927. The marines' presence helped to maintain peace within the unsettled country.

UNITED STATES POLICY UNDER HOOVER

Coolidge's successor, Herbert Hoover, was determined to build good will between the United States and Latin America. Soon after winning the presidential election in 1928, Hoover set off on a ten-week tour of Latin America. In speeches Hoover said that he wanted the United States and the nations of Latin America to be "good neighbors."

Hoover's administration gave solid proof of its good will toward Latin America. In 1930 it issued a memorandum, or statement, that had been drawn up two years earlier by Under Secretary of State J. Reuben Clark. The Clark Memorandum stated that the United States did not have the right to intervene militarily in Latin American nations as it had under the Roosevelt Corollary to the Monroe Doctrine. Latin Americans were pleased with the memorandum, but they waited to see its effect.

The next year Panama, Cuba, and Honduras were shaken by revolutions. Hoover upheld the new policy and did not send troops. Hoover also approved plans to withdraw the marines from Nicaragua and Haiti. "I have no desire," Hoover stated, "for representation of the American government abroad through our military forces."

ROOSEVELT AND THE GOOD NEIGHBOR POLICY

When Franklin D. Roosevelt took office as president in 1933, he adopted Hoover's friendly attitude toward Latin America. "I would dedicate this nation," he said, "to the policy of the good neighbor."

In 1933 Roosevelt sent a delegation to the Seventh Pan-American Conference at Montevideo, Uruguay. Suspicious of United States intentions, the Latin Americans supported a proposal that "no state has the right to intervene in the internal or external affairs of another." Secretary of State Cordell Hull of the United States delegation voted for the proposal.

In 1934 the United States and Cuba signed a treaty canceling the Platt Amendment of 1901. The Platt Amendment had allowed the United States to intervene in Cuba to maintain law and order. In exchange for the cancellation, Cuba agreed that the United States could keep its naval base at Guantanamo Bay.

The next year, Roosevelt followed Hoover's plan to remove the marines from Haiti. For the first time in many years, there were no United States troops in Latin America. And in 1936 the United States gave up its right, by an earlier treaty, to intervene in Panama.

In a speech that year, Roosevelt expressed his belief that the "Good Neighbor" policy was indeed a success:

> Throughout the Americas the spirit of the good neighbor is a practical and living fact. The twenty-one American republics are not only living together in friendship and in peace—they are united in the determination so to remain.

SECTION REVIEW

1. Identify the following: the Five-Power Treaty, the Four-Power Treaty, the Nine-Power Treaty, Dwight W. Morrow, J. Reuben Clark.

2. (a) Why were Americans worried about Japanese moves in Asia after World War I? (b) List two reasons why, by 1921, Americans were concerned about the arms race.

3. (a) What proposal did the American secretary of state make at the Washington Naval Conference? (b) Why did the conference not guarantee peace?

4. (a) What was the purpose of the Geneva Conference? (b) Why did the conference fail? (c) What decision about arms did the United States make after the conference?

5. (a) What agreement did the signers of the Kellogg-Briand Pact make? (b) What criticisms were made about the pact?

6. (a) Name two ways in which the United States was involved in Latin America in 1924. (b) How did Charles Evans Hughes try to reassure Latin Americans of the United States' good intentions toward them?

7. (a) Why did the United States have a particular interest in Nicaragua? (b) What solution was reached for Nicaragua's problems in 1927?

8. (a) Explain the importance of the Seventh Pan-American Conference. (b) What evidence did Roosevelt have that the "Good Neighbor" policy was a success?

A WORLD CHANGED BY WAR

READ TO FIND OUT

— why problems arose regarding European war debts.

— why new tariff agreements did not help the world economy.

— how fascism developed in Italy and Germany.

— how Japan threatened Asia.

— why the United States recognized the Soviet Union.

— why the United States agreed to Philippine independence.

Despite the American talk of isolation during the 1920s, the United States was involved in foreign affairs. There were the conferences and treaties to prevent war and the new policy in Latin America. Even the League of Nations operated in the shadow of American influence.

The United States also played another role in foreign affairs. It became the banker of the world economy. World War I might have soured Americans' international outlook, but it boosted the American economy. In 1919 Woodrow Wilson talked of the changes that war had brought to the United States: "The financial leadership will be ours. The industrial primacy will be ours. The commercial advantage will be ours. The other countries of the world are looking to us for leadership and direction."

THE UNITED STATES AS A CREDITOR NATION

From the earliest colonial days up to the war years, Americans had borrowed money from European nations. Europeans bought American stocks and bonds, and Americans used the money to build farms, railroads, and industries. Then, as World War I loomed, Europeans cashed in their stocks and bonds in order to buy military supplies.

During the war, the United States was not only free of its old debts, but it also loaned about $10 billion to the Allies. As the American economy prospered because of wartime industry, Americans invested in foreign mines and steamships and railroads, especially in Latin America. Now it was the United States and not Europe that loaned money to developing nations. In 1914 the United States had been a debtor nation owing $3.7 billion. By 1919 it was a creditor nation that had loaned some $12.5 billion.

The war left the Europeans with little cash, so they could not pay their debts. The solution, they claimed, was to sell their goods in the United States and thus earn enough money to pay back what they owed. The United States, as creditor, would have to open its market to European goods.

The United States, however, did exactly the opposite. American farmers and factory owners called for protection against imports because imports gave them competition. During the 1920s Congress passed higher and higher tariffs on imports. Europeans could not hope to sell enough goods to pay off their debts.

THE DAWES PLAN

In 1922 Congress set up a debt commission to work out terms of payment with the Allies. The commission tried to make the terms fair by giving each nation 62 years to pay and by charging low interest rates.

Still, payment was a burden for the debtors. Their only hope of paying the United States was to collect reparations from Germany. In the Treaty of Versailles, the Allies had charged that Germany alone had caused the war and so must pay for war damages. In 1921 they set the reparations figure at a huge $33 billion.

However, Germany also had emerged from the war with a shattered economy and wild inflation. By early 1923 Germany had defaulted on its reparations. France and Belgium then sent troops to occupy Germany's Ruhr Valley to take over German mines.

Meanwhile, an international commission was trying to find a way for Germany to pay its reparations. One commission member, American banker Charles G. Dawes, proposed that Germany receive an international loan in order to pay its

As the German economy collapsed following World War I, the government recklessly printed paper money. By November 1923 the mark was valueless.

reparations. The Dawes Plan went into effect in September 1924. American investors took responsibility for over half the loan to Germany.

In 1926 British economist John Maynard Keynes noted how the Dawes Plan actually worked: "The United States lends money to Germany, Germany transfers its equivalent to the Allies, the Allies pay it back to the United States government." Thus, much of the money that circulated through Europe came from and ended up in American hands.

This delicate balance of payments collapsed when the American stock market crashed in 1929. As the United States slid into the Great Depression, Americans stopped investing abroad. As the flow of American dollars overseas declined, Europe also sank into depression.

In the spring of 1931 European nations had to pool their money to keep Austria's largest bank from closing its doors. Germany neared bankruptcy. In June President Hoover approved a one-year moratorium, or delay, on both German and Allied debt payments.

When the moratorium ended, however, Germany could not resume its payments. A few of the Allies made payments on their debts, but others defaulted. By December 1933 all the Allies but Finland had stopped payments.

THE TRADE AGREEMENTS ACT

When President Roosevelt took office in 1933, he was concerned primarily with pulling the United States out of the depression. Yet he also wanted to restore world trade.

Cordell Hull, Roosevelt's secretary of state, had long felt that Congress made a mistake in passing high tariffs. Hull wanted the President to negotiate tariff levels directly with other nations. Roosevelt presented Hull's idea to Congress in March 1934. Congress passed the Trade Agreements Act in June. Under the act, the president could lower existing tariff rates by as much as 50 percent for nations that would reciprocate, or agree, in return, to lower duties on American goods.

The act also contained the "most-favored-nation" principle. According to this principle, when the United States and another nation lowered the tariff on certain items, the United States would also lower its tariff for all other nations producing those items. However, to gain this favored treatment, these nations could not discriminate against American goods. In this way, Hull hoped to persuade other nations to reduce their tariffs on American goods and to expand world trade.

By January 1940 the United States had signed *reciprocal trade agreements* with 21 nations. The agreements won good will abroad, but they made little impact on the world economy. American producers still demanded protection, and tariffs on competing foreign goods were kept fairly high.

THE RISE OF FASCISM IN ITALY

"War and depression—ugly, misshapen, inseparable twins—must be considered together," wrote a senator in 1935. "Each is a catapult for the other." In some nations, war and depression led to the rise of dictatorships.

Italy had emerged from the war bitter and divided. Although one of the victors, Italy had not received all the territory that it wanted. Also, the Italian economy was declining, and jobless workers began to talk of communist revolution. Many Italians, searching for order, were drawn to a new movement called *fascism*.

The word *fascism* comes from the ancient Roman *fasces*, which was a bundle of rods tied around an axe that the Romans carried as a symbol of authority.

The fascists wanted to set up a **totalitarian society**. In a totalitarian society, the state, or the government, controls the economy, the political system, and almost every area of people's lives. In Italy, the Fascist party would have such control, and all other political parties would be banned.

Led by Benito Mussolini, the Fascists attacked communists and labor leaders. In 1922 the Fascist party marched on Rome, seized control of the government, and installed Mussolini as premier. By 1927 Mussolini ruled Italy as a dictator.

When Italy, along with other European nations, slid into depression in 1930, Mussolini provided jobs by building up the nation's armed forces. Italy, he promised, would soon be a mighty power in the Mediterranean and in Africa.

THE RISE OF FASCISM IN GERMANY

In Germany, too, fascism grew out of postwar chaos. The defeated nation was humiliated by the Treaty of Versailles. Thousands lost their savings in the wild inflation of the 1920s.

Then came the worldwide depression. Millions of Germans lost their jobs. Germany's democratic government, the Weimar Republic, seemed helpless. The German Communist party attracted followers, setting off fears of revolution. Many Germans looked to the fascist National Socialist, or Nazi, party to solve the nation's troubles.

The Nazi party was headed by Adolf Hitler, a veteran of World War I. Fiercely proud of Germany, Hitler was embittered by the nation's defeat in the war.

After the war, Hitler had joined a small, strongly nationalist political party. It became the Nazi party, and Hitler became its leader. The Nazis gained strength throughout the 1920s. Hitler promised to create jobs, to tear up the Treaty of Versailles, and to lead Germany into a thousand years of empire. The Nazis, he vowed, would save Germany from communists. Germany would also be saved from Jews, whom Hitler blamed for Germany's defeat in the war and for economic problems. Hard times led many Germans to support the Nazi party. Existing anti-Semitism* in Germany also led Germans to accept Hitler's prejudice.

* anti-Semitism: dislike or hatred of Jews

Hitler, with Goering at his right, marched through Munich with a group of storm troopers. The storm troopers were Hitler's private army of armed, uniformed hoodlums.

HITLER BECOMES CHANCELLOR

By 1933 the Nazis were the nation's strongest party, and Hitler was named chancellor, or prime minister. The following year the German president died, leaving the nation in the hands of its new chancellor.

Hitler moved swiftly to gain total authority over Germany. To manage public opinion, the Nazi party seized control of newspapers, film studios, radio stations, and schools. Hitler established strict controls over banking, factories, and agriculture, and set to work rebuilding Germany's economy and industry. In defiance of the Treaty of Versailles, he began a massive buildup of the German military.

The Nazis preached that Germans were a superior race. Others in Germany—Slavs, gypsies, and especially Jews—were considered inferior. As Germany became a totalitarian state, the Nazis launched a campaign of hatred directed against Germany's Jews.

Laws kept Jews from public office and government service. Jews were also excluded from work in journalism and radio, from farming and teaching, even from practicing medicine. Grocery and butcher shops, bakeries, and dairies would not admit Jews. Drugstores would not sell them medicine. In 1935 all Jews in Germany lost their citizenship.

Under Nazi supervision, a group of Jews in Austria was forced to scrub anti-Nazi emblems and messages from the pavement and walls of a house.

Thousands of Jews fled from Germany to any nation that would have them. Many nations, including the United States, would not ease their immigration restrictions and thus accepted only some of the Jews. Then the German government stopped Jewish emigration. Jews were rounded up and taken to camps to work as slaves in factories, fields, and mines. Many died of the toil.

The purge, or removal, of Jews was only one part of the Nazi blueprint for Germany's future. Hitler wrote that life was "an eternal victory of the strong over the weak." As Germany grew stronger, Hitler looked beyond German borders to other European nations. There, he planned to retake territories that Germany had lost in World War I and to add to Germany areas where Germans lived.

JAPAN INVADES MANCHURIA

Another form of dictatorship arose in Japan after 1930. Instead of a political party seizing control, as in Italy and Germany, the military came to power in Japan. The rivalry between the military and Japan's civilian government had been building throughout the 1920s.

The Washington disarmament treaties and the Kellogg-Briand peace pact angered Japanese military leaders. They felt that, in order to survive, Japan must gain control over much of China, which had raw materials and space for industry. Then a strong Japan could rule all Asia and the Pacific.

In September 1931 Japanese troops rolled into the Chinese province of Manchuria. By early 1932 Manchuria was in Japanese hands. Military leaders renamed the province Manchukuo and began building mines and industries there.

The Japanese invasion violated the Kellogg-Briand Pact, the Open Door policy, and the Covenant of the League of Nations, to which Japan belonged. The American secretary of state, Henry L. Stimson, sent a blunt protest to Japan in January 1932. The United States, he said, did not recognize any territory Japan gained "by the use of force." This policy statement became known as the Stimson Doctrine.

The League of Nations issued a statement similar to Stimson's and sent a commission to Asia to investigate. However, League members and the United States were anxious not to risk war. They took no further action, even when the Japanese bombed the city of Shanghai, killing civilians.

Encouraged by the weak world reaction, the Japanese military grew bolder. At home, it came to dominate the feeble civilian government and the emperor. In 1933 Japan withdrew from the League of Nations. In 1935, defying the Washington disarmament treaty, Japan began to strengthen its naval fleet.

RECOGNITION OF THE SOVIET UNION

One nation that was particularly worried about Japan's actions was Russia, which had been renamed the Union of Soviet Socialist Republics in 1922. The Soviet Union had provinces in Asia and feared that Japan planned to add them to its empire. Seeking allies to curb the Japanese, Soviet leaders looked to the United States.

However, the United States and the Soviet Union had no diplomatic relations. When the Bolsheviks came to power in 1917, the United States would not recognize the new government. Throughout the 1920s Americans refused to acknowledge a government that preached the overthrow of democracy. But the Soviet Union, under the leadership of Joseph Stalin, was becoming too powerful to ignore.

El Lissitzky, *USSR Russische Ausstellung*, 1929. Collection of The Museum of Modern Art, New York.

This poster advertised the Russian Exhibition in Zurich, Switzerland, in 1929. The poster united different pictures into one unit to create a powerful effect.

By the early 1930s the United States began looking at the Soviet Union in a different light. Many business leaders, hoping to revive the American economy, wanted to open trade with the Soviets. Other Americans, including President Roosevelt, thought that the Soviet Union would be a valuable friend against Japanese aggression.

In November 1933 the United States officially recognized the Soviet Union. In response the Soviets made token gestures of good will. They promised to curb Communist propaganda in the United States. They also guaranteed the religious liberty of Americans living in the Soviet Union. For the United States, however, the hoped-for economic gains did not appear. Trade increased only slightly, and the two nations never developed a policy to oppose Japan.

PHILIPPINE INDEPENDENCE

One faraway American possession was quite vulnerable to Japanese expansion—the Philippine Islands. Lying off the coast of China, the Philippines were within easy reach of Japan. Rather than defend them in case of Japanese attack, some American leaders considered giving the Philippines their independence.

There were other American voices proposing Philippine independence, for different reasons. Labor leaders wanted to cut off the flow of Philippine immigrants into the United States. Tobacco and sugar growers wanted to close the market to competing Philippine products, because these products were not restricted by tariffs. In 1934 Congress passed the Tydings-McDuffie Act, promising the Philippines complete independence, to be granted ten years after a constitution had been drawn and adopted. When the work was completed in 1936, the ten-year transition period began and independence was scheduled for 1946.

To many Americans and much of the world, ending control over the Philippines meant that the United States was giving up its interest in Asia. However, formal independence lay several years in the future. The Philippine Islands were still an American outpost in the Pacific, with an aggressive Japan as a neighbor.

SECTION REVIEW

1. Identify the following: the Dawes Plan, Trade Agreements Act, National Socialist party, Stimson Doctrine, Tydings-McDuffie Act.

2. Define the following: fascism, totalitarian state, anti-Semitism.

3. (a) Why were European nations unable to pay their war debts? (b) What was the Dawes Plan?

4. (a) How did Germany feel about war reparations and the Treaty of Versailles? (b) What suggestion did Cordell Hull make in 1933 regarding tariffs passed by the United States?

5. (a) Why were the Italians dissatisfied after World War I? (b) How did Mussolini deal with the depression?

6. (a) List three promises Hitler made to the German people. (b) List three actions Hitler took to gain power in Germany. (c) Explain the Nazis' idea of superior and inferior races. (d) Why did Hitler plan to expand German borders?

7. (a) Why did the Washington disarmament treaties and the Kellogg-Briand Pact anger Japanese military leaders? (b) How did the Japanese military show its strength in 1933 and 1935?

8. List two reasons why the Philippines were promised independence.

EUROPE GOES TO WAR

READ TO FIND OUT

— how the United States maintained neutrality in spite of fascist aggression.

— how the Spanish government became a fascist dictatorship.

— how Japan became increasingly aggressive.

— how Germany's aggression led to war in Europe.

In Europe and Asia, nations were grimly rearming. The disarmament and peace treaties of the 1920s were trampled underfoot. The League of Nations seemed paralyzed.

In the United States, people looked in fear and amazement across the seas, and quickly looked away. "Is there a way to keep America out of war?" one senator asked. He warned, "The world is once again in that precarious condition in which the bad temper of a dictator, the ineptness of a diplomat, or the crime of a fanatic may let loose irremediable disaster."

THE NYE COMMITTEE

In 1934 some Americans tried to figure out how, in 1917, their nation had been drawn into World War I. The business magazine *Fortune* published an article blaming the war on weapons manufacturers. Their aims, claimed the magazine, were to "(a) prolong war, (b) disturb peace."

In April the Senate set up a committee to investigate the armaments industry. An isolationist senator, Gerald P. Nye of North Dakota, headed the investigation. For months the committee investigated the wartime activities of weapons makers and bankers who had loaned the Allies money.

The conclusion was that the arms merchants and bankers had reaped enormous profits by selling arms and providing loans to the Allies. The United States had entered the war, charged the committee, so that profiteers could make money.

Many Americans agreed with the Nye Committee although its evidence was open to question.

The charges were especially easy to accept during the depression, when bankers were unpopular. A cry went up to find some way to keep profiteers from once again dragging the nation into war.

FASCIST AGGRESSION AND AMERICAN NEUTRALITY

Congress responded to the outcry with the Neutrality Act of 1935. Passed in August, the act was intended to keep the United States from taking sides in future wars. It authorized the president to ban any United States arms shipments to *belligerents*, or nations at war. The president also was to warn Americans that if they traveled on ships of belligerents, they did so at their own risk.

Then, in October 1935, Mussolini sent Italian troops into the African nation of Ethiopia. Ethiopia was an independent nation, but it was sandwiched between two Italian colonies. By conquering Ethiopia, Italy would have a solid block of empire in Africa.

The League of Nations promptly declared Italy an aggressor and banned all arms sales to Mussolini's government. Although Roosevelt also considered Italy the aggressor, he invoked the Neutrality Act. Thus, the United States did not take sides.

A photographer with the Ethiopian forces shot this scene of an Italian air raid in October 1935. The Ethiopian infantrymen were frantically running for cover.

Isolationists were pleased with the President's action, but they worried that the United States still might be drawn into war. In February 1936 Congress acted to strengthen American neutrality. The Neutrality Act of 1936 forbade American firms to make loans or to give credit for supplies to any nation at war.

Meanwhile, through the spring of 1936, the march of fascism continued. Italy brutally crushed the last Ethiopian resistance. German troops swept into the Rhineland, the demilitarized zone set up between Germany and France by the Treaty of Versailles.

THE SPANISH CIVIL WAR

In July 1936 a civil war broke out in Spain, and its effects stretched far beyond Spanish borders. Loyalists were fighting for Spain's republican government. The Spanish rebels, led by General Francisco Franco, wanted to install a fascist government. Both Mussolini and Hitler entered the war on Franco's side. The Loyalists received aid from the Soviet Union in the form of supplies and advisers.

On the whole, people in the United States, Britain, and France sympathized with Spain's republican government. However, fearing the outbreak of a world war, these nations decided not to intervene. Since the American neutrality acts applied only to wars between nations, Congress, in January 1937, extended the laws to cover civil wars.

After three years of fighting, Franco's forces overthrew the Spanish government and set up a fascist dictatorship. That was not fascism's only triumph. Hitler and Mussolini formed a political alliance. Mussolini said that the line from Rome to Berlin was the axis around which Europe would revolve. Thus, these nations became known as the Axis Powers. Japan, too, was soon drawn into the alliance. Thus a new world league was born: the Rome-Berlin-Tokyo Axis.

THE THIRD NEUTRALITY ACT

The United States ban on aiding either side in the Spanish civil war worried some Americans. They pointed out that the ban had hurt the Loyalists more than the Fascists. Franco had obtained all the supplies that he needed from Germany and Italy.

Thus, American leaders wanted a law more flexible than the earlier neutrality acts, but one that would still keep the nation out of war. In April 1937 Congress passed the Neutrality Act of 1937. Firms in the United States were still forbidden to sell arms or to give loans to warring nations. However, belligerents could buy other supplies in the United States if they paid cash on delivery and carried the supplies away in their own ships. In addition, Americans were now forbidden, rather than just discouraged, to travel on belligerent ships.

THE "QUARANTINE" SPEECH

The next conflict came not in Europe, but in Asia. In July 1937 Japanese and Chinese troops clashed on a bridge near Peking (Beijing). The fighting quickly spread throughout eastern China.

President Roosevelt feared that he would help Japan and hurt China if he used the Neutrality Act of 1937. Under the act's "cash-and-carry" clause,

Shanghai, a leading Chinese port and industrial city, fell to the Japanese in 1937. Here Japanese troops equipped with the most modern weapons guarded a bridge in Shanghai.

Japan's mighty merchant fleet could acquire huge amounts of American supplies. Thus, Roosevelt decided not to invoke the act, on the grounds that Japan and China were not officially at war.

Still, Roosevelt felt that he must awaken Americans to the threats to world peace. In October he visited Chicago and gave a short speech on world affairs. The world was threatened by a "reign of terror," he said. "Let no one imagine that America will escape." He went on to compare war to an epidemic: "When an epidemic of physical disease starts to spread, the community approves and joins in a quarantine of the patients in order to protect the health of the community against the spread of the disease."

Many Americans applauded Roosevelt's "quarantine" speech. However, isolationists feared that Roosevelt would plunge the nation into war. In Congress, isolationists talked of impeaching the President.

Roosevelt was disappointed by the criticisms. He tried to quiet fears by noting that he was only asking for "moral" condemnation of aggressors.

THE SINKING OF THE *PANAY*

Fearing for the safety of American citizens in China, the United States began to evacuate them. Then, on December 12, 1937, Japanese war planes bombed the U.S.S. *Panay*, one of the evacuating ships, and several American oil tankers. Two Americans were killed and several others wounded. The *Panay* sank.

Americans were outraged. However, Japan quickly soothed American anger with an apology and an offer to pay damages. Most Americans were relieved that the incident had not provoked a war.

In Congress, the sinking of the *Panay* spurred consideration of an amendment to the Constitution. Sponsored by Representative Louis Ludlow of Indiana, the proposed amendment stated that the United States could not declare war without a nationwide vote of approval. A vote would not be required in the case of invasion. According to a national poll, over 70 percent of the American people favored such an amendment.

Under strong White House pressure, Democrats in Congress managed to defeat the measure. However, the Ludlow amendment came within 21 votes of being approved. Clearly, isolationism was strongly supported in the United States.

GERMAN CONQUESTS

While Japan was tightening its hold on China, Hitler began a relentless attack on eastern Europe. In March 1938 Nazi troops swarmed into Austria. In a quick, bloodless conquest, Germany annexed its neighbor. France and Britain fruitlessly protested.

Hitler's next target was the Sudetenland (soo-DAY-tuhn-LAND), a strip of Czechoslovakia in which some 3 million Germans lived. When Hitler demanded the territory, the Czechs prepared to fight. France, Britain, and the Soviet Union all vowed that they would support the Czechs.

In September 1938 British and French leaders met with Hitler in Munich, Germany. Hitler promised that the Sudetenland was "the last territorial claim I have to make in Europe." The British and French agreed to Hitler's demands and persuaded Czechoslovakia to give up the territory. This policy of giving in to the demands of a hostile power in order to keep the peace became known as **appeasement**.

Many nations believed that the Munich agreement had saved Europe from war. However, Hitler soon shattered hopes raised at Munich. In March 1939 Hitler broke his promise as German troops conquered the rest of Czechoslovakia. Germany's Axis allies also were on the march. Italy seized nearby Albania in April 1939. Then Japan occupied the Spratly Islands—French possessions in the Pacific—in June 1940.

GERMANY ATTACKS POLAND

Hitler next turned to Poland, demanding the Polish city of Danzig on the Baltic Sea. Britain and France finally realized that appeasement would not avert war. Late in March, both nations pledged to support Poland if Germany attacked. They also urged the Soviet Union, which bordered Poland, to join them in guaranteeing Poland's safety.

Hitler, too, was courting the Soviet Union. If he attacked Poland, he wanted to be sure that the Soviets would not attack Germany in response. In August 1939 Germany and the Soviet Union stunned the world by signing a nonaggression treaty. In the treaty, each nation pledged not to attack the other. Also, in a secret provision, Germany agreed to divide Poland with the Soviet Union.

On September 9, 1939, the Nazis penetrated Warsaw's defenses and began to destroy the city. The heroic Polish resistance movement drew strength from the ruins.

At 4:45 a.m. on Friday, September 1, 1939, a German battleship opened fire on the port city of Danzig. German dive bombers screamed down out of the skies, machine-gunning Polish troops. Bombs rained on Poland's airfields, destroying planes before they could get into the air. German tanks rumbled across the border.

On September 3 Britain and France, committed to support Poland, declared war on Germany. But they could not save Poland. The German planes and tanks moved like lightning, giving the world a new terror—*blitzkrieg*, or "lightning war."

Two weeks after the German invasion of Poland, Soviet troops attacked from the east. On October 6, 1939, the Polish capital of Warsaw fell, and Poland surrendered. The stricken country was divided between the Germans and the Soviets.

Germany had promised not to interfere if the Soviets took additional territory along their northwestern border. After Poland fell, the Soviet Union demanded naval and military bases in the republics of Lithuania, Latvia, Estonia, and Finland. Lithuania, Latvia, and Estonia agreed to the Soviet demands. The Finns, however, refused, and the Soviet Union invaded Finland. For four months the courageous Finns fought off Soviet forces before finally surrendering. Finland managed to keep its independence, but gave up land to the Soviets.

THE AMERICAN RESPONSE TO WAR

On the same day that France and Britain declared war on Germany, President Roosevelt gave one of his fireside chats on the radio. The nation would remain neutral, he assured his listeners, "But I cannot ask that every American remain neutral in thought as well."

Indeed, Americans were not neutral in thought. In a public opinion poll, 84 percent of the people said that they wanted France and Britain, known as the Allies, to win. As strong as the sympathies were, however, most Americans wanted no part of this war.

Three weeks after Germany invaded Poland, Roosevelt called a special session of Congress to urge an amendment to the Neutrality Act. He felt that the arms embargo, banning the sale of American weapons, would hurt France and Britain. They needed more armaments. Germany, on the other hand, bristled with weapons and did not need American arms.

For six weeks Congress rang with loud debate. Isolationists passionately argued against repealing the arms embargo. If Americans send arms to aid France and Britain, asked one senator, "will we—can we—if the hour of greater need should occur, refuse to send our armies?" Roosevelt replied that no one was suggesting sending Americans to "fight on the battlefields of Europe."

In November Congress passed the Neutrality Act of 1939, the fourth such act. Roosevelt won repeal of the arms embargo. The Allies would be able to buy weapons on a "cash-and-carry" basis.

However, the act retained earlier neutrality provisions. Loans to belligerents and American travel on belligerent ships were still banned. In a final effort to enforce neutrality, the act also forbade American ships to enter combat zones—the seas bordering warring nations.

The United States, together with Latin America, also declared a "safety zone" of several hundred miles around the Americas. Belligerent nations were told to keep their navies out of this zone.

SECTION REVIEW

1. Identify the following: Loyalists, the *Panay*, the Ludlow Amendment.

2. Define the following: belligerents, Axis Powers, appeasement, nonaggression, blitzkrieg.

3. (a) What was the purpose of the Neutrality Act of 1935? (b) What authority did this act give the president?

4. (a) Why did Mussolini send troops into Ethiopia in October 1935? (b) Name two other aggressive actions taken by fascist powers in the spring of 1936.

5. Who supported Franco in the Spanish civil war?

6. (a) What were the terms of the Neutrality Act of 1937? (b) Why did Roosevelt decide not to invoke the act after the Japanese attack on China?

7. (a) How did Japan soothe American anger over the sinking of the *Panay*? (b) Why was the Ludlow Amendment defeated?

8. (a) What promise did Hitler make at the meeting in Munich in September 1938? (b) How did Hitler break his promise?

9. (a) Why did Britain and France declare war on Germany? (b) Name four nations that came under Russian control in whole or in part after the fall of Poland.

10. (a) What argument did isolationists give against repeal of the arms embargo? (b) Explain the terms of the Neutrality Act of 1939.

THE END OF ISOLATION

READ TO FIND OUT

—**how Germany conquered France.**

—**how Britain defended itself against Germany.**

—**how the United States built up its own and Britain's defenses.**

—**how the United States and Britain worked together in the Battle of the Atlantic.**

—**why the United States declared war on Japan, Italy, and Germany.**

During the winter of 1939–1940, the Allies mobilized for war. France fortified its eastern border against Germany. Britain declared a tight blockade of Germany. Germany unleashed its submarines against British ships and mined British harbors. Beyond skirmishes at sea, however, Europe was eerily quiet.

The British called this time "the twilight war." The Germans called it the *sitzkrieg*, or "sitting war," in contrast to their blitzkrieg. Many people were deceived by the relative quiet. News writers in the United States called it the "phony war."

THE FALL OF FRANCE

On April 9, 1940, Hitler shattered the winter lull. In a blitzkrieg as deadly as the earlier attack to the east, German troops now struck north and west. In a single day, the Germans occupied Denmark and key ports in Norway. By the end of the month, Norway was overrun.

In May Hitler's troops stormed through the Netherlands, Belgium, and Luxembourg. British and French troops, which had been sent to Belgium, were forced to retreat. The Nazis pushed onward, sweeping into France. Within a matter of weeks the stunned Allied forces were crushed. At the end of May, some 340,000 French and British troops were trapped against the sea at Dunkirk, in northern France.

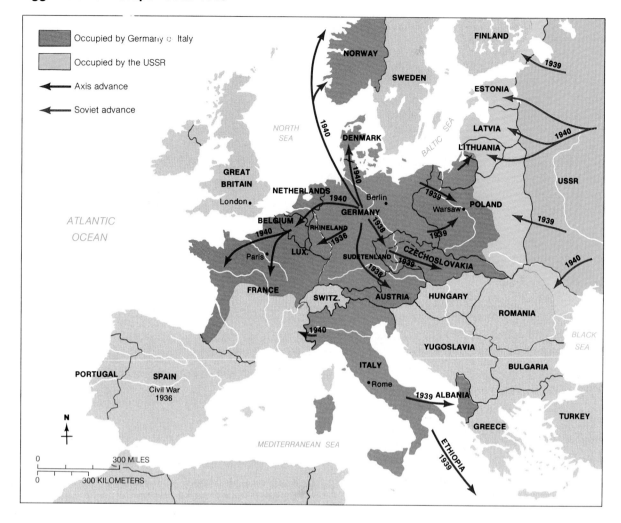

Legend:
- Occupied by Germany & Italy
- Occupied by the USSR
- Axis advance
- Soviet advance

Inspired by their new prime minister, Winston Churchill, the British made a daring rescue of the troops. While the Royal Air Force held off the German bombers, the Royal Navy and hundreds of private boats from Britain ferried soldiers across the English Channel.

For France, however, the battle was nearly ended. In early June Mussolini declared war on France and Britain. He sent Italian troops into France from the south, while the Germans marched toward Paris. On June 22 the French surrendered to Hitler in the same railroad car in the same forest location where Germany had signed the armistice of 1918. Hitler had the railroad car brought there from a museum for the occasion.

France was divided in two. German troops occupied northern and western France. In the southern region, French leader Marshal Pétain (PAY-TAN) set up a German-controlled government at Vichy (VEE-SHEE). However, thousands of people escaped France and carried on the fight against Germany. The headquarters of this Free French resistance movement was in London, under General Charles de Gaulle (duh GŌL).

THE BATTLE OF BRITAIN

Britain now stood alone in Europe, without allies. Prime Minister Winston Churchill urged Britons to fight alone:

RECOGNIZING PROPAGANDA
NAZI NEWSPAPERS

Propaganda is the communication of ideas that further a cause or damage an opposing one. Propaganda appeals to people's emotions.

To recognize propaganda, it is important to understand the devices that are commonly used. One is *name calling*. Another is the use of *glittering generality*, meaningless but high-sounding phrases that cannot be proved or disproved. Another device is *transfer*—connecting something or someone who is admired to the idea the propagandist is promoting. A fourth is *testimonial*—quoting some well-known person. A fifth is *plain folks*—an approach appealing to people's down-to-earth side. *Card stacking* is the use of selected facts to give a misleading impression. The *band wagon* approach encourages doing something because "everyone else is doing it."

The Nazis made use of propaganda to gain power and to stay in power. During the Battle of Britain—when Germans were bombing British cities and the British, in turn, bombed Germany—German newspapers reported the events as follows.

> They [the British] wished, on the orders of Churchill, simply to murder. . . . Albion [Britain] has shown itself to be a murder-hungry beast which the German sword will liquidate in the interest not only of the German people but of the whole civilized world.
>
> *Börsen Zeitung*
> Sept. 19, 1940

> It is a fact that Germany is waging war with clean weapons and in a chivalrous manner.
>
> *Diplo*
> Sept. 20, 1940

> Winston Churchill again yesterday gave British airmen the order to drop their bombs on the German civilian population and thus continue their murder of German men, women, and children.
>
> *Nachtausgabe*
> Sept. 23, 1940

After you have read the quotations from the newspapers, answer the following questions.

1. Of the seven propaganda devices, which ones were being used in the German newspapers?

2. What do you think the propaganda was intended to accomplish? How might readers in Berlin have felt as they read these newspaper pieces?

3. Totalitarian governments are masters in the use of propaganda. Propaganda, however, exists in various areas of society. Look at television to determine whether any of the seven devices are used in commercials. Think of other areas in which you have been exposed to propaganda. Describe them.

4. Why is it important to recognize propaganda? What safeguards against propaganda exist in a free society?

The Battle of France is over. I expect that the Battle of Britain is about to begin. . . . Hitler knows that he will have to break us in this island or lose the war. If we can stand up to him, all Europe may be free and the life of the world may move forward into broad, sunlit uplands. But if we fail, then the whole world, including the United States, including all that we have known and cared for, will sink into the abyss of a new Dark Age.

If Britons held out bravely, Churchill concluded, people for a thousand years would say "this was their finest hour."

While Churchill rallied the British, Hitler boasted that Nazi troops would be in London within three months. To prepare the way for invasion, in July 1940 Hitler sent his air force to bomb British airfields and ports. The German air force heavily outnumbered the small Royal Air Force of Britain. However, the Germans could not match British pilots and planes. The Nazis switched to nighttime attacks, but Britain turned to an invention called radar. Radar pinpointed the German planes so that British pilots could intercept them.

Then, in September, the Germans began bombing British cities, especially London, hoping to demoralize the civilian population. Courageous Londoners took shelter in subway stations, often spending nights there to escape German bombs. British cities were shattered and burned, and thousands of civilians were killed in London alone.

The German blitzes on London left burning ruins and rubble in place of homes and historic buildings. The British endured and cleaned up, their morale high and unshakable.

By December Hitler was forced to postpone the invasion of Britain. In the spring of 1941 Nazi bombs once again battered the island. Again, British pilots took to the skies and fought off the Germans. Finally, Hitler's interest turned elsewhere, and the Battle of Britain subsided.

THE UNITED STATES BUILDS ITS DEFENSES

When the Nazi blitzkrieg began in the spring of 1940, the American mood turned grim. Suddenly Americans were worried about their defenses. In the late 1930s Congress had voted funds to build up the army and navy. Yet by 1940 the armed services had a mere 350 tanks, only 2,806 outmoded airplanes, and combat equipment for just 75,000 soldiers.

In May, President Roosevelt asked Congress for an all-out buildup of the armed forces. Over the next five months Congress voted some $17 billion for defenses. Plans were made for a two-ocean navy and contracts were signed for fighter and bomber planes. Factories tooled up to make machine guns, and the army rushed to modernize.

People also worried that attacks might come from "enemies" at home who supported the Soviet Union or Germany. In June 1940 Congress passed the Alien Registration Act, also known as the Smith Act. This act required all aliens to register at local post offices and to be fingerprinted. The act also made it illegal for anyone, citizen or alien, to urge disloyalty in the military or to call for the overthrow of the government.

At the same time, Congress began debating a bill for a peacetime draft. Citizens had been drafted in the Civil War and World War I, but never in peacetime.

As the Nazis bombed Britain, support for the draft increased. In September the Selective Training and Service Act was passed and signed into law. All men in the United States between the ages of 21 and 35 would have to register, and 2 million would be selected for training.

THE DESTROYER DEAL

While the United States was building up its own defenses, Roosevelt gave a helping hand to Britain. During the summer of 1940 the British lost half of their destroyers to Nazi submarines and bombers. Prime Minister Churchill begged Roosevelt for 50 "overage" United States destroyers.

Roosevelt was certain that Congress would block such a sale, but his attorney general pointed out a legal alternative. Roosevelt could give Britain the ships in exchange for a 99-year lease on British military bases in Newfoundland and the Caribbean. Churchill agreed. On September 3 Roosevelt announced the destroyer deal and stunned the nation.

The deal brought the debate between isolationists and those who favored intervention to a fever pitch. The isolationist America First Committee argued that Hitler posed no threat to the nation. They opposed any kind of aid to Britain, arguing that it would force the United States into war.

The Committee to Defend America by Aiding the Allies, on the other hand, applauded the deal. Only by helping Britain defeat Hitler, they argued, could Americans avoid war. They were delighted that Roosevelt had abandoned strict neutrality.

ROOSEVELT WINS A THIRD TERM

Amid the controversy over the European war, the presidential campaign of 1940 approached. Breaking the tradition of the two-term presidency, Roosevelt accepted the Democratic nomination. He was seeking a third term "to prevent the spread of war."

The Republicans chose Wendell L. Willkie, an Indiana lawyer, as their presidential candidate. Willkie had fought the New Deal's Tennessee Valley Authority in court. Republicans hoped that he would appeal to those tired of Roosevelt's domestic policies. A confident Willkie said he was ready to take on "the Champ."

The real issue of the campaign was the war in Europe. Willkie originally supported Roosevelt's policy of aid to Britain. However, by late October he began to appeal to Americans' determination to stay out of the war. "If you reelect him," warned Willkie, "you may expect war in April 1941." Roosevelt responded, "Your President says this country is not going to war."

Roosevelt won his third term in the November election. Although Willkie ran close in the popular vote, Roosevelt swept the electoral vote 449 to 82. He felt that his victory was also a vote of approval for more aid to Britain.

LEND-LEASE

Britain had been buying arms and supplies from the United States under the "cash-and-carry" clause of the Neutrality Act of 1939. However, by late 1940 Britain was running short of cash, and Churchill begged Roosevelt to help. Roosevelt agreed. He believed that the fate of the United States was tied to the war in Europe.

In December 1940 Roosevelt called a press conference and outlined a simple way to aid Britain. "Let me give you an illustration," he said:

> Suppose my neighbor's home catches fire. . . . If he can take my garden hose and connect it up with his hydrant, I may help him to put out his fire. Now, what do I do? I don't say to him before that operation, "Neighbor, my garden hose cost me $15; you have to pay me $15 for it." . . . I don't want $15— I want my garden hose back after the fire is over.

Roosevelt proposed that the United States lend arms and supplies to Britain. Britain would return or replace them after the war.

In January 1941 Roosevelt's plan, called Lend-Lease, was submitted to Congress. Isolationists mounted fierce opposition, but Congress passed the bill in March. Under the Lend-Lease Act, the president could lend, lease, or sell war supplies to any nation whose defense was vital to the United States.

Within five minutes of signing the bill into law, Roosevelt approved a list of supplies for immediate shipment to Britain. When news of the law reached Britain, American flags were raised over the bomb-cratered streets.

Since the autumn of 1940 British troops had been holding off Mussolini's soldiers on two fronts— in British North Africa and in Greece. In the spring of 1941 Hitler came to Mussolini's aid, conquering Greece and neighboring Yugoslavia. The British troops fled Greece. In North Africa, the Nazis also forced the British to retreat.

The Nazi drive expanded in June. Distrusting Stalin and seeking more territory, Hitler launched an invasion of the Soviet Union.

THE BATTLE OF THE ATLANTIC

During the spring and summer of 1941, Roosevelt had to deal with a problem that went with Lend-Lease. American supplies would be no help to the British unless they reached Britain. And Hitler, to cut the flow of American aid, sent Nazi planes and "wolf packs" of submarines into the Atlantic.

Roosevelt began to help Britain in its Battle of the Atlantic. He ordered the navy to patrol the Atlantic and to broadcast the location of German ships to the British. He also stretched the American safety zone far out into the Atlantic.

In July Roosevelt involved the United States in the battle. American marines were sent to join British troops in occupying the strategic island of Iceland. The United States Navy would convoy, or escort, supply ships as far as Iceland.

In August Roosevelt met Churchill for what one reporter called "the greatest fishing trip that any President of the United States had ever undertaken." In four days of secret talks aboard an American cruiser in the Atlantic, they drew up the Atlantic Charter, a statement of postwar aims. They pledged to seek no territory and to support the right of all people to choose their own government and to be free from want and fear.

As the United States and Britain edged into closer cooperation, the Battle of the Atlantic heated up. In September a German submarine fired on an American destroyer that had been tracking it. Although the destroyer was not hit, Roosevelt ordered the navy to "shoot on sight" all German and Italian warships in the American convoy zone.

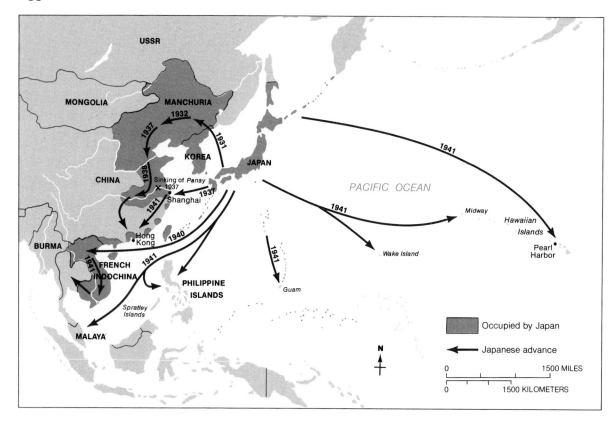

JAPAN ON THE MOVE

While American attention was riveted on Europe during 1940 and 1941, Japan was slashing through Asia. Hitler's blitzkrieg against western Europe in mid-1940 had given Japan a golden opportunity. With France and the Netherlands crushed and Britain under fire, Japan looked hungrily at these nations' colonial possessions in Asia. In August 1940 Japan seized French bases in northern Indochina.

The following month Japan signed the Tripartite Pact with its Axis allies Germany and Italy. Their earlier alliance had been political. This new pact was military. Each recognized the other's conquests. They also pledged that if the United States went to war against one Axis power, the other two would declare war on the United States.

Cautiously, Roosevelt adopted a policy of "slowing Japan up." The United States declared an embargo on war material, such as machine tools, chemicals, scrap metal, and oil, to Japan. The United States also increased its aid to China and fortified its bases on the Philippines and Guam.

Japan and the United States then conducted a series of talks to improve their relations. The talks proved fruitless. In July 1941 Japan occupied the remainder of French Indochina.

Roosevelt responded quickly, freezing all Japanese funds in American banks. Japan, in turn, froze American assets under its control. Once again, the two nations tried to find a way to restore relations.

In November 1941 Japanese diplomats met with Secretary of State Cordell Hull for a final round of talks. The Japanese wanted the United States to cut off aid to China and to end the embargo against Japan. Hull demanded that Japan withdraw from China and renounce the Tripartite Pact.

The talks, according to Hull, went "around and around the same circle." Meanwhile, American cryptographers had broken Japan's secret diplomatic code. From the broken code, known as "Magic," American intelligence experts learned that Japan was planning an attack. However, they did not know where. Most expected it to come at Guam or the Philippines.

PEARL HARBOR

On Sunday, December 7, 1941, the telephone rang on President Roosevelt's desk in the White House. It was Secretary of the Navy Frank Knox, who read a message he had just received from Hawaii: "Air raid, Pearl Harbor—This is no drill."

Americans learned the news in different ways— crackling over the radio, splashed across a newspaper, from the shaking voice of a neighbor. The stark details flooded in.

At 7:55 a.m. some 360 Japanese bombers whined out of the Hawaiian sky. The surprise attack at Pearl Harbor, on the Hawaiian island of Oahu, devastated the United States Navy. Nineteen ships were sunk or damaged, 150 planes were destroyed, and nearly 2,400 soldiers and civilians were killed. Only American aircraft carriers were not in the harbor at the time of the attack. In a sweep across the Pacific, Japan also attacked American bases on Midway, Wake, Guam, and the Philippines, and British bases on Malaya and at Hong Kong.

The Japanese attack on Pearl Harbor was sudden, ferocious, and overwhelming. The Japanese planes blasted American airfields, crippling the air force.

The following day a grim President Roosevelt addressed Congress:

> Yesterday, December 7, 1941—a date which will live in infamy—the United States of America was suddenly and deliberately attacked by naval and air forces of the Empire of Japan.

Roosevelt asked Congress for a declaration of war. Within an hour, with only one no vote, Congress declared war on Japan. Three days later Germany and Italy declared war on the United States, and Congress unanimously voted to go to war against them.

In a fireside chat to the American people, President Roosevelt said, "We are now in this war. We are all in it—all the way. Every single man, woman and child is a partner." Twenty-two years and twenty-five days after the end of World War I, the United States entered World War II.

SECTION REVIEW

1. Identify the following: twilight war, Marshal Pétain, Vichy, Alien Registration Act, Selective Training and Service Act, Lend-Lease, Atlantic Charter, Pearl Harbor.

2. (a) Describe the movements of Hitler's troops in April and May of 1940. (b) How did the British rescue Allied troops trapped at Dunkirk?

3. (a) List the resources of the United States Army early in 1940. (b) List five ways that the United States built up its armed forces in the second half of 1940. (c) What were the provisions of the Selective Training and Service Act?

4. What was the real issue of the campaign of 1940?

5. (a) Explain the provisions of the Lend-Lease Act. (b) Where did Hitler aid Mussolini in the spring of 1941? (c) Why did Hitler break his agreement with the Soviet Union?

6. How did Roosevelt help Britain in the Battle of the Atlantic?

7. (a) What was the Tripartite Pact? (b) What demands did Japan and the United States make of each other in November 1941?

8. (a) Why did the United States declare war on Japan? (b) Why did the United States go to war against Germany and Italy?

SUMMARY

In the years after World War I, most Americans supported isolationism. Yet, the United States did not avoid all foreign entanglements. Anxious to preserve peace, the United States worked to end the postwar arms race and to ease tensions in Asia. The United States also joined with other nations to renounce war.

In Latin America, the United States policy of intervention gradually ended. Hoover worked to build good will with Latin Americans. Roosevelt adopted the same goal, dedicating the United States to the Good Neighbor policy.

In the postwar years the United States played a vital role as a creditor nation. American loans not only allowed Germany to pay reparations but also allowed the Allies to pay war debts. However, the American stock market crash ended the loans, and Europe sank into depression. American attempts to improve the world economy were ineffective. By 1933, all the Allies but Finland had stopped payments on their war debts.

Postwar chaos and depression in Europe led to the rise of fascism. The Fascist party in Italy and the Nazi party in Germany soon established dictatorships and began to build up their armed forces. In Japan military leaders gained control of the government. Japanese troops invaded China.

In the face of aggression by Italy, Germany, and Japan, the United States passed a series of neutrality laws. These laws, Americans hoped, would keep the United States from taking sides in future wars. Then, in 1939, Germany attacked Poland, and Britain and France declared war on Germany.

With the German conquest of France and the Battle of Britain, the United States began to build up its defenses. The United States also provided Britain with ships and supplies. Finally, the American navy began to help the British in the Atlantic.

During 1940 and 1941, American-Japanese relations deteriorated. Continuing talks between Japan and the United States proved fruitless. On December 7, 1941, Japan attacked Pearl Harbor. On December 8, the United States declared war on Japan. Three days later, the United States was also at war with Germany and Italy.

CHAPTER REVIEW

1. (a) In the 1920s why did Americans support isolationism? (b) What change in European-American relations made such a policy difficult for the United States?

2. How did each of the following reflect American foreign policy in the 1920s and early 1930s? (a) the Washington naval conference (b) the Geneva Conference (c) the Kellogg-Briand Pact (d) Coolidge's intervention in Nicaragua (e) the Clark Memorandum (f) the Good Neighbor policy

3. (a) What policies did the United States follow in the 1920s regarding world trade and Allied war debts? (b) Why did the American stock market crash lead to depression in Europe?

4. (a) Explain how totalitarian regimes came to power in Italy and Germany. (b) What form of dictatorship arose in Japan? What encouraged its development?

5. (a) What gains did Americans hope for when the United States recognized the Soviet Union? (b) Why did these gains fail to appear?

6. How did each of the following affect American isolationism? (a) the Nye Committee (b) the Italian invasion of Ethiopia (c) the Spanish civil war (d) the sinking of the *Panay*

Ben Shahn thought that a war poster should have dignity, grimness, and urgency. "French Workers," 1942, was Shahn's first poster for the Office of War Information.

A poster for the Netherlands Government shows the rising sun, an octopus, and a map. It represents the Japanese stranglehold over the Dutch colonies in the East Indies.

7. Explain how each of the following gradually changed American neutrality. (a) the German invasion of Poland (b) the German invasion of northern and western Europe (c) the Battle of Britain (d) the destroyer deal (e) Lend-Lease (f) the Battle of the Atlantic

8. (a) What actions by Japan and the United States led to the deterioration of relations between the two nations from August 1940 to December 1941? (b) How did American and Japanese demands affect the chances of improved relations? (c) What information did code "Magic" contain?

ISSUES AND IDEAS

1. Do you think that the economic policies of the United States in the 1920s hurt world stability? Why or why not?

2. Journalist Dorothy Thompson wrote that one feature of dictatorship was "perpetual aggressiveness." What did she mean? How did events in the 1930s support her statement?

3. The Munich meeting in September 1938 is considered to be a symbol of the policy of appeasement. What were the short-term and long-term results of this policy? Do you believe that the policy was effective? Explain.

4. In July 1940 the Battle of Britain began. (a) As a member of the America First Committee, present arguments why the United States should maintain strict neutrality. (b) As a member of the Committee to Defend America by Aiding the Allies, present arguments why the United States should intervene on Britain's behalf.

SKILLS WORKSHOP

1. *Propaganda.* In May 1940 Hitler ordered German troops into Luxembourg, Belgium, and the Netherlands with the words:

"Soldiers of the West Front!
"The hour of the decisive fight for the future of the German nation has come.
"For 300 years it has been the aim of the English and French rulers . . . to keep Germany weak.
"For this reason all my peace overtures have been rejected and war was declared on us.
"Soldiers of the West Front! The hour for you has now come. The fight beginning today decides the fate of the German nation for the next 1,000 years."

What do you think this message was intended to accomplish? How does it appeal to emotion rather than to reason? In what way are glittering generalities and card stacking used in the message?

2. *Maps.* Look at page 568 of your book. Find the map entitled "Aggression in Europe." What nations had Germany conquered by the summer of 1940? How was the military situation different from the military situation in the early years of World War I? Why do you think Germany was so successful in the early years of World War II?

PAST AND PRESENT

1. In the 1920s nations tried to disarm and to outlaw war in order to preserve peace. What is the United States doing today in the cause of peace? Do you think such efforts can be successful? Why or why not?

2. The real issue of the presidential election of 1940 was the war in Europe. Find out who received your state's electoral votes in the election. How close was the popular vote?

CHAPTER 24

THE SECOND WORLD WAR

1941–1945

THE ALLIES TURN THE TIDE
THE HOME FRONT
THE EUROPEAN FRONT
THE PACIFIC FRONT

During World War II the National Association for the Advancement of Colored People (NAACP) collected letters written by blacks at the front. The pilot who wrote the following letter won the Distinguished Flying Cross for his bravery on this mission. He flew 90 missions during his service and received several other honors, including the Air Medal with eight Oak Leaf clusters.

"We were flying the best fighters in the war, the North American Mustang (Army P-51). . . . I saw a German plane flying along slightly above me and in front of me. . . . I started to follow him, but I saw a German 109 fleeing an American P-51, who in turn was being followed by a German 109. I stopped my pursuit . . . to attempt to rescue the American pilot who evidently didn't realize his plight. The minute I opened up on the German plane, he stopped his chase of the American plane, and attempted to get away. Here the speed of my plane, *Miss Pelt*, named after my fiancée, . . . came in very handy. I overtook him and held my fire until about 75 yards out when I opened up with all four of my fifty cal. machine guns. The German plane lit up like a Christmas tree, . . . As I passed under the burning 109, the pilot bailed out."

In thousands of letters home, Americans told stories of both courage and fear in a long, harsh war. The battlefields were far away from home. Americans fought in island jungles, across searing deserts, through blasted cities, in rough seas, and high above the earth. For many, like the pilot who named his plane after his fiancée, home stayed close in their thoughts.

On a tiny Pacific island a reporter asked a group of marines why they had gone to war. "Home," he found, "seems to most marines a pretty good thing to be fighting for." These marines spoke for Americans in all branches of service.

and parades. In 1941 there were no parades. World War II, said President Roosevelt, would be "the survival war."

ALLIED STRATEGY

On New Year's Day of 1942, representatives of the United States, Britain, the Soviet Union, and 23 other nations met at the White House to form an alliance against "Hitlerism." In time, the alliance, called the Allies, or the United Nations, swelled to 49 nations. Their enemies were the Axis powers—Germany, Japan, Italy. Four other nations—Hungary, Romania, Bulgaria, and Thailand—also were forced to join the Axis powers.

From the start of America's entry into the war, Roosevelt and Prime Minister Churchill of Britain worked closely to plan strategy. They agreed that their major war effort should be in Europe, since they saw Germany as the greatest danger.

Still, Roosevelt did not intend to ignore the Pacific front. While plans were drawn up for an offensive against Hitler, the United States tried to hold off Japan in the Pacific.

JAPAN ON THE MARCH

The Japanese sweep through the Pacific was awesome. By the end of 1941 Japanese troops had conquered the American-held islands of Guam and Wake. Next, Singapore and Hong Kong fell, and, on the Asian mainland, Burma and Thailand fell. Then came more conquest of Pacific islands—the Dutch East Indies, the Solomons, and part of New Guinea. By the spring of 1942 Japan's empire stretched south almost to Australia and west to India.

In the early months of 1942 the American army was involved in a desperate struggle to hold the Philippines. Manila, the capital, fell early in January. General Douglas MacArthur, commander of the American forces in Asia, retreated with his troops to the Philippines' Bataan Peninsula. At an offshore island fortress called Corregidor, MacArthur set up his headquarters.

The American and Philippine forces made a three-month stand at Bataan. However, the Japanese pounded their position. Soon food and medical supplies ran dangerously low. In March President Roosevelt made MacArthur Allied commander in the Southwest Pacific and ordered him to go to

THE ALLIES TURN THE TIDE

READ TO FIND OUT

— how Japan advanced across the Pacific in 1942.

— why the Battle of Midway was a turning point in the war.

— how the British and Americans battled the Germans in North Africa.

— how the Russians turned back the Germans at Stalingrad.

Americans' first reaction to the news of Pearl Harbor was shock. Twenty-four years earlier, when the United States entered World War I, President Wilson had said that the nation was fighting to make the world "safe for democracy." Americans had gone to war in a holiday mood then, with banquets

Allies and Axis

The Allies		The Axis
Argentina	Iran	Bulgaria
Australia	Iraq	Germany
Belgium	Lebanon	Hungary
Bolivia	Liberia	Italy
Brazil	Luxembourg	Japan
Canada	Mexico	Romania
Chile	Netherlands	
China	New Zealand	
Colombia	Nicaragua	
Costa Rica	Norway	
Cuba	Panama	
Czechoslovakia	Paraguay	
Denmark	Peru	
Dominican Republic	Poland	
Ecuador	Russia	
Egypt	San Marino	
El Salvador	Saudi Arabia	
Ethiopia	South Africa	
France	Syria	
Great Britain	Turkey	
Greece	United States	
Guatemala	Uruguay	
Haiti	Venezuela	
Honduras	Yugoslavia	
India		

Officially neutral, Finland accepted German help to counter a Russian invasion. After heavy bombing, the Russians gained ground. Retreating German troops burned Finnish towns.

Australia. As he left, MacArthur promised the Filipinos, "I shall return."

Two months later the Japanese overran the last American defenders at Corregidor. By May 1942 the only places in the Pacific where the American flag still flew were Hawaii and Midway.

AMERICAN VICTORIES IN THE PACIFIC

On April 8, 1942, a group of bombers took off from an American aircraft carrier in the Pacific. Led by General James H. Doolittle, the planes flew hundreds of miles to Japan and bombed the capital of Tokyo. The bombers did little damage, and most of them ran out of fuel and had to crash-land in China. Still, the raid sent American spirits soaring.

The Japanese were astounded and dismayed. They had thought that their islands were safe from Allied bombing. To expand their defenses, the Japanese, in May, sent a fleet of ships into the Coral Sea near New Guinea and Australia. They hoped to cut Allied shipping lanes through the sea and to invade Australia.

However, an American fleet intercepted the Japanese in the Coral Sea. The two-day battle was waged by carrier-based planes. The battleships were never within sight of one another. On May 8 the Japanese fleet withdrew. In the Battle of the Coral Sea, the Americans had managed to stop the Japanese drive toward Australia.

Japan had another target in its offensive—to capture Midway Island, a stepping-stone to Hawaii and the United States mainland. However, American code-breakers learned of the plans and warned the commander of the Pacific fleet, Admiral Chester W. Nimitz. When the Japanese attacked Midway on June 4, the Americans were waiting.

For 4 days American fighters and bombers fought with the Japanese. The sea churned with downed planes. American losses were heavy, but Japan's were worse. It lost 4 of its best carriers and 275 planes.

The Battle of Midway was a turning point in the war with Japan. It ended the Japanese threat to Hawaii and halted Japan's six-month offensive. The United States was once more a naval power in the Pacific.

ALLIED PLANS FOR THE EUROPEAN FRONT

Roosevelt and Churchill jointly planned a major portion of Allied strategy. However, they also consulted the third largest Allied power—the Soviet Union. In time, Roosevelt, Churchill, and Soviet leader Joseph Stalin became known as the "Big Three" of the Allies.

From the beginning, however, American and British relations with the Russians were sensitive. Roosevelt and Churchill opposed communism and distrusted Stalin. Stalin distrusted the British and the Americans and felt that they were not doing enough to help the Russians on the eastern front.

After Hitler's invasion of the Soviet Union in June 1941, the Russians had managed to stall the German drive. Then, during the summer of 1942, the Germans made an offensive strike from the southwest toward Stalingrad. As Churchill noted, the Russians' "vast front [was] flaming and bleeding along nearly two thousand miles."

Maximum Extent of Axis Control 1942

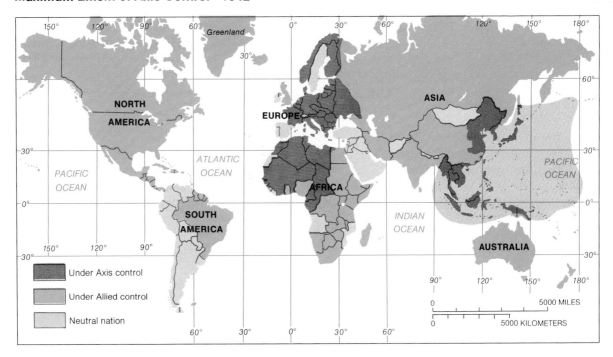

Stalin made two large demands of his allies. He wanted them to launch a cross-channel invasion from Britain into France. This would open a second fighting front, forcing Hitler to transfer troops from the eastern front to a western front. Pressure on the Soviet Union would ease. Stalin also demanded that his allies recognize territory that the Soviets had seized in 1940 and 1941. The Soviet Union now controlled Estonia, Latvia, Lithuania, and parts of Poland, Finland, and Romania.

Churchill and Roosevelt flatly rejected Stalin's territorial claims. Both, however, worried that the Soviet Union might be defeated or that Stalin would make a separate peace with Hitler. To head off disaster on the eastern front, Roosevelt felt that a second front in France was needed.

Churchill disagreed. He felt that the Allies did not yet have enough trained soldiers and supplies for a massive cross-channel invasion. Allied efforts, Churchill argued, should be concentrated on the fighting in French North Africa, where British troops were near defeat.

Roosevelt agreed to the North African campaign, called Operation Torch. The cross-channel invasion was postponed. In August 1942 Churchill flew to Moscow to explain Operation Torch. It was his first face-to-face meeting with Stalin.

The two leaders studied a map of Europe and North Africa. Churchill explained to Stalin that if the British and Americans won in North Africa, they could then strike across the Mediterranean into southern Europe. This should divert the Germans from the Soviet Union.

Churchill then drew a picture of Hitler's Europe in the form of a crocodile. Its snout pointed toward the Soviet Union and its belly rested on the Mediterranean. As Churchill later recorded:

> I . . . explained to Stalin with the help of this picture how it was our intention to attack the soft belly of the crocodile as he [Stalin] attacked the hard snout. And Stalin, whose interest was now at a pitch, said: "May God prosper this undertaking."

VICTORY IN NORTH AFRICA

To win in North Africa the Allies would have to defeat the Africa Korps, Germany's army of heavily armored tanks. The korps was led by General Erwin Rommel, who was nicknamed the "Desert Fox" for his strike-and-retreat tactics.

During 1941 Britain and German tanks had dueled back and forth across hundreds of miles of blazing desert. Then, in May 1942, the Afrika Korps, aided by Italian troops, forced the British to retreat to El Alamein in Egypt. Axis troops were poised to take Egypt's Suez Canal—a vital shipping route—and the Middle East oil fields. It looked as if the Germans would win all of North Africa.

Rommel, however, met his match in British Field Marshal Bernard Montgomery. In late October 1942, strengthened by the arrival of 400 American tanks, British troops stopped the Afrika Korps in the Battle of El Alamein. Montgomery then chased the Desert Fox northwest through Libya toward Tunisia.

Meanwhile, Operation Torch began. On November 8 American and British troops landed on the coasts of Morocco and Algeria, to the east of Tunisia. Commanding the Allied forces was General Dwight D. "Ike" Eisenhower, known for his skill in strategy.

The Allies met initial resistance from the Vichy French, who cooperated with the Germans. However, opposition collapsed within a few days. The Allies then pushed eastward across Algeria into Tunisia, where German forces were massing.

Week by week, the Allied troops battled their way through Tunisia. By May 1943 the Germans were pinned against the sea, trapped by Eisenhower's forces to the west and Montgomery's troops to the east. North Africa at last fell to the Allies.

STALINGRAD

While the British and Americans sliced through North Africa, the Russians grimly held off the Nazis at Stalingrad. With the city close to ruins, the Stalingrad defenders struck back in November 1942. The Russians fought with everything they had—tanks, cannon, infantry, even cavalry. In January the Germans gave up the attack on Stalingrad.

SECTION REVIEW

1. Identify the following: Corregidor, James H. Doolittle, Chester W. Nimitz, the "Big Three," Operation Torch, Afrika Korps, "Desert Fox," Bernard Montgomery, "Ike."

AMERICAN OBSERVERS

MARGARET BOURKE-WHITE
PHOTOGRAPHER

Photographer Margaret Bourke-White was on a crowded troopship headed for North Africa when the torpedo struck. It came almost softly, she remembered, "with a dull blunt thud." Yet everyone knew "this was it."

As the ship began to burn, soldiers and nurses scrambled down rope nets toward quickly lowered lifeboats. Others, not so lucky, were trapped below deck. Soon "the water itself was alive with people swimming, people in lifeboats, people hanging to floating debris." Bourke-White's packed lifeboat drifted for a day and a night on the open sea before being rescued.

When World War II began, Margaret Bourke-White was already a well-known photographer. Born in 1905 in New York City, she had been an adventurous child. She dreamed of traveling around the world. In college she discovered her talent for photography. During the depression, her haunting pictures of the Dust Bowl brought her fame.

2. (a) Where did Roosevelt and Churchill feel that the major war effort should be? (b) What other front was Roosevelt greatly concerned about?

3. (a) How far had Japan expanded its empire by the spring of 1942? (b) Name the two places in the Pacific where the American flag still flew in May 1942.

4. (a) What effect did the bombing of Tokyo in April 1942 have on the Japanese? (b) What was the outcome of the Battle of the Coral Sea? (c) Why was victory at Midway so important to the United States?

5. (a) Name two demands Stalin made of his allies. (b) Why did Churchill disagree to a cross-channel invasion? What was the outcome?

6. (a) In May 1942 why did it look as if Rommel would win all of North Africa? (b) Describe the Germans' position in Africa in May 1943. (c) What were the Russians doing while the British and Americans fought in North Africa?

In 1941 Margaret Bourke-White was the only foreign photographer to cover the German attack on Moscow. In 1942 she went to Europe as a *Life* magazine photographer assigned to the Air Force. After the torpedo attack, she went on to North Africa, where she photographed the Allied campaign. Later she covered the invasion of Italy.

In the spring of 1945 she was with General George S. Patton's Third Army in Germany when the Nazi concentration camps were discovered. "Buchenwald," she said, "was more than the mind could grasp." Though heartsick, she photographed it all, because she wanted the world to know the full horror.

After the war Bourke-White worked for *Life*, covering the independence movement in India and the Korean War. She had always felt "an insatiable desire to be on the scene when history was being made." Through photography, she made it all come true.

THE HOME FRONT

READ TO FIND OUT

— how the United States mobilized for war.

— how industry met the needs of the war.

— how labor and wages and prices were affected by the war.

— how the United States financed the war.

— how Japanese Americans were affected by the war.

— how Americans at home helped the war effort.

The war was a world war in the sense that nations from almost every continent took part. However, only some of the nations became battlefields. Bombs gutted parts of Europe, Africa, Asia, and a scattering of islands. American possessions—Hawaii, Wake, Midway, Guam, the Philippines—were attacked. The United States itself, alone among the great powers, was not scarred by battle.

However, Americans at home were indeed fighting. The Allied armies were fed and supplied by factories, fields, mines, and offices in the United States.

WARTIME AGENCIES

Pearl Harbor had caught Americans unprepared for war. In the late 1930s the United States had made some attempts to build up its defenses. Once it entered the war, however, the nation faced the huge task of mobilization.

To handle all the wartime needs, the government set up a dizzying array of agencies. There were agencies to oversee transportation, housing, information, civil defense, labor, and a dozen other areas. Supervising the whole wartime home front was the Office of War Mobilization (OWM). The OWM acted as an umbrella over all the agencies, coordinating their activities. Its director, James F. Byrnes, operated out of the White House. He was so powerful that he was called the "assistant president."

THE ARMED FORCES

The mobilization of people for military service was itself an enormous task. The War Manpower Commission (WMC) had the responsibility of running the Selective Service System—the draft—and other wartime recruiting and training agencies.

During the war, about 10 million men were drafted into the army. They became known as "GIs." These were the initials for "General Issue"—the words stamped on clothing, rifles, jeeps, and everything else issued to soldiers.

Another 6 million men and women volunteered for the other branches of the military. The navy, marines, and army air corps were all staffed by volunteers.

Women volunteers filled noncombat roles. They joined the Women's Auxiliary Army Corps (WAACS), the navy's Women Appointed for Voluntary Emergency Service (WAVES), the Women's Auxiliary Ferrying Squadron (WAFS), and the Women's Reserves of the Coast Guard and the Marine Corps. Women worked in such roles as clerks, cooks, mechanics, radio operators, and airplane spotters. To free male pilots for battle, women flew planes from factories to military bases and towed targets for gunnery practice.

The armed forces received some of their most enthusiastic volunteers from Indian reservations. Over 30 percent of all able-bodied Indian men joined the services. Some 500,000 Mexican Americans also rushed to serve.

About 900,000 blacks volunteered or were drafted into the services. Most served in all-black units under white officers.

Blacks were often assigned to service units, which were responsible for construction, cooking, and providing troops with weapons and equipment. But many did see combat. Black artillery, antiaircraft, and tank units fought in Europe and the Pacific. Black air units flew more than 15,000 missions. Also, some 4,000 black women served in the various women's corps.

Late in the war, the army needed more infantry and called for black volunteers from service units. Thousands responded. Some 2,500 blacks were accepted, and their platoons fought side by side with white platoons. General Dwight Eisenhower, who had approved the integrated units, remarked, "I do not differentiate among soldiers. I do not say white

A group of World War II American fliers stationed in Italy posed for this photograph. In full flight gear, they were ready for takeoff.

soldiers or Negro soldiers and I do not say American or British soldiers. To my mind, I have had a task in this war that makes me look upon soldiers as soldiers."

WAR PRODUCTION

In January 1942 Roosevelt set up the War Production Board (WPB) to supervise the conversion of industry from peace to war. The last peacetime automobile rolled off a Ford assembly line in February 1942. The auto industry began producing airplanes, engines, and tanks. By the spring of 1942 war factories were operating around the clock in three 8-hour shifts.

Roosevelt set high production goals. The aircraft industry, for example, had produced 6,000 planes in 1939. For 1942, Roosevelt set a goal of 60,000. By 1944 it had become the nation's largest industry, with 2 million workers producing 96,000 planes in a single year.

Industrialist Henry J. Kaiser revolutionized the vital shipbuilding industry. To build warships and the cargo vessels called "Liberty ships," he introduced prefabricated construction,* assembly lines,

* prefabricated construction: construction in standardized sections for shipment and quick assembly

and electric welding. In 1939 it had taken at least three months to build one cargo ship. In 1942 Kaiser workers at the Richmond, California, shipyard reduced the average time to fourteen days.

By 1943 the United States was producing more war equipment than Germany, Italy, and Japan put together. "I think the arsenal of democracy is making good," said a pleased Roosevelt.

Production increased in areas other than industry. To meet demands for food, the Department of Agriculture urged farmers to grow more crops. Farmers fed the United States and its allies, and between 1940 and 1945 farm income quadrupled.

This flood of food and supplies was vital to Great Britain and the Soviet Union. Much of the Soviets' heavy industry had been destroyed by the Germans. With American supplies, the Russians rebuilt entire industries that were safely located beyond the range of German attack. Greater quantities of goods also were sent to the British.

LABOR

Because of wartime production, thousands of jobs became available. Unemployment lines vanished, and suddenly there was a shortage of labor. The

The demands of war industry drew increasing numbers of women to the production lines. A popular patriotic song was entitled "Rosie the Riveter."

hard times of the depression gave way to full employment and prosperity. People who had been jobless for years began earning $100 per week.

Many of the new jobs were held by women. Because so many men were in the military, women began doing jobs that were once considered "men's work," such as driving trucks and operating machines. Over 2 million women found work in war industries, especially in shipyards and aircraft plants. In 1940 women had made up only 1 percent of aircraft workers. By 1945 the figure soared to 65 percent. As one advertisement for women workers stated, "If you can drive a car, you can run a machine."

War industries drew workers from every corner of the nation. Some 27 million Americans moved during the war. It was the biggest migration in the nation's history. Over 1 million people flocked to the shipyards and aircraft plants in the Pacific Coast states. Portland, Oregon, was so crowded that movie houses held "swing-shift matinees" at midnight.

WAGE AND PRICE CONTROLS

Although people suddenly had more money, there was not much to spend it on. Industry was producing war goods, not consumer goods. The demand for the few goods available drove prices higher and higher.

To combat this inflation, Congress set up the Office of Price Administration (OPA) in January 1942. The OPA placed price ceilings, or limits, on rents in areas important to defense and on all goods except farm produce.

The OPA also rationed, or limited distribution of, scarce or war-related goods. The government issued ration books. The books contained coupons with which Americans could buy limited amounts of sugar, coffee, gasoline, rubber tires, nylon, and anything made of metal. Within a year meat, butter, cheese, processed foods, and even shoes were rationed.

Despite the efforts of the OPA, prices continued to rise. Workers protested and demanded wage increases. In April 1943 President Roosevelt, with authority from Congress, issued a "hold-the-line" order to freeze wages and prices.

When the war began, union leaders had promised not to strike if the government would treat workers fairly. However, in May 1943, in protest against Roosevelt's order, John L. Lewis sent his United Mine Workers out on strike. The National War Labor Board (NWLB), which handled labor problems, could not convince the union to go back to work. Roosevelt acted quickly, authorizing a government takeover of the mines. Lewis called off the strike.

The government settled other labor disputes, with groups such as railway workers and employees of the Montgomery Ward mail-order firm. The majority of workers, however, stayed on the job.

Most Americans accepted wartime controls as a necessity. Most felt that, by coping with shortages, they were contributing to the war effort. Skirts were made without pleats to save cloth. Men's "victory suits" had no pockets or cuffs. After all, people told each other, "Don't you know there's a war on?"

FINANCING THE WAR

The cost of the war was staggering. In 1940 the federal government had spent some $9 billion. By 1943 it was spending almost that much every month. By 1945 the annual budget was over $100 billion.

To pay these costs and to curb inflation, the government used several methods. In 1942 Congress passed a revenue act that Roosevelt called "the greatest tax bill in American history." Income tax brackets were broadened to include millions of new taxpayers. Also, the tax rate for those with the highest incomes soared to 94 percent. Employers were compelled to withhold, or deduct, income taxes from workers' paychecks for the government. Thus, the income tax became known as a *withholding tax*.

Taxes on corporations also soared. Companies had to pay income taxes as high as 50 percent. They also paid a special wartime tax of 90 percent on *excess profits*, profits that were higher than what was figured to be a fair rate.

The government also sold war bonds to raise money. By investing, people were told, they could equip soldiers at the front and save money as well. Americans bought over $100 billion worth of bonds.

However, the income from bonds and taxes did not cover all the government's spending. At the end of the war the national debt was $258 billion, six times higher than at the start of the war.

BLACK AMERICANS DURING THE WAR

For black Americans, the war had good and bad effects. Blacks did share in the fruits of the booming war economy, but not without a struggle. Even before Pearl Harbor, defense industries had been rushing to hire workers. Yet black applicants were often turned away.

A. Philip Randolph, head of the Brotherhood of Sleeping Car Porters, decided to protest the discrimination. In May 1941 he called for 50,000 blacks to march on Washington to demand jobs in defense industries.

To prevent the march, Roosevelt met with Randolph to discuss the problems of black workers. In June the President issued Executive Order 8802. The order banned discrimination in the hiring of workers in defense industries or in government. To enforce the order, Roosevelt created the Fair Employment Practices Committee (FEPC).

As the labor shortage grew critical and the FEPC pursued complaints of discrimination, more and more blacks found defense jobs. During the war the number of black workers in government increased from 40,000 to 300,000, and in industry from 500,000 to over 1,200,000. The number of blacks who held skilled jobs doubled.

Blacks were part of the great wartime migration, and some 700,000 of them crowded into industrial cities. Many whites resented black competition for jobs and for scarce housing. Friction between the races sometimes flamed into riots.

In Detroit in February 1942, whites tried to stop blacks from moving into a low-income housing project. Fights broke out and lasted for 2 days. Far more serious riots occurred in the city in June 1943, resulting in 34 deaths. Federal troops had to be brought in to restore order.

Blacks continued to face segregation in restaurants, hotels, and theaters. One black soldier told of being refused service in a midwestern restaurant that was serving German prisoners of war.

Segregation and the outbreaks of violence moved some people to try to improve relations between the races. Some governors called for laws against discrimination. In some cities blacks and whites formed "peace teams" to work for racial equality.

Sixty-five black students found another way to fight segregation. In April 1944 they quietly sat down in a segregated Washington, D.C., restaurant. They were refused service, although most of the white customers did not object to their presence. Several hours later, the restaurant served the blacks.

MEXICAN AMERICANS

Like blacks, Mexican Americans continued to face discrimination during the war. In California and the Southwest, where most lived, industries often denied them job training and promotions. An FEPC investigation into one southwestern oil company found that it had one pay rate for whites and a lower pay rate for blacks and Mexican Americans.

In 1943 racial tensions in Los Angeles, California, led to violence. For five days white soldiers and sailors roamed the streets, attacking Mexican Americans. Such incidents led one marine to say later, "Mexican American soldiers shed at least a quarter of the blood spilled at Bataan. . . . What they want now is a decent job, a decent home, and a chance to live peacefully in the community."

RELOCATION OF JAPANESE AMERICANS

Some Americans whose ancestors had come from Axis nations also suffered during the war. Those of German and Italian descent sometimes faced hostility, but Japanese Americans were confronted with a much harsher situation.

The attack on Pearl Harbor had frightened Americans. People thought that the Japanese might attack the West Coast of the United States. These fears led people on the West Coast to question the loyalty of Japanese Americans.

Fear of sabotage led President Roosevelt, in February 1942, to authorize the War Department to remove people from "military areas." The army thereupon labeled all Japanese Americans living in the Pacific Coast states—about 110,000 people—as a "menace." Two thirds of these people were *Nisei* (NEE-say)—native-born Americans whose ancestors came from Japan. Yet, they were to be removed to "relocation camps" in bleak areas of the western states and Arkansas.

Stunned Japanese Americans hurried to obey the order, with little or no time to settle their affairs. Most had to sell their belongings, homes, and businesses for whatever they could get before being

At the Manzanar, California, relocation camp, a dust storm drove Japanese American internees to take cover. Such storms added to the discomfort of their isolation.

herded off to the camps. One man described a California camp called Manzanar: "The desert was bad enough. The mushroom barracks made it worse. The constant cyclonic storms loaded with sand and dust made it worst. . . . We slept in the dust; we breathed the dust; and we ate the dust."

In 1943 the army began recruiting soldiers from the relocation camps. Those who enlisted served in segregated units. The Japanese American 442nd Regimental Combat Team, for its size and length of service, earned more decorations than any other military unit in American history.

The remainder of the confined Japanese Americans stayed in the camps throughout most of the war. No evidence was ever found to support the charges of disloyalty. Still, in 1944 a Supreme Court decision, *Korematsu* v. *U.S.*, upheld the relocation.

In 1945, when victory in the war seemed certain, the Japanese Americans were freed from the camps. In 1948 Congress passed an act that helped Japanese Americans to recover some of their financial losses.

THE WAR EFFORT

The unfortunate side of the home front was relocation camps, but the bright side was Americans' eagerness to help the war effort. All across the nation, people pitched in.

Americans collected millions of tons of scrap—paper, rags, metal, rubber—to be used in war goods. They gave blood, donated clothing, and sold war bonds.

Because the military and the Allies needed so much food, Americans grew their own. "Victory gardens" sprang up in backyards, in vacant lots, and even in window boxes. In 1943, 20 million victory gardens produced 40 percent of the nation's fresh vegetables.

Many Americans volunteered for civil defense. Air raid wardens patrolled the streets during blackout drills to be sure that no lights were burning that could guide enemy bombers. Airplane spotters identified every plane that flew over their posts.

In early 1943 a British visitor flew in an airliner above the American prairies. "Here, if anywhere, was normality," he noted. "Hundreds of miles of it and not a sight or sound to remind one that this was a country at war." Then his lunch tray arrived. Neatly printed on the butter pat were the words "Remember Pearl Harbor."

SECTION REVIEW

1. Identify the following: Office of War Mobilization, War Production Board, Office of Price Administration, Fair Employment Practices Committee, Nisei, *Korematsu* v. *U.S.*

2. Define the following: price ceilings, withholding tax, excess profits, relocation camps.

3. (a) What was the nation's largest industry in 1944? (b) Why were American foods and supplies vital to the British and the Soviets?

4. (a) How did wartime production affect unemployment? (b) How did the shortage of consumer goods affect prices?

5. (a) How did the federal budget change from 1940 to 1945? (b) List three methods the government used to pay for war costs and to curb inflation.

6. (a) Why did Roosevelt issue Executive Order 8802? (b) How did industries in California and the Southwest discriminate against Mexican Americans?

7. What happened to Japanese Americans living on the West Coast?

8. List five ways in which American civilians helped the war effort.

THE EUROPEAN FRONT

READ TO FIND OUT

—**how the British and Americans conducted the Italian campaign.**

—**how the Big Three coordinated plans at Teheran.**

—**how the plan for D-Day was carried out.**

—**how the Allies continued the offensive in Europe.**

—**what agreements were made at Yalta.**

—**how the Allies gained victory in Europe.**

In January 1943 the tide of the European war was turning in favor of the Allies. The Russians were pushing the Germans out of Stalingrad. The Allies were on the way to recapturing North Africa.

Roosevelt traveled to Casablanca, Morocco, to meet with Churchill. The leaders would plan the next Allied offensive in Europe. They were in close touch with Stalin, who would not leave Russian soil at that critical time. As fighter planes scoured the North African sky, Roosevelt and Churchill conferred in a Casablanca hotel surrounded by barbed wire.

THE CASABLANCA CONFERENCE

Some American advisers at Casablanca were eager to get on with the postponed cross-channel invasion of France. However, the Allies still lacked the necessary equipment—especially landing craft—and German submarines were still a menace in the English Channel. The invasion was again postponed.

Roosevelt agreed with Churchill that the Allies should strike from their bases in North Africa at "the under-belly of the Axis." Sicily, an island at the tip of Italy, was chosen as the first target. The capture of this island would make the Mediterranean safe for Allied shipping. It would also divert the Germans from the Russian front and open the way for the Allies to take all of Italy. The planned attack was code-named Operation Husky.

The two leaders also agreed to keep pressure on the Japanese in the Pacific. However, their first priority would remain the European front.

Finally, Roosevelt and Churchill agreed on the terms of surrender for the Axis nations. As one observer noted, the "ghost of Woodrow Wilson" was at Roosevelt's shoulder. Wilson's Fourteen Points had led the Germans to sign the armistice of 1919 with false hopes of easy terms for peace. Roosevelt wanted no misunderstanding this time. The Allies would demand unconditional surrender.

THE ITALIAN CAMPAIGN

Before dawn on July 10, 1943, some 160,000 Allied troops splashed ashore at Sicily, launching Operation Husky. The amphibious assault was aided by a new type of landing craft, the Landing Ship-Tank (LST). It had a gooey water repellent to protect the motor equipment aboard. In a relentless 39-day campaign, the Allies swept the German and Italian defenders from the island.

Meanwhile, Allied planes rained bombs on Rome. Unhappy with Mussolini, the Italians imprisoned him and formed a new government. They also disbanded the Fascist party. Italy seemed open to attack. From Sicily, the Allies prepared to strike at the Italian mainland.

In early September British forces landed on the southern tip of the Italian peninsula. A few days later an American army under General Mark W. Clark headed for the town of Salerno, north along the coast. On the way, the troops heard that the Italian government had surrendered.

However, when Clark's forces landed at Salerno on September 9, German bombs and tanks nearly drove them back into the sea. After a week of fierce battle, the Americans took Salerno and joined the British forces. The Allies then pushed north to Naples, taking the city in October.

However, Allied visions of an easy victory crumbled. The German army, now numbering 400,000 troops, was determined to hold Italy. The rugged terrain favored the entrenched Germans.

Through a winter of floods and mud, the Allies fought their way toward Rome, 100 miles (161 kilometers) north of Naples. After months of tortuous advance, the Allies decided to bypass the mountain barriers and go around the Germans. They planned to strike behind German lines at Anzio, a coastal city 33 miles (53 kilometers) south of Rome.

American and British troops landed at Anzio in January 1944. The Germans, on high ground, poured artillery fire down on the Allied beachhead. Not until May could the Allies break through German lines. That same month other Allied troops captured Cassino, to the east, after three weary months of attacks.

Finally, in June 1944, the battered Allied forces marched into Rome. However, in the mountains to the north, the Germans prepared for battle. The Allied campaign to conquer all of Italy would continue until the war was almost over.

THE CAIRO AND TEHERAN CONFERENCES

In November 1943, while Allied armies advanced toward Rome, Allied leaders met at two conferences to plan their next campaign. The first conference, at Cairo, Egypt, was attended by Roosevelt, Churchill, and Chinese leader Chiang Kai-shek (CHAHNG KĪ-SHEK). The leaders discussed China's needs and territorial claims in the war against Japan. The Soviets, who were not at war with Japan, did not attend the conference.

From Cairo, Roosevelt and Churchill flew on to join Stalin at Teheran, Iran. At Teheran, Stalin expressed one major concern. He wanted the Germans diverted from the Russian front. The Italian campaign was easing the pressure. Also, the Russians had managed to drive the Germans out of the Ukraine, western Russia, and eastern Poland. Still, Hitler continued to concentrate a good part of his forces against the Soviet Union.

In the four days of talks, Stalin again and again asked the same question. When was the long-delayed cross-channel invasion, Operation Overlord, going to take place? Roosevelt and Churchill, however, were still concerned with the Italian campaign. Operation Overlord, they said, could not be launched until good weather made the English Channel safe for crossing.

Churchill and Roosevelt assured Stalin that the invasion would take place by the summer of 1944. Stalin in turn promised to start a Soviet offensive to coincide with Overlord. He also pledged to join the war against Japan after Germany's defeat.

The invasion at the coast of Normandy in Operation Overlord was an immense, complicated undertaking. A photograph taken on D-Day shows the vast land, sea, and air forces involved. To the Germans the scene must have been awesome.

WINNING COMMAND OF THE SEA AND AIR

The British and Americans had been preparing for Operation Overlord for some time. However, a successful invasion required more than good weather and a massive buildup of troops and supplies. The Allies also needed command of the air and sea. Allied forces crossing the English Channel would be vulnerable to German bombers and U-boats, or submarines.

The Battle of the Atlantic had been raging since 1939. By early 1943 it seemed that the Atlantic Ocean belonged to the Germans. Nazi planes, ships, mines, and some 235 U-boats destroyed millions of tons of Allied shipping. Many Lend-Lease supplies en route to Britain or the Soviet Union vanished.

Then, in the spring of 1943, the Allies began to strike back. The Americans improved their convoy system to escort merchant ships. American scientists developed a device, called sonar, to detect underwater sound. The British had invented radar, a device which located objects by radio waves. Sonar and radar were installed on escort ships to detect U-boats. Allied destroyers and planes could then attack the submarines.

Allied shipping losses quickly decreased. The Allies began destroying U-boats faster than Germany could build them.

In 1942 the Allies also began daily bombing raids on German cities and military and industrial targets. Germany's war production was not much affected, but many cities were bombed into ruins.

Harbors, railroads, and airfields were heavily damaged. Germany also lost many airplanes.

By the spring of 1944, the German air force was outnumbered 30 to 1 by the Allied air forces. On the day of Operation Overlord, General Eisenhower could tell his troops, "If you see fighting aircraft over you, they will be ours."

D-DAY

In the early hours of June 5, 1944, Allied commanders met with weather experts in southern Britain. A storm was raging but the forecasters predicted a period of calm the next day. General Eisenhower, Supreme Commander of the Allied forces, had to make a decision.

Some 176,000 troops, 4,600 ships, and 11,000 aircraft had been assembled for Operation Overlord. However, the invasion depended on a combination of tides, moonlight, clear weather, and secrecy. As Eisenhower wrote:

> The mighty host was tense as a coiled spring. . . .
> Coiled for the moment when its energy should be
> released and it would vault the English Channel in
> the greatest amphibious assault ever attempted.

Eisenhower made the decision to go ahead.

The target was a 50-mile (80-kilometer) stretch of French beach along the coast of Normandy. Shortly after midnight on June 6, paratroopers landed behind German shore defenses to cut rail lines and seize airfields. Silent gliders landed troops, jeeps, and small tanks.

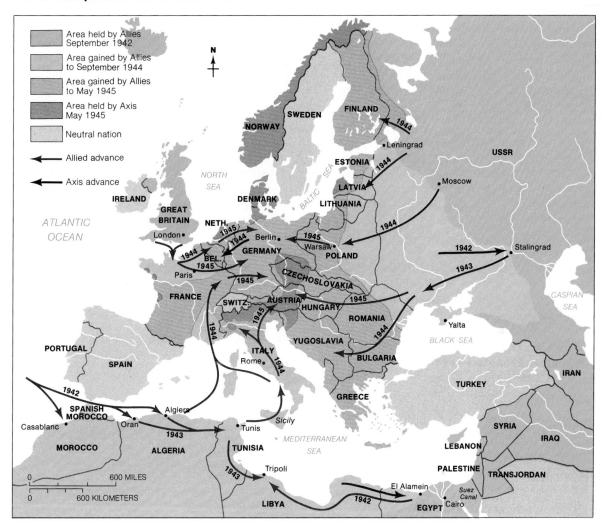

Area held by Allies
September 1942

Area gained by Allies
to September 1944

Area gained by Allies
to May 1945

Area held by Axis
May 1945

Neutral nation

Allied advance

Axis advance

Meanwhile, the huge invasion fleet sailed across the choppy English Channel. Just before a gray dawn, warships began bombing the coast. Allied planes screamed overhead in bombing runs. At 6:30 a.m. troops spilled out of landing craft onto the Normandy beaches. Thus began D-Day.

The Germans were caught by surprise. They had expected an invasion farther north and had concentrated their defenses there. At most sites, Allied troops were able to secure the beaches.

However, at a little strip of beach code-named Omaha by the Allies, a first-rate German unit waited. The water was mined, the beach was mined, and the grass beyond the sand was mined. From cliffs above the beach, German artillery covered every grain of sand.

The landing began. Allied naval guns pounded the cliffs as two divisions of Americans charged, under heavy fire, across an open stretch of beach. Omaha was secured, at a deadly cost. Casualties in the first assault groups were 60 percent.

At day's end, Allied casualties for the total invasion were 10,700. The cross-channel invasion was, however, a success.

THE LIBERATION OF PARIS

Within two weeks of D-Day the Allies controlled the Normandy beachhead. More and more troops and supplies poured across the English Channel. By mid-July the Allies had fought their way inland from the beachhead.

The Germans fell back before the relentless Allied advance. A second Allied invasion force crossed the Mediterranean from North Africa. It landed in southern France and pushed north through the Rhone Valley. Everywhere, Free French forces joined the advancing Allies.

On August 25 laughing and weeping Parisians welcomed Allied and Free French forces into the French capital. A provisional government was set up under Free French leader Charles de Gaulle. Over the next two weeks the Allies swept the Germans from all of France, Belgium, and Luxembourg. However, in September the swift-moving Allies outran their supply lines and stalled along the German border.

Meanwhile, on the eastern front, Stalin had launched his promised offensive. Soviet troops marched westward along an 800-mile (1,290-kilometer) front. By the end of 1944 the Soviets had forced Axis-controlled Romania, Bulgaria, and Hungary out of the war and had freed Yugoslavia from German control.

THE BATTLE OF THE BULGE

However, Germany was not yet defeated. In December 1944 German forces attacked American lines in the Ardennes Forest of Belgium, the weakest section of the whole western Allied front. The Germans overwhelmed surprised American soldiers and pushed through to rear-area supply points.

The lightning German advance—some 50 miles (80 kilometers) into Belgium—created a great bulge in the Allied front. At the little town of Bastogne (bas-TŌN), the Americans grimly dug in to stop the German advance. For 6 days the Germans bombarded the town, and even captured the entire American surgical unit. The Nazis demanded that the Americans surrender. General Anthony C. McAuliffe sent his reply: "To the German Commander—NUTS!—the American Commander."

On the day after Christmas, American reinforcements reached Bastogne and broke the siege. The Americans now took the offensive and within a month drove the Germans back.

The Battle of the Bulge cost the Americans 77,000 killed, wounded, or missing. But the Germans paid more dearly. They lost 120,000 in casualties, about 1,600 planes, and a huge part of their tank force.

THE ELECTION OF 1944

While the Allied offensive raged in Europe, President Roosevelt was running for a fourth term as president. Although exhausted by his 12 years in office, he felt that the nation should not change leaders during a war. Roosevelt's running mate was Senator Harry S. Truman of Missouri.

The Republicans pinned their hopes on Thomas E. Dewey, the energetic governor of New York. Dewey, however, had little to campaign against. Inflation was declining, war production was booming, and the Allies were defeating Hitler.

Voters showed little desire to change leaders. Roosevelt scored another one-sided victory, winning the electoral vote 432 to 99. No president had ever served more than 8 years. Now Roosevelt had won his fourth term.

THE YALTA CONFERENCE

As victory seemed within reach in Europe, Roosevelt, Churchill, and Stalin decided they must meet once again. Plans had to be drawn for postwar Europe and for the Pacific front. The meeting place was Yalta, an old Russian resort town on the Black

At Yalta with Churchill and Stalin, Roosevelt alone showed the strain of the past years. The wartime presidency had been a heavy burden.

Sea. For eight days in February 1945 the leaders of the Allied nations talked.

The Big Three agreed that Germany, after its surrender, would be divided into four zones of military occupation. The zones would be controlled by the United States, Britain, the Soviet Union, and France. The Allied leaders also completed plans, begun at earlier meetings, for a new world organization.

The subject of Poland was discussed at almost every meeting. By the time of the Yalta Conference, the Soviet Union occupied much of eastern Europe, including all of Poland. Stalin insisted that the Soviets had a stake in Poland because they had freed it from the Germans. Also, Stalin claimed that Poland had always been a corridor through which enemies attacked the Soviet Union, and he wanted a secure frontier.

Stalin claimed a large slice of Poland's eastern territory—the area that the Russians had taken in 1939. Poland, Stalin continued, could be compensated with German territory along its western border. Roosevelt and Churchill agreed to Stalin's limited territorial claims in Poland.

However, the Big Three clashed over the government of Poland itself. Stalin supported an existing government in power in the Polish city of Lublin. The British and Americans refused to recognize this Soviet-influenced regime. In a compromise, the Big Three agreed to bring democratic leaders into the Lublin government and to hold free elections at an early date. Democratic governments were also promised for the other eastern European nations occupied by the Soviets.

The Yalta talks also dealt with the war in the Pacific. Stalin pledged to declare war on Japan within three months of Germany's defeat, but he wanted territory in exchange. Both Roosevelt and Churchill felt that Russian help was needed to defeat Japan, and they agreed to Stalin's terms.

Stalin was promised that all territory lost in the Russo-Japanese War would be returned to the Russians. In addition, the Soviet Union would be given Japan's Kurile Islands and southern Sakhalin Island, naval rights in China's Port Arthur, railroad rights in Manchuria, and an occupation zone in Korea. In addition, Roosevelt and Churchill agreed to recognize the Soviet-supported Mongolian People's Republic, which had claimed its independence from China.

The horrors of the German concentration camps are a haunting example of inhumanity. This victim at Bergen-Belsen was trying to delouse his clothing.

THE HOLOCAUST

As the Big Three left Yalta, their nations' armies were closing in on Germany. Soviet troops pushed westward. British and American air forces pounded German targets. Then, in March, Allied troops crossed the Rhine River into Germany.

As the Allies advanced, they discovered a number of concentration camps in which "political prisoners" had been held. Some 12 million civilians from occupied European nations and from Germany itself had died in these camps. Men, women, and children were shot, starved, beaten, tortured in medical "experiments," or gassed in chambers that were disguised as showers.

Six million of those killed were Jewish, victims of the Nazi attempt to destroy all Jews. One third of the Jewish population of Europe had been killed. A horrified world would call this vast destruction of Jewish lives the Holocaust. The names of the camps—Buchenwald, Dachau, Bergen-Belsen, and Auschwitz—would be remembered as evidence of Nazi brutality.

On March 6, 1945, the first American tank entered Cologne, Germany. An important industrial city, Cologne had been a target of heavy Allied bombing.

VICTORY IN EUROPE

As prisoners were liberated from concentration camps by the advancing Allies, the Nazi empire was crumbling. German troops were fighting last-ditch battles. Churchill became worried that the Russians would overrun Czechoslovakia, Austria, and Germany.

Churchill wanted the British and American troops to race to the German capitol of Berlin and to occupy as much of Germany as they could. The Americans felt that such a military decision should be left to General Eisenhower.

Eisenhower decided that his first priority was to thoroughly defeat the Germans. He ordered his troops to spread out and pursue German troops. Thus, the British and Americans advanced only as far as the Elbe River. The Russians, after sweeping into Berlin, met their allies at the Elbe on April 25.

Over the following days the Nazi empire died. On May 1 the German government announced that Adolf Hitler had committed suicide. In Germany, Italy, Austria, the Netherlands, and Denmark, German troops laid down their arms. On May 8, 1945, at Eisenhower's headquarters in a schoolhouse in Reims, France, the German High Command agreed to unconditional surrender.

THE DEATH OF ROOSEVELT

V-E Day—"Victory in Europe"—touched off celebrations throughout Europe and the United States. But one man who had worked so hard for that victory never saw it. On April 12 Franklin Delano Roosevelt died of a cerebral hemorrhage at his retreat in Warm Springs, Georgia.

Stunned Americans wept in the streets. In Britain, a grieving Churchill asked Parliament to adjourn in honor of his friend's memory. On a ship in the Pacific a sailor read a signal flashing the news from a nearby island. "Who," the young sailor wondered, "is president now?"

The sixty-year-old, neat, spectacled vice-president—Harry S. Truman—was president now. Truman quickly went to work. He met with the secretary of state and with war leaders. Then he went to have lunch with Congress.

Later Truman called a press conference. "I don't know if you [people] pray," he said, "but if you do, please pray God to help me carry this load."

SECTION REVIEW

1. Identify the following: Landing Ship-Tank, Operation Overlord, Omaha, Yalta.

2. Name four things that Roosevelt and Churchill agreed on at the Casablanca meeting.

3. (a) How long did it take the Allied troops to sweep the Germans and Italians from Sicily? (b) Why was the fighting at Anzio so difficult for the Allied troops?

4. (a) What issues were discussed at the Cairo Conference in November 1943? (b) At the Teheran Conference, how did Roosevelt and Churchill answer Stalin's question about Operation Overlord?

5. (a) How did the Allies win the Battle of the Atlantic? (b) Why were the Germans taken by surprise on D-Day?

6. (a) How did the Germans create a bulge in the Allied front in Belgium? (b) What was the cost, on both sides, of the Battle of the Bulge?

7. What agreement did the Big Three make about Germany and Poland at Yalta?

8. Why did Eisenhower turn down Churchill's suggestion for the immediate occupation of Berlin?

THE PACIFIC FRONT

READ TO FIND OUT

—**how a final plan was worked out for the Pacific campaign.**

—**why American forces had great difficulty taking South Pacific islands.**

—**how Nimitz led the offensive in the Central Pacific.**

—**how MacArthur recaptured the Philippines.**

—**why the Potsdam meeting was held.**

—**why Japan surrendered in August 1945.**

The war in the Pacific, like the war in Europe, was a long, hard struggle against a mighty enemy. At its height in mid-1942, the Japanese empire included hundreds of Pacific islands. On the Asian mainland, it stretched from Manchuria south to the Malay Peninsula.

Some American troops were sent to the Chinese front to help Chiang Kai-shek resist Japan. However, the primary American thrust against Japan was in the Pacific. American forces would launch dozens of D-Days to take far-flung beachheads.

The Japanese-held islands bristled with defenses. In addition, the islands often held deadly surprises, like snake-infested jungles, malaria-carrying mosquitoes, and enemy snipers lashed into trees.

Nevertheless, one observer wrote, no troops could "ever top in spirit and courage the kids from the streets of American cities, from American farms . . . Sunday-school rooms, pool-rooms, and business offices."

AMERICAN STRATEGY

The Battle of Midway in June 1942 was a turning point in the Pacific war. The Japanese saw that they did not have the naval strength to keep expanding their empire. Instead, they concentrated on holding territory.

When the Allies were ready to take the offensive, the two top commanders in the Pacific differed over the best route to Japan. General Douglas Mac-Arthur favored a South Pacific route that led to the Philippines and then to Japan. The loss of the Philippines was a bitter memory, and he was determined to liberate the Islands.

Admiral Chester Nimitz favored a route through the Central Pacific that would force a showdown with the Japanese fleet. Nimitz had a simple formula for naval war. It was called "subtraction for them and addition for us." He hoped to subtract as many ships and planes as possible from the Japanese fleet. The battered American fleet needed many additions, especially aircraft carriers.

The final Allied plan included both routes to Japan. However, strategists decided, it would be too costly to take each Pacific island. The Allies would seize key islands and, wherever possible, bypass Japanese strongholds. This strategy became known as "island-hopping."

The Central and South Pacific routes would link up in the Philippines. Those islands would then be a springboard for the final part of the Allied offensive—the invasion of Japan.

THE SOUTH PACIFIC CAMPAIGN

The South Pacific campaign began in August 1942. From Australia, American marines struck at Guadalcanal in the Solomon Islands. In the surprise attack, the Americans easily took Japan's newly built airfield. Guadalcanal itself, however, did not fall as easily.

A mountainous island matted with rain forests, Guadalcanal taught the Americans jungle warfare. There was steaming heat, malaria, and rains that could drown a wounded soldier. In the greenish jungle light, troops could barely tell friend from enemy. Often the enemy was invisible, sniping from treetops.

Japanese and American reinforcements poured into Guadalcanal, and the enemies fought for six months to control the island. Finally, in February 1943, the Japanese were driven out. Meanwhile, other Allied forces struck throughout the Solomons.

The marines were aided in these, and other, battles by a special unit of Navaho Indians. Over 400 Navaho marines served as code-talkers in the Pacific. The difficult Navaho language was well suited as a code. Only 28 non-Navaho spoke it.

A code-talker might rush ashore with the assault troops, then transmit to a Navaho on board ship where to direct mortar fire. One newspaper described the transmittal process as follows:

> Huddled over their radio sets in bobbing assault barges, in foxholes on the beach, in slit trenches, deep in the jungle, the Navaho Marines transmitted and received messages, orders, vital information. The Japanese ground their teeth.

While fighting raged in the Solomons, Allies attacked another South Pacific objective—New Guinea. From their New Guinea bases, the Japanese could easily strike across the Coral Sea at Australia. In the autumn of 1942, General Douglas MacArthur led American and Australian troops in a march up the New Guinea coast.

The fighting was grueling. Swamps, jungles, and an enemy that fought to the death took a heavy toll. The Allies won New Guinea by mid-1943, but it cost almost 90 percent of their troops in casualties. Slowly, painfully, the southern route to Japan was being cleared.

THE CENTRAL PACIFIC CAMPAIGN

In the Central Pacific, Admiral Nimitz had to wait for newly built aircraft carriers before launching his campaign. Finally, in the autumn of 1943, Nimitz was ready. He chose the Gilbert Islands, a string of flat coral reefs, called atolls, as the first target.

In November American troops landed on two of the Gilberts. One island was easily taken. The other, named Tarawa (tuh-RAH-wuh), was studded with Japanese gun nests and shelters of concrete, steel, and coconut logs. It took the Americans 3 days of savage fighting to defeat the enemy. "Bloody Tarawa" cost the Americans over 3,000 casualties.

From the Gilberts, Nimitz island-hopped to another coral chain called the Marshall Islands. Hundreds of American planes from carriers and the Tarawa airstrip prepared the way, pounding Japanese air bases in the Marshalls. In January 1944 the troops went in. The Japanese fought fiercely. However, with strong air and sea support, American troops captured two islands within a week. By the end of February the Marshalls were in Allied hands.

The next target for the advancing Americans was the Mariana Islands. The Marianas were vital to both the Japanese and the Allies because they were within bomber range of Japan. The Americans hoped to build bases there for their new long-range bombers, the "superfortress" B-29s.

In June, American and Japanese fleets converged near Saipan (sī-PAN), at the southern end of the Marianas. American fighters took off from aircraft carriers to meet the Japanese planes. American submarines sped toward Japanese carriers. The 2-day battle sent the Japanese limping away. They lost about 400 planes and 3 of their largest carriers. The Americans lost about 30 aircraft.

American troops then fought their way onto the two key Mariana Islands of Saipan and Guam. By the autumn of 1944, B-29s from the Marianas were bombing Japan.

On Guam, once more a United States possession, a radio operator happily tapped out a message to Pearl Harbor. "This news is from Radio Guam. Nothing heard from you since 1941. Greetings."

Amphibious trucks were used to remove the wounded from the Pacific islands. Here casualties from the landing on Guam were being evacuated.

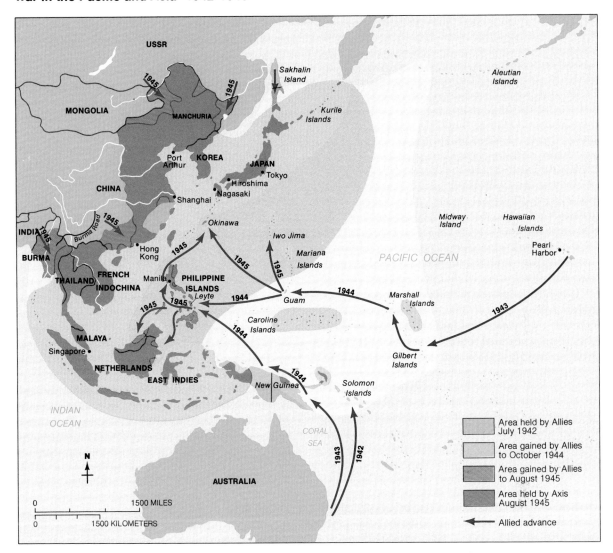

THE BATTLE OF LEYTE GULF

In October 1944 Central Pacific forces under Nimitz and South Pacific forces under MacArthur converged on the Philippine island of Leyte (LAYT-ee). About five hours after the Americans secured a beachhead, General MacArthur waded ashore. "People of the Philippines," he said, "I have returned."

The Japanese, however, were ready to risk the remainder of their fleet to drive him out again. For three days in late October, the Japanese and American fleets clashed in a gulf off Leyte. The Battle of Leyte Gulf was the largest naval battle in history.

In one nighttime engagement American destroyers trapped part of the Japanese force in a narrow strait. The sky lit up as five American ships fired on the Japanese. These warships had been sunk or damaged at Pearl Harbor in 1941 and had been salvaged to fight another day.

As the tide turned against the Japanese, they unleashed a desperate new weapon. *Kamikaze*, or "divine wind," pilots deliberately crashed their explosive-laden planes into American warships. One kamikaze pilot explained before his mission: "I am nothing but a particle of iron attracted by a magnet—the American aircraft carrier."

When the fighting was over, Japan's fleet was in ruins. Japanese power had been swept from the seas.

However, the remaining Japanese-held islands still bristled with defenses.

It took the Americans four hard months of land fighting to advance up the Philippine Islands. In February 1945 the troops at last won the war-torn capital of Manila.

IWO JIMA AND OKINAWA

With the capture of the Philippines, the Allies were now ready to take the last steps to reach Japan. Two islands, Iwo Jima (EE-wō JEE-mah) and Okinawa (ō-kih-NAH-wah), were selected as bases for the final assault. For weeks warships and carrier-based planes shelled little Iwo Jima, about halfway between Guam and Tokyo. Then, in mid-February, marine assault troops landed on the island.

Iwo Jima, a barren volcanic island, was as forbidding as it looked. The Japanese had honeycombed it with caves and laced it with mines. From the lava caves and concrete shelters, Japanese troops poured fire down onto the attacking marines.

The Americans fought bitterly, sometimes hand to hand, for every piece of hard rock. On February 23 they scaled the slopes of the extinct volcano and planted the American flag, but the island was not yet theirs. Iwo Jima did not fall until mid-March, at the cost of over 6,000 marines killed. As Admiral Chester W. Nimitz said, "uncommon valor was a common virtue" during the four weeks of fighting at Iwo Jima.

One more island lay ahead—an island that could provide a base for landings in China or Japan. In April a mighty American armada bore down on Okinawa. Once more American troops had to battle fiercely for scraps of land. Japanese kamikaze pilots screamed out of the sky, sinking 36 ships and crippling dozens more. On June 21 the exhausted Americans, having suffered 50,000 casualties, won their last stepping-stone to Japan.

THE BURMA ROAD

On the Asian mainland, too, Japan was faltering. By 1945 China had retaken a good part of the territory lost to Japan. For three years China's lifeline to the Allies had been American fliers.

American pilots known as the Flying Tigers, under General Claire Chennault, flew war supplies from India to China. The dangerous 500-mile (800-kilometer) route crossed the lofty Himalayas. Then, in late 1944, Allied troops under General Joseph Stilwell hacked a mountain road from India to China. By the spring of 1945 Allied convoys were rolling over the Stilwell Road into China and forcing the Japanese out of Burma and Thailand.

American marines fought yard by yard over bombed, burned, and bloodied ground before they finally raised the flag atop Mt. Suribachi on Iwo Jima.

American supplies trucked over the fantastic Burma Road from India to China helped to defeat the Japanese.

From Allied air bases in China and in the Marianas, bombers flew raid after raid over Japan. Firebombing destroyed some of Japan's biggest cities. American warships shelled Japan from the sea.

After victory in the European war in May 1945, the attacks on Japan increased. The Allies were preparing their invasion of Japan.

POTSDAM

There had been many hard battles on the road to Japan, but the invasion promised to be the hardest of all. The Allies estimated that the fighting would cost at least one million soldiers.

Like Roosevelt, Truman believed that Russian help was vital for the invasion of Japan. To set a date for Soviet entry into the war and to discuss European problems, the Allied leaders met once more in July 1945. The talks were held at an old castle in Potsdam, outside Russian-occupied Berlin. Meeting with Truman and Stalin was the newly elected British prime minister, Clement R. Attlee.

On July 17 Truman received word that an atomic bomb had been successfully exploded in the New Mexico desert the day before. For three years scientists had been working on the top-secret Manhattan Project to build this powerful new weapon. The A-bomb, Truman believed, would force Japan to surrender. Thus the invasion—and Russian help—would not be needed.

The British had assisted in the project and approved the use of the weapon. Truman also told Stalin of the bomb. On July 26 Truman and Attlee issued an ultimatum. Japan must surrender unconditionally or face "prompt and utter destruction."

In Japan a new goverment was ready to discuss peace terms. However, the powerful military insisted on continuing the war and threatened to revolt if the government surrendered. The Japanese made no reply to the Allied ultimatum.

THE DEFEAT OF JAPAN

On the morning of August 6, 1945, a B-29 bomber named *Enola Gay* pierced the Japanese sky over the city of Hiroshima. At 8:15 the atomic bomb was dropped. The shock wave from the blast rocked the *Enola Gay*, and a blinding white flash outshone the sun.

Below, over 4 square miles (6 square kilometers) of Hiroshima—nearly 80 percent of the city—were destroyed. Some 68,000 people were killed instantly. Many thousands more would die of injuries or radiation poisoning. "Every living thing was blackened and dead," said a survivor, "or waiting to die." Still, the Japanese did not surrender.

On August 8 Stalin fulfilled his promise and entered the war against Japan. He sent Russian troops into Manchuria, where they met little opposition. Russians also occupied the southern half of Sakhalin Island, the territory promised to Stalin at Yalta.

On August 9 a second atomic bomb was dropped over Japan. It devastated the city of Nagasaki and killed over 35,000 people. On August 14 Japanese leaders agreed to unconditional surrender, to be effective August 15. V-J Day—Victory over Japan—came 99 long days after V-E Day.

On September 2 tense Japanese leaders came aboard the U.S.S. *Missouri* in Tokyo Bay. There, as Allied officers silently watched, the Japanese signed a formal surrender. Then General Douglas MacArthur spoke by radio to the American people. "Today the guns are silent," he declared. "A great tragedy has ended. A great victory has been won. The skies no longer rain death." However, he noted, if people did not learn to live in peace they would risk again the utter destruction of war. "We have had our last chance," he warned.

AFTERMATH OF THE WAR

After the guns fell silent, the cost of World War II could be counted. About 55 million troops and civilians died in the war. Germany and the Soviet Union lost as much as 10 percent of their populations. Over 400,000 Americans died. Twice that many were wounded, taken prisoner, or missing. Millions in Europe and Asia were left homeless.

Nations spent billions to finance the war and billions to repair property damage. Bombs and artillery devastated cities in Britain, Germany, the Soviet Union, Japan, Holland, Poland, Hungary, and other nations. The United States spent ten times more on World War II than it had on all its earlier wars together.

The war also changed the map of the world. The Soviet Union, in addition to its annexation of the Baltic states, gained land from Finland, Germany, Japan, Poland, and Romania. The United States

NUCLEAR WARFARE
THE DECISION TO USE THE ATOMIC BOMB

In 1982 a Japanese woman described the bombing of Hiroshima. She was sixteen years old at the time.

> I felt I had lost all the bones in my body. . . . I passed out. By the time I woke up, black rain was falling. We thought it was oil, the B-29s coming back to drop oil on us to burn us up. I couldn't see. I thought I was blind, but I got my eyes open, and I saw a beautiful blue sky and a dead city. Nobody is standing up. Nobody is walking around.

The decision to drop the atomic bomb was made in the early summer of 1945. In late May a committee of government officials, generals, and scientists met at the Pentagon. Their job was to advise President Truman on how to use the new weapon that scientists were about to test on the New Mexico desert.

Secretary of War Henry Stimson opened the meeting, warning the group that their advice could "turn the course of history." The group discussed giving a warning demonstration on an uninhabited site. After seeing this "enormous nuclear firecracker," as one scientist called the bomb, the Japanese might surrender. However, the group noted that only two bombs had been produced. With a demonstration, there would be only one left to use if this should be necessary.

The group also worried that the bomb might not work, spurring the Japanese to fight even harder. J. Robert Oppenheimer, the brilliant physicist in charge of the New Mexico project, doubted that a harmless demonstration would "convince the Japanese they ought to throw in the sponge."

The committee then discussed dropping the bomb on Japan itself. They agreed that it would be the quickest way to end the war. They also felt that it would cause fewer deaths in the long run. Six thousand Americans had just lost their lives in taking Iwo Jima. The military estimated that if the United States had to invade Japan, a million American soldiers might die. The continued bombing of Japan by conventional weapons might also cause more deaths overall. A recent firebombing of Tokyo had killed 83,000 people in a single night.

The next day the Pentagon group reached their decision. The atomic bomb should be used in a surprise attack on Japan. "To extract a genuine surrender . . . they must be administered a tremendous shock," Stimson explained. "Such an effective shock would save many times the number of lives, both American and Japanese, than it would cost." Committee member Arthur Compton, a scientist, agreed. "I knew all too well the destruction and human agony the bombs would cause. . . . But I wanted the war to end. I wanted life to become normal again."

When he was told the committee's recommendation, President Truman reluctantly agreed. He, too, could see no other way.

However, at the Chicago laboratory where the first atomic chain reaction had taken place, scientists were deeply concerned. Dr. Leo Szilard, a Hungarian-born physicist, was the strongest op-

In the heart of Nagasaki, twisted, flattened ruins were all that remained after the atomic blast on August 9, 1945. The Japanese answered with unconditional surrender.

ponent of using the bomb against Japan. Szilard had urged President Roosevelt to develop atomic power when it was feared that Germany might have it. Now he and scientist Eugene Rabinowitch were uneasy. "I remember many hours spent walking . . . with Leo Szilard," Rabinowitch said, "arguing about these questions. . . . I remember sleepless nights. . . ."

Szilard, Rabinowitch, and other Chicago scientists prepared a report opposing the use of the bomb on Japan. Although it might save American lives, they thought that it would send a "wave of horror and repulsion" across the world. Instead, they proposed "a demonstration of the new weapon . . . before the eyes of representatives of all the United Nations, on the desert or a barren island." After such a demonstration, the United States could take the lead in obtaining an international agreement on disarmament before other nations developed the bomb.

The Chicago report forced the Pentagon committee to rethink their decision. In mid-June the committee's scientists met in New Mexico. Again they rejected a warning demonstration. "We did not think exploding one of these things . . . over a desert was likely to be very impressive," Oppenheimer explained.

One member of the Pentagon committee did change his mind. Undersecretary of the Navy Ralph Bard came to believe that the Japanese were so weak that they might soon surrender without the bomb. General Dwight D. Eisenhower agreed. "Japan was already defeated," he felt. Bard suggested that the Japanese be told about the bomb and given the chance to surrender. However, he did not know if it would work, and the decision had already been made.

1. What were the Pentagon committee's reasons for recommending a surprise atomic attack on Japan?

2. Why did the Chicago group oppose using the bomb? What did they suggest instead?

3. Do you think the United States should have used the bomb on Japan? If not, what alternatives would you suggest?

received several Japanese island chains to oversee. The great empires of the past—Britain, France, Germany, Japan—would never recover their prewar power.

A new power filled the vacuum left by the war. Straddling Europe and Asia, the Soviet Union was now the strongest nation in that area of the world. Only one other nation had greater power—the United States.

The war also brought another kind of power. Atomic power launched the atomic age. In 1939 a British commander told his regiment that he had begun the war by ordering officers to sharpen their swords. Six years later the war ended with the atomic bomb.

Perhaps the most telling legacy of the war was the memories of those who fought and suffered in it. After the war, an inscription was found on a wall in France:

Austin White   Chicago, Ill.   1918
Austin White   Chicago, Ill.   1945
This is the last time I want to write my name here.

SECTION REVIEW

1. Identify the following: island-hopping, code-talkers, kamikaze pilots, Flying Tigers, Potsdam, Manhattan Project, *Enola Gay*.

2. (a) How did MacArthur and Nimitz disagree on a plan for the Pacific offensive? (b) Explain the final plan for the Pacific offensive.

3. (a) What special lesson did the Americans learn at Guadalcanal? (b) What job did the special unit of Navaho Indians have in the Pacific?

4. Why were the Mariana Islands vital to both the Japanese and the Allies?

5. What was the biggest naval battle in history?

6. (a) What two islands were the bases for the final assault on Japan? (b) Name two routes over which American supplies were delivered to China.

7. (a) What message did Truman receive on July 17, 1945? (b) What ultimatum did Truman and Attlee issue to Japan on July 26, 1945? (c) When did the Japanese agree to unconditional surrender?

8. After the war, which two nations were the most powerful in the world?

Jean Carlu, a French graphic artist working for the United States government, designed "Give'em Both Barrels." His strong, simple images convey the message clearly.

SUMMARY

The United States grimly went to war in 1941. Its position in the Pacific was bleak. By early 1942 Japan had conquered much of eastern Asia and the Pacific, including Guam, Wake, and the Philippines. However, American forces gained victories at the Battles of the Coral Sea and Midway. The victory at Midway was a turning point in the war with Japan. The Allies also won victories in North Africa and at Stalingrad.

At home, Americans mobilized for war. Industries shifted from peace to war, producing planes and ships. Because of increased production, the depression ended, and prosperity returned. Women found employment in war industries, doing new kinds of work. Black Americans also found more and more jobs in industry. However, competition between whites and blacks for jobs and housing led to racial tension. Because of American fears of sabotage, Japanese Americans in the Pacific Coast states were removed from their homes. They were taken to relocation camps where they remained throughout the war.

In 1943 the Allies went on the offensive in Europe with Operation Husky. Allied troops conquered Sicily and invaded Italy, finally taking Rome. In June 1944 the Allies successfuly completed Operation Overlord, the cross-channel invasion of France. Allied armies freed France, and then Belgium and Luxembourg from German control. American troops also stopped a German counteroffensive in Belgium. Meanwhile, Soviet troops launched an offensive into eastern Europe, freeing Axis-controlled nations there.

In February 1945 Allied leaders met in Yalta and made plans for postwar Europe and the war in the Pacific. Three months later, Germany surrendered. The Allies now chose their strategy for the Pacific front and launched an offensive against Japan.

American troops, suffering heavy casualties, slowly retook Japanese-held islands in the Pacific. Japan, however, continued to fight fiercely. In August 1945 the United States dropped atomic bombs on Hiroshima and Nagasaki, and Japan surrendered. World War II, which had cost millions of lives, was over.

CHAPTER REVIEW

1. (a) How was most Allied strategy planned? (b) Why were relations between the Americans, the British, and the Russians sensitive? (c) What issue divided the Allied leaders throughout most of the war?

2. (a) What was Japan's strategy in 1942? (b) How did the Battle of the Coral Sea and the Battle of Midway affect that strategy? (c) Describe the Japanese strategy after 1942.

3. (a) Why was it important for the Allies to defeat the Germans in North Africa? (b) Describe Allied actions in Operation Torch. (c) How did victory in North Africa fit into Allied strategy for Europe?

4. (a) Explain how World War II brought an end to the Great Depression. (b) How did the war affect women? Black Americans? Mexican Americans? (c) Why were Japanese Americans removed to relocation camps? (d) Did Japanese American actions justify the removal? Explain.

5. How did each of the following affect Americans during the war? (a) war industries (b) price ceilings (c) ration books (d) wage and price freezes (e) income taxes

6. (a) Describe the Allied campaign in Italy. (b) Why did the Allies expect an easy victory? (c) Why did the campaign continue until the war was almost over?

7. (a) What agreements were made by the Big Three at the Teheran Conference? (b) Explain how the Allied leaders acted on their agreements.

8. How did each of the following affect the success of Operation Overlord? (a) the Battle of the Atlantic (b) Allied command of the air (c) German surprise

9. (a) List the major agreements reached by the Big Three at Yalta. (b) Why were the agreements significant?

10. Explain the importance of each of the following battles in the war in the Pacific. (a) Guadalcanal (b) New Guinea (c) the Marianas (d) Leyte Gulf (e) Iwo Jima (f) Okinawa

ISSUES AND IDEAS

1. Roosevelt called World War II "the survival war." What did he mean? Do you agree? Why or why not?

2. The role of the federal government in the nation's economy expanded during World War II.

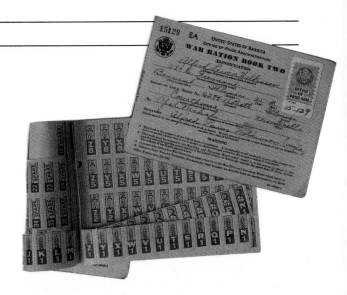

During the war ration stamps were issued to insure that each person would be able to buy a fair share of scarce goods. Most rationing ended in 1945.

Do you agree or disagree? Cite examples to support your conclusion.

3. Do you think that Truman's decision to use the atomic bomb was the most crucial decision of the war? Why or why not?

SKILLS WORKSHOP

1. *Timelines.* Make a timeline of events on the European front, the Pacific front, and the diplomatic front. Below the timelines, describe briefly the relationship between major Allied conferences and campaigns.

2. *Maps.* See page 589 of your book. Find the map titled "War in Europe and Africa." How far did the Soviet offensive reach by February 1945? By that time what Axis-controlled nations were held by Soviet troops? How do you think this military situation affected negotiations among the Big Three at the Yalta Conference?

PAST AND PRESENT

1. How does the map of Europe today reflect changes brought about by World War II?

2. Find out how people in your community aided the war effort.

World War II posters encouraged Americans to enlist, to produce, to save scrap, to buy bonds, to grow vegetables, and to remember.

... we were highly resolved that these dead shall not have died in vain ...

REMEMBER DEC. 7th!

A BEACON
TO THE WORLD

1945–1968

Frédéric Auguste Bartholdi. *Liberty Enlightening the World*, dedicated 1886. Photo by Chuck O'Rear.

1600	1700	1800	1900	2000
• Jamestown founded		• Revolutionary War • Civil War		• Today

UNIT 9
1945–1968

1950 · 1960 · 1970

Truman | Eisenhower | Kennedy | Johnson

POLITICAL

- Taft-Hartley Act
- Army-McCarthy hearings
- Civil Rights Act
- Peace Corps
- Twenty-fourth Amendment: civil rights
- Voting Rights Act

SOCIAL

- Gabriela Mistral: Nobel prize for literature
- Jackie Robinson joins major leagues
- William H. Whyte: *The Organization Man*
- Betty Friedan: *The Feminine Mystique*
- Malcolm X: *Autobiography*
- Martin Luther King, Jr. assassinated

TECHNOLOGICAL

- First nuclear power plant in U.S.
- Russia launches *Sputnik I*
- St. Lawrence Seaway completed
- Laser invented
- John Glenn circles earth
- Rachel Carson: *Silent Spring*
- Dorothy Hodgkin: Nobel prize for chemistry
- First heart transplant

INTERNATIONAL

- Marshall Plan
- India independent
- NATO formed
- Communist victory in China
- Korean War
- Revolt in Hungary
- Gold Coast (Ghana) independent
- Berlin Wall
- Test Ban Treaty
- Six-Day War

1950 · 1960 · 1970

CHAPTER 25

POSTWAR CHALLENGES

1945–1960

POSTWAR RESPONSIBILITIES
THE COLD WAR
CONFLICT IN THE MIDDLE EAST AND ASIA
FOREIGN POLICY UNDER EISENHOWER

In 1945 Eleanor Roosevelt became a member of the United States delegation to the United Nations. She described her experiences in a diary and in letters.

"January 9, 1946. I have spent 9 hours of meetings these last two days to try to frame a resolution on refugees to which the Russians and ourselves can agree. The Dutch, British, and ourselves reach agreement fairly quickly, but the Yugoslavs and Russians start from different backgrounds. Everything must . . . cover their point of view, their needs, no one else's situation is ever considered!

"February 6. Committee meeting was one long wrangle. Finally at one I asked for a vote. The Russians, who always play for delay, asked for a subcommittee to try to get a resolution we could agree upon. It is hopeless as there are fundamental disagreements. . . . At 3:10 we sat down in the subcommittee at Church House and we got up at 6, having agreed on 25 lines!

"February 8. We defeated the Russians on the three points we disagreed on. . . .

"February 13. Yesterday we fought the whole battle over again in the Assembly. . . . The Russians are tenacious fighters. When we finally finished voting at 1 a.m. last night, I shook hands and said I admired their fighting qualities and I hoped some day on that kind of question we would be on the same side, and they were cordiality itself!"

Eleanor Roosevelt's husband, Franklin Roosevelt, had laid the groundwork for the United Nations, a world organization created to build peace. Now she was trying to make it work.

She found, however, that talks between the Americans and the Russians were often "one long wrangle." It was a fitting description. The United States and the Soviet Union would clash again and again in the postwar world.

POSTWAR RESPONSIBILITIES

READD TO FIND OUT

— how emergency aid helped war-torn nations.

— how the Allies dealt with the Axis nations.

— why Russia formed the Soviet bloc.

— how the United Nations was organized.

— why plans to outlaw atomic weapons failed.

At the end of World War II, the United States stood, in Winston Churchill's words, "at the summit of the world." American industry was producing nearly one half of the world's goods. On the seas and in the air the American armed forces were supreme. And the United States alone had the world's most powerful weapon, the atomic bomb.

Below the American summit stood the Soviet Union, second only to the United States in power. The Russians had suffered heavy wartime losses, but they had gained new territories and resources. They also had the world's largest army. And, for the first time, the Russians had no rivals for power in Europe or Asia.

During the war the United States, Britain, and the Soviet Union had formed an uneasy alliance. However, the alliance was held together solely for the purpose of defeating the Axis nations. Could the great powers cooperate in peacetime to shape the postwar world?

EMERGENCY AID

One of the most pressing world needs was emergency aid. In many nations the war left ruined factories, damaged roads and bridges, scorched farmlands, and bombed cities. Starvation and disease threatened millions of people.

The United States had taken the lead in setting up a relief agency in late 1943. Eventually 48 nations joined the United Nations Relief and Rehabilitation Administration (UNRRA). Between 1944 and 1947 the UNRRA rushed food, clothing, and medical supplies to war-torn nations. It helped to restore industries and farms. It also cared for millions of "displaced persons" left homeless by the war.

The United States took responsibility for most of the cost of UNRRA aid. The aid went to both allies and former enemies. Grain, mainly from American farms, was shipped to Europe and Asia. Tractors and plows were sent to hundreds of farms. Pumps and pipes restored Greece's water systems. Missouri mules found new homes on Yugoslavian farms. In its race against starvation and chaos, the UNRRA distributed some 22 million tons (20 million metric tons) of supplies.

POLICY FOR DEFEATED NATIONS

A major task of the wartime Allies was to deal with the defeated Axis nations. Under the Yalta agreements, the Americans, the Russians, the British, and the French divided Germany into four zones of occupation. Germany's capital of Berlin, deep inside the Soviet zone, was also divided by the four powers.

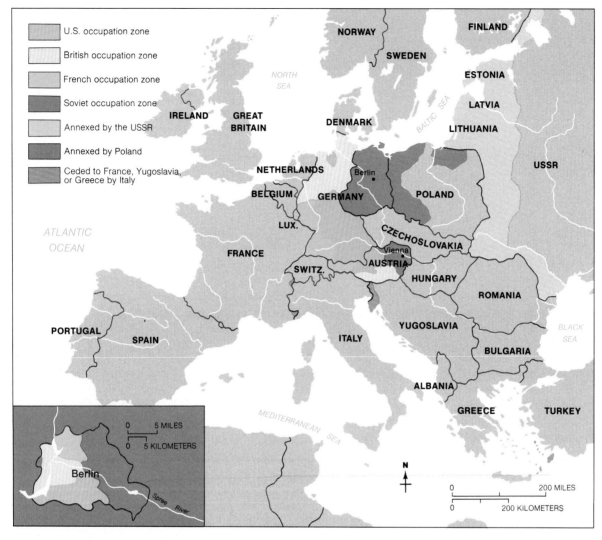

Like Germany, Austria was divided into four occupation zones. Vienna was also divided into four zones. The occupation of both Germany and Austria ended in 1955. After World War II some German territory was transferred to Poland, and Poland's eastern area became part of the USSR.

The occupying governments agreed to disarm Germany. They also pledged to treat Germany as a single economic unit, sharing food and essential supplies among the four zones.

The Russians, however, followed their own policy in the Soviet zone. They shipped German equipment and crops and even German laborers to the Soviet Union. This policy hurt the people of the other zones, who depended on the Soviet zone for food, coal, and other raw materials. Eventually, the burden of feeding people in the non-Soviet zones fell on the United States.

In contrast to Germany, Japan was not divided into zones. Because the United States had played the major role in Japan's defeat, American policies governed the Japanese occupation. General Douglas MacArthur commanded the occupation forces.

MacArthur's first order was to disarm Japan. Military leaders were swept from power, and the army was demobilized. All conquered territories were taken from Japan. All that remained of Japan's once-mighty empire were its home islands.

Like Germany, war-torn Japan needed tremendous aid. The United States fed and supplied

ISAMU NOGUCHI
SCULPTOR OF TWO WORLDS

The celebrated sculptor Isamu Noguchi grew up in two cultures. Half American and half Japanese, he often felt a stranger to both. Noguchi was born in Los Angeles in 1904. His father, a Japanese poet, and his mother, an American teacher and writer, separated when he was a baby. Until he was thirteen, Noguchi lived with his mother in Japan. Then he was sent to school in Indiana, where the lonely boy earned his keep by delivering newspapers and shoveling snow.

After high school he worked for a sculptor, studied art in Paris, then traveled to Japan. While living in a ditchdigger's hut, he learned ceramics from a master potter. Noguchi's experiences in Japan convinced him that art should be a part of everyday life. Returning to the United States, he began to design playgrounds, gardens, clothing, and furniture as well as abstract sculpture.

During World War II, Noguchi was deeply concerned when Japanese Americans were put in relocation camps. As a gesture of kinship, he voluntarily lived in the Poston, Arizona, camp. In 1950 he designed two memorial bridges for Hiroshima's Peace Park. Working "not alone but with history," he created one bridge to represent death, the other, life.

Though Noguchi's childhood had been difficult, it made him strong. It gave him the independence to choose what he needed from East and West. In his sculpture, he combines western abstraction with a Japanese sense of natural form and texture.

Today Noguchi spends part of each year in a Japanese stonecutters' village. He works the rest of the time in his New York studio, equipped with modern power tools. This ability to move between two worlds, Noguchi believes, has helped him "see things without prejudice."

© Arnold Newman

---

the Japanese, and MacArthur urged them to rebuild their peacetime industries. The Americans also drew up a new constitution for Japan, basing power on "the will of the people." The constitution guaranteed political parties, labor unions, free elections, and land reform. It also gave Japanese women the right to vote.*

* In 1951 Japan signed a peace treaty with the United States and 48 other nations. The treaty officially ended the Allied occupation of Japan on April 28, 1952. Japan gained membership in the United Nations in 1956 and became one of the United States' strongest allies.

Italy, which had surrendered during the war, had cooperated with the Allies. It was sustained by UNRRA aid and was not occupied. However, Italy's power was reduced. Its army was limited in size, and it lost all of its African colonies. Also, Italy lost land to France, Greece, and Yugoslavia.

THE SOVIET BLOC

The United States and the Soviet Union clashed on the postwar fate of Eastern Europe. At Yalta, Stalin had promised that free elections would be held there. In 1945 the Soviet army had occupied much of Eastern Europe as it pushed toward Germany.

The Americans wanted to see independent nations with democratic governments in Eastern Europe. The Russians wanted Communist governments there, which they could control. The Russians had suffered heavy losses during the Nazi invasion of the Soviet Union. Also, Stalin did not forget that the Americans, the French, and the British had sent troops into Russia in 1918, during World War I. At that time, the Bolsheviks, who had taken power, made peace with Germany. In response, the Allies sent troops to recover military supplies that they had shipped to Russia. However, Allied troops remained in Russia for two years and aided Russian opponents of the Bolsheviks.

Stalin was determined to have a buffer zone of friendly nations on the Soviet Union's border. When President Truman insisted that free elections be held as promised in Eastern Europe, Stalin bluntly refused. "Any freely elected government in these countries," Stalin explained, "will be an anti-Soviet government and we cannot allow that."

The Soviet Union had already annexed the Baltic states of Latvia, Lithuania, and Estonia. Over a three-year period after the war, the Soviet Union swept much of Eastern Europe under its control. Supported by Russian troops, Soviet-sponsored Communist parties came to power in Poland, Romania, Bulgaria, Hungary, and Czechoslovakia. These nations became known as the **Soviet bloc.**

As communism spread over Eastern Europe, Winston Churchill urged that the British and the Americans adopt a tough policy against the Soviets. "An iron curtain has descended across the continent," he declared. Behind that curtain lay the nations of the Soviet bloc. On the other side were the non-Communist nations of Europe and the United States. These nations became known as the West.

THE UNITED NATIONS

A new international peace-keeping organization, the United Nations (UN), was born during the war. To a great extent, the UN sprang from the heart of Franklin Roosevelt. He had been deeply moved by Woodrow Wilson's quest for peace in 1918 with the League of Nations. Although the League ultimately failed, Roosevelt still believed that international cooperation was possible.

Eleanor Roosevelt's life was dedicated to service. Social work, family, her husband's career, and war work preceded her service in the United Nations General Assembly.

In early 1943 Roosevelt proposed to the British a worldwide organization for maintaining peace. Later that year American, British, Russian, and Chinese representatives signed the Moscow Declaration, agreeing to set up such an organization. As Allied leaders met to plan war strategy, they also made plans to shape the postwar world.

In July 1944 economic ministers from 44 nations met at a mountain resort in New Hampshire called Bretton Woods. There they set up agencies that would work to avoid the economic problems that had developed after World War I. The International Monetary Fund would keep currency exchange rates stable among nations and would promote world trade. The International Bank for Reconstruction and Development, later called the World Bank, would make loans to nations to repair war damage and would aid developing nations. Both agencies later became part of the UN.

A month later, American, British, Russian, and Chinese representatives met at Dumbarton Oaks, a wooded estate near Washington, D.C., to plan the organization of the UN. A major stumbling block was Stalin's demand that each of the Soviet Union's 16 republics, or states, be admitted to the UN as independent nations. At the 1945 Yalta Conference, however, Stalin settled for the admission of two of the Soviet republics as independent nations in ad-

The United Nations

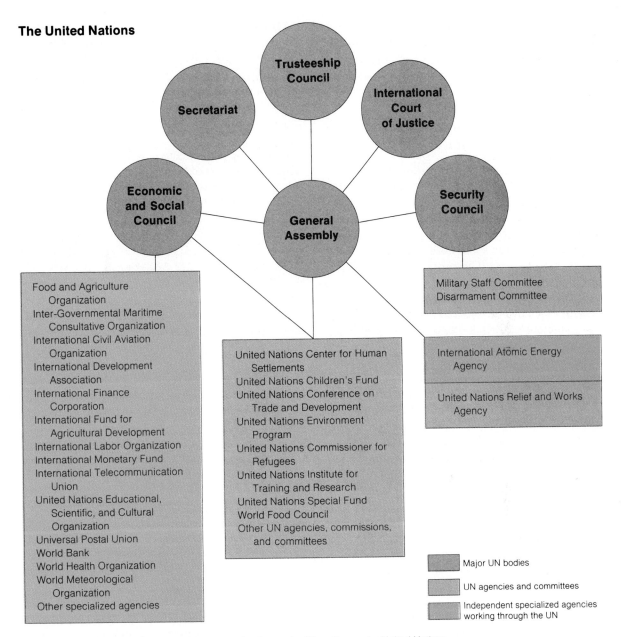

Trusteeship Council

Secretariat

International Court of Justice

Economic and Social Council

General Assembly

Security Council

Food and Agriculture Organization
Inter-Governmental Maritime Consultative Organization
International Civil Aviation Organization
International Development Association
International Finance Corporation
International Fund for Agricultural Development
International Labor Organization
International Monetary Fund
International Telecommunication Union
United Nations Educational, Scientific, and Cultural Organization
Universal Postal Union
World Bank
World Health Organization
World Meteorological Organization
Other specialized agencies

United Nations Center for Human Settlements
United Nations Children's Fund
United Nations Conference on Trade and Development
United Nations Environment Program
United Nations Commissioner for Refugees
United Nations Institute for Training and Research
United Nations Special Fund
World Food Council
Other UN agencies, commissions, and committees

Military Staff Committee
Disarmament Committee

International Atomic Energy Agency

United Nations Relief and Works Agency

Major UN bodies

UN agencies and committees

Independent specialized agencies working through the UN

Although the General Assembly does not supervise the work of the other major United Nations bodies, it is wholly or partly responsible for electing the members of each. The General Assembly is also responsible for the budget of the entire United Nations.

dition to the admission of the Soviet Union. The first UN meeting, to draw up a charter, was set for April 1945 in San Francisco, California.

Roosevelt did not see the outcome of his quest for peace. He died two weeks before the San Francisco conference. However, the conference opened as scheduled on April 25. President Truman gave the opening speech before 800 delegates from 50 nations. Eight weeks later, the delegates completed their work.

In July the Charter of the United Nations was submitted to the United States Senate. Senator Arthur H. Vandenberg of Michigan, an isolationist before the war, urged support for the UN. "World

War III is too horrible to contemplate. It clearly threatens the end of civilization," he declared. "Here is our chance to try to stop this disaster before it starts." The Senate approved the UN Charter by a vote of 89 to 2.

ORGANIZATION OF THE UNITED NATIONS

"We the people of the United Nations," began the Charter, "[resolve] to live together in peace." Thus, the main duties of the UN would be to peacefully settle international disputes and to suppress "acts of aggression." The UN also would work to promote human rights and to solve world problems such as hunger and poverty. The purposes and structure agreed upon have remained the same since 1945.

Each member of the UN is represented in the General Assembly—a "town meeting of the world," where members discuss international problems. Although the assembly has no power to enforce decisions, it can recommend action to the Security Council.

The real power of the UN rests in the Security Council, the peace-keeping body. Fifteen members—originally eleven—sit in the council. The United States, Great Britain, the Soviet Union, China, and France are permanent members and are known as the "Big Five." The nonpermanent members are elected by the General Assembly for two-year terms.

To keep the peace, the Security Council can call on members of the UN to take measures against an aggressor nation. Such measures include suspension of diplomatic relations, economic boycotts, and if necessary, force. Member nations supply armed forces to carry out actions involving force. However, the council can call out UN forces only if all of the Big Five agree. Any one of the five can veto a decision to use force.

In addition to the General Assembly and the Security Council, the UN has four other bodies. The Secretariat handles administrative work. The International Court of Justice decides cases submitted by members and advises the UN on legal matters. The Trusteeship Council supervises "trust territories," colonies lost by defeated nations in the two world wars. Under the Economic and Social Council, various agencies work to improve health, education, and other areas of human welfare.

On October 24, 1945, the Charter of the United Nations went into effect. Senator Vandenberg wrote, "Heaven only knows whether the Charter will work. I *think* it will. If not, *nothing* would. Everything, in the final analysis, depends on Russia."

CONTROL OF ATOMIC ENERGY

One of the first threats to peace that the UN dealt with was the atomic bomb. Late in 1945 leaders of the United States, Britain, and Canada—the nations that had shared in developing the bomb—called for international control of atomic energy. In January 1946 the UN Atomic Energy Commission was set up to study the problem.

At the commission's first meeting Bernard M. Baruch (buh-ROOK), the United States representative, offered an American plan to outlaw atomic weapons. "We must elect world peace or world destruction," he declared. Baruch suggested the creation of a UN agency that would have total control over atomic energy.

Under Baruch's plan, peaceful use of atomic energy would be encouraged. Making atomic weapons, however, would be banned. A UN agency would inspect the atomic facilities of all nations to be certain that atomic weapons were not built. Once the agency established its control, the United States would destroy its own atomic bombs and build no new ones.

Any nation that violated the agreement and built a bomb, explained Baruch, would face penalties, fixed by the UN. None of the Big Five could use its veto to prevent the penalties. This suspension of the veto power would apply only to atomic energy.

The Russians felt that Baruch's plan favored the United States, because it was the only nation that held the secret of the atomic bomb. They vetoed the plan and offered one of their own that called for a ban on atomic weapons and the destruction of American stockpiles. However, the Russians would not allow inspection of their own atomic facilities or suspension of the veto power. The United States insisted on international inspection and control.

Over the next three years the UN Atomic Energy Commission tried, without success, to find a way to control atomic weapons. Meanwhile, the Americans and the Russians moved ahead with atomic research.

On November 1, 1952, American scientists set off the first megaton-class hydrogen weapon. The test was made on Eniwetok, an isolated island in the Marshall chain.

SECTION REVIEW

1. Identify the following: Soviet bloc, Moscow Declaration, General Assembly, Big Five, Bernard M. Baruch.

2. Name three ways in which the United Nations Relief and Rehabilitation Administration helped war-torn nations.

3. How did the Allies divide Germany after the war?

4. What changes took place in Japan after the war?

5. Name eight nations that came under Soviet control as a result of World War II.

6. Name two agencies set up to prevent economic problems after the war. State the purpose of each agency.

7. (a) What are the main duties of the United Nations? (b) Where does the real power of the United Nations rest?

8. (a) What was Bernard Baruch's plan for controlling atomic energy? (b) Why was the plan rejected?

THE COLD WAR

READ TO FIND OUT

— why there was conflict between the United States and the Soviet Union over the Middle East.

— how the Truman Doctrine challenged communism.

— why the United States adopted the Marshall Plan.

— why the United States began the Berlin airlift.

— why the North Atlantic Treaty Organization was formed.

— how the Point Four program helped poor nations.

The United States and the Soviet Union had regarded each other with suspicion ever since the Bolsheviks came to power in 1917. During World War II the Americans and the Russians cooperated as allies, but distrust lay just beneath the surface. After the war, as the two nations emerged as rival superpowers, suspicion welled up again.

Many people hoped that the Americans and the Russians would work together in the United Nations. Instead, the UN became divided into two camps. The Americans and their allies were on one side, the Russians and the Soviet bloc were on the other. The Soviets had no members of their bloc in the Security Council. In danger of being outvoted, they used their veto nine times in 1946.

Less than a year after the war ended, the world crackled with tensions between the superpowers. Henry A. Wallace, who had served in Truman's cabinet, remarked, "The real peace treaty we now need is between the United States and Russia."

THE MIDDLE EAST

The first real conflict between the Americans and the Russians came over the Middle East. This vast region stretches across parts of southeastern Europe, southwestern Asia, and northeastern Africa. It includes the nations of Egypt and Saudi Arabia as well as Turkey and Iran. Part of this highly desert-like region also borders the Soviet Union.

The Middle East holds over half of the world's known oil reserves. World War II had drained the oil resources of both the Soviet Union and the United States. After the war, then, both nations were interested in Middle Eastern oil fields.

Between 1941 and 1945, American, British, and Russian troops had been stationed in the Middle Eastern nation of Iran to protect its oil fields. They also protected a vital supply route to the Soviet Union. After the war ended, the American and British troops withdrew from Iran, but the Russians remained. In late 1945, when a rebellion broke out in Iran's northern province, Russian troops aided the Iranian rebels.

Iran complained of the Soviet action to the UN Security Council in early 1946 and received strong American support. The Russians, however, would not withdraw their troops. Soon they moved more troops into Iran.

In response, the United States bluntly demanded the immediate withdrawal of Russian troops. Finally, the Russians pulled their troops out of Iran, but they won a major concession. A Soviet-Iranian oil company was set up, in which the Russians held 51 percent of the shares.

Soviet interest in the Middle East also extended to Iran's neighbor Turkey. The Soviet Union had long wanted to control the Bosporus and the Dardanelles, the narrow Turkish straits that ultimately connect the Black Sea to the Mediterranean. During 1945 and 1946, the Russians repeatedly demanded that the Turks lease to them bases in the straits. The Russians also demanded two Turkish provinces along the Soviet border. The Turks, supported by Britain and the United States, refused.

American leaders believed that the Soviet Union sought control of Turkey. They worried that if Turkey fell to the Soviets, Greece might be next. This would give the Soviets control of the northeastern Mediterranean. It would also give them a gateway to the entire Middle East.

Greece was bordered by three Communist nations. During the war Greek Communists had tried to overthrow Greece's monarchy. With the help of British troops, Greece ended this threat. However, in 1946 the Communists renewed their fight, supported by Greece's Communist neighbors. Again, Greece relied on the British for help.

Britain, however, decided that it could no longer afford to pour money and troops into Greece. In February 1947 Britain told the United States that it would have to abandon both Greece and Turkey. American leaders saw only one solution. The United States must take over the British role in Greece and Turkey.

THE TRUMAN DOCTRINE

In March 1947 President Truman appeared before a joint session of Congress. A Communist takeover of Greece and Turkey, he said, would threaten world peace and perhaps the security of the United States. He requested $400 million in aid for the two nations, and the authority to send Americans there to oversee the use of the money. Truman told the gathered lawmakers:

> I believe that it must be the policy of the United States to support free peoples who are resisting attempted subjugation by armed minorities or by outside pressure. I believe that we must assist free peoples to work out their own destinies in their own way.

This statement became known as the Truman Doctrine. Some Americans criticized the doctrine for "bypassing the UN," but most Americans

President Truman was a leader whose blunt speech left no doubt about his stand on any issue. He accepted full responsibility for his decisions and actions.

approved the policy. Congress passed the aid bill. With American assistance Greece and Turkey overcame the threat of communism.

The Truman Doctrine was soon linked to an article written by George F. Kennan, a member of the American Foreign Service who was an expert on Russia. The Russians, wrote Kennan, believed that the capitalist world was hostile to the Soviet Union. Soviet policy was designed to counter capitalism by spreading communism. "Its main concern," said Kennan, "is to make sure that it has filled every nook and cranny available to it in the basin of world power."

However, continued Kennan, if the Soviet Union found a barrier in its path, it would retreat. Thus, he felt that American policy must be "a long-term, patient but firm and vigilant containment of Russian expansive tendencies." In effect, *containment* was the basis of the Truman Doctrine. It would guide American policy for years to come.

This American policy of preventing the spread of communism marked the beginning of a new era in world affairs. Bernard Baruch, speaking in South Carolina, gave the era a name. "Let us not be deceived," said Baruch, "today we are in the midst of a cold war." The **cold war**—the conflict between the Soviet Union and the Soviet bloc on one side and the United States and its allies on the other— would be fought not by troops and weapons, but by diplomacy.

A chapel in Naples, Italy, became a depot for shipments of supplies from the United States. These and tons of other supplies helped the Italians survive the postwar years.

THE MARSHALL PLAN

While the United States came to the rescue of Greece and Turkey, another crisis was mounting in Europe. Despite aid from the UNRRA, Europeans were still struggling to recover from the war.

A particularly cruel blow came with the harsh winter of 1946–1947. Blizzards raged through Europe, leaving food and fuel shortages in their wake. In hard-hit Britain, electricity was on for only a few hours each day. Industries throughout Europe shut down, unemployment soared, and currency dropped in value. Thousands of cold, starving Europeans developed the hacking cough of tuberculosis. "What is Europe now?" asked Winston Churchill. "It is a rubble-heap."

In the spring of 1947 the UNRRA—only a temporary agency—ended its relief work. American leaders feared that Western Europe would collapse.

Truman worried that communism would "spread and grow in the evil soil of poverty and strife." Communists had already made solid electoral gains in Italy and France.

In June 1947 Secretary of State George C. Marshall presented a plan to help Europe. He proposed massive American aid in money, food, fuel, and machinery to save Europe from ruin. "Our policy is directed not against any country or doctrine," Marshall explained, "but against hunger, poverty, desperation, and chaos." He invited Europeans, including the Russians, to decide exactly what aid they needed and to present their recovery program to the United States.

In June the British, French, and Soviet ministers met in Paris to make preliminary plans. Midway through the talks, however, the Russian minister was called home. The recovery program, said the Soviets, was an American plot to take over Europe. Soviet-bloc nations would not participate in the program.

In July, 16 European nations met in a general conference to draw up their plan. They created a 4-year recovery program, which would cost between $16 billion and $22 billion. The plan also included an American suggestion to rebuild the industry of the western zones of Germany.

President Truman submitted the European Recovery Program, or Marshall Plan, to Congress in December 1947. Opponents immediately attacked it. The plan, they complained, was a gamble and a "European TVA." Debate dragged on into early 1948.

Then, in February, Soviet actions in Czechoslovakia jolted the United States. Russian-sponsored Communists had been gaining control of Czechoslovakia since 1945. Now they overthrew the democratic government and set up one dominated by the Communists. Communists also seemed to have a good chance of winning a majority in Italy's government in upcoming elections.

"All winter, confidence in peace has been oozing away," wrote a Chicago reporter. "With the Czech coup,* it practically vanished." Fear of the spread of communism gripped the nation. In March Congress passed the Marshall Plan.

* coup (koo): a sudden, forcible overthrow of a government.

To these children in the Russian zone of Germany, eating seemed a serious business. Their food was provided by Americans.

Between 1948 and 1952, the United States committed some $13 billion to aid Europe. Slowly, prosperity returned. Entire cities were rebuilt, railroads were repaired, and new factories sprang up. In France and Italy, the threat of a Communist victory in elections died away.

THE BERLIN AIRLIFT

The American decision to include western Germany in the Marshall Plan touched off a new quarrel with the Soviets. Talks among the Americans, the British, the French, and the Soviets about a government for occupied Germany had broken off in 1947. The United States, Britain, and France decided to continue to plan Germany's future without the Russians. Under the Marshall Plan the United States, Britain, and France merged their zones in order to coordinate economic policies. Then, in June 1948, the three nations announced plans to form a democratic government for all of western Germany.

However, the western sectors in Berlin posed a problem. Berlin was located 110 miles (117 kilometers) within the Soviet zone. The city had been split into four sectors, each controlled by one of the four powers. This meant that the Americans, the British, and the French had to travel through Soviet-occupied Germany to reach their sectors of Berlin.

The Soviets charged that the merging of the western zones violated the four-power control of Germany. On June 24 Russian troops blocked all roads, railroads, and canals between western Germany and Berlin. The western sectors of Berlin were cut off, with only about a month's supply of food and fuel for its 2.5 million residents. Soviet leaders were confident that the blockade would force the United States, Britain, and France to give up their sectors in Berlin.

The military governor of the American zone promptly cabled the United States: "If we mean to hold Europe against communism, we must not budge." Indeed, Truman was determined not to retreat from Berlin. To aid the blockaded city, the Americans and British decided to fly in food and supplies. Thus began the Berlin airlift, or Operation Vittles as it was popularly called. Day after day, transport planes roared into West Berlin at rooftop level. One plane landed every three minutes.

Berlin airlift transport planes flew 277,000 missions in fifteen months. Their noise was a welcome reassurance of continued support.

Clearly, the Russian strategy was not working. In May 1949 the Soviet Union admitted defeat and lifted the blockade. In September the airlift ended. It had run for 11 months, delivering over 2 million tons of food, clothing, medicine, fuel, and other supplies. The grateful mayor of West Berlin renamed the plaza near the city's airport "Airlift Square."

The United States, Britain, and France went ahead with their plans to set up an independent western Germany. On May 23, 1949, the West German Federal Republic was created, with its capital at Bonn. It became known as West Germany. Five months later the Russians organized the East German Democratic Republic, with East Berlin as its capital. There were now two Germanys, one in the West and the other in the Soviet bloc.

NATO

Western Europeans had watched Soviet moves with increasing alarm. Convinced that Western Europe needed to unite, Britain proposed a defensive alliance. In March 1948 Britain, France, Belgium, Luxembourg, and the Netherlands signed the Brussels Pact. In the pact, the nations pledged military aid if any member were attacked. Without American support, however, the alliance had little strength.

After the Soviet blockade of Berlin, many American leaders accepted the idea of a defensive alliance with Europe. The idea was endorsed in the 1948 presidential campaign by both Truman and his Republican challenger, Thomas E. Dewey. After winning his second term, Truman announced plans for an American-European alliance.

In April 1949 representatives of 12 nations met in Washington to form the North Atlantic Treaty Organization (NATO). Signing the treaty were the United States, the five Brussels Pact nations, Canada, Italy, Portugal, Denmark, Norway, and Iceland. Greece and Turkey joined in 1952 and West Germany in 1955.

The treaty stated that an attack against one or more members would be considered an attack against them all. Each member pledged to "assist" attacked nations with "such action as it deems necessary," including armed force.

When Truman sent the treaty to the Senate, it sparked hot debate. Some senators charged that it could force the United States to go to war. But Dean Acheson, Truman's new secretary of state, said that the power to declare war would still rest with Congress alone. Acheson urged Congress to pass the treaty. "We have learned our history lesson from two world wars in less than half a century," he stated. "If the free nations do not stand together, they will fall one by one."

In July the Senate overwhelmingly approved the NATO treaty. This was the first American military treaty with Europe since the alliance with France during the Revolutionary War. The last whispers of isolationism seemed stilled.

ARMING NATO

At the first NATO meeting in September 1949, members made plans to build a military force. They decided on a defensive force strong enough to deter, or discourage, the Soviets from attacking any NATO member. They hoped that American atomic weapons—NATO's "sword"—would deter the Soviets for years. That would give them time to build NATO's "shield," a European force.

However, late in September the Soviet Union announced the explosion of its first atomic bomb. Americans were stunned. Most experts had thought that the Russians would not unlock the secret of the atom for years. Congress quickly voted $1 billion to arm the NATO nations. Some 4 months later Truman announced an American program to build a hydrogen bomb. Such a weapon was potentially 1,000 times more powerful than the atom bomb.

In 1950 United States arms began to flow to Western Europe. The United States also sent additional troops as part of the NATO force. In December General Dwight D. Eisenhower was chosen as Supreme Commander of NATO, with headquarters in Paris. The heart of United States foreign policy was now in NATO. "The defense of Europe is the basis for the defense of the whole free world," Truman said, "ourselves included."

In 1955, as a counterforce to NATO, the Russians formed a military alliance with the Soviet bloc nations. The alliance was called the Warsaw Pact. It included the Soviet Union, Albania, Bulgaria, Czechoslovakia, East Germany, Hungary, Poland, and Romania.

THE POINT FOUR PROGRAM

Not all American aid was directed at strengthening Europe. In his inaugural address in 1949, Truman proposed a "bold new program" to aid the world's developing nations. Because the program was the fourth item in the speech, it was quickly named Point Four.

The Point Four program was intended to help poor nations raise their standard of living by making use of American economic and technical aid. Congress balked at funding such an open-ended program and voted fairly small sums for it. Nevertheless, by 1952 American advisers were to work in 33 nations.

Point Four workers battled malaria in Peru and hunger in India. They built a power plant in Mexico, an agricultural school in Ethiopia, and an irrigation system in Jordan. The program, one Point Four administrator explained, "emphasizes the distribution of knowledge rather than of money. Obviously there is not money enough in the world to relieve the suffering of the peoples of the developing areas, but . . . there is, for the first time in history, enough knowledge to do the job."

SECTION REVIEW

1. Identify the following: Truman Doctrine, George C. Marshall, West Germany, East Germany, Dean Acheson, NATO's "sword" and "shield," Point Four program.

2. Define the following: containment, cold war, coup.

3. Why was the Middle East important to the United States and Russia after World War II?

4. (a) Why did the United States adopt the Marshall Plan? (b) Why did the Soviet bloc not participate in the program?

5. (a) Why did the Soviets blockade Berlin? (b) How did the Americans and the British respond to the blockade?

6. List the nations that formed the North Atlantic Treaty Organization in 1949.

7. (a) How was NATO's military plan upset in September 1949? (b) Name the members of the Warsaw Pact.

8. What was the goal of the Point Four program?

CONFLICT IN THE MIDDLE EAST AND ASIA

READ TO FIND OUT

— how the United Nations tried to solve the problem of Palestine.

— how the Communists triumphed in China.

— why Korea was divided into two nations.

— how the Korean War was fought.

— why Truman dismissed MacArthur.

— how an armistice in Korea was signed.

During World War II Wendell Willkie, the Republican candidate for president in 1940, toured Asia. "I have seen an almost bewildering variety of ways of living and ways of ruling and of being ruled," he wrote. He had seen kingdoms, republics, League of Nations mandates, and colonies. However, everywhere he found that people had something in common: "They all want a chance at the end of the war to live in liberty and independence."

The transition from colony to independent nation could be peaceful, as in the Philippines. On July 4, 1946, the United States fulfilled its prewar promise and granted the Islands independence.

In other places, nationalist groups had to fight to throw off foreign rule. Sometimes, groups struggling to free their country also fought each other. For the world powers, locked in the cold war, the outcome of hot wars in the Middle East and Asia was of vital interest.

THE DIVISION OF PALESTINE

One troubled area was the Middle Eastern land of Palestine. Since World War I, Great Britain had administered this territory under a mandate, or commission, from the League of Nations. Palestine had both Arab and Jewish populations. Each of them was strongly nationalistic. Britain promised that " a national home for the Jewish people" would be set up in Palestine. This would be done, Britain assured the Arabs, without violating Arab rights.

During the 1930s and 1940s, thousands of Jews suffering from Nazi persecution fled to Palestine. This stream of immigrants set off clashes between the Jews and Arabs. Britain, unable to satisfy the claims of either side, earned the anger of both groups.

In 1947 Britain asked the UN to settle the problem of Palestine. The General Assembly recommended that Palestine be divided into a Jewish state and an Arab state. Jerusalem, considered a holy site by both Arabs and Jews, would be an international city under UN control. The Jews accepted the plan, but the Arabs rejected it.

On May 14, 1948, Britain ended its mandate and pulled its troops out of Palestine. That same day the Jews proclaimed the existence of the nation of Israel. President Truman promptly recognized the new nation.

Palestinian Arabs, however, were determined to destroy Israel. The Arab nations of Egypt, Syria, Lebanon, Transjordan (later renamed Jordan), Iraq, Saudi Arabia, and Yemen sent troops to join the Palestinian Arabs. As Arabs and Israelis battled, the UN tried to mediate the war. Finally, in July 1949, a UN team led by American diplomat Dr. Ralph J. Bunche arranged an armistice.

American statesman Ralph Bunche won the Nobel peace prize in 1950 for his work in negotiating peace between the Arabs and the Israelis.

It was an uneasy peace, marred by frequent border raids on both sides. Some 600,000 Palestinian Arabs, refusing to live under Israeli rule, fled to neighboring Arab states. None of the Arab states would recognize Israel's right to exist.

For the United States, the Arab-Israeli conflict was a thorny issue. The United States declared itself a friend of Israel, thus provoking Arab resentment. Yet American leaders also wanted to keep the friendship of the Arab states. George Kennan, an American expert on Russia, worried about still another problem. He warned of the danger of Communist expansion in the Middle East.

CIVIL WAR IN CHINA

Another nation causing the United States worry was China. American concern for China dated back to the Open Door policy of 1899. In the 1890s the great powers had gained control over parts of China. The Open Door policy called for all nations to respect the independence of China while maintaining trade rights.

By the 1920s China was ruled by local warlords, or rulers, who fought each other for power. Many dissatisfied Chinese flocked to the Nationalist party, which was trying to unite the country. The Nationalists also wanted to end the great powers' privileges in China. "China is not the colony of one nation but of all," said a Nationalist leader. "We are not the slaves of one country but of all."

Under Chiang Kai-shek, the Nationalists struggled to win control of China. Chinese Communists fought alongside the Nationalists. However, in 1927 Chiang split with the Communists. A year later he set up a government in Peking (Beijing) which had control over much of the country. The United States quickly recognized the Nationalist government.

The Communists, under Mao Tse-tung (MAH-oh DZUH DOONG), built their own army. The Communists and Nationalists fought each other until Japan invaded China in the 1930s. To resist the Japanese, Chiang and Mao made an uneasy truce. During World War II, however, the truce broke down, and in 1945 civil war erupted.

American leaders supported Chiang and the Nationalist government. However, they hoped to see a unified China as a world power and an ally. In 1945 President Truman sent George C. Marshall to

China to try to join all political parties in a "united and democratic government." Marshall managed to arrange a truce, but it was short-lived.

The civil war continued, and so did American aid to Chiang. But the Communists were growing stronger. The Russians, who had briefly occupied Manchuria in 1945, gave the Communists captured Japanese weapons and supplies. In addition, many Chinese became disillusioned with corruption in Chiang's regime, and they turned to the Communists.

Throughout 1947 and 1948 American leaders argued about what to do in China. Many in Congress insisted that the Nationalists could win the civil war with increased American aid. As Communist successes mounted, however, Truman felt that it would take massive American aid to help Chiang. He preferred to focus on containing communism in Europe and the Middle East.

THE COMMUNIST VICTORY IN CHINA

The final act in the Chinese civil war was played in 1949, when the Communists swept to victory. In October the Communists proclaimed a new government, the People's Republic of China. It was soon known as Red China. The Nationalists fled to the island of Formosa, later renamed Taiwan (TĪ-WAHN).

Americans were dismayed. Many blamed Truman for allowing China to "pass into the Soviet orbit." A study by the Department of State denied that charge. The Nationalists lost, the study concluded, because of the corruption and inefficiency of Chiang's regime.

Still, American leaders refused to recognize the Communist government, which was openly hostile to the United States. The United States continued to consider the Nationalist regime on Formosa as China's legal government. With American support, representatives of the Nationalist regime continued to be the only Chinese delegates seated in the UN Security Council.

Some 25 nations, including the Soviet bloc, Britain, and France, recognized the People's Republic of China. In 1950 Mao Tse-tung visited Moscow and signed a treaty of friendship and mutual aid with the Russians. With this act, the 500 million people of China were allied to the Soviet Union.

A massive parade marched through the streets of Shanghai in 1945 to welcome the Communists. A large banner showed the face of Mao Tse-tung, leader of Communist China.

THE DIVISION OF KOREA

The struggle in China overshadowed unrest in its tiny neighbor Korea. Hooked onto Manchuria like a comma, Korea lies between the Chinese mainland and Japan. Between 1910 and 1945, Koreans had lived under Japanese rule.

During World War II both the United States and the Soviet Union had promised that Korea would become independent. At the war's end the two powers made an agreement for the disarming of Japanese troops in Korea. The Russians would accept the Japanese surrender north of the 38th parallel, and the Americans would disarm Japanese troops south of that line. After the Japanese surrender, the Russians remained in the northern zone, and the Americans stayed in the south.

While the Koreans called for independence, American and Soviet leaders tried to work out a plan to unify Korea. Talks dragged on for two years. The United States and the Soviet Union each feared that the other would gain control of Korea.

Finally, in September 1947, the Americans asked the UN to settle the matter. A UN commission was created to oversee an election in Korea to form a government. Both the Russians and the North Koreans refused to participate in the election.

In May 1948 the commission held the election in the American zone only. The elected assembly drew up a constitution, chose Syngman Rhee (SIHNG-man REE) as president, and proclaimed the Republic of Korea. It was recognized by the UN, the United States and 30 other nations.

In North Korea the Russians held separate elections. The North Koreans then set up the Democratic People's Republic of Korea. Only Communist nations recognized the North Korean government.

Thus, Korea was divided into two nations, one supported by the Soviets and the other by the Americans. Each Korean government claimed to represent all of Korea.

In December 1948 the Soviet Union withdrew its troops from North Korea, leaving tanks and heavy artillery. Six months later American troops left South Korea. The Americans left guns and ammunition, but no tanks or artillery. Through late 1949 and early 1950 North and South Koreans skirmished along the border. The 38th parallel had become another crossroads in the cold war.

STEPS TO WAR

Korea burst into American headlines in June 1950. Early on Sunday, June 25, North Korean troops stormed across the 38th parallel into South Korea. With their Russian tanks and artillery, the North Koreans shattered the lightly armed South Korean forces. The South Koreans retreated southward.

The invasion shocked leaders in the United States. President Truman called the UN Security Council into emergency session. Members called for a cease-fire and the immediate withdrawal of North Korean troops to the 38th parallel. The Soviet delegate, who undoubtedly would have vetoed the resolution, was absent. The Russians were boycotting the Security Council because China's seat was held by a Nationalist, rather than by a representative of the People's Republic.

The next day Truman ordered General Douglas MacArthur to support the South Koreans with American naval and air forces. To keep the conflict from spreading, Truman sent the United States Seventh Fleet to block the Formosa Strait between China and Formosa. The fleet, he thought, would protect Formosa from any Communist attack, and prevent any Nationalist invasion of the Chinese mainland. On June 27 the Security Council supported Truman by urging UN members to assist South Korea in repelling "the armed attack."

However, at the end of the week MacArthur warned Truman that American troops would be needed to stop the North Koreans. Truman acted promptly. On June 30 he approved the use of American forces and ordered a naval blockade of the Korean coast. The American public, Congress, and much of the non-Communist world cheered Truman's actions.

The Security Council also endorsed the American actions. It committed a UN force to fight in South Korea under American command. Truman chose General MacArthur as commander. About 90 percent of the UN force was supplied by the United States and South Korea, although 16 other nations eventually sent troops. However, to most people in the United States, the Korean War was an American war.

THE KOREAN WAR

In midsummer of 1950 American troops marched onto the battlefields of Korea. Most American GIs were unseasoned recruits arriving from occupation duty in Japan. They had no tanks or heavy artillery to use against North Korean forces.

The North Koreans smashed the poorly organized UN forces. By August the UN forces were driven to the southeastern tip of Korea. There, as fresh American troops and weapons arrived, the UN defensive line held. Now MacArthur was ready to take the offensive. He decided to launch an amphibious attack behind enemy lines at Inchon

South Korean women and children fleeing from Communist invaders seemed not to notice the presence of a troop of United States infantrymen going toward the enemy.

United States marines were delayed by an enemy roadblock as they retreated south from the November offensive. They suffered terribly from the subzero cold.

The UN triumph was short-lived. On November 26, hundreds of thousands of Chinese poured across the Yalu and pushed through UN lines. The UN troops retreated over a twisting icy road known as "nightmare alley." Violent snowstorms and steep gorges took as many lives as did Chinese grenades and machine guns. MacArthur's army was driven back into South Korea, with a "bottomless well" of Chinese soldiers in pursuit.

THE TRUMAN-MacARTHUR CONTROVERSY

The UN forces, MacArthur told American leaders in early December, were now "facing the entire Chinese nation in an undeclared war." MacArthur saw only one path to victory. He proposed that UN forces blockade and bomb China while Chiang Kai-shek's Nationalists attacked the Chinese mainland.

Truman and his advisers rejected MacArthur's plan of all-out war. They were certain that such actions would bring the Soviets into the war on China's side and would lead to a third world war. They decided to return to their original, limited goal in the war of driving the Communists out of South Korea.

By March 1951 UN troops had regrouped and were pushing the Communists back into North Korea. Truman decided to seek a cease-fire. MacArthur, however, publicly threatened to attack China. Then he sent a letter to Congress stating his belief that "there is no substitute for victory."

MacArthur's actions, Truman decided, were ruining American efforts to arrange a truce. "MacArthur left me no choice," Truman later wrote. "I could no longer tolerate his insubordination." On April 11 Truman dismissed MacArthur from his command.

Americans were outraged. Pro-MacArthur telegrams flooded the White House, and in Congress there was talk of impeachment. When MacArthur came home, he was welcomed as a hero.

A few weeks later Congress began an inquiry into MacArthur's dismissal. Truman's advisers defended the President's decision. MacArthur, they said, had challenged the President's constitutional right to control the military and to direct foreign policy. Truman's decision was upheld, and the controversy over MacArthur soon died down.

(IN-CHAHN), near the 38th parallel. "We shall land at Inchon, " he declared, "and I shall crush them."

It was not an idle boast. On September 15, American marines captured Inchon in a swift, surprise attack. Then they pushed inland to free Seoul (SŌL), the South Korean capital. Meanwhile, other UN troops sped north, attacking the North Koreans. By October MacArthur's troops were poised along the 38th parallel.

The UN forces had won their goal of sweeping the invaders from South Korea. MacArthur, however, wanted the troops to enter North Korea to destroy the Communist armed forces. Truman agreed. On October 7 the UN called for a "unified, independent and democratic government" of Korea. Thus, the UN had revised its original goal in the Korean War.

As MacArthur's army marched into North Korea, Red China warned that it would not "stand idly by" while its neighbor was invaded. MacArthur assured American leaders that China would not intervene. By November a triumphant MacArthur had reached the Yalu River, which separated North Korea from Chinese Manchuria.

The Korean War 1950-1953

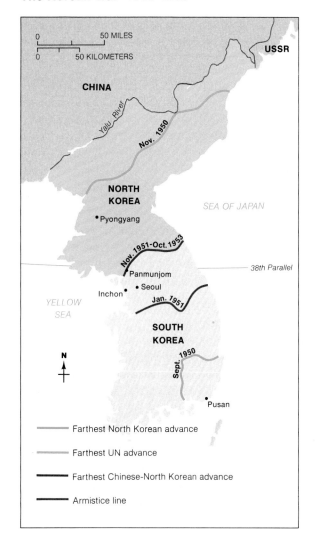

0 | 50 MILES
0 | 50 KILOMETERS

USSR

CHINA

Yalu River

Nov. 1950

NORTH KOREA

•Pyongyang

SEA OF JAPAN

Nov. 1951–Oct. 1953

Panmunjom
• Seoul

Inchon•

38th Parallel

YELLOW SEA

Jan. 1951

SOUTH KOREA

N

Sept. 1950

•Pusan

—— Farthest North Korean advance

—— Farthest UN advance

—— Farthest Chinese-North Korean advance

—— Armistice line

ARMISTICE

In July 1951 representatives of the UN and the Communists began negotiations for a cease-fire. Clouded by suspicion on both sides, the talks dragged on and on. Meanwhile, the fighting continued.

In November 1952 Americans went to the polls to elect a new president. The Korean War was the main issue. Truman had decided not to run. However, the Democratic candidate, Governor Adlai E. Stevenson of Illinois, supported Truman's policy. General Dwight D. Eisenhower, the Republican candidate and popular hero of World War II, promised to go to Korea to end the war. The voters swept Eisenhower into the presidency.

Eisenhower kept his promise and visited the battle front for three days in December. However, he admitted, he found no quick solutions. Only after seven more months of talks did the negotiators sign an armistice, on July 27, 1953.

Under the terms of the armistice, Korea was divided along the battle line, which roughly followed the 38th parallel. This boundary was to be a demilitarized zone between North Korea and South Korea. The armistice also arranged for the return of prisoners of war, and some 3,700 American prisoners came home. However, United States costs in the war were high. More than 54,000 soldiers were killed, about 100,000 were wounded, and about $18 billion was spent.

In the hills of Korea, after three years of fighting, the gunfire stopped. The war was over, but the tension between North and South Korea remained. There would be more clashes, and more casualties, along the 38th parallel.

Still, the United States had managed to contain communism in Korea. And the UN forces had turned back an armed invasion without setting off another world war.

SECTION REVIEW

1. Identify the following: Ralph J. Bunche, Chiang Kai-shek, Mao Tse-tung, Red China, Formosa, 38th parallel, Syngman Rhee, Yalu River.

2. (a) How did the United Nations try to solve the problem of Palestine? (b) How did Arabs react to the creation of Israel?

3. How was the United States caught in the middle of the Arab-Israeli conflict?

4. (a) Why did the Chinese Communists triumph in China? (b) What government did the United States and the United Nations recognize as China's legal government?

5. (a) Name the nations into which Korea was divided in 1948. (b) Describe what happened at the 38th parallel on June 25, 1950.

6. How did Red China react to MacArthur's entry into North Korea?

7. Why did Truman dismiss MacArthur from his command?

8. What were the terms of the Korean armistice?

FOREIGN POLICY UNDER EISENHOWER

READ TO FIND OUT

— how Vietnam was divided into two nations.

— how Poles and Hungarians tried to gain freedom from Soviet control.

— why war broke out in the Middle East.

— how the United States reacted to troubles in Latin America.

— why Berlin remained a source of conflict between Russia and the United States.

— how the "spirit of Camp David" faltered.

Dwight D. Eisenhower won the presidency, in good part, by pledging to end the Korean War. "A soldier all my life," Eisenhower told the voters, "I have enlisted in the greatest cause of my life—the cause of peace." He also pledged a new foreign policy to challenge communism.

The architect of the policy was John Foster Dulles, Eisenhower's secretary of state. Dulles showed the diplomatic command of precise detail. Yet he also had a fondness for expressing policies in dramatic phrases. The President, said one aide, of-ten "smoothed the sharp edges" of Dulles's policies. In the 1950s the bold words of Dulles and the moderation of Eisenhower would shape American foreign policy.

THE DULLES APPROACH

For Dulles, the cold war was more than a power struggle with the Soviet Union. He saw it as a great moral conflict, pitting the forces of good against the evil of communism. He rejected Truman's policy of containing communism. It was a "negative, futile and immoral policy," said Dulles, because it accepted communism where it already existed.

Instead, Dulles wanted to liberate, or free, people in Europe and Asia from the control of the Soviet Union. He felt that this could be done by using "ideas as weapons." The Voice of America, a radio broadcast beamed behind the Iron Curtain, urged people to free themselves from their Communist governments. American aid to non-Communist nations was increased.

Dulles also changed the nation's defense policy. To reduce the strain on the economy, military forces were cut back. The United States would rely instead on less costly nuclear weapons for defense.

By 1953 both the Americans and the Soviets had added the awesome hydrogen bomb to their nuclear arsenals. Scientists in the United States and the Soviet Union were working on bombs that were even more powerful. The two nations found themselves locked in a nuclear arms race.

The Soviet economy is geared to support the production of a huge stock of war machinery. Thousands of tanks such as these invaded Hungary in 1956.

Dulles warned the Soviet Union that the United States would use its atomic weapons to deter agression. The Americans, he said, would "depend primarily upon a great capacity to retaliate, instantly, by means and at places of our choosing." This policy, with its threat to use atomic weapons, became known as "massive retaliation." Dulles believed that the policy would ensure peace.

CONFLICT IN INDOCHINA

Dulles's approach to the cold war was tested during the spring of 1954 in a little country called Vietnam. Vietnam was part of the French colony of Indochina, which also included Laos and Cambodia.

During World War II the French temporarily lost their colony to Japan. Shortly after Japan's surrender, a nationalist group called the Vietminh (vee-ET-MIHN) proclaimed Vietnam an independent nation. Many of the Vietminh, including their leader, Ho Chi Minh (HŌ CHEE MIHN), were Communists.

When France reclaimed Laos and Cambodia after the war, it gave limited recognition to the Vietminh government. However, tensions between the French and the Vietminh soon exploded into warfare. In 1949 France supported the creation of a non-Communist government in southern Vietnam. A few months later the People's Republic of China began aiding the Vietminh. The war quickly turned against the French and their Vietnamese allies.

The United States took a strong interest in Vietnam. From the start, Americans sympathized with the Vietnamese desire for independence. But with China's involvement, American leaders felt that they must help France in the struggle against communism. American aid began flowing to France.

When Eisenhower took office, he approved Truman's policy in Vietnam. Eisenhower's administration feared that if Vietnam fell to communism, other parts of Asia would, like a row of dominoes, also fall. Based on this "falling domino" principle, aid to France was increased. By 1954 American dollars covered nearly 80 percent of France's war costs.

In the spring of 1954 Ho Chi Minh's forces trapped 20,000 French and Vietnamese at the jungle fortress of Dien Bien Phu (DYEHN BYEHN FOO). France pleaded with the United States for military intervention.

When French and Vietnamese forces were trapped at Dien Bien Phu, they received reinforcements of men and supplies by parachute.

Dulles proposed "united action" with the British against the Vietminh. However, both Britain and Congress opposed intervention, and Eisenhower rejected the idea. Dien Bien Phu fell in May. It was a final defeat for the French.

THE DIVISION OF VIETNAM

In July 1954 representatives of Britain, France, the Soviet Union, Communist China, Cambodia, Laos, and Indochina met in Geneva, Switzerland to work out a settlement for Indochina. Observers for the United States also attended.

At the Geneva Conference, Laos, Cambodia, and Vietnam were given their independence from France. Vietnam was divided at the 17th parallel. The Vietminh were given the land to the north, and the non-Communists were given the land to the south. An election was to be held later to create a unified Vietnam.

The election, however, was never held. President Ngo Dinh Diem (noh din ZEE-em) of South Vietnam feared that Ho Chi Minh's North Vietnamese regime would win, and he refused to take part. Thus, Vietnam remained divided. The United States poured aid into South Vietnam, hoping to keep it from falling to communism.

As a barrier to further Communist expansion, Dulles drew up plans for a defensive alliance in Asia. The Southeast Asia Treaty Organization (SEATO) was formed in September 1954. The alliance was made up of the United States, Britain, France, Australia, New Zealand, Pakistan, the Philippines, and Thailand. SEATO members pledged that if one of them was attacked, the others would "act to meet the common danger."

REVOLTS IN THE SOVIET BLOC

Eisenhower had followed a cautious course in Vietnam. Dulles, however clung to his policy of confronting communism. He was certain that the United States had to risk war in order to avoid war.

In a *Life* magazine article, published in January 1956, Dulles explained his view. "The ability to get to the verge without getting into war is the necessary art," he said. "If you are scared to go to the brink, you are lost." Americans were shocked by Dulles's view, which newspapers quickly labeled "brinkmanship." Eisenhower, however, had a more moderate view than Dulles.

In the summer of 1955 American, Russian, British, and French leaders met in Geneva to discuss several cold war problems. Although not one of the problems was settled, the Americans and Russians seemed eager to cooperate with each other. "I have had enough of war," Eisenhower told the Russians. Russian leader Nikita Khrushchev (nuh-KEE-tuh Kroosh-CHAWF), who had come to power after Stalin's death in 1953, spoke of "peaceful coexistence" with the United States. Geneva had produced a slight thaw in the cold war.

The ice cracked a little more in June 1956, when the text of a secret Khrushchev speech was made public. Khrushchev had denounced Stalin's rule as a brutal dictatorship. Krushchev's words seemed to promise more independence to Soviet-dominated nations in Eastern Europe.

In Poland people promptly took advantage of this new mood. In city after city, workers demonstrated against the Communist party and demanded greater freedom from Moscow. Khrushchev reacted with moderation. He gave limited self-rule to the Poles. They in turn reaffirmed their alliance with the Soviet Union.

Waves of restlessness also swept through Hungary. In October, riots broke out in the capital of Budapest and quickly spread. The Hungarians wanted more than limited self-rule. They called for freedom from communism. In November the Hungarians withdrew from the Warsaw Pact and demanded complete independence.

Defiant Hungarians tore down a statue of Stalin and destroyed Communist signs. The Hungarian revolt was crushed in a few days by Russian troops and tanks.

In response, Soviet tanks and troops rolled into Hungary. Hungarian "freedom fighters," armed with little more than rocks and rifles, tried to stop the Russian tanks. Still in control of Radio Budapest, the Hungarians broadcast pleas for help.

In the United Nations, Americans denounced the Soviet actions. Eisenhower urged the Russians to withdraw their troops "in the name of humanity and in the cause of peace." But neither Eisenhower nor Dulles was willing to intervene and to risk war with the Soviets. The Hungarian revolt was crushed.

THE SUEZ CRISIS

While revolt flared in Hungary, conflict grew in the Middle East. The region seethed with rivalries among Arab nations. However, the Arabs were united on one matter—their resentment of Israel—and gunfire often crackled along Arab-Israeli borders. The leader of Egypt, Gamal Abdel Nasser, was a fierce nationalist. He hoped to unite Arabs and to end all foreign influence in the Middle East.

The Soviet Union was eager to extend its influence throughout the Arab world. The United States, which had angered Arabs by its support of Israel, hoped to improve relations with Arab nations. The opportunity came late in 1955.

Nasser had proposed to build a huge dam in Egypt at Aswan on the Nile River. The dam would increase by one third Egypt's croplands. Because Egypt could not finance the costly project, the United States and Britain offered generous loans.

While considering the offers, Nasser talked to the Soviets about a loan. He also increased border raids on Israel and recognized the People's Republic of China. In July 1956 the United States and Britain withdrew their loan offers. Nasser, said Dulles, could "go to Moscow" for the money.

Furious, Nasser seized control of the Suez Canal in Egypt, which was operated by a British-French company. He planned to use income from the canal to pay for the Aswan Dam. However, Britain and France feared that Nasser would bar them from the canal, which was their supply route to Middle Eastern oil fields.

For three months Dulles tried to work out a settlement. Then, in late October, Israeli troops swept into Egypt. They attacked bases from which Arabs had been raiding Israel. Britain and France claimed that the fighting threatened the canal, and they launched their own attacks on Egypt. By early November the British and French controlled the canal, and the Israelis occupied Egypt's Sinai Peninsula.

Eisenhower quickly sought a peaceful solution to the Suez crisis. In a UN resolution, Dulles called for a cease-fire and for withdrawal of foreign troops from Egypt. The Soviet bloc supported the American resolution. Russia even threatened to send troops to help Egypt. So pressured, the British, the French, and the Israelis pulled out of Egypt.

Many Arabs applauded the American stand in the Suez crisis. However, American relations with Britain and France were badly strained.

THE EISENHOWER DOCTRINE

Many Arabs saw the Suez crisis as a triumph of nationalism. Britain and France, the old colonial powers, had been swept from the Middle East. The Soviets saw the Suez crisis as an opportunity to expand their influence, and they sent aid to Egypt and Syria.

American leaders were sharply aware of Soviet actions. "The existing vacuum in the Middle East," said Eisenhower in January 1957, "must be filled by the United States before it is filled by Russia." In March Congress approved a plan that became known as the Eisenhower Doctrine. The plan authorized the president to use armed force to help Middle Eastern nations resist an attack by "any nation controlled by international communism."

The Eisenhower Doctrine was put into practice in 1958. In July an army revolt toppled the pro-Western government of Iraq. The rebels, it was believed, were supported by Egypt, Syria, and the Soviet Union. Leaders of neighboring Lebanon and Jordan feared the same kind of revolt in their nations, and they asked the United States for help.

Eisenhower acted swiftly. He sent 5,000 marines to Lebanon and convinced the British to send paratroopers to Jordan. The Soviet Union, Egypt, and Syria called the American action aggression. However, the Arab states pledged not to intervene in Jordan and Lebanon. American and British troops withdrew.

One more crisis in the Middle East had been settled. However, it was clear that the region would continue to hold a key place in the foreign policies of the United States and the Soviet Union.

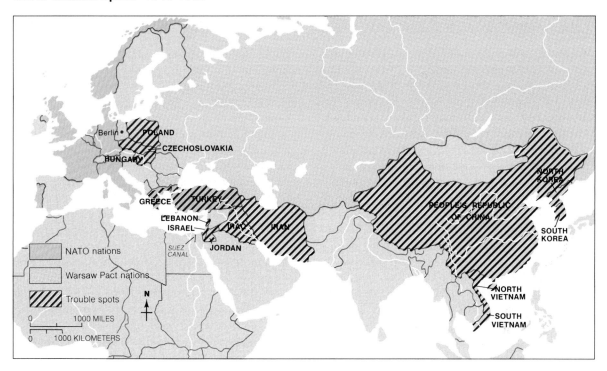

Tension between Communist and non-Communist nations resulted in several mutual defense organizations such as NATO and the Warsaw Pact. In 1955 Turkey, Iraq, Great Britain, Pakistan, and Iran signed the Baghdad Pact, later known as the Central Treaty Organization (CENTO).

RELATIONS WITH LATIN AMERICA

Because of crises in Asia and Europe, the United States often neglected Latin America. The United States was pouring money into Europe and Asia, yet less than 3 percent of its foreign aid went to Latin American nations. Many Latin Americans, beset by economic woes, resented this neglect.

The main concern of the United States in Latin America was to keep communism out of the hemisphere. In 1950 the United States joined Latin American nations in the Organization of American States (OAS). The purpose of the OAS was to settle regional disputes and to maintain peace and security. Members pledged that an attack against one was an attack against all.

In March 1954 the OAS adopted a United States resolution calling international communism a threat to the Americas. Two months later Czechoslovakia shipped a huge supply of arms to Guatemala, whose government was pro-Communist. Dulles declared that this would "endanger the peace of this hemisphere."

The United States quickly sent arms to two of Guatemala's neighbors, Honduras and Nicaragua. In June a group of Guatemalan exiles overthrew the Guatemalan government. The rebels then set up an anti-Communist government, which the United States recognized.

Most Latin Americans resented American support for the new dictatorship in Guatemala, as well as American support for dictatorships in the Dominican Republic and Cuba. In 1958, when Vice-President Richard Nixon visited Latin America, angry crowds lined the streets and showered his car with rocks and eggs.

Worried, the United States moved to improve relations with its neighbors. In September 1958 the United States and Latin America set up the Inter-American Development Bank. The bank would provide credit and other aid to all member American countries. Two years later, the United States pledged $500 million to improve living conditions in Latin American nations. "We are not saints," said Eisenhower. "We know we make mistakes but our heart is in the right place."

THE CUBAN REVOLUTION

Meanwhile, discontent was boiling over in Cuba. In January 1959 rebels led by Fidel Castro, a young lawyer, overthrew the Cuban dictatorship of Fulgenico Batista (bah-TEES-tah). Believing that Castro would set up a democracy, the United States warmly recognized his regime. However, Americans were quickly disillusioned. Castro took over American sugar plantations, giving little payment to the owners. Cuban opponents to Castro were jailed or shot. Civil liberties nearly disappeared in Cuba.

The United States was especially worried about Castro's growing ties to the Soviets. In February 1960 Cuba and the Soviet Union signed a trade agreement that gave Castro generous credit terms. In response, the administration put an embargo on Cuban sugar imports to the United States. As American relations with Castro soured, Soviet influence in Cuba grew.

Fidel Castro talked about freedom for the Cuban people but failed to produce it. Under his dictatorship many Cubans have been denied their civil liberties.

THE BERLIN CRISIS

While the United States was dealing with Latin American relations, its attention was again diverted by a crisis in Germany. Ever since Germany's division in 1947, the two German nations had followed different paths.

The Russians wanted East Germany to demonstrate the superiority of Communist government. However, East Germany suffered from a weak economy, strikes, and poor housing. Between 1949 and 1958, nearly 3 million East Germans fled to prosperous West Germany. In the divided city of Berlin, deep within East Germany, the contrast between the East and the West was even more striking. Thriving West Berlin was known as "the showplace of democracy."

Khrushchev was determined to drive the United States, Britain, and France out of Berlin. Stalin had failed to do this with his blockade in 1948. Khrushchev tried a different course. In November 1958 he demanded that the Americans, the British, and the French withdraw their occupation forces of some 10,000 men from West Berlin and declare it a "free city."*

To gain access to the city, the United States and its allies would have to deal with East Germany, which they did not recognize. Khrushchev gave them six months to agree to his terms.

"We are most solemnly committed to hold West Berlin," announced Dulles, "if need be by military force." Khrushchev warned that an American attack on East Germany would mean war. The tough talk never led to war, but the Berlin problem remained unsolved.

THE SPIRIT OF CAMP DAVID

In the summer of 1959 President Eisenhower decided that he must meet personally with Khrushchev to resolve the Berlin crisis. The President invited the Soviet leader to the United States. The invitation, Eisenhower said, was intended "to melt a little of the ice" of the cold war.

Khruschev arrived in the United States in September and set off on a whirlwind tour of the nation. There were some tense moments, especially when Khrushchev was denied a trip to Disneyland in

---

* free city: a city that is an independent state.

California for security reasons. He soon relaxed, however, and visited farms and factories across the nation.

By the time Khrushchev arrived at Camp David, the presidential retreat in Maryland, he was in a jovial mood. For three days Khrushchev and Eisenhower strolled the grounds and talked. As the meeting ended, the two leaders agreed that all disputes "should be settled not by force but by peaceful means—by negotiation."

The world was warmed by the new "spirit of Camp David." Khrushchev had withdrawn his ultimatum on Berlin. The two leaders now planned a summit conference* with Britain and France to discuss Germany. The date was set for May 1960.

THE U-2 INCIDENT

The spirit of Camp David abruptly ended on May 1, 1960. An American high-flying plane, the U-2, was shot down in Russian air space. Khrushchev announced the news a few days later and accused the Americans of trying to destroy the summit conference.

At first the United States insisted that the U-2 was a weather plane that had strayed off course. Then Khrushchev said that the captured pilot had confessed to being a spy. Also, photographic equipment had held shots of military sites. The Americans conceded that the U-2 was on a surveillance, or inspection, mission over the Soviet Union.

The summit conference took place as scheduled in Paris. There were no handshakes, no friendliness. Khrushchev harshly demanded that the United States end the U-2 flights, apologize for "past acts of aggression," and punish those responsible. President Eisenhower announced that the flights had been suspended, but he rejected Khrushchev's other demands. The following day the Russian leader went home, and the summit meeting collapsed.

Again, the cold war blew with chilly gusts. However, people nervous about this latest Soviet-American clash could take comfort in later words of the two leaders. Khrushchev still expressed his faith in negotiation and called the clash "a passing phase." Eisenhower insisted that "the path of reason and common sense is still open if the Soviets will but use it."

* summit conference: conference of heads of government.

At a meeting of the General Assembly of the United Nations in 1960, Khrushchev rose to make a point. Soviet Minister for Foreign Affairs Andrei Gromyko listened carefully.

SECTION REVIEW

1. Identify the following: John Foster Dulles, Vietminh, Ho Chi Minh, Southeast Asia Treaty Organization, Gamal Abdel Nasser, Organization of American States.

2. Define the following: massive retaliation, "falling domino" principle, "brinkmanship."

3. (a) Why did the United States aid the French in Vietnam? (b) How did the Geneva Conference solve problems in Indochina? (c) Why did the plan for a unified Vietnam fail?

4. What was the outcome of the Hungarian revolt?

5. What stand did the United States take in the Suez crisis?

6. (a) Explain the Eisenhower Doctrine. (b) How was the doctrine first put into practice?

7. (a) What was the main concern of the United States in Latin America? (b) How did the United States try to improve relations with Latin America?

8. (a) How did Khrushchev try to drive the United States and its allies out of Berlin in 1958? (b) What was the "spirit of Camp David"?

SUMMARY

After World War II the United States took on world-wide political tasks. It prepared Japan for a new government, and it occupied one of four parts of a divided Germany. The United States also joined the Security Council of the United Nations.

The United States' role in world politics led to disputes with the Soviet Union. The Soviets refused to yield control over a bloc of nations in Eastern Europe. Nor would the Soviets accept an American plan for banning atomic weapons.

Disputes threatened to become armed conflicts in the Middle East. Soviet-backed forces threatened Greece and Turkey. The United States sent aid under the Truman Doctrine. The aid was part of the developing cold war, fought in Europe with money, supplies, and treaties instead of guns.

When Europe seemed dangerously weak, the United States sent aid under the Marshall Plan. When the Soviets blocked land routes to Berlin, the United States airlifted supplies to the city. The United States and its allies formed NATO to defend Europe. The Soviet Union and its allies countered by signing the Warsaw Pact.

Europe avoided a shooting war, but fighting broke out elsewhere. Arab forces attacked the new nation of Israel in 1948. Civil war in China led to a Communist victory there in 1949, and the People's Republic of China became a Soviet ally. Communist North Korea invaded South Korea in 1950. Determined to halt the invasion, President Truman sent in American troops. Fighting swept back and forth across Korea, settling in 1951 at a battle line near the 38th parallel.

The Korean War ended officially in 1953, after Eisenhower's election as president. Other conflicts involving communism soon arose. Vietnam was divided into two nations, Communist and non-Communist, in 1954. Hungarians tried and failed to free themselves from Soviet control in 1956. War in Egypt in 1956 prompted the Eisenhower Doctrine, an offer to help Middle Eastern nations resist communism. After Castro seized power in 1959, Cuba became a Soviet ally. Attempts to ease the cold war crumbled in 1960 after an American spy plane was shot down over the Soviet Union.

Erik Nitsche. *Exploring the Universe, Nuclear Fusion,* 1958. Collection of The Museum of Modern Art, New York.

Atomic scientists loosed on the postwar world an awesome force. The potential of such power is suggested by an Erik Nitsche poster entitled "Exploring the Universe."

CHAPTER REVIEW

1. (a) How was the division of Berlin after World War II like the division of Germany? (b) How did the division of Germany change in 1948? (c) Why were the land routes to West Berlin cut off between June 1948 and May 1949? (d) Why was West Berlin an embarrassment to Khrushchev in 1958?

2. (a) Explain how the United Nations Security Council differs from the General Assembly. (b) Explain how the Security Council may call out armed forces. (c) Describe how UN forces tried to establish peace in the Middle East after fighting in 1948 and again in 1956.

3. In what ways were the meetings of the UN Atomic Energy Commission, beginning in 1946, like the Geneva Conference of 1927?

4. (a) What did the Soviet Union hope to gain in Iran after World War II? (b) What did the Soviet Union hope to gain in Turkey? (c) How did American policies regarding Iran and Turkey serve the strategy of containment?

5. (a) Explain the difference between NATO's "sword" and its "shield." (b) When did the Soviet Union show that it, too, possessed a "sword"?

6. (a) Name one or more ways in which Truman's Point Four program was like UNRRA aid.

(b) Name at least two ways in which the programs were different.

7. (a) How powerful were the Chinese Nationalists in 1928? (b) How powerful were the Chinese Nationalists in 1950? (c) Why did the word "China" have different official meanings in Washington, D.C., and in London after 1950?

8. Name at least one event related to the Korean War for each of the following months: May 1948, June 1950, September 1950, November 1950, April 1951, July 1953.

9. (a) Explain how a change in Soviet leadership was related to the revolution in Hungary in 1956. (b) Explain how the Soviet Union might have used the falling domino principle to justify its actions in Hungary.

10. (a) Why did events in Guatemala in 1954 cause resentment elsewhere in Latin America? (b) Why did events in Cuba in 1959 cause resentment in the United States?

ISSUES AND IDEAS

1. (a) Why did Senator Arthur H. Vandenberg support American membership in the United Nations in 1945? (b) Would Vandenberg have supported the UN if it had been proposed in the 1930s? Why or why not?

2. (a) Explain how the strategy of containing communism worked successfully from 1947 to 1960. Give examples, including treaties and military actions. (b) Explain how the strategy of containment failed. Give examples. (c) Was the strategy mainly a success or mainly a failure? Explain.

3. General MacArthur proposed that UN forces blockade and bomb Communist China after Chinese soldiers pushed into South Korea. List three or more possible responses by China or by the Soviet Union.

4. Rank the following four regions by their importance to United States foreign policy, from most important to least important: Latin America, the Middle East, Asia, Europe. Give reasons for your choices.

SKILLS WORKSHOP

1. *Maps.* Refer to the map entitled "World Trouble Spots" on page 627. (a) Which of the trouble spots shown border the Soviet Union? (b) Which of the trouble spots shown are members of the Warsaw Pact? (c) How does this map show both successes and failures of the strategy of containment?

2. *Timelines.* Make a timeline of major foreign-policy events from 1946 to 1960. Use four colors to distinguish events taking place in four regions: Europe, the Middle East, Asia, and Latin America.

Dennis Wheeler. *Events, The Reality of A Week, Every Week,* 1963
Collection of The Museum of Modern Art, New York.

EVENTS. THE REALITY OF A WEEK. EVERY WEEK.

A Dennis Wheeler lithograph uses letters from a *Life* magazine cover and a picture of Fidel Castro to reflect the concern of Americans with foreign affairs.

PAST AND PRESENT

1. Interview a veteran of the Korean War or someone who was an adult at the time of the war. Ask the person to recall wartime feelings and impressions.

2. Select a nation that was an international trouble spot between World War II and 1960. Prepare a brief history of the nation in later years. Stress the nation's role, if any, in later conflicts between the Soviet Union and the United States.

CHAPTER 26

DOMESTIC CONCERNS

1945–1960

FROM WAR TO PEACE
QUESTIONS OF LOYALTY
REPUBLICAN LEADERSHIP
YEARS OF ABUNDANCE
CIVIL RIGHTS

On V-J Day, August 15, 1945, writer Edna Ferber walked through New York City and watched Americans celebrate the end of World War II:

"With the old reporter's instinct I walked down Park Avenue from the Seventies, cut over to Fifth, and emerged at 59th Street and the Plaza, opalescent and lovely in the early evening sunset over Central Park. The handsome square was almost peaceful. No din. . . .

"Out to a now crowded Fifth Avenue and cutting across town again and over to Broadway and 45th Street. Here, at last, was New York on the loose.

"They were marching in the middle of that storied thoroughfare, Broadway. This was no organized parade. They were strangers suddenly united by emotion. They simply marched in clumps, men and women, boys and girls, parents with their children. . . .

"As I stood at the curb on Broadway, . . . a young and handsome man in United States Army uniform made his erratic way, slowly and alone, in the street just at the curb's edge. He looked in our faces as we stood massed there, and we stared at him. His arms and hands were outstretched in a gesture of utter wonder and unbelief. . . . He repeated in a quiet and awestruck voice: 'I'm alive. I'm alive! The war's over—and I'm alive!'"

Millions of Americans shared the feeling of the soldier that Edna Ferber saw on Broadway. Eagerly, they turned away from the sufferings of war.

Members of the armed forces rushed home, to begin their lives anew. Factories and workers changed over to peacetime production. By 1950 the economy was booming. The cold war and domestic politics caused many abrupt shocks, but they were cushioned by the nation's growing prosperity.

FROM WAR TO PEACE

READ TO FIND OUT

— what caused postwar economic problems.

— why labor unions went on strike.

— how Congress reduced the powers of organized labor.

— how Truman won the election of 1948.

— how Truman and Congress struggled over the Fair Deal.

When Franklin D. Roosevelt died on April 12, 1945, Vice-President Harry S. Truman became president. "I felt like the moon, the stars, and all the planets had fallen on me," Truman told reporters.

Nevertheless, Truman quickly met the challenging problems of World War II. As commander in chief, he oversaw American troop movements in the final weeks of the war in Europe. He also decided to use the atomic bomb to end the war in the Pacific.

The coming of peace looked just as challenging. Peace would require a huge change in the United States. The nation's economy would have to shift from wartime to peacetime production. Although no one knew what problems this conversion would bring, many Americans feared the return of the Great Depression.

RISING PRICES

During the war the government controlled prices on many goods and on rents in areas near war industries. The government also rationed certain foods, gasoline, and other goods. The price controls and rationing slowed inflation. By V-J Day, August 15, 1945, wartime consumer prices had risen 31 percent. That was exactly one half of the rise in prices during World War I.

After V-J Day, Americans were eager to buy all the goods that they wanted, without restrictions. Except for sugar rationing, which continued until June 1947, the government stopped its rationing programs by the end of 1945. Yet there were still shortages of many goods, and the prices of scarce items seemed likely to skyrocket.

Truman asked Congress to extend price controls to prevent a surge of postwar inflation. Farmers and business leaders, however, asked Congress to end government controls. Congress compromised. In the spring of 1946 it approved a weak program of controlled prices.

Truman judged that the program was not strong enough, and he vetoed the bill. In one month in 1946, from June 15 to July 15, food prices jumped almost 15 percent. Meat became especially costly. One newspaper printed the headlines: "Prices Soar, Buyers Sore, Steers Jump Over the Moon."

Congress promptly passed another compromise bill. This time Truman signed it. Ranchers reacted by refusing to send more cattle to market until the government allowed higher prices. The result was a shortage of meat in the late summer of 1946.

Consumers faced other shortages in 1946. Housing, furniture, new cars, and clothing all were in short supply. Late that year the government lifted all price controls except for those on sugar, rice, and rents.

As industries increased their peacetime production, consumer goods gradually became plentiful. Inflation eased, and by 1948 prices were no longer rising sharply each year.

RISING WAGES

Prices soared after the war not only because goods were scarce. People also had money to spend. They could afford to pay more for what they wanted.

The money came partly from wartime savings. People who worked in defense plants or who served in the armed forces often earned more than they spent during the war. They saved the difference for postwar use.

Veterans also gained money from the Servicemen's Readjustment Act, commonly called the GI Bill of Rights. Passed by Congress in 1944, the act provided unemployment benefits to veterans unable to find work. It also offered low-interest loans to veterans who were starting businesses or buying homes or farms. The act offered money for schooling, too. More than 2 million veterans attended college at government expense after the war.

Americans also had money because of higher wages. While prices rose one third from 1945 to 1948, wages kept pace. Yearly income for a typical family was $2,400 in 1945. That figure soon reached $3,200. Thus, people maintained their purchasing power despite higher prices.

Many wage increases were given in response to the demands of labor unions. Both the AFL and the CIO expanded in the late 1930s and during the war years. By 1945 some 9 million workers belonged to AFL unions. Another 5 million belonged to unions under the CIO. Ten years later the CIO would join the AFL. The combined AFL-CIO would represent almost 17 million workers.

The New Deal, especially the Wagner Act of 1935, had helped to strengthen unions. In a message to Congress in September 1945, Truman proposed to extend New Deal policies. Truman called his proposals the Fair Deal. He asked Congress to raise the minimum hourly wage and to take other steps to benefit working people.

Congress blocked most of Truman's proposals. However, in February it did pass the Employment Act of 1946. This act set up the Council of Economic Advisers to recommend policies that would promote maximum production and employment.

Veterans, too, were caught up in postwar labor turmoil. This group, organized by the CIO Veterans Committee, protested a pay slash resulting from new job training legislation.

LABOR ON STRIKE

Unions wanted more than maximum employment. Workers were demanding wage increases that would help them to keep up with rising prices. In November 1945 auto workers went on a 113-day strike against General Motors. The strike finally was settled with a large pay raise for the workers. Striking steelworkers won a similar increase.

In April 1946 John L. Lewis led 400,000 United Mine Workers out of the coal mines and onto picket lines. The nation's supply of soft coal—its major fuel—began to dwindle. If the supply ran out, the nation's steel mills and railroads would be paralyzed. After 40 days of futile negotiations, Truman declared a national emergency. He ordered troops to seize the mines, ending the strike.

Meanwhile railroad workers threatened to strike. Such a walkout would bring the nation's transportation system to a halt. To prevent the strike, Truman placed the railroads under government control. However, in May 1946 engineers and other railroad workers refused to work. Americans hurried to buy food and fuel while supplies lasted.

On May 25 Truman asked Congress for authority "to draft into the armed forces of the United States all workers who are on strike against their government." Truman intended to order the strikers back to work once they were subject to military command. While he was speaking to Congress, the strikers agreed to return to work.

Truman's actions in the coal and rail strikes cost him widespread support. Union workers were shocked by his strikebreaking tactics. People outside the labor movement blamed the President for letting unions win higher wages by striking. At the same time, consumers blamed Truman for high prices.

In the congressional elections of 1946 the Republican campaign slogan was "Had enough?" In the election the Republicans won majorities in both the Senate and the House of Representatives. When the Eightieth Congress met in January 1947, Truman faced strong political opposition.

John L. Lewis was president of the United Mine Workers from 1920 to 1960. A final triumph in his career was the adoption of the UMW's retirement and health programs.

Residents of industrial areas such as Pittsburgh remained sympathetic toward labor in the 1940s. Attempts to limit union activities were most successful in nonindustrial states.

THE TAFT-HARTLEY ACT

Senator Robert A. Taft of Ohio, son of President William Howard Taft, became a leading figure in the Senate during the Eightieth Congress. Taft believed that Congress was "faced with the job of undoing, step by step, the more serious abuses of the New Deal." In particular, Taft wanted to amend the Wagner Act, which guaranteed workers' rights to organize and to bargain collectively.

On the first day of the Eightieth Congress, Republicans introduced 17 bills aimed at reducing the powers of organized labor. Out of these came the Labor-Management Relations Act of 1947, commonly called the Taft-Hartley Act. It was sponsored by Senator Taft and Representative Fred A. Hartley of New Jersey.

The Taft-Hartley Act set up a 60-day "cooling-off" period before labor or management could end a union contract. During this period federal mediators could try to negotiate a new contract. If a proposed strike threatened the national welfare, the government could delay the strike for an 80-day cooling-off period.

The Taft-Hartley Act also restricted unions. The act outlawed union contributions to national political campaigns. It ended the **closed shop**, a business in which employment was closed to any worker who was not already a union member. The act also al-

ENFORCING EQUAL OPPORTUNITY
THE FAIR EMPLOYMENT PRACTICES COMMITTEE

"In American democracy there is no room or place for racial discrimination," said Frank Paz, a Hispanic leader from Chicago. "Our people do not want any special privileges," he went on. "All they want is the right to enjoy full citizenship."

Frank Paz was speaking in 1945 before a Senate committee that was considering a bill to set up a permanent Fair Employment Practices Committee (FEPC). An FEPC would have the power to investigate discrimination and to enforce equal opportunity in jobs.

Like many people who spoke before the committee, Paz gave examples of discrimination in hiring. "Today in Chicago," he told the senators, "there are signs all over the city asking for workers to work on the streetcars. A boy—and I say boy because he is only 22 or so—by the name of Vilar, decorated with the Purple Heart, discharged, honorably discharged from the United States Army after 3 years and 3 months service in the Pacific . . . applied for a position with this streetcar company." He was refused the job, Paz said, simply because he was a Mexican American.

Others echoed Paz's words. A. Philip Randolph, president of the Brotherhood of Sleeping Car Porters, told of discrimination against blacks in railway jobs. Rabbi Jacob X. Cohen described how Jewish job seekers were refused work because of their religion. Labor leader Donald Henderson said that in Pacific Coast canneries, Filipinos and Mexican Americans were paid far less than other workers doing the same job.

These speakers agreed that an FEPC could do much to end such unfairness. A man or woman who had been refused work on the basis of race, religion, or national background could file a complaint with the FEPC. If the complaint proved true, the FEPC would take legal action to end the discrimination. Americans had just fought a world war to preserve democracy, black leader Roy Wilkins told the committee. An FEPC, he said, would go far to prove "that the Negro, the Jew, the Catholic, the Spanish American, the new citizen, man or woman, who has served his country on the battlefronts, has not fought in vain."

During the next two decades Americans would continue to discuss how to bring about equal opportunity. Bills to create an FEPC were proposed in Congress and endorsed by both political parties. Yet many opposed the FEPC as a solution to the problem. One of the most eloquent was Senator Richard Russell of Georgia.

The FEPC "would destroy natural rights guaranteed every citizen by the Constitution," Russell told the Senate in 1950. The Constitution "is a compact between states, and it limits the powers of the federal government to those expressly conferred by that document." Nowhere, he explained, does it give the government the power to force one citizen to hire another. Yet under the FEPC, exactly that would happen. "If a man refuses to hire or promote," Russell said, "he goes to jail. If he fires an employee contrary to the edicts of this federal agency, he goes to jail."

Russell predicted that the FEPC would become a vast bureaucracy. "Think of the number of lawyers who would be required," he said. "People from all over the country would come to this agency to air their grievances, real or imaginary, . . . at the expense of the American taxpayer." Business people would face "new regulations, investigations, hearings, and litigation, far beyond their time, their energy, or their finances."

Ben Shahn did "The Welders" for the CIO's 1944 voter registration campaign. The poster called attention to the civil rights breakthrough in industry created by wartime demands.

Ben Shahn. *Welders*, 1943. The Museum of Modern Art, New York.

Russell also feared reverse discrimination. The FEPC "is sure to discriminate against the average garden variety American citizen, who cannot claim connection with a minority group," he said. Employers would hire minority persons, even if they were not as qualified, simply to avoid trouble with the FEPC.

The government cannot "legislate tolerance," Russell concluded. By forcing different groups to work together against their will, the FEPC would only increase tension between them. Problems between people are best solved by persuasion and education, not force.

Black educator Mary McLeod Bethune did not agree. Speaking at a congressional hearing, she admitted that an FEPC would no more "do away with prejudice than will laws against murder do away with malice and hate. . . . But the resulting *effects* of prejudice can be outlawed," she said. "Laws against murder prohibit the taking of life. An FEPC would prohibit the taking away of one's livelihood because of race, creed, color, national origin or ancestry."

For twenty years after World War II, equal opportunity in employment was debated in Congress without concrete results. An FEPC was never established. However, the same effect was finally achieved in 1964. Congress passed a sweeping Civil Rights Act, which outlawed all job discrimination. The Equal Opportunity Commission, with powers much like the proposed FEPC's, was created to enforce the act through the courts. Today in the United States job discrimination is clearly against the law.

1. What reasons did supporters give for creating an FEPC? What did they hope that it would accomplish?

2. Why did opponents feel that the FEPC violated the Constitution? What other arguments did they give against it?

3. The Equal Opportunity Commission was created to stop discrimination in jobs. Do you think that such an agency is necessary today? Why or why not?

lowed states to restrict the **union shop**, a business in which all workers were required to become union members after a certain time on the job.

Truman charged that the Taft-Hartley Act would "discriminate against workers." He vetoed the bill in June 1947, but Congress overrode his veto. Truman, however, regained the support of union leaders. They called the Taft-Hartley Act a "slave labor law."

THE ELECTION OF 1948

In June 1948 the Republicans met to name their candidate for president. They chose Governor Thomas E. Dewey of New York. As a candidate for president in 1944, Dewey had made a better showing than any other Republican who had run against Roosevelt. The Republicans chose Governor Earl Warren of California as their candidate for vice-president.

After the Republican gains in the 1946 elections, the Dewey-Warren ticket seemed unbeatable. Truman's administration was linked to inflation, shortages, and strikes. One newspaper columnist suggested, "The most popular, and probably the best, service that Truman could render to his party now is to step aside."

Truman, however, had no intention of quitting. At the Democratic convention in July, Truman won his party's nomination on the first ballot. Senator Alben W. Barkley of Kentucky became the vice-presidential candidate.

However, the convention caused a split in Democratic ranks. Mayor Hubert H. Humphrey of Minneapolis, Minnesota, wanted the party to support the rights of blacks. He fought for a clear civil-rights stand in the party platform. When the delegates narrowly approved this stand, some southerners walked out. They and others formed the States' Rights Democratic, or Dixiecrat, party. In August they named Governor J. Strom Thurmond of South Carolina as their candidate for president.

A few days after the Dixiecrat convention, another party chose its presidential candidate. The new Progressive party nominated Henry A. Wallace, who had been vice-president during Roosevelt's third term. Wallace broke with Truman over American policy toward the Soviet Union after 1945. He wanted a policy that stressed cooperation with that nation. Wallace seemed likely to take liberal votes away from Truman, just as Thurmond seemed likely to take away conservative votes.

Truman campaigned against the Eightieth Congress. Although the Congress had supported the Truman Doctrine and the Marshall Plan, Truman called it the "do-nothing" Congress. He told farmers that Congress's lack of action was the reason for lower grain prices in 1948. He reminded union workers of the Taft-Hartley Act.

Truman traveled 22,000 miles (35,000 kilometers) by train in the fall of 1948. He averaged 10 speeches a day in his campaign. When he attacked the Republicans, the crowds yelled, "Pour it on 'em, Harry!" Yet his campaign did not impress the pollsters—people who study public opinion. Their surveys showed that "Mr Dewey is just as good as elected."

Hundreds of experts were amazed by the election results. Truman won, receiving a little more than 49 percent of the votes to Dewey's 45 percent. Other votes went mainly to Thurmond and Wallace. Truman received 303 electoral votes while Dewey received 189 and Thurmond received 39. Moreover, the Democrats recaptured both houses of Congress.

THE FAIR DEAL

When Truman was inaugurated in January 1949, he renewed his call for the Fair Deal. Since 1945, Congress had blocked most of the Fair Deal measures that Truman had proposed. His plans for civil rights were a primary example.

In 1946 Truman asked Congress to set up a permanent Fair Employment Practices Committee (FEPC). It would seek to end discrimination in the federal government's hiring of employees. The new commission was meant to replace the special FEPC established during the war. Truman's request was defeated in the Senate. Later that year Truman created the President's Committee on Civil Rights. He asked the committee to determine how law enforcement could be "strengthened and improved to safeguard the civil rights of the people."

In 1947 the committee published its report entitled *To Secure These Rights*. The report recommended laws to end discrimination. Early in 1948 Truman sent a special civil-rights message to Congress, calling for new laws, including a new FEPC.

Congress did not pass any laws based on Truman's proposals. When Congress revived registra-

tion for the draft in June 1948, it did not ban segregation in military units. In July Truman issued Executive Order 9981 to end segregation and other forms of discrimination in the armed forces. The order first affected units in combat during the Korean War, beginning in 1950.

Some of Truman's Fair Deal program became law between 1949 and 1952. The Eighty-first Congress raised the minimum hourly wage from 40 cents to 75 cents. It increased social security benefits and extended them to cover an additional 9.2 million people. Congress also approved federal funding for the construction of housing for low-income families. In addition it passed programs to conserve soil, to control flooding, and to bring electricity to rural areas.

Most of Truman's Fair Deal bills, however, were defeated by Republicans and southern Democrats. Truman's plan for government-financed health insurance was rejected as socialism. His proposal for federal aid to education was turned down because of arguments about extending such aid to parochial, or church-supported, schools. His repeated request for an FEPC was refused.

While Truman was struggling with Congress, the states were approving the Twenty-second Amendment. It was proposed by Congress in 1947 and finally ratified in 1951. The amendment limited each future president to a maximum of two terms in office.

SECTION REVIEW

1. Identify the following: GI Bill of Rights, Robert A. Taft, Thomas E. Dewey, Dixiecrat party, Henry A. Wallace, Executive Order 9981, Twenty-second Amendment.

2. Define the following: closed shop, union shop.

3. (a) Give two reasons why prices rose sharply after the war. (b) How did the actions of labor unions affect postwar wages?

4. How did Truman respond to strikes by mine workers and railroad workers?

5. (a) List five provisions of the Taft-Hartley Act. (b) Why did Truman veto this bill?

6. (a) Why did Truman create the President's Committee on Civil Rights? (b) List six Fair Deal bills passed by the Eighty-first Congress between 1949 and 1952.

QUESTIONS OF LOYALTY

READ TO FIND OUT

— why Americans searched for disloyal citizens in the postwar years.

— what security measures were adopted.

— how McCarthyism grew.

During the postwar years, the conflict between the United States and the Soviet Union dominated the nation. Sometimes the clash flared into a hot war, as in Korea. Most of the time, however, the American-Soviet conflict took the shape of a cold war, fought with economic and political weapons rather than troops and bombs.

The cold war was a frustrating struggle, without clear victories and peace treaties. In this war Americans concentrated on more than Communist enemies in Europe or Asia. They also focused on Americans at home who they thought sympathized with communism or who had been members of the Communist party. These Americans were suspected of being traitors, agents for the Soviet Union.

FEAR OF SPIES

Suspicions about traitors were stirred by news from Canada. In June 1946 the Canadian government revealed that it had uncovered a Russian spy ring. The spies included more than twenty Canadian citizens who had occupied "positions of trust." According to Canadian sources, the Russians were running spy rings in other nations, too. Americans began wondering how many secret agents were operating in the United States. Newspapers demanded investigations into the loyalty of government employees.

Truman did not believe that the government could be overturned from within by Communists. However, he created a loyalty review program in March 1947. The program required a check of the loyalty of every employee and every job applicant in the executive branch.

Between 1947 and 1951, the government investigated 3 million of its own employees. More than 2,000 resigned because of the investigations. Another 212 were fired when the Loyalty Review Board determined that "reasonable grounds exist for the belief that the person involved is disloyal to the Government of the United States."

In the summer of 1947 Congress took a further step to tighten security by passing the National Security Act. The act set up the National Security Council and under it the Central Intelligence Agency (CIA). The CIA was given authority to gather information about foreign threats to the United States.

THE HOUSE COMMITTEE ON UN-AMERICAN ACTIVITIES

A congressional committee also went into action. The House Committee on Un-American Activities (HUAC) had been established in 1938 to investigate activities by Nazis, Fascists, and Communists. Now, committee member Karl E. Mundt of South Dakota said, it would focus on "Communists and all who promote the Communist line."

During hearings in 1947 the committee looked for Communists in the film industry in Hollywood. Some performers and screen writers refused to testify. After the hearings, ten such people were blacklisted, or denied work, by the film industry because they had refused to answer questions before the HUAC.

In 1948 the committee made headlines in the case of a former State Department official, Alger Hiss. Hiss had worked for the government from 1935 to 1947 and had been an adviser at the Yalta Conference. According to Whittaker Chambers, a former Communist, Hiss had also been a member of the Communist party in the 1930s.

Hiss denied the charge and sued Chambers for libel. Chambers then made a new charge. Hiss, he claimed, had given copies of Department of State documents to him to be turned over to Russian agents. Chambers led committee investigators to copies of the documents on microfilm, which he kept at his farm in Maryland. For safekeeping, Chambers had recently hidden the microfilm in a hollowed-out pumpkin.

The "pumpkin papers" were widely publicized in the fall of 1948. Because of the statute of

Mr. and Mrs. Alger Hiss are shown leaving a federal court in July 1949 when Hiss's first trial for perjury ended inconclusively. The confusion, fear, and distrust of the cold war years seem to be reflected in the faces of the crowd.

limitations,* Hiss could no longer be charged with spying. However, he was charged with perjury, or telling a lie under oath, for denying that he had given government secrets to Chambers. The jury in Hiss's first trial did not agree on a verdict. In the second trial, ending in January 1950, the jury found Hiss guilty.

The verdict undercut Truman's earlier claim that the government was not threatened by Communists. Republican Congressman Richard M. Nixon, a committee member of the HUAC, charged that the Democrats were more interested in hiding "embarrassing facts than in finding out who stole the documents." The verdict also damaged the reputation of Secretary of State Dean Acheson, who had known Hiss for a long time.

ATOMIC SECRETS

Confidence in America's security already was at a low point. In August 1949 China had fallen to the Communists. In September 1949 Truman announced that the Russians had tested an atomic bomb. America's monopoly on the weapon, expected to last for years, had vanished.

Americans wondered how the Soviet Union had managed to build the weapon so quickly. One

answer came from Britain early in 1950. Klaus Fuchs, a German-born physicist, was convicted by the British of giving atomic secrets to the Russians.

In the United States the Fuchs trial led to the arrest of Ethel and Julius Rosenberg for passing atomic secrets to Soviet agents during World War II. The Rosenbergs were convicted and sentenced to death. In June 1953, after two years of appeals, they were executed.

In 1950 Congress passed a law to reduce the chances of future spying. The Internal Security Act blocked Communists from working in American defense industries. The act also called for registration of members of the Communist party and for their confinement during national emergencies. The new law, sponsored by Senator Patrick McCarran of Nevada, was called the McCarran Act.

In 1952 McCarran helped to sponsor a new immigration law, the McCarran-Walter Act. It included regulations to keep foreign "subversives"* out of the United States. Truman vetoed both McCarran-sponsored measures as too vague and sweeping, but Congress overrode his vetoes.

Many Americans believed that the laws were needed to prevent the Soviet Union from stealing United States military secrets. Other Americans worried that the laws had been passed too late.

---

* statute of limitations: a statute, or law, limiting the length of time during which a person can be charged with a specific crime.

* subversive: a person who seeks to overthrow or undermine a government.

These Americans feared that Communists already held power in the federal government. Their fears were heightened by Senator Joseph R. McCarthy of Wisconsin.

THE RISE OF McCARTHYISM

On February 9, 1950, Senator McCarthy gave a speech in West Virginia. Two radio broadcasters recalled the senator's words: "I have here in my hand a list of 205—a list of names that were known to the secretary of state as being members of the Communist party and who nevertheless are still working and shaping the policy in the State Department."

The next day McCarthy gave a similar speech in Utah. This time he said that there were "57 card-carrying members of the Communist party" in the State Department. McCarthy gave substantially the same speech in Nevada on the day after. Newspapers around the nation began to pay attention to the story. It was the start of sweeping anti-Communist accusations known as McCarthyism.

In 1950, when the trials of Alger Hiss and Klaus Fuchs were making headlines, McCarthy's speeches made sense to concerned Americans. His charges seemed to explain the growth of Communist power. If the Department of State was "thoroughly infested with Communists," as McCarthy stressed in his speeches, then traitors in the United States were to blame for Communist successes.

McCarthy's speeches led to congressional action. A Senate committee led by Millard E. Tydings of Maryland investigated McCarthy's charges against the Department of State. The committee reviewed each individual charged by McCarthy and found no evidence of disloyalty.

In June 1950 Senator Margaret Chase Smith of Maine spoke out against McCarthyism. "The American people," she declared, "are sick and tired of being afraid to speak their minds lest they be politically smeared as Communists or Fascists by their opponents. Freedom of speech is not what it used to be in America." Smith and six other Republican senators signed a Declaration of Conscience against such accusations.

Smith's speech did not stop McCarthy. He questioned the loyalty of Secretary of State Dean Acheson and General George C. Marshall. Even President Truman was not safe from McCarthy's attacks.

By 1951 McCarthy had a large following. If one of his accusations was disproved, he promptly made others, often without evidence. Few public officials were willing to oppose him openly.

SECTION REVIEW

1. Identify the following: Alger Hiss, Whittaker Chambers, "pumpkin papers," Ethel and Julius Rosenberg, McCarran-Walter Act, Margaret Chase Smith.

2. Define the following: blacklist, statute of limitations, perjury.

3. (a) Why were Americans concerned about spies? (b) What did the loyalty review program require? (c) How did Congress tighten security in 1947?

4. On whom did the House Committee on Un-American Activities focus in the 1930s? In the late 1940s?

5. (a) What events in China, Russia, and Britain added to Americans' worry about communism? (b) Name two provisions of the McCarran Act.

6. (a) What charges did McCarthy make against the Department of State? (b) What was the result of the Senate investigation of the Department of State?

After four terms in the House of Representatives, Margaret Chase Smith served in the Senate from 1949 to 1973. She also campaigned for a presidential nomination in 1964.

REPUBLICAN LEADERSHIP

READ TO FIND OUT

—what Eisenhower outlined as the goals of "modern Republicanism."

—how McCarthyism declined.

—why Americans reelected Eisenhower.

Eisenhower was his own ambassador of peace. On a 19-day trip in December 1959, he traveled 22,000 miles, visiting 11 nations. Here he is shown with King Paul I of Greece.

Truman had won an astounding victory at the polls in 1948. There seemed little chance, however, that he could repeat the triumph. The Republicans, aided by claims that their opponents were "soft on communism," made wide gains in the 1950 elections. Meanwhile the war in Korea was at a bitter stalemate.

Truman could have run again. The two-term limit of the Twenty-second Amendment applied only to presidents after him. But in March 1952 Truman announced that he would not be a candidate. For the first time since 1932, the Democratic nomination was open to someone who was not already president.

THE ELECTION OF 1952

In 1952 Truman promoted his own choice for the nomination, Governor Adlai E. Stevenson of Illinois. After three ballots the Democratic convention chose him as their candidate for president. The Democrats nominated Senator John J. Sparkman of Alabama for the vice-presidency.

The Republicans met in 1952 to choose between Senator Robert A. Taft and General Dwight D. Eisenhower. Taft was the favorite of conservative Republicans. Eisenhower, a national hero in World War II, had the support of Republicans who wanted a candidate with wide appeal. Until 1952 Eisenhower had not even identified himself as a Republican. Yet he won the party's nomination on the first ballot. Senator Richard M. Nixon of California became the vice-presidential candidate.

Eisenhower promised that, if elected, he would go to Korea to try to end the war. That promise

helped him to win a landslide victory. He received almost 34 million popular votes, compared to Stevenson's 27 million. Eisenhower gained 442 electoral votes to Stevenson's 89. The Republican party won narrow majorities in both the Senate and the House of Representatives.

EISENHOWER AS PRESIDENT

Eisenhower kept his campaign promise. He traveled to Korea in December, between his election and inauguration. A breakthrough in negotiations occurred later, in the spring of 1953. When an armistice was signed in July, it increased Eisenhower's popularity as a seeker of peace.

Eisenhower's emphasis on peace was respected in part because of his army record. Americans trusted him to understand military threats and alliances. A native of Texas who grew up in Abilene, Kansas, Eisenhower entered West Point in 1911. From then until 1948, when he became president of Columbia University, his career was devoted to military service.

In the White House Eisenhower followed some practices of his military days. He relied heavily on his staff, just as an army commander relies on subordinates. Eisenhower counted on the expert judgment of his cabinet members to help him develop his domestic policies. He also expected others to solve routine problems, leaving him free to consider key issues.

MODERN REPUBLICANISM

Eisenhower's goals, which he called "modern Republicanism," were generally conservative. One aim was to create a balance between the executive and legislative branches of government. The Democrats, Eisenhower believed, had shifted too much power to the president. He intended to restore a proper balance by letting the members of Congress "vote their own consciences." He did not attempt to dominate senators and representatives as Franklin D. Roosevelt had.

Another goal of modern Republicanism was to change the balance between the states and the federal government. Eisenhower believed that the Democrats had shifted too much power to Washington, D.C. He promised to run the federal government by "trying to make it smaller rather than bigger and finding things it can stop doing instead of seeking new things for it to do."

At his urging Congress passed the Submerged Lands Act in May 1953. The act transferred rights to offshore lands, which included valuable oil reserves, to the coastal states.

Another goal of modern Republicanism was to balance the federal budget. Eisenhower and Secretary of the Treasury George Humphrey hoped to do away with deficits, or shortages, in the budget.

The largest item in the federal budget was military spending. Because of the war in Korea, such spending soared, causing a rise in the federal deficit. When the war ended, the Eisenhower administration began to reduce the dollars spent for military purposes. That reduction helped to produce a budget surplus in 1956.

Despite his stress on balanced budgets, Eisenhower did not try to cut costly social programs begun during the New Deal. Instead, he called for a blending of past reforms with new restraints. In April 1953 Eisenhower approved plans for placing social programs in one agency, the Department of Health, Education and Welfare (HEW). Eisenhower named Oveta Culp Hobby, wartime director of the Women's Auxiliary Army Corps, as the first secretary of HEW.

One New Deal program, social security, was expanded in 1954. Amendments to the Social Security Act increased benefit payments and extended coverage to an additional 7.5 million workers, including many farmers.

That year Eisenhower also approved a vast Canadian-American project along the St. Lawrence River. Power plants would be built to provide electricity. Canals would be built to allow oceangoing ships to travel along the river between the Atlantic Ocean and the Great Lakes. The St. Lawrence Seaway was completed in 1959.

Although many goals of modern Republicanism were conservative, most of Eisenhower's practices were moderate. He tried to steer a course "down the middle" to achieve national unity.

THE DECLINE OF McCARTHYISM

Eisenhower tried to deal moderately with Senator Josesph R. McCarthy. When the Republicans took charge of Congress, McCarthy became head of the Senate Permanent Investigating Subcommittee. In this post, McCarthy began hearings on communism in government. His subcommittee investigated the Voice of America, a government agency, and American libraries overseas. No Communists were found, but the hearings damaged reputations and caused the firing of several government workers.

In December 1953 McCarthy began investigating the United States Army. His aide G. David Schine had been drafted into the army that fall. McCarthy claimed that Schine was being treated as a "hostage" to prevent a complete investigation. The army countered that McCarthy had tried to get special treatment for Schine. These charges were

Joseph McCarthy (right) lost his following completely after the public heard the charges of Army counsel Joseph N. Welch (left) in the Army-McCarthy hearings.

aired in special Senate hearings televised to the nation in the spring of 1954.

The Army-McCarthy hearings lasted for 35 days. At times more than 20 million Americans watched as McCarthy rudely interrupted proceedings and made unsupported accusations. By the end of the hearings, McCarthy was discredited.

In December 1954 the full Senate voted to "condemn" McCarthy for conduct that "tended to bring the Senate into dishonor and disrepute." Meanwhile the Democrats won enough seats in the House of Representatives and the Senate to give them control of the next Congress. That ended McCarthy's chance of retaining control of his Senate subcommittee.

McCarthy lost most of his power in Washington, D.C., and soon dropped out of the headlines. He did not attend the Republican convention in 1956, and he died the following year.

A highpoint of the 1950s was Jonas E. Salk's discovery of a vaccine to prevent polio.

ELECTION ISSUES

Democrats who ran for election in 1954 could condemn McCarthyism and expect widespread public support. Democratic candidates also gained support from a controversy involving the Tennessee Valley Authority.

In October 1954 a group of private electric companies, headed by Edgar H. Dixon and Eugene Yates, won a government contract to build a power plant near Memphis, Tennessee. That was on the edge of the area served by the Tennessee Valley Authority. The contract, which Eisenhower favored, prevented the TVA from building its own plant near Memphis. Eisenhower wished to end the TVA's growth. To him the TVA was "creeping socialism." The Democrats, however, argued that the Dixon-Yates contract provided public resources for private profit.

Democratic candidates also blamed the Republicans for economic problems. Eisenhower's budget trimming, including cuts in military spending after the Korean War, triggered a recession in 1953 and 1954. Unemployment rose from less than 3 percent to more than 5 percent of the labor force. The issues of recession, the Dixon-Yates contract, and McCarthyism helped the Democrats regain control of Congress in the 1954 elections.

Despite Republican losses, Eisenhower remained popular. His warm grin and winning manner appealed to most voters. Their admiration outlasted the recession, which ended by late 1954. Their admiration survived the Dixon-Yates controversy, too. After months of arguing by officials in Washington, the city of Memphis decided to build its own power plant. In July 1955 Eisenhower canceled the Dixon-Yates contract.

THE ELECTION OF 1956

The most serious threat to Eisenhower's political career struck suddenly in September 1955. He suffered a heart attack while vacationing in Denver. After a week he began to resume official duties, but he refused to say whether he would run again.

In February 1956 Eisenhower's doctors announced that he was physically fit to campaign. At the end of the month Eisenhower told the nation that he would be a candidate. In August he and Nixon easily won renomination at the Republican convention.

Adlai Stevenson also was renominated for president by the Democrats. Senator Estes Kefauver of Tennessee became the candidate for vice-president after a close contest with John F. Kennedy, a young senator from Massachusetts.

The campaign between Stevenson and Eisenhower centered on military matters. Stevenson wished to end both the draft and further testing of the hydrogen bomb. Eisenhower stressed his administration's record of peace.

In the week before the election two international conflicts dominated the news. Soviet tanks crushed an uprising in Hungary. Also, Britain and France landed troops in Egypt to regain control of the Suez Canal. On election day voters chose the candidate whose military knowledge they trusted.

Eisenhower swept to victory. He won more than 35 million popular votes to Stevenson's 26 million, and 457 electoral votes to Stevenson's 73. Yet the Democrats made gains in the congressional elections, and they kept control of the House of Representatives and of the Senate.

In 1958 the Democrats again made gains in the House and the Senate. They were aided by a recession that began in 1957 and hit its worst point in May 1958. Most voters remembered the Great Depression, and any slip in the economy seemed frightening. Democratic candidates were quick to blame the recession on the Republicans.

The voters forced Eisenhower to work with a Democratic Congress for six of his eight years in the White House. However, the government was not deadlocked. Eisenhower seldom pushed Congress to pass controversial laws. He preferred to let trends and events develop on their own. One great trend was economic growth. Despite recessions, the United States prospered under Eisenhower.

SECTION REVIEW

1. Identify the following: Adlai E. Stevenson, Submerged Lands Act, Oveta Culp Hobby, St. Lawrence Seaway, Dixon-Yates contract.

2. List three goals of Eisenhower's "modern Republicanism."

3. How did Eisenhower deal with social programs begun during the New Deal?

4. (a) How did the Army-McCarthy hearings affect McCarthy's popularity? (b) Why did the Senate condemn McCarthy?

5. (a) Why did Eisenhower oppose the TVA? (b) How was the controversy over the Dixon-Yates contract resolved?

6. (a) On what issue did the presidential campaign between Stevenson and Eisenhower center? (b) What events abroad led American voters to choose Eisenhower?

YEARS OF ABUNDANCE

READ TO FIND OUT

—**how overproduction hurt farmers.**

—**why railroad transportation declined.**

—**how factory production increased.**

—**why many Americans moved to the suburbs.**

—**why education received new emphasis.**

While Democrats and Republicans argued about the economy, experts tracked its performance. In 1953, Eisenhower's first year in office, unemployment fell below 3 percent. In 1958, a recession year, it rose above 7 percent. During most of Eisenhower's time in office, though, the rate held between 4 percent and 6 percent. That was an acceptable level to most Americans, who remembered unemployment as high as 25 percent during the Great Depression.

Inflation, too, was tolerable most of the time. Under Truman, the inflation rate soared after World War II, leveled off for a few years, and then soared again during the Korean War. Under Eisenhower inflation almost ceased for four years. Then it began to rise, exceeding 3 percent in 1958. But wages rose faster than prices. Most Americans enjoyed steadily increasing buying power while Eisenhower was president.

FARMERS' PROBLEMS

Farmers, however, did not fully share in the prosperity of the 1950s. Income from farming declined in most years. At the same time farmers had to pay more for farm equipment, repairs, and taxes. Year by year farm debt increased.

Some 20 million Americans lived on farms in 1953. That number dropped to about 15 million by 1960. The number of farms and the amount of farmland also decreased. Yet farm production rose by more than 10 percent. Farmers were making more efficient use of the land than ever before.

Electricity helped to revolutionize farming. As late as 1945 only about half of all farm homes had electricity. By 1953 electric service reached more than 9 out of 10 farms. Electricity ran home appliances and labor-saving farm equipment.

New gasoline-powered machines assisted farmers in cultivating and harvesting crops. Improved seeds and fertilizers boosted the yield per acre. One worker could produce as much wheat in 1960 as two workers could a decade before. Gains in producing corn and cotton were just as spectacular. The result was an abundance of farm products.

As in the 1920s, the abundance proved to be a trap for farmers. As they produced more, prices fell. Farmers sold more goods, but they received less money. To buy and maintain the machines that they needed, they sank deeper in debt.

At first, Eisenhower's administration offered little help to farmers. Secretary of Agriculture Ezra T. Benson tried a system of flexible government-supported prices in order to discourage farmers from growing crops of which there already was a surplus. But the system failed to reduce surpluses, and it angered farmers. "We've been plagued by one year of flood, three years of drought, and two years of Benson," said a Missourian.

In 1956 the administration tried another approach. Under the "soil-bank" plan, the government paid farmers to turn part of their crop land into pasture or forest. But surpluses continued to mount. Farmers still felt squeezed by high costs and low incomes.

CHANGES IN TRANSPORTATION

Railroads also felt squeezed within a thriving economy. For decades railroads had been the nation's primary haulers of freight. However, their share of the business declined in the 1950s. More and more tons of material were carried by trucks and by oil pipelines.

The potential of long-haul trucking was boosted by the Highway Act of 1956. It committed billions of dollars to building more than 41,000 miles (66,000 kilometers) of new highways. The act established a network of interstate routes to speed trucks and automobiles across long distances.

In 1959 the nation gained two states beyond the reach of the highway system. Alaska, admitted to the union as the forty-ninth state, was separated from the rest of the nation by western Canada. Hawaii, the fiftieth state, was separated from the American mainland by thousands of miles of ocean.

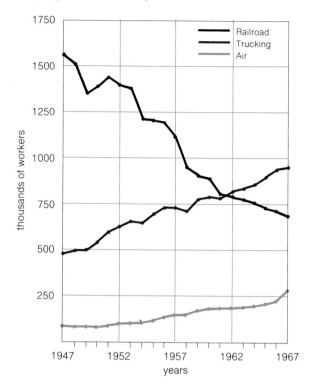

Employment in Transportation 1947–1967

People traveling to or from Alaska and Hawaii went by ship or plane.

Air travel was swifter than ever in the late 1950s. During the decade jet aircraft replaced propeller-driven planes on major air routes. Travelers who once crossed the nation in days by express train now covered the same distance in hours by jet. The railroads lost many long-distance passengers to the airlines.

The railroads also lost local passengers to cars and commuter buses. In 1958 Congress gave the railroads permission to drop hundreds of their unprofitable passenger runs. When this rail service ended, even more people turned to other forms of transportation.

INCREASING PRODUCTION

New developments in industry quickened the pace of production. The developments required about 6 percent more energy each year. This energy came increasingly from oil.

Until 1953 the United States usually produced more oil than it consumed. But the nation's demand for oil kept rising. Electric companies built power plants that burned oil. Homeowners switched from coal furnaces to oil burners. New cars, buses, trucks, and jet planes increased the demand for petroleum products. After 1953 the nation needed to import oil to continue its industrial growth.

In 1957 a new source of electricity began operating. The nation's first nuclear power plant started up at Shippingport, Pennsylvania. Similar plants would be built in the following decades, amid controversy about possible hazards.

Electricity helped to speed up business procedures. In the mid-1950s some large companies began using electronic computers to handle routine paper work. Some industrial firms installed computers to guide the production of steel, chemicals, and petroleum. Whatever their applications, computers could do an astonishing number of calculations per second. As they were improved, computers became smaller and even swifter.

On assembly lines, new electric control boards guided machines that performed each step of production automatically. People hailed the process of automatic manufacturing, or **automation,** as a second Industrial Revolution. Walter Reuther, head of the United Auto Workers, saw its effects in Detroit. In the 1920s workers took a full day to machine*

* machine: to make or finish with a machine.

Behind the quiet beauty of this photograph of a Texas oil refinery in 1949 lay the story of a rising industry.

one engine block. Now, he said, a block moved along an automated line and "fourteen and six-tenths minutes later, it is fully machined, without a human hand touching it."

Reuther and other union leaders did not fight automation as long as management protected workers' jobs and wages. With automation, some union workers shifted to new jobs within a company. Others worked shorter hours or took longer vacations. In 1955 UAW workers even won a guaranteed annual wage from Ford and General Motors. The companies agreed to pay workers during layoffs.

THE MOVE TO THE SUBURBS

New machines and methods also revolutionized the building of houses. During the Great Depression and World War II, little housing had been constructed. Now, in the postwar years, a building boom began, and suburbs sprang up across the nation.

One of the best known suburbs was built by William Levitt. He located Levittown on Long Island, within commuting distance of New York City. Like many suburban developers, Levitt used standard features and designs to lower costs. That allowed him to sell new houses at prices that young married couples could afford.

Young couples, faced with a postwar housing shortage, rushed to buy. With wartime savings or benefits under the GI Bill of Rights, many of them could afford a home of their own. Many young couples also wanted a home in the suburbs for bringing up children. In the postwar years, Americans married earlier and had larger families than in the 1930s. The result was a "baby boom." The nation's birth rate jumped in 1946 and remained high for nearly twenty years.

In massive numbers, Americans left the cities for suburban life. From 1950 to 1955, suburbs grew seven times as fast as the central cities. New housing developments sprawled across acres that had once been cropland or pasture. In their wake came shopping centers, schools, businesses, and new roads to serve suburban Americans.

Not all Americans fled the cities. Rural people, especially from the South, moved to cities in the 1950s. So did immigrants, particularly Puerto Ricans and Mexicans. Most of the newcomers, how-

Births   1930–1970

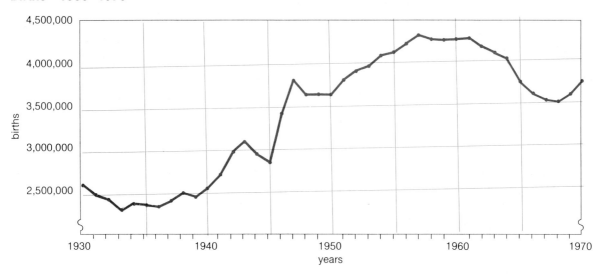

ever, were poor. They could not provide cities with the tax revenue that was lost when wealthier people and businesses went to the suburbs. In the postwar years the central cities were troubled by poverty, crime, and declining public services.

CRITICS OF THE 1950s

Suburban Americans received extended criticism in the 1950s. They were accused of living in a bland world where everyone was much the same as everyone else.

One theme of criticism was sounded by the scholar David Riesman in his book *The Lonely Crowd*, published in 1950. He argued that Americans were too anxious to gain the approval of others. Thus, they conformed to group behavior instead of using individual guidelines.

The theme of conformity was echoed by many writers. The novelist Sloan Wilson wrote *The Man in the Gray Flannel Suit*, published in 1955. It described sameness in business. The social critic William H. Whyte wrote *The Organization Man*, published in 1956. It reported the ways in which people conformed to group behavior at work and at home in the suburbs.

Other writers criticized Americans for their preoccupation with television. Developed before World War II, television initially was a toy for the wealthy. However, in the postwar years inexpensive

television sets were produced, and the popularity of television soared. By 1950 over 4 million families had a TV. Four years later, the "TV dinner" was invented. Americans, critics complained, spent more time watching television than doing any activity except sleeping.

From the air, the homes in Levittown, a suburb of New York, seem to have been planted rather than built. Standard designs cut costs for builders and buyers.

© Arnold Newman

Dutch-born Willem de Kooning, now a major American artist, emigrated to the United States in 1926. His paintings of the 1950s are full of vivid color and characteristic jagged brush strokes.

SPUTNIK AND EDUCATION

The critics of American culture had a new topic to worry about in October 1957. The Soviet Union launched *Sputnik I*, the world's first artificial satellite.* Americans were shocked. The Soviet Union had surpassed the United States in space exploration, an area that seemed likely to have military importance.

Soon the critics suggested a reason for America's lagging performance. The Soviet Union stressed scientific education, but the United States did not. Eventually, warned the critics, the United States would lose the battle of scientific knowledge to the Soviet Union unless American education became more rigorous.

In 1958 Congress passed the National Defense Education Act. The act gave $20 million to the states to improve facilities for teaching science and modern languages. The act provided $295 million for loans to college students.

* artificial satellite: a manufactured object launched by rocket into an orbit around the earth, the moon, or some other body in space.

SECTION REVIEW

1. Identify the following: "soil-bank" plan, William Levitt, "baby boom," *Sputnik I*, National Defense Education Act.

2. (a) Name three ways that farmers increased production. (b) How did overproduction affect farmers? (c) Name two ways that the Eisenhower administration tried to help farmers. How successful were these efforts?

3. Why did railroad business decline in the 1950s?

4. (a) Why did the demand for oil increase in the 1950s? (b) How did electricity affect business procedures?

5. (a) Describe automation. (b) How did union leaders respond to automation?

6. (a) How did builders keep suburban houses affordable to young families? (b) Why did problems in cities increase?

7. Name two criticisms of Americans in the 1950s.

8. What reason did some critics suggest for the failure of the United States to keep up with the Soviet Union in space exploration?

CIVIL RIGHTS

READ TO FIND OUT

— how segregation affected black Americans in the North.

— how Supreme Court rulings helped blacks.

— how blacks organized to work for civil rights.

— how Congress supported civil rights.

In 1945 Pauli Murray, a black graduate of Howard University Law School, wrote a statement of her beliefs. "As an American," she stated, "I inherit the magnificent tradition of an endless march toward freedom and toward the dignity of all." To Murray, discrimination and segregation were a disgrace to that tradition, and she vowed to fight all such practices. "I shall offer one small life," she declared, "for whatever it is worth, to fulfill the prophecy that 'all men are created equal.'"

Many black Americans faced the postwar years with similar determination. They vowed not to give up the gains that they had achieved during the war. And they began to press for the rights guaranteed to all Americans by the Constitution.

SEGREGATION

One of the first targets of black Americans was segregation. During the war thousands of blacks moved to cities outside the South to take jobs in war industries. In many of these cities the black population doubled. Yet segregation remained a fact of life. City neighborhoods where blacks settled became all black as whites moved out. Schools in the neighborhoods became mainly black. The new jobs did not lead to integration in housing or education.

After the war blacks continued to leave the South to find jobs elsewhere. The migrants saw some signs of equality. Outside the South blacks were not barred by law from sitting next to whites on the buses or from using certain public facilities. But the migrants experienced **de facto segregation**—segregation that existed not by laws but by the habits and actions of white people.

Some forms of segregation were ended in the postwar years. In 1947 Jackie Robinson became the first black baseball player in modern times to play in the major leagues. In 1948 Truman banned segregation in the armed forces. In 1949 Congress passed a bill to end discrimination in federal civil service jobs. More far-reaching changes began in May 1954, when the Supreme Court ruled that segregation was no longer legal in public schools.

THE SUPREME COURT AND THE SCHOOLS

The issue of segregation in public facilities had reached the Supreme Court in 1896 in the case of *Plessy* v. *Ferguson*. The Court ruled then that segregation was legal if each group had access to equal facilities. This "separate but equal" doctrine applied to public transportation, public hospitals, and public schools.

In court cases from the 1930s on, the National Association for the Advancement of Colored People (NAACP) tried to prove that public schools for blacks were separate but not equal. Black schools lacked the funds, the equipment, and the trained staffs to match white schools. As a result of the cases, southern states spent more money on all-black schools.

In the early 1950s the NAACP lawyers challenged, in a series of cases, the "separate but equal" doctrine itself. The lawyers argued that separate schools could never be equal, no matter how much money was spent. Segregation in itself, they argued, harmed black students' ability to learn.

One case, *Brown* v. *Board of Education of Topeka*, became the focus of the argument. Oliver Brown and his family had moved into a white neighborhood in Topeka, Kansas. They assumed that their daughter Linda would attend the neighborhood school. Instead, the school board ordered her to attend a distant all-black school. With the help of the NAACP, Brown sued the school board to permit his daughter to attend the local school.

On May 17, 1954, the Supreme Court ruled unanimously in favor of Brown. "In the field of public education," the Court declared, "the doctrine of 'separate but equal' has no place. Separate educational facilities are inherently unequal." Thus, segregated public schools were illegal because of the Fourteenth Amendment, which guarantees all

MARY CHURCH TERRELL
A BLACK WOMAN'S STORY

In 1919 Mary Church Terrell wrote in her diary about her plan to tell the story of her life. "Be sure to be courageous and tell everything," she said. Her story, published in 1940, was the first full-length autobiography by a black woman. In it she told what it was like to be both black and female in a white world.

Terrell told of her birth in Memphis, Tennessee, in 1863, just nine months after President Lincoln's Emancipation Proclamation. She described her schooling in Ohio, where she was the only black in her class and its top student. She continued her studies at Oberlin College, then married and settled in Washington, D.C.

A natural leader, she worked to gain women's suffrage. "A woman," she declared, "had a right to help administer the affairs of the government under which she lived." In the 1890s she joined the fight for an amendment to the Constitution, granting women the right to vote.

Terrell especially worked to improve conditions for her people. In 1895 she became the first black woman to serve on the District of Columbia Board of Education and was a member for eleven years. Soon after, she became president of the new National Association of Colored Women and served three terms.

Terrell wrote and lectured on black history and life. She campaigned against disfranchisement and

Members of the Student Non-Violent Coordinating Committee (SNCC) staged this restaurant sit-in. The SNCC was founded in 1960 by students to speed desegregation in the South.

lynching. In 1952, when she was nearly ninety, she fought discrimination in the nation's capital. Carrying a picket sign in one hand and a cane in the other, she led a group in picketing Washington restaurants that discriminated against blacks.

Mary Church Terrell died in 1954. In her long life this dynamic woman had seen many positive changes for black Americans.

---

citizens the equal protection of the laws. In May 1955 the Court called for schools to act "with all deliberate speed" to comply with the ruling.

INTEGRATING SCHOOLS

The 1954 Court decision provoked years of controversy, especially in the South. School segregation there was written into state laws. Some influential voices in the South urged quick acceptance of school desegregation. But a large chorus of southern voices condemned the Supreme Court.

In September 1957 nine black students prepared to enter Central High School in Little Rock, Ar-

kansas. They would be the school's first blacks. Local offcials expected no trouble. However, Governor Orval E. Faubus of Arkansas ordered the National Guard* into Little Rock to keep the blacks out of the school.

President Eisenhower acted swiftly against the governor's defiance of federal law. He ordered federal troops into Little Rock and put the Arkansas National Guard under federal command. The nine

---

* National Guard: the reserve militia of each state of the United States. In time of emergency, the National Guard may be called upon to serve either the state or the federal government.

On September 25, 1957, by order of the President, paratroopers of the 101st Airborn Division led nine black students into Central High School in Little Rock, Arkansas. Eisenhower was taking a firm stand on civil rights.

black students entered Central High while troops stood guard. In the following weeks the number of troops was gradually reduced, and the crisis faded.

Resistance to the Supreme Court order, however, was far from over. In 1964, a decade after the Court's decision, only about 8 percent of black students in the South were attending integrated schools. In schools outside the South, de facto segregation continued with little change.

THE MONTGOMERY BUS BOYCOTT

Early in the controversy over school desegregation, another civil rights issue burst into the news. It centered on the Montgomery, Alabama, bus system.

The first rows of seats on Montgomery buses were permanently reserved for whites. If those rows filled, blacks in the next seats could be told to give their places to additional white passengers. On the evening of December 1, 1955, a middle-aged black woman was riding home on a bus in Montgomery. She was, she said later, "bone weary" from her day's work as a seamstress. When she was told to move back to make room for whites, she did not get up. She was removed from the bus, arrested, and jailed.

The arrest of the woman, Rosa Parks, set off a two-pronged struggle against segregation on the bus system. Black lawyers challenged the constitutionality of the Alabama state law requiring segregation on buses. Meanwhile, the blacks of Montgomery planned to boycott, or refuse to use, the city buses. By cutting the bus-system revenues, they hoped to force the city to end segregation on buses.

The boycott began December 5, 1955. It was led by a young minister named Martin Luther King, Jr. King believed in *civil disobedience*—nonviolent opposition to unjust laws. He urged the blacks of Montgomery to "protest courageously, and yet with dignity and Christian love." The boycott was maintained for months by thousands of working people who could not afford to be absent from their jobs. They and the boycott leaders set up a system of car pools. When necessary the workers walked for miles to avoid riding city buses.

On November 13, 1956, the Supreme Court struck down the Alabama law requiring the segregation of blacks and whites on public buses. Beginning in December, Montgomery buses were inte-

In December 1956, a year after her historic arrest, Rosa Parks calmly rode in the front of a Montgomery bus.

grated. A local paper reported "a calm but cautious acceptance of this significant change in Montgomery's way of life." The boycott had proved the effectiveness of passive resistance.

CIVIL RIGHTS ORGANIZATIONS

After their victory in Montgomery, the leaders of the bus boycott formed a new organization, the Southern Christian Leadership Conference (SCLC). The goal of the SCLC was to win equal rights for blacks and other minorities in the United States. Its strategy was to use nonviolent protests. Martin Luther King, Jr., led the organization from its founding in 1957.

Admirers in Baltimore, Maryland, shook hands with Martin Luther King, Jr., to congratulate him on winning the Nobel peace prize in 1964.

Under King's leadership, the SCLC began challenging segregation laws in the South. At the same time two older organizations continued working for civil rights. The Congress of Racial Equality (CORE) began as a nonviolent group in 1942. Its founder and leader, James Farmer, encouraged blacks to resist unfair treatment rather than accepting it. CORE members set up community centers, helped establish Freedom Schools for black children, and helped black voters to register. The NAACP, founded in 1909, sponsored programs of education and political action, but it was best known for its work in the courts.

THE CIVIL RIGHTS ACT OF 1957

While black-led civil rights organizations stepped up their efforts to gain equality, the government acted, too. Eisenhower submitted a civil rights bill to Congress to end many forms of discrimination.

For Senator Lyndon B. Johnson of Texas, the bill was urgent. "The Senate simply had to act, the Democratic party simply had to act, and I simply had to act," he said later. "The issue could wait no longer." As Democratic majority leader* in the Senate, Johnson aided in the passage of the bill.

The Civil Rights Act of 1957 was a voting rights law rather than the wide-ranging measure that Eisenhower had proposed. The act set up a Civil Rights Commission to look into possible violations of voting rights of blacks. If the commission found violations, the attorney general could issue court injunctions, or orders, to stop such actions. Although the law did less than Eisenhower wanted, it was the first civil rights law to be enacted since Reconstruction.

SECTION REVIEW

1. Identify the following: Jackie Robinson, *Plessy* v. *Ferguson*, Orval E. Faubus, Rosa Parks, Martin Luther King, Jr.

2. Define the following: de facto segregation, civil disobedience.

3. (a) Why did many blacks migrate to the North after the war? (a) Name two areas in which segregation ended in the late 1940s.

4. (a)What was the "separate but equal" doctrine? (b) How did black lawyers challenge this doctrine?

5. What did the Supreme Court rule in *Brown* v. *Board of Education of Topeka*?

6. (a) Name two steps blacks took in response to the arrest of Rosa Parks. (b) How successful was each of these efforts?

7. Name three black organizations that worked for civil rights.

8. What was the Civil Rights Act of 1957?

* majority leader: the leader of the party with a majority, or the most votes, in the Senate or the House of Representatives.

SUMMARY

The change from war to peace placed great pressures on the American economy. Consumers had money to spend, but peacetime goods were scarce. Congress would not let wartime price controls continue, and prices soared. So did wages, boosted by the demands of labor unions.

To curb the powers of unions, Republicans in Congress passed the Taft-Hartley Act in 1947. Truman campaigned against the act and against the Republican-led Congress in 1948. He and his party won a surprising victory. Still, he was not able to persuade Congress to approve most of the Fair Deal programs that he wanted.

Meanwhile, Communist gains in the world stirred fears about traitors in the United States. The fears grew when Senator Joseph R. McCarthy charged that the Department of State was "thoroughly infested with Communists."

McCarthy's influence peaked after Eisenhower won the presidency in 1952. Then McCarthy appeared in televised hearings and was discredited. Eisenhower, meanwhile, set the government on a moderate course. He wanted a balanced budget, less power for the presidency, and more power for the states.

Eisenhower's personal popularity helped the Republicans regain control of Congress in 1952. Despite his reelection in 1956, the Democrats won control in the next three elections.

The Eisenhower years were generally prosperous, although farmers did not share in the prosperity. Airlines gained more passengers. Factories produced more goods. More and more people moved to the suburbs. Suburbanites were criticized for leading lives of conformity, and educators were criticized, too. After the Soviet Union launched *Sputnik I* in 1957, educators were blamed for neglecting science in American schools.

Civil rights groups prompted changes. In 1954 the Supreme Court ruled in favor of desegregation of public schools. In 1956 black Americans led by Martin Luther King, Jr., achieved the desegregation of public buses in Montgomery, Alabama. Congress passed the Civil Rights Act of 1957 to help guarantee voting rights for blacks.

Ben Shahn. *A Good Man Is Hard To Find*, 1948. The Museum of Modern Art, New York.

A popular song, "A Good Man Is Hard to Find," provided the title for this satirical poster. The dart was aimed at Dewey and at piano-playing Truman.

CHAPTER REVIEW

1. (a) How were people able to maintain their purchasing power after World War II even though prices soared? (b) How did the mine workers' strike of 1946 threaten operations in other industries? (c) Why were Truman's actions in the miners' and railroad workers' strikes unpopular?

2. (a) Explain Truman's basic campaign strategy in 1948. (b) Why were most of Truman's Fair Deal measures blocked in Congress even after the Democrats won in 1948?

3. (a) Describe the difference between the goals of the Loyalty Review Board and the Central Intelligence Agency. (b) Explain why Alger Hiss was not charged with spying in 1948. (c) Explain how Hiss and the people accused by McCarthy differed from the people who were the targets of the Red Scare of 1919–1920.

4. (a) What was the connection between military events in 1952 and 1956 and Eisenhower's election victories in those years? (b) What was the connection between economic events in 1954 and 1958 and the Democrats' congressional victories in those years?

5. (a) Explain how Republican election victories in 1952 added to the power of Joseph R. McCarthy. (b) Explain how McCarthy's added power contributed to his downfall.

6. Explain how abundance proved to be a trap for farmers in the 1950s.

7. Transportation and industry speeded up in the 1950s. (a) Give three examples of the speedup. (b) Tell what effect, if any, each of the three examples had on the nation's demand for oil.

8. (a) Explain how the "baby boom" of the postwar years was both a cause and an effect of the building boom in those years. (b) Explain how the building boom contributed to charges that there was too much conformity in the United States.

9. The National Association for the Advancement of Colored People found it easier to challenge legal segregation in the South than de facto segregation in the North. Why?

10. A Supreme Court ruling ended the segregation of public buses in Montgomery, Alabama. What then was important about the year-long bus boycott in Montgomery?

This lithograph by R. Weaver honors the great American heavyweight boxing champion, Joe Louis. Louis held the world title longer than any other boxer.

ISSUES AND IDEAS

1. Early in 1948 Truman asked Congress to pass civil rights legislation. An opponent said that Truman's request "has inflicted an apparently fatal blow, not only to the unity of the party, but to the unity of the country." (a) How important is unity in American politics? (b) When, if ever, should a president ignore unity? (c) Was Truman wise to ask for civil rights legislation? Refer to specific events in 1948 and after.

2. Compare and contrast conditions for American farmers during the Great Depression and the 1950s.

SKILLS WORKSHOP

1. *Graphs*. Refer to the graph of farms and farm sizes on page 764. (a) About how many farms were there in the United States in 1950? In 1960? (b) About what was the acreage of an average farm in 1950? In 1960?

2. *Maps*. The *total* farmland in the nation decreased in the 1950s. Sketch two maps of an imaginary area having small farms. Show how the *average* farm might increase in area while the *total* farmland decreases. Include landmarks such as roads and streams to make the two maps easy to compare.

PAST AND PRESENT

1. Interview someone who used public transportation for business or vacation trips from your area in the 1950s. Contrast those trips with similar trips now. Find out differences in (a) speed, (b) cost, (c) comfort, (d) equipment, and (e) places to wait for the transportation.

2. The federal interstate highway system has red, white, and blue signs to mark the route. East-west highways have even numbers, and north-south highways have odd numbers. Using a modern road map, find out which interstate highways exist near your community. What route would you choose to drive to Portland, Oregon? Austin, Texas? Green Bay, Wisconsin? Washington, D.C.?

CHAPTER 27

YEARS OF FERMENT

1960–1968

FACING WORLD TENSIONS
A SPIRIT OF CHANGE
NEW PROGRAMS AND PROTESTS
AMERICAN CONCERNS ABROAD

On a summer day in 1963, more than 200,000 Americans gathered at the Lincoln Memorial in Washington, D.C. They listened to speeches about the hope of ending poverty and advancing civil rights. Among the thousands was Emily Rock, a black high school student.

"I have never seen such a crowd of people as there were that day. There was a special feeling of closeness. I have never felt so small and yet part of something so immense, wonderful, and grand.

"I had a feeling of pride for my race and for the whites who thought enough to come. And there was a sense of triumph. We had proved by being orderly, nonviolent, and determined that we were not the kind of people our enemies said we were.

"All around, in the face of everyone, there was this sense of hope for the future—the belief that this march was the *big* step in the right direction. It could be heard in the voices of the people singing and seen in the way they walked. It poured out into smiles."

The hope that Emily Rock felt that day seemed well founded. The national government was working to end segregation in public schools and to secure voting rights for blacks. Martin Luther King, Jr., one of the speakers at the gathering, was optimistic. "I have a dream," he said, "that one day this nation will rise up and live out the true meaning of its creed: 'We hold these truths to be self-evident; that all men are created equal.' . . . I have a dream that my four little children will one day live in a nation where they will not be judged by the color of their skin but by the content of their character."

For Rock and other Americans, such dreams soon were hard to keep in mind. Within months they were crowded out of public attention by the assassination of a president and by a long and bitter war in Southeast Asia.

FACING WORLD TENSIONS

READ TO FIND OUT

— what issues dominated the 1960 presidential campaign.

— why the Bay of Pigs invasion failed.

— how United States military strategy changed.

— how the Cuban missile crisis ended.

In 1960 President Eisenhower prepared to leave office. The nation was prosperous and at peace. Yet many Americans felt a sense of disquiet. A journalist expressed that mood in an article in 1959:

> For the time being our people do not have great purposes which they are united in wanting to achieve. The public mood of the country is defensive, to hold on to and to conserve, not to push forward and to create. We talk about ourselves these days as if we were a completed society, one which has achieved its purposes and has no further business to transact.

This concern with "national purpose" became an issue in the presidential election of 1960.

THE ELECTION OF 1960

By the time the Republicans met to name a candidate for president in 1960, their choice was clear. Vice-President Richard M. Nixon had won all the Republican primaries, unopposed, and had gained President Eisenhower's endorsement. Nixon won the nomination on the first ballot. To run with him, the Republicans chose Henry Cabot Lodge, Jr., a diplomat and former senator from Massachusetts.

The Democratic choice was not so clear. Four senators—John F. Kennedy of Massachusetts, Hubert H. Humphrey of Minnesota, Lyndon B. Johnson of Texas, and Stuart Symington of Missouri—battled for the nomination. However, Kennedy won the nomination on the first ballot. He chose Johnson as his running mate.

In his acceptance speech, Kennedy declared that "too many Americans have lost their way, their will, and their sense of historic purpose." He called for "a new generation of leadership." Kennedy was forty-three years old in 1960. If he won the election, he would become the youngest person—and the first Catholic—elected president of the United States.

Kennedy charged that the United States faced a "missile gap," a Soviet superiority in nuclear weapons. He vowed that if elected he would build up the nation's defenses. Nixon declared that he would "keep the peace for America and extend freedom throughout the world." On domestic issues Nixon and Kennedy also argued about how best to provide aid to education and medical care to the elderly.

In the weeks before the election, Nixon and Kennedy took part in four nationally televised debates. Though neither candidate was a clear winner, Kennedy's poise and ability to match the Vice-President in debate gave him an edge.

The election was very close. Kennedy's total in the electoral college was 303 votes, compared to Nixon's 219. In the popular vote Kennedy received 34,226,731 votes to 34,108,157 for Nixon. Kennedy's margin of 118,000 votes was the smallest in a presidential election since 1884.

THE PEACE CORPS

Although he lacked a strong mandate from the voters, Kennedy called for new beginnings in his inaugural address. He spoke of a "grand and global alliance" to combat "tyranny, poverty, disease, and war itself." He told Americans, "Ask not what your country can do for you—ask what you can do for your country."

Within two months of his inauguration, Kennedy took steps to start the Peace Corps. It provided one answer to people who asked what they could do for their country. They could promote peace by working as volunteers in other nations. Thousands of Americans, young and old, signed up.

The mission of Peace Corps volunteers was to offer their skills to developing nations and to improve international understanding. Volunteers lived in Asia, Africa, and Latin America. They shared their knowledge as teachers, carpenters, farmers, nurses, and workers of other kinds.

The idea of a youth peace army, which was first suggested in 1904, inspired thousands of Peace Corps volunteers. This young American worked as a teacher in Kenya, Africa.

THE ALLIANCE FOR PROGRESS

In March 1961 Kennedy proposed a new program for the development of Latin America. He invited the nations of the Organization of American States (OAS) to form an alliance to foster economic growth and democracy in Latin America. It would be called the Alliance for Progress.

Nineteen Latin American nations and the United States joined the alliance. The Latin American nations agreed to spend $80 billion over 10 years to improve economic and social conditions for their people. The United States pledged to contribute an additional $20 billion.

The Alliance for Progress had uneven results. It did not consistently meet its economic goals. Nor did it lead to the growth of democracy in the hemisphere. Many nations in the alliance shifted away from democracy and toward military rule in the 1960s. Cuba took no part in the alliance at all.

THE BAY OF PIGS

Soon after his election, Kennedy learned that the Central Intelligence Agency (CIA) was involved in a plan to overthrow the government of Fidel Castro in Cuba. Eisenhower had approved the plan in March 1960. Since then, the CIA had trained more than a thousand anti-Castro exiles for an invasion by sea. CIA experts believed that many Cubans would welcome the invaders and would join the fight against Castro.

Kennedy had a choice. He could disband the groups of exiles being trained in Florida and Guatemala, or he could allow the invasion to go ahead. He chose to permit the invasion, but he refused to let United States forces take part in the fighting.

On April 17, 1961, a fleet of small boats landed some 1,500 invaders at the Bahía de Cochinos, the Bay of Pigs, on Cuba's southern coast. Cuban soldiers crushed the invasion within three days and took 1,200 prisoners. There was no popular uprising like the one predicted by CIA experts.

The American role in the invasion quickly became known. Communist nations condemned the United States. So did friendly nations in Latin America and Europe. More than a year later Castro exchanged the 1,200 prisoners for food and medical supplies.

To enraged Berliners the ugly wall built in 1961 to seal off East Berlin was the Wall of Shame. It cut off families and friends and even stopped the city's subway lines. Here a woman hovered forlornly against its cold mass.

THE BERLIN WALL

The uproar over the Bay of Pigs invasion did not stop plans for a meeting between Kennedy and Khrushchev. The two leaders traveled to Vienna, Austria, early in June 1961 for talks on international matters.

Khrushchev focused the talks on the status of Berlin, deep within East Germany. The city was still divided into East Berlin, the Russian sector, and West Berlin, the American, British, and French sectors. However, Germans could travel freely between the two Berlins. As the West German economy boomed, thousands of East Germans fled to West Germany by way of West Berlin.

At Vienna, Khrushchev once again demanded that the Americans, the British, and the French withdraw their troops from West Berlin and declare it a free, or independent, city. To gain access to the city, the United States and its allies would have to deal with East Germany, which they did not recognize. Khrushchev gave them until December to agree to his terms.

The talks between Kennedy and Khrushchev ended in tense suspicion. Kennedy vowed that the United States would not abandon West Berlin. In July, to give force to his position, Kennedy called for an extra $3.5 billion in defense spending.

The next month Khrushchev ordered a barrier of barbed wire set up between East and West Berlin. Soon the wire was replaced with a concrete wall, stretching for miles. The wall was swept by searchlights at night and patrolled by armed guards.

In response to the Berlin Wall, Kennedy ordered 1,500 troops into West Berlin, to support American forces already there. Finally, in October 1961, Khrushchev softened his demand for new arrangements in Berlin by the end of the year.

The status of Berlin, however, continued to be a source of friction in the cold war. Some two years after the wall was built, Kennedy gave a speech in West Berlin. He pledged again the United States' commitment to the city. Then he told a cheering crowd, *"Ich bin ein Berliner"*—"I am a Berliner."

A POLICY OF "FLEXIBLE RESPONSE"

The Berlin crisis heightened fear of atomic warfare. Although Kennedy had talked about a "missile gap" when he campaigned for the presidency, there was no clear evidence that it existed. The Soviets had developed powerful rockets to propel intercontinental ballistic missiles (ICBMs).* The United States possessed long-range bombers and missile-carrying submarines that were armed with nuclear weapons.

Yet Kennedy disliked the United States' reliance on nuclear weapons to stop any kind of Soviet aggression. This was the policy of massive retaliation, begun in Eisenhower's administration. Kennedy wanted the United States to be flexible in its response to Soviet actions, based upon the danger of each action.

Thus, Kennedy and his advisors developed a policy of "flexible response," which stressed the use of troops and conventional weapons as well as nuclear weapons. Kennedy especially wanted American forces, skilled in jungle warfare and guerrilla fighting, to be able to counter Soviet-supported revolutions around the world.

WAR IN THE CONGO

The Berlin crisis slowly faded. It was, however, only one of several international problems. Conflict in other, more distant parts of the world also involved the United States.

One crisis took place in the Congo (now Zaire), in Central Africa. In June 1960 the Congo became independent from Belgium. Elections had been held in May, but none of the nine major political parties won a majority in parliament. The government that was formed lacked unity and broke down within a week of independence. Chaos increased when the provinces of Katanga and Kasai seceded from the new nation.

The government appealed to the United Nations for help. In response, UN troops were sent to the Congo to end the civil war. Violence, however, continued. Early in 1961 Patrice Lumumba, the leader of a party supported by the Soviet Union, was assassinated.

The Soviets blamed the UN and demanded the withdrawal of UN forces from the Congo. Kennedy quickly supported the UN operation. He also declared that the United States would oppose any attempt by the Soviet Union to intervene in the Congo.

* ballistic missile: missile aimed at or before the time of launching.

UN troops stayed in the Congo for four years. Early in 1963 a new Congolese government was formed, reuniting the country. By 1965 the government was in control of the war-torn nation.

CONFLICT IN SOUTHEAST ASIA

Another crisis arose in Southeast Asia. Since 1954 Laos had been recognized as a neutral nation between Communist North Vietnam and non-Communist Thailand. Within Laos a struggle developed among Communist, neutral, and pro-Western leaders. The struggle led to civil war, from 1960 to 1962.

President Kennedy pressed for a compromise in Laos. In July 1962 the three factions formed a coalition government. However, the government did not last, and civil war in Laos broke out again the next year.

When Kennedy took office, the United States already was sending military aid to the Southeast Asian nation of South Vietnam. That nation and North Vietnam had been formed in 1954 at the Geneva Conference. North Vietnam was given to Communists led by Ho Chi Minh. South Vietnam was given to non-Communists. The leader of South Vietnam was Ngo Dinh Diem, whose government received the support of the United States.

The Geneva Conference also scheduled elections for 1956 to unite Vietnam again. Diem, however, feared a Communist victory and refused to let the elections take place. In 1957 guerrilla fighting broke out against his regime. The guerrillas, both Communists and non-Communists, established the National Liberation Front (NLF) to overthrow Diem. Diem called the NLF troops Viet Cong, meaning "Vietnamese Communist."

The United States responded to the fighting by sending money and military supplies to Diem. The United States also sent 700 advisers to help train Diem's army, the Army of the Republic of Vietnam (ARVN).

Aided by soldiers and supplies from North Vietnam, the fighting against Diem increased in 1961. Diem asked Kennedy to send American troops to South Vietnam. In a time of growing Communist activity in Cuba, Berlin, and Laos, Kennedy did not want to let South Vietnam fall to Communists. In November 1961 he ordered a dramatic increase in United States forces there. By the end of the year the number of United States troops stationed in South Vietnam had grown to more than 3,000.

By the end of 1962 there were more than 11,000 United States troops in Vietnam. Officially they were not combat units. Instead they offered combat support—including helicopter transport—and advice and training.

The presence of American troops halted the advance of guerrilla forces in 1962. In February the President's brother Robert Kennedy traveled to Saigon (Sī-GON), the capital of South Vietnam. "We are going to win in Vietnam," he told reporters. "We will remain here until we do win."

THE CUBAN MISSILE CRISIS

Conflicts in Asia affected the balance of world power, but they did not pose a direct threat to the United States. That threat came primarily from Soviet missiles.

Russia's long-range offensive missiles were based in the Soviet Union. Late in 1962 the Soviets moved to install shorter-range offensive missiles in Cuba. Such missiles could reach targets more than 1,000 miles (1,600 kilometers) away. From Cuba, they would be able to hit Washington, D.C.

On October 15, 1962, CIA experts analyzed photographs taken by a U-2 reconaissance plane flying high over Cuba. The photographs revealed the construction of bases for Soviet missiles. Kennedy quickly held secret meetings with his leading advisers. They finally decided that the United States must keep the Soviets from shipping additional offensive missiles to Cuba.

On October 22 Kennedy announced that the United States would set up a naval blockade to intercept "all offensive military equipment under shipment to Cuba." Kennedy demanded the removal of the Cuban missile bases, and he directed United States armed forces to be ready for action.

On October 24 a force of 19 United States warships formed a line in the Atlantic, 500 miles (800 kilometers) from Cuba. They prepared to block a fleet of Russian ships bound for Cuba. Supporting the United States ships were aircraft carriers plus troop ships ready for an invasion of Cuba. The leading Russian ships approached the blockade and stopped. The Soviet fleet reversed course.

The crisis, however, was not over. Some missiles were already in place in Cuba. Kennedy's military

advisers recommended an air strike followed by a full-scale invasion. The President, however, negotiated with Khrushchev.

On October 28 the Soviet Union agreed to withdraw or destroy missiles, launching pads, and other offensive weapons in Cuba. In return, the United States agreed to end the blockade and pledged not to invade the island. In November 1962 the missiles were withdrawn from Cuba.

THE TEST BAN TREATY

While the United States and the Soviet Union built missiles, they also talked about ways to limit the arms race. Such talks had been going on from time to time since the early 1950s. No formal agreements were reached, but the United States, the Soviet

This photograph shows a test Polaris A-3 missile breaking through the Florida waters after launching from a submerged submarine. The missile proved remarkably accurate.

Union, and Britain observed a voluntary ban on atomic testing. They did not explode nuclear devices all through 1959, 1960, and most of 1961.

The Soviet Union resumed atomic tests in September 1961. The United States quickly did the same. Then, following the Cuban missile crisis, a new round of talks began. American, Soviet, and British representatives discussed ways to ban tests of nuclear weapons underground, underwater, in the atmosphere, and in outer space.

The nations did not agree on a method of monitoring, or checking, underground tests. However, they did sign a limited test ban treaty to eliminate tests everywhere except underground. The treaty went into effect in October 1963. Many other nations agreed to the treaty, but France and the People's Republic of China refused to sign.

The treaty did not halt the arms race. President Kennedy worried that "the deadly poisons produced by a nuclear exchange would be carried by wind and water and soil and seed to the far corners of the globe and to generations yet unborn."

SECTION REVIEW

1. Identify the following: Alliance for Progress, CIA, Ngo Dinh Diem, NLF.

2. Define the following: "missile gap," "flexible response."

3. List two issues in the presidential election campaign in 1960.

4. What was the mission of Peace Corps volunteers?

5. What group of nations formed the Alliance for Progress?

6. Why did the CIA think that the invasion of Cuba would succeed?

7. Why did Khrushchev want the United States, Britain, and France to withdraw from Berlin and declare it a free city?

8. List three ways in which American troops aided ARVN soldiers in 1962.

9. (a) How did the United States discover Soviet missile bases in Cuba? (b) What agreements did Kennedy and Khrushchev reach regarding missiles in Cuba?

10. (a) What did the nuclear test treaty of 1963 outlaw? (b) Name two nations that did *not* sign the treaty.

A SPIRIT OF CHANGE

READ TO FIND OUT

—how the United States space program began.

—what economic goals Kennedy pursued.

—how the civil rights movement grew.

—how Supreme Court decisions caused controversy.

—how the Kennedy administration ended.

In April 1962 Kennedy faced a domestic economic crisis when the United States Steel Corporation tried to increase its prices. Kennedy succeeded in preventing the increase.

The baby boom that began after World War II continued into the 1960s. The population of the United States leaped 19 percent in the 1950s, reaching a total of almost 180 million people. By the end of that decade about 70 percent of all Americans lived in towns and cities rather than rural areas.

John F. Kennedy's style as president reflected the national population. He represented big-city sophistication along with a willingness to move and to change. In accepting his party's nomination for the presidency, Kennedy had spoken of a "New Frontier." He called it "the frontier of the 1960s—a frontier of unknown opportunities and perils—a frontier of unfulfilled hopes and threats."

The New Frontier created a mood of "bustle and confidence" in Washington, one observer later recalled. Kennedy called for major reforms in the United States. He urged Congress to pass laws for housing, for medical care for the aged, and for aid to education. He also urged Americans to conquer another frontier—space.

On February 20, 1962, John H. Glenn, Jr., eased into the *Friendship 7* to prepare for blast off. The flight went perfectly, he said later, because of great teamwork.

SPACE PROGRAMS

The Soviet Union had shocked Americans by launching *Sputnik I*, the world's first artificial satellite, in 1957. The Russians shocked Americans again in April 1961 when they placed the first human in orbit around the earth.

Since 1958 the National Aeronautics and Space Administration (NASA) had been working toward placing an American astronaut in space. In May 1961 NASA sent Alan B. Shepard, Jr., on a brief flight out over the Atlantic, but he did not orbit the earth. In July NASA sent Virgil Grissom on another suborbital flight.

NASA succeeded in placing an astronaut in orbit early in 1962. John H. Glenn, Jr., circled the earth three times in a flight lasting almost five hours. After he completed the mission, he received a hero's welcome from Americans, who had watched on television as his craft soared into space.

In 1963 the NASA Mercury missions ended with a 22-orbit flight lasting more than 34 hours. NASA, though, was already planning the Apollo program. Its goal had been defined by President Kennedy in 1961. The United States was committed to "landing a man on the moon and returning him safely to earth" by the end of the decade.

ECONOMIC GROWTH

The early 1960s were a time of solid economic growth. The gross national product (GNP) increased at an average annual rate of more than 5 percent while Kennedy was in office. Inflation also grew year by year, but at a rate close to 1 percent. Unemployment declined from 8 percent of the labor force in 1961 to less than 6 percent in the following years.

Except for one brief dip early in 1961, the economy moved steadily up like a well-tuned car on a smooth grade. Many people credited the economy's performance to ideas derived from the English economist John Maynard Keynes. In the 1920s and 1930s he wrote books that influenced economists in later decades.

Keynesians believed that a government could prevent a severe recession, or decline in business activity, by increasing government spending or by cutting taxes. If a government increased its spending, Keynesians argued, more money would flow into the economy. Additional spending would encourage business investment, increase employment, and enable consumers to spend more.

If a government cut taxes, people would have more money to spend. This, too, would spur investment, employment, and consumer spending. Either way, however, the government would have to spend more money than it received in taxes, adding to its budget deficit, or shortage.

Eisenhower had tried to avoid such deficit spending. However, when the economy declined in 1957 and 1958, he increased government spending in order to prevent a severe recession. This caused a large deficit in 1959. For the year 1960 Eisenhower managed to balance the federal budget. The government took in $92.5 billion and spent slightly less.

Kennedy thought that deficits were sometimes proper. He also was convinced that the government needed to spend more for defense, space programs, and domestic measures. Federal spending rose to nearly $98 billion in 1961 and to $107 billion in 1962. The deficit increased from about $3.5 billion to more than $7 billion.

ECONOMIC MEASURES

Most federal spending went for long-established programs, but some new domestic measures added to the budget. Early in 1961 Congress passed the Area Redevelopment Act. It provided federal loans to new businesses and training for unemployed workers in areas that were depressed. Soon after, Congress passed the Housing Act of 1961. It authorized federal loans for the construction of low-cost housing and mass transportation systems.

Government regulations also affected the economy. In May 1961 a new minimum wage law extended coverage to 3.5 million more workers. They and the 24 million workers already covered were assured a minimum wage rising from the previous level of $1 an hour to $1.25 an hour.

Kennedy fought to stop a price increase in the steel industry. Steelworkers had accepted new wages that did not seem to force an inflationary jump in the price of steel. However, in April 1962 the United States Steel Corporation announced a general price increase of 3.5 percent. Kennedy called the increase "wholly unjustified." His strong opposition caused the steel industry to cancel the price increase.

Later that year Kennedy gained authority from Congress to regulate tariffs. The Trade Expansion Act allowed the president to change tariff rates in order to improve the nation's share of world trade.

America's economic well-being helped the Democrats in 1962. They retained their majority in the House of Representatives and the Senate in the congressional elections.

THE CIVIL RIGHTS MOVEMENT

Black Americans had only a small share in the economic growth of the 1960s. In 1961, when unemployment among whites was 6 percent, unemployment among blacks was more than 12 percent. Both rates fell in the 1960s, but the rate for blacks remained double that for whites.

Black youths of ages sixteen through nineteen had an exceptionally hard time finding jobs. Nonetheless, a spirit of hope grew strong among young blacks at the start of the decade. With this spirit they set out to challenge segregation in the United States.

In February 1960 four black college students sat down at a segregated lunch counter in a variety store in Greensboro, North Carolina. When the students were refused service, they protested by remaining at the counter in a *sit-in*.

The sit-in was inspired by the sit-down strikes of labor unions in the 1930s. Like the Montgomery bus boycott beginning in 1956, the sit-in was a nonviolent technique. In 1960 use of the sit-in spread throughout the South.

By the end of March 1960 more than a thousand protestors, including some whites, had been arrested for sit-ins. In October three major chains of variety stores ended discrimination at their lunch counters in the South.

A new civil rights group sprang up in 1960. The Student Non-Violent Coordinating Committee (SNCC) began at Shaw University in Raleigh, North Carolina. SNCC's first goal was to gain political rights for blacks through voter registration. In this it was aided by the Civil Rights Act of 1960, which provided for referees to help blacks register and vote.

In May 1961 an interracial group of 13 "freedom riders" started a bus trip in the South. The group set out to end segregation in interstate travel—travel between states. Court orders forbade separating blacks from whites in interstate buses and bus stations, but the orders often were ignored. Despite acts of violence against the group, the freedom-ride movement spread.

Marches were another nonviolent technique used in the civil rights movement. Wide publicity helped the marchers bring political pressure to secure rights. The march shown here took place from Selma to Montgomery, Alabama.

VIOLENCE AGAINST CIVIL RIGHTS SUPPORTERS

The hopes of blacks were severely tested in the 1960s. James Meredith, a black veteran of the Air Force, was prevented from registering at the all-white University of Mississippi in 1962. After federal marshals escorted Meredith onto campus to register, a riot erupted. Two people were killed and more than a hundred were injured. Federal troops stayed at the school to protect Meredith until he graduated in 1963.

Martin Luther King, Jr., led demonstrations in Birmingham, Alabama, in the spring of 1963. Marchers protested segregation in restaurants and stores and discrimination in employment. On May 3 Birmingham police turned fire hoses and attack dogs on the marchers. About a week later the local headquarters of the marchers was bombed.

President Kennedy stationed troops near Birmingham to assure order. On June 11 he promised to ask Congress for civil rights laws to ban discrimination in employment on the basis of race. He also promised to ask for laws to ban segregation in public accommodations, such as hotels and restaurants.

On June 12, one day after Kennedy's speech, an NAACP leader, Medgar W. Evers, was shot and killed as he entered his home in Jackson, Mississippi. Evers's death led to rioting in Jackson and to demonstrations in almost every major city in the United States.

THE WARREN COURT

In 1962 the Supreme Court ruled that the public schools of New York State could not legally require students to say an official school prayer. The prayer, the Court declared, violated the First Amendment, which prohibited the establishment of religion in the United States. The Supreme Court decision regarding the separation of church and state was widely criticized.

The Court's ruling on *reapportionment* also caused controversy. In 1962 the Court ruled that states could be required to reapportion, or restructure, their voting districts in order to provide voters equal protection of the laws, under the Fourteenth Amendment. For years people had been moving to cities and suburbs. However, voting districts had not been changed to reflect this movement. Thus, many districts favored rural voters.

In a 1964 case Chief Justice Earl Warren wrote that "legislators represent people, not acres or trees." He held that state voting districts should be approximately equal in population. This "one man, one vote" ruling shifted power away from rural legislators.

The Court also made a series of controversial decisions in the 1960s regarding criminal cases. In 1963 in the case of *Gideon* v. *Wainright* the Court ruled that a person charged with a crime has a right to a lawyer even if the state must pay the lawyer's fee. In 1964 in the case of *Escobedo* v. *Illinois* the Court held that police who question suspects in crimes must tell the suspects that they have the right to consult a lawyer. Otherwise the suspects' statements to police may not be used as evidence.

In 1966 the Supreme Court set more exact guidelines for police questioning. In the case of *Miranda* v. *Arizona* the Court ruled that police must tell suspects that they have a number of rights. These include the right to remain silent, the right to see a lawyer before questioning, and the right to a lawyer even if a suspect is too poor to hire one.

While Earl Warren (front, center) was Chief Justice, the Supreme Court ruled that racial segregation in the public schools was unconstitutional.

These cases occurred at a time when the rate of crime was increasing in the nation. Many Americans accused the Warren Court of hindering the work of state and local police.

THE DEATH OF THE PRESIDENT

On Friday, November 22, 1963, President Kennedy rode in a motorcade through the streets of Dallas, Texas. The sound of rifle shots split the air, and the President slumped forward. He was rushed to a hospital and pronounced dead within an hour. The body of the dead President was taken to the presidential plane. There Vice-President Johnson took the oath of office as Kennedy's successor. Then the plane began its flight back to Washington.

The news flashing out of Dallas stunned the nation. The loss seemed especially bitter because of Kennedy's youth and his limited time in office. The New Frontier had lasted little more than a thousand days.

Dallas police arrested Lee Harvey Oswald, a lonely, emotionally disturbed young man, as the President's assassin. Two days later, while being transferred to another jail, Oswald himself was killed by a Dallas nightclub operator, Jack Ruby. The next day, November 25, Kennedy was buried in a state funeral at Arlington National Cemetery.

SECTION REVIEW

1. Identify the following: John H. Glenn, Jr., James Meredith, Medgar W. Evers, Lee Harvey Oswald.

2. Define the following: sit-in, reapportionment.

3. What were the goals of the New Frontier?

4. What government agency was responsible for sending the first American astronaut into space?

5. How did Kennedy's view of deficit spending differ from Eisenhower's view?

6. Name the first goal sought by SNCC.

7. What did the "freedom riders" of 1961 hope to accomplish?

8. (a) What right did the Supreme Court decision in the case of *Gideon* v. *Wainright* give to a poor person charged with a crime? (b) According to the Supreme Court decision in the case of *Escobedo* v. *Illinois*, what were police required to do when questioning a suspect?

NEW PROGRAMS AND PROTESTS

READ TO FIND OUT

— how Johnson continued the work of Kennedy.

— why Johnson won the election of 1964.

— how Johnson tried to achieve the Great Society.

— what groups in the United States called for justice and equality.

— how frustration affected the civil rights movement.

Lyndon B. Johnson grew up in the hill country of central Texas. He taught school briefly and then entered politics in 1931 to help a Democrat run for Congress.

Johnson became a member of the House of Representatives later in the decade. In 1948 he won election to the Senate. He soon emerged as a leader of Senate Democrats. Senator Hubert H. Humphrey of Minnesota described him as "a genius in the art of the legislative process." Others called him the "Great Persuader."

Johnson's persuasive skill was a great advantage to him when he moved into the White House. So was the memory of John F. Kennedy. Out of respect for the slain leader, Congress approved New Frontier proposals that it had not passed before.

EXTENDING THE NEW FRONTIER

President Johnson stressed that his administration would honor commitments already made. Kennedy had planned a major tax cut to stimulate the economy. In February 1964 Johnson won congressional approval for a $10 billion tax cut. Kennedy had urged passage of a strong civil rights bill. Johnson pushed such a bill through Congress by July.

The Civil Rights Act of 1964 outlawed discrimination in public accommodations and by employers. The bill also strengthened the powers of the federal government to desegregate schools and to protect the voting rights of blacks.

Voting rights of blacks also were affected by the Twenty-fourth Amendment, ratified in January 1964. It banned the use of the poll tax in federal elections. The poll tax was a tax that had to be paid at the polls, or place of voting, in order to vote. This tax had been used so that poor blacks were kept from voting.

During his administration Kennedy had called for a "war on poverty" in the United States. Government studies, released in 1964, made his call an urgent one. According to the studies, 18 percent of the population—some 34 million Americans—lived below the "poverty line," as defined by the federal government.*

Johnson picked up Kennedy's phrase and used it as a rallying cry for new programs to combat poverty. One was the Job Corps. It provided job training for unemployed young men and women in city slums. Another program was the Volunteers in Service to America (VISTA). VISTA volunteers worked in depressed areas of the United States to reduce unemployment and lack of education. Still other programs provided on-the-job training for young men and women.

Congress approved these programs in the Economic Opportunity Act, passed in August 1964. The act set up the Office of Economic Opportunity (OEO) as headquarters for the war on poverty. The OEO was authorized to spend almost $1 billion.

THE ELECTION OF 1964

In 1964 Johnson was the obvious choice for the Democratic nomination for president. He selected Senator Hubert H. Humphrey of Minnesota as his running mate. The two were enthusiastically nominated by the Democratic convention.

Unlike the Democrats, the Republicans were divided over a presidential choice. Nelson A. Rockefeller, the governor of New York, campaigned for the nomination. So did Henry Cabot Lodge, Jr., who had run for vice-president in 1960. Governor William W. Scranton of Pennsylvania also ran.

Rockefeller, Lodge, and Scranton were moderate Republicans from the East Coast. Opposing them

---

* The federal government measures poverty on the basis of income. It identifies the poor as those whose yearly incomes fall below certain levels.

for the nomination was Senator Barry Goldwater of Arizona. He represented the conservative branch of the party. Many members of this branch opposed the social programs of the federal government. They also opposed a foreign policy of negotiation with the Communist bloc.

Goldwater received his party's nomination on the first ballot and chose William E. Miller, a member of Congress from New York, as his running mate. Goldwater's conservatism contrasted sharply with the outlook of Johnson and Humphrey, who favored federal legislation to reform the nation. Thus, Goldwater offered what his supporters had promised—"a choice, not an echo."

In the campaign the Democrats attacked Goldwater for his conservative views. They pointed to Goldwater's votes against the nuclear test ban treaty, against the tax cut, and against the Civil Rights Act of 1964. Above all, the Democrats tried to make Goldwater appear dangerous. They claimed that Goldwater if elected might recklessly start a nuclear war.

The election was a landslide for Johnson. He received more than 60 percent of the popular vote. His margin in the electoral vote was 486 to 52, the second biggest sweep of the century. The Democrats also strengthened their majority in Congress.

In October 1966 President Johnson visited Vietnam to reassure the American troops of support at home. Here he was greeted by troops in Cam Ranh Bay.

THE GREAT SOCIETY

Johnson promised to build the "Great Society" for Americans. It would be based on "abundance and liberty for all." Johnson urgently called on Congress to pass his program.

From April through October 1965, Congress passed more major bills than in any similar period since the New Deal. The Elementary and Secondary School Act granted more than $1 billion to school districts, based on the number of needy children enrolled. The Higher Education Act created federal scholarships for college students.

Congress established the Medicare program to pay medical bills for the aged through the social security system. A Medicaid program, paid for by the state and federal governments, was also set up. It would assist the needy and the disabled not covered by social security.

The Voting Rights Act of 1965 was another Great Society accomplishment. It banned literacy tests—tests to determine whether a person can read or write—that had been used unfairly to keep blacks from voting. The act also authorized federal officials to register eligible voters in states where they faced racial discrimination.

Aided by this and previous laws, civil rights groups stepped up voter registration drives. About 29 percent of southern blacks who were old enough to vote cast ballots in 1964. The figure increased to nearly 48 percent in the congressional elections in 1966.

A housing act provided federal aid for low-income families. The act was administered by the newly created Department of Housing and Urban Development (HUD). A black economist, Robert C. Weaver, became its first secretary.

The Immigration and Nationality Act of 1965 ended the immigration quotas based on national origin, which had existed since the 1920s. The new law opened the way to an increasing number of newcomers from Asia and Latin America.

Environmentalists have worked to outlaw industrial pollution such as this murky yellowish chemical waste foaming into the ocean on the coast of Virginia.

Before it adjourned in the fall of 1965, Congress also passed laws to curb pollution of the environment. The Water Quality Act of 1965 required states to establish and enforce standards for water quality for interstate lakes and rivers. New air quality laws set federal emission standards for new cars produced by American manufacturers.

Legislation for the Great Society slowed in 1966, but it continued. Congress established new safety standards for cars and highways. It created the Department of Transportation to deal with highway, air, and rail traffic. The lawmakers increased the minimum wage, granted educational benefits to veterans, and provided funds for new housing in city slums.

CONSUMERS AND ENVIRONMENTALISTS

Consumers continued to urge Congress to pass laws to make cars and highways safer. They were led by a lawyer named Ralph Nader. In 1965 Nader attacked the auto industry in a book titled *Unsafe at Any Speed.* He argued that many people were killed or injured needlessly because auto makers worried more about style than safety. In response, Congress passed the National Traffic and Motor Vehicle Safety Act of 1966.

Environmentalists also worked for reform in the United States. They pushed for laws to preserve wilderness areas, to beautify cities, and to reduce pollution. They were especially concerned about pollution from pesticides—chemicals used for killing insects and weeds. In *Silent Spring*, a book published in 1962, marine biologist Rachel Carson described the deadly effects of these chemical sprays.

Silent Spring led many people to join the environmental movement. Their pressure on Congress helped to produce laws to ensure that states and federal agencies reduce water pollution. Similar laws were passed to control air pollution and to limit mining and lumbering on public lands.

Congress made protection of the environment a matter of national policy with the National Environmental Policy Act of 1969. It required all federal agencies to consider the impact of their projects on the environment. Late in 1970 the Environmental Protection Agency (EPA) was created to coordinate federal laws against pollution.

WOMEN'S RIGHTS

The Great Society, Johnson believed, "demands an end to poverty and injustice." In the 1960s large groups of Americans set out to gain justice and equality.

One group that fought inequality was technically a majority. In 1965 women made up nearly 51 percent of the population in the United States. Still, they were excluded from most careers with power, prestige, and high pay. Betty Friedan stressed this inequality in her 1963 book, *The Feminine Mystique.* It described the social pressures against women working outside the home.

In 1966 Friedan founded the National Organization for Women (NOW). Within a decade it had

Supporters of equal rights for women are indebted to Betty Friedan. Encouraging women to enter politics, she helped form the National Women's Political Caucus.

some 60,000 members. The organization focused on economic and social issues. Members called for equal pay for equal work, equal opportunities for women in any job, and public day-care centers for the children of mothers who worked.

NOW became a focus of a fast-growing women's rights movement. The movement made use of the Civil Rights Act of 1964. The act barred job discrimination on the basis of race, color, religion, sex, or national origin.

HISPANIC AMERICANS' GOALS

Spanish-speaking people, called Hispanics, also fought inequality. Whether they were newcomers, like Puerto Ricans, or longtime residents, like many Mexican Americans, Hispanic people suffered discrimination in the United States.

Puerto Ricans have a special relationship with the United States. In 1898, after the Spanish-American War, Puerto Rico was annexed by the United States. In the early 1950s Puerto Rico achieved commonwealth status. The island was strongly linked to the United States, yet it was self-governing. Puerto Ricans living on the island could not vote in presidential elections, and they paid no federal income taxes. Yet they were United States citizens who could move to the American mainland without immigration restrictions.

During the 1950s and 1960s Puerto Rico was plagued by high unemployment. Thousands of Puerto Ricans moved to New York City and to other large mainland cities in search of jobs. Many could not speak English. Almost all faced employment problems, poor housing, and prejudice.

Cubans also fled their homeland in the 1960s. Thousands came to the United States to escape the regime set up by Fidel Castro in 1959. Most of these immigrants settled in and around Miami, Florida, and the New York City area. Most also were business people and professionals, and they eased quickly into American life.

Like Puerto Ricans, Mexican Americans also faced discrimination in the United States. Some Mexican Americans could trace their ancestry back to the Spaniards and Mexicans who settled in the Southwest and in California in the 1600s and 1700s. Most, however, were newer settlers. In the early 1900s large numbers of Mexicans escaped political turmoil and poverty by crossing the border into the United States. Only the Great Depression reversed this trend.

During World War II Mexicans once more moved north from Mexico. The war created a demand for labor in the United States. Under a government program, Mexicans could come to the United States for seasonal work on farms and return home when their jobs were finished.

The program continued long after the war. Between 1942 and 1964, some 5 million *braceros* (brah-SEHR-ōs), as the workers were called, were employed in the Southwest. They worked for very low wages and lived in crude farm worker camps. Meanwhile, many Mexicans crossed the border as illegal aliens and became migrant workers. They, too, accepted poor wages and housing in return for jobs.

MEXICAN AMERICAN DEMANDS

Like black Americans, Mexican Americans in the 1960s increased the struggle for their rights. Many Mexican Americans called this struggle the Chicano or "brown power" movement. Most leaders demanded better jobs, higher pay, and good education for their children. Other leaders went even further.

In New Mexico Reies López Tijerina formed an organization to gain certain government-owned lands that he claimed rightfully belonged to Mexican Americans. He based his claim on land grants made before the United States acquired the territory from Mexico. Tijerina wanted the land returned to Mexican Americans.

Rodolfo "Corky" Gonzales also charged the United States with land theft. "Robbed of our land," he said, "our people were driven to the migrant labor fields and the cities." He called for *la raza*, "the race," to renew its self-respect by militant, or aggressive, action.

Cesar Chavez was equally concerned with economic conditions. He set out to gain higher wages and better working conditions for Mexican Americans by organizing a union for farm workers. Like Martin Luther King, Jr., Chavez believed in nonviolent action to achieve his goals.

Beginning in 1965, Chavez led a strike of grape pickers to force the growers in Delano, California, to recognize his union, the United Farm Workers, and to negotiate with it. In 1966 the strikers gained the support of the AFL-CIO. Two years later Chavez organized a nationwide boycott of table grapes not picked by the United Farm Workers.

In 1970 Chavez and his United Farm Workers finally achieved recognition by the growers. But he was unable to build his union into a major economic force. Nor could his farm union affect most Mexican Americans. By 1970 some 80 percent of them lived in cities.

Cesar Chavez never veered from his commitment to a "totally nonviolent struggle for justice." This photograph shows him talking with workers in Lamont, California, in 1973.

INDIAN DEMANDS

Along with blacks and Hispanic Americans, Indians also struggled for equality. Indians received increased federal aid in the 1960s. However, many causes of grievance remained. Indian children on reservations still were obliged to leave their homes if they wanted to go to high school. At the Pine Ridge Reservation in South Dakota, for example, large numbers of children dropped out of school rather than go away. They stayed on the reservation although few houses had electricity and only about half had wells nearby.

Like other minorities, Indians demonstrated to gain public attention. Late in 1969 some eighty Indians captured Alcatraz Island in San Francisco Bay. They demanded that the federally owned island be turned into an Indian cultural center. The demand was rejected, but Indians occupied the island for more than a year.

Meanwhile young Indian leaders started the American Indian Movement (AIM). To dramatize their demands, AIM members occupied the Washington, D.C., offices of the Bureau of Indian Affairs for a half-dozen days in 1972. They called for sweeping reforms in United States policies toward Indian rights and tribal land.

GROWING ANGER IN THE CIVIL RIGHTS MOVEMENT

The minority most involved in direct action were black Americans. Many became increasingly outraged in the 1960s as they became impatient with the slow progress toward equality.

Violence against the civil rights movement embittered many blacks. In the fall of 1963 a black church in Birmingham, Alabama, was bombed on a Sunday. Four little girls were killed. The following year three SNCC volunteers were killed near Philadelphia, Mississippi. In March 1965 Martin Luther King, Jr., led thousands of marchers from Selma to Montgomery, Alabama, to protest restrictions on black voter registration. After the march a white civil rights worker was shot and killed.

Segregation in the North also angered many blacks. Discrimination there was not written into laws, but was just as real as it had been in the South. Schools in northern cities were segregated because neighborhoods tended to be segregated. Businesses often practiced discrimination in hiring. Housing that blacks could obtain was often in poor condition.

For many frustrated blacks, the new civil rights laws did not do enough to bring equality. Children still needed education, the unemployed still needed jobs, and people still needed adequate housing. For some blacks, too, the strategy of nonviolence no longer seemed enough.

In June 1965 a black group in Louisiana, Deacons for Defense and Justice, renounced nonviolence. The group prepared to fight back against white violence. In August a long riot broke out in the Watts area of Los Angeles. Blacks there burned

---

AMERICAN OBSERVERS

MARIA MARTINEZ
PUEBLO INDIAN ARTIST

San Ildefonso, the Tewa Indian pueblo, lies in the sage and mesquite-dotted Rio Grande Valley in northern New Mexico. The land, starkly beautiful, is bordered by blue-violet mountains. The pueblo itself is earth-colored, dotted with flat-roofed adobe houses around a central plaza. Here Maria Martinez, the famed Indian potter, lived for almost a century.

Maria Martinez learned her craft as a child by watching an aunt make pottery in the same way her ancestors had for a thousand years. She was already a skilled artist by 1909, when Dr. Edgar Lee Hewett, an archaeologist, asked her to copy some strange black pots he had found while digging for Indian relics. These pots were more than seven hundred years old, but the secret of their black color had been lost.

Maria Martinez and her husband Julian experimented to rediscover the secret. Eventually they found that when they baked their pots in a fire smothered in cow dung, the smoke turned them a beautiful silvery black. They also learned to coat the pots with an iron-based clay and polish them with stones before baking to enhance their sheen.

For many years Maria Martinez worked to perfect this magnificent black pottery. Gradually her work became known. Pots she once sold for a dollar in the market became museum pieces worth more than a thousand dollars each.

Maria Martinez lived to be ninety-seven years old. Energetic and productive well into her nineties, she preserved the Tewa heritage both as a potter and as a counselor in tribal customs. "When I am gone," she once told her great-grandchildren, "other people have my pots. But to you I leave my greatest achievement, which is the ability to do it."

Today five generations of the Martinez family carry on her work. They also keep alive the dances, music, and other customs of the Tewa people. In her life and in her art Maria Martinez rediscovered and passed on the centuries-old traditions of her ancestors.

Maria Martinez made and polished the beautiful pottery pieces. Her husband Julian painted the elegant designs, often using ancient motifs.

and looted white-owned businesses. The riot caused 35 deaths, more than 1,000 injuries, and $200 million in property damage. More violence erupted in the summer of 1966. Blacks in 16 cities battled police in outbreaks of rioting.

BLACK POWER

Stokely Carmichael, the new head of SNCC, reflected this new mood of militancy. Blacks need political and economic power, he said, "because this country does not function by morality, love, and nonviolence, but by power." Carmichael gave SNCC its new slogan, "black power." Black power stressed pride in being black. It also laid stress on the right of blacks to defend themselves.

Other groups also supported black power. The Black Muslims, led by Elijah Muhammad and Malcolm X, preached that blacks should seek segregation from whites and that they should fight back if attacked. Malcolm X also called for black control of businesses and politics in black communities. Later Malcolm X rejected his separatist views and broke with the Black Muslims. In 1965 he was assassinated. Two of the three assassins were Black Muslims. The *Autobiography of Malcolm X*, published after his death, was widely read.

Like the Black Muslims, the Black Panthers believed that blacks and whites should be separated. They also vowed to meet white violence with black violence. Formed in 1966, the Black Panther party was led by Huey P. Newton, Bobby Seale, and Eldridge Cleaver. Their views alarmed moderate leaders like King. Violence, he felt, could only lead to more violence.

Devastating riots swept through black neighborhoods in Detroit and in Newark, New Jersey, in the summer of 1967. Lesser outbreaks of violence took place in Cincinnati, Buffalo, Boston, Tampa, and a hundred other cities during the summer.

President Johnson ordered a commission to investigate the violence and to recommend ways to deal with it. The commission, headed by Governor Otto Kerner of Illinois, issued its findings early in 1968. The Kerner Report concluded that the nation was rapidly splitting into two parts, black and white. To prevent this split, the report called for economic and social opportunities for black city-dwellers. That would lead toward "common goals of public order and social justice."

A traffic arrest in the Watts ghetto in California set a match to the explosive mood there in August 1965. Five days of death, destruction, looting, and arson followed.

Soon after the report was issued, Martin Luther King, Jr., was assassinated in Memphis, Tennessee, by James Earl Ray, a white escaped convict. King's death caused a new wave of urban rioting as well as an outpouring of public grief.

SECTION REVIEW

1. Identify the following: OEO, Ralph Nader, Rachel Carson, Betty Friedan, NOW, AIM, Malcolm X.

2. Define the following: *braceros.*

3. Name two programs set up by the Economic Opportunity Act as part of Johnson's "war on poverty."

4. How did Goldwater offer voters "a choice, not an echo"?

5. (a) What two medical programs were established by legislation in 1965? (b) What new department of government was established in 1965?

6. (a) Name the Hispanic group able to enter the United States with no immigration restrictions. (b) Describe the Hispanic group with claims of ownership to land in the Southwest.

7. What did black power mean?

8. What orders did Johnson give to the Kerner Commission?

AMERICAN CONCERNS ABROAD

READ TO FIND OUT

— how Johnson reacted to conflict in Latin America and the Middle East.

— why Johnson sent American troops to Vietnam.

— how Johnson expanded the war in Vietnam.

— why opposition to the war grew.

— how the war affected the election of 1968.

President Johnson's domestic programs started with a flourish. The laws passed to win the war on poverty and to achieve the Great Society won initial praise for the President.

Johnson's foreign policy, however, did not start on such a high note. During his first months as president, Johnson was beset by problems in Latin America, the Middle East, and Southeast Asia. As time went on, the conflict in Vietnam came to dominate his attention. The conflict also came to dominate the nation and to divide Americans.

THE DOMINICAN REPUBLIC

While president, Kennedy had tried to improve relations with Latin America. Johnson's actions in the Dominican Republic, however, threatened to revive Latin Americans' distrust of their northern neighbor.

In April 1965 supporters of Juan Bosch tried to overthrow the military government of the Dominican Republic. Soon the nation was close to civil war. Johnson, fearing Communist leadership of the revolt, quickly sent marines to the island to support the existing government.

Johnson's action raised a storm of criticism in Latin America and the United States. Critics argued that the President lacked evidence of the involvement of Communists in the revolt. In addition, they accused the President of bypassing the Organization of American States (OAS), which should have been consulted in the matter.

Johnson kept United States troops in the Dominican Republic for more than a year. By then fighting had ended, and a new regime had been elected.

THE SIX-DAY WAR

Johnson also was concerned with the Middle East. Since the birth of Israel in 1948, the area had been a powder keg. In 1956 it had exploded when Israel, as well as Britain and France, had invaded Egypt. Since that conflict, a UN peace-keeping force had been in the area.

In 1967 the UN force was withdrawn, at Egypt's request. Arab troops began to mass. Suspecting an attack, Israel struck first. On June 5, 1967, Israeli forces invaded Syria, Jordan, and Egypt. Six days later a UN cease-fire was accepted by all sides. By then, Israel held Syria's Golan Heights, all of Egypt's Sinai Peninsula and Gaza Strip, and West Jordan, including the city of Jerusalem.

The cease-fire did not reduce tension. Israel refused to give up its captured territory, and the Arab nations demanded revenge. In later months the Soviet Union supplied planes to build up the Arab air forces, largely destroyed in the war. The United States, meanwhile, sent combat jets to Israel.

AMERICAN INVOLVEMENT IN VIETNAM

President Johnson's major foreign concern was South Vietnam. Since 1961 American advisers and support troops had been pouring into South Vietnam. They helped South Vietnam's soldiers block advances by the National Liberation Front (NLF).

Diem accepted American troops and aid, but was unwilling to accept American advice. Kennedy had pressed Diem to end corruption and to open government positions to Buddhists, who were a majority in the nation. Instead, Diem, a Catholic, repressed Buddhists and political opponents.

During 1963 Buddhists spearheaded widespread opposition to Diem's rule. In November the military overthrew the government of South Vietnam. Diem was assassinated.

The change of government in Saigon encouraged the NLF to increase its attacks. When Johnson became president, he inherited a worsening war and an untried government in South Vietnam.

The Middle East 1967

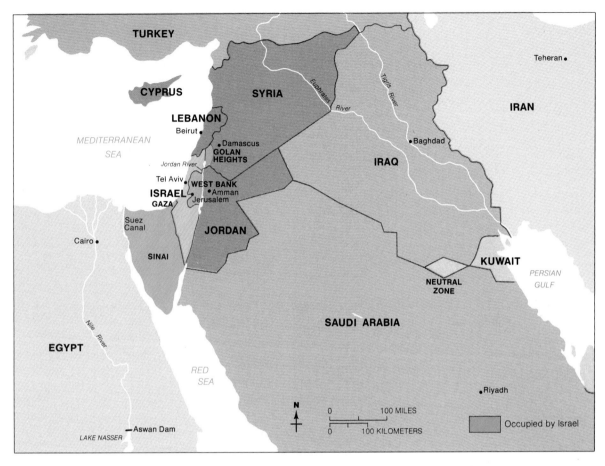

Strategic location, rich oil reserves, political turmoil within each nation, and conflicts among cultures make the Middle East one of the world's most troubled regions.

THE GULF OF TONKIN RESOLUTION

In his first year as president, Johnson did not increase significantly American support to South Vietnam. However, he believed that a Communist victory in South Vietnam would lead to takeovers throughout Asia and in other parts of the world. To prevent that, Johnson was willing to increase America's role in the conflict.

On August 4, 1964, President Johnson reported to congressional leaders that North Vietnamese torpedo boats had for the second time attacked an American destroyer in the Gulf of Tonkin, off the coast of North Vietnam. In response, Johnson had ordered limited air strikes against North Vietnam. He asked Congress for authority to take action in case of further attacks.

On August 7 Congress passed the Gulf of Tonkin Resolution. It allowed the president "to take all necessary measures to repel any armed attack against forces of the United States and to prevent further aggression."

Senator Ernest Gruening of Alaska, who voted against the resolution, called it "a predated declaration of war." Senator Wayne Morse of Oregon said, "We are in effect giving the president . . . war-making powers in the absence of a declaration of war." But every other senator and every representative voted for the resolution.

Later it became known that the first attack on one of the destroyers probably was provoked by South Vietnamese gunboats attacking the North Vietnamese coast. The second attack probably never took place. There were no sightings of enemy ships at the time.

The War in Vietnam 1961-1975

The Vietnam War was a war without battlefronts. Each side held pockets of land here and there throughout the countryside. Vietnam is particularly suited for querrilla warfare. Narrow paths lead through water-covered river deltas, dense tropical jungles, and forest-cloaked mountains.

EXPANSION OF THE WAR

In January 1965 a Viet Cong attack on American military advisers triggered a strong United States response. Using his authority under the Gulf of Tonkin Resolution, Johnson ordered air strikes against North Vietnam. After a similar Viet Cong attack in February, Johnson ordered sustained bombing of the North.

The bombing failed to force North Vietnam to negotiate for peace. In April 1965 Johnson decided to send United States combat troops to fight in Vietnam. By the end of the year some 185,000 American troops were stationed there. Johnson had committed the United States to a land war in Asia.

The war seldom offered fixed battle lines. Instead, ARVN and United States troops used helicopters to make "search and destroy" missions on suspected Viet Cong sites. The Viet Cong, in turn, relied on guerrilla raids and tactics.

Villagers endured pressures from both sides. Those who cooperated with one side might be executed later when the other side returned. Villagers also lost their crops and homes to bombings. Thousands of civilians were killed each year.

Although they sustained heavy losses, Viet Cong troops survived a major battle with American forces late in 1965. When the United States commander, General William C. Westmoreland, asked for more soldiers, Johnson supplied them.

The air war over North Vietnam also increased. By the early months of 1967, American bombers were striking at troop barracks, bridges, rail yards, and other targets. Several targets were near Hanoi (hah-NOY), the capital. Still North Vietnam refused to negotiate unless the United States withdrew from Vietnam and ended all bombing raids.

CRITICS OF THE WAR

In 1967 President Johnson announced that the number of United States troops in Vietnam would be increased to 525,000 by the middle of 1968. Johnson also asked for a 10 percent increase in income-tax rates to help pay for the war. By then the United States was paying $25 billion per year to finance the war. The cost in human lives was high, too. The number of Americans killed, wounded, or missing rose to over 35,000 by 1967.

As the war expanded, some critics argued that the United States could not afford to fight in Vietnam and also to fund domestic programs. One Republican jeered, "The administration some time ago told us we could afford 'both guns and butter,' but now we are lucky if we can afford bread and butter." Martin Luther King, Jr., was more direct. "The Great Society," he said, "has been shot down on the battlefields of Vietnam."

Other critics questioned American intervention in Vietnam. They charged that the fight was basically a civil war in which the United States should have no part. Still others criticized the massive bombing policy of the United States. Bombs, napalm, and chemical warfare, they argued, were destroying the Vietnamese people and land.

Finally, some critics wondered whether the military government of South Vietnam was worth supporting. Robert F. Kennedy noted "the enormous corruption" in the government. He doubted that such a government could have the support of the people of South Vietnam.

Johnson, however, justified the war on a number of counts. The United States, he declared, needed to show that it would honor its commitments to its allies. It also needed to halt Communist aggression and to contain the People's Republic of China. Criticism of the war, Johnson's administration charged, was helping the enemy. "Hawks," people who favored greater military effort, questioned the patriotism of "doves," people who wanted to reduce America's participation in the war.

However, in 1967 there were nationwide protests against the war. The protests increased in 1968, partly because of military events in Vietnam.

THE TET OFFENSIVE

Late in January 1968 Viet Cong and North Vietnamese troops launched a major offensive. They struck during Tet, the lunar New Year in Vietnam.

This photograph movingly records the destruction in a Vietnamese town. The young woman's anguished face spoke for the thousands whose lives were being disrupted.

Field telephones kept American and Vietnamese troops in communication with other units. Sandbagged trenches provided small pockets of defense against enemy fire.

They attacked over thirty towns and cities in South Vietnam, including Saigon. They besieged United States forces at the outpost of Khesanh.

The Tet offensive finally was stopped by United States and ARVN forces after fierce fighting. However, it shattered the confidence of many Americans, who had believed that the war was being won.

Following the Tet offensive, General Westmoreland asked for more than 200,000 additional troops.

Johnson approved about 40,000. Politics at home now placed severe limits on the President's military choices in Southeast Asia.

DEMOCRATIC CANDIDATES

Even before the Tet offensive, Senator Eugene J. McCarthy of Minnesota announced that he would challenge Johnson for the Democratic nomination

ORAL HISTORY
VIETNAM: A VETERAN SPEAKS

Historians use documents—primary and secondary sources—to obtain knowledge of what happened at a particular time. Since the 1940s, they have also been making use of another research tool—*oral history*. An oral history is a person's account of events that he or she has experienced. The account is tape recorded. Then it is often made into a written document.

The following is part of one American soldier's account of his experiences in Vietnam. The veteran, Jonathan Polansky, served in the 101st Airborne Division I Corps in Vietnam from November 1968 to November 1969.

The place where we stayed in the lowlands was a little fishing village called Lang Co. A beautiful, beautiful place, on the coast of the Gulf of Tonkin. It was a peaceful little village, a combination of French and Vietnamese architecture, cement buildings and different shades of blue, little concrete houses.

We were stationed on a bridge to protect the village and the railroad from being blown up. . . .

One day a young lieutenant approached me: "Do you want to teach school?" I said, "Yeah, sure." So he said, "Okay, pick out somebody to go into the village with and talk to the hamlet chief." . . . We talked to the village chief. . . . It would be okay, we could work in the classroom with the kids during the day. . . .

The next three months we worked with the kids, teaching English every day. The classes were made up of kids from five years old all the way to teenagers. Me and J.J. would work out little skits to present to the class, like playing baseball with words. We would stand across the room from each other and throw the word back and forth. We'd pronounce it for the kids and they would go along with us. The

kids would be roaring, they loved us, to see these two jerky Americans, these two animated young fellas. It was a pleasure beyond belief because each day after class we would go through the village and as we'd walk through we'd hear the little kids whisper to their parents, "Schoolteacher, schoolteacher," and we'd be invited into the houses for soda and tea, and all the kids loved us. . . .

While we were guarding the bridge, the VC [Viet Cong] never bothered the village. We left the bridge to go to the Ashau for three months. Completely pulled out. After three months we came back. The village was flattened. There was not a soul in sight. It was flattened by VC destruction. The village was completely burned because all the people were American sympathizers. The only persons left were old bums. . . . I couldn't believe it—the village had been so picturesque, the most beautiful little town. Destroyed. Everything was destroyed. Every living thing was gone. I walked into the schoolhouse. I started crying and crying. It couldn't come together for me. . . .

After you have read the account, answer the following questions.

1. Who is the speaker? Why do you think that he was asked to speak about his experiences? Does he have first-hand knowledge of the events that he describes?

2. What kind of information does the account give that is not in your text? How is this information valuable?

3. Do you think that the experiences described by Polansky are similar to those of other Vietnam veterans? How could you find other descriptions?

for the presidency. McCarthy's main issue was the war in Vietnam. He was outspokenly against it.

When McCarthy traveled to New Hampshire to campaign for election in the first Democratic primary, thousands of college students followed him. His candidacy gave them a way to express their opposition to the war.

Johnson also ran in New Hampshire. He was the winner of the election, but the vote was close enough to show that he could be beaten on the issue of Vietnam. Robert F. Kennedy, then a senator from New York, announced his candidacy a few days after the New Hampshire election.

At the end of March, Johnson proclaimed a halt in American bombing of most areas of North Vietnam. He called on the North Vietnamese to begin peace negotiations. Johnson then announced that he would not run for reelection. In this way, he said, he hoped to end the divisions that had developed in America during his years in office.

Johnson's withdrawal from the race did not bring unity to the Democratic party. Vice-President Humphrey entered the race in April. Kennedy and McCarthy continued to battle in the primaries.

The decisive contest between McCarthy and Kennedy came in California in June 1968. Kennedy won the primary by a clear margin. Moments after he made a victory statement on the night of the election, he was shot and killed. The lone assassin was a young Palestinian named Sirhan Sirhan, who opposed Kennedy's support for Israel.

THE ELECTION OF 1968

The death of Robert Kennedy turned the Democratic convention in Chicago into a contest between political newcomers and party regulars. McCarthy, a newcomer to national campaigning, had challenged his own party's president and won. Humphrey, a party insider and a veteran of many political campaigns, was supported by the President and by most Democratic regulars.

Chicago became a scene of tumult that August. Outside the convention hall thousands of young men and women demonstrated against the war in Vietnam. Some of the demonstrators were eager to provoke the Chicago police, and the police responded with force. Pictures of club-wielding police and taunting demonstrators appeared on television broadcasts across the nation.

In the convention hall, Humphrey was nominated on the first ballot. Senator Edmund S. Muskie of Maine became the vice-presidential candidate.

The Republican convention in Miami was peaceful. The Republican delegates chose Richard M. Nixon, who had been vice-president under Eisenhower and who was now a private citizen. They approved Nixon's selection of Governor Spiro T. Agnew of Maryland as his running mate.

A third party gained wide publicity in the presidential campaign. George Wallace, the governor of Alabama, ran as the candidate of the American Independent party. He campaigned for a military victory in Vietnam and the return of law and order to the nation.

Neither Nixon nor Humphrey created much enthusiasm among voters. Nixon promised to end the war in Vietnam and to restore law and order at home. Humphrey initially defended Johnson's policy in Vietnam. Later, however, he announced that if elected he would stop the bombing completely.

Nixon narrowly defeated Humphrey. Each received close to 43 percent of the popular votes, with the remainder going to George Wallace. The final total of electoral votes was 301 for Nixon, 191 for Humphrey, and 46 for Wallace. Nixon now faced the task of ending the war in Vietnam and patching the deep divisions within America.

SECTION REVIEW

1. Identify the following: Sinai Peninsula, William C. Westmoreland, Hanoi, Eugene J. McCarthy.

2. Define the following: "hawks," "doves."

3. How did Johnson justify his decision to send American troops to the Dominican Republic?

4. Name the three nations invaded by Israel in the Six-Day War.

5. What power did Johnson gain when Congress passed the Gulf of Tonkin Resolution?

6. When did the United States send combat troops to fight in Vietnam? Why?

7. How did the Vietnam War affect the Great Society, according to critics of the war?

8. How did the Tet offensive change American beliefs about the war?

SUMMARY

John F. Kennedy narrowly defeated Richard M. Nixon in the 1960 presidential election. Kennedy promised bold new programs. He started the Peace Corps and the Alliance for Progress. In the cold war, though, he was shocked by the defeat of the Bay of Pigs invasion and by the building of the Berlin Wall. Kennedy then set a policy of "flexible response"—a policy intended to give America more choices in countering Soviet threats.

America opposed Communist forces in the Congo and in Laos. In 1962 America confronted the Soviet Union directly in the Cuban missile crisis, and the Soviets withdrew their missiles from Cuba. Despite this crisis, the superpowers signed a nuclear test ban treaty the following year.

Although the Soviet Union placed the first astronaut in orbit, Americans cheered when John H. Glenn, Jr., circled the earth in 1962. Americans were just as pleased by the nation's smooth-running economy. Yet there were strong conflicts within the nation. Civil rights groups challenged discrimination. The Warren Court sparked controversies through its decisions about school prayer, reapportionment, and the rights of suspects in crimes. Then, late in 1963, the nation was stunned by the assassination of Kennedy.

When he assumed the presidency, Lyndon B. Johnson quickly put through programs Kennedy had wanted. After winning the election of 1964, Johnson extended his success. Congress passed "Great Society" laws to aid education, medical care, low-cost housing, civil rights, and the environment. But many environmentalists wanted stricter laws. Women demanded more opportunities. Minorities, particularly blacks, demanded better opportunities.

In 1965 Johnson sent marines to the Dominican Republic to prevent a change of government. After the Six-Day War, in the Middle East in 1967, Johnson sent jets to Israel. In the meantime, he sent American troops to fight in Vietnam.

Despite the troops, Viet Cong forces launched the Tet offensive early in 1968. Criticism of the war mounted, and Johnson chose not to run for reelection. His vice-president, Hubert H. Humphrey, lost the 1968 election to Richard M. Nixon.

CHAPTER REVIEW

1. How did each of the following increase tension between the United States and the Soviet Union? (a) the Bay of Pigs invasion (b) the Berlin Wall (c) civil war in the Congo (d) Soviet missile bases in Cuba

2. The Kennedy administration used a naval blockade in the Cuban missile crisis. Explain how the crisis illustrated the policy of "flexible response."

3. What steps did the United States take to catch up with Soviet accomplishments in space?

4. What happened to the GNP, inflation, and unemployment while Kennedy was president?

5. Contrast the civil rights sit-ins of the 1960s and the sit-down strikes of the 1930s. What was different about their (a) locations and (b) goals?

6. Explain how each of the following was an attempt to create the "Great Society." (a) Medicare (b) Voting Rights Act of 1965 (c) Department of Housing and Urban Development (d) Water Quality Act of 1965

Roy Lichtenstein is much less of a social critic than many of his fellow pop artists. However, "Blam," done in 1962, conveys a sense of the continuing friction of the sixties.

7. President Johnson promised to work toward "abundance and liberty for all." How would this promise encourage protests by minority groups?

8. How did each of the following influence politics in the 1960s? (a) *Unsafe at Any Speed* (b) *Silent Spring* (c) *The Feminine Mystique* (d) *Autobiography of Malcolm X*

9. The Gulf of Tonkin Resolution transferred power from one branch of government to another. Describe the power and its transfer.

10. Military gains and losses were hard to measure in Vietnam because of the nature of the fighting there. Why?

ISSUES AND IDEAS

1. In 1960 "national purpose" was a campaign issue. Refer to the Declaration of Independence and the Preamble to the Constitution to list phrases that might help define the national purpose in any decade. Then select one of the phrases. Describe how it applied to the decade of the 1960s and to the policies of Kennedy and Johnson.

2. Analyze the reactions to two controversial Supreme Court decisions, one from the 1960s and one from earlier times. In each case, describe (a) what group of people applauded the decision, (b) why those people were pleased, (c) what people criticized the decision, and (d) why those people were displeased. Then decide (e) whether the reactions to the two decisions were at all alike.

3. In 1963 Martin Luther King, Jr., wrote: "For years now I have heard the word 'Wait!' It rings in the ear of every Negro with piercing familiarity. This 'Wait' has almost always meant 'Never.'" Use the case of James Meredith to illustrate how "Wait" threatened to mean "Never." Use the sit-in movement to illustrate a kind of waiting that King approved. What is the difference between the two kinds of waiting?

4. Suppose United States decisions about Vietnam could be changed at just one point from 1954 through 1968. What decision should be changed? Why? What consequences would probably have followed from the change?

SKILLS WORKSHOP

1. *Writing Skills.* Plan a news magazine cover featuring an event described in the chapter. Write a detailed description of the cover.

2. *Maps.* Refer to the map of the Middle East on page 675. Determine the dimensions of the area shown in miles or kilometers. Refer to a map of your own region and determine an area of the same dimensions. Then sketch a map using two colors. Let one color show boundaries and major cities in the area of your own region. Let the other color show a superimposed map of the Middle East, with its boundaries and major cities. Compare the sizes of states in your region with nations in the Middle East.

The peace symbol of the 1960s was created from the semaphore code for the letters *N* and *D*. These letters stood for nuclear disarmament.

PAST AND PRESENT

1. Plan two time capsules, one to hold objects representing life in the 1960s and the other to hold objects representing life in the 1980s. What objects belong in each time capsule? How do the objects in the two capsules differ?

2. Interview a person old enough to remember 1963. Ask the person to recall where he or she was when first hearing of the death of President Kennedy. Ask the same question about the death of Martin Luther King, Jr. Then ask what recent public events seem most memorable.

SHAPING
THE FUTURE

1969–Present

Eero Saarinen. *Gateway Arch*, dedicated 1968. Photo by Edward Bock.

1600	1700	1800	1900	2000

• Jamestown founded   • Revolutionary War   • Civil War   • Today

UNIT 10
1969–Present

	1970	1975	1980	1985	1990
		Nixon	Ford	Carter	Reagan		

POLITICAL

- Twenty-sixth Amendment: 18-year-old vote
- Equal Employment Opportunity Act
- Energy crisis
- Watergate investigation
- Voting Rights Act of 1965 extended
- National Energy Act
- Refugee Act
- Economic Recovery Tax Act
- Voting Rights Act of 1965 extended 25 years
- START talks

SOCIAL

- Some private colleges go co-ed
- Isaac Bashevis Singer: Nobel prize for literature
- Bee Gees inspire "discomania"
- John Lennon killed
- *E. T.* sets box-office records

TECHNOLOGICAL

- James D. Watson: *The Double Helix*
- Moon landing
- First microcomputer
- Apollo-Soyuz Test Project
- Alaska pipeline
- First reusable spacecraft

INTERNATIONAL

- Nuclear Nonproliferation Treaty
- People's Republic of China admitted to UN
- Vietnam cease-fire
- *Mayaguez* incident
- Camp David Accords
- Solidarity strike in Poland
- Hostages return from Iran
- Falklands war
- Civil war in Lebanon

1970	1975	1980	1985	1990

CRITICAL DECISIONS

1969–1976

STRIVING FOR PEACE
YEARS OF DIVISION
REBUILDING PUBLIC CONFIDENCE

In 1968, near the city of Hue in Vietnam, Lieutenant Robert Santos of the 101st Airborne Division led his platoon against troops of the North Vietnamese army:

"I remember walking through the rice paddies that opened up and the small stream and the green on both sides. We were walking down the right side, near the trail, and there was another company on my left flank. All of a sudden [everything] opened up. You have to understand, I've never been a Boy Scout, I've never been a Cub Scout. The closest I came to that was going to my sister's Campfire Girl meetings. I grew up in New York City and Long Island. Watched a lot of movies and read a lot of books. I never fired a weapon. I never got into fights with my buddies. . . . They opened up fire and Wes started going down. You make a connection real quick that someone's being shot and someone's getting hurt. . . .

"I moved, and as I ran forward I heard these noises. Kind of like *ping, ping*—no idea what that noise was. . . . I finally got back after running around, [and] sat down next to the RTO [radiotelephone operator], . . . He said, 'Don't you know what that noise is?' I said no. He said, 'That's the bullets going over your head.' I never knew it. I mean, if I'd known it I probably would've just buried myself and hid. But I didn't know it. I just didn't know it."

For Robert Santos, this clash was the first of many in Vietnam. He went there with the belief that "if I didn't go, someone else would have to go in my place." Still, he longed to return home.

At home, in the United States, the issue of the war in Vietnam bitterly divided Americans. President Nixon worked to reduce American involvement in the war and to change the nation's foreign policy. Yet his administration was swept by scandals. The scandals, like the Vietnam War, plunged Americans into a period of uncertainty and questioning.

est." Virtually all Americans agreed with him. The point on which they could not agree was the meaning of "national interest."

To some Americans, called hawks, national interest demanded that the United States stop the spread of communism in Vietnam—by extended military action if necessary. To opponents of the war, called doves, national interest required the saving of lives and dollars by withdrawing American troops from Vietnam as quickly as possible.

Nixon hoped in time to achieve both aspects of national interest. However, many Americans opposed his policies. Their protests prevented Nixon from fulfilling his campaign pledge to "bring America together."

PLANS FOR VIETNAMIZATION

Over 540,000 United States troops were serving in Vietnam when Nixon took office as president. In June 1969 he announced the first withdrawal of American troops from Vietnam. In the next two months 25,000 soldiers returned to the United States.

In November 1969 Nixon appeared on television to describe to the nation his plans for gradually withdrawing all American forces from Vietnam. The withdrawals, he explained, would depend on the enemy's military actions and on the peace talks going on in Paris. The withdrawals also would depend on the progress of "Vietnamization."

Vietnamization was Nixon's new program to train and equip the Army of the Republic of Vietnam (ARVN) to take major responsibility for fighting the war. United States troops would come home, the President stated, "as the South Vietnamese became strong enough to defend their own freedom."

Opponents of the war were dismayed. President Johnson had sent more American troops to South Vietnam in 1965 because the ARVN had failed to stop the Viet Cong, the anti-government forces. It was not clear that ARVN troops could do better in 1969. These Americans were afraid that Vietnamization would prolong the war instead of end it.

Two weeks after Nixon's speech, 250,000 Americans gathered in Washington, D.C., to protest against the war. Other Americans staged antiwar rallies in cities and on college campuses across the nation. They demanded that the United States end

STRIVING FOR PEACE

READ TO FIND OUT

— how Nixon planned to withdraw American troops from Vietnam.

— how Americans reacted to the invasion of Cambodia and Laos.

— how Nixon changed United States relations with China and the Soviet Union.

— how war in the Middle East threatened détente.

— why Nixon was reelected.

— how the Vietnam War ended.

Conflict over the war in Vietnam hung like a cloud over the nation as Richard M. Nixon took office in January 1969. Early in his term he declared, "I do not want an American [soldier] in Vietnam for one day longer than is necessary for our national inter-

its part in the fighting and withdraw all American forces from Vietnam.

News from Vietnam increased concern about the war. In November 1969 newspapers in the United States reported that American soldiers had killed over four hundred South Vietnamese civilians—elderly men, women, and children. News of the massacre at My Lai, which occurred in March 1968, stunned the nation and led to even more debate about the United States' role in Vietnam. The news also led to the court-martial* of Lieutenant William L. Calley, Jr., for his role in the massacre.

While antiwar protests spread across the United States, two kinds of peace talks were taking place in Paris. Formal talks continued between the United States, North Vietnam, the Viet Cong, and South Vietnam. Meanwhile, secret meetings were held from time to time. They involved the United States, represented by Nixon's foreign policy adviser, Henry A. Kissinger, and North Vietnam.

WARFARE IN CAMBODIA

Nixon was determined to negotiate from a position of strength. He relied on American bombing in Vietnam to put pressure on the North Vietnamese and the Viet Cong to seek peace. Nixon also wanted to deny weapons and supplies to the enemy. The Viet Cong received equipment through Communist forces in Laos and Cambodia, the two nations which bordered Vietnam.

In March 1970 Lon Nol (LAWN NUL), Cambodia's new, pro-Western leader, called on the United States for aid against Communist forces in his nation. Nixon quickly responded. In late April he ordered American and ARVN troops to invade Cambodia in order to seize Communist strongholds and supplies.

The invasion had limited success. American and ARVN troops found large amounts of enemy supplies, but few enemy soldiers. Alerted to the raid, most Communist forces had already fled from their border strongholds. After two months of searching for the enemy, American and ARVN troops returned to South Vietnam. However, the invasion increased conflict in Cambodia between Communists and non-Communists.

*court-martial: a trial conducted under the rules of military justice.

United in their opposition to the war in Vietnam, a quarter of a million American protesters gathered before the Capitol in Washington, D.C., on November 15, 1969.

AMERICAN OPPOSITION TO THE WAR

In the United States opponents of the war reacted strongly to the invasion of Cambodia. Thousands of students on college campuses across the nation protested that Nixon was preparing for full-scale war in Southeast Asia. Some student demonstrations became so violent that colleges called in the National Guard or state police.

On May 4, 1970, National Guard troops were on duty at Kent State University in Ohio. The troops were tired and tense after hours of duty. They opened fire on student protesters, killing four and wounding ten. On May 14 protests at Jackson State

College in Mississippi led to the killing of two students by state police.

The shootings outraged many Americans and led to more protests. Between 60,000 and 100,000 people marched in Washington, D.C., on May 9 to demand an end to the war. But in New York City, construction workers demonstrated in support of Nixon's policies. The war in Vietnam seemed to be dividing the nation in two.

In the congressional election campaigns of 1970, Republicans pictured antiwar protesters as a small but noisy minority. The "silent majority" of Americans, Republicans argued, favored the President's quest for "peace with honor." However, Republicans did not make major gains in the election. They remained a minority in the Senate and in the House of Representatives.

In December 1970 Congress voted to repeal the Gulf of Tonkin Resolution, which had been the legal basis for American military action in Vietnam. Nixon, however, believed that his position as commander in chief gave him the authority to continue military actions in Vietnam.

INVASION OF LAOS

In February 1971 the war once again spilled over Vietnam's borders. ARVN troops, supported by American planes, invaded Laos. Their goal was to cut off supplies on the Ho Chi Minh Trail, the main Viet Cong route from North Vietnam into South Vietnam. After heavy losses, ARVN troops returned to South Vietnam in March. North Vietnamese supplies, however, continued to reach the Viet Cong.

The invasion of Laos sparked new antiwar protests. Democrats in Congress even talked of cutting off funds for the war. But Nixon believed that the invasion was necessary to hasten the end of the war.

Confidence in Nixon's policies in Vietnam was shaken again in the summer of 1971. In June *The New York Times* began publishing classified, or secret, government documents that related the history of the United States' involvement in Vietnam. Known as the Pentagon Papers, the documents showed that the government had not always told the truth to the nation about American actions in Vietnam. The documents referred to the Johnson administration, but they added to the mood of doubt about Nixon's policies.

That summer Daniel Ellsberg, a former aide in the Department of Defense, was charged with stealing the classified documents and turning them over to *The New York Times*. The charges against him, however, were eventually dismissed.

A CEASE-FIRE IN VIETNAM

During 1971 President Nixon had continued air raids on the Viet Cong and the North Vietnamese in Vietnam, Cambodia, and Laos. At the same time, he also had reduced the number of American troops in South Vietnam by more than one half. Some 150,000 United States soldiers still served there at the end of the year. In 1972 Nixon continued to mix air raids against the Viet Cong and the North Vietnamese with the withdrawal of American troops from South Vietnam.

Late in March North Vietnamese troops launched a major offensive against South Vietnam. Nixon countered with intense bombing. American planes attacked the North Vietnamese capital of Hanoi and the port city of Haiphong. The air raids, however, did not stop the North Vietnamese advance.

In May Nixon expanded the American attack in order to cut off the flow of war supplies into North Vietnam from Russia and China. Bombing of military targets, railroads, and supply routes increased. In addition, American and South Vietnamese naval forces blockaded North Vietnam and mined North Vietnamese ports with explosives. These actions would end, Nixon promised, when the North Vietnamese accepted a cease-fire.

By October 1972, just before the presidential election, Henry Kissinger announced a breakthrough in the peace talks with the North Vietnamese. "Within a matter of weeks or less," he told American reporters, "an agreement will be signed." Nixon ordered a halt to American bombing of most areas of North Vietnam. No final agreements, however, were reached, and the peace talks broke off. In December American planes began around-the-clock bombing raids on Hanoi and Haiphong.

In January 1973 the bombing was halted and the talks resumed. On January 27 the United States, North Vietnam, South Vietnam, and the Viet Cong signed an "Agreement on Ending the War and Restoring Peace in Vietnam." The agreement called for an immediate cease-fire in Vietnam, the

A United States Marine helicopter hurriedly evacuated American civilians during Viet Cong fire on Tan Son Nhot Air Base, South Vietnam, in April 1975.

THE FALL OF SOUTH VIETNAM

The cease-fire did not bring peace to Vietnam. The South Vietnamese refused to let the Viet Cong take part in the government. The number of North Vietnamese troops increased in South Vietnam. By 1975 conflict between Communists and non-Communists in South Vietnam as well as Cambodia had increased.

On April 17 Communist forces captured the Cambodian capital of Phnom Penh (NAWM PEHN) and took control of Cambodia. Meanwhile, in South Vietnam, Viet Cong and North Vietnamese forces defeated ARVN troops and swept toward Saigon. Placing responsibility for the defeat of South Vietnam on the United States, President Thieu resigned on April 21. All American civilians in South Vietnam, as well as thousands of Vietnamese, were hastily evacuated by American helicopters by April 29. The next day, the government of South Vietnam surrendered.

withdrawal of all American forces, and the release of all Americans who were prisoners of war (POWs). An international council would supervise the cease-fire. In addition, the South Vietnamese and the Viet Cong would work together to organize elections to determine the government of South Vietnam.

By the end of March over 500 American POWs had been released, and the last American forces had been withdrawn from Vietnam. In this war—the nation's longest and most unpopular—some 46,000 American soldiers had died and 300,000 more had been wounded. Veterans from Vietnam returned to a nation bitterly divided by the war in which they had risked their lives.

Bitterness about the Vietnam War also pushed Congress into action. In November 1973 it passed the War Powers Act over Nixon's veto. The act provided that the president could not send American troops abroad or into situations where warfare seemed likely for more than 60 days unless Congress approved.

The return of American POWs was one happy phase of the bitter conflict in Vietnam. In this photograph, a newly released POW arrives at Travis Air Force Base in California.

The visit of President and Mrs. Nixon to China in February 1972 included parades, banquets, sightseeing, and conferences. Premier Chou En-lai agreed to Nixon's proposals for improved relations. The visit was a personal and political triumph for Nixon.

A CHANGING FOREIGN POLICY

Nixon was a staunch anti-Communist. Yet he and his foreign policy adviser, Henry Kissinger, brought to the nation a new foreign policy toward communism.

To Nixon and Kissinger, the world had changed dramatically since the 1950s. It was no longer divided into two great blocs, or groups, of nations—Communist and non-Communist. Instead, each group had begun to splinter.

As early as 1948, Yugoslavia had rejected the Soviet Union's leadership. It developed its own brand of communism and made its own foreign policy. The split in the Communist bloc widened with conflict between the Soviet Union and the People's Republic of China in the 1960s.

In the non-Communist world, France, under President Charles de Gaulle, had rejected American leadership in the 1960s. De Gaulle worked to create a Western Europe free of either American or Soviet influence. At his request, the North Atlantic Treaty Organization (NATO) moved its headquarters from France, and French troops were withdrawn from the alliance.

Newly developing nations in Asia, Africa, and Latin America—known as the **Third World**—also did not want to take sides with the Soviet Union or the United States. Many Third World nations accepted aid from the superpowers, but preferred to maintain neutrality.

Because of these changes in the world, Nixon and Kissinger worked to ease the cold war. "No one nation," Nixon later said, "should be the sole voice for a bloc of states. We will deal with all countries on the basis of specific issues . . . , not abstract theory."

A NEW CHINA POLICY

Nixon and Kissinger especially worked to improve relations with the People's Republic of China. The United States had never recognized the Communist government of China. Instead, Americans considered the Nationalist regime on Taiwan as China's legal government.

With American support, representatives of the Nationalist regime still were the only Chinese delegates seated in the United Nations Security Council. Such a policy, Nixon believed, was unwise. "We simply cannot afford to leave China forever outside the family of nations," he declared. "There is no place on this small planet for a billion of its potentially most able people to live in angry isolation."

Since the Korean War, the United States and the People's Republic of China had not traded with each other. In 1969 Nixon began to ease trade restrictions. Diplomatic talks between the nations, which had been postponed for two years, resumed in 1970. In 1971 a United States table-tennis team visited Peking (Beijing) and was warmly received.

That year the United States announced that it favored membership for Communist China in the UN Security Council. The United States also noted that Nationalist China had a right to be represented in the General Assembly. However, in October 1971 the General Assembly voted to admit Communist China, seat it in the Security Council, and expel Nationalist China from the UN.

In February 1972 Nixon became the first president of the United States to visit the People's Republic of China. For a week he conferred with Chinese leaders, attended banquets, and saw places of interest. At the end of his visit, Nixon and Premier Chou En-lai (JŌ en-LĪ) agreed on the need for economic, scientific, and cultural relations between their nations. In 1973 the United States and China established diplomatic offices in each other's nation.

DÉTENTE WITH RUSSIA

Nixon also worked to ease tensions with the Soviet Union. His efforts marked the beginning of an era of détente (day-TAHNT), a lessening of hostility between the United States and the Soviet Union.

The most important problem was the arms race, which had speeded up since the Cuban missile crisis in 1962. In 1969 American and Soviet leaders signed the Nuclear Nonproliferation Treaty. The treaty, which was also signed by 60 other nations, banned the spread of nuclear weapons. Nations with the weapons pledged not to give them to other nations. Nations without nuclear weapons pledged not to receive them. However, France and the People's Republic of China did not sign the treaty.

The United States and the Soviet Union also reached an agreement about Berlin, a trouble spot since World War II. In 1971 American, Soviet, British, and French delegates signed the Berlin Accord. This was an agreement to improve communications between the two sectors of the divided city. The

accord led to a 1972 agreement between the four powers that recognized the existence of two nations—East Germany and West Germany. Eventually the United States and East Germany established diplomatic relations.

In May 1972 Nixon also became the first American president to visit the Soviet Union. Nixon and Soviet leader Leonid I. Brezhnev (BREZH-nev) signed several agreements for Soviet-American cooperation in the fields of science, health, and space exploration. The leaders also signed two agreements to limit nuclear weapons.

Groundwork for the agreements had been laid in earlier Strategic Arms Limitation Talks (SALT) between the two nations. One SALT agreement limited the number of offensive weapons for each nation to those already under construction or in use. This agreement would run for five years. The other agreement limited each nation to two defensive, or antiballistic, missile systems.

As a result of Nixon's visit, the United States and the Soviet Union arranged a gigantic grain deal. The Soviets agreed to purchase grain for three years, beginning in 1972. The total price, at least $750 million, made the deal the largest grain-export order in United States history.

THE YOM KIPPUR WAR

The spirit of détente between the United States and the Soviet Union faced a severe test in the Middle East in 1973. Since the Six-Day War in 1967, the region had simmered with hatred and terrorism. Israel refused to return the Egyptian, Syrian, and Jordanian territory captured during the war. The Arab nations refused to recognize the existence of Israel and demanded revenge for their defeat.

On October 6, 1973, the Jewish holy day of Yom Kippur, Egyptian and Syrian troops launched a surprise attack on Israeli-held lands. Originally thrown into confusion by the attack, Israel recovered quickly. Israeli troops soon took the offensive, pushing into Syria and Egypt. The United States sent military supplies to Israel while the Soviet Union supplied Egypt.

By late October all three nations had agreed to a United Nations cease-fire. Scattered fighting, however, continued. The Soviet Union threatened to move troops into the Middle East to supervise the truce. Nixon responded by placing United States armed forces around the world on alert. Suddenly, détente seemed dead as the two powers confronted each other. Then the Soviet Union agreed to the creation of a UN peace-keeping force in the Middle East in which no big power would participate.

With the end of the Yom Kippur War, Henry Kissinger, who had been appointed secretary of state in 1973, worked for further easing of tensions in the Middle East. He began talks with Anwar el-Sadat (suh-DAHT), the new president of Egypt. Since the Six-Day War of 1967, diplomatic relations between the United States and Egypt had been broken.

Kissinger and Sadat agreed to renew diplomatic relations between the two nations. Their talks also led, in January 1974, to agreements between Egypt and Israel to withdraw troops from the positions that they held at the time of the cease-fire.

Later in 1974, Kissinger shuttled, or flew back and forth, between Middle Eastern capitals to promote peace between Israel and Syria. Because of his "shuttle diplomacy," the two nations also signed agreements to pull back their forces from battlefields.

THE ELECTION OF 1972

In August 1972 the Republican convention enthusiastically renominated Nixon for president and Spiro Agnew for vice-president. Republicans were confident of victory. Nixon's dramatic trips to China and the Soviet Union had sent his popularity soaring. Also, by October, Kissinger announced a breakthrough in the peace talks between the United States and the North Vietnamese.

The Democrats, in contrast, did not have a clear-cut choice for president. Senator George McGovern based his campaign for the nomination upon opposition to the Vietnam War. He promised that if elected he would stop the bombing, end the war, and bring United States troops home within ninety days.

Many Democrats battled McGovern for the nomination. Senator Hubert Humphrey of Minnesota, Senator Edmund Muskie of Maine, Governor George Wallace of Alabama, Congresswoman Shirley Chisholm of New York, and others all entered the primaries. Since 1968 the party had reformed its nominating procedures. There were

Israeli prime minister Golda Meir enjoyed an informal talk with Secretary of State Henry Kissinger during a "shuttle diplomacy" visit. Coming to the United States as a refugee from Russia in 1906, Mrs. Meir lived here until she went to Palestine in 1921.

more primaries, and most of them allowed several candidates to gain delegates. Past primaries generally had been "winner-take-all" contests.

By the time of the Democratic convention in July, McGovern had a commanding majority of delegates. He was nominated on the first ballot. As his running mate he chose Senator Thomas F. Eagleton of Missouri.

A few weeks later, reporters discovered that Eagleton had been treated in the past for mental health problems. At first McGovern firmly supported his running mate. But public concern over Eagleton's health grew. Late in July McGovern asked Eagleton to withdraw from the ticket. Then the Democrats chose R. Sargent Shriver, former director of the Peace Corps, to run with McGovern. The Democratic campaign, however, never recovered from its chaotic start.

In the November election, Nixon received 47 million votes, compared to McGovern's 29 million. The electoral vote was overwhelmingly for Nixon, 520 to 17. The sweeping Republican victory, however, did not extend to Congress. The Republicans failed to make major gains in the House of Representatives and in the Senate. The Democrats still controlled Congress.

SECTION REVIEW

1. Identify the following: Henry A. Kissinger, Haiphong, the War Powers Act, Phnom Penh, Chou En-Lai, Anwar el-Sadat.

2. Define the following: "Vietnamization," Ho Chi Minh Trail, détente, "shuttle diplomacy."

3. (a) What four parties met in formal peace talks about Vietnam in 1972? (b) What two parties met in secret peace talks?

4. How were the shootings at Kent State University linked to the invasion of Cambodia?

5. (a) List the provisions of the peace agreement for Vietnam. (b) For what reasons did the agreement fail?

6. How did Chinese representation in the United Nations change in 1971?

7. What was the purpose of the Berlin Accord?

8. How did the Soviet Union threaten the truce after the Yom Kippur War?

YEARS OF DIVISION

READ TO FIND OUT

— **how American astronauts landed on the moon.**

— **how young people revolted against American values.**

— **how the Senate opposed Nixon's court appointments.**

— **what happened to the value of the dollar.**

— **how Nixon fought stagflation and energy problems.**

— **how the Watergate burglary led to the resignation of President Nixon.**

The war in Vietnam divided Americans into hawks and doves, but other issues also created divisions. Concerns about the environment, energy, inflation, and government actions all caused conflicts.

Yet the nation enjoyed a sense of unity early in Nixon's first term. Two American astronauts became the first persons to land on the moon. Their landing and safe return home renewed Americans' pride in their nation's leadership, scientific knowledge, and daring. The mission also fulfilled President Kennedy's goal of "landing a man on the moon and returning him safely to earth" by the end of the decade.

MOON LANDINGS

On July 20, 1969, astronauts Neil A. Armstrong and Edwin E. Aldrin, Jr., left their spacecraft in orbit around the moon and descended to the moon's surface in the lunar module *Eagle*. As they touched down, the astronauts radioed back to the National Aeronautics and Space Agency (NASA), "The *Eagle* has landed."

At the NASA control center, scientists and technicians cheered. They cheered again when they received Armstrong's words as he jumped down from the *Eagle*'s ladder onto the moon's surface. "That's one small step for a man, one giant leap for mankind."

Neil A. Armstrong used a lunar surface camera to photograph fellow astronaut Edwin E. Aldrin, Jr. Aldrin is pictured walking near the lunar module on July 20, 1969.

News of the achievement flashed across the nation. Armstrong and Aldrin had carried television cameras to the moon to transmit pictures to NASA. Broadcast on television, the pictures gave Americans a close-up view of the moon.

Years of preparation had led to the moon landing. In 1966 and 1967 NASA completed 12 missions that developed techniques of joining two space vehicles in flight. Such techniques were needed in the Apollo program, which was directed toward a landing on the moon.

When Armstrong and Aldrin left the moon's surface, they had to meet with their orbiting space-craft, *Columbia*, piloted by Michael Collins. After the two were aboard, Collins fired the *Columbia*'s main engine to leave the moon's orbit and to return to earth.

The Apollo program achieved five other moon landings in the next four years. In 1975, a year of détente, American and Soviet astronauts worked together to complete the Apollo-Soyuz Test Project. Two spacecraft, one from each nation, linked in space during the mission.

Along with missions into space, NASA programs benefited people on earth. NASA research led to improved computers, materials that insulated homes, and devices that generated energy from the sun. NASA photographs of earth produced data about weather patterns and landforms. Communication satellites put into orbit by NASA rockets helped to send information around the world.

However, the space programs were touched by controversy. Their cost—$25 billion—seemed too high to people who wanted the government to spend more on social programs.

THE COUNTERCULTURE

About a month after Armstrong and Aldrin landed on the moon, some 400,000 young people gathered near Woodstock, New York. They took part in a three-day outdoor festival of rock music. The event quickly became a symbol of the "counterculture," the culture of a group of young people in revolt against American values.

People who joined the counterculture believed that American life was dominated by wealth and corruption. They rejected the "Establishment," the large corporations and other major institutions in the United States. The Establishment, they claimed, was to blame for poverty, racial discrimination, and war.

Some of the people of the counterculture became hippies. The hippies of the 1960s wore their hair long, tried drugs, and listened to rock music. Some hippies moved to rural areas and lived off the land as their pioneer ancestors might have lived. Many established communes, where all shared the work and the rewards.

Other members of the counterculture stressed politics. They wanted to change the United States through political action. Many students worked to change first colleges and universities, which they

In dress and occupation, these young people of the counterculture identified with the pioneer spirit. The scarecrow was a type of folk art decoration.

considered part of the Establishment. Students at Columbia University in New York sought more power over school policies by taking over school buildings in 1968. Struggles between the students and police led to the injury of over a hundred people.

Conflicts like the one at Columbia occurred at schools across the nation as students protested school policies, the war in Vietnam, and discrimination against blacks. A number of radical students hoped for revolution, and some took part in terrorist bombings against the Establishment.

After 1969 the counterculture slowly lost momentum. But while it lasted it produced a deep division between the young and the old in the United States. Americans who grew up in the Great Depression and who made sacrifices in World War II were perplexed and angered by the attitudes of hippies and the actions of radical students.

In 1971 Congress proposed the Twenty-sixth Amendment, lowering the voting age to eighteen in all elections. The states quickly ratified the amendment. It answered young people's charge that if eighteen-year-olds were old enough to die in Vietnam, they also should be old enough to vote.

COURT APPOINTMENTS

In 1969 Earl Warren retired as Chief Justice of the Supreme Court. President Nixon named Warren E. Burger to replace him. Burger, a judge from Minnesota, was known as a strict constructionist, a person who favored a conservative interpretation of the Constitution. Nixon counted on him to steer the Court away from the more liberal interpretations encouraged by Warren, especially regarding law enforcement.

The Senate confirmed Burger's nomination in June. Then, in August, Nixon had the opportunity to name another judge to serve on the Supreme Court. Judge Clement F. Haynsworth, Jr., of South Carolina also was a strict constructionist. However, Senate investigators disclosed that Haynsworth had ruled in cases involving corporations in which he held stock. Senators questioned his participation in cases with such a conflict of interest. In November the Senate voted against Haynsworth's nomination.

Nixon quickly named another strict constructionist, Judge G. Harrold Carswell of Florida. Many senators opposed the nomination because of Carswell's unimpressive record and his views toward blacks. In April 1970 the Senate also rejected Carswell.

Nixon attacked the Senate, claiming that Haynsworth and Carswell were rejected because they were strict constructionists and southerners. Finally the President nominated Judge Harry A. Blackmun, another judge from Minnesota. The Senate quickly confirmed this nomination. The conflict, however, left bitter feelings between Nixon and many Senate leaders.

THE DECLINE OF THE DOLLAR

Just as he inherited the war in Vietnam, Nixon also inherited economic problems linked to the war. One problem was the United States **balance of pay-**

ments—the difference between the amount that a nation pays for the goods and services that it imports and the amount that it receives for the goods and services it exports. The nation was paying out more to other nations than it was taking in. These dollars paid for imports, for foreign aid and investments, and for aid to South Vietnam.

In most years since 1950 the nation had a small deficit, or shortage, in its balance of payments. The deficit came mainly from spending for military programs and foreign aid. In terms of trade, the nation enjoyed a surplus year after year, as the dollars received for exports exceeded the dollars paid out for imports. To finance the deficit in the total balance of payments, the United States used its gold reserves.

The United States gold reserves had increased by some $4 billion in the years immediately following World War II. However, they dropped from about $25 billion in 1945 to about $23 billion in 1950. By 1960 the United States gold reserves had been reduced to below $18 billion.

In 1972 the United States balance of payments fell sharply. Some $3 billion was spent for the war in Vietnam. Billions of dollars also flowed out to pay for foreign trade. Americans were buying large numbers of cars, television sets, and other goods made overseas because these were less expensive than American-made products. United States exports were not keeping pace with imports.

Since World War II, foreign nations had set the value of their currency in terms of the United States dollar. The dollar had been given a fixed value in gold, and the United States had agreed to buy all dollars offered to it by foreign governments at that value. Now, with excessive spending in the United States, confidence in the value of the dollar began to decline. To protect their holdings, foreign bankers rushed to exchange their dollars for gold. By the middle of 1971 the United States reserves of gold had fallen to $10.5 billion.

In August 1971 Nixon stopped the exchange of dollars for gold. He also announced a 10 percent reduction in foreign aid and a 10 percent surcharge, or extra charge, on imports. These steps, he hoped, would reduce the deficits in the United States balance of payments. The dollar continued to be a major currency in international trade. It did not, however, regain its place as the single standard by which other currencies were judged.

FIGHTING INFLATION

Nixon also revealed bold plans to fight inflation. Since the United States had sent combat troops to Vietnam in 1965, government spending had sharply increased. As federal spending rose, prices soared and the dollar fell in value.

During his first term, Nixon had tried gradual methods to reduce the rate of inflation. The Federal Reserve Board's policies had raised interest rates, making business loans more expensive. This, Nixon hoped, would decrease the amount of money in circulation. In addition, Nixon cut federal spending in order to slow down the economy.

These methods, however, did little to stop inflation, and they contributed to rising unemployment. From 1966 to 1969, the rate of unemployment had been less than 4 percent. Late in 1970, it climbed to 6 percent.

Inflation hurt numerous wage earners. Workers earned more money than ever in 1970. However, they made no gains in purchasing power because prices were rising as fast as wages. Both workers and employers were caught in an inflationary spiral. After a 71-day strike in 1970, General Motors workers won a 20 percent pay increase over 3 years. To cover the increase, General Motors raised the price of cars. Wages and prices leapfrogged as people struggled to stay ahead. The savings of retired people shrank in value as the purchasing power of each dollar declined.

In August 1971 Nixon announced Phase I of his fight against inflation. He declared a 90-day freeze on wages, prices, and rents. In November he began Phase II—a full year of wage and price controls. The Cost of Living Council was set up to rule on pay raises and price increases. The controls were the first to be imposed in peacetime in the United States. However, they did not cover the prices of all goods. Food costs kept rising, and inflation continued.

In theory, continuing inflation should have meant low levels of unemployment. But unemployment and prices rose together after 1972. The combination of inflation and a stagnant economy offering too few jobs became known as **stagflation**. Nixon tried other wage-price plans, but they also failed.

During 1973 the economy suffered new inflationary pressures. Foreign oil became both scarce and costly. This change caused new tensions and divisions in the United States.

THE OIL EMBARGO

In October 1973 Egypt and Syria attacked Israel, setting off the Yom Kippur War. The United States announced that it would send military supplies to Israel. In response, Arab nations friendly to Egypt and Syria announced that they would halt all oil sales to the United States. Until then the United States had been receiving about a million barrels of oil per day from the Arab nations.

Suddenly heating oil and gasoline became scarce. Americans worried about obtaining enough oil to heat their homes during the winter. Meanwhile they waited in long lines to buy gasoline at local stations.

Early in November, President Nixon called for action against the energy crisis. He asked Congress to lower the speed limit for cars in order to save gasoline. He also asked Congress to approve the construction of a pipeline from Alaska's North Slope, where oil had been discovered in 1968, to the Gulf of Alaska. Construction of the pipeline had been delayed by controversy over its effect on the environment. Finally, Nixon requested greater energy research so that "by the end of this decade we will have developed the potential to meet our own energy needs."

Congress approved a national speed limit for cars of 55 miles (88.5 kilometers) per hour. Congress also approved construction of the Alaska pipeline.

Completed in 1977, it could carry 2 million barrels of crude oil per day from Alaska's oil fields to the Gulf of Alaska. From there the oil was shipped to West Coast refineries.

In the spring of 1974 the Arab nations ended their oil embargo. By summer there were no more lines of cars at gasoline stations. The energy crisis, however, was far from over.

THE ENERGY CRISIS

To energy analysts, the crisis of 1973 was part of a larger pattern. The United States was growing more and more dependent on foreign oil. Imports had grown from about 23 percent of American energy needs in 1970 to 36 percent in 1973. Domestic oil production, meanwhile, was declining. In an emergency, the United States could no longer fill an "energy gap" by increasing its own production.

Other fuels could not easily supply the nation's energy needs. Natural gas was a clean-burning energy source, but its supply appeared limited. Consumption in 1973 was running at twice the rate of new discoveries. Coal was abundant, but it supplied less than 20 percent of the nation's energy in 1973. Increased mining and use of coal were likely to pose environmental problems.

Nuclear power remained a minor energy source, accounting for only 5 percent of all electricity generated in 1973. Solar power—power from the sun—

Beginning at Pump Station 1 in Prudhoe Bay on Alaska's Arctic coast, the pipeline carries oil about 800 miles (1,300 kilometers) across the state. The ice-free port of Valdez on the south central coast is the southern terminal.

OPEC 1970

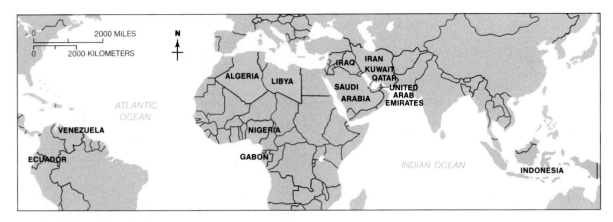

Although OPEC nations produce a significant percentage of the world's crude oil, the leading producer is the Soviet Union. The United States ranks third behind Saudi Arabia. China, Mexico Great Britain, and Canada also produce large quantities of petroleum.

and synthetic, or chemical, fuels seemed unlikely to have a major impact on energy needs in the immediate future. That left oil, and oil was increasingly costly.

The rising cost of oil resulted from a great shift in power in the oil industry in the Middle East. During the postwar years, trading in Middle Eastern oil was controlled by European and American oil companies. They kept the price of oil close to $1.80 per barrel in the 1960s.

Meanwhile major oil-exporting nations worked to gain more power over setting prices. In 1960 five nations—Venezuela, Iraq, Iran, Kuwait, and Saudi Arabia—formed the Organization of Petroleum Exporting Countries (OPEC). Seven other nations joined OPEC in the 1960s, including Libya, Ecuador, and Nigeria.

OPEC nations obtained the technical knowledge to control their own oil operations. In 1970 Libya showed that the price of oil per barrel could be forced up over $2.00. In 1973 OPEC raised the price from $3.01 to $5.12 and then to $11.65. By the end of the decade the price of a barrel of oil exceeded $20.00. That increase contributed to soaring inflation in the United States.

THE WATERGATE BURGLARY

During 1972 Nixon made historic trips to China and to the Soviet Union. He ordered the last American combat troops in South Vietnam to return home. He won a sweeping victory over George McGovern in the presidential election. These might have been the most memorable events of his presidency if five burglars had not been caught in a Washington, D.C., building complex called Watergate.

In 1972 the Democratic National Committee rented offices in Watergate. At 2:30 a.m. on June 17 the burglars were arrested in the offices. They carried a walkie-talkie, lock picks, and devices for electronic eavesdropping. The burglars appeared to be political spies. The question was, Who had planned the burglary?

Ronald L. Ziegler, the White House press secretary, called the break-in a "third-rate burglary." President Nixon stated that no one in the administration was involved. However, two reporters for the *Washington Post,* Bob Woodward and Carl Bernstein, pursued the issue of political spying. They found evidence that John Mitchell, recently retired as Nixon's attorney general, had controlled a fund to pay for spying against the Democrats. Despite their reporting, the Watergate break-in remained a puzzling but minor story as the year ended.

Early in 1973 the question of Watergate burst into the headlines and stayed there. The five Watergate burglars were tried and convicted. E. Howard Hunt, Jr., and G. Gordon Liddy, accused of directing the crime, also were tried and convicted. Hunt had been a White House consultant. Liddy had served in 1972 as a lawyer for the Committee to Reelect the President (CRP).

Late in March the trial judge, John J. Sirica, sentenced all seven defendants to prison. At the same time he read a letter from one of the burglars, James W. McCord. The letter charged that high officials had put pressure on the defendants to plead guilty and to keep silent. Suddenly the "third-rate burglary" was becoming a national scandal.

THE WATERGATE COVER-UP

In the middle of April Nixon announced that a special White House investigation of the Watergate break-in was underway. Later that month he appeared on television to announce the resignations of two of his closest aides, H.R. Haldeman and John Ehrlichman, and of Attorney General Richard Kleindienst. Nixon also announced the firing of his presidential counsel, John W. Dean III.

In May Nixon admitted that his staff had been involved in trying to conceal the truth about the Watergate break-in, but he denied that he had been involved in any way in the cover-up. That month, however, the Senate established the Select Committee on Presidential Campaign Activities to investigate the Watergate burglary and cover-up. The committee, made up of seven senators, was chaired by Senator Sam J. Ervin, Jr., of North Carolina.

For three months Ervin's committee held televised hearings. Americans across the nation watched in fascination as witnesses unraveled the threads of Watergate. One witness identified John Mitchell as a planner of the break-in. John Dean then testified about the cover-up. He claimed that Mitchell, Haldeman, Ehrlichman, and even the President were involved.

Dean also revealed the existence of a White House "Enemies List." It included the names of politicians, journalists, and others who opposed the Nixon administration and who might be the target of harassment. In further testimony Dean described the "Plumbers," a special group that used wiretaps and other illegal activities against opponents of the administration. Meanwhile, in other investigations, the Committee to Reelect the President was charged with forcing large corporations to make contributions to the Republican presidential campaign.

In his testimony, Dean had charged that the President was involved in the cover-up of the Watergate break-in. But the Senate committee needed evidence to confirm or deny those charges. In July

John W. Dean III, former presidential counsel, was the chief witness against Nixon in the Watergate hearings. He gave over four full days of detailed testimony.

1973 Americans learned that the evidence might be at hand. Alexander Butterfield, an assistant to the President, revealed that Nixon's office in the White House contained a tape-recording system. Since early 1971, all of the President's conversations in the Oval Office had been recorded.

THE STRUGGLE FOR THE TAPES

Soon after Attorney General Kleindienst resigned, Nixon had named Elliot L. Richardson to replace him. Nixon told the new attorney general to appoint a special prosecutor to look into the evidence about Watergate. In May Richardson chose Archibald Cox, a Harvard law professor, to serve as special prosecutor.

When Cox learned about the tapes, he obtained a *subpoena*, a written legal order, from Judge John Sirica. The subpoena instructed Nixon to turn over to the special prosecutor the tapes that related to the Watergate burglary and cover-up. Nixon, however, refused to release the tapes. He claimed that as president he had a constitutional right to keep them private.

Despite Nixon's claim to executive privilege, the United States Court of Appeals ruled in October 1973 that he must release the tapes. Nixon still refused, but he offered Cox a compromise. Nixon promised to supply Cox with written summaries of the tapes, with the understanding that Cox would no longer try to obtain the tapes by legal action.

Cox rejected the compromise. The summaries, he knew, would be unacceptable as court evidence. On October 20 Nixon ordered Attorney General Elliot Richardson to fire Cox. Richardson resigned rather than carry out the President's order. So did Deputy Attorney General William D. Ruckelshaus. Finally the next ranking official fired Cox. The resignations and firing quickly became known as the "Saturday Night Massacre."

THE RESIGNATION OF AGNEW

In a separate chain of events, Vice-President Agnew also was under attack. Federal investigators charged that Agnew, while governor of Maryland and vice-president, had accepted bribes from contractors in return for helping them get state government work.

At first Agnew condemned the charges as lies. Then he made an agreement with the Department of Justice. On October 10, 1973, Agnew resigned as vice-president. A few hours later he pleaded "no contest" to a single charge of cheating the government of over $13,000 on his federal income tax payment for 1967. Federal prosecutors dropped other charges against him. Agnew's plea, the judge declared, was "the full equivalent of a plea of guilty." Agnew was fined $10,000 and sentenced to three years of unsupervised probation.*

The Twenty-fifth Amendment, ratified in 1967, set up procedures for choosing the new president or vice-president in case of resignation, disability, or death. Acting under the amendment, Nixon named Representative Gerald R. Ford of Michigan as the new vice-president. Congress quickly approved the nomination.

RESIGNATION OF THE PRESIDENT

The Saturday Night Massacre in October 1973 triggered widespread outrage against Nixon. Sixteen resolutions were introduced in the House of Representatives to impeach, or accuse, the Presi-

dent of "high crimes and misdemeanors." Later that month the House Judiciary Committee, chaired by Peter Rodino of New Jersey, began an investigation of the President's actions. If the House voted to impeach, then the case would be tried in the Senate. If the Senate voted to convict, then the President would be removed from office.

Because of the pressure, Nixon appointed Leon Jaworski, a Texas lawyer, as the new special prosecutor. Nixon also released some, but not all, of the subpoenaed tapes to Judge John Sirica. However, Nixon's lawyers advised the court that two of the tapes demanded by court order had never existed. In addition, investigators found an 18-minute erasure on one of the submitted tapes. The erasure, experts agreed, seemed to be deliberate.

The crisis surrounding the White House worsened in 1974. In March a grand jury* finished its investigation of Watergate. The jury found sufficient evidence to indict, or charge, John Mitchell, John Ehrlichman, H. R. Haldeman, and four other Nixon aides for conspiring to cover up the Watergate break-in. The grand jury named the President a party to the conspiracy, but did not indict him.

In April Special Prosecutor Leon Jaworski requested additional tapes from Nixon regarding the Watergate cover-up. The President refused to provide them, but he released over 1,200 pages of edited transcripts of the tapes. Jaworski, however, insisted on receiving the original tapes. Again, Nixon refused. Jaworski then sued the President. In July 1974 the Supreme Court ordered Nixon to give Jaworski the tapes that he sought. The Court ruled unanimously that the President could not withhold evidence in a criminal case.

Worse was to come for the President. That same month the House Judiciary Committee adopted three articles of impeachment against him. The first article charged that the President had obstructed, or blocked, the investigation of the Watergate break-in. The other articles charged that he had misused presidential powers and that he had illegally withheld evidence from the Senate Judiciary Committee.

Nixon's defenders argued that the President had not committed an impeachable offense. Then,

---

* probation: the suspension of sentence of a person convicted but not imprisoned, on condition of continued good behavior.

* grand jury: a jury of from 6 to 23 persons chosen to investigate accusations of crime and to decide whether there is enough evidence for a court trial.

Nixon released the tapes that he had guarded for so long. They revealed that he had known about the Watergate burglary on June 23, 1972, less than a week after it had happened. The tapes also revealed that he had ordered a halt to an investigation by the FBI. Nixon had been part of the cover-up all along. With these tapes, the President's support in Congress vanished. Impeachment by the House and conviction by the Senate seemed certain.

On August 8, 1974, President Nixon announced his resignation, effective the next day. He was the first president of the United States to resign from office.

REFLECTIONS ON WATERGATE

One of Nixon's favorite domestic programs was *revenue sharing*. Approved in 1972, the program gave federal tax dollars to state and local governments to use as they saw fit, without control from Washington. Nixon hoped that the program would spread power among more local governments.

In the presidency, however, Nixon preferred to concentrate power. This was not a new trend. Since the enactment of the New Deal in the 1930s, the size and power of the executive branch of government had been growing. Massive depression and war had encouraged this change.

Nixon's resignation, a first in United States history, made huge headlines in the newspapers. These editions appeared on August 10, 1974, the day after his resignation.

However, Nixon's actions, even before Watergate, made some Americans fear that the system of checks and balances between government branches was in jeopardy. Nixon's White House Staff was over two-and-one-half times larger than the staff with which Roosevelt fought World War II. Nixon's closest advisers were members of this staff. Unlike cabinet members, they did not have to be confirmed by the Senate. In addition, Nixon defied congressional authority. When Congress appropriated money for programs that he opposed, Nixon *impounded,* or held, the money, refusing to spend it.

With Watergate, the Nixon administration had misused presidential power. More important, it had tried to set itself above the law. Congress and the Supreme Court moved forcefully to challenge this attempt. The checks and balances of the Constitution worked, and the American system of government weathered the crisis.

SECTION REVIEW

1. Identify the following: Clement F. Haynsworth, Jr., OPEC, CRP, John J. Sirica, Sam J. Ervin, Jr., Elliot L. Richardson, Archibald Cox, Leon Jaworski.

2. Define the following: counterculture, balance of payments, stagflation, subpoena.

3. Name the three astronauts involved in the first moon landing.

4. What was the "Establishment," in the view of the counterculture?

5. Why did Nixon choose strict constructionists for the Supreme Court?

6. (a) What did foreign nations do when they lost faith in the dollar? (b) What did Nixon do in response?

7. How did the increase in the price of oil affect inflation in the United States?

8. (a) What was the purpose of the Watergate burglary? (b) How did Nixon become involved in the burglary?

9. What happened in the "Saturday Night Massacre?"

10. (a) How did Leon Jaworski force Nixon to surrender certain tapes? (b) Why did these tapes make Nixon's impeachment and conviction almost certain?

REBUILDING PUBLIC CONFIDENCE

READ TO FIND OUT

— **how Ford's first actions led to new controversies.**

— **how Congress acted to prevent abuses of presidential power.**

— **what steps Ford took to reduce inflation.**

— **what trends affected civil rights.**

— **how Ford continued Nixon's foreign policies.**

— **what factors helped Carter win the presidency.**

In his last hours as president, Richard M. Nixon spoke to members of his cabinet and his staff. Then he left the White House for his home in San Clemente, California. Some ninety minutes later, Vice-President Gerald R. Ford was sworn in as the thirty-eighth president of the United States. He was the first president who had not been elected either as president or vice-president.

Ford faced the large task of rebuilding the nation's confidence in the presidency. He promised "openness and candor" in his administration. "Our long national nightmare is over," he declared.

The new president's reputation seemed to make him the right person to restore confidence. For 25 years Ford had served in the House of Representatives, becoming Republican minority leader* in 1965. He had earned his colleagues' respect by his openness, hard work, and honesty.

Late in August 1974 Ford nominated Nelson A. Rockefeller to be vice-president. Congress carefully investigated Rockefeller, then confirmed his nomination. A four-term governor of New York, Rockefeller was well known in national politics. His appointment added to public confidence in the Ford administration.

---

*minority leader: leader of the party in the minority, or with the smaller number of votes, in the House of Representatives or Senate.

OFFERS OF FORGIVENESS

Soon, however, confidence in the new administration dropped sharply. On September 8, 1974, President Ford gave Nixon "a full, free and absolute pardon for all offenses he committed or may have committed while in office." Nixon, declared Ford, had "suffered enough and will continue to suffer no matter what I do."

Many Americans thought that the pardon was too generous. People also questioned the justice of a pardon for Nixon when his aides were facing trial for their roles in Watergate. In 1975 Haldeman, Ehrlichman, and Mitchell would be convicted of conspiracy, obstruction of justice, and perjury, or telling lies under oath.

To explain the pardon, Ford appeared before a subcommittee of the House of Representatives. He denied that the pardon had been arranged before Nixon resigned. In testimony in October, Ford declared that the pardon came "out of my concern to serve the best interests of my country."

Soon after pardoning Nixon, Ford took another controversial step. He offered amnesty, or a pardon, to thousands of Americans who had evaded the draft by fleeing the country or who had deserted their military units during the war in Vietnam. The amnesty was conditional. Americans who accepted it would have to spend up to two years working in an alternative government service, such as hospitals.

President Ford was eager to restore confidence in the executive office. He had inherited a tangle of domestic problems, starting with a disillusioned citizenry.

Ford hoped that his amnesty program would heal national divisions over the Vietnam War. Instead, it sharpened them. Many Americans who had fought in the war or who had lost loved ones in Vietnam criticized Ford for welcoming back Americans who had refused to fight for their country.

Draft resisters and deserters upheld their right to refuse to fight in a war that they could not, in conscience, support. Amnesty, they argued, should not be conditional upon alternative government service, and few accepted Ford's offer.

Public reaction to Watergate and the pardon of Nixon remained strong. In the 1974 congressional elections, Democrats gained 43 seats in the House of Representatives and 3 in the Senate.

CHANGES IN GOVERNMENT

Even before the elections, Congress acted to curb presidential power. In 1973 Nixon had tried to control federal spending by impounding billions of dollars assigned by Congress to the departments of transportation, defense, and agriculture.

In July 1974 Congress passed the Congressional Budget and Impoundment Act. The act improved congressional budget-making procedures and gave Congress greater control over federal spending. It also set up ways to block a president from impounding funds appropriated by Congress.

In October Congress passed the Campaign Reform Act of 1974. In 1972, the Committee to Reelect the President had misused campaign funds. The Campaign Reform Act was designed to prevent such abuses. The act set limits on individual contributions to a single election campaign. The act also called for the thorough disclosure of sources and uses of campaign money.

Shortly after the elections, Congress passed the Freedom of Information Act of 1974. It strengthened a 1966 law that required federal government agencies to make available to citizens upon request documents and records. In this way, Congress hoped to reverse the trend under Johnson and Nixon toward secrecy in government. The 1974 act, passed over Ford's veto, gave the public greater access to records kept by the government.

Faced with a heavily Democratic Congress, Ford often resorted to the veto. In two and a half years, he vetoed nearly fifty bills. Congress overrode his veto twelve times.

RISING INFLATION

Besides facing opposition in Congress, Ford faced grim economic news. Inflation reached double-digit figures in 1974, exceeding 12 percent. Normally, high inflation meant a booming economy, with low unemployment. But the nation still was caught in stagflation—a combination of high inflation and a stagnant economy. The unemployment rate began to rise rapidly.

In October 1974 the President began a program designed to end inflation. Called WIN (Whip Inflation Now), the program included reduced federal spending, high interest rates, and temporary tax increases on corporate incomes.

Ford's program did not seem to reduce inflation. But it may have made the economy even more stagnant. In November 1974 auto makers announced production cutbacks and massive layoffs. Unemployment rose above 7 percent by the end of the year. Energy costs were increasing. So were interest rates, which meant that fewer Americans could afford to buy homes.

Ford worked to bring about economic recovery. In March 1975 he signed a bill to reduce individual and business taxes by more than $22 billion. Thus, the administration argued, Americans would have more money to invest in business. This would stimulate the economy. From that point the economy did begin a slow recovery, and inflation dipped to less than 10 percent.

Ford also promised to veto bills that he considered too costly. He vetoed a $2 billion health-care bill, but Congress overrode his veto in July. In October he promised to veto "any bill that has as its purpose a federal bailout of New York City." At the time, the city was unable to borrow money. It also was close to defaulting, or failing to make payment, on money previously borrowed. Nonetheless, Congress authorized a federal loan to the city in December.

EXPANDING CIVIL RIGHTS

As always, the percentage of unemployment among black Americans was far higher than the overall percentage. Some 15 percent of black workers could not find jobs in 1975.

In politics, however, blacks could see positive changes. Voter registration among blacks in the

ELIZABETH LOZA NEWBY
A MIGRANT WITH HOPE

For most of Elizabeth Loza Newby's childhood, home was the back of an old army truck. She and her family were migrant farm workers, harvesting crops across the United States. Traveling and living in their truck, they picked cotton in Texas, grapes and lettuce in California, and sugar beets in Nebraska. Like many Mexican American migrants, her family was poor and spoke little English. Their clothes were made of old flour sacks. Often they did not have enough to eat.

When she was seven, Newby encountered prejudice for the first time. Her best friend at a new school was the blonde daughter of the town mayor. "Both of us were totally unaware of our differences," she remembered. Then one day her friend tearfully explained that her father would not let her play with Newby again, because she was "different."

Newby was stunned. Luckily a kind teacher saw what had happened and took her aside. She helped her understand prejudice. "People, all people, fear the unknown," the teacher explained. "By the time she had finished talking," Newby remembered, "I felt I was ready to meet whatever might come."

In 1960, when she was fourteen, her father found a permanent job as a farmhand in Kansas. Despite many obstacles, Newby finished high school, went on to college, and decided to become a writer. In her first book, *A Migrant with Hope*, she described her own harsh childhood and the problems of migrant

Education in schools like this one in Colorado provided the children of migrant workers an opportunity to escape the hardships of their parents' lives.

life. Yet her story was one of hope. She had escaped the cycle of poverty through education, and she believed that it was "the basic answer" for others as well.

Newby hoped that her book would convince people to improve schooling, housing, and working conditions for migrants. "I must seek deliverance for others still traveling the harvest circuit," she wrote. "I cannot escape my responsibility to my people."

South doubled in the 1960s. In 1972, when Nixon won reelection, two southern blacks won seats in the House of Representatives. Andrew Young of Georgia and Barbara Jordan of Texas became the first black representatives from the South since Reconstruction.

In 1975 Congress extended the Voting Rights Act of 1965 for seven years. The original act authorized federal officials to register eligible voters in states where they faced discrimination on the basis of race. The 1975 act was expanded to cover Hispanic Americans, Asian Americans, Indians, and Alaskan natives.

Women working for pay in the 1970s found, as in the past, very few jobs offering high salaries. The average working woman in 1975 made only 57 percent of the pay of the average working man. Some women hoped to correct this inequality with the aid of the Equal Rights Amendment (ERA). Proposed by Congress in 1972, the amendment forbade discrimination on the basis of sex.

To become law, the Equal Rights Amendment needed to be ratified by 38 states. However, the amendment sparked sharp controversy. Some opponents believed that women already had equal rights under the Constitution. Others feared that

Andrew Young visited Nigeria in 1977 while he was United States ambassador to the UN.

Barbara Jordan served in the Texas senate for six years prior to moving to Washington, D.C.

the amendment would make women subject to the military draft or would change in other ways the woman's traditional role in the United States.

DIPLOMACY IN ASIA

President Ford made some changes in the cabinet that he inherited from Nixon. However, Henry Kissinger agreed to stay as secretary of state. Together, Ford and Kissinger continued the foreign policy developed during the Nixon administration.

No American combat troops remained in Vietnam in 1974. However, the United States spent more than $3 billion to support South Vietnam in its continuing struggle against the Viet Cong and the North Vietnamese. Then, in April 1975, after a series of defeats, the South Vietnamese government surrendered. Communist forces marched into Saigon and renamed it Ho Chi Minh City. The surrender of South Vietnam came at almost the same time as the fall of the pro-Western government in Cambodia to Communist forces. In Cambodia, too, Americans were evacuated by helicopter as Communist-led soldiers took over.

Less than a month after the fall of Cambodia, the United States merchant ship *Mayaguez* was seized by Cambodian forces in the Gulf of Siam. President Ford ordered quick military action to free the ship. Marines supported by bombers rescued the *Mayaguez* and its crew of 39. However, 41 American lives were lost as a result of the operation.

In its policy toward China, the Ford administration also followed the policy of the Nixon administration. Accompanied by Secretary of State Henry Kissinger, President Ford visited China late in 1975. The trip was a further step in normalizing relations between the United States and China.

CONTINUING DÉTENTE

The United States and the Soviet Union continued to find areas of agreement during Ford's presidency. Late in 1974 the President traveled to Russia to confer with Communist Party Secretary Leonid Brezhnev. The two leaders signed an arms agreement limiting the total number of offensive nuclear weapons that each nation could have.

In the summer of 1975 leaders from the United States, the Soviet Union, Canada, and 33 other nations met in Helsinki, Finland, and signed the Helsinki Accords. The nations agreed to find peaceful ways to settle disputes in Europe. They also endorsed international cooperation and respect for human rights. Later in 1975 the two superpowers signed a grain agreement committing the Soviets to buy a number of tons of American grain each year, beginning in 1976.

Despite these signs of détente, tension remained in the relations between the United States and the Soviet Union. Americans criticized the Soviet Union's treatment of Jews who wanted to move to Israel and its imprisonment of dissenters, people who criticized their government's policies. The Soviets declared that the United States had no right to interfere in their nation's domestic policies.

THE ELECTION OF 1976

At the time that he was named vice-president, Gerald Ford denied further political ambition. He had no intention, he said, of being a candidate "for any office, president, vice-president, or anything else, in 1976." By July 1975 he had changed his mind. He announced then that he would seek election as president the following year.

Ships from thirty-five nations took part in "Operation Sail 1976"—a Bicentennial celebration in New York harbor.

Ford's main Republican rival was Ronald Reagan, former governor of California and a favorite of conservative Republicans. Ford won the early Republican primaries, but Reagan gained support with victories in the South and the Southwest. At the Republican national convention Ford was nominated on the first ballot by a narrow vote. He chose Senator Robert Dole of Kansas as his running mate.

When the Democratic campaign began, Senator Hubert Humphrey of Minnesota seemed a likely candidate for president. He did not enter any of the primaries, but no other Democrat could match his standing in the party. The primaries, however, produced a tireless campaigner. He introduced himself to voters by saying, "I'm Jimmy Carter, and I'm running for president."

James Earl Carter, Jr., had a varied background. A peanut farmer from Plains, Georgia, he had been governor of the state. Earlier he had been a naval officer who worked on the navy's submarine program. Significantly, Carter was an outsider in national politics. He had no part in the bitter conflicts about Vietnam and Watergate.

Carter entered all 31 Democratic primaries and won 18 of them. He beat back challenges from Governor George Wallace of Alabama, Senator Henry M. Jackson of Washington, and Congressman Morris Udall of Arizona. At the Democratic convention Carter won the nomination on the first ballot. He selected Senator Walter F. Mondale of Minnesota as his running mate.

At the start of September 1976, polls showed a wide lead for Carter. He was popular with workers, southerners, blacks, and farmers. At the time, voters were disappointed in Ford because inflation and unemployment still were high. However, Carter's lead vanished as the campaign went on.

Carter won the election by a narrow margin. He received just over half of the popular vote, compared to 48 percent for Ford. The tally in electoral votes was 297 to 240. In the congressional elections, the Democrats retained their control of the House of Representatives and of the Senate.

As Carter prepared to take office, Ford was praised by his former colleagues in Congress. They spoke of his efforts to rebuild confidence after Watergate. "He was the right [person] at the right time," Democratic leader Tip O'Neill told Congress. "The country couldn't have been better served."

SECTION REVIEW

1. Identify the following: Nelson A. Rockefeller, WIN, Andrew Young, Barbara Jordan, ERA, the *Mayaguez*, the Helsinki Accords.

2. Define the following: perjury, amnesty.

3. What prevented Nixon from being tried as a Watergate defendant after September 1974?

4. What did a draft evader need to do to qualify for amnesty from President Ford?

5. Name the purpose of each of the following: (a) the Congressional Budget and Impoundment Act, (b) the Campaign Reform Act of 1974, (c) the Freedom of Information Act of 1974.

6. (a) How did cutbacks in auto production in 1974 affect unemployment? (b) How was the tax cut of March 1975 expected to help the economy?

7. During Ford's presidency what happened to the Voting Rights Act of 1965?

8. Name two agreements signed in 1975 that continued the policy of détente.

SUMMARY

Before Richard M. Nixon became president, he vowed to "bring America together." The main problem he faced was the war in Vietnam. Nixon planned to withdraw American soldiers from Vietnam, but only after strengthening the South Vietnamese army. He also planned to force a peace settlement through intensive bombing.

Nixon's policies caused controversy. When American troops extended their fighting to Cambodia in 1970, protesters demonstrated in the streets and on college campuses.

In 1971 and 1972 Nixon sharply reduced the number of American troops in Vietnam. In January 1973 an agreement to end the war was signed. Nonetheless, fighting continued. In 1975 Communist forces took control of both South Vietnam and Cambodia.

Nixon opened the way to diplomatic relations with the People's Republic of China with a visit in 1972. In the same year, he visited the Soviet Union, beginning a time of détente. In 1973 Nixon and Secretary of State Henry Kissinger took steps to ease tensions in the Middle East.

Nixon won reelection in 1972 by a large majority. However, his second term was plagued by domestic problems. The Senate rejected two of his nominations to the Supreme Court. The economy worsened as inflation and energy costs soared.

The worst domestic problem grew out of a 1972 political burglary in Washington, D.C. Nixon and several of his aides were accused of covering up the burglary and of misusing presidential powers. In 1974, as the House of Representatives prepared to impeach Nixon, he resigned. Vice-President Gerald R. Ford became the new president.

Ford lost popularity when he gave Nixon a pardon. Congress, reacting to deeds of the Nixon administration, curbed some presidential powers. Congress also opposed many of Ford's calls for legislation. His attempts to reduce inflation were only mildly successful. In foreign affairs, Ford continued the policies of the Nixon years.

A newcomer to Washington, James Earl Carter, Jr., became the Democratic candidate for president in 1976. He won a narrow victory over Ford.

Bob Dylan's songs of social protest made him a symbol to the young people of the Sixties. "Blowin' in the Wind" is one of his best known songs.

CHAPTER REVIEW

1. How was each of the following a turning point in the war in Vietnam? (a) the Gulf of Tonkin Resolution (b) the Tet offensive (c) the "Agreement on Ending the War and Restoring Peace in Vietnam"

2. Contrast the views of hawks and doves about the invasion of Cambodia and about the protests in the United States following the invasion.

3. Both the War Powers Act and the Congressional Budget and Impoundment Act were responses by Congress to actions of the executive branch. (a) What actions? (b) Why did Congress oppose these actions?

4. Henry Kissinger's view of world communism in the 1970s differed from the view of John Foster Dulles in the 1950s. (a) How were the views different? (b) How was the difference shown in American foreign policy toward the People's Republic of China?

5. Student radicals distrusted the Establishment, including government. Explain why they might have objected to President Nixon's policy of Vietnamization.

6. The decisions of the Organization of Petroleum Exporting Countries (OPEC) in the early 1970s affected the United States balance of payments. How?

7. Explain how each of the following events was connected to the next. (a) the arrest of five burglars at Watergate (b) the letter to Judge John J. Sirica from James McCord (c) the hearings chaired by Senator Sam J. Ervin, Jr. (d) John Dean's charges against President Nixon

8. The Watergate investigations were more than struggles between the executive and legislative branches of government. They also were struggles within the executive branch. Explain how this happened.

9. (a) What were Ford's advantages in dealing with Congress? (b) What were his disadvantages, particularly after the elections of 1974?

10. Although the war in Vietnam and the Watergate scandal were over by the time of the 1976 Democratic primaries, they influenced the primaries. In what way?

ISSUES AND IDEAS

1. Early in the 1800s a Prussian military expert, Karl von Clausewitz, wrote that "war is nothing more than the continuation of politics by other means." Apply this statement to the war in Vietnam. (a) What main political goal led to United States involvement in the war in the first place? (b) In what way was this goal served by attacks on North Vietnam during the Nixon administration? (c) How was this goal affected by the outcome of the war in 1975?

2. Neither Nixon nor Ford achieved a comprehensive energy policy for the United States. Analyze the subject by listing some major suppliers of energy, some forms of energy that they supply, and some ways the energy is used. Then tell what a comprehensive energy policy might try to do.

Bicentennial decorations took many forms. Some Americans painted their houses, some painted their faces, and some, as here, painted their cars.

This footprint on the moon documents one of the great achievements of modern science.

3. Foreign policy experts in the United States worried about the Watergate scandal. How could Watergate threaten American foreign policy? Consider national unity and the president's ability to act.

4. Compare the situation of Gerald R. Ford when he took over the presidency to that of Lyndon B. Johnson. Use the comparison to explain why Johnson enjoyed quick success in promoting legislation, but Ford did not.

SKILLS WORKSHOP

1. *Graphs.* Refer to the graph of petroleum consumption on page 769. (a) About how many barrels of domestic petroleum did Americans consume in 1978? (b) About how many barrels of imported petroleum did Americans consume then? (c) What percentage of the total consumption in 1978 depended on imports?

2. *Graphs.* Refer to the graph of petroleum consumption on page 769. Use information from the graph of petroleum consumption to make two circle graphs. On each graph divide petroleum sources into two parts. One part should show domestic production and the other should show imports. Let one graph represent petroleum sources in 1945, and the other graph represent petroleum sources in 1978.

PAST AND PRESENT

1. Describe one example of a current automobile, building, or household appliance designed to save energy. Explain how it saves energy, and if possible tell how its design differs from the design of similar products in the early 1970s.

2. Refer to the business pages of a newspaper or news magazine. Determine the rate at which prices are changing this year. Compare that rate to inflation during Ford's years as president.

CHAPTER 29

NEW DIRECTIONS

1977–1982

ECONOMIC AND ENVIRONMENTAL CONCERNS
STRIVING FOR CIVIL RIGHTS
HUMAN RIGHTS AND FOREIGN POLICY
REAGAN AND THE REPUBLICANS
FOREIGN POLICY UNDER REAGAN

In 1980 thousands of Cubans poured into the United States. Mirella Diaz, part of that wave of immigrants, described her arrival at Key West, Florida:

"The National Guard provided a place to stay, food and clothes, and so many attentions. There was even special attention given for the sick, a mobile hospital. In Cuba, I'd been a slave. I feel more at home on this strange soil. Americans opened their hearts. Everybody clasped our hands like real brothers and sisters. If the young people here would only know how hard it is in other places to be free, filled, clothed, to have everything in hand. How precious freedom is!

I had nothing to eat but as soon as I landed here I felt a peace of mind, just to breathe free and speak free. I still can't believe it. . . .

"It was all so fast. Midnight on Key West. A bus to Miami. One night at the Orange Bowl with six thousand other refugees. There we had breakfast and lunch. . . .

"The first thing I ate were Vienna sausages. . . . Offer me anything and I'll try it."

Diaz would find much to try in American life. She would find stores stocked with goods she had never seen. She would find that many jobs paid amazing salaries.

Diaz would also find that jobs and prices were heated topics in the United States, where the economy seemed to be in chaos. Americans who had never read a newspaper's financial page now talked of interest rates and inflationary cycles.

Americans were also talking about foreign affairs, like the unrest in Cuba that had sent Diaz to the United States. Headlines told of one crisis after another. Americans pulled out their maps, and saw a world linked by sorrow and by hope.

ECONOMIC AND ENVIRONMENTAL CONCERNS

READ TO FIND OUT

— how Carter planned to stimulate the economy.

— how Carter proposed to curb inflation.

— what caused the energy crisis of 1979.

— what environmental crises Americans faced.

— how troubled cities and industries were helped.

January 20, 1977, dawned crisply cold in Washington, D.C. Wind-whipped flags decorated streets and buildings. In the Capitol, James Earl Carter, Jr., took the oath of office as the thirty-ninth president of the United States. He was the first president from the Deep South since the Civil War.

President Carter hoped to begin a new era, "a new national spirit of unity and trust." His first act as president was to pardon almost all of those who had evaded the draft during the Vietnam War. Deserters, however, were not pardoned. Carter hoped that the pardon would help to heal the national wounds left from Vietnam.

President Carter also tried "to stay close to the people." He appeared on television in a version of Franklin D. Roosevelt's "fireside chats." He answered questions on a telephone call-in radio program. He urged people to look on the federal government "as a friend."

THE SLUGGISH ECONOMY

Carter hoped especially for a fresh start in the nation's economic life. The rate of inflation had slowed, but it remained about 6 percent. Business was sluggish, particularly in key industries such as construction. Unemployment hovered around 7 percent.

The economy continued to suffer from an unfavorable balance of trade. The United States was importing more goods than it exported, especially steel, televisions, clothing, shoes, and automobiles.

To change this unfavorable balance of trade, the Carter administration negotiated agreements with Japan, South Korea, and Taiwan. These nations, which were flooding the American market with goods, pledged to reduce exports of some items, such as shoes and color televisions. Not until 1979, however, would American exports exceed imports.

STIMULATING THE ECONOMY

Carter's major economic goal was to stimulate the economy. In early 1977 he asked Congress for funds for public works, jobs for the young and the elderly, and job-training programs. These actions, Carter believed, would put more money into the economy and would create more jobs.

Carter also called for a rebate, or return, of fifty dollars to each taxpayer from the government. Thus, Americans would have more money to spend. Finally, Carter requested tax cuts for businesses in order to encourage them to expand.

Most of Carter's proposals were widely supported in the Democrat-controlled Congress. But many senators and representatives balked at the rebate. It would not do enough, they argued, to boost the economy.

In May 1977, Carter withdrew the rebate plan, and Congress passed his other proposals to stimulate the economy. However, the rate of unemployment dropped slowly.

In the autumn Senator Humphrey and Representative Augustus F. Hawkins of California proposed a "full employment" bill. It set a national goal of reducing unemployment, by 1983, to 4 percent and the inflation rate to 3 percent. It was unclear how these goals would be reached since the bill did not approve new spending or job programs. Nevertheless, Congress passed the Humphrey-Hawkins bill, and Carter signed it in October 1978. Soon after, Congress passed and Carter approved a bill to cut federal taxes by $18.7 billion.

SOARING INFLATION

Despite the goal of reducing inflation, the rate began to rise again in 1977. Everything in the United States seemed to be skyrocketing in cost—including government.

In 1978 Californians passed Proposition 13, an amendment to the state constitution. The amendment sharply cut property taxes. In Colorado, Michigan, New Jersey, and Tennessee, voters limited state and local spending. State legislatures called for an amendment to the Constitution that would require the federal government to balance its budget.

Faced with mounting inflation, Carter changed his economic goals. Instead of requesting an increase in government spending to ease unemployment, he called on Congress to reduce spending to slow inflation.

Carter vetoed bills that he considered inflationary, and he limited wage increases for government employees. He urged business and labor to keep down prices and wages by voluntarily following government guidelines. In 1979 he sent to Congress a "lean" budget for 1980. The President proposed cuts in social services, health care, and environmental programs, as well as a slight increase in military spending.

However, Carter's anti-inflation program met with little success. Congress tacked on increases to

the budget before passing it. Carter's voluntary wage-price controls also failed. By late 1980 the nation was facing an inflation rate of about 15 percent. At the same time, anti-inflation programs were pushing the nation toward recession.

CARTER'S ENERGY PROGRAM

The inflation rate was also increased by America's dependence on foreign oil. By 1977 the United States was importing more than half of its oil. Although the long-awaited Alaska pipeline was completed that year, Alaskan oil would supply only about 10 percent of the nation's needs. In August 1977 Congress voted to create the cabinet-level Department of Energy to deal with conservation and the development of new energy sources.

President Carter, meanwhile, was determined to wean the nation from its dependence on imported oil. In April 1977 he presented a national energy program to Congress. The key to his plan was to discourage the use of oil and natural gas by charging higher prices and by levying taxes.

The federal government controlled the prices of oil and natural gas by setting an upper limit, or

President Carter appealed to many voters because he came new to Washington. He had experience as a Georgia senator and governor but had no ties in the nation's capital.

ceiling. Carter wanted to relax the government price controls on natural gas, allowing the price to rise. He also proposed increased taxes on domestic oil and gasoline, an extra tax on "gas-guzzling cars," and a new tax on industrial use of oil and natural gas.

At the same time, Carter asked for tax breaks, or reductions in taxes, for Americans who conserved energy by insulating their homes and buying small cars. Finally, he urged a shift to other energy sources—coal, nuclear energy, and solar energy.

In October 1978 Congress passed a compromise energy bill based on Carter's proposals. This National Energy Act provided for the gradual lifting of price controls on natural gas. It also approved tax credits—sums deducted from taxes owed—for homeowners and businesses using energy-saving devices. But there were no higher taxes on oil, gas-guzzling cars, and gasoline in order to cut consumption.

THE ENERGY CRISIS OF 1979

In January 1979 the Middle Eastern nation of Iran was shaken by revolution. Iran's production and export of oil came to a halt for a few months, and only slowly resumed. By April the United States faced a gasoline shortage.

During the spring and summer, lines of cars stretched for blocks outside gasoline stations. In panic buying, Americans filled gasoline tanks already half full and stored cans of the precious fuel. Many states responded by rationing gasoline.

The gasoline shortage hurt many businesses. Car sales dropped sharply in May, prompting worker layoffs in some companies. Out-of-the-way shopping centers became nearly deserted. At parks, fairs, motels, and restaurants in most parts of the nation, business declined.

At the same time, the Organization of Petroleum Exporting Countries (OPEC) raised its oil prices by 60 percent. The cost of gasoline—and all oil products—soared. So, too, did the rate of inflation in the United States. Angry Americans demanded that the government do something.

A determined Carter drew up a new energy program. On July 15 he unveiled it to the nation on television. The plan's main goal was to reduce oil imports by 50 percent by 1990. "Never again" Carter vowed, "will our nation's independence be hostage to foreign oil."

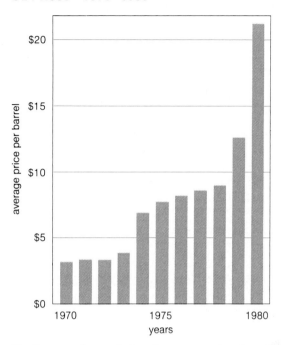

Oil Prices 1970–1980

The figures on the graph show the average value of crude petroleum at the well. Transportation and refining costs are not included. A barrel contains 42 gallons of crude oil.

Earlier that year, Carter had lifted some government price controls on domestic oil in order to allow the price to rise. Rising prices would discourage the use of oil. They also would increase the profits of oil companies. Carter hoped that the companies would use some of this windfall, or unexpected gain, to search for new oil fields. At the same time, however, Carter also called for a "windfall profits" tax on the oil companies' added profits after decontrol.

Now Carter proposed that this tax revenue be used to set up a government energy corporation. It would develop industries to produce synthetic fuels from coal, oil shale, and even crops. Meanwhile, Carter proposed to limit oil imports to their 1977 level and to ration gasoline.

Carter's energy proposals were bogged down for months in congressional committees. In October Congress reluctantly gave Carter limited power to ration gasoline in a shortage. Not until March 1980 did Congress pass a bill to tax the windfall profits of oil companies. Finally in June Congress approved the creation of the United States Synthetic Fuels Corporation to develop fuels to replace oil.

ENVIRONMENTAL ISSUES

American concerns about the economy and energy were related to another concern—the environment. Environmentalists were urging stricter laws to protect the nation's land, water, and air. At the same time, business groups complained about laws requiring antipollution devices. They also charged that environmental restrictions hindered the development of new oil and coal fields.

Both Carter and Congress tried to balance economic and environmental goals. "We will protect our environment," pledged Carter. "But when this nation critically needs a refinery or a pipeline, we will build it."

In August 1977 Congress passed amendments to the Clean Air Act. The amendments extended the deadline for automobile makers and cities to meet tough clean-air standards. Environmentalists scored some legislative victories, too. An August

★ ★ ★ ★ ★ ★ ★ ★ **CRITICAL ISSUES** ★ ★ ★ ★ ★ ★ ★ ★ ★ ★ ★

ENVIRONMENT VERSUS DEVELOPMENT
CRESTED BUTTE'S DILEMMA

The little town of Crested Butte, Colorado, lies in a high Rocky Mountain valley surrounded by a wilderness of mountains, meadows, and forest. At the west end of town looms Mount Emmons, a 12,000-foot peak that townspeople call "the Red Lady" because of its rosy color at sunset.

Until recently Crested Butte was a quiet town of just over a thousand people. Many had moved there from crowded cities in order to live more simply and in harmony with nature. The whole town had been named a national historic site to preserve its wealth of Victorian-style houses, built a hundred years ago during a silver-mining boom.

Then, in late 1977, AMAX, the nation's largest mining company, announced the discovery of eight billion dollars worth of molybdenum, a mineral used in making steel, on Mount Emmons. AMAX planned to spend a billion dollars to mine the "moly," as everyone soon called it. Three thousand workers would be employed to build and run the mine.

Once in operation, the mine would process ten to twenty-five thousand tons of ore daily for twenty to thirty years. Ninety-nine percent of the ore would be "tailings," waste to be dumped on a site that would eventually be thirty times the size of Crested Butte itself. When all the molybdenum was gone, Mount Emmons would be flat.

Most people in Crested Butte reacted with dismay. "We can see a lot of money in moly," the mayor concluded, "but the cost to this community won't be worth it." When the town council voted unanimously to fight the mine, a classic battle between the environment and growth took shape.

The mining company had the law on its side. Mount Emmons was public land, and under United States mining law, companies had the right to mine it. In fact, government policy actively supported the development of underground resources like oil, coal, and minerals to insure a steady supply to the nation's industries.

"We have a national minerals policy that encourages us to go out and find a Mount Emmons and mine it," said a company official. "This is the very best area in the world to look for minerals. I think the question is not *should* we get at these minerals but how do we get at them and do the best possible job." The company promised a modern mine, one that would do the least damage to the environment.

The town questioned federal policy. Was mineral development always more important than historic preservation, clean air and water, and the protection of wildlife? "We can understand the value of Yellowstone and Yosemite," said Crested Butte's mayor. "There are probably tons of mineral deposits in Yosemite and a decision was made in 1890 to preserve it. But what of the value of this valley?"

There were some in town who favored the mine, however. It would be selfish, they argued, for Crested Butte to preserve its way of life at the expense of others. The town "has an obligation . . . to supply molybdenum to the world," said one business leader. Another pointed out that the mine would provide several thousand jobs in a time of high unemployment. "You can't eat scenery," he said.

Others, however, believed that in Crested Butte you almost could. A million and a half hikers,

1977 act put strip mining under federal control. Strip mining, which uncovered coal deposits near the earth's surface, left land hard and scarred. The new law required miners to restore stripped land to close to its original condition.

The conflict between environmental and economic concerns was spotlighted by two crises during the Carter years. One developed at the Three Mile Island nuclear power plant near Harrisburg, Pennsylvania.

Early on March 28, 1979, the plant's cooling system broke down, through a combination of human and mechanical error. The temperature in the reactor core soared, damaging the core. Radiation leaked from the plant into the atmosphere.

Antinuclear groups demanded that the United States end its use of nuclear power. Some 12 percent of the nation's electricity was generated in 72 nuclear reactors. More than a hundred others were under construction.

★ ★

campers, and skiers came to the region each year to escape city life. If the mines ruined the wilderness, people would have no place to go. "What the nation is being asked to do in the West . . . is sacrifice our

W. Mitchell Shaw led the protest against the mining of Mount Emmons. He and others thought it essential to preserve the meadow, the quiet town, and the familiar mountainscape.

national playgrounds," said a townsperson. "The old adage that there's always someplace else to go is just not true anymore."

By 1982 the fight between the company and the town had reached a deadlock. Then AMAX made a surprise announcement. It was postponing mine construction for several years because of a slump in the demand for molybdenum. Some believe that the delay will be longer—that the mine will not be built in this century. Meanwhile, the town has joined with conservation groups to challenge national mining law in court. The question of values—of development versus preservation of the environment—remains unsettled.

"A mine is going to be good for this country," said a mine supporter. "Everything changes. If we didn't change, we'd all be dinosaurs. I don't know how you can stop it. I don't know if you want to. It's federal land. It belongs to everybody."

But a sign in Crested Butte expressed the feeling of most townspeople: "Crested Butte—love it by leaving it the way you found it."

1. Why do people in Crested Butte want to stop the mine on Mount Emmons? What arguments do others give in support of the mine?

2. If you lived in Crested Butte, how would you feel about the mine? Why?

3. Federal mining law favors mining on public land over other uses. Do you think that the law should be changed? Why or why not?

In March 1979 the cooling system at the Three Mile Island nuclear power plant broke down. The results set in motion waves of protest against the use of nuclear power.

Carter, however, did not want to halt the program. "We cannot shut the door on nuclear energy," said Carter. It "is critical if we are to free our country from its overdependence on unstable sources of high-priced oil."

Another environmental crisis occurred near Love Canal in Niagara Falls, New York. In the mid-1900s the canal had been used by a company as a dump for its chemical wastes. Later a school and houses were built on the site. In the mid-1970s scientists found high levels of disease there, related to the chemicals.

New York State then closed the school and promised to relocate over 200 families. The chemical dump, though, had affected many more people. In 1980 some $5 million in federal funds were set aside to evacuate over 700 families from the area of Love Canal. In the same year a tough federal law controlling the disposal of toxic wastes went into effect.

THE TROUBLED CITIES

Solving the problems of energy and of the environment cost money, especially in the cities. Yet many cities were having trouble balancing their budgets as inflation sent costs soaring.

Midwestern and northeastern cities were especially hard hit. People were moving to the suburbs to escape big-city problems such as an increase in crime and a decline in public services. Businesses also joined the flight, taking jobs and tax dollars with them. Unemployment increased. With fewer taxpayers, city treasuries shrank and municipal employees were laid off.

In October 1977 the Carter administration shepherded a major urban-aid bill through Congress. The Housing and Community Development Act provided $12.5 billion to restore neighborhoods and another $1.16 billion to fund low-income housing. Much of this aid went to older cities in the Midwest and Northeast.

Three years later, Carter proposed large cuts in federal spending for 1981. The cuts, designed to slow inflation, eliminated or reduced city-aid programs. City mayors cried out in protest. Carter argued, "Inflation is indeed the most cruel tax of all." The budget was approved by Congress.

INDUSTRY FALTERS

The nation's economic problems were compounded by problems in key industries. The American steel industry, once the world's largest, had lagged behind in adopting new techniques and building new plants. In the 1970s the industry faced stiff competition from Japanese and West German steel makers. As steel imports rose, American plants closed and workers were laid off.

Arson fires left burned shells of apartments near this pile of rubble in the South Bronx, New York. Such vandalism destroys housing and businesses and is costly to cities.

The auto industry suffered a similar fate. It was slow to change from building large cars to small, fuel-efficient models like those built in West Germany and Japan. The energy crisis, inflation, and competition from imported cars dealt the industry record losses in 1980. The Chrysler Corporation escaped bankruptcy only after Congress provided federal aid.

Carter tried a strategy of **deregulation** to help the transportation industries. He proposed to remove most government regulations controlling these industries in order to promote competition and cut the red tape that "hampered [their] free growth and development."

The airlines had been deregulated in 1978. In 1980 the trucking and railroad industries also were deregulated. New laws gave transportation companies more freedom to raise or to lower rates and to set travel routes.

One industry in the United States boomed during the Carter years. Electronics advanced at a dizzying rate. Computers were being made smaller, yet were growing more powerful. Miniature computers called microcomputers were put to use in televisions, testing equipment, information processing, and even in appliances. During the 1970s the United States led the world in computer technology and dominated the international market.

SECTION REVIEW

1. Identify the following: Humphrey-Hawkins bill, Proposition 13, National Energy Act.

2. Define the following: tax break, "windfall profits" tax, strip mining, deregulation.

3. (a) Name three economic problems that Carter faced soon after his inauguration. (b) List three ways that Carter planned to stimulate the economy.

4. What steps did Carter take to fight inflation?

5. (a) Why did Congress create the Department of Energy? (b) What was the goal of the United States Synthetic Fuels Corporation?

6. (a) What caused the gasoline shortage in 1979? (b) How did this shortage affect other areas of the economy?

7. How did Carter plan to improve conditions in troubled cities?

8. Name two major industries that were declining.

STRIVING FOR CIVIL RIGHTS

READ TO FIND OUT

—**what economic gains women made.**

—**how black Americans progressed toward equal opportunities.**

—**how Hispanic Americans worked for equality.**

—**how Indian land claims were settled.**

—**why immigration to the United States soared.**

In November 1977 thousands of women gathered in Houston, Texas, for the first National Women's Conference. Not since 1848, when suffragists met in Seneca Falls, New York, had so many women come together to discuss equal rights.

GAINS AND LOSSES FOR WOMEN

For many women, a key goal was economic equality. About 80 percent of all working women held low-paying jobs, laboring as clerks, typists, and waitresses. Women earned an average of 60 cents for every dollar earned by men.

Still, women made gains during the Carter years. More and more women held professional jobs, working as doctors, engineers, company managers, airline pilots, and college professors. In 1980 women earned half of all master's degrees and one third of all doctoral degrees.

Women entered a previously all-male field in January 1978, when the National Aeronautics and Space Administration (NASA) chose 35 new astronauts. Six of them were women, slated to be mission scientists and flight engineers for NASA's space shuttle program.

President Carter appointed three women to cabinet positions. Juanita Morris Kreps—vice-president of Duke University and a director on the New York Stock Exchange—was named to head the Department of Commerce. Patricia Roberts Harris—professor, diplomat, lawyer—became the head of the Department of Urban Development (HUD).

Sally Ride, pulling the parachute, was selected to be the first woman crew member on a space shuttle mission. Ride was one of eight American women astronauts being trained.

Judge Shirley M. Hufstedler headed the new Department of Education, created in October 1979.

Carter also supported the Equal Rights Amendment (ERA). Passed by Congress in 1972, the act forbade discrimination on the basis of sex. However, in 1977 motions to ratify the amendment were rejected in several states.

The ERA needed approval by 3 more states to reach the total of 38 required for ratification. Fearing that ERA could not be approved by March 1979, the legal deadline, supporters asked for more time for ratification. In October 1978 Congress voted to extend the deadline for 39 months.

GOALS OF BLACK AMERICANS

During the Carter years, blacks continued to strive for equal opportunities. High unemployment and blighted housing were still problems for black Americans. However, there was good news, too. The number of heads of households who owned their own homes rather than renting increased slightly among blacks, from 41 percent in 1970 to almost 44 percent in 1977.

Black college students equaled 9 percent of all college students. That was close to the proportion of blacks in the total population. By 1980 blacks were about as likely as whites to go to college. Blacks also

flocked to the professions, such as medicine and law. History's first three black astronauts were named in NASA's 1978 selection.

More and more blacks entered government at all levels. Black mayors were elected in several major cities, including Los Angeles, Detroit, Atlanta, and New Orleans.

President Carter, in addition to naming Patricia Roberts Harris as HUD secretary, chose blacks for other important posts. Representative Andrew J. Young was appointed ambassador to the United Nations. Lawyer Clifford L. Alexander, Jr., became secretary of the army. In addition, nearly 14 percent of Carter's 258 appointments of federal judges went to blacks.

CONTROVERSY OVER AFFIRMATIVE ACTION

In 1972 the Equal Employment Opportunity Act set up a program of "affirmative action." Under this program, businesses receiving federal funds were required to increase their female and minority workers to proportions matching the local labor market.

All state and most local governments were covered by the program. So were state universities. They were expected to increase their enrollment of minority students. Affirmative action was meant to compensate for past discrimination.

Some Americans complained that affirmative action was simply "reverse discrimination" against whites. In June 1978 the Supreme Court ruled on a reverse discrimination case. Allan P. Bakke, a white, had been denied admission to the University of California Medical School at Davis. Bakke had qualified for admission, but the school had an affirmative action program based on a quota system. This system reserved a certain number of places for minorities.

In *University of California Regents* v. *Bakke*, the Court ruled that Bakke had been rejected because of his race. This violated the Civil Rights Act of 1964. The Court ordered that he be admitted to the medical school. Although the Court rejected the use of quotas, it did rule that schools could consider race or ethnic origin in admitting students. In a later case the Court ruled in favor of affirmative action set up by a voluntary agreement between union and management in the steel industry.

GOALS OF HISPANIC AMERICANS

The second-largest minority group in the United States—and the fastest growing—were Hispanic Americans. In 1980 the Hispanic population was more than 14 million. Most Hispanics in the United States traced their origins to Mexico, Puerto Rico, or Cuba.

Hispanics were very hard hit by stagflation, the combination of inflation and a stagnant economy. Their jobless rate was generally about 4 percentage points higher than the rate for whites during the Carter years. While prices soared, the wages paid to Hispanics lagged far behind the average wages paid to whites.

Many Hispanic Americans saw politics as the best route to economic and social equality. Hispanic groups held voter-registration drives and became active in the Democratic and Republican parties. In 1981 Henry Cisneros won election as mayor of San Antonio, Texas. He was the first Hispanic mayor of a major American city. "I'm not interested in being the first anything," said Cisneros. "I just want to be the best I can be."

Although Hispanics held only four seats in Congress in 1978, they were well represented in the federal government. Eighteen percent of Carter's appointments went to Hispanics.

Henry Cisneros had served three terms on the city council of San Antonio before becoming mayor. He won the support of many of the city's Anglo as well as Hispanic residents.

GOALS OF INDIANS

In September 1977 the Carter administration set up a new government post—assistant secretary of the interior for Indian affairs. The position was created to stress the importance of Indian concerns. Forrest J. Gerard, a Blackfoot, was named as assistant secretary.

In March 1978 the Supreme Court decided the case of *Oliphant* v. *Suquamish Indian Tribe*. At issue was how much sovereignty, or independence, Indian tribes had on their reservations.

A non-Indian living on the reservation in the state of Washington had been tried for assault by a Suquamish tribal court. The Supreme Court ruled that Indian tribal courts did not have the right to prosecute non-Indians for crimes committed on the reservation. The ruling was a blow for those who supported tribal sovereignty.

Another concern of many tribes was how to develop resources on their reservations. About 16 per-

cent of the nation's energy resources lay in Indian lands. The energy-rich tribes, however, were poor in funds. To help these tribes develop their resources, the Department of Energy in 1979 granted them some $2 million.

While some tribes were developing their lands, others were trying to recover lost lands. In 1977 tribes brought suit against several eastern states to regain tribal lands. The states, they argued, had obtained the lands in treaties that violated a 1790 federal law protecting Indian land rights. Carter's administration supported many of these claims in court.

In 1979 the Narragansett Indians and the state of Rhode Island worked out a settlement. Some 1,800 acres (730 hectares) would be returned to the tribe, although much of it could be used only for conservation purposes. In 1980 a claim by the Penobscot, Maliseet, and Passamaquoddy Indians to a huge

Modern technology helps track information on problems new and old. In Washington State, Yakima Chief Totus checked a computer read-out on tribal concerns.

portion of Maine was resolved. The federal government granted the tribes money to buy 300,000 acres (120,000 hectares), a fraction of the claimed land.

One Indian land claim had been dragging on for 58 years. The Sioux wanted to recover the Black Hills of South Dakota, deeded to them by a treaty in 1868. In 1877 Congress had broken the treaty and seized the land after gold was discovered there.

In June 1980 the Supreme Court, in *U.S.* v. *Sioux Nation of Indians*, ruled on the case. The Sioux were awarded more than $100 million in damages and interest. The settlement, however, threatened to drag on for many more years.

A NEW WAVE OF IMMIGRANTS

While Americans struggled for a better life, thousands of people sought the chance to enter the nation. During the Carter years immigrants poured into the United States in the greatest surge since the early 1900s. These new immigrants were overwhelmingly from Latin America and Asia. Many were refugees.

In 1975 South Vietnam, Laos, and Cambodia were taken over by Communist governments. In the

Among the refugees fleeing to the United States from Vietnam in the 1970s was this family. They were photographed with their next-door neighbors in Port Arthur, Texas.

wake of harsh rule, war, and famine, thousands of people fled. Many became "boat people," who set out in small crafts for any nation that would allow them to enter. Large numbers died at sea.

When neighboring countries could not or would not take in the refugees, other nations offered asylum. Under President Carter, the United States stretched its immigration quotas and authorized $455 million to settle over 170,000 Indochinese.

MAXINE HONG KINGSTON
GROWING UP CHINESE AMERICAN

Maxine Kingston was the daughter of Chinese immigrants. Her father first came to the "Golden Mountain," as the Chinese called America, to earn money for his family. Later her mother, a midwife and doctor in China, joined him. Maxine, their first child, was born in Stockton in California's Central Valley, where her parents had opened a laundry.

Because she was born in America, yet with her roots in China, Kingston's childhood was rich but often confusing. To her parents she seemed loud and noisy—American. To other Americans she seemed different—Chinese. When she went to school for the first time, she did not know English and remained silent, even on the playground, for more than a year. Later she became a brilliant student with an extraordinary gift for her new language.

After attending college, Kingston taught school and began to write. Her subjects were her childhood and her Chinese heritage. In her first book, *The Woman Warrior*, she told what it was like to grow up Chinese American. She wove into the book favorite Chinese stories her mother had told her.

In her second book, *China Men*, she described Chinese men in America. She told of her great-grandfathers, who worked in the sugarcane fields of Hawaii. She told of her grandfather, who was paid a dollar a day in the 1860s to help build the transcontinental railroad. She also described her own generation, through her brother who served in Vietnam. Like him, Maxine Hong Kingston called America home, though she knew her Chinese roots would nourish her all her life.

© 1983 Thomas Victor

Refugees from Caribbean nations also piled into boats and headed for the United States. Some 25,000 Haitians, fleeing poverty and a repressive government, reached Florida in 1980. An especially large wave of immigration came in the same year when Fidel Castro allowed 125,000 Cubans to leave their homeland and sail to Florida in a "freedom flotilla." Again, the United States government voted millions of dollars to aid the refugees.

The wave of refugees prompted Congress to revise the nation's immigration laws. The Refugee Act of 1980 tripled the number of refugees allowed into the nation—to 50,000 per year. The annual ceiling for immigrants was also raised—from 290,000 to 320,000.

The refugees, however, were not welcomed by all. Florida officials protested that they could not absorb all the Haitians and Cubans. "We've become a boiling pot, not a melting pot," said the mayor of Miami. Vietnamese fisher folk, many of whom settled in California and the Gulf states, were resented by local fishers.

The immigration and refugee issues heightened the long-burning argument over "illegal aliens"— people living and working in the United States without legal permission. The illegal alien population was thought to be as high as 7 million, and well over half came from Mexico.

Some Americans resented competition from illegal aliens when jobs were so scarce. Because they would work for low pay, the aliens brought down the pay scale for American workers, according to union leaders. However, other people pointed out that illegal aliens, like many immigrants in the past, took the hard jobs that most Americans shunned.

Most of the newcomers to the United States were eager to work hard. The Ilishaevs, a family of seven Jewish refugees from the Soviet Union, held down six jobs. "People all over the world need freedom," said one daughter. "That's the real reason they're coming to this country."

SECTION REVIEW

1. Identify the following: Shirley M. Hufstedler, Patricia Roberts Harris, Henry Cisneros, Forrest J. Gerard.

2. Define the following: affirmative action, "boat people," illegal alien.

3. What happened to the Equal Rights Amendment in October 1978?

4. Name four areas in which blacks made gains during the 1970s.

5. State the issue and the Supreme Court decision in *University of California Regents* v. *Bakke.*

6. (a) Why did some Americans resent job competition from illegal aliens? (b) What argument was used to defend their presence?

7. (a) Was the case of *Oliphant* v. *Suquamish Indian Tribe* a victory or a defeat for tribal sovereignty? Why? (b) Name three Indian land claims settled in 1979 and 1980.

8. (a) During the Carter years, where did most new immigrants come from? (b) How did the Refugee Act of 1980 affect the number of immigrants allowed into the nation?

HUMAN RIGHTS AND FOREIGN POLICY

READ TO FIND OUT

—how Carter stressed human rights.

—how the Panama Canal treaties were negotiated.

—how the United States recognized the People's Republic of China.

—why the SALT II agreement did not go into effect.

—how the Camp David Accords were reached.

—how Iranians took American hostages.

Soon after his inauguration, President Carter wrote a letter to Andrei D. Sakharov. Sakharov, a Soviet physicist and Nobel Prize winner, was an outspoken critic of the Soviet government. He had been warned to cease his antigovernment activities.

"Because we are free," Carter wrote to Sakharov, "we can never be indifferent to the fate of freedom elsewhere." The letter reflected Carter's determination to make concern about human rights a vital part of American foreign policy.

HUMAN RIGHTS

International concern about human rights was not new. The Helsinki Accords, signed in 1975, pledged European nations to respect human rights. Yet violations occurred. Many Czechoslovakians were arrested in 1977 for protesting government restrictions. For decades, people outside South Africa had criticized that government's policy of *apartheid* (ah-PAHRT-hayt), racial segregation by the ruling white minority against the black majority.

Carter hoped to persuade such nations to change their ways. He and Andrew Young, American ambassador to the United Nations, spoke out forcefully against apartheid in South Africa and against similar policies in Rhodesia. The United States supported the negotiations that led Rhodesia—renamed Zimbabwe—to independence in 1980 under black-majority rule.

Carter did not hesitate to criticize the Soviet Union. There, dissidents like Sakharov were censored, arrested, and imprisoned. Carter also condemned Soviet and Cuban intervention in civil wars in the African nations of Angola and Ethiopia. Soviet leaders, in turn, called Carter's support of the dissidents interference in the "internal affairs of the Soviet Union."

THE PANAMA CANAL TREATIES

In 1903 the United States and Panama signed the Hay-Bunau-Varilla Treaty. It allowed the United States to build the Panama Canal and to control it "in perpetuity." But Panamanians resented the treaty, and in the mid-1960s negotiators from the two nations began meeting to plan changes.

In August 1977 the negotiators hammered out two new treaties. The first continued American operation and defense of the Canal until the year 2000, when Panama would assume control. The second treaty guaranteed that naval and merchant ships of all nations would have a permanent right to use the Canal.

Early in September Carter and General Omar Torrijos Herrera, Panama's chief of state, signed the Panama Canal treaties. However, a divided Senate argued heatedly over the treaties. Some senators feared that America was giving up too much control of the Canal.

To please the Senate, Carter and Torrijos added a reservation to the treaties. The United States would retain the right to defend the Canal against any threat, but not to intervene in Panamanian affairs. In the spring of 1978 the Senate barely ratified the two treaties.

RECOGNITION OF THE PEOPLE'S REPUBLIC OF CHINA

For three decades, the United States had recognized the Nationalist Chinese on the island of Taiwan as the rightful government of China. Late in 1978, Carter announced that the United States would establish full diplomatic relations with the People's Republic of China on January 1, 1979.

At the same time, he broke formal diplomatic relations with Taiwan. He also ended the defense treaty between the United States and Taiwan and announced the withdrawal of American troops.

Carter's announcement set off a storm of controversy. Senator Barry M. Goldwater of Arizona declared that the change "stabs in the back the nation of Taiwan." With some members of Congress, he unsuccessfully appealed to the Supreme Court to block the cancellation of the American defense treaty with Taiwan.

In March 1979 the United States and the People's Republic formally exchanged ambassadors. Both nations agreed to cooperate in scientific ventures, and China was granted special trading privileges with the United States.

SALT II

Carter continued talks with the Soviet Union to control the nuclear arms race. The Strategic Arms Limitation Talks (SALT) agreement of 1972 expired the year that Carter took office. That agreement had frozen the numbers of offensive nuclear weapons in the United States and Russia at the level existing in 1972.

Carter was determined to obtain a new arms limitation agreement with the Russians. He proposed a deep cut in the two nations' nuclear arsenals. The Russians, angry about Carter's human rights stand, rejected the proposal. Soviet leader Leonid Brezhnev called it "one-sided" in favor of the United States. Still, Carter assured Russia that American policy was "not designed to heat up the arms race or bring back the cold war."

Carter's efforts finally bore fruit. In late 1977 American and Russian negotiators began a new round of arms control talks. In June 1979 Carter and Brezhnev signed a new strategic arms limitation treaty at a summit meeting in Vienna, Austria. SALT II would limit the United States and Russia each to no more than 2,250 missiles and long-range bombers by the end of 1981.

However, the SALT II agreement failed to pass the Senate. It was not voted down, but debate on the treaty was postponed indefinitely.

THE AFGHANISTAN CRISIS

Relations between the United States and the Soviet Union worsened in late 1979, over a crisis in Afghanistan. Fiercely independent tribes there opposed the pro-Russian policies of the Afghan government. In 1978 the tribes revolted.

In a makeshift prison camp in Afghanistan, guards stood watch over captured Soviet soldiers. The Afghans' tribal dress was a contrast to the Soviet uniforms.

Claiming that the Afghan government had asked for help, the Soviets sent 85,000 troops into Afghanistan by the end of 1979. The Afghan rebels fought the Russians furiously, and more than half of the Afghan army sided with them. When Russians occupied cities, the rebels moved into the mountains and fought as guerrillas.

President Carter responded swiftly to the Russian intervention. He felt that the invasion threatened Pakistan and was "a steppingstone to possible control over much of the world's oil supplies." He placed an embargo on the sale of grain, machinery, and technology to the Soviet Union.

Carter also vowed that the United States would not take part in the 1980 Summer Olympics in Moscow unless the Soviet Union withdrew from Afghanistan. He called on other nations to join the boycott. Eventually, some 65 nations stayed away, including the United States, China, Japan, and West Germany. But the war in Afghanistan continued, and détente seemed more remote than ever.

THE MIDDLE EAST

Afghanistan was not the only trouble spot in the Persian Gulf region. Carter, like his predecessors, tried to ease tensions between Israel and its Arab neighbors.

In April 1977 Carter met with Egyptian president Anwar el-Sadat to discuss American aid to Egypt and peace in the Middle East. The two leaders quickly became friends and spent hours talking together. Carter also met with the leaders of Jordan, Syria, and Israel. But these talks failed to soften Middle Eastern hostilities.

Then, in November 1977, President Sadat stunned the world by announcing that he was ready to go to Israel in the cause of peace. Israeli prime minister Menachem Begin quickly extended an invitation. This would be the first time an Arab leader had visited Israel and, in effect, recognized its existence as a nation.

Later that month, Sadat flew to Israel for face-to-face talks with Begin, despite opposition from other Arab nations. Millions of people throughout the world watched on television the historic meeting of these two leaders. Both nations, in a state of war for thirty years, now agreed to settle their differences.

Soon after Sadat's visit, the Egyptians and the Israelis began peace negotiations, with the United States as mediator. Disagreements quickly arose. The Israelis had built settlements in territories that they had occupied during the Six-Day War in 1967—particularly on the West Bank of the Jordan River and in the Gaza Strip along the Mediterranean. Sadat favored Israeli withdrawal from the settlements. Israeli leaders not only vowed to keep the settlements, but they kept on expanding them to strengthen Israel's defenses.

Another disagreement concerned the fate of the Palestinian Arabs. Sadat insisted that an independent Palestine, created out of the West Bank and the Gaza Strip, was crucial to Middle Eastern peace. Israel argued that such a nation on its borders would threaten Israeli security and refused to consider the possibility.

THE CAMP DAVID ACCORDS

By mid-1978 the Egyptian-Israeli talks were faltering, as each side hurled charges at the other. "Unless there is some major breakthrough, Carter told congressional leaders, "the whole thing will break down." In September Carter made a bold move. He invited Sadat and Begin to Camp David to discuss Middle Eastern peace in the privacy of the Maryland mountains.

For 13 days and nights, American, Egyptian, and Israeli leaders met at Camp David. They prepared two dozen different treaty drafts. Finally, Sadat and Begin reached two major agreements, called the Camp David Accords.

The first stated that the two nations would sign a peace treaty within three months. Then Israel would return the Sinai Peninsula, which it had occupied since 1967, to Egypt in stages. Finally, full diplomatic relations between the two nations would be established.

The second agreement dealt with the West Bank and the Gaza Strip. Palestinians living in those territories would set up a "self-governing authority." Then, during a five-year period, the final status of the territories would be negotiated.

Disagreements over details then arose, and the three-month deadline for signing the peace treaty

Egyptian president Anwar el-Sadat (right) showed the stress of the issues being discussed at Camp David. Israeli prime minister Menachem Begin (left) seemed in deep thought.

passed. Determined to save the accords, Carter flew to the Middle East to renew negotiations. His diplomacy was successful. In March 1979 Sadat and Begin met in Washington, D.C., and signed a treaty ending the state of war between the two nations. Almost all Arab nations responded by breaking diplomatic relations with Egypt.

Israel gradually withdrew from the Sinai Peninsula. In early 1980 Egypt and Israel exchanged ambassadors, and the border between the two nations was formally opened.

However, the Israeli government continued to oppose Palestinian rights to self-rule, and began building new settlements on the West Bank of the Jordan River. Israel also refused to deal with the Palestine Liberation Organization (PLO), which Arabs considered the sole representative of the Palestinian people. Again and again, Egyptian-Israeli negotiations deadlocked on these issues.

REVOLUTION IN IRAN

From the time of World War II, Shah Mohammed Reza Pahlevi ruled Iran. Under the shah's rule, Carter declared, Iran was "an island of stability in one of the more troubled areas of the world."

The shah encouraged the development of Iran into a modern industrial nation. Conservative religious leaders, however, thought that modernization was a threat to Islamic beliefs. Many Iranians also opposed the shah because he banned political parties and used secret police to silence dissent.

Opposition turned to bloody rioting in January 1979, forcing the shah to leave the country. Soon after, the Ayatollah* Ruhollah Khomeini (koh-MAY-nee), an Islamic leader who had been in exile, returned to Iran. Khomeini declared Iran an Islamic republic, governed by the laws of Islam, and he became the leading voice in the nation.

THE HOSTAGE CRISIS

The shah sought asylum in country after country. Finally, in October 1979, Carter allowed him to enter the United States for treatment of cancer.

Militant Iranians feared that the United States was plotting to return the shah to power. On No-

* ayatollah (AH-yah-TŌL-ah): the title of an Islamic religious leader, meaning literally "sign of God."

vember 4, 1979, they stormed the United States embassy in Teheran, taking 53 Americans hostage. They vowed not to release the Americans until the shah was returned to Iran to stand trial for his actions.

Carter bluntly refused to surrender the shah. Iran, in turn, refused to release the hostages, ignoring the rulings of the United Nations Security Council and the International Court of Justice. Carter then stopped American imports of Iranian oil and froze Iranian assets in the United States. He also sent a naval force to the Indian Ocean.

The days of the hostage crisis stretched into weeks and then months. Despairing of a breakthrough, Carter cut off diplomatic relations with Iran in April 1980, and imposed an embargo on American exports to Iran. He also ordered a secret

In January 1981 people across the nation rejoiced at the return of the American hostages from Iran. This crowd gathered in Washington, D.C., to welcome them home.

military mission to rescue the hostages. It failed when a helicopter developed engine trouble before the rescue could be tried.

The fate of the hostages hung like a cloud over the American presidential campaign in the summer and fall of 1980. Republican candidate Ronald Reagan attacked Carter's handling of the crisis. Renominated by the Democrats, Carter hoped for prompt negotiations so the hostages would be released. The shah, who had moved to Egypt, died in July. Still, the situation did not change.

Finally, two days before the election in the United States, Iranians agreed to negotiate. Carter sent an American team to Algeria, whose government served as mediator. After three long months the American, Algerian, and Iranian negotiators reached an agreement. The United States pledged to return most of the Iranian funds that had been frozen in American banks. The United States also promised not to interfere in Iran's affairs and to help Iran recover the shah's wealth.

The agreement went into effect on January 20, 1981, Inauguration Day for Ronald Reagan, the new president. The hostages, on day 444 of their captivity, left Iran just after President Reagan delivered his inaugural address.

SECTION REVIEW

1. Identify the following: Helsinki Accords, Omar Torrijos Herrera, Anwar el-Sadat, Menachem Begin, PLO.

2. Define the following: apartheid, ayatollah.

3. What nations did Carter criticize for violations of human rights? Why?

4. (a) What were the terms of the two Panama Canal treaties? (b) What reservation was added to the treaties?

5. How did Carter change American policy toward Communist China?

6. (a) What limits would SALT II put on armaments in the Soviet Union and the United States? (b) What was the result of Senate debate on SALT II?

7. What were the provisions of the Camp David Accords?

8. (a) Why did Iranians take American hostages? (b) On what terms were the hostages released?

REAGAN AND THE REPUBLICANS

READ TO FIND OUT

—how Reagan won the election of 1980.

—how Reagan planned to create a prosperous economy.

—why the economy slid into recession.

—how Reagan worked to reduce the size of the federal government.

—how deregulation affected American industries.

—why Reagan's policies caused controversy.

The hostage crisis in Iran shook Americans' faith in their government. Many worried that the nation could not deal effectively with crises overseas. The major concern of Americans, however, was the economy. They wanted inflation controlled, taxes cut, and unemployment reduced.

Many people blamed the Democrats for the nation's economic troubles. They felt that traditional Democratic policies and social programs were not working. As the mood of the public shifted toward conservatism, more voters looked with favor on Ronald Reagan—a Californian with a relaxed style and a conservative message.

THE ELECTION OF 1980

Ronald Reagan gained his first fame in the field of entertainment. He began his career as a radio sports broadcaster, then became a Hollywood actor. In the 1940s and 1950s he served as president of the Screen Actors Guild. His interest in politics did not stop there. An effective speaker, Reagan became a campaigner for the Republicans.

In 1966 Reagan won his first election to public office, as governor of California. During his two terms, Reagan's conservative reputation grew. After losing his bid to be the Republican presidential candidate in 1976, Reagan set his sights on the 1980 nomination.

Some Republican leaders feared that Reagan was too conservative for the voters. They also felt that his age—sixty-nine—was a major drawback. During the spring primaries, however, Reagan proved to be eager and energetic.

More important, the nation seemed ready to accept the Reagan philosophy of thrift, hard work, free enterprise, and patriotism. In July 1980 he easily won the Republican nomination. He chose former CIA director George Bush, a rival for the nomination, as his running mate.

The Democrats were in disorder. Senator Edward M. Kennedy of Massachussetts mounted a strong challenge to Carter. Kennedy called for ambitious government programs to aid the economy. Still, the Democrats chose Jimmy Carter as their candidate. Walter Mondale was renominated for vice-president.

A strong third candidate, Representative John B. Anderson of Illinois, ran as an independent. Anderson, who had lost to Reagan in the Republican primaries, gained support from voters unhappy with both Carter and Reagan. He campaigned as a conservative in money matters and a liberal in many social issues.

In October Carter and Reagan met in Cleveland, Ohio, for a debate which was broadcast across the nation. Carter stressed the goals of peace, human rights, and energy independence. His major theme was nuclear arms control.

Reagan's main theme was the economy. "Are you better off now than you were four years ago?" he asked Americans. Reagan announced that he would build up the military, cut other government spending and taxes, and balance the budget. He promised a "new beginning."

On election day only 54 percent of the voters turned out. It was the lowest percentage since 1948. Most experts had predicted a close race. Instead, Reagan beat Carter by a wide margin. Reagan received some 44 million votes, Carter 35.5 million, and Anderson about 6 million. In the electoral college, Reagan received 489 votes, compared to Carter's 49. Anderson received no electoral votes.

The Republicans also did well in congressional elections. They won control in the Senate and picked up strength in the House of Representatives. Aided by conservative southern Democrats, Reagan would be able to count on strong support in Congress.

President Reagan set his usual vigorous pace for the group that accompanied him. With such constant energy, he easily overcame any doubts about his physical fitness.

REAGAN'S NEW BEGINNING

Reagan lost no time in explaining his economic ideas to the American public and in putting them into practice. He believed in "supply-side" economics, a theory of economics designed to deal with the problem of stagflation.

According to supply-side economists, the government can create a prosperous economy by increasing the nation's supply of goods and services. To increase this supply, the government must lower tax rates, making more money available to Americans for investment. The government must also provide businesses with incentives to expand. Then businesses will increase production, employment will rise, more goods will be produced, and the economy will expand.

In his inaugural address, Reagan presented an economic recovery program based on supply-side economics. He planned tax cuts so that people

Demand-Side and Supply Side Economics

Demand-Side	Supply-Side
GOAL	**GOAL**
To balance the economy by regulating the demand for goods and services	To stimulate the economy by encouraging the production of goods and services
APPROACH	**APPROACH**
Adjust the flow of money by raising or lowering taxes, regulating the money supply and credit, and increasing or decreasing government spending	Make money available by decreasing government spending, reducing taxes, reducing government regulations
EXPECTED RESPONSE	**EXPECTED RESPONSE**
Money available to spend will affect demand; business will adjust production to meet changes in demand; production will be encouraged during hard times, slowed during periods of too rapid growth	Personal and corporate savings will be available for investment; business will have money and incentives for investing in plant, equipment and research
RESULTS	**RESULTS**
Economic growth will take place at an even pace; employment will be steady; inflation will be controlled by government money policies	Production will increase; employment will be steady; inflation will be controlled as production keeps up with or exceeds demand

Economists study the problem of how society chooses to use its limited resources—human, natural, and financial—to satisfy people's wants and needs. Economists analyze facts and formulate theories from which policies are developed. They may differ widely in their views.

would have more money to invest. He also planned to end government regulations that interfered with business. At the same time, Reagan expected to slash the federal budget in most areas except military spending. He wanted to balance the federal budget by doing away with large deficits, or shortages of money.

Two weeks after he was inaugurated, Reagan appeared on nationwide television to describe his program in detail. By March the program, soon known as "Reaganomics," was laid before Congress.

As Reagan worked to build support for the program, near-tragedy struck. On March 30 a lone assailant named John Hinckley, Jr., shot the President and three others. Reagan, wounded in the attack, was hospitalized. Americans were quick to express their horror at the shooting and their sympathy for the President.

By mid-April Reagan was back in the White House, campaigning for the tax and budget cuts. Reagan proved to be an expert at political persuasion. He met with blacks, Hispanics, the poor, the elderly, and others who feared the loss of federal aid programs. There would always be a "safety net," Reagan told them, to help the "truly needy" and prevent severe suffering.

Corporations rallied to Reagan's cause. One company in favor of the tax cut even sent a singing telegram to undecided members of Congress.

REAGANOMICS

On July 31, 1981, Congress approved the budget cuts that Reagan had asked for. Some $35 billion was slashed from the 1982 budget, a cut of about 5 percent. More than 200 federal programs were affected.

Many aid programs were cut. The food stamp program, which allows the poor to buy food with government stamps, was trimmed by $1.6 billion. Other reductions came in housing grants, loans to college students, Medicaid, and federal job-training programs. Federal aid to cities was pared slightly. The government's synthetic fuels research project was canceled. The one budget category that won a large increase was defense.

On August 4 Congress passed the biggest tax-cut bill in history. The Economic Recovery Tax Act would reduce taxes by $280 billion over three years. "We're on the right road," said a pleased Reagan.

The keystone of the bill was a 25 percent cut in individual income tax rates over a 33-month period. Inheritance and gift tax rates were also reduced. So were business taxes. There was even a reduction in the tax rate on business incomes up to $25,000—a benefit to small businesses.

Supporters of Reaganomics were delighted. One economist termed the bill "a minor miracle." Critics, however, pointed out that people earning $15,000 a year or less would receive only about 8 percent of the tax-cut dollars. It was a "royal tax cut," benefiting the wealthy, charged one Democrat.

Still other critics believed that Reaganomics simply would not work. With big tax cuts and a large increase in defense spending, they said, Reagan's goal of a balanced budget was impossible. Indeed, many economists feared a growing deficit in the federal budget. To cover the deficit, the government would have to borrow huge amounts of money. Less money, then, would be available to private borrowers, and business would not have money to invest in growth.

Adding to business's gloom was the "tight money" policy of the Federal Reserve Board. Under this policy, the Federal Reserve Board and the nation's banks raised their interest rates on loans in order to make borrowing more difficult. This reduced the amount of money in circulation, causing spending to decline and prices to drop.

RECESSION

By fall 1981 the economy was slipping. Hurt by high interest rates, the already depressed housing and auto industries fell to lower levels. Related industries, such as steel and lumber, also slumped. The rate of business bankruptcies nearly doubled over the 1980 rate. The stock market sank. Once again, the nation slipped into recession.

Reagan responded to the bad news by urging Congress to cut the budget again. Congress, wary of making more cutbacks, refused. When Congress passed its budget resolution in November, Reagan vetoed it and shut down most federal offices for a day. Reluctantly, Congress cut another $4 billion from the budget. Still, the budget deficit for 1982 would reach $111 billion.

There was one bright spot amid the gloom. Inflation, running about 13 to 15 percent in 1980,

Auto Sales 1972–1982

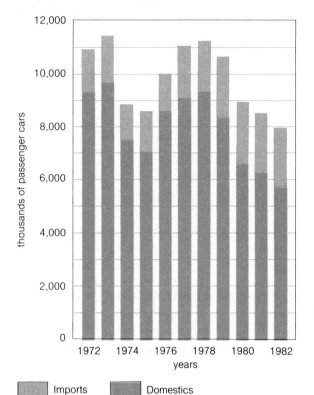

Housing Starts 1972–1982

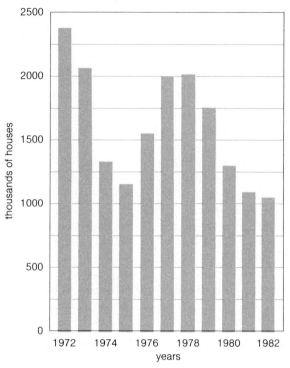

Imports Domestics

Housing starts refers to the beginning of construction on new, permanent, one-family housing. The dip in auto sales and housing starts from 1974 to 1976 reflects, in part, soaring inflation, rising energy costs, high interest rates, and production cutbacks in the auto industry.

dropped to about 9 percent in 1981. Most economists credited the drop to the Federal Reserve Board's tight money policy. Another factor was an oversupply of oil in the world market, which stopped oil prices from rising.

Although worried about the economy, most Americans trusted the President. They were willing to give Reaganomics a chance to work. "It took us 20 years to get into this mess," said a business leader. "We are not going to get out of it in the next 20 months."

BUDGET DEFICITS

The recession deepened in 1982. The economy was stagnant. Unemployment soared to over 10 percent by late summer, the highest rate since 1941. The federal budget deficit, already frighteningly high, seemed likely to go higher. Some experts on eco-

Unemployment 1981–1982

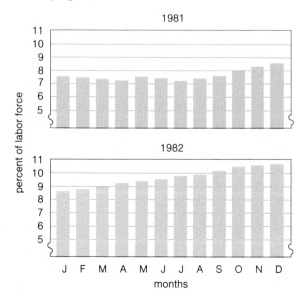

nomics predicted that deficits in the 1983 budget would exceed $200 billion. "Mind boggling," said one Republican.

Through the summer of 1982 Reagan and Congress struggled to work out a budget. Reagan finally threw his support behind a tax increase, reversing his earlier stand. Although opposed by staunch conservatives, the tax bill drew support from a wide range of Republicans and Democrats. In late August it passed, providing a tax increase of $98.3 billion over the next three years.

Most Americans welcomed the bill. It showed the government's determination to reduce the budget deficit and to continue the fight against inflation. Inflation fell below 7 percent by late summer. As inflation fell, the Federal Reserve Board eased its tight money policy. Interest rates declined. Hopeful investors, sensing an economic recovery, sent the stock market booming.

For many Americans, however, the economic signs became real only at the bank, the market, and the office. "I am more worried about Main Street," wrote one man to *Time* magazine, "than I am about Wall Street."

Prime Rate   1981–1982

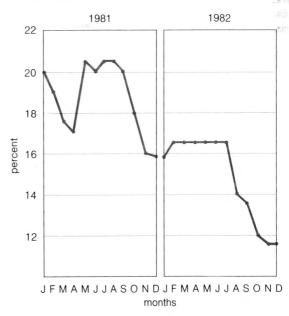

The prime rate represents the average interest rate that major banks charge their most creditworthy commercial customers. Interest rates on other loans tend to be higher.

THE NEW FEDERALISM

While struggling with the economy, President Reagan also worked to reduce the size of the federal government. He had pledged to "take government off the backs" of the people. In various areas, he tried to fulfill the pledge.

In his 1982 State of the Union message, Reagan called for a "New Federalism." This plan would increase the powers of the states by transferring certain programs—especially welfare programs—from the federal government to the states. In addition, federal programs in areas such as education and transportation would be transferred. The states would get some federal money to help cover the costs.

Many governors opposed Reagan's plan. They agreed that services like schools, road building and maintenance, and transit systems should be run by the states. However, the problems of the needy, they said, were often caused by nationwide economic conditions. Therefore, the federal government, not state governments or local communities, should be responsible for welfare.

REDUCED REGULATIONS

To stimulate the economy, the Reagan administration sought to end many regulations on business activity. Some of these regulations were meant to protect the enviroment. The new secretary of the interior, James G. Watt, had spent his career as a lawyer fighting environmental regulations in his native Wyoming and other western states. Watt believed that there was too much protection of public lands and waters. He wanted more private development by industry.

Environmental groups were horrified. The Sierra Club launched a drive to "oust Watt" and collected over a million signatures. But Watt had plenty of supporters. Loggers, miners, and other developers rallied behind him. Many westerners hoped Watt's policy would lead to more jobs in their states. "What we're after," said the *Denver Post*, "is wise use."

Reagan wanted to end other regulations to simplify business procedures. These regulations, he said, involved costs and paperwork that hampered business and pushed up the prices of goods and services.

Government officials reviewed over a hundred regulations, most in the areas of safety, the environment, and consumerism. If the benefit of a regulation did not seem to be worth its cost, it was eliminated. The White House, for example, cut a regulation requiring drug company products to include statements on the possible risks of consuming products.

The administration also stepped up the decontrol of oil and natural-gas prices. And it continued deregulation of the trucking industry, begun by the Carter administration in 1980. Under deregulation, the industry expanded its service and cut its rates. Supporters of the President's deregulation policy pointed to its success in the trucking industry.

CRITICS OF GOVERNMENT CUTBACKS

The President's attempts to lessen the role of the federal government created controversy. One critic claimed that deregulation would "take us back to the nineteenth century and let business regulate itself."

Civil rights groups protested cutbacks in social programs. They argued that reductions in welfare, health care, and housing aid hurt the poor, and that minorities made up a large proportion of the poor. Reagan said that his policies would heal the entire economy and thus help poor people too.

Women's rights supporters faulted Reagan for his opposition to the Equal Rights Amendment. The ERA missed its June 1982 deadline for ratification, still three states short of passage. "The campaign," vowed an ERA leader, "is not over."

However, the women's movement—and a good many of the American people—was pleased with Reagan's appointment of a woman to the Supreme Court. In September 1981 Arizona judge Sandra Day O'Connor became the nation's first female Supreme Court justice. Highly qualified, O'Connor was an ideal choice for this position. The United States Senate confirmed her appointment by a vote of 99 to 0.

In June 1982 Reagan signed a bill that was popular with civil rights groups. It provided a 25-year extension of the Voting Rights Act of 1965. The United States Commission on Civil Rights declared that the law was necessary because minority voters and candidates still faced discrimination.

Agriculture and Industry 1980

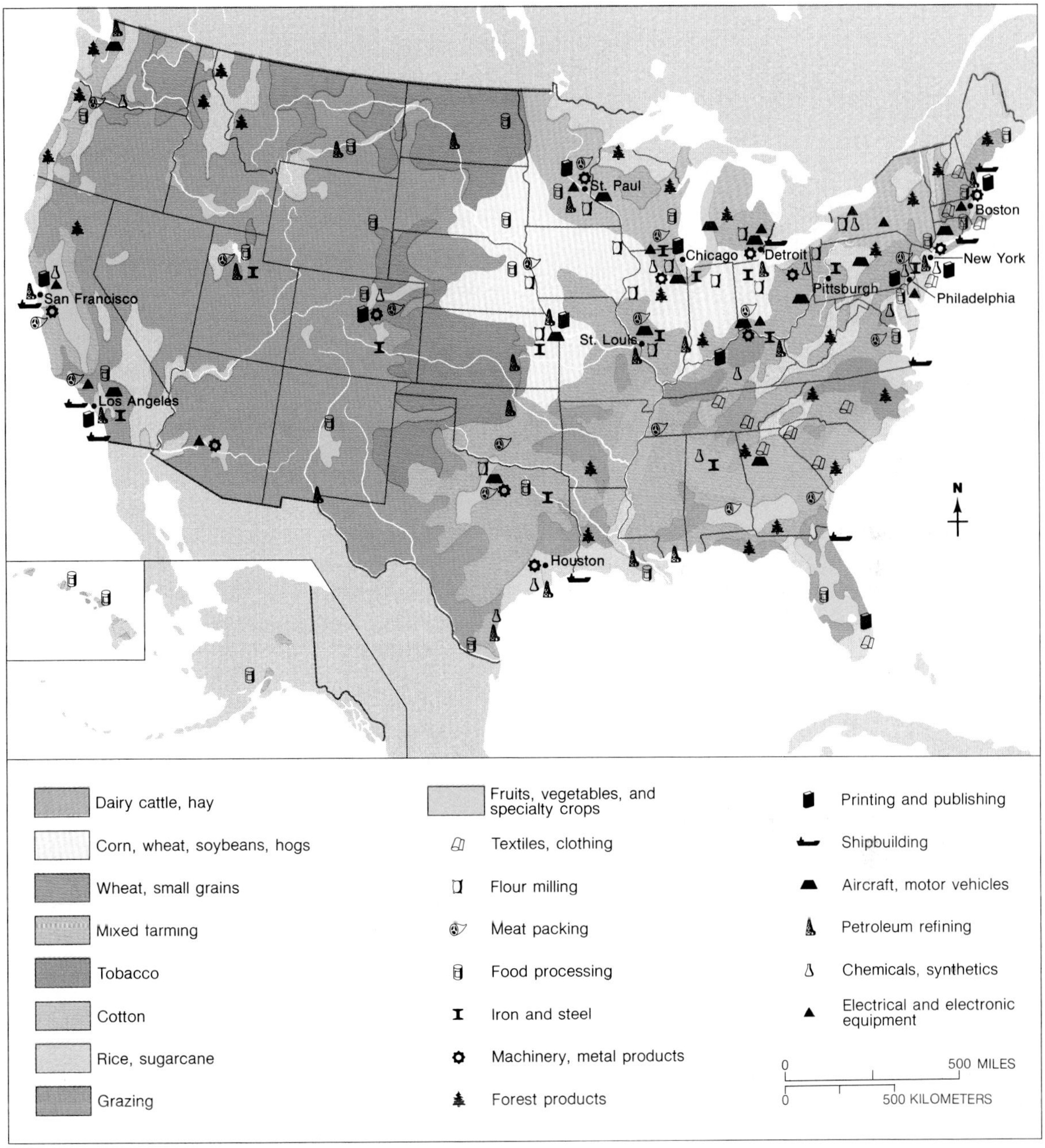

St. Paul
Boston
Chicago
Detroit
New York
San Francisco
Pittsburgh
Philadelphia
St. Louis
Los Angeles
Houston
N
Dairy cattle, hay
Corn, wheat, soybeans, hogs
Wheat, small grains
Mixed farming
Tobacco
Cotton
Rice, sugarcane
Grazing
Fruits, vegetables, and specialty crops
Textiles, clothing
Flour milling
Meat packing
Food processing
Iron and steel
Machinery, metal products
Forest products
Printing and publishing
Shipbuilding
Aircraft, motor vehicles
Petroleum refining
Chemicals, synthetics
Electrical and electronic equipment
0
500 MILES
0
500 KILOMETERS

The application of scientific technology to both agriculture and industry made production more efficient. Farm acreage increased until about 1959, and then began to decline. Yet, farm productivity continued to rise. A greater variety of crops was planted. Industry, which spread from the Northeast to other regions, produced an array of new products.

In general, though, Reagan opposed the claims of consumer and civil-rights groups. He held firmly to his position. He wanted "to reawaken that American spirit of self-reliance, community pride, where the first reaction to a problem isn't 'Let's call Washington.'"

Over a hundred justices were appointed to the Supreme Court before Sandra Day O'Connor became the first woman justice. Here she was accompanied by Chief Justice Warren Burger.

SECTION REVIEW

1. Identify the following: "supply-side" economics, "tight money" policy, "New Federalism," James Watt, Sandra Day O'Connor.

2. (a) What goals did Carter stress during the election campaign? (b) What was Reagan's main election theme?

3. (a) List three provisions of Reagan's economic recovery program. (b) How did he plan to balance the budget?

4. What assurance did Reagan give those who feared the loss of federal aid programs?

5. List five aid programs that were affected by Reagan's budget cuts of July 1981.

6. Describe the American economy in the fall of 1981.

7. Why did the tax-increase bill gain widespread support?

8. (a) List three areas in which government officials tried deregulation. (b) What groups opposed Reagan's efforts to limit the role of the federal government? Why?

FOREIGN POLICY UNDER REAGAN

READ TO FIND OUT

— how Americans divided on the issue of nuclear weapons.

— why martial law was declared in Poland.

— how the United States responded to conflict in Latin America.

— how war erupted in the Middle East.

In foreign policy, Reagan's major goal was to counter the power of the Soviet Union. He worked to strengthen America's ties with old allies and to form new alliances with anti-Communist nations. In a reversal of Carter's foreign policy, Reagan favored ties with anti-Communist nations even when they had poor records on human rights.

THE DEBATE OVER ARMAMENTS

The key to countering the Soviet Union, Reagan felt, was a buildup of United States military strength. After winning huge budget increases, the Department of Defense announced plans to acquire more powerful missiles, long-range bombers, and additional nuclear warheads.*

Most Americans supported a strong defense. However, the military buildup strengthened a growing antinuclear movement both in Europe and the United States. Leaders of the antinuclear movement called for a "freeze," or restriction, on the building of atomic weapons by the United States and the Soviet Union. Nuclear freeze resolutions passed in town meetings, city councils, and state legislatures across the nation.

Critics of freeze resolutions claimed that the Soviets had a stronger nuclear arsenal. A freeze would thus preserve a Soviet advantage. "It's like freezing with their hands at our throat," said one member of Congress.

* warhead: the forward part of a torpedo, missile, etc., that contains the explosive.

This yellow and black sign usually shows people where to find shelters that give protection from radiation. On the umbrella, it was used to protest nuclear power buildup.

War veterans expressed their views at a rally held near the U.S. Capitol. The placards reflect their belief that limitations on nuclear weapons would favor the Soviet Union.

Others, however, declared that each side had more than enough offensive weapons to destroy the other. Admiral Hyman Rickover, who had built up the navy's nuclear fleet, called for cuts in the budget of the Department of Defense. "What's the difference whether we have 100 nuclear submarines or 200?" he asked. "You can sink everything on the oceans several times over with the number we have and so can [the Russians]."

President Reagan faced pressure to resume arms-control talks. The earlier Strategic Arms Limitation Talks treaty (SALT II), concluded by Carter in 1979, had not yet been ratified by Congress. Reagan strongly opposed SALT II, believing that it gave the Soviets an advantage in nuclear weapons. He suggested new negotiations known as Strategic Arms Reduction Talks (START). They began in June 1982 in Geneva, Switzerland.

UNREST IN POLAND

In August 1980 workers at a Polish shipyard on the Baltic Sea put down their tools and went on strike. They won a major victory—the right to form an independent trade union. It was called Solidarity.

By the end of the year Solidarity had 10 million members. The union demanded a voice in government policies and greater freedom for the Polish people. Westerners worried that the Soviet Union would intervene in Poland to crush Solidarity. Instead, the Polish government declared martial law, or rule by the military, as a means of suppressing Solidarity. The government officially suspended the union in December 1981.

President Reagan called on Americans to show their "solidarity with the Polish people." He also limited trade with both Poland and the Soviet Union. The trade restrictions, however, had little impact, and the grip of martial law tightened in Poland.

CONFLICT IN LATIN AMERICA

Two areas of Latin America presented problems to the Reagan administration. Central America was one. In Guatemala and El Salvador, pro-Communist guerrillas were battling anti-Communist governments.

In Nicaragua, a pro-Communist group had already come to power. Reagan announced increased economic aid to the anti-Communist regimes. "It helps our neighbors help themselves," said the President early in 1982.

The United States became most directly involved in El Salvador. Since 1980 civil war had raged in that nation. Rebels fought for redistribu-

Government soldiers are a familiar sight to these Salvadoran children. Their nation, El Salvador, has frequently been plagued by political unrest and violence.

United States hoped to form close ties. Reagan tried to steer a neutral course, and sent Secretary of State Alexander Haig on a peace-keeping mission.

After a month of fruitless talks, Haig announced that the United States would side with Britain. Argentina was clearly the aggressor, said Haig, and the Falklanders wanted to remain British subjects. Joined by 14 western nations, the United States imposed economic sanctions on Argentina. Britain received American military aid. By mid-June, British troops had regained the Falklands.

One loser in the war, many observers felt, was the United States. Although few Latin American nations approved of Argentina's aggression against the Falklands, most supported its claim to the islands. These nations were angry at the United States for supporting Britain.

TENSIONS IN THE MIDDLE EAST

New outbreaks of violence disrupted the Middle East. In 1980 Iran and Iraq, ruled by different Islamic groups, went to war over disputed territory. The war further divided the Arab world, which was already split by religious differences.

The Middle East received a shock in October 1981. President Anwar el-Sadat of Egypt was assassinated by Egyptians who opposed his peace negotiations with Israel and his friendship with the West. Along with a stunned world, the United States mourned Sadat.

The Mideast turmoil prompted American leaders to strengthen ties with friendly Arab states, especially Saudi Arabia. In October 1981 the Senate, urged on by Reagan, approved the sale of advanced military equipment to the Saudis.

The sale further strained American-Israeli relations. They had been tense since June 1981, when Israel bombed a nuclear reactor project in Iraq. The Israelis had flown American-made jets, violating a United States rule that Israel could use American-built equipment only for defense.

Another strain on American-Israeli relations came in December 1981. Israel annexed the Golan Heights, territory it had won from Syria in 1967 and had occupied ever since. Because the high, rocky piece of land borders Syria and overlooks Israel, the Israelis insisted that they needed it to be secure from Syrian attack. The United States rebuked Israel, saying that the annexation was not legal.

tion of land and other reforms. Government troops tried in vain to suppress the revolt. Meanwhile, under pressure from the United States, the Salvadoran government established a land reform program. This outraged many conservative Salvadorans, who began their own war against the rebels. By 1982 an estimated 30,000 Salvadorans had died in the violence.

Besides sending economic and military aid to the anti-Communist Salvadoran government, Reagan also sent about fifty military advisers. Critics were soon comparing the United States' role in El Salvador with the American experience in the Vietnam War. Reagan, however, insisted that aid to El Salvador was vital to counter arms shipments from Cuba and Nicaragua to the rebels.

WAR IN THE FALKLANDS

In April 1982 a crisis erupted in another area of Latin America—the Falkland Islands, off the coast of Argentina. Most of the 1,800 islanders were British subjects, and Britain had long claimed the Falklands as its territory. But Argentina also claimed the islands.

In early April, Argentine troops invaded the Falklands. Outraged, the British sent a huge fleet to recapture the islands.

The United States was caught in the middle of the dispute. Britain was a NATO ally and close friend. Argentina was a nation with which the

CIVIL WAR IN LEBANON

In 1982 the focus of Mideast tensions shifted to Lebanon, Israel's neighbor to the north. Since 1975 it had been divided by civil war between Christian and Islamic factions. The Islamic faction received aid from Syrian troops stationed in Lebanon. The Christians in Lebanon found neighboring Israel a valuable ally.

Complicating the situation were hundreds of thousands of Palestinians living in Lebanon. Some belonged to the Palestine Liberation Organization (PLO). For years, PLO and Israeli forces had battled each other across Lebanon's borders.

In the summer of 1982, Israel launched an invasion of Lebanon. Israel's goals were to destroy the PLO's military bases and to drive the Syrians out of Lebanon. Israel hoped that the Christians would then take control of Lebanon's government.

Within weeks the Israelis had pushed north and laid siege to Beirut (bay-ROOT), the Lebanese capital. Of the 500,000 people trapped in western Beirut, some 6,000 were PLO guerrillas.

Nine cease-fires were set up and then broken during the fighting. Finally, in late August, American negotiator Philip Habib worked out a settlement. A temporary peace-keeping force of American, French, and Italian troops supervised the evacuation of PLO forces from Beirut. Several Arab nations took in the guerrillas.

Yet Mideast tensions remained high. Years of bloodshed between Islamic and Christian forces in Lebanon had produced deep hatred. The bloodshed had become part of the larger struggle between Israel and Syria. The Reagan administration still worked for diplomatic breakthroughs to prevent new outbreaks of violence.

SECTION REVIEW

1. Identify the following: Solidarity, Alexander Haig, Golan Heights, Philip Habib.

2. (a) What was Reagan's major goal in foreign policy? (b) How did he plan to achieve that goal? (c) How did Reagan respond to the antinuclear movement?

3. How did the Polish government respond to the demands of Solidarity?

4. (a) Why did Reagan send aid to El Salvador? (b) Why did some Americans oppose this aid?

5. How was the United States caught in the middle of the Falkland Islands dispute?

6. Why were relations between the United States and Israel strained?

7. (a) What two groups formed opposing sides in Lebanon? (b) What third group complicated the situation?

8. What settlement was reached in Lebanon?

Israeli bombing of Beirut in 1982 destroyed many buildings and filled the streets with huge piles of rubble. American soldiers in the peace-keeping force stood guard among the ruins.

SUMMARY

James Earl Carter, Jr., came to the presidency with the hope of uniting the nation and of restoring Americans' faith in their government. He tried to create a government that was close to the people.

Carter also hoped to stimulate the nation's economy. Congress passed legislation to increase federal spending and to create more jobs. However, the rate of inflation began to rise, and Carter reduced spending, which pushed the nation toward recession. An unfavorable balance of trade and declines in key industries worsened the problem.

Carter tried to end the nation's reliance on imported oil. However, revolution in the Middle East led to gasoline shortages in the United States. At the same time, oil prices soared. In response, Congress approved Carter's plan to create a government energy corporation.

At home and abroad, Carter supported human rights. His administration brought more women, blacks, and Hispanics into government and stressed Indian concerns. It also allowed greater numbers of immigrants to enter the nation.

In foreign affairs, Carter negotiated agreements with Panama, the People's Republic of China, and the Soviet Union. He mediated the Camp David Accords between Egypt and Israel. However, Soviet intervention in Afghanistan chilled détente. In addition, revolution in Iran led to the taking of American hostages. Only after Carter left office were the hostages released.

Ronald Reagan was elected to the presidency in 1980 because of the hostage crisis and the nation's economic troubles. He quickly proposed, and Congress passed, an economic recovery program for the nation. Inflation declined, but the nation slid into a recession. Budget deficits also rose as did the unemployment rate.

In foreign affairs, Reagan worked to counter Soviet power. He built up American military strength and supported anti-Communist governments in Latin America. However, he opened new negotiations with the Soviets to reduce arms. Reagan also tried to negotiate peace in the Falkland Islands and in Lebanon. He lost a valuable ally in the death of Egyptian president Anwar el-Sadat.

CHAPTER REVIEW

1. (a) Explain how each of the following was an attempt by Carter to stimulate the economy: funds for public works, jobs for the young and the elderly, a tax rebate, tax cuts for businesses. (b) How did these measures affect the economy?

2. (a) Describe Carter's actions to reduce inflation. (b) Compare these actions with Carter's actions to stimulate the economy.

3. The main goal of Carter's energy program was to reduce oil imports by 50 percent by 1990. (a) Describe the program that Carter proposed to meet that goal. (b) Which parts of his program were adopted? (c) How did the policies of the Reagan administration affect the program?

4. (a) Compare the views of environmentalists and business groups regarding environmental laws. (b) What was the position of the Carter administration? The Reagan administration? Cite examples.

5. How did each of the following groups gain expanded opportunities during the Carter administration? (a) women (b) blacks (c) Hispanics (d) Indians

6. (a) Describe two goals of Carter's foreign policy toward the Soviet Union. (b) How did these goals contradict each other? (c) How did Reagan change American policy toward the Soviet Union?

Keeping vigil for the hostages in Iran, many Americans tied yellow ribbons on trees and bushes. The idea grew from a popular song, "Tie a Yellow Ribbon Round the Ole Oak Tree."

On July 21, 1981, NASA's *Voyager 2* was 27 million miles (43 million kilometers) from Saturn. A camera, using color filters, shot the three images combined for this photograph.

7. Explain how each event led to the next. (a) admission of China to the UN General Assembly (b) Nixon's visit to China (c) United States recognition of the People's Republic of China (d) cancellation of diplomatic relations with Taiwan

8. How did each of the following contribute to tension in the Middle East? (a) the Six-Day War (b) Israeli settlements on the West Bank and in the Gaza Strip (c) Palestinian Arabs (d) civil war in Lebanon

9. (a) Explain how Reagan carried out his campaign pledges for a "new beginning." (b) How did budget deficits and recession affect his actions? Explain.

10. (a) Why did conflict in Latin America present problems to the Reagan administration? Cite examples. (b) How did Reagan's actions lead to controversy?

ISSUES AND IDEAS

1. Immigrants who poured into the United States in the 1970s faced the same problems that earlier waves of immigrants had faced. Do you agree with this statement? Why or why not? Cite examples.

2. Carter declared that "because we are free, we can never be indifferent to the fate of freedom elsewhere." What did he mean? What problems might arise from a foreign policy based on this view? What benefits? Cite examples.

3. Reagan pledged to reduce the size of the federal government. How did this policy differ from the policies of Democratic administrations between the 1930s and the 1970s? Cite examples.

SKILLS WORKSHOP

1. *Maps.* Look at pages 356 and 731 of your book. Find the maps entitled "Agriculture and Industry 1890" and "Agriculture and Industry 1980." How has agriculture changed since 1890? What new centers of manufacturing developed between 1890 and 1980? How has manufacturing changed since 1890?

2. *Graphs.* Many factors influence the rate of inflation in a nation. Look at page 711 of your book. Find the graph entitled "Oil Prices." In which years did the price of oil rise the most? By how much? Now turn to the Resource Center at the back of your book. Find the graph entitled "The Consumer Price Index and the Purchasing Power of the Dollar." In which years did consumer prices rise the most? By what percentages? How did the price of oil influence this rise?

PAST AND PRESENT

1. Describe efforts in or around your community to conserve energy.

2. Describe how environmental laws have affected industries in or around your community.

Recycling helps to conserve natural resources and to reduce pollution. Glass waste can be recycled and used in making new glass containers and roadbuilding materials.

CHAPTER 30

TOWARD THE NEXT CENTURY

1975–Present

AMERICANS AND TECHNOLOGICAL CHANGE
AMERICANS AND THEIR SURROUNDINGS
AMERICANS ON THE MOVE
THE AMERICAN PEOPLE

On April 14, 1981, the space shuttle *Columbia* completed its first flight. At a postflight briefing, astronaut John W. Young described slides showing the view from space:

"The earth is a beautiful thing. It really is . . . . As you look out the window you can see—the eye can see in three dimensions—the earth forms. The mountains, the valleys, the rivers, and the towns. . . .

"This is a picture of my home town, San Francisco. And the bay there. There's the south—the Ames Research Center is down there somewhere right about there. You can see the bridge right across the bay there if you get up real close—the Golden Gate Bridge. You can't see the Oakland Bay Bridge but you can see that island right in the middle—Treasure Island. Some of the places we used to work at, the Naval Air Station there and San Francisco Airport down in this region right here. That place is as beautiful from orbit as it is close up. . . .

"There's Boston Harbor, that tea party where it all started. Plymouth Rock and a few places like that, and that's really a beautiful picture. You can see all of those places from orbit. I think I saw the *Constitution* down there somewhere."

The world's first reusable spacecraft performed flawlessly. Launched like a rocket, *Columbia* orbited like a spaceship and landed like an airplane. Columbia will be able to haul cargo into space and to serve as an orbiting scientific laboratory. Indeed, the shuttle is being called "the Conestoga wagon of the space frontier."

Columbia stirred memories of earlier leaps into new frontiers. It was like a voyage across the Atlantic to the New World. It was akin to the first transcontinental railroad, which opened the West. And to many Americans, it showed that a pioneering spirit still surged through the nation.

AMERICANS AND TECHNOLOGICAL CHANGE

READ TO FIND OUT

— **what a fully automatic factory is like.**

— **how robots may change work.**

— **why knowledge of computers is important.**

— **how computers affect businesses and homes.**

One of the major forces of change in American history has been technology. In America's first century, the Industrial Revolution made great changes in the labor field by replacing hand tools with machine tools. During the nation's second century, the search continued for ways to produce more goods with less human labor.

By America's third century, computer-run machines were doing routine work in offices and factories. The genius of Eli Whitney, Henry Ford, and others has now been combined with the wonders of modern electronics. Some people are hailing this technological change as the "robot revolution."

THE ROBOT FACTORY

A technician sits at a counterlike desk facing a control panel of dials, buttons, lights, and flickering video images. Familiar factory sounds rise up to this catwalk perch from the work floor below. Air compressors hiss, rivets pop, drills whine.

To the visitor, the sounds are familiar, but the scene is eerie. The night-shift factory is not soaked in bright light. Rather, the noisy work floor is dark. There are no workers. Outside in the vast parking lot sit only the visitor's and the technician's cars.

The technician throws a switch lighting up the entire building, and the two people can now look down on an assembly line in full operation. Some fifty unfinished cars advance on a conveyor belt between two rows of cranelike machines. When the belt stops, the machines bend forward and touch car metal in a shower of sparks. Operating in unison, each of the machines completes a perfect weld.

These robot, or machine, welders bend back and forth again and again—two hundred welds on every car, forty-eight cars every hour. At dawn, the same machines work the day shift. There are no sick days, no paid vacations, no raises.

The work floor is cluttered with other machines doing a variety of tasks. Most are equipped with clawlike "hands," each designed to grip a special tool or a part. The machines move swiftly, precisely. A broken bit on an electric drill causes only a moment's delay. The machine ejects the bit and installs a new one.

After seven months in this computer operated factory, the technician says that the job is both fascinating and unsettling. He considers the self-operating machines to be an industrial miracle. In minutes a technician can program, or instruct, a machine to do a different job simply by changing its packet of computer chips.

Still, the technician finds the work atmosphere strange without people. "The workers used to take a lot of pride in their product," he says. "And there was always a lot of joking and kidding around."

As technology advances, robots will begin to appear in places other than laboratories and factories. You might meet one walking down the street.

CHANGES IN WORK

The Japanese were the first to assemble automobiles that were "untouched by human hands." They used microcomputers developed in the United States as the "brains" of their robots. As the Japanese automated their factories, their nation's industrial production jumped.

To compete, American companies also turned to labor-saving robots. By 1981 the United States had some 5,000 of the "steel-collar workers." Most were in the automobile and aircraft industries. But robots were also assembling refrigerators, mining coal, and even washing windows.

Business owners are delighted with the robots. The hourly cost of a robot is far lower than a worker's hourly wage. And the robots free workers from dirty, boring, and dangerous jobs. Hazardous substances, for example, can be handled by computerized "hands."

Some Americans worry that the workers replaced by robots will not find other jobs. However, says one robot maker, "We're creating a brand-new industry—a bigger one by far than whatever we'll be replacing." Displaced workers can be trained to do skilled jobs in both old and new industries.

Indeed, one executive predicts that by the early 1990s about one half of the American work force will labor in "electronic work stations." The new employee, states the executive, "had better come on the job with computer know-how." A growing number of Americans are gaining that know-how at an early age from home training, in school, or in private tutoring programs.

COMPUTER CAMPS

Under New Mexico's deep blue sky, a dozen teenagers bask in the steamy warmth of a natural hot springs. It seems like the perfect way to spend a lazy afternoon at summer camp. But when a car pulls up, everyone scrambles to be among the first to go back to the ranch house. It is time for a two-hour work session with the computers.

At the adobe ranch house, the students work individually or in small groups. Assignments depend on the students' "computer literacy." Some students are beginners, learning how to program in a computer language called BASIC. The two most advanced students are learning to work with graphics. They are developing a game called "Moon Landing," which uses visual images of a lunar landscape.

"I guess it's not hard to tell that we all want careers that involve computers," says a high school senior from Denver, Colorado. The camp director

Computer-assisted instruction is rapidly becoming part of the typical American school day. Reading is only one of many areas where computers are helpful.

Indicators of an "information revolution" rest on the desks of office workers. The word processor keyboards and television like screens keep company data flowing.

emphasizes the point. "It's going to be harder to find jobs that don't involve computers. Learning how to use them may become almost as basic as reading and writing."

THE COMPUTER AGE

The kinds of jobs that Americans are applying for in the 1980s show the importance of computer skills. One typical want ad in northern California asks for: "PROGRAMMER—Lightning fast programmer, must be able to write bug-free code." However, it is not only the high-technology firms that are seeking people with computer skills. Another ad reads: "TRAVEL AGENT—Experienced. Computer training preferred."

Computer education will give people the skills to answer those want ads. In schools, students are learning computer languages. Computers coach students in math, reading, and history. Computers are also becoming a part of many careers, from engineer to salesperson to test pilot.

The computer boom does not end at the school or office. Across the nation, home computers are used for playing games and doing budgets. By hooking up to information centers called data banks, users can send "electronic mail," check movie reviews, and keep up with the stock market trading on Wall Street. In Columbus, Ohio, people take part in public opinion polls by punching a few buttons on their home computers.

SECTION REVIEW

1. What is a fully automatic factory like?

2. Name three jobs that industrial robots can do besides assembling cars.

3. (a) Why do business owners like robot workers? (b) What new industry is being created by the demand for robot workers?

4. Why is study of computers practical in terms of careers?

AMERICANS AND THEIR SURROUNDINGS

READ TO FIND OUT

— what may replace fossil fuels as sources of power for automobiles.

— how a home can be built to capture the sun's heat.

— what nonfossil fuels can be used to produce electricity.

— how scientists are improving forests.

— how forests contribute to human well-being.

In the spring of 1970, millions of Americans ushered in the new decade by celebrating "Earth Day." They marched under banners protesting pollution. They also picked up trash, planted trees, and joined in other projects to "save the earth." Their goal was to focus national attention on environmental problems.

In the spring of 1979, Americans ushered out the decade by waiting in long lines at gasoline stations. Panicked by a gasoline shortage, drivers rushed to fill their automobile tanks. During the 1970s oil had become an expensive—and sometimes a scarce—product.

In the spring of 1980, the issues of energy and the environment clashed at the Environmental Decade Conference. During the next ten years, many delegates felt, conservation would have to be given less emphasis in order to pursue energy development. Thus, a question ushered in the 1980s. Could Americans both fill their automobile tanks and save the earth?

AN ALTERNATIVE FUEL

Chuck Stone has tried to answer that question by creating an experimental car. This car and its fuel, he believes, will liberate the United States from its dependence on foreign oil. Instead of gasoline,

Stone's car runs on *methanol*, commonly known as wood alcohol.

Although supplies of methanol are still limited, Stone is convinced that it is the "future fuel of America." Methanol can be made from coal, wood, vegetation, garbage, even manure. Stone sells it to his car customers at considerably less than the price of gasoline, and he makes a profit. Although mileage ratings with methanol are not yet as good as with gasoline, the low price cuts driving costs.

Stone convinced officials at the Bank of America in San Francisco, California, of the potential of methanol. Bank of America agreed to convert 150 of the company's vehicles to methanol. They estimate that their savings could top a million dollars per year.

It is possible that a methanol industry would create thousands of new jobs and would free the nation from importing oil. But there is a problem, common to many alternative sources of energy. Methanol cars cannot be produced until there are stations to supply the fuel. And no one will invest in "methanol stations" until there are cars on the road creating a demand.

OTHER FUELS

The idea of using methanol as fuel is not new. Americans have experimented with this and other fuels throughout the twentieth century. Not until 1973, however, did these experiments seem urgent. At that time, the members of the Organization of Petroleum Exporting Countries (OPEC) quadrupled the price of oil. By the 1980s, Americans realized that the era of inexpensive, abundant energy had ended.

Throughout the nation, Americans set to work to develop alternative fuels. An Iowan devised the cheapest alternative—a car that runs on compressed air. Dozens of inventors worked to improve battery-operated cars, which are slow and need to be recharged often. In Florida a retired automotive engineer refined a gasoline engine, hoping to get 90 miles (145 kilometers) per gallon.

One of the promising experiments was *gasohol*. In this fuel gasoline is mixed with alcohol produced from corn, potatoes, or sugarcane. Cars performed well on gasohol. However, some experts declare that more energy is consumed in producing the alcohol than is saved by the use of the fuel.

Solar One, in California's Mojave Desert, is the world's largest solar-powered electrical generating plant. The heliostats (mirrors) reflect sunlight to produce power.

SOLAR ENERGY

"We felt like pioneers," Doreen Callan said about the decision that she and her husband made to build a home using solar energy—energy that comes from the sun. "You gather all the information you can and still you can't learn enough. There's no escaping the feeling that you're plunging into some unknown adventure."

They had bought land in the hilly country of western Massachusetts—the first frontier in America's westward movement over three centuries ago. Partly because of those hills, the winter temperature often drops well below freezing. The Callans would need all the solar heat they could get.

The blueprints showed how the home would be heated. The north side of the first floor would be built into the hill, giving the house natural protection against chill north winds. With the earth as an insulator, the house would have little heat loss. However, there would be few windows along the north wall.

In contrast, the south wall of the house was designed almost entirely of glass, stretching upward to a cathedrallike ceiling. With the winter sun strongest in the south, the glass wall would flood the house with light and heat.

The Callans were told that the floors should be flagstone to hold in the sun's warmth. They agreed to a bare, uncarpeted flagstone floor.

"We were learning to get along with the changes that solar energy demanded," Doreen said, "And that became part of the adventure. We knew that a [nonsolar] house this size would take at least 2,500 gallons [9,500 liters] of oil every year. That's 2,500 gallons we won't be needing."

OTHER ENERGY SOURCES

The Callans used only one of several ways to harness the sun's energy and put it to work. Solar energy today heats a growing number of homes and offices, and powers most of America's satellites and spacecraft. So far, however, the sun provides only a fraction of the energy used by Americans.

Meanwhile, inventors, companies, and government research teams are developing other energy sources. A Californian has taken "an old technology"—the windmill—and updated it with fiberglass blades and a microcomputer brain. This towering windmill produces as much electricity per day as a barrel of oil.

Americans are producing another energy source every day—millions of tons of garbage. At some two dozen "waste transfer stations," trash is burned to generate steam and electricity.

There are still other ways to wrest energy from the earth. The heat escaping from the earth in the form of steam and hot gases produces an enormous amount of energy. Power plants in the United States are beginning to tap this *geothermal energy*. Some Americans also hope to harness the power of the ocean's tides.

These energy sources have real advantages. Americans will not exhaust the supply of sun, wind, tides, steam, or garbage. And, except for trash, these resources do not pollute, or dirty, the environment. However, these energy alternatives can be costly or inefficient.

Many Americans have high hopes for nuclear energy. In 1980 nuclear reactors generated about 12 percent of the nation's electricity. Critics, however, charge that nuclear plants are unsafe, and they point to the accident in 1979 at Three Mile Island as proof.

Until problems are solved in the use of solar batteries, trash, or nuclear reactors, the United States will continue to rely on fuels that are dug from the earth. These *fossil fuels*—coal, oil, and natural gas—still produce most of the nation's energy.

One energy study called coal "a bridge to the future." The United States has nearly 30 percent of the world's coal reserves. But mining coal deep in the earth is dangerous work. Strip mining coal close to the surface scars the land. And burning coal pollutes the air.

Another way to supply the nation with more energy is through conservation. By using less energy today, Americans will have more for the future. Many Americans are conserving. They drive less, and outfit their homes and businesses to save energy. As one power-plant official said, "What's the difference between hanging storm windows and building a new power plant? We get more kilowatt-hours either way." He added, "Conservation's a lot quicker."

REFORESTATION

In northern California there are mountain ranges strung along the Pacific coastline. On the foggy mountainsides of the Coast Ranges grow some of the worlds' biggest trees—the redwoods. Redwoods commonly soar up to 275 feet (84 meters) high, with trunks like massive barrels.

Forester Steve Jolly tramps through this colossal forest, with a shotgun slung under his arm. Jolly is searching for a "Plus tree," a giant among giants. Suddenly, ahead, he sees it. The redwood dwarfs its neighbors by 80 feet (24 meters). Jolly raises his shotgun, takes aim, fires. A small branch crashes to the forest floor. The majestic old redwood has lost only a sliver of its growth. Yet the forest, Jolly hopes, will gain more giants.

Jolly brings his branch back to the nursery. The tip of the branch, full of life, is planted. It soon begins to flower and, in time, will grow cones. The cones will be pollinated and will produce seeds, which will sprout into new plants. Finally, the foresters will plant the seedlings back in the forest. When the seedlings grow into trees, the best of them will be bred.

The outcome of this experiment, foresters hope, will be new kinds of redwoods. These trees will grow faster, bigger, stronger, and straighter than today's giants, even in poor soil. They will be "supertrees."

Since the 1930s reforestation has been a major land-use activity in the United States. Sufficient healthy forests play an essential role in the ecological system.

For over forty years foresters have been operating tree farms and replanting logged lands with seedlings. Through this *reforestation,* they hoped, the nation's supply of trees would keep up with the demand for wood.

ENERGY AND THE ENVIRONMENT

In some 5 million homes Americans feed logs into word-burning stoves. Many of these people switched from gas, oil, or electric heating in order to save money. Firewood, they feel, is a logical alternative energy source.

Burning wood may help to end American dependence on fossil fuels. But the use of firewood—along with lumber, paper, telephone poles, and other wood products—puts a strain on forests.

Few people would argue that no trees should be logged. Still, the forests have uses other than to supply wood. They offer recreation year-round to skiers, hunters, and campers. Those seeking solitude and wilderness beauty come to forests to find these pleasures.

Forests are energy makers. They renew the oxygen supply and produce plant matter on which animals feed. They soak up rainwater, which might otherwise erode or flood the land. Forests are also excellent pollution filters. Pollutants from the air catch in treetops. The leaves are then washed clean by rain, and the pollutants settle safely on the ground.

Like forests, the rest of the environment fills various roles—roles that are not always compatible. That presents Americans with difficult choices. Can they tap the valuable resources of the environment, and at the same time conserve it?

SECTION REVIEW

1. Explain why a large automobile maker probably would not switch over quickly to production of methanol-burning cars.

2. Give reasons for building a solar-heated house (a) set into a knoll, (b) with a south-facing wall of glass, (c) with a floor of uncovered flagstones.

3. How has the old technology of windmills been updated?

4. How do forests (a) provide recreation, (b) prevent erosion, (c) reduce pollution?

AMERICANS ON THE MOVE

READ TO FIND OUT

—why Americans keep moving.

—where Americans have tended to move in recent years.

—how people rebuilt houses and stores in Baltimore.

—how American cities are being renewed.

Americans have always been ready to move. Many of their ancestors crossed an ocean to reach the New World, in search of land, opportunity, and freedom. They soon gained a toehold on the edge of a continent. Year by year, the restless pioneers pushed across the land.

These movers were also builders. Towns sprang up in the wake of pioneers. Americans moved mountains and dug rivers to lace the continent with roads, railroad tracks, and canals.

By the 1900s the untracked frontier was vanishing, but not the movers and builders. In midcentury, poet Archibald MacLeish wrote:

> We have the tools and the skill and the intelligence to take our cities apart and to put them together, to lead our roads and rivers where we please to lead them, to build our houses where we want our houses, to brighten the air, to clean the wind.

Today Americans still pack up and move, still take up a hammer and build, in the hope of a fresh start and new opportunities.

GONE TO TEXAS

"Everything we owned was piled on this broken down old truck," Charlie Rivera wrote. "Chairs were tied over the roof of the cab and odd-shaped items seemed to poke in all directions. Mom worried about losing things on the way. Dad worried about whether the truck could make a trip from the northern border to the southern, from Detroit, Michigan, to El Paso, Texas."

The students in Charlie Rivera's school class were writing about how they came to be in this "new town" just outside El Paso. Charlie's essay told a story typical of the whole class.

His father had worked for an automobile manufacturer in Detroit. One year he was laid off for 18 weeks, the next year for 26 weeks, and then he was fired. The family began talking of moving anywhere that Mr. Rivera might find a job. And they also talked about finding a warmer climate. The fuel bills to heat their eighty-year-old house had become an almost impossible burden.

The Riveras had heard about the Sunbelt states of the South and the Southwest, from Virginia to California. The Sunbelt is the fastest growing region of the nation.

One day Mr. Rivera began talking about Texas. "Our family came from Texas," he said. "We were pioneers there when it was still Spanish. This would be like becoming modern pioneers, entering Texas from the north, and starting a new town."

"But what about jobs?" asked the family. "Is there work in Texas?"

Mr. Rivera happily showed them a letter. "I've been offered a job in . . . a television company."

MOBILE AMERICANS

Every year between 30 million and 40 million Americans pack up and move. That is about the same number as the total immigration to the United States between 1820 and 1950. Every 12 months, then, a great migration takes place. Yet it is scarcely noticed as a historic event because Americans have always moved from one part of the country to another.

During the 1970s people poured out of the older states of the Northeast and upper Midwest. Their goal was the Sunbelt, which offered jobs, sunshine, recreation, and retirement areas. The population of the Sunbelt increased by over 7 million people. All the newcomers, however, began to strain the resources and economy of the Sunbelt. By the early 1980s the southward migration slowed.

The shift in the nation's population means a change in political strength in the House of Representatives. With the 1980 census, 17 House seats shifted from the Northeast and Midwest to the South and West. These regions are now home to more than half the American people.

Americans everywhere are also heading in a direction they have not followed for over a century and a half. They are moving to—not away from—rural areas and small towns. In the 1970s these areas grew faster than cities and their suburbs.

By leaving the cities, people hope to escape urban crime and declining public services. Some follow businesses relocating in rural areas. Some want to live simpler lives close to the land.

While many people are leaving the cities, however, some are moving in. They are known as "urban pioneers."

URBAN PIONEERS

One dollar for a house! The price was not a joke or an advertising gimmick. Doris Shamleffer said that the price persuaded her to become an urban pioneer in Baltimore, Maryland.

"All my life," she said, "I'd felt that Baltimore's row houses were one of the great architectural reminders of our colonial past." The houses share common walls, making a solid form that stretches for an entire block. "But," Shamleffer continues, "I had also watched them falling into greater ruin every year. A lot were abandoned. Others had become depressing slums."

Two housing units in Savannah, Georgia, make a strong case for individual effort at urban renewal. They testify to the need (left) and to the result (right).

The Population Shift to the South and West 1970-1980

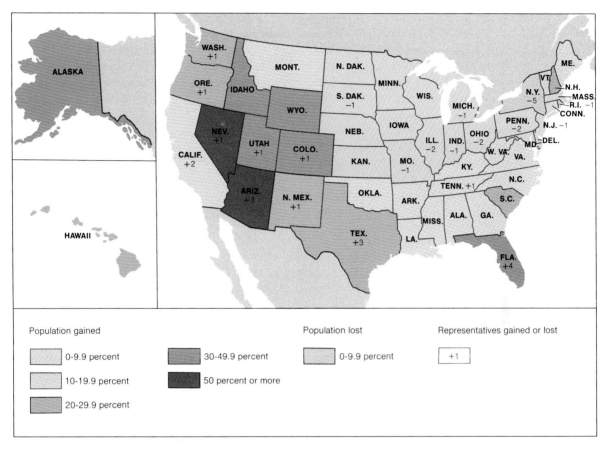

By 1980 more than half of the nation's population lived in the Sunbelt. For the first time the South and the West would have a majority in the House of Representatives. Cities in Florida and Texas grew rapidly. Houston, Texas, was the fastest growing city in the nation.

Like many big cities, Baltimore had been decaying for years. The old shipbuilding city was blighted by rotting wharves, a high jobless rate, and crime. Its population dwindled, and people who stayed called Baltimore "the Survival City."

Then, in the mid-1970s, everything began to change. Neighborhood associations were formed. Many of them represented minority groups—especially black Americans, who are a majority of the city's population. By working with city government, they gained new opportunities for rebuilding Baltimore.

People like Mayor William Schaefer found ways to gain funds for city improvement from the federal government. New street lighting and more police improved safety. A federal grant enabled Shamleffer to buy her one-dollar house. The balance was to be paid off by "sweat equity."

"I'll tell you what 'sweat equity' is," she said. "You learn how to be an electrician, a plumber, carpenter, painter, wallpaper-hanger, plasterer and general handy person. Then you set to work night after night and all day on weekends. Anything you don't know how to do you just ask someone because just about your whole block is being worked on at once."

Not just houses were being saved. Under a program known as "shopsteading," business people were rebuilding run-down stores. And new life pulsed through Baltimore's old waterfront. Useless wharves and warehouses were replaced by Harborplace—a center of shopping and entertainment.

"After years of watching things go downhill people had had enough," concluded Shamleffer. "They began to act and suddenly discovered that everyone else had the same idea."

HOPE FOR THE CITIES

In other parts of the country Americans are beginning to come to the rescue of their cities. In Paterson, New Jersey, abandoned factories are converted into offices. With paint and a hefty private loan, the citizens of Savannah, Georgia, are restoring the city's Victorian houses. Lowell, Massachusetts—the nineteenth-century textile center—is also reviving. City officials lured new businesses to Lowell with grants and low-cost land.

Of course, many cities are still beset by problems. And the flight of people out of cities far exceeds the movement in. But the transformation in Baltimore can happen elsewhere. "Reports of the death of the American city were premature," says one urban developer. "The American city isn't dying. It's being reborn."

In Philadelphia, as in most large American cities, problems of urban renewal await a solution.

SECTION REVIEW

1. (a) Give two reasons why the family of Charlie Rivera decided to move away from Michigan. (b) Give two reasons why the family decided to move to Texas.

2. (a) How did population shifts in the 1970s affect the House of Representatives? (b) How did the population shifts affect rural areas?

3. Why was Baltimore called "the Survival City"?

4. Name three cities that are being renewed, besides Baltimore.

THE AMERICAN PEOPLE

READ TO FIND OUT

— how the American population has increased.

— how new businesses improve their planning.

— what issues concern the elderly.

— how young Americans discover history around them.

In 1790 the United States government conducted its first census. On a summer day census takers set out on horseback to count the scattered American population. The count took 18 months. The government learned that about 4 million people lived in the nation. It also learned how many were free and how many were slaves. That was about the extent of the first census.

For the 1980 census, Americans filled out questionnaires with 19 questions. This avalanche of data was then fed into the Census Bureau computers. The government found that some 226 million people lived in the nation. The census also reported on education, employment, income, kind of homes, and the number of televisions per home.

Still, the major focus of the census was the nature of the population. The 1970s saw some dramatic population shifts. The percentage of Hispanics, Asians, blacks, and Indians in the population surged. The census also looked at age. The number of people under 18 had declined, while the number of people over 65 sharply increased.

Nearly 200 years of change separate the censuses of 1790 and 1980. Yet, today's 226 million Americans are not so unlike those 4 million of an earlier age. They have faith in the future, and the will to make it work.

HOW TO START A BUSINESS

The young salesperson had built a successful career selling health-care products to stores. He worked for a distributor in Los Angeles, California. Lately, however, he had been thinking about striking out on his own. He knew how to sell health products, but he did not know all the steps involved in setting up his own business.

Job counselor Paul Kirschner had the answers. In April 1981, in a San Francisco office, the two talked of finances and marketing. The key to succeeding in a new business, said Kirschner, was to be "realistic." He helped the salesperson draw up a "business plan" for the new health-products company. The salesperson took the plan to the bank and was given a bank loan to go into business.

This person's new career was one more success story for Paul Kirschner. The counselor knows what he is talking about because he has held many executive positions, including business analyst for an engineering firm. Now he is retired. He still goes to work, however, as a volunteer for the Service Corps of Retired Executives.

The Service Corps was started in 1964 by the Small Business Administration, an agency of the federal government. The vast majority of new businesses never succeed beyond the first year. The Service Corps tries to improve these odds. Former executives like Kirschner can steer beginners on the right course.

CONCERNS OF OLDER AMERICANS

The American population is getting older. The 1980 census found that 25.5 million Americans were over the age of 65. That is more than the number of people living in the nation's most populous state, California.

Many older Americans have special concerns. One study ranked the worries of the elderly. Crime headed the list, followed by poor health, poverty, and loneliness. About 15 percent of the elderly need nursing care, and the same percentage live below the poverty line established by the federal government.

Older Americans are beginning to speak out about their needs. In 1970 social worker Margaret Kuhn began a movement that became known as the Gray Panthers. The Panthers made headlines. They argued against cuts in the federal food-stamp program. They demanded lower electricity rates. And they protested proposals to reduce social security payments, upon which many elderly depend.

There is another concern among Americans of retirement age, and that is retirement itself. The

In recent years older Americans have increasingly spoken out for their rights. Margaret Kuhn, founder of the Gray Panthers, defined many goals for these citizens.

majority of older people live independently, are healthy, and want to stay active. Retired people—like Paul Kirshner of the Service Corps of Retired Executives—are finding fulfilling ways of spending their time. Some go to college, to take a few courses or to obtain a degree. Some start a second career, often something quite different from their first.

Many people would prefer not to retire at all. In 1978 Congress raised the mandatory retirement age from sixty-five to seventy for most private businesses and for state and local governments. The retirement age for federal workers was abolished.

Retirement, many feel, should be a choice. Health, pensions, and the nature of the job are all factors affecting that choice. "I don't miss work one bit," says a retired plant manager. "I was bored." Another retired person, with a second career, has a different view. She cites a Hindu prayer: "God give me work for the rest of my life, and life for the rest of my work."

HISTORY LESSONS

On a white-sand beach of western Oahu, Hawaiians recite the chants and eat the foods of their Polynesian ancestors. Then a huge wooden canoe with a single sail is launched, and paddlers take it out to sea. Except for its fiberglass hull, the craft is an exact replica of an ancient Polynesian canoe. Among the proud builders on shore are several high school stu-

FRITZ SCHOLDER
PAINTING INDIANS TODAY

One of artist Fritz Scholder's most famous paintings shows an Indian wearing a traditional buffalo-horn headdress—and eating a strawberry ice cream cone. The painting surprises people accustomed to the stereotyped Indian of "western" art, riding into the sunset on a pony. Scholder's Indians, in contrast, live in today's world, where ancient customs mingle with such modern phenomena as cars, neon signs, and even ice cream cones.

Born in Breckenridge, Minnesota, in 1937, Scholder is part California Mission Indian. As an art student, he experimented with different styles of art. By the time he was in his twenties he was a fine painter of modern abstract art.

In 1964 Scholder began to teach painting at the new Institute of American Indian Art in Santa Fe, New Mexico. "Upon my arrival," Scholder recalled, "I vowed I would not paint the Indian. The non-Indian had painted him as a noble savage and the Indian painter had been caught in a tourist-pleasing cliche." Instead he attended Pueblo ceremonial dances and collected Indian art. Slowly he developed a new vision of how the Indian should be painted.

One winter night in 1967, Scholder decided to experiment. Using techniques from abstract art, he painted his Indian subject in a totally new way. The result was a revolution in Indian art. "My work immediately startled people," Scholder said, "because I, part-Indian, treated the Indian differently."

Today Scholder is the leader of a new movement in Indian art. His own work can be harsh, sad, funny, tortured, ironic. At its heart is a new vitality—a sense that the Indian he paints is not a relic of the past but powerfully alive in twentieth-century America.

Broad strokes and bold colors remove Fritz Scholder's painting from a realistic portrayal of the American Indian.

dents. "Now I really understand the ways the ancient Hawaiians did things," says eighteen-year-old Cathy Kelly.

The students are part of a historical preservation program called Return to the Sea. They work on the canoe, help restore an ancient shrine, and talk with elders about local history. "Someday," says Kelly, "I'd like to transfer what I know to the next generation and keep the Hawaiian heritage intact."

Far from Hawaii's beaches is Virginia, nicknamed the Mother of States because of its rich historic past. Beneath the streets of Alexandria, Virginia, are the skeletons of an earlier age. Volunteers of the Alexandria Archeological Research Center—many of them high school students—probe the past here.

Workers scan promising sites with radar. Then diggers set to work to unearth the artifacts of old Alexandria. One young woman, hands caked with dirt, excitedly finds part of an old bottle. In time, the researchers hope to read the entire history of Alexandria beneath its streets.

Practical skills, as well as tales and remembrances, are passed from one generation to another in the *Foxfire* project. At left, an eyewitness to an event long past shares his knowledge. At right, an experienced potter explains traditional earthenware techniques.

History is preserved in another way in the rugged Ozark Mountains, which slice across the American Midwest. On a typical weekend, students from Missouri's Lebanon High School comb the hills and hollows of the Ozarks. They are seeking folklore and the old-time skills of the mountain people. The students learn how to weave a basket from oak bark, build a mud house, and stitch a quilt.

The folk wisdom is published in the student magazine *Bittersweet*, named for an Ozark berry. *Bittersweet* and many similar student publications trace their roots to the magazine *Foxfire*, started in 1966 at a Georgia high school. All preserve oral, or spoken, history and culture that might otherwise be forgotten.

For these students, the past is part of a continuing story. They follow a trail of artifacts, folk sayings, and other clues to find out what happened before they were born. Their knowledge of the past gives them an understanding of the present. The story—America's story—becomes their own.

SECTION REVIEW

1. (a) What age group declined relative to the entire population in the 1970s? (b) What age group increased?

2. What is a main goal of the Service Corps of Retired Executives?

3. List four major concerns of elderly people in the United States.

4. How are students preserving folk wisdom in the Ozark Mountains?

CHAPTER SURVEY

SUMMARY

Throughout the history of the United States, Americans have searched for ways to produce more goods with less labor. By the 1970s Americans were combining machines with electronics to create fully automatic factories. In these factories robots assembled products such as automobiles or refrigerators. Robots also could free workers from boring, dirty or dangerous jobs involving hazardous substances or high risk.

The "brains" of the robots are microcomputers. For Americans, computers are becoming more and more important. Students are gaining knowledge of computers in computer camps or from other sources. In many areas of business, jobs are demanding computer skills. Computers are also being used in homes for recreation, accounting, and communication.

By the 1970s Americans were also working to find new sources of energy that would not hurt the environment. Americans experimented with new kinds of fuels, such as methanol and gasohol, to run automobiles. They worked on cars that ran on batteries or even on compressed air.

At home, Americans designed buildings that used energy from the sun. They also experimented with other means of producing energy—from the wind, the tides, and the heat escaping from the earth. However, the United States was still forced to continue to rely on fossil fuels.

As in the past, Americans continued to move across the nation. In the 1970s thousands of people left the Northeast and upper Midwest for the Sunbelt. Others moved to rural areas and small towns. Still other Americans became urban pioneers, moving back into cities.

The nature of the American population also changed in the 1970s. The percentage of Hispanics, Asians, blacks, and Indians in the population rose dramatically. The number of people over the age of 65 in the population increased sharply, too.

In the 1970s older Americans began to organize and to speak out about their needs. The government revised retirement policies. Meanwhile, young Americans learned about their past and worked to preserve it.

CHAPTER REVIEW

1. Describe the "robot revolution." Cite examples.

2. Explain how computers have affected each of the following: (a) industry (b) labor (c) careers (d) life at home.

3. (a) Why did American experiments with new fuels become urgent? (b) Summarize the alternative sources of fuel with which Americans have experimented and the problems related to each of them.

4. (a) Explain how Americans have experimented with each of the following as alternative sources of energy: wind, garbage, geothermal energy. (b) What advantages do these energy sources have? What disadvantages?

5. (a) What controversy surrounds the use of nuclear energy? Cite arguments on both sides. (b) Explain why coal is a problem fuel.

6. (a) Describe the development of "supertrees." (b) Why is reforestation important?

7. (a) Why did the Sunbelt become the fastest growing region of the nation? (b) How did rapid growth affect the Sunbelt? The nation?

8. (a) Why did Americans begin to leave the cities? (b) Describe how some Americans expect to change cities. Cite examples.

New technology provides a wonder in miniature. On a surface some one-inch square, eight silicon chips interact to send complex messages to a computer.

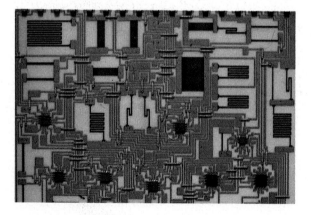

Every pine seedling carefully planted and nurtured will help to guarantee the future balance of America's ecology. Trees clean the air and protect the soil, provide food, shelter, and enjoyment.

9. (a) How have the elderly become politically active as a group? (b) What are their goals?

10. Why are *Foxfire* and *Bittersweet* important to Americans today and Americans in the future?

ISSUES AND IDEAS

1. The director of a computer camp stated that learning how to use computers "may become almost as basic as reading or writing." Do you agree? Why or why not?

2. Do you think that Americans can both fill their automobile tanks and save the earth? Why or why not? Cite examples.

3. Why was the rebuilding of Baltimore by urban pioneers important?

SKILLS WORKSHOP

1. *Charts.* Make a chart of major efforts in the United States since 1973 to deal with energy problems. Under each of your headings— "Developing Energy Resources" and "Conserving Energy"—list government actions and efforts by Americans. Briefly describe each listing.

2. *Maps.* See page 747 of your book. Find the map entitled "The Population Shift to the South and West." Which states gained in population by more than 10 percent between 1970 and 1980? By more than 50 percent? Which states lost population? Which states gained and which states lost representation in the House of Representatives? How do you think this change in representation will affect Congress?

PAST AND PRESENT

1. Americans have always moved from one part of the nation to another. Trace the movements of your parents' families and your own family. Explain why there were moves or why the family stayed in one place.

2. Find out if there are historical preservation programs in or around your community. What kind of history do these programs preserve? How?

Beautifully preserved and restored, a wooden eagle serves as a reminder of both the patriotism and the craftsmanship of earlier Americans. The appearance of many similarly restored objects indicates a renewal of interest in the past, in our American heritage.

REFERENCE SECTION

RESOURCE CENTER

Settlement of the United States

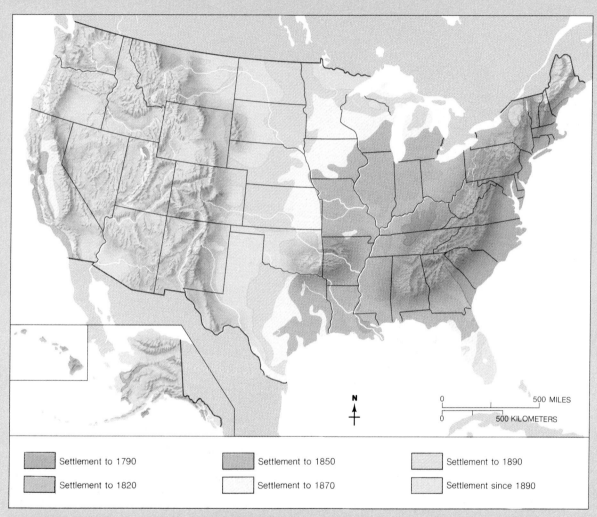

Settlement to 1790

Settlement to 1820

Settlement to 1850

Settlement to 1870

Settlement to 1890

Settlement since 1890

N

0   500 MILES

0   500 KILOMETERS

Territorial Growth of the United States

The Original United States	1783	Treaty with Great Britain	845,882 sq mi	(2,190,834 sq km)
Louisiana Purchase	1803	Purchased from France	831,321	(2,153,121)
Red River Basin	1818	Ceded by Great Britain	46,253	(119,795)
Florida	1819	Ceded by Spain	69,866	(180,953)
Texas	1845	Annexed	384,958	(997,041)
Oregon Country	1846	Compromise with Great Britain	283,439	(734,107)
Mexican Cession	1848	Ceded by Mexico	530,706	(1,374,529)
Gadsden Purchase	1853	Purchased from Mexico	29,640	(76,768)
Alaska	1867	Purchased from Russia	591,004	(1,530,700)
Hawaii	1898	Annexed	6,471	(16,760)

Physical Map of the United States

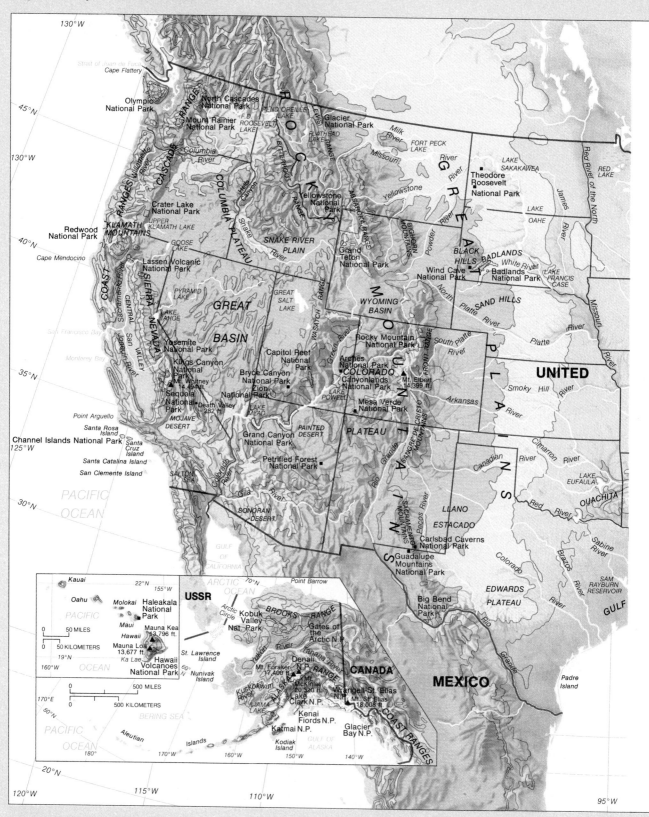

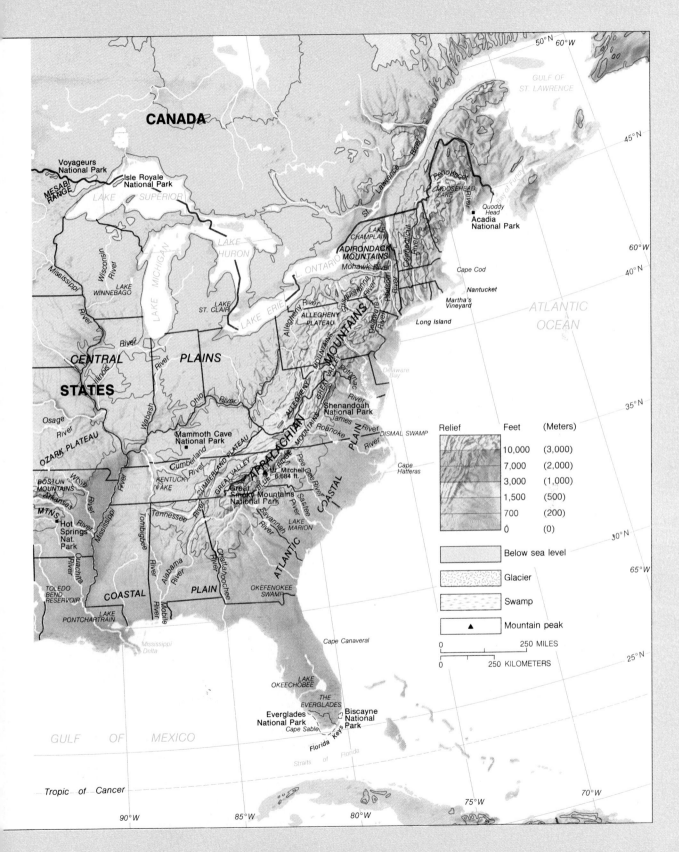

CANADA

Voyageurs
National Park
MESABI RANGE
Isle Royale
National Park
LAKE SUPERIOR

GULF OF
ST LAWRENCE

Penobscot
River
MOOSEHEAD
LAKE

Bay of Fundy

Quoddy
Head
Acadia
National Park

St. Lawrence River

LAKE
MICHIGAN

LAKE
HURON

Wisconsin
River

Mississippi River

LAKE
WINNEBAGO

LAKE
ST. CLAIR

LAKE ONTARIO

LAKE ERIE

LAKE
CHAMPLAIN

ADIRONDACK
MOUNTAINS

Mohawk River

Cape Cod

Nantucket

Martha's
Vineyard

ATLANTIC
OCEAN

Long Island

Connecticut River

Hudson River

Susquehanna River

Delaware River

Delaware
Bay

CENTRAL

PLAINS

STATES

Illinois River

Ohio River

Wabash River

Osage
River

OZARK PLATEAU

White River

Mississippi River

BOSTON
MOUNTAINS

Arkansas River

OUACHITA
MTNS.

Hot
Springs
Nat.
Park

Ouachita River

TOLEDO
BEND
RESERVOIR

LAKE
PONTCHARTRAIN

Mississippi
Delta

GULF   OF   MEXICO

Tropic   of   Cancer

ALLEGHENY
PLATEAU

ALLEGHENY MOUNTAINS

GREAT VALLEY

CUMBERLAND PLATEAU

Cumberland River

KENTUCKY
LAKE

Tennessee River

Tombigbee River

Alabama River

Mobile River

Mammoth Cave
National Park

GREAT VALLEY

APPALACHIAN

BLUE RIDGE MOUNTAINS

Mt. Mitchell
6,684 ft.

Great
Smoky Mountains
National Park

Shenandoah
National Park

James River

Roanoke River

Pee Dee River

Santee River

Savannah River

Chattahoochee River

LAKE
MARION

OKEFENOKEE
SWAMP

Potomac
River

COASTAL

PLAIN

DISMAL SWAMP

Cape
Hatteras

ATLANTIC

COASTAL

PLAIN

Cape Canaveral

LAKE
OKEECHOBEE

THE
EVERGLADES

Everglades
National Park

Cape Sable

Biscayne
National
Park

Florida Keys

Straits   of   Florida

Relief	Feet	(Meters)
	10,000	(3,000)
	7,000	(2,000)
	3,000	(1,000)
	1,500	(500)
	700	(200)
	0	(0)

Below sea level

Glacier

Swamp

▲ Mountain peak

0   250 MILES

0   250 KILOMETERS

50°N
60°W

45°N

60°W

40°N

35°N

65°W

30°N

25°N

70°W

90°W   85°W   80°W   75°W

Political Map of the United States

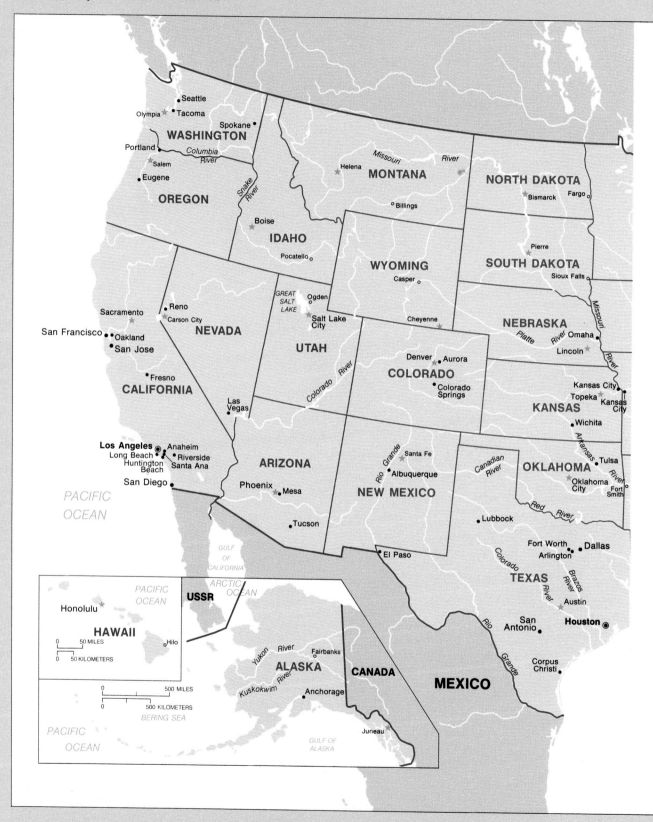

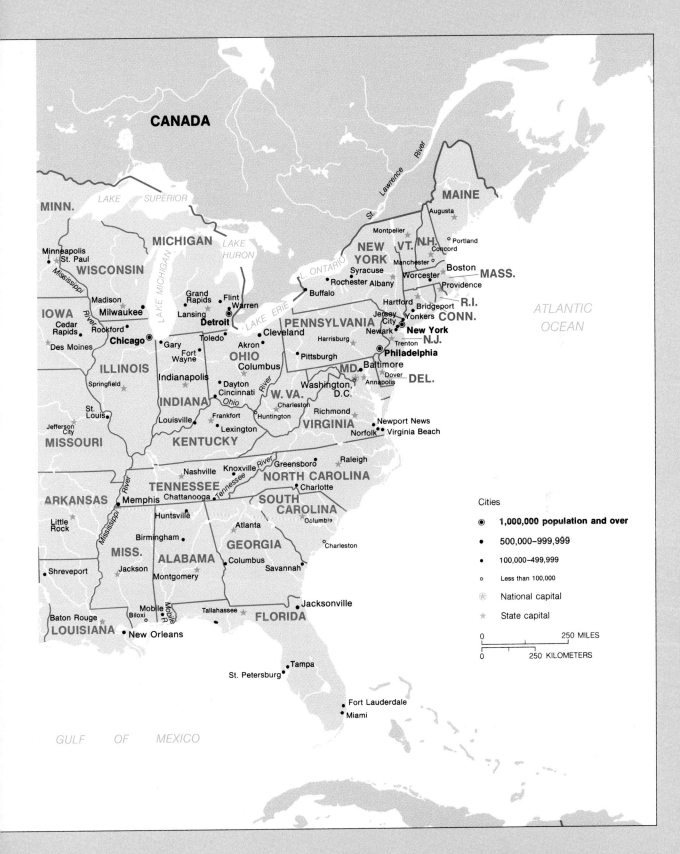

CANADA

MINN.

LAKE SUPERIOR

MICHIGAN

LAKE HURON

MAINE

Augusta

Montpelier

Portland

NEW YORK

VT. N.H.

Concord

Manchester

Minneapolis
St. Paul

WISCONSIN

Madison

Milwaukee

Lansing

Grand Rapids

Flint

Warren

Detroit

LAKE MICHIGAN

L. ONTARIO

Syracuse

Rochester Albany

Buffalo

LAKE ERIE

Worcester

Boston

MASS.

Providence

R.I.

Hartford

Bridgeport

CONN.

ATLANTIC OCEAN

IOWA

Cedar Rapids

Rockford

Des Moines

Chicago

Gary

Fort Wayne

Toledo

Cleveland

Akron

PENNSYLVANIA

Jersey City

Yonkers

New York

Newark

N.J.

ILLINOIS

Springfield

Indianapolis

OHIO

Columbus

Harrisburg

Pittsburgh

Trenton

Philadelphia

Dayton

Cincinnati

Ohio River

W. VA.

Washington, D.C.

Baltimore

MD.

Dover

DEL.

Annapolis

St. Louis

INDIANA

Louisville

Frankfort

Lexington

Charleston

Huntington

Richmond

VIRGINIA

Jefferson City

MISSOURI

KENTUCKY

Newport News

Virginia Beach

Norfolk

Nashville

Knoxville

Tennessee River

Greensboro

Raleigh

ARKANSAS

Memphis

Chattanooga

NORTH CAROLINA

TENNESSEE

Charlotte

Little Rock

Huntsville

SOUTH CAROLINA

Columbia

Mississippi River

MISS.

Birmingham

Atlanta

GEORGIA

Charleston

ALABAMA

Columbus

Savannah

Shreveport

Jackson

Montgomery

Mobile R.

Tallahassee

Jacksonville

Baton Rouge

Mobile

Biloxi

FLORIDA

LOUISIANA

New Orleans

Tampa

St. Petersburg

Fort Lauderdale

Miami

GULF   OF   MEXICO

Cities

◉ 1,000,000 population and over

● 500,000–999,999

• 100,000–499,999

○ Less than 100,000

⊛ National capital

★ State capital

0   250 MILES

0   250 KILOMETERS

The United States in the World

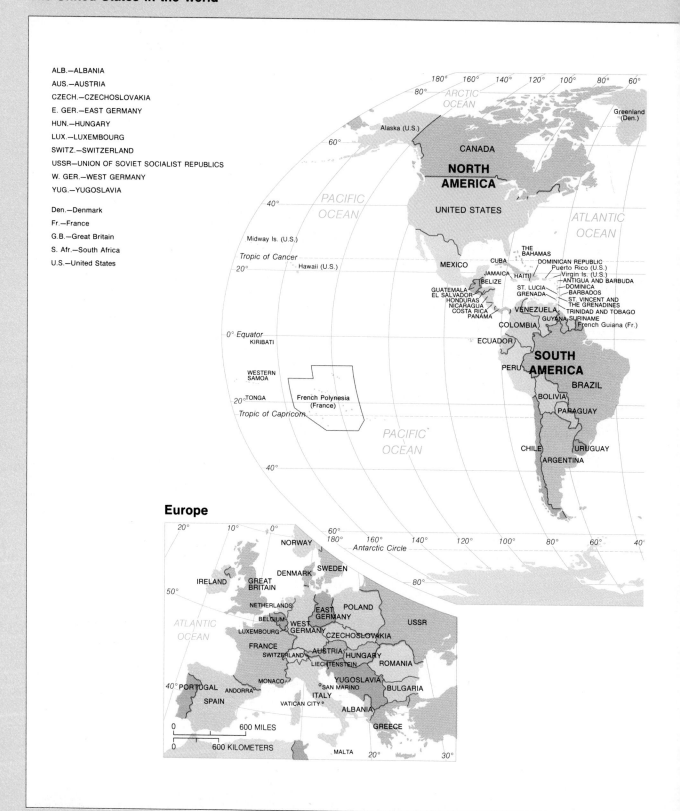

ALB.—ALBANIA
AUS.—AUSTRIA
CZECH.—CZECHOSLOVAKIA
E. GER.—EAST GERMANY
HUN.—HUNGARY
LUX.—LUXEMBOURG
SWITZ.—SWITZERLAND
USSR—UNION OF SOVIET SOCIALIST REPUBLICS
W. GER.—WEST GERMANY
YUG.—YUGOSLAVIA

Den.—Denmark
Fr.—France
G.B.—Great Britain
S. Afr.—South Africa
U.S.—United States

Europe

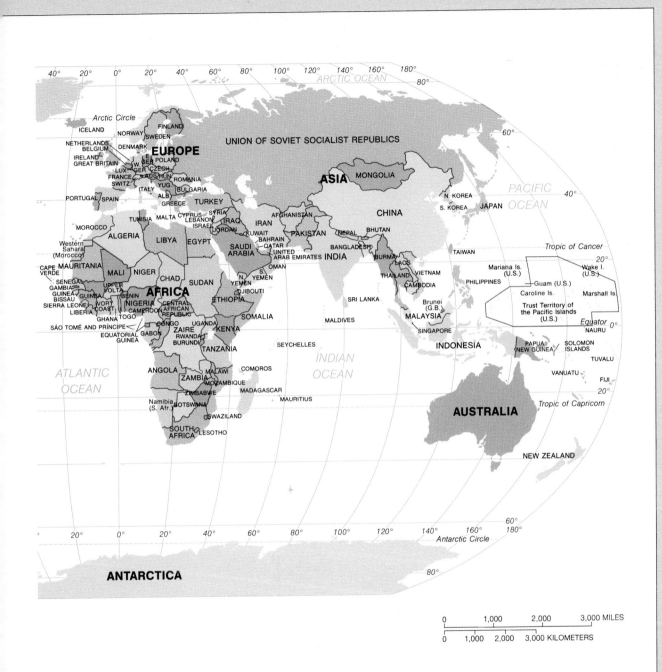

| 0 | 1,000 | 2,000 | 3,000 MILES |
| 0 | 1,000 | 2,000 | 3,000 KILOMETERS |

★ THE AMERICAN PEOPLE ★

Population Growth   1790–1980

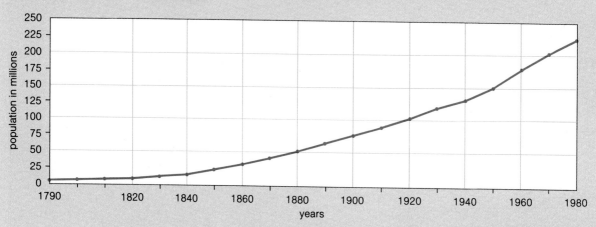

Immigration   1820–1980

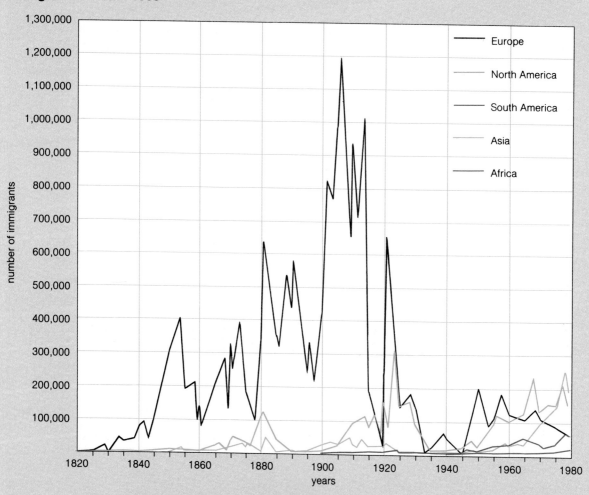

Total Immigration from Leading Countries of Origin   1820–1979

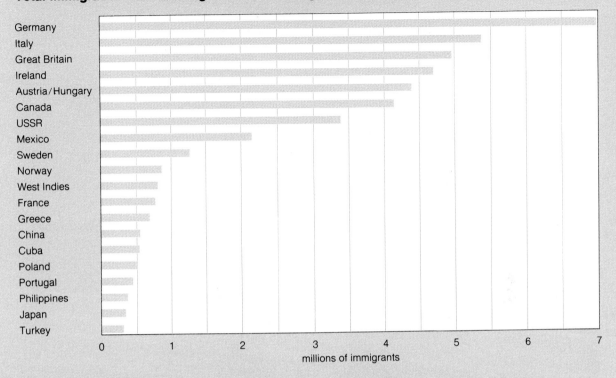

Germany
Italy
Great Britain
Ireland
Austria/Hungary
Canada
USSR
Mexico
Sweden
Norway
West Indies
France
Greece
China
Cuba
Poland
Portugal
Philippines
Japan
Turkey

0   1   2   3   4   5   6   7

millions of immigrants

Racial Origins of Americans   1980

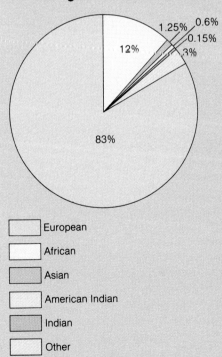

1.25%   0.6%
12%   0.15%
.3%
83%

European

African

Asian

American Indian

Indian

Other

Americans of Hispanic Origin   1980

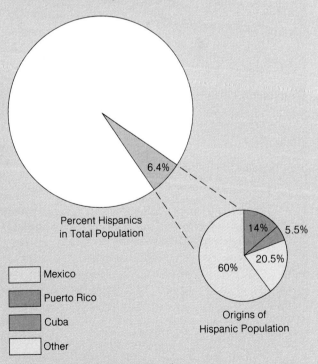

6.4%

Percent Hispanics
in Total Population

14%   5.5%
60%   20.5%

Origins of
Hispanic Population

Mexico

Puerto Rico

Cuba

Other

Persons of Hispanic origin may be of any race.

Population Distribution by Region   1790–1980

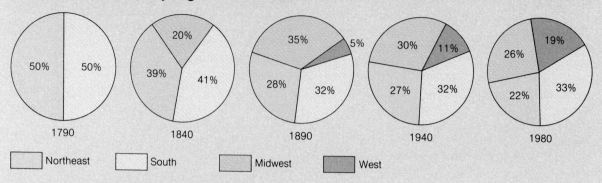

Northeast	South	Midwest	West

1790 — 50% / 50%

1840 — 20% / 39% / 41%

1890 — 35% / 5% / 28% / 32%

1940 — 30% / 11% / 27% / 32%

1980 — 19% / 26% / 22% / 33%

Rural and Urban Populations   1790–1980

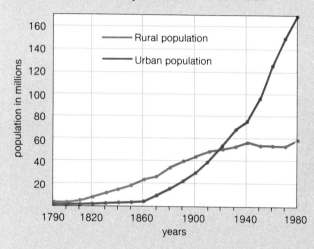

Rural population
Urban population

population in millions

years

Population Distribution in Urban Areas 1950–1980

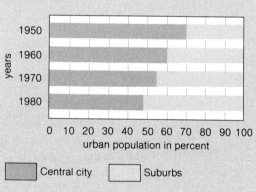

years

urban population in percent

Central city	Suburbs

Number of Farms and Average Farm Size   1850–1980

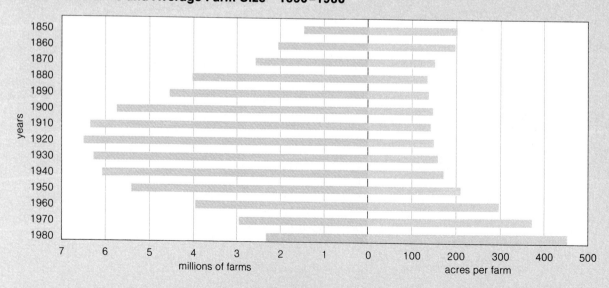

years

millions of farms   acres per farm

Population Density in the United States 1980

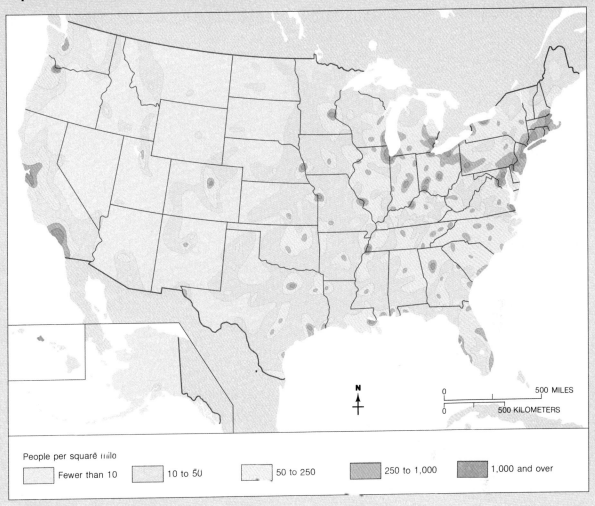

People per square mile

☐ Fewer than 10   ☐ 10 to 50   ☐ 50 to 250   ☐ 250 to 1,000   ☐ 1,000 and over

Population per Square Mile 1790–1980

equals 5 persons

1790
1840
1890
1940
1980

Life Expectancy at Birth 1900–1980

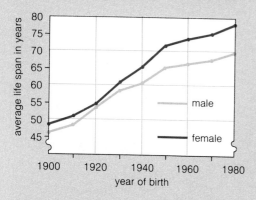

Average Size of Households 1790–1980

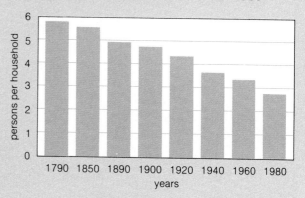

School Enrollment 1890–1980

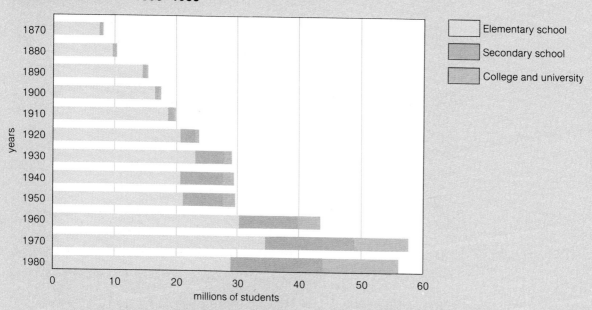

Distribution of Population by Age 1850–1980

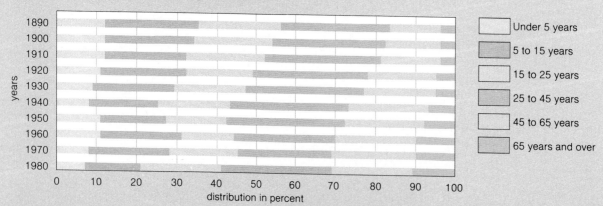

Climates of the United States

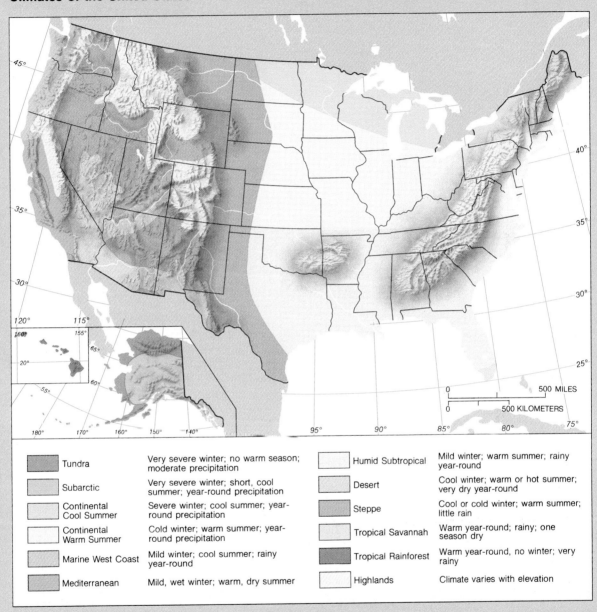

Tundra	Very severe winter; no warm season; moderate precipitation	Humid Subtropical	Mild winter; warm summer; rainy year-round
Subarctic	Very severe winter; short, cool summer; year-round precipitation	Desert	Cool winter; warm or hot summer; very dry year-round
Continental Cool Summer	Severe winter; cool summer; year-round precipitation	Steppe	Cool or cold winter; warm summer; little rain
Continental Warm Summer	Cold winter; warm summer; year-round precipitation	Tropical Savannah	Warm year-round; rainy; one season dry
Marine West Coast	Mild winter; cool summer; rainy year-round	Tropical Rainforest	Warm year-round, no winter; very rainy
Mediterranean	Mild, wet winter; warm, dry summer	Highlands	Climate varies with elevation

The Nation's Crops Ranked by Percent of Farm Sales   1981

Cattle	20.2%	Hogs	6.8%	Eggs	2.5%
Feed crops	12.7%	Vegetables	5.9%	Tobacco	2.3%
Dairy products	12.6%	Fruits, nuts	4.6%	Sheep	.3%
Oilbearing crops	9.8%	Poultry	4.4%	Wool	.1%
Food grains	8.6%	Cotton	3.2%	Others	6.0%

Mineral Resources of the United States

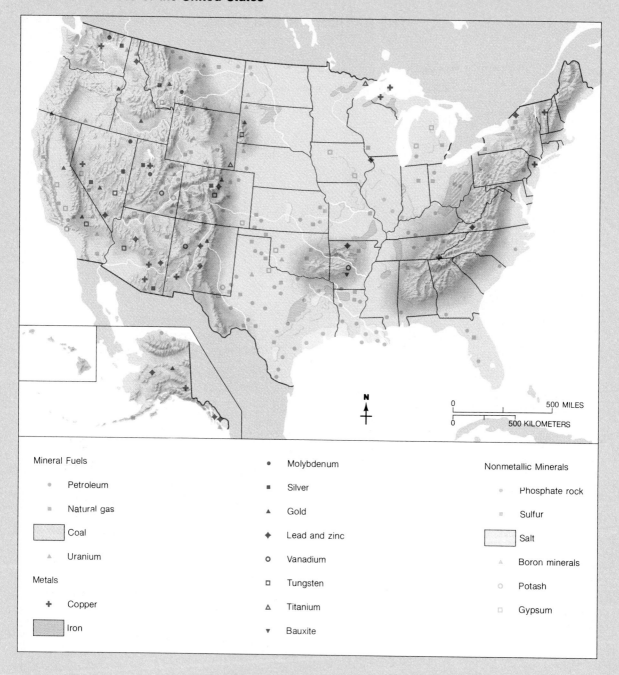

Mineral Fuels

- Petroleum
- Natural gas
- Coal
- Uranium

Metals

- Copper
- Iron

- Molybdenum
- Silver
- Gold
- Lead and zinc
- Vanadium
- Tungsten
- Titanium
- Bauxite

Nonmetallic Minerals

- Phosphate rock
- Sulfur
- Salt
- Boron minerals
- Potash
- Gypsum

Principal Minerals Ranked by Value of Production   1980

Petroleum	$66,670,000,000	Sand and gravel	$2,638,000,000	Salt	$656,200,000
Natural gas	32,670,000,000	Molybdenum	1,344,200,000	Silver	646,600,000
Coal	20,510,000,000	Phosphate rock	1,256,900,000	Gold	582,800,000
Cement	3,801,000,000	Uranium	1,228,000,000	Lead	514,400,000
Stone	3,393,500,000	Clays	898,900,000	Boron minerals	366,800,000
Copper	2,638,000,000	Lime	842,900,000	Potash	353,900,000
Iron ore	2,547,500,000	Sulfer	720,500,000	Zinc	276,300,000

Energy Sources   1980

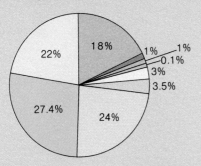

18%
1%
1%
0.1%
3%
3.5%
24%
27.4%
22%

Domestic Production
- Crude oil
- Natural gas
- Coal
- Water power
- Nuclear power
- Geothermal and other sources

Imports
- Crude oil and refined petroleum
- Natural gas
- Others

Energy Use   1980

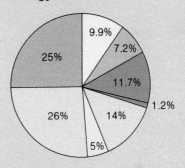

9.9%
7.2%
11.7%
1.2%
25%
26%
14%
5%

Direct Use
- Transportation
- Industry
- Export
- Home and business

Generation of Electricity
- Home use
- Business use
- Industrial use
- Other

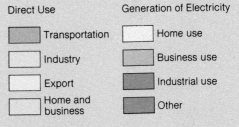

Iron Ore Consumption   1860–1980

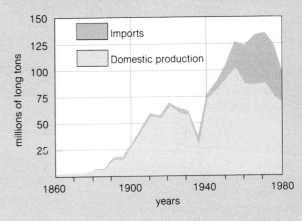

- Imports
- Domestic production

millions of long tons

150
125
100
75
50
25

1860   1900   1940   1980

years

Petroleum Consumption   1860–1980

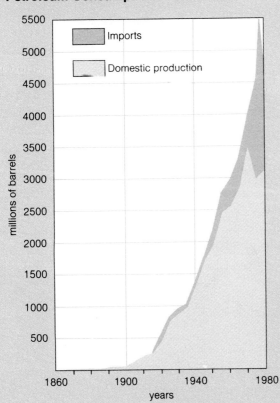

- Imports
- Domestic production

millions of barrels

5500
5000
4500
4000
3500
3000
2500
2000
1500
1000
500

1860   1900   1940   1980

years

Bituminous Coal Consumption   1860–1980

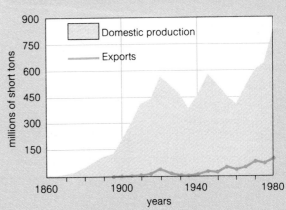

- Domestic production
- Exports

millions of short tons

900
750
600
450
300
150

1860   1900   1940   1980

years

★ AMERICA AT WORK ★

Civilian Labor Force   1890–1980

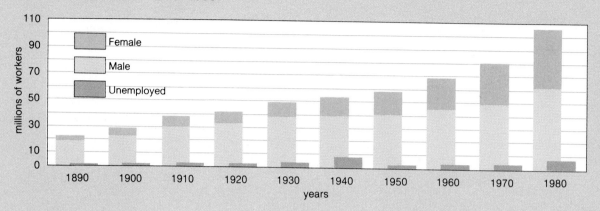

The American Economy 1790–1980

"The American Economy" describes the nation's economic activity, or business cycle. This graph illustrates periods of recession, depression, recovery, and prosperity. The graph was computed from several sources such as indexes of business activity and production, and information about commodity prices, imports and exports, government income and expenditures, banking activities, and stock prices.

Union Membership   1900–1980

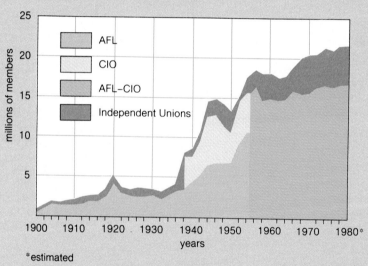

*estimated

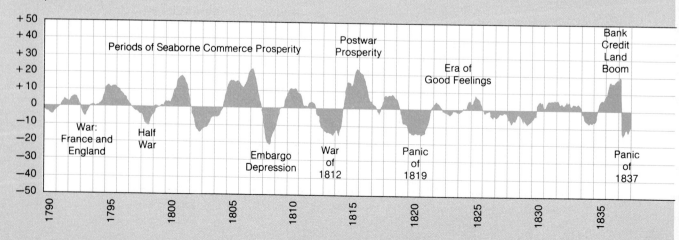

Occupational Groups   1900–1980

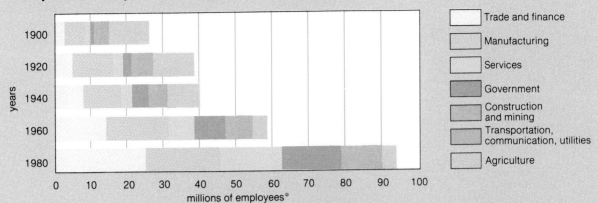

years

millions of employees*

*excludes the self-employed and members of the Armed Forces

Legend:
- Trade and finance
- Manufacturing
- Services
- Government
- Construction and mining
- Transportation, communication, utilities
- Agriculture

Consumer Prices and Purchasing Power   1929–1981

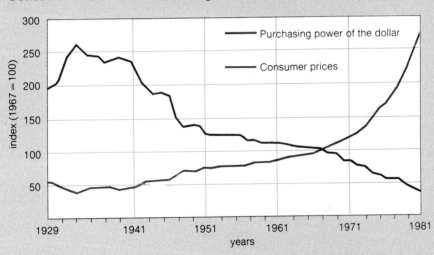

index (1967 = 100)

years

- Purchasing power of the dollar
- Consumer prices

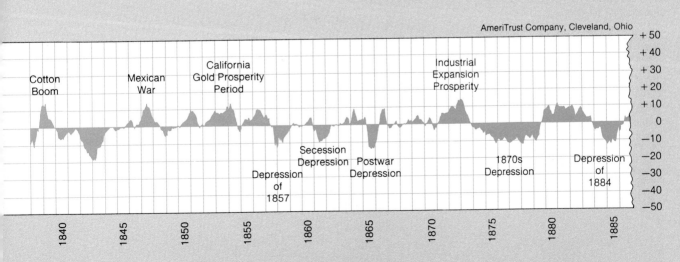

AmeriTrust Company, Cleveland, Ohio

Cotton Boom

Mexican War

California Gold Prosperity Period

Industrial Expansion Prosperity

Depression of 1857

Secession Depression

Postwar Depression

1870s Depression

Depression of 1884

Major Industries: Value of Products, Number of Employees   1980

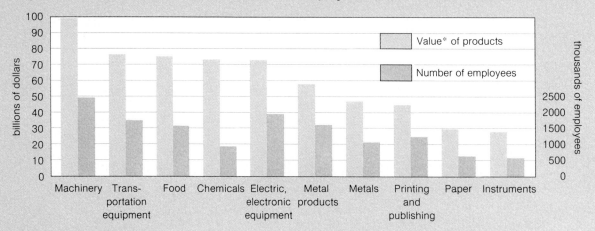

*Value refers to the difference between the cost of production and the selling price.

Gross National Product 1929–1981

Gross National Product per Person   1929–1981

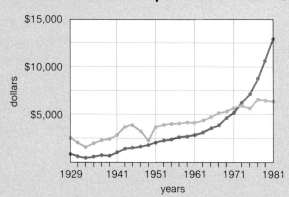

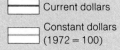 Current dollars   Expressed in terms of the current value of the dollar in each year; the rising values reflect inflation.

Constant dollars   Expressed in terms of a constant value of the dollar (what a dollar could purchase in 1972) to mea-
(1972 = 100)   sure economic growth undistorted by the effects of inflation.

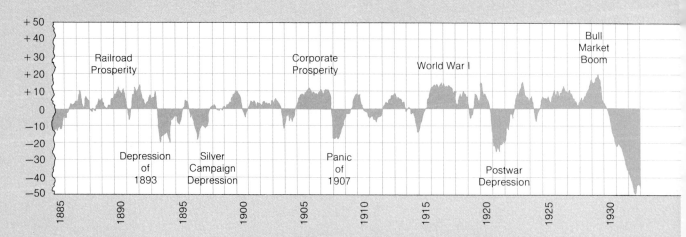

Imports 1830–1980

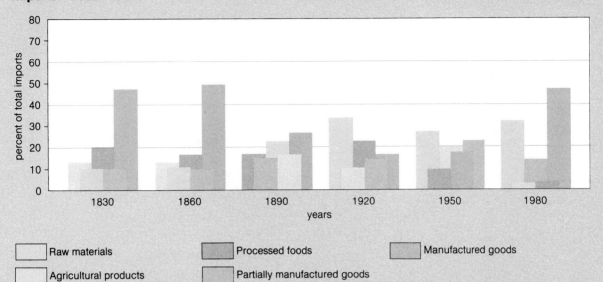

percent of total imports

years

1830   1860   1890   1920   1950   1980

| Raw materials | Processed foods | Manufactured goods |
| Agricultural products | Partially manufactured goods |

Exports 1830–1980

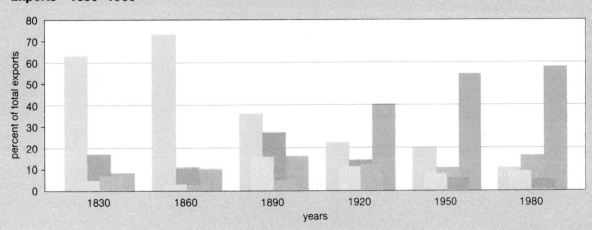

percent of total exports

years

1830   1860   1890   1920   1950   1980

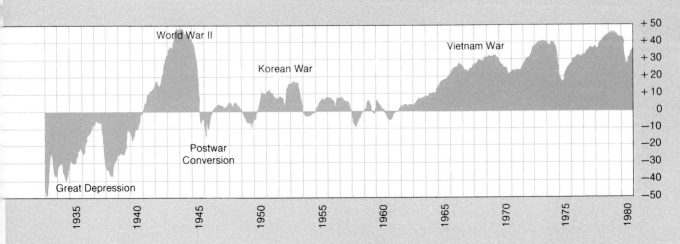

World War II

Korean War

Vietnam War

Postwar
Conversion

Great Depression

+50
+40
+30
+20
+10
0
−10
−20
−30
−40
−50

1935   1940   1945   1950   1955   1960   1965   1970   1975   1980

Populations of the States of the United States 1840, 1890, 1980

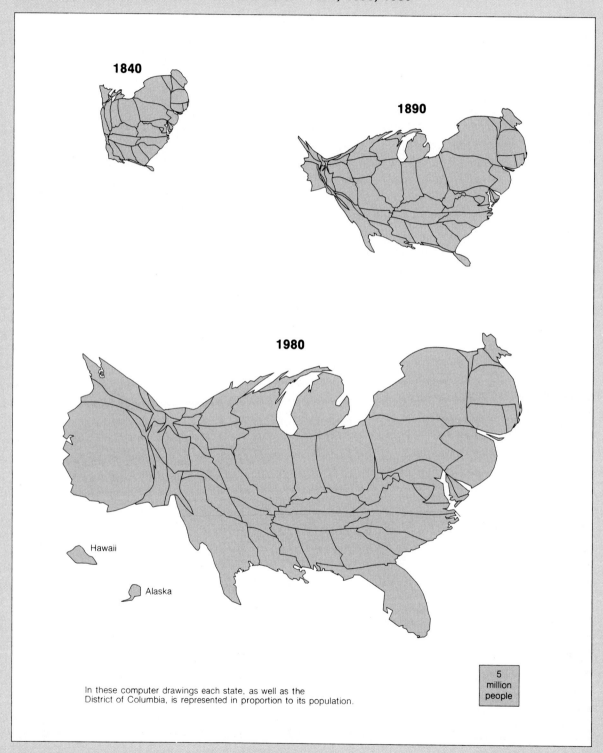

1840

1890

1980

Hawaii

Alaska

In these computer drawings each state, as well as the
District of Columbia, is represented in proportion to its population.

5
million
people

Facts About the States

State	Capital	Date of Entry to Union	Order of Entry	Area in Square Miles (Square Kilometers)		Population in 1980	People per Square Mile*	Percent Urban Population
Alabama	Montgomery	1819	22	51,705	(133,915)	3,890,000	77	60
Alaska	Juneau	1959	49	591,004	(1,530,700)	400,000	1	65
Arizona	Phoenix	1912	48	114,000	(295,260)	2,718,000	24	84
Arkansas	Little Rock	1836	25	53,187	(137,754)	2,286,000	44	52
California	Sacramento	1850	31	158,706	(411,049)	23,669,000	151	91
Colorado	Denver	1876	38	104,091	(269,595)	2,889,000	28	81
Connecticut	Hartford	1788	5	5,018	(12,997)	3,108,000	638	79
Delaware	Dover	1787	1	2,044	(5,295)	595,000	308	71
Florida	Tallahassee	1845	27	58,664	(151,939)	9,740,000	180	84
Georgia	Atlanta	1788	4	58,910	(152,576)	5,464,000	94	62
Hawaii	Honolulu	1959	50	6,471	(16,759)	965,000	150	87
Idaho	Boise	1890	43	83,564	(216,432)	944,000	12	54
Illinois	Springfield	1818	21	56,345	(145,934)	11,418,000	205	83
Indiana	Indianapolis	1816	19	36,185	(93,720)	5,490,000	153	64
Iowa	Des Moines	1846	29	56,275	(145,753)	2,913,000	52	59
Kansas	Topeka	1861	34	82,277	(213,098)	2,363,000	29	67
Kentucky	Frankfort	1792	15	40,409	(104,660)	3,661,000	92	51
Louisiana	Baton Rouge	1812	18	47,752	(123,677)	4,204,000	94	69
Maine	Augusta	1820	23	33,265	(86,156)	1,125,000	36	48
Maryland	Annapolis	1788	7	10,460	(27,092)	4,216,000	429	80
Massachusetts	Boston	1788	6	8,284	(21,456)	5,737,000	733	84
Michigan	Lansing	1837	26	58,527	(151,586)	9,258,000	163	71
Minnesota	St. Paul	1858	32	84,402	(218,601)	4,077,000	51	67
Mississippi	Jackson	1817	20	47,689	(123,515)	2,521,000	53	47
Missouri	Jefferson City	1821	24	69,697	(180,516)	4,917,000	71	68
Montana	Helena	1889	41	147,046	(380,848)	787,000	5	53
Nebraska	Lincoln	1867	37	77,355	(200,350)	1,570,000	21	63
Nevada	Carson City	1864	36	110,561	(286,352)	799,000	7	85
New Hampshire	Concord	1788	9	9,279	(24,032)	921,000	102	52
New Jersey	Trenton	1787	3	7,787	(20,169)	7,364,000	986	89
New Mexico	Santa Fe	1912	47	121,593	(314,925)	1,300,000	11	72
New York	Albany	1788	11	49,108	(127,189)	17,557,000	371	85
North Carolina	Raleigh	1789	12	52,669	(136,413)	5,874,000	120	48
North Dakota	Bismarck	1889	39	70,702	(183,119)	653,000	9	49
Ohio	Columbus	1803	17	41,330	(107,044)	10,797,000	263	73
Oklahoma	Oklahoma City	1907	46	69,956	(181,186)	3,025,000	44	67
Oregon	Salem	1859	33	97,073	(251,419)	2,633,000	27	68
Pennsylvania	Harrisburg	1787	2	45,308	(117,348)	11,867,000	264	69
Rhode Island	Providence	1790	13	1,212	(3,140)	947,000	898	87
South Carolina	Columbia	1788	8	31,113	(80,582)	3,119,000	103	54
South Dakota	Pierre	1889	40	77,116	(199,730)	690,000	9	46
Tennessee	Nashville	1796	16	42,144	(109,152)	4,591,000	112	60
Texas	Austin	1845	28	266,807	(691,030)	14,228,000	54	80
Utah	Salt Lake City	1896	45	84,899	(219,889)	1,461,000	18	84
Vermont	Montpelier	1791	14	9,614	(24,900)	511,000	55	34
Virginia	Richmond	1788	10	40,767	(105,586)	5,346,000	135	66
Washington	Olympia	1889	42	68,139	(176,479)	4,130,000	62	74
West Virginia	Charleston	1863	35	24,231	(62,759)	1,950,000	81	36
Wisconsin	Madison	1848	30	56,153	(145,436)	4,705,000	86	64
Wyoming	Cheyenne	1890	44	97,809	(253,326)	471,000	5	63
District of Columbia				69	(178)	638,000	10,127	100
Puerto Rico	San Juan			3,515	(9,103)	3,188,000	922	67

*Based on land area rather than total area per state

The Federal Budget   1940–1982

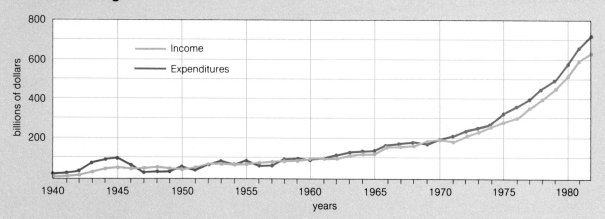

The Federal Budget: Sources of Income   1940–1980

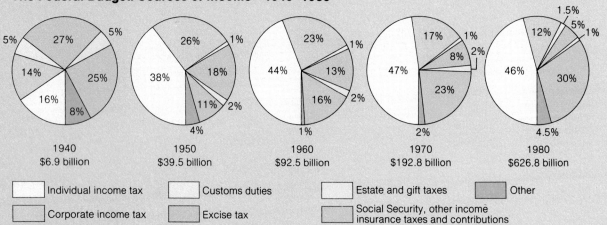

1940
$6.9 billion

1950
$39.5 billion

1960
$92.5 billion

1970
$192.8 billion

1980
$626.8 billion

Individual income tax	Customs duties	Estate and gift taxes	Other
Corporate income tax	Excise tax	Social Security, other income insurance taxes and contributions	

The Federal Budget: Expenditures   1940–1980

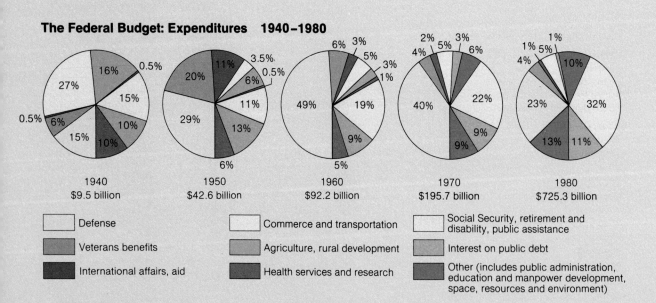

1940
$9.5 billion

1950
$42.6 billion

1960
$92.2 billion

1970
$195.7 billion

1980
$725.3 billion

Defense	Commerce and transportation	Social Security, retirement and disability, public assistance
Veterans benefits	Agriculture, rural development	Interest on public debt
International affairs, aid	Health services and research	Other (includes public administration, education and manpower development, space, resources and environment)

Presidents and Vice-Presidents of the United States

President	Term of Office	Political Party	Born	Died	State Birth—Residence	Occupation other than Politics	Vice-President
1. George Washington	1789–1797	None	1732	1799	Virginia	Planter, soldier	John Adams
2. John Adams	1797–1801	Federalist	1735	1826	Massachusetts	Lawyer	Thomas Jefferson
3. Thomas Jefferson	1801–1809	Republican	1743	1826	Virginia	Lawyer	Aaron Burr George Clinton
4. James Madison	1809–1817	Republican	1751	1836	Virginia	Lawyer	George Clinton Elbridge Gerry
5. James Monroe	1817–1825	Republican	1758	1831	Virginia	Lawyer	Daniel D. Tompkins
6. John Quincy Adams	1825–1829	Nat. Rep.	1767	1848	Massachusetts	Lawyer	John C. Calhoun
7. Andrew Jackson	1829–1837	Democratic	1767	1845	S.C.—Tenn.	Lawyer, soldier	John C. Calhoun Martin Van Buren
8. Martin Van Buren	1837–1841	Democratic	1782	1862	New York	Lawyer	Richard M. Johnson
9. William Henry Harrison	1841	Whig	1773	1841	Va.—Ohio	Soldier	John Tyler
10. John Tyler	1841–1845	Whig	1790	1862	Virginia	Lawyer	
11. James K. Polk	1845–1849	Democratic	1795	1849	N.C.—Tenn.	Lawyer	George M. Dallas
12. Zachary Taylor	1849–1850	Whig	1784	1850	Va.—La.	Soldier	Millard Fillmore
13. Millard Fillmore	1850–1853	Whig	1800	1874	New York	Lawyer	
14. Franklin Pierce	1853–1857	Democratic	1804	1869	New Hampshire	Lawyer	William R.D. King
15. James Buchanan	1857–1861	Democratic	1791	1868	Pennsylvania	Lawyer	John C. Breckinridge
16. Abraham Lincoln	1861–1865	Republican	1809	1865	Ky.—Ill.	Lawyer	Hannibal Hamlin Andrew Johnson
17. Andrew Johnson	1865–1869	Republican	1808	1875	N.C.—Tenn.	Tailor	
18. Ulysses S. Grant	1869–1877	Republican	1822	1885	Ohio—Ill.	Soldier	Schuyler Colfax Henry Wilson
19. Rutherford B. Hayes	1877–1881	Republican	1822	1893	Ohio	Lawyer	William A. Wheeler
20. James A. Garfield	1881	Republican	1831	1881	Ohio	Teacher, lawyer	Chester A. Arthur
21. Chester A. Arthur	1881–1885	Republican	1829	1886	Vt.—N.Y.	Lawyer	
22. Grover Cleveland	1885–1889	Democratic	1837	1908	N.J.—N.Y.	Lawyer	Thomas A. Hendricks
23. Benjamin Harrison	1889–1893	Republican	1833	1901	Ohio—Ind.	Lawyer	Levi P. Morton
24. Grover Cleveland	1893–1897	Democratic	1837	1908	N.J.—N.Y.	Lawyer	Adlai E. Stevenson
25. William McKinley	1897–1901	Republican	1843	1901	Ohio	Lawyer	Garret A. Hobart Theodore Roosevelt
26. Theodore Roosevelt	1901–1909	Republican	1858	1919	New York	Rancher, writer	Charles W. Fairbanks
27. William Howard Taft	1909–1913	Republican	1857	1930	Ohio	Lawyer	James S. Sherman
28. Woodrow Wilson	1913–1921	Democratic	1856	1924	Va.—N.J.	Lawyer, teacher	Thomas R. Marshall
29. Warren G. Harding	1921–1923	Republican	1865	1923	Ohio	Journalist	Calvin Coolidge
30. Calvin Coolidge	1923–1929	Republican	1872	1933	Vt.—Mass.	Lawyer	Charles G. Dawes
31. Herbert C. Hoover	1929–1933	Republican	1874	1964	Iowa—Cal.	Engineer	Charles Curtis
32. Franklin D. Roosevelt	1933–1945	Democratic	1882	1945	New York	Lawyer	John N. Garner Henry A. Wallace Harry S. Truman
33. Harry S. Truman	1945–1953	Democratic	1884	1972	Missouri	Merchant	Alben W. Barkley
34. Dwight D. Eisenhower	1953–1961	Republican	1890	1969	Tex.—N.Y., Pa.	Soldier	Richard M. Nixon
35. John F. Kennedy	1961–1963	Democratic	1917	1963	Massachusetts	Writer	Lyndon B. Johnson
36. Lyndon B. Johnson	1963–1969	Democratic	1908	1973	Texas	Teacher, rancher	Hubert H. Humphrey
37. Richard M. Nixon	1969–1974	Republican	1913		Cal.—N.Y., Cal.	Lawyer	Spiro T. Agnew Gerald R. Ford
38. Gerald R. Ford	1974–1977	Republican	1913		Neb.—Mich.	Lawyer	Nelson A. Rockefeller
39. Jimmy (James Earl) Carter	1977–1981	Democratic	1924		Georgia	Farmer	Walter F. Mondale
40. Ronald Reagan	1981–	Republican	1911		Ill.—Cal.	Actor	George Bush

THE DECLARATION OF INDEPENDENCE

When, in the course of human events, it becomes necessary for one people to dissolve the political bands which have connected them with another, and to assume, among the powers of the earth, the separate and equal station to which the laws of nature and of nature's God entitle them, a decent respect to the opinions of mankind requires that they should declare the causes which impel them to the separation.

We hold these truths to be self-evident, that all men are created equal, that they are endowed by their Creator with certain unalienable rights, that among these are life, liberty, and the pursuit of happiness. That, to secure these rights, governments are instituted among men, deriving their just powers from the consent of the governed. That, whenever any form of government becomes destructive of these ends, it is the right of the people to alter or to abolish it, and to institute new government, laying its foundation on such principles, and organizing its powers in such form, as to them shall seem most likely to effect their safety and happiness.

Prudence, indeed, will dictate that governments long established should not be changed for light and transient causes; and, accordingly, all experience has shown that mankind are more disposed to suffer, while evils are sufferable, than to right themselves by abolishing the forms to which they are accustomed.

But when a long train of abuses and usurpations, pursuing invariably the same object, evinces a design to reduce them under absolute despotism, it is their right, it is their duty, to throw off such government, and to provide new guards for their future security. Such has been the patient sufferance of these colonies; and such is now the necessity which constrains them to alter their former systems of government. The history of the present King of Great Britain is a history of repeated injuries and usurpations, all having in direct object the establishment of an absolute tyranny over these states. To prove this, let facts be submitted to a candid world.

He has refused his assent to laws the most wholesome and necessary for the public good.

He has forbidden his governors to pass laws of immediate and pressing importance, unless suspended in their operation till his assent should be obtained; and when so suspended, he has utterly neglected to attend to them.

He has refused to pass other laws for the accommodation of large districts of people, unless those people would relinquish the right of representation in the legislature; a right inestimable to them and formidable to tyrants only.

He has called together legislative bodies at places unusual, uncomfortable, and distant from the depository of their public records, for the sole purpose of fatiguing them into compliance with his measures.

He has dissolved representative houses repeatedly, for opposing with manly firmness his invasions on the rights of the people.

He has refused for a long time, after such dissolutions, to cause others to be elected; whereby the legislative powers, incapable of annihilation, have returned to the people at large for their exercise; the state remaining in the meantime exposed to all the dangers of invasion from without, and convulsions within.

He has endeavored to prevent the population of these states; for that purpose obstructing the laws for naturalization of foreigners; refusing to pass others to encourage their migrations hither, and raising the conditions of new appropriations of lands.

He has obstructed the administration of justice, by refusing his assent to laws for establishing judiciary powers.

He has made judges dependent on his will alone, for the tenure of their offices, and the amount and payment of their salaries.

He has erected a multitude of new offices, and sent hither swarms of officers to harass our people, and eat out their substance.

He has kept among us, in times of peace, standing armies, without the consent of our legislatures.

He has affected to render the military independent of and superior to the civil power.

He has combined with others to subject us to a jurisdiction foreign to our constitution, and unacknowledged by our laws; giving his assent to their acts of pretended legislation:

For quartering large bodies of armed troops among us;

For protecting them, by a mock trial, from punishment for any murders which they should commit on the inhabitants of these states;

For cutting off our trade with all parts of the world;

For imposing taxes on us without our consent;

For depriving us, in many cases, of the benefits of trial by jury;

For transporting us beyond seas to be tried for pretended offenses;

For abolishing the free system of English laws in a neighboring province, establishing therein an arbitrary government, and enlarging its boundaries, so as to render it at once an example and fit instrument for introducing the same absolute rule into these colonies;

For taking away our charters, abolishing our most valuable laws, and altering fundamentally the forms of our governments;

For suspending our own legislatures, and declaring themselves invested with power to legislate for us in all cases whatsoever.

He has abdicated government here, by declaring us out of his protection, and waging war against us.

He has plundered our seas, ravaged our coasts, burnt our towns, and destroyed the lives of our people.

He is at this time transporting large armies of foreign mercenaries to complete the works of death, desolation, and tyranny already begun with circumstances of cruelty and perfidy scarcely paralleled in the most barbarous ages, and totally unworthy the head of a civilized nation.

He has constrained our fellow citizens, taken captive on the high seas, to bear arms against their country, to become the executioners of their friends and brethren, or to fall themselves by their hands.

He has excited domestic insurrections among us, and has endeavored to bring on the inhabitants of our frontiers, the merciless Indian savages, whose known rule of warfare is an undistinguished destruction of all ages, sexes, and conditions.

In every stage of these oppressions, we have petitioned for redress in the most humble terms. Our repeated petitions have been answered only by repeated injury. A prince, whose character is thus marked by every act which may define a tyrant, is unfit to be the ruler of a free people.

Nor have we been wanting in attentions to our British brethren. We have warned them from time to time of attempts by their legislature to extend an unwarrantable jurisdiction over us. We have reminded them of the circumstances of our emigration and settlement here. We have appealed to their native justice and magnanimity, and we have conjured them by the ties of our common kindred to disavow these usurpations, which would inevitably interrupt our connections and correspondence. They too have been deaf to the voice of justice and of consanguinity. We must, therefore, acquiesce in the necessity, which denounces our separation, and hold them, as we hold the rest of mankind, enemies in war, in peace, friends.

We, therefore, the representatives of the United States of America, in General Congress assembled, appealing to the Supreme Judge of the world for the rectitude of our intentions, do, in the name and by authority of the good people of these colonies, solemnly publish and declare, that these united colonies are and of right ought to be free and independent states; that they are absolved from all allegiance to the British Crown, and that all political connection between them and the state of Great Britain is and ought to be totally dissolved; and that, as free and independent states, they have full power to levy war, conclude peace, contract alliances, establish commerce, and to do all other acts and things which independent states may of right do. And for the support of this declaration, with a firm reliance on the protection of Divine Providence, we mutually pledge to each other our lives, our fortunes, and our sacred honor.

THE CONSTITUTION OF THE UNITED STATES

The text of the Constitution appears to the left below in a version with modernized spelling, capitalization, and punctuation. Brackets in the text mark passages that have been changed or voided by amendments. The words to the right below are comments on the meaning and history of the Constitution.

PREAMBLE

We the people of the United States, in order to form a more perfect Union, establish justice, insure domestic tranquility, provide for the common defense, promote the general welfare, and secure the blessings of liberty to ourselves and our posterity, do ordain and establish this Constitution for the United States of America.

PREAMBLE

The Preamble lists the purposes of the new government, based on the will of the people. Following the Preamble are the first three articles of the Constitution. They divide the powers of government among three distinct branches, creating a system of checks and balances as shown in the chart on page 126.

ARTICLE 1

Section 1

All legislative powers herein granted shall be vested in a Congress of the United States, which shall consist of a Senate and House of Representatives.

Section 2

Clause 1. The House of Representatives shall be composed of members chosen every second year by the people of the several states, and the electors in each state shall have the qualifications requisite for electors of the most numerous branch of the state legislature.

Clause 2. No person shall be a representative who shall not have attained to the age of twenty-five years, and been seven years a citizen of the United States, and who shall not, when elected, be an inhabitant of that state in which he shall be chosen.

Clause 3. Representatives and direct taxes shall be apportioned among the several states which may be included within this Union, according to their respective numbers, [which shall be determined by adding to the whole number of free persons, including those bound to service for a term of years, and excluding Indians not taxed, three fifths of all other persons]. The actual enumeration shall be made within three years after the first meeting of the Congress of the United States, and within every subsequent term of ten years, in such manner as they shall by law direct. The number of representatives shall not exceed one for every thirty thousand, but each state shall have at least one representative; [and until such enumeration shall be made, the state of New Hampshire shall be

ARTICLE 1. The Legislative Branch

Section 1. A Two-Part Congress

The legislative branch is empowered to make laws. Its powers are given to the Senate and the House of Representatives both.

Section 2. The House of Representatives

Clause 1. Elections and Voters. Members of the House are elected every two years by voters who must be qualified to vote in certain state elections.

Clause 2. Qualifications of Representatives

Clause 3. Apportionment of Representatives. The number of representatives from each state is based on the state's population. Originally, indentured servants ("those bound to service") were counted as if they were free. But slaves ("all other persons") were counted at the rate of three fifths. Thus it took 500 slaves to equal 300 free persons in deciding numbers of representatives. When slavery was ended by the Thirteenth Amendment in 1865, the three-fifths rule became meaningless.

The "actual enumeration," or census, was first made in 1790. It has been repeated every ten years since. Today there is no worry that the number of representatives might exceed one for every thirty thousand persons. A typical member of the House now represents about five hundred thousand persons.

entitled to choose three, Massachusetts eight, Rhode Island and Providence Plantations one, Connecticut five, New York six, New Jersey four, Pennsylvania eight, Delaware one, Maryland six, Virginia ten, North Carolina five, South Carolina five, and Georgia three].

Clause 4. When vacancies happen in the representation from any state, the executive authority thereof shall issue writs of election to fill such vacancies.

Clause 5. The House of Representatives shall choose their speaker and other officers, and shall have the sole power of impeachment.

Section 3

Clause 1. The Senate of the United States shall be composed of two senators from each state, [chosen by the legislature thereof,] for six years; and each senator shall have one vote.

Clause 2. Immediately after they shall be assembled in consequence of the first election, they shall be divided as equally as may be into three classes. The seats of the senators of the first class shall be vacated at the expiration of the second year, of the second class at the expiration of the fourth year, and of the third class at the expiration of the sixth year, so that one third may be chosen every second year; [and if vacancies happen by resignation, or otherwise, during the recess of the legislature of any state, the executive thereof may make temporary appointments until the next meeting of the legislature, which shall then fill such vacancies].

Clause 3. No person shall be a senator who shall not have attained to the age of thirty years, and been nine years a citizen of the United States, and who shall not, when elected, be an inhabitant of that state for which he shall be chosen.

Clause 4. The Vice-President of the United States shall be president of the Senate, but shall have no vote, unless they be equally divided.

Clause 5. The Senate shall choose their other officers and also a president pro tempore, in the absence of the Vice-President, or when he shall exercise the office of President of the United States.

Clause 6. The Senate shall have the sole power to try all impeachments. When sitting for that purpose, they shall be on oath or affirmation. When the President of the United States is tried, the Chief Justice shall preside. And no person shall be convicted without the concurrence of two thirds of the members present.

Clause 7. Judgment in cases of impeachment shall not extend further than to removal from office, and disqualification to hold and enjoy any office of honor, trust, or

Clause 4. Filling Vacancies. The "executive authority" refers to a state governor. If a House seat becomes vacant between regular elections, the governor is empowered to call a special election to fill the seat.

Clause 5. Officers; Power of Impeachment. The speaker of the House is the leading officer of the House. Only the House can bring impeachment charges. (See Section 3, clauses 6 and 7, below.)

Section 3. The Senate

Clause 1. Elections. Senators were elected by state legislatures until the Seventeenth Amendment, ratified in 1913. Since then, senators have been chosen directly by the voters of each state.

Clause 2. Overlapping Terms of Office; Filling Vacancies. By dividing senators into three classes, or groups, the Constitution set up a system of overlapping terms in office. Every two years, one third of the senators must vacate office or stand for reelection. Thus the Senate changes somewhat every two years, although senators are elected to six-year terms.

The method of filling vacancies in the Senate was changed by the Seventeenth Amendment. It gave the power of choosing replacements to the voters of each state.

Clause 3. Qualifications of Senators

Clause 4. President of the Senate. The Vice-President serves as president of the Senate, but votes only in case of a tie.

Clause 5. Election of Senate Officers. The Senate elects officers, including a temporary president of the Senate to lead meetings when the Vice-President is absent.

Clause 6. Impeachment Trials. The Senate serves as a jury in impeachment cases. A conviction requires a two-thirds vote of the members present. In 1868 the House impeached President Andrew Johnson, but the Senate acquitted him. In 1974 the House considered impeaching President Richard M. Nixon. Nixon resigned before the House made a final decision about impeachment.

Clause 7. Penalty for Conviction. If an impeached person is convicted, the person will be removed from office (see Article 2, Section 4) and barred from other federal office. The Senate cannot impose further punishment, but the con-

profit under the United States; but the party convicted shall nevertheless be liable and subject to indictment, trial, judgment, and punishment, according to law.

victed person can then be tried in a regular court. The Senate has convicted only four persons, all judges. They were removed from office but not tried in regular courts.

Section 4

Clause 1. The times, places, and manner of holding elections for senators and representatives shall be prescribed in each state by the legislature thereof; but the Congress may at any time by law make or alter such regulations, [except as to the places of choosing senators].

Clause 2. The Congress shall assemble at least once in every year, [and such meeting shall be on the first Monday in December,] unless they shall by law appoint a different day.

Section 5

Clause 1. Each house shall be the judge of the elections, returns, and qualifications of its own members, and a majority of each shall constitute a quorum to do business; but a smaller number may adjourn from day to day, and may be authorized to compel the attendance of absent members, in such manner and under such penalties as each house may provide.

Clause 2. Each house may determine the rules of its proceedings, punish its members for disorderly behavior, and, with the concurrence of two thirds, expel a member.

Clause 3. Each house shall keep a journal of its proceedings and from time to time publish the same, excepting such parts as may in their judgment require secrecy; and the yeas and nays of the members of either house on any question shall, at the desire of one fifth of those present, be entered on the journal.

Clause 4. Neither house, during the session of Congress, shall, without the consent of the other, adjourn for more than three days, nor to any other place than that in which the two houses shall be sitting.

Section 6

Clause 1. The senators and representatives shall receive a compensation for their services, to be ascertained by law, and paid out of the Treasury of the United States. They shall in all cases, except treason, felony, and breach of the peace, be privileged from arrest during their attendance at the session of their respective houses, and in going to and returning from the same; and for any speech or debate in either house, they shall not be questioned in any other place.

Clause 2. No senator or representative shall, during the time for which he was elected, be appointed to any civil office under the authority of the United States which shall have been created, or the emoluments whereof shall have

Section 4. Times of Elections and Meetings

Clause 1. Elections. Each state regulates congressional elections, but Congress can change such regulations. In 1872 Congress required that every state hold congressional elections on the same day.

Clause 2. Meetings. Congress must meet once a year. The Twentieth Amendment, ratified in 1933, changed the first day of the meeting to January 3, unless Congress specifies a different day.

Section 5. Basics of Organization

Clause 1. Members; Attendance. Each house can judge whether new members have been elected fairly and are qualified to serve. A quorum is the minimum number of members who can act for all. Discussion and debate can go on without a quorum, but one is required for voting by either house.

Clause 2. Determining Procedures. Each house can set up its own rules of conducting business.

Clause 3. Written Records. Since 1873 the journals of the House and Senate have been published together in the *Congressional Record.* It appears each day when Congress is meeting. A member of either house may get permission to insert a speech in the published *Record* even though the speech was not actually delivered on the floor of the House or Senate.

Clause 4. Adjournment. Both houses must agree on any adjournment longer than three days.

Section 6. Special Rights and Restrictions

Clause 1. Salaries and Privileges. The members of Congress can by law determine their own salaries. When the members are in session, they cannot be arrested except on certain criminal charges. Thus the work of Congress cannot be disrupted by lawsuits against senators and representatives. In particular, the members of Congress cannot be sued for "any speech or debate in either house." While taking part in the work of Congress, members can write or say anything about anyone without fear of being sued for libel or slander.

Clause 2. Employment Restrictions. Members of Congress cannot create new federal jobs or increase the "emoluments," or payments, for old ones and then leave Congress to take those jobs. Nor can anyone holding a federal job

been increased, during such time; and no person holding any office under the United States shall be a member of either house during his continuance in office.

Section 7

Clause 1. All bills for raising revenue shall originate in the House of Representatives; but the Senate may propose or concur with amendments as on other bills.

Clause 2. Every bill which shall have passed the House of Representatives and the Senate shall, before it becomes a law, be presented to the President of the United States. If he approve he shall sign it, but if not, he shall return it, with his objections, to that house in which it shall have originated, who shall enter the objections at large on their journal and proceed to reconsider it. If, after such reconsideration, two thirds of that house shall agree to pass the bill, it shall be sent, together with objections, to the other house, by which it shall likewise be reconsidered, and, if approved by two thirds of that house, it shall become a law. But in all such cases the votes of both houses shall be determined by yeas and nays, and the names of the persons voting for and against the bill shall be entered on the journal of each house respectively. If any bill shall not be returned by the President within ten days (Sundays excepted) after it shall have been presented to him, the same shall be a law, in like manner as if he had signed it, unless the Congress by their adjournment prevent its return, in which case it shall not be a law.

Clause 3. Every order, resolution, or vote to which the concurrence of the Senate and House of Representatives may be necessary (except on a question of adjournment) shall be presented to the President of the United States; and before the same shall take effect, shall be approved by him, or being disapproved by him, shall be repassed by two thirds of the Senate and House of Representatives, according to the rules and limitations prescribed in the case of a bill.

Section 8

The Congress shall have power:

Clause 1. To lay and collect taxes, duties, imposts, and excises, to pay the debts and provide for the common defense and general welfare of the United States; but all duties, imposts, and excises shall be uniform throughout the United States;

Clause 2. To borrow money on the credit of the United States;

Clause 3. To regulate commerce with foreign nations, and among the several states, and with the Indian tribes;

Clause 4. To establish a uniform rule of naturalization and uniform laws on the subject of bankruptcies throughout the United States;

outside Congress serve at the same time as a member of Congress. This restriction prevents the members of Congress from simultaneously working for other branches of the federal government.

Section 7. Procedures for Making Laws

Clause 1. Tax Bills. All tax bills must begin in the House. However, the Senate can thoroughly revise such bills.

Clause 2. Submitting Bills to the President. After Congress passes a bill, it goes to the President. The bill can then become a law in one of three ways. The President may approve the bill and sign it. Or the President may veto the bill and return it to Congress with objections, but Congress is able to override the President's veto by a two-thirds vote of both houses. Or the President may do nothing, in which case the bill becomes law after 10 days (not counting Sundays), provided Congress is in session at that time.

The bill can fail to become law in two ways. The President may veto it and Congress is unable to override the veto. Or the President may do nothing, and Congress adjourns within 10 days. This method of letting a bill die is called a pocket veto. A President may use it to avoid an open veto of a controversial bill.

Clause 3. Submitting Other Measures to the President. If other measures require agreement by both houses and are in effect bills, they must go to the President. Thus Congress cannot avoid submitting bills to the President by calling them orders or resolutions. When such measures reach the President, they are treated as bills.

Section 8. Powers Granted to Congress

Clause 1. Taxation. Congress can impose "duties," taxes on imported goods. But Congress cannot tax exports. (See Section 9, Clause 5, below.) "Excises" are taxes on making, selling, or using items such as cigarettes within the nation. "Imposts" are taxes of any sort.

Clause 2. Borrowing

Clause 3. Regulating Interstate Trade. This is the "commerce clause," the basis of many federal regulations.

Clause 4. Naturalization; Bankruptcy

Clause 5. To coin money, regulate the value thereof, and of foreign coin, and fix the standard of weights and measures;

Clause 6. To provide for the punishment of counterfeiting the securities and current coin of the United States;

Clause 7. To establish post offices and post roads;

Clause 8. To promote the progress of science and useful arts, by securing for limited times to authors and inventors the exclusive right to their respective writings and discoveries;

Clause 9. To constitute tribunals inferior to the Supreme Court;

Clause 10. To define and punish piracies and felonies committed on the high seas and offenses against the law of nations;

Clause 11. To declare war, grant letters of marque and reprisal, and make rules concerning captures on land and water;

Clause 12. To raise and support armies, but no appropriation of money to that use shall be for a longer term than two years;

Clause 13. To provide and maintain a navy;

Clause 14. To make rules for the government and regulation of the land and naval forces;

Clause 15. To provide for calling forth the militia to execute the laws of the Union, suppress insurrections, and repel invasions;

Clause 16. To provide for organizing, arming, and disciplining the militia, and for governing such part of them as may be employed in the service of the United States, reserving to the states respectively the appointment of the officers and the authority of training the militia according to the discipline prescribed by Congress;

Clause 17. To exercise exclusive legislation in all cases whatsoever over such district (not exceeding ten miles square) as may, by cession of particular states and the acceptance of Congress, become the seat of the government of the United States, and to exercise like authority over all places purchased by the consent of the legislature of the state in which the same shall be for the erection of forts, magazines, arsenals, dockyards, and other needful buildings; and

Clause 18. To make all laws which shall be necessary and proper for carrying into execution the foregoing powers and all other powers vested by this Constitution in the government of the United States, or in any department or officer thereof.

Clause 5. Coining Money. The federal government's printing of paper money derives from this clause.

Clause 6. Punishment of Counterfeiting. The "securities" referred to are government bonds.

Clause 7. Providing Postal Service

Clause 8. Encouraging Authors and Inventors. Through this clause authors receive copyrights and inventors receive patents.

Clause 9. Establishing Lower Courts. Federal courts "inferior to the Supreme Court" include district courts and the United States Court of Appeals.

Clause 10. Punishment of Crimes at Sea

Clause 11. Declaring War. "Letters of marque and reprisal" authorize private ships to attack and seize enemy ships.

Clause 12. Raising Armies

Clause 13. Maintaining a Navy

Clause 14. Regulating the Armed Forces

Clause 15. Calling Out the Militia. Congress can empower the President to call out state militia units, now known as the National Guard.

Clause 16. Maintaining the Militia. The federal government and each state government share in providing funds for the National Guard.

Clause 17. Control of Federal Property. Congress makes laws for the District of Columbia and for federal land on which forts, naval bases, and other federal structures stand.

Clause 18. Carrying Out Granted Powers. This clause, known as the "necessary and proper" clause, gives Congress a basis for dealing with matters not specifically named in the Constitution. The clause also is known as the "elastic clause."

Section 9

Clause 1. The migration or importation of such persons as any of the states now existing shall think proper to admit shall not be prohibited by the Congress prior to the year 1808, but a tax or duty may be imposed on such importation, not exceeding ten dollars for each person.

Clause 2. The privilege of the writ of habeas corpus shall not be suspended, unless, when in cases of rebellion or invasion, the public safety may require it.

Clause 3. No bill of attainder or ex post facto law shall be passed.

Clause 4. No capitation [or other direct] tax shall be laid, unless in proportion to the census or enumeration hereinbefore directed to be taken.

Clause 5. No tax or duty shall be laid on articles exported from any state.

Clause 6. No preference shall be given by any regulation of commerce or revenue to the ports of one state over those of another; nor shall vessels bound to or from one state be obliged to enter, clear, or pay duties in another.

Clause 7. No money shall be drawn from the Treasury but in consequence of appropriations made by law; and a regular statement and account of the receipts and expenditures of all public money shall be published from time to time.

Clause 8. No title of nobility shall be granted by the United States. And no person holding any office of profit or trust under them shall, without the consent of the Congress, accept of any present, emolument, office, or title of any kind whatever from any king, prince, or foreign state.

Section 10

Clause 1. No state shall enter into any treaty, alliance, or confederation; grant letters of marque and reprisal; coin money; emit bills of credit; make anything but gold and silver coin a tender in payment of debts; pass any bill of attainder, ex post facto law, or law impairing the obligation of contracts, or grant any title of nobility.

Clause 2. No state shall, without the consent of the Congress, lay any imposts or duties on imports or exports, except what may be absolutely necessary for executing its inspection laws; and the net produce of all duties and imposts laid by any state on imports or exports shall be for

Section 9. Powers Denied to Congress

Clause 1. Ending the Slave Trade. Congress was forbidden to end the importing of slaves before 1808. In that year, Congress declared that further importing of slaves was illegal.

Clause 2. Suspending the Writ of Habeas Corpus. A writ of habeas corpus is a legal order saying that a person who is held in custody must be brought into court so that a judge can decide whether the person is being held illegally. During the Civil War (a case of "rebellion or invasion"), President Abraham Lincoln suspended the writ of habeas corpus in some areas.

Clause 3. Imposing Certain Penalties. A "bill of attainder" allows a person to be punished without a jury trial. An "ex post facto law" allows a person to be punished for an act that was not illegal when it was committed.

Clause 4. Taxing Individuals Unfairly. A "capitation tax," also known as a "head tax," is paid by individuals directly to the government. This clause requires that any such tax be divided fairly among the states according to their population. The Sixteenth Amendment, ratified in 1913, prevents this clause from being applied to income taxes.

Clause 5. Taxing Exports. Here "exported" means sent out of a state, whether to another state or to another country.

Clause 6. Taxing Trade Unfairly; Allowing Ships to Be Taxed in Trade Between States

Clause 7. Unlawful Spending. The federal government can spend money only when Congress authorizes the spending. Federal spending and receipts must be recorded and published.

Clause 8. Creating Titles of Nobility; Allowing Gifts from Foreign Countries Without Permission. Congress cannot give anyone a title such as duchess or count. Congress has passed laws letting federal officials accept small gifts from foreign countries. Larger gifts become the property of the United States.

Section 10. Powers Denied to the States

Clause 1. Certain Foreign, Financial, and Legal Dealings. Some of these powers are given exclusively to the federal government. Others are denied to any government, state or federal.

Clause 2. Taxing Imports or Exports Without Permission. Except with the consent of Congress, a state cannot tax any goods entering or leaving the state, though the state can charge a small fee to pay for inspection of the goods.

the use of the Treasury of the United States; and all such laws shall be subject to the revision and control of the Congress.

Clause 3. No state shall, without the consent of Congress, lay any duty of tonnage; keep troops or ships of war in time of peace; enter into any agreement or compact with another state or with a foreign power; or engage in war, unless actually invaded, or in such imminent danger as will not admit of delay.

Clause 3. Taxing Ships or Making Military or Diplomatic Arrangements Without Permission. "Tonnage" is the number of tons of cargo a ship can carry. Except with the consent of Congress, a state cannot prepare for war or wage war unless there is a military emergency.

ARTICLE 2

Section 1

Clause 1. The executive power shall be vested in a President of the United States of America. He shall hold his office during the term of four years, and, together with the Vice-President, chosen for the same term, be elected as follows:

Clause 2. Each state shall appoint, in such manner as the legislature thereof may direct, a number of electors, equal to the whole number of senators and representatives to which the state may be entitled in the Congress; but no senator or representative, or person holding an office of trust or profit under the United States, shall be appointed an elector.

Clause 3. [The electors shall meet in their respective states and vote by ballot for two persons, of whom one at least shall not be an inhabitant of the same state with themselves. And they shall make a list of all the persons voted for and of the number of votes for each; which list they shall sign and certify, and transmit sealed to the seat of the government of the United States, directed to the president of the Senate. The president of the Senate shall, in the presence of the Senate and House of Representatives, open all the certificates, and the votes shall then be counted. The person having the greatest number of votes shall be the President, if such number be a majority of the whole number of electors appointed; and if there be more than one who have such majority, and have an equal number of votes, then the House of Representatives shall immediately choose by ballot one of them for President; and if no person have a majority, then from the five highest on the list the said house shall in like manner choose the President. But in choosing the President, the votes shall be taken by states, the representation from each state having one vote; a quorum for this purpose shall consist of a member or members from two thirds of the states, and a majority of all the states shall be necessary to a choice. In every case, after the choice of the President, the person having the greatest number of votes of the electors shall be the Vice-President. But if there

ARTICLE 2. The Executive Branch

Section 1. The Offices of President and Vice-President

Clause 1. The President as Executive; Term of Office. As chief executive, the President is responsible for executing, or carrying out, the laws passed by Congress.

Clause 2. Choosing Electors. This clause sets up the electoral college, the group of people who elect the President and Vice-President. At first the electors were chosen mainly by state legislatures. After 1800 the electors were chosen increasingly by popular vote. Today all electors are chosen in this way.

Clause 3. Voting by Electors. Originally each elector voted for two candidates. Either might become President. As a result, the Republican candidate for President in 1800, Thomas Jefferson, received the same number of electoral votes as the Republican candidate for Vice-President, Aaron Burr. The choice was then left to the House of Representatives, which finally chose Jefferson.

To prevent similar ties between candidates for President and Vice-President, Congress passed the Twelfth Amendment in 1803. The amendment was ratified in June 1804, before the next presidential election. It required electors to cast one ballot for President and a separate ballot for Vice-President.

should remain two or more who have equal votes, the Senate shall choose from them by ballot the Vice-President.]

Clause 4. The Congress may determine the time of choosing the electors and the day on which they shall give their votes, which day shall be the same throughout the United States.

Clause 5. No person except a natural-born citizen, or a citizen of the United States at the time of the adoption of this Constitution, shall be eligible to the office of President; neither shall any person be eligible to that office who shall not have attained to the age of thirty-five years and been fourteen years a resident within the United States.

Clause 6. In case of the removal of the President from office, or of his death, resignation, or inability to discharge the powers and duties of the said office, the same shall devolve on the Vice-President, and the Congress may by law provide for the case of removal, death, resignation, or inability, both of the President and Vice-President, declaring what officer shall then act as President, and such officer shall act accordingly until the disability be removed or a President shall be elected.

Clause 7. The President shall, at stated times, receive for his services a compensation, which shall neither be increased nor diminished during the period for which he shall have been elected, and he shall not receive within that period any other emolument from the United States or any of them.

Clause 8. Before he enter on the execution of his office, he shall take the following oath or affirmation: "I do solemnly swear (or affirm) that I will faithfully execute the office of President of the United States, and will, to the best of my ability, preserve, protect, and defend the Constitution of the United States."

Section 2

Clause 1. The President shall be commander in chief of the army and navy of the United States, and of the militia of the several states when called into actual service of the United States. He may require the opinion, in writing, of the principal officer in each of the executive departments upon any subject relating to the duties of their respective offices. And he shall have power to grant reprieves and pardons for offenses against the United States, except in cases of impeachment.

Clause 2. He shall have power, by and with the advice and consent of the Senate, to make treaties, provided two thirds of the senators present concur; and he shall nominate, and by and with the advice and consent of the Senate, shall appoint ambassadors, other public ministers and consuls, judges of the Supreme Court, and all other

Clause 4. Time of Elections. Congress has decided that presidential elections are to be held every four years on the Tuesday following the first Monday of November. Electoral votes are to be cast on the Monday after the second Wednesday in December.

Clause 5. Qualifications of the President

Clause 6. Presidential Succession. In 1886 Congress specified that the line of succession would go from the Vice-President to members of the cabinet. In 1947 Congress changed the line of succession to go from the Vice-President to the speaker of the House, then to the president pro tempore of the Senate, and then to the cabinet. The Twenty-fifth Amendment, ratified in 1967, prevents a long vacancy in the office of Vice-President. The amendment also establishes procedures in case the President is disabled.

Clause 7. Presidential Salary

Clause 8. The Oath of Office. The Constitution does not say who will administer the oath. Ordinarily it is the Chief Justice of the Supreme Court.

Section 2. Powers Granted to the President

Clause 1. Military Powers; Executive Powers; Reprieves and Pardons. Together, the military powers of the President and of Congress assure civilian control of the armed forces. The President may grant a reprieve to stop punishment after a trial or a pardon to prevent a trial. In 1974 President Gerald R. Ford issued a pardon to Richard M. Nixon, preventing Nixon from being tried on federal charges related to Watergate.

Clause 2. Treaties and Appointments. The President's power to make treaties and appointments can be checked by the power of the Senate to reject them.

officers of the United States whose appointments are not herein otherwise provided for, and which shall be established by law; but the Congress may by law vest the appointment of such inferior officers as they think proper in the President alone, in the courts of law, or in the heads of departments.

Clause 3. The President shall have power to fill up all vacancies that may happen during the recess of the Senate, by granting commissions which shall expire at the end of their next session.

Section 3

He shall from time to time give to the Congress information of the state of the Union, and recommend to their consideration such measures as he shall judge necessary and expedient; he may, on extraordinary occasions, convene both houses, or either of them, and in case of disagreement between them with respect to the time of adjournment, he may adjourn them to such time as he shall think proper; he shall receive ambassadors and other public ministers; he shall take care that the laws be faithfully executed, and shall commission all the officers of the United States.

Section 4

The President, Vice-President, and all civil officers of the United States shall be removed from office on impeachment for, and conviction of, treason, bribery, or other high crimes and misdemeanors.

ARTICLE 3

Section 1

The judicial power of the United States shall be vested in one Supreme Court, and in such inferior courts as the Congress may from time to time ordain and establish. The judges, both of the Supreme and inferior courts, shall hold their offices during good behavior, and shall, at stated times, receive for their services a compensation which shall not be diminished during their continuance in office.

Section 2

Clause 1. The judicial power shall extend to all cases, in law and equity, arising under this Constitution, the laws of the United States, and treaties made, or which shall be made, under their authority; to all cases affecting ambassadors, other public ministers and consuls; to all cases of admiralty and maritime jurisdiction; to controversies to which the United States shall be a party; to controversies between two or more states; [between a state and citizens of another state;] between citizens of different states; between citizens of the same state claiming lands

Clause 3. Temporary Appointments. When the Senate is not in session and cannot confirm appointments, the President may fill vacancies on a temporary basis.

Section 3. Duties of the President

To fulfill the first duty here, the President delivers a State of the Union message to Congress each January. On many occasions, specially in the 1800s, the President has called Congress into special session. No President has needed to adjourn Congress. The duty of receiving ambassadors fits the President's power to make treaties. The duty to "take care that the laws be faithfully executed" places the President in charge of federal law enforcement.

Section 4. Impeachment

Among the "civil officers" who can be impeached are cabinet members and federal judges.

ARTICLE 3. The Judicial Branch

Section 1. Federal Courts

Congress has established district courts and appeals courts under the Supreme Court. Congress also has decided from time to time how many justices serve on the Supreme Court. But Congress can neither abolish the Supreme Court nor remove any federal judges unless they are impeached and convicted. Nor can Congress put pressure on judges by lowering their "compensation," or salaries.

Section 2. Jurisdiction of Federal Courts

Clause 1. Types of Cases. This clause names the types of cases that federal courts can rule on. These include "all cases . . . arising under this Constitution, " which allows the Supreme Court to exercise the right of judicial review as asserted by Chief Justice John Marshall in the case of *Marbury* v. *Madison*. Thus the court can declare a law unconstitutional. First, though, the law must be involved in a lawsuit. The court cannot review a law unless it is presented to the court as part of a case.

under grants of different states; and between a state, or the citizens thereof, and foreign states, [citizens, or subjects].

Clause 2. In all cases affecting ambassadors, other public ministers and consuls, and those in which a state shall be party, the Supreme Court shall have original jurisdiction. In all the other cases beforementioned, the Supreme Court shall have appellate jurisdiction, both as to law and fact, with such exceptions and under such regulations as the Congress shall make.

Clause 3. The trial of all crimes, except in cases of impeachment, shall be by jury; and such trial shall be held in the state where the said crimes shall have been committed; but when not committed within any state, the trial shall be at such place or places as the Congress may by law have directed.

Section 3

Clause 1. Treason against the United States shall consist only in levying war against them or in adhering to their enemies, giving them aid and comfort. No person shall be convicted of treason unless on the testimony of two witnesses to the same overt act, or on confession in open court.

Clause 2. The Congress shall have power to declare the punishment of treason, but no attainder of treason shall work corruption of blood or forfeiture except during the life of the person attainted.

Clause 2. Original Cases and Appeals Cases. Cases of "original jurisdiction" go directly to the Supreme Court. Cases of "appellate jurisdiction" go first to lower courts. Then, if the lower court proceedings are appealed, the cases go to the Supreme Court, under rules decided by Congress. Nearly all cases heard by the Supreme Court begin in the lower courts.

Clause 3. Cases Requiring Trials by Jury. This clause covers trials involving federal crimes. The clause does not require juries in civil cases, which involve individual rights, or in criminal cases under state laws.

Section 3. Treason

Clause 1. Limits of the Crime. To be convicted of treason against the United States, a person must commit an overt act, one that can be seen. Merely talking or thinking about treason is not a federal crime.

Clause 2. Limits of the Punishment. "Attainder of treason" and "corruption of blood" refer to punishing the family of a traitor. Such punishment is banned by this clause.

ARTICLE 4

Section 1

Full faith and credit shall be given in each state to the public acts, records, and judicial proceedings of every other state. And the Congress may by general laws prescribe the manner in which such acts, records, and proceedings shall be proved, and the effect thereof.

Section 2

Clause 1. The citizens of each state shall be entitled to all privileges and immunities of citizens in the several states.

Clause 2. A person charged in any state with treason, felony, or other crime, who shall flee from justice and be found in another state, shall, on demand of the executive authority of the state from which he fled, be delivered up to be removed to the state having jurisdiction of the crime.

Clause 3. [No person held to service or labor in one state under the laws thereof, escaping into another, shall, in

ARTICLE 4. Relations Among the States, the Territories, and the United States

Section 1. Official Acts of the States

Every state must recognize and honor the official acts of other states, and Congress can decide what official proofs (for example, marriage certificates) must be accepted from state to state.

Section 2. Privileges and Liabilities of Citizens

Clause 1. Privileges. No state can discriminate against a citizen of another state except in special cases such as residence requirements for voting or entrance requirements for state colleges.

Clause 2. Liabilities of Fugitive Criminals. If a person commits a crime in one state and then flees to another state and is caught, the governor of the state where the crime took place can demand the person's return.

Clause 3. Liabilities of Fugitive Slaves or Servants. The phrase "held to service or labor" refers to slavery or to consequence of any law or regulation therein, be discharged from such service or labor, but shall be delivered up on claim of the party to whom such service or labor may be due.]

service as an indentured servant. In 1865 the Thirteenth Amendment nullified this clause.

Section 3

Clause 1. New states may be admitted by the Congress into this Union; but no new state shall be formed or erected within the jurisdiction of any other state; nor any state be formed by the junction of two or more states, or parts of states, without the consent of the legislatures of the states concerned as well as of the Congress.

Clause 2. The Congress shall have power to dispose of and make all needful rules and regulations respecting the territory or other property belonging to the United States; and nothing in this Constitution shall be so construed as to prejudice any claims of the United States, or of any particular state.

Section 4

The United States shall guarantee to every state in this Union a republican form of government, and shall protect each of them against invasion, and, on application of the legislature or of the executive (when the legislature cannot be convened), against domestic violence.

Section 3. Admitting New States and Regulating Territories

Clause 1. New States. Congress can add new states to the Union. However, the new states cannot be formed by dividing existing states (as when Maine separated from Massachusetts in 1820) or by combining parts of existing states unless both Congress and the states involved consent to the changes.

Clause 2. Territories. Besides having power over federal property of various kinds, Congress has the power to govern federal land. This land includes territory not organized into states and also federal land within states.

Section 4. Protection of the States

The federal government promises that each state will have some form of representative govenment. The federal government also promises to protect each state from invasion and to send help, when requested, to stop rioting within a state.

ARTICLE 5

The Congress, whenever two thirds of both houses shall deem it necessary, shall propose amendments to this Constitution or, on the application of the legislatures of two thirds of the several states, shall call a convention for proposing amendments, which, in either case, shall be valid, to all intents and purposes, as part of this Constitution when ratified by the legislatures of three fourths of the several states, or by conventions in three fourths thereof, as the one or the other mode of ratification may be proposed by the Congress; provided [that no amendment which may be made prior to the year 1808 shall in any manner affect the first and fourth clauses in the ninth section of the first article; and] that no state, without its consent, shall be deprived of its equal suffrage in the Senate.

ARTICLE 5. Methods of Amending the Constitution

There are two ways to propose amendments to the Constitution. One way is by a two-thirds vote of both the House and the Senate. The other way—which has not yet been used—is by a special convention demanded by two thirds of the states.

Once an amendment is proposed, there are two ways to ratify it. One way is by approval of three fourths of the state legislatures. The other way—which has been used only once, to ratify the Twenty-first Amendment—is by approval of special conventions in three fourths of the states. Congress decides which method of ratification to follow.

The three-fourths requirement for ratification means that 38 states must now approve a proposed amendment before it becomes law.

ARTICLE 6

Clause 1. All debts contracted and engagements entered into before the adoption of this Constitution shall be as valid against the United States under this Constitution as under the Confederation.

ARTICLE 6. Federal Debts and the Supremacy of Federal Laws

Clause 1. Federal Debts. This clause promises that all debts incurred by Congress under the Articles of Confederation will be honored by the United States under the Constitution.

Clause 2. This Constitution and the laws of the United States which shall be made in pursuance thereof, and all treaties made, or which shall be made, under the authority of the United States, shall be the supreme law of the land; and the judges in every state shall be bound thereby, anything in the constitution or laws of any state to the contrary notwithstanding.

Clause 3. The senators and representatives beforementioned, and the members of the several state legislatures, and all executive and judicial officers, both of the United States and of the several states, shall be bound by oath or affirmation to support this Constitution; but no religious test shall ever be required as a qualification to any office or public trust under the United States.

ARTICLE 7

The ratification of the conventions of nine states shall be sufficient for the establishment of this Constitution between the states so ratifying the same.

Done in convention by the unanimous consent of the states present the seventeenth day of September in the year of our Lord one thousand seven hundred and eighty-seven, and of the independence of the United States of America the twelfth. In witness whereof we have hereunto subscribed our names,

George Washington,
President and deputy from Virginia

New Hampshire
John Langdon
Nicholas Gilman

Massachusetts
Nathaniel Gorham
Rufus King

Connecticut
William Samuel Johnson
Roger Sherman

New York
Alexander Hamilton

New Jersey
William Livingston
David Brearley
William Paterson
Jonathan Dayton

Pennsylvania
Benjamin Franklin
Thomas Mifflin
Robert Morris
George Clymer
Thomas FitzSimons
Jared Ingersoll
James Wilson
Gouverneur Morris

Delaware
George Read
Gunning Bedford, Jr.
John Dickinson
Richard Bassett
Jacob Broom

Maryland
James McHenry
Dan of St. Thomas Jenifer
Daniel Carroll

Virginia
John Blair
James Madison, Jr.

North Carolina
William Blount
Richard Dobbs Spaight
Hugh Williamson

South Carolina
John Rutledge
Charles Cotesworth Pinckney
Charles Pinckney
Pierce Butler

Georgia
William Few
Abraham Baldwin

Clause 2. Supremacy of the Constitution and of Federal Laws. The Constitution and federal laws or treaties made under it are the highest laws of the nation. When federal laws are in conflict with state laws or constitutions, state judges must follow the federal laws.

Clause 3. Oaths to Support the Constitution. All federal and all state officials must promise to support the Constitution. However, federal officials must not be required to meet any religious standards in order to hold office. State officials, though, may be required to meet such standards. but since the 1840s no state has set religious requirements for its officials.

ARTICLE 7. Ratification of the Constitution

"Conventions" refers to special conventions held in the states to approve or disapprove the Constitution. Nine state conventions voted their approval by June 21, 1788. The Constitution was signed on September 17, 1787, in the 12th year of the country's independence. George Washington signed first as the president of the Philadelphia convention. He was not elected President of the United States until 1789. Of the 55 delegates to the Philadelphia convention, 39 signed the Constitution.

AMENDMENTS TO THE CONSTITUTION

The first ten amendments, called the Bill of Rights, were proposed as a group in 1789 and ratified in 1791. Other amendments were proposed and ratified one at a time. The dates in parentheses below are the years of ratification.

AMENDMENT 1

Congress shall make no law respecting an establishment of religion or prohibiting the free exercise thereof, or abridging the freedom of speech or of the press, or the right of the people peaceably to assemble and to petition the government for a redress of grievances.

AMENDMENT 2

A well-regulated militia being necessary to the security of a free state, the right of the people to keep and bear arms shall not be infringed.

AMENDMENT 3

No soldier shall, in time of peace, be quartered in any house without the consent of the owner, nor in time of war but in a manner to be prescribed by law.

AMENDMENT 4

The right of the people to be secure in their persons, houses, papers, and effects against unreasonable searches and seizures shall not be violated, and no warrants shall issue, but upon probable cause, supported by oath or affirmation, and particularly describing the place to be searched and the persons or things to be seized.

AMENDMENT 5

No person shall be held to answer for a capital or otherwise infamous crime unless on a presentment or indictment of a grand jury, except in cases arising in the land or

AMENDMENT 1 (1791). Religious and Political Freedoms

Congress cannot establish an official religion, interfere with freedom of worship, or prohibit free speech or other political freedoms. These freedoms are not absolute, though. They are limited by the rights of others. For example, the right of free speech does not include slander—the spreading of false stories to damage another person's reputation. Nor does the right of free speech include words that present what the Supreme Court has termed a "clear and present danger," such as a public speech that provokes a riot.

AMENDMENT 2 (1791). The Right to Bear Arms

For the purpose of maintaining a state militia, citizens may keep and bear arms. However, Congress has prohibited the possession of certain firearms such as sawed-off shotguns and machine guns.

AMENDMENT 3 (1791). The Quartering of Soldiers

In peacetime, soldiers cannot be quartered, or given lodging, in any private home unless the owner consents. In wartime, soldiers can be quartered in any private home, but only as directed by law.

AMENDMENT 4 (1791). Freedom from Unreasonable Searches and Seizures

People and their homes and belongings are protected against unreasonable searches and seizures. As a rule, authorities must go before a court and obtain a search warrant or an arrest warrant before seizing evidence or arresting someone. To obtain a warrant, the authorities must explain why it is needed, where the search will take place, and who or what will be seized.

AMENDMENT 5 (1791). Rights Regarding Life, Liberty, and Property

A person cannot be placed on trial in a federal court for a crime punishable by death or for any other major crime without a formal written accusation by a grand jury. This

naval forces, or in the militia, when in actual service in time of war or public danger; nor shall any person be subject for the same offense to be twice put in jeopardy of life or limb; nor shall be compelled in any criminal case to be a witness against himself, nor be deprived of life, liberty, or property without due process of law; nor shall private property be taken for public use without just compensation.

AMENDMENT 6

In all criminal prosecutions, the accused shall enjoy the right to a speedy and public trial by an impartial jury of the state and district wherein the crime shall have been committed, which district shall have been previously ascertained by law, and to be informed of the nature and cause of the accusation; to be confronted with the witnesses against him; to have compulsory process for obtaining witnesses in his favor, and to have the assistance of counsel for his defense.

AMENDMENT 7

In suits at common law, where the value in controversy shall exceed twenty dollars, the right of trial by jury shall be preserved, and no fact tried by a jury shall be otherwise reexamined in any court of the United States than according to the rules of the common law.

AMENDMENT 8

Excessive bail shall not be required, nor excessive fines imposed, nor cruel and unusual punishments inflicted.

rule does not apply if the person is a member of the armed services during war or a time of public danger.

A grand jury can decide that there is not enough evidence to accuse a person of a crime, or the jury can make a formal accusation based on evidence the jury gains on its own (a presentment) or on evidence presented by a prosecutor (an indictment). The accused person can then be held for trial before a trial jury.

If a person is found not guilty of a certain crime, the person cannot be tried again for the same offense (double jeopardy) in a federal court. This rule does not prevent the person from being tried for the same offense in a state court, however.

A person accused of a federal crime cannot be forced to give evidence against himself or herself. Nor can a person lose his or her life, liberty, or property in federal proceedings except as specified by law. When the government takes private property for public use (through the right of eminent domain), the government must pay a fair price.

AMENDMENT 6 (1791). The Right to a Trial by Jury in Criminal Cases

A person accused of a crime has the right to a prompt, public trial by a jury selected from the district in which the crime was committed. That district must be one that already has been described by law, such as an established city or county. The accused person must be informed of the exact charges and must be allowed to face and question witnesses. The accused has the power to force witnesses to appear in court and has the right to a defense lawyer.

AMENDMENT 7 (1791). The Right to a Trial by Jury in Civil Cases

Common law is based on customs and on decisions made by judges in previous cases. (Statute law, in contrast, is established by legislatures.) Suits at common law usually involve disputes between private parties or corporations, and they usually are tried in state courts. When such suits involve more than $20 and are tried in federal courts, either side can insist on a jury trial, although both sides can agree not to have a jury. Once a jury reaches a decision, that decision cannot be overturned merely because a judge disagrees with the jury's findings about the facts of the case.

AMENDMENT 8 (1791). Bail, Fines, and Punishments

Bail is money or property that an accused person yields to a court as a guarantee that he or she will appear for a trial. The amount of bail varies according to factors such as the seriousness of the crime and the reputation and circumstances of the accused person. Unreasonably high bail is forbidden, and so are unreasonably high fines and cruel and unusual punishments.

AMENDMENT 9

The enumeration in the Constitution of certain rights shall not be construed to deny or disparage others retained by the people.

AMENDMENT 10

The powers not delegated to the United States by the Constitution, nor prohibited by it to the states, are reserved to the states respectively, or to the people.

AMENDMENT 11

The judicial power of the United States shall not be construed to extend to any suit in law or equity commenced or prosecuted against one of the United States by citizens of another state, or by citizens or subjects of any foreign state.

AMENDMENT 12

The electors shall meet in their respective states and vote by ballot for President and Vice-President, one of whom at least shall not be an inhabitant of the same state with themselves; they shall name in their ballots the person voted for as President, and in distinct ballots the person voted for as Vice-President, and they shall make distinct lists of all persons voted for as President and of all persons voted for as Vice-President and of the number of votes for each, which lists they shall sign and certify and transmit sealed to the seat of government of the United States, directed to the president of the Senate. The president of the Senate shall, in the presence of the Senate and House of Representatives, open all the certificates and the votes shall then be counted. The person having the greatest number of votes for President shall be the President, if such number be a majority of the whole number of electors appointed; and if no person have such majority, then from the persons having the highest numbers not exceeding three on the list of those voted for as President, the House of Representatives shall choose immediately, by ballot, the President. But in choosing the President the votes shall be taken by states, the representation from each state having one vote; a quorum for this purpose shall consist of a member or members from two thirds of the states, and a majority of all the states shall be necessary to a choice. And if the House of Representatives shall not choose a President whenever the right of choice shall devolve upon them, [before the fourth day of March next following,] then the Vice-President shall act as President, as in the case of the death or other constitutional disa-

AMENDMENT 9 (1791). Further Rights of the People

The naming of certain rights in the Constitution does not mean that people are limited to those rights only. People may claim other rights as well.

AMENDMENT 10 (1791). Powers Reserved to the States and to the People

The federal government has certain powers under the Constitution. All other powers, except those denied to the states, belong to the states or to the people.

AMENDMENT 11 (1795). Lawsuits Against the States

This amendment came about because the states feared a loss of authority if they could be sued in federal courts by foreigners or by citizens of other states. The amendment prevents such lawsuits from taking place in federal courts.

AMENDMENT 12 (1804). Separate Voting for President and Vice-President

In each presidential election before 1800, the two leading candidates received differing numbers of electoral votes. The candidate with the higher number became President. The second-place candidate became Vice-President.

In 1800, as a result of voting along party lines, the Republican candidates for President and Vice-President received an equal number of electoral votes. To prevent similar ties in later elections, this amendment requires separate electoral voting for President and Vice-President. If no one candidate for President has a majority of all the electoral votes for President, the House of Representatives must choose, by ballot, from the three leading candidates. In the balloting, each state may cast only one vote, no matter how many representatives it has. If no one candidate for Vice-President has a majority of all the electoral votes for Vice-President, the Senate must choose between the two leading candidates.

bility of the President. The person having the greatest number of votes as Vice-President shall be the Vice-President, if such number be a majority of the whole number of electors appointed, and if no person have a majority, then from the two highest numbers on the list the Senate shall choose the Vice-President; a quorum for the purpose shall consist of two thirds of the whole number of senators, and a majority of the whole number shall be necessary to a choice. But no person constitutionally ineligible to the office of President shall be eligible to that of Vice-President of the United States.

AMENDMENT 13

Section 1

Neither slavery nor involuntary servitude, except as a punishment for crime whereof the party shall have been duly convicted, shall exist within the United States or any place subject to their jurisdiction.

Section 2

Congress shall have power to enforce this article by appropriate legislation.

AMENDMENT 13 (1865). Abolition of Slavery

Section 1. Abolition

The Emancipation Proclamation, which took effect in 1863, applied only to the area then controlled by the Confederacy. This amendment bans slavery throughout the United States. The amendment also bans forced labor—"involuntary servitude"—except as legal punishment for crimes.

Section 2. Power of Enforcement

Congress has the power to pass laws enforcing this amendment.

AMENDMENT 14

Section 1

All persons born or naturalized in the United States and subject to the jurisdiction thereof are citizens of the United States and of the state wherein they reside. No state shall make or enforce any law which shall abridge the privileges or immunities of citizens of the United States; nor shall any state deprive any person of life, liberty, or property without due process of law; nor deny to any person within its jurisdiction the equal protection of the laws.

Section 2

Representatives shall be apportioned among the several states according to their respective numbers, counting the whole number of persons in each state, [excluding Indians not taxed.] But when the right to vote at any election for the choice of electors for President and Vice-President of the United States, representatives in Congress, the executive and judicial officers of a state, or the members of the legislature thereof is denied to any of the male inhabitants of such state, being twenty-one years of age and citizens of the United States, or in any way abridged, except for participation in rebellion or other crime, the

AMENDMENT 14 (1868). Citizenship and Civil Rights

Section 1. Citizenship

This section defines state citizenship, preventing states from setting up their own definitions of citizenship in order to exclude blacks or other groups. The section also applies the due-process clause of the Fifth Amendment to actions by state governments. By referring to "equal protection of the laws," the section prevents states from passing laws to discriminate unreasonably against any group.

Section 2. Representation and Voting Rights

Before 1865, each slave was counted as three fifths of a free person in determining the number of representatives a state could send to Congress. This section does away with the three-fifths rule and sets up a different rule. If a state denies the right to vote to male citizens age 21 or over—excepting those who have taken part in a rebellion or other crimes—that state will lose a proportional number of representatives in Congress. The rule, meant to force former slave states to allow black males to vote, has never been enforced. Instead, the Fifteenth Amendment, ratified in 1870, has been used in suits concerning voting rights for blacks.

basis of representation therein shall be reduced in the proportion which the number of such male citizens shall bear to the whole number of male citizens twenty-one years of age in such state.

Section 3

No person shall be a senator or representative in Congress, or elector of President and Vice-President, or hold any office, civil or military, under the United States, or under any state, who, having previously taken an oath as a member of Congress or as an officer of the United States or as a member of any state legislature or as an executive or judicial officer of any state to support the Constitution of the United States, shall have engaged in insurrection or rebellion against the same, or given aid or comfort to the enemies thereof. But Congress may by a vote of two thirds of each house remove such disability.

Section 4

The validity of the public debt of the United States, authorized by law, including debts incurred for payment of pensions and bounties for services in suppressing insurrection or rebellion, shall not be questioned. But neither the United States nor any state shall assume or pay any debt or obligation incurred in aid of insurrection or rebellion against the United States or any claim for the loss or emancipation of any slave; but all such debts, obligations, and claims shall be held illegal and void.

Section 5

The Congress shall have power to enforce, by appropriate legislation, the provisions of this article.

AMENDMENT 15

Section 1

The right of citizens of the United States to vote shall not be denied or abridged by the United States or by any state on account or race, color, or previous condition of servitude.

Section 2

The Congress shall have power to enforce this article by appropriate legislation.

AMENDMENT 16

The Congress shall have power to lay and collect taxes on incomes, from whatever source derived, without apportionment among the several states, and without regard to any census or enumeration.

Section 3. Disqualification of Former Confederate Leaders

Former state and federal officials who had served as leaders of the Confederacy were disqualified from holding state or federal office again, unless Congress voted otherwise. Congress did not completely remove this disqualification until 1898.

Section 4. Legal and Illegal Debts

The payment of the federal debt cannot be questioned, according to this section, but the payment of the Confederate debt by any state or by the United States is illegal. Former slave owners have no legal claim to payment for their loss of slaves.

Section 5. Power of Enforcement

Congress has the power to pass laws enforcing this amendment.

AMENDMENT 15 (1870). Suffrage for Blacks

Section 1. The Right to Vote

Race, color, or "previous condition of servitude"—status as an exslave—cannot be used by any state or by the United States to deny a person's right to vote. For a long time, states were able to use literacy tests and other devices to prevent many blacks from voting, despite this amendment.

Section 2. Power of Enforcement

Congress has the power to pass laws enforcing this amendment.

AMENDMENT 16 (1913). Income Taxes

Before this amendment, Congress was prevented from levying an income tax unless the amount due, state by state, was in proportion to state populations, under Article I of the Constitution (Section 2, Clause 3, and Section 9, Clause 4).

AMENDMENT 17

Section 1

The Senate of the United States shall be composed of two senators from each state, elected by the people thereof for six years; and each senator shall have one vote. The electors in each state shall have the qualifications requisite for electors of the most numerous branch of the state legislatures.

Section 2

When vacancies happen in the representation of any state in the Senate, the executive authority of such state shall issue writs of election to fill such vacancies, *provided* that the legislature of any state may empower the executive thereof to make temporary appointments until the people fill the vacancies by election as the legislature may direct.

Section 3

This amendment shall not be so construed as to affect the election or term of any senator chosen before it becomes valid as part of the Constitution.

AMENDMENT 18

Section 1

After one year from the ratification of this article the manufacture, sale, or transportation of intoxicating liquors within, the importation thereof into, or the exportation thereof from the United States and all territory subject to the jurisdiction thereof for beverage purposes is hereby prohibited.

Section 2

The Congress and the several states shall have concurrent power to enforce this article by appropriate legislation.

Section 3

This article shall be inoperative unless it shall have been ratified as an amendment to the Constitution by the legislatures of the several states, as provided in the Constitution, within seven years from the date of the submission hereof to the states by the Congress.

AMENDMENT 19

Section 1

The right of citizens of the United States to vote shall not be denied or abridged by the United States or by any state on account of sex.

AMENDMENT 17 (1913). Direct Elections of Senators

Section 1. Regular Elections

Article 1 of the Constitution (Section 3, Clause 1) says that senators are to be elected by state legislatures. This amendment gives the power to elect senators to the voters of each state.

Section 2. Special Elections

Any vacancy in the Senate must be filled through a special election called by the state governor. However, the state legislature may let the governor appoint a person to fill the vacancy temporarily, until the election is held.

Section 3. Time of Effect

This amendment takes effect only when it is ratified as part of the Constitution, and not before.

AMENDMENT 18 (1919). National Prohibition

Section 1. The Ban on Alcoholic Beverages

Manufacturing, selling, and transporting alcoholic beverages are to be illegal in the United States and its territories one year after the ratification of this amendment. Exporting and importing alcoholic beverages are to be illegal at the same time. This amendment was repealed in 1933 by the Twenty-first Amendment

Section 2. Power of Enforcement

Both Congress and the states have the power to pass laws enforcing this amendment.

Section 3. Time Limit for Ratification

This amendment is not to take effect unless it is ratified by state legislatures within seven years.

AMENDMENT 19 (1920). Suffrage for Women

Section 1. The Right to Vote

Women and men have an equal right to vote in the elections of the United States and of all the states.

Section 2

Congress shall have power to enforce this article by appropriate legislation.

AMENDMENT 20

Section 1

The terms of the President and Vice-President shall end at noon on the 20th day of January, and the terms of senators and representatives at noon on the 3rd day of January, of the years in which such terms would have ended if this article had not been ratified; and the terms of their successors shall then begin.

Section 2

The Congress shall assemble at least once in every year, and such meeting shall begin at noon on the 3rd day of January, unless they shall by law appoint a different day.

Section 3

If, at the time fixed for the beginning of the term of the President, the President-elect shall have died, the Vice-President-elect shall become President. If a President shall not have been chosen before the time fixed for the beginning of his term, or if the President-elect shall have failed to qualify, then the Vice-President-elect shall act as President until a President shall have qualified; and the Congress may by law provide for the case wherein neither a President-elect nor a Vice-President-elect shall have qualified, declaring who shall then act as President, or the manner in which one who is to act shall be selected, and such person shall act accordingly until a President or Vice-President shall have qualified.

Section 4

The Congress may by law provide for the case of the death of any of the persons from whom the House of Representatives may choose a President whenever the right of choice shall have devolved upon them, and for the case of the death of any of the persons from whom the Senate may choose a Vice-President whenever the right of choice shall have devolved upon them.

Section 5

Sections 1 and 2 shall take effect on the 15th day of October following the ratification of this article.

Section 2. Power of Enforcement

Congress has the power to pass laws enforcing this amendment.

AMENDMENT 20 (1933). Terms of the President, Vice-President, and Congress

Section 1. Ending Dates of Terms

The terms of the President and Vice-President will end on January 20 in their final year. The terms of senators and representatives will end on January 3. Before this amendment, the terms of the President, Vice-President, and Congress ended on March 3. Defeated officeholders had to serve until March as "lame ducks," with scant political power. This amendment, known as the "lame duck amendment," greatly reduces the time during which defeated officeholders remain in office.

Section 2. Meetings of Congress

Congress must meet at least once a year, beginning on January 3 unless Congress chooses a different day.

Section 3. Death or Lack of Qualification of a President-elect

If a President-elect dies before taking office, the Vice-President-elect will become President. If there is a deadlocked election and no President-elect has been qualified to take office, the Vice-President-elect will become President temporarily. If neither a President-elect nor a Vice-President-elect has been qualified to take office by the start of the presidential term, Congress will decide on a temporary President.

Section 4. Death of a Likely President-elect or a Likely Vice-President-elect

If no one candidate for President receives a majority of electoral votes, then, under the Twelfth Amendment, the House of Representatives must choose a President from among the three leading candidates. If one of those three dies before the House makes its choice, Congress can decide how to proceed, under this section of the Twentieth Amendment.

Similarly, Congress can decide how to proceed in case a Vice-Presidential election goes to the Senate and one of the two leading candidates dies before the Senate makes its choice between them.

Section 5. Time of Effect

The first two sections of this amendment take effect on October 15 after the amendment is ratified.

Section 6

This article shall be inoperative unless it shall have been ratified as an amendment to the Constitution by the legislatures of three fourths of the several states within seven years from the date of its submission.

AMENDMENT 21

Section 1

The eighteenth article of amendment to the Constitution of the United States is hereby repealed.

Section 2

The transportation or importation into any state, territory, or possession of the United States for delivery or use therein of intoxicating liquors, in violation of the laws thereof, is hereby prohibited.

Section 3

This article shall be inoperative unless it shall have been ratified as an amendment to the Constitution by conventions in the several states, as provided in the Constitution, within seven years from the date of the submission hereof to the states by the Congress.

AMENDMENT 22

Section 1

No person shall be elected to the office of the President more than twice, and no person who has held the office of President or acted as President for more than two years of a term to which some other person was elected President shall be elected to the office of the President more than once. But this article shall not apply to any person holding the office of President when this article was proposed by the Congress, and shall not prevent any person who may be holding the office of President or acting as President during the term within which this article becomes operative from holding the office of President or acting as President during the remainder of such term.

Section 2

This article shall be inoperative unless it shall have been ratified as an amendment to the Constitution by the legislatures of three fourths of the several states within seven years from the day of its submission to the states by the Congress.

AMENDMENT 23

Section 1

The district constituting the seat of government of the United States shall appoint in such manner as the

Section 6. Time Limit for Ratification

This amendment is not to take effect unless it is ratified by state legislatures within seven years.

AMENDMENT 21 (1933). Repeal of Prohibition

Section 1. Repeal

National prohibition is no longer required by law.

Section 2. Carrying Alcohol into "Dry" States

If a state is "dry"—if it prohibits alcoholic beverages—then carrying alcholic beverages into that state is a federal crime.

Section 3. Method and Time Limit for Ratification

This amendment must be ratified by special state conventions. The amendment is not to take effect unless it is ratified by the conventions within seven years.

AMENDMENT 22 (1951). The Ban on Third Terms for Presidents

Section 1. Number of Election Victories

No person can be elected President more than twice. If a Vice-President or someone else succeeds to the presidency and serves for more than two years, that person cannot then be elected President more than once. This ban does not apply to the person who is President at the time of proposal of this amendment.

Harry S. Truman was President in 1947, when this amendment was proposed.

Section 2. Time Limit for Ratification

This amendment is not to take effect unless it is ratified by state legislatures within seven years.

AMENDMENT 23 (1961). Electoral Votes for the District of Columbia

Section 1. The Number of Electors

The District of Columbia can have the same number of electors it would be entitled to if it were a state. However,

Congress may direct: A number of electors of President and Vice-President equal to the whole number of senators and representatives in Congress to which the district would be entitled if it were a state, but in no event more than the least populous state; they shall be in addition to those appointed by the states, but they shall be considered, for the purposes of the election of President and Vice-President, to be electors appointed by a state; and they shall meet in the district and perform such duties as provided by the twelfth article of amendment.

Section 2

The Congress shall have power to enforce this article by appropriate legislation.

that number cannot be greater than the number of electors from the state with the smallest population. The effect of this amendment is to let residents of Washington, D.C., vote in presidential elections.

Section 2. Power of Enforcement

Congress has the power to pass laws enforcing this amendment.

AMENDMENT 24

Section 1

The right of citizens of the United States to vote in any primary or other election for President or Vice-President, for electors for President or Vice-President, or for senator or representative in Congress, shall not be denied or abridged by the United States or any state by reason of failure to pay any poll tax or other tax.

Section 2

The Congress shall have power to enforce this article by appropriate legislation.

AMENDMENT 24 (1964). Abolition of Poll Taxes

Section 1. Abolition

Neither the United States nor any state can require a citizen to pay a poll tax in order to vote in a presidential or congressional election. The effect of this amendment is to prevent states from using poll taxes—taxes per head, or individual—to keep poor blacks from voting.

Section 2. Power of Enforcement

Congress has the power to pass laws enforcing this amendment.

AMENDMENT 25

Section 1

In case of the removal of the President from office or of his death or resignation, the Vice-President shall become President.

Section 2

Whenever there is a vacancy in the office of the Vice-President, the President shall nominate a Vice-President who shall take office upon confirmation by a majority vote of both houses of Congress.

Section 3

Whenever the President transmits to the president pro tempore of the Senate and the speaker of the House of Representatives his written declaration that he is unable to discharge the powers and duties of his office, and until he transmits to them a written declaration to the contrary, such powers and duties shall be discharged by the Vice-President as Acting President.

AMENDMENT 25 (1967). Presidential Disability and Succession

Section 1. Replacement of the President

If the President is removed from office or dies or resigns, the Vice-President becomes President.

Section 2. Replacement of the Vice-President

When the vice-presidency becomes vacant, the President will choose a Vice-President. The choice must be confirmed by both houses of Congress.

Section 3. Temporary Replacement of the President with the President's Consent

If the President sends Congress notice in writing that he or she is disabled from performing official duties, the Vice-President becomes Acting President. The President resumes office when he or she sends Congress written notice of renewed ability to serve.

Section 4

Whenever the Vice-President and a majority of either the principal officers of the executive departments or of such other body as Congress may by law provide, transmit to the president pro tempore of the Senate and the speaker of the House of Representatives their written declaration that the President is unable to discharge the powers and duties of his office, the Vice-President shall immediately assume the powers and duties of the office as Acting President.

Thereafter, when the President transmits to the president pro tempore of the Senate and the speaker of the House of Representatives his written declaration that no inability exists, he shall resume the powers and duties of his office unless the Vice-President and a majority of either the principal officers of the executive department or of such other body as Congress may by law provide, transmit within four days to the president pro tempore of the Senate and the speaker of the House of Representatives their written declaration that the President is unable to discharge the powers and duties of his office. Thereupon Congress shall decide the issue, assembling within forty-eight hours for that purpose if not in session. If the Congress, within twenty-one days after receipt of the latter written declaration, or, if Congress is not in session, within twenty-one days after Congress is required to assemble, determines by two-thirds vote of both houses that the President is unable to discharge the powers and duties of his office, the Vice-President shall continue to discharge the same as Acting President; otherwise, the President shall resume the powers and duties of his office.

AMENDMENT 26

Section 1

The right of citizens of the United States, who are eighteen years of age or older, to vote shall not be denied or abridged by the United States or by any state on account of age.

Section 2

The Congress shall have power to enforce this article by appropriate legislation.

Section 4. Temporary Replacement of the President Without the President's Consent

If a President is disabled and cannot or will not send written notice to Congress, the Vice-President and a majority of the cabinet or of some other group named by Congress can send such notice. The Vice-President will then become Acting President. The Vice-President will step down when the President sends Congress written notice of renewed ability to serve, unless the Vice-President and others send contrary written notice to Congress in the next four days. Congress then must meet within 48 hours to decide whether the President is still disabled. To reach that decision, two thirds or more of both houses must vote within 21 days that the President is disabled. If they do, the Vice-President remains in office as Acting President. If they do not, the President resumes official duties.

AMENDMENT 26 (1971). Suffrage at Age Eighteen

Section 1. The Right to Vote

Neither the United States nor any state can deny the vote to citizens of age 18 or older because of their age. The effect of this amendment is to lower the voting age from 21, the former minimum in federal and most state elections, to 18.

Section 2. Power of Enforcement

Congress has the power to pass laws enforcing this amendment.

SUGGESTED READINGS

GENERAL BOOKS

Alexander, Rae Pace, and Julius Lester, compilers. *Young and Black in America.* New York: Random House, 1970. Illustrated. 139 pages.

Eight black people, including Frederick Douglass, Richard Wright, and Daisy Bates, tell of early experiences that influenced their entire lives.

Blumenthal, Shirley, and Jerome S. Ozer. *Coming to America: Immigrants from the British Isles.* New York: Delacorte, 1980. Illustrated. 192 pages.

The authors quote extensively from documents that serve to explain why British, Irish, Scottish, and Welsh people became immigrants.

Daniels, George G., editor. *The Spanish West.* Chicago: Time, Inc. 1976. Illustrated. 240 pages.

The volume's pictures and text follow Spanish explorers through what is now Arizona, New Mexico, California, and Texas, and then focus on the lives of Spanish settlers.

DeWitt, Dorothy, editor. *The Talking Sone: An Anthology of Native American Tales and Legends.* New York: Greenwillow, 1979. 213 pages.

These tales and legends are organized geographically, by their places of origin.

Dickinson, Alice. *Taken by the Indians: True Tales of Captivity.* New York: Watts, 1976. Illustrated. 138 pages.

Dickinson combines her own text with accounts by six Indian captives, whose stories span the years from 1676 to 1864.

Fincher, Ernest B. *The Presidency: An American Invention.* New York: Abelard-Schuman, 1977. Illustrated. 210 pages.

Fincher illustrates the powers and limitations of the presidents through specific problems they have faced.

Freidel, Frank. *Our Country's Presidents.* Washington, D.C.: National Geographic, 1977. Illustrated. 278 pages.

Freidel emphasizes the achievements rather than the failures of the nation's leaders. His biographies include brief summaries of the state of the nation during each president's term in offce.

Heuman, William. *Famous American Indians.* New York: Dodd, Mead, 1972. Illustrated. 128 pages.

Biographical sketches center on battles and other exploits of nine Indians: King Philip, Pontiac, Joseph Brant, Osceola, Tecumseh, Sequoyah, Chief Joseph, Crazy Horse, and Sitting Bull.

Hoexter, Corinne K. *From Canton to California: The Epic of Chinese Immigration.* New York: Four Winds, 1976. Illustrated. 304 pages.

Hoexter focuses on individuals who have championed Chinese culture in the United States.

Jordan, Teresa. *Cowgirls: Women of the American West.* Garden City, NY: Doubleday, 1982. Illustrated. 352 pages.

Jordan tells the stories of women who worked the land—raising crops and livestock and riding in rodeos—in the nineteenth and early twentieth centuries.

Lavine, Sigmund A. *Famous Merchants.* New York: Dodd, Mead, 1965. Illustrated. 154 pages.

As Lavine shows, commercial success brought fame to James Cash Penney, John Wanamaker, Frank Woolworth, and a good many others.

Meltzer, Milton, editor. *In Their Own Words: A History of the American Negro.* Three volumes: 1619–1865; 1865–1916; 1916–1966. New York: Crowell, 1964, 1965, 1967. Illustrated. About 200 pages per volume.

This is a fascinating collection of letters, pamphlets, and editorials, all written by blacks, as well as interviews with former slaves and other individuals who gave spoken testimony about black history.

Morison, Samuel Eliot. *Sailor Historian: The Best of Samuel Eliot Morison.* Emily Morison Beck, editor. Boston: Houghton Mifflin, 1977. 431 pages.

Morison's daughter has made the selections, which include portraits of George Washington, Benjamin Franklin, and other American leaders, as well as descriptions of ships and naval battles.

Morison, Samuel Eliot, Henry Steele Commager, and William E. Leuchtenburg. *A Concise History of the American Republic* (an abbreviated edition of *The Growth of the American Republic*). New York: Oxford University Press, 1977. 116 pages.

This book appears in two volumes, one covering the years to 1877, the other covering the years from 1865 to 1976, and both written with a light and humorous touch "for young people of all ages."

Perrin, Linda. *Coming to America: Immigrants from the Far East.* New York: Delacorte, 1980. Illustrated. 192 pages.

Perrin describes Chinese, Japanese, Philippine, and Vietnamese immigrants. She explains the conditions that led them to leave the Far East, the difficulties they found in America, and the ways in which they have adjusted to American life.

Plowden, David, and Richard Snow. *The Iron Road: A Portrait of American Railroading.* New York: Four Winds, 1978. Illustrated. 90 pages.

The photographs by Plowden are matched by Snow's story of the development of railroads and the accompanying development of America.

Sterling, Dorothy. *Black Foremothers: Three Lives.* Old Westbury, New York: The Feminist Press/McGraw-Hill, 1979. Illustrated. 167 pages.

The three are Ellen Craft, Ida B. Wells, and Mary Church Terrell. Craft and her husband made a daring escape from slavery in 1848. Wells and Terrell, born during the Civil War, campaigned for black rights in the years of Jim Crow laws.

Tunis, Edwin. *Frontier Living.* Cleveland/New York: World, 1961. Illustrated. 166 pages.

The period covered is 1725 to 1889–the year when thousands of Sooners rushed into the Oklahoma District. The drawings by Tunis are clear and informative.

Wakin, Edward. *Enter the Irish-Americans.* New York: Crowell, 1976. 189 pages.

Wakin covers the story of Irish immigration from the potato famine to the poetry, politics, and patriotism of Irish Americans.

Wilcox, Desmond. *Ten Who Dared.* Boston: Little, Brown, 1977. Illustrated. 329 pages.

The ten are adventurers and voyagers from Columbus to the first astronauts.

UNIT 1

Alderman, Clifford Lindsey. *Colonists for Sale: The Story of Indentured Servants in America.* New York: Macmillan, 1975. 184 pages.

The lives of most indentured servants were terribly harsh, as Alderman shows in grim case histories.

Bolton, Herbert Eugene, editor. *Spanish Explorations of the Southwest: 1542–1706.* New York: Barnes & Noble, 1963. 486 pages.

Bolton provides diaries, letters, and narratives of explorers, priests, and soldiers who traveled into the Southwest, usually to find gold or to convert Indians.

Caffrey, Kate. *The Mayflower.* New York: Stein & Day, 1975. Illustrated. 329 pages.

Caffrey offers a detailed account of the Pilgrims, including the disputes and negotiations leading to their voyage to the new world.

Chidsey, Donald Barr. *The French and Indian War.* New York: Crown, 1969. Illustrated. 176 pages.

Chidsey describes the war as part of the worldwide struggle between Britain and France.

Galt, Tom. *Peter Zenger: Fighter for Freedom.* New York: Crowell, 1951. Illustrated. 239 pages.

Galt uses Zenger's private letters along with public documents to tell the compelling story of the newspaper editor whose trial became a legal landmark.

Gill, Crispin. *Mayflower Remembered.* New York: Putnam, 1972. Illustrated. 206 pages.

Gill recounts the story of the Pilgrims' expedition. An Englishman, he notes that many English people feel pride in the Pilgrims' accomplishments.

Holbrook, Sabra. *French Founders of North America and Their Heritage.* New York: Atheneum, 1976. 256 pages.

Beginning with Jacques Cartier's first voyage to North America, Holbrook traces the history of French explorers and settlers in the New World.

Jensen, Malcolm C. *Francisco Coronado: A Visual Biography.* New York: Watts, 1974. Illustrated. 58 pages.

Large-scale maps show Coronado's routes north of Mexico, and photographs present Hopi and Zuñi pueblos, sites where Coronado hoped to find gold.

La Fay, Howard. *The Vikings.* Washington, D.C.: National Geographic, 1972. Illustrated. 207 pages.

Here is a detailed account of Viking explorers, explorations, and settlements. The photographs are exceptionally clear and dramatic, and the drawings are full of Viking vigor.

Snell, Tee Loftin. *The Wild Shores: America's Beginnings.* Washington, D.C.: National Geographic, 1974. Illustrated. 203 pages.

Before writing this book, Snell toured the places from which explorers sailed to America as well as the places where they landed.

Tunis, Edwin. *The Tavern at the Ferry.* New York: Crowell, 1973. Illustrated. 109 pages.

Tunis uses "reasonable speculation" and "tradition" to recreate events from 1687 to the time of the Revolutionary War.

Williams, Selma R. *Demeter's Daughters: The Women Who Founded America, 1587–1787.* New York: Atheneum, 1976. Illustrated. 359 pages.

When men were called away for extended times, women took full charge of homes and farms. The author stresses the many contributions of women during the time of the Revolution.

UNIT 2

Adler, Mortimer J., and William Gorman. *The American Testament.* New York: Praeger, 1975. 160 pages.

The authors analyze three key documents in American history: the Declaration of Independence, the Constitution, and the Gettysburg Address.

Akers, Charles W. *Abigail Adams, an American Woman.* Boston: Little, Brown, 1980. 207 pages.

    This biography presents America and the world through Abigail Adams's sharp and discerning eyes.

Borden, Morton. *George Washington.* Englewood Cliffs, NJ: Prentice-Hall, 1969. 154 pages.

    Borden reproduces letters by George Washington from 1753 to 1797, writings about Washington from 1754 to 1814, and later opinions of historians about Washington's character and life.

Bowen, Catherine Drinker. *The Most Dangerous Man in America: Scenes from the Life of Benjamin Franklin.* Boston: Little, Brown, 1974. 274 pages.

    This biography consists of scenes from Franklin's life that interested and amused Bowen.

Chidsey, Donald Barr. *The Loyalists: The Story of Those Americans Who Fought Against Independence.* New York: Crown, 1973. Illustrated. 213 pages.

    Chidsey's style is conversational as he tells the story of those colonists who did not want a revolution and who backed the British.

DePauw, Linda Grant. *Founding Mothers: Women in America in the Revolutionary Era.* Boston: Houghton Mifflin, 1975. Illustrated. 228 pages.

    DePauw quotes from original sources as she covers the roles of women from every stratum of society during the Revolutionary period.

Donovan, Frank. *The John Adams Papers.* New York: Dodd, Mead, 1965. Illustrated. 335 pages.

    The book follows Adams from his days as a student at Harvard to his days in Congress and then to his life as a diplomat and national leader.

Lawson, Don. *The American Revolution.* New York: Abelard-Schuman, 1974. Illustrated. 176 pages.

    This readable account of the Revolutionary War provides unusual details and sketches of personalities.

Munves, James. *Thomas Jefferson and the Declaration of Independence.* New York: Scribner's, 1978. Illustrated. 135 pages.

    In a detailed narrative, Munves treats the seventeen days in 1776 when Patriot leaders worked out the text of the Declaration.

Starkey, Marion. *Lace Cuffs and Leather Aprons: Popular Struggles in the Federalist Era, 1783–1800.* New York: Knopf, 1972. Illustrated. 291 pages.

    Starkey, a specialist on the years of the Federalists, explores the strife and uncertainty of the time.

Walsh, John E. *Night on Fire: The First Complete Account of John Paul Jones' Greatest Battle.* New York: McGraw-Hill, 1978. Illustrated. 185 pages.

    Walsh consulted eyewitness accounts from various sources to piece together the course of fighting between the American ship *Bonhomme Richard* and the English frigate *Serapis* in September 1779. He also judges the skills of the two captains, the American John Paul Jones and his English counterpart.

UNIT 3

Boardman, Fon W. Jr. *America and the Jacksonian Era: 1825–1850.* New York: Walck, 1975. 212 pages.

    Boardman sketches Jackson's political struggles against a wide background of American society and culture.

Chidsey, Donald Barr. *Mr. Hamilton and Mr. Jefferson.* Nashville: Nelson, 1975. 207 pages.

    Chidsey looks at conflicts of personality and principle in the long dealings between Hamilton and Jefferson.

Dangerfield, George. *Defiance to the Old World: The Story Behind the Monroe Doctrine.* New York: Putnam, 1970. 128 pages.

    In explaining the significance of the Monroe Doctrine, Dangerfield shows American leaders in a world of shifting alliances and ambitions.

Lawson, Don. *The United States in the Mexican War.* New York: Abelard-Schuman, 1976. Illustrated. 145 pages.

    Lawson describes pressures that led to war with Mexico, President James M. Polk's role in the conflict, and major battles in the war, from the Alamo to the surrender of Mexico City.

Lloyd, Alan. *The Scorching of Washington: The War of 1812.* Washington, D.C.: Robert B. Luce, 1975. Illustrated. 216 pages.

    Besides giving a narrative history of the war, Lloyd offers short biographies of notable figures of the time and a chronology of major events.

Meltzer, Milton. *Bound for the Rio Grande: The Mexican Struggle, 1845–1850.* New York: Knopf, 1974. Illustrated. 279 pages.

    In explaining the Mexican War, Meltzer describes westward migration, the idea of Manifest Destiny, and the related issue of slavery in the territories.

Meltzer, Milton. *Hunted Like a Wolf: The Story of the Seminole War.* New York: Farrar, Straus & Giroux, 1972. Illustrated. 216 pages.

    The title gives Meltzer's viewpoint. He describes the Seminole being hunted like animals, particularly when pursued by forces under Andrew Jackson.

Miller, Douglas T. *Then Was the Future: The North in the Age of Jackson, 1815–1850.* New York: Knopf, 1973. Illustrated. 270 pages.

    Miller traces the growth of industry in the North and changes in the region's culture and politics.

National Geographic Society. *Trails West*. Washington, D.C.: National Geographic, 1979. Illustrated. 207 pages.

   To prepare this book, present-day writers and photographers traveled like pioneers along the traces of the Santa Fe, Oregon, California, Gila River, Mormon, and Bozeman trails.

Perkins, Bradford, editor. *The Causes of the War of 1812: National Honor or National Interest?* New York: Holt, Rinehart, and Winston, 1962. 120 pages.

   In this collection of essays, various authors argue about the causes of the War of 1812.

Tunis, Edwin. *The Young United States: 1783–1830*. New York: World, 1970. Illustrated. 159 pages.

   The author's goal is to show everyday life in the nation through drawings and through accounts, partly fictional, of ordinary folk.

UNIT 4

Bacon, Margaret Hope. *I Speak for my Slave Sister: The Life of Abby Kelley Foster*. New York: Crowell, 1974. Illustrated. 236 pages.

   Reared as a Quaker in Massachusetts, Abby Kelley became an abolitionist who lectured against slavery during the 1840s and 1850s.

Franklin, John Hope. *Reconstruction: After the Civil War*. Chicago: University of Chicago Press, 1961. 258 pages.

   Franklin takes care to refute some exaggerated claims about the causes and results of Reconstruction, and he shows how former Confederates were able to restore much of the planter culture in the years after the war.

Heidish, Marcy. *A Woman Called Moses*. Boston: Houghton Mifflin, 1976. 308 pages.

   This fictionalized account of Harriet Tubman, written from her own point of view, tells of her escape from slavery and her dangerous journeys to help others escape.

Horan, James D. *Confederate Agent*. New York: Crown, 1954. 326 pages.

   Civil War documents support this account of Captain Thomas H. Hines, who, acting as a secret Confederate agent, attempted to cause a revolution in the northwestern United States.

Jordan, Robert Paul. *The Civil War*. Washington, D.C.: National Geographic Special Publications, 1969. Illustrated. 215 pages.

   Jordan, who visited Civil War battlefields and memorials and who talked to the descendants of soldiers, brings together the past and the present in this history. He documents the course of fighting and the enduring effects of the war.

Khan, Lurey. *One Day, Levin . . . He Be Free: William Still and the Underground Railroad*. New York: Dutton, 1972. Illustrated. 229 pages.

   The author is the great-granddaughter of James Still, brother of William Still. Using records left by William Still, she writes about his life as the "father of the Underground Railroad."

Lewis, Oscar. *The War in the Far West: 1861–1865*. New York: Doubleday, 1961. 263 pages.

   Lewis emphasizes the importance of the West in the conflict between the Union and the Confederacy.

Mitgang, Herbert. *Fiery Trial: A Life of Lincoln*. New York: Viking, 1974. Illustrated. 207 pages.

   The book deals in part with Lincoln's life and career and in part with his beliefs about slavery.

Simmons, Dawn Langley. *A Rose for Mrs. Lincoln*. Boston: Beacon Press, 1970. Illustrated. 197 pages.

   In this biography, Mary Todd Lincoln emerges as a complex and intelligent woman, less bitter and more gracious than she is usually said to be.

Sterling, Dorothy, editor. *The Trouble They Seen: Black People Tell the Story of Reconstruction*. Garden City, NY: Doubleday, 1976. Illustrated. 491 pages.

   Through letters and other documents, this book records the hopes and troubles of blacks from 1865 to 1877.

Thomas, Emory M. *The Confederate Nation, 1861–1865*. New York: Harper & Row, 1979. Illustrated. 400 pages.

   Thomas describes southerners as they worked to set up a nation, form a constitution, engage in foreign relations, and fight against Union forces.

Trelease, Allen W. *Reconstruction: The Great Experiment*. New York: Harper & Row, 1971. Illustrated. 224 pages.

   This book examines both political and social changes after the Civil War.

UNIT 5

Dobie, J. Frank. *Up the Trail from Texas*. New York: Random House, 1955. Illustrated. 182 pages.

   Besides relating tales of cattle drives, based on stories he heard when he was young, Dobie gives the historical background of cowboys and the cattle business in the 1800s.

Fisher, Leonard Everett. *The Railroads*. New York: Holiday House, 1979. Illustrated. 62 pages.

   Fisher tells how Abraham Lincoln, George Armstrong Custer, Buffalo Bill Cody, and many other historical figures were involved with the westward extension of the rails.

Glad, Paul W. *McKinley, Bryan and the People*. Philadelphia: Lippincott, 1964. 222 pages.

    Glad describes the personalities and philosophies of William Jennings Bryan and William McKinley in relation to the election of 1896.

Katz, William Loren, and Jacqueline Hunt Katz. *Making Our Way: America at the Turn of the Century in the Words of the Poor and Powerless*. New York: Dial, 1975. Illustrated. 170 pages.

    A police officer, a farmer, a coal miner, and a hobo are among those whose stories reveal everyday life around 1900.

Latham, Frank B. *The Transcontinental Railroad 1862–69*. New York: Watts, 1973. Illustrated. 90 pages.

    In the 1860s the Union Pacific and the Central Pacific railroad companies overcame great difficulties to complete a transcontinental rail line, as Latham makes clear.

Seidman, Laurence Ivan. *Once in the Saddle: The Cowboy's Frontier, 1866–1896*. New York: Knopf, 1973. Illustrated. 188 pages.

    Seidman presents the heyday of cowboy life, a period of about thirty years.

Weymouth, Lally. *America in 1876*. New York: Vintage, 1976. Illustrated. 320 pages.

    This book begins with the Centennial Exhibition in Philadelphia and then surveys the nation in the centennial year.

UNIT 6

Boardman, Fon W., Jr. *America and the Progressive Era: 1900–1917*. New York: Walck, 1970. 169 pages.

    Boardman's history covers the Spanish-American War, the growth of American sea power, muckrakers, progressives, Theodore Roosevelt, big business, art, and other subjects.

Crane, Stephen. *The War Dispatches of Stephen Crane*. R.W. Stallman and E.R. Hagemann, editors. New York: New York University Press, 1964. Illustrated. 343 pages.

    Stephen Crane covered wars in Europe as well as the Spanish-American War, and his reports describe warfare around the turn of the century.

Hershey, Burnet. *The Odyssey of Henry Ford and the Great Peace Ship*. New York: Taplinger, 1967. Illustrated. 212 pages.

    Before the United States entered World War I, Henry Ford chartered a "Peace Ship" to go to Europe so that he and his associates might convince European nations to stop the fighting and the awful casualties of trench warfare. Hershey, the youngest reporter on board, recalls the Odyssey.

Johnson, Hannah Lyons. *Picture the Past: 1900–1915*. New York: Lothrop, Lee & Shepard, 1975. Illustrated. 96 pages.

    This charming book shows America at the time when the horse and buggy was being replaced by the horseless carriage.

Jones, Virgil Carrington. *Roosevelt's Rough Riders*. Garden City, NY: Doubleday, 1971. Illustrated. 354 pages.

    Jones praises the fighting spirit of the Rough Riders, and he describes the mud and other miseries they confronted in Cuba during the Spanish-American War.

Meigs, Cornelia. *Jane Addams: Pioneer for Social Justice*. Boston: Little, Brown, 1970. Illustrated. 274 pages.

    This sympathetic portrait shows Addams at Hull House in Chicago and in other scenes of social work.

Mother, Ira. *Man of Action: The Life of Teddy Roosevelt*. New York: Platt & Munk, 1966. Illustrated. 93 pages.

    The author quickly reviews Roosevelt as a body builder, student, hunter, soldier, reformer, and politician.

Steinberg, Alfred. *Woodrow Wilson*. New York: Putnam, 1961. 194 pages.

    This study analyzes Wilson's words and personality as well as his political accomplishments.

Tuchman, Barbara W. *The Zimmerman Telegram*. New York: Viking, 1958. 244 pages.

    Like a spy thriller, this history is full of suspense about the secret dealings that hastened America's entry into World War I.

UNIT 7

Allen, Frederick Lewis. *Only Yesterday: An Informal History of the Nineteen-Twenties*. New York: Harper, 1931. Illustrated. 370 pages.

    Allen gives a jaunty review of the manners, personalities, and events of the 1920s.

Alsop, Joseph. *FDR: A Centenary Remembrance*. New York: Viking, 1982. Illustrated. 255 pages.

    Alsop was related to Franklin D. Roosevelt and sometimes visited the President's home in Hyde Park, New York, giving this memoir a personal touch.

Baritz, Loren. *The Culture of the Twenties: 1920–1929*. New York: Bobbs-Merrill, 1970. Illustrated. 436 pages.

    In this anthology, famous individuals analyze war, politics, business, religion, and other topics.

Boardman, Fon W. *America and the Jazz Age: A History of the Twenties*. New York: Walck, 1968. 136 pages.

    Boardman makes it clear that Americans of the time applauded business leaders and celebrities as well as presidents.

Boardman, Fon W. *The Thirties: America and the Great Depression.* New York: Walck, 1967. 157 pages.

In this study Boardman describes the course of the Great Depression, the initiatives of the New Deal, and the political and economic issues involved.

Faulkner, Harold U. *From Versailles to the New Deal: A Chronicle of the Harding-Coolidge-Hoover Era.* New York: United States Publishers, 1950. 388 pages.

Faulkner's careful history illuminates the economics as well as the politics of the time. For example, Faulkner estimates that only about 20 percent of the American people benefited from the boom times of the 1920s.

Latham, Frank B. *FDR and the Supreme Court Fight, 1937.* New York: Watts, 1972. Illustrated. 84 pages.

When Roosevelt announced his plans to reorganize federal courts, he touched off a furious debate. Latham examines FDR's motives and how the long political struggle proceeded.

Lawson, Don. *FDR's New Deal.* New York: Crowell, 1979. Illustrated. 152 pages.

Lawson appraises Hoover as well as Roosevelt, noting Hoover's virtues while showing that the times favored Roosevelt's boldness.

Steinberg, Alfred. *Herbert Hoover.* New York: Putnam, 1967. 255 pages.

John Garner said of Hoover that "if he had become president in 1921 or 1937, he might have ranked with the great presidents." Steinberg's sympathetic treatment of Hoover supports this view.

Tanner, Louise. *All the Things We Were: A Scrapbook of the People, Politics and Popular Culture in the Tragicomic Years Between the Crash and Pearl Harbor.* Garden City, NY: Doubleday, 1968. Illustrated. 356 pages.

This volume gives a panoramic view of the ways in which Americans coped during the 1930s.

UNIT 8

Eisenhower, Dwight D. *Crusade in Europe.* New York: Doubleday, 1948. 559 pages.

Before Eisenhower stepped onto the political stage, he wrote this account of the military operations he directed during World War II. The book offers a view of the development and application of allied strategy against the Axis powers.

Foreign Policy Association. *A Cartoon History of United States Foreign Policy.* New York: Random House, 1967. 252 pages.

The cartoons document foreign policy from the time when the United States rejected the League of Nations to the mid-1960s.

Nevins, Allan. *The New Deal and World Affairs: A Chronicle of International Affairs, 1933–1945.* New York: United States Publishers, 1950. 332 pages.

This book offers a detailed account of the steps that led America to enter World War II, a broad outline of Allied strategy during the war, and a review of the beginnings of the United Nations.

Severn, Bill. *Toward One World: The Life of Wendell Willkie.* New York: Ives Washburn, 1967. 230 pages.

Willkie lost his bid to become president in 1940, but as Severn shows, Willkie supported the main goals of Roosevelt's foreign alliances and he convinced many Americans to turn away from isolationism.

Stokesbury, James L. *A Short History of World War II.* New York: Morrow, 1980. Illustrated. 455 pages.

Stokesbury conveys the magnitude and horror of the drama that began enveloping the world in the 1930s. He gives a vivid account of the intermingling of politics and warfare.

UNIT 9

Archer, Jules. *1968: Year of Crisis.* New York: Messner, 1971. Illustrated. 190 pages.

Archer recalls the sense of crises that gripped the nation in 1968, the year of the assassination of Martin Luther King, riots by urban blacks, a surge of violence by student radicals, and continued fighting in Vietnam.

Coles, Robert. *Uprooted Children: The Early Life of Migrant Workers.* Pittsburgh: University of Pittsburgh Press, 1970. 142 pages.

Coles offers long quotations from migrant children and their parents to reveal the daily events and dilemmas of their lives.

Curtis, Richard. *Ralph Nader's Crusade.* Philadelphia: Macrae Smith, 1972. 136 pages.

This book traces Nader's career since 1965, when he published his investigation of automobiles, *Unsafe at Any Speed.*

Feuerlicht, Roberta Strauss. *Joe McCarthy and McCarthyism: The Hate That Haunts America.* New York: McGraw-Hill, 1972. Illustrated. 160 pages.

Feuerlicht compares McCarthyism to communism in that both scorn freedom of speech for dissenters. She describes the climate of fear in which McCarthyism grew and the tactics that McCarthy used.

Larson, Arthur. *Eisenhower: The President Nobody Knew.* New York: Scribner's, 1968. 210 pages.

Larson argues that Eisenhower deserves far more credit than he has received for his performances as president, especially in the area of foreign policy.

Lynch, Dudley. *Lyndon Baines Johnson: The President from Texas.* New York: Crowell, 1975. Illustrated. 169 pages.

This biography, which offers a balanced view of a controversial president, is particularly vivid in describing the death of President Kennedy and the swearing in of Johnson.

Manchester, William. *Portrait of a President: John F. Kennedy in Profile.* Boston: Little, Brown, 1967. 266 pages.

Manchester interweaves descriptions of Kennedy's presidency with information about his education and his early days in politics.

Robbins, Jhan. *Bess and Harry: An American Love Story.* New York: Putnam's Sons, 1980. Illustrated. 194 pages.

In this portrait of the Trumans, Bess appears as a vital force in shaping her husband's determination to succeed in politics.

Severn, Bill. *Adlai Stevenson: Citizen of the World.* New York: McKay, 1966. Illustrated. 183 pages.

This book presents Stevenson's family background, his career, and his impact on the politics of his time.

Wolfson, Victor. *The Man Who Cared: A Life of Harry S. Truman.* New York: Farrar, Straus & Giroux, 1966. 146 pages.

Plain speech and a direct, no-nonsense approach characterized Truman, and Wolfson uses the same sort of approach in this biography.

UNIT 10

Anderson, Clay, Ronald M. Fisher, Stratford C. Jones, Bill Peterson, and Cynthia Russ Ramsay. *Rural Life in America.* Washington, D.C.: National Geographic Society, 1974. Illustrated. 207 pages.

This book, which emphasizes the beauty and order of rural life, includes memoirs by the authors and interviews with country people.

Drew, Elizabeth. *American Journal: The Events of 1976.* New York: Random House, 1977. 651 pages.

Drew, Elizabeth. *Portrait of an Election: The 1980 Presidential Campaign.* New York: Simon & Schuster, 1981. 495 pages.

In *American Journal* and in *Portrait of an Election* Drew follows the candidates through each election year. She keeps in focus the major political issues as well as the tactics of day-by-day campaigning.

Liston, Robert A. *Presidential Power: How Much Is Too Much?* New York: McGraw-Hill, 1971. 160 pages.

After studying presidents from Franklin D. Roosevelt to Richard M. Nixon, Liston finds that executive power has increased far more dramatically in foreign affairs than in domestic politics.

Michener, James A. *The Quality of Life.* Philadelphia: Lippincott, 1970. 127 pages.

Michener focuses on those aspects of modern life whose quality is often criticized, such as cities, race relations, education, and the environment.

Reeves, Richard. *A Ford, Not a Lincoln.* New York: Harcourt, Brace, Jovanovich, 1974. 212 pages.

The title suggests Reeves's main opinion: Ford, though very likable, did not fully establish his authority as the nation's leader.

Shogan, Robert. *Promises to Keep: Carter's First 100 Days.* New York: Crowell, 1977. Illustrated. 300 pages.

Shogan points out many contradictions in Carter's administration. These include impatience for action verses devotion to methodical planning and liberal ideals versus innate conservatism.

Smith, Hendrick, Adam Clymer, Leonard Silk, Robert Lindsey, and Richard Burt. *Reagan: The Man, The President.* New York: Macmillan, 1980. Illustrated. 186 pages.

The authors are correspondents for *The New York Times.* They provide a serviceable guide to Reagan's outlook and career at the time his presidency started.

Van der Linden, Frank. *The Real Reagan.* New York: Morrow, 1981. 287 pages.

Van der Linden's biography of Reagan, based largely on discussions with Reagan's associates, stresses its subject's successes and achievements.

Walton, Richard J. *The Power of Oil: Economic, Social, Political.* New York: Seabury Press, 1977. 178 pages.

Walton treats both the history of oil and its current importance in world trade.

White, Theodore H. *The Making of the President 1972.* New York: Atheneum, 1973. 419 pages.

White began writing close-up accounts of presidential campaigns in 1960. This work could not include later revelations about Watergate (White covers Watergate in *Breach of Faith: The Fall of Richard Nixon,* published in 1975), but even so White offers an excellent picture of events through 1972.

GLOSSARY

Certain words in the Glossary and in the text have been respelled as an aid to pronunciation. A key to pronouncing the respelled words appears below.

The words in the Glossary are defined to clarify their meaning in the text. The page numbers given refer to the places in the text where the words first appear. The words selected for definition in the Glossary are important in United States history. Other words that need clarification but that have minor historical importance are defined in context or by footnotes in the chapters.

PRONUNCIATION KEY

Like certain other words in this book, the phrase *laissez-faire* has been respelled to indicate its pronunciation: LEHS-ay-FEHR. The small capital letters mean that the first syllable should be spoken with a minor stress. The large capital letters mean that the last syllable should be spoken with a major stress. The vowel sounds shown by the letters *eh* and *ay* in the respelling correspond to the vowel sounds in the key below.

Pronounce a as in hat

ah	father
ar	tar
ay	say
ayr	air
e, eh	hen
ee	bee
eer	deer
er	her
ew	new
g	go
i, ih	him
ī	kite
j	jet
ng	ring
o	frog
ō	no
oo	soon
or	for
ow	plow
oy	boy
sh	she
th	thick
u, uh	sun
z	zebra
zh	measure

abolition: putting an end to slavery in the United States (page 124)

amendment: a change proposed or made in a law, constitution, or other rule of government (page 112)

anarchism: the theory that all systems of government interfere with individual liberties and should be eliminated (page 369)

appeasement: the policy of giving in to the demands of a potential enemy in an attempt to keep the peace (page 565)

arms race: competition between nations in developing and building weapons (page 553)

assembly line: a system of factory work in which goods move along a line where workers each do one step in manufacturing (page 492)

automation: a system of manufacturing in which all or many steps are performed or controlled by machines or electronic devices (page 647)

balance of payments: the difference between the amount of money a nation spends for all its imports and the amount of money the nation receives for all its exports (page 694)

balance of trade: the difference in value between all the imports and all the exports of a country (page 29)

bicameral: made up of two legislative chambers, or houses (page 38)

bimetallic standard: the use of both gold and silver as standards of value for a nation's money (page 395)

black codes: laws passed by southern states after the Civil War, defining and limiting the rights of freed slaves (page 309)

capitalism: a system in which most means of economic production and distribution are privately owned and are operated for profit (page 369)

cash crop: a crop raised to be sold at a profit (page 62)

checks and balances: a system that allows each branch of government to place limits on the other branches (page 125)

civil rights: the rights of a citizen, especially those guaranteed by amendments to the United States Constitution (page 116)

closed shop: a work place in which the employer has agreed to hire union members only (page 635)

cold war: a conflict between nations carried on by economic and political means rather than by direct military action (page 613)

collective bargaining: negotiation between workers as an organized group and their employer or employers, about wages, hours of work, or other labor conditions (page 385)

communism: a system in which the means of economic production and distribution, as well as other property, are owned by society as a whole (page 369)

concurrent powers: powers shared by the national and state governments, under the Constitution (page 125)

confederation: an alliance of people, groups, or states for a common purpose (page 4)

corporation: people joined in an organization that has legal powers to buy, sell, or do other business as if it were a person with individual rights (page 185)

de facto segregation: segregation that exists in fact though not required by laws or official regulations (page 650)

deficit spending: government spending that exceeds government income, resulting in a budget deficit, or shortage (page 546)

deflation: a fall in prices and a corresponding rise in the value of money, caused by reducing the amount of money in circulation (page 390)

delegated powers: powers given entirely to the national government by the states, under the Constitution (page 124)

depression: an economic period marked by sharply reduced business activity, lowered wages and prices, and widespread unemployment (page 84)

deregulation: the ending of government regulation of certain industries, meant to increase competition within the industries (page 715)

direct primary: an election in which candidates for public office are chosen by the vote of the people, not by delegates to a political convention (page 436)

dividend: a share of the profit paid by a company to its stockholders (page 359)

electoral college: a group of people elected by voters to formally elect the president and vice-president of the United States (page 123)

emancipation: release from enslavement (page 124)

embargo: a ban on trade with another nation (page 142)

executive: the person or branch of government responsible for putting laws into effect and for managing the affairs of a state or nation (page 109)

expansionist: a person who favors expanding the territory or power of a nation (page 242)

federalism: a political system formed when states agree to yield powers to a national government while retaining certain powers in local matters (page 124)

free enterprise: an economic system that allows competition among private companies with minimal government regulation (page 358)

frontier: the place where an advancing line of settlements borders undeveloped land (page 66)

general strike: a strike against all industries in a certain city or nation, or against one entire industry (page 383)

gold standard: the use of gold as the one standard of value for a nation's money (page 395)

graduated personal income tax: a tax on individual income, varying so that a person who makes more money pays at a higher rate (page 394)

gross national product: the total value of all the goods and services produced in a nation each year (page 491)

holding company: a company that holds ownership in other corporations, usually to control them (page 364)

impeach: to accuse a public official of wrongdoing before a court with power to try the official (page 126)

imperialism: a policy by which a nation strives to have dominance over the trade and government of other lands (page 403)

indentured servant: a person who signed a contract to work for another for a certain number of years in return for passage to America (page 34)

industrial union: a union open to all employees in a given industry, no matter what kind of work they perform (page 382)

inflation: a rise in prices and a corresponding fall in the value of money, caused by expanding the amount of money in circulation (page 118)

initiative: the right of citizens to propose a new law to legislators or directly to voters (page 436)

injunction: a court order commanding a person or group to do or to cease doing some act (page 387)

interchangeable parts: pieces of machinery so much alike that one can be used in place of another (page 184)

isolationism: a policy of keeping a nation out of foreign alliances or agreements, especially alliances that might draw the nation into war (page 553)

judicial review: the right of the Supreme Court to review an act of Congress in connection with a court case and to decide whether the act is constitutional (page 160)

judiciary: the branch of government responsible for the administration of justice under a system of laws (page 109)

laissez-faire (LEHS-ay-FEHR): referring to the principle that owners of business and industry should operate as they please, without government regulation or control (page 363)

legislature: the group of people responsible for making the laws for a state or nation (page 109)

lobbyist: a person who tries to influence government decisions to favor a certain interest group (page 447)

loose construction: an interpretation of the Constitution that would allow the national government to exercise wide powers under the elastic clause of Article 1, Section 8 (page 137)

mass production: the production of goods in large quantities, especially by machinery (page 184)

mercantilism: a European economic system emphasizing government protection of home industries and a favorable balance of trade in order to accumulate gold (page 29)

metropolis: a large city, usually the most important in a region (page 372)

monopoly: exclusive control of a product or service, or enough control to fix the price (page 361)

nullify: to declare a law void and without effect (page 150)

parity: prices for certain farm products, maintained by a government system of price supports to give farmers a steady level of purchasing power (page 490)

political machine: a political organization which delivers votes to elect certain candidates and in return is given jobs, contracts, and political favors to distribute (page 375)

prohibition: a ban on alcoholic drinks as a result of the Eighteenth Amendment (page 498)

proprietary colony: an American colony granted by the English Crown to a person or group to own and rule (page 42)

protective tariff: a tariff designed to protect domestic businesses by raising the prices of imported goods (page 137)

ratify: to approve, especially to sanction officially (page 112)

rebate: a refund of part of an amount paid (page 359)

recall: the right of citizens to remove an elected official from office by a special election (page 437)

recession: a temporary decline in business activity (page 514)

Reconstruction: the process of reorganizing the Confederate states after the Civil War and readmitting them to the Union (page 307)

referendum: the right of citizens to vote directly for or against certain laws (page 436)

republic: a state or nation in which citizens have authority over government through their elected representatives (page 121)

reservation: an area of land set aside by the federal government for Indians (page 340)

reserved powers: powers kept by the states, under the Constitution, because the powers are neither delegated to the national government nor prohibited to the states (page 125)

royal colony: an American colony ruled by the English Crown through a governor and a council of advisers (page 35)

secede: to withdraw from an organization (page 167)

secret ballot: a person's right to vote without revealing his or her choice of candidates or issues (page 437)

segregation: separation, especially the separation of blacks from other racial groups (page 293)

self-governing colony: an American colony in which citizens had a say in the government by electing representatives to make laws (page 37)

separation of powers: the division of government into separate branches with distinct powers (page 125)

sharecropper: a person who does farm work in exchange for a share of the value of the crop (page 312)

socialism: a system in which the means of economic production and distribution are owned by the government or by workers' groups, not by private individuals (page 369)

Soviet bloc: a group of nations dominated by the Soviet Union (page 608)

sphere of influence: a nation's area of control or strong influence in one or more foreign lands (page 421)

spoils system: a system in which appointive public offices are treated like spoils, or goods seized by force in wartime—the offices with their salaries and opportunities are assigned by the winning party to reward its followers (page 205)

stagflation: an economic condition combining stagnation in business and inflation in the prices of goods (page 695)

states' rights: all the rights neither granted to the federal government nor denied to the state governments under the Constitution (page 150)

strict construction: an interpretation of the Constitution that would prevent the national government from exercising powers not specifically delegated to it (page 137)

strike: an organized refusal to work by employees who hope to force an employer to meet their demands for higher wages, better working conditions, or other changes (page 258)

suffrage: the right to vote (page 203)

tariff: a duty, or tax, placed on imports or exports (page 112)

Third World: nations in Asia, Africa, and Latin America that are not allied with either side in the cold war (page 689)

totalitarian society: a society in which the state or the government controls the economy, the political system, and almost every area of people's lives (page 560)

trade union: a labor union, particularly one open to workers who perform a certain kind of skilled work, known as a craft union (page 382)

trust: a form of business combination, now illegal in the United States, organized to control member corporations and thereby achieve a monopoly (page 361)

union shop: a work place in which the employer has agreed that all new employees must become union members after a certain time on the job (page 637)

veto: to officially reject a bill after it has been approved by lawmakers (page 49)

vigilante (vij-ih-LAN-tee): a member of a vigilance committee, which claims the right to keep order and punish crimes although it is not backed by any legal authority (page 338)

INDEX

The numbers in bold indicate pages on which glossary terms first appear.

816   INDEX

Mexico: immigrants from, 365, 368, 493, 720; independence, 195, 232; preconquest, 2; revolution in, 419–420; Spanish conquest, 2; U.S. issues with, 242, 244, 556

Mexico City, 20, 22; battle of, 245, 246

Meyer, Agnes, 526

Miami, FL, 423

Miami tribe, 143

Michigan: admission, 247; bank holiday in, 526; lumber industry in, 356; Territory, 161, 194

Middle colonies, 57–61, 66–67, 99–103

Middle East, 611–612, 617–622, 625, 676, 691, 722–723; immigrants from, 365; L.B. Johnson and, 674; maps, 473, 675; Reagan policy, 734–735; after World War I, 473

Midway Islands, 404, 573

Midway, battle of, 578, 593

Migrant with Hope, A, Newby, 703

Migrant workers, 543–545

Migration, to North in the *1920*s, 496

Millay, Edna St. Vincent, 496

Miller, William E., 668

Minimum-wage law, 547, 638, 664

Mining industry, 335–337; chart and map, 768

Minneapolis, MN, 373, 376, 430

Minnesota, 346, 356, 360; Farmers' Alliance politics, 393

Minutemen, 91

Miranda v. *Arizona,* 666

Missiles, 657, 659–660

Missions, 22, 232, 236

Missionaries, 230, 404, 405

Mississippi, 69, 161, 194; cotton, 191, 261; readmission, 309, 317; Reconstruction in, 311; secession, 273

Mississippi, University of, 665

Mississippi River, 21, 115, 144; cities, 373; Louisiana Purchase and, 163–164

Missouri, 185, 233, 279–280; admission, 190–192, 194

Missouri Compromise, 192, 243, 264–265, 270

Missouri tribe, 5, 6

Missouri River, 230

Mitchell, Charles E., 511

Mitchell, John, miners' leader, 439

Mitchell, John, attorney general, 697, 699, 701

Mitchell, Maria, 223

Mitchell, William "Billy," 468

Mobile, AL, 69, 255

Modoc tribe, 5, 343

Mohawk tribe, 4, 5

Mondale, Walter, 705, 725

Molasses Act, 69

Money. *See* Currency

Mongolian People's Republic, 591

Monitor, U.S.S., 286, 287

Monmouth Court House, NJ, battle of, 101, 102

Monopoly, Standard Oil, **361**

Monroe, James, 188–196; on black colonization, 191; Florida and, 194; foreign policy, 193–196; on Indian removal, 205; in Louisiana negotiations, 163–164

Monroe Doctrine, 195–196, 406, 407; Roosevelt Corollary, 416–417, 555–557

Montana, 337, 341, 347

Montcalm, Louis Joseph, Marquis de, 74

Monterey, CA, 232, 233, 246

Monterrey, Mexico, 22, 245

Montezuma, 2, 8, 19–20

Montgomery, Bernard Law, 580

Montgomery, Richard, 93–94

Montgomery, AL, 652–653

Montreal, 48

Moon landings, 692–693, 707

Moral diplomacy, 419

Morgan, John Pierpont, 362–363, 439, 442, 482

Morley, Agnes, 337

Mormon Church, 233–235

Mormon Trail, 233 –235

Morocco, 160, 580

Morrill Land Grant Act, 295

Morrill Tariff Act, 282

Morristown, NJ, 100, 101

Morrow, Dwight W., 556

Morse, Wayne, 675

Moscow Declaration, 608

"Most-favored-nation" principle, 559

"Mother Ann," 217

Mott, Lucretia, 224, 225

Mount Holyoke College, 223

Mountain men, 229–230

Muckrakers, 430, 451

Mugwumps, 326, 327

Muhammad, Elijah, 673

Muir, John, 442

Mules and Men, Hurston, 500

Mundt, Karl E., 639

Munich Agreement, 565

Munn v. *Illinois,* 360

Murfreesboro, TN, battle of, 299

Murphy, Frank, 519

Murray, Pauli, 645

Muscle Shoals, 532

Muskie, Edmund S., 679, 691

Muskogean speakers, 4

Mussolini, Benito, 560, 564, 568, 571, 587

My Lai massacre, 686, 687

Nacogdoches, TX, 238

Nader, Ralph, 669

Nagasaki, bombed, 597

Nantucket, MA, 54

Napoleon, 149, 162, 164, 170, 172

Narragansett Indians, 4, 5, 41, 717; Roger Williams and, 38

Narváez, Pánfilo de, 20, 22

Nasser, Gamal Abdel, 626

Nast, Thomas, 323

Natchez Trace, 182

National Aeronautics and Space Administration (NASA), 663, 692–693, 715

National Ass'n for the Advancement of Colored People (NAACP), 431, 576, 650, 653

National Banking Act, 282

National Consumers League, 434

National debt: after the Confederation, 134–136; after World War I, 486; after World War II, 584

National Defense Act, 466

National Defense Education Act, 649

National Energy Act, 711

National Environmental Policy Act, 669

National Gazette, 140

National Industrial Recovery Act (NIRA), 527, 528, 537, 548

National Labor Relations Board (NLRB), 538, 539, 545–546

National Labor Union, 382, 383

National Liberation Front (NLF), 660

National Organization for Women (NOW), 669–670

National parks, 442

National Recovery Administration (NRA), 527, 528, 530, 537, 538, 545

National Road, 181, 182

National Republicans, 198, 199, 213, 214

National Security Act, 639

National Security Council, 639

National Socialist (Nazi) party, 560–561

National Union for Social Justice, 535

National Urban League, 432

National War Labor Board (NWLB), 462, 584

National Women's Conference, first, 715

National Women's Loyal League, 293

National Women's Political Caucus, 670

National Youth Administration (NYA), 537–540

Native Guards of Louisiana, 292

Nativism, 260, 369–370

Natural gas, 730

Naturalization Act, 150, 157

Nauvoo, IL, 233, 234

Navaho tribe, 5, 7, 340, 343; Marines, 593; painting, 21

Naval Appropriation Bill, 459

Navigation Acts, 68–69

Navy/Navies: Dept. of, created, 147; reduction of, 553–555. *See* specific wars

Nazi party, 560–561

Nebraska, 267–268, 346, 347; Farmer's Alliance politics, 393

Nebraska Immigration Ass'n, 347

Netherlands, 24, 36–37, 567; in NATO, 615

Neutrality, in the Treaty of Ghent, 175

Neutrality Acts, 563–564, 566–567, 570; "cash and carry" clauses, 564, 567, 570

Neutrality, Proclamation of, 141–142

Nevada, 232, 337

New Amsterdam, 31, 41

New Bedford, MA, 54

New Deal, 549, 634; first, 525–534; second, 534–539; Supreme Court and, 537, 545–546

New England: colonial, 35–41, 46–47, 53–57; Revolutionary War in, 90–94; secession threat, 167; War of *1812* and, 167, 172, 174–175

New England Confederation, 41

New Federalism, 730

New France, 30, 41, 48, 69

New Freedom, 445, 448

New Frontier, 663, 667

New Guinea, 577, 594

New Hampshire, 109, 112–113, 124, 127, 140, 256; colonial, 40, 41, 47, 48, 58, 67; in Continental Army, 91

New Haven, CT, 40, 41, 48

New Jersey, 45, 47, 48, 58, 67, 112–113

New Jersey Plan, 122–123

New Mexico, 20, 24, 244–246, 347

ILLUSTRATION CREDITS

Cover: © Cabor Demjen/Stock Boston.

Title page: Lee Boltin/National Museum of American History, Smithsonian.

Unit 1: **xvi** Huntington Library, San Marino, California.

Chapter 1: **3** *The Geographer* by Jan Vermeer. Städelsches Kunstinstitut, Frankfurt am Main. **4** New York State Museum. **5** Sisse Brimberg © 1981 National Geographic Society. **6** (top) American Museum of Natural History. **6** (bottom) Nevada State Museum; photo by James LeGoy. **7** © Dan Budnik/Woodfin Camp, N.Y. **8** Museo Nacional de Anthropologia e Historia; photo © Bradley Smith. **9** (left) © Boireau/Rapho. **9** (right) St. Louis Art Museum, gift of Morton D. May. **11** Musée des Tissus, Lyon © Gamet/Rapho. **13** (top) National Maritime Museum, London. **13** (bottom) Detail from *Christopher Columbus* by Sebastiano del Piombo. © Metropolitan Museum of Art, gift of J. Pierpont Morgan, 1900. **14** New York Public Library, Map Division, Astor, Lenox, and Tilden Foundations. **15** With special authorization of the City of Bayeux. **18** New York Historical Society. **21** (top) Archivo de Indias, Seville, Spain; photo © Bradley Smith. **21** (bottom) © Ernst Haas. **25** *Elizabeth I* by M. Gheeraerts the Younger. National Portrait Gallery, London. **26** Bibliothèque Nationale, Paris. **27** Bibliothèque Nationale, Paris.

Chapter 2: **29** *The Mason Children, David, Joanna and Abigail* by an unknown American artist 1670. The Fine Arts Museum of San Francisco, gift of Mr. and Mrs. John D. Rockefeller 3rd. **30** *La Pesche des Sauvages* from the *Codex Canadiensis.* Thomas Gilcrease Institute of American History and Art. **31** (top) National Maritime Museum, London; photo © Michael Holford. **31** (bottom) *Deborah Glen* by Pieter Vanderlyn. Abby Aldrich Rockefeller Folk Art Center, Williamsburg, Virginia. **33** British Museum; photo © Michael Holford. **34** 8631 vol. 7. Huntington Library, San Marino, California. **37** (left) Pilgrim Society. **37** (right) Princeton University Library Department of Rare Books and Special Collections. **39** © Museum of Fine Arts, Boston, Seth Kettell Sweetser Fund. **40** Culver. **42** Massachusetts Historical Society. **43** *Cecilius Calvert* by Soest. Enoch Pratt Free Library of Baltimore. **44** Maryland Historical Society. **46** *Peaceable Kingdom* by Edward Hicks. Abby Aldrich Rockefeller Folk Art Center, Williamsburg, Virginia. **47** New York Public Library. **48** Henry Francis du Pont Winterthur Museum. **50** New York Public Library, Rare Book Division, Astor, Lenox, and Tilden Foundations. **51** 27004 vol. 1. Huntington Library, San Marino, California.

Chapter 3: **53** American Antiquarian Society. **54** Yale University Art Gallery, the Mabel Brady Garvan Collection. **56** New York State Historical Association, Cooperstown. **58** *Pennsylvania Farmerstead with Many Fences* by an unknown American. © 1982 Museum of Fine Arts, Boston, M. & M. Karolik Collection. **59** *Benjamin Franklin* by John Trumbull. Yale University Art Gallery. **60** (left) New York Public Library, Rare Book Division, Astor, Lenox, and Tilden Foundations. **60** (right) Culver. **62** *McCormick Family* by Joshua Johnston. Maryland Historical Society. **63** Map Collection of the Charleston Library Society. **65** (left) National Maritime Museum, London. **65** (right) New York Historical Society. **66** Georgia Department of Archives and History. **68** Mark Sexton/Peabody Museum of Salem. **74** Royal Ontario Museum, Toronto, Canada. **76** Library of Congress. **77** (top) Massachusetts Historical Society. **77** (bottom) *Spring Blessing* by an anonymous American. © 1982 Museum of Fine Arts, Boston, M. & M. Karolik Collection.

Unit 2: **78** Abby Aldrich Rockefeller Folk Art Center, Williamsburg, Virginia.

Chapter 4: **81** Detail from *Surrender of Cornwallis at Yorktown* by John Trumbull, American, 1756–1843, oil on canvas, 13⅞ × 21″, Accession No. 48.217. Detroit Institute of Arts, gift of Dexter M. Ferry, Jr. **82** *Mrs. Ruben Humphreys* by Richard Brunton. Connecticut Historical Society. **83** Library of Congress. **85** American Antiquarian Society. **86** Culver. **87** Library of Congress. **90** *Mrs. James Warren (Mercy Otis)* by John Singleton Copley. © 1982 Museum of Fine Arts, Boston, Bequest of Winslow Warren. **92** *Battle of Bunker's Hill* by John Trumbull. Yale University Art Gallery. **95** Historical Society of Pennsylvania. **97** Library of Congress. **98** Massachusetts Historical Society. **99** *Battle of Princeton* by William Mercer. Historical Society of Pennsylvania. **101** Guilford Courthouse, National Military Park. **103** Life Picture Service. **104** Library of Congress. **106** Massachusetts Historical Society. **107** American Philosophical Society.

Chapter 5: **109** *A View of Mr. Joshua Winsor's House* by Rufus Hathaway. Photo courtesy Stephen Score Antiques. **110** Massachusetts Historical Society. **111** (top) Bettmann. **111** (bottom) Museum of Art, Rhode Island School of Design, gift of Lucy T. Aldrich. **114** (left) Massachusetts Historical Society. **114** (right) *Flax Scutching Bee* by Linton Park. National Gallery of Art, Washington, D.C., gift of Edgar William and Bernice Chrysler Garbisch. **116** William L. Clements Library, University of Michigan. **117** *Tontine Coffee House* by Francis Guy. New York Historical Society. **118** Colonial Williamsburg Photograph. **119** Culver. **122** *The Artist in His Museum* by Charles Willson Peale. Pennsylvania Academy of the Fine Arts. **123** Independence National Historic Park. **124** *Head of a Negro* by John Copley, American, 1738–1815, oil on canvas, 21 × 16¼″, Accession No. 52.118. Detroit Institute of Arts, Founders Society Purchase, Gibbs-Williams Fund. **128** New York Historical Society. **130** New York Historical Society. **131** (top) Massachusetts Historical Society. **131** (bottom) Rhode Island Historical Society.

Chapter 6: **133** detail from *Salute to General Washington in New York Harbor* by L.M. Cooke. National Gallery of Art, Washington, D.C., gift of Edgar William and Bernice Chrysler Garbisch. **135** National Portrait Gallery, Smithsonian. **136** (left) Maryland Historical Society. **136** (right) Library of Congress. **137** Smithsonian No. P64260. **140** *Alexander Hamilton* by John Trumbull, National Gallery of Art, Washington, D.C. **141** New York Historical Society. **143** Detail from *Treaty of Greenville* by an unknown artist 1914.1. Chicago Historical Society. **144** Mount Vernon Ladies' Association. **146** (top) Study for portrait of John Adams by John Singleton Copley. © Metropolitan Museum of Art, Harris Brisbane Dick Fund, 1960. **146** (bottom) Bettmann. **147** Franklin D. Roosevelt Library. **148** Boston Public Library, Print Division. **149** New York Public Library. **151** National Gallery of Art, Washington, D.C., Index of American Design. **152** Library of Congress. **153** Bostonian Society.

Unit 3: **154** Art Institute of Chicago.

Chapter 7: **157** Lafayette College, Alan P. Kirby Collection. **158** (left) New York Historical Society. **158** (right) National Gallery of Art, Washington, D.C., gift of William and Bernice Chrysler Garbisch. **159** National Portrait Gallery, Smithsonian. **162** *Boiling House* from William Clark's *Ten Views of the Island of Antigua.* From the Collection of Mr. and Mrs. Paul Mellon. **163** *A View of New Orleans Taken from the Plantation of Marigny* by Boqueto de Woiserie 1932.18. Chicago Historical Society. **164** Library of Congress. **166** (top) © John G. Zimmerman. **166** (bottom) Missouri Historical Society. **169** *Launching of the Ship Fame* by George Ropes. Essex Institute, Salem, Massachusetts. **171** Fort Malden National Historic Park. **173** New York Historical Society. **174** Maryland Historical Society. **176** New York Historical Society. **177** New York Public Library.

Chapter 8: **179** *Lockport on the Erie Canal* by Mary Keys. Munson-Williams-Proctor Institute, Utica, New York. **180** *Shop and Warehouse of Duncan Phyfe* by John Rubens Smith. © Metropolitan Museum of Art, Rogers Fund, 1922. **183** Lukens Steel Company. **185** *The Red Mill, Yellow Springs, Ohio,* by an unknown artist. The Edison Institute, Henry Ford Museum & Greenfield Village. **186** From *Progress of Cotton.* Yale University Art Gallery, the Mabel Brady Garvan Collection. **187** *St. Louis From the River Below* by George Catlin. National Museum of American Art, Smithsonian, gift of Mrs. Joseph Harrison Jr. **189** *The Virginia Constitution Convention of 1829–1830* by George Catlin. Virginia Historical Society. **190** Historical Society of Pennsylvania. **191** New York Historical Society. **193** Oregon Historical Society. **196** Anchorage Historical and Fine Arts Museum. **197** © Metropolitan Museum of Art, gift of I.N. Phelps Stokes, Edward S. Hawes, Alice Mary Hawes, Marion Augusta Hawes, 1937. **198** Library of Congress. **200** National Archives. **201** New York State Historical Association, Cooperstown.

Chapter 9: **203** Detail from *In the Fields* by Eastman Johnson, American, 1824–1906, oil on board, 17¾ × 27½″, Accession No. 38.1. Detroit Institute of Arts, Founders Society Purchase, Dexter M. Ferry Fund. **205** *Portrait of Andrew Jackson* by Thomas Sully. Detroit Institute of Arts, gift of Mrs. Walter O. Briggs. **206** (top) Woolaroc Museum, Bartlesville, Oklahoma. **206** (bottom) National Portrait Gallery, Smithsonian. **208** National Archives No. 111–B–4669. **210** (left) Dartmouth College Library. **210** (right) Historical Pictures Service. **213** New York Historical Society. **214** *The Cotton Merchants* by Edgar Degas. Fogg Art Museum, Harvard University, gift of Herbert N. Straus. **215** Western Reserve Historical Society. **216** Hancock Shaker Village, Pittsfield, Massachusetts. **217** Index of American Design, National Gallery of Art, Washington, D.C. **218** © Metropolitan Museum of Art, gift of I.N. Phelps Stokes, Edward S. Hawes, Alice Mary Hawes, Marion Augusta Hawes, 1937. **219** © Metropolitan Museum of Art, gift of I.N. Phelps Stokes, Edward S. Hawes, Alice Mary Hawes, Marion Augusta Hawes, 1937. **220** Houghton Library, Harvard University. **221** Department of Special Collections, Wichita State University Library. **222** National Archives Exhibit No. 55. **224** (top) ICHI–11897 Chicago Historical Society. **224** (bottom) Sophia Smith Collection, Smith College. **225** (left) National Portrait Gallery, Smithsonian. **225** (right) Sophia Smith Collection, Smith College. **226** *Indian Seated Overlooking a Lake* by Thomas Cole. Detroit Institute of Arts, Founders Society Purchase, William H. Murphy Fund. **227** New York Public Library.

Chapter 10: **229** *Ute Canyon* by Colman. Bancroft Library, University of California. **230** (left) *Frontiersman* by William Cary. Thomas Gilcrease Institute of American History and Art. **230** (right) Colorado Historical Society. **233** (left) *Mission San Carlos Del Rio Carmelo* by Oriana Day. Society of California Pioneers. **233** (right) *Costumes de Guerre* by Choris. Bancroft Library, University of California. **235** *Winter Quarters* by C.C.A. Christensen. Collection of Brigham Young University, gift of the Christensen Family. **236** *Fandango* by Theodore Gentilz. Library of the Daughters of the Republic of Texas at the Alamo. **240** Library of Congress. **241** University of Texas at Austin. **242** Abby Aldrich Rockefeller Folk Art Center, Williamsburg, Virginia. **243** *Dance on the Sequoia Stump* by F.R. Bennett. New York State Historical Association, Cooperstown. **246** *Taking of Monterey* by W.H. Meyers. Bancroft Library, University of California. **248** California State Library. **249** (top) New York Public Library. **249** (bottom) California Historical Society. **250** © Herbert K. Barnett, courtesy of the Star of the Republic Museum. **251**© Metropolitan Museum of Art, Harris Brisbane Dick Fund, 1939.

Unit 4: **252** From the Collection of Walter Lord.

Chapter 11: **255** Detail from *The Cotton Pickers,* Winslow Homer, U.S. 1836–1918. Los Angeles County Museum of Art: Acquisition made possible through Museum

Trustees: Robert O. Anderson, R. Stanton Avery, B. Gerald Cantor, Edward W. Carter, Justin Dart, Charles E. Ducommun, Mrs. Daniel Frost, Julian Ganz, Jr., Dr. Armand Hammer, Harry Lenart, Dr. Franklin D. Murphy, Mrs. Joan Palevsky, Richard E. Sherwood, Maynard J. Toll, and Hal B. Wallis. **256** *The Railroad Suspension Bridge near Niagara Falls* by an unknown American. © 1982 Museum of Fine Arts, Boston, M. & M. Karolik Collection. **258** Library of Congress. **259** Library of Congress. **260** *Expulsion of Negroes and Abolitionists from Tremont Temple, Boston, 12/3/1860* by Winslow Homer from *Harper's Weekly* 12/15/1860. © Metropolitan Museum of Art, Harris Brisbane Dick Fund, 1928. **261** Library of Congress. **265** New York Historical Society. **267** (left) *Slaves Escaping Through the Swamp* by Thomas Moran. Philbrook Art Center, Laura A. Clubb Collection. **267** (right) Schlesinger Library, Radcliffe College. **269** New York Historical Society. **270** Missouri Historical Society. **271** National Portrait Gallery, Smithsonian. **274** National Portrait Gallery, Smithsonian, on loan from Serena Williams Miles Van Rensselaer. **275** National Archives No. 121–BA–914A. **276** Library of Congress. **277** Library of Congress.

Chapter 12: 279 Library of Congress. **280** Library of Congress. **281** Cook Collection, Valentine Museum. **282** (left) National Archives No. 111–B–82. **282** (right) Cook Collection, Valentine Museum. **283** (left) National Archives No. 111–B–4146. **283** (right) Library of Congress. **284** *At the Front* by George Cochran Lambdin, American, 1830–1896, oil on canvas, 18¼ × 24″, Accession No. 59.314. Detroit Institute of Arts, Founders Society Purchase. **285** Library of Congress. **287** Collection of Oliver Jensen. **288** (left) Cook Collection, Valentine Museum. **288** (right) Library of Congress. **290** ICHI–09460 Chicago Historical Society. **291** Library of Congress. **292** From the original glass plate negative in the Lloyd Ostendorf Collection, Dayton, Ohio. **295** Library of Congress. **296** Schomburg Center for Research in Black Culture, New York Public Library. **297** Rockefeller Collection. **301** *Rebels Defense at Fort Fisher* by Frank Vizetelly. The Houghton Library, Harvard University. **303** Library of Congress. **304** New York Historical Society. **305** General Dynamics, Pierre Laclede Center.

Chapter 13: 307 Library of Congress. **308** Library of Congress. **309** Library of Congress. **310** Library of Congress. **312** National Archives Exhibit No. 116. **313** Library of Congress. **314** Culver. **320** (top) Library of Congress. **320** (bottom) Bettmann. **322** National Portrait Gallery, Smithsonian. **323** Prints Division, New York Public Library. **325** Library of Congress. **326** *Fifth Avenue in 1909* by John Sloan, Private Collecion. **328** Smithsonian No. 72-8046. **329** Edison Institute, Henry Ford Museum & Greenfield Village.

Unit 5: 330 *Homestead* by John Kane (c. 1929?) oil on canvas, 24 × 27″. Museum of Modern Art, New York, gift of Abby Aldrich Rockefeller.

Chapter 14: 333 Detail from *Buffalo Hunt Under the Wolf-Skin Mask* by George Catlin. National Museum of American Art, Smithsonian, gift of Mrs. Joseph Harrison, Jr. **336** (left) Library of Congress. **336** (right) *Californians Catching Wild Horses With Riata* by Hugo Nahl. Oakland Museum, Kahn Collection. **337** Bancroft Library, University of California. **338** Kansas State Historical Society. **340** *Indians Near Fort Laramie* by Albert Bierstadt. © Museum of Fine Arts, Boston, M. & M. Karolik Collection. **341** Smithsonian. **343** (left) Denver Public Library. **343** (right) Library of Congress. **344** (left) Library of Congress. **344** (right) Smithsonian No. 3462-B. **345** Nebraska State Historical Society. **348** Collection of Peter E. Palmquist. **349** Nebraska State Historical Society, Solomon D. Butcher Collection. **351** Alaska Historical Library, Winter & Pond Collection. **352** Buffalo Bill Historical Center. **353** (top) Bancroft Library, University of California. **353** (bottom) © Gary Smith.

Chapter 15: 355 *Brooklyn Bridge* by Joseph Stella. Yale University Art Gallery, gift of collection Société Anonyme. **357** *Manchester Valley* by Joseph Pickett (1914–1918?) oil with sand on canvas, 45½ × 60⅝″. Museum of Modern Art, New York, gift of Abby Aldrich Rockefeller. **358** State Historical Society of Wisconsin, Zimmerman Collection. **359** *Pennsylvania Station Excavation* by George Bellows. Brooklyn Museum, A. Augustus Healy Fund B. **361** Historical Pictures Service. **362** UPI. **363** *J. Pierpont Morgan* by Edward Steichen, photogravure from *Camera Work.* 8⅛ × 6¼″. Museum of Modern Art, New York, gift of A. Conger Goodyear. **365** Library of Congress. **367** (left) Brown Brothers. **367** (right) Library of Congress. **368** *Hester Street* by George Benjamin Luks. Brooklyn Museum, Dick S. Ramsay Fund. **369** Brown Brothers. **370** Los Angeles County Museum of Natural History. **373** *Fifth Avenue at Twilight* by Birge Harrison, American, 1854–1929, oil on canvas, 30 × 23″, Accession No. 10.21. Detroit Institute of Arts, City of Detroit purchase. **374** Library Company of Philadelphia. **375** (left) Museum of the City of New York, Jacob A. Riis collection. **375** (right) International Museum of Photography at George Eastman House. **376** Library of Congress. **377** (left) Museum of the City of New York. **377** (right) Culver. **379** Culver.

Chapter 16: 381 Stefan Lorant Collection. **382** International Museum of Photography at George Eastman House.**384** UPI. **385** Library of Congress/Photo Researchers. **386** *Geography. Studying the Seasons.* From an album of Hampton Institute, 1899–1900, platinum print, 7½ × 9½″. Museum of Modern Art, New York, gift of Lincoln Kirstein. **388** Bureau of Reclamation, National Archives No. 115–UAD–224. **389** Washington State Historical Society. **390** Library of Congress. **392** Washington State Historical Society. **393** Library of Congress. **394** Culver. **395** Historical Pictures Service. **397** Library of Congress. **398** Culver. **399** (top) Library of Congress. **399** (bottom) Culver.

Unit 6: 400 Detail from *Allies Day, May 1917* by Childe Hassam. National Gallery of Art, Washington, D.C., gift of Ethelyn McKinney in memory of her brother, Glenn Ford McKinney.

Chapter 17: 403 National Maritime Museum, San Francisco. **404** Alaska Historical Library, Winter & Pond Collection. **405** (left) *King Kamehameha I* by an unknown artist. Original in Bishop Museum. **405** (right) Brown Brothers. **407** Historical Pictures Service. **408** *Battle of Manila, May 1, 1898,* color print of Japanese origin. Chicago Historical Society. **409** Brown Brothers. **410** (top) UPI. **410** (bottom) Library of Congress. **413** Brown Brothers. **414** Brown Brothers. **417** *Panama Canal* by Charles Sheeler. Citibank, N.A., New York. **420** (left) National Institute of Anthropology and History, Casasola Archive, Hidalgo, Mexico. **420** (right) Library of Congress. **423** (top) Smithsonian No. 72-6726. **423** (bottom) © Bradley Smith *Japan.* **424** Brown Brothers. **426** Bettmann. **427** (top) Library of Congress. **427** (bottom) Historical Pictures Service.

Chapter 18: 429 Historical Pictures Service. **430** Bettmann. **431** Schomburg Center for Research in Black Culture, New York Public Library. **432** *The Banjo Lesson* by Henry O. Tanner. Hampton Institute's Archival and Museum Collection, Hampton, Virginia. **433** Culver. **435** *Park on the River,* William Glackens. Brooklyn Museum, Dick S. Ramsay Fund. **437** Library of Congress. **438** Brown Brothers. **439** Culver. **440** UPI. **441** Brown Brothers. **442** Smithsonian No. 1591. **445** *Grey and Brass* by John Sloan. © Bradley Smith *The USA: A History in Art.* **448** Library of Congress. **450** Brown Brothers. **451** Bettmann.

Chapter 19: 453 *Painting No. 5* by Marsden Hartley (1914–1915), oil on canvas. 39½ × 31¾″. Whitney Museum of American Art, anonymous gift. **454** Bettmann. **455** Bettmann. **458** Imperial War Museum. **459** Manchester (N.H.) Historic Association. **461** BBC Hulton Picture Library. **463** *Smash the Hun* by Edward Hopper. Charles Rand Penney Collection. Photo by Charles A. Stainback. **465** Brown Brothers. **466** BBC Hulton Picture Library. **468** © Association Lartigue/SPADEM. **469** Aerial reconnaissance photograph, Lavannes, World War I, by an unknown photographer, 1917, gelatin-silver print, 6½ × 8⅞″. Museum of Modern Art, New York, gift of Edward Steichen. **471** (left) Brown Brothers. **471** (right) UPI. **474** Brown Brothers. **476** New York Historical Society. **477** Historical Pictures Service.

Unit 7: 478 Detail from *Garage Lights* by Stuart Davis. Memorial Art Gallery of the University of Rochester, Marion Stratton Gould Fund.

Chapter 20: 481 *Rush Hour, New York* by Max Weber. National Gallery of Art, Washington, D.C., gift of the Avalon Foundation. **483** *Bartolomeo Vanzetti and Nicola Sacco* from the Sacco-Vanzetti series of 23 paintings (1931–1932), tempera on paper over composition board, 10½ × 14¼″. Museum of Modern Art, New York, gift of Abby Aldrich Rockefeller. **484** (top) National Archives. **484** (bottom) Culver. **486** Brown Brothers. **488** Culver. **490** *Fall Plowing* by Grant Wood. Deere and Company. **492** Ford Archives, Dearborn, Michigan. **493** Seattle Art Museum, on long-term loan from the collection of Dr. and Mrs. R. Joseph Monsen. **494** University of Louisville Photographic Archives. **496** Brown Brothers. **497** (top) *In Vaudeville* by Charles Demuth (1918). Philadelphia Museum of Art, the A.E. Gallatin Collection. **497** (bottom left) Culver. **497** (bottom right) Bettmann. **498** *The Bootleggers* by Thomas Hart Benton. Reynolda House Museum of American Art. **500** Brown Brothers. **501** Photo from American Heritage Publishing Company. **502** *New York Street Scene* by Joaquin Torres Garcia (1920). Hirschhorn Museum and Sculpture Garden, Smithsonian. **503** (top) Historical Pictures Service. **503** (bottom) Brown Brothers.

Chapter 21: 505 *Aucassin and Nicolette* by Charles Demuth. Columbus Museum of Art, Ohio, gift of Ferdinand Howald. **506** (left) Culver. **506** (right) Bettmann. **507** (top) *Dark Abstraction* by Georgia O'Keeffe. St. Louis Art Museum, gift of Charles E. and Mary Merrill. **507** (bottom) Brown Brothers. **508** Brown Brothers. **510** Brown Brothers. **511** Culver. **512** Popperfoto. **513** UPI. **514** Culver. **515** Library of Congress/Magnum. **516** University of Louisville Photographic Archives. **519** (top) Popperfoto. **519** (bottom) *Women of Flint* by Joseph Vavak. National Museum of American Art, Smithsonian, transfer from Museum of Modern Art. **520** UPI. **521** © The Oakland Museum, the City of Oakland, 1982. **522** Historical Pictures Service. **523** Detroit News.

Chapter 22: 525 Library of Congress. **526** UPI. **529** Library of Congress. **531** Library of Congress. **532** Tennessee Valley Authority. **533** Tennessee Valley Authority. **535** (top) Culver. **535** (bottom) *Scotts Run, West Virginia* by Ben Shahn (1937), tempera on cardboard, 22¼ × 27⅞″. Whitney Museum of American Art. **536** Library of Congress. **537** Brown Brothers. **540** Library of Congress. **541** UPI. **542** UPI **543** Bettmann. **544** Library of Congress. **545** National Archives. **548** Bettmann. **549** (left) Archives of American Art, Smithsonian. **549** (right) Library of Congress.

Unit 8: 550 © William Weems 1978/Woodfin Camp, Washington.

Chapter 23: 553 *Seed for the Planting Shall Not Be Ground Up* by Käthe Kollwitz. Staatliche Museen zu Berlin. **554** Culver. **555** Culver. **556** Edimedia. **559** BBC Hulton Picture Library. **560** UPI. **561** Popperfoto. **562** *USSR Russische Ausstellung* by El Lissitzky (1929) gravure, 49 × 35¼″. Museum of Modern Art, gift of Philip Johnson. **563** UPI. **564** Brown Brothers. **566** DAVA. **570** Brown Brothers. **573** Culver. **574** Library of Congress. **575** Imperial War Museum.

Chapter 24: 577 National Archives No. 80–G–418194. **580** Margaret Bourke-White/*Life Magazine* © 1940 Time Inc. **582** Bettmann. **583** Brown Brothers. **585** National Archives Exhibit No. 156. **588** National Archives No. 26–G2517. **590** Brown Brothers. **591** National Archives No. 208–YE–1A–19. **592** Popperfoto. **594** W. Eugene Smith/*Life Magazine* © Time Inc. **596** (left) W. Eugene Smith/*Life Magazine* © 1945 Time Inc. **596** (right) Imperial War Museum. **598** Popperfoto. **600** Imperial War Museum. **601** (top) Collection of Ann Wilkinson. **601** (bottom) Bettmann.

Unit 9: 602 © Chuck O'Rear/West Light.

Chapter 25: 605 © Elliott Erwitt/Magnum. **607** © Arnold Newman. **608** BBC Hulton Picture Library. **611** Los Alamos National Laboratory. **612** © Planet News/Black Star. **613** Culver. **614** © Kosmos/Black Star. **615** © Fenno Jacobs/Black Star. **617** © Lee Lockwood/Black Star. **619** © Henri Cartier-Bresson/Magnum. **620** UPI. **621** UPI. **623** © Elliott Erwitt/Magnum. **624** Popperfoto. **625** (left) Gillhausen

(Stern)/Black Star. **625** (right) © Stern/Black Star. **628** © Henriques/Magnum. **629** Brown Brothers. **630** *Exploring the Universe, Nuclear Fusion* (1958) by Erik Nitsche, photo-lithograph, 50 × 35¼″. Museum of Modern Art, New York, gift of General Dynamics Corporation. **631** *Events, the Reality of a Week, Every Week* by Dennis Wheeler (1963), photo-offset, 59½ × 46¾″. Museum of Modern Art, New York, gift of Time, Inc.

Chapter 26: 633 *Juke Box* by Jacob Lawrence, American, b. 1917, tempera on paper, 29½ × 21⅛″, Accession No. 53.58. Detroit Institute of Arts, gift of Dr. D.T. Burton, Dr. M.E. Fowler, Dr. J.B. Greene, and Mr. J.J. White. **634** Culver. **635** (top) Culver. **635** (bottom) Library of Congress. **636** *Welders* by Ben Shahn (1943), tempera on cardboard mounted on composition board, 22 × 39¾″. Museum of Modern Art, New York, purchase. **640** UPI. **641** Wide World. **642** © Werner Wolff/Black Star. **643** © Robert Phillips/Black Star. **644** Library of Congress. **647** University of Louisville Photographic Archives. **648** UPI. **649** © Arnold Newman. **651** © Danny Lyon/Magnum. **652** (top) © Burt Glinn/Magnum. **652** (bottom) UPI. **653** © Leonard Freed/Magnum. **654** *A Good Man Is Hard To Find* by Ben Shahn (1948), gouache, 96 × 62″. Museum of Modern Art, New York, gift of the artist. **655** Library of Congress.

Chapter 27: 657 *1960–R* by Clyfford Still (1960). Hirshhorn Museum and Sculpture Garden, Smithsonian, gift of the artist. **658** © Marc and Evelyne Bernheim/Woodfin Camp and Associates, N.Y. **659** © Flip Schulke/Black Star. **661** Department of the Navy. **662** © Art Ricker/Black Star. **663** NASA. **665** © Matt Herron/Black Star. **666** © Dennis Brack/Black Star. **668** George Silk/*Life Magazine* © 1982 Time, Inc. **669** © Dan McCoy/Rainbow. **670** UPI. **671** © Bob Fitch/Black Star. **672** (left) Museum of New Mexico, Santa Fe, photo by Cradoc Bagshaw. **672** (right) © Cradoc Bagshaw. **673** Rentmeester/*Life Magazine* © 1965 Time, Inc. **677** (left) © Dick Swanson/Black Star. **677** (right) © Robert Ellison, Empire News/Black Star. **680** *Blam* by Roy Lichtenstein. Richard Brown Baker Collection, photo from Yale University Art Gallery. **681** © Burk Uzzle/Magnum.

Unit 10: 682 © Edward Bock 1979/Photo Library.

Chapter 28: 685 Arthur Grace/Time Picture Service. **686** © Magnum. **688** (top) © Dirck Halstead/Liaison. **688** (bottom)© Paul Fusco/Magnum. **689** © Wally McNamee 1980/Woodfin Camp, N.Y. **691** © Dennis Brack/Black Star. **693** NASA.

694 © Dennis Stock/Magnum. **696** © Dennis Stock/Magnum. **698** © Mark Godfrey/Archive Pictures. **700** © Alex Webb/Magnum. **701** © Fred Ward/Black Star. **703** © John Messineo/Black Star. **704** (left) © LeRoy Woodson/Woodfin Camp, N.Y. **704** (right) © Dennis Brack/Black Star. **705** © Burt Glinn/Magnum. **706** © Milton Glaser. **707** (top) NASA. **707** (bottom) © Baron Wolman/Woodfin Camp, N.Y.

Chapter 29: 709 © Andy Levin/Black Star. **710** © Arthur Grace/Sygma. **713** © 1981 Steve Northup/Black Star. **714** (top) © Frank Siteman/Stock Boston. **714** (bottom) © Alain Le Garsmeur/Woodfin Camp, N.Y. **716** NASA. **717** © Herman Kokojan/Black Star. **718** (left) © Dirck Halstead/Liaison. **718** (right) © Leonard Freed/Magnum. **719** © Thomas Victor 1983. **722** © Roland Neveu/Liaison. **723** © Sipa Press/Black Star. **724** © Jim Nachtwey/Liaison. **726** © Dennis Brack/Black Star. **732** © Paul Conklin. **733** (left) © Tannenbaum/Sygma. **733** (right) UPI. **734** © 1981 Alon Reininger/Contact. **735** © 1982 James Nachtwey/Black Star. **736** © Jim Nachtwey/Black Star. **737** (top) NASA. **737** (bottom) © Mark Godfrey/Archive Pictures.

Chapter 30: 739 © Craig Aurness/West Light. **740** (left) © J.P. Laffont/Sygma. **740** (right) © Arnold Zann/Black Star. **741** (left) © Paul Conklin. **741** (right) © Chuck O'Rear/West Light. **743** © Sheldon Moskowitz 1982/Liaison. **744** © Mark Godfrey/Archive Pictures. **746** © William S. Weems 1979/Woodfin Camp, Washington. **748** © Cary Wolinsky/Stock Boston. **749** © Elizabeth Crews/Stock Boston. **750** Elaine Horwitch Galleries. **751** © Foxfire Fund. **752** © Dan McCoy/Rainbow. **753** © Dan McCoy/Rainbow. **753** (top) © Erich Hartmann/Magnum. **753** (bottom) © Cabor Demjen/Stock Boston.

Maps prepared by Donnelley Cartographic Services appear on pages 22, 32, 41, 48, 67, 70, 75, 91, 93, 101, 102, 105, 113, 165, 194, 209, 234, 247, 281, 286, 289, 298, 299, 302, 303, 335, 356, 531, 731, 755, 756–757, 758–759, 760–761, 765, 767, 768, and 774.

Maps prepared by John M. Isard Cartography appear on pages 5, 17, 18, 55, 58, 73, 115, 160, 173, 182, 192, 195, 207, 232, 238, 245, 257, 261, 265, 268, 273, 316, 342, 409, 412, 418, 422, 446, 456, 467, 473, 486, 568, 572, 579, 589, 595, 606, 622, 627, 675, 676, 697, and 747.